R. Gupta's®

**Popular Master Guide**

National Testing Agency (NTA)

# UGC-NET/JRF

Junior Research Fellowship & Assistant Professor Eligibility Exam

# EDUCATION

## PAPER II

by

DR. M.S. ANSARI

**2027**
EDITION

RAMESH PUBLISHING HOUSE, NEW DELHI

***Published by:*** O.P. Gupta *for* Ramesh Publishing House

***Admin. Office***

12-H, New Daryaganj Road, Opp. Officers' Mess,
New Delhi-110002 ✆ 23275224, 23245124

**E-mail:** info@rameshpublishinghouse.com
**For Online Shopping:** www.rameshpublishinghouse.com

***Showroom***

• Balaji Market, Nai Sarak, Delhi-110006 ✆ 23282525 📱 9354373464
• 4457, Nai Sarak, Delhi-110006



**Book Code: R-903**

**ISBN: 978-93-87604-57-5**

**Price: ₹ 920**

**Printed at: B.K. Offset, Delhi**

# CONTENTS

---

## Previous Years' Paper

# National Testing Agency (NTA)

## UGC-NET Junior Research Fellowship & Assistant Professor Eligibility Exam

# EDUCATION, JANUARY-2026

(Exam held on 03-01-2026)

## PAPER-II

**1.** Match the List-I with List-II.

| List-I (*Managerial Function*) | List-II (*Description*) |
|---|---|
| A. Plan | I. Implement the plan in practice: build trust and share norms to ensure implementation |
| B. Do | II. Make changes/ improvements based on the data; action may be in process or end process |
| C. Check | III. Strategic/action planning–decide what will be done at district/school or program level |
| D. Act | IV. Collect and analyse formative and summative data on key measures of implementation |

Choose the *correct* answer from the options given below:

1. A-II, B-I, C-III, D-IV
2. A-III, B-I, C-IV, D-II
3. A-IV, B-II, C-I, D-III
4. A-I, B-III, C-II, D-III

**2.** Which statement is not one of Loyd & Loyd's four principles of grading?

1. The system of grading should be clear and understandable
2. Grades should be distributed to match a pre-determined normal curve
3. Grading should be fair regardless of gender, class, race or socio-economic status
4. The system of grading should be communicated to all stakeholders

**3.** What is planning and delivery flow of 'in-service teacher education, under Samagra Shiksha?

A. DIETs to conduct teacher training and BRC/CRC to provide on site support

B. Monitoring feedback by DIET to guide BRC/CRC

C. Inputs from DIETs/BRCs/CRCs

D. SCERT to develop and implement training module

E. SCERT to prepare a combined annual in-service calendar

Choose the *correct* answer from the options given below:

1. C, E, D, A, B
2. A, D, E, C, B
3. E, D, A, C, B
4. A, B, C, D, E

**4.** NCF 2005 described the teacher primarily as a:

1. Controller of the class room
2. Authority to provide facts
3. Authority to ensure memorization of text book by all students
4. Facilitator to construct knowledge

**5.** Given below are two statements: one is labelled as Assertion (A) and the other is labelled as Reason (R):

**Assertion (A):** Robert Stake's Congruence - Contingency model can be categorized under post-modernist approach of curriculum evaluation.

**Reason (R):** This model systematically analyses the congruence between intended and actual antecedents, transactions and results.

In the light of the above statements, choose the ***most appropriate*** answer from the options given below:

1. Both (A) and (R) are correct and (R) is the correct explanation of (A)
2. Both (A) and (R) are correct, but (R) is NOT the correct explanation of A
3. A is correct, but (R) is not correct
4. A is not correct, but (R) is correct

**6.** Who amongst the following can be associated with the functionalist perspective on education?

1. Althusser and Ivan Illich
2. Pierre Bourdieu and Young
3. Durkheim and Parsons
4. Bowles and Gintis and Labov

**7.** Match the List-I with List-II.

| **List-I** (*Steps*) | **List-II** (*Purpose*) |
|---|---|
| A. Analysis of the existing situation | I. Establish targets/ ends that the system should attain |
| B. Setting up goals for the desired situation | II. Appraise current conditions and constraints as a starting point |
| C. Defining mechanism to evaluate achievement of goals | III. Select among alternatives using economic rationality |
| D. Choosing the best solution via cost benefit analysis | IV. Specify criteria/ tools to judge goal attainment |

Choose the ***correct*** answer from the options given below:

1. A-II, B-I, C-IV, D-III
2. A-IV, B-II, C-I, D-III
3. A-III, B-IV, C-I, D-II
4. A-II, B-III, C-IV, D-I

**8.** Select the correct statement(s):

A. Herbartian Model is known for memory level.

B. Bigge and Hunt Model is known for understanding level.

C. Morrison Model is known for reflective level.

D. Malcolm Knowles is known for giving principles of Andragogy.

E. Dynamic Model is known for learner autonomy.

Choose the ***correct*** answer from the options given below:

1. B, C & E only 2. A, B & D only
3. A, D & E only 4. B, C & D only

**9.** Given below are two statements: one is labelled as Assertion (A) and the other is labelled as Reason (R):

**Assertion (A):** Learning analytics can improve institutional decision making at the administrative level only.

**Reason (R):** Learning analytics collects and analyzes learners' data to enhance decision making at multiple levels, including teaching, curriculum design and institutional policy.

In the light of the above statements, choose the ***most appropriate*** answer from the options given below:

1. Both (A) and (R) are correct and (R) is the correct explanation of (A)
2. Both (A) and (R) are correct, but (R) is NOT the correct explanation of (A)
3. (A) is correct, but (R) is not correct
4. (A) is not correct, but (R) is correct

**10.** Sequence the following developments in inclusive education as they unfolded over time:

A. Implementation of differentiated instruction strategies
B. Shift from special education to inclusive education framework
C. Development of collaborative teaching models
D. Adoption of Universal Design for Learning (UDL) principles

Choose the ***correct*** answer from the options given below:

1. B, A, D, C  2. B, A, C, D
3. B, C, A, D  4. A, B, C, D

**11.** Arrange following steps of economic evaluation and financial flow for an educational programme:

A. Cost benefit and cost effective analysis
B. Estimating cost using ingredient method
C. Compute private/social return to justify investment
D. Align funding with budgeting practice
E. Compare alternative on a common outcome metric

Choose the ***correct*** answer from the options given below:

1. A, B, E, C, D  2. B, E, A, D, C
3. D, A, C, B, E  4. E, A, C, B, D

**12.** Under the Samagra Shiksha Framework, which agency is designated as the nodal agency in states for in-service teacher training?

1. DIET  2. IASE
3. RIE  4. SCERT

**13.** Match the List-I with List-II.

| List-I (*Global Initiatives for Inclusive Education*) | List-II (*Primary Objective*) |
|---|---|
| A. Education for All | I. Framing global commitment to inclusive and equitable education by 2030 |
| B. Sustainable Development Goal-4 | II. Advocating for inclusive education systems for learners with disabilities |
| C. Salmanca Statement | III. Ensuring universal access to basic education for all children |
| D. Incheon Declaration | IV. Promoting inclusive, equitable and quality education for lifelong learning |

Choose the ***correct*** answer from the options given below:

1. A-IV, B-II, C-III, D-I
2. A-I, B-III, C-II, D-IV
3. A-III, B-II, C-IV, D-I
4. A-III, B-IV, C-II, D-I

**14.** Match the List-I with List-II.

| List-I (*Commission/ Document*) | List-II (*Recommendation/Idea*) |
|---|---|
| A. Mudaliar Commission | I. Comprehensive programme for teacher education through DIET |
| B. National Education Commission | II. School internship model of 6-10 weeks in a 2-year programme and 15-20 weeks in 4-year programme |

| | | |
|---|---|---|
| C. NPE (1986) | III. | Multi track education at secondary level |
| D. NCFTE (2009) | IV. | Teacher undoubtedly the most important person for education and national development |

Choose the ***correct*** answer from the options given below:

1. A-IV, B-III, C-II, D-I
2. A-I, B-II, C-IV, D-III
3. A-III, B-II, C-IV, D-I
4. A-III, B-IV, C-I, D-II

**15.** F-ratio is:

1. Ratio of the average variability of scores within each group to the variation in the mean of each group from the total or grand mean of all groups.
2. Ratio of the variation in the mean of each group from the total or grand mean of all groups to the average variability of scores within each group.
3. Ratio of the average variability of scores within each group to the between group variance.
4. Ratio of the within group variance to the between group variance.

**16.** Curriculum that emphasizes student choice, self-actualization and happiness in learning reflects:

1. Behavioristic Perspective
2. Cognitive Perspective
3. Humanistic Perspective
4. Sociocultural Perspective

**17.** Arrange the elements of a Model of Teaching in sequence:

A. Syntax
B. Focus
C. Evaluation
D. Support system
E. Social system

Choose the ***correct*** answer from the options given below:

1. B, A, D, E, C
2. B, A, E, D, C
3. C, B, A, D, E
4. A, B, C, E, D

**18.** Bruner has specified four features that a theory of instruction must have, which one of the following is NOT amongst them?

1. Predisposition to Learn
2. Structure of Knowledge
3. Sequence of Instruction
4. Evaluation

**19.** Arrange the following experimental designs in order of highest control of 'threats to internal validity' to lowest control:

A. Time Series Design
B. Static-Group Comparison Design
C. Solomon Four-Group Design
D. One-Shot Case Study
E. One-Group Pretest-Posttest Design

Choose the ***correct*** answer from the options given below:

1. D, E, B, A, C
2. C, E, A, B, D
3. B, D, A, E, C
4. C, A, B, E, D

**20.** Match the List-I with List-II.

| **List-I** (***National Institutes***) | **List-II** (***Cities where they are situated***) |
|---|---|
| A. National Institute for for Rehabilitation, Training and Research (NIRTAR) | I. Chennai |
| B. National Institute for Empowerment of Persons with Multiple Disabilities (NIEPMD) | II. Kolkata |
| C. National Institute for the Empowerment of Persons with Intellectual Disabilities (NIEPID) | III. Cuttack |
| D. National Institute for the Orthopedically Handicapped (NIOH) | IV. Secundrabad |

Choose the *correct* answer from the options given below:

1. A-III, B-I, C-II, D-IV
2. A-I, B-III, C-II, D-IV
3. A-I, B-III, C-IV, D-II
4. A-III, B-I, C-IV, D-II

**21.** Match the List-I with List-II.

| List-I (*Educational Philosophy)* | List-II (*Curriculum Focus*) |
|---|---|
| A. Perennialism | I. Examination of social, economic and political problems, equality of educational opportunity |
| B. Progressivism | II. Constant curriculum, classical subjects, literary analysis |
| C. Essentialism | III. Interdisciplinary subject matter, activities and projects |
| D. Reconstructionism | IV. Mastering the skills, facts and concepts, back to basics movement |

Choose the *correct* answer from the options given below:

1. A-III, B-IV, C-II, D-I
2. A-IV, B-III, C-I, D-II
3. A-I, B-IV, C-III, D-II
4. A-II, B-III, C-IV, D-I

**22.** Which of the following statements is are true?

A. Section 29 of the RTE Act indicates teaching learning through activities.

B. Section 29 of the RTE Act indicates teaching learning through project method only.

C. Section 29 of the RTE Act indicates teaching learning through discovery.

D. Section 29 of the RTE Act indicates teaching learning through exploration.

E. Section 29 of the RTE Act suggests teaching learning in mother tongue.

Choose the *correct* answer from the options given below:

1. A, B, C, D only
2. B, C, D, E only
3. C, D, E, A only
4. D, E, A, B only

**23.** Arrange the following steps as per the Rational Emotive Behaviour Therapy (REBT):

A. Consequences B. Disputing

C. Effect D. Belief system

E. Activating agent

Choose the *correct* answer from the options given below:

1. E, D, B, A, C 2. D, B, A, C, E

3. B, A, C, D, E 4. E, D, A, B, C

**24.** Which statements of the following are true about Spearman-Brown prophecy formula?

A. In the split half method, the reliability coefficient of the whole test can be estimated with the help of reliability coefficient of the half test by using this formula.

B. This formula may be used to estimate the reliability of ratings as well as test scores.

C. It cannot be used to estimate the reliability of paired comparisons.

D. It cannot be used to obtain the effect on reliability by lengthening or repeating a test.

Choose the *correct* answer from the options given below:

1. A and B only 2. B and C only

3. C and D only 4. B and D only

**25.** In case study research the most common form of sampling is:

1. Incidental sampling
2. Snowball sampling
3. Quota sampling
4. Purposive sampling

**26.** Match the List-I with List-II.

| **List-I** (*Type of Ethnography*) | **List-II** (*Characteristics*) |
|---|---|
| A. Realist Ethnography | I. A report of the ethnographer's fieldwork experiences |
| B. Confessional Ethnography | II. A study of the shared patterns of a marginalized group with the aim of advocacy |
| C. Micro-ethnography | III. An objective, scientifically written ethnography |
| D. Critical Ethnography | IV. A study focused on a specific aspect of a cultural group and setting |

Choose the ***correct*** answer from the options given below:

1. A-II, B-III, C-IV, D-I
2. A-I, B-III, C-IV, D-II
3. A-IV, B-I, C-II, D-III
4. A-III, B-I, C-IV, D-II

**27.** Within 'change management' and the cost of quality framework', which of the following combination is correct?

1. Appraisal costs = internal failures such as rework, scrap and downtime
2. Failure costs = only external; exclude warranty claims or customer complaints
3. Cost-Benefit Analysis differs from Cost-Effective Analysis because it measures only qualitative outcome
4. Preventable costs = proactive investments in training, error proofing and system redesign

**28.** Given below are two statements: one is labelled as Assertion (A) and the other is labelled as Reason (R).

**Assertion (A):** SSA and RMSA were closed in 2018.

**Reason (R):** Because the World Bank stopped funding these programmes.

In the light of the above statements, choose the ***most appropriate*** answer from the options given below:

1. Both (A) and (R) are correct and (R) is the correct explanation of (A)
2. Both (A) and (R) are correct, but (R) is NOT the correct explanation of (A)
3. (A) is correct, but (R) is not correct
4. (A) is not correct, but (R) is correct

**29.** Which of the following is not proposed by E.L. Thorndike?

1. The principle of multiple response
2. The principle of equilibration
3. The principle of assimilation
4. The principle of partial activity

**30.** Which statement best distinguishes psychological testing from psychological assessment in practice?

1. Testing synthesizes multiple data sources; assessment is a single standardized instrument
2. Assessment synthesizes data from tests, history and observations to support interpretations; testing is administering one
3. Testing requires theory; assessment is atheoretical
4. Assessment excludes standardized tests by definition

**31.** In the Universal Design for Learning guidelines, which of these is a principle (not just a check point)?

1. Optimize choice and autonomy
2. Multiple means of expression
3. Provide options for perception
4. Nurture joy and play

**32.** In behavioural assessment, explanations should prioritize:

1. Functional relation between environmental events and behaviour with direct evidence
2. Diagnostic labels inferred from traits
3. Personality typologies for parsimony
4. Single - informant reports to reduce bias

**33.** Phoenix Farm and Tolstoy Farm can be associated with:

1. Jiddu Krishnamurti
2. Sri Aurobindo
3. John Dewey
4. M.K. Gandhi

**34.** Arrange the following Instructional Design Models in chronological order of their year of development:

A. ADDIE Model
B. Dick and Carey Model
C. Gagne's Nine Events of Instruction
D. 5Es Model of constructivism

Choose the ***correct*** answer from the options given below:

1. A, C, B, D
2. C, A, B, D
3. C, D, A, B
4. A, C, D, B

**35.** For NAAC accreditation cycles, which of the following is explicitly cited as a minimum institutional requirement for going in for second and subsequent cycles?

1. Submission of SSR only; IQAC is optional
2. Only achieving $B^+$ or above in previous cycle
3. Functional IQAC and timely submission of AQAR
4. Participation in NIRF ranking in the intervening years

**36.** Match the List-I with List-II.

| **List-I** (***Concerns***) | **List-II** (***RTE Act Section***) |
|---|---|
| A. Special Training | I. Section 31 |
| B. Additional Function of National Commission for Protection of Child Rights | II. Section 17 |
| C. School Management Committee | III. Section 4 |
| D. Prohibition of Physical Punishment | IV. Section 21 |

Choose the ***correct*** answer from the options given below:

1. A-II, B-IV, C-III, D-I
2. A-IV, B-II, C-I, D-III
3. A-III, B-I, C-IV, D-II
4. A-I, B-III, C-II, D-IV

**37.** Which of the following book is authored by Jean Piaget?

1. Frames of Mind
2. The Language and Thoughts of the Child
3. The Behaviour of Organisms
4. Cognition and Knowledge

**38.** Vygotsky's concept of private speech refers to:

1. Children's self-talk that guide thinking and action.
2. Internal dialogue that essentially remains without getting vocalised.
3. Secret peer conversation during group learning activities.
4. Secret talk with the teacher in order to avoid embarrassment due to over attention of the peer group.

**39.** In Islamic education, the degree awarded to one who has the special knowledge in religion is ______ and ______ to those who showed excellence in logic.

1. Alim and Fazil
2. Fazil and Alim
3. Talib and Maulvi
4. Maulvi and Talim

**40.** Match the List-I with List-II.

| List-I (*Concept*) | List-II (*Philosophy*) |
|---|---|
| A. Panch-sheel | I. Upnishad |
| B. Panch-kosh | II. Yoga |
| C. Panch-Mahabhut | III. Jainism |
| D. Panch-Mahavrat | IV. Buddhism |

Choose the *correct* answer from the options given below:

1. A-IV, B-II, C-III, D-I
2. A-IV, B-I, C-II, D-III
3. A-III, B-II, C-I, D-IV
4. A-III, B-I, C-IV, D-II

**41.** Which of the following is a CABE sub-committee report?

1. Learning Without Burden
2. Chattopadhayay Committee Report
3. Verma Committee Report
4. Assessment and Implementation of CCE in the context of No Detention Provision

**42.** Arrange the following types of learning in hierarchical order from lower to higher level as proposed by Robert Gagne:

A. S-R learning
B. Chain learning
C. Verbal association
D. Learning of concepts
E. Multiple discrimination

Choose the *correct* answer from the options given below:

1. B, A, C, D, E
2. C, A, B, D, E
3. A, B, C, E, D
4. A, C, B, D, E

**43.** Pick the correct statements:

A. Vedic Studies centers Ghatikas were located all over North India.
B. Nalanda was a Buddhist center of learning.
C. Nalanda received the royal patronage of Hindu Gupta Kings as well as Buddhist Kings like Ashoka and Harsha.
D. The upnayana for women held at the same age that of men.
E. The process of learning in Vedic education is demarcated as Shravan, Manan, Aparigrah and Asteyam.

Choose the *correct* answer from the options given below:

1. A, B, C, D and E
2. B, C and D only
3. A and E only
4. A, B and C only

**44.** Arrange the following chronologically by the year they were launched:

A. DPEP
B. SSA
C. Samagra Shiksha
D. RMSA
E. Navodaya Vidyalaya

Choose the *correct* answer from the options given below:

1. E, D, A, C, B 2. A, B, C, D, E
3. E, A, B, D, C 4. B, A, E, C, D

**45.** Given below are two statements: one is labelled as Assertion (A) and the other is labelled as Reason (R).

**Assertion (A):** Ecological child assessment requires data from multiple informants and settings to capture how behaviour varies across contexts.

**Reason (R):** Children often show marked variability across time and situations: relying on a single informant or setting risks invalid inferences.

In the light of the above statements, choose the *most appropriate* answer from the options given below

1. Both (A) and (R) are correct and (R) is the correct explanation of (A)
2. Both (A) and (R) are correct, but (R) is NOT the correct explanation of (A)
3. (A) is correct, but (R) is not correct
4. (A) is not correct, but (R) is correct

**46.** Match the List-I with List-II.

| List-I (*Taxonomy of Domain Levels*) | List-II (*Activity*) |
|---|---|
| A. Knowledge | I. Use abstraction in novel situations |
| B. Comprehension | II. Recall of specific facts/terms |
| C. Application | III. Translate/express in different form or level of abstraction |
| D. Analysis | IV. Identify relationship/relevance/consistency among parts |

Choose the *correct* answer from the options given below:

1. A-II, B-I, C-III, D-IV
2. A-I, B-III, C-II, D-IV
3. A-II, B-III, C-I, D-IV
4. A-IV, B-II, C-I, D-III

**47.** As per the guideline of SSA framework of 2011, what is the suggested duration of in-service teacher education (Annual) for a working teacher at Elementary level.

1. 10 days
2. 20 days
3. 50 hours
4. 100 hours

**48.** According to Ralph Tyler's Curriculum Development Model the identified general objectives should be refined by filtering them through:

1. Philosophy and Sociology of school
2. School's Philosophy and Psychology of learning
3. Psychology and Sociology of learning
4. Psychology and Spirituality of learning

**49.** Calfee and Masuda argue that 'assessment as inquiry' is best characterized as which of the following?

1. A linear sequence of planning → testing → reporting
2. A static appraisal primarily for accountability
3. An interactive, cyclic process - 'a roller coaster more than an elevator'
4. A one time diagnostic preceding instruction

**50.** Match the List-I with List-II.

| List-I (*Role of Education*) | List-II (*Perspective*) |
|---|---|
| A. Transmission of society's norms and values | I. Marxist |
| B. To foster overall development and to develop talents to the full | II. Functionalist |
| C. To transmit the general ruling class ideology | III. Cultural Deprivation |
| D. Uniform state education would not provide everyone with equal chance. | IV. Liberalist |

Choose the *correct* answer from the options given below:

1. A-II, B-III, C-IV, D-I
2. A-IV, B-I, C-III, D-II
3. A-IV, B-II, C-III, D-I
4. A-II, B-IV, C-I, D-III

**51.** Which of the following correctly represent the uses of ICT in educational evaluation?

A. Automatic test item generation and adaptive testing based on learners previous response.
B. Ensuring instant feedback and analytics through Learning Management Software.
C. Replacing all human judgement by AI based assessment engines for objective and subjective answers.
D. Supporting e-portfolio creation and continuous performance tracking over time.
E. Facilitating large scale online examinations with proctoring and security features.

Choose the ***correct*** answer from the options given below:

1. A, B, C & D only
2. A, B, C & E only
3. A, B, D & E only
4. A, C, D & E only

**52.** Which of the following best illustrates the relationship between learning theories and instructional strategies for a large group in a formal setting?

1. Reciprocal peer tutoring based on Vygotsky's Social Constructivism.
2. Mastery learning modules with formative tests based on Bloom's taxonomy.
3. Programmed learning packages based on Skinner's Operant Conditioning.
4. Experiential project work in small groups based on Kolb's learning cycle.

**53.** Arrange the following five sheaths of consciousness in chronological order:

A. Pranamaya B. Anandmaya
C. Annamaya D. Vijnanmaya
E. Manomaya

Choose the ***correct*** answer from the options given below:

1. C, B, D, A, E 2. A, B, C, E, D
3. C, A, E, D, B 4. A, E, C, D, B

**54.** Choose the characteristics of cooperative learning:

A. For effective cooperative learning, there should be both group goals and individual accountability
B. It emphasizes that learning takes place better in a heterogenous small group environment
C. The notion of cooperative learning is rooted in Bandura's social learning theory only
D. It advocates constructivist perspective for better teaching learning outcomes
E. It provides rigidity in terms of scheduling and grouping

Choose the ***correct*** answer from the options given below:

1. A, B & E only 2. A, C & D only
3. A, B & D only 4. B, D & C only

**55.** Given below are two statements: one is labelled as Assertion (A) and the other is labelled as Reason (R).

**Assertion (A):** In educational management, controlling is closely related to planning.

**Reason (R):** Because controlling ensures the progress of assigned work moves according to the plan, using feedback and collective actions whenever deviation occurs.

In the light of the above statements, choose the ***most appropriate*** answer from the options given below:

1. Both (A) and (R) are correct and (R) is the correct explanation of (A)
2. Both (A) and (R) are correct, but (R) is NOT the correct explanation of A
3. A is correct, but (R) is not correct
4. A is not correct, but (R) is correct

**56.** Which statement appropriately reflects Quality Council of India's (QCI) core mandate relevant to educational quality assurance in India?

1. QCI acts as the national body to develop and operate accreditation programme aligned with international standards
2. QCI directly accredits universities under UGC and issues NAAC grades
3. QCI solely publishes periodical, it has no operational role in accreditation
4. QCI evaluates school brands' curricula and awards CGPA to schools

**57.** Given below are two statements: one is labelled as **Assertion (A)** and the other is labelled as **Reason (R)**.

**Assertion (A):** The Kothari Commission recommended work-experience as an integral part of general education across school stages.

**Reason (R):** Value of work-experience lies in linking education to productivity and modernization so it should be progressively extended to all school.

In the light of the above statements, choose the ***most appropriate*** answer from the options given below:

1. Both (A) and (R) are correct and (R) is the correct explanation of (A)
2. Both (A) and (R) are correct, but (R) is NOT the correct explanation of (A)
3. (A) is correct, but (R) is not correct
4. (A) is not correct, but (R) is correct

**58.** Match the List-I with List-II.

| **List-I** ***(Components of Divergent Thinking/ Cognitive Process)*** | **List-II** ***(Description)*** |
|---|---|
| A. Fluency | I. Enriching an idea by adding details |
| B. Flexibility | II. Producing unique response |
| C. Originality | III. Shifting to alternative ways of thinking |
| D. Elaboration | IV. Producing many ideas |

Choose the ***correct*** answer from the options given below:

1. A-III, B-II, C-I, D-IV
2. A-II, B-III, C-IV, D-I
3. A-IV, B-II, C-I, D-III
4. A-IV, B-III, C-II, D-I

**59.** Arrange the following in order to original Demins's TQM 14 philosophy:

A. Cease dependence on mass inspection
B. Adopt a new philosophy
C. End the practice of conducting business on cost alone
D. Create constancy of purpose
E. Constantly improve processes

Choose the ***correct*** answer from the options given below:

1. B, D, A, C, E
2. D, A, B, E, C
3. D, A, B, C, E
4. D, B, A, C, E

**60.** Which committee or commission recommended to hold single public examination only after completion of secondary education?

1. Mudaliar Commission
2. Verma Commission
3. Kothari Commission
4. Acharya Narendra Dev Committee

**61.** Given below are two statements: one is labelled as Assertion (A) and the other is labelled as Reason (R).

**Assertion (A):** The concept of the single variable provided a sound approach to experimentation in the behavioural sciences.

**Reason (R):** The earliest assumptions of experimental research were based on what was known as the 'law of the single variable'.

In the light of the above statements, choose the ***most appropriate*** answer from the options given below

1. Both (A) and (R) are correct and (R) is the correct explanation of (A)
2. Both (A) and (R) are correct, but (R) is NOT the correct explanation of (A)
3. (A) is correct, but (R) is not correct
4. (A) is not correct, but (R) is correct

**62.** A teacher is designing an online module where learners watch a short video, attempt a quiz, receive automated feedback and then engage in a discussion forum. Which instructional design principle is most clearly demonstrated in the above context?

1. Computer Assised Instruction
2. Programmed Instruction
3. Masteiy Learning
4. Computer Managed Learning

**63.** According to NCFTE (2009), the then existing one-year B.Ed. should be:

1. Retained without change
2. Transformed to a two years programme
3. Replaced with additional 6 month school experience
4. Transformed to four year programme

**64.** Which of the following about the evaluation question proposed by Talmage are correct?

A. The question of idealization value asks - what is the curriculum good for?
B. The question of instrumental value addresses ways to improve a curriculum.
C. The question of intrinsic value deals with both planned and finished curriculum.
D. The question of comparative value asks - is the proposed new programme better than the one it is supposed to replace?
E. The question of decision value deals with whether to retain, modify or discard the new programme.

Choose the ***correct*** answer from the options given below:

1. A, B, E only 2. B, C, D only
3. C, D, E only 4. A, C, D only

**65.** Justice Verma Commission (2012) was constituted in the backdrop of:

1. Irregularities in teacher education through distance mode
2. Irregularities in the admissions of teacher education institutions
3. Irregularities in recognition of teacher education institutions
4. Irregularities in the appointment of teachers

**66.** Which of the following statements are correct?

A. In POSDCORB: P stands for Planning
B. In POSDCORB: S stands for Staffing
C. In POSDCORB: CO stands for Co-ordinating
D. In POSDCORB: R stands for Recording
E. In POSDCORB; B stands for Bench-marking

Choose the ***correct*** answer from the options given below:

1. B, C & D only 2. A, B & C only
3. C, D & E only 4. A, C & E only

**67.** Which of the following pair is NOT a category of Intelligence proposed by Howard Gardner?

1. Spatial & Logical Mathematical
2. Musical & Motivational
3. Interpersonal & Bodily-Kinesthetic
4. Linguistic & Intrapersonal

**68.** Which of the following statement(s) is/are correct?

A. Bodily-Kinesthetic intelligence is one type of Gardner's intelligence
B. Sternberg's theory includes analytical and naturalistic intelligence
C. Analytical intelligence in Sternberg's model involves academic skills and problem solving
D. Creative intelligence in Gardner's theory deals with solving new problems through insight
E. Sternberg's practical intelligence involves to live and work in a context where success is likely and adapting to that context

Choose the ***correct*** answer from the options given below:

1. A, B & E only 2. B, C & D only
3. A, C & E only 4. A, B & D only

**69.** Scientific management's epistemic claim in education administration is most accurately described as which of the following?

1. It treats leadership knowledge as contingent, context dependent praxis rather than objective technique.
2. It promotes the view that leadership knowledge is objective and that specific managerial behaviours reliably produce valuable 'true' results.

3. It rejects the measurability of managerial behaviour in favour of moral judgement.
4. It assumes teacher discretion is superior to any standardized managerial routine.

**70.** Under IEDSS (Inclusive Education for Disabled at Secondary Stage), 2009 financial provisions, the stipend for girl students with disability had an upper limit of:

1. ₹ 100/month 2. ₹ 150/month
3. ₹ 200/month 4. ₹ 250/month

**71.** Match the List-I with List-II.

| List-I (*Theorist*) | List-II (*Theory*) |
|---|---|
| A. Schulman | I. Expansion of knowledge base |
| B. Habermas | II. Pedagogical content knowledge as core of teacher knowledge |
| C. Krishna Kumar | III. Teacher as a meek dictator |
| D. Deng & Luke | IV. Knowledge - constitutive interest and teaching practice, emancipation |

Choose the ***correct*** answer from the options given below:

1. A-IV, B-I, C-III, D-II
2. A-III, B-IV, C-II, D-I
3. A-I, B-II, C-IV, D-III
4. A-II, B-IV, C-III, D-I

**72.** If an e-leaming platform is evaluated using D & MIS model, which of the following would NOT be a part of evaluation?

1. System quality
2. Service quality
3. Pedagogical theories used
4. Net benefits

**73.** Which of the following is NOT one of the 'Panch Mahavrata'?

1. Ahimsa 2. Brahmacharya
3. Yogasana 4. Satya

**74.** Which of the following is NOT true about 'life situation design' of curriculum?

1. students see the relevance of content if it is organized around aspects of community life
2. this design focuses on problem-solving procedures
3. it falls under learner centered design
4. this design is aligned with the idea of Spencer's curriculum for complete living

**75.** Given below are two statements: one is labelled as Assertion (A) and the other is labelled as Reason (R).

**Assertion (A):** Panini and Chanakya are the most famous products of the Nalanda University.

**Reason (R):** Nalanda had a defined procedure of admitting students, and had a splendid library.

In the light of the above statements, choose the ***most appropriate*** answer from the options given below:

1. Both (A) and (R) are correct and (R) is the correct explanation of (A)
2. Both (A) and (R) are correct, but (R) is NOT the correct explanation of (A)
3. (A) is correct, but (R) is not correct
4. (A) is not correct, but (R) is correct

**76.** Given below are two statements: one is labelled as Assertion (A) and the other is labelled as Reason (R).

**Assertion (A):** Educational guidance is prescriptive and remedial in nature to solve the problems faced by students in schools.

**Reason (R):** It's aim is to provide assistance to pupils in their choices and adjustment with relation to school, curriculum and school life.

In the light of the above statements, choose the *most appropriate* answer from the options given below:

1. Both (A) and (R) are correct and (R) is the correct explanation of (A)
2. Both A and R are correct, but (R) is NOT the correct explanation of (A)
3. (A) is correct, but (R) is not correct
4. (A) is not correct, but (R) is correct

**77.** Which phase of CIPP Model focuses on the question - Are the objectives stated appropriately?

1. Context
2. Input
3. Process
4. Product

**78.** During the year 2014 NCTE proposed new norms and regulations for:

A. Two year B.Ed.
B. Two year M.Phil. in Teacher Education
C. Two year M.Ed.
D. Two year B.Ed. through Open and Distance Learning System
E. Two year B.El.Ed.

Choose the *correct* answer from the options given below:

1. C, D, E only
2. A, C, D only
3. E, A, C only
4. A, B, C only

**79.** Which of the following is NOT true about errors in measurement?

1. chance errors and constant errors are not same.
2. constant errors raise or lower all the scores on a test.
3. constant errors affect the reliability coefficient.
4. chance errors are by definition independent and uncorrelated.

**80.** Given below are two statements: one is labelled as Assertion (A) and the other is labelled as Reason (R).

**Assertion (A):** Attitudinal barriers among teachers and school administrators are the most significant challenges to implementing inclusive education.

**Reason (R):** Structural and infrastructural changes in schools are easier to bring about than shifts in deep seated beliefs and prejudices amongst teachers.

In the light of the above statements, choose the *most appropriate* answer from the options given below

1. Both (A) and (R) are correct and (R) is the correct explanation of (A)
2. Both (A) and (R) are correct, but (R) is NOT the correct explanation of (A)
3. (A) is correct, but (R) is not correct
4. (A) is not correct, but (R) is correct

**81.** Arrange the following tests/concepts related to projective techniques in chronological order (oldest to newest).

A. Introduction of the term 'Projective Method' by Frank
B. The Holtzman Inkblot Test
C. The Rorschach Test
D. Word-Association Test by Galton
E. Thematic Apperception Test

Choose the *correct* answer from the options given below:

1. A, E, C, B, D
2. D, C, E, A, B
3. A, D, C, E, B
4. C, A, E, B, D

**82.** Which policy for the very first time used the term 'Child Centric Education' in India?

1. NPE 1968
2. NPE 1978 (Draft)
3. NPE 1986
4. NEP 2020

**83.** Match the List-I with List-II.

| List-I (*Dimension of Curriculum Design*) | List-II (*Description*) |
|---|---|
| A. Continuity | I. Horizontal relationship among topics and themes from all knowledge domains |
| B. Integration | II. Vertical repetition of curriculum component |
| C. Articulation | III. Depth and breadth of content of the curriculum |
| D. Scope | IV. Vertical and horizontal inter-relatedness of various aspects of the curriculum |

Choose the ***correct*** answer from the options given below:

1. A-I, B-II, C-IV, D-III
2. A-II, B-I, C-IV, D-III
3. A-I, B-II, C-III, D-IV
4. A-IV, B-I, C-III, D-II

**84.** The RPwD Act (2016) expanded the number of recognized disabilities from:

1. 5 to 15
2. 7 to 21
3. 10 to 25
4. 12 to 30

**85.** Match the List-I with List-II.

| List-I (*Concept of Cognitivism*) | List-II (*Primary Focus*) |
|---|---|
| A. Information Processing Model | I. Stresses managing intrinsic, extraneous and germane load for effective instruction |
| B. Schema Theory | II. Emphasizes sensory register, short term memory and long term memory |
| C. Cognitive Load Theory | III. Focuses on how prior knowledge structures influence new learning |
| D. Dual Coding Theory | IV. Suggests information is stored in verbal and visual channels, aiding recall |

Choose the ***correct*** answer from the options given below:

1. A-III, B-II, C-I, D-IV
2. A-I, B-II, C-III, D-IV
3. A-II, B-III, C-I, D-IV
4. A-III, B-II, C-IV, D-I

**86.** To put the students of an inclusive class in situations like - to work out the solution of a problematic situation and to construct, create and produce something new, is related with which kind of teaching-learning?

1. Reflective teaching
2. Cooperative learning
3. Co-teaching
4. Brainstorming

**87.** Arrange the following levels in sequence as per the D.L. Kirkpatrick's model of curriculum.

A. Learning
B. Behaviour/Transfer
C. Reaction
D. Results

Choose the ***correct*** answer from the options given below:

1. A, B, C, D
2. C, A, B, D
3. A, D, C, B
4. B, A, D, C

**88.** Following statements describe key milestones in the development of e-leaming. Arrange them in correct chronological order fiom the earliest to the most recent:

A. The open university in Britain leverages the internet to move beyond mail based material

B. Programmed Logic for Automated Teaching Operations (PLATO) is introduced as the first computer based training programme

C. Shareable Content Object Response Model (SCORM) is developed as a standard requirement for major organizations

D. Harvard and MIT begin offering free online classes through platforms like Coursera

E. Business houses begin to widely adopt e-learning for corporate training recognizing its cost effectiveness

Choose the ***correct*** answer from the options given below:

1. A, B, C, D, E 2. B, A, E, C, D
3. B, A, C, D, E 4. A, B, E, C, D

**89.** In a two-tailed test, for a particular degree of freedom, if a null hypothesis could not be rejected at 0.01 level of significance, then at 0.05 level of significance, this null hypothesis

1. will be rejected definitely
2. will not be rejected definitely
3. may or may not be rejected
4. the level of significance does not play any role in null hypothesis testing

**90.** Arrange the following as per revised Bloom's Taxonomy (2001):

A. Creating B. Analyzing
C. Applying D. Understanding
E. Evaluating

Choose the ***correct*** answer from the options given below:

1. A, C, B, E, D 2. D, B, C, A, E
3. C, D, B, E, A 4. D, C, B, E, A

**Directions (Qs. No. 91 to 95):** *Read the following paragraph and answer the questions:*

Colonial educational policy should not be equated with Macaulay's 1835 Minute on Education, though that is done quite often. The Minute had denounced Indian cultures for their alleged poverty and suggested that Western texts alone should be taught at the higher levels of education, primarily through the English language. There were, actually, numerous variations across time and space. The medium of the English language was established only after a bitter debate among Company officials who struggled hard to overcome the opposition of the Orientalists (in the narrower sense of that word) among them. The latter had not wanted the particularly lavish sum of ₹ 1 lakh, assigned to education by the Charter Act of 1813, to be spent on Sanskrit and Perso-Arabic institutions alone. The best-known Indian intervention in that debate, by Rammohan Roy in 1823, clearly wanted a combination of the English medium with emphasis upon scientific education in ways very different from Macaulay's preference for 'liberal', literary training. There were also some advocates for a development of the vernacular media. Notable instances would include William Adam in late 1830s Bengal, he being the author of a famous report on indigenous education: the Company-funded Delhi College in pre-1857 Delhi, which used the Urdu medium and encouraged vernacular translations of books on Western science: the effort to promote vernacular primary education in Urdu and Hindi by Lieutenant Governor Thomson of the North-Western Provinces in the 1850s; and the initial support given by some Bengal official to Iswarchandra Vidyasagar's drive for popular education through the Bengali medium and his founding of some girls' schools in that decade.

**91.** 'Company' in the given passage refers to:

1. Company of all European nations
2. Conipany of English speaking people
3. Company of Queen Elizabeth
4. East India Company

**92.** William Adam, who encouraged vernacular primary education can be hailed as:

1. Benevolent Individual
2. Orientalist
3. Nationalist
4. Christian Missionary

**93.** Raja Ram Mohan Roy advocated education with scientific thrust because:

1. he wanted to counter Macaulay and Woods
2. that alongwith English medium would have liberated and emancipated Indians

3. that would have made better clerks
4. that would have brought English mannerism in Indians

**94.** Orientalists (in narrower sense) means:
1. The individual against education and schooling system of the colonizers
2. The western individual oriented towards Queen rather than the native Kings
3. The one who studies, values and advocates eastern/native's culture, language and art etc
4. The western individual against imperialism and colonialism

**95.** Colonial Education here refers to:
1. The education system evolved by the colonizers to assimilate the colonized.
2. The education system that was prevalent when India got colonized
3. The education system in the country of the colonizer
4. The education system all colonizers had uniformity all over the world

**Directions (Qs. No. 96 to 100):** *Read the following paragraph and answer the questions:*

The term *science* may be thought of as an approach to the gathering of knowledge rather than as a field or subject matter. Science, put simply, consists of two primary functions: (1) the development of theory and (2) the testing of substantive hypotheses that are deduced from theory. The scientist, therefore, is engaged in the use. modification, and/or creation of theory. The scientist may emphasize an empirical approach in which data collection is the primary method, a rational approach in which logical and deductive reasoning is primary, or a combination of these approaches, which is most common. Regardless of the emphasis the scientist begins with a set of ideas that direct the effort and with a goal that entails the development or testing of theory.

By attempting to apply the rigorous, systematic observation analysis used in the physical and biological sciences to areas of social behavior, the social sciences have grown and have advanced humanity's knowledge of itself. The fields of anthropology, economics, education, political science, psychology, and social psychology have become recognized as sciences by many authorities. To the extent that these fields are founded on scientific methodology, they are sciences. Some reject this concept, still defining science in terms of subject matter rather than methodology. Historically their position can be readily explained. Because scientific methods were first used in the investigation of physical phenomena, tradition has identified science with the physical world. Only within the last century has the methodology of science been applied to the study of various areas of human behavior. Because these are newer areas of investigation, their results have not achieved the acceptance and status that come with the greater maturity and longer tradition of the physical sciences.

The uniformity of nature is a reasonable assumption in the world of physical objects and their characteristics, but in the area of social behavior such assumptions are not warranted. Human nature is much more complex than the sum of its many discrete elements, even if they could be isolated and identified. Because human nature is so complex, it is much more difficult to develop sound theories of human behavior than to predict occurrences in the physical world.

**96.** Why prediction of human behaviour is not easy?
1. because human behaviour is the sum total of many discrete elements
2. because it is a newer area of investigation
3. because scientific methodologies can be applied in physical and biological sciences only
4. because human nature is complex

**97.** Which of the following statement is CORRECT according to the paragraph?
1. Scientists use scientific approach for creation of new theories only
2. Commonly, scientists combine rational approach and empirical approach in scientific inquiry

3. Deductive reasoning is always primary in scientific approach
4. Opting between empirical approach or deductive reasoning is mandatory in scientific inquiry

**98.** Applying the approaches of gathering knowledge in physical and biological sciences to the social sciences:
1. has reduced the domain of social sciences
2. has changed the nature of social behaviour by making it uniform
3. has helped in growing up of social sciences
4. should not be promoted to maintain objectivity

**99.** Scientific method has been applied to the study of various areas of human behaviour
1. as an approach to the gathering of knowledge
2. as a field or subject matter
3. to make the study interdisciplinary
4. for observation of the clinica1/biological aspects only

**100.** The assumption of the uniformity of nature in the world of physical objects:
1. makes use of science easy in the areas of social behaviour
2. makes generalizations reasonable in the physical world
3. helped the fields of anthropology and education to be recognized as sciences
4. cannot be tested and verified

## ANSWERS

| 1 | 2 | 3 | 4 | 5 | 6 | 7 | 8 | 9 | 10 |
|---|---|---|---|---|---|---|---|---|---|
| 2 | 2 | 1 | 4 | 4 | 3 | 1 | 3 | 4 | 2 |
| **11** | **12** | **13** | **14** | **15** | **16** | **17** | **18** | **19** | **20** |
| 2 | 4 | 4 | 4 | 2 | 3 | 2 | 4 | 4 | 4 |
| **21** | **22** | **23** | **24** | **25** | **26** | **27** | **28** | **29** | **30** |
| 4 | 3 | 4 | 1 | 4 | 4 | 4 | 2 | 2 | 2 |
| **31** | **32** | **33** | **34** | **35** | **36** | **37** | **38** | **39** | **40** |
| 2 | 1 | 4 | 2 | 3 | 3 | 2 | 1 | 1 | 2 |
| **41** | **42** | **43** | **44** | **45** | **46** | **47** | **48** | **49** | **50** |
| 4 | 3 | 2 | 3 | 1 | 3 | 2 | 2 | 3 | 4 |
| **51** | **52** | **53** | **54** | **55** | **56** | **57** | **58** | **59** | **60** |
| 3 | 3 | 3 | 3 | 1 | 1 | 1 | 4 | 4 | 1 |
| **61** | **62** | **63** | **64** | **65** | **66** | **67** | **68** | **69** | **70** |
| 4 | 3 | 2 | 3 | 3 | 2 | 2 | 3 | 2 | 3 |
| **71** | **72** | **73** | **74** | **75** | **76** | **77** | **78** | **79** | **80** |
| 4 | 3 | 3 | 3 | 4 | 4 | 2 | 2 | 3 | 1 |
| **81** | **82** | **83** | **84** | **85** | **86** | **87** | **88** | **89** | **90** |
| 2 | 3 | 2 | 2 | 3 | 1 | 2 | 2 | 3 | 4 |
| **91** | **92** | **93** | **94** | **95** | **96** | **97** | **98** | **99** | **100** |
| 4 | 2 | 2 | 3 | 1 | 4 | 2 | 3 | 1 | 2 |

# EXPLANATORY ANSWERS

1. This follows the classic PDCA (Plan–Do–Check–Act) improvement cycle used in management and quality assurance—
   - **A–III (Plan):** Planning means deciding objectives, priorities, roles, timelines, and strategies before work begins. It is the stage where "what will be done and how it will be done" is finalised at the appropriate level.
   - **B–I (Do):** Doing means executing what was planned in real conditions, not merely discussing it. It includes building coordination and trust so the plan actually gets implemented on the ground.
   - **C–IV (Check):** Checking is about measuring and verifying performance against what was intended. It requires collecting and analysing evidence/data (both during the process and at the end) to judge implementation.
   - **D–II (Act):** Acting means taking corrective and improvement steps using what the checking stage revealed. It may involve mid-course corrections while work is ongoing or improvements for the next cycle after completion.

2. Loyd & Loyd's principles emphasise clarity, communication, and fairness in grading so that grading reflects actual achievement. Forcing grades into a fixed normal distribution is a norm-referenced "curving" approach that can distort real performance and is not a guiding principle of fair, transparent grading.

   Such a rule can make grades depend on relative rank rather than demonstrated learning outcomes, even when most learners genuinely perform well.

   It can also undermine equity because the distribution is fixed first, and student performance is fitted into it afterward.

3. The flow is from needs/inputs → annual planning → module development → training delivery + support → monitoring feedback loop—

   **C. Inputs from DIETs/BRCs/CRCs:** The planning begins by gathering field-level needs, gaps, and suggestions from the implementing academic structures. This ensures training priorities are grounded in classroom realities and local support requirements.

   **E. SCERT combined annual in-service calendar:** Once needs are consolidated, the state-level body structures the year's schedule and coverage plan. This step sequences trainings across time and locations so implementation is systematic rather than ad hoc.

   **D. SCERT develops/implements training module:** After the calendar, the content and design of training modules are finalised for delivery. It ensures standardisation and alignment with state priorities before large-scale rollout.

   **A. DIET conducts training; BRC/CRC onsite support:** Training is then delivered through district-level institutions with local onsite academic support. This combines structured training with school-level handholding so learning translates into practice.

   **B. Monitoring feedback by DIET guides BRC/CRC:** Post-training, feedback and monitoring inform what support is needed and how it should be adjusted. This closes the loop so follow-up support and future training improve based on evidence from implementation.

4. NCF 2005 places learning at the centre and views children as active constructors of understanding rather than passive recipients of facts. Therefore, the teacher's primary role is to create conditions for inquiry, dialogue, activity-based learning, and meaning-making. In this role, the teacher guides, scaffolds, and supports students' thinking so they build concepts through engagement and reflection, instead of focusing on control, authority, or memorisation as the defining feature of teaching.

5. The Reason accurately states what Stake's Congruence–Contingency (Countenance) model does—systematically examining alignment between what was intended and what actually occurred across antecedents, transactions, and outcomes/results. However, categorising this model as a post-modernist approach is not appropriate because it is fundamentally a

structured, analytic, "intended vs observed" congruence-based evaluation design; post-modernist evaluation is typically characterised more by plural perspectives, negotiated meanings, and strongly interpretive/participatory emphasis as the defining basis of classification.

**6.** Functionalist perspective views education as a system that maintains social order, integration and value consensus. Émile Durkheim explained that education transmits collective norms and prepares individuals for social roles, while Talcott Parsons emphasized role allocation, meritocracy and socialization into universal values. Both see education as contributing to stability and continuity of society. Other thinkers listed belong to critical or conflict perspectives rather than functionalism.

**7.**
- **A–II (Analysis of existing situation → Appraise current conditions):** This step examines present realities, available resources and constraints. It provides the baseline for planning by identifying gaps and limitations.
- **B–I (Setting up goals → Establish targets):** Goals define the intended outcomes or ends to be achieved. They guide the entire planning process and provide direction.
- **C–IV (Defining evaluation mechanism → Specify criteria/tools):** Evaluation requires clear indicators and tools to measure performance. These criteria help assess whether goals are achieved effectively.
- **D–III (Choosing best solution → Economic rationality):** Alternatives are compared using cost–benefit analysis. The most efficient and feasible option is selected for implementation.

**8. A. Herbartian Model → Memory level:** Herbartian steps emphasise presentation and repetition, focusing on retention. Hence, it is linked with memory-level teaching.

**D. Malcolm Knowles → Andragogy:** Knowles developed adult learning principles such as self-direction and experience-based learning. His theory forms the basis of andragogy.

**E. Dynamic Model → Learner autonomy:** Dynamic models emphasise flexibility, interaction and learner-centred processes. They promote autonomy and active participation of learners.

Statements B and C are not correct as given because Bigge and Hunt relate more to reflective/insightful learning, while Morrison's model is associated with mastery learning rather than reflective level.

**9.** The assertion is incorrect because learning analytics is not limited to administrative decision-making. It supports decisions at multiple levels such as classroom teaching, curriculum design and institutional policy. The reason correctly explains that learner data is analysed to improve decision-making across different levels, making it accurate.

**10. B. Shift to inclusive education:** The earliest development was moving from segregated special education to inclusive philosophy. This established the idea of educating all learners together.

**A. Differentiated instruction:** Teachers began adapting teaching strategies to diverse learner needs. Instruction became flexible in content, process and assessment.

**C. Collaborative teaching models:** Co-teaching and teamwork between general and special educators evolved. This strengthened support systems within classrooms.

**D. Universal Design for Learning:** UDL represents a more advanced stage where curriculum is designed to be accessible from the start. It integrates inclusivity at the design level itself.

**11. B. Estimating cost using ingredient method:** Economic evaluation begins with identifying all inputs such as staff, materials and infrastructure, and assigning them monetary value. This provides the total cost base required for any further comparison or analysis.

**E. Compare alternative on a common outcome metric:** Alternatives must be made comparable using a common outcome (e.g., learning gain, pass rate). This ensures that different programmes are evaluated on the same basis before applying economic tools.

**A. Cost benefit and cost effective analysis:** Once costs and outcomes are known, cost-effectiveness and cost-benefit analysis are conducted. These help determine which alternative provides maximum benefit for the given cost.

**D. Align funding with budgeting practice:** After identifying the best option, financial planning is aligned with budget provisions and funding mechanisms. This step ensures feasibility and practical implementation within available resources.

**C. Compute private/social return to justify investment:** Finally, returns such as private and social rates of return are calculated. This helps justify the investment in the programme for long-term economic and social benefits.

**12.** Under the Samagra Shiksha framework, the State Council of Educational Research and Training functions as the key state-level academic authority for teacher education planning. It is designated to steer and coordinate in-service teacher training through the state system, ensuring uniform academic direction. DIETs support training execution at district level, but the nodal role at the state level rests with SCERT.

**13.**
- **A–III (Education for All → Ensuring universal access to basic education):** Education for All focused on expanding basic education coverage so every child could access schooling. Its primary thrust was universalising foundational education access.
- **B–IV (SDG-4 → Promoting inclusive, equitable, quality education and lifelong learning):** SDG-4 explicitly targets inclusive and equitable quality education along with lifelong learning opportunities. It broadens the agenda beyond access to quality and equity across the lifespan.
- **C–II (Salamanca Statement → Advocating for inclusive education systems for learners with disabilities):** The Salamanca Statement strongly promotes inclusion of learners with special needs within regular schools. It is closely associated with disability inclusion through inclusive schooling systems.
- **D–I (Incheon Declaration → Framing global commitment to inclusive and equitable education by 2030):** The Incheon Declaration anchors the Education 2030 agenda as a global commitment framework. It sets the commitment direction and urgency towards inclusive, equitable education by 2030.

**14.**
- **A–III (Mudaliar Commission → Multi track education at secondary level):** The Secondary Education Commission (Mudaliar) emphasised diversified/multi-track courses at the secondary stage. This was aimed at matching education with varied aptitudes and vocational/academic pathways.
- **B–IV (National Education Commission → Teacher most important for education and national development):** The National Education Commission (Kothari) repeatedly highlighted the centrality of the teacher in national progress. The statement directly reflects that emphasis on teacher importance for educational and national development.
- **C–I (NPE 1986 → Comprehensive teacher education programme through DIET):** NPE 1986 led to major restructuring of teacher education support systems at district level. The DIET-based comprehensive teacher education strengthening aligns with this policy direction.
- **D–II (NCFTE 2009 → School internship model of specified duration):** NCFTE 2009 stresses structured school internship as an essential component of teacher preparation. The specified duration pattern is tied to the framework's design of practicum and field engagement.

**15.** In ANOVA, the F-ratio compares how much group means differ from the grand mean (between-group variation) relative to the random spread of scores inside groups (within-group variation). When between-group variation is large compared to within-group variation, the F value becomes larger, indicating the group means are less likely to be equal by chance. This is exactly captured by "between-group variability divided by within-group variability".

**16.** Humanistic approach focuses on learner-centered education, emphasizing personal growth, self-actualization, creativity, and intrinsic motivation. It values freedom of choice, emotional well-being, and meaningful learning experiences. This perspective aims at developing the whole person rather than just cognitive achievement, aligning with thinkers like Maslow and Carl Rogers.

17. **B. Focus:** It defines the objectives and purpose of the teaching model. This step clarifies what learning outcomes are expected.

**A. Syntax:** It describes the sequence of instructional steps. It guides how the teaching-learning process unfolds.

**E. Social system:** It specifies teacher-student roles and interaction patterns. It determines the classroom environment.

**D. Support system:** It includes materials, tools, and resources needed. It ensures effective implementation of the model.

**C. Evaluation:** It assesses the effectiveness of the teaching model. It measures achievement of objectives.

18. Bruner's theory of instruction includes predisposition to learn, structure of knowledge, sequence of instruction, and reinforcement. Evaluation is not one of the four features. His theory focuses on how instruction should be designed to facilitate learning rather than on assessment.

19. **C. Solomon Four-Group Design:** It is a true experimental design with highest control over threats to internal validity. It controls testing effects and includes control and experimental groups.

**A. Time Series Design:** It uses repeated observations over time, helping control some threats like maturation and trends. It is stronger than simple pre-experimental designs.

**B. Static-Group Comparison Design:** It has a comparison group but lacks randomization and pretesting. It has moderate control over validity threats.

**E. One-Group Pretest-Posttest Design:** It measures before and after treatment but lacks a control group. It is vulnerable to history and maturation effects.

**D. One-Shot Case Study:** It includes only treatment and post-test. It has the least control over internal validity.

20.
- **A–III (NIRTAR → Cuttack):** It is located at Olatpur, Cuttack, Odisha. It focuses on rehabilitation training and research.
- **B–I (NIEPMD → Chennai):** Located in Chennai, Tamil Nadu. It works for persons with multiple disabilities.
- **C–IV (NIEPID → Secunderabad):** Located in Secunderabad, Telangana. It deals with intellectual disabilities.
- **D–II (NIOH → Kolkata):** Located in Kolkata, West Bengal. It focuses on locomotor/orthopedic disabilities.

21.
- **A–II (Perennialism → Constant curriculum, classical subjects):** Perennialism emphasizes enduring truths and great works of literature. It focuses on classical subjects and intellectual discipline rather than change.
- **B–III (Progressivism → Interdisciplinary, activities and projects):** Progressivism promotes learning by doing and experiential learning. It integrates subjects and uses projects and activities for understanding.
- **C–IV (Essentialism → Mastering skills, facts, basics):** Essentialism stresses core knowledge and basic skills. It is linked with the "back to basics" approach in education.
- **D–I (Reconstructionism → Social, economic, political problems):** Reconstructionism focuses on social reform and critical analysis of society. It emphasizes equality and solving real-life societal issues.

22. **A. Teaching through activities:** RTE Act promotes child-centered and activity-based learning. It discourages rote memorization and passive learning.

**C. Teaching through discovery:** The Act encourages learning by discovery and exploration. It supports constructivist pedagogy for meaningful understanding.

**D. Teaching through exploration:** Learners are encouraged to explore their environment. This helps develop curiosity and critical thinking.

**E. Mother tongue as medium:** RTE Act recommends mother tongue as medium of instruction at primary level. It supports better comprehension and participation.

Statement B is incorrect because the Act does not restrict teaching to only project method.

23. **E. Activating agent:** This is the external event or situation that triggers the response. It is the starting point of the REBT model (A in ABCDE model).

**D. Belief system:** The individual forms beliefs about the activating event. These beliefs may be rational or irrational and determine reactions.

**A. Consequences:** Emotional and behavioural outcomes arise from the belief system. These consequences reflect how the individual interprets the event.

**B. Disputing:** Irrational beliefs are challenged through logical questioning. This step helps replace faulty thinking with rational beliefs.

**C. Effect:** The final stage leads to new rational thinking and healthier outcomes. It results in improved emotional and behavioural responses.

**24. A. Split-half reliability estimation:** Spearman-Brown formula is used to estimate reliability of the full test from half-test reliability. It corrects the reliability coefficient when test length is changed.

**B. Use in ratings and test scores:** The formula can be applied wherever reliability needs adjustment based on test length. It can be used in both test scores and rating scales.

Statements C and D are incorrect because the formula is applicable for lengthening tests and is not restricted in that way.

**25.** Case study research focuses on in-depth understanding of a particular case, individual or situation. Therefore, samples are deliberately selected based on their relevance and richness of information rather than random selection. Purposive sampling allows the researcher to choose cases that best illustrate the phenomenon under study.

**26.**
- **A–III (Realist Ethnography → Objective, scientifically written):** Realist ethnography presents findings in an objective, third-person voice. It aims at neutrality and scientific description of culture.
- **B–I (Confessional Ethnography → Fieldwork experiences):** Confessional ethnography focuses on the researcher's experiences in the field. It reflects challenges, emotions and methodological issues faced.
- **C–IV (Micro-ethnography → Specific aspect of a cultural group):** Micro-ethnography studies a small, focused cultural situation or interaction. It examines detailed behaviour within a limited setting.
- **D–II (Critical Ethnography → Marginalized groups, advocacy):** Critical ethnography addresses issues of power, inequality and injustice. It aims at social change and empowerment of marginalized groups.

**27.** In cost of quality framework, prevention costs are those incurred to avoid defects before they occur, such as training, quality planning, and system improvement. Appraisal costs relate to inspection and testing, while failure costs include both internal (rework, scrap) and external (warranty, complaints). Cost-benefit analysis deals with monetary outcomes, not just qualitative ones.

**28.** The schemes Sarva Shiksha Abhiyan (SSA) and Rashtriya Madhyamik Shiksha Abhiyan (RMSA) were not terminated but were subsumed into the Samagra Shiksha programme in 2018. This integration was done to create a unified framework covering school education from pre-primary to senior secondary levels, ensuring better resource utilization and continuity. The reason given is incorrect because the restructuring was a policy decision of the Government of India for administrative efficiency and holistic planning, not because of any stoppage of World Bank funding.

**29.** Thorndike's theory of learning (Connectionism) includes principles like multiple response and partial activity. However, equilibration and assimilation are concepts given by Jean Piaget in his cognitive development theory. Since the question asks for the statement not proposed by Thorndike, equilibration is the correct choice as it clearly belongs to Piaget's framework.

**30.** Psychological testing refers to the use of a specific standardized tool to measure particular traits or abilities. Psychological assessment is broader and involves integrating information from various sources such as tests, interviews, observations and case history to form a comprehensive understanding and make informed decisions about an individual.

**31.** In Universal Design for Learning (UDL), there are three core principles—multiple means of engagement, representation, and action & expression. "Multiple means of expression" is one of these principles. The other options like "optimize choice and autonomy" and "provide options for perception" are checkpoints under broader principles, while "nurture joy and play" is not part of UDL guidelines.

**32.** Behavioural assessment focuses on observable behaviour and its interaction with environmental factors. It emphasizes identifying antecedents and consequences (functional analysis) with objective and direct evidence. It avoids relying on abstract traits or labels and instead prioritizes measurable behaviour in context.

**33.** Phoenix Farm and Tolstoy Farm were established by Mahatma Gandhi in South Africa. These communities were based on principles of simplicity, self-reliance, truth and non-violence. They also served as experiments in education and community living aligned with Gandhian philosophy.

**34.** **C. Gagne's Nine Events of Instruction:** Developed in the 1960s, it provided a structured sequence of instructional steps. It is one of the earliest systematic instructional design frameworks.

**A. ADDIE Model:** Emerged around the 1970s as a general instructional design framework. It includes Analysis, Design, Development, Implementation and Evaluation.

**B. Dick and Carey Model:** Developed later in the late 1970s, it provided a systematic approach to instructional design. It integrates objectives, assessment and evaluation in a structured way.

**D. 5Es Model:** Developed in the late 1980s, it is a constructivist model (Engage, Explore, Explain, Elaborate, Evaluate). It emphasizes learner-centered, inquiry-based learning.

**35.** For NAAC accreditation, institutions must have a functional Internal Quality Assurance Cell (IQAC) that continuously monitors quality. Submission of Annual Quality Assurance Reports (AQAR) is mandatory for subsequent cycles. This ensures continuous quality improvement and accountability between accreditation cycles.

**36.**
- **A–III (Special Training → Section 4):** Section 4 of the RTE Act provides for special training for out-of-school children. It ensures they are brought at par with age-appropriate classes.
- **B–I (Additional function of NCPCR → Section 31):** Section 31 assigns monitoring of child rights under RTE to NCPCR. It gives additional functions to ensure implementation of the Act.
- **C–IV (School Management Committee → Section 21):** Section 21 mandates formation of School Management Committees. These ensure community participation and school governance.
- **D–II (Prohibition of Physical Punishment → Section 17):** Section 17 prohibits physical punishment and mental harassment. It protects the dignity and rights of children.

**37.** This book was written by Jean Piaget and focuses on children's cognitive development, especially how language and thinking evolve. The other books belong to different scholars such as Howard Gardner and B.F. Skinner.

**38.** Vygotsky described private speech as self-directed speech used by children to regulate behaviour and guide problem-solving. It is external speech that later becomes internalized as inner speech.

**39.** In traditional Islamic education, "Alim" is a degree given to a scholar of religious knowledge, while "Fazil" is awarded to those who demonstrate excellence in logic and higher studies. These titles reflect specialization in different domains of knowledge.

**40.**
- **A–IV (Panch-sheel → Buddhism):** Panchsheel refers to the five moral precepts in Buddhism. They guide ethical conduct and discipline.
- **B–I (Panch-kosh → Upanishad):** Panchkosh describes five sheaths of human existence. It is explained in Taittiriya Upanishad.
- **C–II (Panch-Mahabhut → Yoga):** Panch Mahabhut refers to five elements—earth, water, fire, air, space. It is used in yogic and philosophical understanding of body and nature.
- **D–III (Panch-Mahavrat → Jainism):** Panch Mahavrat are five great vows in Jainism. They include non-violence, truth, non-stealing, celibacy and non-possession.

**41.** This report was prepared by a sub-committee of CABE (Central Advisory Board of Education) to review Continuous and Comprehensive Evaluation in relation to the no-detention policy. The other reports were prepared by different committees or bodies and are not CABE sub-committee reports.

**42.** **A. S-R learning:** This is the simplest form where a stimulus is directly linked to a response. It forms the base level of learning in Gagne's hierarchy.

**B. Chain learning:** It involves linking multiple S-R connections into a sequence. It is more complex than simple S-R learning.

**C. Verbal association:** It involves chaining of verbal units such as words and sentences. It represents a higher level of symbolic learning.

**E. Multiple discrimination:** Learners differentiate among similar stimuli. This requires higher cognitive processing than chaining.

**D. Learning of concepts:** Concept learning involves abstraction and generalization. It is a higher-order learning compared to discrimination.

**43.** **B. Nalanda was a Buddhist center of learning:** Nalanda was one of the most renowned Buddhist universities in ancient India, attracting scholars from across Asia. It specialized in Buddhist philosophy along with other subjects like logic, medicine and grammar.

**C. Nalanda received royal patronage:** Nalanda flourished under the patronage of Gupta rulers and later kings like Harsha and Pala rulers. This continuous support contributed to its growth as a major center of higher learning.

**D. Upanayana for women at same age:** In early Vedic period, women like Brahmavadinis were allowed Upanayana and Vedic studies. They could undergo initiation similar to men, indicating relative educational equality.

**44.** **E. Navodaya Vidyalaya:** Started in 1985–86 to provide quality rural education.

**A. DPEP:** Launched in 1994 for universalization of primary education.

**B. SSA:** Started in 2001 to universalize elementary education.

**D. RMSA:** Launched in 2009 for secondary education.

**C. Samagra Shiksha:** Introduced in 2018 as an integrated scheme.

**45.** Ecological assessment emphasizes collecting data across multiple settings (home, school, peers) and from multiple informants (parents, teachers). This is necessary because children behave differently in different contexts and situations. The reason clearly explains why multiple sources are essential, making it the correct explanation of the assertion.

**46.**
- **A–II (Knowledge → Recall of facts):** Knowledge level involves remembering previously learned information. It includes recall of terms, facts and basic concepts.
- **B–III (Comprehension → Translation/ interpretation):** Comprehension involves understanding meaning and explaining ideas. It includes translating information into another form.
- **C–I (Application → Use in novel situations):** Application means using learned knowledge in new contexts. It involves applying rules or concepts to solve problems.
- **D–IV (Analysis → Identify relationships):** Analysis involves breaking information into parts. It focuses on relationships, patterns and organization.

**47.** Under SSA (2011) guidelines, in-service teacher training at the elementary level is recommended for about 20 days annually. This duration is meant to strengthen teachers' pedagogical skills and improve classroom practices.

**48.** In Tyler's model, general objectives are refined through two screens—educational philosophy of the school and psychology of learning. This ensures that objectives are meaningful, relevant and achievable according to learner characteristics and institutional values.

**49.** Calfee and Masuda describe assessment as inquiry as a dynamic and continuous process. It involves constant interaction, feedback and revision rather than a fixed linear sequence. This reflects ongoing learning and adjustment.

50. • **A–II (Transmission of norms → Functionalist):** Functionalists view education as transmitting shared values. It helps maintain social stability.
- **B–IV (Overall development → Liberalist):** Liberal perspective emphasizes individual growth and development. It focuses on realizing human potential.
- **C–I (Ruling class ideology → Marxist):** Marxist view sees education as reproducing class inequality. It transmits dominant ideology.
- **D–III (Unequal chances → Cultural Deprivation):** Cultural deprivation theory explains unequal opportunities. It links disadvantage to cultural and social factors.

51. ICT in educational evaluation supports automated item generation and adaptive testing, which personalize assessment based on learner responses and improve measurement precision. Learning Management Systems provide instant feedback, analytics and performance tracking, helping both teachers and learners to monitor progress continuously. ICT also enables e-portfolios, allowing longitudinal tracking of learner growth and reflective learning. Large-scale online examinations with secure proctoring systems ensure scalability, accessibility and integrity of assessments. However, replacing all human judgement with AI is neither feasible nor desirable, especially for subjective assessment requiring interpretation, context and ethical judgement, hence statement C is incorrect.

52. In large group formal settings, structured and individualized learning materials are effective, and programmed instruction based on Skinner's operant conditioning fits this requirement. It uses reinforcement, immediate feedback and small sequential steps to ensure learning. This approach allows learners to progress at their own pace even within a large group. Other options such as peer tutoring, mastery learning or experiential projects are more suitable for small groups or interactive settings, making programmed learning the best fit for large formal instructional contexts.

53. C. **Annamaya:** The outermost sheath related to the physical body. It represents the material existence sustained by food.

A. **Pranamaya:** The vital sheath associated with life energy and breath. It controls physiological functions.

E. **Manomaya:** The mental sheath governing thoughts and emotions. It processes sensory inputs and feelings.

D. **Vijnanmaya:** The intellectual sheath associated with knowledge and wisdom. It involves discrimination and decision-making.

B. **Anandmaya:** The innermost sheath representing bliss and spiritual realization. It is the highest level of consciousness.

54. A. **Group goals and individual accountability:** Cooperative learning requires both collective responsibility and individual performance. This ensures participation and avoids free-riding.

B. **Heterogeneous small groups:** It emphasizes diverse groups for better interaction and peer learning. Students learn from each other's strengths and perspectives.

D. **Constructivist perspective:** Cooperative learning aligns with constructivism, where knowledge is actively constructed through interaction. It promotes understanding through collaboration.

Statements C and E are incorrect because cooperative learning is not based only on Bandura's theory and it promotes flexibility, not rigidity.

55. Controlling is an essential managerial function that ensures activities are carried out according to the plan. It involves monitoring performance, comparing it with standards and taking corrective actions when deviations occur. Since planning sets the objectives and standards, controlling measures performance against them, making the two functions interdependent. The reason clearly explains that controlling uses feedback and corrective actions to align work with planned goals, which establishes the close relationship between planning and controlling.

56. The Quality Council of India (QCI) was established to ensure quality standards across sectors by developing accreditation systems aligned with global benchmarks. It functions through various boards like NABCB and NABL

to accredit certification and inspection bodies. In education, QCI supports quality assurance mechanisms but does not directly accredit universities or assign NAAC grades. Its role is to build frameworks, promote standards and ensure conformity assessment consistent with international practices, thereby strengthening credibility and quality culture.

**57.** The Kothari Commission (1964–66) emphasized the importance of work-experience as an essential component of education to make learning more meaningful and socially relevant. It recommended integrating productive work into the curriculum at all stages of schooling. The rationale behind this was to connect education with real-life productivity, economic development and modernization. The reason clearly explains the purpose behind including work-experience, thus correctly justifying the assertion.

**58.**
- **A–IV (Fluency → Producing many ideas):** Fluency refers to the ability to generate a large number of ideas. It reflects quantity and ease of idea generation.
- **B–III (Flexibility → Shifting thinking):** Flexibility involves changing perspectives and approaches. It shows adaptability in thinking patterns.
- **C–II (Originality → Unique responses):** Originality refers to producing novel and uncommon ideas. It measures creativity and uniqueness.
- **D–I (Elaboration → Adding details):** Elaboration involves expanding and refining ideas. It adds depth and detail to responses.

**59.** **D. Create constancy of purpose:** This is the first principle of Deming's philosophy. It emphasizes long-term improvement.

**B. Adopt a new philosophy:** Organizations must accept modern quality concepts. It promotes change in management thinking.

**A. Cease dependence on mass inspection:** Quality should be built into the process rather than inspected. Prevention is better than detection.

**C. End practice of business on cost alone:** Focus should be on quality and long-term relationships. Not just lowest price decisions.

**E. Constantly improve processes:** Continuous improvement is a core principle. It ensures sustained quality enhancement.

**60.** The Secondary Education Commission (1952–53), popularly known as the Mudaliar Commission, recommended reforms in the examination system to reduce excessive examination burden on students. It suggested that instead of multiple public examinations at different stages, there should be only one public examination at the end of the secondary stage. This recommendation aimed to reduce stress, discourage rote memorization, and promote a more meaningful and continuous learning process. The commission emphasized internal assessment and a balanced evaluation system, thereby making the learning process more student-centered and less examination-oriented.

**61.** The 'law of the single variable' was indeed an early foundational assumption in experimental research, which stated that if all conditions are held constant except one variable, any observed change can be attributed to that variable. This principle worked well in controlled physical sciences and formed the basis of early experimental logic. However, in behavioural sciences, human behaviour is influenced by multiple interacting variables such as environment, cognition, emotions and social context, making it difficult to isolate a single variable in a purely controlled manner. Therefore, the assertion that the single-variable approach provided a sound method for behavioural sciences is not fully correct. Modern research methods in behavioural sciences use multivariate and complex designs, indicating that the strict single-variable approach is limited. Hence, the assertion is incorrect, while the reason is correct.

**62.** The given learning sequence—watching a short video, attempting a quiz, receiving immediate automated feedback, and then proceeding to the next activity—clearly reflects the core features of Programmed Instruction. This approach, developed by B.F. Skinner, is based on the principles of operant conditioning and emphasizes learning in small, structured steps, active learner response, immediate feedback, and reinforcement. Each step builds upon the previous one, allowing learners to progress systematically.

The presence of automated feedback and step-by-step progression aligns strongly with linear or branching programmed learning models. Although technology is used, the focus here is not merely on delivery (as in Computer Assisted Instruction) or management (as in Computer Managed Learning), but on the instructional sequencing and reinforcement mechanism. The absence of a fixed mastery threshold also distinguishes it from Mastery Learning, confirming that the most appropriate principle demonstrated is Programmed Instruction.

**63.** NCFTE (2009) recommended that the existing one-year B.Ed. programme should be extended to a two-year duration. This was proposed to provide deeper engagement with pedagogy, school experience, and reflective practice. The aim was to improve the quality of teacher education by allowing sufficient time for theory, practicum, and professional development.

**64.** **C. Intrinsic value → Planned and finished curriculum:** Intrinsic value focuses on the quality of the curriculum itself. It examines both the design and the implemented outcomes.

**D. Comparative value → Better than previous programme:** Comparative value evaluates whether a new programme is superior. It compares effectiveness with existing alternatives.

**E. Decision value → Retain/modify/discard:** Decision value helps in making policy decisions. It guides whether to continue, revise or discontinue a programme.

Statements A and B are not correct as defined in Talmage's framework.

**65.** The Justice Verma Commission (2012) was constituted to examine issues related to the quality and regulation of teacher education. It was specifically set up in response to concerns about irregularities in recognition of teacher education institutions by regulatory bodies. The commission recommended reforms to ensure transparency, accountability and quality in teacher education.

**66.** POSDCORB is an acronym given by Luther Gulick to describe key administrative functions—Planning, Organizing, Staffing, Directing, Coordinating, Reporting and Budgeting. Thus, P = Planning, S = Staffing, and CO = Coordinating are correct. However, R stands for Reporting, not Recording, and B stands for Budgeting, not Benchmarking. Therefore, only A, B and C are correct while D and E are incorrect.

**67.** Howard Gardner proposed multiple intelligences such as linguistic, logical-mathematical, spatial, musical, bodily-kinesthetic, interpersonal and intrapersonal. "Motivational intelligence" is not one of Gardner's categories. Hence, this pair is not part of his theory, while the other options correctly represent Gardner's intelligences.

**68.** Bodily-kinesthetic intelligence is one of Gardner's multiple intelligences, so A is correct. Sternberg's triarchic theory includes analytical, creative and practical intelligence, not naturalistic intelligence, so B is incorrect. Analytical intelligence involves problem solving and academic abilities, making C correct. Creative intelligence belongs to Sternberg's theory, not Gardner's, so D is incorrect. Practical intelligence refers to adapting to and shaping real-life environments, making E correct. Thus, A, C and E are correct.

**69.** Scientific management, associated with Frederick Taylor, is based on the belief that management can be studied scientifically and that there are objective, universal principles of efficiency. It assumes that managerial behaviour can be measured, standardized and optimized to produce predictable outcomes, reflecting an objective and positivist epistemic stance.

**70.** Under the IEDSS scheme (2009), financial assistance was provided to support students with disabilities at the secondary stage. The stipend for girl students with disabilities was fixed with an upper limit of ₹ 200 per month to encourage their participation and retention in secondary education.

**71.** • **A–II (Schulman → Pedagogical Content Knowledge):** Lee Shulman introduced the concept of Pedagogical Content Knowledge (PCK) as the core of teacher knowledge. It integrates subject matter knowledge with pedagogy for effective teaching.

- **B–IV (Habermas → Knowledge-constitutive interest):** Habermas proposed that knowledge is shaped by human interests—technical, practical and emancipatory. His theory links knowledge, power and emancipation in education.
- **C–III (Krishna Kumar → Teacher as meek dictator):** Krishna Kumar described the teacher in Indian classrooms as a "meek dictator". This reflects authority combined with passivity in pedagogic practice.
- **D–I (Deng & Luke → Expansion of knowledge base):** Deng and Luke emphasized expansion and reconceptualization of curriculum knowledge. They highlighted broader perspectives in curriculum studies.

**72.** The DeLone and McLean Information System (D&M IS) success model evaluates systems based on dimensions like system quality, information quality, service quality, use, user satisfaction and net benefits. It focuses on technological and system performance aspects. Pedagogical theories used are not part of this model, as it does not directly evaluate instructional design or educational philosophy.

**73.** Panch Mahavrata are the five great vows in Jainism—Ahimsa (non-violence), Satya (truth), Asteya (non-stealing), Brahmacharya (celibacy) and Aparigraha (non-possession). Yogasana is related to Yoga practice and is not part of these vows.

**74.** Life situation design is a type of curriculum design that organizes content around real-life problems and social situations. It is considered a society-centered design, not learner-centered. It emphasizes relevance to community life, problem-solving and practical application, and is aligned with Spencer's idea of education for complete living.

**75.** Panini and Chanakya were not products of Nalanda University; they belonged to earlier periods and different centers of learning such as Takshashila. Nalanda University did have a well-developed admission procedure and a vast library, making it a renowned center of learning. Therefore, the assertion is incorrect, but the reason is correct.

**76.** Educational guidance is not primarily prescriptive and remedial; rather, it is fundamentally developmental and preventive in nature, aimed at facilitating the overall growth of the learner. While it may include remedial aspects to address problems, its core purpose is to help students make informed choices, develop abilities, and adjust proactively to educational demands. The reason correctly states that educational guidance assists pupils in making choices related to school, curriculum, and adjustment to school life. This reflects the true aim of guidance, which focuses on support and development rather than merely prescribing solutions. Hence, the assertion is incorrect, but the reason is correct.

**77.** In the CIPP model, Context evaluation is the stage where needs are diagnosed and goals/ objectives are formulated and judged for relevance. It specifically asks whether the objectives are appropriate in relation to identified needs, problems, and priorities of the setting. If objectives are unclear, unrealistic, or misaligned with learner/community needs, that is detected at the context stage itself. Input evaluation comes after this and focuses on plans, strategies, resources, and feasibility for achieving already-framed objectives. Process evaluation monitors implementation while the programme is running, and product evaluation examines outcomes after implementation. Therefore, the question "Are the objectives stated appropriately?" is answered under Context.

**78.** **A. Two-year B.Ed.:** NCTE 2014 regulations extended B.Ed. programme to two years. This was done to enhance quality of teacher education.

**C. Two-year M.Ed.:** M.Ed. was also structured as a two-year programme. It aimed at strengthening research and professional development.

**D. Two-year B.Ed. through ODL:** NCTE provided norms for B.Ed. through Open and Distance Learning. It was regulated with strict eligibility and quality conditions.

Options B and E are not part of these specific regulations.

**79.** Constant errors affect all scores uniformly by raising or lowering them, thus not affecting the consistency of measurement. Reliability is concerned with consistency, and constant errors do not change relative ranking. Hence, the statement that constant errors affect reliability is incorrect. Chance errors, on the other hand, are random and uncorrelated, affecting reliability.

**80.** Attitudinal barriers among teachers and administrators are widely recognized as a major challenge in inclusive education, as beliefs and prejudices influence classroom practices and acceptance of diversity. Structural changes such as infrastructure or resources can be implemented more easily, but changing attitudes, values and mindsets is more difficult and time-consuming. The reason clearly explains why attitudinal barriers are considered more significant, making it the correct explanation of the assertion.

**81.** **D. Word-Association Test – Galton, 1879:** Francis Galton introduced the word-association method as one of the earliest techniques related to projective assessment. It explored unconscious processes through spontaneous verbal responses.

**C. Rorschach Test – 1921:** Hermann Rorschach developed the inkblot test as a formal projective technique. It became one of the most widely used personality assessment tools.

**E. Thematic Apperception Test – 1935:** Developed by Murray and Morgan, it uses ambiguous pictures to reveal underlying motives and conflicts. It extended projective techniques into narrative responses.

**A. Term 'Projective Method' – Frank, 1939:** L.K. Frank formally coined the term "projective method." This provided a conceptual framework for these techniques.

**B. Holtzman Inkblot Test – 1961:** Holtzman developed this as an alternative to Rorschach with improved reliability. It represents a later development in projective testing.

**82.** The National Policy on Education (1986) explicitly emphasized a child-centered approach to education, promoting learning without burden and focusing on the holistic development of the child. It marked a shift from teacher-centered to learner-centered pedagogy in Indian education policy.

**83.**
- **A–II (Continuity → Vertical repetition):** Continuity ensures repetition of content over time. It helps reinforcement and retention.
- **B–I (Integration → Horizontal relationship):** Integration connects subjects across domains. It promotes interdisciplinary learning.
- **C–IV (Articulation → Vertical & horizontal interrelatedness):** Articulation ensures logical sequencing and connections across levels. It maintains coherence in curriculum structure.
- **D–III (Scope → Depth and breadth):** Scope defines the extent of content covered. It includes both range and depth of topics.

**84.** The RPwD Act, 2016 expanded the number of recognized disabilities from 7 (under the earlier Act of 1995) to 21 categories. This expansion ensured wider inclusion and recognition of diverse disabilities.

**85.**
- **A–II (Information Processing → Memory system):** This model explains how information moves through sensory register, short-term memory and long-term memory. It focuses on processing and storage of information.
- **B–III (Schema Theory → Prior knowledge):** Schema theory emphasizes how existing knowledge structures influence learning. It helps in understanding new information.
- **C–I (Cognitive Load Theory → Managing load):** It focuses on managing intrinsic, extraneous and germane load. It aims at optimizing learning efficiency.
- **D–IV (Dual Coding Theory → Verbal and visual channels):** It suggests information is processed through verbal and visual systems. This enhances memory and recall.

**86.** Reflective teaching involves engaging learners in higher-order thinking where they analyze situations, solve problems, and create new ideas or products. In an inclusive classroom, placing students in problem-solving situations and encouraging them to construct or create knowledge aligns with reflective teaching. It promotes critical thinking, inquiry, and self-evaluation, allowing learners to actively engage with content and develop deeper understanding rather than passively receiving information.

**87. C. Reaction:** This is the first level where learners' immediate responses to the programme are collected. It focuses on satisfaction and engagement.

**A. Learning:** This level measures knowledge or skill acquisition. It evaluates what learners have learned.

**B. Behaviour/Transfer:** It examines how learning is applied in real situations. It reflects behavioural change.

**D. Results:** This final level assesses overall outcomes or impact. It focuses on long-term results and effectiveness.

**88. B. PLATO:** Introduced in the 1960s, it was the earliest computer-based learning system. It marked the beginning of e-learning.

**A. Open University using internet:** Later, institutions began integrating internet-based delivery instead of mail. This expanded distance education.

**E. Corporate e-learning adoption:** Businesses adopted e-learning for training due to cost-effectiveness. This increased its practical use.

**C. SCORM development:** SCORM standardized e-learning content and interoperability. It improved compatibility across platforms.

**D. MOOCs like Coursera:** Universities like Harvard and MIT launched MOOCs. This represents modern large-scale online education.

**89.** In hypothesis testing, the 0.01 level of significance is more stringent than the 0.05 level. If a null hypothesis is not rejected at 0.01, it means the p-value is greater than 0.01 ($p > 0.01$). However, the p-value could lie between 0.01 and 0.05, for example $p = 0.03$, in which case the null hypothesis would be rejected at 0.05 level. On the other hand, if the p-value is greater than 0.05 (e.g., $p = 0.10$), it would not be rejected even at 0.05 level. Since we do not know the exact p-value, both situations are possible. Therefore, the null hypothesis may or may not be rejected at 0.05 level.

**90. D. Understanding:** It involves comprehension and interpretation of information. It is the second level after remembering.

**C. Applying:** It refers to using knowledge in new situations. It reflects practical use of learning.

**B. Analyzing:** It involves breaking information into parts and examining relationships. It develops critical thinking.

**E. Evaluating:** It includes making judgments based on criteria. It reflects higher-order thinking.

**A. Creating:** It is the highest level involving production of new ideas. It represents synthesis and innovation.

**91.** The passage clearly situates the debate within the colonial administrative framework referring to the Charter Act of 1813 and Company officials. Historically, such references directly point to the British East India Company, which governed India during that period and was responsible for educational policy decisions. Therefore, "Company" unmistakably refers to the East India Company.

**92.** In the context of the Anglicist–Orientalist debate, those who supported indigenous education systems and vernacular languages were broadly termed Orientalists. William Adam, though originally a missionary, advocated vernacular education and documented indigenous systems of learning in Bengal. His position aligns with the Orientalist perspective that emphasized native languages and traditions rather than exclusive English education.

**93.** Raja Ram Mohan Roy advocated a combination of English medium and scientific education to promote rationality, progress and intellectual advancement. He believed that access to modern scientific knowledge through English would empower Indians and help in social reform, thereby contributing to their intellectual emancipation.

**94.** In the colonial educational debate, Orientalists were those who supported traditional Indian learning, languages like Sanskrit, Persian and Arabic, and indigenous knowledge systems. They opposed the Anglicist view of promoting only Western education and English medium.

**95.** Colonial education refers to the system designed by colonial rulers to serve administrative and ideological purposes. It aimed at creating a class of people who would adopt Western knowledge, language and values, thereby facilitating governance and cultural assimilation within the colonial framework.

**96.** The passage clearly states that predicting human behaviour is difficult because human nature is highly complex and cannot be reduced to simple, isolated elements. Unlike physical sciences, where variables can be controlled and uniformity is assumed, human behaviour involves multiple interacting factors such as emotions, social context and cognition. This complexity makes it harder to develop accurate theories and predictions. Therefore, the correct reason is the inherent complexity of human nature.

**97.** The paragraph explicitly mentions that scientists may use an empirical approach, a rational approach, or a combination of both, and that the combination is most common. This indicates that scientific inquiry typically integrates observation (empirical) with reasoning (rational). The other options are incorrect because scientific work is not limited to theory creation, nor is deductive reasoning always primary, and there is no strict requirement to choose only one approach.

**98.** The passage states that applying scientific methods from physical and biological sciences to social sciences has led to their growth and has advanced knowledge about human behaviour. This approach has helped disciplines like psychology, sociology and education gain recognition as scientific fields. Hence, it has contributed positively to the development of social sciences.

**99.** The paragraph clearly defines science as an approach to gathering knowledge rather than a specific subject area. It emphasizes methodology—observation, analysis and theory testing—rather than content. Therefore, applying scientific methods to human behaviour means using a systematic approach to knowledge generation.

**100.** The passage explains that the assumption of uniformity of nature works well in the physical world, where objects and their properties behave consistently. This allows scientists to make generalizations and predictions with greater confidence. However, such assumptions are not valid in social sciences due to the complexity of human behaviour.

Previous Years' Paper

# National Testing Agency (NTA)

## UGC-NET Junior Research Fellowship & Assistant Professor Eligibility Exam

# EDUCATION, JUNE-2025

(Exam held on 25-06-2025)

## PAPER-II

**1.** Which is NOT a characteristic of narrative research design?

1. Individual experiences
2. Collecting data through rating scale
3. Coding and decoding for themes
4. Collaborating with participants

**2.** 'In order to achieve mastery of a problem, we must receive feedback as to how we are doing".

This statement is related to which principle of Bruner.

1. First Principle
2. Second Principle
3. Third Principle
4. Fourth Principle

**3.** Match the List-I with List-II

| List-I (Platform for MOOC) | List-II (Founder) |
|---|---|
| A. Udacity | I. Eren Bali, Gagan Biyani and Oktay Caglar |
| B. Coursera | II. Harvard University and MIT |
| C. Udemy | III. Daphne Koller and Andrew Ng |
| D. edX | IV. Sebastian Thrun |

Choose the **correct** answer from the options given below:

1. A-III, B-IV, C-I, D-II
2. A-IV, B-I, C-III, D-II
3. A-IV, B-III, C-II, D-I
4. A-IV, B-III, C-I, D-II

**4.** Match the List-I with List-II

| List-I | List-II |
|---|---|
| A. Dharana | I. To cut the relationship of various sense organs from the respective subjects |
| B. Pratyahar | II. To apply the mind to some internal subject |
| C. Dhyan | III. Dhyan becomes stable in Dhyeya |
| D. Samadhi | IV. To concentrate attention on a particular subject of mind |

Choose the **correct** answer from the options given below:

1. A-III, B-I, C-IV, D-II
2. A-II, B-III, C-IV, D-I
3. A-II, B-I, C-IV, D-III
4. A-III, B-IV, C-I, D-II

**5.** Which of the following theoretical perspective mainly emphasizes on hidden curriculum and credentialism?

1. Functionalist 2. Interactionist
3. Conflict 4. Feminist

**6.** Which of the following model of interaction analysis assumes that non-verbal communication can be more effective during interaction in classroom?

1. Flanders' Interaction Analysis
2. R. H. Dave
3. Charles Galloway
4. Malcolm Knowles

**7.** National Curriculum Framework for Integrated Teacher Education Programme in India (2023) was developed by ........ .

1. NCERT 2. NCTE
3. UGC 4. AICTE

**8.** Who has given Fourth Generation Instructional System Development Model (ISD ) to represent complexity of educational technology?

1. Robert Tennyson (1995)
2. Spector (2005)
3. Hartley and Colleagues (2010)
4. David Merrill (2007)

**9.** Which of the following education thinker emphasized on 'Care Ethics'?

1. Paulo Freire
2. J. Krishnamurthy
3. Wollstonecraft
4. Nel Noddings

**10.** Which of the following are the essential characteristics of good research hypothesis?

A. It should be clear and precise.
B. It should be testable.
C. It should be based on ethical consideration.
D. It should be stated in general terms without specifics.
E. It should indicate a relationship between variables.

Choose the **correct** answer from the options given below:

1. A, B, E Only
2. C, B, A Only
3. A, D, C Only
4. C, D Only

**11.** Arrange the following steps in the correct sequence for conducting educational research.

A. Review of related research and literature
B. Data collection
C. Formulation of hypothesis
D. Data analysis and interpretation
E. Identifying the research problem

Choose the **correct** answer from the options given below:

1. E, A, C, B, D
2. A, C, D, B, E
3. C, A, E, D, B
4. B, C, D, E, A

**12.** Arrange the given in chronological order.

A. Indian National Satellite (INSAT)
B. Centre for Educational Technology (CET)
C. Computer Literacy and Studies (CLASS)
D. Satellite Instructional Television Experiment (SITE)
E. SWAYAM

Choose the **correct** answer from the options given below:

1. B, C, D, E, A
2. D, B, E, C, A
3. D, B, A, C, E
4. D, B, C, A, E

**13.** Which of these statements does NOT describe snowball sampling correctly?

A. It is a non-probability sampling technique.
B. It is used when the target population is readily available.
C. Initial participants refer others to take part in the study.

D. It ensures equal chance of selection for all individuals.

E. It is commonly used in sociological and qualitative research.

Choose the **correct** answer from the options given below:

1. A and E Only 2. B and D Only
3. A and C Only 4. B and E Only

**14.** Who stated "Curriculum is a plan or programme for all experiences which the learner encounters under the direction of the school."

1. Oliva
2. Carter V. Good
3. Tyler and Hild Taba
4. Galen Saylor

**15.** Which of the following document does not advocate for inclusive education?

1. National Policy on Disability, 2006
2. Right to Education Act, 2009
3. Rights of Person with Disabilities Act, 2016
4. National Education Policy, 2020

**16.** Arrange the following steps of SWOT analysis

A. Develop strategic actions
B. Prioritize key-factors
C. Analyse external factors
D. Implement and monitor changes
E. Brainstorm and list factors

Choose the **correct** answer from the options given below:

1. B, A, D, E, C 2. C, B, A, D, E
3. E, B, C, A, D 4. A, D, E, C, B

**17.** Which designs are systematic, qualitative procedures that researchers use to generate a general explanation and it leads to process, action or interaction among people?

1. Ethnographic designs
2. Grounded theory designs
3. Narrative research designs
4. Correlational designs

**18.** Match the List-I with List-II

| List-I | List-II |
|---|---|
| A. Pre-experimental design | I. Involves manipulation of independent variable with random assignment |
| B. True-experimental design | II. Lack of randomization and control group |
| C. Quasi-experimental design | III. Examines the interaction effect of multiple independent variables |
| D. Factorial design | IV. Lack of randomization but includes some control |

Choose the **correct** answer from the options given below:

1. A-I, B-II, C-IV, D-III
2. A-II, B-I, C-IV, D-III
3. A-III, B-II, C-IV, D-I
4. A-IV, B-III, C-II, D-I

**19.** Match the List-I with List-II

| List-I | List-II |
|---|---|
| A. Repression | I. Assigning logical or socially desirable motives to what we do so that we seem to have acted rationally. |
| B. Rationalization | II. Excluding from conscious awareness impulses or memories that are too frightening or painful. |
| C. Reaction Formation | III. Assigning our own undesirable qualities to others in exaggerated amounts. |
| D. Projection | IV. Concealing a motive from ourselves by giving strong expression to the opposite motive. |

Choose the **correct** answer from the options given below:

1. A-III, B-IV, C-I, D-II
2. A-IV, B-III, C-II, D-I
3. A-I, B-II, C-III, D-IV
4. A-II, B-I, C-IV, D-III

**20.** Which are the main objectives of in-service education for teachers?

A. To provide financial incentive to the teachers.

B. To help teachers to know their problems and to solve by pooling their resources and wisdom.

C. To broaden the mental outlook of teachers.

D. To increase the professional efficiency of the teacher.

E. To provide the facility away from the place of duty.

Choose the **correct** answer from the options given below:

1. A, E, D Only    2. A, B, C Only
3. B, C, D Only    4. C, D, E Only

**21.** Which of the following statements related to learning theory approach to counselling are INCORRECT?

A. Dollard & Miller relates psychoanalytic methods to reinforcement learning theory.

B. Counselling, according to Pepinskys, aims to strengthen the counselle's behaviour.

C. Eysenck refers to conditioning methods in counselling as "behaviour theraphy"

D. Irrational behaviour is learned and it cannot be changed through learning or relearning.

E. According to Pepinskys, the 'cultural context' does not provide conditions assumed to be antecedent to subsequent learning.

Choose the **correct** answer from the options given below:

1. A and C Only    2. B and C Only
3. B and D Only    4. C and E Only

**22.** Arrange the following four positions of soul from first to fourth.

A. Jagrat    B. Turiya
C. Swapna    D. Pragya

Choose the **correct** answer from the options given below:

1. B, A, D, C    2. C, A, D, B
3. D, C, B, A    4. A, C, D, B

**23.** Which of the following is NOT true about the 'Programme Evaluation and Review Technique (PERT)':

1. It is a network model.
2. It is a project management tool.
3. It is a statistical tool.
4. It is a process-oriented technique.

**24.** Which of the following is NOT a part of formal step of "Syntax" of Herbertian Approach?

1. Presentation
2. Comparison and Abstraction
3. Preparation
4. Focus

**25.** Match the List-I with List-II: CIPP model of curriculum development

| List-I | List-II |
|---|---|
| A. Context | I. To determine the curriculum accomplish the intended goals. |
| B. Input | II. To address curriculum implementation decision that control and manage the plan of curriculum. |
| C. Process | III. To provide information for determining how to utilize resources to meet curriculum goals. |
| D. Product | IV. To study the environment of curriculum implementation |

Choose the **correct** answer from the options given below:

1. A-I, B-II, C-III, D-IV
2. A-III, B-II, C-I, D-IV
3. A-II, B-I, C-IV, D-III
4. A-IV, B-III, C-II, D-I

**26.** For the implementation of Programme of Action (PoA, 1992), how many task forces were constituted on different subjects?

1. 20 2. 21
3. 23 4. 24

**27.** Match the List-I with List-II: CIPP model of curriculum development

| List-I (Statement) | List-II (Thinkers) |
|---|---|
| A. This education ought to be for them a kind of insurance against unemployment. | I. R.N.Tagore |
| B. You cannot teach a child anymore than you can grow a plant. The plant develops its own nature. | II. Sri Aurbindo |
| C. Every child is an inquirer, an investigator, analyser, a merciless anatomist. | III. M.K. Gandhi |
| D. True education consists in knowing the use of any useful material that has been collected to know its real nature and to build along with life a real shelter for life. | IV. Swami Vivekananda |

Choose the **correct** answer from the options given below:

1. A-IV, B-III, C-I, D-II
2. A-III, B-IV, C-II, D-I
3. A-II, B-IV, C-I, D-III
4. A-IV, B-I, C-II, D-III

**28.** Which Commission observed that "one of the most useful methods of enriching rural life is to locate educational institutions in rural areas"?

1. Secondary Education Commission, 1952-53
2. Kothari Commission, 1964-66
3. National Commission on Teachers, 1999
4. University Education Commission, 1948

**29.** Which of the following is NOT true about constructivism theory of instructional design?

1. Learning is more a matter of going from the inside out
2. Learner actively imposes organization and meaning on the surrounding environment and constructs knowledge in this process.
3. Learner receives information from environment, transforms it in many ways and acquires knowledge that is subsequently stored in memory.
4. Constructivism has been felt keenly in the world, partly because it seems to contrast with other foundations such as information processing and Gagne's theories.

**30.** Arrange the given stages of reflection to write good reflective journal:

A. Feelings B. Description
C. Action Plan D. Evaluation
E. Conclusion

Choose the **correct** answer from the options given below:

1. B, A, D, E, C
2. C, A, B, D, E
3. A, C, D, B, E
4. C, B, A, D, E

**31.** Which of the following is "True" about Portfolio?

A. Portfolio contains an index or map
B. Portfolio contains a collection of selected, illustrative material drawn from practice and providing evidence of it.

C. Portfolio generally contains reasonably low validity and very high reliability

D. Portfolio contains commentary discussing the evidence

Choose the **correct** answer from the options given below:

1. A, C, D Only
2. B, C, D Only
3. A, B, C Only
4. A, B, D Only

**32.** Which of the following are salient features of Zero-Base-Budgeting (ZBB)?

A. Adaptability is necessary.

B. It considers an incremental approach.

C. Decision making units need not to be identified.

D. It considers 'choice and withdrawal'.

E. Management hierarchy is not a component.

Choose the **correct** answer from the options given below:

1. A and D Only
2. A and B Only
3. B and C Only
4. C and E Only

**33.** Match List-I with List-II: Match models of curriculum evaluation with establishment year.

| List-I (Curriculum Development Model) | List-II (Year) |
|---|---|
| A. Tylers model | I. 1959 |
| B. States model | II. 1991 |
| C. Scriven model | III. 1949 |
| D. Krikpatrick model | IV. 1967 |

Choose the **correct** answer from the options given below:

1. A-II, B-I, C-III. D-IV
2. A-IV, B-II, C-I, D-III
3. A-III, B-IV, C-II, D-I
4. A-II, B-III, C-IV, D-I

**34.** Which article of UNCRPD stresses the awareness raising to foster respect for the rights and dignity against discrimination:

1. Article 7
2. Article 8
3. Article 13
4. Article 14

**35.** Which are the requirements of effective curriculum transaction?

A. Review of the work in prior.

B. Material organisation as available in the school.

C. Time management.

D. Knowing, observing and understanding children at all times.

E. Individual responsibility.

Choose the most appropriate answer from the options given below:

1. A, B, C, D Only
2. A, C, E Only
3. E, C, A Only
4. B, C, E Only

**36.** Tyler's model of curriculum evaluation obtains the curriculum objectives from following three sources:

1. The student, the society, the subject matter
2. Curriculum, syllabus, course book
3. The teacher, the institute, the Government
4. Course content, teaching method, evaluation strategy

**37.** Jerome Bruner's method of concept attainment has been shaped into a model of teaching by:

1. David P. Ausubel
2. Robert Glaser
3. Bruce Joyce and Marsha Weil
4. Saylor and Alexander

**38.** Identify correct statements:

A. LMX theory is dyadic theory of leadership

B. Variable-value is a type of Poka-Yoke methods.

C. Six-sigma techniques are used basically in martial arts.
D. C.K. Prahlad highlighted the untapped market potential of the world's poorest populations.
E. Fiedler's contingency theory advocates that there is always one best style of leadership.

Choose the **correct** answer from the options given below:

1. A & D Only
2. A & C Only
3. B & E Only
4. B & D Only

**39.** Flander's Interaction Analysis Category System (FIACS) consists of 10 categories (from 1-10). Arrange the given descriptors/ activity of each category in increasing order.

A. Asking questions
B. Lecture
C. Accepts or use of ideas of pupil
D. Pupil talk initiation
E. Praise or encouragement

Choose the **correct** answer from the options given below:

1. B, C, A, E, D
2. E, C, A, B, D
3. C, E, B, A, D
4. D, A, C, E, B

**40.** Which does NOT come under demand factors for finance in education:

1. Demographic factors
2. Economic factors
3. Religious factors
4. Political factors

**41.** Arrange the following steps of Action Research in proper sequence:

A. Formulation of action hypothesis
B. Identification of the problem
C. Collecting data
D. Evaluation of the result of action research
E. Formulation of action design

Choose the **correct** answer from the options given below:

1. B, D, C, A, E
2. C, D, E, A, B
3. B, A, C, E, D
4. A, B, C, D, E

**42.** According to NEP-2020, which of the following recommendations are true?

A. There will be one umberella institution, the National Higher Education Regulatory Council (NHERC).
B. There will be one independent vertical for accreditation, called the National Accreditation Council (NAC).
C. The regulatory regime shall not encourage private philanthropic efforts in education.
D. Within 15 years, all higher educational institutions in India will aim to become independent self-governing institutions.
E. Private higher education institutions will be empowered to set fees for their programmes independently.

Choose the **most appropriate** answer from the options given below:

1. A, B, D Only
2. B, C, D Only
3. B, D, E Only
4. C, D, E Only

**43.** Ethical considerations in Educational Research include:

A. Informed consent
B. Confidentiality of participant data
C. Manipulation of data to support hypothesis
D. Avoidance of plagiarism
E. Providing misleading information to participants

Choose the **correct** answer from the options given below:

1. B, C, E Only
2. A, B, D Only
3. C, A, E Only
4. E, C, A Only

**44.** Match the List-I with List-II:

| List-I (Commission and Committees) | List-II (Year) |
|---|---|
| A. National Commission on Teachers | I. 2007 |
| B. Yashpal Committee Report | II. 1999 |
| C. Justice Verma Committee Report | III. 2012 |
| D. National Knowledge Commission | IV. 2009 |

Choose the **correct** answer from the options given below:

1. A-I, B-II, C-III, D-IV
2. A-II, B-III, C-I, D-IV
3. A-I, B-III, C-II, D-IV
4. A-II, B-IV, C-III, D-I

**45.** Arrange the following keypoints of Bandura's theory in chronological order:

A. Bandura and Walter introduced the concept of modelling behaviour through observation.

B. Bandura proposed the social learning theory, emphasizing observational learning.

C. The concept of reciprocal determinism, where personal environmental, and behaviour factors interact.

D. The example of aggressive children demonstrating how behavioural environment influence each other was used to explain reciprocal determinism.

Choose the **correct** answer from the options given below:

1. A, D, C, B
2. D, C, B, A
3. A, B, D, C
4. A, B, C, D

**46.** Which of the following is NOT related to Soren Kierkegaard?

A. Truth is introvert and subjective.

B. The world is ideas-centred. Entire universe is only an idea.

C. Existence of individuality is reliable and it comes prior to thinking.

D. In order to find self-existence, 'subjective experience' and objectivity both are important.

E. Existential self-experience is necessary.

Choose the **most appropriate** answer from the options given below:

1. A, C, E Only
2. B, D, E Only
3. A, B, E Only
4. B, C, E Only

**47.** Which of the following is NOT a stage of follower readiness according to the situational leadership model given by Hersey and Blanchard (1999):

1. People who are both unable and either unwilling or too insecure to take responsibility to do something
2. People who are able but unwilling or too apprehensive to do what the leader wants.
3. People who are motivated and have appropriate required skills.
4. People who are both willing and able to take responsibility and do what is asked of them.

**48.** The 'Unfreeze-Change-Refreeze' model of organisational development was given by:

1. Blake, Mouton & Bidwell
2. Cummings and Worley
3. Kurt Lewin
4. Michael J. Boyle

**49.** Identify correct statements from the following:

A. Factor cost of education can be exactly put in the same fashion as treated in the case of a firm or an industry.

B. There are no separate price indices for use in educational set up.

C. Educational demand is an external determinant of educational cost.

D. Rate of economic growth does not limit availability of revenues to education.

E. Unit costs have been used in the literature in many ways according to the objectives in view.

Choose the **correct** answer from the options given below:

1. A, B, D Only
2. A, B, E Only
3. B, C, D Only
4. B, C, E Only

**50.** Match List-I with List-II: Match according to NEP 2020

| List-I (Issue) | List-II (Recommendation) |
|---|---|
| A. Recruitment and deployment of teachers | I. Platforms will be developed so that teachers may share ideas and best practices |
| B. Service environment and culture | II. No school stage will be considered more important than any other |
| C. Continuous professional development | III. Transfers will occur in very special circumstances. |
| D. Career management and progression | IV. School complexes could also share counsellors, trained social workers, and technical and maintenance staff etc. |

Choose the **correct** answer from the options given below"

1. A-II, B-I, C-IV, D-III
2. A-III, B-I, C-IV, D-II
3. A-IV, B-I, C-II, D-III
4. A-III, B-IV, C-I, D-II

**51.** "An individual is intelligent in proportion as he is able to carry on abstract thinking." This definition of intelligence is given by:

1. Stern
2. Wagnon
3. Terman
4. David Wechsler

**52.** The central insight in phenomenological analysis is the .............. .

1. Theory of intentionality
2. Theory of knowledge
3. Theory of power
4. Theory of unconsciousness

**53.** Which of the following is correct in context of writing objectives in behavioural terms?

A. Robert Miller's approach (1962) has its origin from biological sciences.

B. Robert Mager's approach gives emphasis on action verbs rather than mental processes.

C. Regional College of Education, Mysore (NCERT-1972) approach for writing behavioural objectives emphasized on mental abilities.

D. Robert Mager concentrates on cognitive, affective and psychomotor objectives.

E. B.S. Bloom has shifted the emphasis from content to objective.

Choose the **correct** answer from the options given below:

1. B, C, E Only
2. A, C, D Only
3. B, D, E Only
4. C, D, E Only

**54.** Match the functions of management

| List-I | List-II |
|---|---|
| A. Planning | I. activates the organizational methods to work efficiently for achieving organizational purposes. |
| B. Organizing | II. to bridge the gap between where we are and where we want to be |
| C. Staffing | III. to provide it with everything useful. |
| D. Directing | IV. manning the organizational structure. |

Choose the **correct** answer from the options given below:

1. A-III, B-I, C-II, D-IV
2. A-II, B-III, C-IV, D-I
3. A-I, B-IV, C-III, D-II
4. A-IV, B-II, C-I, D-III

**55.** PCK framework was given by:

1. Lee Shulman 2. Zongyi Deng
3. Allan Luke 4. Jurgen Habermas

**56.** Which of the following are correct principles of the UN Convention on the Rights of the People with Disabilities.

A. Non-discrimination
B. Accessibility
C. Partial participation
D. Equality of opportunity
E. Segregated approach

Choose the **correct** answer from the options given below:

1. B, C, D Only
2. A, B, D Only
3. A, B, C Only
4. A, C, D, E Only

**57.** Identify correct assertions according to Roger's theory of personality.

A. Self-actualisers are the healthiest one percent of the population.
B. The perceived self influences both the person's perception of the world and his or her behaviour.
C. People are likely to function more effectively if they are brought up with unconditional positive regard.
D. Each of us has an ideal self.
E. Individuals, whose self-concepts match their feelings and experiences, must defend themselves against the truth.

Choose the **correct** answer from the options given below:

1. A, B, C Only 2. B, C, D Only
3. B, D, E Only 4. C, D, E Only

**58.** Who has coined the term 'x-MOOC' in 2012?

1. William and Flora
2. Stephen Downes
3. Lane
4. Sebastian Thurn

**59.** Which of the following statement is NOT true about Idealism?

1. In scheme of curriculum, idealism is not prepared to give any particular preference to any subject.
2. Idealism has talked more of objectives and aims of education and less of devices, methods and organisations.
3. Subjects which have a flavour of personal greatness are greatly emphasized by Idealism.
4. Idealism pay much attention to the present experience of the child in its approach to the problem of curriculum.

**60.** In which stage children are dreamers, with magical thoughts and fantasies in abundance?

1. Formal operational stage
2. Pre-operational stage
3. Concrete operational stage
4. Sensorimotor stage

**61.** Which of the following is NOT related to basic six components of ASSURE model:

1. Require learner participation
2. Analyze teacher
3. Evaluate and revise
4. Utilize technology, media and material

**62.** Arrange the following steps of budget formulation and its role in the implementation of educational programmes in correct sequence.

A. Finance department issues guidelines for budget preparation.
B. Heads of departments instruct subordinate offices and units to prepare budgets.
C. Budget serves as an interim instrument for implementing educational policies.
D. Legislative appraises the performance of departments before voting on expenditure.

Choose the **correct** answer from the options given below:

1. B, A, C, D  2. A, B, D, C
3. C, D, B, A  4. A, B, C, D

**63.** Which of the following disability is caused by Fragile 'X' syndrome?

1. Learning disability
2. Intellectual disability
3. Visual impairment
4. Locomotor disability

**64.** Choose the correct statements:

A. Formal system of schooling is based on the philosophies of idealism and realism.
B. The school's formal social system has hierarchy of positions along which people are assigned different roles.
C. Realism does not recommend the definite curriculum.
D. Informal and non-formal education have their roots in the progressive philosophy of education.
E. Idealism believes that knowledge can be obtained without the help of teacher.

Choose the **correct** answer from the options given below:

1. C, D, E Only  2. A, B, D Only
3. B, D, E Only  4. A, C, D Only

**65.** Match the List-I with List-II

| List-I (Theory) | List-II (Attributes) |
|---|---|
| A. Signaling theory | I. Individuals take actions that will likely increase their future earnings |
| B. Human capital theory | II. Individuals choose a course of action that is most in line with their personal preferences |
| C. Behaviourism | III. Information asymmetry |
| D. Theory of rational choice | IV. Study of politics should begin with society |

Choose the **correct** answer from the options given below:

1. A-I, B-IV, C-III, D-II
2. A-IV, B-I, C-II, D-III
3. A-IV, B-III, C-II, D-I
4. A-III, B-I, C-IV, D-II

**66.** Match the List-I with List-II

| List-I (key terms of model of intellect) | List-II (Description) |
|---|---|
| A. Cognition | I. Altering or restructuring intellectual contents. |
| B. Relations | II. An ordering or classification of relations. |
| C. Systems | III. A connection between concepts. |
| D. Transformation | IV. Recognizing and discovering. |

Choose the **correct** answer from the options given below:

1. A-I, B-II, C-III, D-IV
2. A-II, B-IV, C-I, D-III
3. A-IV, B-III, C-II, D-I
4. A-III, B-II, C-I, D-IV

**67.** Match the List-I with List-II

| List-I (Act) | List-II (Year) |
|---|---|
| A. National Trust Act | I. 1999 |
| B. PWD Act | II. 2009 |
| C. RCI Act | III. 1992 |
| D. RTE Act | IV. 1995 |

Choose the **correct** answer from the options given below:

1. A-II, B-III, C-IV, D-I
2. A-I, B-IV, C-III, D-II
3. A-III, B-II, C-IV, D-I
4. A-II, B-III, C-I, D-IV

**68.** Arrange the following goals of Individualised Education Plan (IEP) in correct sequence:

A. Specific  B. Attainable
C. Time bound  D. Result oriented
E. Measurable

Choose the **correct** answer from the options given below:

1. B, A, E, D, C
2. A, E, B, D, C
3. E, A, B, D, C
4. A, B, C, D, E

**69.** One teacher manages most of the class while other teacher works with small group inside or outside of the classroom. This is an example of which co-teaching method.

1. Alternative teaching
2. Parallel teaching
3. Station teaching
4. One teach one assist

**70.** Which of the following statements is true about Sankhya Philosophy?

1. 'Gya' is matter or Prakriti.
2. Vyakta is consequence of the Karya-karana.
3. Avyakta is Purush.
4. Sankhya asserts that existence of God can be proved.

**71.** Match the List-I with List-II: According to Blake and Mouton's Managerial Grid, Match

| List-I | List-II |
|---|---|
| A. Impoverished Management | I. 5,5 |
| B. Authority-compliance | II. 1,1 |
| C. Middle of the Road | III. 9,9 |
| D. Team/Earn Management | IV. 9,1 |

Choose the **correct** answer from the options given below:

1. A-I, B-II, C-IV, D-III
2. A-III, B-I, C-II, D-IV
3. A-II, B-IV, C-I, D-III
4. A-IV, B-III, C-I, D-II

**72.** According to Unruch and Unruch, arrange the curriculum development steps:

A. Content
B. Goals and objectives
C. Need assessment
D. Evaluation
E. Implementation

Choose the **correct** answer from the options given below:

1. B, C, A, E, D
2. A, B, C, D, E
3. E, B, D, C, A
4. A, E, D, B, C

**73.** Arrange the focus points as given in document of NCF 2005 in correct sequence:

A. Availability of minimum infrastructure and material facilities for better learning environment.
B. Reconstruction of school curricula to emphasize the pedagogic potential of work.
C. Integration of environment concerns into teaching disciplines.
D. Emphasis on promoting peace oriented values in all subjects.

Choose the **correct** answer from the options given below:

1. B, D, A, C
2. D, A, B, C
3. B, D, C, A
4. A, B, C, D

**74.** Arrange the steps of systems approach given by Robb (1974).

A. Specifying appropriate strategies
B. Defining and assigning personnel roles
C. Determining initial behaviour
D. Defining objectives
E. Specifying material, aids and media

Choose the **correct** answer from the options given below:

1. C, D, E, A, B
2. B, A, E, C, D
3. C, B, D, A, E
4. D, C, A, E, B

**75.** Which research is a portrayal and explanation of social groups and situations in their real life contexts?

1. Phenomenology research
2. Ethnography research
3. Grounded theory
4. Case study

**76.** Arrange the following stages of an experiment in a research study.

A. Selecting the relevant variables
B. Designing the experiment
C. Conduct the intervention
D. Assigning the participants to the group(s)
E. Conduct the post-test

Choose the **correct** answer from the options given below:

1. D, E, B, A, C
2. C, D, A, B, E
3. B, D, E, A, C
4. A, B, D, C, E

**77.** Who described the theory of Communicable Action?

1. Zongyi Deng
2. Allan Luke
3. Jurgen Habermas
4. Lee Shulman

**78.** Which of the following is a part of internal compliance monitoring?

1. Maintenance of a process for reporting exceptions.
2. Constant reviewing of the policies and procedures in the organization.
3. Periodically assessing and reassessing the risk of criminal conduct.
4. Implementation of the different standards as well as procedures.

**79.** Which of the following statements are true about educational technology?

A. Educational technology borrowed the term 'systems approach' from management studies.
B. By the mid 1950s, educational technology borrowed the term 'systems approach'
C. Technology of Education implies the use of audio-visual aids.
D. Education technology borrowed the term 'corrective feedback' from cybernetics.
E. In initial phase of development of educational technology, it mainly referred to 'technology in education'

Choose the **most appropriate** answer from the options given below:

1. A, B, C Only
2. A, C, D Only
3. A, D, E Only
4. A, C, D, E Only

**80.** Arrange the following commissions according to their year of establishment in ascending order:

A. Justice Verma Commission
B. National Knowledge Commission
C. National Commission on Teachers
D. National Policy on Education
E. National Education Commission

Choose the **correct** answer from the options given below:

1. E, C, D, B, A
2. D, A, B, C, E
3. C, D, E, A, B
4. B, E, C, D, A

**81.** Malcolm Knowles elaborated the term Andragogy in his famous work:

1. Adult Education: Concept, Theory and Practice
2. The Modern Practice of Adult Education: Andragogy vs Pedagogy
3. Theory and Practice of Andragogy
4. Andragogy Education: Concept, Theory and Practice

**82.** Which of the following statements are INCORRECT regarding benefits of inclusion.

A. Social competence and communication skills of children with diverse abilities are deteriorated in inclusive settings.
B. Children with disabilities demonstrate high levels of social interaction with non disabled peers in inclusive settings.

C. Friendships more commonly develop between children with disabilities and those without disabilities in inclusive settings.
D. Children with disabilities demonstrate high levels of social interaction with disabled peers in inclusive settings.
E. Social acceptance of children with diverse abilities is decreased in inclusive settings.

Choose the **correct** answer from the options given below:

1. A and E Only 2. B and C Only
3. C and E Only 4. A and D Only

**83.** Identify INCORRECT statements.

A. Curriculum is based on the philosophy, goals and values of education.
B. Curriculum refers to all the educational activities of the school in widest possible sense.
C. Curriculum is basically concerned with school subjects.
D. Curriculum is a part of syllabus.
E. Curriculum includes not only indoor activities but also outdoor activities of the school.

Choose the **correct** answer from the options given below:

1. A and E Only 2. D and B Only
3. C and D Only 4. E and B Only

**84.** Which one does NOT belong to inclusive approach?

1. Flexible 2. Diagnostic
3. Individualistic 4. Holistic

**85.** Identify correct statements.

A. A wiki allows multiple users to read and write a web document but editing is not allowed.
B. A vlog uses videos as the primary media source.
C. Microblog services allow user to send text based updates or post short messages.
D. To create a wiki for a course, faculty can use either a campus wide learning management system or an open source programme.
E. A blog consists of series of time stamped entries posted by readers followed by blog's creator.

Choose the **correct** answer from the options given below:

1. A, D, E Only 2. B, C, D Only
3. A, B, C Only 4. B, C, E Only

**86.** Halo Effect is very common constant error committed by raters/teachers in assessment of students through rating scale. This error was first mentioned by Wells in 1907 and was named so by ..............

1. Anastasi (1968) 2. Symonds (1925)
3. Murray (1938) 4. Thorndike (1920)

**87.** Match the List-I with List-II:

| List-I (Affective Domain Level) | List-II (Description) |
|---|---|
| A. Organization | I. Willingness to pay attention |
| B. Responding | II. Showing a preference for a value |
| C. Receiving | III. Adopting a constant value system |
| D. Valuing | IV. Participating actively |

Choose the **correct** answer from the options given below:

1. A-II, B-IV, C-III, D-I
2. A-III, B-IV, C-II, D-I
3. A-III, B-IV, C-I, D-II
4. A-II, B-III, C-IV, D-I

**88.** Which is NOT a characteristic of qualitative research?

1. Exploring, developing, understanding a central phenomenon
2. Collecting data based on words
3. Analyzing the data with statistics
4. Writing the report using researcher's subjective reflexivity

**89.** First chairperson of National Council for Teacher Education (NCTE) was .......... .

1. Pankaj Arora 2. Santosh Panda
3. J.S. Rajput 4. M.A. Siddiqui

**90.** Which of the following is NOT a recommendation of National Knowledge Commission (2007) with respect to School Education?

1. Central Legislation for the right to education.
2. More rigidity in disbursal of funds.
3. Decentralization and greater local autonomy.
4. Expansion of functional literacy.

**Direction (Qs. No. 91 to 95):** *Read the passage carefully and answer the questions that follows:*

Phenomenology lies on the opposite side of the explanatory gap from computational theories. It is the study of consciousness from the first-person perspective-how the world appears to me. There is a long tradition of phenomenology in European philosophy and psychology, but it is sometimes dismissed as a legitimate approach to the study of perception, because it is inherently subjective. Scientific approaches are usually considered to require objective methods. However, phenomenological studies can be performed using a variant of standard empirical scientific methods, including hypothesis generation and observation. There are several key differences between conventional psychophysical observations and phenomenological observations. The convention in psychophysics is to keep subjects naïve as to the purpose of the experiment, and give them a well-defined task with highly constrained responses such as "yes" versus "no". In phenomenological experiments subjects are often fully informed about the purpose of the experiment, and their task is kept relatively open with loosely constrained responses. Response classification may occur only after the data have been examined. A key check on validity in phenomenological experiments is intersubjectivity, or agreement among individuals about the nature of their perceptual experience.

**91.** Phenomenology is:

1. a type of quantitative research.
2. an explanatory gap.
3. an example of computational theories.
4. dependent upon researcher's perspective.

**92.** In a phenomenological study:

1. hypothesis generation is never required.
2. empirical scientific methods are not possible.
3. scientific observation is used.
4. aim of the study is kept secret.

**93.** In phenomenology, consensus among persons about a perception relates to the concept of:

1. Validity 2. Reliability
3. Generalisability 4. Usability

**94.** Scientific approach to research .......... 

1. can never be based on personal experiences.
2. usually to be objective in nature.
3. can never be qualitative.
4. always uses some statistics.

**95.** In psychophysics ............

1. subjects are less aware of the purpose.
2. subjects are fully aware of the purpose.
3. tasks have more constrained responses.
4. tasks have less constrained responses.

**Direction (Qs. No. 96 to 100):** *Read the passage carefully and answer the questions that follows:*

The etymology of the word allows us to see the child with a disability as fighting against the odds. How high those odds are depends on many factors, of which type and severity of impairment are two of immediate concern. Irrespective of these factors, the principle of the teacher's role as assisting the young person not to allow the problem to impede development is attractive.

The metaphor does not lie only with the child with the particular disability; in the inclusive classroom it allows a picture of the teacher monitoring the learner, all learners, irrespective of physique, internal bodily systems, psychological adjustment or intelligence. Inclusion does not mean that handicap does not exist. If a disability handicaps performance in any significant way then in those areas a specific attack needs to be made on how the problem can be overcome. This may mean modifying curriculum demands and hence the need for a critical, objective assessment of skills and strengths that can be built up. It may mean devising and teaching strategies the child can use when faced with the situations they find difficult. Focusing on these practical aspects of the learner's needs will have the effect of lessening thinking about the disability and more on the achievement of goals and increasing abilities. It will also change the teacher's attitudes. Inclusion will be seen not as an insurmountable challenge but as a process of learning that affects everyone in the class and school.

**96.** Inclusive philosophy means that:
1. The teacher will not give extra time to a particular learner.
2. The teacher has to use prescribed pedagogies only.
3. The children with profound disabilities should be sent to special schools.
4. Irrespective of the challenge, the teacher will help the learner.

**97.** Inclusion in education refers to:
1. general solutions to all problems.
2. specific solutions to specific problems.
3. believing that disability does not exist.
4. a challenge almost impossible to overcome.

**98.** Challenges faced by a person with disability depend most on:
1. Attitudes of the society.
2. Degree of disability.
3. Socio-economic condition of the family.
4. Behaviour of peers.

**99.** Which of the following is NOT a part of inclusion:
1. Increased thinking about disabilities
2. Modifying curriculum
3. Evaluating strengths
4. Assessing skills

**100.** Inclusive classrooms are:
1. related to children with disability only.
2. free from learner diversity.
3. focused on all learners.
4. usually an eutopia.

## ANSWERS

| 1 | 2 | 3 | 4 | 5 | 6 | 7 | 8 | 9 | 10 |
|---|---|---|---|---|---|---|---|---|---|
| 2 | 4 | 4 | 3 | 3 | 3 | 2 | 1 | 4 | 1 |
| **11** | **12** | **13** | **14** | **15** | **16** | **17** | **18** | **19** | **20** |
| 1 | 3 | 2 | 1 | * | 3 | 2 | 2 | 4 | 3 |
| **21** | **22** | **23** | **24** | **25** | **26** | **27** | **28** | **29** | **30** |
| * | 4 | 4 | 4 | 4 | 3 | 2 | 1 | 3 | 1 |
| **31** | **32** | **33** | **34** | **35** | **36** | **37** | **38** | **39** | **40** |
| 4 | 1 | 3 | 2 | 1 | 1 | 3 | 1 | 2 | 3 |
| **41** | **42** | **43** | **44** | **45** | **46** | **47** | **48** | **49** | **50** |
| 3 | 3 | 2 | 4 | 4 | * | 3 | 3 | 4 | 4 |

| 51 | 52 | 53 | 54 | 55 | 56 | 57 | 58 | 59 | 60 |
|---|---|---|---|---|---|---|---|---|---|
| 3 | 1 | 1 | 2 | 1 | 2 | 2 | 2 | 4 | 2 |
| **61** | **62** | **63** | **64** | **65** | **66** | **67** | **68** | **69** | **70** |
| 2 | 2 | 2 | 2 | 4 | 3 | 2 | 2 | 1 | 2 |
| **71** | **72** | **73** | **74** | **75** | **76** | **77** | **78** | **79** | **80** |
| 3 | 1 | 3 | 4 | 2 | 4 | 3 | 2 | 3 | 1 |
| **81** | **82** | **83** | **84** | **85** | **86** | **87** | **88** | **89** | **90** |
| 2 | 1 | 3 | 3 | 2 | 4 | 3 | 3 | 3 | 2 |
| **91** | **92** | **93** | **94** | **95** | **96** | **97** | **98** | **99** | **100** |
| 4 | 3 | 1 | 2 | 3 | 4 | 2 | 2 | 1 | 3 |

# Explanatory Answers

**1.** Narrative research design focuses on understanding the personal and lived experiences of individuals.

It collects data mainly through interviews, life stories, journals, and autobiographies.

Researchers work closely and collaboratively with participants to build authentic narratives.

They later code and analyze the stories to identify common themes and patterns.

This design is qualitative and emphasizes depth, meaning, and context rather than numbers.

Collecting data through rating scales is a quantitative method and not part of narrative research.

**2.** Jerome Bruner proposed four major principles of instruction to guide how students learn effectively.

- The fourth principle emphasizes that feedback is essential for achieving mastery in learning.
- This principle states that learners need information about their performance to know how well they are progressing.
- Feedback helps them identify mistakes, correct them, and reinforce correct responses.
- It ensures that learning becomes a self-monitoring process where students continually improve their understanding.

Thus, the statement about receiving feedback to achieve mastery relates to Bruner's Fourth Principle.

**3.** MOOC stands for Massive Open Online Course, and several major platforms offer such courses globally.

- Udacity was founded by Sebastian Thrun, who was a Stanford professor and played a key role in Google's self-driving car project.
- Coursera was founded by Daphne Koller and Andrew Ng, both Stanford professors known for promoting online education.
- Udemy was founded by Eren Bali, Gagan Biyani, and Oktay Caglar to allow instructors to create and sell their own courses to learners worldwide.
- edX was created by Harvard University and MIT as a non-profit platform offering high-quality courses from top universities.

Therefore, the correct matching is A-IV, B-III, C-I, D-II.

**4.** These four are advanced limbs of Ashtanga Yoga that focus on mental control and meditation.

- Dharana means concentration, where the mind is fixed on a single point or thought, which is the first stage of meditation.
- Pratyahar means withdrawing the senses from external objects so that the mind turns inward and avoids distractions.
- Dhyan means continuous meditation, where the mind flows steadily towards one chosen object, showing deep focus.

- Samadhi is the final state, where the meditator becomes completely absorbed in the object and unites with it, achieving total stillness.

So, the correct match is A-II, B-I, C-IV, D-III.

5. The conflict perspective views education as a means to maintain social inequality and class divisions. It highlights the hidden curriculum, which teaches unspoken norms and values supporting the dominant class. It also emphasizes credentialism, where degrees are valued more than actual skills or knowledge. This system benefits the elite and limits opportunities for the marginalized groups in society. It views education as a tool to reproduce existing social hierarchies and power structures.

   Therefore, the perspective that fits is the conflict perspective.

6. Flanders' Interaction Analysis Model is used to analyze classroom verbal behavior between teachers and students. It mainly focuses on verbal communication categories like teacher talk, student talk, and silence. However, Charles Galloway's model emphasizes that non-verbal communication can be even more effective during classroom interaction. His model recognizes gestures, facial expressions, eye contact, and body language as crucial to classroom communication. It suggests that non-verbal cues often convey meaning more clearly and instantly than words.

   Hence, the model assuming non-verbal communication to be more effective is Charles Galloway's model.

7. The National Curriculum Framework for Integrated Teacher Education Programme (NCF-ITEP) 2023 is a key policy document in India. It aims to reform and standardize teacher education to improve quality in school education. This framework has been developed and published by the National Council for Teacher Education (NCTE). The NCTE is the statutory body responsible for planning and coordinating teacher education in India. NCERT creates school curriculum, while NCTE focuses on teacher education curriculum and policy.

   Therefore, the NCF-ITEP 2023 was developed by NCTE.

8. Instructional System Development (ISD) models explain how educational technology can be designed and implemented. The Fourth Generation ISD model represents the complexity and dynamic nature of modern educational systems. It was proposed by Robert Tennyson in 1995 to handle non-linear and adaptive learning environments. This model integrates systematic planning, feedback loops, and real-time adjustments in instruction. It contrasts with earlier linear ISD models that followed fixed steps.

   So, the correct answer is Robert Tennyson (1995).

9. Nel Noddings is an educational philosopher who emphasized the concept of 'Care Ethics' in education. Her approach highlights the importance of relationships, empathy, and nurturing in teaching. She believed caring is a moral foundation and should guide teacher-student interactions. This contrasts with purely cognitive or authoritarian approaches to education. Her work stresses that emotional support and moral sensitivity are vital for holistic learning.

   Therefore, the thinker associated with care ethics is Nel Noddings.

10. A good research hypothesis guides the study and must have specific key qualities.

    - It should be clear and precise so that it is easily understood and interpreted.
    - It must be testable so researchers can verify or falsify it through data.
    - It should also indicate a relationship between variables to guide analysis.

    Ethical basis (C) is important in research conduct but not a defining feature of a hypothesis.

    General vague statements (D) are weak and not desirable in a hypothesis.

    Hence, A, B, E are correct.

11. Educational research follows a systematic and logical sequence of steps.

    - The first step is identifying the research problem to know what will be studied.
    - Then comes the review of related literature to understand existing knowledge and gaps.

- Next is the formulation of hypothesis to make a tentative prediction.
- Then researchers do data collection followed by data analysis and interpretation.

So, the correct sequence is E, A, C, B, D.

**12.** These are major milestones in India's use of educational technology over time.

- The Satellite Instructional Television Experiment (SITE) began in 1975 to broadcast educational content.
- Then the Centre for Educational Technology (CET) was set up to promote technology in education.
- Later, the Indian National Satellite (INSAT) system was launched for communication and education.
- Then came the Computer Literacy and Studies in Schools (CLASS) project to promote computer education.
- Finally, the SWAYAM platform was launched for online courses.

Thus, the correct order is D, B, A, C, E.

**13.** Snowball sampling is a non-probability sampling technique used for hard-to-reach populations. In this method, initial participants refer other participants, creating a chain of recruitment. It is commonly used in qualitative or sociological studies where subjects are difficult to find.

It is not used when the population is readily available because other simpler methods would work better.

Also, it does not give equal chance to all individuals because selection depends on referrals.

So, the statements (B) and (D) are incorrect about snowball sampling.

**14.** The quote "Curriculum is a plan or programme for all experiences which the learner encounters under the direction of the school" was stated by Ralph W. Oliva. Oliva viewed curriculum as a comprehensive plan covering all academic and non-academic experiences students go through under school guidance. He emphasized that curriculum is not just subjects or textbooks, but every planned activity and experience that contributes to learning. This includes classroom learning, co-curricular activities, guidance programs, and all teacher-directed experiences. In contrast, Carter V. Good defined curriculum as a set of prescribed subjects, and Tyler and Hilda Taba focused on curriculum as a structured process to achieve objectives. Galen Saylor described it as the totality of learner experiences under school supervision, but this specific quote is from Oliva.

**15.** The question asks which document does not advocate inclusive education, but in reality all the listed documents support it.

- The National Policy on Disability (2006) clearly promotes inclusive education by ensuring access, support services, and equal participation for children with disabilities.
- The Right to Education Act (2009) guarantees free and compulsory education to all children including those with disabilities, promoting inclusion in schools.
- The Rights of Persons with Disabilities Act (2016) makes inclusive education a legal mandate and ensures accessibility and reasonable accommodations.
- The National Education Policy (2020) emphasizes inclusive and equitable education for all learners, aiming to remove barriers to learning.

Hence, none of the listed documents go against inclusive education — the question is flawed as all advocate for it.

All four documents support inclusive education.

**16.** SWOT analysis is a strategic planning tool to evaluate Strengths, Weaknesses, Opportunities, and Threats.

- The first step is to brainstorm and list all internal and external factors.
- Next, prioritize the key factors based on their impact on goals.
- Then, analyse the external factors like opportunities and threats in the environment.
- After analysis, develop strategic actions to address the key issues.
- Finally, implement and monitor the changes to ensure effectiveness.

Thus, the correct order is E, B, C, A, D.

**17.** Grounded theory designs are systematic qualitative research procedures. They are used when researchers aim to generate or build a theory grounded in data from the field. This design leads to explanations of processes, actions, or interactions among people. Data collection and analysis occur simultaneously in a continuous comparative manner. It is often used in sociology, education, and health studies to build new theories.

Therefore, the correct answer is grounded theory designs.

**18.** Experimental research designs differ mainly in the extent of randomization and control they use.

- Pre-experimental designs are very basic; they lack randomization and control groups, so internal validity is weak.
- True-experimental designs involve manipulation of the independent variable with random assignment of participants, giving strong internal validity.
- Quasi-experimental designs include some control features but lack full randomization, often used in real-world settings where random assignment is not possible.
- Factorial designs are advanced experiments that study the interaction effects of two or more independent variables simultaneously.

Therefore, the correct matching is A-II, B-I, C-IV, D-III.

**19.** Defense mechanisms are unconscious strategies used by the ego to reduce anxiety from unwanted thoughts or impulses.

- Repression means pushing painful or frightening memories or impulses out of conscious awareness to avoid distress.
- Rationalization means justifying one's behavior with logical or socially acceptable reasons to appear rational even if they are not the real motives.
- Reaction formation means expressing the opposite of one's true motive very strongly to hide the real one, such as being overly kind to someone you dislike.
- Projection means attributing one's own undesirable traits or feelings to others in exaggerated amounts to avoid acknowledging them in oneself.

So, the correct match is A-II, B-I, C-IV, D-III.

**20.** In-service education helps teachers improve their knowledge, skills, and professional attitudes.

- It helps them recognize their problems and solve them collectively through shared wisdom.
- It aims to broaden the mental outlook of teachers to keep pace with educational changes.
- It also works to increase the professional efficiency of teachers through continuous learning.
- It does not aim to give financial incentives or provide facility away from duty.

Thus, the correct set is B, C, D only.

**21.** The learning theory approach to counselling applies principles of learning, reinforcement, and conditioning to change behavior.

- Pepinskys did not focus only on strengthening the counsellee's behavior; he emphasized understanding cultural and contextual factors influencing learning, so (B) is incorrect.
- Irrational behaviour can be changed through learning and relearning using approaches like Rational Emotive Behavior Therapy (REBT), so (D) is also incorrect.
- Pepinskys highlighted the importance of cultural context in learning, so saying it does not affect learning (E) is incorrect.
- Dollard & Miller did relate psychoanalytic concepts to reinforcement learning, and Eysenck did refer to conditioning-based counselling as "behaviour therapy", so (A) and (C) are correct.

Therefore, the incorrect statements are B, D, and E — but this exact combination is missing from the given options, so the question is flawed.

None of the given options—Correct set is B, D, and E

**22.** Indian philosophy describes four positions (states) of the soul (consciousness).

- Jagrat is the waking state where the mind is active and senses are functioning.
- Swapna is the dream state where the mind is active but senses are inactive.
- Pragya is the deep sleep state where both mind and senses are inactive.
- Turiya is the fourth transcendental state of pure consciousness beyond waking, dream, and sleep.

Hence, the order is A (waking), C (dream), D (deep sleep), B (turiya).

**23.** The Programme Evaluation and Review Technique (PERT) is mainly used for planning and scheduling complex projects where activity times are uncertain. It is a network model that represents the sequence and dependencies of activities visually. It is a project management tool widely used for coordinating and controlling large-scale projects. It is also considered a statistical tool because it uses three time estimates (optimistic, most likely, pessimistic) and a formula to calculate expected time.

However, PERT is not a process-oriented technique; it is event-oriented, focusing on milestones or events that mark the completion of activities.

Therefore, the statement that it is process-oriented is NOT true about PERT.

**24.** The Herbartian approach to teaching follows five formal steps called the syntax. These are Preparation, Presentation, Comparison and Abstraction, Generalization, and Application. Preparation introduces the topic and links prior knowledge. Presentation gives new material, and Comparison/Abstraction helps find similarities.

Focus is not one of the formal Herbartian steps; it is not part of this syntax.

Therefore, the option Focus is not included in the steps.

**25.** The CIPP model of curriculum evaluation was proposed by Stufflebeam.

- Context evaluation studies the environment and needs where the curriculum is implemented.
- Input evaluation gives data on how to utilize resources to achieve goals.
- Process evaluation monitors curriculum implementation and decisions during execution.
- Product evaluation checks if curriculum outcomes meet intended goals.

Hence, the correct match is A-IV, B-III, C-II, D-I.

**26.** The Programme of Action (PoA), 1992 was created to implement the revised National Policy on Education (NPE), 1986. To achieve this, the government constituted 23 task forces on different subjects related to education. These task forces were composed of educationists, experts, and government representatives. Each task force was assigned a specific area of the NPE to examine and prepare a detailed implementation plan. The reports submitted by these task forces were used to frame the final PoA presented in the Parliament.

Thus, the correct number of task forces is 23.

**27.** These statements are from prominent Indian educational thinkers.

- (A) "This education ought to be for them a kind of insurance against unemployment."
— M.K. Gandhi (III)

Gandhi's Nai Talim or Basic Education aimed to equip students with productive craft-based skills for self-reliance and to prevent unemployment.

- (B) "You cannot teach a child anymore than you can grow a plant. The plant develops its own nature." — Swami Vivekananda (IV)

Vivekananda believed knowledge is inherent in the child, and the teacher's role is only to remove obstacles, letting the child's nature unfold naturally.

- (C) "Every child is an inquirer, an investigator, analyser, a merciless anatomist."
— Sri Aurobindo (II)

Aurobindo emphasized encouraging children's natural curiosity and investigative spirit to promote self-driven learning.

- (D) "True education consists in knowing the use of any useful material... and to build along with life a real shelter for life." — R.N. Tagore (I)

Tagore promoted holistic education connected to real-life skills and harmony with the environment.

So, correct matching is A-III, B-IV, C-II, D-I.

**28.** The observation, "one of the most useful methods of enriching rural life is to locate educational institutions in rural areas," is from the Secondary Education Commission, 1952–53 (Mudaliar Commission). In its report, the Commission explicitly recommended establishing institutions in rural locations to strengthen rural communities and ensure they are not disadvantaged compared to urban areas. This specific wording does not originate from the University Education Commission (1948) or the Kothari Commission (1964–66), though those bodies also discussed rural concerns in other contexts.

Therefore, the Commission that made this statement was the Secondary Education Commission (1952–53).

**29.** Constructivism views learning as an active process where learners build their own understanding. It says learning goes from inside out, meaning learners use prior knowledge to construct new meaning. They actively impose organization and meaning on their environment rather than passively receiving information.

Option 3 states learners receive information, transform it, and store it, which reflects an information processing theory, not constructivism.

Constructivism contrasts with such theories because it emphasizes knowledge construction, not just storage.

Hence, statement 3 is NOT true about constructivism.

**30.** Writing a reflective journal follows a structured order to promote critical thinking.

- It begins with a Description of the event or experience in detail.
- Then comes Feelings where the writer reflects on their emotions during the experience.
- Next is Evaluation to judge what was good or bad about the experience.
- Then Conclusion to summarize what has been learned.
- Finally, an Action Plan is made to improve future practice.

Thus, the correct order is B, A, D, E, C.

**31.** A portfolio is a purposeful collection of a learner's work that shows effort, progress, and achievement over time.

- It usually contains an index or map to organize its contents clearly.
- It includes a collection of selected, illustrative materials drawn from practice as evidence of learning.
- It also contains a commentary or reflection discussing the evidence to show self-assessment and growth.

However, portfolios are known to have high validity but often lower reliability, not the other way around, so (C) is incorrect.

Hence, the correct set is A, B, D only.

**32.** Zero-Base Budgeting (ZBB) is a budgeting method where every expense must be justified from zero each period.

- It requires adaptability because it questions all existing and new expenditures.
- It involves choice and withdrawal, meaning activities can be continued or discontinued based on their justification.

It does not follow an incremental approach like traditional budgeting (B).

Also, decision-making units must be identified and management hierarchy is part of the system, so (C) and (E) are incorrect.

Thus, the correct answer is A and D only.

**33.** These are important models of curriculum evaluation with their years of establishment.

- Tyler's model is one of the earliest and came in 1949 focusing on objectives-based evaluation.
- States model was developed in 1967 emphasizing curriculum alignment with standards.

- Scriven model emerged in 1991 and focused on goal-free evaluation.
- Kirkpatrick model of training evaluation came in 1959 with four levels of evaluation.

Thus, the correct match is A-III, B-IV, C-II, D-I.

**34.** The United Nations Convention on the Rights of Persons with Disabilities (UNCRPD) is a global treaty promoting disability rights. Article 8 specifically focuses on awareness-raising to combat stereotypes and promote respect for rights and dignity of persons with disabilities. It calls on governments to conduct public awareness campaigns and encourage media to portray positive images. It also promotes training for professionals to respect rights and dignity.

Article 7 is about children, 13 about access to justice, and 14 about liberty and security.

Therefore, the correct answer is Article 8.

**35.** Effective curriculum transaction ensures that the planned curriculum is delivered to students meaningfully and successfully.

- Review of prior work helps the teacher gauge students' existing knowledge and link new content with it.
- Material organisation ensures that textbooks, tools, and resources are available and arranged for smooth teaching.
- Time management allows teachers to plan lessons so the whole curriculum is completed within the academic schedule.
- Knowing, observing, and understanding children helps tailor teaching to students' learning styles and needs.
- Individual responsibility is more a student outcome than a teacher requirement, so it is not part of curriculum transaction.

Correct options is A, B, C, D Only

**36.** Tyler's model of curriculum evaluation is one of the earliest and most influential models. He stated that curriculum objectives should be derived from three main sources — the learner (student), the society, and the subject matter. The student's needs and interests help in making learning relevant and engaging. The society's needs and demands ensure the curriculum serves social and cultural development. The subject matter provides the disciplinary knowledge that must be taught for academic growth.

Thus, the correct answer is student, society, and subject matter.

**37.** Jerome Bruner's concept attainment approach emphasizes discovery and inductive thinking. This method was later structured as a model of teaching by Bruce Joyce and Marsha Weil. They developed it as part of their models of teaching framework to encourage conceptual understanding. The model trains learners to observe examples and non-examples to form concepts. It develops analytical and categorization skills in students through guided discovery.

Thus, the correct answer is Bruce Joyce and Marsha Weil.

**38.** Checking options:

- Leader-Member Exchange (LMX) theory is indeed a dyadic leadership theory that focuses on the unique two-way relationships between a leader and each team member, making this statement correct.
- Variable-value is not a type of Poka-Yoke method — the actual types are contact, fixed-value, and motion-step methods, so this is incorrect.
- Six-Sigma is a quality improvement and defect reduction technique used in business, not in martial arts, so this is incorrect.
- C.K. Prahlad correctly highlighted the bottom of the pyramid market opportunity among the world's poorest populations, so this is correct.
- Fiedler's contingency theory states that leadership effectiveness depends on the situation, not one best style, so this is incorrect.

Therefore, the only correct statements are A and D.

**39.** Flanders' Interaction Analysis Category System (FIACS) classifies classroom verbal behavior into 10 categories from teacher talk to pupil talk.

- Category 2 is Praise or encouragement, where the teacher reinforces or motivates students. Category 3 is Accepts or uses ideas of pupils (C), showing teacher acknowledgment of student contributions.
- Category 4 is Asking questions to stimulate student thinking, and Category 5 is Lecture (B) which is teacher giving content.
- Category 7 is Pupil talk initiation where students voluntarily initiate ideas or questions.

Arranging these categories in increasing order gives E (2), C (3), A (4), B (5), D (7).

**40.** Demand factors for finance in education influence how much funding is required. They include demographic factors like population and enrollment growth, economic factors like income levels and employment trends, and political factors like government policies and priorities. Religious factors do not generally determine the demand for educational finance in public systems.

Therefore, the factor that does not come under demand factors is religious factors.

**41.** Action research is a systematic process used by teachers to improve their own practice.

- **Identification of the problem:** This is always the first step. The researcher recognizes and clearly defines a specific problem or area needing improvement.
- **Formulation of action hypothesis:** After identifying the problem, a tentative hypothesis is framed to predict a possible solution or explanation that can be tested through action.
- **(Implied — Designing the intervention / action plan):** Based on the hypothesis, a strategy or plan is created that outlines the steps and methods to tackle the problem effectively.
- **Formulation of action design:** This involves detailing the specific activities, resources, and timeline to implement the planned intervention in a systematic manner.
- **Evaluation of the result of action research:** After implementing the plan, data is collected to evaluate its effectiveness, analyze the outcomes, and decide on further actions if needed.

Hence, correct sequence is B, A, C, E, D.

**42.** Checking options:

**A. NHERC as "one umbrella institution" — Incorrect.** NEP-2020 creates one umbrella institution called the Higher Education Commission of India (HECI) with four independent verticals under it. NHERC is only the first vertical (the single-point regulator), not the umbrella itself.

**B. Independent vertical for accreditation (NAC) — Correct.** NEP-2020 explicitly establishes the National Accreditation Council (NAC) as the second vertical of HECI and a "meta-accreditor" overseeing an ecosystem of accrediting institutions

**C. Regulatory regime shall not encourage private philanthropy — Incorrect.** NEP-2020 states the regulatory regime shall encourage private philanthropic efforts, while curbing commercialization through audit/disclosure and other checks.

**D. Aim for self-governing HEIs within 15 years — Correct.** NEP-2020 provides a 15-year phased pathway: HEIs will work through graded accreditation and autonomy so that in about 15 years all HEIs aim to become independent, self-governing institutions/degree-granting clusters.

**E. Private HEIs empowered to set fees independently — Correct (with safeguards).** NEP-2020 introduces a progressive fee-determination regime that empowers private HEIs to set programme fees independently, within laid-out norms/upper limits, and with requirements for transparency and social obligations (freeships/scholarships, no arbitrary hikes during a student's enrolment).

Hence, correct options is B, D, E only.

**43.** Ethical considerations in educational research protect participants and ensure research integrity.

- Informed consent means participants agree voluntarily after being fully informed.
- Confidentiality ensures their personal data is kept private and secure.
- Avoidance of plagiarism maintains academic honesty and gives credit to original authors.
- Manipulating data and providing misleading information are unethical practices.

So, the correct ethical elements are A, B, and D only.

**44.** These are major Indian commissions/committees and their years of establishment.

- National Commission on Teachers was set up in 1999 to review teacher education.
- Yashpal Committee Report came in 2009, focusing on higher education reforms.
- Justice Verma Committee Report came in 2012, addressing teacher education reforms.
- National Knowledge Commission was established in 2007 to improve knowledge infrastructure.

Thus, the correct match is A-II, B-IV, C-III, D-I.

**45.** Albert Bandura made key contributions to social learning theory in a sequence.

- First, Bandura and Walters introduced modelling behaviour through observation.
- Then, Bandura proposed the Social Learning Theory emphasizing observational learning and imitation.
- Later, he introduced the concept of Reciprocal Determinism where behaviour, person, and environment influence each other.
- Finally, he used examples of aggressive children (Bobo doll experiments) to explain how environment and behaviour interact.

So, the chronological order is A, B, C, D.

**46.** Soren Kierkegaard emphasized individual existence, inward truth, and subjective experience as central to human life.

- The world is ideas-centred belongs to idealism, not existentialism, so it is not related to Kierkegaard.
- Subjective experience and objectivity both are important also does not fit, because Kierkegaard stressed subjective truth over objectivity in matters of existence and faith.
- A truth is subjective, individuality before thinking, and existential self-experience all align with his philosophy.

Since none of the answer options show only B and D, the correct response is that none of the given options is correct.

**47.** Hersey and Blanchard's situational leadership model (1999) links leadership style to follower readiness.

The stages are:

- R1: Unable and unwilling/insecure
- R2: Unable but willing/confident
- R3: Able but unwilling/insecure
- R4: Able and willing

People who are motivated and have appropriate required skills (option 3) does not match any original wording — it blends R3 and R4.

Hence, this is NOT a defined stage of follower readiness.

**48.** The 'Unfreeze–Change–Refreeze' model is a classic model of organizational change and development. It was given by Kurt Lewin, a pioneer in social psychology. Unfreeze prepares people for change by challenging existing beliefs. Change involves adopting new behaviors, processes, or mindsets. Refreeze stabilizes these new practices as the new norm.

Hence, the correct answer is Kurt Lewin.

**49.** Let's analyze each statement:

A. Factor cost in education can't be measured like firms/industries → Incorrect, because education has intangible outputs.

B. There are no separate price indices for education → Correct, cost analysis relies on general indices.

C. Educational demand is an external determinant of educational cost → Correct, it affects needed resources.

D. Economic growth does limit revenue availability → So this statement is incorrect.

E. Unit costs have been used in many ways for different objectives → Correct.

Hence, correct are B, C, and E only.

**50.** According to NEP 2020 recommendations for teachers:

A. Recruitment and deployment → Transfers only in very special circumstances to ensure stability.

B. Service environment and culture → School complexes can share counsellors and staff to improve support.

C. Continuous professional development → Platforms for teachers to share ideas and best practices.

D. Career management and progression → No school stage will be considered more important than any other.

This matches the correct sequence A-III, B-IV, C-I, D-II.

**51.** The statement "An individual is intelligent in proportion as he is able to carry on abstract thinking" defines intelligence in terms of the ability to think conceptually and symbolically rather than concretely. This definition was given by Lewis Terman, a prominent American psychologist who helped revise the Stanford-Binet Intelligence Scale. Terman believed abstract reasoning was a core feature of human intelligence and used this idea as the basis for measuring intelligence through tests. His approach focused on mental age and IQ as indicators of cognitive ability.

Therefore, the correct answer is Terman.

**52.** Phenomenological analysis is a qualitative research approach focusing on understanding human experience as it is lived. The central insight in phenomenology is the theory of intentionality, which states that consciousness is always directed toward something (an object or experience). This means experiences are not isolated but always involve a relationship between the subject and the world. This idea was originally emphasized by Edmund Husserl, the founder of phenomenology.

Thus, the correct answer is theory of intentionality.

**53.** Writing objectives in behavioural terms makes them observable and measurable.

- Robert Mager emphasized using action verbs rather than mental processes to clearly state what learners will do.
- Regional College of Education, Mysore (NCERT-1972) focused on mental abilities in behavioral objectives.
- B.S. Bloom shifted the emphasis from content to objectives by classifying learning into cognitive, affective, and psychomotor domains.
- Robert Miller's biological origin theory and Mager covering all three domains are incorrect in this context.

So, the correct combination is B, C, E only.

**54.** The functions of management are key processes in achieving organizational goals.

- Planning is about bridging the gap between where we are and where we want to be.
- Organizing involves providing the structure with everything useful for achieving objectives.
- Staffing is about manning the organizational structure with competent personnel.
- Directing is about activating organizational methods to work efficiently.

Thus, the correct match is A-II, B-III, C-IV, D-I.

**55.** PCK (Pedagogical Content Knowledge) is a concept explaining the blend of content knowledge and pedagogical skills teachers need to teach effectively. It was first introduced by Lee Shulman in 1986. He argued that good teaching requires not just knowing the subject but also knowing how to make it understandable to students. PCK bridges the gap between what is taught (content) and how it is taught (pedagogy).

Therefore, the correct answer is Lee Shulman.

**56.** The UN Convention on the Rights of Persons with Disabilities (UNCRPD) outlines key guiding principles to protect and promote the rights of persons with disabilities.

These include non-discrimination, which ensures equal treatment; accessibility, which ensures equal access to services and environments; and equality of opportunity, which ensures fair chances for participation.

Partial participation and segregated approach are contrary to the spirit of inclusion promoted by the UNCRPD.

The convention strongly advocates full participation and inclusion in society.

So, the correct principles among the options are A, B, and D only.

**57.** Carl Rogers' theory of personality (humanistic approach) emphasizes the self-concept and conditions of worth.

- He stated that the perceived self influences one's view of the world and behavior.
- He also emphasized that unconditional positive regard helps individuals function more effectively and everyone has an ideal self they strive toward.

- Self-actualisers being the healthiest 1% is from Maslow, not Rogers.
- Defending against truth if self-concept matches experience is the opposite of Rogers' concept of congruence, so it is false.

Thus, the correct assertions are B, C, and D only.

**58.** The term 'x-MOOC' refers to massive open online courses designed for large-scale content delivery and assessment, often lecture-based. It contrasts with 'c-MOOC' (connectivist MOOCs), which emphasize collaborative knowledge creation. The term 'x-MOOC' was coined in 2012 by Stephen Downes, a Canadian educational theorist and one of the pioneers of MOOCs. He used it to distinguish the newer, structured MOOCs from the earlier connectivist models.

Therefore, the correct answer is Stephen Downes.

**59.** Idealism emphasizes ideas, moral and spiritual development, and eternal truths in education. It gives preference to subjects that develop mind and character, like literature, philosophy, and arts (so statement 3 is true). It focuses more on aims of education than on methods (2 is true) and does not give equal preference to all subjects (1 is false). However, Idealism does not prioritize present experiences of the child (4 is false) — this is more aligned with pragmatism or progressivism.

Therefore, the statement not true about idealism is 4.

**60.** In Jean Piaget's cognitive development theory, the pre-operational stage (ages 2–7) is when children are imaginative, egocentric, and full of magical thinking and fantasies. They engage in pretend play and struggle to distinguish reality from imagination. Formal operational (11+ years) involves abstract thinking, and concrete operational (7–11 years) involves logical reasoning about concrete events. Sensorimotor (0–2 years) is focused on sensory and motor experiences.

Thus, children are dreamers with magical thoughts mainly in the pre-operational stage.

**61.** The ASSURE model is an instructional design framework with six steps: Analyze learners, State objectives, Select methods/media/materials, Utilize media and materials, Require learner participation, and Evaluate and revise.

These steps guide teachers in planning and delivering effective technology-integrated lessons.

The step "Analyze teacher" is NOT part of the six components — it focuses on analyzing the learners, not the teacher.

All other given options are real parts of the ASSURE model.

So, the correct answer is Analyze teacher.

**62.** The correct sequence for budget formulation and its role in implementing educational programmes is indeed A → B → D → C.

- First, the Finance department issues guidelines to set the framework and ensure all departments follow national priorities.
- Then, Heads of departments pass these instructions to subordinate offices to prepare detailed budget proposals.
- Next, the Legislature appraises departmental performance and votes on expenditure to approve the budget.
- Finally, the Budget serves as an instrument to implement policies by releasing funds for planned educational programmes.

Hence, correct sequence is A, B, D, C.

**63.** Fragile X syndrome is a genetic condition caused by a mutation on the X chromosome. It is the most common inherited cause of intellectual disability. It leads to delayed development, learning difficulties, and cognitive impairments. It does not typically cause visual or locomotor disabilities. While it can involve learning issues, the main classification is intellectual disability.

So, the correct answer is intellectual disability.

**64.** Formal education systems are traditionally based on idealism and realism philosophies, emphasizing structured content and discipline. They also have a formal social hierarchy assigning roles, like principals, teachers, and students.

Realism does recommend a definite curriculum is false because it stresses organized, real-world knowledge.

Informal and non-formal education align with progressive philosophy, focusing on flexible, learner-centered methods.

Idealism does not claim knowledge can be gained without teachers (E is false), as it values teacher guidance.

So, the correct statements are A, B, and D.

**65.** Signaling theory deals with information asymmetry — people signal their abilities (like degrees) to employers.

Human capital theory says individuals invest in education to increase future earnings.

Behaviourism is unrelated to politics but focuses on learning through conditioning, while Theory of rational choice says people act based on their personal preferences.

The given attribute "Study of politics should begin with society" does not fit these theories and is likely a distractor.

So, the correct match is A-III, B-I, C-IV, D-II.

**66.** J.P. Guilford's Structure of Intellect (SOI) model describes different dimensions of human intelligence.

- Cognition refers to the ability to recognize and discover new information.
- Relations mean identifying connections between concepts.
- Systems refer to the ordering or classification of relations into larger structures.
- Transformation involves altering or restructuring intellectual content to create something new.

Hence, the correct matching is A-IV, B-III, C-II, D-I.

**67.** These are major legislations related to education and disabilities in India with their years:

- National Trust Act was enacted in 1999 to support persons with autism, cerebral palsy, and intellectual disabilities.
- PWD (Persons with Disabilities) Act was passed in 1995 as India's first comprehensive disability rights law.
- RCI (Rehabilitation Council of India) Act came in 1992 to regulate training of rehabilitation professionals.
- RTE (Right to Education) Act was enacted in 2009 guaranteeing free and compulsory education to children.

So, the correct match is A-I, B-IV, C-III, D-II.

**68.** The Individualised Education Plan (IEP) goals must follow the SMART framework.

- They should be Specific to clearly define what is expected,
- Measurable to track progress,
- Attainable to ensure they are realistic for the child,
- Result-oriented focusing on outcomes, and
- Time-bound with a clear deadline.

So, the correct order is A, E, B, D, C.

**69.** In co-teaching models, alternative teaching is when one teacher handles most of the class while the other works with a small group. This method is often used for remediation, enrichment, or targeted support within or outside the classroom. Parallel teaching splits the class into two equal groups taught simultaneously. Station teaching rotates students between different stations run by both teachers. One teach, one assist has one lead teacher and one providing support.

So, the correct answer is alternative teaching.

**70.** Sankhya philosophy, one of the six orthodox Indian philosophies, is dualistic — it accepts two eternal realities: Purusha (consciousness) and Prakriti (matter). Prakriti evolves into Vyakta (manifest world) through the process of karya-karana (cause-effect), so Vyakta is the consequence of karya-karana (2 is true). 'Gya' is not matter (1 false), Avyakta is unmanifest Prakriti, not Purusha (3 false), and Sankhya is atheistic and does not prove God's existence (4 false).

Thus, the only correct statement is 2.

**71.** Blake and Mouton's Managerial Grid evaluates leadership styles on two axes — concern for people and concern for production.

- Impoverished Management scores 1,1 showing minimal concern for both people and production.
- Authority-compliance is 9,1 with high production concern but low people concern.

- Middle of the Road is 5,5 showing moderate concern for both.
- Team/Earn Management is 9,9 showing high concern for both people and production.

So the correct match is A-II, B-IV, C-I, D-III.

**72.** According to Unruch and Unruch, curriculum development follows a systematic sequence to ensure it is purposeful, relevant, and effective.

- **Goals and Objectives:** This is the first step where the overall aims and intended learning outcomes of the curriculum are defined to give direction.
- **Needs Assessment:** Once goals are set, an analysis is conducted to determine the specific educational needs of the learners and the context in which they learn.
- **Content:** After identifying needs, appropriate content is selected and organized to meet the goals and address the assessed needs.
- **Implementation:** The planned curriculum is then delivered in real educational settings, turning the plan into practice.
- **Evaluation:** Finally, the curriculum is evaluated to measure its effectiveness and identify areas for improvement.

So, the order is B, C, A, E, D.

**73.** The correct order of the NCF 2005 focus points is B $\rightarrow$ D $\rightarrow$ C $\rightarrow$ A, progressing from broad pedagogical reforms to logistical support.

- First, Reconstruction of curricula to emphasize the pedagogic potential of work shifts learning from rote memorization to meaningful, work-linked experiences.
- Next, Promoting peace-oriented values across all subjects integrates empathy, harmony, and cooperation into teaching.
- Then, Integration of environmental concerns into teaching disciplines embeds sustainability and ecological responsibility in education.
- Finally, Ensuring availability of minimum infrastructure and facilities provides the physical foundation needed to support all these reforms effectively.

Hence, correct sequence is B, D, C, A

**74.** Robb (1974) systems approach gives a stepwise method to design instruction.

- It starts with defining objectives to know expected outcomes,
- then determining initial behaviour to understand learner's current level,
- next specifying appropriate strategies to reach objectives,
- then specifying material, aids and media to support the strategies,
- and finally defining and assigning personnel roles to carry it out.

So, the order is D, C, A, E, B.

**75.** Ethnography research is the portrayal and explanation of social groups in real-life settings. It involves long-term observation, interviews, and participation in a community or culture. Phenomenology studies lived experiences, while grounded theory builds theories from data. Case studies focus on an individual or single unit, not an entire social group. Ethnography captures the culture, norms, and behaviors of groups as they naturally occur.

So, the correct answer is ethnography research.

**76.** The correct sequence of stages in conducting an experiment is:

- First, researchers select the relevant variables that will be studied.
- Next, they design the experiment by planning procedures and controls.
- Then, they assign participants to groups, such as control and experimental groups.
- After this, they conduct the intervention to apply treatments or conditions.
- Finally, they conduct the post-test to measure the outcomes.

Hence, correct sequence of stages is A, B, D, C, E.

**77.** The theory of Communicative Action was proposed by Jürgen Habermas. He emphasized communication as a form of social interaction aimed at reaching understanding and consensus. This theory highlights rational communication as essential for democratic decision-making and social coordination. It focuses on discourse ethics, where all participants have an equal chance to contribute and critique. Habermas's work contrasts with strategic action, which is goal-oriented and instrumental.

**78.** Constant reviewing of the policies and procedures in the organization is indeed a part of internal compliance monitoring. This involves routinely checking that organizational policies are being followed and remain effective, ensuring they align with legal and regulatory requirements. It helps identify gaps, inconsistencies, or outdated procedures and allows timely corrective actions to maintain compliance. Monitoring is an ongoing process, while reporting exceptions or implementing policies are separate functions. Risk assessment, though related, is done periodically, not continuously like monitoring.

**79.** Checking options:

- (A) True — Educational technology borrowed the 'systems approach' from management studies to design instruction as an organized process with inputs, processes, and outputs.
- (B) False — The systems approach was applied to education mainly from the 1960s–70s onward, not by the mid-1950s.
- (C) False — Technology of Education refers to the systematic application of scientific and psychological principles to teaching and learning, not just the use of audio-visual aids (which belongs to "technology in education").
- (D) True — The concept of 'corrective feedback' came from cybernetics, supporting programmed instruction and adaptive learning.
- (E) True — In its initial phase, educational technology meant 'technology in education', i.e. the use of media tools like film, radio, and projectors as aids to teaching.

Hence, correct statements is A, D, E Only

**80.** The commissions and policies are arranged in ascending order by their year of establishment:

- National Education Commission (Kothari Commission) - Established in 1964, submitted its report in 1966, and laid the foundation for modern educational planning in India.
- National Commission on Teachers - Formed in 1983 under Prof. D.P. Chattopadhyaya to examine teachers' roles, status, and conditions.
- National Policy on Education (NPE) - Announced in 1986 (revised in 1992) to provide a comprehensive framework for educational development.
- National Knowledge Commission - Set up in 2005 under Sam Pitroda to strengthen education, research, and knowledge infrastructure.
- Justice Verma Commission - Constituted in 2012; apart from legal reforms, it gave crucial recommendations to improve teacher education.

So, the correct chronological order is: E, C, D, B, A.

**81.** Malcolm Knowles is considered the father of adult learning theory and introduced the concept of Andragogy, which emphasizes how adults learn differently from children. He highlighted that adult learners are self-directed, bring prior experience, are goal-oriented, and need to see immediate relevance in learning. His well-known book "The Modern Practice of Adult Education: Andragogy vs Pedagogy" (1970) elaborated this concept in detail. Knowles contrasted pedagogy (teacher-centered) with andragogy (learner-centered). This work marked a shift in adult education, encouraging educators to focus on autonomy and life experience in teaching adults.

**82.** Checking options:

- (A) False — Research shows that inclusion improves social competence and communication skills of children with diverse abilities, not deteriorates them.
- (B) True — Children with disabilities often show higher levels of social interaction with non-disabled peers in inclusive settings.
- (C) True — Inclusive settings promote friendships between children with and without disabilities.
- (D) True — Children also interact actively with other children having disabilities in inclusive environments.
- (E) False — Social acceptance of children with diverse abilities is generally increased, not decreased, in inclusive settings.

Hence, incorrect statements is A and E Only

**83.** Checking options:

- (A) True — Curriculum is indeed based on the philosophy, goals, and values of education.
- (B) True — It refers to all educational activities of the school in the broadest sense.
- (C) False — Curriculum is not just about school subjects; it covers all planned experiences.
- (D) False — Curriculum is broader than syllabus; syllabus is a part of the curriculum, not the other way around.
- (E) True — Curriculum includes both indoor and outdoor activities as part of holistic development.

Hence, incorrect statements is C and D Only

**84.** Inclusive education emphasizes collaboration, flexibility, and holistic development, ensuring that all learners, regardless of ability, are supported in the same environment. Individualistic approaches, on the other hand, focus only on one learner in isolation, which contradicts the essence of inclusion that promotes group participation and collective growth. Inclusive approaches are flexible to diverse needs, diagnostic to identify challenges, and holistic to develop the whole child. Individualism can create separation and undermine inclusion efforts. Therefore, it does not belong to the inclusive approach.

**85.** Checking options:

- (A) False — Wikis allow multiple users to read and edit documents; saying editing is not allowed is incorrect.
- (B) True — A vlog is a type of blog that uses video as the primary content.
- (C) True — Microblogs let users post short text-based updates, like on Twitter.
- (D) True — Teachers can create a wiki using an LMS or open-source platforms for collaborative learning.
- (E) False — A blog has time-stamped posts made by the creator, not by readers.

Hence, correct statements is B, C, D Only

**86.** The Halo Effect is a common rating error where a teacher's or rater's overall impression of a student (positive or negative) influences the rating of specific traits or abilities. Although Wells first mentioned this phenomenon in 1907, it was Edward Thorndike in 1920 who gave it the name "Halo Effect" while studying rating biases in military evaluations. This bias can result in inflated or deflated scores on various unrelated dimensions simply because of one dominant general impression. It reduces the accuracy and objectivity of assessments. Recognizing and controlling the Halo Effect is crucial to ensure fairness in student evaluation.

**87.** This question is based on Krathwohl's Affective Domain taxonomy which describes how learners internalize values and attitudes.

- **Receiving–Willingness to pay attention:** It is the lowest level, where learners are just willing to listen or notice.
- **Responding–Participating actively:** This is the stage where learners actively respond through participation and engagement.
- **Valuing-Showing a preference for a value:** At this level, learners accept and show commitment to certain values.
- **Organization-Adopting a constant value system:** Learners organize values into a system, prioritizing them consistently in their behavior.

Hence, correct matching is A-III, B-IV, C-I, D-II

**88.** Qualitative research focuses on exploring and understanding human experiences, perceptions, and meanings in depth. It collects data in words, images, or observations, not numbers, and emphasizes context and rich description rather than measurement. It often uses interviews, focus groups, observations, and document analysis as methods of data collection. Data analysis in qualitative research involves coding, theming, and interpreting narratives, not statistical techniques.

Hence, analyzing data with statistics is a characteristic of quantitative, not qualitative research.

**89.** The National Council for Teacher Education (NCTE) was established as a statutory body in 1995 to oversee standards, procedures, and processes in teacher education in India.

J.S. Rajput became its first Chairperson, playing a crucial role in setting the early framework for teacher education reforms and policies. His tenure laid the foundation for regulatory mechanisms, accreditation norms, and quality improvement initiatives in teacher education.

**90.** The National Knowledge Commission (2007) made several recommendations to improve school education quality, access, and governance.

Key recommendations included:

- Enacting central legislation for the right to education.
- Promoting decentralization and greater local autonomy in decision-making.
- Expanding functional literacy to strengthen foundational learning skills.

However, it did not recommend more rigidity in disbursal of funds; rather, it emphasized flexibility and transparency in fund utilization to improve efficiency.

**91.** Phenomenology is the study of consciousness from the first-person perspective, focusing on how the world appears to the individual experiencing it. It is positioned opposite to computational theories, which are based on objective and measurable data. This approach is inherently subjective and depends on the perspective of the researcher or participant.

**92.** Although phenomenology emphasizes subjective experience, it still uses empirical scientific methods in its studies. Phenomenological studies can include generating hypotheses and conducting systematic observations of participants' experiences. Therefore, scientific observation is a possible and essential part of phenomenological research.

**93.** In phenomenological research, a key check for the validity of results is intersubjectivity. Intersubjectivity refers to the agreement among different individuals about the nature of their perceptual experiences. This shared consensus helps ensure that the findings are credible and trustworthy.

**94.** A scientific approach to research is generally considered to be objective in nature, focusing on unbiased and measurable observations. It aims to reduce personal bias and relies on methods that can be independently verified. This objectivity helps distinguish scientific approaches from purely subjective methods.

**95.** In psychophysics, subjects are usually kept unaware of the exact purpose of the experiment to avoid bias. They are given well-defined tasks that have a limited set of possible answers, such as "yes" or "no". These tasks are therefore considered to have highly constrained responses.

**96.** Inclusive philosophy emphasizes supporting every learner, regardless of their disability or challenge. The teacher's role is to ensure that the problem does not hinder the student's overall development. This means adapting methods to help the learner overcome obstacles and succeed.

**97.** Inclusion in education recognizes that disabilities can create specific challenges for learners. It involves finding targeted strategies to overcome these particular difficulties. Thus, it promotes specific solutions to specific problems rather than one-size-fits-all methods.

**98.** The challenges faced by a person with a disability depend greatly on the type and severity of the disability. The passage highlights that these two factors are of immediate concern in determining the level of difficulty. Other factors like attitudes or socio-economic status matter too but are secondary here.

**99.** Inclusion shifts the focus away from constantly thinking about the disability and toward building skills and strengths. It involves modifying curriculum, evaluating strengths, and assessing skills to support learning. Therefore, increased thinking about disabilities does not align with inclusion.

**100.** Inclusive classrooms are not only for children with disabilities but for all learners with diverse needs. They aim to support everyone—regardless of physical, psychological, or intellectual differences. This approach benefits the whole class, not just specific groups.

Previous Years' Paper

# National Testing Agency (NTA)

## UGC-NET Junior Research Fellowship & Assistant Professor Eligibility Exam

# Education, January-2025

(Exam held on 3-01-2025)

## PAPER-II

**1.** Kolb's experiential learning model follows the cycle:

(*a*) Formation of abstract concepts and generalisation
(*b*) Students make their own observations
(*c*) Concrete experience
(*d*) Testing implications of the concepts in new situations
(*e*) Reflections

Choose the ***correct*** answer from the options given below:

A. (*b*), (*a*), (*c*), (*d*), (*e*)
B. (*c*), (*b*), (*e*), (*a*), (*d*)
C. (*c*), (*a*), (*e*), (*b*), (*d*)
D. (*b*), (*c*), (*a*), (*e*), (*d*)

**2.** A Teacher uses Socratic method to help students in developing critical thinking skills during a lesson on global warming. This method best aligns with which theorist's principle?

A. Skinner
B. Piaget
C. Vygotsky
D. Bruner

**3.** From the given events of instruction of Gagne, Arrange these in a sequence.

(*a*) Provide Reinforcement
(*b*) Stimulate Recall of Prior learning
(*c*) Describe goal and inform the learner of the objectives
(*d*) Provide guidance for learning
(*e*) Gain attention

Choose the ***correct*** answer from the options given below:

A. (*d*), (*c*), (*a*), (*b*), (*e*)
B. (*e*), (*b*), (*c*), (*d*), (*a*)
C. (*d*), (*e*), (*c*), (*a*), (*b*)
D. (*e*), (*c*), (*b*), (*d*), (*a*)

**4.** Arrange the following steps of Inference as propounded by the Nyay School of Indian Philosophy.

(*a*) Conclusion
(*b*) Reason
(*c*) Proposition
(*d*) Example
(*e*) Application

Choose the ***correct*** answer from the options given below:

A. (*e*), (*d*), (*b*), (*c*), (*a*)
B. (*c*), (*b*), (*e*), (*d*), (*a*)
C. (*c*), (*b*), (*d*), (*e*), (*a*)
D. (*e*), (*c*), (*d*), (*b*), (*a*)

**5.** Match List-I with List-II.

| List-I | List-II |
|---|---|
| (*a*) Market economy | I. Government controlled |
| (*b*) Service of a Teacher | II. Functioning of a mechanism |

| | |
|---|---|
| (*c*) Centrally planned economy | III. Skill |
| (*d*) Positive economy | IV. Private Controlled |

Choose the ***correct*** answer from the options given below:

| | (*a*) | (*b*) | (*c*) | (*d*) |
|---|---|---|---|---|
| A. | IV | I | II | III |
| B. | I | III | II | IV |
| C. | IV | III | I | II |
| D. | I | IV | II | III |

**6.** In 1848, Savitri Bai Phule along with her husband Jyotiba Phule and Fatima Sheikh opened the first girls' school. The School's name was:

A. Zubeida School
B. Phule Shikshan Mandir
C. Bal Gandharva Vidyalaya
D. Pune Vidyapeeth

**7.** Which of the following statement is NOT related to Freudian Psychoanalytic Approach?

A. Id refers to the raw, unorganised, inherited part of personality
B. Super ego has two sub parts : Conscience and the Ego-ideal
C. Ego defence mechanisms have adaptive value
D. Super ego helps to control ego impulses

**8.** Match List-I with List-II.

| **List-I** | **List-II** |
|---|---|
| (*a*) Right of Children to Free and Compulsory Education (RTE) Act | I. 2005 |
| (*b*) Commission for Protection of Child Rights Act | II. 2009 |
| (*c*) National Council for Teacher Education (NCTE) Act | III. 1956 |
| (*d*) University Grant Commission (UGC) Act | IV. 1993 |

Choose the ***correct*** answer from the options given below:

| | (*a*) | (*b*) | (*c*) | (*d*) |
|---|---|---|---|---|
| A. | I | II | IV | III |
| B. | III | II | IV | I |
| C. | II | I | IV | III |
| D. | III | IV | II | I |

**9.** Which amongst the following theory affirms that inequality is socially constructed and can be eradicated?

A. Rational Choice Theory
B. Theory of Systems Analysis
C. Marxism
D. Conservatism

**10.** Match List-I with List-II.

| **List-I** | **List-II** |
|---|---|
| (*a*) Q Methodology | I. Hartshorne and May (1929) |
| (*b*) 'Guess Who' | II. Bradley Efron |
| (*c*) Student's distribution | III. Stephenson (1953) |
| (*d*) Bootstrap Method | IV. William Sealy Gosset |

Choose the ***correct*** answer from the options given below:

| | (*a*) | (*b*) | (*c*) | (*d*) |
|---|---|---|---|---|
| A. | II | III | IV | I |
| B. | III | I | IV | II |
| C. | IV | III | II | I |
| D. | III | IV | I | II |

**11.** Which of the following statement is NOT correct about Vygotsky's Socio-cultural theory of child development?

A. Child's cultural development appears twice: First on social level and later on individual level.
B. Human activities take place in cultural settings.
C. Intra Psychological function comes first then Inter Psychological.
D. Development is transformation of socially shared activities into internalized process.

**12.** Match List-I with List-II.

| List-I | List-II |
|---|---|
| (*a*) ADDIE | I. Selecting media |
| (*b*) ASSURE | II. Living books, narration and habits |
| (*c*) Dick and Carey | III. Systematic instructions : step by step framework to assess training and education material |
| (*d*) Mason | IV. Learner analysis and engagement |

Choose the ***correct*** answer from the options given below:

| | (*a*) | (*b*) | (*c*) | (*d*) |
|---|---|---|---|---|
| A. | III | IV | I | II |
| B. | I | III | IV | II |
| C. | II | IV | III | I |
| D. | III | I | IV | II |

**13.** Match List-I with List-II.

| List-I | List-II |
|---|---|
| (*a*) Maslow | I. Psychoanalytic Approach |
| (*b*) Erickson | II. Humanistic Approach |
| (*c*) Sheldon | III. Life Span Approach |
| (*d*) Freud | IV. Constitutional Approach |

Choose the ***correct*** answer from the options given below:

| | (*a*) | (*b*) | (*c*) | (*d*) |
|---|---|---|---|---|
| A. | II | I | IV | III |
| B. | II | III | IV | I |
| C. | I | II | III | IV |
| D. | II | III | I | IV |

**14.** Match List-I with List-II.

| List-I | List-II |
|---|---|
| (*a*) Perceptual Reasoning | I. Similarities, Vocabulary, Information |
| (*b*) Working Memory | II. Digit Span, Arithmetic |
| (*c*) Processing Speed | III. Block Design, Matrix Reasoning, Visual Puzzles |
| (*d*) Verbal Comprehension | IV. Symbol Search Coding |

Choose the ***correct*** answer from the options given below:

| | (*a*) | (*b*) | (*c*) | (*d*) |
|---|---|---|---|---|
| A. | II | III | IV | I |
| B. | II | IV | I | III |
| C. | II | I | III | IV |
| D. | III | II | IV | I |

**15.** As per the intent of NEP-2020, All stand alone Teacher Education Institutions (TEIs) will be required to convert to multidisciplinary institutions by the year ______.

A. 2035 B. 2030
C. 2047 D. 2040

**16.** According to Jainism, following are required to attain Moksa:

(*a*) Samyak Darshan
(*b*) Samyak Drishti
(*c*) Samyak Jnan
(*d*) Samyak Charitra
(*e*) Samyak Sankalp

Choose the ***correct*** answer from the options given below:

A. (*a*), (*c*) and (*d*) only
B. (*b*) and (*e*) only
C. (*a*), (*b*) and (*c*) only
D. (*c*), (*d*) and (*e*) only

**17.** Which of the following value is enshrined in the preamble of the Constitution?

A. Individualism
B. Progressivism
C. Cosmopolitianism
D. Secularism

**18.** The National Commission on Teachers (1983) provided criteria for selection of trainees for becoming teachers. This commission was headed by:

A. R.N. Chattopadhyaya
B. D.S. Kothari
C. V.K.R.V. Rao
D. D.P. Chattopadhyaya

**19.** Needs of curriculum development include:

(*a*) Sports and games

(*b*) Acquisition of knowledge

(*c*) Cultural activities

(*d*) Proper use of time.

Choose the ***correct*** answer from the options given below:

A. (*a*) and (*c*) only
B. (*b*) and (*c*) only
C. (*b*) and (*d*) only
D. (*a*) and (*b*) only

**20.** An inclusive curriculum means:

A. Separate curriculum for children with disabilities
B. One curriculum for all students
C. Separate curriculum for children without disabilities
D. A flexible curriculum

**21.** Which of the following statements are correct about 'Taylorism'?

(*a*) It is also known as 'scientific management'

(*b*) Initial name for this approach was 'shop management'

(*c*) The theory was developed initially within manufacturing industries

(*d*) It was given by Samuel Taylor

Choose the ***correct*** answer from the options given below:

A. (*a*), (*b*) and (*c*) only
B. (*b*), (*c*) and (*d*) only
C. (*d*) and (*b*) only
D. (*a*), (*c*) and (*d*) only

**22.** In monitoring of policy, ensuring policy programmes are completed on schedule and within budget. In process of policy monitoring, arrange the following steps:

(*a*) Establish expectations against which the implementer or policy maker monitors the policy delivery process.

(*b*) Analysis of cause of deviation from planned policy delivery process.

(*c*) Observing performance indicators on all parameters.

(*d*) Taking corrective action in case of deviation from policy delivery process.

(*e*) Application of resources to the policy delivery process.

Choose the ***correct*** answer from the options given below:

A. (*a*), (*e*), (*c*), (*b*), (*d*)
B. (*b*), (*c*), (*d*), (*e*), (*a*)
C. (*c*), (*d*), (*e*), (*a*), (*b*)
D. (*d*), (*e*), (*c*), (*a*), (*b*)

**23.** Match List-I with List-II.

| **List-I (Approach)** | **List-II (Key Question)** |
|---|---|
| (*a*) Ethnography | I. How do the origins, characteristics and culture of different societies compare to one another? |
| (*b*) Ethology | II. What is the experience of an activity or concept from these particular participant's perspective? |
| (*c*) Ethnomethodology | III. How do people make sense of their everyday activities in order to behave in socially accepted ways? |
| (*d*) Phenomenology | IV. What are the cultural patterns and perspectives of this group in its natural setting? |

Choose the ***correct*** answer from the options given below:

| | (*a*) | (*b*) | (*c*) | (*d*) |
|---|---|---|---|---|
| A. | II | III | I | IV |
| B. | IV | III | I | II |
| C. | III | I | IV | II |
| D. | IV | I | III | II |

**24.** Nalanda University was first established during Gupta regime. It was a known ______ centre of learning.

A. Jain  B. Vedic
C. Buddhist  D. Samkhya

**25.** As per the gazette notification of 2021, w.r.t. ITEP, which of the following degree will be the outcome of the four-year Integrated Teacher Education Programme:

A. B.A. B.Ed/B.Sc. B.Ed/B.Com. B.Ed
B. ITEP
C. B.Ed
D. BA.Ed/BSc.Ed/BCom.Ed

**26.** The competency based model of curriculum focuses on:

A. Time spent on acquiring skills
B. Mastering specific skills
C. General knowledge skills
D. General life skills

**27.** Put the five stages of the 'Design for Six Sigma' in a correct order:

(*a*) Design the process at a high level before moving onto a more detailed version.
(*b*) Verify that the final iteration of the product or process is approved by all customers and clients.
(*c*) Define realistic goals that suit customer requirements.
(*d*) Analyse multiple options and alternatives for the customer along with the estimated total life cycle of the project.
(*e*) Measure and identify the customer's critical to quality requirements and translate these into project goals.

Choose the ***correct*** answer from the options given below:

A. (*c*), (*e*), (*d*), (*a*), (*b*)
B. (*e*), (*c*), (*a*), (*d*), (*b*)
C. (*c*), (*e*), (*a*), (*d*), (*b*)
D. (*a*), (*b*), (*e*), (*c*), (*d*)

**28.** Which of the following is NOT a basic principle of curriculum development?

A. Principle of Totality
B. Principle of Leisure
C. Principle of Maturity
D. Principle of Flexibility

**29.** Unruch and Unruch outlined five steps of curriculum development. Arrange these in proper sequence.

(*a*) Content
(*b*) Evaluation
(*c*) Goals and Objectives
(*d*) Implementation
(*e*) Needs Assessment

Choose the ***correct*** answer from the options given below:

A. (*c*), (*e*), (*a*), (*d*), (*b*)
B. (*c*), (*a*), (*e*), (*d*), (*b*)
C. (*e*), (*c*), (*d*), (*a*), (*b*)
D. (*e*), (*d*), (*c*), (*a*), (*b*)

**30.** Write the following steps of sampling procedure in a correct order.

(*a*) Preparing sampling frame
(*b*) Applying the sampling technique
(*c*) Administer the tool
(*d*) Define the universe to be studied

Choose the ***correct*** answer from the options given below:

A. (*a*), (*d*), (*b*), (*c*)
B. (*d*), (*a*), (*b*), (*c*)
C. (*a*), (*d*), (*c*), (*b*)
D. (*d*), (*a*), (*c*), (*b*)

**31.** Prominent feature of Dick and Carey Model that distinguishes it from ADDIE Model is:

A. Emphasis on evaluation
B. Clear learner analysis
C. Inclusion of formative evaluation at each step
D. Sequential and Linear Design Process

**32.** The main curricular areas as per NCFTE-2009 are:

(*a*) Curriculum and Pedagogy
(*b*) Educational technology
(*c*) Foundation of Education
(*d*) School internship
(*e*) Learner assessment

Choose the ***correct*** answer from the options given below:

A. (*a*), (*c*) and (*d*) only
B. (*b*), (*c*) and (*e*) only
C. (*c*), (*d*) and (*e*) only
D. (*a*), (*c*), (*d*) and (*e*) only

**33.** Which of the following DOES NOT align with the concept of inclusive education?

A. Aiming for Mainstreaming
B. Catering to diverse learning needs
C. Catering to Plural society
D. Considering Individual differences

**34.** The Jurisprudential Inquiry model requires a fair amount of teacher directed activity and directed instruction. Component activities of the model include:

(*a*) Facts about social problems
(*b*) Framework for analysing social issues
(*c*) Competence in social dialogue
(*d*) Comfort in expressing opinion
(*e*) Analysing personal values and behaviour

Choose the ***correct*** answer from the options given below:

A. (*a*), (*b*) and (*d*) only
B. (*b*), (*c*), (*d*) and (*e*) only
C. (*c*), (*d*) and (*e*) only
D. (*a*), (*b*) and (*c*) only

**35.** Arrange the sequence of direct teacher talk category in Flanders' Interaction Analysis:

(*a*) Accepts feeling
(*b*) Praises or encourages
(*c*) Asks questions
(*d*) Using pupils idea

Choose the ***correct*** answer from the options given below:

A. (*b*), (*a*), (*d*), (*c*)
B. (*a*), (*b*), (*c*), (*d*)
C. (*c*), (*a*), (*b*), (*d*)
D. (*d*), (*a*), (*c*), (*b*)

**36.** As per NEP-2020, School teachers are expected to spent how much time for continuous professional development?

A. 40 hours
B. 60 hours
C. 50 hours
D. 45 hours

**37.** Swami Vivekanand in his famous speech in Chicago, 1893 conceptualised 'Universal Acceptance'. Which of the following statement encapsulates his philosophy about religion and human nature:

A. The ultimate goal of all humanity is to see the divinity in oneself and in others.
B. All religions are merely path to the same truth, one must transcend religious dogma to realize the awareness of all.
C. The true spirituality is renunciation from all worldly affairs.
D. Every human is an embodiment and manifestation of the divine and thus all forms of worship are equally valid.

**38.** The concept of 'randomness' is based on which of the following assumption?

A. While individual events cannot be predicted with accuracy, aggregate events can.
B. While aggregate events cannot be predicted with accuracy, individual events can.
C. While individual events cannot be studied with accuracy, aggregate events can.
D. Sampling errors are not predictable with randomization.

**39.** Which of the following statements are correct regarding 'Poka-Yoke'?

(*a*) The term poka-yoke originated with the Japanese Baka-yoke.

(*b*) The contact method of poka-yoke identifies defects through physical attributes.

(*c*) The fixed value method of poka-yoke is used in a process with non-recurring activity.

(*d*) The motion-step method of poka-yoke determines whether prescribed steps are completed in order.

Choose the ***correct*** answer from the options given below:

A. (*a*), (*b*) and (*c*) only
B. (*b*), (*c*) and (*d*) only
C. (*c*), (*d*) and (*a*) only
D. (*a*), (*b*) and (*d*) only

**40.** Match List-I with List-II.

| List-I | List-II |
|---|---|
| (*a*) Organisational Development | I. Procedure is monitored and improvement effected by means of statistical technique |
| (*b*) Statistical Quality Control | II. Planned change process which is continuous learning exercise |
| (*c*) Statistical Process Control | III. Benefit should exceed costs of development |
| (*d*) Sustainable Development | IV. Variance from standard measures is tracked applying statistical and engineering techniques |

Choose the ***correct*** answer from the options given below:

| | (*a*) | (*b*) | (*c*) | (*d*) |
|---|---|---|---|---|
| A. | III | IV | II | I |
| B. | II | IV | I | III |
| C. | III | I | IV | II |
| D. | II | I | IV | III |

**41.** Keeping in consideration wide range of special education and related services, most schools provide a continuum of services. Arrange the following in order of increasing severity of disabilities.

(*a*) Full-time separate classroom

(*b*) Regular classroom with supplementary instruction and services

(*c*) Regular classroom

(*d*) Special school

(*e*) Regular classroom and Resource room

Choose the ***correct*** answer from the options given below:

A. (*c*), (*e*), (*b*), (*d*), (*a*)
B. (*c*), (*b*), (*e*), (*a*), (*d*)
C. (*c*), (*a*), (*b*), (*e*), (*d*)
D. (*c*), (*d*), (*e*), (*b*), (*a*)

**42.** The term 'Triadic Reciprocal Causation' is associated with ______.

A. Freud Theory
B. Piaget Theory
C. Bandura Theory
D. Erikson Theory

**43.** Match List-I with List-II.

| List-I | List-II |
|---|---|
| (*a*) Gramsci | I. Pragmatism |
| (*b*) Charles S. Peirce | II. Feminism |
| (*c*) Jean Francois Lyotard | III. Maxism |
| (*d*) Nel Noddings | IV. Post modernism |

Choose the ***correct*** answer from the options given below:

| | (*a*) | (*b*) | (*c*) | (*d*) |
|---|---|---|---|---|
| A. | IV | II | III | I |
| B. | III | I | IV | II |
| C. | IV | III | II | I |
| D. | III | IV | I | II |

**44.** A National Curricular and Pedagogical Framework for Early Childhood Care and Education (NCPFECCE) for children up to the age of 8 will be developed by:

A. D.P.E.P. B. N.C.T.E.
C. N.C.E.R.T. D. S.C.E.R.T.

**45.** On the recommendation of which of the following committee on transformative reforms in accreditations, the executive committee of NAAC had proposed launching of reforms in two phases-Binary Accreditation and Maturity Based Graded Level?

A. Dr. D.P. Singh Committee
B. Dr. Ganesh Kannabiran Committee
C. Dr. Radhakrishnan Committee
D. Dr. Subhas Roy Committee

**46.** Philosophical Model of Teaching comprising Insight (Plato), Impression (Locke), and Rule (Kant) was propounded by:

A. R.S. Peters B. Paul Hirst
C. D.W. Hamlyn D. Israel Scheffler

**47.** The four fold valuation of Indian Culture when arranged in hierarchical order can be represented by following chronology:

A. Dharma - Arth - Kama - Moksha
B. Moksha - Dharma - Arth - Kama
C. Kama - Arth - Dharma - Moksha
D. Arth - Kama - Dharma - Moksha

**48.** Which of the following is TRUE about Learning Theories?

(*a*) Kurt Lewin was one of the founding father of Gestalt Psychology.
(*b*) Albert Bandura described Human Behaviour and learning on the basis of three key concepts Life spaces, Vector, insight
(*c*) Kohler's book related to experiments on chimpanzees was 'Mentality of Apes'
(*d*) Skinner opposed the "no stimulus, no response" mechanism in the evolution of behaviour.
(*e*) A positive reinforcer is any stimulus the removal or withdrawl of which decreases the likelihood of a particular behaviour.

Choose the ***correct*** answer from the options given below:

A. (*a*), (*c*), (*d*) only
B. (*b*), (*d*), (*e*) only
C. (*a*), (*c*), (*e*) only
D. (*a*), (*b*), (*e*) only

**49.** Which of the following are TRUE about inclusive education?

(*a*) It is a part of a wider strategy to develop an inclusive society.
(*b*) It acknowledges that not all children can learn in a general class.
(*c*) It involves restructuring school-cultures.
(*d*) Diversity is a rich resource to support the learning for all.
(*e*) Schools should not be expected to change according to learning needs of all children.

Choose the ***correct*** answer from the options given below:

A. (*a*), (*c*) and (*e*) only
B. (*b*), (*c*) and (*d*) only
C. (*b*), (*d*) and (*e*) only
D. (*a*), (*c*) and (*d*) only

**50.** Etymologically, the term 'Curriculum' is derived from the Latin word:

A. Curricular B. Caricature
C. Curious D. Currere

**51.** According to the leader-member exchange theory, the sub-group of Low-quality exchanges is viewed as:

A. Out-group B. In-group
C. Advisors D. Followers

**52.** The first written examination to test spelling achievement of students was used by:

A. Joseph M. Rice B. R.M. Thorndike
C. Binet-Simon D. DuBois

**53.** As per NEP-2020, National Educational Technology Forum will have the following functions:

(*a*) Envision strategic thrust areas in educational technology

(*b*) Articulate new directions for research and innovation

(*c*) Establish a state of art 'Technology Centre' in Gujarat

(*d*) Provide independent evidence based advice to Centre and State government on technology based intervention

(*e*) Allocate research projects in field of educational technology from 2026.

Choose the ***correct*** answer from the options given below:

A. (*a*), (*c*), (*d*), (*e*) only
B. (*a*), (*b*), (*d*) only
C. (*b*), (*d*), (*e*) only
D. (*a*), (*d*), (*e*) only

**54.** Put the steps of construction of summated rating attitude scale in a correct order.

(*a*) Selection of final items
(*b*) Calculation of item wise critical ratio
(*c*) Item writing
(*d*) Administration for final try out
(*e*) Pre try out

Choose the ***correct*** answer from the options given below:

A. (*e*), (*c*), (*d*), (*b*), (*a*)
B. (*c*), (*e*), (*b*), (*d*), (*a*)
C. (*a*), (*d*), (*e*), (*c*), (*b*)
D. (*c*), (*e*), (*d*), (*b*), (*a*)

**55.** Which of the following statement is NOT correct about PERT?

A. PERT was developed primarily to simplify the planning and scheduling of large and complex projects.
B. In a PERT chart, 'Nodes' represent the activities or tasks and 'Arrows' represent events or milestones in the project.
C. PERT may utilize three 'time estimates'.
D. PERT was developed between 1950-60.

**56.** Which of the following statements are INCORRECT?

(*a*) Rehabilitation Council of India Act was passed in 1992.

(*b*) Persons with Disabilities Act was modified in 2010.

(*c*) UNCRPD talks about compulsory inclusive education.

(*d*) National Policy on Disabilities originated from RTE Act 2009.

(*e*) National Curriculum Framework was prepared in 2005.

Choose the ***correct*** answer from the options given below:

A. (*a*) and (*c*) only
B. (*b*) and (*d*) only
C. (*b*) and (*e*) only
D. (*a*) and (*b*) only

**57.** In 1987, N.C.E.R.T. launched the 'Project on Integrated Education for Disabled (PIED)' in conjunction with:

A. UNESCO
B. WHO
C. Asian Development Bank (ADB)
D. UNICEF

**58.** Arrange chronologically the programmes/ schemes for Education.

(*a*) Sarva Siksha Abhiyan (SSA)
(*b*) Operation Blackboard (OB)
(*c*) District Primary Education Programme (DPEP)
(*d*) Rashtriya Madhyamik Siksha Abhiyan (RMSA)
(*e*) Samagra Shiksha Abhiyan

Choose the ***correct*** answer from the options given below:

A. (*a*), (*c*), (*b*), (*d*), (*e*)
B. (*c*), (*b*), (*a*), (*e*), (*d*)
C. (*b*), (*c*), (*a*), (*d*), (*e*)
D. (*d*), (*b*), (*c*), (*a*), (*e*)

**59.** The four basic leadership styles identified by Bill Reddin were:

A. Telling, Selling, Participating and Delegating
B. $M_1$, $M_2$, $M_3$ and $M_4$
C. DMAIC, DMADV, CTQ, POSDCORB
D. Related, Integrated, Dedicated, Separated

**60.** Which statements define educational finance at the micro and macro levels?

(*a*) Macro finance is framed for the needs used of an individual, small industries and small business units.
(*b*) Macro finance includes drafting policy, subsidies, multiyear expansion plans.
(*c*) The main aim of micro finance is to help economy grow and to generate employment.
(*d*) Macro finance has direct effect on whole economy and indirect effect on the whole population.
(*e*) Micro finance is an endless activity.

Choose the ***correct*** answer from the options given below:

A. (*a*) and (*e*) only
B. (*b*) and (*d*) only
C. (*b*), (*c*) and (*d*) only
D. (*a*), (*b*) and (*e*) only

**61.** Match List-I with List-II.

| List-I | List-II |
|---|---|
| (*a*) The Salamanca Statement | I. 1992 |
| (*b*) The Rehabilitation Council of India Act | II. 1995 |
| (*c*) The Persons with Disabilities Act | III. 2006 |
| (*d*) National Policy for Persons with disabilities | IV. 1994 |

Choose the ***correct*** answer from the options given below:

| | (*a*) | (*b*) | (*c*) | (*d*) |
|---|---|---|---|---|
| A. | IV | II | I | III |
| B. | IV | I | II | III |
| C. | II | III | IV | I |
| D. | II | IV | I | III |

**62.** Match List-I with List-II.

| List-I | List-II |
|---|---|
| (*a*) Arthapatti | I. Conchshell is not a bone according to vedas |
| (*b*) Abhava | II. A chair is not a table |
| (*c*) Upamana | III. He does not eat in day time; he is fat. He eats in night |
| (*d*) Sabda | IV. This cow is different from domestic cow must be a nilgai |

Choose the ***correct*** answer from the options given below:

| | (*a*) | (*b*) | (*c*) | (*d*) |
|---|---|---|---|---|
| A. | II | IV | III | I |
| B. | I | III | IV | II |
| C. | I | II | IV | III |
| D. | III | II | IV | I |

**63.** A job application 'Portfolio' is a:

A. Finished Portfolio
B. Documentation Portfolio
C. Progress Portfolio
D. Working Portfolio

**64.** The measurement of human abilities/personality/interest encounters problems in:

(*a*) Selecting attributes of variables
(*b*) Developing Educational devices/Test
(*c*) Quantifying the attributes
(*d*) Determining operations to isolate the attributes
(*e*) Preparing standard scores

Choose the ***correct*** answer from the options given below:

A. (*a*), (*b*), (*d*) and (*e*) only
B. (*b*), (*c*), (*d*) and (*e*) only
C. (*a*), (*b*), (*c*) and (*d*) only
D. (*a*), (*c*), (*d*) and (*e*) only

**65.** The principles of designing in-service teacher education programmes, as per NCFTE-2009 include:

(*a*) Content and Pedagogic approach
(*b*) Educational attainment approach

(*c*) Structural space approach
(*d*) Addressing teachers as learners

Choose the ***correct*** answer from the options given below:

A. (*b*), (*c*) and (*d*) only
B. (*a*) and (*d*) only
C. (*a*), (*b*), (*c*) and (*d*)
D. (*a*), (*c*) and (*d*) only

**66.** Match List-I with List-II.

| List-I | List-II |
|---|---|
| (*a*) Mastery decisions | I. Summative |
| (*b*) Average IQ | II. Formative |
| (*c*) Evaluation of Capacity | III. Criterion referenced |
| (*d*) Guiding future instruction | IV. Norm referenced |

Choose the ***correct*** answer from the options given below:

| | (*a*) | (*b*) | (*c*) | (*d*) |
|---|---|---|---|---|
| A. | I | III | IV | II |
| B. | III | IV | I | II |
| C. | II | III | I | IV |
| D. | III | II | I | IV |

**67.** Teachers and counsellors are often interested in using tests to determine their students' strengths and weaknesses, the areas where they are doing well and those where they are doing poorly. Which of the following test can be used for the purpose?

A. Formative Evaluation
B. Achievement Evaluation
C. Summative Evaluation
D. Criterion Referred Evaluation

**68.** Which of the following is NOT true?

A. Segregation is integral to special education.
B. Integrated education provides partial opportunities for participation.
C. Inclusive education recognises rights but not realises all of them.
D. Inclusive education is least restrictive.

**69.** According to human capital theory, the main benefit of investing in education is:

(*a*) Higher wages
(*b*) Individual Growth
(*c*) World Ranking of Country
(*d*) Empowerment of People
(*e*) Productivity

Choose the correct answer from the options given below:

A. (*b*), (*c*) and (*d*) only
B. (*a*) and (*c*) only
C. (*b*) and (*d*) only
D. (*a*) and (*e*) only

**70.** Which of the following web 2.0 tool is most effective for collaborative learning in e-learning platform?

A. Wiki
B. Blog
C. Podcast
D. Video Conferencing

**71.** 'QUAN→QUAL' represents a mixed method research design which is:

A. Concurrent Explanatory
B. Concurrent Exploratory
C. Sequential Explanatory
D. Sequential Exploratory

**72.** Which of the following statements are True?

(*a*) Alfred Adler disagreed with Freud's idea that the cause of human emotionality was 'unconscious conflicts'.
(*b*) Aaron Beck developed Cognitive Psychotherapy in 1960's.
(*c*) Cognitive Behaviour Therapy (CBT) came into usage around early 1950's.
(*d*) In ABC Model, 'C' represents the resultant emotion or behaviour.
(*e*) In ABC model, 'A' represents assimilation.

Choose the ***correct*** answer from the options given below:

A. (*a*), (*d*), (*b*) only
B. (*a*), (*c*), (*d*) only
C. (*e*), (*d*), (*b*) only
D. (*a*), (*b*), (*e*) only

**73.** Arrange the following in reverse chronological order.

(*a*) National Commission on Teachers
(*b*) Kothari Commission
(*c*) Justice J.S. Verma Committee
(*d*) National Knowledge Commission
(*e*) Radhakrishnan Commission

Choose the ***correct*** answer from the options given below:

A. (*d*), (*b*), (*a*), (*c*), (*e*)
B. (*a*), (*b*), (*c*), (*e*), (*d*)
C. (*b*), (*a*), (*c*), (*d*), (*e*)
D. (*c*), (*d*), (*a*), (*b*), (*e*)

**74.** Pick the correct statements.

(*a*) Education is a subject matter of the Central list.
(*b*) The state of Karnataka has established its own state education policy commission to review NEP 2020 and to give alternative policy for the state.
(*c*) The government of India spends six percent of GDP on education.
(*d*) With multiple entry-multiple exit of NEP 2020 one can drop after two years of MBBS with a diploma in nursing.
(*e*) NEP 2020 promotes private participation in education through the philanthropy.

Choose the ***correct*** answer from the options given below:

A. (*a*), (*b*), (*d*) and (*e*) only
B. (*a*), (*b*), (*c*) and (*d*) only
C. (*b*) and (*e*) only
D. (*a*), (*c*) and (*d*) only

**75.** Match List-I with List-II.

| List-I | List-II |
|---|---|
| (*a*) Curriculum as a plan | I. Crow and Crow |
| (*b*) Curriculum as an Experience | II. B.F. Skinner |
| (*c*) Curriculum as a subject matter | III. Tyler and Hilda Taba |
| (*d*) Curriculum as an objective | IV. Doll |

Choose the ***correct*** answer from the options given below:

| | (*a*) | (*b*) | (*c*) | (*d*) |
|---|---|---|---|---|
| A. | I | IV | III | II |
| B. | II | III | I | IV |
| C. | III | I | IV | II |
| D. | IV | II | III | I |

**76.** Which of the following is NOT correct?

A. Qualitative research often avoid stating hypotheses before data are collected.
B. A positivist believes that qualities of natural phenomenon must be verified by evidence after considering them as knowledge.
C. The quantitative framework in educational research involves the application of the scientific method to try to answer questions about education.
D. Quantitative research usually tests a specific hypotheses, qualitative research often does not.

**77.** The University of Calcutta, Bombay and Madras were established in 1857 on the recommendations of Wood's despatch in 1854. Who was the viceroy of India, when these were founded?

A. Lord Canning  B. Lord Dalhousie
C. Lord Wellesley  D. Lord Bentick

**78.** Arrange the following as per the competency based curriculum model:

(*a*) Identification of general competencies
(*b*) Assessing competencies
(*c*) Organizing competencies into specific themes
(*d*) Creating learning experiences
(*e*) Evaluating the effectiveness of curriculum

Choose the ***correct*** answer from the options given below:

A. (*a*), (*b*), (*c*), (*d*), (*e*)
B. (*a*), (*e*), (*b*), (*c*), (*d*)
C. (*a*), (*c*), (*d*), (*b*), (*e*)
D. (*a*), (*c*), (*d*), (*e*), (*b*)

**79.** T-score of a particular score in a data set is 50. If each score of the data set is multiplied by 10, what will be the new T-score of that particular score?

A. 500 B. 5
C. 50 D. 0

**80.** Arrange the following according to their licensing and usages flexibility.

(*a*) Creative Common Share Alike (CC BY-SA)
(*b*) Public Domain (PD)
(*c*) Creative Common Non directive (CC BY-ND)
(*d*) Creative Common by (CC BY)
(*e*) Creative Common Non-Commercial (CC BY-NC)

Choose the ***correct*** answer from the options given below:

A. (*a*), (*c*), (*e*), (*b*), (*d*)
B. (*b*), (*d*), (*a*), (*e*), (*c*)
C. (*d*), (*e*), (*a*), (*c*), (*b*)
D. (*e*), (*d*), (*a*), (*c*), (*b*)

**81.** Selection and placement decisions typically involve prediction about future learning based on present characteristics of the individual. A test that is used for the said purpose is:

A. Criterion reference test
B. Attitude test
C. Aptitude test
D. Frame test

**82.** Main features of the grass root approach of curriculum change are:

(*a*) Small scale experiments
(*b*) Bottom-up approach
(*c*) Democratic process
(*d*) Goal-setting by the practitioners
(*e*) Face to face problem solving

Choose the ***correct*** answer from the options given below:

A. (*a*), (*b*) and (*c*) only
B. (*b*), (*c*) and (*d*) only
C. (*a*), (*c*) and (*d*) only
D. (*b*), (*d*) and (*e*) only

**83.** Which statement(s) out of the following is/are true:

(*a*) A valid test will also be reliable as well
(*b*) A reliable test will also be valid always
(*c*) A valid test may be or may not be reliable
(*d*) A reliable test may be or may not be valid
(*e*) There is no relation between reliability and validity of a test

Choose the ***correct*** answer from the options given below:

A. (*a*) and (*b*) only
B. (*b*) and (*c*) only
C. (*a*) and (*d*) only
D. (*e*) only

**84.** Arrange the following in chronological order.

(*a*) Sargent plan
(*b*) Royal Rescript on Education
(*c*) Hartog Committee Report
(*d*) Hunter Commission
(*e*) Stanley's Despatch

Choose the ***correct*** answer from the options given below:

A. (*b*), (*c*), (*a*), (*d*), (*e*)
B. (*a*), (*c*), (*d*), (*e*), (*b*)
C. (*b*), (*e*), (*d*), (*c*), (*a*)
D. (*a*), (*d*), (*e*), (*c*), (*b*)

**85.** Which of the following statements are true about hypothesis?

(*a*) A good hypothesis is based on sound reasoning that is consistent with theory or previous research.
(*b*) A deductive hypothesis is a generalization based on specific observations.
(*c*) 'Tenth grade biology students who are instructed using interactive multimedia achieve at higher level than those who receive regular instruction only' is an example of non-directional hypothesis.

(*d*) Qualitative researchers may develop guiding hypothesis for the proposed research.

Choose the ***correct*** answer from the options given below:

A. (*a*) and (*b*) only
B. (*b*) and (*c*) only
C. (*c*) and (*d*) only
D. (*a*) and (*d*) only

**86.** Which of the following are features of MOOCs?

(*a*) Open access to learning content
(*b*) Optional certificate
(*c*) Limited enrolment
(*d*) Low completion rate
(*e*) Lack of interactivity

Choose the ***correct*** answer from the options given below:

A. (*b*), (*d*), (*e*) only
B. (*a*), (*d*), (*c*) only
C. (*a*), (*b*), (*d*) only
D. (*b*), (*a*), (*e*) only

**87.** Which of the following is NOT a test of Creativity?

A. Remote Associate Test
B. Sharma's Divergent Production Ability Test
C. Minnesota Test of Creative Thinking
D. Guilford Test of Product Improvement

**88.** Online Repository for accessing full academic articles and research papers completely free of charge is:

A. Researchgate B. JSTOR
C. PubMed D. Google Books

**89.** Match List-I with List-II.

| List-I | List-II |
|---|---|
| (*a*) Programmed Instruction | I. Benjamin Bloom |
| (*b*) Mastery Learning | II. B.F. Skinner |
| (*c*) Simulation | III. Tom Good |
| (*d*) Direct Instruction | IV. Carl Smith |

Choose the ***correct*** answer from the options given below:

| | (*a*) | (*b*) | (*c*) | (*d*) |
|---|---|---|---|---|
| A. | I | III | II | IV |
| B. | II | IV | I | III |
| C. | II | I | IV | III |
| D. | III | II | IV | I |

**90.** Match List-I with List-II.

| List-I | List-II |
|---|---|
| (*a*) Mental Retardation | I. Achievement-potential discrepancy |
| (*b*) Learning disabilities | II. Impulsive behaviour |
| (*c*) Autism spectrum disorder | III. Intelligence Quotient |
| (*d*) Attention-deficit-hyperactivity disorder | IV. Social skills deficit |

Choose the ***correct*** answer from the options given below:

| | (*a*) | (*b*) | (*c*) | (*d*) |
|---|---|---|---|---|
| A. | III | I | IV | II |
| B. | II | I | IV | III |
| C. | III | IV | I | II |
| D. | IV | I | II | III |

**Direction (Qs. No. 91 to 95):** *Read the following passage carefully and answer the questions based on it:*

When many cultures co-exist in a given geographical area, without one dominating the other, it is known as "cultural pluralism". There is a common national culture in India, but at the same time the various communities have the freedom to maintain and develop their own cultural and religious traditions, so long as they are not detrimental to the unity and general welfare of the nation. This is cultural pluralism in the Indian context. Nehru (1946) described the "unity in diversity" within India when he said, it is fascinating to find how the Bengalis, the

Marathas, the Gujuratis, the Tamils, the Andhras, the Oriyas, the Assamese, the Canarese, the Malayalis, the Sindhis, the Punjabis, the Pathans, the Kashmiris, the Rajputs and the great Central block of the Hindusthani speaking people, have retained their peculiar characteristics for hundreds of years.... have remained distinctively Indian. Indian Culture is grand and unique and has fostered other cultures. We can call Gandhi the embodiment of Indian cultural Heritage. He was the one who highlighted India's culture and spoke of its characteristics of magnanimity, flexibility and above all of its synthesis. The history of the country's culture goes back to the ancient past or we can certainly line it up at least with the Dravidian era. Later on, many other cultures came in contact with the Indian Culture and easily merged themselves into it according to the circumstances and conditions that prevailed in India. In the same context, Gandhiji regarded the homogeneity of the Indian environment as the basis of this synthesis.

**91.** When the majority culture dominates in a society of multiple cultures, it is:

A. Cultural pluralism
B. Communism
C. Majoritarianism
D. Sectarianism

**92.** Which of the following is NOT true?

A. India has a common national culture
B. India has a pluralistic culture
C. The pathans have retained their peculiar characteristics over time
D. Majoritarian culture should dominate minority cultures in India

**93.** The embodiment of Indian Cultural heritage is perceived in:

A. Mahatma Gandhi
B. Jawahar Lal Nehru
C. Subhash Chandra Bose
D. Rabindra Nath Tagore

**94.** India is land of:

A. A pervasive dominant culture
B. Multiple cultures
C. Individualistic identities
D. Earliest civilizations

**95.** According to Gandhi ji, which of the following is a characteristic of Indian culture?

A. Individuality B. Majoritarianism
C. Magnanimity D. Metamorphosis

**Direction (Qs. No. 96 to 100):** *Read the following passage carefully and answer the questions based on it:*

Althusser argues that no class can hold power for any length of time simply by the use of force. Ideological control provides a far more effective means of maintaining class rule. If members of the subject class accept their position as normal, natural and inevitable, and fail to realize the true nature of their situation, then they will be unlikely to challenge ruling class dominance. Physical force is an inefficient means of control compared to winning over hearts and minds. The maintenance of class rule largely depends on the reproduction of ruling class ideology. Thus Althusser argues that 'the reproduction of labour power requires not only a reproduction of its skills, but also, at the same time a reproduction of its submission to the ruling ideology'. This submission is reproduced by a number of 'Ideological State Apparatuses' which include the mass media, the law, religion and education. Ideological State Apparatuses transmit ruling class ideology thereby creating false class consciousness which largely maintains the subject class in its subordinate position. In pre-capitalist society, Althusser sees the church as the dominant ideological state apparatus. In capitalist society it has largely been replaced by the educational system.

**96.** Which of the following is NOT an ideological state apparatus?

A. Religion B. Media
C. Education D. Class

**97.** Schools:

A. Reproduce ruling class ideology
B. Reproduce communities
C. Reproduce popular culture
D. Reproduce states control

**98.** For the longest possible duration to hold power, the most efficient is:

A. Media control
B. Economic control
C. Religious control
D. Ideological control

**99.** False class consciousness does not make people:

A. accept their position
B. accept the working class ideology
C. accept the insubordination
D. accept church, media and education

**100.** Subject-members take their position as:

A. ascribe, ideological and submissive
B. normal, natural and inevitable
C. prescribed, predetermined and necessary
D. given, required and adhered

# ANSWERS

**1. (B):**

(*c*) **Concrete experience:** This is the first step in Kolb's experiential learning cycle, where learners engage in hands-on experience.

(*b*) **Students make their own observations**: After the experience, learners reflect on what happened.

(*e*) **Reflections**: Learners analyze their observations and understand patterns.

(*a*) **Formation of abstract concepts and generalization**: Based on reflections, learners develop theories and concepts.

(*d*) **Testing implications of the concepts in new situations (d)**: Finally, learners apply the learned concepts in different contexts to validate their understanding.

**2. (C & D):**

- The **Socratic method** is a teaching approach based on **dialogue and inquiry**, where the teacher asks questions to guide students in developing critical thinking skills.
- **Lev Vygotsky's theory** focuses on **social interaction and scaffolding** in learning. His concept of the **Zone of Proximal Development (ZPD)** explains that learners benefit from guided discussions that help them construct knowledge collaboratively.

A teacher using the **Socratic method** in a lesson on **global warming** facilitates student thinking by encouraging dialogue and reasoning, which aligns with Vygotsky's principles.

- **Jerome Bruner's constructivist theory** also supports the **Socratic method** through **discovery learning and inquiry-based teaching**. He emphasized **scaffolding**, where a teacher provides structured guidance to help students reach deeper understanding. His belief in **active learning and inductive reasoning** supports the idea that students should derive concepts through questioning and exploration, making the **Socratic method** a suitable approach for developing critical thinking in a global warming lesson.

**3. (D):**

(*e*) **Gain attention:** First, the instructor captures learners' focus.

(*c*) **Describe goal and inform the learner of the objectives:** The teacher explains what will be learned.

(*b*) **Stimulate recall of prior learning:** Learners connect new information with existing knowledge.

(*d*) **Provide guidance for learning:** The teacher offers support and strategies to help learners.

(*a*) **Provide reinforcement:** Finally, the teacher reinforces learning through feedback and encouragement.

**4. (C):**

(*c*) **Proposition:** A statement or hypothesis is presented.

(*b*) **Reason:** A logical reason is given to support the proposition.

(*d*) **Example:** An example is provided to substantiate the reason.

(*e*) **Application:** The reasoning and example are applied to the case at hand.

(*a*) **Conclusion:** Based on the previous steps, the final conclusion is drawn.

**5. (C):**

**IV. Market economy - Private Controlled:** A market economy is driven by private individuals and businesses with minimal government intervention.

**III. Service of a teacher - Skill:** Teaching is a skill-based profession that requires expertise.

**I. Centrally planned economy - Government controlled:** In a centrally planned economy, the government controls production and resource allocation.

**II. Positive economy - Functioning of a mechanism:** Positive economics deals with objective analysis and the functioning of economic mechanisms without value judgments.

**6. (B):**

- In 1848, Savitri Bai Phule, along with her husband Jyotiba Phule and Fatima Sheikh, established the first school for girls in India.
- The school was named "Phule Shikshan Mandir."
- This initiative was revolutionary at a time when girls' education was highly discouraged in Indian society.
- Fatima Sheikh also played a key role as India's first Muslim female teacher, supporting the Phules in their mission to educate marginalized communities.

**7. (D):**

- Freudian psychoanalytic theory divides personality into three parts:
  1. **Id** – The primitive, instinctual part focused on pleasure.
  2. **Ego** – The rational part that mediates between the id and reality.
  3. **Superego** – The moral compass, enforcing societal norms.
- Superego does not control ego impulses directly, rather, it acts as an internal moral guide, influencing ego's decisions.
- The ego balances between id's desires and superego's morality rather than being controlled by the superego.

**8. (C):**

- **Right of Children to Free and Compulsory Education (RTE) Act (a) - 2009 (II)**: This act ensures free and compulsory education for children aged 6 to 14 years.
- **Commission for Protection of Child Rights Act (b) - 2005 (I)**: This act was enacted to safeguard children's rights and establish the National Commission for Protection of Child Rights (NCPCR).
- **National Council for Teacher Education (NCTE) Act (c) - 1993 (IV)**: This act regulates teacher education and training programs in India.
- **University Grants Commission (UGC) Act (d) - 1956 (III)**: This act was enacted to establish and regulate the UGC, which oversees higher education in India.

**9. (C):**

- Marxism, developed by Karl Marx and Friedrich Engels, argues that social inequality is not natural but rather created by economic and class structures.
- The theory highlights how the bourgeoisie (capitalist class) exploits the proletariat (working class), creating social divisions.

- According to Marxist theory, inequality can be eliminated through class struggle, revolution, and redistribution of wealth.
- Socialist and communist movements have been influenced by Marxist thought, advocating for a classless and equal society.

**10. (B):**

- **Q Methodology (*a*) - Stephenson (1953) (III)**: Developed by William Stephenson, this method is used for studying people's subjectivity, opinions, and viewpoints.
- **'Guess Who' technique (*b*) - Hartshorne and May (1929) (I)**: A psychological test developed by Hartshorne and May to assess children's social behavior and honesty.
- **Student's t-distribution (*c*) - William Sealy Gosset (IV)**: Developed by William Sealy Gosset, who published under the pseudonym "Student," this statistical distribution is widely used for hypothesis testing in small samples.
- **Bootstrap Method (*d*) - Bradley Efron (II)**: Developed by Bradley Efron, this statistical technique estimates the sampling distribution of a statistic by resampling with replacement.

**11. (C):**

- Vygotsky's Socio-cultural theory states that learning occurs first at a social level (Inter-psychological) and then gets internalized at the individual level (Intra-psychological).
- The Zone of Proximal Development (ZPD) explains that children learn through interaction with more knowledgeable others before developing independent understanding.
- The given statement is incorrect because Inter-psychological (social learning) comes first, followed by Intra-psychological (internal processing), not the other way around.

**12. (D):**

- **ADDIE (*a*) - Systematic instructions: step-by-step framework to assess training and education material (III)**: ADDIE stands for Analysis, Design, Development, Implementation, and Evaluation, a structured instructional design model.
- **ASSURE (*b*) - Selecting media (I)**: The **ASSURE model** is used for designing learning experiences, including choosing appropriate instructional **media and technology**.
- **Dick and Carey (*c*) - Learner analysis and engagement (IV)**: This model emphasizes instructional system design with a focus on learner analysis and continuous engagement.
- **Mason (*d*) - Living books, narration, and habits (II)**: Charlotte Mason's approach focuses on learning through storytelling, narration, and habit formation.

**13. (B):**

- **Maslow (*a*) - Humanistic Approach (II)**: Maslow's Hierarchy of Needs is a humanistic theory, focusing on self-actualization and motivation.
- **Erikson (*b*) - Life Span Approach (III)**: Erikson's Psychosocial Development Theory outlines stages of development throughout life, making it a life span approach.
- **Sheldon (*c*) - Constitutional Approach (IV)**: William Sheldon's theory associates personality with body types (ectomorph, mesomorph, endomorph), known as the constitutional approach.
- **Freud (*d*) - Psychoanalytic Approach (I)**: Freud's Psychoanalytic Theory focuses on unconscious drives, childhood experiences, and personality structures (Id, Ego, Superego).

**14. (D):**

- **Perceptual Reasoning (*a*) - Block Design, Matrix Reasoning, Visual Puzzles (III)**: These tasks assess non-verbal reasoning skills and spatial perception.
- **Working Memory (*b*) - Digit Span, Arithmetic (II)**: This measures a person's

ability to hold and manipulate information in short-term memory.

- **Processing Speed (*c*) - Symbol Search, Coding (IV)**: It evaluates how quickly an individual can process and respond to visual information.
- **Verbal Comprehension (*d*) - Similarities, Vocabulary, Information (I)**: It assesses language understanding, word knowledge, and reasoning abilities.

**15. (B):**

- According to National Education Policy (NEP) 2020, all standalone Teacher Education Institutions (TEIs) must become multidisciplinary institutions by 2030.
- The goal is to integrate teacher education with general education to improve the quality and effectiveness of teacher training.
- By 2030, only multidisciplinary institutions will be permitted to offer teacher education programs, ensuring interdisciplinary learning.

**16. (A):** Jainism teaches that attaining Moksha (liberation) requires following the Three Jewels (Ratnatraya):

1. **Samyak Darshan (Right Faith)** – Having true belief in Jain teachings.
2. **Samyak Jnan (Right Knowledge)** – Acquiring correct knowledge of reality.
3. **Samyak Charitra (Right Conduct)** – Practicing ethical behavior and non-violence.

**Samyak Drishti** and **Samyak Sankalp** are not traditionally listed as essential requirements for Moksha in Jain philosophy.

**17. (D):**

- The Preamble of the Indian Constitution enshrines the values of Justice, Liberty, Equality, and Fraternity, including Secularism.
- Secularism ensures that the State does not favor any religion and guarantees religious freedom to all citizens.
- The 42nd Amendment Act (1976) explicitly added the term "Secular" to the Preamble, reinforcing India's commitment to religious neutrality.

**18. (D):**

- The National Commission on Teachers (1983) was established to set guidelines for the selection and training of teachers in India.
- It was headed by D.P. Chattopadhyaya and emphasized teacher education reforms to enhance the quality and effectiveness of teaching.
- The commission provided recommendations on qualifications, training, and professional development for teachers.

**19. (C):** Curriculum development is essential for holistic education and should address both cognitive and practical needs.

(*b*) **Acquisition of knowledge:** A core component of any curriculum, ensuring students gain essential academic skills.

(*d*) **Proper use of time:** Curriculum must be structured to optimize students' learning and productivity.

**Sports and games (*a*)** and **Cultural activities (*c*)** are important for development but are not primary needs in curriculum development.

**20. (B):**

- An inclusive curriculum ensures that all students, regardless of abilities or disabilities, learn together under the same curriculum.
- It promotes equal opportunities while allowing flexibility to meet diverse learning needs.
- This approach is aligned with the principles of Universal Design for Learning (UDL), ensuring education is accessible and beneficial for all learners.

**21. (A):**

- Taylorism is also known as "Scientific Management" and was developed by

Frederick Winslow Taylor to improve efficiency in industrial work.

- The initial name for this approach was "Shop Management", as it focused on maximizing productivity in manufacturing industries.
- Taylorism introduced time and motion studies, standardization of tasks, and financial incentives to increase efficiency.
- Statement (*d*) is incorrect because Taylorism was given by Frederick Winslow Taylor, not Samuel Taylor.

**22. (A):**

(*a*) **Establish expectations**: Setting clear benchmarks for policy implementation.

(*e*) **Application of resources**: Allocating required materials, manpower, and finances for policy execution.

(*c*) **Observing performance indicators**: Monitoring and tracking progress against predefined parameters.

(*b*) **Analysis of deviations**: Identifying gaps or discrepancies in policy implementation.

(*d*) **Taking corrective action**: Implementing necessary changes to address deviations and improve outcomes.

**23. (D):**

- **Ethnography (*a*) - What are the cultural patterns and perspectives of this group in its natural setting? (IV)**: Ethnography involves immersive study of communities to understand cultural and social practices.
- **Ethology (*b*) - How do the origins, characteristics, and culture of different societies compare to one another? (I)**: Ethology examines the behavior of humans and animals in an evolutionary and comparative context.
- **Ethnomethodology (*c*) - How do people make sense of their everyday activities in order to behave in socially accepted ways? (III)**: It studies how social order is created through everyday interactions.
- **Phenomenology (*d*) - What is the experience of an activity or concept from these particular participants' perspectives? (II)**: Phenomenology explores subjective human experiences.

**24. (C):**

- Nalanda University, founded during the Gupta dynasty, was an ancient Buddhist center of learning.
- It attracted scholars from Tibet, China, Korea, and Central Asia, making it a global hub for Buddhist studies, philosophy, and medicine.
- Famous scholars like Xuanzang and I-Tsing studied at Nalanda.
- The university had a vast library, structured learning methodologies, and a curriculum based on Buddhist scriptures and various disciplines.

**25. (A):**

- As per the Gazette Notification of 2021, the four-year Integrated Teacher Education Programme (ITEP) leads to the degrees B.A. B.Ed, B.Sc. B.Ed, or B.Com. B.Ed.
- ITEP aims to prepare quality teachers by integrating subject knowledge with pedagogical skills.
- This program aligns with the National Education Policy (NEP) 2020, which seeks to enhance teacher training and multidisciplinary education.

**26. (B):**

- The competency-based model of curriculum focuses on students mastering specific skills rather than just spending time on learning.
- It emphasizes outcomes-based learning, ensuring that students achieve a set level of competence before progressing.
- This model is widely used in professional and vocational education, where learners must demonstrate proficiency in real-world applications.

**27. (A):**

(*c*) **Define realistic goals**: Setting measurable objectives aligned with customer needs.

(*e*) **Measure and identify critical quality requirements**: Understanding key factors influencing customer satisfaction.

(*d*) **Analyze multiple options**: Exploring different design alternatives and assessing their feasibility.

(*a*) **Design the process**: Creating an initial framework and refining it through iterative improvements.

(*b*) **Verify the final iteration**: Ensuring the final product meets customer expectations and obtaining approval.

**28. (B):** The basic principles of curriculum development include Totality, Maturity, and Flexibility, which focus on comprehensive learning, developmental appropriateness, and adaptability.

Principle of Leisure is not a recognized fundamental principle in curriculum development, as curriculum is primarily structured to meet educational goals rather than focusing on leisure activities.

**29. (A):**

(*c*) **Goals and Objectives**: Establishing learning goals to provide direction for curriculum design.

(*e*) **Needs Assessment**: Identifying learners' requirements and the relevance of the curriculum.

(*a*) **Content**: Selecting and structuring the subject matter based on goals and assessment.

(*d*) **Implementation**: Delivering the curriculum in an educational setting.

(*b*) **Evaluation**: Assessing the effectiveness of the curriculum and making necessary adjustments.

**30. (B):**

(*d*) **Define the universe to be studied**: Identifying the target population for research.

(*a*) **Preparing sampling frame**: Creating a list of individuals or elements that will be sampled.

(*b*) **Applying the sampling technique**: Choosing and implementing a suitable sampling method.

(*c*) **Administer the tool**: Conducting data collection using surveys, interviews, or other research tools.

**31. (C):** The Dick and Carey Model is a systematic instructional design model that differs from the ADDIE model primarily due to its integration of formative evaluation at every stage.

Formative evaluation helps in continuous assessment and improvement of instructional design.

The ADDIE model also includes evaluation, but it is mainly in the final phase, whereas Dick and Carey emphasize formative evaluation throughout the process.

**32. (A):** NCFTE-2009 (National Curriculum Framework for Teacher Education) outlines the key curricular areas for teacher education..

The main curricular areas include:

(*a*) **Curriculum and Pedagogy:** Focus on teaching strategies and subject matter.

(*c*) **Foundation of Education:** Includes educational psychology, philosophy, and sociology.

(*d*) **School Internship:** Practical training in a real classroom environment.

Educational Technology (*b*) and Learner Assessment (*e*) are significant but are not listed as main curricular areas in NCFTE-2009.

**33. (A):** Inclusive education means integrating all students into the same learning environment while accommodating diverse needs.

Mainstreaming refers to placing students with disabilities in regular classes only when they can meet standard expectations, which is not truly inclusive.

True inclusion ensures equal participation of all students without segregation or conditions.

**34. (D):** The Jurisprudential Inquiry Model is a teaching method that engages students in social problem-solving and critical thinking.

Key component activities include:

(*a*) **Facts about social problems:** Understanding real-world social issues.

(*b*) **Framework for analyzing social issues:** Developing a structured approach to examine problems.

(*c*) **Competence in social dialogue:** Engaging in meaningful discussions and debates.

While expressing opinions (*d*) and analyzing personal values (*e*) are important, they are not the primary focus of this model.

**35. (*)**

**36. (C):** According to NEP-2020, school teachers are expected to spend 50 hours per year on Continuous Professional Development (CPD). CPD includes workshops, training programs, skill enhancement sessions, and learning new pedagogical methods to improve teaching quality.

This initiative aims to ensure lifelong learning and keep teachers updated with new educational techniques and technological advancements in the field.

**37. (B):** Swami Vivekananda, in his famous Chicago speech of 1893, emphasized the idea of universal acceptance and religious harmony.

He stated that all religions lead to the same ultimate truth and that spiritual awareness transcends religious dogma.

He urged people to respect all religious traditions and embrace a universal, inclusive approach to spirituality rather than being confined to rigid religious beliefs.

**38. (A):** The concept of randomness is based on the assumption that individual occurrences are unpredictable, but when observed over a large dataset, patterns emerge.

This is the foundation of probability theory, where random events balance out over time, allowing for accurate predictions at an aggregate level.

This principle is widely used in statistics, economics, and physics to analyze large-scale trends despite individual unpredictability.

**39. (D):** Poka-Yoke, a Japanese term meaning "mistake-proofing", is a technique used in manufacturing and quality control to prevent errors.

(*a*) The term originated from the Japanese "Baka-yoke", which means fool-proofing but was later changed to a more polite term "Poka-Yoke".

(*b*) The contact method identifies defects through physical attributes, such as ensuring proper positioning of parts.

(*d*) The motion-step method ensures that all steps are completed in the correct sequence, preventing procedural errors.

(*c*) The fixed-value method is used for recurring activities, not non-recurring processes, making it incorrect.

**40. (B):**

- **Organizational Development (*a*) - Planned change process which is a continuous learning exercise (II):** Organizational Development (OD) is an ongoing process aimed at improving effectiveness and adaptability.
- **Statistical Quality Control (*b*) - Variance from standard measures is tracked applying statistical and engineering techniques (IV)**: SQC is used to monitor and control product quality through statistical methods.
- **Statistical Process Control (*c*) - Procedure is monitored and improvement effected by means of statistical technique (I)**: SPC involves real-time monitoring of production processes to detect and correct variations.
- **Sustainable Development (*d*) - Benefit should exceed costs of development (III)**: Sustainability ensures that economic growth and environmental preservation are balanced by ensuring the long-term benefits exceed the costs.

**41.** **(B):** Continuum of services in special education follows a hierarchy from least restrictive to most restrictive settings.

**(c) Regular classroom:** Students with mild disabilities learn in the same environment as other students.

**(b) Regular classroom with supplementary instruction and services:** Additional support is provided while students remain in a general education setting.

**(e) Regular classroom and Resource room:** Students receive specialized instruction in a separate resource room for part of the day.

**(a) Full-time separate classroom:** Students with significant disabilities are taught in a separate classroom for all subjects.

**(d) Special school:** Reserved for students with severe disabilities, requiring specialized instruction and support.

**42.** **(C):** The term "Triadic Reciprocal Causation" is associated with Albert Bandura's Social Cognitive Theory.

It describes how three factors—personal characteristics (beliefs, self-efficacy), behavior (actions), and environment (social influences)—interact continuously to shape human learning and development.

This theory emphasizes observational learning, self-regulation, and reinforcement in behavior formation.

**43.** **(B):**

**(a) Gramsci - Marxism (III)**: Antonio Gramsci, an Italian philosopher, contributed to Marxist theory, focusing on cultural hegemony and class struggle.

**(b) Charles S. Peirce - Pragmatism (I)**: Peirce is known as the father of pragmatism, emphasizing practical consequences as a key component of truth.

**(c) Jean Francois Lyotard - Postmodernism (IV)**: Lyotard criticized grand narratives and advocated for plurality and skepticism in knowledge.

**(d) Nel Noddings - Feminism (II)**: Nel Noddings developed the "Ethics of Care", a feminist approach to ethics and education.

**44.** **(C):** As per NEP 2020, the National Curricular and Pedagogical Framework for Early Childhood Care and Education (NCPFECCE) will be developed by NCERT.

This framework will focus on play-based, activity-based, and discovery-based learning for children up to the age of 8 years.

It aims to enhance early childhood development and foundational literacy and numeracy skills.

**45.** **(C):** The NAAC (National Assessment and Accreditation Council) introduced reforms in accreditation based on recommendations from the Dr. Radhakrishnan Committee.

**The proposed reforms include:**

- **Binary Accreditation**: Institutions are either Accredited or Not Accredited.
- **Maturity-Based Graded Level Accreditation**: Institutions are evaluated on a progressive scale based on quality improvement.

These changes aim to enhance transparency, credibility, and efficiency in higher education accreditation.

**46.** **(D):** Israel Scheffler propounded the Philosophical Model of Teaching, incorporating the three philosophical insights:

- **Insight (Plato):** Learning is based on deep understanding and reasoning.
- **Impression (Locke):** The mind is shaped by experience and sensory input.
- **Rule (Kant):** Learning follows structured principles and logical reasoning.

This model integrates rationalism, empiricism, and formalism into educational theory.

**47.** **(*)**

**48. (A):**

(*a*) **Kurt Lewin was one of the founding fathers of Gestalt Psychology:** Lewin contributed to Gestalt psychology and field theory, emphasizing perception and group dynamics.

(*c*) **Kohler's book related to experiments on chimpanzees was 'Mentality of Apes':** Wolfgang Kohler conducted insight learning experiments with chimpanzees and published his findings in "The Mentality of Apes" (1925).

(*d*) **Skinner opposed the "no stimulus, no response" mechanism in the evolution of behavior:** B.F. Skinner challenged reflex-based behaviorism, promoting operant conditioning, where behavior is influenced by reinforcement rather than just stimulus-response mechanisms.

(*b*) **and** (*e*) **are incorrect**:

- Albert Bandura's theory is based on observational learning, not life spaces, vectors, and insight.
- A positive reinforcer increases behavior rather than decreasing it upon removal.

**49. (D):**

(*a*) **It is part of a wider strategy to develop an inclusive society:** Inclusive education promotes equity and access to education for all.

(*c*) **It involves restructuring school cultures:** Schools must adapt their practices, policies, and attitudes to support diverse learners.

(*d*) **Diversity is a rich resource to support learning for all:** Inclusion values diverse abilities and backgrounds as strengths in the learning process.

(*b*) and (*e*) are incorrect:

- Inclusive education assumes all children can learn in a general classroom with appropriate support.
- Schools should adapt to meet the learning needs of all children rather than expecting students to fit into a rigid system.

**50. (D):** The word "Curriculum" is derived from the Latin word "Currere," which means "to run" or "a course to be run."

In education, curriculum refers to the structured learning experiences, subjects, and activities designed to facilitate student learning and development.

The term evolved from its original meaning of a "racecourse" to signify a structured educational journey.

**51. (A): Leader:** Member Exchange (LMX) Theory classifies employees into two groups based on their relationship with the leader:

- **In-group:** Members who have high-quality relationships, receive more responsibilities, and have greater trust from the leader.
- **Out-group:** Members who have low-quality exchanges, limited communication, and fewer opportunities for career growth.

Employees in the Out-group have less access to leadership support and developmental opportunities, making their work experience less enriching compared to In-group members.

**52. (A):** Joseph M. Rice conducted one of the earliest large-scale assessments of student spelling achievement in the 1890s.

He used a written examination to test students' spelling proficiency, marking one of the first instances of standardized testing in education.

His work was influential in shaping educational assessments and the development of objective testing methods.

**53. (B):** As per NEP-2020, the National Educational Technology Forum (NETF) has been established to improve technology integration in education.

**Functions of NETF include:**

(*a*) **Envision strategic thrust areas in educational technology:** Identifying emerging trends in educational tools and technology.

(*b*) **Articulate new directions for research and innovation:** Encouraging advancements in technology for education.

(*d*) **Provide independent evidence-based advice to the Centre and State governments:** Helping policymakers implement technology-driven educational reforms.

(*c*) and (*e*) are incorrect: NETF does not establish a Technology Centre in Gujarat nor allocate research projects from 2026.

**54. (D):**

(*c*) **Item writing:** The first step involves developing statements or questions that will measure attitudes on a given topic. These items must be clear, unbiased, and reflective of varying perspectives.

(*e*) **Pre try-out:** Before full-scale testing, the initial items undergo a preliminary trial to identify any ambiguities, biases, or inconsistencies in the responses.

(*d*) **Administration for final try-out:** The refined set of items is administered to a selected sample group to test its effectiveness in measuring attitudes accurately.

(*b*) **Calculation of item-wise critical ratio:** Statistical analysis is conducted to determine the discriminatory power of each item, ensuring only the most effective items remain.

(*a*) **Selection of final items:** Based on statistical evaluation, the final set of items is selected to construct the final version of the attitude scale.

**55. (B):** PERT (Program Evaluation and Review Technique) is used for planning and scheduling complex projects.

The correct representation in a PERT chart is:

- Nodes represent events or milestones.
- Arrows represent activities or tasks.

The given statement is incorrect because in PERT charts, arrows represent tasks, while nodes represent milestones, making the statement factually inaccurate.

**56. (B):**

(*b*) **Persons with Disabilities Act was modified in 2010:** Incorrect. The Persons with Disabilities (Equal Opportunities, Protection of Rights and Full Participation) Act, 1995 was repealed and replaced by the Rights of Persons with Disabilities (RPWD) Act, 2016, not modified in 2010.

(*d*) **National Policy on Disabilities originated from RTE Act 2009:** Incorrect. The National Policy for Persons with Disabilities was adopted in 2006, before the Right to Education (RTE) Act, 2009. It was formulated to ensure equal opportunities, protection of rights, and full participation of persons with disabilities in education, employment, and other fields.

**57. (D):**

- In 1987, the NCERT launched the Project on Integrated Education for Disabled (PIED) in collaboration with UNICEF.
- The project aimed to promote inclusive education by integrating children with disabilities into mainstream schools.
- PIED served as a foundation for the Inclusive Education policies implemented later in India.

**58. (C):**

(*b*) **Operation Blackboard (OB) (1987):** Aimed at providing minimum essential facilities in primary schools, including teaching-learning materials and better infrastructure.

(*c*) **District Primary Education Programme (DPEP) (1994):** Launched to improve primary education in districts with low literacy rates.

(*a*) **Sarva Shiksha Abhiyan (SSA) (2001):** A flagship program for universal elementary education for all children aged 6-14 years.

(*d*) **Rashtriya Madhyamik Shiksha Abhiyan (RMSA) (2009):** Focused on enhancing access to quality secondary education.

(*e*) **Samagra Shiksha Abhiyan (2018):** Integrated SSA, RMSA, and Teacher Education into a single comprehensive program for school education.

**59. (D):** Bill Reddin identified four basic leadership styles:

- **Related:** Leaders focus on team cohesion and personal relationships.
- **Integrated:** A balance between task completion and relationship-building.
- **Dedicated:** Emphasis on goal achievement, structure, and discipline.
- **Separated:** Leaders minimize involvement in tasks and relationships, leading to a hands-off approach.

These styles focus on situational adaptability and organizational needs.

**60. (C):**

(*b*) **Macro finance includes drafting policy, subsidies, multiyear expansion plans:** Correct. Macro finance involves long-term financial planning, such as government policies, subsidies, and funding for large-scale projects.

(*c*) **The main aim of microfinance is to help the economy grow and to generate employment:** Correct. Microfinance supports small businesses, self-employment, and rural economic growth.

(*d*) **Macro finance has a direct effect on the whole economy and an indirect effect on the whole population:** Correct. Macro-financial decisions impact inflation, GDP, and employment rates, ultimately influencing the entire population.

(*a*) and (*e*) are incorrect:

- Macro finance does not cater to individuals or small businesses; that is the role of microfinance.
- Microfinance is not an endless activity; it is structured around short-term and medium-term financial aid.

**61. (B):**

(*a*) **The Salamanca Statement - 1994 (IV):** The Salamanca Statement (1994) was adopted at the World Conference on Special Needs Education organized by UNESCO, emphasizing inclusive education for all children, including those with disabilities.

(*b*) **The Rehabilitation Council of India Act - 1992 (I)**: This act was passed in 1992 to regulate the training of rehabilitation professionals and ensure the provision of high-quality services for individuals with disabilities.

(*c*) **The Persons with Disabilities Act - 1995 (II):** This act was enacted in 1995 to protect the rights of persons with disabilities, ensuring equal opportunities and access to education, employment, and social security.

(*d*) **National Policy for Persons with Disabilities - 2006 (III):** The policy, formulated in 2006, aimed at empowering persons with disabilities by ensuring inclusive education, employment, and social justice.

**62. (D):**

(*a*) **Arthapatti - He does not eat in the daytime; he is fat. He eats at night (III):** Arthapatti (postulation or presumption) is a logical reasoning method used to explain something not directly observed.

(*b*) **Abhava - A chair is not a table (II):** Abhava (absence or negation) is a form of reasoning where knowledge is derived from the absence of something.

(*c*) **Upamana - This cow is different from a domestic cow; it must be a nilgai (IV):** Upamana (comparison or analogy) is used to establish similarity between an unknown object and a known one.

(*d*) **Sabda - Conchshell is not a bone according to Vedas (I):** Sabda (verbal testimony) refers to the authority of reliable sources, such as scriptures or expert statements.

**63. (A):** A Job Application Portfolio is considered a Finished Portfolio because it is a final, refined version of a candidate's work, skills, and achievements.

It includes resumes, certifications, work samples, recommendation letters, and other credentials that demonstrate the candidate's qualifications for employment.

**64. (C):**

(*a*) **Selecting attributes of variables**: Identifying relevant psychological traits like intelligence, personality, or interests for measurement.

(*b*) **Developing Educational devices/Test:** Designing standardized tests and assessment tools to measure attributes.

(*c*) **Quantifying the attributes**: Converting psychological attributes into measurable numerical values.

(*d*) **Determining operations to isolate the attributes**: Establishing experimental and statistical methods to isolate and analyze specific attributes.

(*e*) **Preparing standard scores is not a major issue**, as standardized scoring systems like z-scores and percentiles are commonly used.

**65. (B):**

(*a*) **Content and Pedagogic approach**: NCFTE-2009 emphasizes a holistic approach that integrates content knowledge with effective pedagogical strategies.

(*d*) **Addressing teachers as learners**: The framework recognizes that teachers are lifelong learners and should be continuously engaged in reflective practices and professional development.

(*b*) and (*c*) are not considered primary principles in designing in-service teacher education programs as per NCFTE-2009.

**66. (B):**

(*a*) **Mastery decisions - Criterion referenced (III)**: Mastery decisions involve assessing whether a learner has achieved a specific level of competency, which is evaluated using criterion-referenced assessments.

(*b*) **Average IQ - Norm referenced (IV)**: IQ tests are typically norm-referenced, meaning they compare an individual's score to the performance of a representative sample.

(*c*) **Evaluation of Capacity - Summative (I)**: Evaluating capacity often takes place at the end of a program or course to assess overall ability, which aligns with summative assessments.

(*d*) **Guiding future instruction - Formative (II)**: Formative assessment is used to provide feedback and guide instructional strategies for future learning.

**67. (A):** Formative evaluation is used by teachers and counselors to identify students' strengths and weaknesses during the learning process.

It helps in adjusting teaching methods, addressing areas where students struggle, and providing targeted support to enhance learning.

This type of evaluation is ongoing and provides continuous feedback rather than a final judgment of performance.

**68. (C): Inclusive education recognizes rights but not realizes all of them:**

- Inclusive education ensures that all students, regardless of ability, have the right to learn together in the same environment.
- However, in many cases, practical implementation is incomplete, meaning that while rights are acknowledged, they are not fully realized in practice due to lack of infrastructure, trained teachers, and policy execution gaps.
- True inclusion requires more than just policy recognition; it demands active efforts in providing equal access and support for all learners.

**69. (D): According to Human Capital Theory,** investing in education results in:

(*a*) **Higher wages:** Education improves skills and knowledge, leading to better employment opportunities and increased income.

(*e*) **Productivity:** A more educated workforce contributes to economic growth and efficiency, increasing overall productivity.

(*b*) **Individual Growth and (*d*) Empowerment** are benefits of education but not the primary focus of Human Capital Theory, which emphasizes economic returns.

(*c*) **World Ranking of Country** is not a direct consequence of investing in education under this theory.

**70. (A):** Wikis are the most effective Web 2.0 tools for collaborative learning in e-learning platforms because they allow multiple users to:

- Edit and contribute content in real-time.
- Engage in collaborative writing, discussions, and knowledge sharing.
- Track revisions and build on each other's ideas.

Unlike blogs, podcasts, or video conferencing, wikis provide a dynamic, interactive, and ongoing collaborative learning environment.

**71. (C): Sequential Explanatory**:

- **'QUAN → QUAL'** represents a Sequential Explanatory mixed-method research design.
- In this design, quantitative data is collected and analyzed first, followed by qualitative data to explain or elaborate on the quantitative findings.
- This method is commonly used when quantitative results need further interpretation through qualitative insights.

**72. (A):**

(*a*) **Alfred Adler disagreed with Freud's idea that the cause of human emotionality was 'unconscious conflicts' – Correct.** Adler believed that behavior is goal-directed and influenced by social factors rather than just unconscious conflicts.

(*b*) **Aaron Beck developed Cognitive Psychotherapy in the 1960s – Correct.** Beck is the founder of Cognitive Therapy (CT), which evolved into Cognitive Behavioral Therapy (CBT).

(*d*) **In ABC Model, 'C' represents the resultant emotion or behavior – Correct.** In Albert Ellis' ABC Model,

- **A (Activating Event):** An external event.
- **B (Beliefs):** Thoughts about the event.
- **C (Consequences):** Emotional or behavioral responses.

(*c*) **and (*e*) are incorrect**:

- CBT came into usage around the 1960s, not the early 1950s.
- 'A' in the ABC model represents Activating Event, not assimilation.

**73. (D): Reverse chronological order:**

- **Justice J.S. Verma Committee (2012):** Reviewed teacher education reforms.
- **National Knowledge Commission (2005):** Aimed at improving higher education and research.
- **National Commission on Teachers (1983-85):** Focused on teacher training and development.
- **Kothari Commission (1964-66):** Provided major educational reforms in India.
- **Radhakrishnan Commission (1948-49):** Addressed higher education reforms.

**74. (C):**

(*b*) **The state of Karnataka has established its own state education policy commission to review NEP 2020 and to give an alternative policy for the state – Correct.** Karnataka formed a committee to evaluate NEP 2020 and propose modifications.

(*e*) **NEP 2020 promotes private participation in education through philanthropy – Correct**. The policy encourages private funding, donations, and philanthropic contributions to enhance education infrastructure.

(*a*), (*c*), and (*d*) **are incorrect**:

- Education is on the Concurrent List, not the Central List.
- India does not spend 6% of GDP on education yet (as targeted).
- NEP 2020 allows multiple entry-exit, but dropping out of MBBS with a diploma in nursing is not an official provision.

**75. (C):**

(*a*) **Curriculum as a plan - Tyler and Hilda Taba (III)**: They emphasized curriculum as a structured and pre-planned approach to education.

(*b*) **Curriculum as an experience - Crow and Crow (I)**: Focuses on learning through experiences and interactions.

(*c*) **Curriculum as a subject matter - Doll (IV)**: Views curriculum as a set of knowledge and subjects to be taught.

(*d*) **Curriculum as an objective - B.F. Skinner (II)**: Behaviorist approach where learning is based on predefined objectives and measurable outcomes.

**76. (B): A positivist believes that qualities of natural phenomenon must be verified by evidence after considering them as knowledge**:

- Positivism is a research philosophy that emphasizes empirical evidence and observation as the foundation of knowledge.
- A positivist does not "consider" something as knowledge first and then verify it; instead, they gather evidence first and then establish it as knowledge based on empirical validation.
- The given statement is incorrect because positivists rely on scientific methods to validate knowledge rather than assuming knowledge beforehand.

**77. (A):** The Universities of Calcutta, Bombay, and Madras were established in 1857 following the recommendations of Wood's Despatch (1854).

Lord Canning was the Viceroy of India from 1856 to 1862 and was responsible for implementing these universities under the British administration.

These universities were modeled after the University of London and aimed to promote higher education in India.

**78. (C):** The **Competency-Based Curriculum (CBC) model** follows a structured approach:

(*a*) **Identification of general competencies:** Defining broad skills that students need to develop.

(*c*) **Organizing competencies into specific themes: Structuring competencies into subject-specific or skill-based categories.**

(*d*) **Creating learning experiences:** Designing activities and instructional strategies to teach competencies.

(*b*) **Assessing competencies:** Evaluating students' abilities through various assessments.

(*e*) **Evaluating the effectiveness of curriculum:** Reviewing curriculum impact and making necessary improvements.

**79. (C):** The **T-score formula** is:

$$T = 50+10ZT$$
$$= 50 + 10ZT$$
$$= 50+10Z$$

- Multiplying every score in the dataset by 10 does not change the standardized score (Z-score) because scaling affects the mean and standard deviation proportionally.
- Since the T-score is derived from the Z-score, and the Z-score remains unchanged, the new T-score remains 50.

**80. (B): Licensing and usage flexibility** is ranked from the **most open (least restrictive) to the most restrictive**:

(*b*) **Public Domain (PD):** Completely free, no restrictions.

(*d*) **Creative Commons Attribution (CC BY):** Requires credit but allows modification and redistribution.

(*a*) **Creative Commons Share-Alike (CC BY-SA):** Allows modifications but requires sharing under the same license.

(*e*) **Creative Commons Non-Commercial (CC BY-NC):** Restricts use for non-commercial purposes only.

(*c*) **Creative Commons No Derivatives (CC BY-ND):** Allows redistribution but no modifications.

**81. (C):** Aptitude tests are used for selection and placement decisions as they measure an individual's potential to learn or perform in a given area.

These tests help predict future learning ability based on current cognitive, verbal, numerical, or technical skills.

They are commonly used in educational settings, career counseling, and job placement.

**82. (B): The Grassroot Approach of Curriculum Change** is characterized by:

(*b*) **Bottom-up approach:** Changes originate from teachers and practitioners rather than policymakers.

(*c*) **Democratic process:** Encourages participation of teachers and students in decision-making.

(*d*) **Goal-setting by practitioners:** Teachers and educators define the objectives based on classroom needs.

(*a*) **and** (*e*) **are incorrect** because while small-scale experiments and face-to-face problem-solving may occur, they are not defining characteristics of the model.

**83. (C):**

(*a*) **A valid test will also be reliable – Correct**, because validity requires reliability. If a test is valid, it consistently measures what it is intended to measure.

(*d*) **A reliable test may be or may not be valid – Correct**, because a test can be reliable (consistent results) but not valid (not measuring the intended concept).

(*b*) **is incorrect** because a reliable test is not necessarily valid.

(*c*) **is incorrect** because a valid test must be reliable, but reliability alone does not ensure validity.

(*e*) **is incorrect** because there is a direct relationship between reliability and validity in test construction.

**84. (C): Chronological order of educational policies and reports:**

(*b*) **Royal Rescript on Education (1854, Japan):** Issued by Emperor Meiji to modernize Japan's education system.

(*e*) **Stanley's Despatch (1859):** Focused on Indian education reform under the British administration.

(*d*) **Hunter Commission (1882-83):** Reviewed primary and secondary education in India.

(*c*) **Hartog Committee Report (1929):** Studied quality improvement in Indian education.

(*a*) **Sargent Plan (1944):** Proposed a universal education system for India post-independence.

**85. (D):**

(*a*) **A good hypothesis is based on sound reasoning that is consistent with theory or previous research – Correct**, as hypotheses should be grounded in existing literature and logical reasoning.

(*d*) **Qualitative researchers may develop guiding hypotheses for the proposed research – Correct**, though qualitative research is often exploratory, it may still have guiding hypotheses to shape the research direction.

(*b*) **is incorrect** because a deductive hypothesis moves from general theory to specific observations, not vice versa.

(*c*) **is incorrect** because the statement is a directional hypothesis (predicts one group will achieve higher than another), not a non-directional one.

**86. (C):**

(*a*) **Open access to learning content:** MOOCs (Massive Open Online Courses) provide free access to educational content, making learning accessible to a large audience.

(*b*) **Optional certificate:** Many MOOCs offer optional paid certificates for learners who wish to validate their learning.

(*d*) **Low completion rate:** A common challenge with MOOCs is low completion rates, as learners often drop out due to lack of motivation or self-discipline.

(*c*) **and** (*e*) **are incorrect:**

- **MOOCs have unlimited enrollment,** making them accessible to thousands or even millions of learners.
- **Many MOOCs include interactive elements such as discussion forums, quizzes, and peer assessments,** so they do not inherently lack interactivity.

**87. (D):** The Guilford Test of Product Improvement is not a recognized creativity test.

**Tests of Creativity include:**

(A) **Remote Associate Test (RAT):** Measures divergent thinking and creative problem-solving.

(B) **Sharma's Divergent Production Ability Test:** Evaluates creative thinking based on fluency, originality, and flexibility.

(C) **Minnesota Test of Creative Thinking:** Assesses individuals' ability to generate unique and original ideas.

**88. (A): ResearchGate** is an online repository where researchers share full-text academic articles for free.

It allows open access to research papers, peer-reviewed journals, and scholarly discussions. JSTOR and PubMed require subscriptions for most articles, while Google Books does not specialize in academic research papers.

**89. (C):**

(*a*) **Programmed Instruction - B.F. Skinner (II):** Skinner developed programmed instruction based on behavioral reinforcement principles.

(*b*) **Mastery Learning - Benjamin Bloom (I):** Bloom introduced Mastery Learning, where students progress after demonstrating proficiency in each stage.

(*c*) **Simulation - Carl Smith (IV):** Smith worked on simulation-based learning techniques, which help students practice real-world scenarios.

(*d*) **Direct Instruction - Tom Good (III):** Tom Good emphasized Direct Instruction, where teaching is structured and explicit.

**90. (A):**

(*a*) **Mental Retardation - Intelligence Quotient (III):** Intellectual disabilities are measured using IQ tests.

(*b*) **Learning Disabilities - Achievement-potential discrepancy (I):** Learning disabilities occur when there is a gap between a student's potential and actual performance.

(*c*) **Autism Spectrum Disorder - Social skills deficit (IV):** Autism affects social communication and interaction.

(*d*) **Attention-Deficit Hyperactivity Disorder - Impulsive behavior (II):** ADHD is characterized by hyperactivity, inattention, and impulsive behavior.

**91. (C): Majoritarianism** occurs when the dominant culture of the majority suppresses or marginalizes minority cultures.

This contradicts cultural pluralism, where different cultures coexist without one overpowering another.

**92. (D): Majoritarian culture should dominate minority cultures in India**:

- This statement is not true because India follows cultural pluralism, where all communities have the freedom to maintain their traditions without the dominance of one over another.
- Indian culture embraces diversity, and its unity is based on synthesis rather than uniformity.

**93. (A):** Mahatma Gandhi is regarded as the embodiment of Indian cultural heritage due to his emphasis on synthesis, flexibility, and inclusivity in Indian culture.

His philosophy promoted unity, non-violence, and the coexistence of diverse traditions.

**94. (B):** India is a land of multiple cultures where various linguistic, religious, and ethnic communities coexist.

The concept of "Unity in Diversity" highlights India's ability to preserve distinct cultural identities while fostering national unity.

**95. (C):** Gandhiji emphasized magnanimity as a core characteristic of Indian culture, highlighting its ability to embrace and integrate diverse influences.

Indian culture has been historically open to new ideas, traditions, and philosophies while maintaining its fundamental values.

**96. (D):** Class is not an ideological state apparatus but rather a social structure.

Ideological State Apparatuses (ISAs), as per Althusser, include institutions like religion, media, and education that shape public ideology to maintain the dominance of the ruling class.

**97. (A):** Schools serve as ideological state apparatuses, helping to reproduce ruling class ideology by instilling values, discipline, and social norms that maintain the existing power structure.

**98. (D):** According to Althusser, ideological control is the most efficient way for the ruling class to maintain power because it ensures that people accept their positions without resistance.

Physical force and economic control are less effective in comparison to controlling beliefs, values, and education.

**99. (C):**

- False class consciousness occurs when individuals fail to recognize their oppression and accept their subordinate position in society without questioning it.
- This concept, as explained by Althusser, ensures that the subject class remains in a state of compliance, believing their position to be unchangeable and justified.
- As a result, they accept their insubordination instead of challenging the dominance of the ruling class.

**100. (B):** Subject-class members accept their social position as something that is "normal, natural, and inevitable", meaning they do not question the system or attempt to change it.

This is a key aspect of ideological control, as it prevents rebellion or resistance against the ruling class.

Previous Years' Paper

# National Testing Agency (NTA)

## UGC-NET Junior Research Fellowship & Assistant Professor Eligibility Exam

# EDUCATION, AUGUST-2024

(Exam held on 22-08-2024)

## PAPER-II

1. Choose the correct order for the steps involved in the process of construction of a standardized test:

(*a*) Writing the items
(*b*) Pre-try out
(*c*) Dress-rehearsal
(*d*) Planning of the test
(*e*) Final try out

Choose the ***correct*** answer from the options given below:

A. (*a*), (*d*), (*b*), (*c*), (*e*)
B. (*a*), (*d*), (*c*), (*b*), (*e*)
C. (*d*), (*a*), (*b*), (*e*), (*c*)
D. (*d*), (*a*), (*c*), (*b*), (*e*)

2. Which of the following statements is correct about null hypothesis?

A. The null hypothesis relates to a statistical method of interpreting conclusions about sample characteristics that are inferred from the variable relationships observed in samples.
B. The null hypothesis relates to a statistical method of interpreting conclusions about population characteristics that are inferred from the variable relationships observed in samples.
C. The null hypothesis relates to a statistical method of interpreting conclusion about population characteristics that are inferred from the variable relationships observed in populations.
D. The null hypothesis related to a statistical method of interpreting conclusions about sample characteristics that are inferred from the variable relationships observed in population.

3. Which of the following statements are ***incorrect***?

(*a*) Thorndike's theory is atomistic theory of intelligence.
(*b*) Evaluation is the primary mental process which means retention of what is recognized.
(*c*) Group of specific abilities known as 'S' factor is universal inborn ability.
(*d*) According to Faculty theory of intelligence, mind is made up of different faculties like reasoning, memory, discriminations and imagination etc.
(*e*) Structure of Intellect Model of Intelligence was given by Spearman.

Choose the ***correct*** answer from the options given below:

A. (*a*), (*b*) and (*c*) only
B. (*b*), (*c*) and (*e*) only
C. (*b*), (*c*) and (*d*) only
D. (*a*), (*c*) and (*d*) only

**4.** Which of the following statements are TRUE?

(*a*) Bismillah – a ritual was performed at the age of 4 years 4 months and 4 days in Muslim Education.

(*b*) Pabbaja – a ritual performed at the age of 8 years in Buddhist education.

(*c*) Upasampada – a ritual post-education for permanent membership of a Sangh in Buddhist education.

(*d*) Upanayana – a ritual to begin education at the 8, 11, 12 and 15 years of age for Brahmins, Kshatriyas, Vaisyas and Shudras.

(*e*) Ballabhi and Jagdalla – Centres of Vedic education.

Choose the ***correct*** answer from the options given below:

A. (*a*), (*b*) and (*c*) only
B. (*a*), (*b*), (*d*) and (*e*) only
C. (*d*) and (*e*) only
D. (*b*), (*c*), (*d*) and (*e*) only

**5.** The Dave Committee report is especially focussed on:

A. Minimum Levels of Learning (M.L.L.) at Secondary Level
B. Minimum Levels of Learning (M.L.L.) at Primary Level
C. Art and Craft Education at Primary Level
D. Early Childhood Education

**6.** Pick the INCORRECT match:

(*a*) Education and Schooling are ideological state apparatuses – Althusser

(*b*) Education is for Cultural and Social Reproduction - Bourdieu

(*c*) School is a miniature society – Parsons

(*d*) Education helps the individual to grow and achieve her potentials – Marx

(*e*) Education for democracy is thus education freed from the authoritarian relationships – Dewey

Choose the ***correct*** answer from the options given below:

A. (*a*) only B. (*d*) only
C. (*b*) and (*c*) only D. (*c*) and (*e*) only

**7.** Which of the following is true regarding 'grounded theory' research?

(*a*) Axial coding is the process of relating sub-categories to a category.

(*b*) It includes continuous comparative analysis of cases.

(*c*) Selective coding continues the axial coding at a higher level of abstraction.

(*d*) The size of sample is determined by the theoretical saturation of categories

(*e*) It is a substitute of experimental research.

Choose the ***correct*** answer from the options given below:

A. (*a*), (*b*) and (*c*) only
B. (*a*), (*b*), (*c*) and (*d*) only
C. (*b*), (*c*) and (*d*) only
D. (*a*), (*c*) and (*d*) only

**8.** Which of the following are NOT steps of Instructional Technology?

(*a*) Selection of Instructional material
(*b*) Suggestions for improvements
(*c*) Selection of Appropriate Alternative
(*d*) Reinforced Practice
(*e*) Description of Restrictions

Choose the ***correct*** answer from the options given below:

A. (*a*), (*b*) and (*c*) only
B. (*b*), (*c*) and (*d*) only
C. (*a*), (*c*) and (*d*) only
D. (*c*), (*d*) and (*e*) only

**9.** The correct hierarchy of needs given by Maslow is:

(*a*) Safety Needs
(*b*) Prestige Needs
(*c*) Physiological Needs
(*d*) Self Actualization Needs
(*e*) Needs for Belongingness

Choose the ***correct*** answer from the options given below:

A. (*a*), (*c*), (*e*), (*d*), (*b*)
B. (*c*), (*a*), (*e*), (*b*), (*d*)
C. (*a*), (*c*), (*b*), (*e*), (*d*)
D. (*a*), (*b*), (*c*), (*d*), (*e*)

**10.** It is a learning platform that brings together an integrated environment, a range of resources that enable the learners and teachers to interact online and includes content delivery and tracking.

A. SPSS
B. METAAI
C. SWAYAM
D. R

**11.** The correct sequence of the five steps of Morrison's teaching model is:

(*a*) Recitation
(*b*) Organisation
(*c*) Assimilation
(*d*) Presentation
(*e*) Exploration

Choose the ***correct*** answer from the options given below:

A. (*d*), (*c*), (*a*), (*b*), (*e*)
B. (*b*), (*a*), (*c*), (*d*), (*e*)
C. (*e*), (*d*), (*c*), (*b*), (*a*)
D. (*e*), (*d*), (*c*), (*a*), (*b*)

**12.** Match the List-I with List-II

| | List-I | | List-II |
|---|---|---|---|
| (*a*) | Taxonomy of Educational Objectives: The classification of Educational Goals, Handbook I: Cognitive Domain | (*i*) | Krathwohl *et al.* |
| (*b*) | Taxonomy of Educational objectives: The classification of Educational Goals, Handbook II : Affective Domain | (*ii*) | Anderson & Krathwohl |
| (*c*) | Developing and Writing Behavioural Objectives | (*iii*) | Bloom *et al.* |
| (*d*) | A Taxonomy for Learning, Teaching and Assessing: A Revision of Bloom's Taxonomy of Educational Objectives | (*iv*) | Dave |

Choose the ***correct*** answer from the options given below:

| | (*a*) | (*b*) | (*c*) | (*d*) |
|---|---|---|---|---|
| A. | (*iv*) | (*ii*) | (*iii*) | (*i*) |
| B. | (*iii*) | (*i*) | (*iv*) | (*ii*) |
| C. | (*iii*) | (*ii*) | (*i*) | (*iv*) |
| D. | (*ii*) | (*i*) | (*iv*) | (*iii*) |

**13.** Which component is NOT a part of RMSA initiative?

A. Construction of new classrooms
B. Provision of scholarships
C. Establishment of laboratories
D. Appointment of additional teaching faculties.

**14.** A teacher conducts an assessment in her class and then adjusts the next lesson to meet the students' needs. She is doing:

A. Assessment of learning
B. Assessment for learning
C. Assessment as learning
D. Assessment through learning

**15.** The congruence-contingency model of curriculum evaluation was given by:

A. Tyler
B. Stake
C. Seriven
D. Kirkpatrick

**16.** 'Core Design' is an example of:

A. Learner-centered curriculum
B. Problem-centered curriculum
C. Subject-centered curriculum
D. Core-curriculum

**17.** Which of these accurately reflect the limitations of cost benefit analysis in education?

(*a*) Difficulty in quantifying non-monetary benefits.
(*b*) Short-term focus on costs.
(*c*) Overemphasis on quantitative data.
(*d*) Inclusion in intangible cost.
(*e*) Lack of consideration for long-term outcomes.

Choose the ***correct*** answer from the options given below:

A. (*a*), (*b*) and (*e*) only
B. (*a*), (*d*) and (*e*) only
C. (*a*), (*c*) and (*e*) only
D. (*a*), (*b*) and (*d*) only

**18.** Which of the following in NOT a principle of guidance?

A. Holistic development of an individual
B. Recognition of individual needs and differences
C. Non-cognizance of individual differences
D. Acceptance of individual needs

**19.** The correct sequence of consequential leadership style of Managerial Grid is:

(*a*) Country Club
(*b*) Team Management
(*c*) Impoverished Management
(*d*) Authority – compliance
(*e*) Middle-of-the Road

Choose the ***correct*** answer from the options given below:

A. (*a*), (*b*), (*e*), (*c*), (*d*)
B. (*b*), (*c*), (*d*), (*a*), (*e*)
C. (*d*), (*a*), (*b*), (*c*), (*e*)
D. (*c*), (*a*), (*d*), (*e*), (*b*)

**20.** Curriculum was defined by _______ as "a plan for actions or a written document, which includes strategies for achieving desired goals or ends".

A. Galen Saylor (1970)
B. Tanner & Tanner (1980)
C. Tyler and Hilda Taba (1962)
D. Oliva (1982)

**21.** Which of the following is NOT true about critical thinking/critical pedagogy?

A. The focus is to understand the oppressions of the individual, group and society which might be self-imposed.
B. The focus is to understand the oppressions of the individual, group and society which might be created via external forces.
C. According to Freire dialogue is capable of generating critical thinking.
D. According to Freire dialogue does not need any pre-requirement in the classroom.

**22.** Which of the following statements are TRUE?

(*a*) Medical Model of disabilities find its base in psychology.
(*b*) Human Rights Model of disabilities talks about equity.
(*c*) Charity Model of disabilities treats people with disabilities as incapable.
(*d*) Economic model of disabilities considers disabilities as burden.
(*e*) Religions model of disabilities relates disabilities with God's Wrath.

Choose the ***correct*** answer from the options given below:

A. (*a*), (*b*) and (*d*) only
B. (*b*), (*c*) and (*d*) only
C. (*b*), (*c*) and (*e*) only
D. (*c*), (*d*) and (*e*) only

**23.** What leads to curriculum change?

(*a*) National priorities
(*b*) Placement in jobs
(*c*) Socio-cultural contexts
(*d*) Availability of effective teachers
(*e*) Ideology of the government

Choose the ***correct*** answer from the options given below:

A. (*b*) (*c*) and (*e*) only
B. (*b*) (*c*) and (*d*) only
C. (*a*) (*c*) and (*e*) only
D. (*a*) (*b*) and (*e*) only

**24.** The term 'Andragogy' was coined by:

A. Malcolm Shepherd Knowles
B. Edward C. Linderman
C. Johann Heinrich Pestalozzi
D. Alexander Kapp

**25.** This theory affirms that education is a sequence of selection between binary options of available long-term utility and short-term risk of failure.

A. Rational Choice Theory
B. Systems Analysis Theory
C. Signalling Theory
D. Human Capital Theory

**26.** Match the List-I with List-II

| List-I | List-II |
|---|---|
| (*a*) External criticism | (*i*) Pre-Experimental design |
| (*b*) The time series design | (*ii*) Quasi Experimental design |
| (*c*) Internal criticism | (*iii*) Accuracy or worth of the source |
| (*d*) The static group comparison design | (*iv*) Authenticity or genuineness of data |

Choose the ***correct*** answer from the options given below:

| | (*a*) | (*b*) | (*c*) | (*d*) |
|---|---|---|---|---|
| A. | (*iv*) | (*ii*) | (*iii*) | (*i*) |
| B. | (*iii*) | (*i*) | (*iv*) | (*ii*) |
| C. | (*iii*) | (*ii*) | (*iv*) | (*i*) |
| D. | (*iv*) | (*i*) | (*iii*) | (*ii*) |

**27.** Which amongst the following is NOT a Marxist theorist of Sociology of Education?

A. Emile Durkheim
B. Althusser
C. Gramsci
D. Bowles and Gintis

**28.** Following are significant milestones in the field of inclusive education. Arrange them chronologically:

(*a*) National Education Policy
(*b*) Salamanca Statement
(*c*) United Nations Convention on Rights of the Persons with Disabilities (UNCRPD)
(*d*) Sarva Shiksha Abhiyan
(*e*) National Policy on Disabilities

Choose the ***correct*** answer from the options given below:

A. (*b*), (*c*), (*a*), (*e*), (*d*)
B. (*b*), (*e*), (*c*), (*a*), (*d*)
C. (*b*), (*d*), (*e*), (*c*), (*a*)
D. (*b*), (*c*), (*a*), (*d*), (*e*)

**29.** Which of the following is NOT a part of curriculum development?

A. Choosing appropriate transaction strategy
B. Exploring relevant learning experiences
C. Identifying effective teachers
D. Progressive testing of the achievement of objectives

**30.** Match the List-I with List-II

| List-I | List-II |
|---|---|
| (*a*) Contextual competency | (*i*) Including various concepts of Education and Learning |
| (*b*) Conceptual competency | (*ii*) As regarded general, subject-wise, state-wise, dimensions |
| (*c*) Evaluation competency | (*iii*) Comprising a wider view of the development of education in society and teacher's role in it. |
| (*d*) Transactional competency | (*iv*) Preparation, selection, and use of tools and tests |

Choose the ***correct*** answer from the options given below:

| | (*a*) | (*b*) | (*c*) | (*d*) |
|---|---|---|---|---|
| A. | (*iii*) | (*iv*) | (*ii*) | (*i*) |
| B. | (*iii*) | (*i*) | (*iv*) | (*ii*) |
| C. | (*iii*) | (*ii*) | (*i*) | (*iv*) |
| D. | (*iii*) | (*i*) | (*ii*) | (*iv*) |

**31.** Among the following which is NOT an advantage of SWOT:

A. It is easy to understand
B. It is easy to communicate
C. Data collection, evaluation and decision-making are easily confused
D. Applicable to many levels in an organisation.

**32.** The correct sequence of the steps for developing as Instructional Design is:

(*a*) Assessment
(*b*) Delivery of Instructions
(*c*) Deciding Instructional Goals
(*d*) Need Analysis
(*e*) Task Analysis

Choose the ***correct*** answer from the options given below:

A. (*a*), (*c*), (*d*), (*b*), (*e*)
B. (*c*), (*a*), (*d*), (*e*), (*b*)
C. (*d*), (*c*), (*e*), (*b*), (*a*)
D. (*a*), (*b*), (*d*), (*c*), (*e*)

**33.** Which of the following statements are true about 'hypothesis'?

(*a*) The minor premise of the older deductive method was gradually replaced by hypothesis.
(*b*) Snow (1973) described six levels of theory, with the first level being hypothesis formation
(*c*) For the hypothesis to be testable, the variables must be operationally defined.
(*d*) The most common use of hypothesis is to test whether an existing theory can be used to solve a problem.
(*e*) The hypothesis focuses the investigation on indefinite targets.

Choose the ***correct*** answer from the options given below:

A. (*a*), (*b*), (*c*) and (*d*) only
B. (*b*), (*c*), (*d*) and (*e*) only
C. (*b*), (*c*) and (*d*) only
D. (*c*) and (*d*) only

**34.** Which of the following statements are TRUE as per Functionalist Perspective on Sociology of Education?

(*a*) The major function of education is the transmission of society's norms and values.
(*b*) School serves a function that cannot be provided either by family or peers.
(*c*) School is a focal socializing agency.
(*d*) Educational system is a part of superstructure and reproduces ruling ideology.
(*e*) Mass education began in industrial society and is an established requirement of an industrial society.

Choose the ***correct*** answer from the options given below:

A. (*c*), (*d*) and (*e*) only
B. (*a*), (*c*) and (*d*) only
C. (*b*), (*c*), (*d*) and (*e*) only
D. (*a*), (*b*), (*c*) and (*e*) only

**35.** Schooling reproduces norms and values. Norms and values are simply epiphenomenal expressions of the ruling class. This idea can be associated with:

A. Realism
B. Pragmatism
C. Marxism
D. Post modernism

**36.** The tenth category of Flander's Interaction analysis is related to:

A. Teacher Talk
B. Pupil Talk
C. Accepting the ideas of pupil
D. Silence of Pause or Confusion

**37.** According to which commission, a majority of stand-alone Teacher Education Institutions - over 10,000 in numbers - are not even attempting serious teacher education but are essentially selling degrees for a price?

A. Radhakrishnan Commission
B. Mudaliar Commission
C. Kothari Commission
D. J.S.Verma Commission

**38.** What is the primary focus of Poka-Yoke model in educational leadership?

A. Eliminating financial inefficiencies
B. Preventing errors in educational process
C. Enhancing student-teacher communication
D. Developing innovative teaching materials

**39.** Match the List-I with List-II

| List-I | List-II |
|---|---|
| (*a*) Type of curriculum change | (*i*) Systems |
| (*b*) Factor affecting curriculum change | (*ii*) Perturbations |
| (*c*) Approach to curriculum change | (*iii*) Learning communities |
| (*d*) Strategy for curriculum change | (*iv*) Aspirations of people |

Choose the ***correct*** answer from the options given below:

| | (*a*) | (*b*) | (*c*) | (*d*) |
|---|---|---|---|---|
| A. | (*ii*) | (*iv*) | (*i*) | (*iii*) |
| B. | (*i*) | (*ii*) | (*iv*) | (*iii*) |
| C. | (*iv*) | (*iii*) | (*ii*) | (*i*) |
| D. | (*iii*) | (*ii*) | (*i*) | (*iv*) |

**40.** The Dynamic Model of Learner Autonomy is:

(*a*) a tool for self-assessment
(*b*) a tool for choosing appropriate pedagogy by the teacher in classroom
(*c*) given by Tassinari
(*d*) to be followed in fixed ascending order.

Choose the ***correct*** answer from the options given below:

A. (*a*) and (*b*) only
B. (*a*) and (*c*) only
C. (*b*) and (*c*) only
D. (*b*) and (*d*) only

**41.** Those who are soft and round, such personalities are categorized by Sheldon as:

A. Ectomorphic B. Mesomorphic
C. Asethetic D. Endomorphic

**42.** The correct sequence of functions of management is:

(*a*) Directing
(*b*) Organising
(*c*) Planning
(*d*) Controlling
(*e*) Staffing

Choose the ***correct*** answer from the options given below:

A. (*c*), (*b*), (*a*), (*e*), (*d*)
B. (*c*), (*b*), (*e*), (*a*), (*d*)
C. (*a*), (*c*), (*b*), (*e*), (*d*)
D. (*a*), (*d*), (*b*), (*e*), (*c*)

**43.** A class teacher administered Thematic Apperception Test (TAT) to a group of students to assess their:

A. Achievement
B. Awareness
C. Attitude
D. Personality

**44.** Who is known as the Father of Management Process?

A. Elton Mayo
B. Abraham H. Maslow
C. Henry Fayol
D. Edger Henry Schein

**45.** Islamic philosophers divide natural/universal expressions in five types?

(*a*) Common Accident
(*b*) Species
(*c*) Property
(*d*) Difference
(*e*) Genus

Choose the ***correct*** answer from the options given below:

A. (*e*), (*a*), (*c*), (*b*), (*d*)
B. (*e*), (*b*), (*d*), (*c*), (*a*)
C. (*a*), (*b*), (*d*), (*e*), (*c*)
D. (*e*), (*d*), (*c*), (*b*), (*a*)

**46.** Which of the following is NOT a quadrant of MOOCs?

A. e-Tutorial
B. e-Content
C. Web resources
D. Assessment by the Tutor

**47.** Match the List-I with List-II

| List-I | List-II |
|---|---|
| (*a*) Existentialism | (*i*) Reality is ultimately mental |
| (*b*) Idealism | (*ii*) Education as a means of proletariat emancipation |
| (*c*) Critical Thinking | (*iii*) Essence preceeds in natural world |
| (*d*) Marxism | (*iv*) All education is concerned with reason and logic |

Choose the ***correct*** answer from the options given below:

| | (*a*) | (*b*) | (*c*) | (*d*) |
|---|---|---|---|---|
| A. | (*iii*) | (*iv*) | (*i*) | (*ii*) |
| B. | (*ii*) | (*iv*) | (*iii*) | (*i*) |
| C. | (*iii*) | (*i*) | (*iv*) | (*ii*) |
| D. | (*ii*) | (*i*) | (*iii*) | (*iv*) |

**48.** Which of the following statements are TRUE for Signalling Theory of Economics of Education?

(*a*) Michael Spence is one of the theorist.
(*b*) Individuals have different levels of innate productivity
(*c*) Education helps to enhance the innate levels of productivity.
(*d*) Education helps to identify different levels of productivity.
(*e*) More years of schooling lead to more productivity

Choose the ***correct*** answer from the options given below:

A. (*a*), (*b*) and (*d*) only
B. (*c*) and (*e*) only
C. (*b*), (*c*), (*d*) and (*e*) only
D. (*a*), (*b*), (*c*) and (*d*) only

**49.** Mass education, or the idea that anybody and everybody can learn owes its genesis to:

A. Colonialism B. Modernism
C. Postmodernism D. Reformism

**50.** According to Hackney and Cormier (2005), the correct sequence of steps of counselling process is:

(*a*) Goal Setting
(*b*) Problem Assessment
(*c*) Evaluation, Termination or Referral
(*d*) Relationship Building
(*e*) Counselling Intervention

Choose the ***correct*** answer from the options given below:

A. (*d*), (*b*), (*a*), (*e*), (*c*)
B. (*b*), (*a*), (*d*), (*c*), (*e*)
C. (*a*), (*b*), (*d*), (*c*), (*e*)
D. (*a*), (*d*), (*b*), (*e*), (*c*)

**51.** When for a particular degree of freedom, a null hypothesis could not be rejected at the .05 level of significance then:

A. It will definitely be rejected at the .01 level of significance
B. It may or may not be rejected at the .01 level of significance
C. It will definitely not be rejected at the .01 level of significance
D. The given information is insufficient to decide upon.

**52.** Match the List-I with List-II

| List-I | List-II |
|---|---|
| (*a*) Pre-Scientific Management Era | (*i*) Frederik W.Taylor |
| (*b*) Classical Manage-ment Era | (*ii*) George Elton Mayo |
| (*c*) Neo-Classical Era | (*iii*) Ernest Dale |
| (*d*) Modern Management Era | (*iv*) Charles Babbage and Robert Oven |

Choose the ***correct*** answer from the options given below:

| | (*a*) | (*b*) | (*c*) | (*d*) |
|---|---|---|---|---|
| A. | (*i*) | (*iii*) | (*iv*) | (*ii*) |
| B. | (*iv*) | (*i*) | (*ii*) | (*iii*) |
| C. | (*ii*) | (*i*) | (*iii*) | (*iv*) |
| D. | (*i*) | (*ii*) | (*iv*) | (*iii*) |

**53.** Match the List-I with List-II

| List-I | List-II |
|---|---|
| (*a*) Outcome-based Integrative Model | (*i*) Evaluating quality of education at school |
| (*b*) CIPP Model | (*ii*) Systematic and Comprehensive evaluation |
| (*c*) Scriven's Model | (*iii*) Clear learning Outcomes |
| (*d*) Tyler's Model | (*iv*) Objective Four-step process |

Choose the ***correct*** answer from the options given below:

| | (*a*) | (*b*) | (*c*) | (*d*) |
|---|---|---|---|---|
| A. | (*i*) | (*ii*) | (*iii*) | (*iv*) |
| B. | (*i*) | (*iii*) | (*iv*) | (*ii*) |
| C. | (*iv*) | (*i*) | (*ii*) | (*iii*) |
| D. | (*iii*) | (*i*) | (*ii*) | (*iv*) |

**54.** Identify the impact of C.K. Prahlad's theory on curriculum design in teacher education:

(*a*) Enhancing value through innovative curriculum elements.

(*b*) Aligning curriculum with the long-term goals of Educational Institution.

(*c*) Focusing on high-income student populations to maximize returns.

(*d*) Integrating core competencies into curriculum development

(*e*) Addressing the needs of underserved student groups within the curriculum.

Choose the ***correct*** answer from the options given below:

A. (*a*), (*b*), (*d*) and (*e*) only

B. (*a*), (*c*), (*d*) and (*e*) only

C. (*a*), (*b*), (*c*) and (*d*) only

D. ((*a*), (*b*), (*c*) and (*e*) only

**55.** Correct sequence of five quality indicators used in Education given by Ogawa and Collum:

(*a*) Description (*b*) Monitoring

(*c*) Policy Relevance (*d*) Evaluation

(*e*) Value Judgement

Choose the ***correct*** answer from the options given below:

A. (*a*), (*d*), (*b*), (*e*), (*c*)

B. (*a*), (*b*), (*e*), (*c*), (*d*)

C. (*a*), (*c*), (*b*), (*d*), (*e*)

D. (*a*), (*e*), (*d*), (*b*), (*c*)

**56.** The Paideia Proposal by Mortimer Adler involves:

(*a*) Providing all children with the same quality of schooling.

(*b*) A school curriculum that is primarily liberal and humanistic.

(*c*) Having different objectives for different students.

(*d*) The curriculum consisting of only one kind of learning.

(*e*) Remedial and compensatory interventions for individual differences.

Choose the ***correct*** answer from the options given below:

A. (*b*), (*c*) and (*e*) only

B. (*b*), (*c*) and (*d*) only

C. (*a*), (*b*) and (*d*) only

D. (*a*), (*b*) and (*e*) only

**57.** These are dominant trait of one's personality which may dominate personality to such an extent that the person may become known for those traits only.

A. Secondary Traits B. Learning Traits

C. Cardinal Traits D. Central Traits

**58.** Match the List-I with List-II

| List-I | List-II |
|---|---|
| (*a*) Children with Learning Disabilities | (*i*) Associated speech problems |
| (*b*) Children with hearing Impairment | (*ii*) Braille |
| (*c*) Children with Intellectual Disabilities | (*iii*) Achievement Potential Discrepancy |
| (*d*) Children with Visual Impairment | (*iv*) Intelligence Quotient |

Choose the ***correct*** answer from the options given below:

| | (*a*) | (*b*) | (*c*) | (*d*) |
|---|---|---|---|---|
| A. | (*i*) | (*iii*) | (*iv*) | (*ii*) |
| B. | (*iii*) | (*iv*) | (*ii*) | (*i*) |
| C. | (*iv*) | (*ii*) | (*iii*) | (*i*) |
| D. | (*iii*) | (*i*) | (*iv*) | (*ii*) |

**59.** Which of the following statements are ***incorrect***?

(*a*) Asynchronous interaction takes place in real time.
(*b*) A blog offers interaction with reflective comments and also the ability to interlink related ideas.
(*c*) Synchronous, interaction gives freedom to the learner to learn at his/her own pace and as per the availability of time at his/her disposal.
(*d*) Question Mark Perception is a software which provides scope for submission of answers to multiple choice questions.
(*e*) Calibrand Marker is an Intranet based workflow application through which assessment can be carried out for formative tests.

Choose the ***correct*** answer from the options given below:

A. (*b*), (*c*) and (*d*) only
B. (*a*), (*c*) and (*d*) only
C. (*c*), (*d*) and (*e*) only
D. (*a*), (*b*) and (*c*) only

**60.** In his work during nineteenth century, Charles Darwin,

A. used the inductive method of Bacon.
B. used the deductive method of Aristotle.
C. integrated the deductive method of Aristotle and the inductive method of Bacon
D. discarded the deductive method and the inductive method completely

**61.** Choose the correct order of events for a true experimental design:

(*a*) Random selection of total sample units
(*b*) Exposure to the treatment
(*c*) Identification of population
(*d*) Random assignment of treatment to one group
(*e*) Random division of sampled units into two (one for experimental and one for control) groups

Choose the ***correct*** answer from the options given below:

A. (*c*), (*a*), (*e*), (*d*), (*b*)
B. (*c*), (*e*), (*a*), (*b*), (*d*)
C. (*c*), (*e*), (*a*), (*d*), (*b*)
D. (*b*), (*c*), (*e*), (*a*), (*d*)

**62.** Problem-based Learning (PBL) approach is used for curriculum development as it results in:

A. Reducing the gap between curriculum and syllabus
B. Enhancing the employability of learners
C. Filling the gap between academics and practioners
D. economic growth of the country

**63.** Identify the challenges involved in service teacher education programme.

(*a*) Resistance to change
(*b*) High motivation among teachers
(*c*) Insufficient time allocation
(*d*) Strong institutional support
(*e*) Lack of Resources

Choose the ***correct*** answer from the options given below:

A. (*a*), (*c*) and (*e*) only
B. (*a*), (*b*) and (*e*) only
C. (*a*), (*c*) and (*d*) only
D. (*a*), (*b*) and (*d*) only

**64.** Which of the following is NOT correct about ANOVA?

A. The F-ratio is computed in ANOVA.
B. It is a ratio between 'between-groups variance' and 'within-group variance'.
C. The 'between-groups variance' represents the sampling error in the distributions.
D. F-ratio is named after Sir Ronald Fisher.

**65.** Match the List-I with List-II

| List-I | List-II |
|---|---|
| (*a*) Linear Programming | (*i*) Wrong response also helps in diagnosis of weaknesses of the learner |
| (*b*) Branching Programming | (*ii*) Science of control and communication |
| (*c*) Mathetics Programming | (*iii*) Based on operant conditioning learning theory |
| (*d*) Cybernatics | (*iv*) Based on connectionist theory of learning |

Choose the ***correct*** answer from the options given below:

| | (*a*) | (*b*) | (*c*) | (*d*) |
|---|---|---|---|---|
| A. | (*iii*) | (*i*) | (*iv*) | (*ii*) |
| B. | (*i*) | (*iii*) | (*ii*) | (*iv*) |
| C. | (*iii*) | (*ii*) | (*iv*) | (*i*) |
| D. | (*iv*) | (*iii*) | (*i*) | (*ii*) |

**66.** Which of the following are the assumptions of Knowles' theory of Andragogy?

(*a*) Readiness to learn
(*b*) Internally motivated (Motivation to learn)
(*c*) Self-concept
(*d*) Mandatory guidance

Choose the ***correct*** answer from the options given below:

A. (*a*), (*b*) and (*c*) only
B. (*b*), (*c*) and (*d*) only
C. (*a*), (*c*) and (*d*) only
D. (*a*) and (*b*) only

**67.** Negative reinforcement is:

A. the same as punishment
B. not generally liked by the organism
C. meant for decreasing the probability of the occurrence of a behaviour
D. resulting in directly opposite behaviour

**68.** Identify those which best represent the benefits of implementing six-sigma in teacher education?

(*a*) Improved teacher effectiveness.
(*b*) Enhanced student-learning outcomes.
(*c*) Increased Administrative work load.
(*d*) More efficient use of Resources.
(*e*) Greater standardization of teaching practices.

Choose the ***correct*** answer from the options given below:

A. (*a*), (*c*), (*b*) and (*e*) only
B. (*a*), (*b*) and (*e*) only
C. (*a*), (*b*) and (*d*) only
D. (*a*), (*c*), (*d*) and (*e*) only

**69.** Match the **List-I** with **List-II**

| List-I | List-II |
|---|---|
| (*a*) Method of difference | (*i*) Assumption of experimental research |
| (*b*) Law of single variable | (*ii*) Threat for experimental validity |
| (*c*) While individual events cannot be predicted with accuracy, aggregate events can | (*iii*) Assumption of randomization |
| (*d*) Interaction effect of testing | (*iv*) Mill's Canon |

Choose the ***correct*** answer from the options given below:

| | (*a*) | (*b*) | (*c*) | (*d*) |
|---|---|---|---|---|
| A. | (*ii*) | (*i*) | (*iv*) | (*iii*) |
| B. | (*iii*) | (*i*) | (*iv*) | (*ii*) |
| C. | (*iv*) | (*i*) | (*iii*) | (*ii*) |
| D. | (*i*) | (*iv*) | (*iii*) | (*ii*) |

**70.** Which of the following does not come under the updated D & MIS Success Model (2003)?

A. Information Quality
B. System Quality
C. Net Benefits
D. Organisational Impact

**71.** Match the List-I with List-II

| List-I | List-II |
|---|---|
| (*a*) Permissive style | (*i*) The 9.9 Managerial Style |
| (*b*) Most desirable leadership behaviour | (*ii*) Scientific Management |
| (*c*) Replacement of old rules to thumb method | (*iii*) Laissez Faire |
| (*d*) Principle of span of control | (*iv*) Ian Hamilton |

Choose the ***correct*** answer from the options given below:

| | (*a*) | (*b*) | (*c*) | (*d*) |
|---|---|---|---|---|
| A. | (*iii*) | (*i*) | (*ii*) | (*iv*) |
| B. | (*i*) | (*ii*) | (*iii*) | (*iv*) |
| C. | (*iv*) | (*iii*) | (*ii*) | (*i*) |
| D. | (*iii*) | (*ii*) | (*iv*) | (*i*) |

**72.** Which of the following have direct relevance for inclusive education?

(*a*) UNCRPD
(*b*) Project on Integrated Education for the Disabled (PIED)
(*c*) NEP, 2020
(*d*) NPE, 1986
(*e*) Universal Design for Learning

Choose the ***correct*** answer from the options given below:

A. (*a*), (*b*) and (*c*) only
B. (*a*), (*c*) and (*e*) only
C. (*a*), (*b*) and (*d*) only
D. (*a*), (*d*) and (*e*) only

**73.** Arrange the following theorists chronologically:

(*a*) Functionalist - Durkheim
(*b*) Open System Theory - Bertanlaffy
(*c*) Symbolic Interactionist - Mead
(*d*) Conflict Theorist - Weber
(*e*) Conflict Theorist - Marx

Choose the ***correct*** answer from the options given below:

A. (*e*), (*b*), (*c*), (*a*), (*d*)
B. (*a*), (*b*), (*c*), (*d*), (*e*)
C. (*a*), (*d*), (*b*), (*c*), (*e*)
D. (*e*), (*a*), (*d*), (*c*), (*b*)

**74.** The function of search engine to scour the internet for content, looking over the code/content for each URL they find, is called:

A. Indexing
B. Crawling
C. Ranking
D. URL

**75.** Match the List-I with List-II

| List-I | List-II |
|---|---|
| (*a*) Classical Conditioning | (*i*) The response is made first, then reinforcement follows |
| (*b*) Operant Conditioning | (*ii*) When learners have difficulty with new material, go back to the concrete anchors (Advance organisers) |
| (*c*) Discovery Learning | (*iii*) A stimulus is presented in order to get a response |
| (*d*) Meaningful/ Verbal Learning | (*iv*) Anybody can learn anything at any age, provided it is stated in terms they can understand. |

Choose the ***correct*** answer from the options given below:

| | (*a*) | (*b*) | (*c*) | (*d*) |
|---|---|---|---|---|
| A. | (*ii*) | (*iv*) | (*i*) | (*iii*) |
| B. | (*i*) | (*iii*) | (*iv*) | (*ii*) |
| C. | (*i*) | (*ii*) | (*iii*) | (*iv*) |
| D. | (*iii*) | (*i*) | (*iv*) | (*ii*) |

**76.** Which of the following statements are correct?

(*a*) Gagne has classified learning into Six (06) types in a hierarchical order.
(*b*) The study of instrumental conditioning started from the puzzle box experiments on cats by Skinner.

(*c*) The law of disuse states that other things being equal, when a modifiable connection between stimulus-response (S-R) is not made over a period of time, the strength of that connection is weakened.
(*d*) Hull's theory of learning is called 'Drive-Reduction Theory'.
(*e*) Shaping is the most important mechanism used in classical conditioning

Choose the ***correct*** answer from the options given below:

A. (*a*) and (*c*) only
B. (*b*) and (*d*) only
C. (*a*) and (*e*) only
D. (*c*) and (*d*) only

**77.** Which of the following CC licenses of OER allows others to distribute, change, remix and build upon your work, even commercially, as long as they credit you for the original work.

A. CC BY - NC - SA
B. CC BY - NC
C. CC BY
D. CC BY - SA

**78.** Arrange following categories of children in order of increasing IQ:

(*a*) Slow learners
(*b*) Moderate Mental Retardation
(*c*) Mild Mental Retardation
(*d*) Profound Mental Retardation
(*e*) Severe Mental Retardation

Choose the ***correct*** answer from the options given below:

A. (*d*), (*e*), (*b*), (*c*), (*a*)
B. (*e*), (*d*), (*c*), (*b*), (*a*)
C. (*d*), (*b*), (*c*), (*e*), (*a*)
D. (*e*), (*c*), (*a*), (*d*), (*b*)

**79.** Which model of leadership relies on reward and punishments to motivate followers?

A. Transformational B. Democratic
C. Transactional D. Servant

**80.** The main difference between Galloway's system of interaction analysis and Flander's interaction analysis is:

A. Augmentation and integration of non-verbal communication aspects by Galloway.
B. Removal of verbal communication aspects by Galloway
C. Removal of non-verbal communication aspects by Galloway.
D. Augmentation and integration of non-verbal communication aspects by Flander.

**81.** Select the ***correct*** statement in the following:

A. The state spends six percent of GDP on education.
B. Education is a subject matter of the state government.
C. The state of Karnataka has established its own State Education Policy Commission to review NEP and give alternative policy for the state.
D. Education Cess levied goes to the accounts of the State Government.

**82.** Match the List-I with List-II

| List-I | List-II |
|---|---|
| (*a*) Hierarchically structured chronologically graded education system | (*i*) De-schooling |
| (*b*) Set of learning experiences free of time and space limitations | (*ii*) Non-formal Education |
| (*c*) Lifelong process whereby every individual learns from daily experiences | (*iii*) Formal Education |
| (*d*) Education out of the confines of school for diverse needs and interests | (*iv*) Informal Education |

Choose the ***correct*** answer from the options given below:

| | (*a*) | (*b*) | (*c*) | (*d*) |
|---|---|---|---|---|
| A. | (*iii*) | (*i*) | (*ii*) | (*iv*) |
| B. | (*iv*) | (*ii*) | (*iii*) | (*i*) |
| C. | (*ii*) | (*iii*) | (*i*) | (*iv*) |
| D. | (*iii*) | (*ii*) | (*iv*) | (*i*) |

**83.** 3 × 3 factorial design of experiment represents:

A. Three independent variables with three dependent variables.

B. Two independent variables with three conditions of each.

C. Three independent variables with three conditions of each.

D. Three independent variables with two conditions of each.

**84.** Match the List-I with List-II

| List-I | List-II |
|---|---|
| (*a*) Web conferencing | (*i*) Asynchronous Interaction |
| (*b*) Formative Assessment | (*ii*) As a learning and assessment tool, it may comprise artifacts and also expresses a reflective dimension. |
| (*c*) Digitalized Course Materials | (*iii*) Synchronous Interaction |
| (*d*) e-Portfolios | (*iv*) Typically conducted during the development of a programme |

Choose the ***correct*** answer from the options given below:

| | (*a*) | (*b*) | (*c*) | (*d*) |
|---|---|---|---|---|
| A. | (*iii*) | (*iv*) | (*i*) | (*ii*) |
| B. | (*ii*) | (*iii*) | (*iv*) | (*i*) |
| C. | (*i*) | (*ii*) | (*iii*) | (*iv*) |
| D. | (*iii*) | (*iv*) | (*ii*) | (*i*) |

**85.** Arrange the following chronologically:

(*a*) Hunter Commission

(*b*) The Education Dispatch

(*c*) Grant's Plan

(*d*) Establishment of Universities at Calcutta, Bombay and Madras

(*e*) Charter allocating one lakh rupees

Choose the ***correct*** answer from the options given below:

A. (*c*), (*b*), (*e*), (*d*), (*a*)

B. (*a*), (*c*), (*d*), (*e*), (*b*)

C. (*a*), (*e*), (*c*), (*b*), (*d*)

D. (*c*), (*e*), (*b*), (*d*), (*a*)

**86.** Organise sequentially the components of an effective curriculum development process:

(*a*) Defining course goals.

(*b*) Developing assessment items to measure student progress.

(*c*) Identifying key issues and trends in the content area.

(*d*) Determining the success of the program.

(*e*) Identifying resource materials

Choose the ***correct*** answer from the options given below:

A. (*c*), (*b*), (*a*), (*e*), (*d*)

B. (*b*), (*a*), (*e*), (*d*), (*c*)

C. (*a*), (*b*), (*c*), (*d*), (*e*)

D. (*c*), (*a*), (*e*), (*b*), (*d*)

**87.** Match the List-I with List-II

| List-I | List-II |
|---|---|
| (*a*) Function of school and universities should be different | (*i*) Kothari Commission |
| (*b*) Schools should play a crucial role in developing democratic citizenship | (*ii*) University Education Commission |
| (*c*) Education plays a crucial role in national development | (*iii*) Yashpal Committee Report |
| (*d*) Learning must not be a burden on the learner | (*iv*) Secondary Education Commission |

Choose the ***correct*** answer from the options given below:

| | (*a*) | (*b*) | (*c*) | (*d*) |
|---|---|---|---|---|
| A. | (*iii*) | (*ii*) | (*iv*) | (*i*) |
| B. | (*iii*) | (*i*) | (*ii*) | (*iv*) |
| C. | (*ii*) | (*i*) | (*iv*) | (*iii*) |
| D. | (*ii*) | (*iv*) | (*i*) | (*iii*) |

**88.** Who was the Chairperson of National Commission on Teachers (1983)?

A. Prof. Yashpal
B. Dr. Ram Murti
C. Sam Pitroda
D. Prof. D.P. Chattophadhyay

**89.** Which of the following is related to Web 2.0?

A. Read only pages
B. Semantic Integration and Data Interoperability
C. Social Networking and User Generated Content
D. Advance Virtual Reality

**90.** According to Gutherie which is NOT an important characteristic of strategic leadership?

A. Vision
B. Inspiration
C. Symbolic
D. Strategic Orientation

**Directions (Qs. No. 91-95):** *Read the passage and answer the following questions:*

Freedom does not exist without order. The two go together. If you cannot have order, you cannot have freedom. The two are inseparable. If you say: "I will do what I like. I will turn up for my meals when I like; I will come to the class when I like" – you create disorder. You have to take into consideration what other people want. To run things smoothly, you have to come on time. If I had come ten minutes late this morning. I would have kept you waiting. So I have to have consideration. I have to think of others. I have to be polite, considerate, be concerned about other people. Out of that considerations, out of that thoughtfulness, out of that watchfulness, both outward and inward, comes order and with that order there comes freedom.

You know, soldiers all over the world are drilled every day, they are told what to do, to walk in line. They obey orders implicitly without thinking. Do you know what that does to man? When you are told what to do, what to think, to obey, to follow, do you know what it does to you? Your mind becomes dull, it loses its initiative, its quickness. This external, outward imposition of discipline makes the mind stupid, it makes you conform, it makes you imitate. But if you discipline yourself by watching, listening, being considerate, being very thoughtful - out of that watchfulness, that listening, that consideration for others, comes order. Where there is order, there is always freedom. If you are shouting, talking, you cannot hear what others have to say. You can only hear clearly when you sit quietly, when you give your attention.

**91.** If a teacher wants her students to obey orders without thinking, she is making her students:

A. Rationalists
B. Conformists
C. Progressive
D. Authoritarian

**92.** According to the given paragraph. Freedom without order is:

A. Invaluable
B. Indiscipline
C. Invalid
D. Non-existent

**93.** Being on time, punctuality brings:

A. Discipline
B. Inward Imposition
C. Order
D. Conformity

**94.** Conformism and imitation are the learning outcomes of the pedagogy that believes in:

A. External Discipline

B. Internal Discipline

C. Freedom of Learners

D. Individual Difference

**95.** A teacher shouts, "Pindrop Silence in the Class'. She is:

A. Making her students considerate of orders

B. Making the students thoughtful and watchful

C. Making outward imposition of discipline

D. Making order in the class to make her students free

**Directions (Qs. No. 96-100):** *Read the passage and answer the following questions:*

Inclusive education means that all people – regardless of their gender, religion, cultural and social origin, cognitive, physical, and psychological preconditions – are entitled to equal access to higher education, and that existing entry barriers have to be removed. This broad understanding of inclusive education is fixed to the Curriculum Framework as a cross-cutting theme.

As a pedagogical approach with the essential principle of appreciation and acknowledgement of diversity, the scientific foundation and acceptance or inclusive education has increased since the 1990s. At school it is about "the appropriate non-hierarchical and democratic response to the existing heterogeneity of students". (See Boban; Hinz, 2003: Index fur Inclusion).

The implementation of inclusive education is one of the big challenges to our education system and its stakeholders. Institutions of formal and non-formal education and their activities should be designed in a way that the learning environment adjusts to the students and respects the individual personalities with their different preconditions. Such an orientation towards the students requires a high personal commitment but also differentiated material and activating methods of education which support the individual and at the same time cooperation.

**96.** Inclusive education:

A. Negates cultural diversity

B. Celebrates teacher's authority

C. Celebrates heterogeneity of students

D. Negates social needs

**97.** It is necessary for these institutions to be inclusive:

A. Institutions of formal education only

B. Institutions of informal education only

C. Both the institution of formal and informal education

D. Institutions of non-formal education only

**98.** In inclusive education, an orientation towards the students requires:

A. A high personal commitment only

B. Non-differentiated materials

C. Passive methods of education

D. High personal commitment along with differential material

**99.** Inclusive education mainly focuses on education of:

A. Children with disabilities

B. Children with challenging behaviours

C. Children with learning difficulties

D. All children

**100.** Inclusive education is a pedagogical approach having a principle of:

A. Acceptance of learning difficulties only

B. Appreciation of diversity

C. Acceptance of group dynamics

D. Appreciation of singularity

# ANSWERS

1. **(C):** The correct order for constructing a standardized test begins with Planning of the test, where the scope, purpose, and content of the test are determined. This is followed by Writing the items, where the actual questions or problems are developed. The Pre-try out phase is where these items are initially tested in a small group to refine them. The Final try out involves a larger group testing to finalize the test's usability and reliability. The process ends with the Dress-rehearsal, which is the final validation before the test is officially administered.

   Hence, correct order is (*d*), (*a*), (*b*), (*e*), (*c*).

2. **(B):** The null hypothesis relates to a statistical method of interpreting conclusions about population characteristics that are inferred from the variable relationships observed in samples: The null hypothesis ($H_0$) is a statistical assumption that there is no significant difference or relationship between specified populations, any observed difference being due to sampling or experimental error. This hypothesis is tested against an alternative hypothesis ($H_1$), which posits that there is a significant effect or relationship. The null hypothesis thus concerns inferences about population characteristics based on sample observations, aiming to establish whether observed relationships in the sample can be generalized to the population.

3. **(B):** The incorrect statements are:
   - Evaluation is the primary mental process which means retention of what is recognized, which incorrectly defines evaluation, typically associated with judgment, not retention.
   - Group of specific abilities known as 'S' factor is universal inborn ability misinterprets Spearman's theory which posits that the 'S' factor varies by activity and is not universal.
   - Structure of Intellect Model of Intelligence was given by Spearman is incorrect as this model was proposed by J.P. Guilford, not Spearman.

   Hence, incorrect statements are (*b*), (*c*) and (*e*).

4. **(A):** True statements are:
   - Bismillah – a ritual was performed at the age of 4 years 4 months and 4 days in Muslim Education, which is a ceremony marking the beginning of a child's education.
   - Pabbaja – a ritual performed at the age of 8 years in Buddhist education, marks the ordination of novices.
   - Upasampada – a ritual post-education for permanent membership of a Sangh in Buddhist education signifies full ordination and acceptance into the monastic community.

   The other statements and contain inaccuracies or generalized facts.

   Hence, true statements are (*a*), (*b*) and (*c*).

5. **(B):** The Dave Committee focused on establishing Minimum Levels of Learning (M.L.L.) at the Primary Level. This initiative was aimed at defining clear learning outcomes that children should achieve at different stages of primary education, thereby ensuring a basic minimum standard of education and facilitating systematic assessment and evaluation of student progress.

6. **(B):** Karl Marx did not specifically focus on education helping the individual to grow and achieve her potentials; his views on education were more aligned with its

role in class struggle and the criticism of the capitalist system. The other options correctly match the theorists with their views: Althusser identified educational institutions as part of ideological state apparatuses, Bourdieu discussed education's role in cultural and social reproduction, Parsons likened schools to miniature societies emphasizing socialization, and Dewey highlighted the importance of democratic, non-authoritarian educational environments.

**7. (B):** Grounded theory research involves several key processes, including: Axial coding, which relates sub-categories to a category, and the use of continuous comparative analysis of cases. Selective coding, which continues the axial coding at a higher level of abstraction, and the determination of sample size by the theoretical saturation of categories, are also integral parts of grounded theory methodology.

The notion that it is a substitute for experimental research is incorrect, as grounded theory is a qualitative research method distinct from experimental methodologies.

**8. (D):** Steps of Instructional Technology typically involve systematic planning, development, and evaluation of educational practices, but do not generally include Selection of Appropriate Alternative, Reinforced Practice, or Description of Restrictions as formal steps. These activities might be part of broader educational strategies or methods but are not specific stages in the process of Instructional Technology.

Hence, (*c*), (*d*) and (*e*) are not steps of Instructional Technology.

**9. (B):** According to Maslow's hierarchy of needs, the correct order is: Physiological Needs as the most basic, followed by Safety Needs, Needs for Belongingness, Prestige Needs, and finally reaching Self-Actualization Needs at the top. This sequence reflects Maslow's theory that lower needs must be satisfied before higher-order needs can influence behavior.

Hence, the correct order is (*c*), (*a*), (*e*), (*b*), (*d*).

**10. (C):** SWAYAM (Study Webs of Active Learning for Young Aspiring Minds) is a platform designed by the Government of India to provide an integrated learning environment. It offers courses from school to postgraduate levels and enables interactions online between learners and teachers, including content delivery and tracking. This matches the description of a learning platform that brings together various resources for online interaction and education.

**11. (C):** Morrison's teaching model consists of the following sequence:

- Exploration is where students are introduced to the new content in an engaging manner to spark interest.
- Presentation involves the teacher formally presenting the new information.
- Assimilation is where students process and internalize the new knowledge.
- Organization requires students to organize and make sense of the learned content.
- Recitation allows students to articulate what they have learned, reinforcing their understanding.

Hence, correct sequence are (*e*), (*d*), (*c*), (*b*), (*a*).

**12. (B):** Correct matching is:

- Taxonomy of Educational Objectives in the Cognitive Domain was developed by Bloom and others.

- The Affective Domain taxonomy was expanded by Krathwohl *et al*.
- Developing and Writing Behavioural Objectives was authored by Dave.
- A Taxonomy for Learning, Teaching, and Assessing, which revised Bloom's original taxonomy, was written by Anderson and Krathwohl.

**13. (B):** The Rashtriya Madhyamik Shiksha Abhiyan (RMSA) initiative primarily focuses on the structural and functional enhancement of secondary education in India, including construction of new classrooms, establishment of laboratories, and appointment of additional teaching faculties. Provision of scholarships, although part of broader educational initiatives, is not a central component of the RMSA framework, which is more focused on infrastructural and staffing enhancements at the secondary level.

**14. (B):** When a teacher uses assessments to adjust teaching strategies and lesson plans based on the outcomes, this is referred to as Assessment for learning. It is a formative approach where the emphasis is on using assessment insights to immediately impact teaching methods and support students' learning processes more effectively, rather than merely evaluating what students have learned after instruction.

**15. (B):** The congruence-contingency model of curriculum evaluation, which assesses the effectiveness of a curriculum by examining the fit between the intended outcomes and the actual outcomes, was developed by Robert Stake. This model focuses on how well the educational outcomes align with the educational goals and the needs of the students, making it a valuable tool for evaluating the efficacy and impact of educational programs.

**16. (B):** Problem-centered curriculum: 'Core Design' is an approach that focuses on real-world problems and challenges, encouraging students to engage deeply with the subject matter through problem-solving and critical thinking. This method is categorized under a problem-centered curriculum, where the learning process is centered around solving specific problems, often integrating multiple subject areas or disciplines.

**17. (C):** Limitations of cost benefit analysis in education include the difficulty in quantifying non-monetary benefits, such as personal satisfaction, happiness, or societal well-being, which are crucial in educational outcomes but hard to measure in monetary terms. There is often an overemphasis on quantitative data, which might neglect qualitative aspects of education that are important for holistic understanding. Lastly, there is a lack of consideration for long-term outcomes, as cost benefit analysis may not adequately predict or value the long-term benefits of educational investments.

Hence, correct options are (*a*), (*c*) and (*e*).

**18. (C):** Non-cognizance of individual differences: Guidance as a principle inherently recognizes and accommodates individual differences, needs, and circumstances. It is based on the understanding that each individual is unique and thus requires tailored support and direction. Therefore, Non-cognizance of individual differences is not a principle of guidance, as it contradicts the fundamental ethos of recognizing and responding to individual differences.

**19. (D):** The Managerial Grid, developed by Blake and Mouton, categorizes leadership styles based on concern for people and concern for production. The correct sequence starting from least effective to most effective in terms of overall organizational health would be: Impoverished Management, which shows low concern for both people and production; Country Club, high concern for people but low for production; Authority – Compliance, high concern for production but low for people; Middle-of-the-Road, moderate concern for both; and Team Management, high concern for both people and production, representing the most effective leadership style.

Hence, correct sequence is (*c*), (*a*), (*d*), (*e*), (*b*).

**20. (C):** Curriculum was defined by Ralph Tyler and later expanded by Hilda Taba as a plan for action or a written document that includes strategies for achieving desired educational goals or ends. This definition emphasizes the importance of having a structured approach to education that is purposefully designed to meet specific educational objectives and outcomes.

**21. (D):** According to Freire dialogue is capable of generating critical thinking: Critical thinking and critical pedagogy, as discussed by Paulo Freire, emphasize the role of dialogue in fostering critical consciousness among learners. Dialogue in Freire's framework is not merely conversational; it requires critical thinking and reflection as prerequisites, which help in understanding and challenging the structures of oppression. Freire argues that only through such reflective and critical dialogue can individuals achieve deeper understanding and emancipation.

**22. (C):** True statements regarding disability models include: The Human Rights Model of disabilities, which emphasizes equity and the rights of individuals with disabilities, treating them as full members of society with equal opportunities. The Charity Model of disabilities indeed often perceives people with disabilities as needy or lacking, deserving pity rather than rights. The Religious Model of disabilities, often rooted in historical and cultural contexts, sometimes relates disabilities to divine will or punishment.

Hence, correct options are (*b*), (*c*) and (*e*).

**23. (C):** Factors leading to curriculum change include National priorities, which influence educational objectives to align with the country's needs and goals. Socio-cultural contexts also play a significant role, as changes in societal values and norms necessitate updates in curriculum content and methodology to remain relevant and effective. Additionally, the Ideology of the government can drive shifts in curriculum to reflect the current political and philosophical stance of those in power, impacting educational focus and structure.

Hence, correct options are (*a*) (*c*) and (*e*).

**24. (D):** The term 'Andragogy', which refers to the method and practice of teaching adult learners, was coined by Alexander Kapp in 1833. Malcolm Shepherd Knowles popularized the term much later and developed it as a theory of adult education, but the original coining of the term is attributed to Kapp.

**25. (A):** This theory posits that individuals make decisions based on the anticipated benefits and costs, selecting options that maximize their advantages while minimizing potential risks. In the context of education, Rational Choice Theory suggests that decisions about educational pathways and investments are made after evaluating the long-term utility of educational achievements against the short-term risks of failing or not achieving the expected returns. This approach helps explain various educational behaviors, including the pursuit of higher education, choices of study fields, and participation in professional training.

**26. (A):** Correct matching is:

- External criticism assesses the authenticity or genuineness of data, verifying the source's reliability before its contents are examined.
- The time series design is a type of Quasi-Experimental design that involves repeated measurements over time.
- Internal criticism deals with the accuracy or worth of the source, examining the credibility of the information provided.
- The static group comparison design is a Pre-Experimental design, where two groups are compared without randomization.

**27. (A):** Emile Durkheim, a foundational sociologist, is not a Marxist theorist. His work focused more broadly on the functions of society and social institutions like education, which he viewed as means of socializing individuals and maintaining social solidarity. Althusser, Gramsci, and Bowles and Gintis, however, are all associated with Marxist perspectives in the sociology of education, emphasizing how education systems reproduce class structures and serve capitalist interests.

**28. (C):** Chronological order is:

- The Salamanca Statement in 1994 emphasized the importance of inclusive education for all children, particularly those with special needs.
- The Sarva Shiksha Abhiyan was launched in India in 2001 to make education accessible to all children.
- The National Policy on Disabilities came in 2006, further emphasizing rights and access to education.
- The United Nations Convention on Rights of the Persons with Disabilities (UNCRPD) in 2006 strengthened global commitments to inclusive education.
- The National Education Policy in India was introduced in 2020, building on these foundations to further enhance educational inclusivity.

**29. (C):** Identifying effective teachers is not directly a part of curriculum development. Curriculum development typically involves determining what will be taught and how it will be taught, which includes choosing appropriate transaction strategies (A), exploring relevant learning experiences (B), and progressively testing the achievement of objectives (D). The selection and development of teachers are related to the implementation of the curriculum rather than its development.

**30. (B):** Correct matching is:

- Contextual competency involves a broader understanding of the educational landscape, including the teacher's role in societal development.
- Conceptual competency refers to including various concepts of education and learning, which is essential for developing and delivering educational content.
- Evaluation competency involves the preparation, selection, and use of assessment tools and tests, crucial for measuring educational outcomes.
- Transactional competency pertains to general, subject-wise, and state-wise educational dimensions, focusing on the practical aspects of curriculum delivery.

**31. (C):** The SWOT analysis, known for its straightforward approach, easily communicates strengths, weaknesses, opportunities, and threats of a project or organization. It's widely recognized for its simplicity in structuring and understanding strategic situations. However, it is not inherently designed to confuse data collection, evaluation, and decision-making;

rather, it aims to clarify these aspects by categorizing information into four distinct quadrants, thus enhancing decision-making clarity at various organizational levels.

32. **(C):** The correct sequence for developing an Instructional Design is:
    - Need Analysis, where the specific needs that the instruction aims to meet are identified.
    - Deciding Instructional Goals is crucial as it sets the objectives that the instruction intends to achieve.
    - Task Analysis then breaks down what learners need to know or do to meet these goals.
    - Delivery of Instructions is the phase where the actual instructional activities occur.
    - Assessment evaluates whether the instructional goals have been met.

    Hence, correct sequence is (*d*), (*c*), (*e*), (*b*), (*a*).

33. **(C):** In hypothesis development, it's true that for a hypothesis to be testable, it must have operationally defined variables, which allow empirical measurement and testing. Snow (1973) did categorize theory levels, starting with hypothesis formation at the first level. Hypotheses are commonly used to test the applicability of theories in solving new or existing problems. However, the minor premise in classical deduction was not simply replaced by hypotheses, and hypotheses do not focus investigations on indefinite targets but rather guide research with specific inquiries.

    Hence, correct options are (*b*), (*c*), and (*d*).

34. **(D):** According to the Functionalist Perspective on Sociology of Education, education is seen primarily as a means of transmitting society's norms and values, supporting the socialization process. Schools also serve unique functions that neither family nor peers can provide, such as formal education and certification. As a major socializing agency, schools play a central role in shaping societal functions. The statement about the educational system being part of the superstructure that reproduces ruling ideology aligns more with Marxist perspectives, not Functionalist. Mass education, which began in industrial society, is indeed viewed as a necessity for maintaining the needs of an industrial society.

    Hence, correct options are (*a*), (*b*), (*c*), and (*e*)

35. **(C):** The perspective that schooling reproduces the norms and values as expressions of the ruling class ideology aligns with Marxist theory. Marxism views educational institutions as mechanisms through which the dominant class maintains social control by indoctrinating subordinate classes with its ideology, thereby perpetuating its dominance and perpetuating class distinctions. This viewpoint critically assesses the role of education in reinforcing societal inequalities rather than simply transmitting neutral knowledge.

36. **(D):** Silence or Pause or Confusion: The tenth category of Flander's Interaction Analysis specifically relates to periods of Silence or Pause or Confusion within the classroom setting. This category captures moments when there is no verbal interaction, which can be due to various reasons such as thinking, confusion, or a pause in the conversation. These pauses are significant as they can indicate moments of cognitive processing or confusion that might need addressing by the educator.

**37. (D):** The J.S.Verma Commission pointed out that a majority of stand-alone Teacher Education Institutions, numbering over 10,000, are not engaged in serious teacher education but are instead essentially involved in the commercial transaction of selling degrees for a price. This observation highlights a critical issue in the field of teacher education where the quality and integrity of teacher preparation are compromised.

**38. (B):** Preventing errors in educational process: The primary focus of the Poka-Yoke model in educational leadership is on preventing errors in the educational process. Originally a Japanese concept applied in manufacturing to prevent mistakes, its principles have been adapted in various fields, including education, to design systems and processes that help in avoiding errors and enhancing the efficiency and effectiveness of operations.

**39. (A):** Correct matching is:

- Type of curriculum change pertains to Perturbations, which are disturbances that necessitate changes.
- Factors affecting curriculum change include the Aspirations of people, reflecting societal desires that influence educational content and methods.
- Approach to curriculum change is categorized under Systems, emphasizing systematic, structured changes.
- Strategy for curriculum change involves Learning communities, where collaborative environments foster shared learning and innovation in curriculum development.

**40. (B):** The Dynamic Model of Learner Autonomy, as proposed by Tassinari, serves as a tool for self-assessment, enabling learners to evaluate and enhance their autonomous learning behaviours and skills.

This model is not strictly followed in a fixed ascending order, nor is it solely a tool for choosing pedagogy by the teacher in the classroom, though it can inform pedagogical decisions indirectly through its impact on learner self-assessment.

**41. (D):** According to William Sheldon's classification of body types, individuals who are soft and round are categorized as Endomorphic. This body type is characterized by a higher proportion of body fat, less muscle, and a softer appearance, which Sheldon associated with sociable, relaxed, and comfortable personalities.

**42. (B):** The correct sequence of functions of management is:

- Planning, where objectives and the courses of action are determined.
- Organising follows, where the structure of the organization is built and resources are arranged.
- Staffing comes next, involving the selection and training of the appropriate personnel.
- Directing is the function where the management provides active leadership and ensures communication.
- Controlling involves setting performance standards and measuring actual performance to ensure the achievement of organizational objectives.

Hence, correct sequence is (*c*), (*b*), (*e*), (*a*), (*d*).

**43. (D):** The Thematic Apperception Test (TAT) is used primarily to assess an individual's personality. It involves presenting ambiguous images to individuals and asking them to tell a story based on each image. The content of their stories is then analyzed to uncover underlying themes, attitudes, and potential conflicts within the subject's personality, thereby providing insights into their emotional functioning and personality traits.

**44. (C):** Henry Fayol is known as the Father of Modern Management due to his development of the management process theory. Fayol outlined five primary functions of management: planning, organizing, commanding, coordinating, and controlling, which have been fundamental in shaping modern management practices.

**45. (B):** Islamic philosophers, when classifying natural/universal expressions, typically follow an order beginning with Genus, which is the general category or family that entities belong to. Species follows, which specifies the differences within the genus. Difference then highlights the unique characteristics that distinguish one species from another within the same genus. Property is the attribute that a species always possesses. Finally, Common Accident is a characteristic that may or may not be present and does not define the species.

Hence, correct options are (*e*), (*b*), (*d*), (*c*), (*a*).

**46. (D):** MOOCs (Massive Open Online Courses) typically feature quadrants such as e-Tutorial, e-Content, and Web resources, which include videos, readings, and interactive content respectively. However, "Assessment by the Tutor" is not typically categorized as a separate quadrant in the structure of MOOCs, which usually emphasize automated assessments or peer evaluations rather than direct assessments by a tutor.

**47. (C):** Correct matching is:

- Existentialism posits that essence precedes existence in the natural world, stressing individual choice and responsibility.
- Idealism asserts that reality is ultimately mental, valuing the role of ideas over material conditions.
- Critical Thinking is concerned with reason and logic, focusing on analytical and evaluative skills.
- Marxism views education as a means of proletariat emancipation, analyzing education's role in societal structures.

**48. (A):** The Signalling Theory of Economics of Education, developed by Michael Spence, argues that educational attainment serves as a signal to employers about an individual's level of ability or productivity. It posits that individuals have different levels of innate productivity, and that education itself does not necessarily enhance these innate levels but rather helps to signal these differences to potential employers.

This theory does not inherently claim that education enhances productivity, nor does it state that more years of schooling lead to increased productivity.

Hence, true statements are (*a*), (*b*) and (*d*).

**49. (B):** The idea of mass education, suggesting that education should be accessible to all, is fundamentally linked to the ideologies of Modernism. This period emphasized progress, enlightenment, and the belief that education could improve individuals and societies universally, reflecting an optimistic view of human potential and the transformative power of education.

**50. (A):** According to Hackney and Cormier (2005), the counselling process begins with Relationship Building, where establishing trust and rapport is critical for effective therapy. This is followed by Problem Assessment, where the counselor and client explore and define the client's issues. Goal Setting comes next, where objectives for the counselling sessions are agreed upon. Counselling Intervention involves the application of therapeutic techniques to address the issues. Finally, Evaluation,

Termination, or Referral concludes the process, assessing progress and determining the next steps, whether ending the therapy or referring to other services.

Hence, correct sequence is: (*d*), (*b*), (*a*), (*e*), (*c*)

**51. (C):** It will definitely not be rejected at the .01 level of significance: When a null hypothesis cannot be rejected at a .05 level of significance, it means there is not enough evidence against the hypothesis at that level of probability. Since the .01 level of significance is more stringent (requires stronger evidence to reject the hypothesis), it is not possible to reject the hypothesis at this level if it was not rejected at the higher .05 level. The probability of rejecting the null hypothesis decreases as the level of significance becomes more stringent.

**52. (B):** In the historical progression of management thought:

- The Pre-Scientific Management Era includes early figures like Charles Babbage and Robert Owen, who laid foundational ideas for the management field.
- The Classical Management Era is epitomized by Frederick W. Taylor, who is known for his principles of scientific management.
- The Neo-Classical Era is associated with George Elton Mayo, who introduced human relations into management theory.
- The Modern Management Era often relates to thinkers like Ernest Dale, who contributed to contemporary organizational and management practices.

**53. (D):** For the educational evaluation models:

- The Outcome-based Integrative Model focuses on achieving clear learning outcomes.
- The CIPP Model, proposed by Stufflebeam, is a comprehensive framework for evaluating the quality of education at school.
- Scriven's Model emphasizes systematic and comprehensive evaluation of educational programs.
- Tyler's Model is known for its objective, four-step process in curriculum development and assessment.

**54. (A):** C.K. Prahlad's theories, notably on core competencies and strategic focus, can influence curriculum design in teacher education by emphasizing innovation, aligning educational goals with the institution's long-term objectives, integrating essential competencies into the curriculum to enhance educational effectiveness, and addressing the specific needs of underserved student groups. His work suggests leveraging core strengths to create value, which in educational settings translates to enhancing curriculum relevance and inclusivity.

Hence, correct options are (*a*), (*b*), (*d*) and (*e*).

**55. (A):** The correct sequence of five quality indicators used in education according to Ogawa and Collum:

- Description, which involves defining what will be evaluated.
- Evaluation follows, assessing the described elements' performance or quality.
- Monitoring is continuous observation to ensure that standards are maintained over time.
- Value Judgement involves assessing the worth or value of the educational outcomes.
- Policy Relevance examines how the findings relate to and inform educational policies. This sequence reflects a comprehensive approach to assessing and enhancing educational quality, from defining parameters to applying findings to policy.

Hence, correct sequence is (*a*), (*d*), (*b*), (*e*), (*c*).

**56. (D):** The Paideia Proposal by Mortimer Adler emphasizes the idea of providing all children with the same quality of schooling, advocating for an equitable educational system. It promotes a school curriculum that is primarily liberal and humanistic, focusing on broad-based, general education that fosters critical thinking and well-rounded development. Additionally, it supports the use of remedial and compensatory interventions to address individual differences among students, ensuring that all have the opportunity to succeed regardless of their starting points or inherent abilities.

Hence, correct options are (*a*), (*b*) and (*e*).

**57. (C):** Cardinal traits are those dominant personality traits that may define a person's behavior so strongly that they become known primarily for these traits. These traits overshadow other personality aspects, forming a significant identity marker for individuals. Examples might include traits like narcissism or altruism, which can dominate all other aspects of a person's personality.

**58. (D):** Correct matching is:

- Children with Learning Disabilities are often characterized by an Achievement Potential Discrepancy, which means there is a significant gap between their expected and actual learning achievements based on their cognitive ability.
- Children with Hearing Impairment frequently face Associated Speech Problems due to the impact of hearing loss on the acquisition and development of spoken language.
- Children with Intellectual Disabilities typically have issues related to Intelligence Quotient, affecting their cognitive functions across various domains.
- Children with Visual Impairment often use Braille as a tool for reading and writing.

**59. (B):** The incorrect statements are:

- Asynchronous interaction takes place in real time is false because asynchronous interaction occurs without the need for participants to be engaged at the same time.
- Synchronous interaction gives freedom to the learner to learn at his or her own pace is incorrect as synchronous learning involves real-time, scheduled interaction.
- Question Mark Perception is a software which provides scope for submission of answers to multiple choice questions might be inaccurately described regarding its specific functionality or the name might be slightly incorrect.

Correctly, a blog offers interaction with reflective comments and interlinks related ideas, and Calibrand Marker is indeed used for assessment in formative tests.

**60. (C):** Integrated the deductive method of Aristotle and the inductive method of Bacon: Charles Darwin effectively integrated both the deductive and inductive methods in his scientific work, particularly in his formulation of the theory of evolution by natural selection. He used the deductive method to propose hypotheses based on theoretical assumptions, and the inductive method to gather and analyze vast amounts of empirical data from his observations and experiments, which solidified his theories. This blend allowed him to develop a robust scientific framework that has stood the test of time.

**61. (A):** The correct sequence for a true experimental design is as follows:

- Identification of the population is the first step, where the overall population from which the sample will be drawn is defined.
- Random selection of total sample units occurs, ensuring each member of the population has an equal chance of being selected.

- Random division of sampled units into two groups, one for experimental and one for control, is carried out to ensure unbiased distribution.
- Random assignment of treatment to one group is then performed to one of these groups, usually the experimental group.
- Exposure to the treatment is administered to the experimental group while the control group receives no treatment or a placebo, completing the experimental setup.

Hence, correct sequence is (*c*), (*a*), (*e*), (*d*), (*b*).

**62. (C):** Problem-based Learning (PBL) is utilized in curriculum development primarily because it helps bridge the gap between academic knowledge and practical application. This educational strategy focuses on real-world problems that demand solutions utilizing both theoretical understanding and practical skills, thereby aligning academic learning with the practical demands and challenges faced by professionals in the field.

**63. (A):** The main challenges involved in service teacher education programs:

- Resistance to change, where teachers may bc hcsitant or skeptical about new methods and technologies.
- Insufficient time allocation is another significant hurdle, as teachers often find it difficult to fit in professional development alongside their teaching responsibilities.
- Lack of Resources can also pose a challenge, as adequate funding, materials, and support are crucial for the success of these programs.

High motivation among teachers and strong institutional support are generally positive aspects and not challenges.

Hence, correct options are (*a*), (*c*) and (*e*).

**64. (C):** The 'between-groups variance' represents the sampling error in the distributions: This statement is incorrect about ANOVA (Analysis of Variance). The 'between-groups variance' in ANOVA does not represent the sampling error but rather the variability among the different group means and is used to test if at least one group mean significantly differs from others. It essentially reflects the impact of the independent variable(s) on the dependent variable across different groups, not sampling error. Sampling error pertains to the differences caused by random selection of samples.

**65. (A):** Correct matching is:

- Linear Programming is based on operant conditioning learning theory, which involves learning from the consequences of behavior.
- Branching Programming suggests that a wrong response also helps in the diagnosis of weaknesses of the learner, making it a diagnostic learning approach.
- Mathetics Programming, based on connectionist theory of learning, involves understanding the connections between stimuli and responses.
- Cybernetics is the science of control and communication, which involves understanding how systems, including learning systems, are controlled and communicated within.

**66. (A):** According to Knowles' theory of Andragogy, the assumptions include:

- Readiness to learn, where adults become ready to learn when they experience needs and interests that learning will satisfy.
- Internally motivated reflects the assumption that adults are primarily motivated to learn by internal drives and curiosity.

- Self-concept as adult learners are described as self-directed and responsible for their own choices in education.

Mandatory guidance is not an assumption of Andragogy, as this approach emphasizes self-direction rather than mandatory guidance.

Hence, correct options are (*a*), (*b*) and (*c*).

**67.** **(*)**

**68.** **(C):** Implementing six-sigma in teacher education can lead to improved teacher effectiveness by optimizing teaching methods and processes. Enhanced student-learning outcomes can result from more efficient and effective teaching strategies. More efficient use of resources is also a typical benefit, as Six Sigma focuses on reducing waste and increasing efficiency in processes. Increased administrative workload and greater standardization of teaching practices are not necessarily benefits; the former is often viewed as a drawback, and while standardization may occur, it is not a primary goal of Six Sigma.

Hence, correct options are (*a*), (*b*) and (*d*).

**69.** **(C):** Correct matching is:

- Method of difference is associated with Mill's Canon, which identifies the cause of a phenomenon by comparing instances where the phenomenon occurs and does not occur, differing only in one condition.
- Law of single variable aligns with the assumption of experimental research, emphasizing the control of variables to isolate effects.
- The statement that while individual events cannot be predicted with accuracy, aggregate events can pertains to the assumption of randomization, which is fundamental in experimental design to ensure unbiased results.
- Interaction effect of testing represents a threat for experimental validity, as it can influence the outcomes of an experiment by the mere act of testing.

**70.** **(D):** In the updated DeLone and McLean Model of Information System Success (2003), the model includes dimensions such as Information Quality (A), System Quality (B), and Net Benefits (C). Organisational Impact (D) is not listed as a separate dimension in this updated model; rather, the model focuses more generally on the impact of information systems on success metrics, which can include but is not specifically limited to organizational impact.

**71.** **(A):** Correct matching is:

- Permissive style is synonymous with Laissez Faire, a management approach that grants autonomy to individuals or teams.
- The most desirable leadership behavior is identified as The 9.9 Managerial Style, which effectively balances productivity and people management.
- Replacement of old rules with systematic methods aligns with Scientific Management, which emphasizes efficiency through scientific approaches to task management.
- The Principle of span of control was significantly expounded upon by Ian Hamilton, focusing on the limits of effective management and supervision.

**72.** **(B):** UNCRPD, NEP, 2020, and Universal Design for Learning have direct relevance for inclusive education. UNCRPD provides a framework for promoting the rights and inclusion of persons with disabilities. NEP, 2020 emphasizes the inclusion of all students, including those with disabilities, and promotes the implementation of inclusive education policies. Universal Design for

Learning is an educational framework that supports educational practices to accommodate individual learning differences, enhancing accessibility for all students.

Hence, correct options are (*a*), (*c*) and (*e*).

**73. (D):** Chronologically, Marx, who lived from 1818 to 1883, comes first and is known as a conflict theorist. Durkheim, a functionalist, lived from 1858 to 1917. Weber, another conflict theorist, lived from 1864 to 1920. Mead, known for symbolic interactionism, lived from 1863 to 1931 but his theories gained prominence after Weber's. Bertalanffy, known for Open System Theory, was active later, with significant contributions in the mid-20th century.

Hence, chronological order is (*e*), (*a*), (*d*), (*c*), (*b*).

**74. (B):** The function of a search engine to scour the internet for content by looking over the code/content for each URL they find is called Crawling. Crawling is the process by which search engines discover updated content on the web, such as new sites or pages, changes to existing sites, and dead links.

**75. (D):** Correct matching is:

- Classical Conditioning is a learning process that involves a stimulus presented to get a response.
- Operant Conditioning is based on the principle where the response is made first, then reinforcement follows.
- Discovery Learning aligns with the idea that when learners have difficulty with new material, going back to concrete anchors like advance organizers helps.
- Meaningful/Verbal Learning reflects the concept that anybody can learn anything at any age, provided it is stated in terms they can understand.

**76. (D):** The law of disuse states that other things being equal, when a modifiable connection between stimulus and response (S-R) is not made over a period of time, the strength of that connection is weakened. This principle is associated with the theories of Edward Thorndike, not Skinner. Hull's theory of learning is indeed called 'Drive-Reduction Theory', which suggests that learning is driven by basic needs, and behaviors are developed through repetitive actions that reduce these drives.

Hence, correct options are (*c*) and (*d*).

**77. (C,D):** Both the CC BY and CC BY-SA licenses allow others to distribute, change, remix, and build upon your work, even commercially, as long as they credit you for the original creation. The CC BY license requires attribution alone, while the CC BY-SA additionally requires that derivative works be licensed under identical terms, meaning any adaptations must also be shared alike.

**78. (A):** Arranging the categories of children in order of increasing IQ:

- Profound Mental Retardation as having the lowest IQ
- Severe Mental Retardation
- Moderate Mental Retardation
- Mild Mental Retardation
- Slow learners who typically have higher IQs compared to those with mental retardation but may still be below average in intelligence.

Hence, correct order is (*d*), (*e*), (*b*), (*c*), (*a*).

**79. (C):** Transactional leadership is based on a system of rewards and punishments. It is a management style that focuses on the supervision, organization, and group performance; it is centered on the concept that managers give something to subordinates, like a salary, in return for something else, like the work performed. This approach heavily relies on setting clear objectives and goals for employees, with rewards that are contingent on achieving objectives.

**80. (A):** Galloway's system of interaction analysis differs from Flanders' interaction analysis primarily in its augmentation and integration of non-verbal communication aspects. Galloway's model includes not just verbal interactions but also takes into account non-verbal behaviors and interactions, which provides a more comprehensive analysis of classroom dynamics and teacher-student interactions.

**81. (C):** Karnataka has initiated a unique approach by establishing its own State Education Policy Commission. This commission is tasked with reviewing the National Education Policy (NEP) and proposing an alternative education policy specifically tailored for the state. This move reflects a proactive approach to address local educational needs and align them with broader national goals.

**82. (D):** Correct matchig is:

- Hierarchically structured chronologically graded education system corresponds to Formal Education, which is characterized by a structured educational pathway including primary, secondary, and tertiary levels.
- A set of learning experiences free of time and space limitations aligns with Non-formal Education, which includes education outside the traditional school system, such as adult education and continuing education.
- Lifelong process whereby every individual learns from daily experiences matches Informal Education, which occurs through daily interactions and experiences without formal curriculum.
- Education out of the confines of school for diverse needs and interests is associated with De-schooling, a concept that involves breaking away from traditional school structures to meet varied educational needs and interests.

**83. (B):** A 3 × 3 factorial design of experiment represents a study setup that involves two independent variables, each of which has three different conditions or levels. This type of design allows researchers to examine the effects of each independent variable on the outcome, as well as the interaction effects between the variables, providing a comprehensive understanding of their influences.

**84. (A):** Correct matching is:

- Web conferencing involves Synchronous Interaction, where participants interact in real-time.
- Formative Assessment is typically conducted during the development of a programme, allowing for ongoing adjustments based on student performance.
- Digitalized Materials refer to Asynchronous Interaction, where the interaction does not happen in real-time but can be accessed at any time.
- e-Portfolios, as a learning and assessment tool, comprise artifacts and also express a reflective dimension, facilitating ongoing evaluation of a learner's progress and development.

**85. (D):** Chronological order is:

- Grant's Plan, which was an educational strategy for India, began in 1835.
- Charter allocating one lakh rupees for education in 1835 as well.
- The Education Dispatch, also known as Wood's Dispatch, was introduced in 1854, outlining the framework for education in India.

- The establishment of Universities at Calcutta, Bombay, and Madras occurred subsequently in 1857.
- Hunter Commission, which reviewed education in British India, was set up later in 1882.

This order reflects the historical development of educational policies and institutions in colonial India.

**86. (D):** An effective curriculum development process generally follows these steps:

- Identifying key issues and trends in the content area helps set the context and foundation for what needs to be addressed in the curriculum.
- Defining course goals follows, where specific objectives for the curriculum are established.
- Identifying resource materials is necessary to determine the tools and materials needed to achieve the course goals.
- Developing assessment items to measure student progress is then undertaken to ensure that the objectives can be effectively evaluated.
- Determining the success of the program assesses the overall effectiveness and impact of the curriculum after its implementation.

**87. (D):** Correct matching is:

- The function of schools and universities should be different is a principle emphasized by the University Education Commission.
- Schools playing a crucial role in developing democratic citizenship was highlighted by the Secondary Education Commission.
- The role of education in national development was a key focus of the Kothari Commission.
- The idea that learning must not be a burden on the learner was advocated by the Yashpal Committee Report.

**88. (D)**

**89. (C):** Web 2.0 is associated with technologies and web platforms that facilitate interactive information sharing, interoperability, user-centered design, and collaboration. It is characterized especially by social networking sites and applications and user-generated content, which allow users to interact, collaborate, and share content online in previously unprecedented ways.

**90. (C):** According to Gutherie, Symbolic is not listed as an important characteristic of strategic leadership. Strategic leadership typically involves vision, inspiration, and strategic orientation, focusing on setting directions, inspiring others, and aligning organizational goals with effective strategies. Symbolic elements might be part of broader leadership qualities but are not emphasized as core components of strategic leadership per Gutherie's definition.

**91. (B):** If a teacher wants her students to obey orders without thinking, she is making her students conformists. Conformity involves aligning one's thoughts and behaviours to what is expected or demanded by others, often at the expense of one's own opinions or preferences. This is reflected in the passage where the author discusses how such an approach to discipline can dull the mind and hinder independent thought and initiative.

**92. (D):** According to the passage, freedom without order is non-existent. The author emphasizes that order and freedom are inseparable and that one cannot truly exist without the other. The idea is that without a structured framework or consideration for others, what one might consider freedom can actually lead to chaos and disorder, which ultimately restricts true freedom.

**93. (C):** Being on time and showing punctuality, as mentioned in the passage, contribute directly to creating order. By considering others and adhering to agreed-upon times, individuals facilitate a smooth functioning of group activities, thus promoting order in the environment around them.

**94. (A):** Conformism and imitation are learning outcomes of a pedagogy that relies on external discipline. The passage critiques this form of discipline, highlighting how it suppresses individual initiative and intelligence, leading students to simply follow orders and mimic behaviours without engaging in critical thinking or developing personal insights.

**95. (C):** When a teacher shouts, "Pindrop Silence in the Class," she is imposing discipline from the outside. This is a form of control that does not necessarily encourage students to understand the value of quietness and attentiveness on their own. Instead, it forces them to conform to the teacher's immediate demand, which aligns with the passage's discussion of how external discipline can make the mind conform and imitate rather than truly understand or choose to behave in a considered way.

**96. (C):** Inclusive education, as defined in the passage, emphasizes that all people, regardless of various differences, are entitled to equal access to higher education. It is inherently about celebrating the heterogeneity of students, recognizing and valuing the diverse backgrounds and abilities that students bring to the educational environment.

**97. (C):** The passage clearly states that both formal and non-formal education institutions and their activities should be designed to adjust to the students and respect their individual personalities with their different preconditions. This underscores the necessity for inclusivity across all types of educational institutions, not just formal but also non-formal settings, to ensure a comprehensive approach to inclusive education.

**98. (D):** Implementing inclusive education requires a high personal commitment from educators and stakeholders, along with differentiated material and activating methods of education. This approach ensures that the learning environment is tailored to meet the diverse needs of all students, supporting both individual learning and cooperative learning experiences.

**99. (D):** Inclusive education is focused on the education of all children, not just those with disabilities, learning difficulties, or challenging behaviours. The principle of inclusive education is to ensure equal access and remove entry barriers for all students, recognizing and accommodating the diverse spectrum of student needs across the entire student population.

**100. (B):** Inclusive education is described as a pedagogical approach that fundamentally values and appreciates diversity. This approach is based on the essential principle of recognizing and valuing the differences among students as a positive and enriching aspect of the educational experience, rather than as a challenge to be overcome.

Previous Years' Paper (Solved)

# National Testing Agency (NTA)

## UGC-NET Junior Research Fellowship & Assistant Professor Eligibility Exam

# EDUCATION, DECEMBER-2023

(Exam held on 08 December, 2023)

## PAPER-II

**1.** Given below are two statements:

**Statement I:** Collection of learner's work on a variety of tasks is meant for keeping a record of their performance and is known as portfolio.

**Statement II:** Portfolio is an essential part of learner's performance.

In the light of the above statements, choose the **most appropriate answer** from the options given below:

A. Both Statement I and Statement II are correct
B. Both Statement I and Statement II are incorrect
C. Statement I is correct, but Statement II is incorrect
D. Statement I is incorrect, but Statement II is correct

**2.** Which of the following are examples of learning management systems:

(*a*) Moodle (*b*) Canvas
(*c*) Edupuzzle (*d*) Schoology

Choose the **correct** answer from the options given below:

A. (*a*), (*c*), (*b*) Only
B. (*a*), (*b*), (*d*) Only
C. (*c*), (*a*), (*d*) Only
D. (*b*), (*c*), (*d*) Only

**3.** Arrange the following in chronological order:

(*a*) Post modernism
(*b*) Transcendentalism
(*c*) Empiricism
(*d*) Analytical Philosophy
(*e*) Rationalism

Choose the **correct** answer from the options given below:

A. (*e*), (*b*), (*c*), (*a*), (*d*)
B. (*b*), (*d*), (*a*), (*c*), (*e*)
C. (*b*), (*c*), (*e*), (*a*), (*d*)
D. (*e*), (*c*), (*b*), (*d*), (*a*)

**4.** The Virtual University for Small States of Commonwealth (VUSSC) in 2000 was initiated by:

A. Inflibnet
B. Commonwealth of Learning
C. Delnet
D. IGNOU

**5.** Reactive change:

A. is a change brought about by a sudden or unplanned event
B. involves reimplementation of a change in the same organisational unit
C. involves changes that are generally new and familiar
D. is a systematic deliberate change in the way part or all of an organization functions

**6.** Given below are two statements:

**Statement I:** According to realists, curriculum follows a hierarchical order with the abstract subjects at the top and the transitory subjects at the bottom.

**Statement II:** Pragmatist curriculum would focus on experiences and subjects that land themselves to philosophical dialogue and acts of choice making.

In the light of the above statements, choose the **most appropriate answer** from the options given below:

A. Both Statement 1 and Statement II are correct
B. Both Statement I and Statement II are incorrect
C. Statement I is correct, but Statement II is incorrect
D. Statement I is incorrect, but Statement II is correct

**7.** Which of the following is not an aspect of 4P model of creativity as given by Rhodes?

A. Person B. Peers
C. Process D. Press

**8.** Which of the following is correct?

(*a*) CIPP model for curriculum evaluation is developed by Daniel Mento in 1949
(*b*) Tayler's curriculum model is a four part linear model
(*c*) CIPP model for curriculum evaluation is based on "how can we determine whether the purposes are being attained?"
(*d*) CIPP model for curriculum evaluation involves the steps and resources needed to meet the new goals and objectives and might include identifying successful external programes and materials as well as gathering information
(*e*) Tayler's model for curriculum evaluation provides decision makers with information about how well the programme is being implemented

Choose the **correct** answer from the options given below:

A. (*b*) and (*e*) Only
B. (*a*) Only
C. (*e*) Only
D. (*b*) and (*d*) Only

**9.** Which statement is correct in relation to scales of measurement?

(*a*) Ratio scale is having an absolute zero point
(*b*) Interval scale is having an absolute zero point
(*c*) Ratio scale is used in mental measurement
(*d*) Interval scale is mental measurement
(*e*) All the characteristics of ratio scale are included in the interval scale

Choose the **correct** answer from the options given below:

A. (*a*) and (*c*) Only
B. (*b*) and (*d*) Only
C. (*a*) and (*d*) Only
D. (*d*) and (*e*) Only

**10.** Under the heuristics, which of the following is a strategy for the solution of the problems stands for the identification of the difference between the current state and the one that is desired in relation to the nature and solution of the problems and then taking action to reduce this difference for arriving at the solution of the problem:

A. Means-end Analysis
B. Using an Analogy
C. Sub-goal Analysis
D. Working Backward

**11.** If a phenomenon changes over time, what kind of research should be undertaken to study it?

A. Experimental Research
B. Longitudinal Research
C. Ex-post facto Research
D. Ethnographic Research

**12.** Teaching-learning process and learning strategy in adult education should be based on ............. .

(*a*) Experience based learning
(*b*) Self directed learning
(*c*) Readiness to learn
(*d*) As per the formal education system
(*e*) Rigid learning environment

Choose the **correct** answer from the options given below:

A. (*a*), (*b*), (*c*) Only
B. (*a*), (*b*), (*c*) and (*e*) Only
C. (*b*), (*c*), (*d*) and (*e*) Only
D. (*c*) and (*d*) Only

**13.** Which are correct facts relating to reliability and validity of research tool?

(*a*) Consistency is necessary for reliability
(*b*) Validity is the precondition for reliability
(*c*) A reliable test is always valid
(*d*) A valid test is always reliable
(*e*) There is no relationship between reliability and validity of a test

Choose the **correct** answer from the options given below:

A. (*a*) and (*b*) Only B. (*a*) and (*c*) Only
C. (*a*) and (*d*) Only D. (*a*) and (*e*) Only

**14.** Given below are two statements: one is labelled as Assertion (A) and the other is labelled as Reason (R).

**Assertion (A):** Psychomotor domain of learning helps the children to acquire skills on certain aspects to create something by their own.

**Reason (R):** Psychomotor domain of learning is very much linked with cognitive and affective domains as it helps the children to understand the concept and to develop a right attitude for working on that concept for developing skills.

In the light of the above statements, choose the **most appropriate answer** from the options given below:

A. Both (A) and (R) are correct and (R) is the correct explanation of (A)
B. Both (A) and (R) are correct, but (R) is not the correct explanation of (A)
C. (A) is correct, but (R) is not correct
D. (A) is not correct, but (A) is correct

**15.** Arrange the leadership styles in the Blake and Mouton's managerial grid in order of their concern for people from the least concern to the most concern:

(*a*) Country Club Management
(*b*) Authority Obedience Management
(*c*) Impoverished Management
(*d*) Team Management
(*e*) Middle of the Road Management

Choose the **correct** answer from the options given below:

A. (*c*), (*d*), (*b*), (*a*), (*e*)
B. (*d*), (*a*), (*b*), (*c*), (*e*)
C. (*b*), (*e*), (*c*), (*a*), (*d*)
D. (*b*), (*c*), (*d*), (*a*), (*e*)

**16.** Identify the situation involving sychronous and asychronous communication:

(*a*) Taking to someone in your room
(*b*) Checking email
(*c*) Reading an email
(*d*) Participating in web conferencing

Choose the **correct** answer from the options given below:

A. sychronous (*a*), (*d*) asychronous (*b*), (*c*)
B. sychronous (*a*), (*b*) asychronous (*d*), (*c*)
C. sychronous (*c*), (*a*) asychronous (*d*), (*b*)
D. sychronous (*d*), (*a*) asychronous (*b*), (*c*)

**17.** Match List-I with List-II.

| **List-I** | **List-II** |
|---|---|
| (*a*) Measurement | I. Value Judgement |
| (*b*) Assessment | II. Standardized test |
| (*c*) Evaluation | III. Quantitative description |
| (*d*) Norm | IV. Qualitative description |

Choose the **correct** answer from the options given below:

| | (*a*) | (*b*) | (*c*) | (*d*) |
|---|---|---|---|---|
| A. | IV | I | II | III |
| B. | III | IV | II | I |
| C. | II | I | IV | III |
| D. | III | IV | I | II |

**18.** The difference between the values of "Parameter" and "Statistics" is called as:

A. Type-I Error

B. Type-II Error

C. Sampling Error

D. Error in Calculation

**19.** ………… is the stable body of information that we know about ourselves and other people as thinkers.

A. Self Regulations

B. Meta Cognitive Knowledge

C. Knowledge about Self

D. Self Cognition

**20.** Match List-I with List-II.

| **List-I (Models)** | **List-II (Goals for which most applicable)** |
|---|---|
| (*a*) Anxiety Reduction | I. Direct, spontaneous expression of feeling in social situations |
| (*b*) Assertive Training | II. Social behaviour, skills |
| (*c*) Managing Behaviour | III. Substitution of relaxation for anxiety in social situations |
| (*d*) Relaxation | IV. Reduction of stress |

Choose the **correct** answer from the options given below:

| | (*a*) | (*b*) | (*c*) | (*d*) |
|---|---|---|---|---|
| A. | I | III | II | IV |
| B. | IV | I | III | II |
| C. | III | I | II | IV |
| D. | III | II | IV | I |

**21.** Which of the following is correct?

(*a*) Intellectual Academic Approach to curriculum propagates for curriculum areas in arts, music, literature etc.

(*b*) Behavioural-Rational Approach to curriculum is also known as logical positivist, conceptual, rational-scientific and technocratic approach

(*c*) Humanistic Aesthetic Approach to curriculum also refers to as traditional encyclopedic or knowledge oriented approach

(*d*) Systems Managerial Approach to curriculum focuses on programmes, schedules, materials, personnel and resource

(*e*) Reconceptionalist Approach to curriculum looks at schooling and education from a broader perspective and discusses education from a historical and philosophical angle

Choose the **correct** answer from the options given below:

A. (*a*) and (*b*) Only

B. (*e*) Only

C. (*b*) and (*d*) Only

D. (*b*) and (*c*) Only

**22.** Given below are two statements:

**Statement I:** The entire process of teacher education lies in its curriculum, designs and transaction modes as well as the extent and its appropriateness.

**Statement II:** The curriculum is essential component for every stream.

In the light of the above statements, choose the **most appropriate answer** from the options given below:

A. Both Statement I and Statement II are correct

B. Both Statement I and Statement II are incorrect

C. Statement I is correct, but Statement II is incorrect

D. Statement I is incorrect, but Statement II is correct

**23.** Which of the following can not be associated with 'Discipline'?
A. Authority
B. Punishment
C. Reward
D. Child Centeredness

**24.** In an educational research, variable under study are being manipulated and controlled, what kind of research it is?
A. Quasi-Experimental Research
B. Experimental Research
C. Ex-post Facto Research
D. Mixed Method Research

**25.** Match List-I with List-II.

| List-I | | List-II |
|---|---|---|
| (*a*) Stratified random sampling | I. | Error in Sampling |
| (*b*) Purposive sampling | II. | Sample |
| (*c*) A representative proportion of the population | III. | Non-probability sampling |
| (*d*) Difference between the estimate of parameter and statistics | IV. | Probability sampling |

Choose the **correct** answer from the options given below:

| | (*a*) | (*b*) | (*c*) | (*d*) |
|---|---|---|---|---|
| A. | IV | III | I | II |
| B. | III | IV | II | I |
| C. | IV | III | II | I |
| D. | III | IV | I | II |

**26.** Given below are two statements:

**Statement I:** Nai Talim was suggested by the Zakir Hussain Committee at Wardha.

**Statement II:** Nai Talim suggested that all education must be in English to make independent citizens.

In the light of the above statements, choose the **most appropriate answer** from the options given below:
A. Both Statement I and Statement II are correct
B. Both Statement I and Statement II are incorrect
C. Statement I is correct, but Statement II is incorrect
D. Statement I is incorrect, but Statement II is correct

**27.** When judgements are based on the information present in our memories, we are using the:
A. Heuristic
B. Confirmation Bias
C. Representative Heuristic
D. Availability Heuristic

**28.** What is the nature of Educational Research?
(*a*) Educational research is empirical in nature
(*b*) Educational research should be systematic
(*c*) Educational and Physical science research findings are measured in the same scale
(*d*) Educational research should be valid
(*e*) Educational research should be reliable

Choose the **correct** answer from the options given below:
A. (*a*) and (*b*) Only
B. (*a*), (*b*) and (*c*) Only
C. (*d*) and (*e*) Only
D. (*a*), (*b*), (*d*) and (*e*) Only

**29.** Match List-I with List-II.

| List-I (Leadership style) | | List-II (Characteristics) |
|---|---|---|
| (*a*) Autocratic Leadership | I. | Inspires and motivates followers to achieve a shared vision |
| (*b*) Democratic Leadership | II. | Leader provides little guidance or structure, allowing subordinates to make most decisions |
| (*c*) Laissez faire Leadership | III. | Leader makes decisions without input from subordinates |
| (*d*) Transformational Leadership | IV. | Encourages participation and input from group members in decision making |

Choose the **correct** answer from the options given below:

| | (*a*) | (*b*) | (*c*) | (*d*) |
|---|---|---|---|---|
| A. | III | I | IV | II |
| B. | III | IV | II | I |
| C. | III | IV | I | II |
| D. | III | II | I | IV |

**30.** Match List-I with List-II.

| List-I | List-II |
|---|---|
| (*a*) Choleric Type | I. Active, cheerful and optimistic |
| (*b*) Melancholic Type | II. Humble, sad, depressed |
| (*c*) Sanguine Type | III. Slow, dull, and unemotional |
| (*d*) Phlegmatic Type | IV. Energetic, full of ambition and courage but easily excitable to anger |

Choose the **correct** answer from the options given below:

| | (*a*) | (*b*) | (*c*) | (*d*) |
|---|---|---|---|---|
| A. | I | II | III | IV |
| B. | III | I | II | IV |
| C. | IV | II | I | III |
| D. | IV | I | III | II |

**31.** The types of Cerebral Palsy are:

(*a*) Diplegia (*b*) Rickets
(*c*) Orthotics (*d*) Hemiplegia
(*e*) Ataxia

Choose the **correct** answer from the options given below:

A. (*a*), (*d*) and (*e*) Only
B. (*d*) and (*e*) Only
C. (*c*) and (*d*) Only
D. (*a*), (*b*), (*c*) and (*d*) Only

**32.** The University Education Commission is also known as:

A. Mudaliar Commission
B. Radha Krishnan Commission
C. Kothari Commission
D. Secondary Education Commission

**33.** Match List-I with List-II.

| List-I (Concept) | List-II (Explanation) |
|---|---|
| (*a*) Mainstreaming | I. A legal requirement specifying that students with disabilities should be educated in typical classrooms to the maximum extent possible |
| (*b*) Full Inclusion | II. A document outlining educational goals and services for a student with a disability |
| (*c*) Least Restrictive Environment (LRE) | III. Placing students with disabilities in regular education classes for a portion of the day |
| (*d*) Individualized Education Program (IEP) | IV. Inclusive education model where students with disabilities are fully integrated into regular classrooms |

Choose the **correct** answer from the options given below:

| | (*a*) | (*b*) | (*c*) | (*d*) |
|---|---|---|---|---|
| A. | III | IV | I | II |
| B. | III | I | IV | II |
| C. | IV | III | I | II |
| D. | II | III | IV | I |

**34.** Light, Sound, Love, Truth are all examples of:

A. Tangibles B. Intangibles
C. Innovations D. Goal Orientation

**35.** Which is the component of affective domain as per Krathwohl et.al?

(*a*) Comprehension (*b*) Emotion
(*c*) Feeling (*d*) Attitude
(*e*) Values

Choose the **correct** answer from the options given below:

A. (*a*), (*b*) and (*c*) Only
B. (*b*), (*c*), (*d*) and (*e*) Only
C. (*b*) and (*c*) Only
D. (*d*) and (*e*) Only

**36.** Given below are two statements: one is labelled as Assertion (A) and the other is labelled as Reason (R).

**Assertion (A):** Counselling is a face to face relationship between the guidance worker and the person who seeks a special kind of guidance.

**Reason (R):** Counselling is an intimate interpersonal relationship in which one person by virtue of his special training and skills is recognized as the helper while the other person is recognised as an individual or group with a problem who can benefit from the former.

In the light of the above statements, choose the **most appropriate answer** from the options given below:

A. Both (A) and (R) are correct and (R) is the correct explanation of (A)

B. Both (A) and (R) are correct, but (R) is not the correct explanation of (A)

C. (A) is correct, but (R) is not correct

D. (A) is not correct, but (R) is correct

**37.** Which is a correct statement relating to the types of assessment?

(*a*) Criterion Referenced Test is related to Formative Assessment

(*b*) Criterion Referenced Test is related to Summative Assessment

(*c*) Norm Referenced Test is related to Formative Assessment

(*d*) Norm Referenced Test is related to Summative Assessment

(*e*) Summative assessment is terminal in nature

Choose the **correct** answer from the options given below:

A. (*b*) and (*e*) Only

B. (*b*) and (*c*) Only

C. (*a*) and (*d*) Only

D. (*a*), (*d*) and (*e*) Only

**38.** The foundational principles of cost benefit analysis in education includes:

(*a*) Explicit Valuation

(*b*) Intrinsic Value of Freedom

(*c*) Consequential Evaluation

(*d*) Pricing the Intangible

(*e*) Additive Accounting

Choose the **correct** answer from the options given below:

A. (*c*) Only

B. (*a*) and (*b*) Only

C. (*a*), (*c*) and (*e*) Only

D. (*b*), (*c*) and (*d*) Only

**39.** Given below are two statements:

**Statement I:** The concept of quality in education is solely determined by the availability of modern technology and resources.

**Statement II:** Quality in education encompasses a broad range of factors including curriculum teaching methods, assessment and learning environment in addition to technology and resources.

In the light of the above statements, choose the **most appropriate answer** from the options given below:

A. Both Statement I and Statement II are correct

B. Both Statement I and Statement II are incorrect

C. Statement I is correct but Statement II is incorrect

D. Statement I is incorrect but Statement II is correct

**40.** Given below are two statements: one is labelled as Assertion (A) and the other is labelled as Reason (R).

**Assertion (A):** Ethical leadership is not relevant in education as ethical standards are not applicable to administrative roles.

**Reason (R):** Ethical leadership in educational administration is essential because it emphasizes making morally sound decisions and serving as a role model for ethical behaviour.

In the light of the above statements, choose the **most appropriate answer** from the options given below:

A. Both (A) and (R) are correct and (R) is the correct explanation of (A)
B. Both (A) and (R) are correct, but (R) is not the correct explanation of (A)
C. (A) is correct, but (R) is not correct
D. (A) is not correct, but (R) is correct

**41.** Given below are two statements: one is labelled as Assertion (A) and the other is labelled as Reason (R).

**Assertion (A):** Buddhism is a nastik school of philosophy.

**Reason (R):** Astik-nastik in Indian philosophy is about faith in vedas.

In the light of the above statements, choose the **most appropriate answer** from the options given below:

A. Both (A) and (R) are correct and (R) is the correct explanation of (A)
B. Both (A) and (R) are correct, but (R) is not the correct explanation of (A)
C. (A) is correct, but (R) is not correct
D. (A) is not correct, but (R) is correct

**42.** Erotetic teaching relies on .......... as a central pedagogic technique.

A. Questioning B. Homework
C. Activity D. Lecturing

**43.** Given below are two statements: one is labelled as Assertion (A) and the other is labelled as Reason (R).

**Assertion (A):** Teacher should use a wide variety of online assessment tools and technique to assess children.

**Reason (R):** No single online tool is capable of providing information about a child's progress and learning in different areas of developments.

In the light of the above statements, choose the **most appropriate answer** from the options given below:

A. Both (A) and (R) are correct and (R) is the correct explanation of (A)
B. Both (A) and (R) are correct, but (R) is not the correct explanation of (A)
C. (A) is correct, but (R) is not correct
D. (A) is not correct, but (R) is correct

**44.** According to WHO statistics (2011) arrange the following from most prevalent to least prevalent communication related disabilities:

(*a*) Communication related Disabilities
(*b*) Mobility related Disabilities
(*c*) Hearing related Disabilities
(*d*) Vision related Disabilities
(*e*) Cognition related Disabilities

Choose the **correct** answer from the options given below:

A. (*e*), (*a*), (*c*), (*d*), (*b*)
B. (*b*), (*d*), (*c*), (*a*), (*e*)
C. (*a*), (*c*), (*e*), (*b*), (*d*)
D. (*c*), (*a*), (*b*), (*e*), (*d*)

**45.** "Students of high intelligence will significantly do better in their academic achievement", which type of hypothesis is it?

A. Directional Hypothesis
B. Non-directional Hypothesis
C. Null-Hypothesis
D. Concurrent Hypothesis

**46.** Which of the following can be associated with Gandhi?

(*a*) Sabarmati Ashram
(*b*) Nai Talim
(*c*) Geetanjali
(*d*) Santiniketan
(*e*) Craft based education

Choose the **correct** answer from the options given below:

A. (*a*), (*b*) and (*e*) Only

B. (*c*) and (*d*) Only

C. (*a*) and (*e*) Only

D. (*b*) and (*d*) Only

**47.** The advantage of digital libraries as compared to traditional libraries is:

(*a*) Effective use of technology

(*b*) Difficult cataloguing

(*c*) Accessible anytime anywhere

(*d*) Easily linked to other resources

(*e*) A resource can be simultaneously used by multiple users

Choose the **correct** answer from the options given below:

A. (*a*), (*b*), (*c*), (*d*) Only

B. (*a*), (*c*), (*d*), (*e*) Only

C. (*a*), (*b*), (*d*), (*e*) Only

D. (*c*), (*e*), (*b*), (*a*) Only

**48.** This theory of intelligence consist of one factor - a fund of intellectual competency - which is universal for all the activities of an individual?

A. Anarchic Theory

B. Monarchic Theory

C. Sampling Theory

D. Hierarchical Theory

**49.** Match List-I with List-II.

| List-I (Books) | List-II (Authors) |
|---|---|
| (*a*) Emotional Intelligence: Why It Can Matter More Than IQ | I. Darwin C |
| (*b*) Emotion, Obesity and Crime | II. Young, P.T. |
| (*c*) Emotion In Man and Animal | III. Goleman, D. |
| (*d*) The Expression of the Emotions in Man and Animals | IV. Schachter,S. |

Choose the **correct** answer from the options given below:

| | (*a*) | (*b*) | (*c*) | (*d*) |
|---|---|---|---|---|
| A. | II | I | IV | III |
| B. | III | IV | II | I |
| C. | I | II | III | IV |
| D. | IV | III | II | I |

**50.** Which of the following are post independence commissions on education?

(*a*) Kothari Commission

(*b*) Hunter Commission

(*c*) Calcutta University Commission

(*d*) Nai Talim

(*e*) National Knowledge Commission

Choose the **correct** answer from the options given below:

A. (*b*) and (*c*) Only

B. (*a*) and (*e*) Only

C. (*a*), (*c*) and (*e*) Only

D. (*b*), (*c*) and (*d*) Only

**51.** Which is not true in case of Flander's Interaction analysis?

A. Interaction means participation of teacher and students in the process of teaching

B. Teacher evaluates the students through assignment

C. It helps to know whether the teacher is effective or not

D. Teacher influences students through lecture, asking questions, criticizing, giving directions etc.

**52.** Which of the following is not a social function of Schooling as understood by the Deschooling movement?

A. Custodial Care

B. Social Role Selection

C. Indoctrination

D. Social Change

**53.** Match List-I with List-II.

| List-I (Books) | List-II (Authors) |
|---|---|
| (*a*) Pedagogy of Oppressed | I. John Dewey |
| (*b*) Deschooling Society | II. Paulo Freire |
| (*c*) Democracy and Education | III. Bertrand Russell |
| (*d*) Education and Social Order | IV. Ivan Illich |

Choose the **correct** answer from the options given below:

| | (*a*) | (*b*) | (*c*) | (*d*) |
|---|---|---|---|---|
| A. | II | IV | I | III |
| B. | I | II | III | IV |
| C. | II | I | IV | III |
| D. | III | IV | I | II |

**54.** The International Classification of Functioning, Disability and Health (ICF) conceptualise a persons level of functioning as a dynamic interaction between his or her:

(*a*) Health Conditions
(*b*) Environmental Factors
(*c*) Personal Factors
(*d*) Economic Factors
(*e*) Innovative Factors

Choose the **correct** answer from the options given below:

A. (*a*) and (*b*) Only
B. (*a*), (*b*) and (*c*) Only
C. (*c*), (*d*) and (*e*) Only
D. (*d*) and (*e*) Only

**55.** According to Thurston, the primary factor in intelligence is:

(*a*) Spatial Ability
(*b*) Associative Memory
(*c*) Problem Solving
(*d*) Perceptual Speed
(*e*) Reasoning

Choose the **correct** answer from the options given below:

A. (*b*) Only
B. (*a*) and (*c*) Only
C. (*a*) and (*e*) Only
D. (*e*) Only

**56.** A zero rejection policy was adopted under:

A. National Policy of Education, 1986
B. Persons with Disability Act, 1995
C. Sarva Shiksha Abhiyan, 2001
D. National Curriculum Framework, 2005

**57.** Arrange the following in traditional manner of writing lesson plan

(*a*) Previous knowledge
(*b*) Specific Aims
(*c*) Home Work
(*d*) Content Delivery
(*e*) Recapitulation

Choose the **correct** answer from the options given below:

A. (*b*), (*a*), (*d*), (*e*), (*c*)
B. (*a*), (*c*), (*e*), (*d*), (*b*)
C. (*c*), (*a*), (*d*), (*b*), (*e*)
D. (*d*), (*e*), (*a*), (*b*), (*c*)

**58.** Arrange the following steps of AADIE model framework in the correct sequence:

(*a*) Design
(*b*) Analysis
(*c*) Implementation
(*d*) Evaluation
(*e*) Development

Choose the **correct** answer from the options given below:

A. (*c*), (*b*), (*a*), (*e*) and (*d*)
B. (*b*), (*a*), (*e*), (*c*) and (*d*)
C. (*b*), (*c*), (*e*), (*a*) and (*d*)
D. (*b*), (*d*), (*e*), (*a*), and (*c*)

**59.** Arrange the steps involved in scientific procedure of problem solving behaviour in correct order:

(*a*) Collection of relevant information about problem
(*b*) Problem understanding
(*c*) Problem awareness
(*d*) Verification of the concluded solution
(*e*) Hunch for possible solution

Choose the **correct** answer from the options given below:

A. (*a*), (*b*), (*c*), (*d*), (*e*)

B. (*b*), (*c*), (*a*), (*d*), (*e*)

C. (*c*), (*b*), (*a*), (*e*), (*d*)

D. (*b*), (*e*), (*c*), (*a*), (*d*)

**60.** Mention the correct sequence of the following education commissions in post Independent India

(*a*) The Secondary Education Commission

(*b*) National Commission on Teachers

(*c*) Acharya Ramamurti Committee

(*d*) The University Education Commission

(*e*) The Kothari Commission

Choose the **correct** answer from the options given below:

A. (*d*), (*a*), (*e*), (*b*) and (*c*)

B. (*a*), (*c*), (*d*), (*e*) and (*b*)

C. (*d*), (*b*), (*a*), (*c*) and (*e*)

D. (*a*), (*c*), (*d*), (*b*), and (*e*)

**61.** Which of the following affects curriculum change?

(*a*) Placement in Jobs

(*b*) Religious Sentiments

(*c*) Availability of Competent Teachers

(*d*) Important to Nation

(*e*) Socio Cultural Context

Choose the **correct** answer from the options given below:

A. (*a*) and (*d*) Only B. (*b*) and (*c*) Only

C. (*d*) and (*e*) Only D. (*c*) and (*e*) Only

**62.** "Assessment for learning" emphasises:

A. Assessment to enhance learning

B. Assessment to know the mastery of the content

C. Assessment to certify the learners

D. Assessment to grade the learners

**63.** Which of the following are method of knowing according to Nyay philosophy ?

(*a*) Perception (*b*) Inference

(*c*) Arthapatti (*d*) Smriti

(*e*) Abhava

Choose the **correct** answer from the options given below:

A. (*c*) and (*e*) Only

B. (*c*) and (*d*) Only

C. (*a*) and (*b*) Only

D. (*b*) and (*e*) Only

**64.** Professional norms of teacher education are developed by:

A. NCTE B. IGNOU

C. UGC D. NCERT

**65.** The types of planning techniques are:

(*a*) Critical Path Method

(*b*) Cost Benefit Analysis

(*c*) Planning, Programming and Budgeting System

(*d*) Managerial Quality

(*e*) Programme Evaluation Review Technique

Choose the **correct** answer from the options given below:

A. (*a*) and (*d*) Only

B. (*c*), (*d*) and (*e*) Only

C. (*b*), (*d*) and (*e*) Only

D. (*a*), (*b*), (*c*) & (*d*) Only

**66.** Which of the following are associated with Rousseau?

(*a*) Emile

(*b*) Social contract

(*c*) Back to nature

(*d*) Man is born as Slave

(*e*) Knowledge is based on reason only

Choose the **correct** answer from the options given below:

A. (*a*), (*b*) and (*c*) Only

B. (*d*) Only

C. (*a*) and (*d*) Only

D. (*e*) Only

**67.** We are caught in narratives and metanarratives and they sit on our judgements. We must be incredulous towards metanarratives. This sentence can be associated with:

A. Idealism B. Structuralism

C. Postmodernism D. Realism

**68.** A six Sigma process is one in which too much percentage of the products manufactured are statistically expected to be free of defects.

A. 95.99966%  B. 99.99966%
C. 98.99966%  D. 96.99966%

**69.** Order the sequence of steps followed in educational research:

(*a*) Selection of research problem
(*b*) Selection of research method
(*c*) Formulation of research question
(*d*) Data collection and analysis
(*e*) Reporting the results

Choose the **correct** answer from the options given below:

A. (*a*), (*b*), (*c*), (*d*), (*e*)
B. (*a*), (*c*), (*b*), (*d*), (*e*)
C. (*a*), (*d*), (*b*), (*c*), (*e*)
D. (*b*), (*a*), (*c*), (*d*), (*e*)

**70.** According to Thorndike, following is one of the secondary laws of learning:

A. Law of Readiness
B. Law of Exercise
C. Principle of Partial Activity
D. Principle of Effect

**71.** Which apex body is regulating integrated teacher education programme in the country?

A. NCERT  B. NCTE
C. NIEPA  D. UGC

**72.** Which of the following are 'Astik' schools of Indian philosophy?

(*a*) Buddhism  (*b*) Jainism
(*c*) Samkhya  (*d*) Nyay
(*e*) Charvak

Choose the **correct** answer from the options given below:

A. (*a*) and (*b*) Only
B. (*a*), (*b*) and (*e*) Only
C. (*c*) and (*a*) Only
D. (*c*) and (*d*) Only

**73.** Which of the following is most important for inclusive teaching learning:

A. Educational Technologies
B. Teaching Technologies
C. Assistive Technologies
D. Communication Technologies

**74.** Which is the sequence of taxonomy of cognitive domain as per Anderson and Krathwohl's taxonomy (2001)?

(*a*) Remembering  (*b*) Understanding
(*c*) Analysing  (*d*) Applying
(*e*) Evaluating

Choose the **correct** answer from the options given below:

A. (*a*), (*b*), (*c*), (*d*), (*e*)
B. (*a*), (*c*), (*b*), (*d*), (*e*)
C. (*a*), (*b*), (*d*), (*c*), (*e*)
D. (*a*), (*b*), (*d*), (*e*), (*c*)

**75.** Match List-I with List-II.

| **List-I (Books)** | **List-II (Authors)** |
|---|---|
| (*a*) Shaikshik Gyan Aur Varchasva | I. Gijubhai Badheka |
| (*b*) Shiksha Mein Badlav Ke Sawal | II. Sadhna Saxena |
| (*c*) Shiksha Aur Jan Andolan | III. Krishna Kumar |
| (*d*) Divaswapn | IV. Anil Sadgopal |

Choose the **correct** answer from the options given below:

| | (*a*) | (*b*) | (*c*) | (*d*) |
|---|---|---|---|---|
| A. | IV | III | I | II |
| B. | II | IV | III | I |
| C. | III | II | IV | I |
| D. | III | IV | II | I |

**76.** Which policy suggested to confer autonomous status to SCERT, NCTE and set up State Board of teacher education?

A. Programme of Action on NPE 1986
B. National Policy on Education 1986
C. National Education Policy 2020
D. National Commission on Teacher 1983

**77.** Following is not a category of learning as per Gagne's classification of learning:
A. Stimulus Response Learning
B. Chain Learning
C. Ideational Learning
D. Verbal Associate Learning

**78.** Which is not a benefit to use reflective journal as an assessment tool in pedagogy of education?
A. Reflective writing can enable students to demonstrate complex learning outcomes including critical thinking
B. Students can demonstrate analysis, creativity and originality
C. Students may not fully understand what is required of them in reflective writing
D. Reflection in and of itself can be a powerful learning process

**79.** Carl Rogers proposed the following types of Counselling:
(*a*) Rehabilitation Counselling
(*b*) Substance Abuse Counselling
(*c*) Non Directive Counselling
(*d*) Education Counselling
(*e*) Directive Counselling

Choose the **correct** answer from the options given below:
A. (*a*) and (*b*) Only
B. (*c*) and (*e*) Only
C. (*c*) Only
D. (*d*) Only

**80.** Taylor Postcard Frame is used for:
A. Writing large character Braille on one side of the paper
B. Writing large character Braille on both side of the paper
C. Writing small character Braille on one side of the paper
D. Writing small character Braille on both side of the paper

**81.** Screening measures that can assist in the diagnosis of Autism Spectrum Disorder (ASD) include:
(*a*) Autism Behaviour Checklist (ABC)
(*b*) Development Behaviour Checklist (DBC)
(*c*) Self Confidence Checklist
(*d*) Psycho Educational Profile Revised (PEP - R)
(*e*) Hand Flapping

Choose the **correct** answer from the options given below:
A. (*a*), (*b*), and (*d*) Only
B. (*a*) Only
C. (*b*), (*c*) and (*d*) Only
D. (*b*), (*c*), (*d*) and (*e*) Only

**82.** Arrange the following in chronological order:
(*a*) University Education Commission
(*b*) Secondary Education Commission
(*c*) Acharya Rammurti Committee
(*d*) National Education Commission
(*e*) Birla Ambani Report

Choose the **correct** answer from the options given below:
A. (*a*), (*b*), (*d*), (*c*), (*e*)
B. (*b*), (*a*), (*c*), (*d*), (*e*)
C. (*a*), (*d*), (*b*), (*e*), (*c*)
D. (*b*), (*e*), (*c*), (*d*), (*a*)

**83.** Given below are two statements:

**Statement I:** All valid tests are reliable but all reliable tests are not valid.

**Statement II:** Split-half method is used to determine reliability of a test.

In the light of the above statements, choose the **most appropriate answer** from the options given below:
A. Both Statement I and Statement II are correct
B. Both Statement I and Statement II are incorrect
C. Statement I is correct, but Statement II is incorrect
D. Statement I is incorrect, but Statement II is correct

**84.** What is not related to education?

(*a*) Direct benefit
(*b*) Indirect benefit
(*c*) Investment in people
(*d*) Human Resource development
(*e*) Public funding

Choose the **correct** answer from the options given below:

A. (*a*) Only
B. (*b*) and (*c*) Only
C. (*c*) and (*d*) Only
D. (*b*) and (*e*) Only

**85.** Disability represents:

A. Disturbance in perception
B. Disturbance at a personal level
C. Disturbance in social functions
D. Disturbance in medical conditions

**86.** Important approaches of cost analysis in education are:

(*a*) Cost Benefit
(*b*) Cost Feasibility
(*c*) Cost Utility
(*d*) Cost Empire
(*e*) Cost Counting

Choose the **correct** answer from the options given below:

A. (*c*), (*d*) and (*e*) Only
B. (*a*), (*b*) and (*c*) Only
C. (*a*) and (*c*) Only
D. (*b*), (*c*), (*d*) and (*e*) Only

**87.** If a teacher through her teaching enables the students to learn, comprehend, understand the related concepts and perform behavioural actions based on learning, the teaching level is ............. .

A. Memory Level Teaching
B. Understanding Level Teaching
C. Application Level Teaching
D. Reflective Level Teaching

**88.** Match List-I with List-II.

| **List-I** | | **List-II** |
|---|---|---|
| (*a*) E Learning | I. | Hyper media based instruction programme which utilizes the attributes and resources of the world wide web to create a meaningful learning environment where learning is fostered and supported |
| (*b*) Virtual Learning | II. | It is synonymous to web based learning where learning is fostered via hypertext transfer protocol (http) in internet or intranet |
| (*c*) Web Based Instruction | III. | A wide set of application and processes including computer based learning, web based learning, virtual classroom and digital collaboration |
| (*d*) Online Learning | IV. | The educational process of learning over the internet without having face to face contact |

Choose the **correct** answer from the options given below:

| | (*a*) | (*b*) | (*c*) | (*d*) |
|---|---|---|---|---|
| A. | I | III | II | IV |
| B. | III | IV | I | II |
| C. | IV | I | III | II |
| D. | IV | III | II | I |

**89.** Creativity emphasizes more on testing of:

A. Similar Thinking
B. Progressive Thinking
C. Convergent Thinking
D. Divergent Thinking

**90.** The correct sequences of stages of curriculum evaluation is:
(*a*) Planning
(*b*) Regular Monitoring
(*c*) Goal Specification
(*d*) Validation
(*e*) Field Testing

Choose the **correct** answer from the options given below:
A. (*a*), (*b*), (*c*), (*d*), (*e*)
B. (*e*), (*d*), (*a*), (*c*), (*b*)
C. (*c*), (*d*), (*a*), (*b*), (*e*)
D. (*c*), (*a*), (*d*), (*e*), (*b*)

**Directions (Q.No. 91-95):** *Read the following passage carefully and answer the questions that follow.*

What passes for knowledge is of two kinds: first knowledge of facts ; second, knowledge of the general connection between facts very closely connected with this distinction is another: there is knowledge which may be described as "mirroring", and knowledge which consists in capacity to handle Leibinitz's monads 'mirror' the universe, and in this sense know it ; but since monads never interact they cannot handle any thing external to themselves. This is the logical extreme of one conception of "knowledge". The logical extreme of the other conception is pragmatism which was first promulgated by Marx in his Thesis on Feuerbach (1845) the question whether objective truth belongs to human thinking is not a question of theory, but a practical question, the truth, i.e. the reality and power of thought must be demonstrated in practice ........ philosophers have only interpreted the world in various ways, but the real task is to alter it.

**91.** Philosophers have only interpreted the world in various ways ......... this sentence closely sounds akin to:
A. Satyamev Jayte
B. Ekam sat vipra bahudha vadanti
C. Asato ma sadgamaya
D. Jnanam param balam

**92.** In Philosophy of education, who is considered as the father of pragmatism:
A. Bertrand Russell B. Leibinitz
C. Karl Marx D. John Dewey

**93.** There is smoke on the hill, there must be the fire. This knowledge is:
A. Knowledge of facts
B. Knowledge of reality
C. Knowledge of truth
D. Knowledge of general connections

**94.** Leibinitz's monads know the universe as they ............. it:
A. Reflect B. Image
C. Mirror D. Analyse

**95.** According to the paragraph, the real aim for knowledge is to:
A. Interpret the world
B. Alter the world
C. Practice the power in world
D. Know facts and general connections

**Directions (Q.No. 96-100):** *Read the following passage carefully and answer the questions that follow.*

The Education Commission (1964-66) reviewed Indian education in its totality and gave special attention to women's education. It said, "The problem of women's education has been examined by a number of committees - the National Committee on Education of Women 1959, the committee on differentiation of curricula between boys and girls 1961, the Bhaktvatsalam Committee 1963 which studied the problem in six states where the education of girls is less developed, We fully endorse the recommendations of these committees". Inspite of this it made following recommendations (i) education of women should be regarded as a major programme for some years to come to close the existing gap between men and women in this regard (ii) special schemes should be prepared for this purpose and funds should be provided on priority basis and (iii) both the centre and in the states there should be special machinery to look after the education of girls and women.

**96.** The Education commission (1964-66) was headed by:

A. S. Radhakrishnan
B. Prof. Yashpal
C. UKRV Rao
D. Daulat Singh Kothari

**97.** Girls and women's education must be given priority for:

A. Companionable wives
B. Empowerment of women
C. Teaching daily economics of home
D. To teach own children

**98.** The National Committee on Eduaction of women was set up in 1959. It was chaired by:

A. Indira Gandhi
B. Durgabai Deshmukh
C. Hansa Mehta
D. Sarojini Naidu

**99.** The biggest hindrance in women and girls education is:

A. Lack of interest in education by women
B. Household work
C. Economic loss
D. Patriarchy and its implications

**100.** The paragraph mentions a committee on differentiation of curricula between boys and girls (1961), this committee was headed by:

A. Durgabai Deshmukh
B. Vijay Laxami Pandit
C. Hansa Mehta
D. Rajkumari Amrit Kaur

## ANSWERS

| 1 | 2 | 3 | 4 | 5 | 6 | 7 | 8 | 9 | 10 |
|---|---|---|---|---|---|---|---|---|---|
| C | B | D | B | A | C | B | D | C | A |
| **11** | **12** | **13** | **14** | **15** | **16** | **17** | **18** | **19** | **20** |
| B | A | C | A | * | A&D | D | C | B | C |
| **21** | **22** | **23** | **24** | **25** | **26** | **27** | **28** | **29** | **30** |
| C | A | D | B | C | C | D | D | B | C |
| **31** | **32** | **33** | **34** | **35** | **36** | **37** | **38** | **39** | **40** |
| A | B | A | B | B | A | D | C | D | D |
| **41** | **42** | **43** | **44** | **45** | **46** | **47** | **48** | **49** | **50** |
| A | A | A | B | A | A | B | B | B | B |
| **51** | **52** | **53** | **54** | **55** | **56** | **57** | **58** | **59** | **60** |
| B | D | A | B | * | C | A | B | C | A |
| **61** | **62** | **63** | **64** | **65** | **66** | **67** | **68** | **69** | **70** |
| C | A | C | A | D | A | C | B | B | C |
| **71** | **72** | **73** | **74** | **75** | **76** | **77** | **78** | **79** | **80** |
| B | D | C | C | D | A | C | C | C | C |
| **81** | **82** | **83** | **84** | **85** | **86** | **87** | **88** | **89** | **90** |
| C | A | A | A | B | B | D | B | D | D |
| **91** | **92** | **93** | **94** | **95** | **96** | **97** | **98** | **99** | **100** |
| B | D | D | C | B | D | B | B | D | C |

# EXPLANATORY ANSWERS

1. **(C):** Portfolio assessment is a compilation of a learner's work across a variety of tasks and activities, showcasing their progress, achievements, and abilities over time. This method is highly regarded in educational settings for its holistic approach to evaluating student performance and learning outcomes. It allows educators to assess not just the final outcomes but also the process of learning, including the development of skills, understanding, and reflection on the learning journey. Portfolio assessment is not merely for record-keeping; it serves a broader purpose by facilitating a reflective learning process for students, enabling them to identify their strengths and areas for improvement. It supports formative assessment practices by providing ongoing feedback that guides learners in their future learning endeavors. Therefore, Statement I correctly describes the nature and purpose of a portfolio, emphasizing its role beyond simple record-keeping to include reflective and formative aspects of student learning.

   Statement II asserts that the portfolio is an essential part of learner's performance. This statement is somewhat subjective and depends on the educational context and philosophy. In many modern educational frameworks, portfolios are indeed considered crucial for a comprehensive evaluation of a student's performance, offering a nuanced view that traditional testing methods may not capture. They are particularly valued in contexts that prioritize learner-centered approaches, skills development, and process-oriented learning. However, the essentiality of portfolios can vary across different educational settings and disciplines. In some contexts, portfolios may be one of several key components of assessment, alongside tests, projects, and other forms of evaluation. Therefore, while portfolios play a significant role in assessing learner performance, labeling them as universally "essential" may not fully capture the diversity of educational practices and assessment strategies. Thus, Statement II, while reflective of a progressive view on education, might be considered less universally applicable than Statement I, leading to the conclusion that Statement I is correct, but Statement II's universality is debatable.

2. **(B):** Learning Management Systems (LMS) are software applications or web-based technology designed to plan, implement, and assess a specific learning process. Moodle, Canvas, and Schoology are all well-known examples of LMSs used widely in educational institutions and corporate settings for delivering online courses, managing classroom activities, and facilitating communication between teachers and students. These platforms provide a suite of tools to create, manage, and deliver educational content, track student progress, and foster interaction and collaboration among users.

   - **Moodle:** Moodle is an open-source learning platform used by educators to create online courses, administer assessments, track student progress, and facilitate communication between instructors and learners. It offers a wide range of features such as discussion forums, wikis, quizzes, and assignment submissions. Moodle is highly customizable and widely adopted by educational institutions worldwide.

- **Canvas:** Canvas is a cloud-based learning management system (LMS) developed by Instructure. It provides a user-friendly interface for instructors to design and deliver online courses, manage course content, facilitate communication through announcements and messaging, and assess student learning through assignments, quizzes, and discussions. Canvas is known for its intuitive design and mobile-friendly interface, making it a popular choice among educators.
- **Schoology:** Schoology is a learning management system (LMS) that offers a centralized platform for course management, communication, collaboration, and assessment. It enables instructors to create and organize course materials, engage students with multimedia content, facilitate online discussions, administer assessments, and provide feedback. Schoology integrates with various educational tools and resources, making it a versatile platform for both K-12 schools and higher education institutions.

Edupuzzle, on the other hand, is an example of an educational technology tool that complements LMSs rather than being an LMS itself.

3. **(D):** The chronological arrangement of the given philosophical movements and approaches is a reflection of their historical development and the evolution of philosophical thought over time. Rationalism and Empiricism are two foundational approaches in the history of philosophy that primarily emerged in the 17th and 18th centuries, laying the groundwork for modern philosophical inquiry. Rationalism, with philosophers like Rene Descartes, posits that reason is the primary source of knowledge, independent of experience. Empiricism, championed by figures such as John Locke and David Hume, argues that knowledge comes from sensory experience. Transcendentalism, a philosophical and social movement, arose in the early to mid-19th century, mainly in the United States. It emphasized individual intuition and the inherent goodness of people and nature, reacting against the intellectualism and rationalism of the time. Analytical Philosophy, which began in the late 19th and early 20th centuries, focuses on the analysis of language and concepts, marking a significant shift in philosophical methodology with an emphasis on clarity and argumentative rigor.

   Postmodernism, emerging in the mid-20th century, challenges the foundational concepts and grand narratives of modernism, including the notions of objective truth, reason, and universal morality. It emphasizes relativism, skepticism towards grand theories, and the role of language and culture in shaping understanding.

   The chronological order (*e*), (*c*), (*b*), (*d*), (*a*) reflects the historical progression from the foundational debates about the sources of knowledge and the nature of reality (Rationalism and Empiricism), through the individualistic and nature.

4. **(B):** The Virtual University for Small States of the Commonwealth (VUSSC) was initiated by the Commonwealth of Learning (COL). The COL is an intergovernmental organization created by Commonwealth Heads of Government to promote the development and sharing of open learning and distance education knowledge, resources, and technologies. VUSSC is a network aimed at empowering small states of the Commonwealth to develop, share, and adapt flexible learning materials and programmes that are of direct relevance to their needs. The initiative was established to leverage information and communication technologies to increase access to quality education and

training resources, helping these states to expand their educational offerings and improve their human capital development. The COL's role in initiating VUSSC reflects its broader mission to support member states in harnessing the potential of distance education and technology-enhanced learning to improve educational outcomes and facilitate lifelong learning opportunities.

5. **(A):** Reactive change is characterized by responses to unanticipated problems or opportunities, rather than being part of a preconceived plan. It occurs after an external event has already taken place, requiring an organization to react in order to survive, adapt, or take advantage of new circumstances. This type of change is not initiated by the organization's desire to move towards a specific future state through strategic planning, but rather as a direct consequence of a sudden shift in the external environment. Examples of triggers for reactive change include technological advancements, competitive pressures, legal regulations, or economic downturns. Reactive changes are typically more hurried and less strategic than proactive changes, as they aim to address immediate issues or challenges. This approach can lead to short-term solutions that may not align with long-term strategic goals, making it a less desirable mode of change management. However, in situations where swift action is required, reactive change can be necessary to navigate crises or capitalize on unexpected opportunities.

6. **(C):** Statement I accurately reflects the realist perspective on curriculum design. Realists advocate for a curriculum structured around a hierarchy of disciplines, prioritizing abstract, theoretical knowledge such as mathematics and science, which are seen as representing universal truths about the natural world. According to realism, these subjects hold intrinsic value for developing the intellect and understanding reality, and they should form the foundation of education. This hierarchical approach emphasizes the importance of systematic knowledge acquisition, starting with fundamental principles and advancing to more complex ideas.

   Statement II correctly describes the pragmatist approach to curriculum development. Pragmatism, as a philosophical foundation for education, emphasizes learning through doing and the importance of experiences that are relevant to the learner's life. Pragmatist educators focus on curriculum that fosters problem-solving skills, critical thinking, and the application of knowledge in real-world contexts. The emphasis is on learning by engaging with content that is directly applicable to students' lives, encouraging active participation and reflective thinking. For pragmatists, education should prepare students for effective action in a changing world, making subjects that lend themselves to philosophical dialogue and choice-making essential components of the curriculum. This approach reflects a belief in the value of experiential learning and the development of adaptable, thoughtful individuals who can navigate the complexities of modern society.

7. **(B):** The 4P model of creativity, as proposed by Mel Rhodes in 1961, identifies four components that contribute to the creative process: Person, Process, Product, and Press (environment). These components encompass the wide range of factors that can influence creativity, from the characteristics and abilities of the individual (Person), the mechanisms or procedures of thinking and producing ideas (Process), the outcome of the creative effort (Product), to the environmental factors that can affect creative expression (Press). Peers are not

explicitly mentioned as a separate category in Rhodes's 4P model. While the interaction with peers can indeed influence creativity, within the framework of the 4P model, such influences would likely be considered part of the "Press" (environment) component, which encompasses the broader social and cultural context in which the creative activity occurs.

**8. (D):** The CIPP model for curriculum evaluation, developed by Stufflebeam, is an approach that focuses on four components: Context, Input, Process, and Product. This model is designed to guide decision-making and assessment throughout the entire program or curriculum development process.

- The statement about Tayler's curriculum model being a four-part linear model is accurate, reflecting the structured approach to curriculum design that emphasizes sequential stages in the development and evaluation process.
- The description of the CIPP model focusing on determining whether the purposes are being attained relates closely to its purpose-driven, evaluative approach, which indeed seeks to assess the effectiveness and outcomes of educational programs. However, the precise wording of this statement may not perfectly capture the full scope of the CIPP model's evaluative focus.
- The detailed explanation of the CIPP model involving steps and resources for meeting new goals and objectives aligns with the Input and Process components of the model, emphasizing the importance of planning and implementing educational programs in a way that is informed by evidence and aimed at achieving specific educational outcomes.

Therefore, option D, which includes statements (*b*) and (*d*), is correct as these statements accurately reflect aspects of the CIPP model and Tayler's curriculum model.

**9. (C):** The statements about scales of measurement correctly identify the characteristics of ratio and interval scales.

- Ratio scales are indeed characterized by the presence of an absolute zero point, which allows for the measurement of true zero quantities and the comparison of absolute magnitudes of measurements. This feature enables calculations of ratios, making statements about how many times one object is as much as another meaningful.
- Interval scales, unlike ratio scales, do not have a true zero point. They measure the difference between values, but because there's no true zero, ratios between numbers on an interval scale are not meaningful. The temperature scale (in degrees Celsius or Fahrenheit, for instance) is a common example of an interval scale where differences between points are meaningful, but having "zero" does not mean "none" of something.
- The statement that ratio scales are used in mental measurement is incorrect; mental measurements often involve ordinal or interval scales, depending on the nature of the construct being measured.
- Interval scales can indeed be used in mental measurement, as they are suitable for measuring concepts where equal intervals between scores represent equal differences in the property being measured, but without the need for an absolute zero point.

Therefore, option C, which includes statements (*a*) and (*d*), is correct, accurately reflecting the properties of ratio and interval scales.

**10. (A):** Means-end analysis is a problem-solving strategy that involves identifying the difference between the current state and the desired state, then creating and implementing a plan to reduce this difference. This heuristic approach breaks down the problem into smaller, more manageable parts, each of which represents a step towards the end goal. By continuously assessing the difference between the current state and the goal, the problem solver can make decisions about the best actions to take to move closer to the solution. This method is particularly useful in complex problem-solving situations where the path to the goal is not immediately clear, allowing for strategic planning and step-by-step progress.

**11. (B):** Longitudinal research is the most appropriate approach for studying phenomena that change over time. This type of research involves repeated observations of the same variables (e.g., individuals, groups) over a period of time, extending from days to years. By observing how specific variables change over time, researchers can identify patterns, trends, and potentially causal relationships between variables. Longitudinal studies are particularly valuable in fields such as psychology, sociology, and education, where researchers seek to understand how characteristics, attitudes, behaviors, and conditions evolve. This approach contrasts with cross-sectional research, which looks at a phenomenon at a single point in time, and experimental research, which manipulates variables to determine cause-and-effect relationships under controlled conditions.

**12. (A):** Teaching-learning processes and learning strategies in adult education are most effective when they are based on principles that recognize the unique characteristics of adult learners. These principles include:

- **Experience-based learning:** Adult education should leverage the rich experiences that adult learners bring to the educational setting, using these as a foundation for new learning.
- **Self-directed learning:** Adults tend to be more autonomous in their learning pursuits and benefit from educational approaches that allow them to take control of their learning process.
- **Readiness to learn:** Adult education should align with the immediate needs and interests of adult learners, acknowledging that adults are most ready to learn when they perceive that the knowledge or skills being taught are directly applicable to their personal or professional lives.

These principles highlight the importance of flexibility, relevance, and learner-centered approaches in adult education, contrasting sharply with the more rigid, curriculum-driven approaches typical of formal education systems designed for younger learners. Therefore, options (*a*), (*b*), and (*c*) correctly describe the foundation upon which effective adult education should be built, focusing on the learner's experience, autonomy, and situational readiness to learn.

**13. (A):** In the context of research methodology, reliability and validity are two crucial aspects of a research tool's effectiveness.

- **Consistency is necessary for reliability:** Reliability is essentially about the consistency or stability of measurements. It reflects the extent to which the same results are obtained under repeated measurements in similar conditions. For a measure to be considered reliable, it must produce consistent results when administered multiple times under the same or similar conditions. In other words, if a measurement procedure yields different results each time it is administered, it cannot be considered reliable. Consistency is crucial because it ensures that the variability in the results is due to the construct being measured and not due to random error or inconsistency in the measurement process. Therefore, consistency is indeed necessary for a measure to be reliable. Without consistency, it is difficult to have confidence in the accuracy and stability of the measurements obtained.

- **A valid test is always reliable:** Validity refers to the degree to which a test measures what it claims to measure or the accuracy of the inferences drawn from the test scores. A valid test accurately represents the construct or concept it intends to measure. It assesses the intended domain or content area in a meaningful and relevant manner. If a test is valid, it means that it is effectively capturing the construct of interest and providing accurate information about it. Now, for a test to be valid, it must also be reliable. This is because reliability is a prerequisite for validity. If a test is measuring the intended construct accurately (valid) it should consistently produce similar results when administered repeatedly under the same conditions (reliable). In other words, if a test is producing inconsistent results across different administrations or conditions, it undermines its validity because it suggests that the test scores are influenced by factors other than the construct being measured. Therefore, a valid test must also be reliable to ensure that the measurement process is consistent and trustworthy.

**14. (A):** The psychomotor domain of learning focuses on physical skill acquisition and the development of motor abilities. It encompasses activities that require physical movement, coordination, and the use of motor-skill areas.

- Assertion (A) is correct because the psychomotor domain indeed facilitates the acquisition of physical skills, allowing learners to create or perform something tangible using their bodily movements and coordination.
- Reason (R) correctly identifies the interrelation between the psychomotor domain and the other domains of learning (cognitive and affective). The cognitive domain involves understanding and knowledge acquisition, while the affective domain relates to emotions, attitudes, and values. The integration of psychomotor activities with cognitive learning enhances understanding and application of concepts, and when aligned with affective outcomes, it promotes a comprehensive learning experience that encompasses thinking, feeling, and doing.

Thus, both statements are correct, and (R) provides a valid explanation for (A) by highlighting how the development of physical skills is enriched and made more meaningful through cognitive understanding and affective engagement. This integrated approach supports the holistic development of learners, making (A) the correct option.

**16. (D):** Situation involving sychronous and asychronous communication:

- **Synchronous (a), (d) asynchronous (b), (c):** This option identifies situations involving synchronous communication as (a) talking to someone in your room and (d) participating in web conferencing.

Both of these activities involve real-time interaction where participants engage simultaneously.

Asynchronous communication is identified as (b) checking email and (c) reading an email. In both cases, communication occurs without the need for immediate responses from the other party. Checking email involves sending and receiving messages that are not time-sensitive, and reading an email does not require real-time interaction with the sender.

- **Synchronous (d), (a) asynchronous (b), (c):** This option also correctly identifies (a) talking to someone in your room and (d) participating in web conferencing as synchronous communication activities. In both situations, participants engage in real-time interaction.

  Asynchronous communication is identified as (b) checking email and (c) reading an email. Again, these activities involve communication that does not require immediate responses and can occur at different times, making them asynchronous.

**17. (D):** The correct matches between List-I (terms) and List-II (definitions) are based on their standard meanings in the context of educational and psychological measurement:

- Measurement refers to the process of obtaining a quantitative description, often by assigning numbers to objects, traits, or performances according to specific rules.
- Assessment is a broader term that can encompass both quantitative and qualitative descriptions of performance but is often associated with the gathering and interpretation of data to make decisions.
- Evaluation involves making value judgments about the quality, effectiveness, or worth of a program, practice, or performance. This process often integrates both quantitative and qualitative data.
- Norm refers to a standard or average performance against which individual performances can be compared, typically derived from the statistical analysis of a large group's performance on a standardized test.

Thus, the correct answer is (D): (*a*)-III, (*b*)-IV, (*c*)-I, (*d*)-II.

**18. (C):** The difference between the values of a "Parameter" and a "Statistic" is referred to as "Sampling Error."

- A Parameter is a value that describes a characteristic of an entire population (e.g., the mean income of all households in a country).
- A Statistic is a value that describes a characteristic of a sample drawn from a population (e.g., the mean income of households in a sample of 1,000 drawn from the population).

Sampling error arises because a sample is only a part of the population, and the statistic obtained from the sample might not perfectly represent the true parameter of the entire population. This error reflects the discrepancies that can occur due to the variability inherent in which individuals or items are included in the sample. It is not due to mistakes in calculation, but rather the natural variation observed when a sample does not perfectly represent the population from which it was drawn.

**19. (B):** Meta-cognitive knowledge is the understanding and awareness of one's own thought processes. It involves knowing about the ways we learn, process information, and the strategies that work best for us as learners. This type of knowledge includes understanding our strengths and weaknesses in learning, how we think and solve problems, and our awareness of our own learning processes. Meta-cognitive knowledge is critical for effective learning and problem-solving because it allows individuals to regulate and adapt their strategies to improve learning outcomes. It is a higher-order thinking skill that enables learners to plan, monitor, and assess their understanding and performance. Meta-cognitive knowledge goes beyond simply knowing facts or information; it involves a deep understanding of how we think, learn, and apply strategies to master new information or skills.

**20. (D):** Matching the models with the goals for which they are most applicable:

- **Anxiety Reduction: Substitution of relaxation for anxiety in social situations:** The Anxiety Reduction model aims to replace anxious responses with calm ones by teaching individuals relaxation techniques. These techniques help individuals manage their anxiety in social situations by inducing a state of relaxation. By substituting feelings of relaxation for feelings of anxiety, individuals can cope better with social interactions and reduce their overall level of anxiety.
- **Assertive Training: Direct, spontaneous expression of feeling in social situations:** Assertive Training focuses on teaching individuals to express themselves confidently and effectively in social situations. This model encourages direct and spontaneous expression of feelings, thoughts, and needs in interpersonal interactions. By learning assertiveness skills, individuals can communicate openly and honestly, express themselves authentically, and establish healthy boundaries in social interactions.
- **Managing Behaviour: Social behaviour skills:** The Managing Behaviour model focuses on identifying and modifying maladaptive social behaviors to improve social skills. This model helps individuals develop a repertoire of effective social behaviors and interpersonal skills. By learning to manage their behavior in social situations, individuals can enhance their social functioning, build positive relationships, and navigate social interactions more successfully.
- **Relaxation: Reduction of stress:** The Relaxation model aims to reduce stress and promote overall well-being by teaching individuals relaxation techniques. These techniques, such as deep breathing, progressive muscle relaxation, and meditation, help individuals achieve physical and mental relaxation. By incorporating relaxation into their daily routine, individuals can alleviate stress, tension, and anxiety, leading to improved health and reduced overall stress levels.

**21. (C):** The correct matches based on the descriptions given:

- Intellectual Academic Approach to curriculum typically focuses on the development of intellectual abilities and academic skills, not specifically advocating for areas in arts, music, literature, etc., making statement (*a*) incorrect in this context.
- Behavioural-Rational Approach to curriculum is indeed known as logical positivist, conceptual, rational-scientific, and technocratic approach. This approach emphasizes measurable outcomes and

often relies on behavioral objectives to guide curriculum development, making (*b*) correct.

- Humanistic Aesthetic Approach to curriculum is centered on personal growth, creativity, and the development of the whole person, which contrasts with a traditional encyclopedic or knowledge-oriented approach, making statement (*c*) incorrect.
- Systems Managerial Approach to curriculum focuses on the efficient organization and management of educational resources, programs, schedules, materials, and personnel, aligning with statement (*d*) and making it correct.
- Reconceptionalist Approach to curriculum does indeed take a broader perspective on education, critically examining its purposes and practices from historical, sociological, and philosophical viewpoints, making statement (*e*) correct in general but not included in the selected option based on the provided choices.

Therefore, the correct answer is C: (*b*) and (*d*) Only, as these statements accurately reflect the described approaches to curriculum development.

**22. (A):** Both statements I and II highlight fundamental aspects of education and teacher education specifically.

Statement I articulates the comprehensive nature of teacher education, emphasizing that its effectiveness is contingent upon the curriculum, its design, the methods of delivery (transaction modes), and the relevance and adequacy of these components. This holistic view recognizes that teacher education is not just about the content being taught but also how it's designed, delivered, and whether it meets the needs of prospective teachers. The curriculum in teacher education must be relevant, up-to-date, and appropriate to prepare teachers for the challenges of the classroom. This includes both theoretical knowledge and practical skills.

Statement II underscores the universality of the curriculum's importance across all educational streams. Regardless of the field of study, the curriculum serves as the backbone, providing structure, direction, and content for the educational process. It ensures that learners are exposed to essential knowledge and skills in a coherent and organized manner. This statement affirms the curriculum's foundational role in achieving educational objectives across diverse subjects and disciplines.

Given the correctness and relevance of both statements to their respective contexts, the most appropriate answer is A: Both Statement I and Statement II are correct.

**23. (D):** Discipline in educational settings often involves guidelines, rules, and measures to maintain order and facilitate a conducive learning environment. While authority, punishment, and reward are directly associated with maintaining or enforcing discipline—authority establishes the basis for rules and guidelines, punishment may be used as a consequence for violating these rules, and rewards can incentivize adherence to them—child centeredness is not directly associated with discipline in the same manner.

Child centeredness refers to educational approaches and philosophies that prioritize the interests, needs, and well-being of children above all else. This approach emphasizes the importance of considering the individual child's learning styles, interests, and developmental stages in the educational process. While a child-centered approach can influence how discipline is conceptualized and applied in educational settings, making it more empathetic and supportive rather than punitive, it is not a direct component of discipline itself. Therefore, the correct answer is D: Child Centeredness, as it is the least directly associated with the traditional concept of discipline.

24. **(B):** Experimental research is characterized by the manipulation and control of variables to determine cause-and-effect relationships. In this type of research, the researcher actively changes one or more independent variables to observe the effect on one or more dependent variables, while controlling for extraneous variables to the extent possible. This manipulation and control of variables allow for conclusions about causality, distinguishing experimental research from other types, such as quasi-experimental, ex-post facto, or mixed-method research, where such direct manipulation may not occur, or other methods are integrated into the study design. Therefore, the correct answer is B: Experimental Research, as it specifically involves the manipulation and control of variables under study.

25. **(C):** Matching the terms in List-I with their corresponding descriptions in List-II:

- Stratified random sampling is a type of probability sampling where the population is divided into different subgroups or strata, and samples are randomly selected from each stratum to ensure a representative proportion of the population is included. This method enhances the representativeness of the sample, making IV (Probability sampling) the correct match for stratified random sampling.
- Purposive sampling involves selecting samples with a specific purpose in mind, which is a characteristic of non-probability sampling methods. Samples are chosen based on the researcher's judgment and the study's objectives rather than through a random selection process, making III (Non-probability sampling) the correct match for purposive sampling.
- A representative sample accurately reflects the characteristics of the population from which it is drawn. This concept is essential in probability sampling to ensure that the sample's composition mirrors the broader population's diversity, making II (Sample) the correct match for a representative proportion of the population.
- The difference between the estimate of a parameter (a value describing a characteristic of the population) and the actual statistic (a value obtained from the sample) is known as sampling error. This error arises due to the natural variability in selecting a sample from a population, making I (Error in sampling) the correct match for the difference between the estimate of parameter and statistics.

Therefore, the correct answer is C: (*a*)-IV, (*b*)-III, (*c*)-II, (*d*)-I.

26. **(C):** Nai Talim, also known as the Basic Education system, was indeed suggested by the recommendations arising from discussions at the Wardha Education Conference in 1937, which was led by Mahatma Gandhi, not the Zakir Hussain Committee. The Zakir Hussain Committee later elaborated on the principles and implementation of this educational approach. Nai Talim emphasized learning through productive work and the integration of intellectual and manual labor, aiming to develop the whole person and prepare individuals for self-reliance in a free and cooperative society.

Statement II is incorrect because Nai Talim advocated for education to be imparted through the mother tongue, not English. It was based on the principle that education should be holistic and directly relevant to the environment in which the learner lives, contrasting sharply with the assertion that all education must be in English.

Therefore, the correct answer is C: Statement I is correct (with the clarification that Nai Talim was associated with Gandhi and further detailed by the Zakir Hussain Committee), but Statement II is incorrect.

**27. (D):** When judgments are made based on the ease with which examples come to mind, it is an example of the availability heuristic. This cognitive shortcut helps people make decisions or solve problems quickly and efficiently by relying on immediate examples that come to a person's mind. The availability of certain types of information in our memory can significantly influence the judgments and decisions we make, often leading us to overestimate the likelihood of events that are more memorable or vivid, regardless of their actual probability. This heuristic demonstrates how people's perceptions of reality can be shaped by the frequency and vividness of experiences they can easily recall, rather than by all possible information on the subject.

Therefore, the correct answer is D: Availability Heuristic.

**28. (D):** The nature of educational research encompasses several critical characteristics that ensure its effectiveness, accuracy, and relevance:

- Educational research is empirical in nature, meaning it is based on observed and measured phenomena and derives knowledge from actual experience rather than from theory or belief.
- It should be systematic, implying a structured, methodical approach to inquiry where procedures and practices are used consistently to ensure the research is comprehensive and coherent.
- Validity in educational research refers to the extent to which the research accurately reflects or assesses the specific concept that the researcher is attempting to measure. It's about the truthfulness of the research findings.
- Reliability involves the consistency of a research study or measuring test. A research instrument or procedure is considered reliable if it produces the same results under consistent conditions.

The statement that educational and physical science research findings are measured on the same scale (*c*) is not necessarily true, as the methodologies, tools, and scales used in educational research can be quite distinct from those in the physical sciences due to the differences in the nature of the phenomena being studied.

Therefore, the correct answer is D: (*a*), (*b*), (*d*), and (*e*) Only.

**29. (B):** Matching each leadership style with its characteristic:

- **Autocratic Leadership:** Leader makes decisions without input from subordinates: Autocratic leadership is characterized by a leader who maintains full control over decision-making and provides little to no opportunity for input from subordinates. The leader makes decisions independently, with minimal consultation or involvement of others.
- **Democratic Leadership:** Encourages participation and input from group members in decision making: Democratic

leadership involves a leader who actively seeks input and participation from group members in the decision-making process. The leader values and considers the opinions and perspectives of team members before making decisions, fostering a sense of inclusivity and collaboration within the group.

- **Laissez-faire Leadership:** Leader provides little guidance or structure, allowing subordinates to make most decisions: Laissez-faire leadership is characterized by a hands-off approach, where the leader provides minimal guidance or direction to subordinates. In this style, individuals are given significant autonomy to make decisions and manage their own tasks without much interference or oversight from the leader.
- **Transformational Leadership:** Inspires and motivates followers to achieve a shared vision: Transformational leadership focuses on inspiring and motivating followers to work towards a common vision or goal. Leaders employing this style inspire and empower their team members, fostering enthusiasm, commitment, and innovation. They encourage individuals to transcend their self-interests for the collective good and strive for excellence.

Therefore, the correct answer is B: (*a*)-III, (*b*)-IV, (*c*)-II, (*d*)-I.

**30. (C):** Matching the temperament types with their characteristics according to classical temperament theory:

- Choleric Type is known for being energetic, full of ambition and courage but can be easily excitable to anger, making IV the correct match.
- Melancholic Type is often described as humble, sad, or depressed, matching with II.
- Sanguine Type is characterized as active, cheerful, and optimistic, making I the correct match.
- Phlegmatic Type is known for being slow, dull, and unemotional, which matches with III.

Therefore, the correct answer is C: (*a*)-IV, (*b*)-II, (*c*)-I, (*d*)-III.

**31. (A):** Cerebral Palsy (CP) is a group of permanent movement disorders that appear in early childhood. The types of CP include:

- Diplegia refers to a type of CP where both sides of the body are affected, usually the legs more than the arms.
- Hemiplegia refers to CP affecting one side of the body (either the right or the left side).
- Ataxia is a type of CP characterized by a lack of muscle coordination during voluntary movements, such as walking or picking up objects.

Rickets is a bone condition that affects children due to vitamin D deficiency, and Orthotics are devices used to support or correct musculoskeletal deformities and anomalies; neither is a type of CP.

Therefore, the correct answer is A: (*a*), (*d*), and (*e*) Only.

**32. (B):** The University Education Commission (1948-49) is also known as the Radhakrishnan Commission, named after its chairman, Dr. Sarvepalli Radhakrishnan. The commission was established to report on Indian university education and suggest improvements and extensions that might be desirable to suit present and future needs of the country.

**33. (A):** Matching the concepts with their explanations:

- **Mainstreaming:** Placing students with disabilities in regular education classes for a portion of the day: Mainstreaming refers to the practice of placing students with disabilities in regular education classrooms alongside their non-disabled peers for at least part of the school day. This approach allows students with disabilities to participate in typical classroom activities and interact with their peers, promoting social inclusion and providing opportunities for academic and social growth.

- **Full Inclusion:** Inclusive education model where students with disabilities are fully integrated into regular classrooms: Full inclusion involves the complete integration of students with disabilities into regular education classrooms for all aspects of the school day and curriculum. In a fully inclusive setting, students with disabilities receive all instruction and support within the general education classroom, with accommodations and modifications made as needed to ensure their success.

- **Least Restrictive Environment (LRE):** A legal requirement specifying that students with disabilities should be educated in typical classrooms to the maximum extent possible: The Least Restrictive Environment (LRE) is a legal principle outlined in the Individuals with Disabilities Education Act (IDEA) that mandates students with disabilities should be educated in the least restrictive environment appropriate to their individual needs. This means that students should have the opportunity to learn alongside their non-disabled peers to the maximum extent possible, with access to the general education curriculum and appropriate support services.

- **Individualized Education Program (IEP):** A document outlining educational goals and services for a student with a disability: An Individualized Education Program (IEP) is a legal document developed for each student with a disability who is eligible for special education services. The IEP outlines the student's unique learning needs, educational goals, and the services and accommodations necessary to support their academic progress. It is designed to ensure that students with disabilities receive a free and appropriate public education tailored to their individual strengths and challenges.

Therefore, the correct answer is A: (*a*)-III, (*b*)-IV, (*c*)-I, (*d*)-II.

**34. (B):** Light, Sound, Love, and Truth are all examples of intangibles. These are concepts or experiences that cannot be physically touched or measured in the traditional sense but are very real in terms of their presence and impact on human life. Intangibles play a significant role in various aspects of life, including emotional experiences, values, and the understanding of natural phenomena. Unlike tangible items, which have a physical presence and can be directly observed with the senses, intangibles are understood through their effects, manifestations, or the feelings they evoke.

**35. (B):** The components of the affective domain as per Krathwohl et al. include:

- **Emotion:** Emotions are subjective experiences characterized by feelings such as joy, sadness, anger, fear, or surprise. They are typically brief and intense reactions to specific stimuli or situations. Emotions play a crucial role in influencing cognition, behavior, and decision-making. In the context of education, understanding and managing emotions are important for fostering social and emotional learning, empathy, and emotional regulation.

- **Feeling:** Feelings are similar to emotions but are broader and encompass a wider range of subjective experiences. Unlike emotions, feelings can be more enduring and may involve complex combinations of emotions. Feelings can include both positive and negative experiences, such as contentment, satisfaction, discomfort, or unease. They often arise from personal interpretations of situations, relationships, or events and can influence attitudes, behaviors, and overall well-being.
- **Attitude:** Attitudes refer to individuals' evaluations, beliefs, or predispositions toward objects, people, ideas, or situations. Attitudes can be positive, negative, or neutral and can influence behavior and decision-making. They are formed through experiences, socialization, and interactions with others and are relatively stable over time. Attitudes play a significant role in shaping perceptions, preferences, and responses to various stimuli and can impact learning, motivation, and interpersonal relationships.
- **Values:** Values are deeply held beliefs, principles, or standards that guide individuals' thoughts, actions, and behaviors. They reflect what individuals consider important, meaningful, or desirable and serve as guiding principles for decision-making and goal-setting. Values are shaped by cultural, familial, religious, and societal influences and can vary greatly among individuals and communities. They provide a framework for moral reasoning, ethical decision-making, and personal identity development.

Therefore, the correct answer is B: (*b*), (*c*), (*d*) and (e) Only.

**36. (A):** Both statements about counseling correctly describe its nature and purpose:

Assertion (A) emphasizes counseling as a face-to-face relationship, highlighting the personal and direct interaction between the counselor (guidance worker) and the client (person seeking guidance). This aspect of counseling is fundamental, as it establishes the basis for a therapeutic relationship that facilitates guidance and support.

Reason (R) elaborates on the nature of the counseling relationship by specifying the roles within this interaction: one individual, possessing specialized training and skills, acts as the helper, while the other, facing a problem, is in a position to benefit from this assistance. This statement underscores the professional and supportive dynamics of counseling, where expertise is applied in a personal context to address specific needs or issues..

Since Reason (R) provides a deeper understanding and justification for the face-to-face relationship described in Assertion (A), indicating why such a relationship is structured the way it is, it can be considered the correct explanation of (A). Thus, the correct answer is A: Both (A) and (R) are correct, and (R) is the correct explanation of (A).

**37. (D):** In the context of educational assessment:

- Criterion-Referenced Tests (CRTs) are designed to measure student performance against a fixed set of predetermined criteria or learning standards. They can be used in both formative and summative assessments, but their association is not limited exclusively to one type over the other. CRTs are particularly useful in formative assessment when identifying specific learning objectives students have mastered or need to focus on. Therefore, option (*a*) is relevant.

- Norm-Referenced Tests (NRTs) compare a student's performance against a norm or average taken from a larger group. While NRTs can be used in various contexts, their relation to formative or summative assessment is not inherently exclusive to one type. However, they are often associated with summative assessments to rank or grade students.
- Summative assessment is terminal in nature, which means it is typically conducted at the end of a unit, course, or educational program to evaluate cumulative student learning. This makes statement (*e*) correct.

Given the above explanations, options (*a*), (*d*), and (*e*) correctly relate to the types of assessment, with an emphasis on the adaptability of criterion-referenced tests and the terminal nature of summative assessment. Therefore, the correct answer is D: (*a*), (*d*), and (*e*) Only.

**38. (C):** Cost-benefit analysis in education evaluates the economic worth of educational programs by comparing their costs with the benefits they generate. The foundational principles include:

- **Explicit Valuation:** Assigning explicit monetary values to the costs and benefits of educational programs, even when those benefits are not directly traded in markets.
- **Consequential Evaluation:** Assessing programs based on the outcomes or consequences they produce, focusing on the tangible results that can be measured and valued.
- **Additive Accounting:** Summing up all relevant costs and benefits over time to make informed decisions about the investment in educational programs.

While "Intrinsic Value of Freedom" and "Pricing the Intangible" could be considered in broader evaluations of educational programs, they are not typically foundational principles of cost-benefit analysis, as cost-benefit analysis focuses more on tangible, measurable outcomes and the explicit valuation of those outcomes.

Therefore, the correct answer is C: (*a*), (*c*), and (*e*) Only.

**39. (D):** Statement II accurately captures the multifaceted nature of quality in education. Quality education is determined by a broad range of factors including, but not limited to, the curriculum, teaching methods, assessment practices, and learning environment. Technology and resources are important, but they represent only a part of what constitutes quality in education.

Statement I, which claims that the concept of quality in education is solely determined by the availability of modern technology and resources, is overly narrow and neglects the importance of other critical elements such as pedagogical approaches, curriculum relevance, teacher effectiveness, and the overall learning climate.

Thus, Statement II provides a more comprehensive view of quality in education, making the correct answer D: Statement I is incorrect, but Statement II is correct.

**40. (D):** Assertion (A) is incorrect because ethical leadership is highly relevant and crucial in education, including administrative roles. Ethical standards are fundamental to guiding behavior and decision-making in educational leadership, ensuring that actions and policies are conducted in a manner that is fair, just, and respectful to all stakeholders. Ethical leadership in education involves adhering to principles of integrity, equity, justice, and respect for diversity, which are essential for creating a positive educational environment and for modeling ethical behavior to students and staff.

Reason (R) is correct because it highlights the importance of ethical leadership in educational administration. Ethical leadership involves making decisions that are morally sound, promoting a culture of integrity, and serving as a role model for ethical behavior within the educational community. This is crucial for building trust, fostering a positive learning environment, and ensuring that educational practices reflect values of fairness, respect, and responsibility.

Given the contrasting nature of the statements, where (A) incorrectly dismisses the relevance of ethical standards in educational leadership and (R) correctly affirms the importance of ethical leadership, the correct answer is D: (A) is not correct but (R) is correct.

**41. (A):** Both Assertion (A) and Reason (R) are correct, and (R) provides the correct explanation for (A).

Assertion (A) states that Buddhism is considered a nastik (nastika) school of philosophy in the traditional Indian context. This is correct because Buddhism does not accept the authority of the Vedas, which is a primary criterion used in classical Indian philosophy to distinguish between astik (astika, "orthodox") and nastik (nastika, "heterodox") schools. The distinction is not necessarily about belief in God but rather about the acceptance of the Vedas as authoritative.

Reason (R) explains that the classification of astik and nastik in Indian philosophy is based on the acceptance or rejection of the Vedas' authority. Since Buddhism does not accept the Vedas as authoritative, it is classified as nastik. This explanation directly supports why Buddhism is considered a nastik school of philosophy, making it the correct explanation for (A).

Therefore, the correct answer is A: Both (A) and (R) are correct, and (R) is the correct explanation of (A).

**42. (A):** Erotetic teaching is centered around the use of questioning as a central pedagogic technique. This approach involves engaging students through questions to stimulate critical thinking, foster deeper understanding, and encourage exploration of ideas and concepts. Questioning is used to provoke student thought, prompt inquiry, and facilitate active learning and dialogue within the classroom. By employing questions effectively, educators can guide students to construct knowledge, explore possibilities, and develop their analytical and problem-solving skills. Hence, the correct answer is A: Questioning.

**43. (A):** Both Assertion (A) and Reason (R) correctly highlight the importance and rationale for using a diverse range of online assessment tools in education.

Assertion (A) suggests that teachers should use a wide variety of online assessment tools and techniques to assess children. This approach is beneficial because it allows for a more comprehensive and nuanced understanding of students' learning and progress across different areas. Different tools can capture different facets of learning, catering to diverse learning styles and intelligences.

Reason (R) supports this assertion by explaining that no single online tool can provide complete information about a child's progress and learning in all areas of development. This is because learning is a multifaceted process that involves various skills, competencies, and domains. Different tools are designed to assess different aspects of learning, such as cognitive abilities, conceptual understanding, skills application, and emotional and social development.

Given that (R) directly justifies the need for a diverse range of assessment tools as stated in (A), the correct answer is A: Both (A) and (R) are correct, and (R) is the correct explanation of (A).

**45.** **(A):** The statement "Students of high intelligence will significantly do better in their academic achievement" is an example of a Directional Hypothesis. This type of hypothesis specifies the expected direction of the relationship between variables. In this case, it predicts that higher intelligence (an independent variable) is associated with better academic achievement (a dependent variable), suggesting a positive relationship between the two. Directional hypotheses are specific and assertive, indicating not only that a relationship exists but also the nature of that relationship, which in this scenario is posited as positive.

**46.** **(A):** Mahatma Gandhi is associated with several educational and philosophical concepts that have had a significant impact on India and beyond. Among the options provided:

- Sabarmati Ashram was one of the residences of Mahatma Gandhi. It served as one of the main centers from where Gandhi led the Indian independence movement.
- Nai Talim is a principle of education formulated by Gandhi, emphasizing the importance of manual labor and the integration of intellectual and practical work.
- Craft-based education is also associated with Gandhi's educational philosophy, which focused on the development of skills and self-reliance through engaging in crafts and productive work as part of the curriculum.
- Geetanjali is a collection of poems by Rabindranath Tagore, and Santiniketan was founded by Tagore as a place of learning, which later became Visva-Bharati University. These are associated with Tagore, not Gandhi.

Therefore, the correct option is A: (*a*), (*b*), and (*e*) Only.

**47.** **(B):** Digital libraries offer several advantages over traditional libraries, thanks to their use of technology. These advantages include:

- Effective use of technology to manage and provide access to digital resources.
- Accessible anytime, anywhere, providing users with the flexibility to access information and resources beyond the physical constraints of traditional library buildings.
- Easily linked to other resources, allowing for seamless integration with external information sources and databases.
- A resource can be simultaneously used by multiple users, overcoming the limitations of physical copies that can only be accessed by one person at a time.

Difficult cataloguing is not considered an advantage of digital libraries; in fact, digital libraries aim to simplify and enhance the cataloging process through metadata and digital management systems.

Therefore, the correct option is B: (*a*), (*c*), (*d*), (*e*) Only.

**48. (B):** The theory of intelligence that consists of one factor, often referred to as a general intelligence factor or "g", is part of the Monarchic Theory of intelligence. This theory suggests that there is a single, overarching cognitive ability that underlies and supports more specific skills and abilities. The concept of "g" was proposed by Charles Spearman in the early 20th century, and it posits that individual differences in intelligence are largely due to this single dominant factor, which influences performance across a wide range of cognitive tasks. This general factor is considered universal for all the activities of an individual, affecting various specific abilities.

**50. (B):** The post-independence commissions on education in India include:

- Kothari Commission, officially known as the Education Commission (1964-66), was appointed by the Government of India to examine all aspects of the educational sector in India, suggest improvements, and formulate a national policy for education.
- National Knowledge Commission was established in 2005 by the Prime Minister of India to provide recommendations for improving the knowledge infrastructure in the country, focusing on areas such as education, research, and innovation.
- The Hunter Commission and the Calcutta University Commission are associated with the pre-independence era, focusing on different aspects of educational reform during British rule in India. Nai Talim is a principle of education proposed by Mahatma Gandhi, emphasizing craft-based, holistic education, rather than a commission.

Therefore, the correct option is B: (*a*) and (*e*) Only.

**51. (B):** Flanders' Interaction Analysis is a system developed by Ned A. Flanders for analyzing teacher-student interactions within the classroom. This method is used to observe and categorize the types of interactions that occur between teachers and students to improve teaching effectiveness. Key aspects of Flanders' Interaction Analysis include:

- Interaction indeed means the participation of both teacher and students in the process of teaching, making it a fundamental aspect of the analysis.
- It is designed to assess the effectiveness of teaching by analyzing the nature and quality of interactions, rather than through assignments directly. Thus, "Teacher evaluates the students through assignment" is not a core component of Flanders' Interaction Analysis, making option B the incorrect statement in the context of what Flanders' Interaction Analysis primarily focuses on.
- The system does help to determine whether the teacher is effective or not by providing a structured way to observe and analyze classroom interactions.
- Teacher influence through lectures, asking questions, criticizing, giving directions, etc., is part of what is observed and analyzed in Flanders' Interaction Analysis.

Given these points, the correct answer is B: "Teacher evaluates the students through assignment" is not true in the case of Flanders' Interaction Analysis, as the method is more about observing interactions than evaluating student performance through assignments.

**52. (D):** The Deschooling movement, most notably associated with Ivan Illich's critique of institutionalized education, identifies several functions of schooling that it critiques for being more about maintaining the status quo rather than fostering genuine learning or enlightenment. Among the options given:

- Custodial Care, Social Role Selection, and Indoctrination are indeed recognized as social functions of schooling critiqued by the Deschooling movement. These functions relate to the way schools act as caretakers during work hours, sort individuals into different social roles through tracking and evaluation, and indoctrinate students into specific values and norms, respectively.
- Social Change, however, is not typically critiqued as a social function of schooling by the Deschooling movement. In fact, advocates of deschooling often argue that traditional schooling systems are insufficient for promoting true social change, which is contrary to the often conservative, status-quo-preserving functions attributed to formal education systems. The Deschooling movement itself advocates for radical reforms or alternatives to traditional schooling precisely to enable more profound social change.

Therefore, the correct answer is D: Social Change, as it is not considered a critique by the Deschooling movement but rather a potential outcome they might argue is stifled by traditional schooling systems.

**53.** **(A):** The correct matches between the books (List-I) and their authors (List-II) are:

- "Pedagogy of the Oppressed" is a seminal work by Paulo Freire, which critiques traditional education systems and advocates for a more emancipatory approach to teaching and learning, making II the correct match.
- "Deschooling Society" is written by Ivan Illich, in which he argues against the institutionalization of education and promotes the idea of learning webs as alternatives to traditional schools, making IV the correct match.
- "Democracy and Education" is authored by John Dewey, where he explores the relationship between education and democratic society, emphasizing the importance of experiential learning, making I the correct match.
- "Education and Social Order" is by Bertrand Russell, not directly matched here but given the options, the closest association to education and its societal implications among the authors listed would align with the philosophical breadth of Russell's work, although "Education and Social Order" as a title is not as widely recognized in direct association with him as the other works are with their authors.

Given the matches provided in the options, the correct answer is A: (*a*)-II, (*b*)-IV, (*c*)-I, (*d*)-III.

**54.** **(B):** The International Classification of Functioning, Disability and Health (ICF) by the World Health Organization conceptualizes a person's level of functioning as a dynamic interaction between:

- **Health Conditions:** The diseases, disorders, and injuries that can affect functioning.
- **Environmental Factors:** The physical, social, and attitudinal environment in which people live and conduct their lives. These can be either facilitators or barriers to functioning.

- **Personal Factors:** The particular background of an individual's life and living situation, encompassing features of the individual that are not part of a health condition or health states.

Economic Factors and Innovative Factors are not explicitly named components of the ICF framework. The ICF focuses more on the direct interactions between health conditions, environmental contexts, and personal attributes in determining levels of functioning and disability.

Therefore, the correct answer is B: (*a*), (*b*), and (*c*) Only.

**56. (C):** Sarva Shiksha Abhiyan (SSA) is a Government of India flagship program aimed at providing universal access to education for children aged 6 to 14 years. One of the fundamental principles of SSA is the implementation of a zero rejection policy, ensuring that no child is denied admission to school due to reasons such as disabilities, poverty, gender, or social background. The zero rejection policy under SSA emphasizes inclusivity and aims to ensure that every child has the opportunity to receive quality education, regardless of their circumstances. It focuses on removing barriers to education and promoting equal access and participation for all children, including those with disabilities or from marginalized communities. By adopting the zero rejection policy, SSA strives to achieve its goal of universalizing elementary education and promoting the holistic development of every child, thereby contributing to the overall educational empowerment and social inclusion of all sections of society.

**57. (A):** In the traditional manner of writing lesson plans, there is a logical sequence that educators often follow to ensure a coherent and structured delivery of content. This sequence typically includes:

- **Specific Aims:** Stating the objectives or goals of the lesson, what the teacher aims to achieve.
- **Previous Knowledge:** Assessing what students already know related to the lesson's topic, to build upon existing knowledge.
- **Content Delivery:** The main body of the lesson where new information, concepts, or skills are introduced and taught.
- **Recapitulation:** Summarizing the lesson to reinforce learning and ensure understanding of key points.
- **Home Work:** Assigning tasks or exercises for students to complete outside of class, to practice and apply what they have learned.

These steps are designed to facilitate effective learning by preparing students for new information, engaging them in the learning process, and reinforcing their understanding.

Therefore, the correct answer is A: (*b*), (*a*), (*d*), (*e*), (*c*).

**58. (B):** The ADDIE model is a framework that guides the process of instructional design. It is an acronym for Analysis, Design, Development, Implementation, and Evaluation, representing the five phases involved in the process of creating educational and training programs. The correct sequence according to the ADDIE model is:

- **Analysis:** Identifying the instructional problem, the goals and objectives, the learners' needs, and the learning environment.

- **Design:** Specifying how to meet the instructional goals and objectives, including the creation of the instructional strategy, learning objectives, and choosing the right delivery methods.
- **Development:** Creating the instructional materials.
- **Implementation:** Putting the plan into action and delivering the instructional materials to the learners.
- **Evaluation:** Assessing the effectiveness and efficiency of the instruction and its impact on learners.

Therefore, the correct answer is B: (*b*), (*a*), (*e*), (*c*) and (*d*).

**59. (C):** The scientific procedure of problem-solving behavior typically involves the following steps in order:

- **Problem Awareness:** Recognizing that a problem exists.
- **Problem Understanding:** Comprehending the nature of the problem and its specifics.
- **Collection of Relevant Information about the Problem:** Gathering data and information related to the problem.
- **Hunch for Possible Solution:** Formulating hypotheses or potential solutions based on the information collected.
- **Verification of the Concluded Solution:** Testing the hypotheses or potential solutions to verify their validity and effectiveness in solving the problem.

Therefore, the correct answer is C: (*c*), (*b*), (*a*), (*e*), (*d*).

**60. (A):** The correct sequence of the mentioned education commissions in post-Independent India, based on their years of establishment, is:

- **The University Education Commission:** Also known as the Radhakrishnan Commission, was established in 1948-49 to report on Indian university education and suggest improvements.
- **The Secondary Education Commission:** Established in 1952-53 to examine the entire field of secondary education in India.
- **The Kothari Commission:** Officially known as the Education Commission, was established in 1964-66 to formulate a national policy for education.
- **National Commission on Teachers:** There were two National Commissions on Teachers, one formed in 1964-66 and the other in 1983-85.
- **Acharya Ramamurti Committee:** Established in 1990 as a review committee for the National Policy on Education, 1986.

Therefore, the correct answer is A: (*d*), (*a*), (*e*), (*b*), and (*c*).

**61. (C):** Curriculum change can be influenced by various factors that reflect the needs, values, and priorities of society and the educational system. Among the options given:

- **Important to Nation:** National priorities and policies can significantly influence curriculum changes. Educational content may be adjusted to reflect the nation's economic, technological, social, or political goals.
- **Socio-Cultural Context:** The social and cultural values, norms, and issues prevalent in society can drive changes in the curriculum to ensure it is relevant, inclusive, and responsive to societal changes.

While placement in jobs, religious sentiments, and availability of competent teachers can impact aspects of the educational system, the direct factors that typically lead to curriculum change on a broader scale are more aligned with national importance and socio-cultural contexts.

Therefore, the correct answer is C: (*d*) and (*e*) Only.

62. **(A):** "Assessment for learning" emphasizes the use of assessment as a tool to enhance and support learning. It involves ongoing feedback during the learning process to help students understand their strengths and areas for improvement, and to guide them in how they can improve their learning strategies and understanding. This approach is formative in nature, aiming to support the learning process rather than just measuring its outcomes or providing grades.

63. **(C):** According to the Nyaya philosophy, a classical school of Indian philosophy that emphasizes logic and epistemology, the methods of valid knowledge (pramana) include:

- **Perception:** Direct sensory observation or experience.
- **Inference:** Logical deduction based on observation and reasoning.

The other options, such as Arthapatti (presumption), Smriti (memory), and Abhava (non-existence), are not specifically listed as methods of knowing in the Nyaya philosophy. Nyaya traditionally recognizes perception and inference as primary means of acquiring valid knowledge, along with comparison (upamana) and verbal testimony (shabda) as additional pramanas.

Therefore, the correct answer is C: (*a*) and (*b*) Only.

64. **(A):** The National Council for Teacher Education (NCTE) is responsible for developing professional norms for teacher education in India. NCTE is a statutory body established by the Government of India to oversee standards, procedures, and processes in the teacher education system. Its primary role includes formulating policies and programs to ensure the maintenance of norms and standards in the teacher education system, including the accreditation of teacher education institutions and ensuring quality education for teachers.

65. **(D):** The types of planning techniques are:

- **Critical Path Method (CPM):** CPM is a project management technique used to determine the longest sequence of dependent tasks and identify the critical path, which helps in scheduling project activities efficiently.
- **Cost Benefit Analysis:** Cost Benefit Analysis is a systematic approach to evaluating the costs and benefits of a proposed project or course of action in order to determine whether it is economically feasible and to compare different options.
- **Planning, Programming, and Budgeting System (PPBS):** PPBS is a management tool used to integrate planning, programming, and budgeting processes in organizations to ensure that resources are allocated efficiently and effectively in alignment with organizational goals and priorities.
- **Managerial Quality:** Managerial Quality might encompass various techniques or practices aimed at improving managerial effectiveness and efficiency, such as leadership development, performance management, and organizational culture enhancement. It focuses on ensuring that managers possess the necessary skills, competencies, and qualities to lead and manage effectively.

Therefore, the correct answer is D: (*a*), (*b*), (*c*) and (*d*) Only.

**66. (A):** Jean-Jacques Rousseau, a Genevan philosopher, writer, and composer of the 18th century, is associated with several key ideas in educational and political philosophy:

- **Emile:** A treatise on the nature of education and on the nature of man. Rousseau emphasizes education that fosters rather than restricts children's natural instincts and learning through experience.
- **Social Contract:** Rousseau's work on political philosophy in which he theorizes about the best way to establish a political community in the face of the problems of commercial society, which he had already identified in his discourse on inequality.
- **Back to Nature:** This is a theme that runs through Rousseau's work, reflecting his belief that society corrupts the innate goodness of man and that one should look to nature as a source of inspiration and morality.

"Man is born as Slave" misrepresents Rousseau's famous claim that "Man is born free, and everywhere he is in chains," suggesting instead that society corrupts man's natural freedom.

"Knowledge is based on reason only" does not accurately represent Rousseau's views on education and knowledge, which emphasize emotion and the development of the whole person as much as rationality.

Therefore, the correct answer is A: (*a*), (*b*) and (*c*) Only.

**67. (C):** The statement about being caught in narratives and metanarratives and the recommendation to be incredulous towards metanarratives is closely associated with Postmodernism. Postmodernist thinkers argue that metanarratives (large, overarching stories or perspectives that claim to explain large aspects of human experience and history) are often tools of power and domination and cannot objectively explain everything they claim to. Instead, postmodernism encourages skepticism towards these grand narratives, advocating for an appreciation of smaller, localized, or individual narratives. This view reflects a postmodernist skepticism towards universal truths and grand theories, emphasizing the complexity, relativity, and constructed nature of knowledge.

**68. (B):** A Six Sigma process is one in which 99.99966% of the products manufactured are statistically expected to be free of defects. This translates to a goal of having no more than 3.4 defects per million opportunities. Six Sigma is a set of techniques and tools for process improvement, developed by Motorola in 1986, and it aims for near-perfection in manufacturing or business processes.

**69. (B):** The sequence of steps followed in educational research typically begins with the identification of a gap in knowledge or a specific problem that needs investigation. The correct order is:

- **Selection of research problem:** Identifying and defining the issue or area that the research will address.
- **Formulation of research question:** Developing specific questions that the research aims to answer, based on the selected problem.
- **Selection of research method:** Deciding on the methodology or approach to use in answering the research questions.
- **Data collection and analysis:** Gathering and analyzing data to answer the research questions.

- **Reporting the results:** Summarizing the findings and explaining their implications in a report or publication.

Therefore, the correct sequence, starting with the selection of the research problem and ending with reporting the results, is B: (*a*), (*c*), (*b*), (*d*), (*e*).

**70. (C):** Edward L. Thorndike, an American psychologist, formulated several primary laws of learning, such as the Law of Effect, the Law of Readiness, and the Law of Exercise, which are considered foundational in understanding the learning process. These laws describe how individuals learn from the consequences of their actions, the importance of being mentally ready to learn, and how practice strengthens learning, respectively.

The Principle of Partial Activity, however, is not commonly listed among Thorndike's primary laws of learning. Instead, it appears to be more closely related to concepts within his overall framework of connectionism and learning theories but is not identified as one of the "secondary laws of learning" directly attributed to Thorndike in a widely recognized manner. Among the options provided, none are traditionally recognized as Thorndike's "secondary laws of learning" in the classical sense; his most emphasized laws are the primary ones mentioned above. In the context of Thorndike's work, detailed exploration of his secondary principles or laws would delve into more nuanced aspects of his theories, such as the law of effect's emphasis on the strengthening or weakening of connections based on consequences.

Given the options listed and considering Thorndike's most well-documented contributions to learning theory, it's essential to clarify that the primary laws are the most recognized. If considering secondary principles or nuances in Thorndike's theories, a thorough review of his work would be necessary for precise attribution.

**71. (B):** The National Council for Teacher Education (NCTE) is the apex body responsible for regulating and overseeing teacher education programs in India. This includes integrated teacher education programs. NCTE sets the standards and norms for teacher education to ensure quality education for teachers across the country.

**72. (D):** In Indian philosophy, "Astika" schools are those which accept the authority of the Vedas and "Nastika" schools are those which reject the authority of the Vedas. Among the options given:

- Buddhism and Jainism are considered Nastika schools because they do not accept the authority of the Vedas.
- Charvak is also a Nastika school, known for its materialistic and skeptical philosophy.
- Samkhya and Nyaya are Astika schools, as they accept the authority of the Vedas and are part of the orthodox Hindu philosophy.

Therefore, the correct answer is D: (*c*) and (*d*) Only, as both Samkhya and Nyaya are considered Astika schools.

**73. (C):** Assistive Technologies are the most important for inclusive teaching and learning environments. These technologies are designed to support students with disabilities and ensure that they can participate fully in educational activities alongside their peers. Assistive technologies can include software, devices, and equipment that help overcome learning barriers. This might involve tools for visual or hearing impairments, mobility aids, specialized computer software for learning disabilities, and more. By leveraging assistive technologies, educators can create a more accessible and equitable learning environment for all students, regardless of their physical or cognitive abilities.

**74.** **(C):** Anderson and Krathwohl's revision of Bloom's Taxonomy of Cognitive Domain (2001) organizes cognitive learning objectives in a hierarchy, starting from basic to more complex levels of thinking. The correct sequence, according to their revised taxonomy, is:

- **Remembering:** Recalling or recognizing information.
- **Understanding:** Comprehending the meaning of the information.
- **Applying:** Using information in new situations.
- **Analyzing:** Breaking information into parts to explore understandings and relationships.
- **Evaluating:** Making judgments based on criteria and standards.

Therefore, the correct sequence according to Anderson and Krathwohl's taxonomy is (*a*), (*b*), (*d*), (*c*), (*e*).

**76.** **(A):** The Programme of Action on the National Policy on Education (NPE), 1986, suggested several measures to improve and reform various aspects of the Indian education system, including teacher education. It recommended conferring autonomous status to the State Councils of Educational Research and Training (SCERTs), the National Council for Teacher Education (NCTE), and the establishment of State Boards of Teacher Education to oversee and improve the quality of teacher education programs. These recommendations were aimed at decentralizing education governance and enhancing the quality and effectiveness of teacher education through greater autonomy and focused oversight.

**77.** **(C):** Robert Gagne's classification of learning outcomes includes several categories, such as:

- **Stimulus-Response Learning:** Learning to respond to a given stimulus in a specific way.
- **Chain Learning:** Learning sequences of actions or events.
- **Verbal Associate Learning:** Learning verbal connections between concepts or terms.

However, **Ideational Learning** is not listed among Gagne's specifically defined categories of learning outcomes. Gagne identified several types of learning, including signal learning, stimulus-response learning, chaining, verbal association, discrimination learning, concept learning, rule learning, and problem-solving, but "Ideational Learning" as a category is not part of Gagne's taxonomy.

**78.** **(C):** Reflective journals as an assessment tool in the pedagogy of education offer numerous benefits, including:

- Allowing students to articulate and explore their learning experiences, demonstrating complex learning outcomes like critical thinking.
- Enabling students to show their ability to analyze, be creative, and introduce original ideas through their reflections.
- Serving as a powerful learning process in itself, where the act of reflection fosters deeper understanding and personal growth in learners.

However, Students may not fully understand what is required of them in reflective writing, represents a challenge rather than a benefit of using reflective journals as an assessment tool. This challenge underscores the need for clear guidance and support from educators in helping students understand how to engage effectively with reflective writing tasks.

Therefore, the correct answer is C: Students may not fully understand what is required of them in reflective writing.

**79. (C):** Carl Rogers, a pivotal figure in the development of psychotherapy and humanistic psychology, introduced the concept of non-directive counseling, now more commonly known as client-centered or person-centered therapy. This approach is characterized by its focus on the client's ability to lead the process of therapy while the counselor adopts a non-directive role, facilitating an environment where the client can explore their feelings and thoughts in a supportive, non-judgmental space. Unlike directive counseling, where the therapist might guide or advise the client towards specific outcomes, or other forms of specialized counseling like rehabilitation, substance abuse, and educational counseling, non-directive counseling is grounded in the belief in the individual's innate capacity for self-healing and growth. The therapist in this approach actively listens and reflects the client's own words back to them, providing empathy and unconditional positive regard. This creates a safe space for the client to gain clarity, make decisions, and pursue change at their own pace. Rogers' theory posits that everyone has the potential for personal growth and change, given the right conditions, and this belief is at the heart of non-directive counseling. This approach has been influential in shaping the therapeutic landscape, emphasizing the client's perspective, feelings, and inherent self-worth, diverging from more prescriptive or advice-giving methods of counseling.

**80. (C):** The Taylor Postcard Frame serves as an essential tool in braille transcription, specifically designed to emboss small character Braille onto paper, often in a postcard-sized format. Its functionality lies in ensuring precise alignment and spacing of braille cells on one side of the paper, guaranteeing accuracy and readability for individuals with visual impairments. By securely holding the paper in place and providing guidance for the placement of braille dots, the frame assists transcribers in producing clear and legible tactile information. This aids in creating various materials, including postcards, notes, or small informational documents, in braille, thereby enhancing accessibility and communication opportunities for individuals who depend on tactile reading methods for information access and communication. The Taylor Postcard Frame serves as an essential tool in braille transcription, specifically designed to emboss small character Braille onto paper, often in a postcard-sized format. Its functionality lies in ensuring precise alignment and spacing of braille cells on one side of the paper, guaranteeing accuracy and readability for individuals with visual impairments. By securely holding the paper in place and providing guidance for the placement of braille dots, the frame assists transcribers in producing clear and legible tactile information. This aids in creating various materials, including postcards, notes, or small informational documents, in braille, thereby enhancing accessibility and communication opportunities for individuals who depend on tactile reading methods for information access and communication.

**81. (C):** Screening measures that can assist in the diagnosis of Autism Spectrum Disorder (ASD) include:

- **Development Behaviour Checklist (DBC):** The Development Behaviour Checklist (DBC) is a screening tool used to assess behavioral and emotional problems in children and adolescents. While it is not specific to autism, it can help identify behavioral patterns or difficulties that may be indicative of autism spectrum disorder (ASD). The DBC assesses a range of behavioral domains, including disruptive behavior, anxiety, social relating, and self-absorbed behavior, which are relevant for evaluating developmental concerns such as ASD.
- **Self Confidence Checklist:** The Self Confidence Checklist is not typically used as a screening measure for Autism Spectrum Disorder (ASD). Instead, it assesses an individual's self-confidence level and may be used in various contexts, such as educational or counseling settings, to evaluate self-esteem and self-perception. As it is not specific to ASD symptoms or behaviors, it is not considered a relevant screening tool for diagnosing ASD.
- **Psycho Educational Profile Revised (PEP - R):** The Psycho Educational Profile Revised (PEP-R) is a diagnostic assessment tool specifically designed to evaluate the developmental skills and behaviors of individuals with autism spectrum disorder (ASD). It assesses various domains, including cognitive abilities, language and communication skills, social interaction, and adaptive behavior. The PEP-R provides valuable information for diagnosing ASD and developing appropriate interventions and educational programs tailored to the individual's needs.

Therefore, the correct answer is C: (*b*), (*c*) and (*d*) Only.

**82. (A):** The chronological order of the listed commissions and reports related to education in India can be determined by looking at the years they were established or published. The University Education Commission, also known as the Radhakrishnan Commission, was established first in 1948-49 to report on Indian university education and suggest improvements. Following this, the Secondary Education Commission, often referred to as the Mudaliar Commission, was set up in 1952-53 to examine the country's secondary education system and recommend changes. The National Education Commission, also known as the Kothari Commission, was formed in 1964-66 to develop a national system of education that would increase the quality of education in India. The chronology of the Acharya Ramamurti Committee and the Birla Ambani Report is more nuanced; however, for the purpose of this answer and based on the available options, it seems there may be some confusion with these names as they are not as widely recognized in the standard list of educational commissions and reports in India. Given the options, the Acharya Ramamurti Committee, which could be referring to a committee on educational reforms in the late 20th century, and the "Birla Ambani Report," which does not directly correlate to a well-known education commission or report, might not fit neatly into this chronological order. Therefore, the most accurate chronological order given the first three significant and identifiable commissions would be (*a*) University Education Commission, (*b*) Secondary Education Commission, (*d*) National

Education Commission, with (*c*) and (*e*) being more difficult to place accurately without specific years or more commonly recognized names in the context of Indian education reforms.

**83. (A):** Both statements provided are correct within the context of psychometric principles regarding tests and measurements. Statement I, "All valid tests are reliable but all reliable tests are not valid," addresses the concepts of validity and reliability in psychological testing. Validity refers to whether a test measures what it is supposed to measure, while reliability refers to the consistency of the test results. A test must be reliable to be valid because if it produces inconsistent results, it cannot accurately measure what it claims to measure. However, a test can be reliable without being valid; it might consistently measure something, but not necessarily what it is intended to measure. Thus, the statement correctly encapsulates the relationship between validity and reliability.

Statement II, "Split-half method is used to determine reliability of a test," is also correct. The split-half method is a common technique used in psychometrics to assess the internal consistency reliability of a test. By dividing the test into two parts (e.g., even and odd items) and comparing the scores from these two halves, one can evaluate the consistency of the test results. If the two halves of the test yield similar results, the test is considered to have high internal consistency, indicating reliability. This method is especially useful for tests that are designed to measure a single construct or ability, ensuring that all parts of the test contribute equally to what is being measured.

**84. (A):** When examining the options provided in relation to education, all except for "(*a*) Direct benefit" can be directly related to educational objectives, outcomes, or processes. Education is widely recognized for its direct and indirect benefits, investments in people, contributions to human resource development, and reliance on public funding.

- Direct benefits of education include measurable outcomes such as academic achievement, qualifications obtained, and specific skills or knowledge gained. These benefits are directly related to the individual's participation in educational programs.
- Indirect benefits might include broader socio-economic improvements, increased civic engagement, and improved health outcomes, which are less directly measurable but significant outcomes of educational investment.
- Investment in people, or human capital theory, posits that education increases the productivity and efficiency of individuals, which is a fundamental aspect of educational rationale.
- Human Resource development involves developing and enhancing the skills and knowledge of people within an organization or society, in which education plays a critical role.
- Public funding for education is a common method for supporting educational systems, ensuring access to education for a broad segment of the population.

Given this context, direct benefits are intrinsically related to education as they represent the immediate outcomes of educational processes. Therefore, stating that direct benefits are not related to education would be incorrect. All other options listed are aspects or consequences of educational systems and processes.

**85. (B):** Disability can be understood as a disturbance at a personal level that affects an individual's ability to perform certain activities in a manner or within a range considered normal for a human being. It encompasses a wide range of conditions, including physical, mental, intellectual, or sensory impairments. These conditions can interact with various barriers in the environment, hindering full and effective participation in society on an equal basis with others. While disturbances in perception, social functions, and medical conditions can all be aspects or consequences of disabilities, the essence of disability is its impact on the individual at a personal level. It's the personal experience of these disturbances and the barriers they present in everyday activities and societal participation that define the concept of disability. This personal-level disturbance can manifest in challenges with mobility, communication, learning, self-care, and social integration, requiring a nuanced understanding and approach to support, accommodation, and inclusion.

**86. (B):** Important approaches to cost analysis in education include Cost Benefit, Cost Feasibility, and Cost Utility.

- Cost Benefit analysis in education evaluates the economic return on investment in education, comparing the costs of educational programs or policies against the benefits they generate, often expressed in monetary terms. This approach helps policymakers and educators understand the long-term value of educational investments to society.
- Cost Feasibility analysis focuses on assessing whether the planned educational programs or interventions are financially viable and sustainable given the available resources. It involves a detailed examination of the costs associated with implementing and maintaining these programs against the available budget or funding.
- Cost Utility analysis is a method used to assess the value of educational interventions in terms of their effectiveness and the utility or satisfaction derived from them, often considering various outcomes beyond just financial gains, such as improvements in educational quality or accessibility.

The term "Cost Empire" does not correspond to a recognized approach in educational cost analysis, and "Cost Counting" seems to be a misinterpretation or misnomer of cost accounting or simply tallying costs, which on its own does not constitute a comprehensive approach to analyzing costs in the context mentioned. Therefore, the most accurate options related to the approaches of cost analysis in education are Cost Benefit, Cost Feasibility, and Cost Utility.

**87. (D):** Reflective Level Teaching is the most advanced among the options provided, aiming not only for students to remember information (Memory Level Teaching), understand concepts (Understanding Level Teaching), or apply what they have learned to solve problems (Application Level Teaching) but also to engage in a deeper level of thinking that involves reflection on the learning process itself. Reflective Level Teaching encourages students to think critically about the material, question assumptions, make connections between new and existing knowledge, and reflect on their own understanding and learning processes. This level of teaching promotes a higher order of cognitive skills, including analysis, synthesis, and evaluation, enabling students to not just learn and apply information but to also understand and appreciate the underlying principles, critically evaluate their knowledge and beliefs, and develop the ability to learn how to learn. Reflective Level Teaching fosters autonomy in learning, encouraging students to become self-directed learners who can adapt their knowledge to new situations, engage in lifelong learning, and contribute meaningfully to their fields of study or professional practices.

**89. (D):** Creativity emphasizes more on Divergent Thinking. Divergent thinking is a thought process or method used to generate creative ideas by exploring many possible solutions. It involves thinking in a way that is not necessarily linear but rather branching out to various directions, allowing for the generation of multiple solutions for a given problem. Unlike convergent thinking, which aims at finding a single, correct answer to a problem, divergent thinking encourages the exploration of many different possibilities and perspectives. This type of thinking is essential for creativity, as it fosters the ability to see connections between seemingly unrelated concepts, come up with original ideas, and approach problems in innovative ways. Divergent thinking is characterized by a free-flowing, spontaneous generation of ideas, often facilitated by brainstorming sessions, and is crucial in creative fields where innovation and originality are valued.

**90. (D):** The correct sequence of stages of curriculum evaluation involves the following steps:

- **Goal Specification:** The first step in curriculum evaluation is to clearly specify the goals and objectives of the curriculum. This involves defining what the curriculum is intended to achieve in terms of student learning outcomes, skills, and knowledge.
- **Planning:** Once the goals are specified, the next step involves planning the curriculum, including deciding on the content, teaching methodologies, resources required, and assessment strategies.
- **Validation:** This stage involves evaluating the curriculum design to ensure it is capable of achieving its goals. Validation may involve expert review, pilot testing, and adjustments based on feedback.
- **Field Testing:** After validation, the curriculum is field-tested on a small scale to assess its effectiveness in a real-world educational setting. This stage allows for practical evaluation and identification of any issues that need to be addressed.
- **Regular Monitoring:** The final stage involves ongoing monitoring of the curriculum as it is fully implemented. This includes regular assessment of student performance, feedback collection from teachers and students, and making necessary adjustments to ensure the curriculum remains relevant and effective.

Therefore, correct sequence is (*c*), (*a*), (*d*), (*e*), (*b*).

**91. (B):** The sentence "Philosophers have only interpreted the world in various ways..." closely aligns with the Sanskrit aphorism "Ekam sat vipra bahudha vadanti," which translates to "Truth is one, sages call it by various names." This aphorism from the Rig Veda emphasizes the idea that the ultimate truth or reality is one, but it can be interpreted and described in many different ways by wise people or philosophers. The sentence from the passage resonates with this idea by suggesting that philosophers have offered various interpretations of the world, akin to the way sages have described the one truth in many ways. This comparison highlights the diversity of philosophical thought and the understanding that while interpretations may vary, they all attempt to grapple with the underlying reality or truth of the world.

**92. (D):** In the Philosophy of education, John Dewey is considered the father of pragmatism. Although Karl Marx's ideas influenced pragmatic thought, especially with his emphasis on practice and the material conditions of life shaping consciousness, it is John Dewey who is most prominently associated with the development and articulation of pragmatism as a philosophical school of thought. Dewey's pragmatism focused on the idea that the value of ideas is determined by their practical effects and applications, emphasizing experience, experimentation, and the role of education in fostering democratic citizenship. His work profoundly influenced educational theory and practice, advocating for experiential learning and the development of critical thinking skills.

**93. (D):** The statement "There is smoke on the hill, there must be fire" exemplifies knowledge of general connections. This type of knowledge involves understanding the causal or correlational relationships between phenomena. In this case, the observation of smoke leads to the inference of fire based on the general connection that smoke typically indicates the presence of fire. This is not merely knowledge of specific facts (the presence of smoke) but an application of a broader understanding of how facts are generally connected (smoke usually comes from fire).

**94. (C):** According to Leibniz, monads "mirror" the universe. Leibniz's monads are metaphysical entities that reflect the universe in a pre-established harmony without physically interacting with each other. Each monad is a unique, indivisible entity that contains within it a reflection of the entire cosmos. This mirroring concept is fundamental to understanding Leibniz's philosophy, where monads serve as the basic building blocks of reality, each representing a microcosm of the universe through their internal states.

**95. (B):** The passage suggests that the real aim for knowledge is to "alter the world." This idea reflects a pragmatic view of knowledge, emphasizing that the true test of ideas, theories, and thinking lies in their ability to effect change in the practical world. It critiques the notion that philosophy should only interpret or understand the world, arguing instead that the purpose of engaging with knowledge and thought should be to make tangible improvements and transformations in the world. This perspective aligns with Marxist and pragmatic philosophies, which stress the importance of applying knowledge to address and solve real-world problems.

**96. (D):** The Education Commission (1964-66), also known as the Kothari Commission, was headed by Dr. Daulat Singh Kothari. This commission was pivotal in shaping the direction of education in India, focusing on a comprehensive review of the educational system and making significant recommendations for its improvement, including special attention to women's education.

**97. (B):** Girls and women's education must be given priority for the empowerment of women. Empowering women through education enables them to gain access to opportunities, make informed decisions about their lives, contribute to economic growth, and participate more fully in society. Education is a fundamental tool for achieving gender equality and improving the status of women in society.

**98. (B):** The National Committee on Education of Women, set up in 1959, was chaired by Durgabai Deshmukh. This committee played a crucial role in evaluating the state of women's education in India and recommending measures to improve and expand educational opportunities for women.

**99. (D):** The biggest hindrance in women and girls' education is patriarchy and its implications. Patriarchal structures and attitudes create barriers to education for women and girls, including gender biases, societal norms that prioritize men's education, and restrictions on women's mobility and autonomy. These challenges can limit access to education and contribute to disparities between men and women in educational attainment.

**100. (C):** The committee on differentiation of curricula between boys and girls (1961), chaired by Hansa Mehta, was established to address the disparities in educational content and approaches based on gender in Indian education. Its primary focus was to examine how educational materials and methods could better cater to the needs and potentials of both boys and girls, ensuring equal opportunities and outcomes in education. Through its work, the committee aimed to create more inclusie and gender-sensitive curricula, fostering an environment where education could empower all students regardless of gender, thus contributing to broader societal progress and gender equality.

# UGC-NET/SLET
# EDUCATION

# UNIT-I

★ *Relationship of Education and Philosophy*
★ *Western Philosophies and Education*
★ *Western Philosophers and Education*
★ *Indian Philosophies and Education*
★ *Indian Philosophers and Education*
★ *Logical Empiricism and Logical Positivism*

# Relationship of Education and Philosophy

## INTRODUCTION

Education and philosophy are so inseparably linked that all the educationists were philosophers and vice versa. For this very reason Socrates (470–399 BC) calls himself a philosopher. If we go into detail about the nature and functions of education, it looks as if putting the ideas of philosophers into practice is nothing but education. What the prophets and exponents of religions would have thought better for the common people, their disciples might have given these ideas into practical shape. How these thoughts touched the minds of these prophets is a question yet to be debated, but one thing is very clear that there have always been such people who made it incumbent on themselves to think persistently what to do and what not to do and why it is to be done in a particular way. By answering the question how to do, education makes the process of life complete and meaningful.

So, before coming to discuss any point of education it is better to know what is philosophy and how and why it is related to education.

## MEANING OF PHILOSOPHY

The word philosophy has been derived from two Latin words *Philos* and *Sofia*. Philos means love and *Sofia* means wisdom or knowledge. Thus philosophy means love for wisdom. The person who has love for wisdom or truth may be called as philosopher provided that this love is in active form. If this love for wisdom is in active form, the person will be restless in search of truth and facts behind any phenomenon.

Plato in his book **Republic** says, "He who has a taste for every sort of knowledge and who is curious to learn and is never satisfied may be termed as philosopher."

Practical meaning of philosophy is somewhat different from this etymological meaning. Man undergoes a lot of experiences in his life from birth to death coupled with variety of problems related to knowledge, reality and cosmos. In order to solve these problems he ponders over them rationally by utilizing his experiences. All these exercises enhance his wisdom. In this way every man is a philosopher at his own level but technically philosophers are designated only those people who can guide others by influencing their ideas and actions with their own.

Indian concept of philosophy *(Darshan)* is rather different. It has been derived from the Sanskrit word "Drishti" meaning "to see". This perception is not physical. It is rather metaphysical or intutional in nature. It leads a man to the realization of truth (Atman). Thus truth is the direct realization of self. Intution of self (Atman) is nothing but liberation from the bond of this mundane life (Moksha). Thus, Darshan is actually conducive to achieving Moksha.

In the words of **Max Muller,** "Philosophy was recommended in India not for the sake of knowledge but for the highest purpose to discover and follow the way to the other shore (heaven) across the troubled ocean of *Sansar* (world)."

### Definitions of Philosophy

- **Plato (428-348 BC) :** Knowledge of eternal nature of things which is in fact knowledge of true nature of different things is philosophy.
- **Aristotle (384-322 BC) :** Philosophy is a science which discovers the real nature of supernatural things.
- **Henderson :** Philosophy is an attempt to conceive and present an inclusive and systematic view of the universe and its main place in it....It is a

rigorous, disciplined and guarded analysis of some most difficult problems which man has ever faced.

- **S. Radhakrishnan :** Darshan is a logical exposition of the nature of reality.
- **Bertrand Russell :** Philosophy like other studies aims primarily at knowledge.

Thus philosophy can be defined practically in the following words:

"Rational approach of answering unsettled questions and redefining various entities of the universe in its own way is philosophy. Methods to be followed for this purpose are thinking, intution and experiences. And aim of all these exercises is the enhancement of knowledge."

It is clear from the above definitions that all the sciences that have taken birth so far originated into philosophy. Philosophy determines not only the direction of knowledge but it also establishes the aims of education (life) in a particular society. Aims of education vary as much as there is variation in the individual and socio-political philosophy of the people. Thus, task of a philosopher or educationist never comes to an end. Philosophy is actually the base of all educational thoughts.

### Nature or Origin of Philosophy

Several views regarding the origin of philosophy are given below:

1. According to Plato, philosophy finds its origin in wonder or curiosity created in the mind of man. (this curiosity motivates him to think in diverse ways.)
2. According to the exponent of modern western philosophy, Descartes (1596-1650 AD), philosophy originated from the feeling of skepticism in the mind of man. (Man tries to discover proof to confirm his doubts.)
3. Third view is that human mind is restless. It is always active in the search of truth or reality. When man faces miseries or difficulties in this world, he is shaken and he tries to find the ways and means to solve these problems. Thus, all the scientists and scholars of social sciences are philosophers first.
4. Philosophy finds its origin into religion. God would have never left the man without guidance when he was created. Thus guided principles—what is right or wrong, what is proper or improper, what is heaven or hell and so on which can lead a man to a right direction is philosophy.

## SCOPE OF PHILOSOPHY

Till the medieval period only persons of highest learning and great scholars were known as philosophers. Even today this subject is considered the highest discipline of knowledge. But modern western philosophy changed this viewpoint by relating it to real worldly life. Now philosophy solves the real problems of life first then it touches the metaphysical world. Thus, scope of philosophy has increased manifold. Its three major categories (branches) are given below:

### 1. Metaphysics (Belief about values):

The thing which is beyond our physical reach is metaphysics. It has five parts-

(a) ***Theology*** : It deals with nature and existence of God, his wishes and commands, his power and his relation to the universe, especially to humans.

(b) ***Concept of Soul*** : Here we study the purpose and role of living organisms, existence of soul and its relation to the mortal body.

(c) ***Science of Universe*** : It deals with the origin and end of the universe, its mortal and immortal elements and theories explaining to these.

(d) ***Science of Creation*** : How this universe has been created and how will it come to an end etc, are discussed here.

(e) ***Cosmology*** : It deals with the creation of cosmos and other living and non living things.

### 2. Epistemology (Belief about knowledge):

Here we study about human intelligence and his capacity to acquire knowledge, nature and verification of evidence and knowledge and various methods of knowledge acquisition.

### 3. Axiology (Belief about reality):

It covers different types of values and ideals of life. Three things are included in this branch of philosophy.

(a) ***Logic*** : It determines real nature of a thing and conclusion is drawn through inductive and deductive methods. Imagination and reasoning dominate in this method of enquiry.

**(b)** ***Ethics*** **:** It is concerned with the conduct of man in the society by demarcating a line between good and bad. The Question of why a man should behave in a particular manner is answered here.

**(c)** ***Aesthetics*** **:** It is concerned with the problems of beauty. On what criteria and standard beauty or ugliness is judged is the main area of study here.

Thus we see that the scope of philosophy is the entire sphere of life ranging from this world to the other world. That is why every discipline of knowledge takes the help of philosophical thoughts and problems of life studied systematically. Whenever we try to define any concept related to any subject of study, we become a philosopher.

## BRIEF CHRONOLOGY OF WESTERN PHILOSOPHICAL THOUGHTS

### Early Ancient Period

The period before Socrates is called early ancient period. Important philosophers of this period are as follows:

- **Thales (6th Cen BC) :** He might be considered as the father of ancient western philosophy. According to him, the world has originated from water.
- **Pythagoras (572-497 BC) :** He tried to synthesise mathematics with divine knowledge (religion). He divided the society into several classes on the basis of their mental capacities and jobs that they do.
- **Heraclitus (536-470 BC) :** He opined that the world had originated from fire. He also said that everything in the universe goes on changing so rapidly and orderly that we cannot plung into the same water again.
- **Protagorus (480-410 BC) :** His philosophy is pragmatic in nature. According to him, man is the measure of all things.

### Later Ancient Period

Great thinkers like Socrates, Plato, Aristotle etc. dominated the scene during this period. Their basic ideas about the universe are given below:

- **Socrates (470-399 BC) :** He expressed his ideas in the form of a teacher taught dialogue and developed a unique method—questioning method of teaching. He believed that knowledge that already exists in soul is real and it is determined by dialogue and discourses.
- **Plato (428-348 BC) :** He has explained the relationship between man and the universe very systematically.
- **Aristotle :** He has mostly elaborated the ideas of his great teacher Plato but in the light of natural and universal laws.

### Medieval Period

This is the period of religious (Christian) philosophy. Important philosophers of this period are as follows-

- **Augustine (354-430 AD) :** He was the first main Christian philosopher who believed that only God is real and he is the creater of all elements of the universe.
- **Thomas Acquinas (1225-1274) :** He also had firm belief in Christianity. He believed that fundamentals of all religions are true. The concepts of vices and virtues are also real. Man should save himself from sin by following the tenets of religion. .

### Modern period

If the history of philosophy, modern period believed to be started systematically in the 15th century. It is the period that has given us many new philosophical thoughts like Naturalism, Pragmatism and Existentialism. Chief contributors of the period are summarized below:

- **Erasmas (1466-1536) :** Modern period of philosophy begins with this Dutch writer whose main topic of discussion was marriage. In his book **Philosophy of Marriage,** he tried to prove that system of marriage is a foolish proposition. He even attacked the religion recognizing this system.
- **Descartes (1596-1650) :** He gave for the first time a scientific base to the subject philosophy as he was a well known scientist and mathematician. Thus he disbelieved everything that could not be proved by scientific enquiry. He believed that matter and mind are the two essential elements for the knowledge of the universe. Thus, he propounded the *Theory of Dualism.*

- **John Locke (1632-1704) :** He is an empiricist. His philosophical discourse is restricted to matter only. According to him learning is possible only through sensory experiences.
- **Berkeley (1685-1753) :** According to him, whatever is visible is universe. In this way all physical aspects of the universe are reducible to mental phenomena i.e., we can think of whatever is visible.
- **Rousseau (1671-1741) :** He is the chief propounder of Naturalism. He says that nature plays an exquisite role in manifesting reality and knowledge.
- **Kant (1724-1804) :** He criticized Rousseau by saying that discovery of knowledge is not nature but conscious self (human mind) that is more important. True knowledge is obtained only by coordinating mind with nature. Nature without mind cannot discover truth or knowledge.
- **John Dewey (1859-1952) :** The chief propounder of Pragmatism believed that only that which could be experimented is real and utility is the criteria of knowledge.

## CONCEPT OF EDUCATION

The basic problem that all living creatures face after taking birth is the problem of adaptation to environment mentally, physically, emotionally, socially and professionally. Some creatures have some natural capacities which help them adapt to their environment and no systematic education is needed for this purpose. But case of human is different. He is the most dependent being of all the living beings known. His family and the society educates him formally as well as informally to make him self dependent. The intellectual power and wisdom that man has over and above other animals help him to receive education. It is the education that helps him to adapt to the environment.

The process of education begins immediately after the child is born. His mother teaches him first how to breast feed. By using trail and error technique, the child comes to learn how to suck milk from the breast of the mother. As the child's exposure expands the number of his formal and informal teachers also increases. This process continues till his last breath in some way or the other. Thus, whole life of a man is centred around his wisdom or intelligence making him superior to all other living beings in the process.

Today, society and social needs have become very complex. There is always a new challenge as soon as we take the second breath. Newer and newer inventions and discoveries have taught the man to have more and more control over nature. Social relations have also become very complex. Apart from this, search from good to better in order to make the life more easy and comfortable has also revolutionised the human life at its peak. All these factors have led to the creation of formal education in schools, colleges and universities. In order to make education a systematic and healthy process, the knowledge of philosophical thoughts and social awareness becomes necessary.

Following procedure is followed while imparting formal education in schools:

*(i)* Society and the nation take the responsibility of imparting education to the people to bring about an adaptable change in them. For this purpose, human and physical resources are arranged.

*(ii)* The entire educational material is condensed and divided into subjects.

*(iii)* Subjects and its contents are selected keeping in view the age, ability, intelligence, needs and specific interest area of learners coupled with the needs of society and the nation.

*(iv)* Then education is imparted by the teacher who knows how to bring about maximum change in learners in lesser amount of time, energy and resources.

*(v)* Lastly, evaluation is done in order to give them the certificate of adaptability like degrees of B.A. B.Sc, B.Ed. etc.

### Meaning of Education

The word "Education" has three roots in Latin language.

*(i)* Educatum—to train/Art of teaching.

*(ii)* Educere—to draw out (inner powers)

*(iii)* Educare—to bring up/to develop.

Thus drawing out the innate capacities of the individual to develop his personality to the full by training or teaching is **Education.**

From the above etymological concept of education, following characteristics of education can be drawn:

*(i)* Education is a continuous process that starts with life and ends with death. It is because innate capacities are not restricted to age. At every moment of life man has some innate capacities.

*(ii)* Innate capacities when come in contact with the outer environment develop some beliefs and values in the individual. Thus, education is concerned with beliefs and values also.

*(iii)* When man is trained or taught, he acquires certain skills. Thus, education is a skill that a person acquires after practice.

*(iv)* Education is the enrichment of human knowledge and experiences by going through the process of thinking, experimentation and drawing conclusion.

*(v)* Education is a process of developing personality of the individual to enable him to adapt to the changing physical and social environment.

*(vi)* Individual is composed of body and soul. So, education is concerned with the physical and spiritual development both.

In order to understand the concept of "Education" three meanings of the word, 'Education' are given below:

**1. General meaning:** The instructions and knowledge given in schools is known as education by the ordinary people. In this process, teachers impart knowledge to students with specific aims. Here teacher dominates the scene and learners are only passive listeners who receive only what is given to them. When the process is over, they receive the certificate of pass or fail at the end of the year or course.

This concept of education is very narrow in the sense that it is only the communication of information by the teacher and acquisition of knowledge by students. Here no emphasis is given on all round development of child's personality. As a result, this type of education fails to prepare a child capable of facing future challenges and hardships.

**2. Technical meaning:** Education consists of all those experiences in and outside the school which affect the individual in any way during his life time. It is essentially the process of developing personality, shaping behaviour and modifying character related to the person being educated.

Thus, education is a life long conscious as well as unconscious process which is also not restricted to the boundaries of time, place or person. Every time when we are not asleep, we receive some education in the form of knowledge or experience.

The place where exchange of experiences takes place is technically a school and any person who plays more active role in the process is a teacher.

**3. Functional Meaning:** Functionally, education is the full exploitation of inherent capacities of the individual for new experiences and developing his personality in such a way that enables him to apply the acquired knowledge and experiences in his real life for the betterment of the self, society and the nation.

Thus, education can make an individual a perfect and complete man in his own boundaries though the highest degree of perfection or completeness will never be achieved. It is because only Brahma (God) is real and perfect.

## Definitions of Education

Various definitions of education have been grouped as under:

### Education as a modification of behaviour:

- **Prof. Drever :** Education is a process in which and by which knowledge, character and behaviour of the young are shaped and moulded.
- **John Dewey :** Education is a process different from the process of preparation for future life. It is a gradual repetition of experiences and feelings.

### Education as a process of personality development:

- **Mahatma Gandhi :** By education I mean the alround drawing out of the best in child and man-body, mind and spirit.
- **R.N.Tagore :** Education means to enable the child to find out the ultimate truth, making truth its own and giving expression to it.

**Education as a process of drawing out the innate powers:**

- **Socrates :** Education means the bringing out of ideas of universal validity which is latent in the mind of every man.
- **Pestalozzi :** Education is a natural, harmonious and progressive development of man's innate powers.

**Education as a process of adjustment to environment and society:**

- **Brown :** Education is a consciously motivating process whereby changes in behaviour are produced in the person and through the person within the group.
- **T. Raymont :** Education is the process of development which consists the passage of human being from infancy to maturity, the process whereby he adapts himself gradually in various ways to his physical, social and spiritual environment.

### Characteristics of Education

If we analyse the above definitions we can infer the following characteristics of education:

1. **Education—a life long process :** It is not limited to the education imparted in the school complex for a specified period of time but it is a life long process and obtained anywhere from the more experienced persons.
2. **Develops the inherent power of a child :** Education is not a thing that is forced into the mind from outside. It rather works as catalyst to develop the innate capacities of a child through outside experiences of the environment.
3. **A dynamic process :** Education and its nature changes according to the changing needs of the society and the individual. Thus, it is a meaningful and purposeful activity.
4. **A tripolar process :** Education is a process in which a more matured person works on less matured one with the help of the curriculum. Thus, a teacher is free to act only within the boundaries of the curriculum and students gain knowledge plus experiences from their teacher.
5. **A process of modifying behaviour and character formation :** It moulds the behaviour and character of the child in desirable manner.
6. **A direct and indirect process both :** When teacher and taught are in direct contact, education is a direct process but when pupils receive it from a distance, it is an indirect process.
7. **Enrichment of experiences :** Every individual has his own range of experiences which may be right or wrong. Through the process of education these experiences are directed towards the goal of life.
8. **A process of alround development of the individual :** Personality of an individual has three equally important dimensions—physical, mental and spiritual. A healthy mind lies only in a healthy body and body alienated from soul is dead. The man away from spirituality is like beasts whose activities of life are confined to fulfilling physical needs only. The process of education coordinates these three dimensions of the individual and makes him an accountable man.
9. **A process of adjustment to environment :** When we don't get what we desire to get, we become maladjusted in the society. By teaching various skills to the individual, the process of education brings about social adjustment. Similarly, the individual and the environment are most of the time antagonistic to each other, e.g., severe cold forces us to wear warm clothes. Through the process of education the lessons of adjustment are taught.

## FUNCTIONS OF EDUCATION

### General or Individual Functions of Education

*(a)* Development of innate power of the individual
*(b)* Alround development of the individual
*(c)* Modification of behaviour and character formation
*(d)* A tripolar process
*(e)* Enrichment of experiences
*(f)* A life long process

**Note :** *All these functions have already been discussed under the head of " Characteristics of Education" So we are coming to the next.*

*(g)* ***Controlling, guiding and sublimating the instincts*** : According to Mc Dougall, every infant is born with some basic instincts which

determine the nature and types of activities that he gets into. These instincts also gain strength with age. If they are not controlled and guided in a desired direction, activities of the individual will also be uncontrolled and directionless.

Moreover, some undesirable instincts need be sublimated in order to flush out acceptable activities. Education performs all these functions in the interest of the society and the individual.

(h) ***Preparation for adult life*** : The responsibilities of the child increases with age. When he is fully grown up, he needs a job to support his family. He is also expected to develop a good social relation with his relatives, neighbours and the people at large. All these skills are taught to him through the process of education and he is prepared to lead a responsible life in the society.

(i) ***Preservation and transmission of culture*** : An individual is born in a society where various cultures, traditions and religious ideals exist. Each nation is proud of its culture and traditions, so they are preserved by education for the present generation and transmitted for the next one.

(j) ***Realisation of Brahma (self)*** : The wordly life is a temporary one. Assimilating the soul with Brahma is the main aim of our life. Education helps us know the methods of realization of self.

## Social and Civic Functions

Important such functions of education are given below:

(a) ***Enhancement of social efficiency*** : Social efficiency of a nation depends upon the individual efficiency which in turn depends upon the standard of education created for them. Social efficiency is the pre requisite for prosperity and economic growth of a nation. Education performs this function in and out side the school.

(b) ***Modification of the environment*** : An individual is not only expected to adapt to the environment by changing his habits and behaviour but he should also modify the environment according to his specific needs. Education develops in him the skills to modify the environment physically and ideologically. For example, communal feeling creates social tension. This type of feeling is reduced by teaching the universality of religions.

(c) ***Creation of a Civilized Society*** : Education helps a man know how to behave different people in different ways. For this purpose, rules of conduct and norms of ethics are taught to him. This makes the whole society civilized.

(d) ***Citizenship training*** : For being a country good, its citizens should also be good and responsible. Education tells them how to exercise their rights and how to perform the duties. They are not only imparted leadership training but fellowship feeling is inducted into their minds through actual experiences.

(e) ***Social reforms*** : Education annihilates the unfounded beliefs, senseless traditions, evil customs and unsound social practices. In this way education becomes a major reform process also.

(f) ***Vocational efficiency*** : Education provides us vocational and professional knowledge. This makes us self reliant and competent to perform a job. This increases our income which in turn increases our satisfaction.

(g) ***Reconstruction of experiences*** : Man undergoes a number of experiences when he comes in contact with the physical and social environment. These experiences sometimes lead him to wrong direction due to lack of maturity in the self. Through education these experiences are reorganized in a positive manner and then they are reconstructed for future action.

(h) ***National integration and development*** : India is a country of diversity of religions, languages, castes, cultures and life styles. If these diversities are not brought under check, the whole nation will be disintegrated resulting in huge loss of property and human lives. Thus for the purpose of snatching the nation to the track of development, education should bring about unity in this diversity. This can be done only by altering the ordinary society into educated and enlightened one.

(i) ***Emotional integration*** : For achieving national integration, emotional integration is first needed.

It removes the narrow feeling of hatred, enmity, jealousy and rivalry among the groups. Emotional integration is brought about by imparting fellow feeling and sense of cooperation in the individuals.

(j) ***Moral training*** : We cannot make a society good only by invoking laws. The role of law in disciplinary affairs is very limited. It is only confined to physical aspects of life. Validity of a witness is another problem to enforce a law. Morality, on the other hand, is a self imposed discipline which is guided only by spirits. Thus, high moral values and ideals are taught through education by citing the examples of priests, prophets and justice loving rulers.

(k) ***Supply of skilled manpower :*** A number of skills and techniques are needed to perform various types of productive and non productive tasks in the society. Such skilled and semi skilled workers are supplied by formal and non formal educational institutes.

(l) ***Adaptation to environment :*** (*It has already been discussed*)

## VARIOUS FORMS OF EDUCATION

**1. Formal-Informal and Non-Formal Education:** The education which is imparted at a particular place under controlled environment is called formal education. Here aims and methods of teaching are predetermined, curriculum (dozes of knowledge) is fixed, duration of teaching time is controlled by the time table of the school and discipline is exhibited everywhere in the system. Once the education is over, the students are given pass or fail certificate or degree. Education imparted in schools and colleges is termed as formal education.

Informal education is a natural and unconscious process. Here learner does not know that he is receiving any particular education at any particular time. The nature of contact between sender and receiver is also informal. Aim of education, curriculum, method of teaching, place and time of learning—everything is undetermined. As a result, no certificate or degree is issued at the end of the programme. Family, neighbourhood, play ground, church, social and religious organizations, peer group etc. are important informal agencies of education.

Non-formal education is that education which is systematically imparted to learners according to the time table suitable to them and certificate or degree may also be issued at the end of education. Adult education centres, Anganwadi, library, museum, art galleries, extension lectures, symposia and seminars etc. are termed as non-formal agencies of education. Here aims, curriculum and methods of teaching are fixed but teaching is not controlled by evaluation. However, when process is controlled by evaluation, a degree or diploma is also issued. Distance education is a better example of this.

**2. General and Specific Education :** The education which is compulsarily imparted to students upto a certain stage or grade irrespective of mental aptitude, interest and particular needs of students in a formal setting is termed as general education. For example, Education imparted upto class tenth is general in India. Here students do not have freedom to opt a subject according to their own choice till class X. This education is expected to sharpen the general mental abilities of the child to make his life successful.

Specific education has specific aims and curriculum based on the specific needs, interest and aptitude of students. This type of education prepares the students for specific streams and areas of life, such as, PCM, PCB or Arts group education or business education, other vocational or technical education and so on.

**3. Technical or Professional Education :** Technical education is given for the purpose of equipping the students with a particular technique suitable to a particular trade or job, such as polytechnique, home science, para medical training etc. Practical aspects of education dominates over theoretical aspects here.

Professional education is wider than technical education in scope. It prepares the students to run various types of professions in life, e.g., medical education , management education, B.Ed. and M.Ed. courses etc. Professionals know their jobs well as compared to the ordinary people. This education also requires training but sufficient amount of theoretical knowledge is also given.

**4. Individual and Collective Education :** Individual education is that education which is imparted to students individually and separately on the basis of their specific interest, aptitude and needs. Here teacher can easily adjusts himself to the individual needs and capacities of a child. This education is more psychological in its nature and scope.

Collective education is imparted to the group or classes of students. This is more formal than the individual education. Children of different intellectual abilities and interests are grouped in a class and then they are taught by a group of teachers one by one according to the pre-specified time frame. This education is more philosophical in its nature and scope. School education is an example of collective education.

**5. Direct and Indirect Education**: *(It has already been discussed).*

## SCOPE OF EDUCATION

The above definitions and functions of education clarify that the process of education is not different from the process of life. They are rather complementary to each other. So the scope of education is pervasive to the whole life of human being. Since we come across a number of problems when we live in the society, education helps us in reaching the solution to these problems through experiences. But the spectrum of these experiences is so wide and divergent that it is impossible for us to acquire all the experiences of life. For this very reason we divide these experiences into parts and sub parts, we can call them as subjects and papers respectively and then we select any subject and paper on the basis of our own interest and need. These divisions and sub divisions of experiences have made education an independent discipline in itself. Thus, education is now not only a process of life but also a subject. The scope of education from these two points of views is being discussed under the following heads.

### Scope of Education as a Subject

(a) ***Educational Psychology*** **:** Child faces a number of problems related to education and development and their solutions require to take the help of psychology. Educational psychology studies various stages of physical, social, mental and emotional development of a child and their implication to the process of education. Learning theories of psychology are also applied to the teaching-learning environment for making the learning possible. Problems related to personality, intelligence, memory, adjustment etc. are also studied for fuller understanding of a child.

(b) ***Educational Philosophy*** **:** Nature and purpose of education is determined on the basis of the philosophy of nation and the people. For this purpose, various philosophical thoughts and their impact on education and life are studied. Thus, educational philosophy determines the direction as well as amount of education imparted to the individuals.

(c) ***Educational Sociology*** **:** Under this division we study the society and its impact on education on one hand and impact of education on culture and society on the other. Thus, sociological bases are provided to education and objectives of socialization of a child are achieved.

(d) ***Educational Technology*** **:** This branch of study helps the teacher to achieve the most with the least possible time, energy and resources. Various teaching strategies and techniques are applied on students and their performances are evaluated keeping in view the pre-determined objectives and then final result is obtained.

(e) ***Educational Administration*** **:** Success of the process of education whether it be formal or non-formal depends entirely on the efficient administration. For this purpose, principles of educational administration, supervision and control of schools, appointment of teaching and non-teaching staff, qualifications and duties of teachers, and evaluation of school performance etc. are studied and reforms and changes are made on the basis of system analysis.

(f) ***Educational Measurement and Evaluation*** **:** Under this division, we study why and how evaluation in education is done, how much degree of achievement may be a guarantee for success and how much degree of error in measurement is acceptable. Thus, evaluation works as a supplement to the whole educational processes.

(g) ***Special Education*** : This discipline refers to the methods of imparting education to deviant groups of the society, handicapped or backward and talented or superiors. Relative importance of special and integrated education is also studied here.

(h) ***History and problems of education*** : Under this division we study the nature and patterns of education from the ancient period to the 21th century and their related problems.

### Education as Process of Life

It would not be incorrect to say that *Education is life itself.* It is because education covers all the spheres of our lives through experiences. The scope of education as a process of life can be well understood from the individual and social functions of education which has already been discussed in this very chapter. Students are also advised to go through the meaning and characteristics of education. If you are interested to have a detailed knowledge of how education is related to life, you are advised to go through the book "Society and Education" by John Dewey.

## INTER-RELATIONSHIP OF PHILOSOPHY & EDUCATION

Education and philosophy are so much inter-dependent on each other that it is very difficult to separate them practically. They may be termed as the two sides of the same coin. They are inter-dependent on each other in the following ways:

1. **Philosophy determines the direction of education :** Education is a conscious, dynamic and purposeful process. Philosophy determines the goal of life which is consciously adapted by education and thus aims of education and its nature are determined. When these aims of life change with the passage of time, philosophy of life again changes these educational objectives.
2. **Philosophy shapes the aspects of education :** There are two aspects of education—theoretical and practical. How much emphasis should be given to either of these aspects is determined by philosophy. Higher payment and higher status given to men of latter in the society as compared to technocrats and professionals testifies to the fact that philosophy still dominates on educational scenes.
3. **Education is the dynamic side of philosophy :** Philosophy equips us with thoughts or ideas and these thoughts are put into practice by education. Thus, a combination of theory and practice makes the process of life complete.
4. **Education gives birth to new philosophy also :** Herbart holds the opinion-"Education has no time to make holiday till all the philosophical questions are once for all cleared up".

When we go through the process of education, we come across various types of problems which need to seek the help of philosophers to solve them. Philosophical debates are held for this purpose. This can cause new philosophy to emerge.

## PHILOSOPHY AND VARIOUS DIMENSIONS OF EDUCATION

### Philosophy and Educational Values

Most of the educational values such as accountability to man and unseen God, honest and impartial attitudes towards all humans, purification of souls, independent thinking over the creation of the universe etc have been derived from religion. Philosophy has given a rational and logical shape to these values by giving answers of "How and Why" questions. Thus there is a close relationship between philosophy and educational values and much more importance is given to mental development of the child along with spiritual development.

### Philosophy and Science

Science is a systematic knowledge based on observation and experimentation and conclusions are drawn on the basis of data collected. When we interpret the data, relationship between facts and events and respective cause and effects etc are also established. Then conclusions are presented in the form of principles and theories. Philosophy also does the same job. It also discovers the facts first. Then it formulates the principles and laws on the basis of observation, experimentation and analysis of data collected. From this point of view, there is no difference between the two. That is why we see that Aristotle, the originator of modern science was himself a philosopher; Descartes, the great mathematician of his time was a well recognized philosopher; Kant, a famous scholar of geography and physics was a great philosopher and so on.

But there are some big differences between philosophy and science as well, they are given below:

*(a)* The scope of science is limited to the physical world but the scope of philosophy is the entire universe, seen and unseen both.

*(b)* Philosophy starts where the science ends. Science can interpret only the natural phenomena of a thing but philosophy can elaborate the supernatural phenomenon also.

*(c)* Philosophy is said to be the coordinator of all sciences, thus it works as a gap filler. Science elaborates the fact or events separately, though they have very much in common. Thus, philosophy is a generalized study and science is a specialized study.

*(d)* The aim of science is to discover the facts of concrete nature which are real in themselves but the aim of philosophy is more comprehensive in nature. It discovers the concrete as well as abstract facts and accepts a truth only when it is fully examined. Thus synthesis dominates in philosophy while analysis dominates in science.

*(e)* Science is concerned only what the nature of a thing is but philosophy is concerned with what is as well as what ought to be. Thus, philosophy starts when science fails.

## Philosophy and Aims of Education

Contribution of philosophy in the determination of aims of education is very significant, such as,

*(a)* Philosophy gives valuable advice regarding the determination of aims of education by studying the view points of various persons and groups.

*(b)* Philosophy helps the people in establishing their real view about life and metaphysical world. Once such views are established, education is imparted to them accordingly.

*(c)* By interpreting these views philosophy makes it clear as to which of these views are beneficial for us and which of them are harmful.

*(d)* Philosophy explains which of educational aims will bear fruitful or harmful results keeping in view the attitude of the society and the individual toward life.

With this perspective some examples of Indian and western philosophical thought on educational aims are cited below:

**(A) Ancient Period:**

1. The people of Sparta were constantly attacked by their enemies. So their philosophy of life came to be known as a constant struggle against the enemies. Due to this, developing the passion of patriotism, courage and fearlessness and making the citizens physically strong and healthy were the main aims of education. Weakness of body was considered a vice and sacrifice of life for the sake of nation was regarded as highest virtue.
2. People of Athens had beauty of physique and character and aesthetic sense for beautiful objects as their philosophy of life. Therefore, their aim of education was the development of fine character and personality.
3. The ancient western philosophers like Socrates, Plato and Aristotle considered the discovery of truth as the ultimate goal of life. Therefore, their aim of education was spiritual development along with mental training.
4. Indian philosophers were of the view that knowledge and realization of Brahma or supreme soul is the ultimate aim of life. Thus the aim of education is not merely to acquire material success in life. Material success is only a sort of illusion which arises out of ignorance. The real aim of education is spiritual development through meditation, yoga and discourse.

**(B) Medieval Period:**

1. Emergence of new religion such as Islam was the main feature of this period. Islam considered that the worldly life is the cultivation of life hereafter and propagation of Islam is the means to achieve this end. This philosophy was interpreted by ulemas and saints in different ways. Some of them believed that Islam was to be propagated by subjugating the non Islamic kingdoms. Military

power was necessary for this. So the aim of education was to acquire more and more physical strength and technology of warfare. Others believed that Islam could be propagated only by the lasting influence of conduct and character on the masses. So character formation should be the chief aim of education.

2. In Europe, people stood up against the hegemony of christianity and criticized catholism. They wanted freedom of thoughts and expression which was denied by the church. Thus, their aim of education was to develop critical insight and imagination through reason and experimentation.

**(C) Modern Period:** Philosophy of life drastically changed in the modern period. As a result revolutionary changes were brought about in the field of education as well. Some examples are cited below:

1. The philosophy of inborn capacities of a child was propounded by Locke and he argued that education should develop the inherent qualities and capacities of children.
2. Psychological and scientific tendencies influenced the philosophy of the people very powerfully and thus education was made child centred and aim of education was to develop scientific temper among children.
3. Fast industrial development revolutionased the way and standard of life and philosophy of attainment of wordly pleasures-eat, drink and be merry, emerged. This philosophy of life emphasized vocational aims of education.
4. Philosophy of pragmatism emerged in America and spread all over Europe in no time. With this philosophy child centred purposive education dominated the scene and the aim of education was to recognize and develop the child according to his needs, interests and aptitudes.
5. Countries having strong democratic waves consider inculcation of democratic values and principles among individuals as the main aim of education.
6. Countries like Russia, China and Muslim kingdoms of the world exploite education as an instrument of indoctrinating enforced obedience and rigid discipline.

## Philosophy and Curriculum

The activities which are organized for the students and experiences which are provided to them in order to attain the goals of education is called curriculum. When philosophy determines the goals of education it must also determine the curriculum to achieve those aims. But the problem is that the life span of man is very short and the knowledge and experiences accumulated so far is very vast. As a result, nobody can acquire all the experiences and knowledge howsoever hard working he is. Besides, universe continues to change what is true and believed today may not be necessarily true or believed tomorrow. Philosophy solves all these problems of curriculum construction and development in the following ways:

(*a*) Philosophy evaluates all the human experiences and knowledge from the point of view of usefulness and gives its judgement as to what should be taught and at what stage.

(*b*) Since humans can not accumulate all the experiences in their life span, philosophy divides these experiences into sections and subsections and determines what portion of knowledge a person should study on the basis of his needs and interest.

(*c*) Capacity to digest a particular amount of knowledge develops with age and maturity. By taking the help of psychology, philosophy determines how much titbits of knowledge and experiences should be provided to an individual at different stages of his life.

(*d*) It also gives us knowledge of what is worth teaching and what is not. Thus, philosophy talks in terms of values of life and ethics of education.

(*e*) It also tell us which part of the curriculum should be given special emphasis and why.

(*f*) Since knowledge and experiences change with time, philosophy adapts itself to the changing needs and modifies the curriculum accordingly.

## Philosophy and methods of Teaching

Philosophy is way of thinking and way of working both. So when philosophy changes, method of teaching also changes.

The process of carrying the related knowledge and experiences to the reach of students is called method of teaching. The discovery of a method to perform any activity or work is primarily the function of science but how and why to use a particular method is the scope of philosophy because philosophy correlates the method with the aim first then clearance regarding the use is given. That is why, different philosophers have propounded different methods of teaching in accordance with the aim. Some examples are given below:

*(i)* Idealists like Socrates, Plato and others advocated conversation and lectures as methods of teaching.

*(ii)* Naturalists like Rousseau and others maintained that child should be given maximum freedom in the class. So they advocated Dalton Plan, learning by doing, Montessori Method and so on as methods of teaching.

*(iii)* Bacon opined that observation and experimentation would be the best methods of teaching.

## Philosophy and Educational Administration

There are five basic areas of educational administration—establishment of schools, management of schools, finance, supervision and organizing co-curricular activities in schools. Philosophy contributes to these gigantic tasks in the following ways:

*(a)* Decision regarding the establishment of schools is taken after studying the specific needs of the society concerned. Then site is selected keeping in view the aims of education set by the society and the nation. After that physical facilities contributing to the teaching learning process are arranged. Finally the inner and outer decoration of the school, keeping in view the nature of aesthetic sense of the local people is made.

*(b)* Management of the school is the second important thing. Whether school should be run by the government or should it go to the private managing committee to run, this decision is also taken by the philosopher. Role of management is very significant regarding teaching learning process as it frames the policies regarding the appointment of teachers and admission of students. For example, if managing committee have pragmatic view of life, it will appoint only those teachers to teach who are pragmatic in behaviour and thought.

*(c)* Finance is the third most important problem related to educational administration. If people of a particular area are rich and they are willing to contribute to the development of education, school can be established without state's or outside help. Contrary to this if a school is to be established in a poor locality, the state will have to own the financial responsibilities of the school. All these decisions are taken by none but philosophers.

*(d)* The fourth aspect of educational administration is supervision and control. Through this process, the maximum utilization of physical and human resources are ascertained. Honest and unbiased attitude toward life will make this process a success and corrupt behaviour will spoil the whole process.

*(e)* The nature of co-curricular activities are also decided by the philosophy of life of those engaged in educational administration.

## Philosophy and School Discipline

Discipline of the school is also determined by the philosophy of life. There may be three types of disciplines in schools:

**(a) Repressionistic Discipline :** In this type of discipline, child is repressed by despotic attitude of the teacher. He is not allowed even to think freely. Children are expected to abide by the rules and regulations of the school without questioning why. Corporal punishment teachnique is used to enforce disciplinary rules. This type of discipline is adopted by those who believe in classical idealism.

**(b) Impressionistic Discipline :** Some philosophers believe that no child is good or bad in behaviour. His behaviour is shaped by those who come in contact with him. So teachers can easily influence the thinking and behaviour of children. Here self discipline is taught to children by lofty character and good conduct of teachers and nothing is imposed on them from outside. There is no scope of corporal punishment or creating sense of fear in the minds of children.

(c) **Emancipatory discipline :** This type of discipline is based on the philosophy of Naturalism which believes in the inherent goodness of the nature of a child. Here child is allowed to learn by the laws and rules of natural consequences and so nothing is dictated to him from outside. Full freedom is given to him to develop his thinking and reasoning power.

Which type of the above disciplines should a school follow, depends upon the philosophical foundations of the society which the school represents. If democratic values are followed by the society, the repressionistic discipline will be unsuitable to them because students are not habitual to these types of behaviour and they will revolt against the authority. Actually a combination of all these disciplines may be suitable to any school as compared to a single philosophy of discipline.

## Philosophy and Evaluation system

In order to see whether educational objectives have been achieved or not, evaluation is done. Thus, evaluation is a monitoring system and students, teachers and school are continuously evaluated in order to ascertain the maximum utilization of resources and develop sense of responsibility among all individuals concerned.

Evaluation also talks in terms of changes in behaviour of individuals. Whether these changes in behaviour are acceptable to the society or not, is exclusively determined by philosophy. It determines the criteria of goodness and thus promotion is given on the basis of grades. For example, those who score 33% marks in the examination are considered liable to be promoted to the next class. It is the philosophy that has fixed this criteria.

Similarly, when idea of sense of responsibility is added to performance, evaluation becomes philosophy. For example, when a teacher is found guilty for the poor performance of his students and he is punished for that, evaluation becomes the dynamic side of philosophy.

## Specific Branches of Philosophy and its relationship with education

There are some specific branches of philosophy which are deeply related with education. The relationship of some of these with education is given below:

**(a) Epistemology :** In epistemology, truth and unture of knowledge is examined. It also discusses how true knowledge can be obtained, i.e., means of acquisition of knowledge. Philosophers have contradictory view- points with regard to nature and means of acquiring knowledge. Idealists believe that true knowledge is obtained by thinking, meditation and discourse while pragmatists are of the view that true knowledge is obtained by observation, experience and experimentation. Kant tried to coordinate these two views and said that outer environment is an important source of knowledge but it is mind that can give it a definite form.

Contribution of epistemology to education can be understood by the following points:

*(a)* It tells us what knowledge should be given to students and how.

*(b)* It tells us what part of knowledge should be given to students at a particular stage of life.

*(c)* It tells us how various concepts of knowledge should be organized for students so that it may become meaningful to them.

*(d)* Development and transfer of knowledge need language and logic which can be developed by epistemology only.

**(b) Metaphysics :** The scope of metaphysics is the whole universe but it mainly discusses how we can acquire the knowledge of ultimate reality or final truth, i.e., Brahma. If a person does not believe in God, he would not mind whether the knowledge acquired by him is true or false. But the person who believes in God would always endeavour to acquire true knowledge only. Thus, metaphysics acquaint the man with the reality and purpose of life. It has helped education in the following ways-

*(a)* It tells us that there is a definite purpose of this universe. So education should be such as to make the educant accountable to the ultimate reality.

(*b*) It tells us how we can discover ultimate reality by the process of education.

(*c*) Through metaphysics we learn to believe many unseen nature of things through intutions and meditations.

(*d*) It lessens the effects of pessimism by giving the idea of second life which is nothing but the union of soul with God.

(*e*) It also tells us that only physical things are not real. Unseen elements of the universe can also be real.

**(c) Ethics :** Ethics is related to good and bad or desirable and undesirable behaviour of man. There are two groups of philosophers explaining this. The group of pessimists headed by Berkeley is of the view that everything in the world is necessarily evil but there is no better planet than the earth in the whole universe. On the other hand group of optimists led by Hegel opines that there are both virtues and vices in the world. On the basis of criteria of goodness, ethics evaluates human behaviour and thus it is a value judgement.

Decision regarding goodness or badness of a thing is taken only after careful consideration. Ethics helps education in this regard in the following ways:

(*a*) Only those things which are good, virtuous or desirable from any point of view are included in the curriculum.

(*b*) Only virtuous behaviour is allowed to get practised. Thus, character is built on ethical lines.

(*c*) Values become very important along with material well being and survival of a nation entirely depends on it. For example, sacrificing life for the sake of the nation is a value. It is very much emphasized in education though it does not have any concurrence with the material well being.

Thus we see that the role and contribution of philosophy is very much evident and significant in every aspect of education.

## OBJECTIVE QUESTIONS

**1.** The person who has love for wisdom (truth) may be called as philosopher provided that
(*a*) he has logical power
(*b*) his love is in the active form
(*c*) his knowledge is correct
(*d*) none of the above

**2.** The person who is curious to learn and is never satisfied may be termed as philosopher. It is the opinion of
(*a*) Plato (*b*) Socrates
(*c*) Descartes (*d*) John Locke

**3.** Which of the following statements is/are correct?
(*a*) Philosophers are designated only those who can guide others by influencing their ideas and actions
(*b*) Darshan in Sanskrit refers metaphysical or intutional perception that leads to Moksha
(*c*) Darshan is a logical exposition of the nature of reality
(*d*) All of these

**4.** The purpose of all philosophical exercises is
(*a*) The enhancement of knowledge
(*b*) To provide base to all educational thoughts.
(*c*) To remove the doubts and wonders of the people
(*d*) All of the above

**5.** The person who tried to synthesise mathematics with divine knowledge was
(*a*) Socrates (*b*) Pythagoras
(*c*) Protagorus (*d*) Aristotle

**6.** Dialogue method of discovering the truth was discovered by
(*a*) Saint Augustine (*b*) Plato
(*c*) Heraclitus (*d*) Socrates

**7.** 'Philosophy of Marriage' was written by
(*a*) Erasmas (*b*) Satre
(*c*) John Locke (*d*) None of these

**8.** Match the following:

| | A | | B |
|---|---|---|---|
| (*i*) | Republic | (A) | Descartes |
| (*ii*) | Emile | (B) | Rousseau |
| (*iii*) | Modern theory of dualism | (C) | John Dewey |
| (*iv*) | Experimentalism | (D) | Plato |

| | (i) | (ii) | (iii) | (iv) |
|---|---|---|---|---|
| (a) | A | B | C | D |
| (b) | D | B | A | C |
| (c) | D | A | B | C |
| (d) | A | C | D | B |

9. Adaptation to environment while facing its adversaries is
   (a) Education (b) Teaching
   (c) Moulding (d) All of these
10. Which of the following statements regarding education is correct ?
   (a) Education is a continuous process starting from the first breath of life to the last
   (b) Drawing out the innate capacities of man to enable him to adapt to the social environment
   (c) Education is the other name of personality development
   (d) All of the above
11. If education is a tripolar process, which is the third element after students and the teacher?
   (a) School (b) Parents
   (c) Curriculum (d) None of these
12. Controlling and sublimation of instincts are done through the process of education. It is the opinion of
   (a) McDougall (b) Bruner
   (c) RN Tagore (d) MK Gandhi
13. In the 21st century, education is considered
   (a) as a preparation for future life
   (b) as a source of gaining material wealth
   (c) as a symbol of status
   (d) all of the above
14. Formal education differs from non-formal education in which of the following points.
   (a) Formal education is controlled by definite time-table
   (b) Certificate is not issued after education is over
   (c) Curriculum is pre determined in formal education
   (d) None of these
15. Which of the following is not an agency of informal education?
   (a) Church
   (b) Social organization
   (c) Art galleries
   (d) All of these
16. Education in India prepared by Central Board is general up to class
   (a) Xth (b) XIIth
   (c) VIIIth (d) IXth
17. Professionals are preferred to general people in every field today because
   (a) they can do their job better
   (b) they can adopt research oriented technique to solve a problem
   (c) their theoretical knowledge is more sophisticated than mere technical people
   (d) All of these
18. Education is lame without philosophy because
   (a) ideas and concepts are judged by philosophy
   (b) education goes in the direction of goals of life and philosophy determines those goals
   (c) philosophy can give birth to new sciences
   (d) all of the above
19. Education and philosophy are inter related in which of the following points?
   (a) Most of the educational and moral values have been derived from philosophy
   (b) Both of them discuss the validity of laws and principles and their applications.
   (c) Philosophy is a generalized study of all sciences
   (d) All of the above
20. Philosophy dominates over science in which of the following ways?
   (a) Science discusses what the nature of reality is and philosophy discusses what it is and what it should be both
   (b) Analysis dominates in science while synthesis dominates in philosophy
   (c) Philosophy is a generalized study while science is a specialized one
   (d) All of these
21. Which of the following societies had deep aesthetic sense in the ancient period?
   (a) Athens (b) Sparta
   (c) Arab (d) Indian
22. Mundane life is the cultivation of the world hereafter. It is the philosophy of

(*a*) Christianity (*b*) Islam
(*c*) Athens (*d*) Sankhya

**23.** In the medieval period people rose up against the catholic church because
(*a*) church denied them the freedom of thought and expression
(*b*) church banned scientific experimentation
(*c*) both of these
(*d*) none of these

**24.** Who propounded the philosophy of inborn capacities of a child?
(*a*) John Locke (*b*) John Dewey
(*c*) Kant (*d*) None of these

**25.** The process of carrying the related knowledge and experiences to the reach of students is called
(*a*) curriculum
(*b*) teaching
(*c*) method of teaching
(*d*) none of these

**26.** The child is not permitted even to think freely in the class. This is the example of
(*a*) Impressionistic discipline
(*b*) Repressionistic discipline
(*c*) Emancipatory discipline
(*d*) None of these

**27.** Emancipatory discipline in the school system is approved if the society is
(*a*) Idealistic
(*b*) Realistic
(*c*) Closed
(*d*) Open and free

**28.** Students are evaluated in the school in order to
(*a*) Ascertain the maximum utilization of resources
(*b*) Check the sense of responsibility among the persons concerned
(*c*) Promote the students to the next higher class
(*d*) All of these

**29.** In evaluation, criterion of acceptability of behavioural change in learner is determined by
(*a*) the school
(*b*) educational technology
(*c*) philosophy
(*d*) none of these

**30.** Purpose of the creation of the universe and its relation to man and God is discussed in
(*a*) Metaphysics
(*b*) Ethics
(*c*) Epistemology
(*d*) None of these

**31.** The group of pessimists in ethics is headed by
(*a*) Kant
(*b*) Berkeley
(*c*) Hegel
(*d*) None of these

**32.** There is only one subject matter of education that is life in all its maifestation who said this
(*a*) TP Nunn
(*b*) Whitehead
(*c*) John Dewey
(*d*) None of these

**33.** Formal education is different from non-formal in which of the following points.
(*a*) Formal education has fixed points of entry and exit
(*b*) Formal education works out on the principle of wedding out failures
(*c*) Both of these
(*d*) None of these

**34.** Who said this "Education is man making. It is that by which character is formed, strength of mind is increased, intellect is expanded and by which man can stand on his own feet"
(*a*) Vivekanand
(*b*) Tagore
(*c*) Dayanand Saraswati
(*d*) None of these

**35.** Which of the following is not the function of education?
(*a*) Development of personality
(*b*) Preservation, transmission and advancement of culture
(*c*) Leadership training
(*d*) Economic prosperity

**36.** Destiny of India is being shaped in the class rooms. It is the opinion of
(*a*) Education Commission
(*b*) Hunter Commission
(*c*) Hurtog Committee
(*d*) None of above

## ANSWERS

| 1 | 2 | 3 | 4 | 5 | 6 | 7 | 8 | 9 | 10 |
|---|---|---|---|---|---|---|---|---|---|
| (b) | (a) | (d) | (d) | (b) | (d) | (a) | (b) | (a) | (d) |
| **11** | **12** | **13** | **14** | **15** | **16** | **17** | **18** | **19** | **20** |
| (c) | (a) | (d) | (d) | (c) | (a) | (d) | (d) | (d) | (a) |
| **21** | **22** | **23** | **24** | **25** | **26** | **27** | **28** | **29** | **30** |
| (a) | (b) | (a) | (a) | (c) | (b) | (d) | (d) | (c) | (a) |
| **31** | **32** | **33** | **34** | **35** | **36** | | | | |
| (b) | (b) | (c) | (a) | (d) | (a) | | | | |

# Western Philosophies and Education

## INTRODUCTION

From Plato's Idealism to post World War II philosophy of Reconstructionism there existed a number of philosophical thoughts that influenced the society and education during their respective periods. All these philosophies vitiated human thoughts and behaviour to such an extent that we are not led by any particular philosophy today. The ideals that have been framed by these thoughts leading to democracy at the top are still with us and we are now able to survive in the world absolutely because of this ideal of democracy. This ideal of democracy is now being challenged by terrorism, a latest philosophy of late 20th century resulting in disintegration and chaos in the society once again. The need of a new Marx is again felt with much intensity to redefine the class struggle to bring about political parity rather than social parity in the society.

Some dominating philosophical thoughts and their contribution to education and social change are discussed here.

## IDEALISM

Idealism contends that the material and physical world known to science is an incomplete expression of reality, that it exists but to observe and requires to complement at a higher type of reality, a spiritual reality ---- *Rusk*

### Meaning

Born out of ideas and ideals, Idealism means that material objects and physical world are myth. They are only the means to reach the spiritual reality. When these ideas and ideals are put into practice, the body—the mythical object gets united with the spirit of God—the real object. As the holy scripture, Quran says "Everything in the universe is destructible except God who will last forever. This lord is almighty and praise worthy"(Al-Rehman). From this meaning of Idealism we can draw the conclusion how can a thing that is destructible be real, e.g., the ideas of a chair makes it a chair. When chair is destroyed with the passage of time, idea of he chair still remains in our mind. We can give it another name say plate but this plate or chair will still holds the meaning of a thing to sit in. We can give different names to supreme power say God—Allah, Ishwar, Brahma, and so on, but his reality is always unchangeable. Thus idea is real.

As far as attributes of God are concerned, they are constructed by the man himself on the basis of imagination and meditation. These attributes are also real because hey are product of ideas.

Now the question arises why to believe in Idealism. The answer is very simple. It is only the role of contrast that has caused the physical universe to exist. For example, electricity passes out when plus charge touches the minus charge, offspring is produced when male comes in contact with female, distinction of a thing is possible when darkness touches light and so on. Therefore, if there exist physical world to observe, there must exist metaphysical world to meditate and unity between the two makes the process of life complete and it is done by putting the ideas into practice.

### Chief Contributors of this Philosophy

Idealism influenced many great philosophers from time to time. Some of these great philosophers are Socrates, Plato, Descartes, Berkeley, Fichte, Hegel, TP Nunn etc.

### Various forms of Idealism

Different idealistic philosophers have understood this philosophy in different ways. Some interpretations are given further:

*(a)* **Personalistic (Subjective) Idealism :** The exponent of this kind of Idealism is Berkeley. He accepts only the existence of mind. Even attributes and qualities are mental and if they are mental, they will necessarily be subjective i.e., each one considers an object in one's own way and defines it. Thus, attributes which are transformed into objects are very much personal in nature. We observe only the attributes not the object.

*(b)* **Absolute Idealism :** Exponents of this kind of idealism are Fichte and Hegel. According to them only self (soul) is the absolute reality. As far as physical world is concerned, all events in the universe is governed by some absolute laws. So, only absolute laws are real. Progress in this world is the result of thesis, anti-thesis and synthesis. As soon as a viewpoint comes into light, its contradiction also comes to the scene. Then these two ideas are synthesized into one, then it is again opposed and thus the process of progress goes on till we reach the absolute truth.

*(c)* **Objective Idealism :** Plato is the originator of this kind of Idealism. According to him, reality of spirit is not because it is realized by someone but it is independent of realization. If God is real, he will always remain real whether anybody considers him real or not. Independent existence of reality is the source of all souls.

*(d)* **Phenomenal Idealism :** Kant is the first exponent of this kind of philosophy. According to him, whatever knowledge we have acquired about physical or metaphysical world is not actually and absolutely real. It is only the phenomenon of the reality. Original or absolute reality can not be known as it is beyond our capacity. For example how God, heaven or hell actually can not be known by anybody.

## Characteristics and Principles of Idealism

Important principles and characteristics of this philosophy clarifying the concepts of reality, knowledge and values are as follows:

*(a)* **Classification of substances :** Idealism studies the entire existence of the universe which is made up of a number of substances. On the basis of similarity and dissimilarity, idealists have classified these substances into various groups. They are matter, otherness, diversity, motion and motionless according to Plato. Kant has classified these substances into four groups attribute, result, system and association. Indian philosopher Vaishishka has classified them into matter, action, attribute, special, general and common. They are of only two types according to Descartes—nature and soul or inanimate and animate.

*(b)* **Supremacy of ideas over objects :** Source of knowledge are ideas not objects. Mind or soul is the ultimate reality while objects which can die out are myth. According to Plato, "Ideas are the ultimate cosmic significance. They are rather the essence which give form to cosmos. These ideas are eternal and unchanging". From the reality of mind we can also conclude that we can arrive at final truth through debate and discussion. The debating parties convince each other to give up the falsehood and consensus is arrived at. Many controversies of the physical world are done away with by using this method even today.

*(c)* **Classification of the world :** Idealists have divided the world into two forms—material and spiritual. Here only spiritual world is real and material world is unreal because it is mortal. Thus, self realization, i.e., realization of soul is the aim of human life.

*(d)* **Superiority of man to nature :** It studies man with much emphasis because it is man who has higher power, i.e., intelligence. He can mould and modify his surroundings and circumstances according to his needs. He can rise up higher and higher and attain divinity provided that intellectual power is guided by a Guru.

*(e)* **Nature of mind and epistemology :** Mind is neither lifeless nor mechanical. It is a living being as well as rational. It has its indepent existence away from body. Physical world is only a manifestation of mind and there always exists a harmony between nature and man. So, knowledge obtained through mind is real. It never dies. When any old knowledge is replaced by a new knowledge, old knowledge also remains alive in its original form.

(*f*) **Values and role of soul:** Physical world is the means and spiritual world is the end according to Idealism. So, the aim of man is to attain divinity through spiritual progress. These spiritual values are permanent and they never change with the change of time. For example, abusing a man is immoral. It will remain immoral for all the times to come. According to J.S. Ross, truth, beauty and goodness are seen to be absolutes, each existing in its own right and entirely desirable in itself.

(*g*) **Self realization (The purpose of all creations) :** This universe has not been created without purpose. The creator who is God has given it life from his own life and thus the purpose of man who is the centre of all creations in the universe is to know his God, to follow his wishes and to leave this world to attain divinity. Self realization is the method of attaining divinity. If the existence of God has some purpose, his creation must also have some purpose.

We can conclude their beliefs regarding knowledge, reality and value in the following words:

- Truth (Reality) is mind itself which is just the manifestation of God. So only God (Spirit is true.)
- Knowledge is what we acquire by using our mind. Only this knowledge is real.
- Values are permanent because they are derived from soul (God). It is God who decides what is good or bad. Thus, values are also related to mind.

## Educational Implications of Idealism

**1. Aims of education -** Idealism propounds the following aims of education:

(*a*) *Beautification of personality :* Human personality is to be beautified and exalted by ideas and ideals according to this philosophy. These ideas and ideals are adopted even in adverse type of environments. So, the role of will power also becomes important in shaping the personality. If will power is guided by pious ideas and ideals of religion or philosophy and proper environment is also created, human personality will develop in the desired manner and its darkness is removed. Thus, the aim of education should be to develop the personality of the child by creating congenial environment and by raising his will power through accepted ideas and ideals. Development of personality is nothing but the realization of the self (soul) and negation of the unreal (destructible objects). Education exposes the unreal nature of the physical world and makes an individual know the reality of the spiritual world.

(*b*) *Development of spirituality :* Physical or material attainments are only the means to achieve the ends, i.e., development of spirituality. First of all, a child knows only his physical self. Then he comes to know the social self. These two self cannot be ignored by anybody. They are however, not the real self. Real self is spiritual self which is to be developed by education by giving him moral and social training and by arousing his spirituality. At this stage, he will be able to perceive God, and he will be glad . In the final stage he will harmonise his self with God and both will become one. As a result he will see his God everywhere and in every physical particles.

(*c*) *Moral and intellectual training :* Truth is that which is established by mind . When we discuss a matter, we come across various views and counter views. We cease to debate the topic, when we are convinced by the counter argument. This is possible only when we are morally matured and pious. Negating an idea just due to prejudiced attitude is wrong according to Idealism. The aim of education is to train the child morally and mentally together.

(*d*) *Preservation, transmission and advancement of culture :* Mental capacities of man develop cultural, social and artistic values in the individual as well as social life of man. His achievement in science and technology due to his creativity are also added to these cultural and social values resulting in the enrichment of culture. The aim of education should be to conserve this culture if it is true and transmit it for the benefit of the next generation. These two functions of education are essential because cultural heritage belongs to the whole humanity. This heritage is also advanced by applying mental processes in the situation. Since, this philosophy believed in the unchangeable nature of truth and values, efforts are kept on to establish a harmonious relationship between man and God.

(e) *Creation of an ideal society:* Physical as well as social environment is the product of vices. Education aims at reforming the society by creating spiritual environment there.

**2. Curriculum:** Idealists consider thoughts, feelings, ideals and values more important than the child. Besides, they pay attention to the entire experiences of humanity-past and present rather than individual experiences of man. This makes the scope of their curriculum very wide. According to this philosophy curriculum should be so constructed and developed as to enable the child in knowing, willing and doing. For example, teaching of different subjects will develop the knowing faculty of the mind, teaching of arts, music and dance will develop willing faculty and teaching of science will develop doing capacity of the mind. The development of knowing will help the child to discover the truth, the development of willing will enable him to realize beauty and development of doing will make him competent in physical and material activities for achieving goodness.

Thus, we see that Idealism is not in favour of any particular subject. Every subject that can make the child intelligent and spiritualistic and that can help him discover universal and absolute laws is important for Idealists. Several schemes of curricula propounded by different Idealist philosophers are given below:

(a) *Plato's Scheme :* Language literature, History, Geography, Maths, Science etc. are taught for intellectual training. Arts, Music, Poetry etc. are taught for aesthetic training and Religion, Ethics, Metaphysics etc are taught for moral and spiritual training.

(b) *Herbart's Scheme :* He gave priority to subjects like Literature, History, Arts, Music, Poetry and Political Economy to promote moral values and ideals and Science subjects were given less importance.

(c) *TP Nunn's Scheme :* He classified human activities into two groups. In the first group he puts physical, social, moral and religious activities which needed Physical Education, Culture, Sociology, Ethics and Religion to study. Literary and aesthetic-higher activities are kept in the second category which needed Arts, Literature, Music, Handicrafts, History, Geography, Science and Mathematics to study.

(d) *Ross's Scheme :* He classified human activities into physical and spiritual. Physical education and life skills are taught for physical development. He divided spiritual activities into intellectual, moral, aesthetic and religious again, Literature, Science, Maths, History, Geography etc are taught for intellectual development, Ethics for moral development, Fine Arts and Music for aesthetic development and Metaphysics plus religion for religious development.

**3. Method of teaching:** Any teaching method can be chosen keeping in view to the demand of the situation and educational aims according to Idealists. Due to this reason, Socrates adopted question answer method, Plato followed discussion and debate methodology, Aristotle advocated inductive deductive method, Herbert advocated instruction and lecture method, Froebel stressed upon play way method and so on. The only thing that is important here is that we have to reach the goal without compromising our spirituality.

**4. Status of the child:** This philosophy does not take the child for granted. It considers him more than a body. So, his spiritual development is taken at the top and this is achieved through self realization.

**5. Status of the teacher:** The status of a teacher is very high, and glorious almost equal to God in Idealism. His main role in the class is to develop child's personality in right direction through self realization. So, he himself must know the essentials of self realization in theory and practice. The personality of the teacher should be so impressive from idealistic point of view that he need not say much about this. He should create congenial atmosphere for the child by his own activities and planned experiences. Above all, he should guide the students with love, affection and sympathy.

**6. Discipline:** Idealism keeps the child fully under control. If he does any thing wrong, he is immediately punished but no reward is given for committing good deeds because doing good is the prerequisite for spiritual development. The habit of self discipline is also developed by impressing the child with the exemplary activities and behaviour of the teacher. Thus, Idealism favours impressionistic as well as repressionistic type of discipline in the school. Teacher always treats the child like his son whose task is to rectify the child any how and by whatever means.

**7. Education and society:** The society intends to shape the school according to its needs and all types of assistance is given to schools for this purpose. School on the other hand, removes the evil practices prevailing in the society through education. School accepts all assistance from the society, it however, does not allow any interference in its affairs from the society. School plays the role of a leader and reformer for the society through its students and teachers. It guides the people of the society every now and then and its guidance is given due importance.

**8. Influence (Merits) of Idealism:** This philosophy has influenced every society since the very cradle of the civilization. Its impact can also be seen on every other philosophy that took birth after it. It has influenced the social values and traditions in the following ways:

*(i)* It has helped in the determination of educational aims to a large extent. Educational aims such as personality development through self realization and creation of an ideal society etc have helped to a great extent in the construction of curriculum even today.

*(ii)* Its concept of moral education is recognized by all societies of the world.

*(iii)* It stresses on the ideal character of the teacher that is the very important need of the hour in order to bring about desirable change in the behaviour of students.

*(iv)* It advocates intimate relationship between teachers and students. Student-teachers ratio is being reduced today in order to develop this affinity between the two.

*(v)* Every one has now started to define values, truths and reality in one's own way keeping one's compatibility into mind. This is the main cause of social and cultural tension today. If we go back to the Idealistic concept which considers values and reality eternal and absolute, most of our cultural and social problems may be solved.

*(vi)* It recognizes the individuality of a child and tries to stimulate his creative potentialities. Most of the educational systems have adopted this view in framing curriculum and method of teaching.

*(vii)* The concept of discipline based on impressionistic type of discipline was accepted by all modern Indian philosopher like Vivekananda, Gandhiji etc.

## Criticism of Idealism

This philosophy can be criticised on some superficial grounds in the following ways:

*(i)* It neglects the present realities and prepares the child for the future world only. This criticism is baseless, because idealism has always considered the present world as means to achieve the end, i.e., the next world. So there is no question of negligence of the present world.

*(ii)* It takes only the ultimate aim of life into account. This criticism is also baseless. Idealism considers other related aims only as means to achieve this end.

*(iii)* It gives much more importance to thinking and intellectual process as compared to physical activities. It may be a defect of this system.

*(iv)* Values are not absolute. They change as the time changes. Those who have criticized this philosophy on this ground forget that the very individual conception of values has deteriorated the society today. These people criticize this philosophy because of its absolute

and unchangeable concepts but they themselves believe in absolute freedom of man in a democracy. Thus, their criticism becomes irrational.

*(v)* Teachers are given priority over students here. This criticism is really significant.

*(vi)* This philosophy stresses on cramming and rote memory. This criticism is absolutely wrong. No discourse can take place without higher level of intellectual abilities.

*(vii)* They talk about the reality and existence of God but none of them has given any proof about it. Besides, they also seem incompetent to differentiate the visible and dream world. This criticism is really notable and it is the real weakness of the philosophy.

## NATURALISM

Naturalism is a doctorine, which separates nature from God, subordinates spirit to matter and sets up unchangeable laws to be supreme. ----*Ward*

### Meaning

A philosophy, which considers nature (or matter) as every thing and denies any existence of spirit, can be understood only in the perspective with which it rose. A cry against the despotic behaviour of religion and state toward the common people was always the motivating force behind the growth of this philosophy in every age. Thus, Naturalism has gone through the process of evolution in 2500 years. Several forms of Naturalism have emerged during this long period. We will discuss some of these forms first before coming to its fundamental principles.

### Various forms of Naturalism

**1. Atomistic Naturalism :** It is the oldest form of Naturalism. Democritus (460-360 BC) and Epicurus (340-270 BC) are its chief exponents. This philosophy says just as when we go on dividing a thing, a situation comes when further division is not possible. Similarly when we go on discussing a thing, a situation comes when further discussion is not at all possible. This ultimate indivisible unit or situation is called atom. The universe is composed of such atoms, which are different from each other in colour, form, quality and shape. Democritus added that heavy atoms fell down more quickly than the lighter ones and began to unite with each other on the way. Thus, the creation of the universe is a natural process. There is no role of any metaphysical power here. Epicurus amended the view by saying that atoms have motion and they combine with each other by changing their motion during fall.

**2. Scientific Naturalism:** This form of Naturalism is the product of early modern period. It was the period when scientific experiments were going on at a fast speed. These experiments proved that both heavy and light atoms fall down with the same velocity. They also divided atoms into electron, proton and neutron and ultimate unit of substance is not atom but energy of electric or electronic power which is embodied in nature itself. This energy is the creator of the nature. Thus, Scientific Naturalism is totally against the philosophy of atomistic naturalism as far as, them are almost similar. This we can see in two sub forms of Scientific Naturalism.

*(a)* *Physical Naturalism :* According to it, nature and matter are the same thing. Nature is what that has physical existence and can be experienced directly by our senses. Thus, the study of metaphysics is not the subject of this philosophy. Only physical objects are real. According to it, there is no difference between nature and consciousness. Human activities and experiences are studied in terms of material objects and natural laws. So, all material objects come to the category of consciousness. Since all natural laws are governed by cause and effect relationship, study of this relationship is a conscious study. Thus, by denying the existence of non material objects, it has denied the existence of God or soul. It is the energy wave which activates the body, not soul and this energy wave is also dependent on natural laws.

*(b)* *Biological Naturalism :* This philosophy is based on Darwin's theory of evolution. According to it man is product of evolution from lower creatures by a gradual process. Darwin put forward three principles to explain his theory. First is adjustment to environment i.e., each unit of species tries to adjust to the force of environment in its life. Second is

struggle for existence, i.e., it struggles for existence in the process of adjustment. Third principle says that in the process of adjustment and struggle, only the fittest survives and others die out.

**Darwin** has also recognized the theory of change in the nature of living being and theory of use and disuse of organs. According to this theory, if environment changes the nature of man also changes and if any organ is not used for a longer period, it stops functioning. This is the biggest change in man. Due to this change, the theory of natural selection becomes operative. Darwin further explains that traits are of two types, original and acquired. Original traits are transmitted to the next generation by genes but acquired traits are not transferred at all.

Darwin propounded these theories only in the form of hypotheses but he translated them in such a systematic manner that they were accepted and were later applied in education.

**3. Mechanical Naturalism :** According to Herbert Spencer, the main exponent of this philosophy, the world is like a machine. Man is a small part of this huge machine. So, he also behaves very much mechanically. As far as the evolution of this universe is concerned, he says that the world is composed of a kind of ethereal dust called Nebula. In the beginning, the entire solar system was full of nebula and water. Having been separated due to the motion of the solar system, they began to revolve round the other centres. Later on with cooling down of the atmosphere they also cooled and gradually converted into planets. Thus, creation is ethereal and its development is mechanical and purposeless.

This machine is still moving. In the movement of this machine, there is no role of any mental or spiritual power. Since, man is also a part of this huge machine, his movement is also governed by external stimuli or forces of nature. These laws are temporary one. We have to discover the eternal laws with the help of science. This philosophy led to the development of psychology as science.

**4. Historical Naturalism :** According to this philosophy, human history is the history of man's struggle on this earth. Accumulation of wealth is the main cause behind all these struggles and wars. Thus, wealth or matter is real and its accumulation is a natural phenomenon. This philosophy later led to the rise of communist philosophy in the 20th century.

The common feature in all the above philosophies is that only matter is real. Mind is also a form of matter. Every material object is governed by temporary natural laws. We can find out the reality of matter (or nature) by sense experience and experimentation. If man goes away from nature, his survival will be at stake. The existence of any supernature is only a myth.

## Chief Contributors of Naturalism

Like Idealism, naturalism has also influenced many philosopher in such a great extent. Some of these great philosophers who contributes to this philosophy are—Aristotle, Comte, Bacon, Rousseau, Darwin, Lamark, Huxley, Spencer, J.B.Shaw etc.

## Principles and Characteristics of Naturalism

1. **Harmony with nature :** Every matter including man is governed by natural laws. We should not endeavour to change the route of these laws artificially, i.e., natural light and air is more important than artificial light or air. The personality of the child should be developed but only on natural track. Nothing should be imposed artificially on him. If we try to make the child cultured and civilized, his whole personality will be disintegrated. Nature is our friend. We should go in the direction in which nature is going. The process of evolution is slow but natural. Child acquires the necessary traits from the environment slowly and systematically.
   In the absence of harmony with nature, humans will fall a prey to different diseases in the process of struggle for existence and medical (artificial) treatment will be required to get rid of these diseases. Thus, revolt against natural laws hampers the natural development of humans.
2. **Freedom :** In the words of Rousseau, *"Man is born free and I find him in chains everywhere."* These chains are of different forms, political, social and cultural. Despotic rulers are not allowing him to do anything freely. Man is bound with cultural and social tabbos also and he has

rented his destiny in the hands of some supernatural power. He has become the slave of artificial life style also, i.e., "big cities are not proper dwelling places. They are rather grave yards." Since man is born free, he must be allowed to live freely according to his natural impulses and inborn tendencies. If such freedom is not given, his struggle for existence will be weakened and his survival will become more difficult than ever. Freedom consists of freedom of thought, expression and activity.

3. **Mechanical behaviour of man :** Man is a small but compete machine in the large machine, the universe. His behaviour is not conscious, it is rather mechanical. If stimuli is given, response will be there. Response can be accelerated by giving natural stimuli.
4. **Reality of matter :** Matter is not the creation of any supernatural power. Physical and chemical reactions have given life to it. This matter can be experienced by our senses, so it is real. Soul or spirit (God) can not be experienced by our senses so it is not real. Thus, only the life of this world is real. Man should try to make this life happy.
5. **Status of man :** All the innate tendencies and capacities of man are determined by natural laws. So, he is not absolutely independent in his activities, he will remain free only if he does not voilate the laws of nature. e.g., sexual desire is an innate tendency, killing this tendency by unnatural means will hamper the process of development. In spite of that, man is the supreme creation of nature because he is evolved out of lower animals.
6. **Unchangeable laws of nature :** Natural laws are permanent and are governed by cause and effect relationship. There is no God here to control it. Darwin also proves it but in opposite way by admitting that change in nature of man is brought about by changes in the environment.
7. **Belief about knowledge :** Only that knowledge is real which is obtained from experience and experimentation. Intution or philosophical discoveries is not real knowledge. Thus, this philosophy stresses the study of science subjects only.

## Educational Implications of Naturalism

Naturalism when applied to education means putting the child at the centre of all educational processes and natural laws will be the teacher to teach the child according to his own nature. Nature of a child is of two types, physical nature and biological (psychological) nature. Former is external and later is internal. For the natural development of the child, the external laws of nature should correspond and coincide with the internal nature of the child. It means that child should be given full freedom to develop his innate tendencies and natural capacities. External environment will not hamper this natural process at all.

Thus, Naturalism was a reaction to Idealism, Humanism and Formalism which insisted on bookish knowledge to be enforced into the mind of the child from outside. The credit of introducing Naturalism into education goes to Comenius and Francis Bacon but Rousseau and Spencer brought this movement to the zenith.

The implication of Naturalism in education can be studied under the following heads:

**1. Principles of Education:** This philosophy has propounded the following principles of education:

(a) *Follow nature :* According to Rousseau, education is not to prepare the child for his future life but to develop him in the present according to his natural abilities and instinct. The help of physical nature is taken for this purpose. Thus, nature is the best teacher of the child. So, instead of artificial environment, natural environment in the school is created for this purpose.

(b) *Self learning :* Child should be given opportunity for learning through sense experiences in the lap of nature. Bookish knowledge is only secondary.

(c) *Child centred education :* This phrase was first used by John Adams. "Child is the centre of teaching learning process." Here every activity is directed to him. The role of the teacher is only of a guide. Even curriculum is not given more importance than the child.

(d) *Progressive manner of education :* As a child develops physically and mentally, curriculum is also developed progressively. There are four stages of child development infancy, childhood, adolescence and adulthood according to Rousseau. The load of the curriculum is distributed according to the age and mental level of a child.

(e) *Complete freedom of the child :* Child is given full freedom to develop according to his natural tendencies. He is not tied with artificial rules and regulations of the school. He is given full opportunity to observe and experience the matter that exists before him.

(f) *Training of senses :* Sense organs are the gateways of knowledge. Only that knowledge is real which is acquired through senses. So these sense organs are trained in such a way that acquisition of knowledge becomes a natural process.

(g) *Materialistic education :* Spiritualistic education is of no use for a child. Matter (wealth) is everything for him because it can give him pleasure and comforts. Child should contribute to scientific inventions and discoveries to enhance his comforts and reduce his miseries.

(h) *Negative education :* See Rousseau's Negative education in previous chapter.

**2. Aims of Education:** It is very difficult to establish any definite aim of education according to this philosophy. The reason is that nature is neither definite nor certain. That is why when Rousseau says that the aim of education should be to establish harmony between man, nature and substance, the task of an educator becomes very difficult. How can unchangeable nature of subjects be harmonized to a changing nature of man? This is really a challenging task. Another difficulty of establishing aims of education is that all Naturalists do not have consensus over the aims of education. Different philosophers have propounded different aims of education. Some of these aims which are totally individualistic in nature are given below:

(a) *Preparation of child for struggle of life :* According to biological Naturalism, the aim of education is to prepare the child for struggle in order to adapt to the environment, only then he will be able to survive.

(b) *Attainment of comforts and pleasure :* According to physical naturalism, the aim of education is to develop the child to attain material comforts through scientific inventions and discoveries.

(c) *Sublimation of instincts :* Mc Dougall opposed the view of physical Naturalism and said that the aim of education is not to attain pleasure but to sublimate the uncontrolled instincts. If it is not sublimated, the man may distort the natural environment by artificial means and it will be very dangerous for him.

(d) *Conditioning of reflex action :* According to mechanical Naturalism, the aim of education is to establish reflex action of children by conditioning. When senses and other organs are trained, child's responses get controlled and conditioned. Thus, without jeopardizing the freedom of the child learning by conditioning is taught to him.

(e) *Adjustment to environment :* According to Lamark, environment is not always conducive to natural living of the child. So, the aim of education is to strengthen the capacity of the child to adjust with hostile and changing environment.

(f) *Development of physical and natural powers:* Naturalism does not believe in any form of Idealism as well as the spirituality explained by it. According to Spencer, the aim of education is to develop the physical and natural powers of the child through experience and experimentation. For this purpose, child is made physically healthy and strong.

(g) *Progressive and unrestricted development. :* The aim of education is to put away all barriers that are there in the path of natural development of the child and provide him maximum opportunity for progressive development.

(h) *Self-learning:* Self learning through self study, experience or experimentation is very important here. Bookish knowledge based on hypothetical ideas is not supported by this philosophy at all. The aim of education is to create environment for self learning.

**3. Curriculum :** Naturalism considers child and his natural development more important than the curriculum. Important characteristics of Naturalistic curriculum are given below-

*(i)* The purpose of education is to develop the child fully according to his innate tendencies and abilities. So, wide range of curriculum is needed.

*(ii)* It favours only that education which is directly related to life. So subjects taught should be useful for each stages of life.

*(iii)* Teaching of literary subjects is useless because they can not give any material satisfaction or pleasure.

*(iv)* Moral or religious education is also not needed for a child. This education does not prepare him for material life.

*(v)* Curriculum should be constructed keeping in view the life stages of the child and his aptitude. So, different things will be taught at different age. Thus, physical education in infancy and training of senses in childhood is emphasized. Subject education should start only in adolescence.

*(vi)* No books will be recommended in the early period of education. Natural development of the child will be encouraged through physical exercise and activities.

**4. Status of the child :** At the time of birth, the child is fully free from evils. It is the society and the environment that vitiate and corrupt him later on. Thus there is no role of nature in corrupting the child. If child again is back to nature and he is given full opportunity to develop according to his natural tendencies, he will again be free from evils. Proper education is needed for this purpose. Child is always made supreme in the educational system and everything is done in his interest keeping his needs and abilities into account. By doing so, Naturalism favours individualistic education. It means individual is always superior to society.

**5. Status of the Teacher:** Natural development of the child is possible only when he is allowed to develop freely in a natural environment without creating any hindrance from outside (teacher). Thus, the role of the teacher is only secondary for students. He is only accepted as a necessary evil in the class. The lesser a teacher speaks in the class, the better. The interference of the teacher should be minimum in the class.

The teacher's role is like that of a gardener who prepares the earth for proper development of plants only. Teacher only creates conducive learning environment in the class. Then like a silent spectator he sees the children grow. Teacher is fully impartial in his attitude and he is capable of judging the abilities of his students. He is affectionate and sympathetic to his students and participates with them in games, sports and other recreational activities like a friend. The actual teacher of the child is nature.

**6. Method of Teaching:** Education is fully child centred in Naturalism. So, following teaching methods are adopted:

*(a)* *Use of learning theories :* Learning is very much mechanical according to Naturalism. The role of mind is all the time secondary. So, teacher applies all the learning theories in his teaching such as conditioning theories, trial and error, etc.

*(b)* *Learning by doing :* Children are taught through activities keeping in view their specific interests and abilities. Lectures are not used at all to teach them and books are used only as means.

*(c)* *Learning by experiences :* This philosophy considers only perceptual knowledge as real. This knowledge is obtained from sense experiences in the natural environment. The child comes in contact with nature, he gets inspiration from it and in the process he learns directly.

*(d)* *Self learning :* Here the role of the teacher is only a guide. He only creates full conducive environment and everything is learnt by the students themselves. Children learn according to their aptitudes and interests and they are least interfered in doing so.

*(e)* *Progressive method :* Teaching method is also determined by stages of development of the child. Activity is emphasized in the period of infancy. Then teacher gradually shifts from doing to knowing in the later stages of development.

(f) *Learning by play :* Learning is made play not a work by the teacher. Everything is taught with the help of games.

(g) *Individual teaching :* Individual attention is paid on children in the class. Each child is important for the teacher.

**7. Discipline:** Here child is not punished for any of his mistakes. He is punished by the nature if he ignores laws of nature. Thus, natural tendencies are the basis of students' behaviour and self discipline is the best discipline approved by Naturalists. It is based on theory of natural consequences of an act. It means that if child neglects some work, he will face the consequences of his negligence. For natural and independent development of the child, the policy of least interference by the teacher is followed.

## Influence of Naturalism

Naturalism was the philosophy which influenced not only education but also society, polity and science. Some examples are cited below:

(a) *Development of child psychology :* Naturalism for the first time emphasized the development of the child according to his natural tendencies, needs and aptitudes. Thus this philosophy led to the rise of psychology as a full fledged subject. People started conducting experiment on children and lower animals and findings of lower animals were also applied to children.

(b) *Rise of scientific study of society :* Man was for the first time given very much importance. People started studying the impact of society and environment on man and vice versa. This led to the interference of the church in the individual life of man declined.

(c) *Rise of democracy :* Rousseau advocated liberty, equality and fraternity as three guiding principles for man which were completely denied by the despotic rulers and the church. Under the impact of Naturalism people rose up against the sociopolitical system. This later led to the rise of democracy, a new philosophy of life of, the modern world.

(d) *Scientific tendency in education :* After declaring only perceptual knowledge as real, Naturalism motivated the people to come closer to science subjects and experiments in Physics, Chemistry, Biology and Astronomy gained momentum. This led to many new inventions and discoveries at that time.

(e) *Introduction of child centred activity method:* Activity, play-way and experience based methods of teaching were accepted in schools. Physical education and sports activities were included in the curriculum and individuality of the child and individual differences were considered important principles in teaching learning process. All these things made the process interesting and natural Kinder Garten and Montessori schools were opened exactly on the line of Naturalism.

(f) *Change in the concept of school discipline :* Discipline was imposed by repressive methods and by using corporal punishments in schools before the rise of modern Naturalism. Students were denied the freedom of expression and action in schools. This philosophy developed the concept of self discipline which was established by natural consequences of action.

## Criticism of Naturalism

Several defects in this philosophy have been pointed out by different thinkers and educationists. Some of them are given below:

(i) It is one sided and incomplete. It describes what not to do in detail but what ought to be done is generally overlooked.

(ii) Here achievement is evaluated on the basis of result but whether the result is good, satisfactory or poor, can not be determined by this philosophy. For this purpose we will have to go to Idealism back.

(iii) It neglects spiritualism altogether and puts emphasis on nature only. Thus, material attitude of the people toward life may make the people selfish and self centred which is very dangerous for a society like ours.

(iv) Mental side of man is more powerful than physical (mechanical) side. Its height and depth is unlimited. So, by giving importance to natural tendencies only, Naturalism narrows, down the scope of life.

*(v)* It also lacks educational aims and talks about the natural development of the child only.

*(vi)* Naturalism does not give any importance to the experiences gained by the previous generations and stresses on the personal experiences only. Thus a child might repeat all those mistakes which were committed by his precedors. Moreover, he will be able to acquire only a small fraction of the vast knowledge accumulated so far on the basis of his own experiences.

*(vii)* It stresses on the present needs of the child only and neglects his future needs and problems.

*(viii)* It stresses on the activities and experiences of the child and ignores the bookish knowledge.

*(ix)* It gives unrestricted freedom to the child which may develop arbitrary behaviour in the child in the long run. In such case, child will not consider others at all and will decide arbitrarily.

*(x)* It gives very little importance to teachers in the class. This attitude is not considered healthy and sound in modern democratic countries where various social and moral qualities are also to be inculcated by the teacher.

*(xi)* It ignores the development of the society altogether.

*(xii)* It makes the child only a machine.

## REALISM

Realism is the doctorine that states that objective reality or material universe exists independent of the conscious mind, its nature and properties are affected by being know. —*C.V.Good*

### Historical Background

Realism is an old philosophy in the sense that Aristotle propounded his ideas on its basis. In India too Samkhya system, Charvak Darshan, Vaishishka philosophy, Jainism, Buddhism, all opposed the existence of God or soul and considered only material world to be real on the ground that this can be perceived by our senses. Thus, all these thoughts are based on Realism.

But Realism developed as a formal school of philosophy only in the 17th century as a protest against the philosophy of Idealism. The fast scientific and technological progress was the feeding ground for this philosophy. Upto the end of the 17th century, people had lost faith in all the ancient and medieval ideals of life. The reason was that Idealism had failed to inculcate that capacity in men which could enable them to face the real challenges and problems of life and thus it was not giving them material pleasure. Several other powerful movements like scholasticism, Renaissance, Reformation, Humanism etc also started during this period. These movements addressed the problems of worldly life very powerfully and the solutions proposed by these movements motivated the people a lot to adopt a realistic attitude towards life. Since science was advancing by leaps and bound during this period and for solving the real day to day problems of men, people accepted Realism as a philosophy of life with pleasure. The main factors, behind the growth of this philosophy was the breaking of the old superstitious beliefs and traditions by the scientific inventions and discoveries. Thus, we can say that the very impact of science on Naturalism (materialism) gave rise to Realism.

### Meaning of Realism

To do away with the world of imagination, dream or intution is the general meaning of Realism. A Realist is one who believed in what he is at present with all his strengths and weaknesses and does not dwell in the world of utopia. Technically Realism believed in that knowledge only which is acquired by our senses. If anything found to be true on the basis of observation or experimentation, only then it is taken to be true. Mind has actually no role to play in determining the reality of an object, i.e., objects are real independent of mental phenomenon. If we are able to perceive a thing by our senses, it is real.

The extreme form of Realism reduces the mind itself to an object of matter.

### Chief Contributors

The chief protagonists of this philosophy are Irasmus, Rebellias, Milton, Lord Montaigne, John Locke, Francis Bacon, Comenius and Bertrand Russell, etc.

### Definitions of Realism

*(a)* *Bulter*, "Realism is the reinforcement of our common acceptance of this world as it appears to us."

According to this definition reality is what we perceive and our common perception gets reinforced with the help of this philosophy through observation and experimentation.

(b) *J.S. Ross:* "The doctorine of Realism asserts that there is a real world of things behind and corresponding to the objects of our perception." According to this definition reality is a bit deeper than the phenomenal world. That we perceive generally is not actually real. The reality of an object is perceived and ascertained by close observation, examination and experimentation of the object.

## Forms of Realism

Various forms of Realism and the education proposed by them are given below :

**1. Humanistic Realism:** This form of Realism emphasizes the general human welfare through education by saying that human beings are the fundamental realities in the material world. So realities of the material objects must be examined in terms of human realities. Meaning thereby, the education imparted to the people should be realistic, only when it can solve the day to day problems of men and thus promote human welfare. Several contributors of this form of Realism are as follows:

(a) *Irasmus :* The English philosopher condemned unrelated and narrow education system and advocated broad, liberal and useful education.

(b) *Rebellias :* The French philosopher opposed academic and theoretical type of education and laid emphasis on the practical, physical, social and moral education. He advocated that the education should be such as to prepare the individual to face the problems of life with courage and solve them successfully. For this purpose curriculum should be reorganized and method of teaching should be changed. Rebellias gives no place to logic, grammar or literature in the curriculum. As far as pedagogy is concerned, instead of drill or cramming, scientific and psychological methods and techniques should be adopted.

(c) *John Milton :* The great English poet and philosopher expressed his ideas in his book **Tracts of Education** by saying "I call therefore a complete and generous education that which lifts a man to perform justly, skillfully and magnanimously all the offices both private and public of peace and war." In his book he opposed mere academic education and insisted that education should give the knowledge of objects and things. Physical and practical education is a must for this purpose. He structured a curriculum for the children and youth in the age group of 12-21 years. In this structure he categorized curriculum into main and subsidiary subjects. Language, literature, moral science etc. are main subjects and physiology, agriculture, sculpture etc. are subsidiary subjects.

Milton is different from most of Realist in two ways.

- He believes in God.
- He opposes education of the masses.

**2. Social Realism:** Social Realists are the base of this philosophy which is judged on the relative strength of merits and demerits of an action. The thing which is socially useful to us is only real.

The aim of this philosophy is to make human life happy and successful by fulfilling the social needs. This philosophy opposed the mere academic or bookish knowledge and advocated practical education that can be useful to the individual in any way. Thus, education must promote the working efficiency of the individual. For this purpose, History, Geography, Arithmetic, Diplomacy law, Warfare, Horse riding Gymnastic exercises, Dancing etc are included in the curriculum.

The chief contributors to this philosophy are as follows:

(a) *Lord Montaigne:* His ideas on education can be traced in three books written by him. These books are **Pendentry, Of the Education of the Children** and **Affection of fathers to their children.** According to him, the purpose of education is to develop intelligence and self discriminating power of children. This education prepares the child to a high level that he does not accept anything without understanding it. Knowledge for the sake of knowledge is useless according to him. It must be useful and purposeful for the sake of social life. He upheld the view of learning by self experiences. For this purpose, he prescribes tours and excursions of children. In the school children should learn their own mother tongue, then they should learn the language of their neighbours and finally other languages like Greek or Latin may be taught.

(b) *John Locke :* His thoughts on education can be seen in his famous book **Some Thoughts Concerning Education**. According to him, the aim of education is to inculcate virtue, wisdom and capacity to learn in children. Unlike John Milton, he also opposed the education of the masses and restricted education to the higher strata of the society. He believed that the mind of the child is a clean slate on which the experiences of the age is written. Locke emphasized the education through the medium of mother tongue and insisted that only that education should be given to a child which is individually or socially useful for him.

**3. Sense Realism:** According to this philosophy knowledge primarily comes through senses not from words. So senses of a child should be used to the maximum in the process of education. It otherwise means that truth can only be gained by observation and experience, i.e., by the contact between external object and the senses. The child is given full opportunity to observe and study natural phenomenon (laws) after coming in contact with external objects. Thus, we see that sense Realists were greatly influenced by the scientific researches and inventions and they gave a solid practical base to education through their philosophy. The main aspects of this system are given below:

(*i*) Mother tongue as the medium of instruction.

(*ii*) More importance to study of nature through the study of science subjects instead of languages and humanities.

(*iii*) More emphasis on practical and utilitarian education.

(*iv*) Psychological method of teaching.

(*v*) Deductive method is more important than inductive method.

Some of the contributors of this philosophy are given below:

(a) *Mulcaster :* The English philosopher had been headmaster in different schools for 37 years. He advocated that the aims of education should be mental and physical development of the child through observation of natural laws. He emphasized that education should be child centred and imparted through mother tongue. As far as method of teaching is concerned he says that psychological method of teaching should be used. He divided the curriculum into two stages. At the primary stage, mother tongue, reading, writing, music, painting etc., may be taught but at the secondary stage only science subjects should be given priority.

(b) *Francis Bacon :* The educational thoughts of this famous English writer and philosopher can be found in his books namely, **The New Atlantis**, and **Advancement of Learning**. He opined that the object of all knowledge is to give man power over nature. He condemned the present system of education and advocated a change and reorganization in this system on scientific and inductive lines. In other words Bacon popularized inductive method of teaching in his time as against deductive method of Aristotle. He gave more importance to science and observation of nature as against literature, religion or philosophy.

(c) *Comenius :* He asserted that ultimate end of man is eternal happiness. So, a child should be a moralist or God fearing. And since this is the right of all children to get eternal happiness, so character of education should be universal and liberal. By criticizing the inductive method of Bacon he proposed natural method of teaching. According to him, knowledge comes not only through the senses alone but intelligence and divine inspiration can also play an important role in gaining knowledge. He propounded nine rules regarding method of teaching.

(*i*) Teaching method should be simple.

(*ii*) The purpose of learning should be told to children.

(*iii*) Children should be given only useful knowledge.

*(iv)* Teaching should be done very effectively.

*(v)* General rules should also be explained.

*(vi)* The material should be taught in parts and step by step in a sequence.

*(vii)* Chronology should be followed.

*(viii)* Subject matter should be discussed very clearly.

*(ix)* Teacher should never cease his efforts till learning is achieved.

*(x)* Some other ideas of Comenius are as follows:

- Nature does its work according to a time table and stage. So, we must follow nature.
- Mother tongue should be taught first.
- The curriculum should be integrated from lower to a higher level.
- Corporal punishment to children must be avoided.

**4. Neo Realism:** According to this form of Realism, rules and procedures of science are also changeable. So, there is no permanent nature of truth or reality. Truths or values are valid in certain circumstances. Because of this reason the usefulness of a knowledge or value also changes with the change of time :

Important exponents of this branch of Realism are given below:

*(a)* *Whitehead :* Education should give the child full knowledge of an organism who is movable and immovable, conscious and unconscious. Along with the scientific values one should know other values also.

*(b)* *Bertrand Russell :* He emphasized the sensory development of the child since the very period of infancy. He was in favour of analysis method of teaching. He did support liberal education and strongly opposed religious education.

## Principles and Characteristics of Realism

1. **Nature of universe :** Universe is not only external but it is governed by the inexorable law. It seems less true in social sciences as compared to natural sciences, it is because that man has not yet perfected techniques of ascertaining and stating the laws of social phenomenon.
2. **Reality differs from truth :** Reality is concerned to what actually is and truth is its image. The test of truth is its correspondence to reality. If ideas work, it is because they are true to reality and not vice-versa.
3. **Values :** Morals are either enforced by social processes or are self enforcing through their natural consequence (close to Naturalism). Character education has therefore no authority external to nature. Meaning thereby, values are derived from the lows of nature. So moral ethics should not be imposed on a person from outside.
4. **Nature of truth :** According to this philosophy, the phenomenal world (matter) is real. There is no world beyond this material world. Thus, realism is the antithesis of subjective Idealism.
5. **Belief about knowledge :** Senses are the gateway of knowledge. The impression and sensation which are results of contact between external objects and the senses is nothing but knowledge. Thus, knowledge based on observation or experience is always real. Bertrand Russell in his book **Analysis of Mind** writes that ultimate constituent of matter are not atoms but sensations. I believe that stuff of our mental life consists wholly of sensations and images.
6. **Opposite of Idealism :** Here there is no scope of imagination without experimentation at all. There is no existence of God, soul or heaven according to this philosophy. They are merely the product of human imaginations. Only matter is real because it can be experienced through our senses.
7. **Nature of man and mind :** Man is a part of the material world so, he is also real. Hc is cndowed with sense organs and the mind which help him in attaining knowledge so, they are also real, being material in nature.
8. **Emphasis on experimentation :** This philosophy lays much emphasis on experimentation and observation for acquiring knowledge. Moreover, no experience can be accepted as true unless it is analysed and classified in totality.
9. **Belief about values :** Values are not permanent. They also change with the change of time. These values are not derived from religion. They are rather social acceptability based on experiences.
10. **Different from Naturalism :** Both Naturalism and Realism believe in the reality of matter and

material world but there are differences between the two also such as,

(i) Naturalism believes in ultimate reality of matter but the reality of Realism is not ultimate. It is rather phenomenal.

(ii) Naturalism always follows nature but Realism can manipulate natural laws also.

(iii) Values do not change in short period in Naturalism, but in Realism, values can always change

**11. Realism differenciated from Pragmatism :** Both Pragmatism and Realism emphasize the role of experience and experimentation for gaining knowledge but Realism is different from Pragmatism in the sense that Realism believes in traditions and facts with which the real knowledge is linked up while in Pragmatism true knowledge of the material world is gained by activity related experiences.

## Educational Implication of Realism

**1. Nature and Characteristics of Education :**

(a) *Based on science :* The realists advocate the inclusion of science subjects in place of academic subjects in the curriculum. It is because only that knowledge is real which can be proved by scientific experiments.

(b) *Based on present life of the child :* Here the present life of the child is the focal point of the educational system and the purpose is to make it comfortable. The life of the world hereafter is not the subject matter of Realism. So, this philosophy opposed traditional ideals and values and is concerned with the practical problems of day to day life. Due to this reason, subjects discussing the mundane life of the people are included in the curriculum.

(c) *Emphasis on application of knowledge:* Mere academic knowledge is not enough according to this philosophy. It should be applied to real life situations by experience and experimentation. If practical work is given to a child only then he can solve the practical problems of his life. Thus, Realism opposes bookish knowledge based on rote memory.

(d) *Material education :* It opposes all sorts of spiritual or metaphysical education of Idealists and believes in material education. This philosophy snatches a man from the world of ideas and makes him enter a practical world. Action rather than thinking is important here.

(e) *Freedom of the child :* The child has to put ideas into practice, for this purpose he should be given freedom of experience and experimentation. Child will proceed from ignorance to knowledge slowly through his own efforts.

(f) *Vocational education :* The aim of education according to Realism is to help a man to lead a happy life. This is possible only when the needs of bread and butter are fulfilled by education. Education must enable man to succeed in his vocation. For this purpose, vocational subjects are specially included in the curriculum.

(g) *Activation of senses :* According to Realism knowledge is acquired through sense organs. So, senses of the child are trained very effectively. Such type of education is given to children which can activate their senses and thus the horizon of experiences are expanded.

(h) *Simultaneous development of individuality and society :* For the purpose of creating a well satisfied society, individuality of a child is not neglected here. Individuals through their own development develop the society.

**2. Aims of Education :** Education should serve the following aims according to Realism :

(a) To prepare the child for a happy and successful life by solving the real problems of life successfully.

(b) To enable a child to accumulate material gains as much as possible.

(c) To make the child practical in his behaviour.

(d) To help the child to accept the bitter realities of life on one hand and to enable him to change it into pleasant realities.

(e) To develop the physical and mental power of the child.

(f) To train the child to use his senses to the maximum level possible.

(g) To bring the child closer to nature.

(h) To acquaint the child with physical and social environment in which he lives.

(*i*) To enable the child to earn his livelihood through vocational and practical education.

(*j*) To enable the child to observe nature with more penetrating mind so that he may visualize the deep reality along with the phenomenal one.

**3. Curriculum :** Here only those subjects or activities are included in the curriculum which prepare the child for his real worldly life. For this purpose science and vocational subjects are primarily and preferably taught and secondary place is given to Arts and Humanities. Realists opine that mother tongue is the base of all the educational activities. So, language must go side by side of vocational subjects. Moreover, specific interest and abilities of children are also taken into account while selecting a particular subject for them.

**4. Method of Teaching:** Following methods of teaching are proposed by Realists :

(*a*) Observation, sense experiences, and self experimentation, i.e., the knowledge of objects and external phenomena is imparted through senses.

(*b*) Action or experimentation rather than thinking, i.e., practical instead of bookish knowledge is emphasized.

(*c*) Audio-visual aids are also used in order to activate senses.

(*d*) Inductive method, means that objects or its models are shown to the child first then its interpretation is made.

(*e*) Travelling and excursion in order to enhance experiences.

**5. Role of the Teacher:** Here role of the teacher is neither as high as an Idealist nor as negligible as a Naturalism. The teacher should have full command over the subject on one hand and he should know his pupils fully on the other. He presents the subject matter before his pupils very clearly and systematically by using psychological and scientific methods, then he invites his pupils for self observation and experimentation. He must also know what amount of knowledge should be given to children at a particular time and why it is to be given.

**6. Discipline:** Realists believe in self discipline in the educational system which is established by synthesizing impressionistic and emancipatory forms of discipline.

## Merits of Realism (Influence)

Realism, though could not influence traditional system of education very much, yet it proved to be a foundation stone of Pragmatism in the 19$^{th}$ and 20$^{th}$ centuries. Some of its merits are given below:

1. It emphasizes that education should be practical rather than theoretical and directly useful for life for an individual. Thus, education, was for the first time linked with practical problems of life such as problem of food, cloth and shelter.
2. Because of the influence of this philosophy science subjects found an important place in the curriculum. People began to believe that no country can progress without the knowledge of science.
3. Realism encourages scientific experimentations which lead to new inventions and discoveries in science and technology.
4. It also brought about revolutionary changes in the method of teaching, inductive method, heuristic and experimental methods and correlation devices are now very much accepted and used by educators today.
5. This philosophy rejected repressionistic discipline and advocated a synthesis of impressionistic and emancipatory disciplines which is now accepted by the people with consensus.
6. Objectivity in teaching or evaluation that we see today is very much due to the contribution of this philosophy.

## Criticism of Realism (Evaluation)

1. It denies the existence of metaphysical world in toto but it fails to answer several questions such as
   - Is there any power behind the physical world?
   - Is this physical world absolute and supreme?
   - What are the limits of this physical world and so on?
2. Realism regards the senses as gate way of knowledge when senses come in contact with physical objects. But how illusion occurs when senses are so powerful sources of knowledge.

This is the question that Realism is unable to answer.

3. It does not believe in imagination or emotions. The fact, however, is that without imagination no scientific invention takes place.
4. It takes only worldly pleasure into account. This belief is also unsounded because many people commit suicide only due to lack of spiritual bliss.
5. Realism accepts facts and truths as they are i.e., if there is any injustice or corruption in the society, there is no need to change them.
6. If science subjects are given very much preference to Arts and Humanities, it may create imbalance in the curriculum.
7. Realism does not give any importance to ideals and values. How can a valueless society survive for long is a big question.

## HUMANISM

Putting the man at the top in thinking and action, removing all sorts of discriminations meted out to man and doing only what is in the interest of human being are the ideals with which this philosophy was coined.

— *M.S. Ansari*

### Meaning

Different philosophers have elaborated Humanism in different ways such as :

*(i)* Humanism is a proper adjustment in life. No other human being is harmed by his fellow being at any stage or circumstances of life.

*(ii)* Humanism is for the purpose of creating interest in all spheres of life. Renunciation is not adopted by those who believe in this philosophy.

*(iii)* Humanism means religious freedom given to all human being and nothing is imposed externally on them.

*(iv)* Humanism means to express feeling about all human happenings.

*(v)* Humanism asserts that man is the centre and measure of all human activities in the world.

*(vi)* Humanism means that criterion of all human activities is human welfare and human betterment.

### Forms of Humanism

**1. Rational Humanism :** It says that essence of human nature is rational in character. Rationality, i.e., doing anything after careful consideration, is the distinguishing feature between man and other creatures of the universe. Reason (mind) thus separates man from other living beings. This form of Humanism is also called scientific Humanism.

Scientific humanism advocates scientific methodology and approach in solving various life relate problems leading to the welfare of man. In the field of education, it recommends two types of education—instrumental and positive. Its chief exponents are Herbert Spence and Thomas Huxley.

Important characteristics of this form of Humanism are as follows :

*(i)* Man is the centre and measure of all activities. Whatever is to be done will be done in the interest of man.

*(ii)* Man will not be discriminated on the basis of race, religion or nature.

*(iii)* International friendship is the third feature of Scientific Humanism.

**2. Buddhist Humanism :** Buddha has explained his Humanism in terms of four noble truths already explained in the chapter "Indian Philosophies and Islamic Traditions". There is only one way to get rid of this suffering and that is the adaptation of eight fold paths given by Mahatma Buddha.

Buddha advocated that man should be non violent (free from all violent activities or killings) first in order to adopt eight paths of life and second in order to establish a pain free society.

### Basic Principles of Humanism

Humanism as a philosophy has a definite notion regarding man, his problems and the universe. Some of the fundamental principles of this philosophy are given below:

1. **Nature and its role :** According to Humanism all necessary materials of life are received by us from nature which is very powerful and wide. Our very existence also depends on nature. Existence of humanity is not possible without nature. It is because of power of nature that man

achieves success in Arts and Science and moulds the culture in his own way. Thus, we can say that human life, earth and the universe are the manifestation of nature.

2. **Opposition of supernaturalism :** Humanists so firmly believe in nature and its manifestation that they strongly oppose supernaturalism of any kind. There is no role of god or any supernatural power in the creation of this universe. It is nature that brings about continuity of every changing events.
3. **Concept of man :** Man is a part of as well as gift of nature. As a result he is governed by natural laws. If it is so, human body and personality can not be separated from each other. Since man is a part of nature, he is very powerful. He is creating the world in his own way. He is trying to bring heaven on earth by conquering the great forces of nature, such as, he is trying to build home on the moon as well as on Mars. All these things reflect that nature in the form of man is very powerful.
4. **Mind and its role :** According to Humanism human thinking is the result of reaction between living system and environment. Human thinking is a natural process just like the process of respiration, digestion and locomotion. Thus, mind can not be separated from the functioning of brain. Actually, mind is brain in action.
5. **Human problems can be solved :** Man is fully competent to find solutions to his problems on the basis of his intelligence and scientific method. Fate has no role to play in determining the direction of human life. We achieve every thing that we want by hard work.
6. **Freedom of man :** According to this philosophy, man can achieve happiness and pleasure only in this world as there is no existence of other world. So he should be given full freedom to achieve this happiness through economic, cultural and moral progress. Every human being in the world is unique. His thinking is entirely individual, independent of others. Because of this individuality he takes interest in a particular thing or object and tries to adjust himself to that thing. How man gives priority to a particular thing or object and adjust himself with it, is the result of freedom given to him.
7. **Opposition to religions :** Humanism does not approve any particular religion but it takes human principles and values of all the religions into account. The purpose here is to avoid cultural or religious conflict and to bring about a peaceful and happy society.
8. **Social peace through democracy :** The purpose of Humanism is to establish national and international democracy in order that permanent peace in the world might be established. Lessons of responsibility, freedom and tolerance, etc. are taught to every body thus democracy and international peace are two guiding principles that Humanism talks about.
9. **Emphasis on science and scientific attitude :** Humanism finds solutions of all human problems through scientific method and enquiry. Adoption of scientific attitude is a must even while studying social science. This attitude is more important than collection of information. Thus, ideas are not imposed here. People are convinced scientifically to adopt a particular idea or principle. If on the other hand, a person is not using scientific method and attitude, he will have to face objections of the people regarding his inferences on a particular issue.
10. **Human welfare :** Maximum human welfare is the prime motive of this philosophy. This is achieved by establishing peace in the society, by putting tolerable ideas and principles, by increasing the number of democratic institutions and by rational thinking. This welfare increases the general socio economic standard of the people.

Thus, Humanism wants to make this earth heaven of peace and beauty and to increase the happiness of man on this earth, which is actually the birth right of man. This happiness will be brought about by the man himself. Any supernatural force has no role to play in this regard. Thus, Humanism makes a man optimistic, courageous and active. It reminds man every time that his happy home is this world only. So he has to make his destiny on this earth on his own efforts. While doing so he confronts with the other fellow being and their destinies but he never transgresses his limit. As a democratic member of the society he does not create any barrier in the ways of achieving happiness by others. He rather creates conducive circumstances for the collective survival of all humans on the earth.

Morality of Humanism includes service to humanity. That is why human welfare is the other name of this philosophy.

This philosophy believes in the equality of all humans irrespective of caste, creed, colour or race. Universal brotherhood (international understanding) which is called *Vasudhaiva Kutumbakam* in India is the theme of this philosophy.

## Ethics of Humanism

*(i)* Humanism wants that man should accept different gifts of life happily. He should not be self contended and avoid worldly pleasure.

*(ii)* Human life should automatically be so splendid and full of charm as is the notion of immortality i.e., charm of life should never come to an end.

*(iii)* Humans should accept different types of joys, beauties, braveries, and ideals of this earth. Learning the life of Sanyasi or Saint is opposed by this philosophy. This philosophy later led to the rise of consumerism in the late 20th and 21st centuries.

*(iv)* Humanism believes in love of beauty and beauty of love both. Love of beauty means a man must have aesthetic sense to admire the beauty spreading everywhere on the earth. Beauty of love means deep social relations between humans in which there is no scope of selfishness. Everyone is always ready to cooperate with his fellow being.

*(v)* People should have positive thinking and attitude regarding life.

*(vi)* Humanists want that all the people of the world should continue to enjoy the materials of the world abundantly. Man belongs to this world, so he does not need the pleasure of other world. He does not consider sexual relation in itself as a sin. He establishes this relation on a higher plane and enjoys the life. An example may illustrate the difference between sin and pleasure. If sexual intercourse is made without the consent of the other party, it is sin and if sexual relationships are established amicably, then it is pleasure.

*(vii)* Humanism does not accept any supernatural interpretation of morals and values. It accepts morality only on the basis of human virtues and happiness.

*(viii)* Only intelligence and scientific method should be used to find the solution of a problem. Solution obtained through the principles of any religious book, help of any superpower or prayers, etc, are actually misleading.

*(ix)* No worldly object is good or bad in itself. The criteria of goodness or badness of an idea or object lie in the fact that how far it is useful or harmful for man or society.

*(x)* According to humanism, truth is verified on the basis of human experience. Experience is the guiding principle of truth. It is not derived from religious books or holy scriptures.

*(xi)* According to this philosophy, from the point of view of human experience, today is as important as tomorrow. It is because human experiences are inter linked.

*(xii)* Human nature is essentially flexible, changeable and worthy of being educated. So human nature can be readjusted and sublimated and this process of adjustment and sublimation continues from birth to death. Thus, according to this philosophy every bad man can be made good by education and thus, society can be made good.

*(xiii)* There is no contradiction between man and the society according to this philosophy. Social and harmonious creative tendencies are developed in man through skillful training. If there is any arrogant tendency in the personality which is rebelling against the social norms, this can also be removed and modified by tactful regular training.

*(xiv)* The life of man should be happy and prosperous and this is possible only when his economic condition is good. For this purpose industrial and technological progress should be emphased. By making man prosperous and happy, society can also be made happy.

*(xv)* In today's age of nuclear technology and ecological disturbance due to air or water pollution and terrorist activities across the globe Humanism is still determined for the good and welfare of humanity as a whole. According to it, hatred should be reduced by love and confidence and environment of war should be replaced by the atmosphere of peace.

*(xvi)* Humanism is optimistic, firm and persevering from the point of view of human welfare. In order to achieve this end Humanism wants that man should apply self restraint in order to bring peace and happiness on this earth. Some desires should be given up for this purpose.

## Democratic Ideals of Humanism

This philosophy is very close to democracy. Some of the democratic ideals propounded by this philosophy are given below:

1. It wants to make the best possible applications of democracy in all spheres of life, such as inculcating sense of responsibility among the people, treating all humans on equal footing without the discrimination of caste, creed or colour and so on.
2. It advocates full freedom given to men that is very essential for the development of man and the society.
3. It wants to develop men in social context which is very essential to do good to all humanity, i.e. the general welfare of the society.
4. According to it, people should develop so much ability that they are themselves able to plan for their future happiness and progress. It is also an important principle of democracy.
5. Democracy is not a political ideology only. It is rather an ideal of life which covers all human spheres such as economic, religious, social, educational and the like.

## Educational Implications of Humanism

**1. Meaning of Education:** Education is that sorts of activity which brings about justice, equality and progress through peace, mutual cooperation and tolerance among the people.

**2. Aims of Education:**

1. To prepare useful and peace loving workers and other resources necessary for human good.
2. To provide equitable facilities for development without the distinction of caste, creed, colour, race or sex or without the discrimination of poor, rich, backward or forward.
3. To patronize educational efforts in the interest of social welfare instead of individual well being.
4. To inculcate kind feeling in the youth.
5. To develop scientific temper and rational attitude among the people.
6. To make the people conscious toward Arts and Literature which will develop in them a capacity for realizing the goodness and beauties of life.
7. To improve the standard of living of the people through economic and cultural development.
8. To develop thinking power of children.
9. To help the children to understand the nature more closely and more minutely and also its role.
10. To turn the children into hard working adults who believe in their struggle and strife rather than fate.

**3. Educational Administration:**

1. If this philosophy is adopted by a society, schools, colleges, universities and research institutes will get heavy financial aid from the government. With the help of these funds they will prepare useful workers and other resources necessary for human welfare.
2. Democratic principles will be followed in the administration and the management of schools and colleges. For this purpose the procedure of admission and appointment will be made fair and transparent.
3. Educational facilities will be extended from primary to adult stage and quality will be maintained.

**4. Curriculum:**

1. The study of social sciences will be emphasized here. Political science, History and Economics will be made the focal point of study, along with science subjects.
2. Ethics will also be given an important place in the curriculum. It will develop kind and soft feeling among children and will make them reliable and creditable citizens of the country.
3. Science and scientific methods will be brought more in practice. Even social sciences will be taught through scientific methods.
4. In order to inculcate love for beauty, Arts and Literature will also be included in the curriculum.

**5. Method of Teaching:**

1. Scientific and psychological methods will be used in teaching learning process.
2. Children will learn the subject matter with fuller understanding instead of cramming them. Teacher will focus to develop thinking power of children.
3. The conflicts between science and social science will be removed by developing reflective thinking in children and both will lbe given almost equal weightage.
4. Heuristic and discovery methods of teaching will also be used. Students will mostly learn by self experiences.

**6. Discipline:**

1. Students will be given full freedom of expression in educational institutions. Nothing will be imposed on them from outside. Self discipline will be encouraged in the schools.
2. Students and teachers will also be given freedom to form organizations of their own choice and they will join them willingly.
3. There will be no atmosphere of pressure, fear or punishment in the school. It will increase creativity of children there.

## PRAGMATISM

Pragmatism is a temper of mind and an attitude. It is also a theory of nature of ideas and truth and it is a theory about reality. *–William James*

### History in Brief

The seeds of Pragmatism can be traced in ancient Greek Sophists who believed that "Man is the measure of all things". Modern Pragmatism was introduced by American philosopher G.S. Pearce in 1878 by saying "Our beliefs are really the rules of our action" Meaning thereby actions depend on our beliefs. This philosophy was given practical and solid base by another American philosopher William James. Pragmatism was later refined by John Dewey of America and Schiller of England. To understand this philosophy fully we must know the recent past history of America where this philosophy actually flourished.

In the 16th and the 17th centuries in Europe the Roman Catholics treated out the Protestants in a very cruel and inhuman manner. As a result, hundreds of thousands of oppressed people left their native land and migrated to America in search of freedom, safety and peace. When these migrants reached America they found new types of problems and difficulties there due to changed circumstances. Their old ideals and values were helpless in solving these problems. This made them think in a new way for solving these problems. This new type of thinking led them to new types of activities. They learned through these activities and experiences. The correctness of these activities was judged on the basis of their consequences. If the result of these activities was found good and useful, the activities were also considered good and useful otherwise these activities were discarded and new activities came to the front for experimentation. Upto the beginning of the 19th century this philosophy become so powerful that it pushed all old ideals, beliefs and values to the background and influenced American way of thinking and action to a great extent. American democracy is actually very much indebted to this philosophy.

### Meaning

Etymologically, the world Pragmatism has been derived from the Greek words "Pragma" means action and "Pragmatikos" means practicability or utility. Thus, it is a philosophy based on action or experimentation and criteria of an action or experimentation is its utility.

Technically, Pragmatism is a philosophy in which activity or experiments is done first and on the basis of its result, idea or principle is formed. That is why this philosophy is also known as "Experimentalism". If this result is useful to the individual and the society, the idea derived from action is adhered to, otherwise it is rejected. Because of this reason, this philosophy is also called "Consequentialism".

**J.S. Ross** has very rightly defined this philosophy in the following words. "Pragmatism is a humanistic philosophy maintaining that man creates his own values in the course of activity and that reality is still in the making and awaits its parts of completion from the future, that an ascertainable extents of truth are man made products." According to this definition,

*(i)* values are nor fixed or predetermined. They are created by man in the course of activity. As a result values are always changing.

*(ii)* reality or truth is in the making. It has not achieved its final shape yet. Thus, unlike values reality is also continuously changing. As a result, reality and values are not universal. They differ from place to place, from time to time and from circumstances to circumstances depending on the nature of experience or experimentation.

*(iii)* truths are not divine, they are rather man made products. Man can determine his own destinity by determining his truth.

*(iv)* no truth is absolute. A phenomenon is true to the extent it is useful to the society.

## Forms of Pragmatism

There are three forms of Pragmatism given below:

1. **Humanistic Pragmatism :** According to this variety of Pragmatism, only those ideas (principles) are true which can satisfy the needs, aspirations, and ends of human beings. Thus, human welfare is the base of this philosophy.
2. **Experimental Pragmatism :** According to this form of Pragmatism, only those ideas (principles) are true which can be verified and proved by experiments. If an idea is not useful or practicable on the basis of activity or experiments, it will not be accepted.
3. **Biological (Instrumental) Pragmatism :** This form of Pragmatism considers the power or capacity of a human being valuable. This power enables a man to adjust in the society and with the environment. It also enables him to change his environment according to his needs and objectives. John Dewey and William James are the chief exponents of this philosophy. Thus, this form of Pragmatism has its roots into Darwin's theory of evolution and natural selection. According to it, there is always struggle for existence seen in the physical and social environment. Each organism tries to adjust with his environment according to his power and strength. In this process weaks are decayed and only the fittest survive.

## Principles of Pragmatism

Fundamental principles of Pragmatism are given below:

1. **Changing nature of truth :** According to this philosophy, truth, reality, goodness or beauty etc. are all relative terms. These concepts are not predetermined or absolute. They change with the change in person, place, time or circumstances. That is to say truths are many and they are all in the making to reach the ultimate truth. What is true today, may not necessarily be true or good to others and so on. Truth is actually that which can be experimented or verified by human activity. Thus, change is an important characteristics of this philosophy.
2. **Useful result is the criterion of truth :** If truth is considered fixed and certain, it will hamper the progress of the world according to Pragmatism. It is the change that will lead to progress. Progress is after all a value word and values are instrumental. They are measured by their efficiency in giving ends. In other words values of a particular end must, therefore, be judged instrumentally in comparison to the other ends. Thus, truth based on activities are measured in terms of consequences or result. If it is able to solve human problems and gives desired result only then it is accepted otherwise rejected. In other word, we can say that truth is not absolute or permanent. How far an activity is able to achieve the objective is the degree of truth.

3. **The solution of the problems is the criteria of truth :** Human life is full of problems. Experiments are carried out to solve these problems. The success of these experiments brings us to the point of truth. In short, truth is that which solves the problems of life.
4. **Knowledge is the result of action :** Knowledge is somethings which is sought out in action, i.e., ideas are born out of activities. Man learns by various types of activities that he is engaged on his long path of life. Information becomes knowledge when it is judged to be relevant to the solution of a particular problem.
5. **Social rather individual values :** Man is a social being. He is born in a society, lives there and dies in a particular society. So, his existence without society is meaningless. Due to this reason, social values and ideals are important instead of individual ones and social values are nothing but democratic values. These values are freedom, equality, tolerance, responsibility and justice.
6. **Utility of ideas :** Reality of an idea or principle lies in its utility or usefulness. Any idea or principle which is useful to us is proper and right otherwise it is wrong. Thus, this philosophy is very much subjective because an idea or thing which is useful for me may not necessarily be useful for others.
7. **Importance of man power :** Man is a very powerful and dominating organism in the universe. By virtue of his power, he can change his environment and make it useful and conducive for his development and development of the society.
8. **Emphasis on present:** This philosophy does not look into the domain of the past. It rather wants to solve present problems on the basis of present experiences. It does not give importance to the experiences of the previous generations. That is why it opposes old customs, traditions and taboos. It believes in the present realities of life and wants to make the people think and act in a realistic way.
9. **Principle of pluralism :** Every one in the society tests the truth on the basis of his own way of experimentation. Thus, there comes many truths not one. If truths are many, everyone must be given full freedom to follow one's own path. Since the world is in the process of reconstruction and development, the nature of reality also changes with the change of time, Homosexual marriages which were once considered sin are now approved by at least some people. All these things make the society pluralistic. So, everyone in the society must be fully accommodative and considerate to adjust in the society.
10. **Flexibility is necessary for progress:** Nothing is fixed and final in the world, everything is changing. Even human life and its ideals are changing. Due to these changes humans confront various types of problems and when he starts some activities to solve these problems, certain new ideas come to the fore. All these things show that flexibility is needed everywhere. This flexibility brings out progress and development in the society.

## Difference between Pragmatism and Idealism

Pragmatism differs from Idealism in the following ways :

1. Pragmatism does not recognize any supernatural power such as God. Thus, it totally negates spiritualism. It believes in individual consciousness only. Idealism, on the other hand, is based on spiritualism, metaphysics and eternal and absolute truth (God).
2. Environment, feelings and human activities, are the basis for the development of culture according to Pragmatism. Idealism on the other hand, believes that mind, ideal behaviour and theoretical knowledge are the basis of development of culture.
3. Morality and ethics are fixed and permanent in Idealism but they are always changing in Pragmatism.
4. Truth is only one according to Idealism but there are many truths based on different experimentations according to Pragmatism.
5. Pragmatism considers physical world as real. Thus, it gives importance to physical comforts

and joy while explaining human welfare. Idealism, on the other hand, considers physical world as perishable and spiritual world as real. Thus, spiritual satisfaction is given importance here.

6. According to Pragmatism, knowledge, reality, everything changes with the change of time, place or circumstances but Idealism believes in fixed and permanent nature of reality.
7. According to Pragmatism, only that power is real which can solve the complex problem of man and it is the power of man itself. Idealism considers that power as God.
8. Pragmatism judges the idea on the basis of its social usefulness while Idealism believes that ideas itself are real.
9. By following predetermined beliefs and single truth of idealism the society becomes arbitrary according to Pragmatism, as a result progress of man is obstructed. Thus, Pragmatism is progressive and optimistic while Idealism is stationary and rigid.

## Difference between Pragmatism and Naturalism

Pragmatism differs from Naturalism too on the following points :

1. Pragmatism recognizes ideals and beliefs on the basis of experiments but Naturalism totally negates the ideals and beliefs.
2. Feelings are given importance in Pragmatism but they find no place in Naturalism.
3. Naturalism gives importance to mechanical ideas while Pragmatism gives importance to useful ideas based on experiments.
4. Pragmatism does not give any importance to aims of education. Social aims are to some extent given importance. While in Naturalism the aim of education is to develop the child according to his nature, i.e., individual aim is emphasized.
5. Pragmatism is a positive approach while Naturalism is a negative approach.
6. Naturalism considers physical laws to be universal. Pragmatism talks mostly of social laws which are always changeable. Even physical laws can change.

## Educational Implications of Pragmatism

**(A) Meaning of Education :** There are two fundamental beliefs of pragmatists. First is that no principle or idea is valid and true for all times. They must go through the process of change. The second belief is that real value of a thing lies in its utility and usefulness for human welfare.

On the basis of these beliefs they hold the view that no education process can be regarded as final and useful for all times to come. It must change according to the changing needs and circumstances of the society. Activity or experimentation is the method testing usefulness. So, education is that process of life which prepares a man to test knowledge or truth on the basis of its usefulness by activity or experience especially in a social environment and its ultimate purpose is to solve social problems of man.

On the basis of these very ideas Pragmatists believe that education is not the dynamic side of philosophy but philosophy itself is evolved from education. Education is not the preparation of man for his future life but it is life itself. It always involves experience, experimentation and free thinking.

**(B) Characteristics of Education :** Following are the main characteristics of Pragmatist education:

1. *Education is life :* Real knowledge can not be gained without experience, activity or experiments. Education provides a child more and more opportunities to get involved in such activities and experiences. As a result he creates his own values and ideals and makes his life richer and happier.
2. *Educaion is growth:* Society is undergoing a process of continuous change. These changes create new problems in the society. Nature and organization of education also change to cope with these changes and to solve the social and individual problems. When it happens so, growth and development take place. According to this philosophy, every child is born with inherent tendencies, aptitudes and capacities which are drawn out and developed by education by giving him full freedom to develop his inherent potentialities.

3. *Education is a continuous reconstruction of experience :* Knowledge is actually not obtained from books. Real knowledge is gained by activity or experiences conducted by the child himself. When he goes through one experience, new problems of life lead him to go through another experience and thus the process goes on till final truth is obtained. In this way the area of his knowledge is widened gradually. These experiences help him to adjust with the other people of the society in a more democratic manner.
4. *Education is a social process:* Man is a social animal. He lives in the society and he will continue to live there. So, he should be educated through the medium of the society so that he may develop in him the desirable social qualities. Any individual type of education given to a child may be of no use for him.
5. *Education is a social responsibility:* Education is the process of life that makes the citizens of a country democratic in their attitude and behaviour. So, it is the birth right of each individual to get education. Each individual can not get education on its own. So state takes the responsibility to provide education to all its citizens.

**(C) Aims of Education :** Pragmatism does not believe in any pre-determined and fixed aim of life. When aims of life is indeterminate and changeable with the variation of time, place or persons, there can never be pre-determined and fixed or general aim of education. The aim of education is different for different people in different countries at different spans of life. The only thing that is required from education is growth and creation of new values and ideals for adjustment in the society according to specific interest, aptitude and need of the child. So, education must create environment for the democracy to flourish. If maximum opportunities and free environment are available to the individual, his growth will also be maximum.

Thus, specific aim of education is the gaining of such capacities by the individual which enable him to determine his beliefs, fulfil his needs and grow to the maximum level possible by solving the real and social problems of life in a free and democratic environment.

**(D) Curriculum Construction:** Following principles must be taken into account while constructing curriculum for children :

1. *Principle of Utility:* Only those subjects, activities and experiences should be included in the curriculum which have direct relevance and usefulness to fulfilling the specific needs of children. Languages, Physical education, Geography, History, Science, Mathematics, Agriculture and Home Science (for girls) may be most suitable subjects in all societies. Vocational and technical education should also be included in the curriculum in order to enable a child to earn his living.
2. *Principle of Interest :*All things should not be taught to all children. It is against the principle of democracy if anything is imposed on them. Students should be given full freedom to opt their choice of subjects according to their specific interest. According to John Dewey, these interests are of four types I-Interest in conversation, II-interest in investigation, III-interest in construction and IV- interest in creative expression. Keeping these varieties of interest into account, reading, writing, counting, arts, crafts and natural sciences may be taught at the primary stage. At the secondary stage, more optional subjects will be included in the curriculum. Abilities of students will also determine the interests.
3. *Principle of Activity or Experience:* Pragmatism condemns cramming and teaching of academic subjects and advocates practical subjects. For this purpose independent, purposeful and social activities should be included in the curriculum to help the students to fulfil their needs along with the fulfillment of the needs of the society. Such activities and experiences will make the children good citizens and men of high moral character.
4. *Principle of Integration :* All subjects and activities should be integrated in order to make the knowledge as one unit. The subjects which are taught after dividing them into units for

convenience must have to be integrated at the end. In order to develop clear understanding in children subjects should also be correlated at various grades of study. According to this philosophy, all knowledge is like a tree and different subjects are its branches.

**(E) Methods of Teaching :** The philosophy prescribed the following methods of teaching:

1. *Child centred teaching:* Each child is different in intelligence, abilities and interest. As a result, no single and fixed method of teaching can be useful to all. Methods of teaching are changed keeping in view these individual differences of children but in all these methods child is made the pivot of all educational activities.
2. *Activity centred teaching:* Instead of emphasizing thoughts, ideas and rote learning Pragmatism has given rise to different activity centred and experimental teaching methods. These activities and experiences are organized for the child in such a way that he is able to solve his own problems as well as the problems of the society. Thus, Pragmatism synthesizes theory and practice by these activities. The child takes part in these activities and experiences himself and nothing is imposed on him from outside. It develops the creative power of the child which is very useful for the progress of the state.
3. *Problem centred teaching:* A number of relevant problems are put before children and teaching is done through these problems. The child is initiated by the teacher to solve these problems through self activities and experimentation. Project method of Kilpatrick is very suitable for this.
4. *Purposive and progressive teaching:* The child must be able to achieve some goals of life through the process of education-self learning or experiences. Since purpose of life is not constant, process of education should also change to coincide the changing goals of life. Teacher guides the students to change their activities and experience accordingly. In this way, the process of search from good to better never stops.
5. *Integrated approach of teaching :* All subjects are taught in a correlated and integrated manner to make the knowledge a single unit. Activities and experiences of the child are also integrated from the lower level to the higher ones in a chain.

**(F) Discipline :** Social and self discipline based on the specific interest, abilities and needs of children is prescribed by this philosophy. Such discipline is brought about by giving them full freedom to get involved in purposeful experiences and collective activities. By performing these activities, the child himself becomes self restrained and cooperative and sense of morality (responsibility) is automatically developed in him. The role of the teacher is very important here not as a dictator but as a friend, philosopher and guide in the class.

## Merits of Pragmatism (Influence)

1. Its main contribution lies in formulating several child centred teaching methods such as problems solving method, project method etc. In all those methods activities and experiences are given preference to bookish knowledge and thought. It is very useful to the system of education in the $21^{st}$ century.
2. Here child is kept at the top. He is developed mostly by his own efforts and self experiences.
3. This philosophy is very useful and practicable to any changing society as we see today. Values and ideals are changing very fast and education has to run after it.
4. This philosophy has popularized democratic ideals in all pluralistic societies. It has, no doubt increased the tolerance level of the people that is very essential for progress. In those countries where this level is low terrorism or separatism has raised its head. It has affected the social lives of the people very badly as is the case of India, Pakistan, Sri Lanka, Israel etc.
5. This philosophy talks about increasing the social efficiency of children through individual freedom. It is a useful approach of life.
6. Democracy has also got its place in education due to the influence of this philosophy
7. This philosophy has developed progressive and optimistic attitude in the people. The fastest

growth of America in the world is very much indebted to this philosophy.

8. Usefulness of knowledge propounded by Pragmatism is very much acceptable today. It can save our time from getting so vast amount of irrelevant and haphazard knowledge.

## Criticism of Pragmatism (Evaluation)

Pragmatism can be criticized on the following grounds:

1. Pragmatism completely ignores the aims of education. Without predetermined aims everything goes on certain assumptions. Can this he a practical approach to deal with the problem of life?
2. Pragmatism gives priority to activity and experiences and intelligence is put at the secondary place. Human being is different from animals only because of his intelligence. So ignoring ideas or thoughts is similar to putting the man at animal instincts again.
3. All truths are not changeable. Some truths are eternal and universal. Ignoring these truths means creating some new problems before the society.
4. This philosophy also ignores spirituality and supernatural power. Belief in any super power is deeply rooted in man by nature. As a result, only few people will accept this philosophy for a long period of time.
5. This philosophy wants to make a man socially efficient. How can this be possible without taking the help of universal morality and ethics.
6. This philosophy only takes the present and the future into account and neglects the past. If the experiences of our forefathers are not given due importance, it will take to much time to acquire knowledge on the basis of present experience only.
7. It is very difficult to construct curriculum on the basis of this philosophy because noting is fixed and everything is based on activity and experiences.
8. Truths are many according to this philosophy and every one arrives at his own truth on the basis of his own experiences. If this is so, there will be a total chaos in the society because everyone will try to put his own truth at the top.

# RECONSTRUCTIONISM

## Sources of the Philosophy and its Bases

1. **William Montaigne:** According to him the primary contribution of philosophy to civilization has been to speculate upon the possibilities inherent in man as a scientist, artist, politician and man as man. He also wants to design novel cultural pattern upon the solid base of scientific knowledge of nature and man.
2. **Utopianism:** It means future looking orientation on the basis of present. Here imagination is constructed into a far reaching idealization of social possibilities.
3. **Modern Utopianism:** The group leader of this philosophy is Thomas More. He was a great renaissance leader, a severe critique of feudalism and an advocate of liberal order for the society. The title of his work is **Utopia** in which he pictures a society which emphasizes communal rather than individual prosperity.
4. **Fracois Babeuf:** He was interested in eradicating evils already generated by the young capitalist culture. This group emerged when revolution against the feudalism got completed. He believed that if people received equal share in the resources of the country, only then economic and political problems can be solved.
5. **Saint Simon:** He deviated from Babeuf by assuming natural inequalities of talents and these talents should be guaranteed to develop freely.
6. **Foureir :** According to him, soundly organized society must be adapted according to the passion of man.
7. **Marx and Engles :** They believed in the idea of a classless society. Their works were later developed and described as Marxism.
8. **H.G.Wells :** He advocated within limits the accumulation of private property as the population of inferior individuals rival with superiors.
9. **Thorstien Veblen and Bourne :** They belonged to the 19th century. Veblen was the leader of movement in 1930s in America named the movement of technocracy. He said that only social engineer was sufficiently trained and skilled to operate the industrial political machine.

10. **Lewis Mannford :** He was a severe critique of the ugly modern metropolis and prepared blueprint for its reconstruction in the light of technological demands.
11. **John Dewey :** The chief exponent of Pragmatism suggested the name of this philosophy in the title of his book **Reconstruction in Philosophy**.
12. **Theodore Brameld (1950) :** He laid the foundation of social reconstruction through education.
13. **I.B.Berkson (1958) :** He said that although the school itself should not take the lead in the social reform but it should cooperate with the movement already active in the society.

From the other ideas of different philosophers it is clear that old Reconstructionism was the result of frustration from fast rising capitalism, and economic and social inequalities arising out of industrialization and mechanization of life and modern Reconstructionism was the result of frustration from World's Great Economic Depression of 1930s and two great World Wars which resulted into mass poverty, social and economic inequalities, insecurity of life and property due to absence of peace and pessimism in attitude and behaviour. It is actually an interpretation of and response to contemporary problems, i.e., to reconstruct the society in order to meet the cultural crisis of our time.

## Fundamental Postulates

**(A) Belief About Reality:** This philosophy is hostile to any metaphysics that tries to establish the primacy of supernature over that of nature and is especially antagonistic to objective system of pre established order whether it be of Realist or Idealist variety. It talks in terms of social reality-particularly group experiences which have been ignored by the progressivists.

The concept of reality has been discussed under the following heads:

**1. Cultural determinants of human experiences:**

*(a) Group conflicts*: Conflicts between nations take place when one nation favours his economic interest more than his due and deprives the others and the interest of war becomes more powerful than that of peace. Similarly civil war occurs when arbitration or national police are too weak to curb or calm the people and economic or religious factors motivate one group to stand against the other. Terrorism in India is an example.
Cultural conflicts take place when some people discriminate any culture on any ground like race, language, caste or traditions. Thus, group conflicts are the real phenomenon. It may be called social reality. It ranges from war at one extreme to mere contempt at the other.

*(b) Group allegiance:* At international level, patriotism and nationalism arise through war between nations. At national level group solidarities develop when we force a group to live in segregation or we persecute it on any ground. Religious and cultural beliefs are less contributory in group allegiance. This reality is another social reality.

*(c) Group conditioning:* This philosophy may also be called social behaviourism because it says that groups are conditioned to behave as they do by the effect of cultural forces. Communal riots of Gujarat of 2002 is an example.

*(d) Moral man and immoral society:* Group behaviour may become immoral and cruel more oftenly than the individualistic behaviour. Man as an individual does not behave like that but only in exceptional situation because morality dominates in him. For example, during communal riots, we see that mob of the people comprising of neighbours also kill their neighbours but individually they protect them.

**2. History as reality:** History is a basic fact of reality. Every next period emerges from the preceding ones and leads into later ones in such a way as to be influenced by the former and to influence the later. It has no pre determined good but it depends on the choices, failures and successes as men make during the process.

Important principles of cultural history as reality are given below:

*(a) Social struggle :* In history social and power struggle has been a real phenomenon of all ages between slaves and free people, between vassals and lords, between workers and masters and so on. These

struggles generate new arrangements like communism, capitalism, democracy etc of today.

(b) *Expansion of freedom and contraction in history:* People struggle because of economic motivation and to win a greater share of wealth and freedom. But sometimes this struggle takes place when some people want to restrict the freedom of others in order to satisfy their vested interest. Thus, we see that history is a two way process.

(c) *Society as organism :* This philosophy believes that objectives needed in social arrangements constitute an organic whole and every action of the individuals is determined on that unified goal.

**(B) Belief About Knowledge :** Knowledge seeking process is entirely natural and does not depend on supernatural or mystical devices. In psychological term thoughts are integrated with emotional and muscular functions. According to this philosophy mind is not a thing but a way of dealing with human situations and social problems.

Following principles have been propounded by the exponents of this philosophy regarding belief about knowledge.

1. **Goal seeking knowledge :** Ends and means both are necessary to acquire knowledge and both are motivated and generated by the fundamental goals we want to achieve.
2. **Role of prehension :** Prehension means unity, the organic wholeness of natural events. It is a unified kind of awareness that precedes and succeeds apprehension i.e. it is the analytical awareness of an event by which we recognize its consequent parts. Meaning thereby events are analysed to determine its consequences on the basis of prehension.
3. **Role of ideology :** Ideology has two important functions (I) It serves to rationalize the cultural practices and habits (II) All ideologies are historical. They too emerge, mature and die out. They are the devices by which the institutions of any culture is preserved. They are indispensable for knowledge.
4. **Role of utopia:** It is the utopia that may look forward as well as backward. It may deny the prevailing ideology of a given time and may become the ideologies of next age if it looks radically to the future.
5. **Role of truth seeking as social consensus:** Truth of these experiences is most vital in the social life of any culture determined not merely by the needful satisfaction they produce but also by the extent to which they are agreed upon by that largest number of people concerned. Thus we are arrive at truth here by social consensus.

**(C) Belief About Values:** Values are opposition to any theory that deviate from set values absolutely. It is the negative approach. Positive approach is that values are wants or satisfaction, hence they are rooted in the goal seeking activities of individuals or group. They are tested by evidence communication and social consensus. As a result, values are never absolute or fixed forever. In axiology it is called social self organization. The same is described as democracy in political science where decision is always taken on social self realization.

Democracy, the determining factor of values has been explained by this philosophy in the following ways:

1. **Meaning of majority rule:** Social institutions are run by the majority of people on the basis of general agreement. It is not simply a quantitative judgement but a qualitative as well. Decisions are taken after through discussion.
2. **Meaning of minority rights:** The prime political function of the minority is to criticize through additional or corrective evidence and communication. The evidence should be supported by facts and experimentation. Through this process values will always be rectified.
3. **Meaning of public policy:** The majority can not decide all varieties of truth or value on the same degree like fundamental truths of physics and mathematics becasuse values or truths are to be measured on objective standard. The majority can only determine the central distinguishing characteristics of every policy and policy is nothing but consensus of values in political purposes of given period of time.
4. **Meaning of popular government:** When these policies are implemented through legislation and

social practices, popular governments are formed. This process can be called as the assimilation of values.

## Educational Implications of Reconstructionism

It is an aloof theory of means and ends if we talk about it from educational point of view. We decide here where we have to go and how can we go there. This is a prerequisite for learning. The directions given by this philosophy regarding education are summarized below.

**(A) Aims of Education:** Education pattern will be developed to achieve the following aims:

1. To replace an economy of scarcity by an economy of abundance. It will raise general standard of living.
2. To make the state a constructive and integrating servant rather than a necessary evil.
3. To make the science supportive to common welfare.
4. To create environment for free expression of arts in order to develop creativity..
5. To reorganize education from compulsory school level to the adult stage.
6. To train human being to share equality in all rights and obligations as a citizen.
7. To achieve all those objectives which a democratic society sets up.

**(B) Curriculum :** Core curriculum is adopted here from elementary to higher education. It is developed in the form of chain learning, i.e., the curriculum in each year borrows from the preceding one, inherits its problems as well as solutions. The curriculum prescribed for various grades of education is given below:

**1. Elementary Stage :** Pattern of education is 5+7+4. Here, 5 stands for nursery, (Age 1-5 years), 7 stands for lower primary, (age 6-12 years), 4 stands for Upper primary, (age 13-16 years). Thus 16 years of age is required to complete elementary education.

It means that all children below six years of age are eligible to be admitted in Nursery schools. These schools are supported and controlled by the government. Here mother remains full time with her child. Post and pre natal care is also provided to all mothers in public institutions.

At the lower primary stage learning by doing i.e., activity centred method along with the support of the environment and living situations of the child are preferred here. Social self realization like nutrition, health, group experiences etc are taught and learning through social consensus is also brought at this stage according to the age level of the child. Standard of education and learning will be very high from the very early stage.

At the upper elementary stage, most of the characteristics described above is applicable here too. This learning prepares the child to study in the secondary school. Thus, all introductory syllabi of secondary school are taught at this stage.

**2. Secondary Stage :** Four years of secondary education starts at the age of 16.

***First Year Course*** : It has two main objectives.

*(i)* To provide motivation and orientation of the total plan of the entire secondary programme.

*(ii)* To examine the need for goals that are required in the spheres of economic political reconstruction.

The first objectives can be achieved by cooperative examintion of contemporary culture and its empirical relations to students. For this purpose past is studied for its motivation of present and the future. Past is also compared with present to decide what would be better in future. In this way children arrive at a crude consensus about common values. At least one third of the year will be allotted for this purpose. Economics, Political science and Arts are also taught at this stage.

Eight months will be fixed to achieve the second objectives. At this stage the study of subjects to achieve the first objective becomes more intensive and systematic. Children study the problems of the community like income, employment, saving, labour organization, taxes , organization of local government, leading political parties, public services and other related issues. History is also taught to the students at this stage so that they are able to understand the evolution of business enterprises, technological development and cultural changes. These curricula will enable the students to evaluate the whole programme from the point of view of utility.

Other materials capable of integration include foreign language, methematics and commerce. Students engaged in vocational training are also made conscious of the economic and political problems Work experience is an essential aspect of entire programme.

***Second Year Course*** **:** It also has two main objectives.

*(i)* To specify the main problems, needs, methods and goals in the area of Science.

*(ii)* To do likewise in the area of Arts.

The year starts with the recapitulation of the previous knowledge and anticipation of the further one. For this purpose a project report is prepared in the summer vacations of the first year.

In order to achieve the first objective, science is seen to be primarily a methodology rather than a body of knowledge. Social functions of science is also taken into account along with the other functions. Science is regarded as a great instrument of public welfare and students study it in the very perspective.

Study of Mathematics is enlarged at this stage but the study of Algebra, Geometry and Statistics is not required for average students. The teaching of foreign language continues to enable the students to learn the scientific progress of the other nations. Practical training is also given along with theoretical knowledge.

With the study of Arts they go deeper into the history, psychology, sociology and philosophy of Arts. Thus, the gap between science and Arts is automatically reduced. Moreover, other subjects of the first year gets continued.

***Third Year Course*** **:** It deals with a review of education of the first two years. All the courses and subjects of these two years continue in the third year also but with a higher standard. However, one full day in a week is set aside for specialized subject or training.

A novel learning experience is also provided to the students to sample and assess the whole learning programme now in operation. Here efforts are made to impart knowledge of at least following topics to students.

- Personal and family relations
- Relation between the sexes
- Relation between younger and adults
- Relational between races
- Relation between nationalities
- Relation between economic classes
- Relation between religions

***Fourth Year Course*** **:** During this year students devote 60% of their time in the direct study of guiding themes and committed subjects and 40% time is devoted for training. General assembly and group discussion meets take place on an average of 3 days weekly.

Theory of means and ends is taught with reference to various subjects at this stage. Ideas are taught in an aggressive manner so that they can discard other ideologies forcefully. Students are made familiar with the total purpose of education, i.e. what can they do now and what should they do after graduation.

**(C) Methods of Teaching :** The exponents of this philosophy have advocated the following methods of teaching.

1. **Learning through evidence :** The process of learning takes place from a great variety of indirect sources like Science, History, Economics, Religion etc and each individual and group is directly made aware of the experiences of these subjects
2. **Learning through communication :** Both kinds of evidence—direct and indirect are subjected to communication. Direct sources of communication are text books, lectures, pictures etc and indirect sources are reciprocal expression among students and teachers.
3. **Learning through agreement :** Agreement is the next step when students would have learned as much as possible from their members. This process continues till the final agreement or social consensus is arrived at.
4. **Learning through group dynamics :** It is a feasible resource for developing, refining and testing social consensus, group mind and other concepts.
5. **Learning through problem solving :** Life related problems must be solved through

education. For this purpcse students are taught through this method so that they can easily solve their social problems.

6. **Learning through action :** Students devote at least one third of their time in training. Training is nothing but putting theory into practice through activities and experiences.

## Merits and Influence of the Philosophy

1. It has discussed in detail how to solve social problems through evidence and consensus.
2. This philosophy is very much helpful in solving the social problems of today.
3. It has given democracy a practical and rational shape.
4. It has given a detailed programmed of education.
5. This philosophy talks in terms of material prosperity which can reduce frustration from the minds of the people.

## Criticism of the Philosophy

1. It talks a lot but gives only a little.
2. Most of its values discussed were already in practice in democratic countries. Thus, this philosophy is only an elaboration of democracy in heavy terms.
3. Society can not be reconstructed and improved without spiritual and fixed values and final truths.
4. This philosophy is totally failure to meet the challenges of fundamentalism and terrorism.

# EXISTENTIALISM

This is also a post world war philosophy developed out of frustration from war. Though this was first originated in the 19th century and the reason was again the frustration from war. The individuality of man was very much negated in the two world wars. In order to re-establish the supremacy of man as an individual again, this philosophy came into being. This philosophy prefers man to nation, body to intelligence and physical world to nature. It also opposes industrial age, science, objectivity etc that all have made man a tool in the hands of industrial society and political system. Existentialism believes that everything should serve man and not vice versa. Thus this philosophy was propounded in opposition to materialism in the form of Marxism, Realism and Naturalism.

## Postulates of the Philosophy

1. Man is a supreme organism. He should not be exploited in the interest of the society or the nation. Society or political system is a must but society should not give secondary place to man. Society is for man and not vice-versa.
2. This philosophy will never achieve old age, i.e., it is limited to time. According to it, **struggle** for existence was there when man was first evolved and it is continued even today. Man tries to become victorious at all costs.
3. French novelist **Jean Paul Satre** in his novels broke all traditions and taboos and picturised a man free from all bondages. This man would act according to its own wishes and nothing will be imposed on him.
4. It believed in the inner and immediate realization of self consciousness. There is a basic desire for the existence of individuality in man. If this individuality is recognized, his life becomes purposeful, meaningful and easy. Man becomes conscious of this self if he is given importance. Thus, developing self is an important function of this philosophy. So long as this self is not realized by man he can not acquire real knowledge. Real knowledge is what that is obtained by applying consciousness.
5. Existence does not mean mere living. It rather means complete, strong, self conscious, responsible and progressive life of man.
6. Mechanical and industrial life of today has snatched individual freedom from man and hence he is deprived of realities, of life.
7. In this scientific and technological age, man is leading a solitary and frustrated life full of anxieties, fear and guilty consciousness. The purpose of this philosophy is to remove frustration, fear, sense of guilt and worries of man by recognizing his individuality and giving technological progress a secondary place.

## Chief Exponents of the Philosophy

**1. Soren Kierkegeard :** Danish Philosopher expressed his views on existentialism in his essays and writings. He is an existentialist who has faith in God. The main beliefs of Kierkegeard are given below:

(a) *Truth is internal and subjective :* We do not accept any truth only for mental satisfaction but we want to realize it in our inner life. Every truth should satisfy our self (soul) and not our mind alone. In this scientific and industrial age we want to satisfy others with the objectivity of truth. It endangers the existence of individuality (self consciousness). On the other hand, by subjective truth we will first of all satisfy ourselves. If truth is made internal and subjective every individual will be allowed to act, think and feel freely in his own way.

(b) *Existence of individuality is reliable and prior to thinking :* Physical and conscious existence is prior to thinking, i.e., willing is more important than intelligence. Doing is real and thinking is unreal. The objective knowledge of Science, History, Mathematics gives an idea of truth only. This idea alone can not help anyone to live a real life. If this idea is given a concrete shape taking the individuality of man into account, he will be able to live a real life. Kierkegeard says " I think because I exist." I that exist is always subjective. So, truth changes from person to person on the basis of his individual existence. It means that I should be given importance rather than we. If 'I' is lost, the existence of 'we' will come into being. It is wrong.

Same is the case with morality and religion. They are also expressed in subjective terms taking 'I' factor into account. Morality and religion can not be sought in outside world. They are present in the inner self of man. They can be found by establishing a contact between God and soul. There is no universal and objective religion present in the world.

(c) *Self consciousness is nature of knower :* Existence is always subjective. It is nothing but self existence. Instead of knowing the objective world, it should only be felt subjectively and enjoyed. Cognitive aspect of knowledge side is not purposeful. Volition is more important than cognition to arrive at moral reality. Thus, truth and reality are subjective in nature. They depend on the nature of knower. It means that what you think is not correct but what I think is true only. Nobody should impose his views on others. When we arrive at self existence, we indirectly honour the existence of others by giving up our selfishness and by opening the path of happiness for others.

(d) *Existential self realization is necessary :* Subjective existentialism is necessary. Without it we can not realize the sufferings of others. If I have not got the experience of starvation, how can I know the pains of starving people. If we think about death objectively, thinking it in the context of others, we will remain confined to rituals like grave, condolence, lamenting and cremation ceremony etc. It will not give us true realization of death. But if we think about death subjectively, our imagination, feeling, behaviour every thing will be affected and shaken by the reality of death. Thus, for realization of truth and reality, subjectivity is a must.

The conflicts of inner self may also be overcome by self realization of consciousness. When we think introvertly, "what I am and what I should be" this introversion motivates us and we actively proceed to achieve the ideal. Thus, self realization is a motivating force also.

(e) *Existence of Individuality is needed for religious and moral development :* Just as shadow gives us the idea of existence of light, similarly disappointment leads to the hope of attainment of God. When we struggle for our existence, we go through the process of penance, sacrifice and forbearance of troubles and finally through decisive manifestation (by considering the same for others) guilt feeling is apprehended and removed from the mind.

Thus, a religious person develops the faith in the existence of God in this world itself and engages himself in the welfare work faithfully. It is because a religious person relates his self not only to others but also to God by remaining subjective and introvert throughout his life. According to Kierkegeard, God is a spiritual existence. He can not be realized only in the existence of self. He can not be experienced like physical objects. The relationship between God and man should be expressed by worship. Once this relationship is established, three types of feeling emerges in man—aesthetic, moral and religious.

Aesthetic feeling is of the lowest order. It is related to outward beauty of the universe. It admires God and his creation. Moral feeling is of the second order. It is related to the inner self and think for the welfare of others. Religious feeling is the top order feeling, moral feeling gets perfected through this feeling. Once this feeling is developed man mingles his existence with that of God and thus the process of realization of self gets completed.

**2. Karl Jasper :** German Philosopher, propounded restrained and balanced form of Existentialism. His ideas are summarized below :

(a) *Search of existence is universal :* A person is known as philosopher who adopts existential view point as a part of life. For satisfaction of thirst of truth he recapitulates the three thousand years of his history of Indian, Chinese and Western philosophy. The philosophic view points prevailing at different times were developed in their own environment for search of same absolute truth but they did not succeed because of some shortcomings. The shortcoming of the modern age is the progress based on the modern science. Technical and industrial progress has brought an end to self realization of mankind.

(b) *Self existence is comprehensive and is the result of idea or mind :* Self existence is an object of knowledge from objective to subjective process. We feel the existence of living being only with our insight and intelligence. With the help of mind, the individual gets the sudden light of permanent knowledge. Though this light of knowledge does not add anything to our apperception but its contribution is that it activates the living being to realize the existence.

Self is realized through the process of objectivity. It is because objective knowledge is obtained through self satisfaction mentally when a person ponders over it subjectively. As soon as self is realized the objective knowledge also becomes subjective and comprehensive because it becomes devoid of the objects at this state. Now the person who already knows the object requires to know the idea only. Thus, we see that subjective realization starts from objective knowledge.

The person becomes able to solve his problems by becoming subjective from objective. The ideas of these mental states are true. These views are not universal because they are not objective. Subjective knowledge rather than objective knowledge is real.

Three things are required for self realization, knowing, willing and doings. At the knowing stage the man gets objective knowledge but when he reaches willing and doing stages his knowledge becomes subjective and the process of attaining knowledge gets completed.

On the basis of above discussions we can say that science and philosophy are inseparable. Science is purely objective and its concepts are universal. Philosophy, on the other hand is subjective and is based on a definite, methodical and scientific knowledge of matter. Science is a precondition of philosophy. It searches only objective truth and philosophy, on the other hand is in search of absolute truth. It does not want to become universal by being confined to objective knowledge of physical objects. Those who want to bring philosophy to the level of objective science, they do not understand the seriousness and real function of philosophy according to Karl Jasper. In order to achieve the ultimate truth we must synthesize science and philosophy.

(c) *Self existence of man is true:* According to Karl Jasper either this living world which surrounds man should be taken as true or only the existence of man is true. When the self of man is added to the spiritual world, the human existence gets perfection. Man realizes his existence as a living being only when he establishes his relationships with the physical and spiritual world both. Physical world is objective and the spiritual world is subjective. Man can not achieve self realization without being subjective and without establishing a relationship with the spiritual world. Man is not an object. He is a conscious power which has its own existence.

Self existence of man is basic, free from objectivity and has the following characteristics:

*(i)* He is dissatisfied with his physical achievements and wants something more that is subjective.

*(ii)* He is dedicated to reach the absolute truth.

*(iii)* He is hungry for achieving unity with spiritual world.

*(iv)* He is conscious for immortality

*(v)* He wants to describe his existence.

In short, man's existence is extensive and divine. He is the carrier of God's will and he can realize it only by becoming introvert. Once man realizes his existence fully, he surrenders before God and performs all the duties levied on him. He receives divine instructions from his inner self. The whole universe is the language of God and it can be realized only by becoming subjective.

According to Jasper scientific, industrial economic, political and military environment of today has made man so much helpless that he is not able to realize his honour, his freedom and his power by becoming introvert. He is so much afraid of the objectivity of modern science that he does not want to leave physical comforts. Even religion is so full of false show and superstitions that man can not realize his self existence through it. The world created by man himself has become a curse for him. He has lost his subjective personality in it and he has been cut off from his self.

*(d)* *Reality of the physical world :* Karl Jasper says that self existence is to be realized in this very physical world. This world is also real to some extent and life is tied with it. We can realize our self and preserve it only by engaging ourselves in the worldly affairs but the purpose will always be to attain spiritual happiness. This process of self realization is not an easy task. Physical world tries to destroy and intimidate the self of man but man struggles for his existence by becoming conscious of his power of self. This self is counter productive and an expression of God. So, the aim of Existentialism is to attain mental peace which can be achieved only by struggling with opposite forces active in the physical environment.

According to Karl Jasper if we consider the self wholly subjective, it is also wrong. Complete subjectivity will make us proudly. We have not to ignore the existence of others for preserving and realizing our own self. We should preserve our self only by establishing affectionate and cooperative relationship with others. It is because 'I' and 'You' both are the manifestation of divine existence.

**3. Martin Heidegger :** Greek philosopher took the help of history in explaining his views. He wanted to change extrovert people of Greece into introverts by his philosophy of Existentialism. He is also of the view that self can be preserved by the coordination of objective as well as subjective knowledge. His ideas are summarized below :

*(a)* *Self consciousness can be realized :* Man can study the existence of living being by becoming introvert and can realize his self consciousness by peeping into his inner self. The expression of self existence in man can be seen through his efforts and conduct. Science studies the living being objectively while theology studies living being subjectively. The specific, individualistic and valid study of inner self of living being is done by theology. According to Heidegger, man can realize his existence only by coming in contact with the objective world in which he lives. His attraction for this world or its substance is the basis of his self existence. By observing his mental inclination which is changeable also, one can know what kind of relation he has with the objective world. The proof that he is influenced by this objective world is that he expresses different types of emotions at different times such as curiosity, restlessness, happiness, sorrow and fear. If he loses interest in this world, he becomes indifferent to its substances. The consciousness

of self and tendency to struggle for it gets expression due to his interest in the objective world.

According to Heidegger, it is the characteristics of self that it gets manifested itself, gets open itself and gets expressed itself. It is the basis of individuality of man and its general form is found in all persons.

(b) *Essence of truth is freedom of self expression:* Human knowledge is not the result of interaction between mind and object. It is obtained through inner vision which gets manifested from the self itself. This knowledge gives expression of the relationship between self mind and object. It requires freedom. If freedom is not given to self, knowledge does not get expressed and the being does not get self consciousness.

The insight of man should be so developed that he becomes conscious to know what is existence of his being and how it is. Human behaviour and behavioural life of man are based on this truth and freedom. Here only those aspects of truth are emphasized which are practicable.

Err is the nature of man. He commits mistakes only because he is extrovert. As soon as he becomes introvert, this err is reduced. An ordinary man does not realize truth. He always lives in the unreal world. It is because he can not make himself introvert so easily, by becoming conscious of his self. But as soon he begins to think what is his living being the light of truth begins to grow in him. He begins to get pleasure of freedom for self expression and this is the essence of truth.

(c) *Being is different from non-being :* We can realize being only when there is non-being. It is non being that gives the idea of existence of being. He further says that existence of being depends on the existence of non-being same as the existence of light depends on shadow. Every living being is created out of non-being. For example, fear is an experience of non-being. When some one tries to change our being into non-being (dead) fear is created. If there is no danger to our existence, we shall not make an effort for our being (existence). Thus, being is created out of non-being. In this sense objective world is considered to be unreal and we come to the understanding of truth or reality by taking our self from objectivity to subjectivity.

(d) *Absolute truth is obtained from non-being :* When our being is threatened by the objective world, we realize our being (absolute truth). In order to save our being courage is developed in us. This courage which struggles with our non-being is the gift of our being. In this struggle we give expression to our being. This process of struggle gives us a sort of mental and spiritual peace. This self satisfaction makes a man introvert. For his being man sacrifices his self. At this point, Heidegger is very close to Marxism which advocates the sacrifice of self for social being.

Through the process of self realization, man recognizes his potentialities and he selects a suitable way for preservation of his being. In this process be gives up all those physical objects which work as a hindrance in the realization of his self due to objectivity.

This is the real world in which man hears the voice of his soul and the echo of his insight. He expresses his echo in such a language that is serious, meaningful and effective. His language is translated into action. Thus, thinking and action combined together reflect the existence of his being.

Heidegger further says that "being" begins to rise high by getting its existence and it is later assimilated in the super being (God). This secret is not known to everybody. Only that man who can preserve and nourish his being can maintain the externity of his existence and he will finally enter the subjective world of being by rising high above the limits of objective physical knowledge. The being that was imperfect upto now is perfected now. Thus, a man perfects his being while living in this very physical world.

## Educational Implications

**(A) Meaning of Education :** Existentialism is not a philosophy for revealing the truth, reality and values of the objective world. It is a doctrine of discussing the existence of self. A man becomes considerate to the personality of others only on the basis of his subjectivity. How he feels for himself is felt for others.

Thus, education according to this philosophy is to give special importance to individuality of man in educational system and to develop the self of all individuals. If education is not provided according to this self, man will not attain perfection.

Education according to this philosophy is the development of self (spirituality) while living in the very physical world to the level where he can attain divine existence. This philosophy can be considered a bridge between religion and the modern life of the 21st century.

**(B) Aims of Education:**

1. To educate each and every individual of the society in order to develop his insight and feeling for the development of his inner self.
2. To provide opportunities for all round development of the personality. Education should develop individuals physically, mentally, emotionally and spiritually.
3. To turn everybody from objective to subjective in feeling and behaviour. We can know the sufferings of others by our own sufferings. So, we must be subjective to the phenomenon. But this subjectivity will be free from prejudice because of the development of spirituality. Thus, education should make a man subjective and should make him conscious for his individuality or self.
4. To acquaint man with his destination, by giving him understanding of his "being" and this will, ultimately lead him to his heavenly abode. By this aim of education existentialism accepts the principle of liberal education.
5. To develop the ability of perseverance and tolerance in man so that he may live and adjust in the modern world without compromising his individuality and subjectivity.
6. To provide maximum freedom to the individual to develop his thinking power.

**(C) Curriculum :** By discarding the objectivity of physical knowledge and experiences Existentialism does not give any importance to objective subjects like natural sciences and mathematics. This philosophy opposes that scientific, industrial and technical environment which does not allow the individuality of man to develop. It wants to develop scientific and technological knowledge for the service of man. Due to this reason, philosophy has given preference to science. It wants to change the thinking of man in such a way that he may evaluate every situation in his own context rather than in the context of others. For this purpose Humanities and Social sciences are given very much importance.

Since objective knowledge is the means of arriving at subjective knowledge, so natural sciences are also studied but with the spectacles of subjectivity.

In order to develop subjectivity and inner self of man, subjects of moral sciences and theology are also included in the curriculum.

While developing and constructing the curriculum the individual nature of child and his specific interest are also taken into account. This very point makes this philosophy different from Idealism. Otherwise this philosophy is just like the reinterpretation of idealism in new terms.

**(D) Method of Teaching :** This philosophy has not actually propounded any specific method of teaching. It simply lays stress on developing the self of the individuals in whatsoever manner it is possible. Emphasis given on certain points regarding methods of teaching are given below.

1. *Individualistic teaching :* Existentialism wants to develop the self of each individuals separately so teaching proposed by this philosophy is very much individualistic in nature. The social system of this philosophy is highly democratic and laissez-faire in nature.
2. *Use of reflective thinking :* In order to develop the subjectivity of the individuals reflective thinking is very much used. Efforts are made to develop thinking power of the child and acquaint him with his existence.
3. *Opposition of experimental sciences :* This philosophy takes the objective science only as means to reach the end that is the subjectivity of knowledge. As a result knowledge based on experiments is not relied upon. It is not necessary

to satisfy others with the knowledge according to this philosophy. The learner should, first of all, satisfy himself. This is the approach approved by this philosophy.

4. *Heuristic method :* This method can be used very easily by those who believe in this philosophy. Individual discovers here his own truth by applying his intellect.

**(E) Discipline:** Students are given importance here without lessening the importance of the teacher. It is the teacher who creates environment for students in which they change their extroversion into introversion. Students achieve self realization under the mature guidance of their teacher. Teacher must also be subjective in his approach only then he will be able to make his students subjective.

As far as students are concerned, they are also given full freedom to develop their self by changing their objective knowledge into subjective one. But these children are trained in such a manner that they do not become selfish, autocratic or irresponsible due to their subjectivity. Their subjectivity will lead them to understand the subjectivity of others. They are also given education according to their specific interest and abilities.

**(F) Religious Education :** Existentialism is actually a link philosophy between religion and the modern age. It is the modern scientific age that has made man a machine and a tool in the hands of science and political group. His interests in the religions is now lessening at a fast rate. This philosophy tried to bring the man closer to the religion without compromising the scientific and industrial progress. The similarities between the religion and Existentialism are given below:

1. Both believe in the limited existence of man in this world. Worries of man are created due to this limited existence. Since his stay in this world is very temporary, he must realize his own self as well as the self and subjectivity of others. Thus both want to make man considerate and cooperative.
2. Both believe that it is the function of education to give man an understanding of his imperfect powers and limited existence and the purpose of education is to make him perfect by subjectivity and introversion.
3. Both believe in universal nature of education given to all individuals.
4. Both believe that modern man should be given the knowledge of that eternal existence which can help him to gain perfection through religious education. Hence, religious education must be imparted to students in schools.

The only difference between the two is that existentialism advocates a deep faith of man in the preservation and progress of his being. Thus, this philosophy approves individual progress. Religion, on the other hand, advocates social being or progress instead of individual being. The existence of the individuals may be compromised when social being is considered important.

## Merits of the Philosophy (Influence)

1. The last century and the 21st century have made man so much materialistic and selfish that he was lost in the shine and glory of industrial and material progress. At this juncture, a philosophy of this kind was very much needed.
2. Industrial and material world was neglecting the individuality of man completely. He had become only a tool in the hands of science and technology. Existentialism once again recognized the individuality of man and all round development of his personality.
3. Man is very much dynamic and progressive. His interest in the objective world is also very much on the increase leaving the religion aside. By emphasizing the limited existence of man, this philosophy brought the man closer to religion again.
4. It wants to make a man perfect and subjective. It enables him to realize the suffering of others on the basis of self realization. The feeling of hunger is felt only when a person is hungry.

## Criticism of Existentialism

1. This philosophy is actually an old wine in a new bottle. What was illustrated by Reconstructionism in social context, have been elaborated by this philosophy in individual context with weak arguments as compared to the former philosophy.

2. It talks too much but gives little. Most of its points were discussed by Naturalism and Idealism in a different language. What is actually new in this philosophy is very difficult to ascertain.
3. The ideas of arriving at perfection through subjectivity and introversion is misleading. If one has subjective attitude towards a problem how can his views be accepted by others in today's objective world.
4. Negligence of objectivity and over emphasis on subjectivity make the philosophy a game of arguments only. Because of this reason, this philosophy has not gained popularity so far.
5. Values have not been properly discussed by this philosophy.

## MARXISM

The revolutionary ideas propounded by German Philosopher, Karl Marx (1818-1883) and Friendrich Engels (1820-1895) are technically known as Marxism (Communism). This philosophy was later modified by Lenin (1870-1924) and was given the name of Socialism. In spite of some differences between Communism (a classless society) and Socialism (a society of equal distribution of the means of production) their fundamentals are the same. We are giving here the ideas of Karl Marx and Lenin separately.

### Karl Marx (1818-1883)

1. The philosophical view of Marxism is that man's defining characteristics is his creativity. It is his creativity that enables him to exert labour on objects in order to satisfy his needs. But man does not labour merely for himself as an individual. He rather labours as a species. As a result a labour class is formed. All of men's works from food to art, houses to government form the human world. In this way man becomes a productive power as a species. This proletariat class works in the interest of the bourgeosis class for his two end meals. Thus, creativity of man is sold for a few pieces of bread.
2. In a capitalist society this proletariat class invests its creative energies (labour) while the bourgeosis class pays him wages in exchange for the product of his energy. Thus human world created by proletariat class itself becomes alien to this class. It is rather owned by bourgeosis class. As a result, workers do not get the fruits of their labour properly and they are exploited by their masters.
3. It is the class not the individual that is the basis of the state, i.e., state is run not by the individuals but by a particular class. Initially it was aristocrats. Now it is bourgeosis which is exploiting the proletariat (labour class).
4. This class works cohesively, i.e., the will of the class is the real view of all the people in the class. It is because character, behaviour, interests and ideas of each individual in the class are determined by the values of the class. Individual has no existence outside his class.
5. The bourgeosis have gained control over the means of production altogether. They are using the government machinery to fulfil their vested interest. Therefore, the major portion of income and wealth goes to them and workers get only a little.
6. In the **Communist Manifesto**; published by Marx and Engels in 1848, it was stated, "the history of all hitherto existing societies is the history of class struggle. History is a practical struggle between the exploiting class and the exploited class. All battles in history have been fought for gaining control over the means of production and wealth".
7. In order to preserve his material life, man must interact with nature through a set of relations called the means of production. These relations are chosen by man in each stages of history. These historical stages evolve themselves in a dialectical manner, i.e., each stage is being succeeded by a contrasting one with which it interacts creating a synthesis of the two. This synthesis will constitute a third stage and so on. In each stage the prevailing means of production stipulate a set of relationship between man and nature on one hand and between man and man on the other. The most recent historical stage is that of Capitalism which did not exist in the beginning of history. Capitalism's success is based on the ability to increase productive capacity by generating

enormous quantities of surplus values. Capitalism has turned the entire class of human being into commodities. By doing so it is digging its own grave. Once this stage gets completed, capitalism will also come to an end. In Capitalism the proletariats are so thoroughly deprived of their human rights that they will at last unite themselves for a common goal of liberating themselves from exploitation and overthrow Capitalism by a revolution that is natural.

8. No natural cooperation or reconciliation is possible between these two classes of the society. It is because the class which is enjoying the maximum facilities from the means of production and establishment of the state is not prepared to give up any thing in favour of others. In order to save itself from any kind of adversaries, it misuses the administrative machinery of the state. Therefore, in order to remove these socio-economic disparities and exploitation, revolution is the only way open for proletariat. For this purpose **class war** is necessary and it is to be fought until the powers of the state come in the hands of the proletariats.
9. After the revolution is over and power comes in the hands of workers, a transition period will start. Great political and social disturbances will be seen in the society during this period but soon the situation will become normal and a classless society will be formed. This society will be based on mutual cooperation, economic equality and social justice. The means of production will be in the hands of workers and every person in the society will enjoy the benefits of productive(creative) energies equally. And finally the society will be free from all sort of exploitations.
10. As far as religion is concerned it has no role to play in the affairs of humans. Means of production and creative energies are only real things. Religion or church is also an important means of exploitation in the hands of the aristocrats and the priest. It is actually a barrier in the way of creating a classless society. It is because it is religion that is dividing people in various classes and exploiting the worker class. There is no existence of God, heaven or hell. They are all man made ideas. Values are determined by the ruling class that is the working class in a communist state. Similarly, there is nothing more real and true than the means of production or material. Man does everything for his material benefits.

## Lenin Nikoli (1870-1924)

Lenin transformed the revolutionary ideas of Karl Marx according to the demands of early 20th century. His ideas are summarized below:

1. Working class is not able to bring about revolution by itself. This class must be guided by professional class of the revolutionaries (intellectuals and military men).
2. Imperialism and Colonialism have accelerated the tendency of exploitation of the poor by rich. The imperialist countries are providing some facilities to the exploited people in their own countries in order to check them from rising against the imperialist power. But these imperialist countries are assisting revolutionaries in other countries in order to protect the interest of Capitalism and Colonialism. Moreover, due to mutual rivalries between colonial powers, they provide arms and ammunitions to the exploited people of their own land in order to protect themselves from the rival powers. This exploited class would eventually realize a day that these imperialist powers are misutilizing them for fulfilling their own selfish interest. As a result of these activities, the exploited people of various countries will unite together a day by throwing away the shackles of separate national boundaries. They will rise up against their masters and overthrow them with the help of arms and ammunitions already supplied to them. Once it happens international communism will be established.
3. Communist revolution would start from his country Russia because the situation there is fully ripe for a revolution.
4. Communist revolution will not come automatically through the unity amongst the exploited people but it will have to be brought out deliberately. It will need some people of

revolutionary ideas who will be prepared to sacrifice themselves completely for making the revolution a success. The successful people will chalk out a plan for other countries in order that exploited people in those countries may also rise in revolt.

5. After the revolution is over, the proletariat dictatorship will determine an outline for a new communist society. It will not transfer power to the general people because they lack the ability of decision making and judgment. If the political power is delegated to them, the very purpose of revolution would be defeated.

## Nature of Socio-Political system based on Communism

Important features of socio-political system of a Communist-Socialist-Marxist society are given below:

1. Individual is regarded as a treasure of state. Individuality of the self is completely ignored. If state needs any sacrifice from any individual, he will have to extend it for the security and existence of the state. Individuals are only to serve the state and nothing more than that. Whatever is decided by the state, the individuals will have to abide by it. State is always supreme.
2. It is the state, which will control the family, and the community by deciding about cultural, economic, social, religious and political lives of the people. Even political, social or religious organizations will not be allowed to function without the permission of the state. Means of production and system of distribution will be totally in the hands of the state. Each member of the society will be paid by the state according to his creative energies and nothing will accrue as a private property out of these creativities.
3. Recreational means and health facilities will be in the hands of the state fully. It is the state that will decide what to think and what to do in the interest of the state, i.e., interest of the state will always be kept at the top. Thus, individuals will be given very limited freedom in socialism.
4. State will always endeavour to bring about social equality in the society in whatever manner it is possible. If some people own huge private properly it will be confiscated by the state.
5. Central planning is also an important characteristic of a communist totalitarian state. Individuals cannot plan for themselves individually. They are rather planned by the state. The assumption behind this principle is that if planning is made by the state, there is least chance of injustice meted out to any one.
6. Practicability is important rather than ideas. Whatever we think it must be translated into action. State does not need ideas but material objects for its progress and strength.
7. Communism divides individual freedom into two classes, negative freedom and positive freedom. Freedom granted to the individuals under other political systems is negative freedom because the aim of this freedom is to serve the ends of a special class of the society i.e., the exploiting class. The freedom granted to the individuals under communism is the real or positive freedom because the purpose of this freedom is to serve the group of which the individual itself is a member.
8. Creating a classless society is the ultimate aim of the state. Equality of opportunities is to be provided to each individual for this purpose.
9. Communist organization is the highest authority. The leaders of this organization determine the destiny of the whole nation. If there are differences in the organization they are resolved through discussions and deliberations. A member of the organization can express his different opinion only to the extent he is permitted by the leader. Opinions of the masses are not taken into consideration. Even press and media are given only a restricted freedom as they may be the voice of people. They are rather used to propagate the policy and philosophy of the state.

## Fundamental Beliefs (Characteristics) of Marxism

1. **Superiority of matter to mind or idea :** Like Realism it also presupposes a physical reality independent of mind. It studies human nature in a materialistic way. If a child does not do well in the school he is sent not to a psychologist to be tested but to a physician to be attended.

2. **Centrality of economic activity :** Mode of production determines the character of social and political institutions and value of goods is measured by the labour expanded on them. So labour must be given an important place in all social activities including education.
3. **Equality of manual or mental labour :** Physical labour is no less important than mental work. There is no artificial dualism between the work of hand and that of head. Consequently, this philosophy also rejects the dualism between the cultural and vocational curriculum. There should be close relationship between school and the factory.
4. **Dominating role of the school :** School is treated as a deliberate instrument for popularizing state policy. In fact, school is a weapon in the hands of the ruling class and teachers are like soldiers in the battle for Communism.
5. **Subjective nature of truth**. Truth is not objective and universal. The subjective nature of truth is affected by the vested interest of the state. Truth is that which is considered true by the state and which can benefit the state on any way.
6. **Values :** They originate in social class thinking. There is no divine nature of morality or values at all.

## Educational Implications of the Philosophy

A. **Meaning of Education:** Education is the medium through which economic and military development of a country takes places and a classless society (Communism) is created.

Keeping this idea of education into account in Russia Education was given a top priority and its control, organization and implementation was handed over to the most trusted leaders of the country and from primary to higher level it was completely centralized. This centralization brought about uniformity in the standard of education.

B. **Aims of Education:**

1. *Mass education :* Each and every individual of the country will be given equal opportunity to receive education. For this purpose state should shoulder the entire responsibility of imparting education to the people
2. *Physical and mental development of the individual on the collective basis :* Development of the individual is the responsibility of the state and this responsibility will be fulfilled by the state through the agencies of education. Individual will be made strong through this process. And if individuals are strong, state will also be strong.
3. *Preparing state serving citizens :* Education will make the people fully obedient and law abiding. The sense of sacrifice and feeling of patriotism will be developed in them. As a results they will be ready to give up everything even their lives for the sake of the state if it is needed in any time in future.
4. *National reconstruction and progress :* A nation can be made strong militarily and economically through education, especially through science and vocational education. People will study those subjects for this purpose which give them objective knowledge.
5. *Creating feeling of dignity of manual labour :* Majority of the people exercise their manual potentialities to earn their living. Dignified feeling of manual labour is created in children through vocational and trade education since the primary stage.
6. *Social training :* Society or the state is important in socialism, so ,adequate social training is given to children to help them adjust in every society. It is because they have after all to propagate communism in all corners of the world.
7. *Bringing about equality and justice in the society:* Class struggle is an eternal truth. Once it is removed by communism it has to be preserved by the people and it is possible only when people are just and honest and they do not intend to exploit the others. Education provides maximum opportunities to all the individuals to get education according to their ability and interest. As a result equality in the society is maintained.
8. *Bringing full employment situation :* It is the responsibility of the state to provide employment to each and every citizen of the country. They are given education according to the job requirement of the country. Scientific, vocational and professional educations are emphasized for

this purpose. Efforts are always made by the state to make the country self reliant and developed.

9. *Giving priority to less privileged class :* Education targets the less privileged and backward class of the society first. Once they are educated and employed, the general standard of living of the country will automatically increase.

10. *Developing progressive and rational thinking :* It is the religion that is responsible for creating injustice and inequality in the society. Traditions, customs and taboos also carry the country to the backward track. So education should enlighten the people to think rationally. It should remove superstitions from the minds of the people and make them progressive in ideology and action.

### C. Curriculum Construction & Stages of Learning:

1. *Religious Education :* Religion is given no place in education as it cannot solve the objective problems of the physical world. Instead of religion, study of history is emphasized for inculcation of patriotism and love for nation. Similarly, study of science and technology is emphasized for making the people progressive in thinking and action.

2. *Primary Education :* Marxism believes in universal education, so primary and pre-primary educations are given most importance. Eight years free and compulsory primary education upto the age of 15 years is given to children by trained and competent teachers. Vocational and technical education also starts from this stage. Students are given practical experiences of industries and agriculture here.

3. *Secondary Education :* After the completion of compulsory primary education only those adolescents are permitted to go for secondary education who are really fit and competent for it. This education is of three years duration. At this stage special provisions are made for vocational and technical education. Specialized training in agriculture, industries, management, health services and technology is also given in specialized institutions. Students who have not been selected for secondary education may go through correspondence courses for their further studies.

4. *Higher Education :* After secondary education special provisions are made for few selected students to go for university education. After secondary education all adults have to take to some vocations and jobs and those desirous of further education may join evening classes and correspondence courses. After that a few of them are permitted to take admission in universities for three years higher education. The duration of this education is of three years and admission is given only on the basis of screening tests. Approval of communist party is also necessary for admission in universities.

5. *Language Education :* This philosophy does not neglect the study of languages. Language is considered a great cementing force in binding the entire nation into one fold. Three language formula is adopted for all the students here.
   - *(i)* A National Language i.e., Russian in USSR and Chinese in China.
   - *(ii)* A Regional Language
   - *(iii)* A European Language

Education is provided free of cost at all stages of learning.

**D. Methods of Teaching :** Following methods of teaching are advocated by this philosophy.
- *(i)* Lecture and text book method
- *(ii)* Tutorial method and seminars
- *(iii)* Project and problem solving methods

**E. Discipline:** Discipline is authoritarian in nature here. Students are given only limited freedom in the class, school and the society. Interest of the nation is always kept at the top. Even project method of teaching is used under strict disciplinary control. The place of the teacher is not very high here. Teacher is only a worker of the state and is directly accountable to the communist party.

## Merits (Influence) of the Philosophy

1. Many reforms made by democratic countries of the world are very much indebted to this philosophy such as equality of opportunities in education and employment, equitable distribution

of income and wealth, owning of key industries by the state, universalisation of education etc.

2. Interference of religion into politics was reduced in almost every country of the world due to the impact of this philosophy.
3. This philosophy for the first time tried to solve the basic problems of man, i.e. food, cloth and shelter. Marx and Lenin addressed these problems very pragmatically and genuinely and gave practical solutions of them.
4. By denying the role of metaphysical world in the affairs of man it motivated the people to go through the material progress by the use of science and technology.
5. The concept of creating a classless society was very much relevant in the 19th and 20th centuries. Though it failed to create a classless society anywhere in the world yet poor and unprivileged class received due attention by the state in almost every part of the world.

## Criticism of the Philosophy

The philosophy can be criticized on so many grounds such as:

1. All the forecastings regarding the creation of a classless society through class struggle made by Marx and Lenin have already been proved to be wrong today. Socialism was banished from Russia and East European countries in 1991 and China also did away with this philosophy to a great context in 2002 after accepting the membership of WTO.
2. This philosophy considers material achievements as real and neglects spiritual aspects of life altogether. As far as values are concerned it is totally silent regarding it. Thus, it once again brought man to the level of beast by limiting his activities to earn a living and consuming it.
3. The individuality of man and his self is totally discarded by this philosophy which later led to the rise of Existentialism which explained individuality and self in an extreme way. Every decision regarding the life of man is taken by a central authority, i.e., what to do, how to do and why to do and so on are determined by the state. All these make the man a refined slave.
4. By denying the private property and advocating state ownership of means of production it want to establish a classless society based on economic equality and justice. But no such societies ever existed in any communist country of the world.
5. Marx reduces the role of capital in the process of production and gives priority to the role of labour. In today's industrial age can this be possible? High-tech machines are used in the process of production to reduce cost and to compete in the global market. We cannot go in the reverse direction once again.

## DEMOCRACY

Democracy is not technically a philosophy in the sense that it does not technically discuss reality, knowledge and values as other philosophies do. But since this ideology has influenced human way of thinking so profoundly that it is generally taken as the philosophy of life by the modern man today. It has its origin into politics but its area of action is the whole society including all social institution. It is the only ideology that has influenced educational process the most. It is a value in itself and determines the human ideals. Even religions are interpreted in terms of democratic values and ideals. Philosophies are also evaluated on the basis of democratic principles. Thus, we can say that democracy is not only a political system but a way of life and a basis of human coexistence.

### Meaning

The word democracy has been derived form two Greek words, *Demons* means power and *Cratic* means public. Thus, democracy means power of the public.

American Ex-president Abraham Lincon also defined democracy in political terms as "Democracy is a government of the people, by the people and for the people". In this sense democracy means a government in which people rule over themselves by their own elected representatives.

### Definitions

1. **Seely :** Democracy is a government in which everybody has its share.
2. **Bode :** Democracy is a way of life and a way of life means a determining influence in every area of life.

3. **Radha Krishnan** (University Education Commission) : Democracy is a way of life and not a mere political arrangement. It is based on the principle of equal freedom and equal rights for all regardless of race, religion, sex or economic status.

**Explanations:** We can derive the following conclusions from the above definitions of democracy.

*(i)* In democracy every person irrespective of caste, creed, colour or sex has his own say.

*(ii)* All members of the society are equally weighted.

*(iii)* People run the government themselves through their elected representatives.

*(iv)* Freedom and rights are associated with duties and responsibilities and thus a fully committed citizen is prepared.

*(v)* Democracy is a way of life also. By making the people considerate, tolerant and justice loving through education, democracy opens a new window of universal brotherhood. Each human is judged only on the basis of his ideals, values and peace loving behaviour and not on the basis of his social status or economic power.

*(vi)* Democracy makes the earth a heaven by creating equal opportunities for all.

## Forms of Democracy

**A. Political democracy:** The chief characteristics of this democracy are as follows:

*(i)* Political power is not concentrated in the hands of a single despot or few selected aristocrats. People elect their own representatives through voting and decide their destiny themselves.

*(ii)* Every member of society has equal right to vote and weightage of votes of all citizens are equal. They exercise their rights freely without any fear or pressure.

*(iii)* The law of the land is equally applicable to all citizens irrespective of caste, creed, colour or race.

*(iv)* Accountability is maintained at every step of power sharing such as executive is responsible to legislature and legislature is accountable to the public and so on.

*(v)* People elect their representatives for a specified period of time and their re-election will only depend on the performance according to expectations of the people. Thus power also changes with the change of values and expectations.

**B. Economic democracy :** Main characteristics of economic democracy are cited below:

*(i)* Economic power will not be concentrated in the hands of few hourgeosis. Every citizen rich or poor will equally benefit from the fruits of production and distribution. Thus, economic prosperity of the nation as a whole is taken into account.

*(ii)* A number of choices are available for citizens for earning their living. They can choose any profession, trade, or job on the basis of their interest or abilities.

*(iii)* Equal opportunities are provided to all citizens along with supportive schemes for weaker sections of the society.

*(iv)* Economic organization is made cooperative without compromising its competitiveness.

*(v)* Problems of unemployment and exploitation are reduced to the minimum by installing welfare schemes and adopting preventive measures.

**C. Social Democracy :** This form of democracy is valued on the following grounds:

*(i)* All types of distinctions based on caste, creed, colour or sex are abolished and equality is maintained at all costs. Prohibitory laws are made to restrict anyone to discriminate any one on any ground, e.g., none can stop a Dalit to take water from a public tap.

*(ii)* Equal educational opportunities are provided for all citizens and thus government takes full responsibility of imparting education to children.

*(iii)* Maximum freedom is given to the people so that they can develop according to their interests and abilities. In this way, no one is allowed to deny the freedom of others in any way.

(iv) Fraternity and universal brotherhood is maintained by maintaining justice in the society.

(v) Individuals are allowed to form their own organizations in order to enable them to develop as group also.

## Principles of Democracy

1. **Freedom and Responsibility:** In the absence of freedom, no individual will be able to develop his inherent capacities to the fullest. So complete freedom of the action and expression is given to each and every individual of the society. He can speak, criticize, suggest and discuss the matter in his own way. He can criticize and condemn even the head of the state if he strides on wrong track. But freedom propounded by democracy is not absolute like that of Naturalism or Existentialism. It does not mean uncontrolled, indisciplined and arbitrary behaviour of an individual. It is because this freedom is always linked with responsibilities, i.e., full consideration of the freedom of others. In other words I am as much free as the other people so my freedom ends at the nose of others. This binding duty makes the concept of freedom meaningful and practicable.
2. **Equality :** Without discriminating the individuals on the basis of caste, creed, colour or sex equality of opportunities are provided in the matters of education, employment, adaptation of profession or trade, legal procedures, welfare schemes, civic amenities and so on. Equality does not here mean the denial of differences that is a factual phenomenon. Equality only means that if I and you have the same thing, it will be weighted equally and if there is only one opportunity, either of the two will be chosen on the basis of toss. It otherwise means that individual differences will not hinder the progress of persons in the society. Equal pay for equal work is a good example of equality.
3. **Fraternity:** It is the feeling of oneness and brotherhood on human ground only. Each individual is respected in the society as a man not as a Hindu, Muslim or Christian or as Indian, Pakistani or European. Since, democracy has to promote the welfare of all, this feeling and its translation into action are must. Common goals of the society are achieved only by this principle But this principle is adopted by the people only when the previous two principles come into practice.
4. **Justice:** Justice is a must for the success of democracy. Justice means three things:

   (i) Demanding not more than due.

   (ii) Assigning not more than due

   (iii) Receiving not more than due.

There are three forms of justice:

(i) Social justice-unbiased legal and educational structure and religious cultural system.

(ii) Economic justice- giving the people what is their due, especially money, wealth and jobs.

(iii) Political justice- taking honest political decisions and a humanistic foreign policy.

When justice prevails in the society, individuals need not suppress or repress his conscious self. He leads a contended and free from fear life in the society. Independent judiciary will help in establishing justice in the society.

## Democratic Values in the Context of Truth, Beauty and Goodness

Real democracy is manifested not merely in elected legislature, responsible executive and independent judiciary but it lies in the hearts of the people and manifests in their attitude and behaviour. The guiding values and ideals of democracy are given below:

1. As an integral part of the society each individual is respected by others and his capacities and powers are freely allowed to flourish without any hindrance from other individuals or group.
2. Each individual must be tolerant enough in order to be considerate for the contradictory views and behaviours of others. Differences of opinions are fundamental realities of life. So nobody should think that only he is right and the person or persons who does not agree with him are wrong.
3. People reach at consensus through discussion and dialogue. In the absence of consensus the opinions of the majority (more than 50% of the total number of people present and voting) is

followed without isolating the minority votes. For this purpose middle path is adopted. Thus, middle path is a fundamental reality.

4. A discrimination free peace loving society is established in democracy. Peace and social self are essential for the existence of the self.
5. A true democracy is dynamic in nature and change is its fundamental characteristics. This change is necessary for progress. Some truths and values are always changing and individual has to adapt to them by changing his attitude and behaviour.
6. Change in the society is brought about through persuasion and not by compulsion. This persuasion is the cause of change in public opinions.
7. Opposition is real. Without opposition democracy will not survive. But this opposition should be guided by general welfare of people. For this purpose, honest and justice loving opposition is needed.
8. Knowledge is what that is obtained through consensus, discussion and rational establishment of theory. An idea or opinion is not true unless its practical implementation is not proved good.
9. Individual is for the society and society, in turn, promotes the good of the individual. Thus, both of them are complementary to each other. If society develops, individual will also develop and vice versa.
10. Universal brotherhood through progress and peace is the ultimate good of democracy. It is because unity of human soul is real and unity of soul with divine soul is real knowledge and the practice of this unitary idea is the real value.

## Educational Implications

If we look at the principles and values of democracy, we see that establishment of democracy as an institution and human behaviour very much depends on the enlightenment of the people and enlightenment is possible only through education. Only an educated man can be expected to follow these principles and assimilate these values in his life. It otherwise means that democracy can not survive in an ignorant society of illiterate people. Their ignorance to their rights will lead to dictatorship of some shrewd people and their apathy and indifference to their duties will lead to anarchy.

Now the question arises what should be the shape, and nature of education and how it should be structured in a democratic society? How will a teacher behave in the class and how much sensitive the administration of education will be to the needs, capacities and interests of children and the society?

### A. Principles of democratic education:

1. *Equality of educational opportunities :* Every citizen in the country is given equal opportunities to receive education and economic and social hindrances are removed by giving them special protection and by creating awareness.
2. *Fullest development of individuality :* Each and every individual is given maximum opportunity to develop his individuality fully. Here his inherent and environmental individual differences are also taken into account.
3. *Universalisation of education :* Free and compulsory education is given to all its citizens at least upto elementary or secondary stage. This education will make the people conscious of their rights and duties and remove their ignorance. Education is the birth right of each individual in a democracy. So, state takes the total responsibility of providing education to its citizens by bearing its expenses upto a certain necessary level.
4. *Adult and women education :* Those individuals who lag behind in education due to certain reasons are also taken up through non formal system of education. Night schools, short term courses, Sunday classes and the like scheme are launched for grownup adults and women separately so that they may not remain ignorant to their basic rights and responsibilities.
5. *Education for disabled :* Disabled are one who can not be accommodated in normal setting of education under normal provision. Special provisions are made for these people and special facilities are provided to them either in normal schools or in special schools and the object is to bring them at par any how.

6. *Child centred education :* Child is always supreme in democracy in comparison to teachers. Hence, his attitude, interest, inherent powers and needs are all the time given priority. Curriculum, methods of teaching, discipline, everything is determined on the basis of it.
7. *Social training :* Differences of opinions due to freedom of expression, if not tolerated by the people, will create hatred and enmity. Due to this reason, social training through schools and colleges is a must. Democratic values and ideals are taught to students through not only text books and activities but through the behaviour of the teacher as well. In this way school is considered as miniature society.
8. *Political training* : This type of training is given to students through students union students council, group activities and clubs. Students learn techniques of ruling through these institutions.
9. *Teacher's participation :* Teacher is not merely a policy implementer as he is in a communist society. His participation in curriculum construction, educational planning, administration and conducting researches in the field of education is fully regarded and encouraged. Thus, suitable autonomy is given at each level of educational administration.
10. *Diagnostic and intelligence testing :* In order to hold the teachers responsible for their carelessness and negligence, intelligence and diagnostic tests of students are also conducted. If there is no defect in the student and even then he fails, the teacher must take full responsibility of his failure.
11. *Physical and health education :* In democracy, schools don't prepare such students who are able to exercise their mental abilities only. But in order to save the country from despots, physically fit citizens are also needed. Students are given physical and health education at all levels.

**B. Aims of education :** Education should achieve the following aims according to this philosophy-

1. *Self realizations :* It include the following aims.
   - Development of power of speech
   - Development of logical power
   - Development of reading and writing skills in at least mother tongue
   - Knowledge of life related mathematics
   - Sensory motor development
   - Health awarenessss
   - Development of taste of recreation
   - Utilization of leisure time
   - Development of values of life
   - Development of introversion and subjectivity
2. *Establishment of proper human relations :* I' includes the following aims:
   - Feeling of respect for others
   - Development of friendly relations
   - Feeling of cooperation and social welfare
   - Development of good behaviour
   - Feeling of tolerance
   - Preservation of family
   - Feeling of mutual co-existence
   - Development of worthy interests
   - Feeling of justice
   - Sense of social responsibility
3. *Self Reliance :* It consists of the following aims.
   - Inculcation of vocational efficiency
   - Professional training
   - Researches for agricultural and industrial development
   - Talent search and assignment of task
   - Upliftment of weaker sections by providing extra facilities
   - Market training
   - Development of sensitivity to the interest of consumers
   - Inculcation of professional ethics
   - Job oriented education
   - International understanding
4. *Political and social awareness :* It includes the following aims:
   - Sensitivity to fundamental rights and duties.
   - Knowledge of democratic institutions like legislature, executive and judiciary
   - Inculcation of liberal ideas
   - Protection of national property
   - Obedience to the law of the land
   - Leadership training
   - Development of understanding to solve national and international problems

- Knowledge of propaganda and facts
- Development of decision making power
- Knowledge of constructive role of opposition

**C. Curriculum:** In a democratic country curriculum is developed for the purpose of propagating democratic values and putting democratic principles into practice. Enabling the students to live a successful living is the ultimate target of the curriculum. This curriculum has following characteristics.

1. *General curriculum upto a certain level :* Each and every person can not be taught everything but there are some fundamental titbits of knowledge that every citizen in the society must acquire. In India, education upto class Xth is general in nature. Every pupil has to study everything without the provision of option upto class Xth. Through this education democratic and social values are actually taught with scientific temperament.
2. *Diversified curriculum :* Interests, abilities, needs and attitudes of children are different so different options are made available to them on the basis of their individual differences, such as arts, commerce, science management etc. A number of co-curricular activities are also organized for this purpose
3. *Flexible :* Needs of the individual and the society also change with the change of time. It is because a democratic society is always dynamic. Keeping this change into account, curriculum is also revised and changed from time to time.
4. *Vocation based :* The purpose of education is to enable the children to earn their living also. As a result, vocational subjects are especially included in the curriculum after class Xth.
5. *Equal weightage on the subjects of science, humanities and social sciences :* In democracy no specific stream of education is given preference to other streams. Speaking power and logical thinking are developed by the subjects of humanities, social and political awareness is developed by the subjects of social sciences and scientific temper is developed by the study of natural sciences.
6. *Activity centred :* Children are encouraged to search and test the truth on the basis of their own experiments and experiences. Hence practical works go side by side the theoretical knowledge and emphasis is gives on learning by doing.
7. *Secular :* In democracy no religion is given special weightage. All religions are rather equally treated. Hence, religious education is not imparted in government institutions but private educational ventures are fully allowed to fulfil the needs of the people.
8. *Forward looking :* Curriculum is also made visionary so that it can fulfil not only the present needs of the people but also the future requirements. Thus, it prepares the children for future life.

**D. Method of teaching :** Child reigns supreme in democracy so all methods of teaching in democracy are children centred. Important methods are given below:

1. *Learning by doing :* Activity, experiences and experiments are preferred in democracy to mere bookish and theoretical knowledge. Laboratory and experimental methods are used for this purpose.
2. *Self learning :* Children are motivated to go through self learning under the guidance of an able teacher. Montessori method, Heuristic method and Daltan plan are commonly used methods here.
3. *Problems solving method :* Life related actual problems are assigned to students and they are required to solve them by discussions or experiments. It requires thinking and logical power.
4. *Discussion method :* Each child is free to express his views here. Subject matter is discussed in the class and conclusion is arrived at through discussion, and debate.

**E. Discipline:** Instead of repression or suppression, self discipline through impression and experiences is advocated in democracy. Important characteristics of discipline are given below:

1. Principal or teachers do not behave like police officers. They are rather friends, philosopher and

guide in the school and they mould the behaviour of children through their friendly and affectionate behaviour.

2. Only those programmes and activities are included in the curriculum which cater to the needs and interests of children. It develops self discipline among them.
3. Children are given full freedom to discuss the problems and to participate in various activities of the school. Thus, individuality of a child is always given importance. This develops self confidence in them.
4. Students are fully permitted to run their unions and clubs in the school. They can also participate in various co-curricular activities in the school. In this way their extra energy causing indiscipline is released. Leadership and followship qualities are also developed through these activities and it is much helpful in establishing self discipline in the school.
5. Students are taught responsibilities and duties along with rights. This develops self restraint and considerate feeling in them. Indiscipline is mainly caused due to lack of these qualities.
6. Democratic behaviour of the teacher also plays an important role in maintaining discipline. What is taught by 100 words can be taught by a single behaviour of the teacher.
7. Teachers always keeps the individual differences of children into account and gives them full chance to flourish on the basis of; their inherent potentialities.
8. Teacher is also conscious of rights and duties towards the individual and the society hence he always keeps himself alert in the class.

### Merits (Influence) of Democracy :

1. This philosophy of life is very much suitable to the modern changing world.
2. This philosophy and its honest practice can be used to change the minds of extremists and separatists.
3. It is very suitable to create an environment in which knowledge can be increased very rapidly.
4. It is very close to human nature. That is why its acceptability is universal.
5. Deviation from this philosophy will lead to despotism and autocracy.
6. Every peace loving nation adopts this philosophy because of its merits.

## FUNDAMENTALISM

### Introduction

This philosophy also originated in the West by those people who had deep faith in democracy and in its principles but wanted to impose it on others without their consent. The origin of this philosophy dates back to 1993 when Islamic Salvation Front-a political-religious party in Algeria could not take over the government even after its mandate in general elections and military officials backed by France and U.K. captured power. The reason was simple enough. Europe wanted its own variety of democracy established there. Hence, it supported the military take over there. Since then this very practice has been repeated in many countries such as Uzbekistan, Chychenia, Afghanistan, Iraq etc. The reaction to this fundamentalism gave birth to religious fundamentalism which is no less dangerous than democratic fundamentalism. The practical form of this fundamentalism is terrorism which is menacing the whole humanity today. We can survive on this earth until the period these terrorists reach the nuclear weapons. Once they are able to develop such weapons, everything will be extinguished. We will not go into the perspectives of this ideology and its repercussions into detail here. We will only discuss the ideology or philosophy of fundamentalism only.

### Meaning

The word fundamentalism technically means sticking to the fundamentals of life with rigidity. A fundamentalist is one who is not considerate to others because of ideological differences and he can go to any extent to make his opponent subservient to him. Nazism and Fascism of the recent past and American Republican ideology at present are good examples of democratic fundamentalism and Al Qaida, Hamas, LTTE etc. are examples of religious fundamentalism.

### Forms of Fundamentalism

1. **Democratic Fundamentalism :** A democratic fundamentalist is one who has so strong faith in

his own democratic ideals that anyone who slightly deviates from his own principles and beliefs is considered sinful and fundamentalist thinks it necessary to mould him in whatsoever manner it is possible whether by menace, incentive, coercion or war. This type of fundamentalists use democratic institutions to fulfil their vested interests and welfare of the masses is generally neglected. They only serve the interest of a particular group or class of the country. This type of fundamentalism may later change into colonialism.

2. **Religious Fundamentalism :** A religious fundamentalist is one who does not approve any philosophy except that of his own religion and opposes any ideology by giving its anti thesis or action. He wants to establish a theocratic state. The physical world is denied and considered only a phenomenon of the real spiritual world by him. Thus religious fundamentalism is a world denying philosophy that considers the man only as a means to achieve the religious supremacy that is the end. Political power is necessary to achieve this end. This power is not taken over by election or popular votes but by force or compulsion. The only such state established so far was Afghanistan of Talibans. American, democratic fundamentalist state overthrew their government by force and now the conflicts between these two types of fundamentalism has taken the form of gorilla wars in many parts of world. The germs of this philosophy have entered in India also and separatist movements active in Jammu & Kashmir and in the North East are the examples of such clashes.

## Principles of Fundamentalism

1. **Extreme form of self existence :** This philosophy does not believe in the free existence of others. Others may exist on this earth but only as subjugated and slave organisms. Their thinking and actions will always be guided by the political power.

2. **Strong belief in conflicts and wars :** This philosophy believes that weak and strong people as well as weak and strong nations cannot exist as separate and free entities. The weak must have to bow before the strong at least socially and economically. If it does not happen automatically, war will be waged against the weak. If fundamentalists are not in a position to wage a face to face battle, they will use the technique of suicide attack. This will also make them victorious in the life hereafter. If they are killed in the attack, they will directly be sent to paradise to live a well satisfied life there. Under the influence of this philosophy, American soldiers in Iraq and else where in the world are sacrificing their lives and same thing is done by religious fundamentalists in all parts of the world also.

3. **Extremist nature of faith in religion :** Fundamentalists have so strong faith in religion that they discards other beliefs altogether. They are not considerate even to those people who have some slight variation in their beliefs. There voices are suppressed by using force. They need not convince others on any matter. They do what they think right in their own way.

4. **Politics is the applied form of religion:** Religion and politics are not separate according to this philosophy. They are rather one and the same thing in the sense that religion is related to individual life of a man but it necessarily guide the social and political lives of the people in the society as a whole. Fundamentalists use the religion and energy as power to run the political machine.

5. **Superiority of society over individuals:** According to this philosophy, society and social values are given preference to individual ones. Individuals of the society are only parts of the big machine of the society. Thus, social interest is taken into consideration instead of individual interest.

6. **Centres of powers are many not one :** Authority is not in a single hand here. It is rather distributed among few powerful persons in the society. These people decide the destiny and future of all the individuals in the society.

**7. Belief about reality :** According to it, only divine power (God) and the life hereafter is real. Whatever right or wrong is done by the people here, it is evaluated in terms of spiritual world and the purpose is always to make the society good and the people happy and prosperous.

**8. Belief about knowledge :** True knowledge is what that can be experimented in the laboratory and field. The knowledge given by holy scriptures are also true because they can also be experimented in the laboratory and the field.

## Educational Implications

**A. Aims of education:** The aims of education enumerated by fundamentalists are given below :

1. *To make the society economically and militarily strong :* This is essential for establishing political supremacy in the world.
2. *To make the people morally high :* Moral values are given special emphasis in fundamentalism. Students studying in Madarsas and missionary schools are kept very high on moral and ethical grounds.
3. *To develop strong adherence to social principles of religion in the people :* This philosophy wants to prepare such individuals who are not very much inclined to rituals but they are rigid and conservative to social values and principles of religion.
4. *To develop creative powers of the individuals in the field of science :* Scientific Experiments are the means of acquiring military power. So science subjects are taught in such a way as to develop creative potentialities in children.
5. *To develop oratory skills :* Masses are convinced by thrilling speeches and cermons of what is needed and what is not needed. Hence by developing language and oratory skills the will of the masses are suppressed.

**B. Curriculum:** Reading, writing and computer are taught at the lower primary stage along with the teaching of environment and sociology. Foreign languages are added at upper primary stage in Madarsas. Thus education upto secondary level is general in nature. Specialized knowledge of health, technology, management, defence etc. are given. Thus, students are taught everything that is anyhow useful to build a strong society and the nation.

**C. Methods of teaching :** Fundamentalists do not stick to any particular method of teaching. The only thing that they emphasise is the achievement of objectives in whatsoever manner it is possible thus, lecture method, activity method, laboratory or experimental method, problem solving method, etc. all are used according to the demand.

**D. Discipline :** The place of the teacher is very high here. Everything for the students are decided by him. Students are not given very much freedom to think and act in their own way. Limited freedom is permissible for students.

## Dangers of the philosophy

This philosophy is preparing such people who want to bring everything under their control at the expense of rights of others. Such a philosophy is likely to divide the whole world into exploited and exploiting classes once again in the same way as it was doing in the 19th century. Its repercussion may be that millions of people will lose their lives in the near future if no compromise is made between real democracy and this philosophy.

# OBJECTIVE QUESTIONS

**1.** Filtration theory of education was supported by
(*a*) Russell (*b*) Milton
(*c*) Dewey (*d*) Kant

**2.** Which of the following is not the work of Russell
(*a*) Outline of Philosophy(1928)
(*b*) Education and the Social Order (1932)
(*c*) Impact of Science on Society (1952)
(*d*) Democracy and Education (1946)

**3.** It is rational nature of man that makes him above other living creatures in the world. It is called
(*a*) Neo realism
(*b*) Sense realism
(*c*) Rational Humanism
(*d*) None of these

**4.** The aim of education advocated by Realistic humanism is

(a) Cultivation of intellect for making man rational
(b) Developing human values in man
(c) Both of these
(d) None of these

5. The philosophy closer to Idealism is Scholastic Realism because it advocates that
(a) God is central to its metaphysical theology and nature is his manifestation
(b) Truth is eternal and unchanging
(c) Both of these
(d) None of these

6. Neo Realism states that
(a) True knowledge essentially comes through senses
(b) Knowledge should essentially benefit humans
(c) Both of these
(d) None of these

7. Which of the following phrases conforms Sense Realism
(a) Observation and contact as the legitimate sources of knowledge
(b) Inductive method of teaching
(c) Emphasis on nature study and natural sciences
(d) All of the above

8. Which of the following philosophies supports education for the masses
(a) Sense Realism (b) Pragmatism
(c) Existentialism (d) All of these

9. Indian philosophy close to Realism is
(a) Jainism (b) Samkhya
(c) Advaite Vedanta (d) Both (a) & (b)

10. Anektavad principle of Jainism implies
(a) Flexible outlook in the pursuit of knowledge and truth
(b) Liberal attitude towards the people and matter
(c) Both of these
(d) None of these

11. Which of the following philosophies opposes bookish knowledge as the sole source of knowledge
(a) Naturalism (b) Realism
(c) Pragmatism (d) All of these

12. Real knowledge comes from the social contact of man with material things. It is the belief of
(a) Humanism (b) Socialism
(c) Social Realism (d) None of these

13. Material and physical universe is an incomplete expression of reality. It is the idea of
(a) Idealism (b) Buddhism
(c) Islam (d) Both (a) & (b)

14. Man is above all living and non living creature because of the rational mind given to him. It is the belief of
(a) Idealism (b) Islam
(c) Both of these (d) None of these

15. Maya is indescribable i.e., it is neither true nor false. This is the belief of
(a) Jainism (b) Advaite Vedanta
(c) Realism (d) All of these

16. Education of Advaite Vedanta is different from western Idealism in which of the following points.
(a) Enabling the child to realize his real nature which is divine
(b) Moksha can be obtained through knowledge
(c) Learning is restricted to the present world not to the world hereafter
(d) All of these

17. The ultimate aim of education according to Naturalist is
(a) Adaptation to changing environment
(b) Development of the child in a free environment
(c) Bringing the child back to nature
(d) All of these

18. The criterion of judging values and reality in Pragmatism is
(a) Utility and usefulness
(b) Changing needs of the society
(c) Rational discourses
(d) None of these

19. The biggest reality according to Pragmatism is
(a) Consequences of action
(b) Progress and change
(c) Adaptive power of humans
(d) None of these

20. Which of the following tenets does not belong to Pragmatism
(a) Idea devoid of action are meaningless
(b) Experiment is needed for verification of truth
(c) Only that knowledge is significant which has any relevance to man

(*d*) If individual is developed, society will automatically develop

**21.** Pragmatism considers education
(*a*) As an interactive process that takes place in a social matrix
(*b*) As the reconstruction of experiences to benefit the society as a whole
(*c*) As a responsibility of the state to take it to the last man of the society
(*d*) All of the above

**22.** Pragmatism is also known by the name of
(*a*) Pragmatic Naturalism
(*b*) Instrumentalism
(*c*) Experimentalism
(*d*) All of these

**23.** Which of the following is not the postulate of Humanism
(*a*) Man is competent to solve all his problems by applying reason and scientific methods.
(*b*) Man is the maker of his own destiny.
(*c*) Achieving happiness on earth is the birth right of man.
(*d*) Supernatural hand is also there to punish those who hinders in getting happiness.

**24.** Harmonious blending of all the philosophies and their implication in the classroom according to need of the society is called
(*a*) Sociological tendency in education
(*b*) Eclectic tendency in education
(*c*) Modern tendency in education
(*d*) None of these

**25.** Founder of Existentialism was
(*a*) Kierkegeard (*b*) Satre
(*c*) Jasper (*d*) Augustine

**26.** Which of the following philosophies gives much more importance to man
(*a*) Humanism (*b*) Existentialism
(*c*) Both of these (*d*) None of these

**27.** The philosophy antagonistic to Marxism is/are
(*a*) Existentialism (*b*) Naturalism
(*c*) Both of these (*d*) None of these

**28.** Individual and self evaluation in the school is advocated by
(*a*) Idealism (*b*) Existentialism
(*c*) Realism (*d*) None of these

**29.** Match the following

| **(I) Role of the teacher** | **(II) Philosophy** |
|---|---|
| (A) Guide and helper | (i) Marxism |
| (B) Instructor | (ii) Existentialism |
| (C) Autocrat | (iii) Pragmatism |
| (D) Disciplined inition | (iv) Idealism |

| | A | B | C | D |
|---|---|---|---|---|
| (*a*) | (iii) | (iv) | (i) | (ii) |
| (*b*) | (i) | (ii) | (iii) | (iv) |
| (*c*) | (iv) | (iii) | (ii) | (i) |
| (*d*) | (ii) | (iii) | (iv) | (i) |

**30.** Which of the following is exclusively advocated by Humanism
(*a*) Freedom of propagation and follow of religion
(*b*) Man is the centre and measure of all activities in the world
(*c*) Happiness of man is to be increased in whatever manner it is possible
(*d*) All of these

**31.** Which of the following philosophies believe in eternal and absolute values
(*a*) Idealism
(*b*) Humanism
(*c*) Both of both
(*d*) None of these

**32.** Downfall in history according to Humanism, is due to
(*a*) Class struggle
(*b*) Decline in moral standard and values
(*c*) The downfall of educational standard
(*d*) All of these

**33.** Modern Humanism believes in
(*a*) Universal brotherhood
(*b*) Internationalism
(*c*) Human welfare at all costs
(*d*) All of these

**34.** Modern democracy is very much indebted to which of the following philosophies.
(*a*) Humanism
(*b*) Naturalism
(*c*) Existentialism
(*d*) All of these

**35.** Humanism as a modern philosophy emerged in
(*a*) 17th century (*b*) 19th century
(*c*) 20th century (*d*) 15th century

## ANSWERS

| 1 | 2 | 3 | 4 | 5 | 6 | 7 | 8 | 9 | 10 |
|---|---|---|---|---|---|---|---|---|---|
| *(a)* | *(d)* | *(c)* | *(a)* | *(c)* | *(a)* | *(d)* | *(d)* | *(d)* | *(c)* |
| **11** | **12** | **13** | **14** | **15** | **16** | **17** | **18** | **19** | **20** |
| *(d)* | *(c)* | *(a)* | *(c)* | *(b)* | *(d)* | *(a)* | *(a)* | *(b)* | *(d)* |
| **21** | **22** | **23** | **24** | **25** | **26** | **27** | **28** | **29** | **30** |
| *(d)* | *(d)* | *(d)* | *(b)* | *(a)* | *(c)* | *(c)* | *(b)* | *(a)* | *(d)* |
| **31** | **32** | **33** | **34** | **35** | | | | | |
| *(c)* | *(b)* | *(d)* | *(d)* | *(a)* | | | | | |

# Western Philosophers and Education

## SOCRATES (469–399 BC)

### His Life Sketch

- He was born in Athens in 469 BC.
- His father was a sculptor and his mother was a midwife. He chose the occupation of his father for earning his livelihood when he grew up.
- He was having some unrest in his mind regarding the physical and metaphysical world. So he would visit the people at market and other places and discuss them the matters related to war, politics, marriage, love, poetry, science, religion etc. Gradually he lost his interest in the physical world.
- He was kind, gentle and witty and had great sense of humour.
- His acceptability as the wisest man of Athense created many enemies around him and finally a complaint against him was lodged in the court accusing him of corrupting the youth and propagating atheism. And he was given poison to consume to embrace death after trial.
- Many of his followers persuaded him to escape the jail but he declined saying that everyone must obey the laws of the state even at the cost of one's death.
- He was perhaps the most beloved teacher of his time though he never claimed to be a teacher.
- The chief contribution of Socrates is that he aroused the young men from that false self satisfaction which was the chief cause of their miseries and through his dialectic method he led them to self examination and self criticism.

### His Philosophical Thoughts

**1. His dialectic method :** "There are two things which we might attribute to Socrates—his inductive discourses and his universal definitions of concepts."-**Aristotle**

Socrates never wished to influence and convince the people by his ideas. He only wanted to correct their ideas by making them philosopher themselves. He was of the view that knowledge already exists in the soul and when man takes birth he forgets it. The purpose of a philosopher is to bring out this latent knowledge only. Thus, he inculcated in them the love for philosophy or love for wisdom by his unique approach known as **numetic approach**.

Dialectic was the method of discovery of valid and objective definitions of concepts commonly used in daily life. Through this method Socrates brought out the defects in the meaning and definition of concepts and persuaded the people through discourses and questioning method to modify and rectify the concepts.

The salient features of this method are as follows-

(a) *Skeptical methodology:* Skeptical methodology means critical examination of the problem concerned by creating artificial doubt about the validity of the current beliefs. In this method Socrates would pretend himself to be an ignorant person about the real meaning of a concept and want that other people might enlighten him on the subject. This pretence of ignorance is known as "Socratic Irony".

(b) *Conversational:* Socrates used dialogue method for the development of ideas. A dialogue is a process of exchange of ideas on a certain topic between two or more persons to arrive at definite conclusions. Through this method Socrates brought latent ideas in the mind of men to the surface.

(c) *Conceptual and semantic:* He was interested to deliver the correct and precise definition of the concepts. The meaning of concepts was derived from the general and universal features of a thing.

(d) *Inductive enquiry:* Socrates asked questions one by one and on the basis of answers given by his interlocutors he would develop the general features of a thing and finally the concept was defined.

**2. His theory of knowledge :** Socratic ideas were actually a threat for sophists who believed that there was no objective truth and morality and that each view was only the opinion of a particular person. Therefore, superiority of an opinion over others is not because of its inherent character but due to the manner and force with which it is argumented and proved. Thus, according to them, truth is subjective, particular and contextual. Thus, this philosophy was very damaging for the society in the long run. Every one could have his own ideas about morality and character and he could logically prove it as well.

By acknowledging the diversity of opinions about a subject, Socrates opined that in order to reach the truth, man must be skeptical regarding all sorts of opinions first. Then he should cut through the false layers of prejudices by cross questioning and reach the objective, universal and real nature of truth, e.g., speaking the truth is a universal and objective concept. Its opposite can not be accepted on the basis of logical argumentation.

**3. His theory of concepts :** Socrates believed that knowledge was based through the medium of concepts. Concept is an idea based on the general and common characteristics of all members of a group. It is contrary to a percept which is an idea based on the particular characteristics of a thing. For example, "Inflation" is a concept based on the general trend of price rise in almost all the commodities for a longer period of time. If price of only few commodities are rising, it will not be termed as inflation.

Socrates tried to construct and define concepts by using the process of induction and by giving familiar examples. This provisional nature of definitions was tested by discovering the exceptions. This process is carried on till a satisfactory definition is arrived at. Thus in order to establish the universality of knowledge, Socrates emphasized the importance of precise, clear and universally acceptable definitions of concepts.

**4. His philosophy of Virtue :** Socrates believed that knowledge should enlighten the path of each man's life. Thus, knowledge should reform the conduct of man which is of highest value and Summum Bonum of life. According to him knowledge is virtue itself. No one does anything wrong knowingly. For example, strong people oppress the weaker ones due to ignorance about its consequence in this world as well as in the world hereafter. Thus, he believed that right knowledge was the key to right conduct.

**5. His principles of wisdom :** There are four fundamental principles given by him in this regard.

(a) *Virtue or knowledge is the goal of life :* Some people believe that attaining pleasure is the goal of life. Some people believe that abiding by the rules framed by elders is the goal of life. But Socrates believed that gaining knowledge was the highest goal of life. It is because knowledge is the sine quo non of all virtues. If we know what is right, we cannot commit wrong. So, in order to be good, we must know what is right or good.

Socrates believed that wrong could not be done knowingly because will or desire, subservient to reason would not permit it. It would surely be moulded by knowledge. Moreover, according to him known bad is superior to unknown bad, killing a man with a gun deliberately is an unknown bad because the killer does not know how wrong it is from ethical or social point of views. So he will again do the same in future. But killing a man accidentally is a known bad and it will not be repeated in future.

(b) *Virtues can be taught:* According to him virtue is knowledge and since knowledge is a system, it can be taught to the people. We sometimes give up many bad practices just after hearing a lecture.

(c) *Virtue is one :* Traditional Greek philosophers held the view that there were four virtues—wisdom, courage, temperance and justice but Socrates said that there was only one virtue, that was knowledge itself.

(d) *Virtue is ecstasy :* According to Socrates, happiness in life is not possible without virtue. Virture is nothing but knowledge.

**6. His philosophy of death :** According to him, death is really the greatest blessing that a man can have. So there is no need to fear it.

## His Education Thoughts

1. **Aim of Education :** The aim of education derived from his thoughts is to train the individual to arrive at true knowledge by clarifying, concepts regarding mind and spirit.
2. **Method of Teaching :** He propounded four methods to arrive at true knowledge.
   (a) Discussion and discourse.
   (b) Question-Answer method
   (c) Skeptical enquiry
   (d) Inductive reasoning and logic
3. **Curriculum :** Anything that helps the individual to know the real nature of the universe may be taught.
4. **Discipline :** Socrates was not a formal teacher. So nothing can be derived from his thoughts regarding discipline.

## PLATO (427-347 BC)

## His Life Sketch

- His father Ariston was a skillful player. Education at that time was imparted through games, music, poetry and philosophy, so Plato was also educated on these lines.
- His life can be divided into three stages. In the first stage he received education from various teachers. Then he came in contact with Socrates—a great philosopher of that time. Plato was greatly influenced by his ideas and his simple style of living though he himself belonged to a rich family influenced by sophist philosophers. His second life started after the death of Socrates when he visited Italy, Egypt and Asia Minor and roamed in these countries for about ten years. He also studied the ideas of Pythagoras in Italy. In the last stage of his life he returned to Greece and established his Academy. Here he taught mathematics and philosophy for about 40 years.
- The main source of his philosophical ideas is his famous book "**Republic**".
- He took much more interest in the political field because political conditions of the state at that time were very deplorable and Plato was disappointed with it.

## His Philosophical Thoughts

**1. His belief about knowledge :** There are three sources of knowledge according to him:

(a) Knowledge is obtained through five senses-hearing, seeing, smelling, touching and tasting but this form of knowledge is not real.

(b) Knowledge is obtained through personal experiences but the opinion of the people regarding an object or event may differ due to individual differences of experiences. So this form of knowledge is also not real.

(c) Knowledge obtained through mind is real. This knowledge is abstract and can not be experienced like any concrete object. This idea is very much similar to that of Socrates who believed that knowledge is already present in the mind in the form of impressions. When a person is born, this knowledge is activated via mind.

Thus, according to Plato, concrete world is unreal. Only metaphysical or idealistic world is real. The world of idea is real because it is everlasting, formless and unchangeable. Plato also believed that all ideas are joined together with a divine thread and manifest the purpose of God.

**2. His belief about body and soul :** As a spiritual thinker Plato tried to distinguish the body from soul. He said "as the essence of the universe man, is a combination of body and soul. Body is full of vices because of its physical components and soul is full of virtues because of the following metaphysical components":

(a) *Desire :* Its centre is abdomen. All bodily desires originate from here.

(*b*) *Courage :* Its centre is heart. It is the source of encouragement for all activities.

(*c*) *Reason :* Its centre is mind. It is neither destroyed nor does it change its form. It arouses wisdom. When this wisdom is aroused, body loses its existence.This wisdom dwells in the divine power of God before birth. After birth soul becomes its abode. Due to this very wisdom soul comes to know about truth, beauty and goodness. This wisdom also guides the desire and courage and everything comes to right. A man can become happy and contended only after the realization of this wisdom.

Moreover, desire and courage are born with the body, so they are destroyed with annihilation of the body. This makes them unreal. But wisdom remains alive with the soul even after death, so it is real.

**3. His moral ideals :** Plato wanted to make all citizens of the state ideal and virtuous. His moral ideals are as follows:

(*a*) Morality means achieving virtues. These virtues are in the form of quality of soul. Patience, justice, self restraint, comprehension, memory and high ideals based on the nature of man are some of the qualities of soul.

(*b*) Desire can be controlled by self restraint. Quality of heart is patience and quality of intelligence is knowledge. Knowledge or wisdom is the supreme virtue of man. Virtue is that which gives us spiritual pleasure and vice is that which gives us spiritual pain. When self restraint, patience and knowledge are harmonized in man, justice is emerged.

(*c*) Justice motivates him to do noble deeds. Thus unlike his teacher Socrates he considers goodness (human welfare) as the aim of life which can enable a man to achieve highest delight.

(*d*) Human welfare and achievement of delight are the greatest truths of the world which are to be nourished by all objects of the world.

(*e*) Desire can give us only mundane pleasure which are useless from spiritual view points. So desires must be fully controlled to achieve spiritual delight.

(*f*) Body is the source of all evils but it should be developed because it is the means of spiritual success.

## His Educational Thoughts

Plato wanted to solve social and individual problems of his time through education. He gave equal importance to individuals and society and made them complementary to each other.

His main ideas are given below:

(*a*) It is the duty of the state to provide education. It is merely education that can produce worthy warriors and noble citizens. So it is the duty of the state to produce Ideal citizens through education.

(*b*) Education cannot be separated from the culture of the state.

(*c*) It is the duty of every citizen to live and die for his country. Education should develop **patriotism** in him.

(*d*) There are three types of people found in a country and education pattern should be developed accordingly.

First are desire-dominated people who are concerned to physical pleasure and material gains. For this purpose, they engage themselves to agriculture, industry and trade. They should be educated in their respective fields. Second type of people are those who are courageous and brave. Thus they lie in the second virtue of soul. They are interested to protect the state from enemies and establish peace. They should be given military and warfare education. Third category of people has wisdom-the highest level of soul. They are the administrators and rulers. They should be given such a high education as to develop in them the potential of justice and goodness.

(*e*) In an ideal state education is the means of the progress of the state as well as the individual. It is only the education that can remove the defects in the political system and bring about an ideal state. Therefore, education should not be left in the hands of the family. According to Plato, it was the main reason for the downfall of Athens. State must own all the responsibilities of education.

(f) Educational principles of Plato are founded on four pillars—ability, knowledge, service and diplomacy. Ability means education according to the ability of learners. Knowledge means goodness. Only that education is regarded good which enables the child to love that which is good and hate that which is bad. Service means education should develop the passion of patriotism in youth and diplomacy means the art of ruling and administration.

(g) As far as functions of education are concerned, Plato opined that education should unite the people to serve the state unitedly and make them ideal citizens full of patriotism. They should be given only that amount of freedom that might not make them indisciplined. From this point of view, he was a socialist. The second important function of education is to inculcate wisdom among the learners so that truth can be ascertained and adopted properly. The third function is that education should coordinate body and mind in such a way as to develop qualities of soul among the individuals. The fourth function of education is to make the individuals skilled, strong and healthy which will, in turn, make the country strong and self reliant.

## His Programme of Education (Curriculum)

There can be two forms of education according to him. First is that education which makes the individual adapted to his daily life, like the education of trade, commerce and agriculture. This is of a low degree education. It does not develop wisdom in man and he is drifted away from justice. Second is that education which enables the individuals to serve the state in any way. This form of education creates wisdom in him which is necessary for practicing justice and goodness. This is of a high degree education. Plato's unique programme of education is summarized below:

(a) **Education from birth to six years :** During this period attention should be paid on physical development of the child along with inculcation of healthy habits. The child should be allowed to act according to his desires, i.e., the lowest level of soul. At this stage, the love for national culture and traditions should also be developed by telling stories of the national events. In the sixth year, he should be taught music, poetry, dance and religion. Teaching of riding and shooting should also start at this stage and ideals of justice and cooperation should be developed through these activities. Elementary knowledge of mathematics should also be included in the curriculum at the age of six years.

(b) **Education from 6-13 years of age :** Proper education of games and elementary military training along with the knowledge of mathematics and religion should be systematically given at this stage. Proper age of schooling according to him is 6 years (see his book Republic). Special emphasis should be given on reading, writing and cramming of poems but these poems should not be based on false imaginations like many poems of the national poet **Homer**.

(c) **Education from 13-16 years :** Religious hymns and national songs should be taught along with other subjects at this stage. Efforts should be made to develop logical power of the child.

(d) **Education from 16-20 years :** Special emphasis should be given on physical and military education during this period. There is no need of any literary education here.

(e) **Education from 20-30 years :** If the person is intellectually sound, he should go through scientific study during this period.

(f) **Education from 30-35 years :** Those who are interested in administrative services at the age of thirty, should be taught philosophy, logic, oratory, ethics and psychology.

Thus we see that Plato does not include vocational or technical education in the formal system of education though he is not opposed to them. These types of education may be imparted at home.

(g) **Education for women :** He does not make any distinction between men and women. Therefore, he has not given any separate system of education for women.

## His Aims of Education

His primary aim of education was to awaken the wisdom of man and his secondary aim was to strengthen the state by strengthening the individuals. According to him, individuals were for the state and not vice versa.

## Criticism of Plato

Plato's ideas on education can be criticized on the following grounds:

*(i)* He denied the freedom of the individual. There is not much option available for the people even on the course of educational activities.

*(ii)* He makes the family free from the total responsibility of education of the child.

*(iii)* He coerces the children to do good deeds, which is psychologically wrong and very far from the principles of motivation.

*(iv)* He advocates same type of education for men and women. If women had been given priority in certain fields, it would have been better.

*(v)* He does not include industrial and technical training in the curriculum, though this is the backbone of every economy today.

*(vi)* He divides the soul into three parts—desire, courage and reason. Then he relates desire directly with body. This, technically, seems to be wrong.

*(vii)* His idea of starting military education in early childhood period also seems to be impracticable.

## JOHN AMOS COMENIUS (1592-1670)

He believed in self experienced realism. His philosophical ideas are summarized below:

### 1. His Belief about Knowledge

*(a)* There are three sources of knowledge according to him—Intution, observation and idea.

*(b)* Every person may be made noble through education. Thus, he favoured the idea of universal education. It is not the privilege of rich people only but it is also the right of poor children to receive education. Once the scope of education is universal, the knowledge of all subjects—physical or metaphysical, is real.

*(c)* Nature has put the seeds of knowledge, virtues and devotion to God in all persons. The purpose of education is only to nourish them to help the people grow in a proper way.

*(d)* State should take full responsibility of education. It should not be left at the mercy of family and parents.

*(e)* While imparting knowledge help from nature should also be sought. Thus, his ideas are similar to those of Rousseau. Character of education is universal nevertheless, only students of high moral character should be admitted to the universities.

### 2. His Aim of Education

**Education has three aims:**

*(a)* Giving knowledge to a person for a successful living

*(b)* Arousing wisdom for moral development and character formation.

*(c)* Making the individual to be fully devoted to God.

### 3. His Method of Teaching

*(a)* Students should be given examples first then generalization(rules) should be taught. (Inductive method)

*(b)* Language need not be taught via grammar, i.e., knowledge of grammar is not necessary for learning a language. For language teaching, proper environment of that language should be created. It should be taught in such a natural way as walking is taught to a child.

*(c)* Education in the school should be made interesting so that students may not shun the schools or classes.

*(d)* The behaviour of the teacher should be sympathetic in the class.

*(e)* Rewards should be given for motivating the students.

*(f)* Corporal punishment and chiding create hatred in the mind of the child toward education, teacher and school. It must, therefore be avoided.

*(g)* Physical as well as educational atmosphere of the school should be attractive and congenial to teaching-learning process.

*(h)* Teaching of children should begin at the earliest age (opposed to the idea of Rousseau).

*(i)* It is proper to teach in the begining of the day as faculties of children remain active and fresh in the morning.

### 4. His Views on Curriculum

*(a)* Mother tongue should be taught first. Once the foundation of mother tongue gets solidified, other languages may be taught.

*(b)* Curriculum should be integrated, i.e. knowledge of class first should be the base for class second, the knowledge of class second should be the basis for class third and so on.

*(c)* Books should be prepared very carefully keeping in view the life stages of children and teachers themselves should play active role in the preparation of these text books.

*(d)* Contents related to knowledge, virtues and devotion to God should be included in the curriculum.

### 5. His Ideas on Education System in Schools

Comenius was very much disappointed with the system of education in schools. He found the following important defects in schools of his time:

*(a)* They fully lacked the three aims of education mentioned by him.

*(b)* Children were frightened of these schools because of their poor educational environment.

*(c)* They had become slaughter houses of minds where nothing was done to develop physical faculties of a child.

*(d)* Children were taught in a repressive atmosphere forcibly.

*(e)* Teaching of mother tongue was neglected and the whole time was wasted in learning Latin grammar and literature.

*(f)* Words and rules were taught first and teaching of concrete things were given least importance.

*(g)* No uniform system of education was there in schools. Every school and the teacher had his own method of teaching and curriculum.

Comenius gave **nine** basic principles for educational reforms. They are:

*(i)* Teach the child in direct language and clear words.

*(ii)* The thing to be taught should have practical utility.

*(iii)* Eliminate the complexity of education.

*(iv)* The purpose of whatever is to be taught should be clearly stated.

*(v)* General rules should be explained by examples.

*(vi)* Everything of a subject should be taught in a proper sequence.

*(vii)* All subjects should be taught in a proper order.

*(viii)* Teaching should not be stopped until the child understands clearly.

*(ix)* Mutual differences in subjects should also be made clear.

These nine principles are also the part of **teaching strategies** propounded by him.

### 6. His Programme of Education

(Ideas on School Administration) :

There are four types of school organizations based on the age of students according to him.

*(a)* **Infancy schools :** Children from birth to six years of age should be educated in these schools. The organization of these schools are the responsibility of parents themselves.

*(b)* **Childhood schools :** Children from 6 to 12 years of age should be educated in these schools and their medium of education will be mother tongue.

*(c)* **Adolescence schools :** Learners from 12 to 18 years of age are educated in these schools. Latin language and literature will be mainly taught here.

*(d)* **Adult schools :** Such schools are meant for learners above 18 years of age. Everything related to practical life will be taught here.

### Criticism of Comenius

His educational ideas can be criticized on the following grounds. The credit of much of these criticisms mainly goes to a well known philosopher of that time.

*(i)* He has not given any systematic educational system for children. He only categorized the learners on the basis of their age but failed to deal with each group properly.

*(ii)* The idea as a source of knowledge is not new. It was very systematically explained by Socrates two millennium ago.

*(iii)* He preferred the study of science to that of culture and he wanted to prepare such individuals who are devoted to God. These two ideas are very much contradictory to each other.

(iv) He is of the view that man should learn everything thus, he is unable to estimate the knowledge and the capacity of human mind to acquire knowledge.

(v) It is not necessary to explain general rules first.

(vi) He is of the view that essence of a language should be taught to the child. This is also not necessary. There are many words in a particular language that we do not know and there is no need of knowing them as well.

## JEAN JACQUES ROUSSEAU (1712-1778)

### His Life Sketch

- He lost his mother just after his birth. His father brought him up but he could not look after him and Rousseau fell a prey to all sorts of bad habits.
- He originally belonged to Geneva and the beauty of that place lured him to use it. This made him a careless man.
- When he got matured, he hated the society for its evils and artificial traditions and wanted to reform it on the line of Naturalism.
- He could not get any love from the family or society. So he wanted everybody to shun the society and live with nature. Due to this reason we see a strong tendency of pessimism in his philosophy.
- Out of five books, *The progress of Arts and Sciences*, *New Heloise*, *Confessions*, *Social Contact* and *Emil*, the last two brought great name and fame for him.
- His ideas on education can be seen in **Emile**. It is a novel whose hero is Emile and heroine is Sofia. In this book Rousseau keeps Emile away from society and culture and leaves him under the guidance of an ideal teacher in a natural environment and Emile is educated in an atmosphere of natural beauty. There are five broad chapters in the book. The first four chapters describe the education of Emile in infancy, childhood, adolescence and adulthood and the last chapter deals with the education of Emile's wife-Sofia.
- People reacted against his book, "Emile" very sharply. France and Switzerland banned it and it was put into fire at many places in Europe. Consequently Rousseau had to leave France for England in 1766.
- After eleven years of exile he returned to France and wrote his last book, **Confessions.**

### His Philosophical Thoughts

**1. His naturalism:**

(a) God had made all humans good but when they come in contact with the society, they become spoiled. In order to change them again into good, we should bring them back to nature.

(b) In the beginning of human civilization man was happy and good but now he is unhappy. If he goes back to nature, he will again be happy and good. Thus, a child be educated and developed according to his natural tendencies. Family, society or school has almost no role to play in this process.

(c) He did not like old values and traditions of the society. According to him, social reform can be brought about by destroying these values.

(d) There are three main forms of Naturalism—social, psychological, and physical. In his social Naturalism, he devices education as a method to mould the society. He opined that we could not become a man and citizen both at the same time. Out of two options we should become a man only. Thus, individuality of a man is honourred by him. Psychological Naturalism means that the child should be given chance to develop on the basis of his inner feeling and natural tendencies and experiences gained from contract with others are harmful and unnatural. By Physical Naturalism Rousseau meant that child should be given chance to come in contact with plants, birds, animals and other physical objects of the nature and learn in the process. This learning will make him free from evils.

(e) He opposed the organization of education on social foundations. Thus, he opposed school education in its formal sense and advocated individual basis of education.

(f) He opposed to all sorts of habit formations in the child, it is because this can make a child traditional.

Thus we see that Rousseau's Naturalism is full of many unnatural and impracticable ideas and he himself realized it but he put these ideas with such a force that it influenced not only the society of Europe but also the educational system of that period.

**2. His negative education:** In the seventeenth century Europe, man was considered bad by nature. So, efforts were made to change the nature of man by imparting religious education. Rousseau went contrary to this by believing the infalibility of man and proposed the idea of negative education. By this education he means not teaching truth or virtues to a child but shielding his heart from evils and mind from errors. Features of his negative education are given below:

*(a)* Nothing against the interest, aptitude or age of the child should be taught. He should be given full freedom to choose his own curriculum.

*(b)* The education of a child should be based on his natural tendencies and stages of development by using different organs and senses of the child. Mind should be less taxed for this purpose. Mind should be left inactive till the child develops discretion power in him. Thus, he emphasized the training of senses by keeping the mind idle.

*(c)* Child should be protected from outside environment to keep him alien to vices. In this way, there will not be any need to impart knowledge of virtues to the child. Virtues may be taught at the later stages of his life.

*(d)* The child should not be taught anything at all especially from books. Small children should learn from nature itself.

Thus by his negative education, Rousseau opposed not only the mental development of the child but he also opposed moral and spiritual development.

His negative education can be criticized on two grounds:

*(i)* He stresses the training of senses by keeping the mind inactive. But how can these sense organs function without utilizing the mind is a big question.

*(ii)* He wants to keep the child away from society in order to save him from evils. But it is not a fact that a child learns in a more natural way by living with his peer groups and friends.

## His Educational Thoughts

**1. His aims of education:** He emphasized on the following aims of education:

*(a)* We are born weak and we want strength. We are poor and we want help and so on. Whatever we do not have is to be given by education is the ultimate aim of education.

*(b)* To establish harmony between man, objects and nature is the second aim.

*(c)* Child attains pleasure by using his organs and senses and by applying his strength. So, the aim of education is to develop his various powers by helping him in his natural activities.

*(d)* Books are not an end of education. They are only means and child is the end. The aim of education is to develop the child to the fullest for his complete and happy living.

**2. His self education:**

*(a)* He opposes the imposition of ideals and morals into the mind of the child from outside. Children should learn these things through activities. It is because children are more interested in activities rather than sitting idle and hearing lecture. At this stage, he has enough power to assimilate himself to the environment. He does not make any distinction between construction and destruction. His only concern is to bring about change in the form through any activity.

*(b)* Rousseau says if Emile is given the chance of self study, he will use his own reason. He will not be dependent on the experiences of others. Just as body becomes strong through physical exercise, mind also becomes strong through self study. In self education, child can proceed further according to his own physical and mental capacities.

*(c)* Only that knowledge gets retained for a longer period of time which is learnt from self experiences. We should accept the experiences of others only after using our own wisdom. Blind followship is not acceptable at all. In other words, a child should not learn a thing because he has

been asked to do so. He should only learn it in the process of self study.

(*d*) Special attention should be given on physical development of the child. If he is physically healthy, his impulses will also be healthy.

Thus according to Rousseau, a child should not be taught the truth directly. He should only be guided to discover the truth himself.

Rousseau's self education has been criticized on the following lines:

(*i*) If a child is not taught what is constructive and what is destructive, he may harm himself, e.g., touching of fire or electric wire is harmful.

(*ii*) It we do not rely on the experiences of others, we will always have to start the task from the very beginning. Thus, new inventions and discoveries will take much longer period of time.

(*iii*) When we study books, we are benefitted from the experiences of others. How can we keep a child away from this.

(*iv*) Just as physical exercise is necessary for physical development, similarly, mental exercise is necessary for mental development.

(*v*) His belief that reason sleeps during childhood is not sound. Intelligence tests have proved that mental development starts from the age of early childhood.

**3. His programme of Education (Curriculum):** He had divided his whole programme of education (curriculum) on the basis of development stages of humans. It is given below.

(*a*) *Infancy (From zero to five years) :* At this stage, instead of giving him controlled information of various subjects, it is better to pay attention to the development of child's body and his sense organs. He should be allowed to play with whatever thing he likes. His dress should be so comfortable that he does not have to face any difficulty in the free movements of his body organs. Child should be brought up by his mother and she should never force him to do any work. His toys should be cheap, ordinary and natural like leaves, plants, flowers, stones etc. According to Rousseau, Emile should be given negative education during infancy.

(*b*) *Childhood (5-12 years):* He opposes the use of any textbook during this period. Child should be given chance to learn everything through observation and experiences. These experiences develop sense organs, which will lead to the development of mind and his power of reasoning. He should he given full freedom to use his senses in the natural environment. The eyes of the child should be trained to measure height, weight and distance, Music educates his ears, flowers educates his nose and so on. For training the senses, natural problems should be placed before him and he will reach the solution himself. Geometry may be taught during this period and the inclusion of history, geography and languages in the curriculum is not proper. As far us moral education is concerned, it should not be given to a child as long as he fully understands the meaning of morality. Limited amount of moral education may be given through activities.

(*c*) *Adolescene (12-15 years)* During this period natural curiosity in the child develops, so he should be taught natural sciences and languages, mathematics, music, painting and social sciences, etc. This is a good period of education according to Rousseau. But here too the use of sense organs should be preferred to books. Industrial and professional experiences are also necessary at this stage to earn livelihood. As far as teaching of geography is concerned it should not be taught through maps, as maps develop wrong conception in the minds of children regarding the shape of the earth. The students should be exposed to the natural environment as much as possible.

(*d*) *Adulthood (15-20 years) :* Sex organs become active along with the maturity of mind and intellect during this period among boys and girls. It is the proper time to teach them social and moral obligations. It is because they can now recognize what is right and what is wrong. But these things should not be taught by lectures of a teacher only. The youth should rather go to the society and visit the hospitals, prisons and orphanages in order to see the evils and miseries of the society directly.

But they should not visit these places frequently because of two reasons:

(i) Seeing the miseries of the world again and again may frustrate them.

(ii) Seeing the evils of the society again and again may turn them into evil persons.

(e) *Women education :* He is willing to give full freedom to the boys but he always wants to keep the girls under strict control. He proposes that type of education for women which can enable them to best serve the men. They should, all the time, give love, respect and happiness to men. According to Rousseau, women are least interested in reading and writing, so, they should be given such type of education as to make them efficient in house works, such as cooking, weaving tailoring etc. Religious education should not be enforced on them. If it is to be given to them, it should be made interesting and fully understandable to them. Philosophy must not be taught to them because they cannot understand it.

**4. His principles of education (method of teaching):** Rousseau believed in self experiences of a child by the use of sense organs and other powers. For this purpose, child should be given full freedom and teacher should work only as a guide. Rousseau proposed following principles of education to be used in a classroom:

(a) *Learning by games :* Rousseau advocated play, way method instead of oral or verbal teaching. The child should be allowed to play and explore the environment in whatsoever way he likes and he will learn in the process.

(b) *Learning through natural objects :* Whatever a child wants to know, he should be given that knowledge through natural objects rather than books. He should be kept away from books upto 12 years at least.

(c) *Learning by self experiences :* Sense organs rather than mind are the important medium of experiences and learning. They are trained in such a way as mental faculties are automatically developed.

(d) *Learning by doing :* Rousseau insisted on practical education rather than theoretical one through this principle. It is this method that can make the gained knowledge permanent and useful. Even social sciences should be taught through this method and child should be brought to the society for practicals.

**5. His discipline:** Rousseau advocated complete freedom and absence of any restraint for the child. The child should be left free in the environment to develop his natural powers. There is no scope of giving any type of punishment to the child. When a child commits mistakes, he suffers from pain and when he does something good, he feels pleasure. Hence, natural process of feedback instills discipline in him. This is the naturalistic theory of punishment. Thus, there is no need of lecturing the child about the codes and ethics of life at all. Self discipline is learnt in the process of experimentation and experience.

**Influence of Rousseau :** Rousseau's ideas influenced the educational system and the society of Europe to a great extent but only after his death. Here are some examples:

(i) Child was given recognition in the educational institutions.

(ii) Experimentation in natural sciences gained momentum which led to lots of inventions and discoveries in the later period.

(iii) The study of plants and animals were included in the curriculum.

(iv) French revolution may be considered an important outcome of his ideas.

Rousseau's philosophy influenced other philosophers of Europe also. Some examples are given below:

(i) Education is not the preparation of life but life itself, Dewey accepted this principle of Rousseau.

(ii) Education of a child should start only when his natural impulses are fully matured. Pestalozzi accepted this principle and Froebel put it into practice.

(iii) Pestalozzi and Froebel are also agree with the idea that physical labour alone can keep a man healthy.

(iv) Children should not be taught religion because they do not understand it at this stage. Basedow and Pestalozzi accepted the principle.

(v) Children should be educated through nature. Herbert Spencer accepted this principle.

(vi) Child expresses himself through activities. Dewey's philosophy is based on this principle.

(vii) Interest of a child changes according to his age. This principle has been accepted by all modern philosophers.

(viii) The aim of education is to strengthen different organs of the child. Pestalozzi's **principle of development according to power** and Herbert's **multi sensory principle** are based on this philosophy.

(ix) If a child has logical power, it should be utilized in researches and solving the daily problems. This principle has been accepted by Dewey.

## JOHN HENRICK PESTALOZZI (1746-1827) & PSYCHOLOGICAL TENDENCY IN EDUCATION

### Meaning of Psychological Tendency

Rousseau was the first thinker of Europe who diverted the attention of educationists from the subject matter and the teacher to the child and made him pivot of the process of education. Though he went to the extreme in developing a new educational system, yet he influenced later philosophers like Pestalozzi, Spencer and Froebel very much who carried out experiments after experiment to modify and mould the then education system on psychological and scientific lines.

The psychological tendency in education means education based on the psychology of the child and he will be educated according to his inherent potentials, interest and needs keeping in view his life stages and thus education will become a natural process of life for the child.

Important characteristics of this tendency are given below:

(i) Education of a child will be according to his psychology and psychological principles.

(ii) Curriculum and the teacher are meant for the child and not vice versa. So his interests and abilities will be taken into account in the process of education.

(iii) Child must be studied first while organizing curricular and co-curricular activities. Thus, knowledge of the child is a must here.

(iv) Child is not an adult. So recognition of his childish nature and activities will be given by educators.

(v) There is no scope of control or compulsion there. Child will be given full freedom in his natural surroundings.

(vi) Individuality of a child is recognized here and he is treated with love, affection and sympathy by his teachers. His individuality is not compromised from the point of view of social obligations and customs.

(vii) Education will be started from the period of early childhood to provide a solid foundation for later education.

(viii) The process of education (life) will be made interesting in order to motivate the child to learn more and more.

(ix) No two individuals are alike in the world. These differences are caused by heredity, environment, sex, intelligence, socio economic conditions and so on. Teachers and curriculum framers will keep these individual differences into account.

(x) Teacher is only a guide and helper here. He cannot impose anything from outside. His presence is only for the purpose of creating conducive environment to learning.

### Life Sketch of J.H. Pestalozzi

- He was born in Zurich, Switzerland.
- He lost his father when he was five years old and he was brought up by his liberal minded and loving mother.
- He received his early education in his native village, then he joined University of Switzerland for higher education. Here he got a chance to read Rousseau's Emile. He wanted to become a social reformer but after reading this book he came to the conclusion that one must be an educationist first before one decides to become a social reformer.
- He expressed his ideas in magazines and newspapers but government did not like them and sent him to jail.

- After he was released from prison, he took to agriculture for livelihood, but he failed in this profession. Then he opened a school to impart free education to children on charitable funds but due to financial crisis he had to close the school also.
- He started writing books and worked as an editor of a magazine, named "Swiss Journal" to earn his living.
- His famous book "Leonard and Gertrude" was published in 1788. This look brought him name and fame.
- In 1798, he was given an opportunity to conduct experiments in Stanz but he failed here again.
- In 1799, he opened a boarding school to train teachers. This training school became so famous that people from different countries took admission here and received training. Herbert and Froebel also received training from this very school.

### His Philosophical and Educational Thoughts

He has derived most of his ideas from Rousseau's "Emile". He was the first who gave a scientific base to the ideas of Rousseau by carrying out experiments on children. *He is Rousseau minus, negative education.* Following are his ideas of education.

1. **His theory of development according to powers**: Educational principles of Pestalozzi can be traced out from this theory. It is based on five principles.
   (a) *Harmonious development of innate powers :* Child is endowed with certain innate physical, mental, social and emotional powers by birth. Education should exploite these powers and develop them in a harmonious manner.
   (b) *Internal growth of powers :* Just as a plant develops gradually and internally, a child also develops gradually from within. So, the task of a teacher is not to enforce anything from outside into his mind, but to create such a conducive educational environment which will promote the spontaneous development of powers of the child.
   (c) *Development is a natural and gradual process:* As long as a child develops his needs, interest and attitudes change with age. So, curriculum should be organized in accordance with his changed needs, interests, and requirements of his particular stage. Easy subjects should be taught in the beginning in order to develop his thinking and reasoning power. He should be dragged to more and more difficult subjects and experiences gradually.
   (d) *Nourishment for developing power :* Just as plants need water, soil and light for its growth, similarly, a child also needs love, care and sympathy to nurture his innate powers. He should be treated in the school in such a way as to make him feel at home and among his lovers.
   (e) *Chennalisation of powers :* Each child differs in his attitudes and interests. So imparting religious education to all irrespective of their attitude and interest is wrong. Mass education full of varieties for all on the basis of their interests and needs should be given.
2. **Meaning of education :** Education is a natural, harmonious and progressive development of man's innate powers.
3. **Aims of education:** The aim of all instructions is and can be nothing but the development of human nature by the harmonious cultivation of its powers and talents and the promotion of manliness of life.
4. **Curriculum :** He included language, mathematics, history, geography, psychology, music, agriculture and craft in the curriculum in addition to the study of those incidents and experiences which children come across themselves.
5. **Method of teaching:** He was against rote memory and experimentless verbal teaching. He was of the opinion that child himself seeks out the knowledge and develops self learning skills. He invented his own method of teaching called **Aunshaung**. It means a child acquires knowledge within no time by his own efforts, observations and experiences provided that he is properly guided by the teacher.

6. **Discipline :** He is against the repressionistic type of discipline in the school and recommended a mixture of impressionistic and emancipatory discipline. It will create self discipline among students.

## FREDRICK WILLIAM A. FROEBEL (1782-1853)

### His Life Sketch

- He was born at Oberweisback in Germany.
- His father married to another lady after his mother's death in his childhood and Froebel become a neglected child. As a result he roamed about jungles all day long. It developed in him a love for nature.
- He was admitted to a school by his maternal uncle when he was ten years old.
- He inherited religious mentality from his father who was a clergyman. This mentality later developed into idealism.
- He was sent to Jena University at the age of 18 but he had to leave it due to financial stringency and thus he could not complete his education.
- He decided to become a teacher at the age of 20. For this purpose he went to Pestalozzi's school in Yerdon where he learnt as well as taught for two years.
- When he left Yerdon, he opened his own school at Keilhau exactly on the line of Pestalozzi but this school failed.
- He wrote his famous book **Education of man** in 1826. This book brought great name and fame to him.
- He opened a school for small children at Blankenburg named "Kinder garten" means garden of kids. This school was a great success and many such schools were opened across the country.
- In 1851, government closed all kinder gartens under the impression that Froebel is spreading revolutionary ideas in the country through these schools. This was a great setback for Froebel and he almost collapsed.
- He was the man to put Pestalozzi's ideas into practice. Thus, psychological tendency in education matured during his time.

### His Philosophical Thoughts

1. **His theory of development of the individual:** According to him, "mind unfolds from within according to a predetermined pattern. The development and formation of the whole future life of each being is contained in the beginning of its existence". Each child is born with some innate tendencies and they inspire him to realize God. The spiritual development of the race also depends upon this individual nature of development and it is a continuous process. According to him, all things are developing according to specific divine laws and so there should be no external interference in the process of development.

   Thus, we see that his theory of development is similar to but more comprehensive than his teacher's theory (Pestalozzi's theory) and it makes him a Naturalist.
2. **His unity of existence:** All things of the universe have different entities, yet they all have originated from God. Thus, all the objects, howsoever different they look in appearance are essentially the same. Because of this reason each individual undergoes and recapitulates the same level of spiritual development. Thus, he is not in conformity with Pestalozzi here who recognizes individual differences of men. His is rather a pure idealist.

### His Educational Thoughts

1. **Aims of education:**

   *(a)* Man is originally good in nature but it is the environment that makes him bad. The purpose of education is to awaken this spiritual nature of man.

   *(b)* Divine power operates behind the whole world. This power expresses itself in the conscious state of nature as well as man. The purpose of education is to enable the child to realize this divine presence and to identify himself with nature.

   *(c)* To enable the students to realize the fundamental unity of all living being with God is the third aim of education.

   *(d)* To develop the students according to their nature is the last aim. Full freedom to explore

the environment is given to them for this purpose. It means all educational programmes are arranged according to the needs and nature of learners.

2. **Programme of education:** He has given different programmes of education for different stages of development .

(a) *Infancy :* It is a period of sensory development. Only sense organs are used to acquire any sort of knowledge. Education of a child does not starts here.

(b) *Childhood :* It is a period in which internal is made external i.e., whatever innate tendencies a child has, they are expressed through activities. Attention, **watchfullness**, and action, less directed to the body than to the mind are some other characteristics of this period. Actual education begins at this age. During this period, objects are identified with their names and words are uttered clearly. So, clear concepts about the objects should be given as Froebel writes **"the name created the thing for the child".** The names also define the object by connecting it with some familiar things.

Since internal is made external through activities during this period, play way can be an important method of instruction for them. But play of the child must not be purposeless activity. It must be directed and controlled by the use of definite materials to be presented in orderly sequence. Froebel says, "Without rational and conscious guidance, childish activity degenerates into useless play instead of preparing him for those tasks of life for which he is destined."

(c) *Adolescence :* It is a period in which external is made internal, just opposite of childhood. Whatever a child perceives in his environment, he thinks over them and internalizes them. Thus, curriculum centred rather than child centred education is needed here. Through the process of education, knowledge and comprehension of life are connected with making the internal, external and vice versa and a harmony is brought about between the two. Here interest in the process rather than interest in the product is created. Froebel says, "If activity brings joy to the child, the work will give delight to the boy". It means work is given in the form of delightful activity or play to the child but work is always self selected not imposed by the teacher. If we compare childhood and boyhood, we can say that in childhood he initiates domestic activities. But in boyhood he is involved into neighbourhood, occupation and his development is determined by his widening range of environment. Through these activities he will mostly solve practical problems of his life.

3. **Curriculum:** As far as curriculum for this period is concerned subjects like drawing, painting, gardening and nature study are taught along with formal subjects like religion and philosophy, natural sciences, mathematics and languages. All these subjects should possess internal unity and high degree of correlation.

4. **Method of teaching:** His method of teaching is based on four basic principles.

(a) *Principle of self activity :* Self activity means those activities which a child does in accordance with his own interest and liking. He is imposed nothing from outside. He initiates the play as well as work himself.

(b) *Principle of learning by games :* Child takes much interest in play activities and games. So, whole curriculum is organized through games.

(c) *Principle of sociability :* Self activities are expressed in a good social environment. For this purpose activities are organized through group plays. Group plays develop mutual love, sympathy, cooperation and fellow feeling along with the feeling of competition among them.

(d) *Principle of freedom:* Full freedom is given for the expression of activities and educational development of a child. He is not interfered from outside at all.

5. **Discipline :** His concept of discipline is the same as that of Pestalozzi. Self discipline is learned through self activities and outside interference. Compulsion and control are avoided. Social

discipline is more important than individual discipline according to him, which is brought about through group activities and teamwork.

## His Kinder Garten

The special school which Froebel opened in 1843 at Blankenburg to educate the children is called Kinder garten—Garden of small kids. He put his educational ideas into practice through this school. Important features of this school are as follows:

1. He provided full and free opportunities to children for the expression of their self activities.
2. Child was educated and guided on the principle of self experience, observation and socialization in school.
3. Child expresses himself through activities and plays. He is given chance to do so. Take the example of a ball. By means of a ball, child perceives his life, his power, his activity and his senses. This idea was put into practice in kinder garten.
4. Mother's play and nursery rhymes together with gifts, and occupation were used as means of educating the child.

   **Mother's play and nursery rhymes** is a small book which contains fifty songs. These songs establish affectionate bond between his sense organs and helps in the physical, mental and spiritual development of the child.

   *Gifts:* They personify the play things of the child, Froebel believes that children will be able to appreciate the symbolism involved in them. In his scheme of gifts he has given a scheme of 20 gifts. They are spherical, cylindrical and cubic objects given to a child one by one in a sequence. Abstract thinking is also developed through these gifts. For example, spheres and cubes can develop the concept of opposite which child perceives every-where around his life.
5. When thinking power of a child is fully developed through these gifts, he was led to other occupational activities like paper cutting, wood craft, picture drawing, making a garland, sewing, carpet knitting, singing, dancing etc. In this way activities are transformed into playful work.

*Merits of Kinder Garten :* His kinder garten is very much recognized by the educationists because of its following merits:

(i) It is a child centred education, though importance of curriculum is not neglected.

(ii) Creativity and self thinking power can be developed in children through this system.

(iii) Child will not lose interest here till the last moment of learning process.

(iv) Child will learn many social qualities such as love, sympathy, fellow feeling, cooperation etc through group activities.

(v) Sense organs can be easily activated through playthings (gifts).

(vi) His concept of externalizing the internals in the childhood and internalization of externals in adolescence is very unique and practiced in K.G.

*Demerits of Kinder Garten System :* Some demerits of this system are also given below:

(i) Many children in their early age do not comprehend the principles of internalization and externalization emphasized by Froebel.

(ii) Froebel's pictures, rhyms and gifts are not suitable for all places for all periods of history. Modification in them is necessary.

(iii) Since these gifts are provided in a sequence according to definite rules, hence, services of specialised teachers are necessary which is really a tough tasks in India.

(iv) Educating children through these activities may cost much time and energy. In today's age when knowledge doubles in just five years, how can this method be applicable.

## HERBERT SPENCER (1820-1903) & SCIENTIFIC TENDENCY IN EDUCATION

18th and 19th centuries were the period of great scientific inventions and discoveries which changed the life style of the people and made the daily life easy and comfortable. This change in life style also led to a drastic change in thinking style and ideology. People began to realize the importance of science subjects in the curriculum. It was a challenge before the Greek and Latin literatures which were supposed to be the backbone of all sources of knowledge and education. When people advocated for the inclusion of science subjects in the curriculum, classical educationists and philosophers naturally opposed it and a conflict started between the two. In the 19th century Spencer came in support of scientific tendency. He presented his ideas with such force that it was impossible for the educators to neglect them. As a result, science subjects began to occupy an important place in the curriculum. Oxford and Cambridge universities of England opened department of science as a separate discipline and science subjects were included in the curriculum of secondary education as well.

## Meaning of Scientific Tendency

Including subjects of science in the curriculum and a scientific approach based on cause and effect relationship for the solution to the problems of life in order to make the life complete, considerate and comfortable is called scientific tendency. When this tendency is applied to education, there developed the following characteristics in the process of education:

*(i)* It opposes the study of literary subjects, which can not give us any physical comforts directly. It advocates the study of those subjects which are directly useful to our daily life.

*(ii)* Scientific tendency in education opposes any theoretical knowledge without practicals.

*(iii)* It prefers curriculum or subject matter to methods of teaching.

*(iv)* Only the study of natural sciences can make our life happy and comfortable. This is advocated by this tendency.

*(v)* Full freedom should be given to a child to select any subject according to his own choice.

*(vi)* Proper guidance is given to students to select subjects.

*(vii)* Inductive method of teaching is used to teach the students and theoretical knowledge is supplemented with lab experiment.

*(viii)* Real knowledge of nature and natural objects is possible only through the study of science subjects.

*(ix)* Metaphysical world has no role to play in our physical life. Therefore only the knowledge of concrete objects is real.

*(x)* The concept of liberal education is to be propagated which includes vocational and professional education, citizenship training and preparation for life.

*(xi)* Life should have an immediate purpose to serve.

*(xii)* Orthodox thinking is removed.

## Life Sketch of Herbert Spencer

- He was born in Derby, England.
- His father was a learned teacher of physics and chemistry who strongly believed in self education of a child. So, Herbert was initially educated at home.
- At the age of 17, he had acquired good mastery on almost all subjects and he started writing on social and economic problems. His early articles were published in a famous magazine named "Non Conformist".
- He became co editor of a famous journal 'Economist' in 1848.
- His famous book **Social Statics** was published in 1850. In this book he has described the process of social development through natural laws.
- He wrote his another famous book **Essays on Education** in 1861. This book contains four articles, (i) What knowledge is of most worth (ii) Intellectual education (iii) Moral education, (iv) Physical education.
- He has written about 20 books on Biology, Sociology, Psychology and Ethics.
- He divided school subjects into two categories—Science subjects and academic subjects and preferred the former category to the later on utility ground.

## His Philosophical/Educational Thoughts

**1. Aims of Education:** The education aims at preparing a child for a complete living. In order to attain this aim, the child is taught how to develop body and mind and how to manage the affairs of life. Thus a child should be taught what he needs for his successful living, i.e., Science subjects and other subjects with scientific temper are given preference.

**2. Concept of Complete Man and Programme of Education:** A man who bears the following five responsibilities successfully is actually a complete man.

(a) *Self preservation :* Nature has made everything for the service and preservation of man. So it is the duty of man to understand nature and cooperate with it. If we do not pay heed to these natural laws, our preservation will be at stake. For self preservation (good health) students should be taught the laws of physiology and hygiene and their implications on our daily life.

(b) *Earning a living :* For survival of man, earning a living is a must. Science can help a man in this regard. There is no work or vocation which can be learnt without taking the help of science. The need of science is realized in all the activities of our daily life, such as house construction, business, agriculture, shipping, war etc. Thus knowledge of science is essential for a man to prepare him for future life.

(c) *Upbringing of children :* The responsibility of upbringing of children mostly lies on the shoulders of parents. But if parents are not educated and conscious, the personality of children will be spoilt. Due to this reason, the effective role of the school in upbringing the children becomes necessary. It is the school which prepares the child for his life. Thus, receiving education is compulsory for a man.

(d) *Citizenship :* Child is born in a society. So, he must know what are his duties toward the society and the nation, how he is different from other creatures and why it is necessary to adapt to the natural environment. For answering all these and the like questions, man should study history in the light of science. Science is the key to open all the locks of history. In this way, he will study historical facts in such a way that definite conclusions may be drawn from them.

(e) *Worthy use of leisure time :* The problem of utilization of time has arisen due to mechanization of life by science. What a man could do in days, can be done in hours today. Thus, he has a lot of time for leisure. This problem can be solved by studying painting, music, poetry sculpture etc. These subjects will, however, never be considered more precious than science subjects. They are just the subjects of time pass.

Thus, we see that Spencer puts science above all subjects. He says that science develops not only our memory but thinking power also. It is only science that can make us self reliant as well as religious in behaviour.

Spencer's ideas can be criticized on the following grounds:

(i) Science is not everything for man. Literature and Fine Arts are equally important. It is because the later prepares ground and nurture imagination for the former.

(ii) Life of a man cannot be satisfied by physical comforts only. The real comfort is the spiritual one. Literature and Fine Arts are the medium that illuminates the soul.

(iii) Science is always helpless to provide solutions to sentimental problems.

**3. Method of Teaching :** His teaching pedagogy is based upon seven maxims of teaching. They are given below:

(a) *From easy to difficult :* Children should be taught easy material first. Then they should be brought to the difficult materials gradually. It will increase their sustainability to acquire knowledge.

(b) *From known to unknown :* Children should be given new knowledge only on the basis of their previous knowledge. Thus, a relationship will be established between the two and both types of knowledge will become one.

(c) *From definite to indefinite :* Children have definite knowledge about many things. They acquire this knowledge from the environment and nature. Indefinite portion of knowledge should be provided to them on the basis of this definite shape of knowledge.

(d) *From concrete to abstract :* Concrete objects are those things of which child has direct experience, i.e., ball, table, cot etc. Abstract concept of a sphere can be developed with the help of balls or other round objects. Thus, examples should be given first, then generalization should be developed on the basis of these examples. Material aids are also used for this purpose.

(e) *Teach according to the stages of human development :* From infancy to adulthood a man goes through many stages of mental, social, emotional and physical development. Human civilization has also passed through these stages of development. Thus, in the beginning, child should be given opportunity to perceive and analyze an object through his sense organs. As long as he grows, he uses mind and intellect for the perception and anylysis of an object more and more. Thus curriculum as well as method of teaching is adapted accordingly.

(f) *From empirical to rational :* Child takes too much interest in experimenting the objects since the early childhood period. This habit of child should be exploited to imparting rational knowledge as well. They should not be given bookish knowledge as long as they are familiar with the objects of the environment.

(g) *Interest based teaching :* Children should not be taught anything until and unless they take interest in teaching. Interest can be created by changing the teaching techniques and strategies and by giving them motivation.

**4. Moral Education :** Nature is the best judge of morality and conduct. If someone commits any immoral act, he will be punished by the nature itself. There is no need of any external punishment to be given to a child.

Environment also affects moral character of children. If parents are of good moral character, their offsprings are also likely to be moral and good. There should not be any contradiction between words and action at home. If parents have promised to give some reward to the child, it must be given at all costs. Parents and teachers should exhibit ideal behaviour first and then they should expect the same from children.

Spencer is also of the view that there must be similarity between an offence and punishment. The degree of punishment should not be more than that of offence, e.g., if a child has broken a plate, it should be compensated from his pocket money. If he has torn a shirt, he should not be given another shirt till the period of first shirt expires.

**5. Physical Education :** Spencer is strongly in favour of good health for children. He has given following four basic principles for proper physical education and health:

(i) Sufficient amount of food in variation. i.e., the same kind of food should not be given at all times.

(ii) Proper clothing during winter and summer separately.

(iii) Proper time should be given for physical exercises.

(iv) Their mind should not be heavily taxed. It will jeopardize their physical health also.

Thus, we see that all Spencer's ideas are very much practicable and convincing baring a few.

### Criticism of Spencer

(i) We do not find any originality in the ideas of Spencer. Almost all of them have been borrowed from Rousseau, Pestalozzi and Froebel. So, whatever shortcoming is there in the ideas of his precedors, does existing in his own ideas.

(ii) He does not give any importance to humanities and stresses only the study of science. This is also against the principle of choice.

(iii) His programme of education is based on experience and experimentation but the same experiences that earlier people came across are neglected.

(iv) According to him, education is must for a successful life. This may be correct but can this education be limited to the education of science and practicals, is a big question.

## JOHN DEWEY (1859-1952)

### His Life Sketch

- He was born in Burlington, USA.
- He was mainly educated in Vermont and Hopnkins Universities of USA.
- After his education was over, he worked as a teacher in Michigan and Chicago Universities upto 1903.
- He was appointed as professor of philosophy in Columbia University in 1904.
- He was invited by different countries of the world such as Japan, China, Turkey and Russia to give his suggestions regarding the organization of education there.

- In 1919 he delivered a series of lectures at the Imperial University of Tokyo. These lectures were later published in a book form named **"Reconstruction in philosophy"**.
- He has written about fifty books and more than 800 articles on philosophy, education, politics and sociology and many of them have been translated in many languages of the world as well. The names of some of these books are given below.
  *(i)* School and Society
  *(ii)* Child and the Curriculum
  *(iii)* Schools Tomorrow
  *(iv)* Democracy and Education
- No other philosopher and educationist has influenced the world so much as John Dewey. He was considered an expert unparalleled during his life time.

## His Philosophical Thoughts

In the beginning Dewey was influenced by Hegel's idealism but later on the ideas of William James and Herbert Spencer influenced him very much. In spite of that most of his ideas are original at least in their applicability. Important concepts elaborated by him are given below:

1. **Reflective Thinking :** According to him thinking is meaningful only when it is related to problems of life and their solutions. Reflective enquiry is required for the solution of an indeterminate situation (problem). There are five steps involved in reflective enquiry. In the first step problem is realized when some break down in the habitual response is seen. Clarification of the problem is the second step. Through analysis and observation, sufficient data are gathered to formulate the difficulty and define the problem. Formulation of tentative solutions to the problem (Hypothesis) is the third step. Deductive elaboration is the fourth step of reflective enquiry. Here we reason out the implication of various Hypotheses one by one and finally select only few. They are tested in the last step on the basis of data collected. If one of the Hypotheses works out, the determinate situation replaces the indeterminate one and solution is found.
   The implication of reflective enquiry is recognized in all the research works today.
2. **Knowledge and Experience :** Knowledge is what we attain in the context of problematic situation. Thus, it is inferred from the five steps of reflective enquiry which involves operation of controlled observation, experimentation and testing.
   Experience is an intercourse between a living being and his physical and social environment. The important trait of experience is that it is always connected with future. Our future action is improved through experience. Thus, it is nothing else but testing and verification of hypotheses for future improvement of life.
   On this basis we can say that there is no distinction between knowledge and experience. Only that knowledge or experience which is useful for the individual and the society is considered as real by John Dewey.
3. **Philosophy :** The function of philosophy is not to know the world but to control and reform it by solving the problems of man. It should adjust the body of traditional beliefs to scientific tendencies and political aspirations which are novel and incompatible on everyday. Thus, philosophy should understand those problems which are generated due to arising conflicts between democracy, business and science and try to solve them by using reflective enquiry. The task of philosophy is to clarify men's mind regarding the social and moral issues of the world which are always changing with time.
   Dewey says that philosophy is nothing but a general theory of criticism whose task is to criticize and clarify human culture, values and beliefs and redefine it.
4. **Mind :** Mind is a means of controlling the environment in relation to the objectives of life processes and senses are not primarily gateways to knowledge but only stimuli for action. Thus, Dewey tries to establish the supremacy of mind over senses by synthesizing the two.
5. **Experimentation :** Experimentation is a programme of action to determine consequences.

It is not merely an action but a way of introducing intelligence into a situation. Dewey believed that we were living in a hostile environment and we have to adjust ourselves there. Experiment will help us to discover the procedures of the adjustment in the society by eradicating its ills and securing goods. Thus his experimentation is not restricted to biological or physical levels of the individuals only but covers the whole spectrum of the society.

6. **Instrumentalism :** Ideas are not the images or visions of an external objects. They are rather the instrument to facilitate an organism's behaviour to think so. Ideas are only the instruments through which we operate on physical objects. Thus, they are the means to reach the ends. The more we lay stress on ends, the greater, we will pay attention to the means. So the separation of goods into natural and moral may have harmful consequences. The conceptualization of goods depend upon the ideas or instruments with which they are treated. There is no scope of permanent or predetermined truth or morality. It is changeable with time, place or circumstances depending upon the instrument with which they are treated. For example, homo-sexual marriage may be considered a sin today but will it remain sin tomorrow, is a big question? Same is true for all concepts of natural sciences as well.

   Thus John Dewey believes in the philosophy of social change which is inevitable and it will also bring about change in the social and moral problems.

7. **Relativism :** Nothing is absolute in the world. Poverty is studied in the context of richness. Theory is significant in the context of experimentation and so on. So unqualified generalization is misleading, e.g., an economic policy or a plan of action may be good in relation to a particular time and situation but it may be absurd in relation to other situations.

   On the basis of these ideas, he did not believe in any divine power. He rather believed in strong power of man who could choose his own path for his progress and development.

8. **Humanism :** According to Dewey, knowledge is tested by the promotion of human intelligence based on the experience of modern sciences for the sake of bettering human situations. Knowledge obtained from revealed religions does not have any role to play in the practical life of man. Only experiment based knowledge can do something for the welfare of man. So, it is our duty to conserve, transmit, rectify and expand our heritage of values (knowledge) so that our next generation may share it more generously and more securely.

   On the basis of above views of John Dewey, we can conclude that he is a pragmatist on one hand and humanist and experimentalist on the other.

## His Educational Thoughts

**1. Principles of education:**

(a) *Pragmatism :* Any idea, belief or action is measured and given importance on the basis of its results. If its result is useful to the individual and the society, it is accepted otherwise rejected.

(b) *Child centred education :* Every child is given full opportunity and freedom to develop according to his need, ability and interest. Thus school environment is made democratic to the maximum level possible.

(c) *Social utility :* School is a miniature society. So needs of the society should be taken into account. If evils are prevailing in the society, schools should make the society free from these evils. Schools become the natural part of the society only when natural inclinations and activities of the child are reflected by them.

(d) *Self experience :* The child should discover the truth himself by using reflective enquiry and experimentation. He is not to rely on the experiences of others. Truth is that which is useful and useful is that which is truth (tested).

(e) *Correlation of education and society :* Education is what the society needs. Thus society is also reflected by the school. Life of a child is organized according to moral values and moral values are nothing but social values.

(f) *Universal education :* Education should not be restricted to only a few sections of the society. Every citizen of the country should get equal opportunities of getting education. Thus, it is the state that should take the responsibility of imparting education to boys and girls.

(g) *Social change :* Social change is a natural phenomenon. No society can remain static for a long time. So, education should also change according to the changing needs of the society.

2. **Meaning of education:** Education is not the preparation of a child for his future life but it is life itself. Life is not possible without education. Life here means social life, it is because man is a social animal. His activities are directed and determined by the society by living there. So collective activities are organized in the school. Participation in collective activities gives him knowledge of social efficiency and sociability. Collective work enables the child to know the purpose of work and equips him with necessary method and ability to do the work.

3. **Aims of education:** John Dewey has given priority to social aims of education over individual aims but individual aims are not neglected. Following are some important aims prescribed by John Dewey.
   (i) To reform and reconstruct the society through education.
   (ii) To enable the individual to adjust with the changing social environment.
   (iii) To develop the child fully according to his interest, abilities and needs.
   (iv) To create social efficiency in the child from pragmatist point of view.
   (v) To develop democratic values and ideals in the child.
   (vi) To provide educational opportunities to all citizens on equal footing.
   (vii) To instill habit of experimentation in children.
   (viii) To remove the social evils and make the society a good place for living.
   (ix) To enable the child to discover the truth himself.
   (x) To make the child self reliant.

4. **Curriculum:** Curriculum is constructed and developed keeping in view the following principles:
   (a) *Ability and interest of the child :* Child's ability and his personal inclinations should be kept in mind before constructing the curriculum and nothing is imposed on him.
   (b) *Flexibility :* Every society is dynamic. So curriculum should be constructed according to the changing needs of the society. Vision is required for this purpose so that it may last long.
   (c) *Usefulness :* Curriculum must have utility for a child. He should be taught only what is useful for him.
   (d) *Social efficiency :* Curriculum must make a child socially efficient and democratic in his behaviour. He should be able to behave his fellow being so democratically in the society as he was behaved in the school. It should enable the students to get fully adjusted in the society.
   (e) *Experimental :* It should develop the habit of self experience and experimentation in the child. Different kinds of problematic situations are presented before him and he reaches the solution to these problems through activities and experimentation.
   (f) *Life related :* Only those subjects should be included in the curriculum which have direct link to the lives of children. It will make them self reliant and a productive member of the society. Vocational subjects are preferred for this purpose. Subjects of social sciences and humanities are also taught but only after creating some harmony with the subjects of natural sciences.

5. **Method of teaching:** Whatever is to be taught to a child must be correlated with the natural activities of the child. For this purpose, following methods of teaching are adopted:
   (a) *Learning by doing :* Child learns the best when he performs some actions along with the theoretical knowledge of a subject. Teacher guides the students for these activities by which child develops his own natural abilities.

In order to involve him in some activities, he is confronted with practical difficulties and problems of life and he tries to solve them through self experience and experimentation. Thus, project method and problem solving method are advocated by John Dewey.

*(b)* *Collective approach :* Children participate in these activities collectively. It develops in them social efficiency. They are assigned various types of jobs by the teacher and they complete them collectively. When one job gets completed, they are guided by the teacher to choose next one. In this way they are given collective training in the school.

*(c)* *Integrated approach :* A subject is taught only after integrating it with other subjects as well as life. In this way knowledge becomes compact, useful and systematic.

*(d)* *Individual approach :* Each child is unique and different from his fellow flock. Teacher should regard individual differences and teach a child according to his level of understanding and specific interest.

**6. Discipline:** Self discipline is learnt by the students in the proper democratic and social environment of the school. They participate in collective activities and learn cooperation and control. Child is given full freedom to develop his natural abilities. Teacher does not consider himself superior to the child. He works in the class as a supervisor only. He also takes the individual differences of children into account.

**7. His experimental school:** In order to test and implement his educational ideas, Dewey opened his experimental school in Chicago University in 1896. In this school, children in the age group of 4-14 were admitted and then they were regrouped into small groups on the basis of their specific common interest and abilities. Teachers trained in Kinder Garten system of education were appointed to teach in the school. School programme was not restricted to any rigid rules and regulations. Teachers were given full freedom to make necessary changes in the curriculum and the method of teaching according to the need. The task of the teachers was to develop natural abilities of the child in a conducive social environment through problem solving method. When students reached solution to the problems by themselves, the ideas of Dewey were proved correct. When this school became famous, many such schools were also opened across the country. This school was run on the two basic principles given below:

*(i)* Activity method of teaching

*(ii)* Reorganization of experiences.

When a child was motivated to take part in natural activities like, reading, writing, playing or arithmetic, he took full interest in them and got some experiences. These experiences were reorganized to induce him to new tasks. Thus, the process of education was made natural.

**Impact of Dewey's Ideas on Modern Education:** Dewey has influenced not only the USA but the whole world such as:

*(i)* Inculcation of democratic values and social responsibilities have been included in the aims of education today.

*(ii)* Dewey's activity and self experience methods of teaching are very much recognized today. His view that method of teaching should vary with the variation of interests and abilities of children is also accepted today. Kilpatrik's Project Method is the direct result of Dewey's educational thoughts.

*(iii)* Special emphasis on vocational and professional courses and organization of co curricular activities in the school are also indebted to his thoughts. Curriculum is now updated after every five years according to the changing needs of the society. This is also the result of Dewey's contribution to education.

*(iv)* The concept of self discipline and democratic dealing have very much been recognized by schools today.

*(v)* The idea of free and compulsory education from 6-14 years has been derived in India from Dewey's thoughts. For universalisation of elementary education it has been made seventh

fundamental right under the 91st amendment of the constitution in 2001 by amending article 45(A) and article 21 of Indian constitution.

## Criticism of John Dewey

*(i)* Dewey wants to improve the world by experimentation. This idea is not acceptable to Realist who want to see the world as it is.

*(ii)* Dewey rejects the experiences of others and believed in self experience of man. This idea is also not acceptable to Realist.

*(iii)* Dewey advocates full freedom for the child which may spoil his career because of his immaturity and lack of experience.

*(iv)* Truth never changes according to the Idealists. Dewey opposed this and says that it is changeable with time and place. This idea may prove very dangerous for the society.

*(v)* Dewey wants to solve social problems arising out of conflicts of vocation, science and democracy. But the root cause of the problem is not the conflicts of vocation, science and democracy. It is something else. 21st century's terrorist activities across the world testify to this fact.

*(vi)* According to him, education is life itself and it is not possible to determine any objective for it due to continuous change in the pattern of living. This idea is also unbelievable. Changes do take place immediately but they take time. Specific aims of life must be there before the changes occur.

*(vii)* All facts and experiences can not be learnt by instruments. Those who do not take benefit of experiences of others, live in fool's paradise.

## SIR T PERCY NUNN (1870-1944)

## His Philosophical Thoughts

The philosophical thoughts of T.P.Nunn, the professor of philosophy and education in London University are summarized below:

1. **Individual development of man's personality:** According to him, in the beginning, the personality of man is flawless. He becomes good or bad in the society where he is brought up. It is the duty of teachers, parents and members of the society to provide him conducive and healthy environment so that his individual development becomes natural. Education should also be provided accordingly keeping in view his specific abilities and interest.
2. **Self realization :** According to him, development of personality depends on self realization. So, self realization is the main aim of education. It is very important to create such an environment in which spontaneous, natural and complete development of man is possible through self realization.
3. **Classification of mind :** He has classified the mind into two categories Horme and Maeme on the basis of process of mind.

*(a)* *Horme (urge) :* It keeps a man active by propelling him to reach the goal. In order to achieve the goal, he plans and reorganizes his behaviour and experiences. If this urge is not there in the mind, we shall not be driven to reach the goal. This urge controls our conscious as well as unconscious mind.

*(b)* *Maeme (power of conservation) :* This power plays an active role in conserving experiences. Memory and maeme are, however, closely related but the difference between the two is that memory conserves only specific experiences while maeme conserves all the experiences changeable and unchangeable. He calls the later ones as engrains and they are hereditary in nature. All new ideas and experiences affect these engrains and thus a personality is shaped by the composite effect of heredity and environment.

## His Educational Thoughts

If education is organized according to the needs, interests and abilities of a child, only then his natural development and formation of an independent personality is possible. Keeping this fact in view Nunn has given the following ideas regarding education and its role:

1. **Stages of education:**

*(a)* In the first stage of education (upto eight years) child should be educated by Kinder Garten and Montessori methods.

(b) In the second stage of education (8-13 years) child should be given regular and formal education in schools.

(c) In the third stage (13-18 years) children should be educated in secondary schools. This is the age when feeling of manhood in boys and womanhood in girls begins. These emotions should be nurtured in natural ways. This stage is particularly responsible for shaping the future personality of the individual.

2. **Aims of education:** He is of the view that social development should be brought about through personality development of the individuals. Man is a social being and is an inalienable part of the society. So it is the duty of the society and school to create such an environment where individual development of personality is not hindered. If individual is not paid proper attention, his individual qualities might remain latent. Schools should search out these hidden qualities by examining the personality of the individual and should provide them a solid base through education.

3. **Curriculum:**According to him, schools should keep the history of human development, society, nation and culture alive and should try to develop human and national culture. Only then we can bring about harmony between culture, civilization and spiritualism. Therefore, early achievement and social ideals of man should find a place in the curriculum. For this purpose Humanities, History, Geography, Art, Music, and Religion will occupy an important place in the curriculum along with the study of science and mathematics. Thus Nunn's Individualism is very much titled to Idealism.

4. **Discipline:** According to him, man is free by birth, so he should be given full freedom for his natural development. The real freedom is that which helps in the harmonious development of man and society both. But this freedom should not be unchecked. If behaviour of the child does not coincide the behaviour of the society, it should be controlled. Discipline here, does not mean the rules imposed from outside. Discipline is established by such laws as students abide by themselves. Teacher must also exhibit discipline to inculcate discipline among students. Thus, Nunn favours the impressionistic nature of discipline in the class.

5. **Pleasant nature of education :** Education should be provided in the form of play rather than work, i.e., efforts must be made to make it interesting to the maximum level possible.

## BERTRAND RUSSELL (1872-1970)

### His Life History

- He was born in Trelleck (Wales).
- He lost his parents at the age of 3 and was brought up by his grand father.
- He took admission in Trinity College in 1890 because of his deep interest in philosophy and religion.
- He was appointed fellow of Trinity College in 1891.
- His first book **Principles of Mathematics** was published in 1903.
- In the post world war period he took part in *Conscription Fellowship* an anti war movement, and was fined one hundred pounds by the government. When he did not pay the fine, his personal library was confiscated. He was sacked from his job also.
- He was offered to teach philosophy in Harward University but government did not issue him visa. He wrote an article in **Tribune** opposing and criticizing the policy of the government and he was jailed for six months. During his period of imprisonment, he wrote his famous book. **An Introduction to Mathematical Philosophy.**
- He was invited by the government of China in 1920 to deliver lectures on Philosophy.
- He was also awarded with Nobel Prize for literature in 1950. Some other famous books written by him are given below :

(a) On Education (1926)
(b) Outlines of Philosophy (1928)
(c) The consequence of Happiness (1930)
(d) Scientific Outlook (1931)

(*e*) Education and the Social order (1932)
(*f*) An enquiry into meaning of truth(1940)
(*g*) Human knowledge—its Scope and Limits (1948)
(*h*) New Hope for A Changing World (1951)
(*i*) The Impact of Science on Society (1952)

## His Philosophical Thoughts

1. **Logical Atomism :** He has given very much importance to logic in arguing and proving his ideas. He had no faith in prevailing beliefs as they were obsolete and tested them on the principles of logic. In this way, he was able to bring about great changes in the ideas of ethics, epistemology and axiology. He was of the view that through arguments and logic we could reach the ultimate depth of an idea and take self decision.
2. **Psychological Reform :** According to Russell, creating talent of man is very important. It should be exploited to the reach of the logical truth. By doing so, creativity of man can also be sharpened. He took great interest in basic problems of man and tried to give a happy solution to these problems. That is why he is known as **psychological reformist** also.
3. **Human Welfare :** He was a staunch supporter of world peace and hated all atomic weapons. He raised his voice against use of atom bomb in Japan during World War II. Feeling of human welfare was deeply rooted in his philosophy.
4. **Democracy and Science :** Democratic system of today excels in science. Democracy can not be developed without the progress of science. Science created self imagination and free thinking in man. So it can be an important means of developing democratic values in man. Vice versa is also correct. Unless we are given full freedom to think and act properly, we can not discover or invent anything.

## His Educational Thoughts

**1. Aims of Education:**

(*i*) Russell accepts the view that aim of education should be to prepare a worthy and noble man and to create a lofty society. But what should be the criteria of being a man good and a society lofty. This problem can be solved by using logic and wisdom. So, important aim of education is to develop logical power and wisdom in the individuals.

(*ii*) To develop the individual in such a way that he becomes a competent and acceptable member of the society is the second aim of education. Child is not the means. He is rather end and teachers and curriculum are the means. So, means should be adopted only after understanding the end. End is always above the state. So, his individuality should never be denied.

(*iii*) Natural individual differences exist from person to person. Therefore, similar type of education can not be imparted to all individuals. Their specific interests and abilities must be kept in mind in the process of education. It is because nation needs variety of people to serve it, such as, farmers, doctors, teachers, artisans, vocationals etc.

(*iv*) Character formation is the fourth important aim of education.

**2. Character Formation :** Education should develop following four qualities of character in children:

(*a*) *Vitality :* It is related to health and age. A man should posses health according to the norms of his age. As the man grows in age, his vitality increases but after a certain age, it starts diminishing especially in the old age. Mental health too depends on physical health therefore, vitality must be kept in mind when a child stays in the school. The important symptom of vitality is that child should feel pleasure in doing a work. Frustration should not overpower him.

(*b*) *Courage :* It is not easy to give a universal definition of courage, we can, however, understand the boldness of a courageous person by seeing his behaviour displayed in fearful and adverse situations. His wisdom and decision making power are not lost in such situations and he acts fearlessly after applying his wisdom and intellect. This courage is developed through education and when it is fully developed, it is exhibited by the child in his thinking, speech and action.

*(c)* *Sensitivity :* It also develops gradually with age. Take the example of liking and hatred. At the age of five, children begin to enjoy social recognitions given to them. This joy from social recognition goes on increasing with age. As a result, they hate contempt and take particular interest in praise. The desire for social recognition works as a strong motivating force in modifying his behaviour. Education should develop this desire until their behaviour becomes acceptable to the society. Sympathy is another example of sensitive feeling. In the beginning, it is shown for relatives and friends and child may weep at their sorrows. This narrow concept of sympathy is changed into broader one by education and efforts are kept on as log as child expresses sympathy even for those persons who he does not know at all. If a child is able to show sympathy even at the slightest possibility of troubles, it means that development of sympathy has taken place in him.

*(d)* *Intelligence :* It is a power acquired due to the presence of curiosity instinct in man. Curiosity is the basis for all mental processes. Man should posses higher level of curiosity, i.e., earnest curiosity to acquire any sound knowledge. It is the curiosity that develops love for knowledge in man. It is a motivating force for knowledge as well. Education should develop this earnest curiosity in man in desired direction. Only then development of intelligence is possible.

Above are the four important elements that are needed for the development of personality of an individual. By the age of six all important traits very much come up in children. Their role is very significant for future development of the personality. So, this period should be utilized very carefully by parents and Kinder Garten teachers.

**3. Acquisition of Knowledge and Personality Traits: (Principles of Education):**

*(a)* *Curiosity :* Mental training of a child starts when he attains the age of six. Even moral ideals should be evaluated from mental point of view. Curiosity is the base for all processes of mental development. This curiosity exists in the child by nature. If this does not exist in the child because of environmental influences, it is the duty of the teacher to arouse curiosity by teaching methods and techniques. For the purpose of satisfying this instinct of curiosity, child is acquainted with certain skills suitable to his instinct. The curiosity of the child should never be suppressed even if it is undesirable from moral point of view. It may be sublimated by guidance and counseling.

*(b)* *Unbiased Behaviour :* Some of our religious and traditional beliefs make us prejudiced. This negative trait in man begins to decline with the increase in age. It is because child starts to realize the real situations of life and society by becoming rational and open minded. Teacher should try to develop this trait to the maximum level because without it, acquisition of knowledge is not possible.

*(c)* *Confidence :* It makes the child active and motivated for the next knowledge. Teacher should develop confidence in the child.

*(d)* *Perseverance :* Continuous and persistent efforts are necessary for success in every affair of life without the exception of acquision of knowledge. All scientific inventions and discoveries are the result of perseverance. This quality can be developed in the child by citing the examples of successful industrious persons in the world and by making the aspiration level of the child high.

*(e)* *Attention :* Attention and concentration level are very low among children and it develops with age. Teacher should develop this quality by adopting novel methods and techniques of teaching and by using other material aids.

*(f)* *Practice :* It is very much needed for making the knowledge fixed.

*(g)* *Reality :* Reality in ideas and action helps the child to reach the truth. This reality may be pleasant as well as unpleasant. The child

should be trained to bear the unpleasant situations also coupled with making the education itself interesting and meaningful.

**4. Discipline**

(i) Teacher should work as a guide and friend in the class. Children should be educated through Froebel and Montessori's methods of education. This will make teaching a natural process rather than compulsion.

(ii) Children should be assigned work according to their abilities and interest so that they may take full interest in doing it. If a child is unable to do a work, the reasons must be ascertained and removed.

(iii) Children should be motivated by using praise technique rather than punishing them.

**5. Programme of Educational (Curriculum)**

(a) *Nursery education :* Pre primary education must be given in Nursery schools. The qualities acquired during this period shapes the entire personality in the later period of a child's life. So, this period is very crucial for a child. Every child poor or rich, rural or urban, should be given opportunities to receive nursery education in schools. It is only the nursery schools that can take the responsibility of developing healthy habits during infancy. Parents cannot do this due to lack of knowledge and training. Physical and health education is also necessary at this stage, e.g. if a child suffers from indigestion, he may be mentally sick also. Medical treatment on psychological lines is needed then.

(b) *Education during 6 to 14 years :* Education should be given according to the specific characteristics of a particular age. Similarly, interest and needs of different persons also differ. These differences must be taken into consideration in the process of education. Some common things are give below:

- The development of reading and writing skills must be completed at the end of six years along with sense perception, knowledge of general principles of dancing, singing and painting.
- Mental activities should start only after the age of seven. It is the age to start elementary mathematics.
- Teaching of history and geography should also start at this age. All these books should be decorated with pictures, stories and maps to clarify how man lived and hunted animals in the past, how a country is different from other countries in soil, rainfall and temperature, what crops are cultivated in different regions and so on.
- Individual and collective dance and chorus songs should also be practiced during this period.
- In the later part of this period, interesting literature should be taught to them. It can improve reading and writing skills of children.
- Teaching of modern languages also starts during this periods. If they are taught more than one language, it is better.
- Knowledge of regular mathematics and science starts at the age of 12. Since these subjects are very uninteresting, interest should be created in children externally.

In short we can say that general education is required upto the age of 14 and there is no need of any specialization upto this age.

(c) *Education during 14 to 18 years :* Specialized education should be provided during this period. There are three groups of specialization here.

- Classical Languages
- Mathematics and Science
- Modern Humanities

Child will select any of these specialized groups on the basis of his specific interest and abilities and along with the study of these subjects he will also study physiology, anatomy and hygiene which are subjects directly useful for life. All children of any group should also be taught how to adjust with other people in the society by getting them involved in social, political and religious activities.

(d) *University education :* According to him, university education has two important aims.

(i) To prepare trained men and women for various vocation, jobs and professions.

(ii) To expand knowledge by research.

Keeping the above aims in view, university education need not be given to all. It should be given to only those students who are willing it and they are capable also. But the problem may arise as to how should these students be selected? Admission test may be conducted for this purpose.

Another problem is too high cost of this education to accommodate the poor students in the university. For this purpose, scholarship provisions must be made so that gifted children may not be deprived of this education due to their poverty. Current JRF test conducted by UGC is based on this idea.

Even after admission, if a student does not fulfil his obligations and is unable to satisfy his teachers, he should not be allowed to stay in the university. University must be made an abode for hardworking, intelligent and active persons.

As far as appointment of teachers in the universities is concerned, only those teachers who have real interest in teaching and research, who are hardworking and are prepared to sacrifice everything for the development of education should be appointed. These teachers should be paid handsomely and they should be given leave of at least one year in their service period for higher studies and research.

The ultimate aim of universities is to carry out researches. This work must be done by the teachers in the universities.

**6. Method of Teaching**

*(i)* The children should be taught through activity method. Learning by Doing is the best method.

*(ii)* Children should be attracted to problems of life and they will solve these problems themselves, i.e., problem solving method.

*(iii)* Individual activities should be given more importance than class work. In this way child gets chance of development according to his ability and nature. (Opposed to Dewey)

*(iv)* Self study is given preference to lecturing in the class. Students are also instructed to write a statement of what they have studied. When knowledge is put in written form by the students, it will be very easy for them to crame it. Teacher can also evaluate the students by these statements and proper guidance can be given.

*(v)* Intellectual discussion is another method of teaching. During discussions students should never be checked when they criticize a matter or thing.

*(vi)* Independent thinking is developed by applying scientific enquiry and wrong beliefs are changed by this method.

*(vii)* Students are advised to study two types of books. First type of books give necessary knowledge to all of them and second type of books give them knowledge according to their abilities and interest.

*(viii)* For the purpose of evaluating the students question papers are set in such a manner that only those who have studied the subject matter thoroughly are able to answer the questions.

## OBJECTIVE QUESTIONS

**1.** Rousseau's aim of education was

*(a)* to develop the child according to his innate tendencies and capacity

*(b)* to develop good as well as bad sense of the child

*(c)* to help the child in the acquisition of moral values by action

*(d)* all of these

**2.** Which of the following methods is not supported by Rousseau

*(a)* Laboratory method

*(b)* Heuristic method

*(c)* Project method

*(d)* Learning by doing

**3.** The philosopher supporting utopian tendencies is/are

*(a)* Comenius *(b)* Pestalozzi

*(c)* Kant *(d)* All of them

**4.** Pestalozzi wanted to establish a/an

*(a)* scientific society *(b)* ethical society

*(c)* modern society *(d)* primitive society

**5.** Which of the following ideas has not been given by Pestalozzi

(*a*) Growth of the child is more important than achievement
(*b*) Even wrong conclusions if drawn by the child himself is acceptable
(*c*) Fun games should be introduced in education
(*d*) Mental development of the child through education

**6.** Dewey differs from other philosophers of 20th century in his concept of
(*a*) Mind
(*b*) Experimentalism
(*c*) Activity centred education
(*d*) All of these

**7.** The test of truth and reality according to Dewey is
(*a*) Usefulness through experimentation
(*b*) Social significance
(*c*) Individual benefits
(*d*) a & b both

**8.** Those desires and norms whose gratification hinder the economic efficiency of man is called
(*a*) Negative morality
(*b*) Positive morality
(*c*) Instrumentalism
(*d*) None of these

**9.** The concept of neutral monoism was given by
(*a*) T P Nunn (*b*) Russell
(*c*) Kant (*d*) Satre

**10.** Regarding method of teaching Russell advocates
(*a*) Maximum use of senses for learning
(*b*) Scientific way of dealing the subject matter
(*c*) Analysis as method of teaching
(*d*) All of these

**11.** Which of he following philosophers supports child centred education
(*a*) Froebel
(*b*) John Dewey and Plato
(*c*) Maria Montessori
(*d*) All of these

**12.** Who among of the following is not the exponent of Humanistic Realism
(*a*) Milton (*b*) Aristotle
(*c*) Erasmus (*d*) Rebellay

**13.** Whitehead and Russell support
(*a*) Neo Realism (*b*) Sense Realism
(*c*) Social Realism (*d*) Humanistic Realism

**14.** According to Comenius "Ultimate end of man is eternal happiness" so, education should aim at
(*a*) making the child God fearing
(*b*) helping him to enjoy life
(*c*) using the senses more and more
(*d*) none of these

**15.** "The world is continuously evolving toward a greater degree of perfection that is God". It is the opinion of
(*a*) Russell (*b*) Aristotle
(*c*) Comenius (*d*) Hegel

**16.** There is a distinction between matter and form and their existence is independent of mind. This idea makes Aristotle
(*a*) A Realist (*b*) A Humanist
(*c*) Existentialist (*d*) Pragmatist

**17.** According to Aristotle, education should aim at enabling man to attain his rational self and raise his level by increasing his divinity
(*a*) by living with the matter
(*b*) by realizing the rational self
(*c*) by forsaking the matter that restricts his upward movement
(*d*) b & c both

**18.** Ultimate aim of education according to Aristotle is
(*a*) The realization of complete happiness
(*b*) Search of matter and its details
(*c*) Both of these
(*d*) None of these

**19.** Which of the following ideas does not belong to Aristotle
(*a*) Virtues are of two kinds—intellectual virtues developed by teaching and moral virtues developed from habits.
(*b*) Virtues are to be judged by their consequences.
(*c*) Happiness lies in he best activity which is nothing but contemplation.
(*d*) Equality according to proportion to enable every man to enjoy his own must be there in the society.

**20.** According to Aristotle, children should be given knowledge of difficult subjects through direct experiences. This is an approach
(*a*) from known to unknown
(*b*) from general to particular

(*c*) from unknown to known
(*d*) none of the above

**21.** Which of the following philosophers has influenced modern system of education very much
(*a*) Aristotle (*b*) Dewey
(*c*) Pestalozzi (*d*) All

**22.** "There is a real world of things behind and corresponding to the objects of our perception". This definition of Realism was given by
(*a*) Ross (*b*) Milton
(*c*) Erasmus (*d*) Nunn

**23.** The role of teacher is minimum in
(*a*) Naturalism (*b*) Realism
(*c*) Marxism (*d*) Pragmatism

**24.** Emile was written in
(*a*) 1782 (*b*) 1772
(*c*) 1762 (*d*) 1600

**25.** Which of the following philosophers put Rousseau's educational ideas into practice
(*a*) Pestalozzi (*b*) Froebel
(*c*) Montessori (*d*) All of them

**26.** Which of the following is the work of Pestalozzi.
(*a*) Evening hours of a hermit
(*b*) Leonard and getrude
(*c*) The swan song
(*d*) All of these

**27.** Which of the following books is similar to Emile
(*a*) Evening hours of a hermit
(*b*) Leonard and getrude
(*c*) The swan song
(*d*) All of these

**28.** Arrange the Pestalozzi's stages of intellectual development given below in sequence
(*i*) Function of mind starts with impression
(*ii*) Sense impression makes form and qualities of things clear
(*iii*) Images of things are transformed into ideas
*Codes:*
(*a*) *i, ii, iii* (*b*) *ii , i , iii*
(*c*) *iii, i, ii* (*d*) *iii, ii, i*

**29.** Anschaung in English means
(*a*) First hand experience of the child
(*b*) Personal experience of the child
(*c*) Face to face knowledge of objects
(*d*) All of these

**30.** Pestalozzi is distinguished from other Naturalists in his contribution of
(*a*) stress on curriculum
(*b*) teacher training
(*c*) ability grouping
(*d*) all of these

**31.** Which of the following is not the work of Froebel?
(*a*) Education of man
(*b*) Pedagogies of Kinder garten
(*c*) Essays on education
(*d*) Reminiscences

**32.** The idea that there is unity between man, nature and God was given by
(*a*) Plato (*b*) Aristotle
(*c*) Froebel (*d*) b and c both

**33.** The idea of natural goodness of man is supported by
(*a*) Prophet Mohammad
(*b*) Rousseau
(*c*) Froebel
(*d*) All of these

**34.** Maria Montessori (1870-1952) was basically a
(*a*) Lady doctor (*b*) Teacher
(*c*) Social worker (*d*) None of these

**35.** The fundamental concept behind Montessori method is
(*a*) that individuality of the child should not be crushed through collective teaching
(*b*) students can be motivated for learning by games
(*c*) Both of these
(*d*) None of these

**36.** By stressing sense training of the child, Montessori comes closer to
(*a*) Realism (*b*) Pragmatism
(*c*) Marxism (*d*) Naturalism

**37.** Which of the following is not the work of Maria Montessori
(*a*) Emile
(*b*) The discovery of the child
(*c*) Education for a New World
(*d*) Reconstruction in Education

**38.** In Montessori's system of education, the role of a teacher in the class is like a
(*a*) Guide
(*b*) Directress

(c) Well prepared instructor
(d) Helper

**39.** Montessori's method can be criticized on which of the following grounds?
(a) it neglects play activities of children
(b) it is centred around didactic apparatus
(c) it is costly because method of teaching changes with the topic
(d) all of these

**40.** Montessori and Froebel are not alike in which of the following points
(a) Sense training for sharpening mind
(b) Recognition of individuality of the child
(c) Development of child on idealistic pattern of life
(d) Play activities of the child

**41.** For which of the following books Russell was awarded noble prize in 1950
(a) Marriage and moral
(b) Principle mathematica
(c) Education
(d) None of these

## ANSWERS

| 1 | 2 | 3 | 4 | 5 | 6 | 7 | 8 | 9 | 10 |
|---|---|---|---|---|---|---|---|---|---|
| (d) | (c) | (d) | (b) | (d) | (a) | (d) | (a) | (b) | (d) |
| **11** | **12** | **13** | **14** | **15** | **16** | **17** | **18** | **19** | **20** |
| (d) | (b) | (a) | (a) | (b) | (a) | (d) | (a) | (b) | (a) |
| **21** | **22** | **23** | **24** | **25** | **26** | **27** | **28** | **29** | **30** |
| (d) | (a) | (a) | (c) | (d) | (d) | (b) | (a) | (d) | (d) |
| **31** | **32** | **33** | **34** | **35** | **36** | **37** | **38** | **39** | **40** |
| (c) | (d) | (d) | (a) | (a) | (a) | (a) | (b) | (d) | (d) |
| **41** | | | | | | | | | |
| (a) | | | | | | | | | |

# Indian Philosophies and Education

## INTRODUCTION

Kautilya in his book **Arthshastra** has mentioned only three philosophical systems prevailing in ancient India. These systems are Samkhya, Yoga and Lokayata. But actually there are nine systems. Six of them represent the astika or orthodox schools of thought and three of them represent nastika or heterodox schools.

*(i)* **Astikas :** They believe in God and the other world. They also believe in infallibility and supreme authority of Vedas.

*(ii)* **Nastikas :** They do not believe in God, Vedas and the other world. Two religions representing this school of thought are Buddhism and Jainism. Since Buddhists and Jainists have their own holy scriptures, they considered the followers of Vedas as Nastikas.

## SOURCES OF INDIAN PHILOSOPHY

### Vedas, the Origin of Indian Philosophy

The word Veda means knowledge. It is revealed knowledge according to orthodox. Some people believed that principal Veda is only one which was later divided into four—Rig Veda, Sam Veda, Yajur Veda and Atharva Veda. Among them Rig Veda is the oldest and Atharva Veda is the latest. These Vedas are in the poetic forms called hymns (mantras). There are 1028 mantras only in Rig Veda. All these mantras have been grouped in 10 stanzas. In its bulk Rig Veda is equal to the poems of Homer. Its age is around 2000-2500 B.C.

Actual reading of Rig Veda shows that these mantras are the simple expression of our everyday desires, such as desire for cattle, food, rain, safety, victory, health, progeny etc. Thus they are not philosophical discussions in technical terms. They are only the materialistic or pragmatic explanations of human values and life.

In spite of these we find a fine explanation of God, soul and religion in some of these mantras. All these vedic mantras have been divided into four parts. The first three parts contain mantras pertaining to worship and rituals for yagya and the last part is called Upanishads.

If we go into details of these four Vedas we see that Rig Veda is mostly concerned with rituals and a major portion of other three Vedas primarily deals with magic. For example, second part of Sam Veda is a regular handbook of magic in which the employment of various melodies for magic purposes is taught. Atharva Veda is also a compilation of primitive magical charms to secure the fulfillment of a variety of worldly desires. As far as Yajur Veda is concerned, it mentions many deities in its hymns no doubt but the purpose of these hymns is not to please Gods but to coerce them with the help of magic for materialistic purposes and benefits.

### Brahmanas

They are the second source of philosophical thoughts after Vedas. They are in prose and were written much later than Vedas. Morals have found no place in Brahmanas as they propagate materialism. The sacrifice *(Bali)* which regulates the relationship between man and God is a mechanical operation and is very much emphasized here.

### Upanishads

Only that part of Vedas which contains logical and philosophical discussions on various subjects are called Upanishads. According to Upanishads, God is immortal, omnipotent and omnipresent. He has finite and non finite both forms. Soul is also immortal and it is an integral part of the universe. Ultimate goal of man's life according to Upanishads is salvation or Moksha.

The word "Upanishad" means secret knowledge and it has been derived from three words Upa-Ni-Shad means to sit down near some one. Upnishads were written after Brahmanas. The main Upanishads are 13 in number. All of them are in poetry except two. They belong to the pre Buddha period. Only two Upanishads--Maitri and Mandukya could be of post Buddha period. They are in prose. Thus, we see that Upanishads are not the contribution of one or few persons but they are the product of creative speculations of the generation of several centuries. King Janak of ancient India was a great Upanishadic Philosopher.

### Bhagwat Geeta

It is the fourth important source of Indian Philosophy. According to Geeta soul is immortal and ultimate aim of man's life is salvation. This salvation can be achieved by using three means—Bhakti, Gyan and Karma. Among them Nishkam Karma (Selfless action) is the best and the easiest way of achieving salvation.

## SHASHT DARSHAN (VEDIC PHILOSOPHIES)

The theistic Indian Philosophy has been divided into six parts known as Shasht Darshan. The sources of these philosophies are Vedas, Brahmanas, Upanishads and Geeta. Vedas are considered revealed sources and other sources are actually the interpretations of Vedas. They are described below:

### Vedanta

It took its stand on Upanishads that is why it is called Vedanta (Veda+Ant). This philosophy claims to have systematized the philosophical content of it. This philosophy was elaborated by the work Vedants Sutra and Brahma Sutra. According to it ultimate reality is Brahma. Only he is eternal and real and everything else is myth. Soul is an integral part of God so it is also real. All knowledge flows from Vedanta, so it can remove all ignorance. If man sees any plurality in the universe, it is because of this ignorance. An important branch of this system is Advaite Vedanta propounded by **Shankaracharya.**

Advait literally means non dualism. According to this philosophy, Brahma, the ultimate reality is identical with the self. Everything is unreal except God or Self (soul). Vaishnavites conceived this God Vishnu and Shavites conceived him Shiva but he is only one Brahma.

Shankara was basically an idealist and his chief aim was to refute the philosophical postulates of Mimansa and Samkhya. He argued that knowledge and action are totally opposed to each other and action or karma is a serious impediment in the way of gaining knowledge. It is because karma has duality in many ways such as body, this world and so on. If one is engaged in karma, it means he is seriously involved in physical world or bodily desires which is nothing but duality. This duality makes the realization of self or Brahma (reality) difficult. So karma must be rejected in all its forms. It is the knowledge of self or realization of Brahma that can lead a man to salvation.

Brahma has been discussed in detail in **Brahmasutra:** The Brahmasutra has been interpreted by different philosophers in different ways. Some interpretations are given below:

***(a)*** **Bhaskara's doctorine of difference cum non-difference :** Soul is both different and non-different from God just like waves and the ocean. Thus difference is sometimes seen and sometimes it is not seen.

***(b)*** **Ramanuja's doctorine of qualified non-dualism :** Highest reality is God but this reality can be understood only by his attributes. Whatever exists is contained within God but within this unity are distinct elements of plurality because of many attributes of God. These attributes may be described as types of God. Above all, devotion to God is an important means of achieving salvation.

***(c)*** **Samkara's mayawada (doctorine of ignorance) :** Pure knowledge brings freedom from ignorance and therefore liberation is achieved. This liberation totally depends on the grace of God and devotion is an important way of achieving this grace.

(*d*) **Nimbaraka's doctorine of dualism–cum–non-dualism :** The relation of God to individual soul is that of dualism–cum–non–dualism just like the air which have different forms and behaves differently in different conditions. The jiva and the world are distinct from Brahma only in the sense that they are developed and evolved from the qualities, force or power of Brahma and thus relationship between animate and inanimate forms of the universe is established. This doctorine also emphasizes devotion as a means of achieving salvation.

(*e*) **Madhawa's doctorine of plane dualism :** God is the efficient cause of all creations. God is none else but Vishnu. Whenever he becomes incarnate, he has Vayu (Air), the air god as his son. Madhawa, himself was considered as incarnation of Vayu who came to the earth to destroy the followers of Samkara. Thus dualism here means the distinction between independent supreme being (Brahma) and dependent principle of life (Jivatma). Madhawa also led great emphasis on devotion as a path to salvation.

(*f*) **Chaitanya's doctorine of difference–cum–non-difference :** This philosophy is based on the principle that all men are equal in the eyes of God as all of them have originated from same God.

## Mimansa

This philosophy put forward a number of arguments to prove that entire Veda is infallible and real. Rituals and Yagya have been entirely emphasized by this philosophy. "Brahama Sutra" is the source book of this system.

This book contain 2500 aphorisms compiled by Jaimini. The chief propounders of this system are Sabara, Prabhakara and Kumairila. However because of the strong' differences between Prabhakara and Kumairila Bhatta two separate schools of thoughts came into being called Prabhakara school and Bhatta school. Both of these schools are atheistic in the sense that they do not believe in god, mahapralay or creation of the world. They however, believed that all Vedic instructions are real and only those karmas (actions) are religious which are mentioned in Vedas. It is because only Vedas are reliable for them.

Thoughts of chief contributors of this system are given below:

(*a*) **Sabara :** There is no evidence of the existence of God. Sense perception does not prove the existence of God at all, and other sources of knowledge are after all based on sense perception.

(*b*) **Prabhakara :** Individual things of the world have their beginning and their end but this does not mean that the world as a whole is ever created or it will be destroyed any time in future. There is only the constant process of becoming and passing away.

(*c*) **Kumairila :** He rejects the idea that God is the creator of everything. He says how a disembodied soul can create anything. For creation he must have body.

## Samkhya

Ausuri, Panchshikha, Sunak and Sananda were great teachers of this system. This philosophy is very old and its pervasive impact can be seen in Mahabharat, Kanak Samhita, Manusmriti and Puranas. Basic ideas and chief characteristics of this system are given below:

(*a*) There is no proof of the existence of God.

(*b*) Creation of the universe is the result of cause and effect. Brahma has not created this. Prakriti and Purush are the two main elements of this creation. Prakriti is a combination of three qualities—Sat, Raj and Tam. This Prakriti is eternal and unconscious. Purush (matter) is also eternal but it is conscious and it is a cooperative element of Prakirti. When three qualities of Prakirti came into contact with Purush, the universe was created.

(*c*) Effect is only a modification of the cause. What was found in the effect was already contained in the cause. For example, sugarcane crop can produce only sugarcane and nothing else.

(*d*) Everything in the universe is an unstable composition of three kinds of substances, technically called as Gunas (attributes):

- Sat (exhibiting qualities of illumination and joy)
- Raj (exhibiting qualities of movement, excitement and pain)

- Tam(exhibiting qualities of destruction, heaviness and sloth)

Moreover, among these three primeval matters Sat contains intelligence, Raj contains energy and Tam is the cause of inertia.

*(e)* In the earliest stage of Prakirti, these three attributes-Sat, Raj and Tam were in equilibrium. Evolution is the result of loss of equilibrium in these states of nature. The evolution of the universe has gone through the following stages:

- From disturbed equilibrium arose Mahabat or Buddhi.
- From Mahabat arose Ahankar (ego).
- From ego arose Manas (mind), five sense organs, five motor organs and five subtle elements.
- Five subtle elements changed into five Mahabhutas like earth, water, air, fire, and sky.

On the basis of above discussions we can conclude that Samkhya system is purely a materialistic philosophy. It profoundly opposed the idealistic philosophy of Vedanta.

### Yoga

Except for the admission of God this system is essentially the same as Samkhya. That is why Patanjali's philosophy is called Samkhya with God. This system was so meaningful that Mahavira devoted himself 12 long years and Buddha devoted himself for 6 long years to the yogic practices. It is a physiomental training for the realization of truth. There are eight aspects of yogic training-*(i)* Yam *(ii)* Niyam *(iii)* Pranayam *(iv)* Dhyan *(v)* Dharma *(vi)* Pratyahar *(vii)* Asan *(viii)* Samadhi.

### Nyaya

This philosophy is realistic. It says that Brahma is the creator of the universe. He is our saviour as well as destroyer. Soul is immortal and its conscious form is life. When body dies, soul again becomes unconscious. This system has proved the existence of God in many ways. It has also given four proofs of mind- assumption, comparison, perception and word in atomic form.

### Vaisheshika

This system is very much similar to Nyaya system. This has divided the wordly materials into seven parts—action, quality, matter, special, ordinary, abundance and scarcity.

## HETERODOX OR NON VEDIC PHILOSOPHIES

### Buddhism

This religion is mainly attributed to Mahatma Buddha, a young lad of Sakya tribe in the 5th century BC. Buddha preached his religion and philosophy till 483 BC when he died at the age of 80.

The oldest Buddhist literature consists of speeches, sayings and traditions of Buddha, poems, tales and rules of conduct. They all are compiled into three Pitakas written in Pali language.

*(a)* **Vinaya Pitak** (Basket of discipline) : It is for the purpose of regulating daily life and conduct of monks and nuns.

*(b)* **Sattaya Pitak :** It is in prose and poetry both. It explains Buddhist religion and its rituals.

*(c)* **Abidhamma Pitak** (basket of Higher Religion): Its topics for discussion are the same as Sattya Pitak but in a more scholarly manner.

**Four Noble truths of Buddha**

*(a)* *Everything is suffering:* Such as birth is suffering, old age is suffering, sickness is suffering, death is suffering, to be united with unloved is suffering, to be separated from the loved is suffering and so on. Thus, the world is full of miseries and sufferings. In one sentence we can say that this world is ocean of griefs.

*(b)* *Suffering has a cause:* Lust and desire are the main cause of sufferings.

*(c)* *Suffering can be removed:* If we give up all sorts of desires, suffering is automatically removed.

*(d)* *Path is there to extinguish suffering*: Sacred eight fold path should be adopted for this purpose. These eight fold path are as follows:

*(i)* Right faith

*(ii)* Right resolve

*(iii)* Right speech

*(iv)* Right action

*(v)* Right living
*(vi)* Right efforts
*(vii)* Right thought
*(viii)* Right self concentration

**Explanation :** Right speech, right action and right living lead to physical control; Right effort and contemplation lead to mental control; (Samadhi) Right belief and resolve lead to insight (prajna) and prajna leads to salvation.

## Historical background of the philosophy

It was the age when India was first witnessing the rise of ruthless rulers of Magadha and Kosala who were treating their subjects like slaves. Society was also divided into a number of castes and classes mostly antagonistic to each other. The people of lower castes were inhumanly treated by the people of upper castes and Upanishadic religion was also supporting this.

At this very period of social chaos and religious intolerance Buddha asked his pupils to turn away from the opinions relating to the beginning and end of the universe, nature and attributes of God etc because they were of no use for the common people. That was why Buddha would remain silent when he was asked metaphysical questions. He also postulated that belief in God is not a necessary pre-requisite of a religion.

The lives of the people at the time of Buddha was so full of suffering that he asked the people to adopt *Pabbaja* and *Upsampada* ordinations i.e., to go out of the actual society and lead a life of renunciation by becoming monks.

## Basic Philosophy of Buddhism

Basic postulates of this philosophy are given below-

*(i)* Desires should be completely given up
*(ii)* Samghas—the life of a monk should be adopted
*(iii)* Nirwan—it is a state in which suffering is completely removed.
*(iv)* Dwadasa Nidan—there are 12 main causes of suffering. This is known as theory of natural causation of suffering
*(v)* Denial of soul as a substance : Transient sensation and thoughts along with the physical frame with which they are associated are real and idea of reality of soul or Brahma is superstition. Thus, this philosophy strongly opposed Vedanta.
*(vi)* Description of Personality : It consists of five factors (Scandhas) namely Rupa, Vijnana, Veduna, Sanjana and Sanskara. The first is related to physical body while the other factors are psychological.

Keeping in view the above ideas and thoughts we can say that this philosophy of life emerged as a reaction against Upanishads.

## Three Buddhist Sects

1. **Sarvastvalians** : This sect believed in the universal existence of every thing—past, present and future.
2. **Hinayanists** : Hinayana is an abusive name coined by their rivals Mahayanists. They believed in the Nirvana of the individual rather than of the collective whole.
3. **Mahayanists** : There are two subsects of Mahayanists.

*(a)* *Yogacara:* Its general philosophical conclusion was the same as that of Berkeley in Europe. It says that since we cannot jump out of our own idea and can know an object through the mind, so only ideas are real and material world is unreal. Berkeley also said the same thing but with the admission of God. The greatest representative of this school Vasubandhu says, "All this world show is nothing but mere manifestation of consciousness and has no reality at all apart from these consciousness. The thing that appears as contents of conscioueness is unreal".

*(b)* *Madhyamica:* This Mahayana sect of Buddhism was given special protection by king Kanishka of ancient India. It tried to establish the primacy of the spirit over the body by proving the unreality of the material world. This school propounded a new philosophy known as **shunyawad**. The leader of this philosophy was **Nagarjun**.

The central point of Madhyamica philosophy is the same as that of Upanishadic idealism. That is why it is called a link philosophy between Upanishads and Advaita Vedanta. Its shunyavada is totally a world denying philosophy. Nagarjun said that the empirical world is there because of our ignorance and with the dawn of knowledge, it would no longer exist.

The detailed description of Mahayana philosophy can be seen, in Mahayana Sutra written in hybrid Sanskrit.

## Jainism

Historically this religion is older than Buddhism but its philosophical thoughts were developed much later than that of Buddhist thoughts.

The two sects of Jainism are as follows-

*(a)* **Swetambara :** Wearing clothes of white colour.

*(b)* **Digambara :** Their ideal is to go absolutely naked. These two sects do not differ at all in their doctrines. The difference is there only in their ritual observances. Mahavira was the greatest prophet of this religion but he was not the founder of Jainism. He was supposed to be the last in the long line of successive prophets called *Thirthankoras*. The principal source of the systematic exposition of jain philosophy is Tattavardhigm Sutras written by Umasvati.

## Doctorines of Jain Philosophy

1. **Anekta Veda :** It is sometimes referred as doctrine of non dualism. According to it reality is not of a permanent nature. It underwent the processes of production, continuation and estruction. Any material being continues forever to exist as matter. This matter, however, may assume any shape and quality but it will always remain matter, e.g. clay is a material thing. We can make so many material things from this matter.
2. **Syad Veda :** Syad means may be or somehow. An assertion or statement and its opposite both may be somehow true but each is only partially true.
3. **Doctorine of Seven Mayas :** Maya here means the ways of expressing things i.e., judgement. There are seven possible ways of passing judgement upon any thing.
   *(i)* it exist
   *(ii)* it does not exist
   *(iii)* it exists as well as exist not
   *(iv)* it is indescribable
   *(v)* it exists but it is indescribable
   *(vi)* it does not exist but it is indescribable
   *(vii)* it exists as well as exists not and it is indescribable.
4. **Substance Classification :** All substances were divided into two broad classes:
   *(i)* *Non souls* : It is of five types, Kala (time), Akash (Space), Dharma (religion), Adharma (non religion) and Padgala (matter). Space, dhárma and adharma are necessary conditions for the subsistence of all other things. Dharma is like water to the fish which enables it to move. Adharma is like shadow for the travelers which lures them to take rest. But neither of them use any coercive method for action. Padgala (matter) was conceived in terms of four well known elements namely earth, water, fire and air.
   *(ii)* *States of matter* : This doctorine made a clear cut distinction between two states of matter. First state is subtle which is super sensuous and second state is gross state which can really be perceived.
5. **Universality of Souls :** Everything in the universe has soul.
6. Natural qualities of souls are perfect knowledge, intution (faith) highest bliss etc. but these qualities are weakened by defilement of karma.
7. The highest goal of man is to get rid of karma and to stop the influx of any new karma.
8. Right faith, right knowledge and right conduct are conducive to liberation.

Thus this philosophy totally goes against the philosophy of Geeta.

## Charwak Darshan

This philosophy is also atheistic like Buddhism or Jainism but materialistic. The main postulates of this philosophy are as follows :

*(a)* It does not accept God or soul.

*(b)* It describes the body itself as soul which is composed of different physical elements. This body dies away when these elements are destroyed.

(c) Consciousness which is produced by the combination of physical elements is a natural phenomenon.

(d) Universe is composed of four basic elements—earth, water, fire, and air.

(e) Sense perception is the only method of acquiring knowledge.

(f) When body dies, soul also dies.

(g) The pleasure in life is the best ideal because nothing is left after death.

Thus, this philosophy is very much similar to Realism, which takes knowledge obtained by sense perception as real.

## NATURE OF EDUCATION ACCORDING TO ADVAITE VEDANTA

According to Shankaracharya the principle of monotheism should be made the main basis of education. To realize the elements of Brahma (God) should be the principal aim of education. In order to achieve this aim, ignorance (Agyan or Maya) must be dispelled. When ignorance is removed the unity between Brahma and Atma (God and Soul) will be realised. Therefore according to Shankar true education is that which helps one to realize the unity between Atma and Paramatma (Soul and God) between Nar and Narayan (man and God). Thus Shankar regards knowledge (Gyan) as the objective of education. To Shankar education is a tripolar process in which the teacher (Guru), the student (Shishya) and the subject matter (Pathyakram) are the three major sides.

### Aims of Education According to Advaite Vedanta

Education must enable one for performing the four Purusharths—Artha, Dharma, Karma and Moksha, i.e., valour, righteous duties, worldly pleasures and salvation. Artha stands for achievement of enough property through the other three Purusharthas. Advaite Vedanta particularly emphasizes the fourth Purushartha, i.e., the Moksha. It is for the attainment of the fourth Purushartha that the other three Purushartha have to be employed. Self realization or realising one's unity with God, i.e., merging oneself into God, is the ultimate end of education or all Sadhana. In other words, we may say that the ultimate aim of education is to guide the student toward attainment of spirituality (Moksha).

### Christianity

Basic tenets of Christianity are given below.

(i) God, the creator of the universe, is one who speaks through his son Jesus Christ.

(ii) Love for humanity is above rituals. Service of humanity is synonymous to service of God. Under privileged, poor and sick people of the society should be targetted by welfare programmes more than others.

(iii) Perseverance and forgiveness in attitude and action are necessary. Retaliation of any sort is not permissible.

(iv) Celibacy is the best method of reaching spiritual zenith and pleasing God.

(v) There is a life hereafter and heaven or hell will be allotted to humans on the basis of their good or bad deeds.

(vi) Medium is necessary for becoming closer to God. Nobody can realize self (God) without taking the help of Bishops.

(vii) Forgiveness is the ultimate virtue. "If you forgive others for the wrongs they have committed against you, your father in heaven will also forgive you."

(viii) Goodness brings goodness. Education should make people good for all.

(ix) Charity by action and wealth is needed to get good rewards in heaven. This life is only a temporary one. So, wealth or worldly things should not be accumulated here.

(x) Jesus Christ was born on 25th December to end darkness from this earth. Christmas is observed on this day.

(xi) Crucification of Jesus took place on the third Friday of April. It is observed as Good Friday, a day of mourning and abstinence.

(xii) Jesus Christ is also believed to come back a day on the third day of Good Friday (Sunday) again. This day is observed as Easter Sunday.

### Educational Implication

Christianity takes life in a negative and pessimistic manner. That is why we see that Europe could not come out of the dark age till it stopped following

Christianity as a philosophy of life. When people rose up against this philosophy, revolted against it and restricted religion to the private affairs of man, modern scientific age began and knowledge based on experience and experimentation got recognition and weightage.

The only contribution of Christianity in modern age is that it provoked the people to expound two philosophies, namely, modern idealism and humanism.

## ISLAMIC TRADITIONS

### Introduction of the Religion

The word "Islam" has been derived from Arabic word "Sallam" meaning peace, complete submission (to God) and unbreakable (by stones of ignorance). Its latest version as we see Islam today was introduced in Mecca in 610 AD by Prophet Mohammad (the person to be praised). He was called *Sadique* (truth speaking) and *Ameen* (completely honest) before his prophethood (at the age of 40) by the people of Mecca. Mohammad was born in Mecca in the family of Hashim in 570 AD. He was always in search of truth and used to go to Hira mountain till he was appointed appostle by his God.

After ten years of struggle in Mecca, Mohammad migrated to Madina where he was welcomed by the local people and Mohammad succeeded there in establishing Islam as a system. He became the head of state in Madina and efforts were made to spread Islam in all corners of the world. After his death, Abu Bakar succeeded him and every thing was smooth and peaceful till the reign of Ali who was not accepted as religious leader and political head by a large section of Muslim community which resulted into two civil wars—Jamal and Siffeen in which about 120000 Muslims were killed on both sides. Those who supported Ali in these wars declared themselves as Shia-ne-Ali (friends of Ali). Their political philosophy later turned into a religious one and Islam was divided into two sects—Shia and Sunni. Sunni sect of Islam was interpreted by different schools of thoughts but only four of them—Hanafi, Maliki, Humbali and Shafai are recognized by Sunni Muslims. Hanafi school of thought is most popular in Indian sub continent.

### Fundamental Beliefs and Tenets

*(i)* Faith in Allah, the prophets, the day hereafter, the angels, the holy books like Quran, Taurait, Zaboor and Injeel (Bible), faith in unseen objects mentioned in Quran and faith in good or bad destiny of life etc.

*(ii)* The purpose of Islam is to create peace in the world and to establish sovereignty of God on earth.

*(iii)* All human races are the descendents of only one father (Adam) and mother (Eve). Islam stunds for equality of all humans irrespective of caste, creed and colour.

*(iv)* Source of Islamic teaching is Quran and traditions and life of the Prophet Mohammad. Prophet's saying and life style were compiled into six books of Hadises in the very beginning. These six books are Bukhari, Muslim, Ibne Maja, Tirmazi, Nisai and Abu Dawood.

*(v)* God is only one. He has no son and polytheism of any type is not acceptable to God.

*(vi)* Means and ends both should be pious and purpose of creating muslims on earth is to establish peace and justice among humans irrespective of caste, creed or colour.

*(vii)* Five fundamentals of Islam are Faith, Namaz, Zakat, Ramazan and Hajj. Namaz is for God, Zakat is for helping poor and needy, Ramazan (fast) is for self purification and Hajj is for establishing universality of Islam.

*(viii)* Wiping out evils and flourishing good in the society are the important duties of muslims on earth. It will be done in the same way as Prophet used to do during his life time.

*(ix)* Protecting neighbours on individual basis and subjugated people on collective basis.

*(x)* Abiding by the law given about legitimates and illegitimates.

*(xi)* Right faith is essential for right action. Whether action is right or wrong will be judged on the basis of beliefs given in Quran and traditions of Prophet.

*(xii)* Jihad (Holy war) becomes incumbent on muslims when people are not allowed to follow the fundamentals of Islam. Killing of innocent

people even for the establishment of Islamic rule in the society is terrorism not jihad.

## Educational Tenets of Islam as given in the Holy Quran

The Holy Quran was revealed to Prophet Mohammed at intervals over a period of twenty-three years, partly while at Mecca,and partly while at Madina. Mecca-Madina are the places of Hajj pilgrimage, undertaken by devout muslims all over the world every year. In India these visits are highly subsidized by the State, and are a matter of discontent and controversy. All the holy shrines of Sunni muslims are located in Saudi Arabia, and those of the Shias, in Iraq. Karbala and Najaf are the two holy places of Shia Muslims. They are located in Iraq.

Quran begins with the very first words revealed to Mohammed,

"Read : in the name of the Lord who createth.

Created Man from a clot.

Read : Any thy lord is the most bounteous who teacheth by the pen.

Teacheth Man that which he knew not"

Man has the potential to raise himself to any level by following the teaching of the Lord, and has the capacity to understand and act upon his tenets. He, therefore, is an intelligent being capable of action, Islam as such is a religion of action and vibrance and does not abandon man. Man will be judged on the basis of his action and faith.

Education should, therefore, help man to rise to the prescribed level and potential. All this is possible through the teaching of the Holy Quran that ordains man to read and teach.

## Educational Implications of Islam

1. Education is sacred as it was Allah Himself who educated the first man.
2. More emphasis on reading and writing.
3. Islam recommended knowledge and education Prophet Mohammad declared.

   "Seeking knowledge is a religious duty for every Muslim, man and woman."

   "Seek knowledge from cradle to grave". Thus, Islam considers education as a continuous, life long process, much the same way the present day progressive educationists do. Islam had the vision of education that stood through the test of time and turbulation. There was no gender discrimination in education; women were as much entitled to education as the men were.
4. Education was not restricted to what went within the school premises alone : it had a wider meaning of education to include all kinds of experiences.

## Beliefs about Knowledge, Reality and Values

1. True knowledge is what that is given in Holy Book. It can be experimented by scientific methods but its finality can not be challenged.
2. Knowledge based on reason and experimentation is also true but only for the period till it is repudiated or rejected by other reasons and experimentations.
3. Physical objects as well as metaphysics like day of resurrection, heaven, hell etc all are real. Intutional knowledge is not real until it is substantiated by Quran and traditions.
4. Values are not changeable. They are fixed and rigid. They can not be manipulated on will. The authority in religion can manipulate them in the light of Quran and Hadith.
5. Islam is not against modernism provided that modernism is not against Islamic values and tenets.
6. No body can change any line of Quran and Hadith. Thus, fundamental truths can not be altered at all.
7. There may be many sects following Islam but belief in fundamentals will always be the same. Thus, plurality is permitted but with certain restrictions on it. This makes the truth fixed and unchanging. If anybody happens to give up Islam any time by rejecting its fundamental beliefs, he can not come back to the religion again any time in life. If Islamic government is there, the person will be beheaded by the judicial system of the state. Thus, rigidity is the chief characteristics of Islam.

## History of Compilation of Quran

Quran was revealed to the Prophet in parts in 22 years, 2 month and 23 days. The sequence of its verses is the same as was made by the Prophet himself. When any verse or surah was revealed to him, prophet immediately asked the writer to write it on the due place. Prophet himself did not know how to write. That was why he was called Ummy.

During Prophet's time some other people also copied the verses and kept them safe. There were many people in the society who memorized the whole Quran from beginning to end. During the regime of Abu, Bakre, about hundreds of Hafizs (those who memorized Quran fully) were killed in the battle of Yamama and the safety of Quran in intact form was feared. Seeing this Abu Bakre appointed Zaid son of Thabit to collect all the copies of Quran and its parts from the whole of Madina. Witness of two persons was also necessary to make any part of Quran valid and reliable. In this way, the whole of Quran was substantiated by a number of sources and one complete copy of Quran was prepared. This gigantic task was completed in two years and the copy was kept by Caliph Abu Bakre himself. After the death of second Caliph Omar, the copy was transferred to **Hafsah**, the widow of the Prophet.

During the regime of third Caliph Usman, several copies of this Quran were prepared by the order of the state and they were sent to different corners of the Islamic state for the use of the people. The phonetics of these copies of Quran was absolutely based on the phonetics of Quraish. These copies of Quran are known as Mashaf-e-Usmani.

### History of Compilation of Hadithes

During Prophet's time, instructions were given to the people by the Prophet orally. Prophet did not know how to write. Similarly, only few people were allowed to note down the sayings and actions of the Prophet. People, however, remembered the instructions, activities and decisions of the Prophet orally because of their fast and sharp memory.

Because of the above reasons only few written traditions of the Prophet are found during Prophet's time. Well known Hadith (tradition) writers were Abdullah s/o Omar, Abdullah s/o Maswood, Ali, Omar s/o Hazam etc.

People were allowed to write Hadithes in order to save the people from false Hadithes created by non believers of that time. These false Hadithes could misguide the people of that time.

The person who compiled a number of Hadithes after the demise of the Prophet was Ibn-e-Shahab Zohri. Imam Shafai, Imam Malik and Imam Ahmad were other persons who compiled Hadithes with great efforts.

Hadithes were systematically compiled by six learned scholars by following all the norms of compilation in which the narator of the Hadith as well as its sources both must be trustworthy on the technique of Asma-u-l-Rijal. The six compilations of Hadithes compiled by these scholars are known as Saha-e-Sitta.

## OBJECTIVE QUESTIONS

**1.** Pitaks were compiled in written form in
(*a*) 80 BC (*b*) 140 BC
(*c*) 2000 BC (*d*) 560 AD

**2.** The stories and legends on the life of Lord Buddha have been compiled in
(*a*) Tripitakas (*b*) Jatakas
(*c*) Both of these (*d*) None of these

**3.** Founder of Buddhism got Nirvan in
(*a*) 460 BC (*b*) 563 BC
(*c*) 663 BC (*d*) 483 BC

**4.** Buddha got enlightenment under a Pipal tree in Bodh Gaya at the age of
(*a*) 35 (*b*) 40
(*c*) 29 (*d*) 50

**5.** Which of the following does not belong to the four noble truths identified by Buddha?
(*a*) Life is suffering
(*b*) Desire is the cause of suffering
(*c*) Salvation is necessary
(*d*) Suffering can be extinguished

**6.** Buddhist philosophy mainly aimed at
(*a*) ending the suffering of the people
(*b*) making a caste free society
(*c*) coping with only physical problems of the world
(*d*) all of these

**7.** The philosophy of Madhyam Marg (Middle path) has been supported by

(a) Islamic religion (b) Buddhism
(c) Both of these (d) None of these

8. Non violence as a belief is accepted mainly by
(a) Buddhism (b) Jainism
(c) Christianity (d) All of these

9. Aims of education according to Buddhism is
(a) Nirvan through eight fold paths
(b) Pleasing God
(c) Extinction of sufferings
(d) None of the above

10. Which of the following was not approved by Buddha as method of instruction?
(a) Oral instruction and discussion
(b) Meditation
(c) Craft centred instruction
(d) Educational tours

11. Which of the following is not the part of Vedas?
(a) Rhythmical sentences-mantras
(b) Prayer details Brahmanas
(c) Books of forest dweller-aranyakas
(d) Samhitas

12. Which of the following statements about Vedangas is correct?
(a) They are six in number
(b) They give knowledge about 64 sciences
(c) They are in the form of prose.
(d) All of these

13. The approach of Hinduism is
(a) Pragmatic and empirical
(b) Rational and realistic
(c) Both of these
(d) None of these

14. Ultimate values proclaimed by Vedic religion is/are
(a) Dharma only
(b) Artha and Kama both
(c) Moksha and Kama both
(d) All of the above

15. Tamso ma jotirgamay means
(a) Bringing from disbelief to faith
(b) Bringing from darkness to light
(c) Both of these
(d) None of these

16. Goddess of Shakti is worshiped in
(a) Durga puja (b) Dushehra
(c) Holi (d) None of these

17. Theory of representative knowledge was accepted by
(a) Advaite Vedanta (b) Yoga
(c) Samkhya (d) All of these

18. The knowledge which is obtained by the interaction between a subject and an object is called
(a) Saskin Jnana (b) Vrtti janana
(c) Antah karan (d) None of these

19. According to Advaite Vedanta the levels of reality (satya) are
(a) two (b) three
(c) four (d) nine

20. Aims of education, according to Vedantic philosophy is
(a) Material gain
(b) Liberation from the worldly life
(c) Moral development of the child
(d) Both b & c

21. In Advaite Vedanta, **sarvana** refers to
(a) Ultimate truth which is learnt only through the study of revealed text
(b) True knowledge which is obtained only with the help of a guru
(c) Both of these
(d) None of these

22. Janana yoga-methodology realising moksha needs everything except
(a) Experimentation (b) Sarvana
(c) Manana (d) Nidhidhyasana

23. Which of the following does not come under the three levels of reality in AdvaiteVedanta?
(a) Pratibhasica satta (b) Pratihara satta
(c) Vyaviharica satta (d) Parmarthica satta

24. Jainism is similar to Buddhism in which of the following aspects?
(a) Repudiation of Vedas
(b) Pessimism
(c) Non violence as a philosophy
(d) All of these

25. The person who has successfully subdued his passions and obtained mastery over himself, according to Jainism is called
(a) Jina (b) Jiva
(c) Mukta (d) None

**26.** Vardhaman is the real name of
*(a)* Buddha *(b)* Mahavira
*(c)* Bhaskara *(d)* None of the above

**27.** Jain philosophy discards
*(a)* Karma *(b)* Yoga
*(c)* Meditation *(d)* None of these

**28.** Which of the following philosophies are most tilted to individualism?
*(a)* Jainism *(b)* Samkhya
*(c)* Buddhism *(d)* None of these

**29.** Aim of education according to Jainism is/are
*(a)* To enable the child to discriminate pap and pun
*(b)* Attainment of triratna
*(c)* Development of personality
*(d)* All of these

**30.** According to Jainism, knowledge is obtained through
*(a)* Senses *(b)* Meditation
*(c)* Both of these *(d)* None of these

**31.** When three qualities of Prakirti come in contact with Purush, universe was created. This is the belief of
*(a)* Samkhya *(b)* Buddha
*(c)* Mimansa *(d)* None of these

**32.** Dwadasa Nidan explains that .
*(a)* There are twelve causes of sufferings
*(b)* There are 12 paths to remove sufferings
*(c)* Both of these
*(d)* None of these

## ANSWERS

| 1 | 2 | 3 | 4 | 5 | 6 | 7 | 8 | 9 | 10 |
|---|---|---|---|---|---|---|---|---|---|
| *(a)* | *(b)* | *(d)* | *(a)* | *(c)* | *(d)* | *(c)* | *(d)* | *(a)* | *(c)* |
| **11** | **12** | **13** | **14** | **15** | **16** | **17** | **18** | **19** | **20** |
| *(d)* | *(d)* | *(c)* | *(d)* | *(b)* | *(a)* | *(d)* | *(b)* | *(b)* | *(d)* |
| **21** | **22** | **23** | **24** | **25** | **26** | **27** | **28** | **29** | **30** |
| *(c)* | *(b)* | *(d)* | *(a)* | *(a)* | *(b)* | *(a)* | *(a)* | *(d)* | *(c)* |
| **31** | **32** | | | | | | | | |
| *(a)* | *(a)* | | | | | | | | |

# Indian Philosophers and Education

## MAHATMA GANDHI (1869-1948)

### His Life Sketch

He was born on October 2, 1869 at Porbandar, Gujarat. He was married to Kasturba Gandhi at the age of 13. After passing Matriculation in 1887 he was sent to Bhavanagar for further studies but he could not stay there because of the dull and monotonous environment of the college. Then he was sent to England for the study of law. Before leaving for England he vowed before his mother that he would not touch meat, wine and woman during his stay in England. He established a vegetarian club in England to popularize this cult of life.

He passed his Bar at Law in 1891 and returned to Mumbai to start his Law practice there but his practice failed and he went to South Africa in 1893 to look after the business of an Indian Company there. The racist regime of South Africa was very much discriminatory against the coloured people including Indians. He put up a tough fight for the rights of his countrymen and the rights of black Africans there.

He decided to adopt Brahmacharya in 1906 for the sake of better dedication to the service of humanity. He founded the Tolstoy Farm where he and his co-workers lived a life of self discipline and dedication. He returned to India in 1915 and started a non violent movement and Satyagrah against the British masters here. He established his famous Sabarmati Ashram at Ahmedabad in 1917 which was the centre of politics, economic reforms and spiritual upliftment for almost four decades.

He actively participated in the war for freedom since a little before the end of the World War first. Since then he led the whole nation through Indian National Congress till the attainment of freedom in 1947. He launched three important movements during his leadership.

(*i*) Civil disobedience Movement.

(*ii*) Non cooperation Movement.

(*iii*) Quit India Movement.

When India got independence in 1947 communal riots broke out across the country. Millions lost their lives in these riots and many more would have lost their lives if Gandhijee had not acted very firmly. He was shot dead by a fundamentalist named Nathu Ram Godse on January 30, 1948 and thus the greatest apostle of peace and non-violence received his martyrdom by violence.

### His Philosophical Thoughts

1. **His socialism :** He believed in a classless society by decentralizing powers to village panchayats and parishads and by raising the economic standard of lower sections of the society. He wanted to create exploitation free society by increasing the employment opportunities for the poor. His socialism is different from that of Marx in the sense that Marx believed in the supremacy of mater while Gandhijee was the staunch supporter of spiritualism. Other differences between the two are given below:

   (*a*) He did not believe in the incumbency of class struggle like Marx.

   (*b*) He did not believe that state's ownership of means of production would end exploitation.

   In spite of these he had a strong faith in socio-economic equality of man.

2. **His non-violence:** He believed that if a person is resorted to violence to brutal forces, it only showes his weakness. Violence creates more violence and disruption in the society. If our cause

is really true we need only Satyagrah (request for truth) and people will sooner or later surrender to it. Thus, non-violence is a powerful weapon for strong minded people. He explained the meaning of Ahinsa in the following words.

"Ahinsa is complete absence of ill will against all that live. In its dynamic condition it means conscious suffering. Non-violence, in its active form, is goodwill towards all life. It is pure love". Thus, non-violence is complete self restraint against all evils.

3. **His ethics :** There must be only one system of morality according to which the private as well as public life of the individual should be moulded, directed and controlled. Truth, non-violence and purity of means are three values on the basis of which, the life of a person should be organized. If we want to achieve something very good, means adopted to achieve this end must also be very good based on truth and non-violence. These are universal values needed by every human being. If these values are followed, the contradiction between words and action will be removed.

4. **His religion :** He was strong follower of Hinduism though he was opposed to traditions and conventions. In spite of it he wanted to find out the basic truths of all religions that was truth, love for humanity and equality of man. That was why he did not oppose any religion in his life. He even recited the verses of Quran and Bible in his daily prayers.

   The aim of religion according to him is to make a Hindu a better Hindu, to make a Muslim a better Muslim, to make a Christian a better Christian and so on.

5. **His political ideas :** His political ideas are summarized below :

   *(a)* That government is the best that governs the least. Thus, he favoured decentralization and purely federal form of the government.

   *(b)* Welfare state is a must to create a classless society.

   *(c)* He did not believe in representative form of democracy as it promotes corruption and hypocrisy. His concept of democracy was metaphysical. He believed that each and every member of the society should have his say in political matters and state affairs through local government. Thus, according to him, the law and role of majority has little application in matters of conscience.

   *(d)* He believed in Panchayati Raj system to carry the fruits of freedom to the masses. Thus, real state will emerge from below and every village will be organized on cooperative basis. This idea of Gandhijee was put into practical shape in India only in 1993.

   *(e)* Charkha should be used to revive the entire economic life of the people of villages. By the word Charkha he strongly favoured the installation of cottage industries. He wanted to make the masses economically strong and such a strength is necessary for political strength and progress of the country. Such was his economic beliefs.

6. **His concept of truth :** His aim of life was to realize God. He firmly believed that it is God who has created this universe. It is mortal. Only God is immortal. Truth is the only method to realize this immortal God. According to him, there is no difference between truth and God. God is the ultimate truth. Truth does not mean the truthfulness of words or speech only but it is applicable to all aspects of human life by purity of means and action. Every one must try to find out this truth.

7. **Means and ends :** The ends pre-exist in means. So right means must be employed to realize the right and noble ends, e.g., achieving freedom is a noble cause but it can not be achieved by violence. Purity of means is equally necessary even in social affairs of life.

8. **Satyagrah :** Gandhijee explained Satyagrah as holding fast to death. Here the opposite party is not given any pain-mental or physical. Pain is rather borne by the satyagrahi with such an everlasting impression that opposite party is automatically persuaded to accept the truth. Thus, it is the change on opponent's hearts by means of self suffering with strict adherence to truth.

## His Educational Thoughts

Gandhijee was not technically an educationist like Tagore or Aurobindo but his views on basic education testifies to the fact that he was a social educator. He advocated social revolution (reform) to go hand in hand with any political revolution and education is an important means to bring about any social revolution and reform. His educational ideas are summarized below :

### A. Principles of Education

1. Education of children upto 14 years of age should be free, compulsory and universal.
2. Mother tongue should be the medium of instruction and english should not be given any importance in the curriculum.
3. Making the people literate is not making them educated, education is a much higher process. It should develop human values in the child and should enable the child to realize the ultimate truth (God) through non violence and purity of means.
4. Education should develop all powers of the child to adjust in the community to which he belongs.
5. Education should develop the total personality of the child, his mind, body and soul.
6. To enable the child to earn his living, craft should be the medium of instruction. It is a must for the economic self reliance of the child. These crafts should be correlated with the local industries, i.e., the crafts for a child should be locally chosen. The main aim of basic education is to purify the heart and mind of the people and create a society free from all exploitations and aggressions.
7. Child should also be given work experience through practical training. Theoretical knowledge without getting it into practice is useless.
8. Schools should be made a place of activity for the child. All work experiences should be given to the child in schools.
9. Education should make responsible, useful and dynamic citizens.
10. Inculcation of universal moral values through education in the child is the pre-requisite for achieving any success in the field of education.

### B. Meaning of Education

In the words of Gandhijee, "Literacy is neither the beginning nor the end of education. This is only a means through which man or woman can be educated. By education, I mean an all round drawing out of the best in the child's and man's body, mind and spirit."

Thus, we see that Gandhijee distinguished between literacy and education. Literacy is a must for receiving any type of education and it will lead to all round development of child's personality. This will be possible only when education is imparted through local crafts.

### C. Aims of Education

Gandhijee has classified educational aims into two categories given below :

**I. Immediate Aims of Education :**

(a) *Vocational aims :* A child should learn a productive craft to meet his future economic and bread-butter needs of life. After education, he will be able to earn his living by starting his own vocation or by joining an industry. By this aim of education Gandhijee does not want to turn the child into a physical labourer. He only wants that the child should be self reliant and not a parasite on others after education. At the time of Gandhijee, Khadi and Charkha was an important vocational field. Today it can be the computer industry and programming.

(b) *Cultural aim :* Education must make a child Indian in behaviour and attitude. He must be identified with the culture he belongs to. In the words of Gandhijee

"I consider the cultural aspect of education as more important than its academic one. Culture is the main foundation and an essential and special part of education. Hence, all types of human activities must bear the imprint of culture and refinement."

Thus Gandhijee strongly favoured cultural function of education.

(c) *Perfect development aim :* Gandhijee wants an alround development of individual's personality by developing his mind, body and soul. Physical abilities are needed for his economic life, mental abilities for individual and social life and development of soul is essential for realization of God.

(d) *Character development aim :* Education must build a man of strong character. For this purpose essentials of all religions should be taught to him. Character building is the essential basis of educational development according to him.

(e) *Liberation aim :* He advocates two kinds of liberation. One was the liberation from all kinds of economic, social, political and mental slavery. Second kind of liberation is the liberation of the soul from worldly persuits and devote itself to higher form of spiritual living. Both these two types of liberations should be provided by education to the child.

**II. Ultimate Aim of Education:**

Ultimate aim of education according to him is actually the realization of God through self restraint and perseverance. Education must keep all other aims under this aim.

## D. Curriculum

Gandhijee's scheme of education is known as "Basic Education". Important characteristics of this education are as follows:

(a) *Education through handicraft :* In this scheme of education an attempt is made to establish a direct relationship between knowledge and life. Every thing is taught to the child through the medium of crafts. His crafts is also sold in the market and thus child is made an earning member of the society. Even language is taught through crafts. Thus, craft is made the centre of education. This is actually called Wardha scheme of education.

(b) *Child centred education :* Child is made the centre of education along with crafts selected for him. Craft is used to develop the personality of the child comprehensively.

(c) *Systematic organisation of knowledge :* Knowledge through crafts is organized very systematically here. Nothing is imposed on the child against his wishes. Child is not only taught to spin and weave but he is also taught how cotton is produced and what are ideal conditions for its cultivation and so on.

(d) *Flexible curriculum :* Teachers and students are free to work according to their interests and local needs. Necessary changes may be introduced by the teacher on his own if need arises.

Basic education curriculum is designed for children from 7-14 years. The structure of curriculum is given below:

- General Science for boys and Home Science for girls.
- Co-education upto class fifth only.
- Important crafts included in the curriculum are Spinning and Weaving, Carpentary, Agriculture, Fruits and flower cultivation, Book Craft, Leather work, Pisiculture, or any craft needed locally.
- Mother tongue, the medium of instruction.
- Mathematics to develop calculation ability.
- History, Geography and Civics in all classes.
- Painting and music since the beginning.
- PT, Drill and sports.
- Subjects included in General Science are Physics, Chemistry, Biology, Hygiene and Nature study.
- Hindi for that area where it is not the mother tongue of the people. English has not been given any place in the curriculum.
- Religious education also does not occupy any place in the curriculum. Self realization is the greatest religion according to Gandhijee. Character of the child will be built by the ideal character and behaviour of the teacher.

## E. Method of Teaching

By discarding subject centred education, Gandhijee, for the first time advocated craft based child centred education. He said that local crafts should be made the medium of education so that child might develop his body, mind and soul in a harmonious manner. The likely methods of teaching to further craft centred education are given below:

(a) *Learning by doing :* Every thing is taught to the child by activity and practical works of crafts. Even alphabet are taught through the practice of arts. For this purpose, children are given Art training first.

(b) *Learning by experience :* Children are not taught everything by the teacher. Knowledge is organized very systematically for them and then they learn many of the thing through their own experiences. Efforts are also made to establish correlation between teaching methods and learning experiences.

(c) *Project method :* Students are also assigned various projects by the teacher. They complete the projects by the cooperation of their fellow being. This project is evaluated on the basis of the usefulness and beauty of the items prepared by them.

## Influence of Gandhijee's Philosophy and Scheme of Education :

1. Job oriented technical and vocational education gained recognition and popularity under the influence of this philosophy. Such educations are introduced in India after class Xth. This shows a slight departure from the scheme of Gandhijee but basic philosophy of both are the same after all.
2. Gandhijee advocates a scheme of education based on the essential values of Indian Culture and civilization. Such education will essentiality keep Indians to remain Indian in spirit and modernisation will not effect their Indianness.
3. Gandhijee keeps the dignity of labour at the top. Only white collar jobs should not be regarded a sign of high status. A carpenter or a toy seller is equally high in status in the society as far as realization of God through the practice of truth and non violence is concerned.
4. Gandhijee was Idealist in his soul but Naturalist and Pragmatist in action. He translated all his ideas and ideals into practice by a harmonious blending of these philosophies. Thus, his views taught us that there is no need to stick to a single philosophy in life.
5. His realization of God is done neither in a temple performing rituals nor in jungles practicing isolated-meditations. A man can reach and realize his God while doing his menial and manual jobs. Thus, Gandhijee for the first time blended religion with our routine life. We can remain staunch Hindu or Muslim while living a *Grihast* life.
6. Gandhijee advocates the development of a child according to his interest, abilities and needs. Thus, his pragmatic views are very much acceptable to a democratic society.

## Criticism :

Gandhijee's scheme of basic education has been criticised on the following grounds:

1. School will require so many crafts according the local needs and specific interests of children. It will require a number of teachers trained in specific crafts to teach in the school. This is actually a real challenge before this scheme because the cost of this type of education will be very high.
2. It is very difficult to correlate a craft with other crafts and to give all necessary informations to the child through the crafts only.
3. This scheme takes eight years to get completed. Skills obtained during this period may be outdated after the completion of education.
4. It is very difficult to prepare study materials of this scheme. Organisation of materials is another difficulty before a teacher.
5. It is almost impossible to provide work experiences of so many crafts especially in schools located in big cities.
6. Developing character and personality through crafts alone is only a theoretical proposition. No school in India has got any success in this regard.
7. This Scheme of education may be suitable for the children of poor class families but those who are interested in higher studies will not be benefitted after receiving this type of education.
8. This scheme of education is very costly for a poor country like India.

## RAVINDRA NATH TAGORE (1861-1941)

### His Life Sketch

- He was born in Kolkata in a rich and educated family.
- He was taught Sanskrit, Indian philosophy and Astronomy first by his father Davendra Nath Tagore.
- He received higher education from Bengal Academy but he left the Academy before the completion of his course because of its dull and rigid nature of education.
- He was sent to England in 1877 to study law. Here too he was fed up with the system and returned to India without degree.

- He used to write articles for Bengali magazine since very early age.
- He became famous because of his stories, novels and poems. He became famous as a philosopher and a painter too and people began to address him as Gurudev in reverence.
- He translated his **Geetanjali** into English also which brought him noble prize and world wide recognition.
- He was also conferred the honorary degree of Doctor of Literature by Calcutta University.
- He was endowed with knighthood in 1915 by the British government which he returned after the massacre of Jalianwala Bagh.
- He established his famous Vishva Bharti on 22nd September 1921. The aim of this university was to bring about a synthesis between East and the West. For the development of this university he worked hard for 20 years and provided it a solid foundation.

## His Philosophical Thoughts

1. He very successfully incorporated Idealism into Naturalism.
2. He believed in the absolute and immortal existence of God. But his God was a superman and he considered this world as his best creation.
3. He also believed in the philosophy of liberation. He said, "We should try to search for God and thus realize that truth which will liberate us from material bonds of existence and which is capable of illuminating the whole world with its divine light."
4. God is one and it is He who has created human being and material world (nature). We perceive a unity in him and through him the fraternal bonds between all human beings and the external nature.
5. He was a Humanist and regarded man as a reflection of God. As such there is no distinction between man and man at all.
6. He wanted to elevate human soul by establishing a close relation with God. For this, moral and mental progress of man is a must.
7. He strongly favoured social reforms, national and communal integration and opposed untouchability of all forms.
8. He wanted to study nature by observation and experiments both. Nature is very much reflected in his poetry, novels, stories and paintings.
9. There is a fundamental unity between nature and man. Nature is nothing but reflection of God in physical form. Education should promote this unity through love of nature.
10. He opposed the rigid and lifeless system of current education and insisted that education should acquaint the child with the voice and missions of the individual in national and international perspectives.
11. Child should enjoy complete freedom to develop according to his nature. Nature is an effective and powerful teacher of the child.
12. Education is a vehicle of social reform if education is to prepare the child to serve the humanity.
13. A child should be educated according to the realities of life. It should prepare the child to face the real challenges of life.
14. He translated his ideas into practice by establishing Shantiniketan at 120 Kolkata where Arts and culture are flourishing in the same way as it was suggested by Tagore. Thus we see that Tagore is a man of practice also.

## His Educational Thoughts

**1. His Principles of Education:**

*(a)* Mother tongue should be the medium of instruction.

*(b)* Child should be given full freedom during his education. If he is given opportunities for self expression, his creativity will prosper.

*(c)* Child should be educated in the lap of nature away from the crowded environment of towns and cities.

*(d)* In order to develop sense of social service in the child, he should be provided opportunities for social contact.

*(e)* Foreign education can do nothing in awakening national spirit. Children will come to know about national ideals, values and culture through national education.

*(f)* Education should bring about all round development of child's personality.

(g) Children should not be compelled to acquire bookish knowledge, knowledge acquired from original sources is the best.

(h) Education should not make children to become successful farmers, clerks or craftsmen but it should develop them as a complete human being.

**2. Meaning of Education :**

Tagore is of the view that God reveals himself through nature more effectively than through man made institutions. So a child must be educated in a natural environment so that he may develop a deep love for nature on one hand and love for other living being on the other, Tagore said, "That education is highest which not only imparts information and knowledge to us but also promotes love and fellow feeling between us and other living being of the world"

**3. Aims of Education :**

Tagore was not technically an educationist in the sense that he has not written any book on this subject. Following aims of education have been derived from his speeches and short writings.

1. Physical development of the child through education should be given the first priority. Children should be motivated to participate in activities like swimming, climbing trees and plucking fruits from trees, games and sports etc. He also prescribes healthy diet given to students.
2. In order to promote mental development of the child their curiosity should be aroused through activities, self experiences and self learning.
3. Promotion of moral and spiritual development of the child is also necessary to realise the superman who is God. Children must know the importance of mutual cooperation, tolerance, courtesy etc.
4. Drawing out of inner and latent faculties of the child is another aim of education. For this purpose children should be given full freedom to exploit nature to the maximum level possible. Meaning thereby the individuality of the child should never be crushed by traditional, rigid and lifeless rules and regulations of the school system.
5. Each child has so many creative powers. They should be developed by providing conducive natural environment to him.
6. Education should also develop international understanding and sensitivity in the child. It is because individual child is a part of nature not a part of particular society or culture.

**4. Curriculum :**

Curriculum should be such as to develop the child physically, mentally, morally, socially and spiritually. For this purpose, curriculum based on activities and broad self experiences in real life situations is needed. Efforts should be made to give bookish knowledge as less as possible. Moreover, along with the teaching of formal subjects co-curricular activities like, dancing, music, painting, singing, designing, sewing, cutting, knitting, games, sports and cooking (for girls) should also be included in the curriculum. In short, a child should be taught every thing that he needs. That is why we see that History, Geography, Agriculture, Nature study, Field study, Horticulture, Gardening, Fine Arts, Music, Sculpture, Vocational, Professional and Technical subjects—everything is taught in Vishva Bharti.

**5. Method of Teaching :**

Tagore was totally against the dull and mechanical methods of teaching prevailing in his time. He advocated that methods of teaching should be full of life and vitality. They should be based on real problems of life. Child should be given more and more opportunities to investigate the phenomenon by his own activities and experiences and gain knowledge directly. Important methods prescribed by him are as follows :

(a) *Teaching While Walking :* If children are sitting idle in the class, their minds will also be passive and dull. On the other hand if they are slowly walking, minds will be alert. If something is taught to them while walking they will easily grasp them.

(b) *Discussion Method :* Education is that which solves the real problems of life. So problems must be put before children for open discussion. They will think over the problems logically and finally solve them.

(c) *Activity Method :* Activities must be incorporated in all subjects. Tagore advocated that learning of handicrafts is necessary for all students. Physical exercises and games must be made the part of activities in schools.

6. **Discipline :**

Child is given full freedom for his activities and experiences without lowering down the status of the teacher in the class. The teacher considers the children innocent and behaves them with great love, affection and sympathy. He is not a dictator in the class to impose bookish knowledge. He rather creates a conducive environment and children learn themselves with the help of nature. Thus, along with the students teacher is also all the time active in the class or outside the class with his students.

## COMPARISON BETWEEN RAVINDRA NATH TAGORE AND GANDHIJEE

1. Unlike Gandhijee Tagore also did not believe in any particularism. He only wanted to develop the soul of man without disregarding his body and nature. That was what Gandhijee emphasized by his principles of truth, nonviolence and purity of means.
2. Both wanted to blend the culture of the East with the knowledge and progress of the West. Here vision of Tagore is more impressive and dominant than that of Gandhijee.
3. Tagore was a poet and Artist while Gandhijee was a politician and saint. So it is very difficult to compare them. Tagores sees beauty in every thing of nature while Gandhijee wants to use nature as less as possible.
4. Both of them had almost similar goals but their approaches were different, e.g., Gandhijee practiced fully disciplined and regulated life while Tagore favoured a natural life of an ordinary man.
5. Gandhijee was born in a middle class Vaishya family of Gujarat while Tagore belonged to an aristocrat Brahmin family of W. Bengal. So, life styles of both of them were also very different. This difference in life styles is very much manifested in their ideas.
6. The truth and non-violence forcefully explained in the philosophy of Gandhijee does not exist in Tagore.
7. There is no difference in private and public lives of Gandhijee which were the real explanations of his philosophy but we see a thick curtain before the private life of Tagore.
8. Both were extremely religious with different visions.
9. There is full agreement between the two as far as realization of ultimate truth (God) is concerned. But in order to attain this ideal both adopted their own distinct way. Though neither of two sought God in the privacy of a temple, in the solitude of a cave or in the piety of rituals. Both of them sought God in the hearts and minds of the people and in the service of humanity.
10. Gandhijee's willingness and capacity to suffer was much greater than that of Tagore.
11. Unlike Gandhijee Tagore did not believe in a classless society.
12. Tagore has not put up any political philosophy like that of Gandhijee.

## AUROBINDO GHOSH (1872-1950)

### His Life Sketch

He was born in 1872 in Kolkata. He was sent to England to study there at the age of 6 where he grew up with the adherence of European culture. He mastered Greek and Latin languages to study the works of ancient European philosophers, social engineers and poets. He also learnt French, German and Italian languages. He passed Indian Civil Service Examination held in England in 1890 but could not appear in the horse riding test. As a result, he was disqualified for the job and returned to India in 1893.

In India he studied Sanskrit language and literature and also served for 14 years in the State of Baroda. After the Bengal partition disturbances, he resigned from his job and joined the national movement for India's struggle for freedom. He roused the nationalist feeling among Indians through his firy speeches and three news papers namely, **Bande Matram, Karma Yogi** and **Dharm**. He was sent to jail several times because of his political and nationalist activities.

Once he was in Alipur jail, he realized the presence of God in his dream. He was so much fascinated with the divine vision that after his release from the jail in 1915, he shunned all his political activities immediately and lived a retired life in Pondicherry as a seer. He opened an Ashram there which is known as Aurobindo Ashram today. He spent the rest of his life in the Ashram doing yoga, sadhna, and meditation and for his spiritual advancement he kept least touch with this material world. He preached his philosophy of dharma, education, spiritual advancement, brahmacharya and yoga across the country. He died in 1950 as a great saint.

## His Philosophical Ideas

Philosophical ideas of Aurobindo mostly taken from his weekly newspaper 'Karma Yogi', are summarized below :

1. He was basically an idealist. His idealistic philosophy of life is based on the philosophy of Upanishads. He streesed a lot on the spiritual penance.
2. Yogic practices, Sadhna and Brahmacharya are necessary for the promotion and development of human soul.
3. Growth and development is not a long jump or high jump process. It is always guarded by a certain principle. The aim of this principle of growth is to achieve all the divine powers through yoga and meditation. This principle of growth continues to operate in all conditions and in all times and places, i.e. acquisition of divine power is universal. It is not restricted to a particular community or country.
4. The principle of growth states that a man can attain the status of a superman himself by virtue of his supreme development of mental power. Thus a man grows from knowledge to more knowledge and from enlightenment to more enlightenment step by step. When he reaches at the top he experiences the supreme happiness and the divine bliss. Here man develops insight into all creations and the inner spirit of cosmos which are actually the creation of God. Thus, he does not consider God as superman like Tagore. God is above all the creatures.
5. The main aid of a teacher is his conscience. This conscience has four stages namely *(i)* Consciousness, *(ii)* Mind, *(iii)* Intelligence, *(iv)* Knowledge. Education should develop all these stages as much as possible.
6. A man does not possess a physical spirit only. He is endowed with higher mental abilities, Godly intelligence and a very high spiritual soul element. In order to realize these potentialities, he should develop his power of thinking, concentration and deep meditation together with the other divine faculties to the fullest.
7. Real education is that which makes the child free and creative. This education is provided in a free environment. Here efforts are made to develop interest, creativity, mental power and aesthetic senses of the child. All these finally leads to the development of his spiritual power. In other words, we can say that physical development leads to mental development of the child and mental development leads to highest spiritual development.
8. Humans are the elements and gifts of divine power (nature). This power has given them full freedom to develop by coming in contact with the environment.

In short we can say that Aurobindo, with the admission of spirituality or God, is a Humanist whose main aim is to make the society good in all respects.

## His Educational Ideas

**(A) Meaning of Education:** According to him, education should be according to mental and spiritual needs of children and demands of the country. Thus education should be in accordance with the changing needs of our real modern life so that children may face the present challenges of life with ease.

According to him, "Education to be true must not be a machine made fabric but a true building or living evocation of the powers of mind and spirit of human being."

**(B) Aims of Education:**

*1. Physical purity and development* : According to him, it is body which performs all religious functions, so it must be fit and purified. Without physical progress and purity, spiritual development is also not possible.

2. *Training of senses :* Senses are the important sources of knowledge so they must be trained to the full. And they can be fully trained only when nerve, chitta and manas are pure. This purity of senses or mind is achieved through education.
3. *Mental development :* Mental development means the development of all mental faculties such as memory, thinking, reasoning, special relationship, imagination, discrimination and generalisation etc.
4. *Development of morality :* According to him, without moral and emotional development mental development of the child may prove to be harmful. Moral development of the child requires development of emotions, habits and temperament. These three factors are purified and sublimated by education. In order to develop emotions, hearts of children should be so developed as to show extreme love, sympathy, cooperation and consideration for all living beings. For this purpose, the ideal of a teacher should be so high that children can reach higher and higher stages of moral development by mere imitation.
5. *Development of conscience :* Conscience has four levels according to him, namely- Chitta, Manas, Intelligence and Knowledge. All these levels should be developed harmoniously step by step. Before reaching the highest level, a teacher makes it sure that spiritual development has been achieved otherwise such a knowledgeable person will create chaos in the society.
6. *Spiritual development :* This is actually main aim of education according to Aurobindo. Every individual has some element of divinity in him. The teacher should first of all, find it out, then nourish it through yogic exercises and adoption of Brahmacharya.
7. *Development of hidden potentialities :* Every child has some latent physical, mental, and spiritual potentialities. The task of the teacher is to draw out these potentialities in a harmonious manner. This turns the child into a complete man, i.e., superman.

**(C) Curriculum :** Only those subjects and activities are to be included in the curriculum which the students are interested in. Such subjects and activities must also posses creativity and educational expression. After all curriculum must be able to make a child into a superman. Ghosh has prescribed five principles of curriculum construction which are as follows :

*(i)* Curriculum should be interesting for the child.
*(ii)* It should consist of those subjects and activities which can promote mental and spiritual development of the child.
*(iii)* It should be able to motivate the children for learning.
*(iv)* It should be able to activate the creative potentialities of children.
*(v)* It should be so up-to-date and enriched that it can make the child a superman.

Keeping the above principles into account, Aurobindo has prescribed following subjects to be included in the curriculum at various levels of education.

- *Primary Stage :* Mother-tongue, English, French, Literature, National History, Arts, Painting, General Science, Social Studies and Arithmetic.
- *Secondary Stage :* Mother tongue, English, French, Arithmetic, Arts, Physics, Chemistry, Biology, Physiology, Health Education and Social Studies.
- *University Education :* Indian and Western philosophies, History of Civilization, English Literature, French Literature, Sociology, Psychology, History of Science, Physics, Chemistry, Zoology, Botany and International relations.
- *Vocational Education :* Arts, Painting, Photography, Sewing, Sculptural drawing, Typing, Shorthand, Cottage Industries, Carpentary, Mechanical and Electrical Engineering, Nursing, Indian and European Music, Drama and Dancing.

**(D) Method of Teaching :** Following principles should be followed by the teacher in the teaching learning process.

1. *Freedom to the child :* Free environment should be created for children so that they may gain more and more knowledge by their own efforts. If any restriction is imposed on them it will retard their natural growth and development.
2. *Mother tongue, the medium of instruction:* Children should be imparted education through their mother tongue. It will increase their grasping capacities and they will learn even difficult subjects easily.
3. *Sympathetic attitude towards children :* Utmost love and sympathy should be shown by the teacher for his pupils in the class. This will reduce tension of learning from the minds of pupils.
4. *Principle of interest :* Children can be motivated in the class only when education is given to them according to their specific interests. For this purpose, teacher should first study the varied interests of his pupils.
5. *Principle of self experience :* Children should be given freedom to initiate them to learn by their own efforts and experiences. This type of learning is very useful for their future life. So, the activities of the teacher should be kept to the minimum.
6. *Principal of learning by doing :* Aurobindo gave very much emphasis on the activities of pupils. Whatever they learn from books, it should be supplemented by experimentation. Montessori method of teaching for primary classes and practice of drawing in secondary classes are suitable methods of teaching according to him.
7. *Principle of group learning :* According to him, teaching and learning is a cooperative process. So, there must be full cooperation between teacher and his pupils on one hand and among pupils themselves on the other.
8. *Education according to the nature of children :* Each child has been gifted by nature some mental and spiritual potentialities. Teacher should try to develop these potentialities to the maximum level possible. In this way, the elements of divinity present in the child will give him some divine power.
9. *Principle of need of the child :* While imparting education specific needs of the child must be taken into account. These needs can be found out by studying their interests and attitudes.
10. *Sensory approach :* Senses are the gateway of knowledge. So, senses of children should be trained properly to acquire knowledge and experience. From this point of view Aurobindo is a Realist.

**(E) Discipline :** According to Aurobindo, the child has his own interest and potentialities. To develop these divine gifts fully is the chief purpose of education. For this purpose, child is given full freedom to express and act without any restriction imposed on him. Teacher does not interfere in the self experience of his pupils. He is not an instructor or task master. He is only a helper and guide in the class. His business is to suggest not to impose. He actually does not impart knowledge. He rather shows his pupils the way to acquire knowledge that is within themselves.

In conclusion we can say that Aurobindo was a philosopher who integrated Western philosophy with the Indian one. Because of this reason his philosophy led the people from extreme materialism to spiritualism. He vehemently condemned Western materialistic education and said that it could not sustain Indian beliefs and culture. Aurobindo wants to make the Indian society good and happy by making the individuals good through education, so he can also be called a Humanist with God, though he is essentially an Upanishadic Idealist.

## SWAMI VIVEKANAND (1863-1902)

### His Life Sketch

He was born in Kolkata. His real name was Narendra Nath Dutta. He inherited religious temperament and farsighted intelligence from his father. He was sent to school at five years of age. He studied History, Literature and Philosophy since very early age. Herbert Spencer and J.S.Mill were his favorite Philosophers and Wordsworth was his favorite poet. One day his headmaster Mr. Heasty introduced him to Shri Ram Krishna Paramhansa and Narendra Nath remained in his contact for about six years. Here he got initiated into the saintly order and was given the title of Swami Vivekananda. When Swami Ram Krishna Paramhansa died in 1876, Swami Vivekanand established Ram Krishna Mission to proceed the unfinished religious assignments of his Guru further. He spread the message of his Guru that was actually the principle and practice of Vedanta in Asia, Europe and America.

As a philosopher he proved that the ancient philosophy of Vedanta could successfully meet the challenges of today and solve the modern problems very effectively. He was actually the person who synthesised the Idealistic philosophy of the West and creative Vedantic philosophy of Hindu religion. He preached universal brotherhood and interpreted Humanism in his Idealistic manner. He died young.

## His Philosophical Thoughts

Philosophical ideas of Vivekanand are summarized below :

1. Human life is a constant struggle between the strong and the weak. In this struggle of life only victorious will be able to survive and the defeated will die out. So, every individual should prepare himself for this struggle and face all the challenges boldly and confidently.
2. Fear and lack of confidence are the root cause of miserable conditions of Indians. He said, "We do any work in fear, we speak in fear, we even think in fear. It appears that we are born in a land of enemies and not of friends. This abject condition is due to our disconnection from the philosophy of Vedanta."
3. Boldness and courage are needed to bring about peace in the society. A coward and an indifferent person can do nothing in his life. The world can be uplifted and made free from sins by brave men only. So we should become brave in our temperament and dynamic in our approach. He would often say, "I have no fear. Tell this to everybody – have no fear. Tell him (people) fear is sin, fear is hell, fear is unrighteousness, fear is wrong life."
4. Service of humanity is the prime object of life. We can serve humanity by becoming fearless and by making ourselves fit for struggles of life.
5. Swami Vivekanand propagated Indian nationalism by glorifying ancient Indian culture and preached spiritualism. His spiritualism was not the renunciation of worldly life. Everybody can nourish this spiritualism by living in the society and serving the humanity. He believed that every living being has a soul. To identify this soul is true religion.
6. All knowledge—worldly or spiritual are latent in the human mind. It is dormant and covered with a veil of darkness and ignorance. Once this darkness or ignorance is removed, the light of knowledge shines out brightly.
7. All learning is self learning. Knowledge is latent. Thus, it is not taught by anybody. The external teacher only guides, suggests and helps. All the rest is done by the students themselves. It is the teacher who encourages and guides the students to find out the hidden treasure of knowledge that lies inactive within the individual.
8. He condemned the education of his time as wicked, useless and artificial. According to him, real education is that education which prepares a man for struggle of survival. It is not merely passing examinations and getting degrees. Education must develop character, intelligence and self reliance in the individuals. Thus, Vivekanand advocates simultaneous development of body, mind and spirit.
9. Knowledge of Western technology and industrial education is a must for the national progress of the country. He vehemently condemned the theoretical and academic knowledge and said "You will have to be practical in all spheres of work. The whole country has been ruined by mass theories".
10. Concentration is needed for acquiring knowledge. For this purpose practice of Brahmacharya is necessary.
11. For self discipline purity of thought, speech and action is needed.
12. Human development is possible through service and sacrifice. Unless people are ready to serve

their fellow being and sacrifice their lives for the sake of others, peace and prosperity will not be achieved in the society.

13. Religious education should be imparted through sweet impressions and fine conduct of the teacher not through books.
14. Any improvement in the condition of the masses can be brought about only through education, so mass education scheme should be launched. Boys and girls should be given the same type of education but religious education should be imparted to women especially. It is because the role of character formation of children especially lies on their shoulders.
15. Education should be imparted according to the nature of the child and his natural propensities.
16. He was very sad to see the deplorable condition and poverty of the masses. He said, "Great national sin is neglecting of the masses and it is one of the causes of our downfall. No amount of politics would be of any avail until the masses of India are well educated, well fed and well cared for.

## His Educational Thoughts

**(A) Meaning of Education :** Education is not the tit-bits of knowledge or information inserted into the minds of children by force. According to Swamijee if education means information only, then libraries could be the greatest saints of the world and encyclopaedia had become seers and rishis. "Education is actually the manifestation of perfection already reached in a man." Thus, merely passing examination or receiving degree is not education according to him. Education is that process which prepares a man for struggle of existence by making him self reliant and by developing his character and intelligence. It is, in fact, a life long process.

**(B) Aims of Education:**

1. *Making a man perfect :* Education makes a man perfect by diagnosing the perfection which is already present in him. All material and spiritual knowledge is already present in man but it is covered with a veil of ignorance. Education should remove this veil and bring him to the level of self actualization.
2. *Developing the child physically and mentally :* After studying Geeta the child becomes able to promote national growth. It is because by knowing the philosophy of Karma propounded by Geeta he becomes a fearless and physically strong citizen of tomorrow. Mental development of the child is promoted by the study of Vedanta and modern sciences.
3. *Moral and spiritual development of the Child:* According to Swamijee, a nation's greatness is measured not only by its parliamentary institutions and mere material well being but by the greatness of its citizens morally and spiritually. Education should foster these qualities in them.
4. *Character formation :* Brahmacharya should be practiced for building a strong character. Education should prepare such men who have no contradiction between their words and deeds.
5. *Development of faith and shraddha in God and oneself :* Education should prepare such a people who are always prepared for self surrender, sacrifice and renunciation of material comforts for the benefit of others. Others are always given priority to oneself according to him.
6. *Development of oneness feeling :* According to him, material and spiritual worlds are essentially one and the same. If there appears any distinction, it is because of the illusion. Education must remove this illusion. Moreover, material world itself is full of so many diversities which is dividing the humanity on various lines. Education must develop an insight into the people that they can perceive the ultimate unity in such diversities.
7. *Preparation of bold citizens :* Fear is the main cause behind all social and individual problems. Education should remove this fear and make the citizens bold and brave to face the challenges of life.
8. *Scientific and technological progress :* Renunciation of Swamijee does not mean total renunciation of the world. We have to live in this world and struggle for our survival. Material and technological progress is a must for this. Education of Western science and technology is to be given due emphasis for this purpose.

**(C) Curriculum :** In order to achieve the above mentioned aims those subjects and activities should be included in the curriculum which can bring about material progress along with spiritual development. For material progress he advocated the study of Languages, Geography, Science, Political science, Economics, Psychology, Arts, Agriculture and Industrial and Technical subjects along with the subject of Physical Education. This education must neither be theoretical nor bookish. It should rather be practical. For spiritual development he prescribed the study of Religion, Philosophy, Puranas and Upanishads and the company of saints and seers. Religious education should be imparted through sweet impressions and fine conduct of teachers rather than through books.

**(D) Method of Teaching :** He prescribed the same ancient methods of instruction which were in practice in Gurukuls. In that system Guru and his disciple lived in close association like the members of a family. Other characteristics of this method are given below :

*(i)* Practice of Yoga for controlling mind and emotions.

*(ii)* Deep meditation for the development of mind.

*(iii)* Self learning-Guru will work as a guide and helper only.

*(iv)* Activities for developing creative potentials.

*(v)* Lecture and discussion methods for elaborating essential facts.

*(vi)* Behavioural change through a fine model presented by the teacher.

*(vii)* Individual guidance by the teacher given to students.

**(E) Discipline :** He emphasized child-centred education in which child is given full freedom for activity and self learning. He should be given full opportunity to develop in a natural environment. According to Swamijee, each child is his own teacher. He has knowledge latent in his mind. The task of the external teacher is only to guide and inspire the child so that his inner knowledge is brought out.

## HUMANISM OF AUROBINDO AND VIVEKANAND—A COMPARATIVE STUDY

### Similarities

1. Both of them want to maximize human welfare. They believe that humans should be ready to give up their own comforts for the goods of others. A nation can progress only when the masses are well educated and well fed.
2. Both of them favours religious freedom given to individuals.
3. Both of them consider man as the centre and measure of all human activities in the world. So they always talk in terms of all round development of man.
4. Humanism believes that all necessary materials of life are received by us from nature. Nature is so powerful that our existence is not possible without nature. Even culture is moulded by man by the power of nature. Aurobindo and Vivekanand calls this nature as divine power. Humans are the gifts and elements of divine power.
5. Both of them believe that man should be given full freedom to achieve happiness and this is possible. by economic, moral and cultural progress.
6. Both of them want to make a man optimistic, bold and active.
7. Both of them believe that democratic ideals and ways of life are essential for collective survival of all humans on this earth. It is because democratic member of the society does not create any barrier in the way of achieving happiness by others.
8. Both of them are of the view that worldly pleasures and comforts should not be avoided. They want to make a strong and brave man to face the challenges of life.
9. Both of them want to train senses as they are the gateway of knowledge. Thus, they believe in education based on experience and experimentation.
10. Humanism of Aurobindo or Vivekanand is not the attainment of material pleasure without any check. Their humanism creates self restraint and disciplined man.
11. Both of them believe that hatred among the people can be reduced by love and confidence and love and confidence can be created by selfless service.

12. Both of them wants to develop self discipline through the purification of thoughts, expressions and action.
13. Both of them believe that knowledge without spirituality will bring about chaos in the society. Thus very purpose of human welfare will be at stake. Due to this reason we say that their Humanism covers the veil of Idealism.
14. Both of them advocate vocational and technical education for material well being of citizens.
15. Both of them advocate full freedom of the child given in the class and teachers work only as a guide or helper.

**Differences**

1. Aurobindo wants to make a man superman by virtue of supreme development of his mental power. A man grows from knowledge to more knowledge step by step and when he reaches at the top, he experiences the supreme happiness. Thus Aurobindo's approach is very much individualistic in nature. Vivekanand, on the other hand, wants the betterment of the masses through education and material progress. Though he at the same time emphasizes the spiritual progress of the individuals also.
2. According to Aurobindo, man is endowed with higher mental abilities that is intelligence. In order to realize these potentialities he should develop his power of thinking and concentration. Man can solve his problems by using his intelligence. Vivekanand, on the other hand, says that man can solve his problems by becoming bold. Only then humanity can be served and solutions to our social problems is arrived at.
3. According to Aurobindo, every individual in the world is unique. So his thinking is also individualistic in nature. Because of this individuality, he takes interest in a particular thing or object and tries to adjust with it using his intelligence and creative power. All these finally lead to the development of his spiritual power. Swamijee, on the other hand, says that human life is a constant struggle between the strong and weak and only strong survives in this struggle. This strength is achieved by physical development and material progress.
4. Aurobindo talks of individual peace and happiness while Vivekanand talks in terms of social peace and happiness.
5. According to Vivekanand, solutions to all human problems can be found out through scientific methods. Even social sciences should be studied by scientific attitude. It otherwise means that there is solutions to all problems of man. Aurobindo, on the other hand, advocates meditation and yoga for the solution of human problems.
6. Dharma dominates in the philosophy of Aurobindo and Karma dominates in the philosophy of Vivekanand though both of them wants to make this earth a heavenly place for living.
7. Morality, according to Vivekanand, is the service of humanity and character formation. Strong character is built by practicing Brahmacharya and Brahmachari by his selfless efforts can serve the humanity well. Morality according to Aurobindo, is the purification of mind and body. This purification leads to spiritual development of man and that will in turn give happiness to him.
8. Vivekanand wants to raise the socio-economic standard of the masses by his philosophy while Aurobindo does not give much importance to economic well being. But both of them believe that if man is happy, society will automatically be happy.
9. According to Aurobindo, for the development of morality in children their hearts are so trained as to show extreme love, sympathy, cooperation and consideration of all living being on the earth. These concepts are also advocated by Vivekanand by his scheme of mass welfare and mass education. These are the social qualities needed by all humans to bring about justice and peace in the society.
10. Vivekanand was immensely attached to the poor people of the country. He wanted to remove their deprivation by motivating the political leaders and encouraging the poor to struggle hard for existence. Aurobindo, on the other hand, sublimated the frustration of the poor people by yogic exercise and Sadhna.

## OBJECTIVE QUESTIONS

1. Tagore's aim of education was :
   (a) Self realization through meditation.
   (b) Self realization by establishing affinity between man, nature and God.
   (c) Self realization through yoga.
   (d) Self realization through nature study.
2. Tagore's belief that man is the centre and measure of all activities in the universe makes him a :
   (a) Naturalist (b) Humanist
   (c) Existentialist (d) Idealist
3. The dimensions of reality, according to Tagore is three-man, nature and
   (a) God (b) Matter
   (c) Rational thinking (d) None of these
4. Which of the following beliefs makes Tagore an Idealist :
   (a) Development of spirituality
   (b) Bread butter aims of education
   (c) Utilitarian aim of education
   (d) None of these
5. According to Tagore, knowledge should he communicated to children in
   (a) An environment of nature
   (b) A social and friendly environment
   (c) An environment where free action is permitted
   (d) All of these
6. Parentheistic relationship between man and nature makes him, according to Tagore, a
   (a) real man (b) cosmic man
   (c) happy man (d) none of these
7. Which of the following beliefs of Gandhijee makes him a liberal Idealist?
   (a) Truth is God and vice versa, Satyagrah (request for truth) is the only way of self realization
   (b) Non-violence (absence of ill will against all living being), is the means of Satyagrah
   (c) Both of these
   (d) All of these
8. Gandhijee believed in
   (a) Education through crafts
   (b) Education through mother tongue
   (c) Education for self reliance
   (d) All of these
9. By correlating schools with the local industry Gandhijee supports :
   (a) Existentialism (b) Marxism
   (c) Pragmatism (d) None of once
10. Which of the following philosophers supports self discipline :
    (a) Gandhijee (b) Tagore
    (c) Vivekanand (d) All of others
11. Which of the following approaches makes Gandhijee different from Shankaracharya : (Shankara did not have these beliefs)
    (a) Manual labour for self realization
    (b) Satyagrah for self purification
    (c) Both of these
    (d) None of these
12. Real education prepares a man for struggle for existence and social service. It is the opinion of :
    (a) Vivekanand (b) Tagore
    (c) Gandhijee (d) None of them
13. Who among the following was a staunch supporter of practical and technical education:
    (a) Gandhijee (b) Vivekanand
    (c) Both of them (d) None of them
14. "Arise, awake and stop not till the goal is achieved" is the call given by :
    (a) Tagore (b) Vivekanand
    (c) Gandhijee (d) None of these
15. Aurobindo's conscience has :
    (a) four levels (b) three levels
    (c) five levels (d) two levels
16. Vishva Bharti was established by Tagore in
    (a) 1913 (b) 1911
    (c) 1901 (d) 1902
17. Tagore was honoured with Knighthood by British government in:
    (a) 1911 (b) 1915
    (c) 1917 (d) 1902
18. Man is a part of nature. It is believed by :
    (a) Aurobindo (b) Radhakrishanan
    (c) Tagore (d) None of these
19. Tagore believed in
    (a) eternal and absolute values
    (b) values created by nature

(*c*) values created by man
(*d*) all of these

**20.** Which of the following is not the principle of education given by Tagore
(*a*) Freedom for self expression and creativity
(*b*) Knowledge based on experimentation
(*c*) Active communication between nature and man
(*d*) Internationalism

**21.** Which of the following is not the work of Gandhijee :
(*a*) India wins freedom
(*b*) India of my dream
(*c*) Tasks before India
(*d*) Towards new education
(*e*) Medium of instruction

**22.** Non violence is preferred to violence by Gandhijee because :
(*a*) it is needed for moral and spiritual victory
(*b*) it is needed to show love for living being which is actually love for God
(*c*) it shakes the opponent's will and destroys his morales
(*d*) all of these

**23.** Gandhijee despised industrialization because :
(*a*) He did not want to make India a rich country
(*b*) He was obsessed with the inequalities of income and wealth
(*c*) Indian condition was not suited to industrialization
(*d*) All of these

**24.** Gandhijee dreamed of a :
(*a*) Sarvodaya Samaj
(*b*) Saral Samaj
(*c*) Brahmo Samaj
(*d*) None of these

**25.** The philosopher who advocated a reunion between the spirituality of the East and materialism of the West was :
(*a*) Tagore (*b*) Vivekanand
(*c*) Gandhijee (*d*) None of them

**26.** Out of four paths of liberation, i.e., Karma, Bhakti, contemplation and knowledge which is the best path of liberation :
(*a*) Karma alone
(*b*) Bhakti alone
(*c*) Karma and Bhakti both
(*d*) Any of the four depending on the nature of man.

**27.** Which of the following is the belief of Vivekanand
(*a*) Teacher is necessary to lead to the path of salvation
(*b*) Strength is life and weakness is death, so, stand firm like a rock
(*c*) Patriotism and universal brotherhood
(*d*) All of these

**28.** Which of the following is an important cause of misery of Indian masses
(*a*) Ignorance
(*b*) Lethargy (Inertia)
(*c*) Narrow mindedness and casteism
(*d*) All of these

**29.** "If education was identical to informations, the libraries would be the greatest saints of the world and encyclopaedias the greatest rishis". Who said this :
(*a*) Swami Vivekanand
(*b*) Tagore
(*c*) Gandhijee
(*d*) Aurobindo

**30.** Vivekanand recommends that education by which
(*a*) Character is formed
(*b*) Strength of mind is increased
(*c*) One can stand on one's own feet
(*d*) All of the above

**31.** According to Vivekanand which of the following is most needed in the acquisition of knowledge.
(*a*) Concentration of mind
(*b*) Drill
(*c*) A real guru
(*d*) All of these

**32.** Vivekanand favoured that religious education in school which :
(*a*) is based on Upanishads
(*b*) includes essentials of all religions
(*c*) is purely secular
(*d*) none of these

**33.** To propagate revolutionary ideas among Indians, Aurobindo started :
(*a*) Inqilab
(*b*) Swadeshi

(*c*) Bandematram
(*d*) None of these

**34.** Aurobindo Ashram is in
(*a*) Pondicherry
(*b*) Tamil Nadu
(*c*) Annamalai
(*d*) None of these

**35.** **Karmyogi** a weekly paper was edited by
(*a*) Gandhijee
(*b*) Swami Dayanand
(*c*) Tagore
(*d*) Aurobindo

**36.** Who among the following favoured development of senses as aim of education
(*a*) Tagore
(*b*) Aurobindo
(*c*) Vivekanand
(*d*) Gandhijee

## ANSWERS

| 1 | 2 | 3 | 4 | 5 | 6 | 7 | 8 | 9 | 10 |
|---|---|---|---|---|---|---|---|---|---|
| (*b*) | (*b*) | (*a*) | (*a*) | (*d*) | (*b*) | (*c*) | (*d*) | (*c*) | (*d*) |
| **11** | **12** | **13** | **14** | **15** | **16** | **17** | **18** | **19** | **20** |
| (*c*) | (*a*) | (*c*) | (*b*) | (*a*) | (*c*) | (*b*) | (*c*) | (*a*) | (*b*) |
| **21** | **22** | **23** | **24** | **25** | **26** | **27** | **28** | **29** | **30** |
| (*a*) | (*d*) | (*b*) | (*a*) | (*b*) | (*d*) | (*d*) | (*d*) | (*a*) | (*d*) |
| **31** | **32** | **33** | **34** | **35** | **36** | | | | |
| (*a*) | (*b*) | (*c*) | (*a*) | (*d*) | (*b*) | | | | |

# Logical Empiricism and Logical Positivism

## LOGICAL POSITIVISM

Positivism is a word synonymous to empiricism. Logical positivism is that logical knowledge which is based on direct experience. Thus pure scientific knowledge which can be proved by experimentation comes under this category. We may call it scientific empiricism. The term empiricism was coined by Hume (1711-1776). His empiricism means psychological analysis of human experiences in the form of primary feelings and effects.

### Origin of the Philosophy

In 1928, some scientists, mathematicians and philosophers formed a club in Viena. In this club philosophers like Carnep, Russell, Wittgenstein etc. were prominent members. The similar type of club was also established by C W Morris in USA. Viena Club was converted into International Congress by some disciples of Russell,. Prominent among them was G.E.Morre. The main purpose of this Congress was to popularize logical analysis on the basis of scientific experiences.

Hume was a prominent logical positivist of this centre. The other philosophers who interpreted history on scientific lines were Russell, Whitehead and Karl Marx but the person who popularized the movement of logical positivism was Wittgenstein.

### Main Thoughts of the Philosophy

Carnep is of the view that philosophical thoughts should be analysed logically by using scientific methods.

Wittgenstein gave the idea that world is an essence of fact not an essence of any object. He criticized science by saying that science is not an organized form of names but an organized form of sentences.

However, the main purpose of above philosophers was to prove the futility of metaphysics. They tried to give a scientific base to philosophy rejecting metaphysics. Thus the basic purpose of logical positivism is to prove metaphysics as meaningless.

Viena club was established to serve this very purpose and it was to be done by providing a safe base to science subjects in order that they become a basis of subjects like philosophy and by proving the futility of metaphysics.

### Logical Positivism and Language Analysis

The views of this philosophy on language are as follows:

I. Language gives a symbolic representation of experiences based on facts, *i.e.*, language represents facts.

II. Language may be broken into logical statements, called assumptions. These assumptions can be broken (analysed) into primary assumptions.

III. Primary assumption is a photo copy of automatic facts. This picture may further be broken into atoms (smaller facts).

IV. Fact is nothing but matter. It can prove the assumption true.

V. If all the assumptions can be broken into primary assumptions, facts and atoms then ultimate aim of all assumptions is a fact empirically established.

## How is Metaphysics Rejected by this Philosophy ?

According to logical positivism, metaphysics is that branch of philosophy which is related with the meaning of nature and existence. If philosophy is to make meaningful, nature must be analysed logically and since it is not possible so metaphysics is futile.

According to logical positivism there are two ways of knowing.

I. Knowing by experience
II. Knowing by intelligence

Knowledge of physical world is obtained by experience and it is not difficult to test its truth. Knowledge based on intelligence can be tested by logic. Logical positivism has adopted a course which is called the measure of its reliability

## Measure of Reliability

Only that truth is meaningful which can be ascertained through analysis or experiment. Philosophy is neither a system of stating a thing nor a science. Philosophy uses analysis as a method. It is regarded as a queen of sciences. Science can never take the place of philosophy because of its limitations.

Philosophy, on the other hand, can establish the truth directly and indirectly both. For example, we can not see an atom directly but the existence of an atom is established through indirect experience. In this way all statements explaining an atom are meaningful because the existence of any atom can be proved indirectly with the help of science. Thus, we see that science supplements the task of philosophy and procedure of establishing the truth gets completed.

## Futility of Metaphysics

According to logical positivism metaphysics can be rejected on the following grounds :

I. Metaphysics believes that principles of reality are beyond realization. If it is not realized directly or indirectly, its existence is doubtful.
II. When any clause, phrase or word is meaningless the whole sentence becomes meaningless. Since metaphysics does have meaningless words or clauses so the whole system becomes futile.
III. When words are not meaningful in a particular context, the whole sentence becomes meaningless.

## New Functions of Philosophy

Taking science as a base and with the help of logical analysis, philosophy has to perform the following functions according to logical positivism.

1. Philosophy should accept only those things (atoms) as true which can be verified practically. The nature of philosophy is objective similar to natural science not subjective.
2. Philosophy should analyse those sentences also which have already been ascertained by scientists, so that their form and relationship can be established. Thus, philosophy has to analyse all assumptions and principles in order to give them a new form and sequence.
3. It should compose new metaphysics by using deductive method. Inferences drawn are of two types:
   *(a)* Intelligence or preceding facts.
   *(b)* Experience or following facts.

If inference is based on experience rather than on intelligence, this inference will be synthetical and probable. Logical positivism supports analysis rather than synthesis. Hence, use of intelligence will also be necessary for arriving at definite truth.

## Modified Forms of Logical Positivism

The philosophy of logical positivism was gradually modified by philosophers. Modified ideas of the philosophy are given below:

I. The earlier logical positivists refute metaphysics from every angle but later philosophers did not refute it altogether.
II. Principle of verification of truth was accepted on the basis of logical analysis of sentence only. This principle was also opposed by later logical positivists.
III. When it is said that meaning of assumption is based on verification, then the question arises

what is verification? Does it mean that the truth of assumption will be established with the view of its meaning in the context of conceptual knowledge. If it is so, how can we understand a thing which has not come under direct observation. For example, incidents of the past can never be observed practically. Due to this difficulty later philosophers believed that it is not necessary to verify all assumptions by perception. Logical verification of the assumption is enough to ascertain a truth.

## Reinterpretation of Science by this Philosophy

Following three principles have been given by this philosophy in this regard. These are:

1. Because of the changes or mistakes committed in observations, any logical statement or concept can not be considered as true or false without imposing some conditions (assumption) on it. A probability is found between the two limits of truth and falsehood.
2. According to the principle of repetition of probability, probability is based on supervised repetition of facts of some incidents. The greater the number of times a probability is proved true, the greater will be the amount of fact in a probability.
3. The third principle is based on simple logic. Its main characteristics are as follows :
   *(a)* The principle of probability should be followed in ascertaining truth.
   *(b)* Logical relationship that is found between two assumptions is nothing but probability.
   *(c)* If any two assumptions are "a" and "b" respectively, there can be three types of logical relationship between them as has been made clear from the sketches given below:

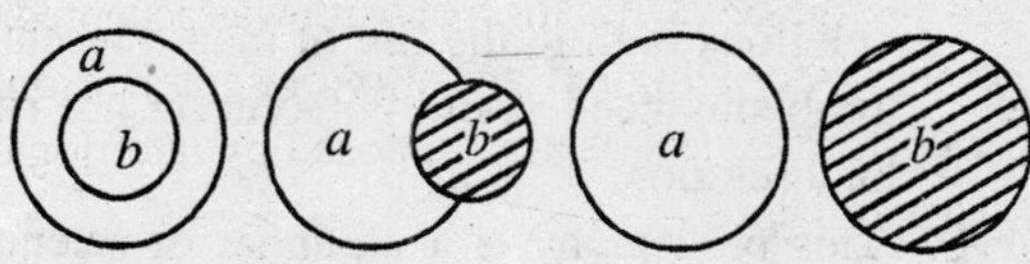


In the first relationship, if

- All kings are men (assumption a)
- All kings are conscious (assumption b)
- Some men are conscious (conclusion)

If this conclusion is drawn assumption (b) becomes constant.

In the second relationship 'b' is neither completely separate from 'a' nor it is completely covered by 'a' Such logical relationship which exists between two assumptions (between absolute truth or absolute falsehood is called probability.

In the third situation both a and be are separate. Here a and b both may be opposite assumptions as.

All kings are men (assumption a)

All kings are unconscious (assumption b)

Thus we see that this philosophy establishes the relationship between assumptions in various ways and conclusions are drawn on the basis of the relationship.

## View Points of Modern Logical Positivism

The main points of this philosophy has been given by Wittgenstein. They are given below:

1. Language is a means of coming to the reality and every assumption is a picture of some atomic facts.
2. Language is a medium and way of expressing behaviour.
3. It is the language that is used in questioning, thinking, abusing, welcoming, praying, estimating and making fun of others. It is very important medium of communication.
4. There can be no common form or essence of all languages.
5. There are no definite atomic and simple elements of reality equivalent to words and early assumptions e.g., a black spot on the floor is only a colour but it may be a mixture of several parts. Similarly, an atom may also be a compound of several qualities.
6. The attitude that we adopt toward an idea or object may be different from that of others towards the same idea or object. As a result, subjectivity may be involved in getting the reality of an idea or object.
7. Our knowledge of reality and the description of a thing through language can give rise to several

probabilities and possibilities, ie. even language can change the nature of reality.

8. The function of philosophy is not to propound a principle but to remove doubts and dissatisfaction created by mind.
9. New problems are created when we relate words with past or future because they are not before us. We should therefore use the words in the context of the present and in the context of our daily life only in order to solve a problem and get satisfaction.
10. We have to use words in the context of our daily life, so, a list of daily use of words should be prepared. It can give us the form of grammar to philosophy.

## Focal Points of the Philosophy

I. Verification or reliability is the measure. On this measure meaning may be proved true or false. Only that statement is meaningful which can be verified by experience or perception. According to verification principle, if a statement is meaningful, it would certainly be verified and become a part of our experience directly. Thus, in order to arrive at true knowledge mathematical and language analysis techniques should be used apart from using empirical technique of science.

II. This philosophical thought makes it clear how basic ideas, hypothesis and procedures can be verified in the field of knowledge and evolution and how they can be classified.

III. The contribution of this philosophy is very significant. Some of its methods have been adopted by the philosophy of scientific Humanism.

## Educational Implications of the Philosophy

I. This philosophy is very much helpful in establishing language grammar.

II. Empirical view points of the philosophy is very much helpful in testing scientific principles on logical ground.

III. It has also helped us in studying history by logical analysis.

IV. This philosophy does not verify absolute values. Only relative values are significant after verification.

V. Only those ideas are given importance in education which are verified. Verification makes them distinct. Even scientific laws and principles need to be logically verified.

VI. Conclusion should be drawn by using intelligence and reasoning. Mere empirical knowledge is not enough to believe.

VII. Only those facts should be placed before children which are verified. Only this knowledge is reliable.

VIII. The aim of education is to develop reasoning and intellectual power of children and to help them verify every bits of knowledge.

IX. It emphasizes on objective knowledge and ignore subjectivity. This objective knowledge can be obtained only by adopting empirical attitude.

X. The purpose of education is to develop purposive behaviour in children. They have to study only those things which have any purpose to serve in their daily life.

XI. Education should bring perfection in man. This is possible only when we adopt verifying attitude towards any idea.

XII. This philosophy does not give much weightage to past and future and restricts students to the present only. Only present is the source of happiness.

XIII. According to logical positivism self criticism should not be encouraged among students in schools because it creates mental tension, unrest, fear, frustration and nervousness.

XIV. Scientific and logical attitude must be developed in children through education. There is no place of superstition or unfounded religious faith in the life of man. Present day problems need scientific solution not rituals of a religion.

XV. This philosophy is a grammar of science. It emphasizes analysis of the language and denies all traditional philosophical ideas. It makes scientific statements logical on the basis of language analysis.

XVI. It also gives a rational foundation to our expression. Our expression becomes scientific when our argument is supported by empirical facts and anylysis of language.

XVII. The training of anylysis of language work is very valuable from educational point of view, because it provides means for the following:

(a) It gives recognition to propaganda work.

(b) It determines those definitions which are acceptable to others.

(c) It makes understanding of difference between knowledge and evaluation easy.

(d) It is useful in manifestation of secret word-interpretation and expressing its factual hollowness.

(e) It gives a sort of strength in accepting a good thing.

## Criticism of the Philosophy

Logical positivism has been criticized on the following grounds.

1. Utility or meaningfulness of a sentence can be accepted temporarily on the basis of verification only when assumptions *a* and *b* are not related to each other. Can this happen always is a big question.
2. Metaphysics is rejected by this philosophy because of its general approach to ideas but when the same generality is seen in science, science is not rejected.
3. This philosophy rejected all kinds of subjective knowledge and thus, it treats the society like a big machine and humans as its parts. This is nothing but the denial of individuality of man.
4. According to this philosophy, soul has no place in the life of man because it can not be seen directly or indirectly. This makes the scope of philosophy very narrow.
5. Logical positivism is nothing but the reinterpretation of different concepts and ideas with the help of language analysis.
6. This philosophy proves the futility of those very principles on which it is based by accepting indirect method of knowing a thing to some extent.

## OBJECTIVE QUESTIONS

**1.** Which of the following denotes empiricism ?
(a) Physical verification of objects or ideas
(b) Psychological analysis of human experiences
(c) Both of these
(d) None of these

**2.** Logical Positivism denies metaphysics because
(a) later can not be verified
(b) Later is related to values
(c) Later determines values
(d) All of these

**3.** In Logical Positivism values are
(a) Real
(b) Fixed
(c) Absolute
(d) Relative

**4.** Viena club aimed at
(a) Reinterpreting philosophical terms
(b) Popularizing logical analysis on the basis of scientific experiences
(c) Both of these
(d) None of these

**5.** Which of following methods of teaching is supported by this philosophy
(a) Analysis
(b) Experimentation
(c) Logical argumentation
(d) All of these

**6.** According to this philosophy students should be given
(a) Less chance of self criticism
(b) Less chance of going into past or future

(*c*) More chance of logical analysis of objects or ideas
(*d*) All of these

**7.** Logical positivism is more close to
(*a*) Scientific Humanism
(*b*) Objective Idealism
(*c*) Neo Realism
(*d*) Mechanical Naturalism

**8.** All logical positivists are at consensus at
(*a*) Opposing metaphysics
(*b*) Analyzing the statements on logical principles
(*c*) Both of these
(*d*) None of these

**9.** If any word or phrase becomes meaningless in a concept, what will happen
(*a*) The concept will also become meaningless
(*b*) The meaning of the concept will change
(*c*) Both of these
(*d*) None of these

**10.** Method of teaching proposed by Logical Positivism is—
(*a*) Discussion and argumentation
(*b*) Problem solving
(*c*) Learning by doing
(*d*) All of these

## ANSWERS

| 1 | 2 | 3 | 4 | 5 | 6 | 7 | 8 | 9 | 10 |
|---|---|---|---|---|---|---|---|---|---|
| (*c*) | (*a*) | (*d*) | (*c*) | (*d*) | (*d*) | (*a*) | (*c*) | (*d*) | (*a*) |

# UNIT-II

- ★ *Education and Sociology*
- ★ *Agencies of Education*
- ★ *Education as a Social Sub System (Education and Society)*
- ★ *Education and Culture*
- ★ *Education and Socialization of Child*
- ★ *Education, Social Stratification and Social Change*
- ★ *Education and Social Mobility*
- ★ *Equality of Educational Opportunities and Education of Disadvantaged Sections of the Society*
- ★ *Education and National Integration*
- ★ *National Values Enshrined in Our Constitution*
- ★ *Modernization and Education*

1

# Education and Sociology

## INTRODUCTION

French philosopher August Comte used the word Sociology for the first time in his lectures in 1837. He recognized it as a separate subject and put it at the top of all sciences. It is because sociology can actually synthesize all sciences into a composite science that can be used for the reconstruction and reformation of the society. Because of these views Comte is known as the Father of sociology. He advocated scientific study of society, its consciousness, role of its agencies etc. for the first time.

## Meaning of Sociology

Technically the word sociology means the scientific study of society. It is the man, the smallest unit of the society who does this job. He takes birth in a society as a social being, he remains here throughout his life, he affects the society by his ideas and actions and is affected by the society after all. Individual philosophy gets assimilated in the society when philosophy of the society is powerful. On the other hand, when individual philosophy is very strong, it can change the total philosophy of the society by a revolution.

Thus, we see that when man thinks and acts individually it is philosophy but when this individual thinking and action is accepted and followed by the society as a whole in the form of culture or tradition it becomes the subject matter of sociology. In this way the scope or subject matter of sociology is very wide. Whatever is related to man as a group of men is the subject matter of sociology. Since education is also a social process, it is also the subject matter of sociology. When education reaches its highest peak, it loses its identity and becomes synonymous to sociology. Education and sociology are different to each other only in approaches not in ends. The approach of education is micro while the approach of sociology is macro. Education aims at making the society better by modifying the behaviour of man in a desirable manner while sociology makes the society better by changing the group behaviour of men in a desirable manner.

## Subject Matter (Characteristics) of Sociology

We have discussed the subject matter of education in the previous chapters. Now the subject matter of sociology is given below :

*(i)* Sociology studies social elements and social processes in a scientific manner. These processes and elements are the results of social interactions among humans on one side and among humans and non-humans on the other.

*(ii)* Change is an important characteristics of social elements and social processes because of the dynamic nature of humans. Sociology analyses these changes scientifically and predicts about the future behaviour of humans on the basis of these changes.

*(iii)* Sociology studies the multidimensional behaviour of humans manifested in a group of individuals. Since individual behaviour is always affected by the behaviour of the group and vice versa, group behaviour is given more importance than individual behaviour in sociology. In this sense sociology is more comprehensive than philosophy.

*(iv)* Sociology studies all those institutions that exist in a society such as family, religion, state, social or reform organizations etc. It prepares norms and guidelines for each of them.

*(v)* When man lives in a group, he comes across a number of problems there. Sociology studies those problems objectively by analyzing their possible causes and then gives tentative solutions to these problems. Once these suggestions are brought into practice for a long

period of time sociological theories come into being.

*(vi)* Sociology also studies those elements and factors which necessarily affect human being. Actually man is governed by these customs, traditions, dogmas, beliefs and culture as a whole. Since these factors and elements are not universal any where, Sociology also studies the possible causes of differences such as geographical conditions, standard of living, levels and roots of scientific inventions and so on.

*(vii)* Sociology studies social institutions with reference to their characteristics and functions which differ from place to place, generation to generation and institution to institution.

*(viii)* The chief purpose of sociology is to develop certain social qualities in man which are basic for his survival as a social being such as friendship, cooperation, sympathy, sacrifice for others and mutual coexistence.

*(ix)* Sociology also studies possible causes of social disintegration and cultural enmity and suggest for their removal with the help of education.

*(x)* Sociology studies social norms and legal prospects in the context of these norms. It believes that everything can not be made good by just invoking laws. Social norms can play more important roles than legal provisions in making the society better.

It is clear from the above discussion that education and sociology both are inter-related and inter dependent on each other in many ways. Sociology without education is like a body without soul and education without sociology is like a vehicle without wheels. So, it is better to synthesize both by new name Educational Sociology or Sociology of Education.

## EDUCATIONAL SOCIOLOGY

The combined approach of education and sociology is necessary because of the following reasons :

*(i)* The larger aims of sociology can not be achieved without integrating the process of education into it.

*(ii)* Without studying the social problems on a micro level that is done through education we can not propose for a macro solutions.

*(iii)* Educational sociology studies social processes and interactions very objectively and without which pure educational problems can not be solved.

*(iv)* Educational sociology studies social activities and social institutions in the context of future social needs also, so, it is very much helpful for the process of education.

*(v)* Educational sociology gives equal weightage to the development of the individual as well as the society.

George Payne is regarded as the Father of Educational sociology. In his book **Principles of Educational Sociology** he has discussed the influene of education upon group life and the effects of group life upon education. In addition to Payne, other sociologists like John Dewey, Fredrick Lepay, Maciver, Davis, Clark, Ottaway, etc. have also contributed a lot in the development of educational sociology.

### Definitions of Educational Sociology

1. **Brown:** "Educational sociology is the study of interaction of the individual and his cultural environment."
2. **Ottaway:** "Educational sociology starts with the assumption that education is an activity which goes on in the society and the society in turn determines the nature of education."
3. **Good:** "Educational sociology is the scientific study of how people live in social group especially including the study of education that is obtained by living in the social groups and education that is needed by the members to live effectively in the groups."

On the basis of above definitions we can say that sociology and education are the need and requirement of each other on almost equal basis.

### Aims and Importance of Educational Sociology

1. Man is a social being. He has to learn the lesson of social adjustment in the school with the help of his teachers and school mates. Educational

sociology recognizes the social nature of man and plans accordingly.

2. As a social being all men are equal. They can not be discriminated on the basis of birth, occupation, beliefs and place of living. Educational sociology recognizes this fundamental principle and makes education accessable to all persons without distinction. He is given opportunities to receive education to the maximum level of his capacity.
3. School is an integral part of the society. It is rather the reflection of the society. Whatever changes we want to bring about in the society, its foundation is laid in the school. It is because small and immature representatives of the society will lead the society in future when they are matured.
4. Individual is necessarily affected with the social elements. Educational sociology studies these impacts objectively and apply them in the educational environment of the school.
5. Culture which is the most important element of society is formally preserved and transmitted in the school. Educational sociology analyses the desirable and undesirable aspects of culture by comparing them with the national and international culture.
6. Educational sociology helps the philosophers in constructing curriculum keeping in view the socio economic tendencies and demands of the society.
7. By the help of educational sociology individuals endeavour to create and sustain those institutions which are conducive to social growth.
8. Educational sociology helps us to provide sound social bases for educational researches. Sociological researches in education have special significance.
9. Educational sociology studies the causes of social and group conflicts which is to be removed by imparting suitable education.
10. Educational sociology paves the way for independent living of the child in the society.

## Scope of Educational Sociology

Educational sociology is bipolar and reciprocal process. It studies the influence of educational process on sociology on one hand and the effects of sociological process on education on the other. Educational sociology especially covers the following fields:

1. Mutual relationship among students and their impact on education.
2. Mutual relationship between two groups, teachers and students and their impact on teaching learning process.
3. The place of a teacher in society and its relative impact on teaching learning process.
4. Social problems and its impact on education and life.
5. Social organizations and their role on educational and school administration.
6. School and its relationship with society and other small organization.
7. Effects of social patterns and culture on education.
8. Progress of democratic values in educational institutions.
9. Role of education in socialization and social change.
10. Curriculum construction in a changing society.
11. Conflicting ideals and education.
12. Mass media, social mobility and education.
13. National integration and education.
14. Terrorism and fundamentalism in relation to social change.
15. New world order and its impact on education in future.
16. Education for under privileged classes of the society.
17. Educational challenges before the middle and lower middle classes.

# OBJECTIVE QUESTIONS

**1.** Education is a

(*a*) Biological necessity

(*b*) Social necessity

(*c*) Psychological necessity

(*d*) All of these

**2.** Adjustment function of education mainly refers to

(*a*) Social adjustment

(*b*) Biological adjustment

(*c*) Adjustment to nature
(*d*) None of these

**3.** The word "Sociology" was for the first time used by Comte in
(*a*) 1937 (*b*) 1854
(*c*) 1837 (*d*) 1890

**4.** Educaion is an/a
(*a*) Interpretation of society
(*b*) Social sub system
(*c*) Modification of the whole society
(*d*) All of these

**5.** Educational sociology is the study of the interaction of the individual with his cultural environment which includes other individuals, social group and pattern of behaviour. This definition was given by
(*a*) Auguste Comte (*b*) George Payne
(*c*) Brown (*d*) None of these

**6.** Human behaviour is determined by
(*a*) Biological factors (*b*) Psychological factors
(*c*) Social factors (*d*) All of these

**7.** Which of the following is not a biological factor affecting human behaviour ?
(*a*) Nutrition
(*b*) Neuro muscular reaction
(*c*) Growth and matrutiy
(*d*) Reproduction

**8.** Which of the following living being takes longest time for cultural assimilation?
(*a*) Humans (*b*) Birds
(*c*) Animals (*d*) None of these

**9.** Which of the following functions of education is determined and guided by Educational Sociology?
(*a*) Adjustment with social environment
(*b*) Cultural assimilation and enrichment of culture
(*c*) Development of new social pattern
(*d*) All of these

**10.** Educational sociology contributes
(*a*) to the formulation of educational aims
(*b*) to the development of curriculum.
(*c*) to the establishment of school discipline
(*d*) all of these

## ANSWERS

| 1 | 2 | 3 | 4 | 5 | 6 | 7 | 8 | 9 | 10 |
|---|---|---|---|---|---|---|---|---|---|
| (*d*) | (*a*) | (*b*) | (*b*) | (*c*) | (*d*) | (*b*) | (*a*) | (*a*) | (*d*) |

# Agencies of Education

## INTRODUCTION

If we accept John Dewey's definition of education that education is life, we will surely hold the view that every moment of our life gives us education in some form or the other. Only thing needed is that we must be conscious of this movement and try to develop ourselves physically, mentally, socially, spiritually and so on. Whatever a child learns from the environment after interacting with other human being, it modifies his behaviour. If this modification is desirable it is called positive education otherwise it is termed as negative one. The sources from which a child receives education are technically termed as agencies of education.

From this point of view, the role of educational institution as an agency of education is very limited, almost one fourth in the first half of the life and the destiny of man is necessarily possessed by other agencies. However, this limited role of schools and colleges is so powerful that other agencies of education are directly or indirectly controlled and guided by these educational institutions. Through all agencies of education, education is concerned with the preservation, transmission and advancement of experiences from one generation to the next for the sake of linking past, present and future.

These agencies may be formal, informal and non-formal. Here are some basic differences between the three:

| S.No. | Formal | Informal | Non-formal |
|---|---|---|---|
| 1. | Fully controlled educational environment | Free and uncontrolled natural educational environment | Partially controlled environment |
| 2. | Preplanned achievements of specific and general aims | No preplanned scheme for aims and objectives | Preplanned achievement of only narrow aims of education |
| 3. | Direct education and full interaction between teacher and the taught | Indirect education and no interaction between the two | Direct, and indirect education and interaction is not necessary |
| 4. | Place and duration of work both are fixed | Neither place nor duration of work is fixed | Only place is fixed but duration of work can vary from time to time |
| 5. | Guided and supervised by experienced and professional persons | No guidance or supervision is here | It is also guided and supervised by experienced persons |
| 6. | Curriculum, time table and approaches are fixed | Nothing is fixed here | Only curriculum is fixed here |
| 7. | Mid term appraisal is done here | No pain of achieving aims | Appraisal is done only in the end |
| 8. | Examination is conducted at the end of each unit of task and degree, diploma or certificate is issued | No examination as a result no degree, diploma or certificate is issued here | Informal examination is conducted at the end of whole task. Degree or diploma may be issued (example of correspondence courses) |
| 9. | It is always for specified age group | It is unrelated to age group | It is generally run for grown up people and adults. |
| 10. | Books are used as means here | No book is generally used here | Books are often used to take the task with interest |

Agencies of education can also be classified from one more angle i.e., active and passive.

Active agencies are those which act on and react to the growing child. Here child is also active and can influence the working of the agency also.

Passive agency refers to one way process of educating the learners. Here, child is not in a position to influence the agency at all and remains only as a passive recepient.

School family, community, religion, state, social and recreational clubs sports and games activities, aangan wadi centres etc. are some active agencies while cinema, mass media, market, social functions, library, museum, art galleries etc. are passive agencies.

## SOME IMPORTANT AGENCIES OF EDUCATION

### School (An Active and Formal Agency)

**Meaning :** Technically school is a place where teachers under a preplanned system (definite curriculum and examination system) give specific doses of knowledge and experiences to students of the school under a fixed time table and once this process is over with the help of students interaction, students as well as teachers are evaluated to certify the degree of success that they have achieved.

**Definition of school:**

1. According to John Dewey, School is a special environment where a certain quality of life and certain types of activities and occupations are provided with the object of securing child's development along desirable lines".
2. According to J.S. Ross, "Schools are institutions developed by civilized men for the purpose of aiding in the preparation of the young for making them well adjusted and efficient members of the society."

**Characteristics of schools:** On the basis of above definitions we can derive the following characteristics of schools –

1. School is a special environment not merely a building to be used for teaching learning process.
2. Here life related activities and experiences are provided to students to make the quality of life better.
3. With the help of these activities and experiences the development of child is brought about on desirable lines.
4. Schools are established by all civilized societies. Here young children and adults are prepared to get adjusted in the society.
5. Schools make the students efficient and productive members of the society. Thus schools work as miniature societies.
6. Schools always work on the lines of general welfare of the people in whatsoever manner it is possible.
7. The role of school changes with the change and demand of the time.
8. School is an institution established by the society for the purpose of preparing the young to participate in that society. Thus, school is a social institution whose fundamental character is determined by the society it serves.

### Need and Importance of the School

(i) *Fast growth of knowledge :* Knowledge is growing very fast today. It can not be preserved, transmitted or advanced by ordinary and non specialized agencies. Schools and colleges, can easily perform this function.

(ii) *Fast going life of the people :* Members of the family (society) have become so much busy in their economic or political activities that they are unable to spare time for this specialized social work. So separate agency must be there to perform this function

(iii) *Special knowledge :* Knowledge and experiences are not so general today as it was in the past. Only a specialized and fully trained person can perform this job. Hence, establishment of schools becomes necessary.

(iv) *Popularization of mass education :* Education is not the privilege of the rich and well to do people of the society but it is the right of all citizens irrespective of their ethnicity, culture, race or sex as has been accepted by all democracies of the world. Such a vast nature of task can not be left at the mercy of unorganized efforts of the people, hence, organized system of education is necessary for this purpose.

(v) *A bridge between family and society :* Whatever values and ideals are taught to children in the family, they are practiced in the society through the schools first. Thus, these values and ideals do not remain confined to the four walls of the home. In the schools child comes in contact with so many children belonging to different families. As a result he learns so many new values and ideals. Out of them unwanted values and ideals are washed away by the school by its own values and ideals and thus a fully refined and acceptable child is prepared in the school.

(vi) *Special environment for specialized job :* We have to develop a child at a very fast speed keeping in view the modern needs and challenges of the society. Schools can provide such an environment where everything goes on as a preplanned and a well organized manner.

(vii) *Harmonious development of child's personality:* No other agency of education whether it be family or church or it be mass media or the like can maintain harmony among all phases of development more than the school. Over emphasis on any phase at the cost of other phases or aspect will destroy the personality of the child. It is the school that can do this job in a planed and systematic manner.

(viii) *Cultural pluralism need :* Children belonging to different culture, creed, caste or strata come to school to study there. They mix up with each other in a friendly atmosphere just in order to achieve the common goals. They develop the emotions of sympathy, cooperation, tolerance, respect for others etc. in the context of the school environment here.

(ix) *Citizenship training :* Schools are the best place to train children for an ideal citizenship. They learn their rights and duties, political values and ideals, social norms and ethics and so on through activities and experiences. Schools are the necessity of the state and vice versa. State can also propagate its own philosophy through schools very easily.

(x) *Economic and social significance:* Education has become very much professionalised today. So it is the duty of the school to prepare such children who can earn their living after education in future. Moreover, child is made more and more social in his outlook and behaviour through schools. Thus, schools develop in him the sense of social responsibilities also.

(xi) *A conducive place for learning :* A child can not learn so easily and comfortably in his family or religious institution as he can do in schools because of its preplanned physical and social environment. A number of co curricular activities can easily be organized in school, which is not so easily possible in other agencies.

(xii) *Cheap education:* A number of children are collectively taught in regular classes in schools which is not possible in a family, club or church. This reduces the cost of education and wastage of time or energy. This makes the task of the state easy.

## Types of Schools

**(A) Traditional Schools:** Traditional schools are those:

1. Where religious priests and seers work as teachers and emphasis is made on making the people religious rather than enlightened.
2. Where readymade tit-bits of knowledge are given to children in a fully controlled and strict environment and individual differences of children and their varied interests and attitudes are not taken into account.
3. Where creative and imaginative powers of students are strangled by autocratic teachers and administrators.
4. Where teaching of classical subjects and discipline are given priority to the experience of 21st century.

**(B) Modern and Progressive Schools :** Such schools came into being under the influence of democracy and socialism in the life of the people. They are purely child centred where child's aptitude, interest and needs are given priority to other matters and by the process of education children are made self reliant, fully adjustable and energetic. Other characteristics of such schools are given below:

1. Child is given more importance than subject matter, teachers and classical values or ideals. The objective of harmonious and comprehensive development of the personality of the child is put at the top.
2. Activity and experiences are given more importance than mere transfer of knowledge from teachers to students. Children are not passive learners here. They are rather motivated to get involved in self learning and experimentation. Thus, students create their own ideals and values themselves.
3. Practical and pragmatic knowledge replaces bookish and theoretical knowledge. To do better always is the maxim of life here. Curriculum centres round the individual and social lives of children in these schools and looking forward is always stressed.
4. Rights and responsibilities are taught to children in these schools to make them useful and constructive citizens. By discarding their dogmatic attitudes, liberal and considerate nature of life is inculcated in them. Purpose of these schools is not to make the children religious but to enable them to fulfil their social and human responsibilities.
5. Such schools are developed as centres of social and scientific progress. They strengthen the ties between the individual and the society. Communities are identified with these schools and not vice versa.

## Functions of Schools

Functions of schools may be classified as formal and informal functions on the basis of current activities of schools :

**(A) Formal Functions:** Important formal functions of schools are given below:

(i) *Development of minds of children :* Schools are mainly centres of learning and research. Their chief function is to develop mental faculties of children through knowledge, activities and experiences. Such a function is performed keeping in view the interest, abilities and needs of children. When it is done by the schools it brings about new inventions, discoveries and experiences to the front by utilizing the creative potentials of children.

(ii) *Cultivation of a dynamic and adaptable life:* Physical as well as social environment is full of so many adversaries for the living organisms. Humans are always taught to do struggle for their survival. Such techniques and potentials are professionalised in humans by these schools to make their lives easy, adaptable and useful to the environment.

(iii) *Preservation, transmission and advancement of culture :* These functions are performed by the schools by producing books, by conducting researches and by motivating students for activities and experiences. These are very important functions of schools for the development of civilization.

(iv) *Vocational education for livelihood :* Earning livelihood becomes a problem for a poor or middle class child when he is devoid of any skills. Such skills are provided through training by these schools which help them get employment after education.

(v) *Reconstruction of society through newer experiences :* Society always undergoes a process of change and a number of new problems are created in the process. Schools actively participate in the reconstruction of society by solving these problems. They are actually research centres for reconstruction of experiences.

(vi) *Modification of child's behaviour :* Many delinquents and truants are moulded in schools by setting ideals of the teachers. Thus, schools mould the behaviour of children in order to make them acceptable for the family and the society.

(vii) *Citizenship and social training :* Students are also taught how to live and behave in the society on one hand and how to perform the duties of citizens here. They have to run their own government through their elected representatives. Schools create in them the civic and political awareness which is very essential for the survival of democracy.

**(B) Informal Functions :** Important informal functions of schools are given below :

(i) *Character formation :* Parents do not have time to look after their wards today. Schools take this responsibility and special care is made to build the character of the child on ethical or social lines.

(ii) *Physical development :* This function is also performed by the schools today. Games, sports and other co curricular activities are also organized in the school complex along with the inculcation of formal knowledge and experiences.

(iii) *Spiritual development :* The most touching reality is that everything on this earth will perish a day and only soul will remain as the ultimate reality. This reality must be realized by the child because he is not a beast restricted to the activities of taking food and reproduction. Schools make him think the purpose of his existence on this earth.

(iv) *Emotional development :* Emotions are properly developed by the school. For this purpose child is given full opportunity to think and act freely in the school and to release his pent-up feeling. Aesthetic sense is also created in him by the school.

## INDIAN SCHOOLING SYSTEM; A CRITICAL APPRAISAL

Indian schools are not doing very well as far as their functions and responsibilities are concerned. Their main drawback is that they are traditional and are least interested to reconstruct them according to the changing demands of 21st century.

In the words of **Khwaja Gulamus Sayyadain,** "In our schools today only formal education of Geography and Science is imparted to children. Some schools are much below the standard and where initiatives and enthusiasms of students for work are crushed."

The situation is not so dismal in many schools as has been explained by K.G. Sayyadain today. Some of the short comings that we still see today are given below:

- Many schools are still following the British pattern of education today. Only curriculum of these schools is of Indian origin. Thus, students educated in these schools develop some unique type of superiority complex in them.
- They are fully isolated from other agencies of education. Thus, desired results are not being brought about.
- Teachers of many government schools are not performing their duties honestly due to lack of supervision and control. Abolition of evaluation system from the elementary schools has multiplied this problem today. Since students do not have to fail so the shoulders of teachers are also made free from bearing any responsibility.
- No mechanism of checking poor performance in schools is there in India. A teacher of a government school is not liable to be punished even if all his students fail in the examination.
- Where there is any sensitivity to maintaining standard of education, the emphasis is only on subject matter not on the child.
- The individuality of the child is generally neglected and all students irrespective of their interest and abilities are homogeneously meted out in the class.
- Emphasis on activity and practical knowledge is minimum. Even public schools are not performing this function honestly.
- All round development of child's personality is not promoted. Even mental development is limited to cramming of subject matter without taking them to the understanding or reflective levels of teaching.
- The environment of the school is dull, lifeless and rigid. Everything in the school is done in a mechanical fashion. Even physical environment of the school is not made attractive and living.
- Many schools lack essential resource facilities like proper laboratory and library what to talk of playground, common room, or school canteen.
- Teaching strategies followed by teachers are also traditional and autocratic. Whatever is written in the book if dictated by the teacher to the students, they think that their job is over. Majority of teachers do not do even this amount of job.
- School curriculum is constructed by the government either at the central or state level.

Schools are not given any freedom to modify them according to their local conditions and requirements. In Indian scenario it is better in my opinion. It is because if schools are given this freedom to mould curriculum according to their local needs, they may spoil the whole thing to fulfil their own vested interest.

- Methods of teaching prevailing in the schools are faulty, unscientific and unpsychological in general.
- No conscious efforts are being made in those schools to do anything for character formation. The whole Indian society is becoming corrupt by and by because moral development of children are neglected in the early stages of their lives. The materialistic and selfish attitude developed by these money making business shops of education are mainly responsible for it.
- In India vocational or technical education is given only after class Xth. This is benefiting only about half of the population because 50% students leave their schools before reaching this stage.
- The schools are either killing the creative potentials of children or are totally indifferent to them.
- Availability of trained teachers in these schools is not a problem. But are these so called trained personnel really trained, is a question. Training colleges are only selling degrees to them and no action research in education is being carried out in these training colleges. We are only copying the researches of the west and irrationally applying them in Indian situations. The opening of training colleges to private ventures has made the situation even worse.
- No coordination is seen among various schools. The concept of Sahodaya is not existing here. Even government schools are totally independent of each other.
- The education imparted in schools does not have anything to do with the real life situations. Absence of link between education and life is making the education unuseful and unproductive.
- Children learn many varities of behaviour in schools but their behaviours are not given any weightage in real life. Students will gain almost nothing without high percentage of marks.

### Suggestions For Reform

If we flush out these drawbacks from the schools, they will become exemplary for the whole nation as well as for the generation to come. One word suggestion is that all these drawbacks must be removed.

## FAMILY (AN ACTIVE BUT INFORMAL AGENCY)

**Meaning:** It is the oldest and fundamental unit of human society. It consists of husband, wife, children along with all other young and old dependents. In ancient period slaves and servants were also considered a part of the family. Interdependence of each member of the family, physically and emotionally on each other compels them to be united. Family might be considered the smallest miniature society.

### Definitions

1. According to Machiver and Page, "The family is a group defined by sex relationship sufficiently precise and enduring to provide protection and upbringing of children".
2. Burgess and Locke have opined as, "A family is a group of persons united by the ties of marriage, blood or adoption constituting a single household interaction and in inter communication with each other in their respective social role of husband and wife, father and mother, son and daughter, brother and sister etc creating and maintaining a common culture".

In broad sense a family may be defined as a group of people living in four walls of a house comprising of grandfather, grandmother, father, mother, brothers, sisters, sons, daughters, servants, tenants, nephew niece, uncles, aunties etc. Each family is identified because of its unique habit of clothing, talking, eating, meeting, and living. Thus, each family has its own specific culture.

### Characteristics of a family

On the basis of above definitions the following characteristics of a family can be derived :

1. The basis of inter relation between members of a family are sex, culture, economic and emotional dependence and so on depending upon the nature of ties.

2. Once sex relationship is established between members of the family, the size of the family will increase. In order to ascertain this relationships, two members of opposite sexes each from two different families will have to be tied.
3. Family takes full responsibility of preservation and upbringing of children at least till the period they become an independent productive member of the family.
4. Members of the family are united naturally by the ties of marriage, blood or adoption. Economic and emotional interdependence and common culture also help them to get united.
5. They get interacted with each other because of their respective social roles and inter communication among them is a natural process.
6. Sexual relationship among opposite sexes of the family is developed on the basis of marriage in a systematic manner under pre defined rules of the society.
7. In order to develop better interaction and ties, each member of the family contributes something to others.
8. Properties of the families are shared jointly and division if needed is made on the basis of predefined rules and regulations.
9. Family is universal human phenomenon. It is found in every society across the world, though cultural ties may differ from society to society.
10. Family is the smallest unit of the society and a number of such units constitute the society. Thus, structure and characteristics of the society very much depend upon those of the families.
11. Innate tendencies determined by genetic characteristics differ from family to family especially in case of big joint families.
12. Family exerts most important influence on the development of a child's personality. These impressions are permanent to a lager extent. These influences are genetic and acquired both.
13. Small members of the family are taught socially desirable values and culture by the family first. Thus, family plays very crucial role in making the young ones a useful member of the society.
14. Family is a permanent institution of the society. If any member of the family departs from it, he will create his own family sooner or later. Similarly, if any member of the family dies, new members are also added to the family by new births of children.

## Types of families

Family can be classified into two categories.

1. *Unitary Family :* A unitary family is one in which a single couple with its offsprings lives. Its smallest size is comprised of two members husband and wife without offspring.
2. *Joint Family :* A joint family is one in which at least one extra member of the family lives with a unitary family such as brothers or sisters of the couple, parents or grandparents etc.

### Causes of disintegration of joint families :

1. Industrialization led the people to different corners of the country for jobs. As a result, couple started living separately from its origin.
2. Urbanization is also leading the people to settle in big and cosmopolitan cities.
3. Materialistic attitude towards life is another cause. Everybody wants to fulfil his own vested interest by earning more and more money and consuming the whole alone.
4. Family welfare programmes are motivating the people to have only one or two children. These motivated people do not want to feed the cricket team of their unmotivated brothers.
5. Consumerism crept into the minds of the people is leading the people to be separated from their roots. More and more consumption is possible only when family is small.

### Merits of joint families :

1. Joint families make social cohesion strong. Head of the family had full control over the young ones in the past. Such heads could easily unite the whole society by their authoritative control over their respective families.
2. Tension for earning a living was not so high in the past. If some people in the family were earning members, it was considered enough.
3. A joint family could exercise its physical or military powers very easily.
4. An individual could obtain more social values and ideals in the large spectrum of the family.

5. Joint families give more emphasis on saving rather than on consumption. This approach was a good approach when production was not made on so large scale as it is done today.

**Effects of disintegration of joint families : (Merits of Unitary families) :** Unitary or separate families are gaining ground at a very fast speed today. The main advantages of these families are given below:

1. Families toil for their own offsprings. As a result, couple is highly motivated to earn more, save more and consume more in future.
2. Size of the families is decreasing which is a good sign for a highly populated country like India. Besides, good quality of education can also be provided to offsprings.
3. A small modern family can not fulfil all the physical, mental, emotional or moral requirements of its children which have led to the rise of specialized institutions to do the job well. Thus specialized training to children can be given.
4. It has reduced group rivalries in villages and more freedom given to children in social affairs is enabling them to utilize their creative potential fully. Practice of equality has also increased in the society. Thus, fragmented small families are useful for a democratic country like India.
5. The practice of inter caste marriages and other social relations is gaining popularity because of unitary families. This is good sign for a society of 21st century. This tendency will crush down caste based inequalities and discriminations in the long run.
6. The moral, social and economic life of the individual have come under the control and guidance of social institutions. The individuals are now to a great extent free to avail the opportunities on his own.

   The only dominating demerit of these families is that their role in imparting informal education to children has gone down to a great extent because father or mother has no time to give it to their children.

## Family and Education

Family can very much contribute to the education of its children in the following ways:

(i) *Conditioning of values and ideals :* The child begins his life under the fostering affection and care of his parents. He receives the first lesson of life in his family. These habits, ideals, and patterns of behaviour received by the child from the family last throughout his life. Thus an individual can not do away with the influence of his family throughout this life. All these things will have direct bearing on the process of education set for a child.

(ii) *Advancement in child's vocabulary and experiences :* All the members of the family act for and react to the child's activities and in this process of give and take child learns many things. His vocabulary also increases in the process of action and reaction. In short, the foundation of a child's future life is laid in the family itself.

(iii) *Reorganization of experiences :* Child learns many experiences from the members of the family. Some of these experiences are good and some are bad, some are pleasant and some of them are painful to him. He recognizes those experiences, if his individuality is respected and he is given love and affection from the family. This reorganization of experiences is very useful for his future life.

(iv) *Natural education :* No preplanned education is given to the child at home. Everything goes on in a natural way. Thus, child learns many things in the family without any deliberate effort.

(v) *Inculcation of social and human values :* Child learns sympathy, cooperation, honesty, truth, justice, feeling of love and many other social and human values at home. When they are formally taught in schools it becomes very easy for him to understand and practice them.

(vi) *Educational effects of family environment :* In the words of K.G. Sayyadain, " The education of man depends on the environment that he enjoys. If these environments are based on good customs and traditions of the family, they will spread beneficial influence on his ideas and development and his education will be useful not only to him but to the whole community.

## Functions of the family

Important function of the family are given below :

(i) *Reproductive function :* The most important function of the family is to reproduce the offspring to maintain continuity of human existence. This function is performed only after marriage. Sexual relations are not established in India without such marriages. Marriage gives a certificate to the new born child that he is the product of a particular couple and he will be identified with that couple throughout his life.

(ii) *Upbringing function :* After reproducing a child the couple takes full responsibility to bring up the child to satisfy his emotional and physical needs. Parents and other members of the family take care of health and other well being of the child . Child is motivated to walk and run, to take food according to his age and to adopt the habits of hygiene and cleanliness in the family. Along with physical development, adequate opportunities and experiences are also provided to the child to train his mental faculties to enable him to earn his livelihood in future. Child also learns a variety of emotions and its expressions from his family when he comes in contact with the members of the family.

(iii) *Social functions :* Child has to live and adjust in the society throughout his life. For this purpose, social values ideals, customs and traditions, cooperative attitude, belongingness, etc. are also taught to him. He is also brought up in a particular religious environment so that he may not lose his cultural identity in future. Teaching of religious lessons becomes more important in the context of secular India because such an education is not to be given in the educational institutions recognized and maintained by the state.

(iv) *Moral development function :* Children are taught what to do and what not to do, what to listen and what not to listen first of all in the family. They are equipped with the acceptable norms and values of the family and the community and thus parents build the character of their offsprings in the manner they like.

(v) *Economic functions:* Once the child attains the age of five he is given opportunity to purchase the small bits from the near by shops. He also learns those vocations and occupations that he visualizes in the family. If members of the family belong to service sector, child gives more emphasis on receiving education to earn his living in future.

(vi) *Educative functions :* This topic has already been discussed in detail in under the chapter "Family and Education".

**How to make the family an effective agency of education ?**

In order to ensure maximum level of physical social, religious, economic and educational development of children, a family is expected to adopt the following measures in the interest of the child :

(i) *Physical environment* **:** Neat and clean health conducive environment should be there in the family. The house should also be open enough to welcome air and sunlight to make the family disease resistant.

(ii) *Social environment* **:** Social environment of the family should be such that child gets maximum opportunity to develop. Family members should be truth loving, honest, cooperative and considerate. They should not be accustomed to filthy habits to infect the young ones of the family. Children should also be given adequate freedom to play and explore the environment themselves.

(iii) *Emotional environment* **:** Child should be regarded as a human not a commodity of future consumption. Environment of love, affection, sympathy, justice etc. should be there in the family. If there are more than one child in the family, all of them should be equally treated by members. The members of the family should talk to the child to the maximum level possible. High level of conversation is a must not only for emotional satisfaction of the child but it is also conducive to his language development in future.

(iv) *Availability of basic needs* **:** Food, cloths and shelter are the basic needs of every human being. Family should do the best to provide nutritious food, environment friendly clothes and a comfortable house for the child. A child born on a footpath is subjected to any atrocities in the society and thus his fundamental right of shelter is denied. If parents are unable to provide these basic needs to their young ones, they should not go for marriage and hence reproductive function.

(v) *Spiritual and aesthetic environment* : For permanent emotional satisfaction, the spiritual and aesthetic environment should also be made good and close to nature. Their dresses should be according to the current fashion of the society. Conscious efforts should be made to get them involved in religious ceremonies and practices. Moreover, if they want to listen music and song or play it, they should not be hindered at all.

(vi) *Activity based environment :* Children are least interested in reading or listening but they are highly motivated for doing something, i.e., writing, drawing a sketch, playing with toys, breaking the articles, etc. All these things increase their practical knowledge. They should be given opportunities for these practicals to the maximum level possible.

(vii) *Educative environment :* A child has to learn many things in today's age of science and technology. Hence, education of the child should start from the family. Even after sending him to the school this responsibility of parents toward a child continues. They must look after him what he is doing in the school and how can be helped at home to achieve high academic numerals in the school.

## COMMUNITY (AN ACTIVE BUT INFORMAL AGENCY)

### Meaning

The word "Community" etymologically means to serve together for a common goal. Technically community is a group of people either living together on a geographical place of land or tied with each other with common ideals and ways of living to achieve the common objectives—physical or metaphysical. A community may be big or small depending on the number of people joining the group ranging from four or five persons to hundreds of millions. Consensus on at least one particular ground to achieve the common goal is the criterion of certifying a group to a community. Thus villages, towns, cities, Muslims, Hindus, Christians, Indians, Americans, Europeans, consumers, producers, financers, all are communities within their circles.

### Definitions

1. **K.Davis defines community as**, "Community is the smallest territorial group that can embrace all aspects of social life"
2. **According to Ginsberg**, "By community is to be understood a group of social beings living a common life including all the infinite variety and complexity of relations which result from common life or constitute it."

## Characteristic Features of a Community

On the basis of the above definitions we can say that community has the following characteristics :

1. The word community is applicable to three types of groups of people I- People living in a particular territory, II- People having common beliefs, III-People following common ideals, values and way of life. All these groups of people are communities in their respective field. Territorial concept is the broadest sense of the community.
2. A community must have some common goals to achieve and through these goals they will reach the final goal.
3. A community shares common ways of living, working and experiences.
4. Social lives of all the persons in the community are common and the same.

## Types of community experiences

(i) Home and family relationship
(ii) Neighborhood
(iii) Play ground and clubs
(iv) Nature such as, plants, animals, birds, growing crops, rivers etc.
(v) Religious institutions
(vi) Work experiences
(vii) Civic life
(viii) Street activities
(ix) Travel and tour
(x) Group activities.

## Community and Education

A child who is attached to his family is also attached to the community which he belongs to. It is because each family unit is an integral part of the community. The influence of the community on the personality of the child is indispensable and continuous. Community helps the child in his teaching learning process in the following ways :

1. *Establishment of schools and vocational centres*: Education of whatsoever type, is a must for progress and socio-economic growth. If community is not providing right type of education to its members, it will remain stagnant resulting to lagging behind the other communities. Community moulds education according to its socio-economic and political needs. For achieving these objectives it establishes schools, colleges and a number of vocational and technical institutions as we see in India. Many types of NGOs run their educational institutes on their own with or without any assistance from the government. If these institutions are run on welfare grounds, only nominal fees are charged in these institutions from the students. In this way, community works almost as a formal active agency of education.

2. *Social and adjustment training* : Community moulds the patterns of behaviour and ways of thinking of its members informally. Community organizes fairs, festivals, conferences, cultural functions and so on to propagate its own distinct culture. Children actively participate in these programmes and they learn many desirable activities through these processes of social contacts and group dynamics such as languages, pronunciation, style of speaking, manners, behaviours and traditions. Community maintains its distinctive identity in the society through these activities.

3. *Transmmission, preservation and advancement of culture* : Community performs these functions in two ways *(a)* Establishing formal educational and cultural institutions *(b)* Organizing cultural programmes for its members of and on. Through these formal and informal activities, the members of the community come in contact with the members of other communities. As a result, culture is not only preserved and transmitted to children but many new chapters of cultural affluence are also added to the individual as well as community life. These avenues and opportunities reduce inter community cultural differences as well.

4. *Local self government and child's development:* No awareness campaign of the government can be made a success without the participation of the community. When NGOs actively took part in National Literacy Mission in 1990s and AIDS Awareness campaign in 2000s only then government achieved a bit success in these campaigns. Similarly, health of the people can not be improved simply by opening hospitals and health care centres in the country. It is because preventive measures are all the time more powerful than curative measures and hence role of the community becomes very significant. Moreover, community also organizes local bodies which look after the sanitation problems, supply of water and maintenance of roads and community health services. It constructs parks and gardens to provide clean atmosphere to people and establishes gymnasiums to provide exercise facilities to people. Once these facilities are availed by children, they develop physically and when they listen the speeches of political leaders and see the local, state or general elections, they become politically matured also.

5. *Mental development of the child :* Community opens libraries and reading rooms for its members and organizes symposia, seminars and conferences on education and science. All these activities give children the opportunities to develop their mental faculties to the maximum level possible.

6. *Religious and moral development of the child:* Community organizes various religious functions and festivals now and then and children also participate in so many religious rituals and practices. They learn many religious traditions and social norms from these activities and they build their character on the basis of them. Community tries to make the social environment good by these activities. Contrary to this if

environment is ethically vulnerable, the members of the community will be addicted to many bad habits such as stealing, robbery, drug addiction etc.

## Significance (Merits) of Community ..ole

The role of the community in shaping and moulding the behaviour of the child and making the social environment conducive to learning is significant in the following ways :

1. Education provided by the community is the need of the hour in today's age of liberalisation and privatization. It is because Government is gradually withdrawing its role from the field of education.
2. Community provides only that type of education which it thinks useful to it.
3. Community education gives real and practical experience to the child which is useful for living.
4. Informal education provided by the community is based on the principle of activity and direct experiences.
5. For transmission and preservation of cultural heritage, the role of the community is always necessary.
6. Democratic values and ideals can easily be imparted to children by various activities of the community.
7. Community emphasises to make its members productive and self reliant. Thus, economic prosperity can also be brought about through community participation.

## Negative role of the community as an Agency of education

If community is not enlightened enough and sensitive to needs and interests of its members, it can damage the total process of education in the following ways :

1. It can provide very poor quality of education to children if the community itself is uneducated on modern lines.
2. If moral standard of the community is low, corruption and malpractices may also creep into the sanctity of education.
3. It can fulfil its own narrow ends and vested interests by manipulating the process of education.
4. If leaders of the community are narrow minded and conservative, they can propagate superstitious beliefs and dogmatism in the society.
5. Community centred education can create communal feelings in the society resulting in social chaos, hatred and intolerance.
6. If repressionistic discipline and rigid curriculum are followed by the community, it will crush the natural and free development of the child.
7. Excess involvement of the community in the personal affairs of the people is a big impediment to the development of national character as is the case of Afghanistan and Algeria today.

## How to make community an effective agency of education ?

Some suggestions are given below to make the community an effective and constructive agency of education.

1. Community should present ideal examples of sacrifice, cooperation, co living and social service before children.
2. Liberal and open minded people can do something for the betterment of the humanity in general. Community should encourage these types of people for leadership role.
3. Community should not run educational institutions on communal lines. Indians are only one community and poverty and deprivation are their biggest foes. So, process of education should be carried on in the national perspectives.
4. Community should recognize and respect the individuality of the child. Especially his innate tendencies, interests and abilities must be taken into consideration and nothing should be forcefully imposed on him.
5. Inter caste marriages and other relations must be encouraged by the community in order to minimize social inequalities and caste or creed distinction.
6. Community should make the social environment as good as possible so that character of the child may be build up on desirable lines.
7. More and more community schools should be established for the education and care of the child. The task of education should not be left on the government alone.

8. In order to preserve and transmit culture, community should organize cultural activities and educational conferences at short intervals.
9. There must be maximum coordination among all agencies of education and in order to ensure it a coordination cell could be set up.
10. State's patronage and control are must for making community educational programmes a success.

In admission of students and appointment of staff transparency must be maintained by the community. Worth and willingness should be the criteria not money and muscle power.

## CHURCH OR RELIGION (AN ACTIVE AND INFORMAL AGENCY OF EDUCATION)

**Meaning :** In the narrow sense religion means belief in and practice of rituals, participation in religious ceremonies and performing time bound prayers at religious places. Individual considers his own religion only right and discards other religions and its rituals in toto.

In broad sense religion is a way of life for all human being with purity of mind and heart. This religion does not instigate a person to show hatred to others on ideological grounds. Followers of such religion shower love, sympathy and aid to others by compromising their selves in the larger interest of humanity. Such a religious person is always a piece of consolation for others. He performs rituals but not at the cost of humanity. In short, realization of self (God) through social, moral, spiritual and human values and ideals is true religion. In the words of Iqbal-the composer of *Sare Jahan Se Achchha*

"Slaves of God are many having their abode in wood.

I am the slave of thee who is the lower of manlihood"

### Definitions

1. **Kant:** "Religion is the recognition of all our duties as divine commandments."
2. **Harold Hoffding:** "The essence of religion is faith in the conservation of values."
3. **Gisbert:** "Religion is the dynamic beliefs in and submission to God or Gods on whom man feels dependent."
4. **Prophet Mohammad:** "Religion is a way of life that ensures the well being of the humanity as a whole".

### Characteristics and Importance of Religion

On the basis of above definitions of religion we can derive the following characteristics and their significance for human being :

1. Humans have to pay off many duties while living in the society. Considering these duties as commandments of God is actually religion. Thus it is religion that tells us how to pay off our duties toward humanity as a whole.
2. The faith that we have in values and ideals is religion. But having mere faith is not enough. This faith must be translated into action.
3. It is the nature of man that he creates his God to be dependent on Him especially on the occasions of frustrations and failures. Man shows full submission to his God on these occasions. Thus, religion is a kind of consolation mechanism.
4. Religion ensures human welfare in general irrespective of caste, creed or colour.
5. Religion inculcates in man the essential social and moral values like courtesy, tolerance, sympathy etc.
6. Religion is a way of purifying mind and heart that is very essential for achieving mental peace.
7. Religion is actually hope of achieving permanent bliss (parmanand) in the very distant future. Thus, religion develops self confidence in us.
8. Cultural and social values are mostly derived from religions. These values undergo changes when we confront to the physical objects of the world. These processes of adjustment and readjustment go on throughout our life.
9. Religion channelizes our sexual instincts also. Through religious instructions we give up behaving like beasts and legalizes our sexual relations in the society through marriage.
10. Man is not expected to be civilized without religion. If God had not existed, man would have created him in order to live a civilized and controlled life.

## Religion and Education

Education is an active and practical aspect of religion. Both are inter-related to each other in the following ways:

1. Educational and social values are derived from religion. An effective educational system incorporates only those values and ideals in education which are common to all religions.
2. Philosophies are the logical and dynamic interpretation of religions and aims of education are derived from these philosophies. Thus, education is indirectly indebted to religion.
3. Without religion education is just the attainment of material comforts. It is religion that takes us to spiritual satisfaction.
4. Religion is the way of life and what else is education.
5. Education modifies human behaviour and build his character in accordance with ideals and values set by the religion.
6. Religion and education both teaches us the lessons of tolerance, sympathy, courtesy, cooperation, social service and sacrifice for and respect of others. Principle of justice is followed in all these matters.
7. Sense of duty and responsibility which are inalienable parts of democratic life are taught by religion and education both.
8. Preservation, transmission and advancement of culture are important functions of education and this culture is basically rooted in religions
9. Idealism and Existentialism, these two philosophies have close affinity to religion. Every educational system is recognizing these two philosophies to fight against the menacing philosophy of fundamentalism.
10. Religion is not opposed even in secular countries like India or France. The reason is that they recognize their role in the individual lives of their citizens.

## Two aspects of Religion

Religion has two aspects, individual and social. Religion is deeply rooted in the individual life of man by nature. If there is some deviation from religion it is because of the irreligious social environment. Religion can play a good role in regulating our social lives also but it is a tough task because of the diversity of religions.

A middle approach is that we should make the society religious by making the individuals religious without touching their social dogmas. Society should be guided only by those principles which are common to all religions. This may be the real implication of secularism in a country like India. Society here means the society as a whole not the society of Muslims, Hindus, Christians etc. Every individual should be left free to act in his own boundaries freely provided that these individuals are not crossing over the boundaries of others. This is the real spirit of religion. It has been well explained by Quran in the following words :

"Religion is only one. It is man who has manipulated this religion to fulfil his own vested interest". This one religion is actually the realization of divine power.

## Religious Education in Schools

**Arguments for the motion :**

1. Child without moral and spiritual values may be very dangerous for the society in future and the root of these values is but religion. So religious education should be included in the curriculum.
2. Acts of sacrifice, social service and charity can be incorporated in the behaviour of the child through this education.
3. Students come to know about so many personalities of high character in this type of education and these people can be a source of motivation for them.
4. Religious education teaches the lesson of human equality and social justice. This is the touching need of a fragmented society like India. There is no scope of caste based differences in religions especially in Islam and Christianity.
5. Culture which is an integral part of our social system can easily be preserved by religious education.
6. Humans of today are very much dissatisfied with the material affluence and they are looking for mental peace in night clubs and five star hotels. These places are awarding them HIV infections and nothing else. Religious education can easily make them tension free by making them self restraint.

7. Religious education brings a child close to his religion and a truly religious person is absolutely harmless for the society in general.
8. Rituals taught by this education regulate the life of the child round the clock.
9. Corruptions of the society can be removed by religious education.
10. We can inculcate self restraint and devotion to job through religious education.

All these things are possible only because a truly religious person is always afraid of absolute divine power and his accountability to that power will work as a supervisor before him.

**Arguments against the motion:** There are some practical difficulties in imparting religious education in schools. They are as follows :

1. *Selection of religion and its various sects :* There are so many religions on this earth and each religion has many sects extremely at variance with each other. Which religion and which sect to be chosen for this purpose is really a challenge before us. If all of them are included in the curriculum on optional basis, it will incur too heavy costs to afford.
2. *Narrow mindedness :* Interpreters of religions have made the religious fundamentals very complex and rigid. This rigidity and complexity can develop narrow mindedness in children.
3. *Negation of the present world :* Religious education gives so much emphasis on the world hereafter and present world gets ignored. This denial of world is really a danger for human excellence through inventions and discoveries.
4. *Wastage of time :* Religious education without practice is useless. And if both are included in the curriculum it will cost too much time and energy. As a result, school will not be able to complete the courses of modern curriculum.
5. *Problem of ideal teachers :* Religious education can not be imparted by ordinary teachers. Experts in the field will be needed for this purpose. If such experts are recruited from pure religious background, their adjustment in the school system will be very difficult.
6. *Problems of curriculum construction :* Religious education is a vast area in itself. So the whole subject matter can not be included in the curriculum. What part of this education should be incorporated in the modern education and what should be the criteria of selection are some of the unanswered questions so far.
7. *Opposition from some guardians :* Religion is not the priority of many people today. Hence, if this type of education is included in the curriculum, many guardians, may rise against it.
8. *Against the spirit of the constitution :* Article 22 of the Indian constitution states that no religious education can be imparted in any government school. Even those public schools which are recognized by the government can do so only at the will of guardians. Only those institutions can impart religious education which are founded by any trust or society exclusively for this purpose. Thus, if we want to include this education in the curriculum, we will have to amend the constitution first on solid ground. We will have to amend not only this Article but a number of several other Articles too.

## Suggestions to overcome the difficulties

Imparting religious education in original sense is not actually the solution to all our social problems. Schools are not temples, mosques or Madarsas. They should impart religious education with the following adaptations :

1. Unity of all religions should be emphasised in the education of schools as Gandhijee has rightly pointed out-
   "Fundamental principles of ethics are common to all religions. They should be certainly taught to students."
   For this purpose a committee of experts from different religions should sit together to identify those common points. These points should be explained with the help of examples from all religions simultaneously. This will develop a critical and comparative insight in children.
2. Moral, spiritual and social values from all religions should be borrowed judiciously and should be taught to students through languages and subjects of sciences. There is no need of teaching Moral science as separate subject. This is the opinion of Education Commission (1964-66) also.

3. A responsible and justice loving society can be created by practice of religion and not by making students learned in religious field. Stories of religious personalities of the past and ideal characters of a teacher will motivate them to put the religion into practice. Hence, social and educational system should be reorganized from this point of view.
4. There are many superstitions found in every religion. They are big impediments in the way of progress. They should not be made the part of curriculum at any level. Even metaphysical principles should be taught rationally and scientifically.
5. Religious rivalries, or crusade should be excluded from the curriculum of religious education so that communalism might not raise its head in the society.
6. Thee are many unanswered questions in every religion. They should not be touched upon at all.
7. Efforts should be made to ensure that secular fabric of the nation should not be destroyed by this education. If it happens so, democratic set up of the society may change and majority may inflict mental or physical casualties on minorities.

## STATE (AN ACTIVE AND NON FORMAL AGENCY OF EDUCATION)

### Meaning

State is a powerful super structure of the society as a whole whose laws have to be abided by all its members without question. There are four fundamental elements necessarily found in a state :

- **Territory :** State has well defined territory where its members live in and this territory can not be changed in the short run.
- **Population :** A piece of land without any population can not be termed as state.
- **Government :** A state has a government also. This government frames laws for its people to bring about peace in the society.
- **Sovereignty :** The members belonging to the same territory will run the government, otherwise it will cease to be a state. It will rather be a colony.

These four elements are there in the definition of the state given by **Garner** as below :

"State is a community of persons more or less numerous, permanently occupying a definite portion of a territory, independent of a foreign control and possessing an organized government to which the inhabitants render a habitual obedience."

### Types of State

***Totalitarian State :*** Communist states or kingdoms come under this category. In such states political, social or economic powers are entirely concentrated in the hands of one or few persons in the state. This type of states have absolute control over education also. Here individual freedom or privacy of citizens is not recognized by the state. All the citizens have only to think and do what state wants to make them so without any questioning. Thus destiny of individuals is totally in the hands of state. In the field of education, what to teach, how much to teach, why and how to teach, everything is decided by the state without any regard to individual's ability, innate inclination and needs.

***Democratic State :*** Here everything is decided by the members of the state themselves through their representatives. State also distributes its absolute power among its citizens through decentralization. The citizens plan for their own and execute the plan themselves. Individuals here are fully free to decide what to teach, how and why to teach and how much to teach. Private institutions are fully allowed to choose their own track.

### State and Education

There are three approaches supported by philosophers regarding the relationship between state and education. They are given below –

1. **Individualism :** John Locke, J.S. Mill, Bentham etc. are supporters of this ideology. According to this approach, the function of the state is to protect and guide its people only and not to interfere in their personal affairs. Education is entirely a personal matter. So, state should not interfere in the sphere of education at all. This doctorine is also known as "Doctorine of Laissez Faire".
2. **Collectivism :** Mathew Arnold, Carlyle, Ruskin, Marx etc. are the supporters of this ideology. According to this ideology, the function of the state is not to protect its citizens from external or internal dangers only but also to control their

behaviour and activities through education in the larger interests of the state. Individuality of the people is totally denied here.

3. **Golden mean approach :** In between the two extremes of individualism and collectivism there is a middle path supported by modern thinkers and democrats. According to them, the task of education is so important for the individual as well as the state that there must be full cooperation and coordination among all the agencies of education-family school, church and community and only state can play this dynamic role because of its super structure and legal powers. All the agencies are allowed to perform their educational functions, with full freedom but supervision is necessarily done by the state to bring about social justice. Besides, welfare states also take the responsibility of educating the masses and the poor on its own. Government schools and colleges etc. are run for this purpose.

While supporting this balancing approach Raymond has rightly said–

"The function of the state is to protect and promote not to absorb or take the place of family and the individual. In the sphere of education it is the state's right and duty to protect the interior right of the family and the church. Similarly state ought to make good the deficiency due to incapacity, unworthiness or other defects of parents and generally to protect according to rules of reason and the faith, the moral and religious education of the young by removing any public impediments".

## Arguments in Favour of State Control Over Education

1. Universalisation of education is possible if state takes full responsibility of educating the masses and without education democracy may not be a success.
2. Uniform education and education of national character is possible only when education is centralized by the state.
3. National integration in a country of diverse culture and religion is very much needed to get the whole country united. It is possible only when all citizens of the country are given same type and quality of education under the supervision of the state.
4. State can better visualize the need of the country as a whole with respect to the changing requirements of the time and age and it can plan accordingly. Individuals are not supposed to do so.
5. Business and industries have expanded a lot today. If citizens are uniformly educated they can adjust anywhere in the country very easily.
6. In a country like India where education is beyond the reach of 30% population on their own, state will have to take the initiative. Same is the case with many underdeveloped and poor countries.
7. If state lessens its role regarding education, religion, the second important agency of education will increase its role and fundamentalism in the society will develop.

## Arguments Against the State Control of Education

1. State interference in education can politicize education also.
2. State can indoctrinate its own ideology into the minds of children.
3. By neglecting the individuality of children state can crush creativity also.
4. Only those teachers will be appointed to teach the boys who are subservient to the state fully and this can make the schools prisons for children.
5. Freedom of preparing individual cultures will not be there in such system. It will lead to cultural deprivation in the country.
6. All round development of personality of children is not possible here.
7. Child will not be able to receive education according to his own interest and needs.
8. Democracy may not survive in this system because everything will be imposed from above just in order to bring about equality of socialistic nature. That is why this system failed in erstwhile U.S.S.R. and Eastern Europe.
9. This type of education will prepare only slaves not citizens.

## Educational Functions of State

A democratic state is supposed to perform the following functions regarding education:

1. **Educational planning :** Educational planning is made after consultation with educators, philosophers and educationists. This planning is made not only for government schools and colleges but also for private ones and a national framework of education is made.

2. **Construction of comprehensive scheme of education:** Equal educational opportunities are provided to all citizens without the distinction of caste, creed, colour or sex and special provisions are made for weaker sections of the society in order to bring them at par. This scheme of education is communicated to all levels of educational administration by the government.

3. **Construction of curriculum :** Curriculum is constructed by the government through its authorized bodies and it is followed by all educational institutions with minor additions(not subtraction) according to the local needs. Emphasis is given here on free development of personality of the child.

4. **Inculcation of democratic values :** Democratic values and ideals are included in the curriculum and scheme of education very intelligently. These values and ideals mould the children in such a way that they are able to serve the country in the best manner possible without ignoring their own interests. State also takes the help of mass media and cultural centres in this regard.

5. **Provision of educational institutions :** At least 5% of the gross domestic product (GDP) is spent on education in a democratic state. Government establishes its own educational institutions, give financial assistance to high performing private institutions, supervises and controls privately managed institutions and motivates the NGOs to open more and more educational institutions across the country. Uniformity of standard is also maintained everywhere.

6. **Adult education campaign :** There are many citizens who lag behind in education in their childhood due to certain reasons. Adult education centres are run for these people to provide them education through evening or night classes on non-formal basis. Adults are educated through mass media also in the country.

7. **Self reliance through education :** Only that education is given to citizens which can help them earn their livelihood. For this purpose, a variety of vocational and professional courses are also run along with the education of pure academic subjects. Thus needs of the individuals and the society is simultaneously taken into consideration for this purpose.

8. **Training and appointment of teachers :** Teaching is a critically challenging job not a play. It requires especially trained teachers for this purpose. Such training is given by the state through specialized agencies and when they are fully trained they are appointed to further the mission to its final stage. Transparency is always maintained in these admissions and appointment of teachers is made on the basis of worth and willingness only. Even privately managed institutions have to follow clear cut guidelines of the state in this regard.

9. **Military education to children :** In order to protect the country from foreign invasion and insurgency, military education is provided to all children. These trained children will defend the country once they are grown up.

10. **Scholarship facilities to talented and poor students :** In order to maintain high standard of education, scholarships are given to talented students after standardized tests and interview. Such scholarships are also made available for poor students so that their poverty may not work as a barrier in their way to progress.

11. **Appointment of commissions and committees:** In order to review educational aims, curriculum, method of teaching and examination system commissions and committees are also appointed by the government and their recommendations are accepted and implemented.

12. **Incentive to educational researches :** Research in any field of education is an expensive and time taking process. So individuals are least likely to be interested to carry forward this task.

State takes initiative in this regard to solve educational problems and to improve the situation in the best interest of the society.

**Negative role of the state**

Liberty must be guaranteed by the state. A state may become the enemy of liberty in three ways.

(i) *By disloyalty :* State or those in power are not faithful to the public. They are corrupt as is the case today.

(ii) *By excess :* Government or those in power are treating the people with heavy hand. It is not heeding to the demands of the people in general.

(iii) *By inefficiency :* Government is not efficient resulting in socio political chaos.

If such is the case in any country, education will work as the most abused weapon in the hands of the state or those in power.

# OBJECTIVE QUESTIONS

**1.** School, state, church, museum, library and art galleries are formal agencies of education because
(a) they have been established with specific educational objectives to achieve.
(b) they have fixed time table and place for their activities.
(c) their supervision and evaluation procedures are fixed.
(d) all of these

**2.** In informal agencies of education
(a) formalities of rules and regulations are reduced to the minimum
(b) learners need not do efforts for learning here
(c) no formal evaluation is done
(d) all of these

**3.** Informal agencies of education may be criticized on which of the following grounds
(a) It imparts vague and unsystematic knowledge
(b) It does not enforce discipline
(c) Professional skills cannot be developed here
(d) All of these

**4.** Which of the following is not an active agency of education
(a) family
(b) religious and social organizations
(c) factory and workshop
(d) state

**5.** Mass media, cinema and library are passive agencies of education because
(a) learner can not react to the feedback system of these agencies directly
(b) they provide informal education
(c) they can not come closer to the educant
(d) all of these

**6.** Which of the following is a non commercial agency of education (CFJ Brown's classification)
(a) NGOs
(b) Church
(c) Non Welfare Clubs
(d) Scouting

**7.** Education of a child really begins
(a) Once he takes birth
(b) Once he attains the age of three
(c) Once he is admitted to post nursery schools
(d) Once he learns to speak

**8.** Family is the original social institution from which all other institutions emerged, who said this
(a) Brown (b) Ballard
(c) Machiver (d) None of them

**9.** Basis of relationship in the family is
(a) sexual intercourse
(b) blood
(c) breast feeding
(d) all of these

**10.** Which of the following informal systems is most effective for socialization
(a) Playground (b) Public library
(c) Family (d) Church

**11.** Social functions of the family are more important than economic or civic functions because
(a) even sick and old people and widows are cared in the family
(b) it teaches manners and traditions to children
(c) both of these
(d) none of these

**12.** Common people in India got the opportunity of schooling during
(*a*) Medieval period (*b*) British period
(*c*) Buddhist period (*d*) b and c both

**13.** The future of a nation is decided in
(*a*) schools
(*b*) big factories
(*c*) the military headquarters
(*d*) all of these

**14.** Which of the following is not the primary function of schools
(*a*) reorganization and reconstruction of human experiences
(*b*) all-round development of the child
(*c*) to make the children self reliant
(*d*) advancement of culture

**15.** Which of the following is an important responsibility of schools toward home
(*a*) supplementing the educative functions of the family
(*b*) enabling the child to appreciate the role of the family
(*c*) equipping the child with social norms
(*d*) all of these

**16.** Character and nature of education in schools must be revised and reviewed very frequently because
(*a*) society is dynamic and changes very frequently
(*b*) demographic composition of the society changes
(*c*) both of these
(*d*) none of these

**17.** In a democratic country, school should reflect
(*a*) National aspirations
(*b*) Community related local aspirations
(*c*) Both of these
(*d*) None of these

**18.** A corrupt society like India's can best be reformed by
(*a*) schooling system
(*b*) judicial system
(*c*) legislative system
(*d*) all of them as a joint effort

**19.** Which of the following characteristics does not belong to a community
(*a*) group of people serving each other
(*b*) people belonging to a particular religion
(*c*) a group of people living in a geographical place of land
(*d*) people having common ideals of life

**20.** The best teacher in a village school is he who
(*a*) carries community experiences to the class room
(*b*) prepares instructional programmes in the interest of the community
(*c*) carries classroom experiences to the community
(*d*) all of these

**21.** Difference between the nature of activities of school and state lies in
(*a*) the enforcement of law (state) and rules (school)
(*b*) enforcement of law guided by the judiciary in case of the state
(*c*) organizational structure, i.e., State is a political and school is a sovereign social organization
(*d*) Taking pain for the development of citizens

**22.** Which of the following is not included in human development Index-progress index of a nation
(*a*) education
(b) health
(*c*) political stability
(*d*) per capita income

**23.** Universalisation of education is the concept adopted by
(*a*) modern state (*b*) democratic state
(*c*) totalitarian state (*d*) religious state

**24.** Which of the following agency regulates education ?
(*a*) Church (*b*) State
(*c*) School (*d*) Library

**25.** Secular education in India means
(*a*) an education cpposed to religion
(*b*) an education indifferent to religion
(*c*) an education emphasizing equality of religions
(*d*) none of these

**26.** In the three stages of family life cycle, begining family, expanding family and contracting family, role of education becomes dominant in which of

the following stages
(*a*) first stage
(*b*) third stage
(*c*) second stage
(*d*) first and second stage

**27.** Adjustment problem is most seen between husband and wife in which stage of family cycle.
(*a*) Expanding family
(*b*) Contracting family
(*c*) Begining family (*d*) Both (a) and (c)

**28.** Sex education to adults is needed in order to
(*a*) get them adjusted in their own families
(*b*) reduce mis-conceptions about sex and its related problems
(*c*) both of these
(*d*) none of these

## ANSWERS

| 1 | 2 | 3 | 4 | 5 | 6 | 7 | 8 | 9 | 10 |
|---|---|---|---|---|---|---|---|---|---|
| (*d*) | (*d*) | (*d*) | (*d*) | (*a*) | (*c*) | (*a*) | (*b*) | (*d*) | (*c*) |
| **11** | **12** | **13** | **14** | **15** | **16** | **17** | **18** | **19** | **20** |
| (*c*) | (*d*) | (*a*) | (*d*) | (*d*) | (*a*) | (*c*) | (*d*) | (*b*) | (*d*) |
| **21** | **22** | **23** | **24** | **25** | **26** | **27** | **28** | | |
| (*b*) | (*c*) | (*a*) | (*b*) | (*c*) | (*c*) | (*d*) | (*c*) | | |

# Education as a Social Sub System (Education and Society)

## SOCIETY

### Meaning of Society

Society is simply not an assembly of few or more people. An assembly of people will be termed as a society if following conditions are fulfilled-

I. Mutual contact between its member on a formal basis
II. Exchange of ideas among people
III. Some rules and regulations for the preservation of rights of every member
IV. Certain norms must be there to be followed by the people so that duties may be performed
V. Permanency and continuity must also be there. Society undergoes some changes no doubt but these changes will not be such as to finish the society by its root. The institutions which are formed and then they die out are only the units of the society. They are not society in itself.

School is also a society or social sub system because it fulfills all these five conditions.

On the basis of these characteristics we may define a society in the following words :

"A society is a group of people living in a geographical area with almost common values, ideas and culture. These people follow the accepted norms to consider the right of others".

Thus, we see that there is no particular size of a society. It may be so small consisting of three persons only i.e., first person, second person, and the third person and so big consisting of millions of people i.e. a country, a religious community or a particular race living in a particular area. A big society may have so many units and subunits to run the society smoothly and a person may acquire the membership of so many social units at a time. The sphere of the society is so wide that all the activities of men come under it.

### Need and importance of the society

1. Man is a social animal. He does not like to live a solitary life. He needs someone to interact. Without this interaction his communication ability will not last long.
2. Man is tied with some relationship through his family in the society. He is someone's father and someone is his uncle or nephew. Such relations are necessary for social cohesions.
3. Motivation of life is derived from these blood relations. If there is none for whom I have some love or bond, I would not have any craze for life.
4. All the people have some common interests which are preserved by them while living in a society.
5. Every human wants to perform something extra ordinary or unique. This is possible only in a social environment.
6. The existence of a society reduces the vulnerability of a man. If he does not belong to any society he may be easily finished by his rivals.
7. Culture and traditions are the product of the society. A man can not behave against the self established ideals and traditions in the society.

### The relationship between society and education

It is the society that determines and formulates the pattern of education keeping its particular needs into account. Education generally does not deviate from the ideals of the society. Thus, fundamental character of the education system is determined by the society it serves. The other way round is also correct in the sense the education preserves the ideals of the society and its culture and brings about reform if there is any deviation seen by the people. Thus, education is instrumental in shaping the pattern of the society as well. The examples of various societies and the pattern of education set by them are given below:

1. **Ancient Indian society :** Religion especially rituals and yajnas were dominating in the society. So education was mostly religious in character emphasizing character building and religious ceremonies. Vedic mantras were mostly taught to the selected class of the society because education was confined to Brahmins.
2. **Medieval societies of the world** : It was the age when international rivalries were on its peak. Strong nations had extreme desire to colonialise the weak onces by putting them down. So emphasis was given on military training and advancement of warfare technology.
3. **Modern society** : It is very much open and free in its structure. Mental as well as physical activities are not crushed here. This freedom of thinking and action is also reflected in the educational system. The variety and number of choices which are available today were beyond our imagination in the past.
4. **Idealistic society :** In such a society emphasis is given on adherence to ideals and progress of ideas. As a result, most part of the educational processes revolve round the mental and spiritual activities.
5. **Materialistic society :** In such a society only material affluence is given importance. In such a society education prepares a child to become a money earning member of the society. People recognize economic activities only.
6. **Pragmatic society** : In such a society only that part of knowledge is given to the child which is useful for him in any way. He is not taught irrelevant or spiritual materials. New values are created through education to adapt to the changing values of the society.
7. **Fascist society :** In such a society racial supremacy and state dominance is emphasised in order to propagate extreme form of nationalism. Education prepares the child to sacrifice everything that he has to protect and extend the national boundaries.

## Duties and Functions of the Society Towards Education

Important educational functions of the society are as follows :

1. **Formulating ideals and values for education :** The ideals and values which are to be achieved by education are determined by the society. The formulation of these values will depend upon the nature and type of the society, thus, education reflects the needs of the society.
2. **All round development of children :** Society wants to develop its members to the fullest extent. Society performs this function by establishing various units and sub units such as schools, colleges, religious centres, welfare organizations different types of clubs etc.
3. **Vocational training :** Society has to make its members productive and self reliant. For this purpose, they are given various types of vocational training through various social sub systems. This helps them to participate in the activities of the society actively and confidently.
4. **Civic training** : It is the duty of the society to make its members socially responsible and politically aware. They are taught their rights and duties through various formal and non formal agencies of education and through active participation in civic life.
5. **Inculcation of principles of justice :** Everyone wants to gain more from the society by sacrificing less. By doing so, he usurps the due of others using unjust and unfair means. Lesson of justice and fairness is taught to him by the society. This process starts from the family and is furthered by other agencies. If this is not given due importance, the survival of the society itself will be at stake.
6. **Development of aesthetic sense :** Members of the society must admire what they see in physical form. This aesthetic sense is developed by getting them involved in painting, arts, music, drama, dance etc. Mass media plays very important role in this regard.
7. **Tolerance :** Society is very much pluralistic due to the rise of many religions and languages today. Everyone considers himself right because of the excessive liberty given to him. For the proper

development of this attitude everyone must be tolerant enough to regard others without any narrow mindedness. This function is performed by the society by establishing secular, social and political institutions.

8. **Adaptation of social changes:** Society is not static. It is always changing. Whatever changes take place in the society over time are transferred to education to adapt to it. As a result, education pattern, policies and programmes also change.
9. **Establishment of schools :** This is the most important and direct function of the society. A child remains in the schools and colleges more than 12-16 years devoting maximum time to his school obligation. So schools and colleges can be used as most important agency to bring about all those changes in the child that a society wants to do. For this purpose, it establishes educational institutions constructs curriculum for children, appoints trained teachers and provides financial assistance to them for their best running.
10. **Establishment of public libraries :** Grown up people who have left the schools after education need certain academic and peaceful places to satisfy their minds. Libraries may be suitable places for them. Society establishes these libraries and equip them with variety of books, newspapers, journals, magazines etc.
11. **Formation of clubs** : Recreation in the form of games, sports and cultural activities are intensely needed by all humans. This need is satisfied by the society by establishing cultural and games clubs.
12. **Coordinating various agencies of education :** There are so many agencies engaged in fulfilling the educational needs of the people. There must be full coordination among all of them to achieve higher level of growth. This functions is performed by the society by its most powerful unit, i.e., state. It is the state that brings all these efforts into a single thread.

## Impact of education on society

Education is supportive to the enrichment of the society in the following ways :

1. **Preservation, transmission and advancement of culture :** Every society has its customs and traditions, moral, cultural and religious values, cultural heritage of the past etc. and society is always proud of them. Education plays a leading role in the preservation of them. They are transmitted to the next generation by various agencies of education. During the process of education certain new knowledge is also added to them by researches and experiences of the people. This makes the culture advanced.
2. **Social awakening :** While living in the society, the individual comes across certain social problems. He is confronted with certain inhuman attitude and unfriendly behaviour. He comes to know through education that social values and norms are very essential for a peaceful society. He finds the way of solving social problems through education.
3. **Political awareness:** Though education individual comes to know about various political ideologies operating in the world and their impact on the society. Knowledge of rights and duties given to the people and their implementation by law enforcing agencies can make the society better.
4. **Contributive to economic prosperity:** Education provides various types of vocational and professional training. Education is also responsible to new inventions and discoveries and advancement of technology. All these things increase the income of the people directly or indirectly and thus society becomes rich.
5. **Social mobility and social change :** A man can achieve higher and higher social status through education. The ward of a rickshaw puller can become a D.M. and thus his status can change. Besides, whatever social, economic or scientific development takes place in any part of the world is immediately brought to the country through education. This social change is necessary for the social development of man.
6. **Socialization of the child :** The child comes in contact with many other children of the society and learn many desirable attitudes and

behaviours. He also observes the behaviour of his teachers and adopts them as ideals. He can learn many ideals and values from his books also. All these things help in the socialization of a child.

7. **Social reforms** : Man is by nature creation of evils. He is always vulnerable to evils prevailing in the society. Education makes him conscious of these evils. His behaviour is shaped in such a way that he does not get involved in evil activities. Collective reform of the society is also possible only through education.

## Indian Society and its Characteristics

Indian society is unique and different from other societies of the world with respect to following characteristics:

**1. A Stratified Society :** Strata suggest an ordered hierarchy of superiority or inferiority along with differences. Indian society is divided into different strata just like layers of rocks. Each stratum has its unique position. This stratification is made on the basis of birth. Take the example of Hindu society. Brahmins who are born out of the mouth of Brahma are at the top. Then comes Khashtriyas who have taken birth from the arms of Brahma, Vaishya occupies the third place in the society. They have taken birth from the stomach of Brahma. Shudras, the product of Brahma's feet occupy the lowest status in the stratification system. According to Manusmiriti, Brahmins own the responsibility of education, Khashtriyas are to defend the country, the occupation of Vaishyas should be trade and agriculture and Shudras are there to serve all the others.

Apart from these four major divisions, every caste is divided into a number of sub castes, and each of them has different rank in the society. For example, rank of Tripathi is not the same in the society as that of Chaturvedi, a Mittal differs from a Bansal, and so on. In this way the Hindu society have thousands of social divisions, on the basis of birth.

Case of Muslims is not much different from Hindus. They are mostly Hindu converts. When they embraced Islam in the pre-medieval period they also brought their social divisions to Islam. Thus, Muslim society formed by them also get fragmented. For example, almost all thakurs adopted the title of khan. All Brahmins put themselves at the top by choosing the title of Seyyids and so on. Thus, almost the same stratification is seen in Muslim society as well.

These divisions are so deeply rooted in the society that a vaishya can not think of establishing marital relations with a Brahmin. Even a sub caste of the root caste is very much socially away from other sub castes of the same root. There is a slight change in Muslim society in this regard. This society is actually grouped into two major castes. High castes people and lower caste people. Inter caste social relations are possible here but only within the group. The combination of high and low is not possible at all.

This stratification is not limited to castes only. Occupational and economic stratifications are also disintegrating the society. Certain occupations are given high status in the society and some are ranked at the lowest. A rickshaw puller who is earning more than Rs. 5000 per month is lower than a potter who is on the other hand earning less than Rs. 2000 per month just because of differences in the occupational status. Similarly, manual labour is rated low as compared to mental work and social relations between these two groups are rarely seen.

Some people say that castes were born out of occupational groups in the past but this is only partially correct. It is because we see many people belonging to higher castes when they adopt the occupation of lower castes people, do not lose their status in the society because of their occupation.

These rigid stratifications are actually disintegrating the society socially, emotionally and culturally resulting in disintegration of the nation.

The emergence of private sector in the production process as a dominant force has created one more grouping in the society. It is the new division of society into two classes—government employees and employees of the private sector. Later is rated low in the society because of low pay scale and lack of pension benefits. Similarly, liberal policies of employment towards women have created a new class. If husband and wife both are employed, they are rated high in the society as compared to single earning member families.

One thing that is clear from the above discussion is that caste based distinction is social in nature and mostly related to birth while class based distinction is economic in nature and mostly related to occupation. However, the impact of these distinctions is so powerful that no social reformer has been able to wash them out in India since the ancient period. Society is still the same as it was thousands years before. This gulf is widening even further because of the wrong methods of reservations given to different sections of the society. Had economically and socially backward families of all communities in India been identified and registered separately, caste based differences must have been narrowed down to a great extent. We are issuing separate certificates to physically challenged people after thorough investigation but we are reluctant to do so in case of socially and economically backwards. Is it rational to give reservation in jobs and admissions to descendants of Mayawatijee (had she got married and had children). I leave this question for readers and is it justified to leave Kashmiri Brahmins on the mercy of their cruel destinies. I leave this question for politicians.

**2. A Closed Society:** In the context of Indian society it can very rightly be said that there are so many entrance gates here but no exit at all. Once we enter into this society we can not go out. Some examples in this regard are given below-

*(i)* We do not accept humans as one community with same redness of bloods, with same number of hands, legs, mouth, eyes, nose etc. We first personify them as Hindus, Muslims, Christians, Jews etc. on the ground of personal beliefs. Bengalis, Assamese, Biharis, Kashmiris etc. on the ground of speech or vocal differences. Tiwari, Varanwal, Agarwal, Chauhan, Pasi etc. on the ground of birth, and Julahas, Charmkars, Nais, Washermen etc. on the ground of occupation and so on. Indians are not considerate enough to regard humans as humans only.

*(ii)* Social barriers are so strong in India that inter caste or inter creed marriage are generally considered as a social crime. Thus, mixing of one sub social system with others becomes very difficult.

*(iii)* 50% of the total population is still unwilling to give up the occupations of their forefathers and the traditions attached to them.

*(iv)* Indian society is slave of customs and traditions. It is not willing to accept this fact that these traditions and customs were made by man not by God, so man can change them also.

*(v)* People of India are sticking to so many superstitions and dogmas though no scientific theory or logic can prove them. Take the example of Ganga Ishnan. We believe that whatever sins we commit throughout the year is automatically washed away if we take a dip into Ganga. Is this type of belief helpful in removing the evils from the society. Such types of beliefs are actually barriers in the way of social reforms.

*(vi)* So many restrictions are imposed by the family, the smallest unit of the society on its members. Many of these restrictions hinder free thinking and independent action.

*(vii)* People of India have been made accountable to so many superiors and systems. It has turned them into rebellion and they do not feel accountability at all.

*(viii)* Everyone in the society wants excess of his due without extra efforts. Our social system is making us parasite on others. This is a serious challenge for economic progress and prosperity and without economic prosperity openness is not possible.

**3. A Static Society :** Indian society is very much averse to change. If any change is accepted, it is done only unwillingly. Resistance is always shown for every type of change. If someone advocates for change, he is opposed and some times punished. Change which is the law of nature is very much essential for social prosperity.

**4. A Corrupt Society :** Barring few people, the whole Indian society is corrupt. A professor or a school teacher is corrupt by not teaching his students honestly and devotedly a businessman is corrupt by giving fake advertisement and charging monopolistic prices, politicians are corrupt by demanding large amount of money from beaurocrates which the later loot from ordinary people, police is corrupt by doing excess and by distorting the cases at bribes and so on. If any resistance is shown against it by honest people of the society, they are penalized socially, mentally, physically as well as economically. The more dismal side of the picture is that we have given up hope and bowed down before this devil. Some innocent people of the society are waiting for a divine messenger or incarnate to come but both these approaches are wrong in my opinion.

## Difference between Caste, Class and Ethnicity

Before coming to the solutions of these problems it is better to define caste, class and ethnicity and technical differences between them :

1. Caste is related to birth and it has its origin into superstitious beliefs. Classes are created while living in the society. Ethnicity refers to group of people of different racial or national origin. For example Aryans came to India from Central Asia. Arabs came to India from Arab Peninsula, Pakhtoons came to India from Afghanistan and Iran. All of them are different ethnic groups.
2. The rules of caste demand that an individual be born, live and die in one caste while social mobility in a class system permits an individual during his life time to move up or down through the several social strata.
3. There may be so many castes found in a particular ethnic group, superior or inferior to each other.
4. Vertical mobility is not possible in social classes depending on caste. Only horizontal mobility is possible there. For example, if a member of Dalit community becomes a professor his status will rise in his own class or caste only. Other high social class people will not consider him high as far as social status is concerned. Thus, we see that caste permits no mobility across caste line while class permits some degree of mobility across class line. Both types of mobilities are possible in class based division.
5. Social classes arise out of language, locality, occupation or specialization when these things are associated with a status hierarchy. Ethnic classes are created when political powers remain in their hands for a very long period of time. For example, Mughals and Turks ruled India for a very long period. They were regarded very high on social hierarchy which is fading day by day because they have lost political power today.
6. A system of social classes involves three things
   *(a)* Hierarchy of status groups
   *(b)* Recognition of superior inferior stratification
   *(c)* Some degree of permanency of the structure

Ethnic classes on the other hand involves better places of living, differentiation of physique or complexion and permanency of the highest degree in the structure of classes.

As far as education is concerned it is the only hope of making the society an integrated, peaceful and paradise looking one. Every type of distinction based on caste, ethnicity or class can be brought to the minimum by education. A corruption free open society can also be created with the help of education. Education can also turn the society into a dynamic one. There are so many agencies of education that can play a significant role in this regard. School is the most important and formal agency of all. We will discuss the role of schools only because social system and school system are very much similar in their composition. School is a social sub system because of the following reasons.

*(i)* Schools have definite populations
*(ii)* They have a clearly defined political structure and social interactions
*(iii)* They exhibit social relationship
*(iv)* They are run by a we feeling
*(v)* They have a particular culture that is definitely their own

Because of the great deal of similarity between school and the society school can play a very important role in removing the defects that is there in our social system. The thinking and behaviour of the children can be changed in a desirable manner by changing the curriculum and by giving them instructions under the supervision and control of ideal teachers. There are several other measures that can be very helpful in this regard. Some of them are given below:

1. **Modification of curriculum :** Curriculum refers to total activities and experiences given to children in the school environment. They should be taught the lessons of equality, tolerance, and respect of others. They should be made clear that taking birth in different families or regions does not make any one inferior or superior. These are

actually the tactics used by religious leaders and educated class of the society to exploit the masses. It was the education in the past that had made some people superior in the society. The reason was that educated men interpreted the religion and society in their own way. Religion is misinterpreted by these shrewd people even today. If curriculum is constructed from this point of view for each grade of schooling and for each subject, differences on the basis of castes, clan, class, or ethnicity can be reduced to the minimum.

2. **Equality of educational opportunities** : People are by nature unequal in their capacities to learn. So equalities of educational opportunities does not refer to equalizing native capacities through education but it refers that environmental circumstances are to be equalized in such a way that every member of the society gets equal chance to receive education in the best manner possible. In a democratic welfare society it is not simply enough to equalize the chance but together with this action, hurdles if any must also be removed so that uneducated family really get access to education. For example, if they are too poor to buy books or to bear other expenses, they must be assisted by the government to overcome these difficulties. Similarly, if they are too poor to spare their earning child to attend the school, their poverty must be removed by the government. Once the people of the society in general are educated and their children study with those of so called upper strata of the society, they will come to know about their rights and status in the society.

3. **Teaching by enlightened teachers :** The defects of Indian societies can be removed only if children are taught by especially trained enlightened teachers of the society. Such teachers will not come from heaven. They will be prepared in well devoted training colleges. One or two years teachers training will not serve the purpose. At least five years integrated training courses especially meant for the purpose are needed to prepare separate category of teachers to teach in primary, upper primary, secondary and senior secondary classes. These pupil teachers should be taught all schools subjects afresh but with different angles. Out of these teachers only those teachers should be recruited to teach in schools who are really competent and committed to their job and remaining lot should be rejected after a trial and probation of two or three years.

4. **Equality of employment opportunities** : Whosoever is educated in the society should have equal access to job. Equality here does not mean rigid nature of merit criteria i.e. 60% of a poor boy is considered at par with the same number of marks scored by rich boy. Naturally the education of first generation will be weak academically as compared to the next generations. These weaknesses must be compensated by giving reservation to the first and second generations in employment. Once the backward class students cross the educational barrier, the extra benefit given to them should be pulled away and they should be treated with the remaining class people equally.

5. **Honest and efficient educational administration:** All educational policies can be implemented only if educational administration is fair in its dealing and transparent in action. For this purpose, educational administration should be strict in control and slightest deviation from the norm should be dealt with very firmly.

6. **Employment generating education :** Money is that power which can hide all stigmas. Stigma of caste, ethnicity or class is also shortened when the person becomes educated, employed and earns his living in the society. If education given to children is such that they can get employment in future, they will not be under rated by the society after two or three generations.

7. **Incentives to mobility** : Many of the social inequalities are automatically reduced when people belonging to different cultures are mixed up and stay with each other for a longer period of time. If people do not know my caste in other areas of the country, there will be no question of social distinctions at all. People should be rated on the basis of their action and behaviour not on the basis of their birth or domicile. This tendency should be developed in the society.

8. **Incentive to inter caste marriages** : No barrier should be there in the way of inner caste marriage. It should rather be encouraged by the state. Relevant materials regarding this should be included in the curriculum.

9. **Industrialization and urbanization :** It has been noted that agrarian and rural societies are very closed, rigid and narrow minded. So, efforts should be made to bring the villages closer to cities either through rural migration to cities or through setting up new industries in villages.

10. **Giving least weightage to religious show off :** There are many people in the society who are not religious in real sense but they pose to be religious by putting on caps or by using tilaks on their foreheads. Such a tendency should be discouraged by education and mass media.

## OBJECTIVE QUESTIONS

1. A society is identified by its
   (a) economic progress
   (b) military power
   (c) culture
   (d) all of these
2. School works as a social sub system for
   (a) transmission of culture
   (b) preservation of culture
   (c) advancement of culture
   (d) all of these
3. "Society is nothing but a process of interaction among people." Who said this?
   (a) Lapier (b) Cuber
   (c) Reuter (d) Payne
4. Conflicts in the society occurs when
   (a) interest of the people do not match
   (b) justice is not maintained
   (c) undue domination of a section prevails
   (d) all of these
5. Remarkable change/changes brought about in Indian society is/are
   (a) evolution of a strong middle class
   (b) rise of a new capitalist class
   (c) employment guarantee to poors
   (d) all of these
6. The most influential social engineer in the country is
   (a) the social worker (b) the teacher
   (c) priest (d) none of them
7. Which of the following statements regarding the relationship of society and education is not correct
   (a) Society determines the model and structure of education
   (b) Education changes the ideals of the society
   (c) Education can reduce regional disparities
   (d) The best school reflects the worst society
8. The best model of schooling is
   (a) close interaction between education of society
   (b) Self reliant society by education
   (c) Reflection of openness by schools
   (d) All of these
9. All of the following have a role in determining the direction of school except,
   (a) State (b) Society
   (c) Religion (d) None
10. Which of the following is not the characteristics of Indian society
    (a) Status is determined by birth
    (b) People are liberal to embrace any religion
    (c) Occupation and profession determine the status of a person
    (d) People are open minded
11. Caste distinction in India is rooted in
    (a) Culture (b) Religion
    (c) Both of these (d) None of these

## ANSWERS

| 1 | 2 | 3 | 4 | 5 | 6 | 7 | 8 | 9 | 10 | 11 |
|---|---|---|---|---|---|---|---|---|---|---|
| (c) | (d) | (c) | (d) | (d) | (b) | (d) | (a) | (d) | (b) | (b) |

# Education and Culture

## CULTURE

### Meaning of culture

The word culture has been understood by different people in different ways. Some people regards culture as a universal attitude towards life. Some people think that it is a way of living, talking and behaving, some people are of the view that sum of all customs and traditions of the society is culture, some people relate it to the progress of art, music, architecture and literature etc. and there are many other people who restrict it to the mastery of different languages. The more a person knows different languages, the more he is cultured.

Actually human being are born with a cultural environment which consists of:

I. Tools, buildings, equipments, machines and other material objects, which man has made out of his physical environment for his comforts and use.

II. The meaning which are attached to things and their various qualities together with the knowledge, institutions, social practices, symbolic systems and all other creations of man.

III. Beliefs, customs, attitude, mutual association and all religious or social organizations.

IV. Style of living, dressing and participations in various social sub-systems.

### Definitions of culture

1. Tylor, "Culture is the complex whole which includes knowledge, beliefs, arts, morals, laws, customs, and other capacities and habits acquired by man as a member of the society.
2. Machiver "Culture is the expression of our nature in our mode of thinking and living in our everyday intercourses, in art, in literature, in religion, in recreation and enjoyments".

### Characteristics of culture

On the basis of meaning and definitions of culture given above we can derive the following characteristics of culture :

1. *Culture is acquired :* Culture is not inherited from forefathers. It is rather acquired in social situations. When a child takes birth, he is like a clean slate but when he grows he acquires different ideals, attitudes, skills, beliefs, knowledge, habits, traditions and style of living and thinking in social contacts.
2. *Variability in culture is natural :* Every individual in the society has his innate tendencies, interests, and capacities due to genetic differences of nature. When acquired culture gets interacted with this nature, variation in culture is created. That is why we see slight differences in cultural attributes everywhere.
3. *Culture has distinct entity :* Different societies of the world have different cultural patterns because of the differences in beliefs, material or spiritual progress, attitude towards life, geographical conditions and physical environment.
4. *Culture can be observed* : Culture can be visualized or seen in its physical form. Even nonmaterial or metaphysical cultures can be seen when they are translated by people into action. For example, a God fearing society will also be just and honest in its manifestation of behaviour that can be observed.
5. *Culture is man made or revealed :* Most part of human culture is made by man himself. Only that part of culture which is related to beliefs or rituals may be revealed. But these too do not reach man directly. God sends messengers or incarnates himself to acquaint the human being with this culture.

6. *Culture is dynamic .* When a particular culture is transmitted to the next generation the recipient generation modifies it according to its own needs and then this modified form of culture is transmitted to the third generation. This process of modification never stops and thus continuous enrichment in culture is also seen. A certain rigid part of culture may however, be kept preserved at every stage of transmission.
7. *Culture has utility :* A person is identified with the culture he lives in. His culture determines and formulates his behaviour desirable and acceptable to the society. Culture is actually learnt by the mutual interactions in the society. This interaction can be made smooth and natural by education. In short, cultural enrichment is the sign of progress.
8. *Acquisition of culture is an automatic process:* Man is a social being. When he gets interacted in the society, he acquires its culture. As soon as he grows, enrichment in his culture increases. Thus, no one is fully cultured in absolute term. This relative significance of culture testifies to the fact that (I) every man can be changed through education (II) cultural discrimination of a man or a group is immoral i.e. culture of a man or group can be improved.
9. *Culture is necessary :* Culture is necessary for man because of the following reasons.
   - *(a)* Every human being is born in a particular geographical climate. He has to adjust to that climate. This is possible only when he creats a culture according to that particular climate.
   - *(b)* Society is divided into different classes, castes, ethnicity or religions. Man has to adjust himself to that sub social system. So, he learns the particular culture of that social sub system to get adjusted there.
   - *(c)* Man always tries to enhance his comforts by new inventions and discoveries. Everyone in the society should know about them in order to take the benefits of them.
   - *(d)* The personality of a man is shaped by the culture he adopts from the society. Thus, culture has direct impact on social, mental, physical and spiritual development of a man.
10. *Culture is the sum total of man's life experiences:* Whatever knowledge or experiences a man acquires in life is his culture provided that they are manifested in the social contacts.

## Types of Culture

1. **Individual and communal culture :** Interests, attitudes, liking, modes of thinking or behaviour etc. differ from person to person. As a result they do not adopt the social or national culture in toto. They rather adopt it after some modification. This is called individual or personal culture. Communal culture, on the other hand, is the result of religious beliefs and represents the whole community.
2. **National or local culture :** Each nation has some distinct national traits and attributes of character including values, ideals, mode of thinking and living etc. Such national traits are known as national culture. Local culture is restricted to a particular locality, area or geographical boundary. It is influenced by geographical climate, local beliefs and traditions and standard of living of the people of that area.
3. **Material and non material culture :** Material culture includes those man made physical objects which man has created for his physical comforts, such as clothes, buildings, food items, machines and equipments, means of transport and communication etc. Non material culture includes beliefs, traditions, values ideals, language etc. They are accepted and followed by at least one sizeable section of the society.
4. **Universal and particular culture :** Universal form of culture includes those ideals, beliefs, values, languages, customs, traditions etc. which are adopted by all members of the society across the world such as truth, honesty, cooperation, sympathy, love for children etc. Particular form of culture is that culture which is adopted by a particular section of the society.
5. **Optional form of culture :** It is that culture which is neither universal nor particular. It is optional in the sense that it is not adopted by many people. The person who adopts more and more optional

elements of culture, is called more and more cultured. It is necessary for the progress of human civilization.

## LEVELS OF CULTURE

*(i)* culture of the academic group including technocrats
*(ii)* culture of ruling class and politicians
*(iii)* culture of agricultural community
*(iv)* culture of labour class
*(v)* culture based on religions, regions etc.

### Cultural lag

Due to rapid progress of scientific inventions and discoveries and technological advancement material aspects of culture has gone ahead of non material aspects. The difference between material and non material aspect of culture is called cultural lag.

### Cultural system

Individual participates in the cultural system in terms of positions he occupies in the society sometimes he occupies more than one position in the society, i.e., a head of a family and worker in a factory. In such cases he exhibits different cultural patterns in different situations. It is clear that system persists while individuals who occupy different places within it may come and go.

Similarly, if a teacher is concerned with individuals having child status, his task will be to help the individuals to acquire a new status or to learn to play the roles expected of him at present as well as in future. Thus, we see that culture always changes with the change in the status.

### Acculturation

An individual takes birth in a particular society or culture. In that society he comes in contact with different people and is influenced by its environment. Individual tries to adjust himself according to the recognized beliefs. values, ideals and way of life of that society. This process is known as acculturation.

People belonging to different cultures also go through the process of acculturation by changing their own culture. This is possible only when the culture in which they live is stronger and more influential than their own culture.

There are three important **methods of acculturation** :

1. *Organized activities and experiences :* Through these activities and experiences culture is taught to children in schools. They learn desirable element of culture through these activities and adopt them in their lives.
2. *Imitation :* Child sees different people around him and observes their activities. He imitates these activities willingly and the process of acculturation goes on day by day. He learns style of talking, language, behaviour etc through imitation.
3. *Active participation and practice :* The last stage of acculturation is practice. Child actively participates in various activities without any compulsion and when this participation is repeated many time, the child becomes the part of that culture.

### Relationship between education and culture

Meaning and concepts of culture testifies to the fact that education and culture is intimately connected. In broad sense culture is not a part of education but it is education itself. Cultural pattern of a society determines its educational system. Educational system simultaneously affects the culture of that society by shaping and influencing the thinking and behaviour of individuals. For example if cultural pattern of a society is materialistic, its educational system will also be framed in the same way. Similarly, if there is cultural conflicts in the society, it can be wiped out only by education. We will study the inter relationship between the two here.

**(A) Influence of culture on education :** Cultural pattern affects education in the following ways:

*(i)* *Formulating educational aims :* Whatever ideals, values and beliefs people in the society have, the aims of education will be to preserve them. Local aims will be derived from local culture and national aims will be derived from national culture. Thinking and pattern of behaviour of the people and their standard and style of living will also play an important role in determining educational aims.

(ii) *Constructing curriculum :* Culture is not genetically inherited, it is rather acquired. So, curriculum will be constructed to acquire the desired culture by the people. Culture becomes the need of the society in the sense that its acquisition increases material or spiritual comforts. Curriculum will be so developed as to increase these comforts.

Besides, all elements of culture is not universal. Some of them are optional. As a result, culture differs from society to society. This variability of culture will also be accommodated in the curriculum to increase the adjustability of people in the society.

(iii) *Organizing co curricular activities :* Culture is not to be preserved only. It has to be transmitted to the next generations. For this purpose, various literary, cultural and games activities are organized in the school campus.

(iv) *Methods of teaching :* Whether the culture of the society is accommodative or impenetrable also determines the behaviour of the teachers and their methods of teaching. Whether education will be teacher centred, curriculum centred or child centred will depend on whether the cultural pattern of the society is autocratic or democratic. If the society follows democratic culture, teacher will teach the students according to their needs, interest and aptitude. On the other hand, if culture of the society is influenced by Idealism or Communism, the behaviour of the teacher will be very rigid.

(v) *Reconstruction of education and society :* Culture or sub culture of a society always changes with the change of time. These changes are also taken into consideration while formulating educational plans. Thus, continuous review in the educational system becomes necessary for us.

(vi) *Discipline :* No other aspect of education is so directly affected by culture than discipline. Problem of indiscipline is generally seen in those societies where education is not given priority by the people i.e., culture of the labour class. Children belonging to these cultures are dealt with very strictly in a repressionistic manner. On the contrary, children representing cultured societies are very much cooperative to the school discipline. So, they are democratically treated by their teachers.

(vii) *Research activities :* Culture or sub culture of the society determines the directions as well as dimensions of researches. For example if people believe that AIDS can be treated by magical hyms or Quranic verses recited by Maulana, no efforts will be made to find out the causes or remedies of the killer disease. On the other hand if people believe that there is no disease on this earth which does not have a definite cure, they will work hard to discover the cure of this disease.

(viii) *Development of arts, music and literature :* Arts, literature and music reflect the culture of a particular age. We can study the culture of the past on the basis of these things and can relate them to the present in order to predict about future. Thus it is culture alone that binds past, present and future into a single time unit. This, phenomenon of culture can reduce many of the social or cultural conflicts that we see today.

(ix) *Effects on teacher's behaviour :* Teacher of the class is the practical being and living form of a culture. Whatever culture he has acquired from the society is fully reflected through his behaviour in the society. Thus a teacher can make the process of acculturation very easy and natural. He tries to inculcate those ideals and values in children which he considers good. Thus a teacher can modify and transform the culture of his students by his own behaviour.

(x) *School system as a whole :* School exists for the purpose of inducting the young into the culture to which school belongs. For this very reason, linguistic and religious minorities establish their own educational institutions to preserve and transmit their culture. The total activities and programmes of the school are organized according to the cultural pattern of the society.

**(B) Functions of education towards culture:** Culture is also influenced by education in the following ways :

(i) *Cultural enrichment of children :* All individuals in the society do not have same amount of experiences because of the differences in family and society experiences. They lack many important elements of culture when they enter the school. These elements are imparted to them through education.

(ii) *Preservation transmission and advancement of culture :* Already has been discussed as an active agency of education)

(iii) *Removing cultural conflicts :* There are several cultures found in the world. Even a nation may have different cultures. Because of these differences, followers of one culture look down upon the representatives of other culture. For example, followers of one culture may allow their women folk to walk without veil while many people consider this veil necessary for their female society. This attitude may create cultural conflicts when one group considers its culture better and tries to impose it on people of the other cultures. Only education can remove these cultural conflicts by making the people tolerant. Children will be taught good and common elements of all cultures and their prejudices will be removed. Children will learn many good elements of different cultures either through books or through imitating the behaviour of their teachers.

(iv) *Cultural reforms :* Culture is always dynamic in nature. So many new things are added to culture every time. But all these additions or modifications are not always desirable for the good of the society. Education analyses the culture scientifically and brings out all those undesirable elements which are not conducive for their development.

(iv) *Maintaining the continuity of culture :* No society can survive without its culture. Cultural identity is a must for creating self consciousness in man. Education saves a sub culture from the dominance of a powerful culture and thus it maintains the continuity of culture through its diverse activities and programmes. This move is not against cultural integration among different societies. It only means to safeguard one culture from the dominance of other culture.

(vi) *Removing cultural lags.:* Material culture generally grows at a faster rate than non material culture. It creates ideological conflicts in man in his internal behaviour. Education redefines the concepts, beliefs and ideals according to the changing needs and thus cultural lag is removed.

(vii) *Development of a composite culture :* When different cultures come in contact with each other a composite culture is created due to exchange of cultures. In this type of culture something is given to other cultures and something is taken from them. This culture may be more acceptable as compared to a particular culture imposed on people by force as is the case of India. Education can play a significant role in creating such cultures and in integrating the whole nation into one unit.

## OBJECTIVE QUESTIONS

**1.** "The greatness of a nation is to be measured not by its material power and wealth but by the inter cultural relationship of its people". Who said this?

(a) Dr. Radha Krishnan
(b) More
(c) Vivekanand
(d) None of them

**2.** In a culturally pluralistic country which type of education is suitable

(a) education developing tolerance to other cultures
(b) Education free from culture
(c) Education emphasizing national culture
(d) both (a) & (b)

**3.** Which of the following qualities a teacher should have for developing inter cultural understanding in children

(a) He should have knowledge about the origin of various cultures and sub cultures
(b) He should be very progressive and open minded
(c) He should be able to relate the subject with national culture
(d) All of these

4. Which of the following is not included in the material culture of a country
   (a) Warfare technology
   (b) Houses
   (c) Software technology
   (d) Industrial growth
5. Which of the following comes under non material culture
   (a) group behaviour pattern, i.e., Dance, music, drama,etc.
   (b) ideals of life and moral values
   (c) literary and scientific progress
   (d) all of these
6. Which of the following is an important characteristics of culture
   (a) Culture is cumulative form of all non material aspects
   (b) Culture is the cumulative product that people have acquired in centuries
   (c) Culture can be preserved and transmitted
   (d) All of these
7. Which of the following is the characteristics of culture
   (a) continuity
   (b) unconscious adoption
   (c) growth and change
   (d) all of these
8. When a person adopts any thing from a dominant culture, it is called
   (a) Universalization of culture
   (b) Acculturation
   (c) Cultural Lag
   (d) None of these

**ANSWERS**

| 1 | 2 | 3 | 4 | 5 | 6 | 7 | 8 |
|---|---|---|---|---|---|---|---|
| (a) | (d) | (d) | (c) | (d) | (d) | (d) | (b) |

# Education and Socialization of Child

## SOCIALIZATION

### Meaning of Socialization

It is a process by which an individual is made social, socially acceptable and emotionally matured enough to deal with others in a friendly manner. By this process, society develops an individual according to the needs of its ideals, beliefs, customs, traditions, norms and social laws. This is done when an individual interacts with other individuals of the society. Thus social exposure is necessary for socialization.

But the problem is that when process of socialization starts it is confronted with individual needs, interests, attitudes and behaviour. As a result, process becomes very difficult. Due to this reason individual is motivated to adopt social values and ideals willingly so that he may shun the individuality and mix up with the society. Some compromise is also made by the society in order to make this process easy and possible. When individual acquires these qualities he is made well adjusted with the family, with neighbours, with other social institutions and with the society as a whole. He develops such a confidence and capability in him through this process that he does not remain hesitant to interacting with others.

For example, when a child sees his parents to take to any of their friends he observes how they talk and behave with each other. He then interacts with his age mates of the family and repeats the same. Thus, a child learns something from every member of the society desirable and undesirable. His parents teach him what are desirable social elements and why are they essential.

### Definitions of Socialization

1. J.S. Ross, "Socialization is the development of we feeling in association and the growth in the capacity and will to act together."
2. Bugardus, "Socialization is the process whereby persons learn to behave dependably together on behalf of human welfare and in doing so they learn experiences, social self control, social responsibility and balanced personalities."

### Characteristics and importance of socialization

*(i)* It is a conscious process. The child learns that he is given something and the giver also knows that he is giving something useful to the child.

*(ii)* It is a slow process of habit formation and it takes too much time to complete. One single effort should not be considered sufficient.

*(iii)* This process makes the child social and socially acceptable.

*(iv)* It develops we feeling in children when they are grown. Thus it is very necessary for all types of social activities and for establishment of social institutions.

*(v)* Socialization is necessary in order to live in the society at ease. For example, if a child abuses everybody in the society, he will not be tolerated by the other people and everyone may take action against him.

*(vi)* By this process an individual becomes a real part of the society.

### Motivating factors involved in socialization

Following factors play a motivating role in the process of socialization :

1. *Rear and care :* Careful upbringing of the child is very helpful in the process of socialization. If family environment is not soothing for the child and he is not getting proper care and attention from his parents, he may develop anti social

tendencies in him. It happens when family is broken or there is tension between father and mother or child is orphan from any side. Such children are vulnerable to social maladjustment.

2. *Sympathy and love :* You can bring about drastic change in a child just by a word of sympathy and love. During infancy and early childhood a child is fully dependent on his family and other relatives. If child is treated sympathetically and lovingly by his kith and kins, he will behave others in the same manner. Manners and etiquettes learnt in the family are manifested in the society in a natural way.
3. *Co-operation :* Co-operation given to the child creates we feeling in him. He comes to know that any difficult task can be fulfilled very easily if cooperative efforts are there for the task. In this way child also extends his hands of cooperation for other members of the society.
4. *Forbidding :* Society including the family and neighbourhood is full of evils also. Child is forbidden to do something so that he may not develop undesirable tendencies in him. If he is allowed to be punished by nature because of his wrong actions, the process of socialization will be delayed. For example, he is forbidden to touch the belongings of others, to abuse others or to address elders with rough words.
5. *Advice :* A child generally acts in accordance with the suggestions given to him from his well wishers. If suggestions are timely given to him and he does not face the evil consequences of his wrong actions, it plays very important role in the process of socialization.
6. *Identification :* Child sometimes identifies the person or persons whom he likes more and he tries to behave in the same way as the person identified by him had behaved in the past. For example, if child sees his father greet the guests with respect, in the absence of his father he will also greet him in the same way. Young girls also identify themselves with their mothers by putting on veils.
7. *Imitations :* Child imitates many behaviours of his family members, peer group, neighbours or teachers without receiving any instructions from them. If child is given good environment, he will imitate good habits and behaviour. This imitation is the most powerful method of socialization today. We can teach many desirable things to children by films, T.V. or internet and child will imitate them.
8. *Informal group teaching :* Sometimes elders and older people of the families collect all children of the family and tell them stories and sagas. Many desirable habits are developed in children through these stories. Children take much interest in such stories and they are automatically motivated to get socialized.
9. *Reward and punishment :* When a child acts according to the norms and ideals of the society as he was instructed before he was rewarded by the family materially or verbally. People appreciate him and approve his behaviour. On the contrary if he does something wrong from social point of view, he is punished.
10. *Strict supervision:* For a successful socialization strict supervision by the family is necessary. Child may commit many thing wrong just in order to get pleasure of doing. Hence if his activities are properly monitored, he will not be able to develop anti social behaviour in him.

## Agencies of socialization.

Following agencies take part in the process of socialization of a child:

1. *Family :* It is the first and the most important agency of socialization. Child spends maximum period of time here. In the family child comes in contact with his parents, brothers, sisters, uncles, aunties, cousins, grandparents. etc. and he learns many habits and behaviour from them. Love, sympathy, cooperation, tolerance, consideration and so many qualities are learnt in the family first. Child also learns many ideals, customs and traditions, first of all from his family. Family is actually his first school and mother is his/her most loving teacher.
2. *Neighbourhood :* When a child grows a little older, he goes to the houses of his neighbours and plays there. He interacts there not only with young ones but also with the matured members of the house. If **neighbourhood** is good and

cultured, socialization will be positive, otherwise child will learn many undesirable habits and behaviour from his neighbours.

3. *Schools :* At the age of four, child starts attending schools also. Here he comes in contact with many children of different communities and culture. He also comes in direct touch with teachers in the class and peons in the campus. He also participates actively or as a spectator in various cultural activities and social function there. All these factors affect his personality in different ways and process of socialization goes further.
4. *Relatives :* Relatives, also visit the family of the child though occasionally but child leans many social habits and ideals from them. Since there is close intimacy between the child and his relatives, child does not show any shyness in exposing himself. Thus, his behaviour is easily modified in a desirable manner.
5. *Playground :* Apart from his school, child also visits nearby playing fields where he plays different games with his age mates and peers. He learns many desirable qualities such as cooperation, fellow feeling, team spirit, tolerance, discipline, honesty, integrity, supremacy of rules and regulation and so on from these games.
6. *Scouting for boys and guiding for girls :* The purpose of these activities is to serve the people by helping them in their troubles. These are regular part of activities of the school. These activities also create feeling of sacrifice in children. Co-operation and self dependence are the basic principles of scouting and guiding. These activities also make the child courageous and risk bearing.
7. *Caste, clan and community :* Each caste, clan or community has its own customs, traditions, style of walking or talking and manner of behaviour. Children learn many important things from these units of the society also. These are better places of exposure for an immature child and his caste or community or clan may tolerate many undesirable behaviour of the child easily.
8. *Religions :* A child goes to temples, churches or mosques with his parents or family members. He participates in various rituals and ceremonies there. He listens the sermons of the priest and interacts with other devotees. All these things contribute to his socialization .
9. *Social functions and parties :* Child takes part in various social functions and parties with his family members. He learns many important things from these places also such as style of walking or talking, manner of taking food, methods of serving the guests etc.
10. *Peer group, friends and age mates :* No child likes to be confined at home. He visits the houses of his friends and age mates and invites them to his home also. He talks to them, plays with them and walks with them in the neighbourhood and local markets. All these interactions help the child to get socialized.

## Factors Resisting Socialization

There are so many factors that hinder the process of socialization. They are given below-

*(i)* Indifferent attitude towards a child
*(ii)* Strict control on a child
*(iii)* Mobility restrictions imposed on a child
*(iv)* Prejudices against a child
*(v)* Frequent uses of punishment measures on small mistakes
*(vi)* Insecure social or family environment
*(vii)* Broken families
*(viii)* Social or economic disparities restricting the interactions
*(ix)* Stubborn attitude of the child
*(x)* Physical or mental disabilities
*(xi)* States of deprivation in the family
*(xii)* Insulting the child by elders
*(xiii)* Frequent failures in attempts
*(xiv)* Lack of education
*(xv)* Excess dependence of the child on others
*(xvi)* Lack of courage and inability to take initiatives

## Role of the Teacher in Socialization

Teacher is the most important figure after parents with whom a child identifies himself very much and gives him the most weightage in the society. His wordings are many times considered final by little kids. A teacher can augment this process in the following ways.

*(i)* Teacher comes in contact with the parents of the child and collect informations about

interests, attitude and special needs of the child. He then accommodates the social needs, norms and ideals with the needs, interest and capacities of the child. By doing so he reduces the resistance of the child towards socialization.

*(ii)* He acquaints the child with the cultural heritage of the country along with the current culture and sub cultures. Transmitting the cultural values to the child makes the process of socialization easy.

*(iii)* He treats the child so sympathetically and affectionately that child comes to accept him his well wisher and ideal. When it happens, child imitates the habits, behaviour and ideals of his teachers.

*(iv)* Teacher teaches social ideals and norms by organizing games, sports and other co curricular activities for the child. Child participates in these activities and learns many things through group interactions himself.

*(v)* School subjects are also taught to the child in social context so that child may understand the demand of the society as well.

*(vi)* He also uses reward and punishment techniques for approving the desirable behaviour and for discarding the undesirable one respectively.

*(vii)* Teacher does not exhibit any prejudice against any child. He treats all the children rich or poor, fairly and does not discriminate them on the basis of their castes or creeds. In this way, every idea given by the teacher becomes acceptable to children.

*(viii)* He provides maximum opportunities of interaction to children belonging to different strata of the society. This helps the children learn something from each other.

*(ix)* School is a social subsystem so if a child is adjusted in the school, he is likely to be adjusted in the society also. Teacher makes the school environment fully adjustable for children.

*(x)* Healthy competitions also lead to effective socialization. Teacher develops in children feeling of healthy competition.

### Difference between Socialization and acculturation :

*(i)* Socialization is related to social adjustment and acculturation is concerned with adjusting with a particular culture only. Thus, socialization is general and acculturation is particular in character.

*(ii)* Socialization is restricted to values, norms and ideals only while acculturation extends to knowledge, beliefs, progress, etc. also.

*(iii)* Informal agencies of education are sufficient enough to complete the process of socialization and the role of formal agency is only desirable here but acculturation is a life long process and involvement of all the agencies of education is necessary.

## OBJECTIVE QUESTIONS

**1.** The process by which an individual learns to behave in accordance with social norms and culture is called

*(a)* Acculturation *(b)* Socialization

*(c)* Assimilation *(d)* None of these

**2.** Socialization is a

*(a)* behaviour raining in social situations

*(b)* adjustment training to social environment

*(c)* social training for adoption of culture

*(d)* all of these

**3.** Process of socialization of a child will become slow if

*(a)* he is not allowed to go to neighbourhood due to social evils rampant there

*(b)* child can not communicate due to language barriers

*(c)* child is handicapped and he is hated by the society

*(d)* all of these

**4.** Which of the following is not the means of socialization

*(a)* segregation *(b)* imitation

*(c)* counseling *(d)* association

**5.** How is the process of socialization similar to that of teaching

*(a)* Both requires interactions

*(b)* Both are an automatic processes

*(c)* Both starts from the family

(d) Both (a) and (b)

6. Process of socialization increases when the child is brought to
   (a) participate in co curricular activities
   (b) attend classes
   (c) do experiment in the laboratory
   (d) all of these
7. Which of the following play a vital role in the process of socialization
   (a) Group activities in the school
   (b) Cooperation
   (c) Competition
   (d) All of these
8. By the process of socialization, we make the child
   (a) Cultured
   (b) Acceptable to the society
   (c) Aware of the social norms
   (d) All of these

## ANSWERS

| 1 | 2 | 3 | 4 | 5 | 6 | 7 | 8 |
|---|---|---|---|---|---|---|---|
| (b) | (d) | (d) | (a) | (d) | (a) | (d) | (d) |

# Education, Social Stratification and Social Change

## SOCIAL CHANGE

### Meaning of Social Change

Change simply means deviations from the existing patterns. Thus social change means changes in the structure and functions of social system. Since culture can not be separated from the society, social change refers to cultural changes also.

By social change we mean those changing activities which have changed the form and structure of the society so drastically that these changes look distinct and visible.

### Causes of Social Change

Change is a natural phenomenon. All things, including ideas, culture, civilization and human activities, are changeable. The situation that existed 20 years ago, does not exist today and it will not remain so after ten or twenty years.

Important factors responsible for social change are given below:

1. Human beings come across a number of newer and newer problems every day. In order to solve these problems they think and act in divergent ways and thus they happen to deviate from the existing pattern.
2. Style of living also changes due to changes in technology and increase in income. Thus, social change occurs.
3. When scientific inventions and technological researches take place, some conflicts between culture and science are seen. These conflicts motivate the people to bring about social changes.
4. Man always tries to make his life easier and comfortable. For this purpose he carries out inventions and discoveries. When he is successful in his efforts his outlook toward the society also changes. As a result social changes take place.
5. Time is itself an important factor of social change. Humans get bored of old values, ideals or culture with the passage of time. Hence, they bring about some modification in them. This is done by philosophers who redefine the society and its ideals in the present context.
6. When physical environment changes man also changes his style of living to adapt to new environment.

### Various Definitions and Concepts of Social Change

1. Sir Jones, "Social change is a term used to describe variation in or modification of any aspects of social process, social interactions and social organizations".
2. Gillin, "Social changes are variations from the accepted modes of life whether due to alterations in geographic conditions, cultural equipments and composition of the population or ideology or whether brought about by diffusion or invention within the group".
3. Brown, "Social and cultural changes are the same thing. Cultural change is a sizeable part of social change".
4. According to Chopin, cultural changes means three things (a) changes related to material culture (b) changes related to nonmaterial culture (c) changes related to both.
5. According to Spencer, "Social changes are uniform, gradual and progressive".
6. According to Listerward, Social change is related to changes in social aims and aspirations of the individuals.

7. According to Oghurn, there is no distinction between social change and cultural change. Cultural change is of two types i.e. change in material culture and change in non material culture. Material culture is concerned with all those things and objects which man has made for his comforts and happiness, i.e., means of transport and communications, refrigerator, A.C. etc. Non material culture is concerned with human ideas, values, ideals, habits, customs, traditions etc. Changes in the material culture occur first then it brings about changes in the non material culture.

In short we can say that social change is the change in any of the cultural attribute material or nonmaterial. This change is so distinct that we can easily come to the conclusion that society in general has deviated from its accepted norms. Man, an active part of the society brings this change.

## How Changes Occur?

When man confronts with social or individual problems or he wants to make his life easy, he starts thinking to solve them. His imagination coupled with the action and experiments cause some inventions and discoveries to occur. These inventions and discoveries change his style of living because he wants to get the pleasure of them. Under this condition he tries to change his values and ideals also to adapt to the new environment. As a result, a totally new society in its culture comes into existence.

These changes are sometimes so slow that man does not realize these changes and when he opens his eyes he sees a totally different world before him. These changes are realized when philosophers and students of sociology studies the past and present comparatively. On the other hand, sometimes these changes are so fast that they are initially resisted by a larger section of the society. But gradually these resistance are weakened and society adopt the new system and ideals. For example, use of loudspeakers in prayers was considered unlawful and sinful by majority of Muslims some 40 years ago but now it is widely used even in mosques.

## Causes of Resistance to Social Change

Following factors play a negative and resisting role in the process of social change :

1. *Cultural inertia* : It means adherence of the people to those blind beliefs, customs, traditions and rituals which have come down to them from their forefathers with so blindly and in a rigid manner that they consider every thing wrong and unlawful against these beliefs, customs and traditions. These conservative and rigid people are averse to any change. They also think that if they deviate a little from these accepted norms, they will be punished by divine power, evil spirits or persons of supernatural powers.
   The inertia makes the society to remain backward in many respects. For example, in the dark age Europeans and Indians considered sea voyage unlawful and the person doing so was liable to be punished by nature. This absurd belief kept most part of the world undiscovered. Willingness to social change is actually the precondition for any scientific or technological advancement.
2. *Mindset :* Some minds are very apprehensive and skeptical to any new things because it may disturb their life routine. Such people think that new things will be injurious to them physically or spiritually. For example, when tea culture was introduced in India it was strongly opposed by the masses but with the passage of time tea has now gained the status of hosting the guests with honour. If this tea is not served for the guest they are often heard saying, even tea was not asked.
   The reason of this mindset is that many changes are not good to the society in many ways. Hence, people show skepticism to all changes. If changes are supported by scientific experiments and people adopt scientific temper towards a change, such a mindset can easily be changed.
3. *Vested interest of some people :* Generally changes are opposed by those people who have some of their vested interest in the prior position. The privileged section of the society especially religious or political leaders of the country fear that social changes may harm their leadership and followers will be independent of their fabricated thread. If people are enlightened enough, they may adopt their independent attitude

toward their affairs. For example, elite class of Indian society especially politicians do not want the masses to be educated. Hence, minimum efforts are done by them to popularize quality education for the poor people.

4. *High degree of isolation :* Those people of the society who live in an isolated manner away from the rest of the society for a long period of time, resist to social changes. These people try to remain in isolation and do not want to mix up with the other people. They are so conditioned to their old traditions and habits that they hate new ones. For example, when I was principal in a CBSE affiliated school in Ambedkar Nagar, New Delhi I built a public toilet of 30 rooms especially to be used by Harijans, by using the development fund of local MP. When I visited the place after three months again I found that these latrines were used to store the household fuels. Most of them were not used even once as toilet. We can see so many isolated localities of Dalits in many parts of the country even today.
5. *Forced imposition of a new culture :* A culture howsoever fine it is if imposed by some people by force it is vehemently opposed by the people. Common Civil Code (C.C.C.) is the necessity of India today to bring about cultural and social harmony but if it is imposed by force it will be opposed. If its invoking as a law is made optional and people are given choice to tried either by C.C.C. or by Hindu or Muslim Laws, most of the people will opt C.C.C. gradually.
6. *Cultural lags :* Most of Indians living in cities have become Europeans in their life styles but they are rigid Indians in their ideology and behaviour. Similarly, fast growth of material culture has left the non material culture far behind. These incomplete cultural change made the people contended to be what they are now. Moreover, if something is bad in a culture, its good elements are also discarded. The reason is that totality is generally upheld as compared to various parts of things.

## Relationship of Education and Social Change

Social changes are necessary for all types of progress and development but these changes adversely affect our universal as well as local values and ideals many time. In both the cases the role of education becomes very significant. Besides, factors resisting to social change can be controlled or modified only by education.

Social changes also widens the scope and credibility of education physically as well as ideologically. People come to know many new ideas and objects by social changes. Thus, process of human progress continues unabated.

We will elaborate this inter relation of education and social changes in the following lines :

**(a) Education prepares the ground for social changes:**

*(i)* All inventions and discoveries which are the starting elements of social changes take place due to education. These inventions and discoveries are essential for human progress.

*(ii)* Educational philosophers and men of letters introduce many new ideas and concepts to the society. People study them and are influenced by them sooner or later.

*(iii)* Education makes the attitudes of the members of the society liberal and considerate which is very essential for greeting social changes.

*(iv)* Educational aims are formulated keeping in view the needs and demands of the society. Thus, bringing social changes are necessarily integrated to aims of education.

*(v)* Education has two important functions to do. Firstly, it preserves the present material and non material culture and secondly, it adds something more to this culture every time and thus it makes the society dynamic all the time.

*(vi)* Education motivates the people to realize the importance of social change in their individual as well as social lives and thus it increases people's participation in the process.

**(b) Education makes the resistance to social changes passive and dormant :** Six forms of resisting factors to changes can be made inactive or powerless by education. Unscientific beliefs and irrational attitudes of the people towards customs and traditions can be changed by proper education. Mindset of the people can also be changed to accept new ideas and objects for the ease of human life. Those who have some vested interest in any particular culture, their influence can be reduced by awakening the masses through education. Those who are living in isolation for centuries or decades can be brought to social mainstream by educating them properly and once they are enlightened and educated they would cease resisting to social changes. Education also makes the people accommodative and considerate. These educated people will not try to impose some culture on others by force. This will make the process of social change natural. And above all cultural lags can be removed only by education. Education can change the thinking pattern of the people at a very fast rate and in a drastic manner.

In short, we can say that education prepares the mentality of the people to welcome and adopt the desirable social changes and this is not done by compulsion. People are rather convinced logically about the utility and desirability of the new culture.

**(c) Education evaluates the social change and removes its undesirable elements :**

*(i)* People attached to the process of education evaluates all social changes by analyzing their merits and demerits. The desirable elements are proposed for the society and undesirable ones are discarded. Thus, education lays down the criteria and norms of values and ideals in the context of which social changes are evaluated.

*(ii)* Education gives right direction to utilizing pleasure and satisfaction derived from new inventions and discoveries. This is done by studying their impacts on society and culture at present. This social change gives us many new topics for researches.

*(iii)* Social changes are brought about in the society in two ways. First is the gradual change which is brought about by planned and systematic efforts. Second is the change brought about by movement and revolution. First method is based on democratic principles and is done in a peaceful manner and second method is based on fascism and advocates blood shed, hatred and pressure. Education prepares the ground for both depending on the need and circumstances.

*(iv)* Education also analyses old customs and traditions in view of the present context and lifeless knowledge or experiences are weeded out in the process thus education overhauls the system all the time.

**(d) Education transmits and popularize the culture-past and present-education land culture.**

**(e) Social change determines the nature and functions of education :**

*(i)* Social change brings about changes in the style of living of the people also along with changes in their attitude. As a result, direction and functions of education also change.

*(ii)* When culture changes, nature and pattern of education also changes to adapt to the changing needs and demands. For example, science and technology is given very much importance today because this is the fast developing age of science and technology. As a result of this, science and technology is given maximum weightage in the curriculum.

*(iii)* When social changes take place, society develops and creates many social institutions to popularize these changes. Schools and colleges are most prominent of all social institutions. These institutions motivate the people to adopt these changes.

## SCHOOLS AND SOCIAL CHANGES

Society runs many institutions to bring about social change. School is one of them. It is the most important and active formal institution of education. It is social sub system or a miniature society in itself. Hence, it can play very important role regarding desirable social changes. These are as follows:

*(i) Reflection of social order :* Nature, functions and organizational set up of the school depends upon the prevailing social order. Whatever ideals, values, customs and traditions are adhered by the society, they are reflected in the functioning of the school. School tries its best to preserve them; if some changes occur in the social system, school changes its programmes accordingly. It is also expected from the school that if there is

something undesirable in the new social order, it must resist to them and remove the unwanted elements from the system.

(ii) *Reflection of national policy of education :* Whatever policy is framed by the nation, it must reflect in the school system. School not only adopt those policies but it also implement them sincerely so that national objectives may be achieved and national culture may be developed. For example, if national policy is to popularize birth control measures through education, school would include related subject matter in the curriculum.

(iii) *Minimizing the role of resisting factors to social change :* There are six important factors that strongly resist to social changes. School minimizes their role by changing the attitude of the people. This is done not only by the modification of the curriculum but by the role and active participation of teachers. Actually school prepares the mind of the child to accept those changes willingly. Scientific attitude toward a pattern is developed for this purpose.

(iv) *Preparation of accommodative generation :* School modifies the behaviour of the child to adjust in the society according to its changing needs. We can not change the behaviour of a matured person but we can do it very easily when it is the case of young ones. They remain in the school for more than 12 years. Whatever they learn there they put them into practice in the society. That is why it is said that process of reconstruction of a society or revolution in it starts at least 20 years before its real shape.

(v) *School increases the speed of social changes:* Whatever inventions or discoveries take place in the society, its foundation are laid in the school. School prepares the child to contribute something to material culture. For this purpose, creative and talented children are identified and selected. They are given proper educational environment there.

(vi) *Employment oriented education :* In order to increase the productivity of the county and to raise the standard of living of the people school runs professional and technical courses. Once they are grown up they are easily employed in the economy. Their employment increases their earning and hence standard of living. This high standard of living is very conducive to social change.

(vii) *Maintaining continuity of culture :* School transmits the existing culture from one generation to the next and since it is a regular function of the school, so, whatever changes occur in the society any where, they are also transmitted to the next generation immediately. In this way continuity of culture is maintained.

(viii) *Role of the teacher :* Teacher can initiate and promote social changes only when he knows about it and he is also well versed with the needs and aspirations of the society. He must also know the types and directions of changes. All these things are taught to him by training him especially for the purpose. Once the teacher knows about all these things he moulds the process of social change in such a manner that it becomes acceptable to the whole society. He also protects the society from uneven, undesirable and harmful social changes.

# OBJECTIVE QUESTIONS

**1.** Which of the following will promote social change

(*a*) liberalization (*b*) globalization

(*c*) privatization (*d*) all of these

**2.** LPG (Liberalization, Privatization and Globlization) policy in India was adopted since

(*a*) 1990 (*b*) 1991

(*c*) 1995 (*d*) 2000

**3.** Social change refers to

(*a*) cultural change

(*b*) change in social structure

(*c*) change in social ideals

(*d*) all of these

4. Which of the following types of social stratification is seen in India
   (a) caste based stratification
   (b) occupational stratification
   (c) income based stratification
   (d) all of these
5. Which of the following is the characteristic of social change?
   (a) it is a slow but continuous process
   (b) it is an automatic and universal process
   (c) social change is affected by material and non material culture both
   (d) all of these
6. Social education refers to
   (a) education arousing national awareness
   (b) education accelerating social mobility
   (c) education encompassing social change
   (d) all of these
7. Which of the following is an important technological factor of social change?
   (a) improvement in communication and transport
   (b) mechanization of daily life
   (c) opening domestic markets for international trade
   (d) all of these
8. Which of the following functions of education is not related to social change
   (a) education should also change with the social change
   (b) education should accelerate the process of social change
   (c) education should check undesirable social change
   (d) all of these
9. Process of defining different categories of people in the society is called
   (a) social stratification
   (b) social mobility
   (c) socialization
   (d) none of these
10. Which of the following is not the characteristic of social stratification
    (a) permanent grouping and ranking of the society
    (b) birth distinction
    (c) social and economic inequality
    (d) group behaviour according to the norms and ideals of the class
11. Which of the following does not specify Max Weber's concept of social stratification
    (a) educational status
    (b) income and wealth
    (c) political power
    (d) social prestige
12. Which of the following stratifications jolted during British rule
    (a) occupational stratification
    (b) caste based stratification
    (c) educational stratification
    (d) both (a) and (b)
13. Which social class led the freedom movement in India
    (a) Feudal class (b) Upper class
    (c) Middle class (d) Proletariat class

## ANSWERS

| 1 | 2 | 3 | 4 | 5 | 6 | 7 | 8 | 9 | 10 |
|---|---|---|---|---|---|---|---|---|---|
| (d) | (b) | (d) | (d) | (d) | (d) | (d) | (b) | (a) | (b) |
| 11 | 12 | 13 | | | | | | | |
| (a) | (d) | (c) | | | | | | | |

7

# Education and Social Mobility

## SOCIAL MOBILITY

### Meaning of Social Mobility

Social mobility refers to change in the social status of a person or a group in the context of others. It is commonly seen in stratified society where people are categorized into different status groups, and they try to change their status by their efforts. For example, if a poor Dalit child becomes IPS after education, his social status will definitely change. How far this change is recognized by the people of other castes is another issue but he will surely achieve high status in his own caste. Thus social mobility means the movement of an individual in a social structure. It does not refer to physical movement of a person or group from one place to another. It is only migration. Similarly, material change(becoming from poor to rich) is also not social mobility in real sense. It is only rise of standard of living but when this material change is linked with social status it becomes social mobility. For example, becoming a professor from the post of lecturer is social mobility.

**P.A. Sorokin** has defined social mobility in the following words:

"Social mobility is either horizontal or vertical. Horizontal mobility is the process of making changes in the same status level while vertical mobility is the process of changing from one status to another either to a higher or lower level".

### Types of Social Mobility

Sorkin has divided social mobility into two categories:

**(A) Horizontal Mobility:** In every society some groups of people enjoy higher position and some of them are given lower status. When transformation of a person takes place within the group it is called horizontal social mobility. Social status of a person does not change in horizontal mobility or this change is so insignificant that it is given no importance. It means that position of a person may change but his salary, grade, prestige, privileges, etc. remain unchanged. For example, there are so many types of vendors we see in the street. If a groundnut seller starts selling cloth in the same fashion it will not change his social status. It will only be horizontal mobility.

Various sub forms of horizontal social mobility is given below :

1. *Inter group race, sex or age based mobility :* Mobility that we see within the same age or sex group is called horizontal mobility. The reason is that nobody can change his race or ethnicity and age or sex by his own efforts. For example, no man can become a woman or no child can become an adult even if he desires so. Similarly, no person can change his caste or ethnicity at any cost. Hence, if society is so stratified on these grounds into different layers, the status of the people will remain the same. But when these groups grow and develop as social groups due to interactions, horizontal mobility will be seen. If mindset of the people dividing the society on these grounds changes due to education, this mobility will also be helpful in social mixing.
2. *Occupational mobility :* Change from one occupation to another of the similar nature or status is called occupational mobility. For example, if a tailor changes his occupation and opens a show room it will not increase his status in the society. In closed societies even this mobility is not easily possible because of the restrictions imposed by the society. Sometimes a particular class of the society is associated with its occupation so firmly that it is not willing to change. As a result, this class is identified with its occupation. Indian society is becoming open day by day in this respect.

3. *Religious mobility :* All regions do not differ at all, as far as social status is concerned. So, conversion from one religion to another is horizontal mobility. This type of mobility is more seen in men than women, in urban population than in rural one and in educated class than uneducated one. But this mobility becomes vertical when a section of the population which is highly discriminated in his own community embraces a religion of those who give them equal status in the society and the community. Conversion of Dalits to Islamic religion is an example of it.
4. *Political mobility :* Several people change their party loyalties because of certain reasons. It generally does not change their social status. But when an ordinary member of central or state legislative council joins a ruling party and occupies a ministry, this becomes vertical mobility. This mobility is very common in India.
5. *Territorial mobility :* Leaving a territory or country by a group of people and entering into another territory for residing is called territorial mobility. This mobility becomes vertical when these migrants are looked down upon by the original inhabitants and thus migrants lose their prior social status as is the case of Afghan refugees in Pakistan or Iran. Migrating of village population to cities for jobs is not included in social mobility but when the whole village or several villages migrate together to other socially safe areas of the country to avoid social tortures it is called sub territorial social mobility, such as migration of Kashmiri Brahmins and their settlement in different parts of the country.
6. *International mobility :* Encouraged by better living conditions and better prospects of life many people migrate from under developed countries to developed ones. This is an example of international mobility. But this mobility is economic more than social.

**(B) Vertical Mobility:** All social groups or sub groups do not enjoy the same position in the society. Some of them are considered high and some are low with respect to social prestige. If an individual or group is able to change his social status by his own efforts and he rises up in the hierarchy it is called vertical mobility. No body wants to go to the lower status, so he always endeavours to maintain his social status but when others supercede him in the race of life, he automatically pushed down to the lower status. For example, Zamindars enjoyed very high position in the society but rise of the new industrial groups in India have pushed them down. Thus vertical mobility refers to both achieving higher or lower status in the society. Example of Dheeru Bhai Ambani can be citied here. He started his career as a petrol pump worker in Yaman but achieved a very high status in India by establishing Reliance Group.

In the words of Sorokin, " By vertical mobility I mean the relations involved in a transition of an individual from one social stratum to another."

He has categorized this mobility into two sub parts:

1. *Ascending mobility :* In this type of mobility a person belonging to lower strata of society enters into higher stratum by his efforts. Promotion of a clerk to an officer or promotion of a school teacher to a university teacher are examples of ascending vertical mobility. But when any stigma is attached to him because of his caste, ethnicity or parental professions, this vertical ascending mobility raises his status in his own community only. Other sections of the society do not regard him so high. But this situations do not last long. When this mobility is upheld for two or three generations in a row, the person belonging to lower stratum of the society really achieve higher status, as we see the cases of Dalits and Backward classes today. They are not only ruling different states of the country today but they are also influencing the national policies and programmes.
2. *Descending mobility :* Descending mobility means going down of a person or group of persons from higher position, prestige or status to lower position, prestige or status. It is generally not consciously done by any person or group but when others surpasses him in status or prestige because of their efforts, the earlier position of the person or group is lost automatically.

In short, we can say that vertical mobility is actually a relative phenomenon.

## Dimensions of Social Mobility

Social inertia and related mobility are seen in the following areas :

1. *Occupational divisions :* Society is stratified on the basis of occupations and economic status. Some occupations are given high social status and some are considered low. For example, rickshaw pulling is considered an occupation of low status as compared to that of a vendor. Similarly there are many occupations of the same social prestige. Because of these two different natures of occupation horizontal as well as vertical mobility is seen simultaneously. Income is not the criteria of these stratification. For example, many occupations of low social prestige can accrue larger income than that of high social prestige.
2. *Class divisions :* Society may be divided into rich, poor and middle classes. A number of sub divisions within the class may also be there. These stratifications are rigid at some places but in many parts of the world social interactions among these groups are seen. But any person can go to higher social classes if he is able to increase his income to that level. Thus, vertical mobility is not impossible here. Anybody can change his status on his efforts.
3. *Stratification based on consumptions :* According to Lipset and Zitterber, there is a difference between occupational status and economic status. Business status of different individuals is ranked according to the income that they earn while economic status of a person is determined on the basis of his consumption volume and pattern. Consumption is positively correlated to standard of living. Society is also divided on the basis of their standard of living. Besides, standard and style of living also depend on education. If a person is educated, his standard of living may be high despite his comparatively low income. On the other hand, an uneducated rich man may adopt a very low standard of living. Social mobility is not difficult here. Anybody can change his status on his will here.
4. *Caste ranking :* Such type of ranking generally has its origin into religion and beliefs. Division of the society on the basis of caste or sub caste is so rigid that social mobility becomes very difficult here. Only horizontal mobility is possible through marriages.
5. *Power ranking :* Persons of the same power impact form a power group. These powers may be social and political both. Groups belonging to ruling class are generally given high status in the society. This power division is not of permanent nature in social or political system. Social mobility is not difficult here.

## Factors Affecting Social Mobility

There are many factors that affect social mobility in positive and negative ways. Negative factors (factors resisting to social change) have already been discussed in the previous chapter. Here we will discuss only positive factors that enhance social mobility in any way. Some of them are given below:

1. *Structure of the society :* Societies may be of two types, closed societies and open societies. Thinking of the people in closed societies are very backward and narrow. People weigh everything on the basis of traditions and old customs. Thus chances of social mobility are very low in such societies. In open societies on the other hand, individuals have full freedom to do or adopt anything in whatever manner they like. For example, any person belonging to any caste or creed can marry to any woman of whatever caste or creed she belongs to. No one in the society cares for it. Thus open societies are very conducive to social mobility. Urban societies are somewhat open but rural societies are very closed in structure in the context of India.
2. *Religious beliefs and superstitions :* The thing which is associated to religion becomes rigid. If religions followed by the people are unscientific in majority of affairs, social mobility will be very difficult. For example, the status of a Mulla or Pandit is always ranked high because of beliefs. Similarly, people visit to pilgrimage and participate in many superstitious rituals. All these make social mobility difficult. On the other hand, religions interpreted scientifically increase social mobility.

3. *Demographic structure :* Migration of the people from villages to cities and towns increases social mobility because of the open environment and better future prospects there. Similarly, if a person is having less number of offsprings to support, it will raise his standard of living. As a result, upward social mobility will be there. Composition of population also affects social mobility. If there are large number of old people to check small number of young population, social mobility will be restricted and vice versa will increase it.
4. *Economic factors :* Some of these factors are given below:
   *(i)* Industrialization increases social mobility because it raises general standard of living of the people.
   *(ii)* Liberalisation and globalization also increase social mobility because people belonging to different countries of the world come in contact with each other.
   *(iii)* If income of the people increases it will increase social mobility. This increased income will increase the investment volume of the country and general social mobility will be positively affected.
5. *Political factors :*
   *(i)* If a person has freedom to run any business or to adopt any trade and profession social mobility will increase.
   *(ii)* Political stability in the country may also affect social mobility in the sense that development programmes will not be disturbed before their completion.
   *(iii)* If ruling party and opposition both are at variance with each other, no parliamentary business will go on. Thus social mobility will be at stand still.
   *(iv)* In a democratic country even a peddler can become a P.M. or a Minister if he wins the election.
6. *Education :* Education plays the most dominant role in increasing social mobility. A layman or a man of the street can become a lecturer or a D.M. only after education. Thus his status will automatically go up. Education in itself is a social status. An educated man or a scientist is generally held in high esteem by the society. Teachers who earn less than businessmen are given high status in the society only because of education.
7. *Aspiration level of the people :* If people in the society are ambitious to raise their status in the society, social mobility will be positive. This ambition or aspiration level of the people depend on the trend prevailing in the society and achievement level of certain groups. If all sections of the society are stagnant economically and socially, no social mobility will be seen.

## Relationship between Education and Social Mobility

Education is contributive to social mobility in the following ways :

1. It can raise individual status in the society. An educated person receives recognition, prestige, honour, and position in the society because of his education.
2. Education can provide good employment opportunities. It will raise the income of the people on one hand and their consumption level on the other. This will make their standard of living high and high standard of living is positively correlated to social mobility.
3. An individual can cross his caste barrier through education very easily. Education makes the people so liberal and broad minded that they do not regard caste division of the society very important.
4. Education abolishes rigidity of social structure and removes discrimination based on birth, sex or ethnicity. Once the bonds of social stratification is loosened, social mobility automatically goes up.
5. Education is a process through which ideals and values continuously change and new values and ideals are formed. As a result, criteria of social status also change.
6. Education motivates the people to change occupations to earn more and more profits. Once it happens social mobility is seen.

7. Education is also an important means of gaining power by qualifying civil services examination. Even a poor student can quality IAS or IPS and achieve high status in the society. In the olden days power of politics or administration was generally inherited and it was not possible for general public to enter into this field. But it is not the case today. Any person can occupy any position in the society with the help of education.
8. Mass media-the specialized branch of education has increased the rapport among the people. It is the pre requisite of all social mobilities.
9. In the olden days, the status of teachers was very high. It is still very high today but only those teachers are revered by the masses who are very devoted, laborious and honest.
10. Fifth pay commission has increased the salaries of different categories of teachers very much. Especially primary and secondary teachers are drawing almost double salary drawn in the past. This has increased their horizontal social mobilities if not vertical mobilities.
11. Education has widened the scope and dimensions of life. We can adopt any profession out of millions.
12. Education from primary to university level is also stratified. An individual will gain vertical social mobility according to his level of education.
13. Individuals are given so many options to choose any one of them as far as curriculum and subject matter is concerned. They choose their subjects of interest on the basis of their interest and thus social mobility is seen. For example, science subjects are rated high by the society today as compared to humanities and social sciences so subject stratification is also there in education.
14. Those who are engaged in research studies, inventions and discoveries, they are rated high in the society. Any person can go to this level of education according to his efforts. Higher the academic achievement greater will be the social mobility.
15. All universities are not equal in educational standard. Some of them are rated high by the people of the society and thus selection of a good university or college for higher studies increases social mobilities. This diversification in the standard of education of different universities has very well been recognized by National Aassessment and Accreditation Council (NAAC) which is now gracing universities and colleges of India on the basis of their performance. MJP university was rated as B + in 2004

Social mobility also affect education in the following ways:

*(i)* If status of the individual is high, he will send his wards to reputed public schools and private colleges.

*(ii)* Social mobility is a continuous process. If it is drastic in nature in the society, it will change education also, especially curriculum.

*(iii)* Educational stratification that we see in India today is the result of fast social mobility. There are millions of government primary schools on one hand where education is imparted in deplorable buildings free of cost and on the other hand, well furnished public schools are imparting education at high costs.

*(iv)* Tendency of private tuitions is also the outcome of fast social mobility. Because of this tendency teachers do not take interest in teaching in their schools but explcit students at their homes.

# OBJECTIVE QUESTIONS

**1.** Socio-economic status of a person can change due to

*(a)* Change in income
*(b)* Education
*(c)* Promotion in job
*(d)* All of these

**2.** Which of the following works as a powerful barrier against vertical mobility in India

*(a)* Caste *(b)* Class
*(c)* Occupation *(d)* Jobs

**3.** All of the following are examples of horizontal social mobility except

*(a)* Promotion of a peon to the post of clerk
*(b)* From shop keeping to supply trade
*(c)* An SC student becoming IAS
*(d)* A farmer becoming a primary teacher

4. Which of the following societies is conducive to vertical social mobility
   (a) Closed society (b) Open society
   (c) Pluralistic society (d) None of these
5. A closed society is one where
   (a) Inter caste marriages are prohibited due to difference in status
   (b) People are orthodox and rigid
   (c) Both of these
   (d) None of these
6. Which of the following steps have been aken after independence to promote social mobility?
   (a) Political and social equality
   (b) Equality before law
   (c) Equality of educational opportunity
   (d) All of these
7. In which of the following ways education can promote social mobility
   (a) It can help to change occupation
   (b) It can enable us to get administrative power
   (c) It can make the person liberal in his attitude and thinking
   (d) All of these

## ANSWERS

| 1 | 2 | 3 | 4 | 5 | 6 | 7 |
|---|---|---|---|---|---|---|
| (d) | (a) | (a) | (b) | (c) | (d) | (d) |

# Equality of Educational Opportunities and Education of Disadvantaged Sections of the Society

## INTRODUCTION

Education, which was monopolized by the socially privileged class of the society in the ancient and medieval period and by economically strong sections of the society during the British period, was for the first time opened to all without discrimination of caste creed, or colour when India got independence in 1947. But this was not enough for educational equality. A large section of Indian society was so poor that it could not avail the opportunity because of the following reasons:

*(i)* They were not motivated to receive education because of social factors.

*(ii)* They could not afford the cost of education because of their poverty.

*(iii)* Their wards were the earning members of the family even from their tender ages. Sending them to school was a sort of direct economic loss.

*(iv)* Women and girls were socially confined within the four walls of the family. They were considered as private property of males of the society. Leaving them in the open either for schooling or for any other purpose was thought as raid for usurping this property.

*(v)* Very few employment opportunities were available after education. So, poor people could not take the risk of unemployment. Teaching of vocational skills within the family was a safe procedure to make youth earning members of the family.

*(vi)* Even primary schools were not there in villages. Children had to walk miles to attend schools. Only well off families could afford the cost of private schooling and conveyance.

## CONSTITUTIONAL PROVISIONS FOR WEAKER SECTIONS

1. **National objectives declared in the preamble :** India was declared a sovereign, socialist, secular, democratic republic whose objectives will be to provide equality, liberty, fraternity and justice. It means that every citizen of the country irrespective of caste, creed or colour will have his say in the political, and social affairs of the country. Equal opportunities will be available to all of them in the matters of education and employment.
2. **Fundamental rights :** Right to equality, right to freedom and right to education upto class VIII are three rights given to citizens which are safeguarded by judiciary and nobody and not even government can deny them of these rights.
3. **Article 46 :** The state shall promote with special care the education and economic interest of the people particularly, the scheduled castes and scheduled tribes and shall protect them from social injustice and all forms of exploitations.
4. **Article 15 :** Nothing in this article or in clause (2) of article 29 shall prevent the state from making any special provisions for the advancement of socially and educationally backward classes of citizens or for scheduled castes and scheduled tribes.

5. **Article 15(3) :** Nothing in this article shall prevent the state from making any special provision for women and children.
6. **Article 16(4) :** State can make any special provision for SCs and STs and can provide reservation to them in government jobs.
7. **Article 330 :** Reservation provision is there for scheduled castes in public services.
8. **Article 15 (1) :** No citizen shall be discriminated on the ground of caste, creed colour or sex. Thus women were for the first time given status equivalent to men.
9. **Article 39 :** Men and women will be given equal rights by the state in getting means of livelihood and equal pay for equal work formula will be followed. Thus, discrimination against women were abolished in the matters of employment and pay.
10. **Article 51(a) :** It is the duty of every citizen to respect women and to remove every such tradition which goes for dishonour of women.
11. **Reservation in privately managed educational institution Act 2005 :** At the order of the government even private educational institutions were asked to give 12.5% reservation of admission seats for SCs, 7.5% for STs and 27% reservation of seats for OBCs. These institutions went to the Supreme Court against this GO and got 100% relief and thus order of reservation of seats for SCs and STs in engineering, medical or management colleges was abolished. At this move, Indian parliament brought a bill in the winter session of parliament in 2005 in order to provide reservation facilities to weaker sections of the society even in private educational institutions. Finally, the bill was passed.
12. **Women Reservation Bill :** Women reservation bill is also pending in parliament for the last few years in order to give 33% separate reservation to women in education and employment.
13. **Development Schemes for SCs and STs :** Since socio educational problems of these sections of the society are deeply rooted in economic problems, government has launched a number of such schemes which can improve their economic conditions. Once economic conditions are improved, social and educational conditions will automatically improve. Some of these schemes and development programmes are described below:
    *(i)* Most of the Indian states are providing them books and stationery, free uniform, school bags everything free of cost.
    *(ii)* Scheduled castes students have been exempted from paying any school fee upto graduation level. If they have taken admission in a private school or college even then their tuition fee is paid by the state government.
    *(iii)* Free coaching facilities for competitive examinations have also been made available for them by some states.
    *(iv)* Post metric scholarship scheme have been launched in many states to provide them economic support for higher education.
    *(v)* Dr. Ambedkar National Scholarship Scheme was started for talented students of SCs and STs from 2002-03. The purpose of this scheme is to identify the talented students in scheduled castes and tribes through a national level test and to support them economically for higher education and research.
    *(vi)* Sarva Siksha Abhiyan is another programme started in the last decade for the children of SCs and STs. The purpose of this programme is to promote 100% enrolment of those students who belong to SCs and STs in schools.
    *(vii)* 457.29 crore rupees were spent on 21 lakh students belonging to scheduled castes in the ninth five year plan for their higher education including professional and technical education.
    *(viii)* 118.10 crore rupees were spent for the construction of hostels for students (boys and girls) belonging to scheduled castes in the ninth plan.
    *(ix)* Special component plan : was started in 2002-03 for upliftment of scheduled castes people.
    *(x)* All above facilities have also been made available for the children belonging to scheduled tribes and tribals of Asam, Meghalya, Tripura and Mizoram and have been

given preference with some additional reservation facilities over others in the matters of education and employment.

*(xi)* Panchsheel principles were accepted in 1956 for the development of tribal communities.

*(xii)* Establishment of special financial institutions for tribals like Tribal Cooperative Marketting Development Mahasangh (1987) and National Scheduled Castes and Scheduled Tribes Finance and Development Corporation (1989).

*(xiii)* Establishment of separate ministry for tribals (1999).

**14. Development schemes and programmes for women :**

*(i)* **Kanya Vidya Dhan Yojna :** This programme was started by UP Government in 2004 to promote higher education among girls. Under this scheme a cash composite amount of Rs 20000 are given to all those girls who secure more than 60% marks at intermediate level. Now all girls living below poverty line are given this scholarship after passing intermediate whatsoever may be their percentage of marks in the exam.

*(ii)* **Hostel facilities :** 102 hostels were constructed for 8000 working women in the ninth plan in order to provide them cheap residence away from home.

*(iii)* **National Women's Fund:** This fund was created in 1993 in order to provide loans to women at cheaper rate of interest. Once their economic condition is improved they will go for the education of their sons and daughters.

*(iv)* **National Women's Commission:** It was established in 1992 in order to protect the rights of women in general.

*(v)* **Kasturba Gandhi Education Plan :** This programme was started on August 15, 1997. The purpose of this plan is to establish educational institutions in those areas where women's literacy rate is very low.

*(vi)* **Balika Samriddhi Yojna :** This plan was started in 1997. Under this plan Rs. 500/ are given to the family at the birth of a daughter. When that daughter goes to school, a scholarship of Rs. 300/ per year is given to the child upto class VIII. This amount is raised to Rs. 1000/ per anum in class IXth and Xth. This plan is basically for girls living below poverty line.

*(vii)* **Maulana Azad National Scholarship Scheme:** Maulana Azad Education Foundation New Delhi was established during VIIth five year plan for the promotion of Girl's education in the country. Foundation started Maulana Azad National scholarship scheme on August 1, 2003. The purpose of this scheme is to identify talented girls among minorities and to provide them special scholarship facilities for their education.

*(viii)* **Mid day Meal Scheme :** Mid day Meal Scheme was started in Primary Schools to provide free lunch to school going children. This scheme was started in 1995-96.

*(ix)* **Girls' Empowerment Scheme :** The purpose of this scheme is to accelerate authority and self knowledge among unmarried girls. Under this scheme, drop out girls living below poverty line are selected. These girls are put in aangan-wadi centres for six months where they get education and vocational training both, and become self dependent and empowered before marriage.

*(x)* **Sarva Siksha Abhiyan :** This scheme was started just before tenth five year plan. The purpose of this scheme is to provide primary education free of cost for children in the age group of 6-14 years. This scheme also aims at improving primary education through community participation in order to impart quality education to children. Girls, and children belonging to SCs and STs have especially been targeted under this scheme. For the success of this scheme, a National Mission has also been set up in 2000. The Chairman and Vice Chairman of this mission are Prime Minister and Minister for Human Resource Development respectively.

**15. NPE (New Education Policy) (1986) and Education for women's Equality:**

*(i)* Education will be used as an agent to change the status of women. National Education system will play a positive and interventional role in the empowerment of women. It will foster and establish new values in the society through redesigned curricula, text books, the training and orientation of teachers, decision makers and administrators and through the active involvement of educational institutions.

*(ii)* Women's studies will be promoted as a part of various academic courses and educational institutions will be encouraged to take up active programmes to further women's development.

*(iii)* Illiteracy among women will be removed by encouraging their enrolment in formal educational institutions and obstacles inhibiting their access to elementary education will also be removed by providing special support services and effective monitoring.

*(iv)* Major emphasis will be laid on women's participation in vocational, technical and professional education at different levels. They should not be discriminated on the ground of sex in these institutions at any step.

*(v)* Women's participation in non traditional occupations and new emerging technologies will be promoted.

**16. NPE and Education of SCs and STs:** NPE's view points regarding the education of SCs and STs are given below-

*(i)* Incentives should be given to poor families to sent their children to schools regularly till they reach the age of 14.

*(ii)* Prematric scholarship schemes should be introduced for children of families engaged in occupations such as scavenging, flaying etc. Such scheme should start from class first. All children of such families regardless of income will be covered by this scheme and time bound target will be fixed for the purpose.

*(iii)* Constant micro planning, monitoring and verification should be ensured so that enrolment, retention and successful completion of courses by these students do not fall at any stage and provision of remedial courses should also be made to improve their prospects for further education and employment.

*(iv)* Recruitment of teachers from these communities should be made on priority basis.

*(v)* Hostel facility should be provided to SC and ST students at district headquarters in a phased manner.

*(vi)* Schools and adult education centres should be opened in such places where these students can easily avail the facilities.

*(vii)* Constant innovation in methodologies and approaches is also necessary to increase the participation of SC and ST students in the educational process.

## OBJECTIVE QUESTIONS

**1.** A list of scheduled castes was first prepared in India in

*(a)* 1935 *(b)* 1941
*(c)* 1948 *(d)* 1950

**2.** The population of scheduled castes in India according to the 2001 cencus is

*(a)* 20 crores *(b)* 16.66 crores
*(c)* 25 crores *(d)* 13 crores

**3.** Literacy rate in scheduled castes is

*(a)* 37.41% *(b)* 41.2%
*(c)* 65% *(d)* 48.2%

**4.** The highest percentage of scheduled castes lives in

*(a)* MP *(b)* AP
*(c)* UP *(d)* Bihar

**5.** How much percentage of population belonging to scheduled castes live below poverty line

*(a)* 51% *(b)* 37%
*(c)* 41% *(d)* 48%

**6.** Representation of scheduled castes people in government jobs including IAS, IPS and IFS at present is

*(a)* 20% *(b)* 17%
*(c)* 12% *(d)* 26%

**7.** The largest concentration of scheduled tribes (94.5%) live in

(a) Mizoram (b) Nagaland
(c) Meghalaya (d) None of the above

**8.** Administration of pure tribal areas is mentioned in Article
(a) 51 (b) 222(a)
(c) 251 (d) 244(2)

**9.** Education of tribal people has been especially stressed in
(a) the tenth plan
(b) NPE 1986
(c) NPE (revised) 1992
(d) None of these

**10.** The percentage of women population in India at present is
(a) 47% (b) 48.3%
(c) 46.6% (d) 49%

**11.** National Mother Security Scheme was started in
(a) 1995 (b) 1999
(c) 1997 (d) 2003

**12.** National Women Commission established in 1992 is a/an
(a) constitutional body
(b) advisory body
(c) autonomous body
(d) none of the above

**13.** Constitution of India was adopted on
(a) 26 Jan. 1950 (b) 26 Nov. 1949
(c) 15 Aug. 1947 (d) 26 Aug. 1948

**14.** Which of the following sections of the society is getting lion's share in central government jobs
(a) Scheduled castes (b) Scheduled tribes
(c) Minorities (d) Upper castes people

**15.** What is the percentage of population of schedule castes people in India?
(a) 16.20% (b) 20%
(c) 32% (d) 12%

**16.** What is the percentage of backward children in normal class:
(a) 5% (b) 10%
(c) 15% (d) 20%

## ANSWERS

| 1 | 2 | 3 | 4 | 5 | 6 | 7 | 8 | 9 | 10 |
|---|---|---|---|---|---|---|---|---|---|
| (a) | (b) | (a) | (c) | (b) | (a) | (a) | (d) | (c) | (b) |
| **11** | **12** | **13** | **14** | **15** | **16** | | | | |
| (d) | (a) | (b) | (a) | (a) | (b) | | | | |

# Education and National Integration

*"We should not become parochial, narrow minded, provincial, communal and caste minded because we have a great mission to perform. Let us, the citizens of India bring about the integration of the Indian people. We have to build up this country into a mighty nation, mighty not in the ordinary sense of the word, but mighty in thought, mighty in action, mighty in culture and mighty in its peaceful service of humanity".*

— Jawaharlal Nehru

## NATIONALISM

### Meaning of Nationalism

When nation is kept above religion, politics, caste, ethnicity, language or culture and individual feel emotionally associated with the country (nation), it is called nationalism. Individual is more for the nation and not vice-versa. Every individual's duty is bound to uphold the sovereignty and integrity of the nation. When such feeling runs in the veins of citizens, they do not find it difficult to sacrifice what they have, especially life, property and the self for the nation.

Thus, nationalism is that feeling which inspires all its citizens to rise above their narrow differences and work in unity for the development of the nation. The nationalism actually means whole hearted devotion to the nation, sense of duty towards it and unquestioning faith in its glorious future.

**Brubacher** differentiates it with patriotism in the following words:

"Nationalism is a term that has come into prominence since the renaissance and particularly since the French revolution. It ordinarily indicates a wider scope of loyalty than patriotism. In addition to ties of place nationalism is evidenced by such other ties as race, history, language, culture, and tradition".

In extreme form of nationalism, aggressive attitude towards other nations economically, politically or militarily is expressed by the people. Such people keep their nation higher than the other nations in language, culture and system of governance. In order to manifest their nationalism, they interfere with the internal affairs of other nations generally. Political party in power motivates the people to behave so. American nationalism is a glaring example of aggressive nationalism in the 21st century. Chinese nationalism comes at the third place after Britain.

### Demerits of Extreme form of Nationalism

We do not support this extreme form of nationalism because of the following reasons.

*(i)* It is actually a threat to world peace because once it envisages sharp reactions from other nations, wars take place between nations or groups of nations'.

*(ii)* It is against the spirit of humanity. How can a nation be above or below the other nations.

*(iii)* Expansion of territories which was the trend till the first quarter of 20th century is not a realistic approach today because weapons of mass destruction if used in wars today, they will annihilate the whole living being on the earth.

*(iv)* It creates hatred among citizens of different nations. I have the right to exist as much as you have. If hatred is created among human being and they are sharply divided among different nations, international relations in trade commerce, diplomacy or culture will not be possible.

*(v)* Exchange of technology, culture or ideas will not take place in the presence of this type of nationalism. Sooner or later it will be defeated by collective efforts.

(vi) If this type of nationalism grow in any society, higher concentration is laid on defense related activities. These activities are very costly today because of excessive use of technology in such activities. The result will be that lesser efforts will be done for the improvement of living conditions of poor. Thus about half of the same country will suffer from its own maladies.

(vii) It is against the principles of democracy and if it survives for a longer period of time, it brings about autocracy or dictatorship in politics.

## Merits of Genuine form of Nationalism

Genuine form of nationalism is supported because of the following reasons:

(i) If nation is kept above religion, politics, caste, culture etc. it is possible to maintain national unity and integrity.

(ii) Those who have vested interests and do everything to fulfil them can easily be identified on the basis of these norms.

(iii) It develops sense of loyalty and patriotism among the people of the country. Such feeling helps the country to achieve fast economic growth.

(iv) It creates a positive feeling of sacrifice towards the country. When any alien power invades the country the whole country gets united and the enemy is defeated by the force of unity.

(v) It removes social tension in the nation as well because feeling of love and cooperation is created by this form of nationalism.

(vi) It can also reduce the tendency of juvenile delinquency among the youth because every member of the society gets emotionally attached to the nation.

(vii) Uniform educational policy for the whole nation can be adopted which is very essential to reduce regional disparities in the country.

(viii) A national language can be developed sooner or later. It is very essential to maintain the tempo of nationalism in the country.

(ix) People will rise above their narrow political or party differences.

(x) Social progress will also be seen in every part of the country.

(xi) This feeling of nationalism will increase love and cooperation among the citizens. As a result, exc9hange of economic activities will be high and it will increase economic development of the country.

(xii) If this form of nationalism is inculcated in the people by education, it may eradicate corruptions from the public life. Citizens try to do for the honour of the nation and not for its defame.

# NATIONAL INTEGRATION

## Meaning of national integration

When all citizens of a country irrespective of their caste, creed, colour, race, culture or language get united to act as a cohesive force it is called national integration. National integration is not an idea but is an action taken collectively in the interest of the nation. Thus it is very synonymous to nationalism discussed earlier. The only difference between the two is that national integration is the process and nationalism is its output. A person who is disintegrating the nation by any of his activities he can never be a nationalist. From this point of view all those who are disintegrating the nation by creating hatred are none than anti-nationalists.

## Problem of National Integration

Problem of national integration does not arise in those countries where there is only one culture, language or religion prevailing. Unity on at least one point is necessary for all mutual, social or national relations. In a country like India problem of national integration is serious because of the following reasons :

(i) There exist thousands of castes including sub castes.

(ii) There are hundreds of languages spoken and dialects change after every ten miles.

(iii) So many cultural patterns are adopted by the people.

(iv) Almost all the ethnicities of world are found here.

(v) A number of religions followed by the people of India are very much antagonistic to each other.

(vi) Political parties in the country are emerging like herbs.

*(vii)* The elite and highly educated classes are not willing to leave the room for ordinary classes of the society.

*(viii)* Thousands of people are killed in communal riots but government machinery stands like a silent spectator.

*(ix)* Fruits of socio economic development is not distributed equitably.

## Important Sources of National Disintegration

Important obstacles in the way of national integration are as follows:

1. *Religion based partition of the country :* The whole India was divided into two nations, Bharat and Pakistan in 1947. The criteria of partition was that Muslim majority areas were given to Pakistan and Hindu majority areas were gone into the hands of India. Minorities were not to vacate their dwellings according to this criteria and baring a few lakh populations in either sides. All the minorities remained in their original places and they did not migrate. Minorities were not to be distributed in 1947. It was only the division of majority areas. All those muslims who did not migrate to Pakistan do belong to this country. Hence, if their loyalties are questioned by ignorant people, it erects a wall of hatred and distance between the two communities increases.
2. *Presence of so many religions :* There are so many religions followed in India, e.g., Hinduism, Islamic religion, Christianity, Judaism, Jainism, Buddhism, Parsi religion and so on and there are a number of sects and subsects in each religion too. Such as there are mainly two sects in Islam—Shiaites and Sunnis. Sunnis are divided into four subsects—Hambali, Muliki, Shawafai and Ahnaf. Ahnaf sect is further divided in India into two schools of thoughts—Barelli school of thought and Deobandi school of thought—both are highly at variance with each other. Then similar nature of divisions are also seen in other religions of the country. These ideological differences sometimes inspire the followers to translate these differences into action and enmity among them is created. Law is not there in India to regulate the citizens in their private affairs. Religious hatred are seen when different sects and sub sects practice social and collective congregation and transgressions into other sects and sub sects take place. Such a crime is punishable in India no doubt but procedure of prosecution and conviction is very complex.
3. *Communalism :* It is the biggest enemy of our secular character. Communal feelings are raised by the majority community against the minorities mostly to gain political mileage. Many unsettled issues which could not be settled even during the Mughal or British rules are being raised for final settlement through mass mobilization and when status quo is jeopardized, minorities lose patience resulting in blood shed and loss of property. Court is here to settle all such issues but it is by passed by ignorant fellow beings.
4. *Caste differences :* There are a number of castes and hundreds of sub castes found in India. Castism is not a challenge against any nation if it is upheld for the purpose of distinction and keeping genetic heritage distinguishable. But when it is recognized as a basis of social stratification and translated into untouchablity or genetic vulgarity it becomes a menace for the progress of the nation. This problem is intensified when leaders of different social groups mobilize the members of the groups to act selfishly disregarding the interest of the nation. Such a temperament is seen not only in the localities but also in educational institutions, offices and production units. The new trend of castism is seen in politics today and parties are formed on caste or creed lines and once the leader is elected for legislative bodies he is only obliged to serve his own community or caste.
5. *Regional aspirations :* After independence many new states were organized and reorganized on lingual basis such as Tamil Nadu, Andhra, Gujarat, Maharashtra etc. Then demand for a separate Punjabi states arose and Punjab came into being. Several other states were also organized on the same line. This division of country into different states in order to maintain its federal character have created regional feeling by intensifying regional aspirations. Creation of Jharkhand, Uttaranchal and Chhattisgarh is not

the end of the chapter. Agitations are on to open new chapters even now. These regional aspirations get intensified when any group or section of a larger group is neglected politically or economically. Such ignorance creates majority phobia among them. As a result, weaker sections of the society gets united to fight against the prevailing system. Then this regionalism is turned into extremism and terrorism as is the case of Assam, Nagaland and J&K. When such feelings are suppressed by force, this action leads to another reaction and a vicious circle of disintegration continues.

6. *Absence of one common language :* We speak so many languages in India and out of them 20 have been included formally in the schedule of our constitution. When constitution came into force Hindi was adopted as National language and English as an official language. It was also affirmed that efforts will be made to popularize Hindi as an official language and lingua franka within 15 years. But Hindi speaking people are only a little over 50% even today. English and many regional languages dominate in many states. English is still being used as a medium of higher education in almost all universities of India. Common man is still miles away from one common language acceptable to the whole country. Language, the most important element of social cohesion is still beyond our reach. If we really want to bring the whole population emotionally attached to each other, we will have to put Hindi at the top.

7. *Cultural disparities :* India is a country of so many cultures and mostly contradictory to each other. Some people protect birds and animals and some kill them to be used as food. Some people bury dead bodies and there are some people who cremate dead bodies by burning and throwing the ashes into the river. Mughal rulers tried to popularize an acceptable composite culture and Britishers further enriched it by introducing modernity into it but all these efforts lay in vain when some people tried to impose ancient Indian culture on others. People reacted sharply against it and cultural conflict got intensified. Since culture is directly related to customs and traditions, cultural differences will necessarily divide the society.

8. *Economic and Social disparities :* If society is bitterly divided into poor, middle or upper classes and poor class think that he is not being given his due share in the economy, this class will not assimilate into the society properly. He will form his own group for all practical purposes, though formation of such groups need not be on papers. In 1947 such disparities were very high and about 50% population was technically poor but today only 26% of the population live below poverty line. Gloomy side of the picture, however, is that poor and rich are not rising up in the economy proportionally. The gap between the rich and the poor is increasing day by day. Those who are rich they educate their children in reputed public schools to secure administrative and other high positions in the society. Poor, on the other hand, take shelter in government schools for education and is then pushed backward in the race. This social inertia is an unhealthy sign for national integration. Nation is not for a few privileged classes but it is for all on equal basis.

9. *Unworthy political and social leadership :* Days are gone when Gandhijee, Nehru, Maulana Azad, Sardar Patel, Molvi Hifzurrahman and the like figures were the leaders of the country. Today political leaders are probably a bit less than pick pockets whose entire efforts lie in making their private lives luxurious and accumulating wealth for their unknown future generation. Because of this reason they are not revered by the whole nation collectively and their voices are not adhered to unanimously. They maintain their leadership in their particular groups and do not extend their role to other groups at the cost of their survivals. They only want to grab powers either by using money or muscle power. Social leaders are also not there to unite the whole society on humanitarian ground.

10. *Non secular education :* Education which moulds the behaviour of the child since his childhood is not free from cultural dominance. If decision regarding the dominance of a particular

culture is taken on the ground that the sentiments of the majority are to be pacified, it is technically wrong. It is because if such subject matter is to be studied by all people of the country then why the minority is to be loaded with a material which does not belong to them. If any one needs something extra, it may be given to him in extra time outside the school time table. In the regular time table only that thing should be taught which is acceptable to all so that no unwanted reaction is shown by anyone. If representation of a particular culture is felt necessary, then other cultures should also be equally represented as every thing belongs to one India. Had this type of secularism been adopted in Education since 1947 Indians should have got rid of any disintegrating forces upto now.

11. *Unfair selection in public jobs :* This was not actually a big problem of national integration in 1950s and 1960s but it may be kept at the top now. Selection of a candidate for a government job is made on the basis of so many considerations other than worth. This problem is multiplied when least efforts are made to increase the worth of backward communities. This treatment leads to frustration among youth. Youth generation needs jobs to support their families. If job reservation is given to woman, it will deteriorate the social positions of the youth further because women are not expected to support the family and jobless youth will have no option but to do or die in frustration.
12. *Multiparty system :* Regional aspirations are flourishing because of multiparty system. When a party is not able to secure a simple majority at the central or state level, small parties support it to form coalition government. These unstable governments do not adhere to the national norms and personal vested interest disintegrate the nation.

## Educational Measures to Ensure National Integration

If we want to make India a united and powerful country, education can do a lot in this respect. Education can mould and condition the behaviour of citizens in a comprehensive manner. A child, since the very beginning of his life can be prepared and taught the points of consensus that exist in the social lives of Indians. There is no single point at which people from across the country can be united except the point of common territory. It must be inculcated in them that recognition as citizens of a powerful nation is possible only when they are united in their action and thought. This single point of concurrence can be translated into reality through education in the following ways:

1. All text books that are taught in schools and colleges should be scrutinized. If there is any dominance of any particular culture or religion it should be reduced to parity. India belongs to all its citizens not to some groups or religions. Permission maybe given to run cultural institutions on private basis without any assistance and recognition by the government. There may be some anti national elements in text books especially in states. They should be removed after scrutiny.
2. Masses should be motivated to participate in national festivals. These festivals should be organized by government agencies, NGOs and educational institutions. India's freedom fighters should be remembered on regular basis and their anniversaries should be celebrated by doing more work not by holidays. This will increase economic growth of the country.
3. In history books all rulers should be treated only as rulers not as the representative of a particular community. If someone is tyrant, he will not distinguish between you and me.
4. Dramas, discussions, debates and other cultural activities advocating national character of Indian society should be organized across the country. Mass media can play a very significant role here but it is possible only when people associated with these activities are especially trained by education. If the editor of a news paper is narrow minded, if not anti national, his attitude will surely be reflected in his news paper. So, we first of all, prepare nationalist editors then we should expect something positive from mass media.
5. Fairness in admission and employment is also necessary to develop a national thinking among the people. They should realize that nation is all the time ready to protect them.

6. Moulding the behaviour of children is not so easy. It requires especially trained teachers to perform this esteemed job. For this purpose the role of teacher's training colleges becomes important. They cannot fulfil this requirement through one or two years training courses like B.Ed. or BTC. These teachers should be trained for at least six years just after high school or intermediate to teach students upto high school.
7. Before appointing a person in the field of educational administration he should be properly tested regarding his attitude towards problems of national importance. Other appointments of administrative and higher posts should also be done on this very basis.
8. Efforts should be made to provide students opportunities of interacting with different cultures in the schools.
9. Non formal education programmes should be reorganized keeping in view the needs of national character. Literacy kits should be prepared from integration point of view.
10. Three language formula—Hindi as a national language, English as an official language and one regional language should be strictly followed in all government and private schools. At least nine periods in a week should be allocated for teaching Hindi.

These ten points programmes are very much in concurrence with the recommendations of **Kothari Commission** (1964-66) which reacted to this problem in the following words.

"Educational system must make its contribution to the development of habits, attitudes and qualities of character which will enable its citizens to bear worthily the responsibilities of democratic citizenship and to **counter act** all those fissiparious tendencies which hinder the emergence of a broad national and secular outlook".

## National Integration Committee

It was set up in 1967 under the chairmanship of Mrs. Indira Gandhi, late prime minister of India. The first meeting of this committee was held in 1968 in Sri Nagar. In this meeting it deliberated and expounded the main aims of education with reference to national development. It also appointed three sub committees to tackle various problems related to national integration. Such as problems of achieving communal harmony, problems of regionalism and to reorganize educational system to achieve unity in diversities. These sub committees put their suggestions before the National Integration Committee and these recommendations were accepted in toto. NIC also realized that this huge task could not be fulfilled by the government alone. Active participation of enlightened citizens will be necessary for this purpose. Important suggestions given by NIC are given below:

*(i)* Children should be made familiar with all aspects of national life and culture.

*(ii)* Children should be properly informed about the important events and happenings related to national movements during freedom struggle.

*(iii)* Education should be reorganized in such a way as to bring about unity in diversities and to inculcate in children qualities of communal harmony and human well being.

*(iv)* Efforts should be made to increase the sense of sacrifice for nation in children.

## Other Measures to Ensure National Integration

1. *Honest and unbiased attitude towards all citizens:* Partiality, nepotism or corruption in public life leads to frustration in the masses. These frustrations develop antisocial or anti national attitude among them. It is because those in power in any way are identified with the country and reaction against them spreads to the nation as well. So, it is very essential that those in power should be honest and impartial in their attitude and behaviour. Stern action should be taken against them if they show dishonesty or prejudice against any one. Seven fundamental rights given to citizens should be imprisoned to the constitutional provisions. If justice is not maintained in the society it will develop the feeling of castism, communalism, regionalism and separatism among the people.
2. *Protection of minorities :* Many people belonging to minority communities lose their lives and

property during communal riots. This develops in them a sense of insecurity which further leads to isolation in national roles. So efforts should be made to protect them in hostile situations. If we take the example of Muslims, they are extremely backward educationally and socially. They should be protected against the ruthless competition of survival also.

3. *Purification of politics :* Politics has become a safe shelter for criminals and corrupt people today. Cleansing campaign should be launched against these people by making judiciary active and powerful. Once it happens masses will rise up in support of these campaigns and everything will be correct in no time. To check illegal properties, assets more than income Act should be amended and consumption norms should be prepared to assess the consumption level and pattern of the people. If everything is clear in advance we can prosecute any corrupt official or leader very easily. Corruption and nepotism should be made non bailable offense just like POTA in the recent past. It is because these things create terrorist or separatist feeling. Terrorists or separatists are not born.
4. *Strict adherence to secularism:* If any religion or religious community is supported by the state directly or indirectly more than its due, it will jeopardize national integration. State must keep itself at equal distance from all religions. It will again require justice loving political leaders and such leaders can not be produced without taking the help of education.
5. *Emotional integration :* National integration is not possible without emotional integration.
6. *Development of morality and character :* In the above discussion we see that most of the problems of national integration are directly linked with degenerating individuals and the society in morality and character. A high charactererd religious man never thinks of doing any harm against the society or the nation. The physical strength of the nation lies in the spiritual prosperity of the society.

## OBJECTIVE QUESTIONS

**1.** Preamble of the Indian constitutions declares India a
   (*a*) Socialist republic (*b*) Democratic republic
   (*c*) Secular republic (*d*) All of these

**2.** Democracy in India is grounded on which of the following principles
   (*a*) Liberty and equality
   (*b*) Fraternity
   (*c*) Justice
   (*d*) All of these

**3.** The largest amendment in Indian constitution was made in
   (*a*) 1972 (*b*) 1976
   (*c*) 1975 (*d*) 1992

**4.** At which of the following levels of education, privatization is most successful?
   (*a*) Primary level
   (*b*) Secondary level
   (*c*) Higher education level
   (*d*) Technical education level

**5.** For success of democracy in India which of the following things is required at present
   (*a*) Fair and transparent education and employment policies
   (*b*) Abolition of reservation in education and employment
   (*c*) Tolerance and co existence
   (*d*) All of these

**6.** Secularism in India means
   (*a*) State keeps equal distance from all religions
   (*b*) An irreligious society
   (*c*) An irreligious state
   (*d*) Equal weightage to all religions

**7.** The policy of universalisation of elementary education is a
   (*a*) Socialistic concept
   (*b*) Capitalistic concept
   (*c*) Autocratic concept
   (*d*) None of these

**8.** Education is included in which of the following lists
   (*a*) Union list (*b*) State list
   (*c*) Concurrent list (*d*) Residual list

**9.** Privatization in education and economy got momentum since

(a) 1991 (b) 1995
(c) 2002 (d) 1999

**10.** If there is any controversy on any matter of education between centre and any state what will be the final settlement

(a) State legislation will be accepted as education was in the state list before 1976
(b) Law made by the parliament will prevail.
(c) Both the laws will be rejected and matter will be decided by Supreme Court
(d) Both centre and state will choose separate line of action

**11.** Central government maintains the quality and standard of education in the educational institutions of national importance like central universities, IITs, IIM etc. through

(a) University Grant Commission (UGC)
(b) All India Council of Technical Education (AICTE)
(c) Central Council of Indian Medicine
(d) All of the above

**12.** Which of the following is not included in the entry 13 of the union list

(a) Educational and cultural relations with foreign countries
(b) Maintenance of IIM
(c) Participation in International conferences
(d) International association for culture

**13.** Vocational and technical training of workers comes under

(a) Concurrent list (b) State list
(c) Union list (d) None of them

**14.** No citizen shall be denied admission in any educational institution maintained by the state or receiving aid out of state fund on grounds of religion, race, caste, language or any of them. It has been stated in

(a) Article 29 (i) (b) Article 29(ii)
(c) Article 31 (d) Article 30

**15.** Primary education in the mother tongue has been safeguarded in Article

(a) 29 (b) 350
(c) 220 (d) 351

**16.** Central government can implement any policy on education ignoring State's wishes because

(a) Education is in the union list
(b) Education is in the concurrent list
(c) India has parliamentary democracy
(d) None of these

**17.** Central government must consult the state before beginning any legislation on any subject included in the concurrent list. This recommendation of Sarkariya Commission was accepted by Inter State board in

(a) 1995 (b) 1986
(c) 1992 (d) 1991

**18.** Democratic socialism enshrined in our constitution means

(a) reduction of inequalities of income through monetary and fiscal measures
(b) absence of class distinction
(c) mixed economy.
(d) both (a) and (b)

**19.** Which of the following is not needed as the qualification of a legislator

(a) He must be a citizen of India
(b) He must not have a criminal record
(c) He must be at least matriculate
(d) both (a) and (b)

**20.** Which of the following is an important characteristic of Indian democracy

(a) Every citizen in India has the right to develop his personality according to his own choice
(b) Equality of educational opportunities but special safeguard to weaker sections of the society
(c) Linguistic or religious minorities can run their own educational institutions in order to protect their culture and language
(d) All of these

**21.** What you love and what you want for yourself, you must desire the same for others also. This is the opinion of

(a) Justice Venkatchaliah
(b) Prophet Mohammad
(c) Both of these
(d) None of these

**22.** The purpose of democracy in India is to end

(a) Political inequalities

(b) Social inequalities
(c) Economic inequalities
(d) both (a) and (b)

**23.** In order to strengthen national unity and integrity through education which of the following points has been recommend by Education Commission (1964-66)
(a) Common school system for public education
(b) Making social and national services obligatory for all students
(c) The development of an appropriate language policy
(d) All of these

**24.** Which of the following is an important characteristic of new social order
(a) Privatization of education including higher education
(b) Increased role of women in education and employment sectors
(c) Pressure and vote bank politics
(d) All of these

**25.** In the present political and social scenario in India positive autonomy is
(a) essential for the survival of democracy
(b) is the approach through which terrorism can be sublimated
(c) is needed to raise quality of education
(d) all of these

**26.** Illegal, arbitrary and unreasonable action of the executive is checked by Supreme Court under
(a) power of judicial review
(b) advisory jurisdiction
(c) the saviour and interpreter of the constitution
(d) none of these

**27.** Functional literacy programme has been started for
(a) factory workers
(b) illiterate farmers
(c) tribal people
(d) all of them

**28.** Autonomy in the field of education can be dangerous for total education system if
(a) It is absolute as is the case of educational institutions maintained by minorities
(b) It lacks accountability on the part of the authority
(c) It is not guided by certain necessary laws
(d) All of them

## ANSWERS

| 1 | 2 | 3 | 4 | 5 | 6 | 7 | 8 | 9 | 10 |
|---|---|---|---|---|---|---|---|---|---|
| (d) | (d) | (b) | (a) | (d) | (a) | (a) | (c) | (a) | (b) |
| 11 | 12 | 13 | 14 | 15 | 16 | 17 | 18 | 19 | 20 |
| (d) | (b) | (a) | (a) | (b) | (b) | (d) | (a) | (d) | (d) |
| 21 | 22 | 23 | 24 | 25 | 26 | 27 | 28 | | |
| (c) | (d) | (d) | (d) | (d) | (a) | (b) | (d) | | |

# 10

# National Values Enshrined in our Constitution

Education, the most important and dominating face of human life have very well been addressed by framers of our constitution under fundamental rights and directive principles of state policy. Supreme Court of India have elaborated all these articles in different ways from time to time. We will discuss here all the relevant articles one by one in the context of education only.

## FUNDAMENTAL RIGHTS

### Article 14 (Right to Equality in General)

According to this fundamental right, state shall not deny any person to equality before law or equal protection of laws within the territory of India.

It means that whatever opportunities are available in the country it will be made equally accessible to all citizens irrespective of caste, creed, colour, sex or on any other ground. If opportunities are few and aspirants are many, impartial and fair admission test will be conducted for this purpose to select the required number of candidates according to merit.

While explaining this article Supreme Court states:

"Interview or viva-voce should not be exclusive test for admission to government medical or engineering colleges (or any other government schools or colleges) or for appointment to government service. For admission to government colleges marks fixed for the interview should not exceed 15% of the total marks and for appointment to government services marks fixed for interview should not be more than 25% of the total marks".

This provision has been made by the Supreme Court just in order to reduce subjectivity and discrimination in matters of admission and appointments.

Supreme Court has also made it clear that private educational bodies receiving grants from the government are obliged to act fairly in accordance with the fundamental rights as well as the rules and regulations framed by the government. The grant being public fund, such educational bodies are bound by all the rules and regulations framed by the government and recognizing authority in the matters of recruitment of staff and teachers, their condition of service, syllabi, standard of education and so on and in the matters of admission, they have to follow the rules of merit also. Moreover, private educational institutions receiving grants from the government cannot charge any fee higher than what is charged in government institutions.

Education is not a commodity to be sold and purchased like other articles in the market. So no individual can run a college or school like a business firm to earn more and more profit. If education becomes an article of profit, only few people will be able to receive it because of its high costs. So educational institutions must be run by society or trust. While elaborating this point Supreme Court stated:

"A professional college shall be permitted to be established and administered only by a society registered under the societies registration act of 1860 or by a public trust, religious or charitable trust. No individual firm or company or other body of individuals, will be permitted to establish or administer a professional college."

This ruling of the Supreme Court is applicable to public schools also.

### Article 15(1) (Right to Equality in Particular)

This Article is actually the explanation of the Article 14. It provides that state shall not discriminate any citizen on ground of religion, race , caste, sex, place of birth or any other ground.

This Article is restricted to the discrimination by the state only not by the private individuals.

Thus discrimination in any form has been made illegal by this Article.

## Article 15(3) (Provisions for Women, SCs, STs, OBCs)

Under this Article special provisions have been made for women, socially and educationally backward classes of citizens (SCs and STs) and other backward classes. According to this article state is asked to do something special for these groups of people. Reservation of seats in admission or employment is given to these people by the state. State also provides special scholarship facilities to them. If persons belonging to SCs and STs study in private educational institutions, their total fees are paid by the government.

## Article 16

### (Equality of Opportunity in Matters Relating to Public Employment)

Under this Article all citizens are given equal opportunities to secure any public job irrespective of their caste, creed, race, sex, place of birth or place of residing.

If citizens fulfil the eligibility criteria they can apply for any public post and their recruitment will be made on the basis of merit only with the exception of special provision made for SCs, STs, OBCs etc. Under article 16(4) general merit list will be prepared first. If a person belonging to special category comes under this category, his candidature will be treated as general. After that separate reservation list will be prepared.

While interpreting this article Supreme Court has rejected the view that backwardness under article 16(4) should be both social and educational. Social backwardness is sufficient enough for the purpose of reservation. If person belonging to any reserved category are not educationally backward even then they are entitled to reservation on social grounds only.

One important thing that Supreme Court holds is that the reservation in favour of backward classes under article 16(4) should not exceed 50% of the total seats to be appointed. It can be done only in extra- ordinary situations. The rule of 50% should be applied to each year not of the total strength of the cadre.

Article 16(4) is however silent regarding the matters of promotions on reservation ground. In order to remove this difficulty an amendment in the constitution was made in 1995 according to which state has been empowered to make provisions for reservation in matters of promotion in favour of SCs and STs.

## Article 19(1) (Right to Freedom)

According to this Article, all citizens shall have the right.

I. to freedom of speech and expression
II. to assemble peacefully without arms
III. to form associations and unions
IV. To move freely throughout the territory of India
V. To reside and settle in any part of the country
VI. To practice and carry on any profession, occupation, trade or business

All these freedoms given in the constitution are not only concerned directly with our life but also concerned indirectly to the process of education.

Without freedom of speech and expression no teaching learning process can go on smoothly. If we do not criticize the present system on the basis of past records, how can we make our future better. Teachers and students can express themselves freely in the class on the basis of this very freedom.

Peaceful assembling is the second freedom and it is seen everywhere in the school complex.

Students' unions in the school campus and many of the students' or teachers' associations are formed as a collective approach to achieve the ends. If such freedoms were not there, there would have been total lack of cooperation among teachers and students in their respective groups. This freedom makes the teachers and students, from across the country united.

Indian citizens can go anywhere to reside temporarily or to settle either for the purpose of education, employment or business. Through this freedom even those people who belong to very backward regions can be educated to the highest level. Teachers from across the country can be made available anywhere in the country to teach. Schools and colleges can also be established in any part of the country but they will not come under the category of trade or business as Supreme Court opinions.

Thus article 19(1) provides a unitary structure to education as well as other spheres of life.

Supreme Court has interpreted, the freedom of speech and expression by saying that only peaceful and orderly demonstration are also the manifestation of feelings of an individual or group. So they are just the communication of one's ideas to others. If a demonstration is violent or disorderly, only then it will be restricted.

While interpreting freedom to form association Supreme Court has held that if state has taken over an educational institution on certain ground it does not mean that state can take over that society also which owned the institution as its only property. These two things are different. Moreover, this right does not mean that an institution has the right to be recognized by the government. Government can linger on the recognition of the society or deny it.

Similarly, freedom of profession, trade or business does not exempt a person from minimum qualification necessary for that profession or business. State can prescribe certain qualification to carry on a particular profession or trade, eg, a person can not become the principal of his own school without fulfilling the criteria set by the government or any of its agency.

## Article 21 (Right to Life and Personal liberty)

Right to education has been derived from this article on the ground that education flows from the right to life. Supreme Court has held the view that every child upto the age of 14 years has fundamental right to get free education. So in the light of this article several other Articles like article 45 and 46 along with 21 of the constitution were amended to make education a seventh fundamental right in 2001. Now every child has fundamental right to get free and compulsory education upto the age of 14 years.

Supreme Court also holds the view that right to higher education of citizens after the age of 14 is not absolute but subject to the economic capacity or development of state.

## Article 24
## (Prohibition of Employment of children)

According to this Article, no child below the age of 14 years shall be employed to work in any factory, mine, construction industry or in any other hazarduous industry.

Several acts have been enacted for this purpose. Child labour act 1986 is the latest and the most important of all. Moreover, after including right to education into the category of fundamental rights, children are now given full facilities to take admission in schools and receive free education there. Mid day meals are also provided to them under mid day meals scheme to motivate them to go to schools. Examination reforms have also been brought about to bring down wastage and stagnation in primary schools.

## Article 25
## (freedom of conscience and profession, practice and propagation of religion)

Subject to public order, morality, health or any other provision related to fundamental rights all persons are equally entitled to freedom of conscience, and the right freely to profess, practice and propagate religions. Freedom of conscience includes that the person has the right to entertain beliefs and doctrines concerning matters which he considers to be conducive to his spiritual well being.

In Sanjay Dutta's case Supreme Court has observed that freedom to religion is the core of Indian culture. Even the slightest deviation may shake the social fabric.

Freedom of religion also includes the freedom to practice rituals and ceremonies which are essential and integral parts of religion. But this freedom of religion is not absolute. It is subject to four types of restrictions.

*(i)* Public order may not be disturbed by it. In the name of religion no body can be permitted to aid noise pollution or violate noise pollution norms. Even if there be a religious practice to use loud speaker, it should not adversely affect the rights of others. This is the interpretation of the article by the supreme court.

*(ii)* Religion shouldn't adversely affect the morality of citizen. No such religion will be allowed to exist which is absolutely immoral in beliefs or action.

*(iii)* Health of the person should not be damaged by the practice of religion.

*(iv)* Practice or propagation of religion should not jeopardize other fundamental rights.

Religion as an active agency of education makes the task of education easy and reachable. Such freedom given to people can help them to obtain more and more education through religion.

### Article 26
### (Right to Religious Denomination)

Religious denomination means a collection of individuals having common faith, common organization and designated by distance name. This article guarantees certain rights to every religious denomination subject to public order, morality and health.

Under section (a) of this article every religious denomination shall have right to establish and maintain institutions—educational and other types for religious and charitable purposes.

This fundamental right is very conducive to preserving and transmitting particular culture for the purpose of maintaining cultural identity. This is very much needed in a country of diverse religions and cultures. Each religious sect is maintaining and administering educational institutions like Madarsas and Maths for the purpose of preserving and transmitting its own culture to the people of its sects.

### Article 28
### (Attendance at Religious Worships in Educational institutions)

Article 28 mentions three types of educational institutions-

*(a) Educational institutions wholly maintained out of state fund.* In such institutions no religious instructions shall be provided. This article however does not prohibit moral education dissociated from any doctrine of religious denomination. Teaching and philosophy of any great saint of India may be taught as a part of academic study. According to this, a person can take part in religious worships on his own even if the place of worship is located in the premises of the institution. But he cannot be forced by the authority to do so.

*(b) Educational institutions administered by the state but established by a trust-* These are also government institutions. Here religious instruction can be given if trust or managing committee desires to do so but separate instructions will be given to separate religious sects. Hindus can not be compelled to study Quran and Muslims cannot be compelled to study Geeta and so on.

*(c) Educational institutions recognized by the state or receiving aid out of the state fund :* Here no person shall be required to take part in any religious instruction or to attend any religious worship that are conducted in such institutions without his consent (will). Thus secular character of the institution will always be maintained.

Thus, we see that India is not opposed to any religious instruction or ceremonial participation at all. It is rather supportive to them but under the boundaries of right to freedom and equality. Because of this freedom given to all religions they are prospering by leaps and bounds in their own circles without touching or frustrating the others.

### Article 29-(1)
### (Minority Right to Conserve Language, Script or Culture)

Any citizen having a distinct language, or culture of its own shall have the right to conserve the same. People belonging to majority community also have this right.

In order to preserve culture, language or a particular script, people of India in general and minorities in particular can establish their own educational institutions, form their own associations and cultural groups and organize collective activities for this purpose.

Supreme Court holds the view that right to conserve the language includes right to agitate for the protection of the language. If being of any language is in danger, people of India can launch agitation in order to protect it from extinction.

## Article 29(2)
## (Right against Discrimination in Matters of Admission in Educational Institutions)

According to this article, no citizen will be denied admission into any educational institution maintained or aided by the state on the basis of caste, creed, language, race or region. But reservation of seats for the students of a particular area on any special ground is not the violation of this Article.

Supreme Court has interpreted this article by saying that state funded minority institutions are entitled to prepare their community candidates to maintain the minority character of the institution but they must leave at least 50% seats for other communities for the purpose of general merit selection.

## Article 30(1)
## Right of Minorities to Establish and Administer Educational Institutions)

Under this Article linguistic or religious minorities have the right to establish and administer educational institutions of their own choice to preserve their culture or language.

In Indian context this fundamental right given to minorities is essential for establishing communal and cultural harmonies. Minorities will not feel alienated or suppressed in the society. They can chalk out plans for the upliftment of their own community and establish such schools and colleges. State will also grant them aids to run these institutions smoothly.

Supreme Court has interpreted the article by saying that right to administer the educational institutions is not absolute right but it is subject to regulatory power of the state. State can regulate them by invoking laws but these regulations will not jeopardize the welfare of the minorities in any way. Because of this reason Supreme Court has held the view that the G.O. which provides that non Kannada teaching schools shall teach Kannada language from first standard is rational. Thus, we can say that state can direct the management of these institutions to follow the policies made by the government in the larger interest of the society, such as adoption of three language formula or maintenance of minimum standard or following the state curriculum.

Supreme Court also holds the view that the regulations which completely takes away the autonomy of the educational institution will not be valid. However, regulations made for regulating the terms and conditions of service of teachers or other employees with the object to maintain the educational standard will not be the violation of the Article. Similarly, taking prior approval of the director of education before the suspension of a teacher by any minority institution to provide protection to the teacher is not the violation of the Article.

According to this Article, a university can not deny affiliation to any educational institution on the ground that it is managed by a minority community. However, a university, in granting affiliation can impose certain restrictions for maintaining the requisite educational standard. A minority can claim to administer an institution only when it has established it. For example, A.M.U. has been established by a statute of parliament not by the Muslim Minority so Muslim minority can not claim to administer the A.M.U. any time in future.

Important religions minorities are Muslims, Christians, Parsis, Jews, Sikhs, Jains, Arya Smaji's, Brahm Samajis etc in India. Minorities are those which are less than 50% of the population of a state and form a distinct and identifiable group of citizens.

## Article 30 (2)
## (Right Against Discrimination in Matters of Granting Aids to Educational Institutions)

According to this section of the Article, while granting aids to educational institutions state shall not discriminate any of them on the ground that it is under the management of a minority. The state, however, can impose certain reasonable conditions for the grant of aid but that condition should not be such as to destroy the minority character of the institution.

Thus minority institutions receive grants from the government under this article and they are not discriminated on the basis of their particular religion, language or culture. These educational institutions are sometimes given priority in granting aids by the government.

## DIRECTIVE PRINCIPLES OF STATE POLICY

### Article 37

According to article 37, directive principles are not enforceable by any court like fundamental rights. Courts are not entitled to compel the government to carry out the directive principles but they are however, fundamental in the governance of the country and state is under duty to apply them in making. They are actually essential for bringing about socic-economic justice in the society.

### Article 41
### (Right to Work, Education, Public Assistance in Certain cases)

State shall make within the limits of its economic capacity and development effective provision for securing the right to work, to education and the public assistance in cases of unemployment, old age, sickness or disablement.

Right to education upto 14 years of age at elementary level is now fundamental right. Other two rights are only guidelines for framing policies by the government. Right to education upto 14 years of age has been included in the list of fundamental rights by an amendment in the article 21, 41 and 45.

### Article 343

Under this article Hindi was declared official language of the union ($CL_1$), English shall continue to be used for official purpose for 15 yrs from the date of commencement of the constitution ($CL_2$), after15 years English may be used for such purposes if Hindi does not take its place ($CL_3$).

### 42nd Amendment of the constitution (1976) and Education

The 42nd amendment of the constitution is so dynamic that it can be described a mini constitution. It also amended the seventh schedule so as to transfer certain subjects from the state list to the concurrent one. Education was one of them. When it was in the state list only state government could make laws regarding it. After transferring it into concurrent list states and centre both can make laws and the provision of the concurrent list of subjects is that if there is any conflict between centre and states regarding any law, the law made by the union government will prevail only.

Before this amendment, education was taken as play thing by some states and proper attention was not given to it due to paucity of funds or lack of will power. Lack of uniformity in the nature and standard of education was also a problem. The value of a high school marksheet of U.P. could not be taken as the same to that of a marksheet of Bihar. Inefficiency of states regarding education was the third problem.

After this amendment the union Government also took much interest and did a lot in this regard and all the above three problems have now been removed to a great extent today. Both states and centre are equally active today as far as education is concerned.

### Article 45 of the Indian Constitution and Objectives of Primary Education

NCERT, mentions the following objectives of education :

1. The first objective is literacy. The child should learn the first language, which would generally be his mother tongue to a level where he can communicate easily with others through articulated speech and writing.
2. The second objective is attainment of numeracy. The child should develop facility in the four fundamental numerical operations and be able to apply these in the life of the community to solve practical problems
3. The third objectives is technocracy. The child should learn the method of the enquiry in science and should begin to appreciate science and technology in the life and world around it.

   These objectives were reviewed by Ishwarbhai Patel Committee and Teacher Education and the Emerging Indian Society (1988) Even the terms primary and elementary are often interpolated however, the National Educational Policy 1986 finally put the official stamp of elementary education to the educational activity for class I to VII/VIII.

Article 45 of the Constitution neither uses the term elementary education nor primary education. It mentions "Compulsory Education for all children until they complete the age of fourteen years".

**Department of Elementary Education and Literacy**

Ministry of Human Resource Development, Government of India has introduced Sarva Shiksha Abhiyan promising education for all children of the school going age. The parliament of India devoted lot of its precious time because nothing much happened till 1990 in this direction as envisaged by the National Education Policy 1986. The programme started around 1990 endeavouring to bring all children to school by 2003 is still a far, distant dream. Besides, Shiksha Vahini, another innovative programme of education on the internet was also introduced recently to make education more conveniently accessible.

## OBJECTIVE QUESTIONS

**1.** Which of the following objectives has not been mentioned in the Preamble of our constitution.

(*a*) Justice and equality
(*b*) Fraternity
(*c*) Right to employment
(*d*) Liberty

**2.** Which of the following terms was added to the Preamble of our constitution in 1976

(*a*) Socialist (*b*) Secular
(*c*) Integrity (*d*) All of these

**3.** Special provisions have been made for socially and educationally backward classes of the nation under article

(*a*) 29 (*b*) 31
(*c*) 15 (*d*) 19

**4.** Religious education is prohibited in government schools and colleges under Article

(*a*) 29 (*b*) 28 (1)
(*c*) 39 (2) (*d*) 15 (a)

**5.** Religious and linguistic minorities shall have the right to establish and administer their own educational institutions under Article

(*a*) 30(1) (*b*) 31(2)
(*c*) 40 (*d*) 41

**6.** Article 351 is about

(*a*) education of tribals
(*b*) promotion of Hindi
(*c*) promotion of secularism
(*d*) English as official language

**7.** Status of central university is given to any educational institution under union list of

(*a*) Entry 65 (*b*) Entry 63
(*c*) Entry 66 (*d*) None of these

**8.** Entry 25 of concurrent list states about

(*a*) vocational and technical training of labour
(*b*) the education of working class
(*c*) the education of disabled
(*d*) none of the above

**9.** Education in the mother tongue at primary stage to children belonging to linguistic minorities has been mentioned in Article

(*a*) 250 (*b*) 350
(*c*) 349 (*d*) 351

**10.** Educational and economic interests of SCs and STs have been safeguarded under Article

(*a*) 46 (*b*) 45(a)
(*c*) 351 (*d*) 52

**11.** Education of union territories is administered by the central government under Article

(*a*) 350 (*b*) 229
(*c*) 239 (*d*) 50

**12.** Education was transferred from state list of subjects to concurrent list in

(*a*) 1976 (*b*) 1972
(*c*) 1980 (*d*) 1950

**13.** The fundamental national values (objectives) has been given in the

(*a*) Preamble of our constitution
(*b*) Articles of our constitution
(*c*) Entries of the lists of subjects
(*d*) All of these

**14.** Indian democracy, socialism and secularism have been explained by

(*a*) the fundamental rights only
(*b*) fundamental rights and other articles of the constitution
(*c*) the preamble of the constitution
(*d*) all of these

**15.** Which type of educational system is prevailing in India

(*a*) Autocratic with red tapism
(*b*) Socialistic

(*c*) Democratic
(*d*) None of the above

**16.** Autonomy given to Universities by the UGC is in accordance with
(*a*) Socialistic principles
(*b*) Democratic principles
(*c*) Idealistic principles
(*d*) None of these

**17.** Guardian of Indian constitution and protector of fundmental rights of citizens is
(*a*) parliament
(*b*) judiciary
(*c*) Supreme Court only
(*d*) none of these

**18.** Out of 343 universities in India how many of them are Central Universities
(*a*) 14 (b) 18
(*c*) 20 (*d*) 22

**19.** In which of following central universities 50% reservation was given to minorities in 2005 but it was later disapproved by Supreme Court
(*a*) AMU Aligarh (*b*) BHU Varanasi
(*c*) DU Delhi (*d*) JMI Delhi

**20.** Literacy rate is expected to raise upto 75%. This is the objective set for
(*a*) Ninth five year plan
(*b*) Tenth five year plan
(*c*) Eleventh five year plan
(*d*) None of these

## ANSWERS

| 1 | 2 | 3 | 4 | 5 | 6 | 7 | 8 | 9 | 10 |
|---|---|---|---|---|---|---|---|---|---|
| (*c*) | (*d*) | (*c*) | (*b*) | (*a*) | (*b*) | (*b*) | (*a*) | (*b*) | (*a*) |
| **11** | **12** | **13** | **14** | **15** | **16** | **17** | **18** | **19** | **20** |
| (*c*) | (*a*) | (*a*) | (*b*) | (*a*) | (*b*) | (*c*) | (*b*) | (*a*) | (*b*) |

11

# Modernization and Education

## MODERNIZATON

### Meaning of Modernization

Modernization is a multidimensional process. It covers the following areas especially:

1. Maximization of physical and technological power to increase productive and warfare potential.
2. Economic prosperity and high standard of living.
3. Adherence to democratic values like liberty, equality and justice in the socio political spheres.
4. Effective realization of creative potentials in a free atmosphere.
5. Open and scientific thinking in dealing with social affairs and making the religion a private matter.
6. Taking social change a natural process and adapting to it naturally without any compulsion.
7. A faded picture of modern India can be seen in the preamble of our constitution and New Education Policy 1986.

### Need for modernization of Indian Society

Modernization of Indian society is needed more than ever because of following reasons:

1. Institutionalization and internalization of constitutional goals and consequent social changes can not take place effectively unless the masses have a desire of change in consonance with these goals. If masses do not go forward in this direction, the fate of India will not change from a traditional to a modern one.
2. Long cherished religious beliefs which are unscientific in any way must be given up in order to become secular, rational, open minded and progressive. Without these values, human values cannot be cherished.
3. Fatalism is fatal for progress. The Indians should believe that nothing is beyond the reach of human if it is supported by hard work and consistent efforts.
4. Modernization will help the people not only to restrict their loyalty to a particular caste, class, community or region but to expand it to the whole humanity even by crossing the national boundaries. Contrary to this, traditionalism will shatter the nation into pieces.

### Characteristics of a Modern Society

A modern society is one which has at least the following characteristics :

1. People in a modern society are always ready to welcome social and cultural changes and adapt these changes naturally.
2. It is a lover of science based technology and material prosperity.
3. Its administrative structure is vast and complex.
4. People in the society have high level of specialized knowledge to be fully benefited from the social structure.
5. Punctuality, hard work, integrity, consistency, loyalty, positive attitude of learning new things, respect for rules and regulation, openness are important economic characteristics of people of a modern society.
6. People here have better capacity to adjust to conflicting and antagonistic situations due to a high degree of tolerance and resistance to social infections.
7. Democracy, secularism, freedom and equality of opportunity prevails everywhere in the society in social, economic and political spheres. Everything runs in the interest of all not few.
8. People are open minded, rational, objective and critical here and creativity has maximum chance to flourish.
9. People develop a mobile personality the ramification of which is a psychic urge to achieve higher and higher material reward.

10. In a modern society, bounties and pleasures are available only for those who are talented, industrious, enlightened, progressive and creative.

## Modernization and social changes

Social change is in most of the cases related to modernization and vice versa. The inter relationship between the two are as follows :

1. Social change means significant change in social structure, the pre-requisite of modernization.
2. Social changes occur in sequential chains, Revolution in information technology has not only increased the rate of change but it has also strengthened these chains.
3. Social change affects the functional aspects of societies in the modern world, e.g., phonography is not only seen in TV screen but also adopted in real life.
4. The course of social change may be gradual or rapid, peaceful or violent, continuous or spasmodic, orderly or erotic. The course of modernization is also the same.
5. Social Change sometimes, takes place in the form of ideological expression of radical nature but modernization is always progressive.
6. Causes of social changes are many such as demographic, technological, economic, cultural, legal, political and administrative. If these factors have an upward trend, modernization will be there.
7. Social tensions and conflicts are also important sources of social change. Modernization helps to overcome these tensions and conflicts on one hand and adapt to that environment on the other.

## Trends of Social Change in India

1. Indian society is undergoing important social changes due to westernization, secularization, industrialization, urbanization, globalization, development of science and technology and fast material progress. All these factors are directly contributing to modernization.
2. One factor that goes against the process of modernization is corruption and usurpation of opportunities by unfair means. The legitimization of these factors in Indian society is really a set back for modernization.
3. Growth with justice is an important characteristics of modernization which is not found in Indian society.
4. Social tensions and conflicts have very rapidly increased in India and modernization has failed to cope with this problem even today.
5. Rapid growth of population, mushroom growth of religious fanaticism, violent growth of caste and region centred politics etc. are such factors which are making the process of modernization very slow.

## Modernization of education in India

## Goals of Indian Education system :

1. Education system has decided to modernize social, economic and political institutions of the society in a natural manner. It is believed that education system can play a major role in bringing about necessary socio-political changes.
2. Development of science and technology necessary for material prosperity, urbanization and industrialization is possible only through the development of education on modern route.
3. Development of new technical and social skills, new values and behaviour in consonance with national, democratic and secular values is needed in younger generation of the country for the purpose of achieving a change oriented society.
4. Cultivation of indigenous resources for the development and reorientation of education.
5. Economic modernization through privatization of higher education and outsourcing.

Problem of Indian education in the context of modernization :

**(A) Orientation of education :** A modernizing society needs reorientation of education in the direction of modern educational goals. Most of the Indian traditions inhibit modernity. Its moral values are anti secular, its social institutions are authoritarian and its political values are opportunistic and corrupt. It is only education that can transform a traditional society into a modern one. For this purpose, reorientation of education is necessary.

**(B) Problem of quantitative expansion of education:** A modernizing society needs a large base of functionally literate people, adequate and regular supply of technicians and professionals and a large number of highly trained people to lead the nation in different fields. For all these purposes, quantitative expansion of education in all fields is necessary. This is possible only when both public and private agencies work together with the motive of welfare not amassing profit. Differential needs of various sections of the society must be taken into account to ensure development with justice. Unless education is diversified enough at different levels by applying differential allocation of resources for different sections of the society, progress with justice is not possible.

**(C) Problem of qualitative expansion :** Better placement of educated people is possible only when education is contributive to economic prosperity and progress. For this purpose qualitative improvement of education is necessary at all levels. It can reduce educated unemployment on one hand and utilize efficient manpower in the productive work on the other.

**(D) Problems of determining priorities :** We have not yet fixed whether we want quantitative or qualitative improvement in education, whether we want economic development through education or vice versa, whether we want to start improvement from primary level or to develop few institutions of higher learning as model base, whether we want improvement through physical facilities and technology of education or through restructuring organization of education at different levels and examination and so on. We are still in complete dilemma without having a clear cut and smooth route of educational development

## Role of the teacher and modernization

The teachers are supposed to play the following roles for the modernization of education and society.

1. Teachers should study literature on modernization so that they might properly appreciate the dimensions of the problem and project the same to their students.
2. The teacher should motivate the students to think, to imagine, to reason out and to arrive at a decision that is free from subjectivity.
3. The teachers should give right sort of guidance to students to select optional subjects in view of the demands of the new age and environment.
4. Teachers can, to a great extent, help the students in resolving the conflicts of traditional and modern values of our society. They can convince them that neither all traditional values are irrelevant and harmful nor all western values can be labelled as modern values.
5. If educators are able to drop their conservatism, they can develop a new educational technology that would raise the productivity of schools on one hand and produce better results without raising the costs. Dropping of conservatism and adherence to modernity require knowledge, understanding, competence and qualities on the part of the teacher, necessary materials and equipments on the part of the institution and better organizational structure and recruitment on the part of educational authorities.

Steps to be taken for modernization of society and education :

1. *Reduction of educated unemployment :* Unemployment is the major source of tension among youths. It can be reduced by providing them education according to the modern needs. Education system should discourage excess production of trained personnel in unneeded skills and should divert its attention to the needed skills by proper planning. Only those persons should be given chance of higher education and research who are really capable for that.
2. *Raising private funds for education :* Limited public resources can not be fully relied on for the expansion of education. Entry of private entrepreneurs into the industry of education and private bearing of cost of education is necessary for quantitative as well as qualitative expansion of education. However, care should be taken to ensure that education should not become the status symbol of the elite class but it should contribute to the development of the country in more than one way.

3. *Expansion of education in rural areas :* Rural population is still dependent on urban areas for getting education. New educational institutions and placement industries should also be opened in rural areas on a priority basis. It is necessary because traditionalism is still very powerful in villages and it can only be removed by education.
4. *Recruitment of educational decision makers :* The controllers and supervisors of the educational system at different levels play a very crucial role in facilitating or obstructing change in the educational system in the desired direction. In order that, right type of persons are recruited in the positions of educational planners, education ministers directors and inspectors of educations, Vice-Chancellor, Chairman and Members of various educational boards and committees etc., The recruitment procedures must be sufficiently impersonal and objective and the basis of recruitment must be merit and achievement of the persons that are relevant to the position involved.

**Differential evaluation of educational institutions**

The quality of educational institutions may be of different levels and the measures that may be suited to improvement to a high quality institutions may not be suited to those that are of a low quality. For example, an ordinary engineering college can not be compared to an IIT in its performance. So, educational institutions should be classified into different categories on the basis of their quality and differential treatment should be given to them.

## OBJECTIVE QUESTIONS

**1.** Which of the following is not a contributory factor for modernization?
(*a*) Reorientation of education.
(*b*) Social changes
(*c*) Conservatism
(*d*) Rapid industrialization

**2.** Which of the following characteristics is possessed by a modern society?
(*a*) Open mindedness
(*b*) Stiff competition for material progress.
(*c*) Upholding justice
(*d*) All of these

**3.** Which of the following characteristics makes India a traditional country even today?
(*a*) Blind loyalty to caste and creed
(*b*) Superstition in the name of religion
(*c*) Regional aspirations and self centred politics.
(*d*) All of these

**4.** All of the following are important agencies of modernization except
(*a*) Religious institutions
(*b*) Adult Education centres.
(*c*) Universities and colleges.
(*d*) Primary schools.

**5.** Which of the following characteristics of Indian society makes it a backward traditional society?
(*a*) Laws against conversion of religion
(*b*) Reservation given to SCs on the basis of religion
(*c*) Castes based marriages
(*d*) All of these

**6.** Which of the following steps should be taken in order to make India a developed country?
(*a*) Maximum exploitation of resources.
(*b*) Education according to the need of the economy.
(*c*) Development oriented politics.
(*d*) All of these

## ANSWERS

| 1 | 2 | 3 | 4 | 5 | 6 |
|---|---|---|---|---|---|
| (*c*) | (*d*) | (*d*) | (*a*) | (*d*) | (*d*) |

# UNIT–III

- ★ *Psychology and Educational Psychology*
- ★ *Growth and Individual Differences*
- ★ *Psychology of Child Development*
- ★ *Theories of Child Development*
- ★ *Learning of Concepts, Reasoning and Problem Solving*

1

# Psychology and Educational Psychology

## PSYCHOLOGY

### Meaning

The word psychology is derived from two Greek words Psycho-means soul and logy means science. Thus in the beginning the psychology was believed to be the science of soul. This definition was popular among the people when psychology was studied as a sub branch of philosophy. Psychology as an independent discipline acquired separate status very recently. Otherwise in most of the periods psychology was the only a tail of big Halley's Comet.

### Philosophy

Since the nature of soul could not be defined in definite terms, this meaning of psychology was opposed by contemporary philosophers. They evolved another definition of psychology saying that psychology is the science of mind.

The second definition was accepted by the people for a very long time, then again the same controversy arose regarding the nature of mind and its definiteness and ultimately this definition too was discarded by the philosophers.

In the third phase the attention of philosophers shifted from thinking to action. Man engages himself in a number of activities from morning till evening. He is conscious why he is doing a particular activity and how is this activity governed by mind. Thus, philosophers defined psychology as a science of consciousness or immediate experience.

But later on this definition too was rejected by the psychologists, on the ground that consciousness is only a small portion of total personality of humans. Behaviours are conscious, subconscious and unconscious, all. Thus, we can not study an individual just by observing his conscious activities only.

This last definition led to the beginning of experimental psychology and psychology was made an independent discipline free from philosophy. Thus, pure psychologists defined psychology "as a science of behaviour."

In order to know what psychology actually is we must analyse these two concepts—science and behaviour separately.

### Science

It is a systematic study of knowledge which may be verified at any time by any number of individuals under given condition. Thus, knowledge obtained by science is not subjective. It is rather objective.

Science actually finds out those conditions and factors that determine the cause or occurrence of a particular event. The methods used for this purpose are observation and experimentation.

Thus, science or scientific study has the following characteristics.

*(i)* It is the process of discovery of truth and this truth can be objectively verified.

*(ii)* Scientific statements are general and systematic. They are put in a systematic order depending on the objectives of research. Thus, scientific study is all the time research study.

*(iii)* For the purpose of reaching truth in science, data are first collected by observation and experimentation. Then these data are interpreted keeping in view the research objectives and hypothesis. Finally, definite conclusions are drawn by using reflective thinking.

(iv) The inference drawn from the researches are put in the form of certain laws. These laws are so solid that they can predict about future course of action.

(v) Scientific laws can be applied to real life situations or they can be used to understand the life itself.

## Behaviour

The term behaviour was popularized by an American psychologist J.B. Watson. He defined behaviour as an action which can be seen and observed in an objective way. This meaning of behaviour includes external and internal stimulations both. Thus human behaviour can be measured objectively according to this definition of behaviour. Whatever is there in our conscious, unconscious or subconscious mind is reflected by our behaviour at proper stimuli. Greater part of this behaviour is observable and we can hide only a little part of it.

## Psychology–A Science of Behaviour

Psychology is a science of behaviour in the following ways:

(i) It uses scientific method to collect data about individuals and the group to analyse present behaviour in order to predict about it for future. Thus, we find out new truth in psychology on the basis of observation and experimentation. Only observable behaviours are studied in psychology and facts are established by objective proofs.

(ii) In psychology we try to find out about those variables which affect our behaviour directly or indirectly. In this way casual relationships are expressed as a system of hypothesis or law.

(iii) We can verify the laws and principles propounded in psychology in the same way as we do in science.

(iv) Almost exact prediction about human behaviour is possible on the basis of present behaviour pattern.

(v) Psychology is expanding our knowledge of the environment in the same way as is done by science through experimentation.

(vi) Scientific enquiry develops a way of thinking that is very much critical and evaluative to present knowledge, values and beliefs and its facticity is also examined and ascertained.

(vii) Psychology also helps us to control behaviour on one hand and understand it on the other. Underlying variables are checked and controlled in order to understand a particular behaviour.

(viii) Psychological principles and laws are applicable to human life situations also just in the similar ways as scientific laws and principles.

(ix) Psychology is a biological and behavioural science both. Psychology as a biological science began with the study of physiology in Germany during the late half of the $19^{th}$ century. In modern times too psychologists are engaged in searching the biological determinants of motivation, memory, mental disorders and learning. Psychology as a behavioural science aims at studying the behaviour of humans sometime directly and sometimes through the behaviour of animals. Man is a social animal. His behaviour and personality are shaped in the environment he lives through the social and physical interactions with the environment. Thus in modern psychology we also study how environment influences the behaviour of the individual and vice versa. Thus, social dynamics are systematically taught in psychology.

(x) Psychology is a social science also because it studies human behaviour in social context. Thus, it is helpful in solving social problems (related to behaviour) very systematically and scientifically. When pure objectivity is maintained in solving these problems, psychology becomes a natural science.

(xi) Psychology is a general science. Its application can be seen in Education, Commerce, Industry, Management, Agriculture and from the very beginning in sports. As a result, psychology takes a variety of forms such as Educational psychology, Management psychology, Human or animal psychology, Abnormal psychology. Social psychology, Military psychology, Clinical psychology and so on.

## Definitions of Psychology

1. *Woodworth :* Psychology is the science of activities of an individual in relation to his environment.
2. *Mc Dougal :* Psychology is a science that gives us better understanding and control of behaviour of the organism as a whole.
3. *Crookes and Stein :* Psychology is the scientific study of behaviour and mental processes of humans and other animals.

## SCOPE OF PSYCHOLOGY

It is clear from the other definitions that scope of psychology is very wide. It covers especially the following areas:

1. It studies all activities of the individual that he does in his environment. Thus all activities of the individual in the society are directly or indirectly studied in psychology.
2. With the help of psychology we are able to understand our behaviour scientifically.
3. Psychology equips us with the knowledge of how to control our behaviour in unconducive situations.
4. Psychology studies not only behaviour but also mental process. There is direct relationship between mental process and behaviour. These relations are also studied in psychology.
5. Since these activities and behaviours are manifested in the environment, Psychology studies environment, physical and social both.
6. Human behaviour can change in different social and physical environments. Therefore, psychology also takes those factors into account which can bring about change in behaviour.

### Methods of Psychological Studies

**Brief history of the recent past :** The first effort of conducting systematic studies in psychology started in 1879 in Germany with the establishment of first laboratory of psychology by W Wundt. He defined psychology as the study of conscious experiences. He exclusively used introspection as the sole method of collecting data.

The next method of collecting data is psychoanalysis used by Sigmund Freud. He for the first time, emphasised the significance of unconscious mind in understanding the behaviour. He collected data from his patients by using the techniques of free association and dream analysis.

In the second cecade of the 20th century psychology developed as an objective science of behaviour by the efforts of Pavlov, Guthrie and Watson. They discarded introspection as well as psychoanalysis methods by saying that these are mentalistic and subjective approaches to understanding behaviour. They developed observation and experimental methods for collecting data. Cognitive field theories of Guthrie gave more importance to observation of behaviour in total situations in which the individual moves while S.R. theories emphasised experimental methods in the laboratory for collecting data.

### Methods of Collecting Data

There are five methods commonly used in psychology to collect data.

**(A) Introspection :** Introspection means self observation or looking within oneself. Here individual introspects observes, analyses and reports his own feeling in different mental situations. For example, researcher here asks the person how he feels when any of his relative dies and how will he behave in such situations.

*Merits of the method :*

1. It is the easiest method of collecting data where no equipments or apparatus is needed. We can ask any body regarding his own experience and record the response.
2. It is based on personal experiences of the person being interrogated. Thus, no mediator or environmental hurdle is there between the researcher and the person being interrogated.

*Demerits of the method :*

1. Human beings are not static like non living things. His mental process constantly undergoes changes. As a result, the gap which is there between the time of happening and time of reporting may distort the information.
2. The data collected by this method is highly subjective. There is no way to prove the reliability

of the facts. Whatever information is supplied by the introspectors is recorded as it is whether it is true or false. That is why conflicting reports are seen by different introspectors under the same conditions.

3. This method can not be applied to children, animals or abnormal people. Thus its scope is very limited.
4. It analyses experiences into images, sensations and feelings. It does not yield adequate representation of the unitary experience in its totality. How can we isolate a particular experience from the total set of experiences. This objection was raised by Gestalt Psychologists.

**(B) Observation :** Observation means looking outside one self. Here the researcher observes the overt behaviour of the individual from our side. As far as observation of overt behaviour is concerned it is the manifestation of covert condition by different activities within the organism. The study of these behaviours give the clue about the mental condition of the organism. For example, if a person is kicking household articles without caring damage of the article, it means that he is in the state of anger. Observation can be of the following types:

1. *Direct and Indirect :* In direct observation, the person directly observes the behaviour of his counterpart but in indirect observation, help is taken by a third person to observe and data is collected on the basis of the report of this third person. Taking the service of a detective to observe the behaviour of someone is indirect observation.
2. *Natural and Artificial :* In natural observation we observe the specific behaviour of children or adults in natural setting. The observant here does not know that someone is observing him. Observing the students in the playground or doing class work is natural observation. In artificial observation, the artificial situations are created to observe the display of behaviour. Here observant fully knows what behaviour should he displayed to be observed by the observer and for how much time will this process go on.
3. *Participant and Non participant :* In participant observation, the observer becomes the part of the group which he wants to observe and observants don't know that they are being observed by some one. Thus they do not hide or manipulate any of their behaviour to be observed. But the problem with the observer is that he has to play double role, the role of an observer and of a performer. As a result, it becomes very difficult for him to record the behaviour. In non participant observation the observer keeps himself a little away from the actual situation. He only becomes a silent spectator.
4. *Scheduled and Unscheduled :* In scheduled observation, what behaviour is to be observed and for how much time and under what situation etc, everything is predetermined and then observed. In unscheduled setting nothing is predetermined. Everything depends on the will of the observer.

*Merits of the Method :*

1. This is the easiest method of studying the behaviour or activities of an individual and if observer is fair in his attitude very reliable result will come out.
2. This method has great application in class room and sports situations. We can easily predict the future behaviour of an individual on the basis of his present behaviour and we can also give suggestions to improve and control the behaviour in certain situations.
3. All judgments in sports competitions are made on the basis of observation.

*Demerits :*

1. This method is applicable only in case of overt behaviour which is manifested by various activities. The behaviour which is governed by internal mental process and is covert in nature cannot be studied by this method.
2. If a person is able to hide his actual behaviour in the presence of an observer, no definite information can be obtained about his psychology.
3. Subjectivity of interpretation is another problems. If observer manipulates the data in his own way the studies will not be reliable. Observer's liking,

disliking, values and his own attitude towards life can affect the result. One more problem is that researcher sees only what he wants to see and his prejudice may make the studies biased.

4. The observer generally neglects the why side of the observing situation.
5. Sampling error is the biggest limitation of this method. If the situation selected for observation is inadequate and unrepresentative to the total situation, the data collected will be incomplete.

*Suggestions for Improvement :* In order to improve the observation as a tool of psychological studies following suggestive measures should be adopted:

1. *Use of mechanical devices (VCRs) :* Generally observations are not immediately recorded on the spot. They are recorded later on by applying recall. As a result certain important informations are left out. This problem can be easily removed by using mechanical devices.
2. *Specific objectives :* Specific objectives of observation in clear and definite terms must be specified by the observer in advance. This will help the observer to remain on the right track during observation.
3. *Schedule :* Observation must have a definite schedule. For how much time a particular person is to be observed must be specified in advance. Statement should also be prepared in advance in order to note down the observed behaviour.
4. *Training :* Observation is well planned technique which is full of a number of complexities. It requires skills on the part of the observer. So observer must be properly trained in this regard. Concentration, keenness and alertness are the important skills for the purpose.

**(C) Clinical Study :** The main objective of this method is to study the individual cases to detect and diagnose their specific problems and difficulties and to suggest remedial measures in order to rehabilitate them to their environment. For this purpose history is taken from the birth of the individual to his present situation and detailed data are collected by direct or indirect questions, medical examinations, intelligence, personality or attitude tests and by observations or introspection in some cases. Background of the individual is also studied and informations collected from all sources are pooled together in a sequential order, in order to prepare a comprehensive case history. Thus, the causes of the problems are located pin pointedly. Clinical Study is of two types :

1. **Clinical case history :** This method is used to know the causes of learning difficulties, emotional disturbances or delinquency or other related problems. Here detailed information about the person is collected by various methods mentioned above and causes of the problems are found out. In preparing clinical case history the informations are collected from the following sources.
   - **Preliminary information** which includes name, age, education, parents' age and their education and occupation, socio economic status etc.
   - **Past History** which includes condition of the mother during pregnancy, his/her physical, social, emotional and mental development after birth, relation between parents and other members of the society, birth order, number of brothers, sisters in the family etc.
   - **Present condition** includes Medical examination , IQ, personality and attitude tests, environment at home, school and the society, observation and introspection of the case etc.
2. **Development case study :** Two approaches are followed for this purpose. First is the longitudinal approach. In this approach we collect a sample of cases of any specific age and observe their developmental characteristics continually from year to year. 24 hours of observation is the ideal situation but we generally do observation for a selected period of time. Regular tests are also applied and assessment is made at regular intervals. Then norms are finalized at different ages on the basis of maximum occurrence of behaviour. Second is cross sectional approach. In this approach we select sample of different age levels. Then characteristics of a particular age are identified after comparing it with those of other ages.

**(D) Survey or Differential Method :** This method is used to know the individual differences among individuals. This method makes use of various techniques of collecting data such as standardized tests, questionnaire, observation, interview and use of statistics in analyzing data.

There are three broad categories of survey method. All of them use sampling method of study.

1. *Field Study :* It is a scientific investigation carried out in the field which involves the direct manipulation of some independent variables. Field studies are conducted in natural situations spread over a wide area and detailed informations are collected after coming in contact with the situation. Door to door survey is also done here.
2. *Development surveys :* These surveys collect information about the pattern of change in the growth and development of a group of individuals over a specified period of time. These surveys can be longitudinal as well as cross sectional. Here a group or a community as a whole is studied.
3. *Differential survey :* They are conducted for establishing typical differences between individuals or group of individuals. For example, if we study the difference in intelligence between Indian and European races, it will be a differential survey.

*Merits of the Method :*

1. Wide range of informations can be collected through these methods.
2. Investigating agencies are involved in these surveys. So, chance of individual prejudices are reduced.

*Demerits :*

1. Sometimes samples chosen are not true representative of the population. Thus, result obtained on the basis of inadequate or wrong sample may be wrong.
2. Sample of behaviour to be investigated may be inadequate especially in case of personality tests. As a result, conclusions drawn are wrong.
3. If subjects to be investigated are not cooperative, they may supply wrong information.

**(E) Experimental Method :** This method was developed in psychology to conduct objective and scientific study of human behaviour. One of the most important contribution of behaviourism is the development of experimental method to understand, control and predict behaviour. It is the most precise planned, systematic and controlled observation.

This method uses a systematic procedure called experimental design. The term experimental design has dual meaning. First meaning is that experimental design follows systematic experimental procedure. Second meaning is that it is a procedure for assigning subjects to experimental situations and appropriate statistical test is used to analyse the data. The findings of an experimental study depend on how accurately the experimental design has been prepared. These experiments are conducted in the laboratory as well as outside the laboratory (field).

1. *Laboratory Experiment :* When a problem is to be studied in a laboratory, experimenter controls all the variables except one under study. Individuals as well as groups are experimented here. The experiments of Pavlov on dogs and Skinner's experiments on rats are examples of laboratory experiments.
2. *Outside laboratory (Field) experiment :* This type of experiments can be divided on the basis of number of groups involved in the experiments and their respective control procedures. The number of groups may vary from one, two, three to many depending on the type of problem. (See chapter 38 for details)

*Merits of the Method :*

1. Experimental method is the most systematic procedure of studying a problem. Here study is carried out in fully controlled situation. As a result, reliable findings are obtained. Such findings can be verified by other investigations also.
2. On the basis of these findings and conclusions pin pointed suggestions can be given.
3. Such experiments provide new avenues of researches on similar problems.

*Demerits:*

1. Here effects of an independent variable is studied in a controlled experimental situation. But whether these changes in behaviour will be similar in normal situation or not is a big question.
2. Experimental data do not provide insight into the total behaviour of the individual. Behaviour is actually an interaction between the organism and the environment. Thus a part of total behaviour may also affect the total behaviour after interaction with the environment.
3. Unlike normal observation, experiments too cannot handle the covert behaviour of the individual in the laboratory.
4. In psychology most of the experiments have been conducted on lower animals. Application of principles derived from these experiments on humans is not a solid base for study.
5. All problems of psychology cannot be studied exclusively by this method. Human being is a complex organism. He cannot be studied as simply as we study the lower animals.

## NEED OF EDUCATION

The basic problem that all living creatures face after taking birth is the problem of adaptation to environment mentally, physically, emotionally, socially and professionally. Some creatures have some natural capacities which help them adapt to their environment and no systematic education is needed for this purpose but case of human is different. He is the most dependent being of all the living beings known. His family and the society educate him formally as well as informally to make him self dependent. The intellectual power and wisdom that man has over and above other animals help him to receive education. It is the education that helps him to adapt to the environment.

The process of education begins immediately after the child is born. His mother teaches him first how to breast feed. By using trail and error technique, the child comes to learn how to suck milk from the breast of the mother. As the child's exposure expands, the number of his formal and informal teachers also increases. This process continues till his last breath in some way or the other. Thus whole life of a man is centred around his wisdom or intelligence making him superior to all the other animals in the process.

Today, society and social needs have become very complex. There is always a new challenge as soon as we take the second breath. Newer and newer inventions and discoveries have taught the man to have more and more control over nature. Social relations have also become very complex. Apart from this, search from good to better in order to make the life more easy and comfortable has also revolutionarised the human life at its peak. All these factors have led to the creation of formal education in schools, colleges and universities. In order to make education a systematic and healthy process, the knowledge of philosophical thoughts and social awareness become, necessary. Following procedure is followed while imparting formal education in schools.

*(i)* Society and the nation take the responsibility of imparting education to the people to bring about an adaptable change in them. For this purpose human and physical resources are arranged.

*(ii)* The entire educational material is condensed and divided into subjects.

*(iii)* Subjects and its contents are selected keeping in view the age, ability, intelligence, needs and specific interest area of learners coupled with the needs of society and the nation.

*(iv)* Then education is imparted by the teacher who knows how to bring about maximum change in learners in lesser amount of time, energy and resources.

*(v)* Lastly, evaluation is done in order to give them the certificate of adaptability like degrees of B.A, B.Sc, B.Ed, etc.

## EDUCATION

### Meaning of Education

The word "Education" has three roots in Latin Language

I. Educatum............to train/Art of teaching

II. Educere...........to draw out(inner powers)

III. Educare..........to bring up/to develop.

Thus, drawing out the innate capacities of the individual to develop his personality to the full by training or teaching is Education.

From the above etymological concept of education, following characteristics of education can be drawn:

*(i)* Education is a continuous process that starts with life and ends with death. It is because innate capacities are not restricted to age. At every moment of life man has some innate capacities.

*(ii)* Innate capacities when come in contact with the outer environment develop some beliefs and values in the individuals. Thus education is concerned with beliefs and values also.

*(iii)* When man is trained or taught, he acquires certain skills. Thus, education is a skill that a person acquires after practice.

*(iv)* Education is the enrichment of human knowledge and experiences by going through the processes of thinking, experimentation and drawing conclusion.

*(v)* Education is a process of developing personality of the individual to enable him to adapt to the changing physical and social environment.

*(vi)* Individual is composed of body and soul. So, education is concerned with the physical and spiritual development both.

In order to understand the concept of "Education" three meaning of the word, education are given below:

**1. General meaning :** The instructions and knowledge given in schools is known as education by the ordinary people. In this process teachers impart knowledge to students with specific aims. Here teachers dominate the scene and learners are only passive listeners who receive only what is given to them. When the process is over, they receive the certificate of pass or fail at the end of the year or course.

This concept of education is very narrow in the sense that it is only the communication of information by the teacher and acquisition of knowledge by students. Here no emphasis is given on all round development of child's personality, as a result, this type of education fails to prepare a child capable of facing future challenges and hardships.

**2. Technical Meaning :** Education consists of all those experiences in and outside the school which affect the individual in any way during his life time. It is essentially the process of developing personality, shaping behaviour and modifying character related to the person being educated.

Thus, education is a life long conscious as well as unconscious process which is also not restricted to the boundaries of time, place or person. Every time when we are not asleep, we receive some education in the form of knowledge or experiences. The place where exchange of experiences takes place is technically a school and any person who plays more active role in the process is a teacher.

**3. Functional Meaning :** Functionally, education is the full exploitation of inherent capacities of the individual for new experiences and developing his personality in such a way that enables him to apply the acquired knowledge and experiences in his real life for the betterment of the self, society and the nation.

Thus, education can make a individual a perfect and complete man in his own boundaries though the highest degree of perfection or completeness will never be achieved. It is because only Brahma is real and perfect.

## Relationship between psychology and education :

Education aims at developing the inherent potentialities of the individual to the maximum level possible through the modification of human behaviour. Once we want to modify the behaviour, we will have to study and analyse it objectively and scientifically. This function is performed by psychology. It is psychology which tells us to hit when the iron is hot in the context of behavioural change. It means that what, how, how much and when to teach a child for maximum amount of learning are known by the study of psychology.

Thus, relationship between two sciences can be understood with the help of the following discussion:

1. *Supremacy of child in the learning process:* Child rather than teacher (education) is important today. Teaching learning process revolves round the child and complete information about the child is obtained from psychology. Thus, psychology is the foundation stone of education. If role of psychology from education is eliminated, child will be spoiled.
2. *Control of behaviour :* Whatever changes in the behaviour is to be brought about is to be done in a controlled environment. For this purpose, the teacher must know the science of behaviour. He must know the developmental stages of children and the specific characteristics pertaining to a particular stage to match the content with the behaviour. If a teacher does not know the science of behaviour he would not be able to bring about desirable changes in learners.
3. *Realization of educational objectives :* Educational objectives are formulated keeping in view the needs, interest and abilities of children. Psychology helps us know not only needs, interests and abilities of children but also their attitudes towards environmental stimuli in different situations. Once these objectives are realized, desirable changes in the behaviour of learners are seen.
4. *Development of new teaching strategies :* Many new teaching strategies have been developed on the basis of psychological theories of learning and development. In these strategies, child and his unique problems are studied first then on the basis of action researches, new strategies based on maximum interaction of the child are developed.
5. *Recognition of individual differences :* No two children are alike in the world in any respect. They differ emotionally, physically, mentally and socially shaping their unique personality structure. In such a situation, all of them can not be treated in the class in a similar manner. If a teacher does so, he will spoil the whole teaching learning process. Knowledge of psychology helps the teacher to formulate his teaching behaviour keeping in view the unique needs, abilities and interests of children in the class.
6. *Curriculum construction :* What and how much content is to teach to a child and at what stage are determined on the basis of psychology of children. It is because learning and maturity of each stage of life is unique to learn something. For example, trigonometric ratios can not be taught to children below 13 years of age due to lack of maturation of the age.
   Similarly, different curricula are also needed for gifted and slow learners, for emotionally and orthopedically handicapped and so on. Knowledge of psychology will help us in this regard also.
7. *Use of audio-visual aids :* Audio-visual materials are used in the class for two purposes, for clarifying the concepts and for motivating the students by enhancing interaction. Which material aid will suit to which group of children is also the subject matter of psychology.
8. *Organization of co-curricular activities :* Co- curricular activities are essential for total development of personality of the child. Knowledge of psychology tells us which activity will suit to which age group of children. Literary and performing arts, music and sports etc. are some such activities.
9. *Improvement of discipline :* Discipline is the pre-requisite of learning. When students of different personality structures are dealt with differently by teachers and the school administration, discipline improves which improves learning in the long run.
10. *Group dynamics :* Students of a class can be divided into different groups on the basis of certain similarities and differences and thus, their group behaviour can be harnessed in the direction of teaching learning process in the class.
11. *Measurement of behaviour :* Whatever advancement we see in psychology is the result of contribution of educational and psychological measurement. Similarly, psychology has also contributed to the development of newer and newer techniques of measurement. With the help of measurement techniques we can also come to know to what extent the changes in the behaviour of learners are desirable.

# EDUCATION PSYCHOLOGY

## Meaning of Educational Psychology

Educational psychology is the application of psychological theories and principles into education and its environment. In educational psychology we study the behaviour of the individual in the teaching learning process on one hand and help of psychological findings is taken to mould and shape the behaviour in the desired manner on the other. When this is done, rate of learning (modification of behaviour) increases which is the ultimate aim of educational psychology.

Thus, we see that educational psychology is an applied discipline by the study of which human behaviour can be understood, predicted and directed to achieve the educational goals of life.

### Definitions

1. **Judd :** Educational psychology is the scientific study of life stages in the development of an individual from the time he is born until he becomes an adult.
2. **Skinner :** Educational psychology utilizes those findings that deal with the experiences and behaviour of human being in educational situation.
3. **Crow and Crow :** Educational psychology describes and explains the learning experiences of an individual from birth to old age.
4. **Stephen :** Educational psychology is the systematic study of educational growth and development of a child.

### Nature and Characteristics of Educational Psychology

As an applied science, educational psychology studies human behaviour in educational setting for the purpose of increasing rate of learning. It is a science in the sense that it studies behaviour in an objective manner and prediction made by it are reliable. It is an art also because behaviour of individuals is modified and moulded in the direction of pre-determined standard. **Science and arts** (nature) of educational psychology are discussed below:

1. It studies human behaviour by applying scientific principles and theories and thus results obtained are objective and reliable.
2. It studies human behaviour in teaching learning environment and the purpose is always to increase rate of learning. This makes educational psychology an art.
3. Why an individual behaves in a particular manner and under what conditions behaviour will be desirable, the study of these aspects makes educational psychology a positive science.
4. It helps in developing new teaching strategies and techniques. This makes educational psychology an applied science.
5. The principles of educational psychology and its theories are universal. It can be applied to any place and at any time under similar situations. This nature of the subject makes it a pure science.
6. When we study casual factors of a particular behaviour, educational psychology becomes a science again.
7. A number of learning theories have been developed in educational psychology on the basis of experimentation on animals. Then results are applied to human being. This approach is again scientific.
8. When educational psychology predicts behaviour on the basis of past records or experimentation, it becomes an art with the scientific bias.
9. Human behaviour is not static in any way. It is all the time vulnerable to change due to the effects of the environment. This makes educational psychology a dynamic discipline. Efforts will always be made to improve the results but findings will never be as accurate as we see in natural sciences.
10. All findings of educational psychology are based on certain limitations. This makes its scope very wide.

On the basis of above discussion we can say that educational psychology is a human science more than a natural or positive science.

### Scope of Educational Psychology

Educational psychology is applied to the teaching learning process of an individual from birth to death. This makes the scope of the subject very wide because education is a life long process full of many complexities and contradictions. Researchers are trying to reduce and eliminate these complexities all the time which is increasing its scope more than ever. Certain important points in this regard are given below:

1. *Study of development stages :* It is essential to study the process of growth and development of an individual and to know how an individual grows and develops. This is very essential for the teacher.
2. *Study of individual differences :* Educational psychology helps to understand individual differences. No two persons or individuals are alike. They differ in the various dimensions of their personalities. They also differ in their abilities and capacities. So study of the individual differences is the scope of educational psychology.
3. *Study of behaviour :* It is through the study of educational psychology that the behaviour of the child in different learning situations can be known. The emotional, social, physical and mental behaviour of the child in different situations of learning can be studied with the help of knowledge of educational psychology.
4. *Guidance and counseling :* Another area of educational psychology, which is emerging, is the area of educational guidance and counseling. In order to become a good guidance worker and a counseller, the knowledge of educational psychology is very essential for the teacher.
5. *Study of personality :* Educational psychology helps to understand the different dimensions of the process of the development of the personality of an individual and defects in the personality can also be studied.
6. *Measurement and evaluation :* An important area of educational psychology is the area of measurement and evaluation. Educational psychology provides new and effective techniques to measure and evaluate the interest, attitudes, personality etc. of the students. Besides this, educational psychology provides much help in the measurement of intelligence of the students.
7. *Condition of learning :* Educational psychology makes a major contribution to study the conditions of learning. The conditions of learning can not be ignored in this scientific age. The total process of learning therefore, has to be studied with reference to the principles of education and psychology.
8. *Group Dynamics and Group Behaviour :* The study of the group dynamics and group behaviour also comes under the scope of educational psychology because a student lives in the group, learns in the group and plays in the group. A child not only affects the group behaviour but is also affected by the group behaviour. Naturally, the area of guidance and counseling finds its place in the contents of educational psychology.
9. *Adjustment :* The process of adjustment of the students is a wide area and the subject of educational psychology can not ignore this fact. The problem of maladjustment, whether in the school or outside the school, social or emotional, can be solved with the help of the knowledge of educational psychology.
10. *Evaluation of teacher :* Educational psychology has also been found useful in the evaluation of teachers. Educational psychology gives information about the different techniques and methods of evaluation which may be helpful in evaluating the teachers.
11. *Research :* Educational psychology and research are related fields. The research in both the fields ultimately affects education. In order to conduct researches in education and training, the principles of educational psychology are applied.

On the basis of above discussion, we can conclude that the boundaries of educational psychology are limitless and changing. It is also difficult to fix limits for the problems of education. Since the educational psychology is in the developing stage, so the boundaries of educational psychology are difficult to be defined.

## Development of educational psychology (ancient and modern contributors)

1. Democritus was the first philosopher who talked about the influence of home on the development of child's personality resulting in the unique nature of development of the child.

2. When Plato and Aristotle talked about education according to different kinds and nature of children, education for character building, different methods of teaching in different situations, the impact of home on personality etc, it were all the elaboration of psychological tendencies in education. Aristotle presented his views more systematically than Plato. He believed in the faculty theory of mind and impressed the world by his ideas for more than 2000 years. Faculty psychology later led to the development of "Formal discipline theory of education".
3. Descartes also founded his ideas on Aristotelian line and believed in the true nature of knowledge.
4. Rousseau is considered as the best imitator of Aristotle. He propounded the concept of negative education, i.e., Education according to the true nature of child.
5. According to John Locke, human mind is not matured and prepared at the time of birth and thus, its function is very slow. But it is at least so much sensitive as to accept the impressions from the external world through the senses.
6. Pestalozzi was the first philosopher who for the first time integrated psychology with education at least on theoretical grounds. He also evolved several methods of learning and developed laws of human development.
7. The pioneer contributions to the development of educational psychology were made by Herbart and Froebel. Their process of education was based on the principles of psychology. They rejected the faculty theory of psychology by stressing the importance of interests and appreciation for learning. Kindergarten method of teaching developed by Froebel is an important landmark in the history of educational psychology. This method emphasizes the early experiences of the child for learning in the later age.
8. William James, a well known pragmatist philosopher published his book **Principles of Psychology** in 1890 in which he advocated functional approach to psychology.
9. J.M.Cattell talked about individual differences on the basic of his contribution in the field of intelligence testing.
10. Binet and Simon systematized the efforts of intelligence testing by preparing standardized intelligence scale.
11. Contributions of behaviorist like Pavlov, Thorndike, Skinner etc. of the $20^{th}$ century can not be denied at all. These psychologists for the first time based their studies on scientific enquiry and experimentation.
12. Last but not the least psycho analysis, field psychology and psychology of exceptional children are other important areas of educational psychology which are contributing a lot to the teaching learning process.

## Contributions (Functions) of educational psychology

Study of educational psychology helps a teacher in the class in two ways : (A) As a function to the theory of education and learning. (B) As a function to the practice of education

**(A) Theory of education and learning :**

1. It tells the developmental characteristics of the child at different stages of life and curriculum as well as method of teaching is formulated on the basis of those characteristics. For example, what suits a child in infancy does not suit in his adolescence or childhood. He enjoys playing with objects or persons in the early childhood but takes no interest in such activities in the later childhood. Thus, a teacher will have to modify his behaviour according to the specific characteristics of the child in the particular age.
2. Educational psychology tells the teacher about different learning problems of the classroom. This knowledge helps him for better classroom management. This knowledge is based on experiments. Once a teacher knows science of behaviour, he can know different types of the problems arising out of different types of behaviours and its adjustability.
3. Each individual is different in personality structure and intelligence. Once a teacher knows these differences he can mould his behaviour in the class accordingly.

4. Psychologists have developed many learning theories and principles to be applied in education. A teacher can create better teaching learning environment in the class by knowing these theories and principles. A teacher can adopt remedial measures also on the basis of these learning theories and principles.
5. Educational psychology has also helped to develop a number of teaching methods, strategies and techniques. These strategies and techniques are essential for better communication in the class. Knowledge of these strategies and techniques helps the teacher to get more in less time by utilizing minimum resources.
6. Psychological principles and theories have also contributed a lot in developing maxims and principles of teaching. Educational psychology has eliminated many traditional practices which have become obsolete on the basis of experiments.
7. By the study of educational psychology, the teacher can know the causes of educational problems of students. He can know with the help of researches which conditions are suitable to learning and how controlled environment is conducive to learning.
8. For better adjustment in the school as well as in the society the teacher and the taught must be mentally healthy. Educational psychology equips the teacher with the knowledge of mental hygiene and various processes of defense mechanism. This knowledge will help the teacher to prevent maladjustment in children.
9. Psychological principles are also helpful in developing curriculum for different stages of learning. It is constructed keeping in view the unique needs and priorities of children at different stages of life.
10. Educational psychology has also constructed a number of tools to measure learning outcomes of children. These tools and techniques help the teacher to know to what extent behavioural changes of learners are desirable. In the light of performance of students, the teacher can evaluate his own methods and procedures also.

**(B) Practice of Education:**

1. Once the above aspects of educational psychology are put into practice it opens new avenue for researches in educational psychology. It helps the teacher in developing new tools and techniques for measuring various types of variables in the class. Better controlling and prediction of behaviour of students are possible with the help of these researches.
2. When a teacher applies principles of educational psychology in his practical life it becomes very easy for him to develop positive attitude among his students. Positive attitude towards teaching can be brought about among teachers also with the help of educational psychology.
3. We see many problems of indiscipline in the class. Causes of many of these problems are psychological in nature. Once a teacher applies his knowledge into teaching learning process, he can easily solve these problems of the class. He avoids corporal punishment meted out to students in the class and uses techniques of rewards and praises for motivating his students. He talks to his students freely in order to know his students well. These and many other techniques applied by the teacher reduces problem of indiscipline in the class.
4. Preparation and use of audio-visual aids in the class is based on solid psychological systems and principles. This applied form of educational psychology helps the teacher to clarify the concept and to intensify the interest of his students.
5. Democratic classroom management is totally based on the application of educational psychology in the class. The application of educational psychology in the class has reduced the distance between the teacher and the taught and it has improved teaching learning environment in the class.
6. While preparing school time table, principal also takes the help of educational psychology. For example, difficult subjects are taught in the morning and easy subjects are taught in the afternoon. Similarly, one easy subject is put in between two difficult subjects and so on.

7. There was a time when undue importance was given to theoretical subjects and only curricular activities in the school. Educational psychology has drastically changed this trend. Almost every subject is now taught with practicum or project work and co curricular activities have now become an indispensable part of school activities everywhere. All these things have helped the students to develop their personality in full.
8. Several innovative ideas have been introduced today to improve teaching learning process in the class. Use of educational psychology has contributed a lot in innovating new ideas. For example, experiments conducted on pigeons by Skinner is now used in the classroom for shaping and moulding the behaviour of students and for correcting maladjusted behaviour of learners. Micro teaching, stimulated teaching, programmed instruction etc are some other examples of innovation here.
9. Educational psychology has also contributed a lot in producing text books for different age groups of children. Beautiful pictures in multi colours are given in the text books which are prepared for small children. Even those books which are prepared for adults have pictorial materials. These and other examples show that text books are now being produced keeping in view the intellectual, social and emotional development of children and their varied nature of interest. Even publishers are also taking the benefit of educational psychology to the maximum level possible.
10. Recommendations of various commissions and committees also show that dignitaries of these commissions and committees have also realized the importance of educational psychology for the upgradation of teaching learning process. For example, Yashpal Committee has recently recommended that there should be no Board examination upto class Xth in order to reduce strain from the minds of learners (Times of India dated 4-9-2005). This type of recommendation is surely based on the findings made in the field of educational psychology.

In short, we can say that educational psychology helps-

- the teacher to improve teaching learning process in the class.
- the principal for achieving better discipline and better academic performance of the school.
- researcher to discover new methods and procedures in the field of education.
- the curriculum developers to construct need based up to date curriculum for students.
- the policy makers to do educational planning in accordance with the current requirements of the society.

On the basis of above discussions we can say that ignoring the role of educational psychology in education is synonymous to spoiling the personality (self) of the child.

# OBJECTIVE QUESTIONS

**1.** Psychology as a science of mind was rejected by philosophers because
(*a*) mind could not be defined in definite terms
(*b*) mind could not be interpreted in behavioural terms
(*c*) both of these
(*d*) none of these

**2.** All are the characteristics of scientific knowledge except
(*a*) it can not be repudiated in future
(*b*) it can be verified objectively
(*c*) it depends on observation and experiment
(*d*) future course of action can be predicted by it

**3.** The first psychologist who systematically studied behaviour was
(*a*) Wundt (*b*) J.B.Watson
(*c*) Pavlov (*d*) None of them

**4.** Psychology is a social science because
(*a*) its laws and principles are applicable to human life situations
(*b*) it studies human behaviour in social context
(*c*) it helps in moulding behaviour of the child according to the need
(*d*) all of these

5. Which of the following is not a subjective method of studying behaviour
(a) observation (b) interview
(c) introspection (d) dream analysis
6. Participant method of observation is suitable for studying the behaviour of
(a) small children (b) criminals
(c) both of these (d) none of these
7. Observation method is used in
(a) classroom situation
(b) sports situation
(c) lab situation
(d) all of these
8. Which of the following techniques (tools) is used in educational survey (to study the problems of education)
(a) tests (b) questionnaire
(c) interview (d) all of these
9. Studying the classroom problems is an example of
(a) field study (b) field experiment
(c) clinical survey (d) none of them
10. Educational psychology helps the teacher in which of the following ways
(a) he can motivate the learners for learning
(b) he can modify his teaching in accordance with individual differences
(c) he studies the personality of learners and then plans his way of action.
(d) all of them
11. The first philosopher who integrated psychology with education at least theoretically was
(a) Pestalozzi (b) John Locke
(c) Aristotle (d) None of them
12. Principles of Psychology of William James was published in
(a) 1890 (b) 1888
(c) 1906 (d) 1913
13. Which of the following is a specialized branch of educational psychology
(a) Measurement and evaluation
(b) Educational technology
(c) Special education
(d) None of the above
14. Psychological principles and theories can be applied in the field of
(a) management
(b) business and trade
(c) medical treatment
(d) all of these

## ANSWERS

| 1 | 2 | 3 | 4 | 5 | 6 | 7 | 8 | 9 | 10 |
|---|---|---|---|---|---|---|---|---|---|
| (a) | (a) | (b) | (d) | (a) | (c) | (d) | (d) | (b) | (d) |
| 11 | 12 | 13 | 14 | | | | | | |
| (a) | (a) | (c) | (d) | | | | | | |

# Growth and Individual Differences

## INTRODUTION

The terms growth and development are generally interchangeably used by experts because both the processes are interrelated and interdependent on each other, ie, no growth is possible without development and vice versa as far as an individual is concerned. In spite of that some psychologists have tried to differentiate the two concepts that are given below-

## MEANING OF GROWTH

Growth is an indicator of increase in bodily dimensions such as height and weight and it is generally confined to quantitative changes

**Arnold Gessell**, an American psychologist has defined growth in the following words.

"Growth is a function of the organism rather that of the environment as such. The environment furnishes the foil and the milieu for the manifestation of development but these manifestations come from inner compulsion and are primarily organized by inherent inner mechanics and by an intrinsic physiology of development. The very plasticity of growth requires that there should be limiting and regulatory mechanisms. Growth is a process so, intricate and so sensitive that there must be powerful stabilizing factors, intrinsic rather than extrinsic which preserve the balance of the total pattern and direction of the growth trend. Maturation is in a sense a name for this regulatory mechanism"

According to this definition, the process of growth has the following **characteristics and dimensions**:

1. Growth is related to quantitative change brought about in the body of an individual. For example, if the height of a person increases from four to five feet, it means that the size of the person has grown.
2. Whatever changes take place in an individual, is the result of heredity and environment both. Growth is related to hereditary or inherent factors while development is related to environmental or extrinsic factors
3. The process of growth starts from within the individual and does not come out till the end.
4. Growth has some limiting and regulatory mechanism. An individual can grow only to a certain limit. If gene has fixed his body size as 6 feet, he can not increase his height to seven feet in any manner. Similarly, growth is a systematic and well regulated process. We can increase our body weight gradually not all of a sudden depending on the kind of food that we take and the type of exercises that we do.
5. Growth is an intricate and sensitive process. So, there must be some powerful stabilizing factors to control it. These factors are present within the body of the organism. These factors not only bring about balance in the total pattern but also gives direction of the growth trend. For example, our hands, legs, neck stomach etc grow in a coordinated style. There is no abnormal pattern of growth found in any part of the body.
6. The mechanism that regulates the process of growth is called maturation. An individual goes to the second step of growth only after the maturation at first stage. These stages are so closely inter linked that we can not isolate one stage from the other perfectly. Where does childhood ends and adolescence starts is very difficult to demarcate.
7. Growth can always be measured in quantitative terms but development can be assessed only qualitatively.

8. The process of growth actually works as a base for the process of development. No development is possible without growth.
9. Food and nutrition will affect growth and development both. If proper food is not available, genetic determinant will not be able to grow the body organs to the required level.

## MEANING OF DEVELOPMENT

It is emerging and expanding of capacities of the individual to provide greater facility in functioning such as development of motor ability from uncertain manipulation to proficiency in games. This development is achieved through the process of growth.

Development refers to interaction of a person with his environmental surroundings whose after product is to increase:

- The strength
- The degree of differentiation
- The organization of personality

Development refers to those effects upon the person's cognitive and emotional systems which strengthen one or more abilities of the person in the desired manner. Thus, development is the qualitative changes in the organism. Environment has very important role to play in the process of development.

### Three concepts of development

1. *Development is maturation :* According to **Arnold Gessell**, the role of physical changes is very important in development. The development from infancy to adolescence is governed by physical changes. When physical growth of the particular stage gets matured only then development in that stage is possible. For example, a growing nervous system changes systematically and automatically and this results in predictable changes in bones and muscles. Thus major changes in the organism are based on maturation.

   According to Gessell, there is internal programming toward physical and cognitive growth and each year is characterized by certain behavioural changes. Development is always guided and controlled by these changes.
2. *Development is learning :* According to **Baer**, "development is the behavioural changes which require programming and programming requires time but not enough of it to call it age."

   Programming here means the sequence of learning which may happen naturally or it may be arranged in the life of an individual with the help of the environment. Thus, according to this definition, development is genetic and environmental both. Whatever we learn in the process of our life is related to development of us.
3. *Development is the synthesis of abilities :* According to **Jean Piaget**, there are four basic elements that take part in the process of development and development is the result of synthesis of all these elements. They are given below:

| | |
|---|---|
| I. Maturation | An automatic and innate process |
| II. Social transmission | Learning through language, schooling or training given by parents |
| III. Experiences | Obtained from the outer environment informally |
| IV. Equilibration | Whatever is learnt or gained internally or externally is equilibrated here. |

### Principles of development

1. *Development is a product of interaction :* Development is a process which is the result of constant interchange of energy within the organism and his environment. Thus hereditary forces interact with environmental forces and the process of development goes further. These two forces are so closely interacted that it is very difficult to isolate the contribution of either of them. The contribution of gene may be 10% as compared to 90% contribution of environment in the process of development.
2. *Development follows an orderly sequence :* The rate of growth and development is different in different individuals depending upon a number of factors but it does follow an orderly sequence in all the individuals. The psychologists have reported three important directional trends in the process of development:

(a) *Cephaulo caudal :* Development starts from head and proceed toward heel. We see that development of head of a child is well advanced as compared to other parts of the body.

(b) *Proximodigital :* Development starts from the central part of the body. Then it spread to other outer or more distant parts of the body. We see that an infant uses his shoulders and elbows first to reach an object and then he uses his fingers and wrists.

(c) *Locomotion* : Locomotion develops in a sequence in all the individuals belonging to different cultures of the world. The rate of development for different infants may be different but every infant will have to pass through these stages at all cost. For example, an infant first learns to crawl, then to sit, then to stand and finally to walk. No infant can walk directly in the first stage.

3. *Development is a continuous process :* Development is a continuous process which begins from the time of conception in the womb of the mother and continues till death. But this process is not always smooth or gradual. Ups and downs are most of the time seen in every stage of development. There are spurts in physical growth and psychological functioning. Sharp growth rate is seen at the time of spurts. For example, a sharp increase in height and weight in the early adolescent period, a fast rise in vocabulary during pre-school period, sudden improvement in problem solving abilities during adolescence and so on.

4. *Development goes from bilateral to unilateral trend :* Infants up to the age of 2.5 years use both of their hands with equal ease. Then they learn to use any of their hands preferably. Similarly, in the beginning of cycle learning we use both the hands to control it but when we become fully experts in cycle learning we can control the cycle single handedly. Thus, development is a process of specialization also.

5. *Inter-relationship of different aspects of development :* Different aspects of development are interdependent and inter related. For example child's social behaviour is interrelated with his physical development. If child is physically handicapped, his emotional development may also be slow with aggressive development in some emotions. Similarly, if social development of an individual is poor, his mental or physical development will also be slow.

6. *Development is individualized process :* All individuals develop in their own way depending on their genetic characteristics and the training received from the environment. Thus, each child has his own rate of physical, social, mental or emotional development. If we observe ten years old children in a society, we find that there are great differences in their height, weight, sociability, emotional expressions and learning readiness. Similarly, the rate of growth is very high during infancy or pre-adolescent period as compared to other periods of life. Thus, rate of growth also changes with the change in stages of life.

7. *Development is positive and negative both :* Up to a certain period of human's life all the faculties of the individual develop but after that retardation starts specially after the age of 70. Physical and emotional retardations are seen during this age with zero social development. Mental development still continues but it too ultimately starts diminishing with the increase in age. Death is nothing but the collapse of all these processes of development.

8. *Development is cumulative :* Development is a cumulative process. Certain changes impress the observer and it looks as these changes are sudden but actually they are not sudden. They are the cumulative effect of all the changes in the individual. The child climbs the steps of the development one by one and then he reaches the zenith. The child first of all learns the words, then he learns the phrases, then sentences and finally he comes to know how the stories or essays are written. Thus, each change in the child is the culmination of his prior growth and experiences.

9. *Development proceed from general to specific :* In all types of development we find the principle of mass differentiation and integration. At the time of birth, the world is like big blooming confusion

for the child. Then by and by his behaviours are refined and become goal directed responses.

10. *Rate of development differs with sex :* There is slight difference in the process of development between boys and girls. Girls mature earlier than boys at least emotionally. Girls are taller and heavier than boys in pre adolescence period but by the end of this period boys surpass them.

## Dimensions of Growth and Development

1. *Physical growth and development :* It refers to strengthening of body and muscles with better proficiency and coordination of motor organs, if a person is able to do heavy work with ease, if he is able to do the task in lesser time, if he is able to do the task with accuracy and if he is able to do the task with neatness and beauty, then it is said that physical growth and development of the person is satisfactory.
2. *Social growth and development :* It refers to improvement and refinement of behaviour of an individual in social situations. If a person is stable in his behaviour even in adverse situations, if the behaviour of the person is fully acceptable to the society and if he is able to influence the society by his behaviour, then it is said that the social growth and development of the person is satisfactory.
3. *Emotional growth and development :* It refers to the accuracy of responses that an individual will exhibit under the influence of his emotions. These exhibited responses will be real as well. For example, if anger is not exhibited at the abuse given by any other person, it means that emotional growth and development is not satisfactory. Expressing sorrow at losses but not so much sorrow as it is beyond control is emotional maturity. If a person gets angry at his insults but he fully controls his anger according to the situation, then it is said that his emotional growth and development is satisfactory. Same is the case with other emotions also.
4. *Intellectual growth and development :* It refers to the ability to draw out conclusion from jumbled informations and to apply the inferences to real life situations in order to make the life happy and meaningful. If a person normally does what he is expected to do, if he is able to mould the situation in his own favour, if he is able to manipulate the situation against the other and if he is not backward in any way in mental operations, then it is said that his mental growth and development is satisfactory.
5. *Language growth and development :* Language is means of expressing, thinking and action. Had we not been given this power, we would not have been able to interact with others and our social existence was not possible. Language may be verbal and non verbal both. Human being uses both types of languages at a time to inform others about his thinking and behaviour and to be informed about their thinking and behaviour. Thus, language development refers to the ability of a person to convince the people what he thinks right.

## Factors Affecting Growth and Development

Many factors affect to these dimensions of growth and development. Some of them affect mental or social growth and development and some factors affect all of them. Important such factors are given below:

1. *Proper Diet :* There is direct relationship between nutrition and physical growth. If diet is not taken according to the physical activities, physical growth will be retarded which will in turn affect the social, mental and emotional growth and development also.
2. *Exercise :* Physical exercise on regular basis will also improve physical growth and development. If a person is slow in his physical activities, his health might be worsened. The more an organ of the body is used, the more it will become strong.
3. *Sanitation and hygiene :* A disease free body is likely to grow more freely. This is possible only when the person is following the norms of hygiene and live in a good sanitary condition. It will save the person from communicable diseases.
4. *Genetic factors :* Genes play very important role in the process of growth and development. Nobody can surpass his genetic characteristics. If a person belongs to a race which is genetically short in height he can not increase his height by taking nutritious food and doing exercises.

5. *Recognition in the society :* If the individuality of a person is recognized in the society and he is given full freedom to grow his potentialities, his physical as well as social growth and development will be maximum. Unnecessary restrictions imposed on a person hampers the process of growth and development.
6. *Sociability :* Social relations also affect growth and development of a person. If a person is discarded by the society and people are biased against him, he will get less chance of socialization. As a result, his social horizon will be limited which will reduce his social learning. This will deteriorate the social growth and development. In that case the person will get less chance of exposure in the society. It will reduce his physical development also. As far as language development is concerned, sociability is a must.
7. *Training :* Growth and development is science in itself. If proper training on scientific lines is given to the individual, he is likely to grow and develop by leaps and bounds. Physical and health education serves this purpose.
8. *Games and sports :* Games and sports are necessary for all types of growth and development. They release pent up feeling of the person on one hand and give more chance of physical activities on the other. They are an important source of recreation as well. All these things are very conducive to physical, social and emotional growth and development.
9. *Protection :* A person must feel secure in the society only then his growth and development will be natural and spontaneous. If an individual is living in a surcharged atmosphere and his life and property is always in danger, he will develop negative thinking. Negative attitude towards life and society is an enemy of growth and development in general.
10. *Manipulation of the environment :* If a person is given full enhance to manipulate the environment, his thinking will expand. It will have a positive bearing on his mental and emotional development.
11. *Free exchange of ideas :* Language development takes place only when a person is exposed in the society. In such an environment free exchange of ideas takes place. It increase word power of a person.
12. *Self contentment :* Human desires have no ends. If first desire of the wants is satisfied, another desire replaces the first, thus man always becomes slave of desires. It creates a tension in the mind of man. On the other, if a man is fully contended with what he has, he becomes tension free. It can improve his process of growth and development to a great extent.

### Determinants of growth and development

There are some psychologist who over emphasize the environmental factors in the growth and development of personality and there is another group of physiologists who claim the superiority of heredity over environment in the development of personality. As a matter of fact, no definite line of demarcation can be drawn between the contribution of these two factors in the process of growth and development. One thing is clear that an individual is by product of his genes and environmental training. The manner in which an individual is similar or different from his fellow being in the performance is due to the combination of these two factors. It should, however be noted that the influence of genes on the personality of an individual may be preliminary in understanding his behaviour. If we are able to trace out the genetic influence, we can mould the environment accordingly. It may save our time and energy in guiding an individual to develop his personality. Thus, genetic factors work as base and only with the coordination with the environmental factors they shape the personality of an individual.

## MEANING OF HEREDITY

All that which we inherit from our parents, grandparents, great grandparents and so on as a free gift is called heredity. It is of two types: (i) Biological heredity and (ii) *Social heredity*

Biological heredity is that which a person inherits from his forefathers in the forms of chromosomes and genes.

Social heredity means all that one generation receives from the preceding generation in the form of social traditions customs and skills.

Person belonging to Rajput race is generally found muscular with strong and wide bones. It is an example of biological heredity. And the son of a carpenter is also likely to be an expert carpenter. It is an example of social heredity.

We will talk in this part only about biological heredity which is determined by genes. These genes are located in chromosomes. A person inherits chromosomes from his forefathers. With the transfer of these chromosomes genes are also transferred which are actually the carrier of heredity. Sex of an individual is also determined by genes. In order to know how traits are fixed by genes, we must first of all know the principles of heredity.

## Principles of Heredity

There are two principles in this regard :

(a) *Principle of resemblance* : This principle states that like begets like. A cat can only give birth to a kitten, a human can only give birth to a baby and so on. According to this principle children generally resemble their parents or relatives.

(b) *Principle of Variability* : Many children do not resemble their parents. There are many instances where intelligent parents have dull children or ugly parents have beautiful children. This variation is universal in nature. That is why we see every individual unique in certain respect. This is called principle of variability of inheritance.

## Mechanism of Heredity

When human sperm and egg unite, they are fertilized into zygote. Each zygote has 23 pairs of chromosomes. Every egg in the body contains the same number of chromosomes. The number of chromosomes in a given species are same but different species have different number of chromosomes.

For example, all humans contain 46 chromosomes. Half of them come from mother and half of them come from father. Within the chromosomes there are thousands of minute particles called genes. They are actually the carriers of hereditary traits from one generation to another.

Chromosomes are made up of long organic molecules whose main substance is deoxyribo nucleic acid (DNA). It is found in the chromosomes as two long strands periodically connected by chemical bonds.

Our heredity information is not found in the two long strands of DNA but in their order of appearance between the two strands of DNA. One pair of chromosomes is related to sex (gender) also. Females have two x chromosomes and male's have an x and a y chromosome. If sperm of x chromosomes unite with the egg of y chromosomes, then the child will be a girl. If on the other hand, the sperm of y unite with the egg of x chromosomes, then the offspring will be a male child.

The story of hereditary influence will not be complete without knowing the influence of genes on our traits. It is because traits are determined exclusively by genes.

Genes are of two types **(i) dominant and (ii) recessive**. We inherit the same qualities of our parents because of dominant genes. If same characteristics are not inherited it means that recessive gene is active there. If marriages between blood relations take place, the recessive genes are developed which can cause many deformities in the body, i.e., offspring may become physically or mentally handicapped.

## Law of Inheritance

Gregor Mendel (1866) discovered the law of inheritance in hybrid peas growing in the garden of an Austrain monastery. His law was found applicable to animals also. His law can be summarized as under.

"If a man who is homozygous for blue eyes marries a woman who is homozygous for brown eyes, the children of the couple will have brown eyes only" (Homozygous condition is that condition in which information concerning a given characteristic differ in the paired gene position)

If a homozygous man marries to a heterozygous woman the distribution of children from the couple will be such that one fourth of them will be homozygous for brown eyes, one half of them, will he heterozygous and one fourth of them will be homozygous for blue eyes.

By this law, Mendel concluded that all genetic informations come to the individual in units rather than in graduated series. In other words, we receive from our ancestors genes controlling the development of specific unitary characteristics not a composite of traits called tendencies.

The second conclusion that can be drawn from this law is that characteristics of men do not remain constant. They tend to vary continuously along a dimension of genes.

## Some studies on Influence of Heredity

How great the role of inheritance is in shaping the personality of an individual by the process of growth and development can be understood by the following studies:

1. **Galton :** He was the first psychologist who conducted studies on the nature and extent of genetic influences in man. He studied 997 eminent British people and found that there were 322 people out of 997 who were also distinguished. He also studied 997 average people and found that only one of them was eminent. He thus concluded that eminent men were found in families which have already one eminent member at least. He also found that decreased instances of imminence were seen when eminent people decreased their relationship with eminent persons. Thus, according to him eminence is inherited from generation to generation.

   He also studied some people of U.S.A. who were given better educational facilities and compared them with the eminent people of U.K. who were given average educational facilities. He found that people of USA were not better performed than that of UK.

2. **Goddard (1914) :** He studied a Kalikak family of USA. Martia Kalikak who was a soldier in the American revolution, developed illegal sexual relation with a feeble-minded lady and an illegitimate child was born. 480 descendents were traced from the family tree of this illegitimate boy. Out of them 143 were feeble-minded, 291 were borderline normal and only 46 were found normal in intelligence.

   After the revolution when Mr. Kalikak married a normal lady a legitimate child was born. 496 descendents were traced from the family tree of this boy. All of them except two were found normal or above normal in intelligence and they became teachers, lawyers, businessmen etc. This study proves that intelligence is inherited from one generation to the next.

   These two studies show that heredity plays an important role in determining the traits. But the conclusions derived from these two studies can not be fully relied upon because of the following reasons:

   *(i)* They do not distinguish between biological and social inheritance. Their studies combine these two factors. So, it is very difficult to isolate the contribution of gene in shaping the personality.

   *(ii)* Testing material used in these studies was not perfect and the survey is also unsystematic and unreliable.

   *(iii)* The researchers were already biased in favour of hereditary factors. So, their conclusions can not be relied upon.

3. **Kellogg and Kellogg :** In order to study the relative influence of heredity and environment they conducted a systematic research by taking their own son and a chimpanzee. Their respective ages were 10 months and 7.5 months. Both of them were brought up in the same environment with similar type of facilities given to them. Their behaviours were systematically studied at regular intervals. It was found that in the beginning the chimpanzee surpassed the son in motor skills of jumping, running, climbing, etc. Chimpanzee also learned some social skills such as eating with spoon and drinking from a glass, but he could learn 93 words only. But later on, the son caught him up in all areas of development except physical strength.

   This study shows that heredity sets a limit for maximum development which can not be improved even by providing the best environment.

## Meaning of Environment

Environment here means social and cultural environment especially. Physical environment also becomes the part of social environment when it is used in the learning process. When an individual lives in a society, in a family, he learns many things from the social and cultural environment. These learnings bring about certain changes in his behaviour. Some of these changes may be of permanent nature. These permanent changes become the part and parcel of his habits. When these habits are converted into values after maturity, they become the representative traits of the individual. Individual is now recognized with these traits.

### Influence of Environment in Shaping the Personality

The role or contribution of environment is no less than that of the heredity. In fact human being is a by product of heredity and environment both. The importance of environment in the process of growth and development can be understood by the following example.

A missionary in (Midnapur) Bihar found two children who were taken by wolves in early children hood. These children were reared in the company of wolves in beast environment. They learned to walk on four feet, ate raw flesh and verbalized like wolves. These children were brought back from the forest and kept in a hospital. One of them died next day and the other could hardly learn elementary things. This study shows that if suitable environment is not provided to a person, his genetic qualities will not flourish at all.

On the basis of studies on heredity and environment with regard to growth and development following conclusions can be drawn:

1. Heredity and environment both play combined role in the development of personality of an individual.
2. Heredity does not determine any trait of the personality in isolation. It only provides a base and then environment develops the trait.
3. Subjective traits of the individual like physique, colour of skin, resistance level of the body etc are determined by the hereditary factors. Certain diseases are also inherited because of low resistability of the body of the individual.
4. Bad environment can surpass good inheritance but good environment is not a substitute for poor heredity. It means heredity sets a limit for the maximum development. Even good training and experiences will not enable the person to cross this limit. On the other hand, even good man by genes can be made corrupt in a bad environment.
5. Training and experiences can improve the traits of an individual to a great extent. Even intelligence level can be improved to some extent.

### Environmental Factors Affecting Growth and Development

Environmental influences begin since the time of conception of the child into the womb of his mother. Mental, physical and emotional conditions of mother also influence the development of foetus in the womb. When child opens his eyes in the physical world, he immediately comes in contact with the environment. Since he takes birth in a society, he is also influenced by a number of social and cultural factors. The impact of some of these factors on his growth and development is given below:

1. **Physical factors of the environment :** Physical and geographical conditions of the environment play an important role in shaping the personality of an individual. People living in deserts, hilly areas and plains have great difference in their body strength, height, structure, mode of living, habits etc. Climate of the region also affects the behaviour, body built and resistance to fight the environmental forces. For example, people living in Siberian region can tolerate lower degree of temperature than those who live in Indian sub continent. Personality traits are also determined by these environmental factors, for example, people living in African continent are more aggressive and get easily annoyed than those living in North America.
2. **Family of the individual :** Personality of an individual develops fully only when interaction between biological inheritance and environmental forces take place. Home is the first place of these interactions. Whatever early changes take place in the nature and pattern of personality formation in the initial life of an individual at home, they are generally upheld in the whole life. In the family, child comes in contact with his parents, grandparents, uncles, aunties and cousins. These people give full

recognition to the child. They also respond him keeping his likes and dislikes. Several empirical evidences support that childhood experiences are decisive determinants of his personality in later life. For example, if a child is deprived of family love and other facilities, he may grow into either an aggressive or totally submissive person in future. Margarets Ribble in 1944 started a series of investigations on the effects of some psychological deprivations in infancy. She studied 600 children in this regard and concluded that lack of adequate cuddling and other close physical contact with some friendly adults can impose serious handicaps on the growing infants. Each and every characteristic of the family affects the personality of the child in future. We are taking here one more example of morale of the family. A low morale home does not present a good model before the child for imitation. Stort in 1939 on the basis of a questionnaire administered on 1800 adolescents concluded three things given below-

- Children coming from homes where good morale pattern dominated were better adjusted, more independent in thinking and action and more satisfactorily related to their parents than those who were average in this dimension.
- Adolescents who came from discarded and nagging families were poorly adjusted in the society.
- Economic factors also influence the development of personality. Poverty of parents and lack of money even to fulfil legitimate needs of their children led to certain kinds of frustrations in adolescents.

3. **School :** School is a miniature society in itself. Here individual stays for almost six hours daily in the early quarter period of his life. His personality is shaped by the school in the following ways.
   - School poses new problems before the child to be acquired and new models for imitation.
   - School provides new knowledge and expands the horizon of the child. These behavioural changes determine the pattern and direction of growth and development.
   - Social interaction with teachers, classmates and peers is possible in schools. These interaction also shape the personality of the individual.

4. **Teacher :** Teacher can play a very crucial role in shaping the personality of the individual. The way the teacher behaves and handles his students and the personality traits exhibited by him have an important effect on the future personality of students. He influences a child in the following ways.
   - The way the teacher carries out his role in the class will affect the emotional climate of the classroom. An authoritarian teacher will establish an autocratic climate and a democratic teacher will create a permissive climate in the classroom. Autocratic climate will tend to create aggression and bostility among students. If climate is democratic, it will develop constructive, thoughtful and cooperative behaviour among students. All good personality traits can be developed by democratic climate in the class. Because of this reason democratic dealing is preferred to autocratic dealing. The more a teacher is democratic in his attitude and behaviour, the more his students will be accommodative to others.
   - Studies have shown that children who repeatedly fail in the class are likely to be cruel, selfish, unfriendly, unhappy, impolite, boastful and quarrelsome. Thus, teacher tries to reduce the occurrence of failures in the class by his dedicated efforts.
   - Whatever model of character is presented by the teacher in the class, it is immediately copied down by the students. If teacher has ideal traits in him, students, are also likely to be idealistic.

5. **Language :** Language is the medium by which the society is structured and experiences of the race are transmitted from generation to generation. The child learns the languages of the society. He learns many experiences and knowledge by these languages. He also communicates the other members of the society by these languages. Thus, by these processes he becomes an integral part of the social environment.

6. **Social roles :** The word role has been derived from the theatre world. In theatres the actors play the role of different characters as the situation demands. Worlds is also a stage and human beings are just actors who play their respective roles. Man is a social animal. He comes in contact with different people in the society. As a result he has to play the role of a father, son, brother, friend, student etc. throughout his life at various stages of his development. Social roles are the process by which an individual interacts with other members of the society. Thus, social roles are the collection of behaviour and relevant attitudes towards others. These roles are learned by individuals through observation and imitation.
7. **Self concept :** Self concepts are the means by which we create our unique image and identity in the society. Self concept in the child is initiated by physical awareness. The other means of developing self concept are how we maintain our social status, how we dress ourselves and how we speak and respond to others. Self concept influences our personality development in two ways. The first is that if people hold us in high esteem, we feel exalted. And the second is that if others hold negative attitude towards us, it creates the feeling of worthlessness and it may lead to self defence or withdrawl from the social situation. If self concept is fully developed in an individual his rate of growth and development will be high.
8. **Identification :** Identification is the process by which we imitate the physical, social or mental characteristics of our model. When a boy identifies himself with his father by coping father's behaviour it means that he wants to be like him. If identifying models are solid physically, mentally or socially, the identification process will also be solid and healthy.
9. **Living standard :** Physical and mental health of a person is directly related to his living standard. If he is getting nutritious food and sufficient amount of time for sports and exercise, his rate of development will be high. People of developed countries are found very advanced because of this reason.
10. **Cultural heritage :** Every society is identified by its cultural heritage which is transmitted from one generation to the next. The transmission of cultural heritage may also be termed as social heredity. The personality of an individual is gradually shaped by the culture he is born in.

    **E.R. Tyler** defined culture in the following words.

"It is that complex whole which includes knowledge, beliefs, morals law, customs and many other capabilities (skills) and habits acquired by man as a member of society."

Thus, culture refers to total life activities of a society. Whatever a person learns from the society by the process of interaction is called culture. In other words, what the people think, feel and do constitute the culture of a society. Biological inheritance is more or less the same all over the world but whatever differences are seen in the process of growth and development of personality among individuals it is because of the differences of social inheritance (culture). We can easily identify people reared in different cultures by the personality patterns they possess. English, Africans, Arabs and Indians can be identified by their cultural background more than by their biological heredity.

No single culture dominates in big countries. Sub cultures within the culture is also seen which brings about social conflicts. This conflict distorts the personality of individuals as well. Culture or sub cultures are silent educators and they mould the personality of individuals very silently.

The influence of cultural forces is so powerful that if three identical twins of a Hindu family are reared in three different cultures such as houses of Muslims, Christians and jews, the impact of their respective cultures will produce three distinct type of personality. These twins will not have any thing of their original Hindu culture.

The influence of culture can also be understood by the following words:

"Culture regulates our lives at every turn. From the moment we are born until we die, whether we are conscious of it or not, constant pressure on us forces us to follow certain types of behaviour that other men have created for us".

Culture influences the personality development of an individual in the following ways:

- Ideas, values, beliefs, customs and traditions are internationalized through the process of learning. A child who takes birth in a particular culture is reared in that very culture. He learns ideas, beliefs, values, customs etc. of his society and thus he acquires distinctive personality characteristics in the process.
- Various cultures are propagated by various institutions. When individual takes part in these activities actively or in a passive manner, he gets attached to these cultural institutions. Thus, his culture is institutionalized. This is the **second stage of culture formation.** When culture of a region reaches this stage it becomes very difficult to wipe it out by other cultures.

# OBJECTIVE QUESTIONS

**1.** Which of the following statements about growth and development is not correct ?
(*a*) Growth generally refers to quantitative changes while development refers to qualitative changes.
(*b*) Growth is a function of the environment
(*c*) Growth is not possible without development and vice versa
(*d*) Growth is determined by intrinsic and genetic factors of the organism

**2.** The limit of growth is fixed by
(*a*) internal factors of the organism
(*b*) nutrition and exercise
(*c*) both of these
(*d*) none of these

**3.** In the following question Assertion (A) is followed by Reason (R)
**Assertion (A):** There is a powerful stabilizing factor to control and coordinate growth.
**Reason (R):** If it is not so body weight will not coordinate to body size.
(*a*) if both A and R are correct
(*b*) if A is correct but R is wrong
(*c*) if A and R are unrelated
(*d*) if both A and R are wrong

**4.** Development is
(*a*) Maturation
(*b*) Learning
(*c*) Synthesis of abilities
(*d*) All of them

**5.** Development takes place when
(*a*) environmental forces work on the organism
(*b*) environmental forces interact with the hereditary forces in an organism
(*c*) both of these
(*d*) none of these

**6.** Which of the following statements about development is correct?
(*a*) Process of development can be improved by exercise and nutrition
(*b*) Development may be positive and negative both
(*c*) Development proceeds from general to specific
(*d*) All of these

**7.** The son of a goldsmith becomes an expert goldsmith. It is an example of a
(*a*) biological heredity
(*b*) social heredity
(*c*) transfer of instinct
(*d*) none of these

**8.** All humans contain .............. chromosomes.
(*a*) 26 (*b*) 36
(*c*) 46 (*d*) 42

**9.** DNA test helps us to know
(*a*) the genetic traits of a person
(*b*) nature of personality and its composition
(*c*) both of these
(*d*) none of these

**10.** The law of inheritance was discovered by Gregor Mendel in
(*a*) 1866 (*b*) 1911
(*c*) 1888 (*d*) 1920

**11.** The traits of Kalikak family of USA were studied by
(*a*) Goddard (*b*) Galton
(*c*) Gregor Mendel (*d*) None of these

**12.** Which of the following statements regarding personality traits is correct?
(*a*) Traits of personality can not be developed in isolation without taking the help of environment.
(*b*) Subjective traits of the individual are determined by genetic factors.
(*c*) Bad environment can surpass good inheritance but good environment is not a substitute for poor heredity.
(*d*) All of these

## ANSWERS

| 1 | 2 | 3 | 4 | 5 | 6 | 7 | 8 | 9 | 10 |
|---|---|---|---|---|---|---|---|---|---|
| (*b*) | (*a*) | (*b*) | (*d*) | (*c*) | (*d*) | (*b*) | (*c*) | (*c*) | (*a*) |
| **11** | **12** | | | | | | | | |
| (*a*) | (*d*) | | | | | | | | |

# Psychology of Child Development

## STAGES OF DEVELOPMENT

From infancy to adulthood human being undergoes the following stages of development.

| | | | |
|---|---|---|---|
| 1 | Infancy | - | 0-2 years |
| 2 | Early childhood | - | 3-6 years |
| 3 | Later childhood | - | 7-12 years |
| 4 | Adolescence | - | 13-17 years |
| 5 | Adulthood | - | 18-25 years |

At each stage of human development, certain physical, intellectual, language, emotional and social changes occur which may be similar or entirely different from the preceding age. We will describe all these stages one by one.

### Dimensions (Areas) of Development

Before coming to the stages of development it is better to know what the physical, intellectual, emotional and social development are:

1. **Physical development :** Important characteristics of physical growth and development are given below:
   - Physical growth is curvilinear not steady or regular. Rapid growth is followed by slow growth and then again rapid growth may be there.
   - Different parts (organs) of the body have its own unique way of development. Whatever changes we see in hands and legs cannot be seen in heart or lung.
   - Physical growth and development is affected by climatic conditions. For example, cold countries have more favourable conditions of growth and development than hot or humid countries.
   - Heredity fixes a limit of physical growth and development. The descendents of five feeted man is not supposed to have a height of more than 6 feet or 5½ feet.
   - Physical growth is very rapid in the infancy and in the later childhood. It is again fast in the start of adolescence.

***Dimensions of Physical Growth :*** Important dimensions of physical growth and development are as follows:

(i) *Height* : A new born baby is 19-20 inches in length at the time of birth. As soon as the baby grows, his height also increases.

(ii) *Weight :* Human baby has a weight of 2.5 kg. – 3.5 kg. at the time of birth. Girl babies are generally lighter than male babies here. When a baby becomes an adult he acquires a weight of 55 kg. at the height 5.5 feet. The weight of boys are generally higher than girls due to increased height. If height is more, weight will also be high.

(iii) *Body proportion :* Some organs of the body are more developed at the time of birth than others. But as soon as the baby grows and reaches to the period of adulthood, proportionate change and growth are seen. For example, head is already somewhat developed at the time of birth but it grows less proportionately than other parts of body.

(iv) *Internal organs :* Internal organs of the body also develop with age. As the child grows, the heart beat which is 100-120 per minute in infancy, becomes regular and normal, *i.e.*, 72 times per minute. Respiration also becomes slower, deeper and regular, food takes longer time to pass the digestive tract, the body temperature becomes stable and so on and all this happens due to growth and development of the internal organs of the body. This increase in efficiency enables the older children and adults to adapt to the environmental changes.

It is pitutory gland which is responsible for growth in the early years of life. Sex gland is also activated under the influence of this gland, and influence the pitutory gland as well. If sex hormones did not restrain the function of pitutory gland the human being would become a giant.

2. **Motor development :** Motor development includes movement of hands, lags, mouth and other related muscles of the body. Important features of motor development are as follows :
   - Motor development occurs in those structures which lie nearest to the main axis especially near the vaist, thighs, legs etc. The child learns to control the muscles of his arms earlier than those of fingers.
   - Bilateral to unilateral trend in the coordination and control of muscles is seen. The child first uses both of his hands then he gradually learns to use only one hand in specialized manner.
   - From general to specific trend in motor development is seen.
   - An orderly sequence of motor development is also seen. **Hurlock** found that motor development in the head region takes place first, followed by the motor development of arms, hands, legs, etc. This trend is not reversed any how.
   - If motor development of the child is delayed by any reason, his emotional and social development will also be delayed or disturbed.

3. **Intellectual development :** Intellectual development includes attending, perceiving, observing, thinking, recalling, analyzing, evaluating, problem solving and the development of language and concepts. These aspects of mind grow and change with age. Generally these activities of mind are inter related. Important features of intellectual development are as follows:
   - Mental development is a continuous but steady process and all activities of mind are inter-related also.
   - As long as the experiences of the child increase, his mental horizon expands. He learns not only to differentiate but to integrate different elements of the physical as well as meta-physical world.
   - Factors affecting mental development are maturation and learning.
   - Mental activities are guided and controlled by nervous system. Brain which is an important part of nervous system plays the key role in the mental development of the child.
   - Sensation and perception are the primary aspects of mental activities. In fact, mental activities start from these two aspects. Sensation is the first step to knowledge which is accompanied by perception.
   - Perceptual experience leads to concept formation. Concept formation takes place on the basis of general and common qualities of an object, e.g., concept of "book" is developed after seeing so many things like books and then we say that books are for reading. Thus, concept is developed on the basis of common qualities of an object. It involves discrimination and generalization both.
   - Concept of an object or idea changes with the change in experiences for example, cold season of December may have different meaning for the people of Kolkata and Srinagar due to difference of experiences.
   - Child's concepts change with the increase in his age. For example, a small child may develop a unique concept of ghost. But when he becomes an adult, his concept of ghost changes.

4. **Language development :** Language development is actually the verbalization of concepts which is learnt by imitation (hearing). If child is deaf, his language development will be zero. Important features of language development are given below.
   - Language is a tool to be used for all types of communication. Without proper language development, no communication from one person to the other is possible.
   - Language is used as a tool in acquiring knowledge. When knowledge increases, vocabulary also increases.
   - Language development starts with mere names of objects or events and when it reaches at its peak it develops ideas into universal concepts.

- Growth and maturity of speech is an important aspect of language development. Four needs of the child motivates him to learn speech.

Desire to secure information more and more (Interrogative sentences).

(a) Desire to give commands or to do requests (Imperative sentences).

(b) Desire to come into social relationship with others.

(c) Desire to express feelings and thoughts (Exclamatory and Assertive sentences)

- There are spurts or rest in the speech development. It is not constant throughout life. Sometmes it is very rapid and sometimes very slow.
- The development of thinking moves from simple to complex and from the concrete to the abstract.
- An individual stops growing intellectually upto the age of 20 years in general.

5. **Emotional development :** Emotion is a strong feeling that is so strong that it can be observed overtly. There are **four qualities of emotional experiences:**

- Every emotional experience involves feeling
- Every emotional experience is accompanied by marked physiological changes
- An emotional experience includes an impulse towards some kind of action, ie, overt response is seen
- Emotion involves awareness or perception of what it is or what it might be that causes these impulses and feelings

Important features of emotional development are as follows :

(a) Emotions start immediately after birth. For example, an infant shows fear, anger, love etc, though his emotions are not clear at this age, according to Sherman.

(b) Children's emotions are very intense as compared to adults. As they grow they begin to exercise restraint over their emotions. They learn to modify and hide their emotions also.

(c) Child's emotions last only for a few minutes and then it ends all of a sudden. The transitory nature of the child's emotions lies in a rapid shift from one emotion to another. When he shows anger, he at the next moment smiles.

(d) In the beginning, the emotional expression is diffused and generalized. It becomes stable, differentiated, selective, moderate and graded as the child grows older.

(e) Emotional development is also determined by the socio-economic background of the child. If a child belongs to a cultured family, he will show more emotional maturity.

(f) Emotional development is affected by the physical development of the child also. For example, if a child is physically weak due to malnutrition or diseases, his emotions will be less stable and less subtle.

6. **Social development :** Human baby is the only organism in the world that takes maximum and longer time to be socially and economically self dependent. He needs help from others more than any other creature. This dependence of the child on others helps him to learn how to interact with others in diverse situations. The more a person is healthy in his social interactions, the more he is said to be socially developed. Important features of social development are as follows:

- Social development starts with the process of socialization, a process which enables a child to acquire his social status according to his age. It is the process of socialization that helps the child to learn social traditions, customs and culture.
- The child increases his social circles gradually. These circles increase further when the child grows with age. It makes very difficult for the child to adjust with different types of people in the society. Thus, social development is actually an adjustment training.
- Social development means to share joy and sorrows with others, to work as a member of a group, to cooperate with others and to develop social perception for the purpose of developing belongingness with the rest of the society.
- The end points of social development is social maturity, ie, to adapt successfully to the social environment without frustration. A socially matured person is one who is fair in his dealing, courteous in his behaviour and honest in his character. His sense of responsibility, his self confidence, and his leadership quality make him distinct from others. He confirms what is

acceptable to others and denies what is antagonistic to him.

## Life Span and Development

**(A) Infancy and development :** Various dimensions of development during the period of infancy are given below.

**1. Physical development :** This period is marked by following characteristics of physical development.

*(i)* Physical development is very rapid during this period. For example size increases ten inches upto second year. Weight also becomes almost double at the age 4½ months, i.e., from 3 kg at birth to almost 6 kg. At the age of 4½ month.

*(ii)* Though sex organs are totally undeveloped and inactive during this period, yet a tendency to sexual development is seen in the second year of life. Child actually passes through three stages of sexual development. First stage, the stage of self love belongs to infancy. Here the child derives pleasure from his body, by sucking his thumbs of hand or legs or by touching his sex organs. The other two stages- homosexual or hetero sexual belong to early childhood.

*(iii)* At the time of birth, boys are heavier than girls. 7% weight loss is seen in the first seven days then the baby start to gain weight.

*(iv)* Study shows that boys are on the average heavier than girls at all age levels except from 11-14 years of age in which girls are found heavier than boys.

*(v)* Head is more developed than other parts of the body at birth. It grows proportionately at lesser speed than other parts of the body. At 6 years, the child gains 90% of the adult size of head.

*(vi)* Facial skeleton is found larger in proportion to cranium from birth to seven years of age.

*(vii)* Nose is proportionately small and flat on the face in the first four years. It gains full size at the age of 13 or 14.

*(viii)* Trunk is found heavy during the period of infancy. It along with legs lengthens gradually.

*(ix)* At birth, the weight of the brain is one fourth of an adult brain. It is one half by the age of 9 months and three fourth by the age of two years.

*(x)* In the first year of the baby the heart beat is very irregular and its speed is very high. As the child grows, the heart beat becomes regular and slower. Other physical changes are given below.

- Food takes longer time to pass through the digestive tract and to reach the intestines.
- Urine bladder can retain urine for a longer period of time.
- Body temperature becomes more stable.
- Composition of blood does not change.

*(xi)* The weight becomes almost three times the birth weight at the end of first year. By the age of 2, it becomes 3½ times the birth weight.

**2. Nervous system :**

*(i)* Nerve cells attain maturity during this period

*(ii)* Brain also grows rapidly and its size and weight increases

*(iii)* Improvement in the functioning and structure of sensory organs is seen. Thus, by the end of this period the child is able to perform all the functions of seeing, hearing, smelling, tasting and touching properly.

**3. Motor development :**

*(i)* Co-ordination and control of bodily movements are seen.

*(ii)* The child starts grasping objects in the fourth month of his life

*(iii)* He sits in the sixth month. He crawls in the seventh or eighth month. He stands with the help of support in the ninth month and in the 12th month he begins to walk slowly without support.

*(iv)* Running begins in the second year of his life

*(v)* Greater muscular involvement is seen during infancy

**4. Language development :**

*(i)* It starts with vocalization in the form of cries or explosive sounds. This vocalization may be described as pre speech form.

*(ii)* The child only cries at the time of birth to express his emotions or desires. This crying is used even in the second year of life to express desires and needs.

*(iii)* He begins to utter few words by the end of the first year like mama, dada etc. Some unintelligible words spoken by the child may be seen in the seventh or eighth month.

*(iv)* Language development properly begins in the beginning of the second year. The rate of language development becomes rapid at the

age of 1.5 years and the child crames any new learnt word just in order to retain it in his mind.

(v) By the end of two years he begins to speak proper but short sentences, though grammatical mistakes may be there.

**5. Intellectual development :**

(i) No clear cut sign of intellectual development is seen during infancy. His capacity to grasp new words is totally based on rote memory, though his cramming is without reason or intellect.

(ii) He lacks abstract understanding. His understanding is exclusively restricted to concrete materials but he thinks that heavier is one which is bigger in size. Thus, a plastic ball of bigger size is heavier than a metal ball of smaller size for the child.

(iii) Sign of creativity is seen at the end of the 2nd year. The infant often engages himself in collecting many articles.

(iv) This is a period of make belief. When he attains the age of 2, he believes in what he is told by his elders.

(v) A baby perceives an unfamiliar object as a form or as a figure. He has an innate tendency to organize his sense field and to perceive the object as a whole but this perception lacks definiteness.

**6. Social development :**

(i) He learns social skills in the company of his mother and fathers. When he is responded by them he learns how to respond to others. Thus, he learns all his social experiences from his family members in the first year but in the second year his horizon expands to his neighbourhood.

(ii) By the end of two years he begins to take the notice of other infants and plays with them.

(iii) He totally depends upon his family members for the fulfillment of his social, psychological and physical needs.

(iv) He expects that every body around him should love him and care him. When this expectation is not fulfilled he becomes irritated and cries.

(v) The baby becomes aware of other persons around him at the age of one month. In the second month, he smiles in response to the attentions of adults and he is able to distinguish his mother and other women. In the third month he waves his hands and legs when he is talked to. In the fourth month, he makes anticipatory adjustment to being lifted by someone. In the fifth month, he attends to the human face and looks in the direction of the person who leaves him. He smiles in response to the person who speaks and plays with him. In the sixth month, he reacts differently to smiling and scolding and shows negative responses to strangers. In the ninth month, he tries to imitate the speech of others. He copies simple acts and gestures of others after observation in the tenth month. In the 12th month, he can refrain from doing things when he is forbidden to do so.

In the second year of life he exhibits fear and dislike for strangers by crying or withdrawing. When the baby attains the age of 18 months, he shows negativism in the form of stubborn resistance to the demands of adults.

(vi) In the first two years, the child's play is self centred. He does not like to be interfered by other children or adults. He plays in his own way. He is generally non-cooperative and has to be handled with patience and tacts. In short, the baby is socially underdeveloped.

(vii) Hurlock has presented the social development taking place during first two years of infancy as under :

| | |
|---|---|
| 1. First month | Understand human and other voices |
| 2. Second month | Recognizes human voices and greets with smile |
| 3. Third month | Recognizes mother and distresses on her being away |
| 4. Fourth month | Recognizes human faces |
| 5. Fifth month | Understands the tone of voices i.e. love and hate |
| 6. Sixth or Seventh month | Welcomes the known with smile |
| 7. 8th or 9th month | Plays with his own shadow |
| 8. 24th month | Participates in elder's work |

**7. Emotional development:**

(i) He is completely egocentric and selfish. When he reaches the age of 2, he even does not want to share his toys.

*(ii)* He is irritated and cries when he is chided by his family members.

*(iii)* His emotions are intense, frequent and totally unstable though emotional reactions become distinct in the beginning of the second year. These emotions are spontaneous and he can not control them.

*(iv)* He cannot hide his feelings thus, his entire emotions are in the overt form.

*(v)* Emotions of anger, fear, disgust, elation, love and affections are seen. For example, when he is loved by his mother, he shows his affection by his activities. Similarly, when he is not attended by his family members, he feels disgusted. He also feels pleasure in the company of his mother or his father.

*(vi)* A number of psychologists are of the view that infants are able to undergo emotional experiences. Emotions of fear, anger, joy, hate etc. are seen in them even in the first year.

*(vii)* During the period of infancy only those conditions arouse emotional responses which affect the child's immediate needs and well being, but when the child grows, his spectrum increases and he becomes responsive to a number of stimuli.

*(viii)* It has been noticed that babies and children show their pronounced emotional disturbance just before eating, sleeping, or waking up. For example, when a baby wakes up after sleep, he cries whether he is hungry or not.

*(ix)* Intellectually dull children are less emotionally disturbed than the normal children.

*(x)* Infants show smiling response to any human face whether familiar or stranger between eight and twenty weeks of age. Negative responses to strangers starts after 20 weeks of age and continues upto 40 weeks.

**(B) Early childhood and development :** Various dimensions of development during the period of early childhood (3-6 years) are as follows:

**1. Physical and motor development :**

*(i)* He acquires many motor skills like catching, throwing, running, jumping, climbing, using simple tools, riding a tricycle etc.

*(ii)* Growth in outer parts of the body especially height, weight, formation of muscles etc. is not as fast as it was during infancy. The child, however begins to assume the body proportion of an adult.

*(iii)* The growth of legs is rapid and it acquires about half of an adult size. The growth of head is, however, very slow and that of trunk is medium.

*(iv)* The height of a three years old child is 38 inches on an average though Indian children may be slightly lower than this size. Similarly, the weight should also be 33 pounds at the age of three. By the age of five years, the average weight of children is 43 pounds and average height for boys is 43 inches.

*(v)* Muscles develop at a very rapid speed due to excess involvement of the child in motor activities.

*(vi)* The rate of heart beat and pulse slow down and blood pressure goes up steadily.

*(vii)* By the age of 5-6 the child acquires 90% of the adult weight of brain. Nerve fibres in the brain areas also come to almost maturity by the end of the period of early childhood. It should be noted that the growth of brain and nerve fibres is very rapid from birth to four years.

*(viii)* Self feeding, self dressing, self bathing, combing the hair, brushing the teeth, playing with toys, using pencils for writing or sketching etc are also seen during this period.

**2. Intellectual development :**

*(i)* Perceptual development begins from mass movement to differentiation. Norms for perceptual development is given in the callout table.

*(ii)* The child perceives those things quickly and clearly which are concerned with his mental set and interest.

*(iii)* The child begins to explore his social environment and acquire new experiences at the age of three.

*(iv)* By the age of six, the child develops clear perception of size, shape, colour, time and distance. He does not consider all bigger objects as heavier too.

| Motor | 2 years | 3 years | 4 and 5 years |
|---|---|---|---|
| Development | Walks without help, jumps, runs | Skips, hops | Free and active movement responds to music |
| Fine motor coordination | Copying | Can match shapes, sees similarities and differences | Can name colours |
| Perceptual | Identifies self, matches colours | Can fit nuts, boxes | Matches shapes and colours, distinguishes names |
| Vocalization | 200 words, uses few words | 900 words, follows commands | Can repeat 4 digits-2000 to 3000 words, can define familiar words |
| Adaptive behaviour | Bowel control | Builds blocks, can draw a man | 4 digits, draws body with details |

*(v)* The child begins to form concepts of physical and social reality. For example, he does not do any thing against the wishes of his family members. If he does so, he hides the same.

*(vi)* The child starts learning many materials by rote memorization. His capacity to retain learnt material increases.

*(vii)* Imagination begins to grow and creativity is seen. He manipulates or breaks his toys to understand its mechanism. But his thinking process is restricted to concrete objects only.

*(viii)* Span of attention increases from 7 minutes to 20 minutes.

*(ix)* His curiosity forces him to explore the environment. He asks so many questions from his elders for this purpose.

*(x)* The child is now able to use symbols in language and mathematics.

*(xi)* The child develops a lot of concepts during this period but many of his concepts cannot be verbalized by him due to limited vocabulary.

*(xii)* During this period, children's concepts of spatial relations, distance and depth are vague. This makes the children awkward in their behaviour. For example they calculate height and distance wrongly.

*(xiii)* By the age of five, they are able to distinguish between past, present and future, ie, between yesterday, tomorrow and day after tomorrow etc.

*(xiv)* The concepts of number and quantity also become clear to them. According to Piaget, children acquire concept of number even before they are able to count.

*(xv)* Children's social concepts are influenced by the nature of inter-personal relationship.

*(xvi)* This stage is also called the stage of fantasy. The child takes shelter into his imaginary world in order to escape the harsh realities of his world at home and neighbourhood. If he is given more chance to interact with people, his social concepts will be rich.

**3. Language development**

*(i)* The child has to master four major tasks in the process of learning to speak properly.

- Comprehension of the speech of others
- Building a vocabulary
- Using and combining words into sentences
- Pronouncing the words correctly

By the end of the period of early childhood, the child is able to master all these four tasks.

*(ii)* Language development of a child actually begins from birth cry. When he is responded by his mother after crying, he comes to understand the meaning and importance of crying.

*(iii)* A ten month old child is able to use one or two words only but by the end of the first year his vocabulary increases to four, as **Smith** has observed. By the end of 2nd year, he can use 272 words. In the third year, his vocabulary increase to 896. when he attains the age of four, he can use 1560 words and at the age of 6 he can use 2562 words as Smith has observed.

*(iv)* Language development of children is not uniform. It depends upon better socio-economic environment at home, better schooling and independent living of the child.

**4. Social development:**

*(i)* Feeling of autonomy develops in children. They try to explore and manipulate their environment independently.

*(ii)* The child learns how to behave, talk and interact with the family members and neighbourhood.

*(iii)* The child may be frustrated if social atmosphere of the neighbourhood is not similar to that of the atmosphere at home.

*(iv)* The child's play no longer remains a solitary play after the age of three. The child selects his playmates and develops casual friendship with them. He learns cooperation, competition, sympathy, jealousy, teasing, bullying, quarrelling, etc. in the company of his playmates.

*(v)* Imitation, timidity, shyness, desire for possession etc. are other forms of social behaviour that develop during this period.

*(vi)* The child who is resistive upto the age of three years becomes cooperative and friendly and seeks approval of adults upto the age of four years. That is why he does not object to exchange his toys with his best friends.

*(vii)* At the age of 5-6 he begins to pride about his parents and boast about other members of his family after six.

*(viii)* Most of the children want to dominate in their respective groups at the age of six. Thus group leader changes every time in the group. In this way, the child learns how to adjust in the society in varied situations.

*(ix)* Children of both sexes play together without any discrimination.

*(x)* They also take part in those games which involve physical energy and motor activity like hide and seek.

*(xi)* They take interest in fairy tales and animal stories in which they want that someone should win in the fighting. They are very much interested to know which animal is stronger and strongest out of so many at the age of 4-5.

*(xii)* Negativism increases during this period. It is believed that the more a child is frustrated by the interference of adults, the more negativistic his behaviour will be.

*(xiii)* Girls have been found more dominating than boys in social and group situations.

**5. Emotional development :** Contributions of emotions are very much recognized in the personal and social adjustment of the individuals. Important features of emotional development during this period are given below.

*(i)* Emotions of the child are exhibited only for a very short period. It means that child shifts from one emotion to another very rapidly. For example, if a three or four years old child who is weeping loudly is given a toffee, he will become pleased at once.

*(ii)* Emotions of children are intense irrespective of the intensity of the stimulus. A very simple stimulus can create a very intense emotional experience.

*(iii)* Children are helpless to hide their emotions and they express them by different activities like crying, throwing objects, nail biting, bullying, thumb sucking and speech difficulties. Emotions of hope, disappointment, fear, anxiety, shame, jealousy, hatred etc. are expressed during this period in different ways.

*(iv)* He is still guided by his innate tendencies and instincts.

*(v)* His moral behaviour is also guided by his emotions-pleasure and pain.

*(vi)* Emotions of submission and elation are alternately seen in the child.

*(vii)* At the age of five his emotions begin to organize into sentiment. The most primitive sentiment is his love for his own self and his love for his toys. Due to this reason, this stage is also called "Narcissism autoerotism" or self love. This word **narcissism** has been derived from Greek language which means falling in love with one self.

*(viii)* The child also develops a deep sentiment of affection for his parents. At the age of 6-7 it is very painful for the child to see his/her father or mother ailing. Here Freud is of the opinion

that girl is very much attached to her father and boy feels more attachment to his mother. Former is called Elektra complex and later is called Oedipus complex.

(ix) The child begins to show "moodiness" expressed in sulking and bad emotions at the age of four. This emotion reaches to its peak during the period of adolescence.

(x) Most of the emotional responses are learned by children by imitating parents and other family members. Thus, emotions are innate but emotional responses are innate and learnt both.

## Educational Implications of the Period of Early Childhood

Early childhood is basically a pre-school period. The formal education of the child begins when he attains the age of five so, sixth year of life of the child is very important from point of view of educating the child. Since success of education of this period will depend on the pre-school education, so, the whole period from 3-6 becomes very important. Following strategies must be adopted by the school to develop the child educationally.

(i) The teacher in the school should first see whether the child has proper physical and motor development. Regular medical and health check up programme should be organized in the school for this purpose.

(ii) Parents should also be consulted if teacher finds some problem in the physical or motor development of the child.

(iii) It is the teacher who will first notice the physical or motor problems of the child. Hence, he should know the norms of physical and social development of children. On the basis of his very report, the child will be sent to the doctor for further diagnosis and investigation.

(iv) Various types of games and play activities should be organized in the school according to the age of children and they should be motivated to participate in those activities.

(v) The child is very active physically during this period. He mostly takes part in those activities, which involve muscular movement. Seeing this, he should be given rich diet to eat. If child is not getting proper nutrition, he will not gain height or weight properly.

(vi) This is a period of taking shift from dependence to self help, so child should be given more and more freedom to do in whatever manner he likes and to manipulate his environment in his own way.

(vii) This is a period of rapid intellectual growth. Hence, he should be sent to pre-primary school for learning through plays.

(viii) He should also be taught religious and moral principles so that he may become an acceptable member of the society.

(ix) He should be given freedom to manipulate objects so that he may develop his creative potentials.

(x) The teacher should narrate the stories of animals before such children. It will develop their vocabulary and imaginative power.

(xi) The child can concentrate for a longer period. Hence, the teacher can teach him any thing systematically. Even mathematics can be taught to him because he can understand symbols.

(xii) Efforts should be made to increase the vocabulary of the child as much as possible so that he can verbalize all the concepts that he knows.

(xiii) In order to save the child from frustration, he should not be interfered by the adults or parents.

(xiv) The child can increase his vocabulary mostly by hearing, so, he should be talked more and more. Better environment created at home means better language development.

(xv) Group activities are most suitable for such children. They should be given chance to get involve in such activities. Through these activities they would learn competition, cooperation, sympathy and the like feeling.

(xvi) The child seeks approval of adults. Adults should not be miserly in giving such approvals. They should rather love him.

(xvii) Girls and boys can be educated in a co-setting. This arrangement will create no administrative problem.

(xviii) If the child disobeys the parents they should not mind it. It is a natural phenomenon and will come down in the later childhood.

(xix) Girls should be preferred to be given the role of group leaders.

*(xx)* A teacher can control intense emotions of the child by his loving behaviour.

*(xxi)* Since children of this age can not hide their emotions, it is very easier for the teacher to deal these children effectively.

*(xxii)* Early childhood is a period in which the child can be emotionally attached to any body who loves him. The emotional attachment with parents may be generalized and extended to teachers in the school. A teacher can exploit this tendency and get the students involved in so many types of tasks.

**(C) Later childhood and development :**

This is the period between the age of 6-12 years. At the end of this period, puberty symptoms begin to grow and the period of adolescence starts. This period is marked by **pseudo maturity** and excellence in different fields. As far as sexual maturity is concerned, it remains completely dormant during this period, but this sex emerges with a great force at the end of this period. Because of the dormant nature of sex, this stage is also called **latency period**. Various dimensions of development during this period are given below.

**1. Physical development :**

*(i)* Steady and slow but uniform growth in the external as well as internal organs are seen.

*(ii)* Milk teeth are replaced by permanent set.

*(iii)* Auscification of bones takes place due to increase in height and weight.

*(iv)* Refinement in motor skills are seen.

*(v)* The child is physically restless during this period. He finds himself engaged in one activity or the other.

*(vi)* The brain acquires the size of an adult.

*(vii)* It is the period of best health of the individual during his whole life. During this period children never get tired. They burn their calories in physical activities and eat to the maximum level possible.

*(viii)* Girls are ahead of boys by two years in height and weight physiologically. Girls at the age of 11 are ahead of boys by at least one year.

*(ix)* Shedding of milk teeth and growth of permanent teeth change the shape of mouth, like flattening of forehead, sharpening nose and broadening of the chest.

*(x)* Important physical characteristics of this period are increased manual dexterity, high muscular strength, increased resistance to fatigue, increased endurance for play activities and so on.

**2. Intellectual development :**

*(i)* The child develops the powers of observation, reasoning and abstract thinking.

*(ii)* He can accumulate huge amount of knowledge in his mind. He can derive information and pleasure from books.

*(iii)* His perceptual ability, memory, and application of mental powers become keener.

*(iv)* The IQ of the child becomes stable and determines his IQ level in future. In short, it is a period of intellectual maturity.

*(v)* Boys love adventure and fairy tales and girls love mild form of romance and biographies.

*(vi)* The child begins to admire things and people around him and he begins to imitate the behaviour of those people who he likes.

*(vii)* The child begins to make clear distinction between himself and the outer world. He starts working on reality principles according to Freud.

*(viii)* The concept of natural laws becomes fully developed at the end of this period.

*(ix)* Capacity of logical thinking and power of reasoning increases.

*(x)* Interest in science fictions and stories reaches at its peak by the end of later childhood.

*(xi)* Courage and loyalty both increase simultaneously.

*(xii)* The child starts day dreaming and he defeats his rivals in his imaginative plays.

*(xiii)* The early imaginary fears are disappeared by the end of 12 years.

*(xiv)* When a child attains the age of ten, he shows high ability of generalization.

*(xv)* Children of this age are concerned with immediate cause and effect relationship and current happening. They live in the realm of present and don't care for future.

*(xvi)* The child begins to understand conceptual problem very well. He can analyse it and can give suggestions for its solutions.

(xvii) The physical growth is slow and steady during this period but intellectual growth and the functioning of mind are very rapid during this period.

(xviii) The child develops clear concepts of length, breath, time and distance.

**3. Sexual development :**

(i) From this angle this stage of the child is called latency period. Generally sexual energy at this age remains dormant but it becomes very active immediately after the age of 12 years.

(ii) Indifferent and antagonistic attitude towards the opposite sex are seen by the age of 10-11. As a result of this attitude, boys do not like to mix up with girls and girls are antagonistic to mix up with boys. Due to this reason upper primary education (from VIth –VIIIth ) in co educational setting is not suited in school.

**4. Emotional development :**

(i) Rapid shift from one type of emotion to another is not seen and the child learns how to control his emotions in a variety of social situations. For example, he avoids weeping in the company of his friends.

(ii) Emotional responses of the child become less diffused and undifferentiated, ie, intensity of emotions is reduced.

(iii) Emotions are expressed even in the absence of concrete materials.

(iv) Fear of animals, ghosts, loneliness and high place that was found in the early childhood, no longer persists in the later childhood.

(v) Certain new fear appear during this stage like fear of failing in the attempt such as games examinations, etc, fear of supernatural objects, such as heaven or hell etc and fear of being ridiculed etc.

(vi) The child gets angry if he is thwarted, teased or prejudiced. If he is compared with other children wrongly, he is interfered in his activities or he is ridiculed by elders, all these things will make the child angry.

(vii) If child thinks that some other children are being favoured by elders, he again gets angry. He becomes jealous of those children who are favoured. Emotion of jealousy is found in girls more than in boys.

(viii) All emotions like joy, love, curiosity, grief and affection appear during this stage in a stable manner. The child can hide his emotions. He expresses only those emotions which are approved socially.

(ix) Emotions are structured into sentiments. Various types of sentiments like religious, moral, patriotic and aesthetic sentiments develop during this period.

(x) Complex of superiority develops during this period. Boys consider themselves superior to girls.

**5. Social development :**

(i) He loves to play in groups and shares his toys with other children. Team spirit and group loyalties are commonly seen in such children in a more matured form.

(ii) Social horizon of the child increases to neighbourhood and school and he looses the shackles of his family ties. He becomes independent of his parents and does many things against their wishes.

(iii) He wants to become hero or leader in the group in the same way as we see in the period of early childrenhood.

(iv) He cares himself more than others. His self centred behaviour sometimes gives rise to rivalries and aggression.

(v) He accepts social norms. He feels pride to be ruled by public opinions. He is so much attached with his group that he can defy even the orders of his parents if they do not match with the norms of the group to which the child belongs. This tendency in children continues upto the age of 17-18.

(vi) Social development of the child mostly takes place in the play ground. The child mostly takes interest in those games which require stiff competition like football, hockey, kabaddi and kho kho.

(vii) Girls mostly prefer indoor games but if they are exposed to outdoor games they enjoy more than boys. Badminton, tennis and skipping are their favorite games.

(viii) When something wrong happens, boys indulge into physical combat and girls into verbal fights or pulling each others hairs. The behaviour of the child is largely influenced by the group to which child belongs.

*(ix)* The age from 10-12 is referred to gang age when children take much interest in gang activities and adhere to gang loyalties. That is why we see that every child in the age group of 10-12 necessarily joins a group and follows its rules and regulations strictly.

*(x)* Sex differentiation becomes sharp,i.e., girls play with girls only. The child does not like to play with girls during this period. He accepts only those girls in his group which are very energetic and courageous.

*(xi)* It is the period of peak unruliness in schools and homes especially when child is thwarted by his peers and relatives. Here, the child rejects many of the standards set by the adults or his family members and tries to live an independent life in his own circle.

*(xii)* Some delinquent acts like bullying, stealing, gang activities etc begin at the end of this period.

*(xiii)* Boys are more rebellion than girls and their groups or gangs are more organized than girls.

*(xiv)* Because of the excess involvement of boys and girls in their respective groups, this period is particularly known as gang age period.

**6. Moral development:**

*(i)* When the child attains the age of six, his capacity to understand relationship increases. He accepts lawful and unlawful social matters, though his concept of right and wrong may be different from his peers.

*(ii)* At the age of 8 he moves from specific response to generalized response and thus his concepts become more generalized. For example, he comes to realize that stealing of any thing is bad whether it be the matter of money or books.

*(iii)* During the period of later childhood morality is defined as performing good acts and maintaining the conventional social order. Children of this age are not deficient of this respect in any way.

*(iv)* At the age of 11-12, moral behaviour is oriented towards authority and maintaining the status quo which is considered to be a primary value. When the child changes his group loyalties, moral values may also change. It is because their conduct is mostly governed by the mores of his group.

*(v)* The development of right and wrong concepts begins at home in the period of early childhood, but it actually matures in the group. That is why we see that the child may float the authority of his parents but he may not go against the wishes of his gang. Such moral behaviour is dangerous only when the group is not following social and moral norms properly.

## Educational Implications of the Period of Later Childhood

*(i)* Suitable freedom should be given to children to develop physically, emotionally and intellectually.

*(ii)* These children like games, sports and group activities very much. School should organize such activities and should make them an indispensable part of the curriculum.

*(iii)* A teacher should not try to compare boys with girls. It is because girls feel themselves superior to boys and vice versa. If a teacher does not follow this maxim, it will create hatred for girls in the minds of boys.

*(iv)* Most of the lessons should be taught to children of this age through group activities.

*(v)* A teacher must be democratic in dealing such children. If anything is imposed on them irrationally, they will not follow it.

*(vi)* It is also necessary for the teacher to express faith in such children. He should not suspect the integrity and honesty of these children without reason.

*(vii)* Many desirable behaviours come to light during this period. Such behaviours should be reinforced regularly.

*(viii)* Children should be allowed to go to neighbourhood to learn community experiences. Remember that only school experiences are not enough.

*(ix)* The parents should not take the gang activities of their sons and daughters with anger. The only thing that is needed is that the gang should be good in behaviour.

*(x)* Certain hobbies are developed during this period. They should be encouraged by teachers and parents.

*(xi)* Interest and liking of boys and girls differ. Hence, they should be assigned different types of works according to their liking.

*(xii)* Children should be motivated to take rich diet in order to develop their muscles and bones.

*(xiii)* Child is never at rest during this period. So, a teacher should always get them involve in certain activities—physical or mental. If child is free, he may be destructive and problematic for the family.

*(xiv)* If a teacher knows the norm of physical growth of these boys and girls, he can guide them accordingly in the class. If the child is not growing on a satisfactory line, the teacher can report to the parents of the child.

*(xv)* If a teacher is successful in developing reading habits as a part of their routine activity in students, they can accumulate huge amount of information and knowledge.

*(xvi)* The teacher should take the child to the laboratory for observation and experimentation. Lab work must start at the age of 12.

*(xvii)* Children of this age should be taught stories full of adventure and romance.

*(xviii)* The tendency of hero worshiping in such children should be exploited by the teacher.

*(xix)* Power of reasoning of the child should be utilized in understanding religion and mythology.

*(xx)* Parents should not forbid the child from doing a particular thing in a straight forward manner. They should give reason to the child why it should not be done.

*(xxi)* The child should be given chance to generalize laws and principles as mush as possible.

*(xxii)* Children of this age do not care much for their tomorrow. Hence, whatever good is done by them should be reinforced immediately.

*(xxiii)* At the age of ten, girls do not like to mix up with boys and vice versa. So, a teacher should guide them separately and co-education at the junior level is not recommended at all.

*(xxiv)* Children can hide any of their emotions at this age. So, a teacher should not study them in hurry and draw conclusion about the child.

*(xxv)* The behaviour of the teacher should be completely unbiased. He should not discriminate any child on any ground. Biased attitude and discrimination make the child angry.

*(xxvi)* The child should be given opportunity to lead at least one group in any curricular or co-curricular activities.

*(xxvii)* Religious and moral educations should properly begin at this stage.

*(xxviii)* Gang activities of children should not be discouraged by the teacher. Such activities are essential for self expression and exposure.

**(D) Adolescence and Development (13-17 years):** The economic and military growth of a country depends on how its young lots have been guided in the school and the society. Whatever inventions and discoveries are made in any country, their seeds are soon in this very period. In fact adolescence is the foundation of a responsible social life. It is the spring of life for the individual.

**1. Meaning of adolescence:** The word adolescence has been derived from Greek word "Adolescere" meaning to grow to maturity. Thus an important feature of adolescence is maturation in emotions, physique, intellect and social behaviour. A lot of changes take place during this transitional period and the man enters into a responsible age.

**Dorthy Rogers** defines adolescence as "a process rather than a period, a process of achieving the attitudes and beliefs needed for effective participation in the society.

**2. Characteristics of adolescence :** The period of adolescence is marked by the following important characteristics:

1. Many of the features of infancy are repeated during this period and the boy gets maturity at the end of this period.
2. This is a period of great stress and strain because a few new instincts and emotions emerge and disturb the personality of adolescent.

3. An attitude of dependence is again seen. The dependence, however, is not on parents but on friends. The criticism of friends, is specially resented. His mingling with his peers increases his feelings of belongingness and to win approval.
4. As regards imaginative activity and Hero-worship, fairy tales get replaced by novels of adventure, travels, history, and other literature. A flash cinema star becomes the Hero that the adult worships. Teachers are liable to be exalted into the position of Hero. Adolescent Hero worship may result in the sentiments of love for the moral qualities of his hero.
5. Gregarious impulses are sublimated into definite form of social behaviour. These altruistic impulses and heart burning desire of the adolescent should be directed by the teacher into fruitful channels.
6. Adolescent is unstable and unadjusted with the surrounding world.
7. At this stage self assertion is stronger. He wants to free himself from bondage of all adult restrains.
8. There is exuberance of imagination. He is intensely self centred and introvert withdrawing himself from the word.
9. Sex instinct is the most prominent feature of the period. It is "Like the over-flow of a great river". So the moral character is chaotic and sublimation is required for the instinct.
10. Intellectual development is reaching its maximum.
11. It is in this stage that scientific, philosophical, humanistic interest begin to shape. Poetry, science and critical thought monopolies the adolescent mind and there are vague doubts and questions in his or her mind about the constitution of the universe and society.
12. There is crystallization of special mental abilities during adolescence.
13. Problems of vocational choice and vocational placement begin to worry the adolescent.
14. Habitual disobedience to parents and elders is a keen desire for self-expression and self-improvement.

## 3. Significance of Studying the Period:

This period is marked with so much complexities and problems that every parent and the teacher must know the minutest detail of this period. The study of adolescence period will help the teachers and parents in the following ways.

1. *Understanding the unique problems of adolescents:* The problems of adolescents are very unique and this is due to lots of changes that take place during this period. The teachers and parents must know these things and their casual factors so that adolescent may be guided educationally, vocationally and socially.
2. *Up keeping the mental and physical health of the boy:* If unique problems of adolescents are not dealt with effectively, they will suffer from many mental and physical diseases. If parents and teachers know how to deal with such problems, they can care and prevent incidence of maladjustment.
3. *Handing responsibilities to adults:* Individuals have to take all the social and familial responsibilities after this age. The teachers and parents must know how to shift responsibilities on their shoulders.
4. *Understanding special needs of adolescence :* This period is marked by very special needs of young boys which is not generally seen before or after the period of adolescence. Teachers and parents must be aware of these needs in order to pave the way for the fulfillment of these needs.
5. *For fulfilling the curiosity of oneself :* The study of psychology of adolescents may be a desire to know something about oneself that is related to his past. If teachers and parents know how they were in the past and how helpless they were in adolescence to control themselves, they will not punish the young boys for their unruly and bullying behaviour.

## 4. Views and theories on adolescence

1. *Rousseau :*
   I. He described the period from 2-12 years as "savage period" when individual works on animal level. There is lack of reasoning and sound judgment in his actions.
   II. From 12-15 years of age the adolescent is able to live almost self dependent life. He gains physical strength to a great extent and shows his personal strength in all his activities.

III. A 15-16 years of age is marked by sex awakening and its uses. The adolescent begins to play new roles in his life. He thinks that he is something so he must be cared by someone.

2. *Stanley Hall :* He was the first psychologist who devoted his time in collecting data on needs and problems of adolescents. Thus, systematic and scientific study of the period of adolescence started with the beginning of the 20th century by this U S psychologist. In order to collect information about adolescents, he not only observed them but analysed the self expression of children through essays written by them and directed interviews.

According to him adolescence is closely related to the period of later childhood. His views on adolescence can best be understood by the following views that he has expressed on the period of later childhood and its likeness with the period of adolescence.

"The years from 8 to 12 constitute the unique period of human life. Height and weight are at their full-Health is at its best. Activity is greater than even before. The child develops his own circle out of home. He develops peculiar endurance and resistance to fatigue. There is greater immunity to exposure, danger and accident. The development is salutatory. It is a period of storm and stress. Important functions previously non existent arise. Every step of the upward way is strewn with wreckage of body, mind and morals. Sex asserts its mastery in field after field and works its havoc in the form of secret vices. The social instincts undergo sudden enfoldment and the new life of love awaken everything is plastic. Character and personality take form. Self feeling and ambitions are increased. It is all marvelous new birth."

Hall's views can, however, be criticized on the following grounds.

I. Hall did not take into consideration the social relationship between adolescents and social environment.

II. He did not take into consideration the individual differences of adolescents. Individuals who deviate from the average in any side have not been touched by Hall.

III. Methods used by him for data collection are not correct. He did not use standardized tools for collecting data as they did not exist at that time.

IV. Hall believed that acquired characteristics of the individual are genetically transmitted to the next generation. This belief is not scientifically proved.

3. *Hollingworth :* Her views are entirely different from Hall. According to her, changes in adolescence is not rapid and sudden. It is a continuous and steady process that does not differ from other periods. Due to this reason it is very difficult to draw a line of demarcation between later childhood and adolescence.

Studies conducted by Ruth Benedict and Margaret Mead concluded that adolescence is a period of normal growth not a period of stress and strain as reported by Hall. Hollingworth is also of the view that stress and strain are caused by cultural factors and socio-economic conflicts prevailing in the society.

4. *Sigmund Freud :* He concentrated more on sexual development that is responsible for all types of development. He does not agree with Hall who says that sexual impulses take birth in adolescence. According to him such instincts exist even at birth. His theory of psycho-sexual development from infancy to adolescence has been given in a tabular form below:

| AGE | STATE | SOURCE OF PLEASURE | TRAITS |
|---|---|---|---|
| First to 18 month | Oral | Mouth, sucking, eating, chewing. | Envy optimism, pessimism. |
| 18 months to 3½ years | Anal toilet training, | Anus, retention, expulsion, control, destruction, messiness, | Stinginess, obstinacy, cruelty |
| 3 to 5 years | Phallic Oedipal | Genital organs, curiosity about self. | Relatedness with others, self-regard, chastity, Gregariousness |
| 6 to 12 years | Latency | Sensory motor, pleasure from knowledge, skills, peer group interaction | Differentiation, social learning |
| Puberty | Genital | Hetero sexual contacts and productiveness | Harmonious blending of pre genital traits. |

## Dimensions of development and adolescence:

**(A) Physical development:** Physical development of the boy is marked by the following characteristics-

1. *Change in height and weight :* Almost all adolescents have spurts of growth. Due to this spurt sudden increase in height is seen among them. This growth in height is associated with pubertal growth ranging from 13 to 17 years of age. Thus some boys and girls show rapid increase in height and weight at 13-14 and some of them come across this stage at the age of 15-16.
   Sex difference is also seen in this characteristics. At the age of 13, girls are taller and heavier than boys but at the age of 15-16 boys are definitely taller and heavier than girls. Both of them however, attain their maximum height at the age of 17-18.
2. *Auscification of bones and formation of muscles:* Bones and muscles both become very strong during this period. The bones no longer remain delicate. They rather become broad and rigid. Muscles of boys also become rigid and strong but muscles of girls still remain soft and delicate.
3. *Changes in body proportions :* Different parts of the body grow at different speeds during this period in order to give a good shape to the human body. For example, pelvis bones of girls become broadened and their wrist become round. Thighs and hips of girls become fat and shoulders of boys become round. The shape of the face also changes and it does not look as big as it was in infancy.
4. *Change in voice :* Clear change in voice of boys and girls is seen during this period and it no longer remains, childish. The voice of boys become hoarse and girls voice become sweeter than ever
5. *Changes in sexual characteristics :* Secondary sex characteristics develop in adolescence. Genital organs in boys including pennis increase in size. Sexual organs of girls like vagina, pelvis, breast etc. also attain full maturity. Marked changes in her gait is also seen and she becomes aware of these changes.
6. *Growth of hair :* Hair growth is also associated with puberty. In case of boys hairs appear on upper limbs and beard. Pubic hair and hair in arms pits appear in both boys and girls at the age of 13-14. Boys have hair on legs, arms, thighs nose, ears and on almost all parts of the body.
7. *Change in internal organs :* All systems of humans such as respiratory, circulatory, digestive, blood pressure, heart beat, pulse rate etc acquire their full growth. Brain is also fully developed upto the age of 18.
8. *Starting of night emissions and menstruation:* Average age of menstruation for girls and night fall for boys is 13-16. It has however, been found that girls and boys of tropical and sub tropical regions mature earlier than cold regions. Sexual feeling among boys and girls start arousing at the age of 13-14. These sex related changes bring about many complexities among boys and girls both. But one thing is clear that girls mature earlier than boys in sexual characteristics.
9. *Growth trend in .notor performance :* Boys are better than girls in showing their performance in running, throwing and jumping. Boys are superior to girls in general in all those activities which involve speed and muscular strength. On the other hand, girls are superior to boys in those activities which are associated with beauty and cleanliness. The importance of physical and muscular strength is given more importance in an aggressive culture than in a sophisticated white culture.
10. *Sex differentiation and power of reproduction:* Clear cut sex differentiation and the development of the powers of reproducing the offspring are the end point of physical development of adolescents. Habit of masturbation also develop in boys during this period. But the development of this habit depends on the exposure of the adolescents to such an environment at particular age.
    Suffice it to say that physical development contributes a lot to social, emotional or mental development. If physical development is delayed, all other types of development is retarded. For example, if a girl is ugly and under developed, she avoids, social situations and thus social development is delayed. Similarly, if a boy or girl is handicapped physically, his mental development will be hampered.

**(B) Mental development :** Mental development of adolescents is marked by the following characteristics :

1. *Increased ability to generalize facts and principles:* Intellectual development in childhood mostly operates on perceptual level but in adolescence it operates on conceptual level. The adolescents can generalize concepts and laws very easily here due to a shift from concrete to abstract thinking.
2. *Increased ability of comprehension :* The understanding level of adolescents is so developed that he can solve complex problems, he can see new relationship between abstract concepts, he can distinguish the positive and negative aspects of a thing and so on.
3. *Increased power of imagination :* Many writers and poets who attain greatness in their later age begin their work in adolescence. High imaginative power can take the adolescents to an unknown world which brings out many imaginative ideas later on.
4. *Development of memory :* Upto the age of 15 the memory of the adolescents is highly developed. Not only his word power increases but he can retain any learnt material for a longer period of time.
5. *Increased power of concentration :* Adolescents can concentrate for a longer period of time on academic and non academic topics. They can be taught in the school for hours and they will not lose attention. They can discuss any topic of their interest for hours.
6. *Hero worshiping :* During this period adolescents are bent toward hero worshipping. These heroes can be the father of the adolescent, the political leaders, film actors and actresses, well known scientists, teachers etc. Adolescents identify themselves with their selected heroes and imitate them.
7. *Decision making power :* The adolescents have to take many decisions in their lives. During this period. They can take quick decision of what to do and what not to do but most of the time their decisions are dominated and overpowered by emotions as a result, their decisions become wrong.
8. *Independent thinking :* Adolescents do not like all the time to be guided and dictated by others. He likes to use his independent thinking in his action. He does not like something to be imposed by others but he prefers his own judgement on matters of controversy. The adolescents have the ability to think independently about their future.
9. *Understanding of moral concepts :* The child without questioning the moral codes obeys them at the wishes of his parents and teachers. But when he enters the age of adolescence, he does not like to follow these principles like a mute. He critically examines these moral codes and asks a number of questions regarding their validity. In this way he is able to differentiate what is good or bad for him
10. *Development of Interests :* Various interests develop in the adolescents. In their interest, recreational interests, social interests, individual interests, vocational interests, religious interests and sexual interest are included. If these interests are not cared for, it can affect the personality of the adolescents.

    One fact to be kept in mind is that out of so many interests given above every adolescent takes special interest in one or two field. This special field of interest must be known by parents and teachers both.

**(C) Emotional development :** The significance of emotions is that they control our behaviour. Emotion in the organism is a dynamic internal adjustment that operates for the welfare and satisfaction of the individual. The adolescence is marked by heightened and uncontrolled emotionality. History is full of many heroic deeds of these adolescents which were done by them under the impact of emotions.

According to **McDougall**, "Emotional development is caused by the basic instincts. The core of emotions are feelings, which get intensified," As a result of these feelings, emotions develop and this is known as emotional development. There are such emotions which are useful for a person and the society. We call them positive emotions such as affection, creativity, happiness etc. Those emotions which are not useful for a person or society are called negative emotions such as anger, fear, jealousy and displeasure.

**Causes of heightened emotionality are many. Some of these causes are given below:**

*(i)* When a child enters the age of adolescence, from home to neighbourhood and schools his social roles and responsibilities increase. He has to adjust to every new situation every moment. This frequent change over of pattern of habits creates emotional tensions in adolescents. His shift from total dependent life to semi independent life in the society makes him disturbed.

*(ii)* If parents are not preparing adolescents to face the real challenges of life, emotionality of adolescents will be heightened. Similarly, if parents treat their sons/daughters in a very strict and harsh manner from the very beginning, the adolescents become rebellion against their parents. They not only quarrel with their parents but with other persons in the society and at home also.

*(iii)* If genuine economic, recreational and social demands of adolescents are not fulfilled by concerned people, the adolescents become hostile to the whole system.

*(iv)* If adolescent is not given lift by members of opposite sex in the family, he/she will not be able to face such situations even outside the family.

*(v)* When a child enters into the gate of adolescence, he is immediately expected by elders and parents to act and behave like an adult for which the child is not intellectually prepared. As a result of this the child internally fights for his real social status and role. This creates emotional conflicts in him and he fails to adjust to the environment.

*(vi)* At the start of adolescence age the attraction for opposite sex is seen but the adolescents do not know how to make friendship with the members of opposite sex and how to maintain it. This tendency creates emotional tensions in adolescents.

*(vii)* Every child is brought up in a particular religious and cultural environment but when he becomes an adolescent, he starts questioning the validity of such beliefs and actions. Most of the time his mind goes against religious injunctions and thus a conflict between id and ego is seen. This is also responsible for heightened emotionality.

*(viii)* Castism and communalism are also rampant in Indian society. Adolescents are very much sensitive to such feelings of hatred and partiality. They want justice in the society which is very rarely found.

*(ix)* Many adolescents fail in the school due to various reasons and repeated failure in a particular class may lead them to even commit suicide.

*(x)* Adolescents at the age of 15-16 begin to think about their future and career. They begin to think what they will do after school. If the adolescent has not got admission in a good professional course, he will be in the state of constant and persistent anxiety which will force him to behave under the stress of emotions.

## Emotional Development of Adolescence is Marked by the Following Characteristics:

1. *Complexity :* In adolescence, the emotional development is very complex composed of many emotions at a time. We can not understand the emotions of an adolescent by his overt behaviour. We will rather have to fathom deep to understand him.
2. *Emotional reactions to abstract :* Children express their emotions to only concrete objects but adolescents can show their emotional expressions to abstract things also thus their emotions are linked with intelligence.
3. *Expanded emotions :* Emotional feelings are expanded in adolescence. The boy gets pleasure not only what he has at present but he gets pleasure from future expectations also. Similarly, the social circle of the boy becomes widened during the period of adolescence. It also increases the scope of emotional expressions.
4. *Intense emotions :* The adolescent stage is the stage of emotional revolution. At this stage many ups and downs occur in the adolescents with regard to emotions. These ups and downs in the adolescents are due to their physical, sexual and emotional changes. During this period their

emotions are so intense that the adolescents can do any activity under the effect of these emotions. If an adolescent loves any body, he or she shows immense love for that individual. Similarly, if he or she has hatred for someone, he or she will exhibit hate for the individual. In short during this period, emotions reach their top.

5. *Uncontrolled Emotions :* The emotions during this period are not under their control. Tensions and anxiety persist among them. There may be various reasons for them. They are emotionally unstable.
6. *Variations in Emotions :* There are distinct fluctuations in the emotions during adolescent period. The adolescents are happy at one moment and become depressed at the other moment. Their mental stage does not remain the same at all times.
7. *Sharing of emotional experience :* The adolescents for the first time come to understand the emotional feelings of others as a result, he can very easily share his emotional experiences with others. This sharing of emotions reaches at its peak when adolescents begin to live for others such as he develops the emotion of patriotism or he falls in love with any girl or he happens to find a good friend in life.
8. *Emotions of the real cause :* Before the beginning of adolescence the child was living in the world of utopia or fantasy. Now he enters into real world. He can very well perceive and appreciate people around him and he is expected to show only those emotions which are real.
9. *Self centred tendency :* Adolescent many times likes to be alone free from all types of disturbances. In such a state of mind he gets pleasure by thinking about that friend who he wants to love. Day dreaming is at its peak during this period.
10. *His emotions can be exploited :* Emotions of adolescents are uncontrolled and intense. Due to this reason, clever people can arouse their emotions very easily and thus a simpleton can be changed into a terrorist just by exploiting his emotions.

## Pattern of Various Emotions in Adolescence:

During this period all emotions get maturity and perfection. The two channels of emotions delight and distress of infancy period get differentiated into a number of emotions. Some of these emotions and their pattern are given below.

I. *Love and affection :* Emotion of love is the result of physiological disturbances caused due to the spurt of puberty and sex. In infancy the emotion of love and affection is directed to animal and inanimate objects and people both but in adolescence, this love is restricted to people only and sometimes it is also directed to the country. It is called patriotism .

Adolescence love is a source of pleasure because it is mostly sexual in nature. During this period, the circle of close relationship of adolescents narrows down and they become closely attached with one another. Association made during this period are lasting and sometimes permanent. Affection for friends is very strong and affection of parents and relatives is very weak during this period. A boy can prefer his girl friend to her mother.

II. *Pleasure and delight :* During adolescence physical health, body structure and physique are permanent sources of joy and pleasure for the adolescerts.

The second situation which calls forth joy is the release of pent up energy. That is why an adolescent gets maximum pleasure in his play field where his pent up energy is released.

Feeling of superiority is the third cause of happiness in adolescents. If an adolescent is very brilliant in his studies or he stands first in any contest, or he is very smart or he is in the state of good health, all these things develop superiority complex in him and he gets delighted.

III. *Feeling of sexuality:* At this stage feeling of homosexuality and heterosexuality develops. In the beginning of this stage the males and females establish relationship with each other and are attractive towards each other. This is called hetero-sexuality. At this age boys and girls try to attract each other by using various methods. This includes the make up of girls too. The boys observe themselves in front of mirror.

If society is orthodox and rigid in thinking and it is not possible to develop hetero-sexual relations, the adolescents come to develop homo-sexual relations. The reason is that it is safer for them to have such relations and society will not object it.

*IV. Worry and anxiety :* Worry is an imaginary fear. It is caused by the repeated rehearsal of the situation feared. If level of this imaginary fear is more it may be termed as anxiety.

Moderate level of anxiety is a must for all successes in life but if level of worry is mild or very low, it will not motivate the person for action and high level of anxiety is frustrating all the time. Worries are generally related to school work or failure in the examination or not achieving success in life according to the anticipation. Only that person can take some responsibility in his life who has some sorts of anxiety.

*V. Fear :* It is an important negative emotion during adolescence. Important fear causing stimuli are as follows—

- fear of material objects like snakes, dogs, wolf, strange noise, ghost, lion etc. Now adolescents do not fear elephants, aeroplane, rockets etc.
- fear of social situations like meeting with people in high offices, fear in the company of strict people, being lonely in the house, sitting at the corner of a high place, facing the audience in recitation or speech, meeting and talking the members of opposite sex, doing any illegal work etc.

The important point here is that most of these fears decrease with the advancing age and an adolescent may be fearless and bold person at the age of 18. It has, however been seen that children of cowardice parents are generally cowardice throughout life. Probably, this emotion can not be eliminated by training. Cowardice or courage is genetically determined emotion.

*VI. Anger :* It is a learned response to environment when antagonism is seen between the individual and the environment **Hebb** wrote about the nature and source of fear and anger in the following words.

"Fight and aggression are two different modes of reaction tending to restore the dynamic equilibrium or stability of cerebral process ........... each of these modes of response tends to restore integrated cerebral action."

### Important Anger Arousing Situations are As Follows:

- Not getting any material object according to the desire and effort
- Prejudice shown by the people resulting in loss of property or status.
- Teasing by elders, step mother, parents, teachers and peers.
- Unfair and insulting treatment by the people.
- Sarcastic remarks, encroachment of rights by brothers, sisters and rivals.
- Thwarting of self assertion, insulting remarks, unwelcome suggestions, not being invited by a so called friend.
- Repeated interference by parents and elders and not allowing the adolescents to go anywhere.

One point to be noted is that anger should be there on legitimate matters but it should be shown only in controlled manner. If anger is used in an uncontrolled way, it may be very damaging for the individual.

## EFFECTS OF EMOTIONS

Emotions is the other name of life. There is no excitement or enthusiasm in life without the development of proper emotions. These emotions can make or mar our career. Their effects on human personality are given below:

**(A) Good Effects :**

I. Emotions can motivate the organism for action. Love, fear, anxiety and curiosity all help us to reach the goal. For example, fear of failure in the examination can motivate the person to study hard, love for children and wife motivate the person to work harder and harder and so on.

II. Emotions are great source of enjoyment too. When we read novels or see movies, we are excited and overjoyed by the happenings.

III. Emotions must be brought up to maturity in order to maintain the self respect of the individual.

IV. Emotions give strength and endurance to our body. An individual can work an extra-ordinary work under the pressure of an emotion and he can not do that task in ordinary condition. For example, an individual can study 15 hours daily to qualify CPMT or IIT if such is the condition of marriage set by a girl. Even fatigue does not set in under the state of emotional excitement.

**(B) Bad Effects :** Uncontrolled emotions can cause the following damages to human bodies.

I. Constant emotional tensions and worries may cause sleepless night, headache, chronic fatigue, insomnia, lack of appetite, indigestion and many varieties of cancer.

II. Emotional tension affects the efficiency of an individual. It can develop unfavourable mood and inconsistency in behaviour.

III. It also affects reason, memory and intelligence. Forgetting increases in emotional state

IV. Constant emotional pressure disturbs learning ability due to poor rate of concentration and accumulation.

V. If we do anything in anger or in the state of over joy, that task is most likely to be disturbed.

VI. Negative emotional pressure for a very long period can mar the personality of an individual and may lead to neuroticism in the long run.

**(C) Social Development:** Several definition of social development are given here first.

1. "Social development means the attaining of maturity in social relationship".

***—Hurlock***

2. "Social development means acquisition of ability to behave in accordance with social expectation."

***—C.L.Kundu and D.N. Tutoo***

3. "By social development we mean increasing ability to get along well with oneself and others."

***—Sorenson***

The foundation of social development is laid by parents at home which starts from socialization in a limited circle of people. But when the child reaches the age of adolescence, his range of social circle increases. The friends and types of peer groups the adolescent has joined shape his personality and social behaviour. The social development of adolescent is also determined by the place and status with which an individual is regarded in the society. For example, if a person is addressed by others by using abusive language all the time, he will avoid social situations to the maximum level possible and his social development will be retarded.

Social development of adolescents is marked by the following **characteristics**:

1. **Limited friend circle :** During this period the adolescents do not like to have so many friends. They select only one or two close friends and share their experience with them. The adolescent participates in all social situations with his friend and learns social skills there.
2. **Relationship with opposite sex :** In childhood, the boys play with boys and girls play with girls. But when he attains the age of adolescence, heterosexual trend in companionship is seen. The boys like to have the company of girls. They get intense pleasure in talking with girls. Kissing, hugging and fucking are also possible if opportunities are available
3. **Common interest groups :** Adolescent boys and girls form their groups based on their common interests and goals. These very common interests bring the adolescents of varied colour and physique together. Groups of boys are larger than girls because boys get more chance to move in the society freely than girls. If girls are also given freedom, their groups will be larger than boys as we see in cosmopolitan cities.
4. **Criteria of friendship :** Adolescents make friendship with those who conform to their standard and possess the personality traits they like. The number of close friends decreases with the increase in age but the affiliation gets stronger and deeper. The adolescents do not like to be interfered by their parents in selecting friends or age mates. The friendship of this period is generally permanent. If a girl is cheated by a boy in the matter of love, the girl can not forget this love throughout life.
5. **Interest in social situations :** Boys and girls very; much like to attend parties, celebrations, fairs and functions where girls expose themselves before boys and vice versa to the extent permission is there.

Besides, adolescent takes interest in talking of various topics. Social, religious and sexual talking plays a cathartic role for adolescence.

Adolescents take much interest in games and sports either as players or spectators and they learn cooperation, sympathy, adoption of rules and regulations and obedience etc, from field.

### Concept of development tasks and special needs of adolescents

When a child reaches the age of adolescence, he develops some special ends and objectives related to the need of that particular age. These ends are called developmental tasks. They are inescapable requirement imposed by the person himself or by the society. An adolescent must be competent to achieve these ends. Failure to achieve competency has a crippling effect on the personality development of the adolescent.

**Havighurst** proposed a system of development tasks for American adolescents. He described in detail the developmental process and its relation to educational objectives. Development task has been defined by Havighurst as a task which arises at or about a certain period in the life of the individual, successful achievement of which leads to his happiness and success with later tasks while failure leads to unhappiness in the individual, disapproval by the society and difficulty with later tasks."

From the above discussions we see that development tasks of adolescents are especially related to **the needs very specific to that particular age.** Such important needs are given below:

1. *Achieving matured social relations :* It is a must for the adolescent to achieve a well matured relationship with both the sexes. A masculine or feminine role that a child has to play is decided at this age. For this purpose he/she needs to learn many things from his/her peers. This learning is harnessed only when the relationship of the adolescent with different types of people are matured and stable
2. *Need for affection, social status and security :* A desire for social approval and social acceptability is universal in all adolescents. If a person is accepted by his friends, peers, teachers, relatives etc. at home, in the neighbourhood and in the school he experiences a great sense of self confidence and security. In order to fulfil this very type of need, they take part in elections or in sports and become captains, members, president, secretary, monitor, in charge of co-curricular activities etc.

   Desire for affection and love from parents, teachers and other responsible positioners of the society is found intense during this period. If such needs are not fulfilled, they get frustrated and sense of insecurity develops in them. There are many situations which tell us that they struggle for their social status and security and avoid being rejected by the people, such as fear of failure in the examination, fear of losing the sympathy of teachers, and parents, fear of being rejected in the society and at home etc. These fears may cause hostility, aggression, anxiety, anger, isolation, frustration and so on.

   Thus, love, affection, and social approval are necessary for the emotional security of the adolescents. If they are deprived of these human rights, they may face emotional problems which may further lead them to anti social and delinquent behaviour.
3. *Need for Independence :* You know that in the early years of life, the child is entirely dependent upon the parents and elders. When he reaches adolescence stage, he is physically, mentally and emotionally well developed and has gathered experiences of the world. Therefore, he thinks of getting freedom from the parents and other members of the society and develops a desire to lead the life in his own way. Some psychologists call this tendency **"psychological weaning"** of the adolescent, whereas others describe this as process of destalization. But both mean that at this stage of development, the adolescent students try to stand on their own feet, try to take their own decision, try to plan their future life independently and try to lead their life themselves. However, for emotional satisfaction of their need for love, affection and sympathy, they still need the support of parents and their elders surely.

The adolescents feel themselves capable of shouldering responsibility of the world. This is why they glamour for adult status to be granted to them by their society. But the society including teachers considers that still they are immature and need protection, directions and control. This state of affairs puts the adolescents in "No Man's land" where they feel that neither they belong to childhood nor to adulthood. This is why at this stage their development has been characterized by indecision, confusion, insecurity, uncertainty of status, fear of coming into class with their parents and elders, feeling of anxiety caused by many restrictions put on them and so on. If the situation is handled properly, this state may develop into various emotional problems.

4. *Participating in adventurous and risky tasks :* The desire for adventure is dominant in all the adolescents. Even cowardice people want at least to see such tasks or to read such stories. Adolescents like thrilling and risky activities, like climbing a tree, beating someone on the way to school, playing more risky shots in the play ground or visiting lonely and haunted places of the locality. These adolescents get satisfaction from such experiences. They accumulate such experiences for further narration and recall. Due to this reason all adolescents have been found reading detective or romantic stories, though excess involvement of adolescents in such activities is very harmful as far as other roles of life is concerned.
5. *Need for maintaining health and body building:* Almost all adolescents want to build their muscles and body. For this purpose, they do various types of exercise and consume highly nutritious food. They join various types of clubs for this purpose also. They also do some exercises for increasing their sexual power.
6. *Need for friendship with opposite sex:* Such type of needs are very strong in this age. Every boy wants the company of a girl and vice versa. If society is orthodox and it is not permissible to have such relations in the society, then homosexuality is adopted by adolescents which is safer for them.

Such needs are aroused due to basic changes taking place in the sex glands. This sex urge may find expression in many ways. They may read sex related stories, they may see nacked films or they may go through the habit of masturbation. If such sex urge is completely suppressed, it may cause serious emotional problems. Mental conflicts, guilty feeling, phobia, anxiety, etc may grow out of this stress. If we call all such sex urges and impulses as sinful and dirty, and suppress them to the maximum, it will retard the growth of the adolescents.

7. *Drug addiction :* This need is not universal in nature and it depends on the environment in which the child is reared. If there is a fashion of drugs, wine or any other types of alcoholic drinks in the society, the adolescents will adopt it. These drugs are also used to escape the real pains of life for the time being but consumption of all such items will lead to depression and paranoid symptoms.
8. *Adjustment of personal appearance:* Personal appearance is an important part of the adolescent's personality. They are concerned about their personal appearance. It influences their personal and social development and very often their social status in the group is determined by their personal appearance. A beautiful and charming face is the centre of affection of the whole group and this makes the adolescent more confident and more secure. Pleasing faces get more affection from their parents, teachers and other members of the society. Besides, persons of good appearance get more approval of the opposite sex. Whereas an unimpressive personal appearance or poor complexion causes a fear of being rejected by the group. No adolescent can tolerate such a situation. That is why they may resort to excessive attention to make up and clothes.
9. *Requirement due to physiological changes :* When a child becomes an adult, many physiological changes especially in the internal organs of the body and sexual organs take place and many of them can cause emotional problems too if not tackled properly. Similarly, if the growth of the adolescent is abnormal in any way,

it may also cause emotional stress and strain. The problem becomes more serious if the adolescent hides his defect. Thus, proper adjustment to these physiological changes is a must.

10. *Need for utilization of excess energy :* Adolescence is a period full of energy and activism. If this energy is not utilized in constructive works, he may take part in Dharna, strike or other forms of violent activities in the college campus. Most of the adolescents feel that they are living in a vacuum or helplessness. This feeling give rise to apathy or aggression towards the old people of the society. Indifferent attitude towards adolescents may also create sense of being oppressed and exploited. Since, adolescents are more idealistic than older people, so they can not tolerate injustice of any type. They can use demonstration and destruction both against the prejudices prevailing in the society.
11. *Need to form a set of values :* Adolescents need to form a set of values to establish good relations with parents, relatives, teachers, and friends. They have to be sympathetic and helpful to their friends. They have to be obedient and respectful with their teachers. Dealing with different people in different capacities differently is tough task which adolescents need to perform. Their behaviour should be so decent that everybody in the society is pleased with them. Failure to learn codes of life, observance of law and other social political and aesthetic norms etc. may pose serious problems of adjustment for these adolescents. If they are not properly adjusted in the society, they would not let the others sit peacefully either.
12. *Need for self support:* Adolescents happen to develop a desire to become independent of their parents. Now they want to be economically self supporting. Therefore, vocational planning comes to the fore front in their minds. In some adolescents vocational aims dominate almost their every thought and action. Uncertainty about getting jobs worries them. In some cases it develops a persistent emotional tension. Some of their emotional problems grow out of their inability to clearly see their vocational goals. In big cities adolescents constantly see growing competitions in the fields of employment. They feel frustrated and react to this situation emotionally. Some adolescents develop worries, anxieties and other emotional problems which may affect their academic programmes and social adjustment.

## Educational Implication of the Period of Adolescence

Keeping in view the peculiar needs of adolescents, their education will have to be moulded and modified in the following way.

1. *Education for proper physical and motor development :* Physical and motor development especially building of the body and formation of muscles is most needed during adolescence. So, proper exercise and suitable games and sports along with proper diet are recommended for them. But their particular interest must be taken into account while framing physical education curriculum for them
   According to medical science, if this stage is left unexercised, flabby constitution of the body for the rest of life is the result.
2. *Arrangement of picnics and excursions:* School should arrange tours and excursions for them to visit historical, geographical and research places and educational institutions. This will give them knowledge, increase their cultural horizon, release their pent up feeling and stresses and channelize their energy.
3. *Training of emotions :* Many negative emotions are injurious for them throughout their life. Even positive emotions are harmful if they are expressed in an uncontrolled manner. So, sublimation or training of these emotions are necessary through literature, art, music and dance. Discussion, debates, essay writing or speech competitions, participation in play or drama or seminars can also help them a lot. So, they should also be organized now and then by the school and the society.
4. *Sex education :* Sex urge is found strong and uncontrolled during the period of adolescence. If proper sex education is not given to them they may adopt many sex practices which are harmful for their life and morals, ie, masturbation,

homosexual relations, unsafe practice of intercourse with girls etc. So, such an education is a must for adolescents.

5. *Educational guidance :* All adolescents differ in their ability and interest. They are helped by the school to s elect subjects according to their mental level and interest. Vocational guidance is also given to them according to their paying capacity and need.
6. *Freedom with vigilance :* Adolescents are given freedom by parents and teachers to the maximum level possible but proper vigil is also made to see what they are doing. If their job is constructive, they are not interfered by the society.
7. *Organization of co-curricular activities :* In order to develop the adolescents physically, mentally, socially and emotionally in a proper manner, various types of co-curricular activities are also organized in the school. These activities will engage them most and they will not have time to destruct the society any way.
8. *Library attachment :* Adolescent should also be brought to the library to study books on various topics. Public libraries should also be established at various places for this purpose. These books will give them knowledge and entertainment.
9. *Democratic atmosphere :* School should maintain democratic environment. Due respect to the students should be given. Such type of co curricular activities be planned and executed which encourage cooperation, and brotherhood among adolescents. They should be given opportunities to participate in such activities so that they may exhibit their talent and develop democratic qualities. By organizing various games and other activities adolescents can be kept away from anger and jealousy.
10. *Religion and moral education :* Adolescents do not get right direction in such matters and they suffer from wrong ideas. As a result of this they lack decision making behaviour. As such, moral, religious and liberal education be imparted so that they may be able to distinguish between right and wrong.
11. *Use of proper teaching method :* Subjects should be taught with proper methods of teaching which are according to their needs and stage of development, so that they can develop their thinking and reasoning powers and can use them in their daily life.
12. *Mature behaviour with the Adolescents :* Adolescents should not be under estimated as a child. They should be treated as adults so that their thinking become mature. They should also be given full respect by elders.
13. *Organization of parent teacher association :* Parent-teacher association should be established in every school, so that the teacher and parents can solve the problems of adolescents.
14. *Facilities for vocational subjects :* Education and training for various vocations can be arranged so that the adolescents may adopt some useful vocations in their future life.
15. *Medical care :* Adolescents are very much anxious of their health and physical development. School should arrange medical check up camps in the schools for these students where they should also be given proper health advices by expert doctors.
16. *Physical and health education :* Keeping in view the special physical and physiological needs of these students physical and health education as a subject should be compulsorily taught in the school in theory and practice both.
17. *Nursing of creativity :* Adolescence is a period in which creative potential is especially seen. For this purpose, they should be provided opportunities to participate in music, dance, arts, etc; and an assignment of preparing science model should also be given to them by the teacher.
18. *Community service :* For proper development of adolescents, a close relationship should be established between the community and the school. Schools should treat them as treasures of the community and the later should feed the school to the maximum level possible. Many athletes and players are identified at this stage. Community should help the school to identify such adolescents so that they can be referred to proper sports clubs for their better training and rehabilitation.

# OBJECTIVE QUESTIONS

**1.** Which of the following characteristics denote infancy period?
- (*a*) Physical growth is curvilinear
- (*b*) Physical growth is rapid
- (*c*) Head grows at relatively slower rate as compared to other parts of the body.
- (*d*) All of these

**2.** Which gland controls the pitutory gland and hence the normal and proportionate growth of the body?
- (*a*) sex gland
- (*b*) thyroid gland
- (*c*) urinary gland
- (*d*) none of these

**3.** Which of the following is not the characteristic of infancy period?
- (*a*) From bilateral to unilateral trend in motor organs
- (*b*) From general to specific trend in motor organs
- (*c*) Emotional/social development is not associated with motor development
- (*d*) Steady mental development

**4.** Which of the following illustrates conceptual development?
- (*a*) Perception is the beginning of concept formation'
- (*b*) Concept changes with changes in experiences
- (*c*) Concept changes with age.
- (*d*) All of these

**5.** There is one thing common in language and physical development what is that?
- (*a*) Spurts of development at different ages
- (*b*) Dependence on experience
- (*c*) Dependence on training
- (*d*) None of these

**6.** Which of the following characteristics is not associated with emotional development?
- (*a*) Emotion is accompanied by physiological changes.
- (*b*) Emotions start immediately after birth.
- (*c*) Intense form of emotions are seen during early childhood period.
- (*d*) Emotions are unrelated to physical development.

**7.** The child acquires about three fourth of the brain weight by the age of
- (*a*) 21/2 years (*b*) 2 years
- (*c*) 6 years (*d*) 8 years

**8.** Social development of an infant depends on
- (*a*) his chance of interaction with others
- (*b*) love and affection shown to the child
- (*c*) the extent to which he is able to attract the attention of others
- (*d*) all of the above.

**9.** In which of the following stages the child looks self centred?
- (*a*) Infancy
- (*b*) Early childhood
- (*c*) Adolescence
- (*d*) Adulthood

**10.** In the period of infancy, emotions are
- (*a*) intense, frequent and unstable
- (*b*) like an open book(overt)
- (*c*) need based
- (*d*) all of these

**11.** Which of the following organs of the body shows rapid growth in infancy?
- (*a*) growth of hands
- (*b*) growth of head
- (*c*) growth of legs
- (*d*) growth of fingers

**12.** The child should have a height of 43 inches and weight of 43 pounds by the age of
- (*a*) three years (*b*) five years
- (*c*) four years (*d*) eight years

**13.** Clear conception of size, weight, colour, time etc., is seen at the age of
- (*a*) six (*b*) four
- (*c*) 4½ (*d*) five

**14.** Which of the following is not the characteristics of intellectual development of early childhood?
- (*a*) increased span of attention
- (*b*) exploration of the environment
- (*c*) ability to verbalize all known concepts
- (*d*) ability to distinguish past, present and future

15. Social development by the end of early childhood is marked by
    (a) the feeling of autonomy
    (b) the end of solitary plays
    (c) the temperament of co-operation and friendliness
    (d) all of these
16. Fictional world of the child starts at the age of
    (a) 5-6 (b) 6-8
    (c) 3-4 (d) 4-5
17. Girls are more dominating than boys in social situations in which of the following periods?
    (a) pre-adolescent period
    (b) early childhood period
    (c) both of these
    (d) none of these
18. In the period of early childhood, child is
    (a) helpless to hide his emotions
    (b) seen shifting his emotions very rapidly and frequently
    (c) guided by his innate tendencies and instincts
    (d) all of these
19. A nursery teacher should organize
    (a) group games in the school
    (b) those games which involve motor organs of the body
    (c) those games which help the child to manipulate the environment
    (d) all of these
20. Later childhood is called latency period because
    (a) creative potentials are dormant
    (b) sex remains dormant
    (c) it is a period of inactivity
    (d) all of these
21. Physical development of later childhood is marked by
    (a) Auscification of bones
    (b) Permanent teeth
    (c) Excessive motor activity
    (d) All of these
22. Girls surpass boys physically in
    (a) infancy
    (b) later childhood
    (c) early childhood
    (d) adolescence
23. The period of later childhood is marked by
    (a) intellectual maturity
    (b) high muscular energy
    (c) hero worship
    (d) all of these
24. Which of the following is not the characteristics of intellectual development of later childhood?
    (a) High interest in science fiction
    (b) Increased logical power
    (c) Careful for future
    (d) End of imaginary fears
25. Children are very much hateful or indifferent to opposite sex at the age of
    (a) 11-12
    (b) 13-14
    (c) 10-11
    (d) 15-16
26. Period of later childhood is marked by
    (a) slow and steady physical growth
    (b) stability in emotions
    (c) anger against injustice
    (d) all of these
27. At the end of later childhood period, the child
    (a) feels himself superior to girls
    (b) becomes independent of his family
    (c) wants to become hero
    (d) all of these
28. The best place of social development for a 12 years old child is
    (a) neighbourhood
    (b) family
    (c) playground
    (d) school
29. Group activities and group loyalties are at its peak at the age of
    (a) 10-12 (b) 13-15
    (c) 8-10 (d) 18-20
30. A teacher should not let a 12 years old child any time free because
    (a) child is always interested to get involve in physical or mental activities
    (b) spurts of creativity are seen at this age
    (c) child is frustrated
    (d) all of these

## ANSWERS

| 1 | 2 | 3 | 4 | 5 | 6 | 7 | 8 | 9 | 10 |
|---|---|---|---|---|---|---|---|---|---|
| *(d)* | *(a)* | *(c)* | *(d)* | *(a)* | *(d)* | *(b)* | *(d)* | *( )* | *(d)* |
| **11** | **12** | **13** | **14** | **15** | **16** | **17** | **18** | **19** | **20** |
| *(c)* | *(b)* | *(a)* | *(c)* | *(d)* | *(a)* | *(c)* | *(d)* | *(d)* | *(b)* |
| **21** | **22** | **23** | **24** | **25** | **26** | **27** | **28** | **29** | **30** |
| *(d)* | *(b)* | *(d)* | *(c)* | *(a)* | *(d)* | *(d)* | *(c)* | *(a)* | *(a)* |

# Theories of Child Development

Theories of child development can be classified into three broad categories. The first is psycho analytic theory propounded by Sigmund Freud and his associates. This theory gives much importance to unconscious motivation developed especially in the early period's of life and it determines the personality of the individual in the later parts of life also. The second is behaviouristic theory of child development which lays stress on the connection between stimulus and response. The major advantage of this category of theories is that it can be experimented and verified in clinical setting and thus these theories are more scientific in nature. The last category is cognitive theory of child development. It is a molar approach of explanation of human development and it takes the total situation facing the mind into account. It lays stress on perception and its organization responsible for learning and development.

Some of these theories are being described below:

1. **Psychoanalytic Theory (Freud) :** According to this theory, every child passes through five stages of psycho-sexual development. These stages are given below.

(a) *Oral stage:* At this stage focus of pleasure is mouth. When child sucks milk from the breast of her mother, he not only quenches his hunger but also gets pleasure by the excitement of mouth.

(b) *Anal stage :* When child attains the age of two the focus of pleasure shifts from mouth to anus. The child obtains pleasure from the activities related to anus during this period. That is why defecating is enjoying for the child.

(c) *Phallic stage :* This period starts at the age of three and lasts at the age of six. Here the focus of pleasure shifts from anus to sexual organs like pennis or vagina. That is why habit of masturbation is common in children. Two special complexes also develop during this period (1) Oedipus complex-here the male child wants his mother more but finds his father as a powerful rival. He wants to destroy this rival but he is unable to do so. (2) Elektra complex-Here female child comes closer to her father and hates her mother.

(d) *Latency stage :* During this period all earlier forms of sexual activities are stopped. The child takes interest in learning skills and in the development of social and religious values. This stage helps the child to develop his super ego on the basis of his ego.

(e) *Genital stage :* The focus of pleasure shifts to the member of the opposite sex by using genital organs here. This stage starts after 13 years.

2. **Ericksons' Theory of Psychosocial Stages :** Erickson has proposed another theory of stages of child development. He divides stages of development into eight phases marked by specific developmental characteristics. The stages are as follows :

| S.No. | STAGE | PSYCHOSOCIAL CRISES |
|---|---|---|
| 1 | Birth to first year | Trust Vs mistrust |
| 2 | 1 to 2 years | Autonomy Vs shame, doubt |
| 3 | 3 to 5 years | Initiative Vs Guilt |
| 4 | 6 to 12 years | Industry Vs inferiority |
| 5 | Adolescence | Identity Vs identity diffusion |
| 6 | Early adult period | Intimacy Vs Isolation |
| 7 | Young and middle adult | Generativity Vs self-absorption |
| 8 | Later adult period | Integrity Vs despair. |

A brief explanation of these stages are given below:

(i) The infant develops a sense of trust in himself as well as in the environment. This trust is developed when he finds others at the beck and call of his physiological needs. Contrary to this, if his needs are not fulfilled by the people around him, he aches and cries. As a result, he loses his faith in the people around him.

*(ii)* When the child attains the age of 1.5 years, he develops the sense of autonomy in him. He does not want help from others. If parents give them reasonable freedom, it will develop confidence in them. Children who are not given such freedom to explore the environment, develop suspicion and doubt about their abilities. When they perform a task they become shy and hesitant. They are afraid of their mistakes which can bring about shame for them.

*(iii)* At the age of three, rapid growth of children in all dimensions is seen. At this age, the child starts to take initiatives on various tasks. The social horizon of the child begins to spread from home to neighbourhood and then to school. At this age, children also begin to develop the sense of right or wrong. Feeling of guilt is developed when they do not follow moral principles and codes given by their parents and teachers.

*(iv)* Fourth stage of development in the life of a child starts at age of six and comes to an end just before adolescence. During this period child utilizes his energies for self improvement and for the conquest of the outer world. He shows his industry and hard labour in all directions with special emphasis to motor field. The child wants to understand different mechanisms of the world through his toys and other usable articles. If the above opportunities are not given to him and the child is still treated as a child of low mind, it develops inferiority complex in him.

*(v)* When the child attains the age of thirteen he begins to fight for his identity in his group. He wants to become a leader in various activities and through this he wants to gain popularity among girls. Contrary to this if he is completely disregarded in the group to which he belongs, his identity is diffused.

*(vi)* Adulthood period starts at the age of 17. In the early years of adulthood, the individual wants to increase his social circle as large as possible. If he is amiable by nature, he is liked by others and if he is selfish, self centred or intolerant or he is hated by others especially by the girls, he starts to live in isolation. Many tragic songs and dramas are written during this period.

*(vii)* In the middle years of adulthood, generativity is seen. The individual exposes himself through any outstanding efforts in any field. He wants to live for others. That is why he is very much interested to see a better and disciplined world around him. The condition of self absorption is seen when an individual does not receive any encouragement for his tasks from anywhere.

*(viii)* Last stage is known for the integrity of the person to his profession, group, organization and institution to which he belongs. When justice is not maintained or an individual is not paid and recognized according to his efforts, his integrity is turned into despair.

3. **Robert Sears' Development Theory:** This theory represents the behavioural approach to the study of child development. According to Robert Sears learning experiences of the child are the result of stimulus-response associations that may result either classical or operant conditioning procedures . Thus according to this theory, development is a process of observable social interaction. The more there is social interaction, the more there is learning which is enhanced by reinforcement also.

There are three broad phases of human development according to this theory which are given below-

*(a)* *Phase (I) Rudimentary behaviour :* Initial behavioural training starts during this period. The period of this stage is birth to sixteen months of age. During this period the infant is activated by his innate needs of hunger, thirst, motor movement, defecation etc. These needs create tension in him and in order to reduce this tension, the infant is motivated for action. When action of the infant is reinforced by positive response, his needs are satisfied. The infant is very much selfish in his behaviour in the beginning and does not care for any social world. But when social

world (parents and relatives) fulfills his needs and infant is reinforced for his action of say crying learning takes place which makes the learner more learned and goal directed.

Since, the infant here depends on someone else for the gratification of needs, the development becomes a process of social interaction. It is a type of operant behaviour here. The social environment in which the child is born greatly influences the development of the child. If child is not reinforced by anybody, *i.e,* his needs are not fulfilled, no development will be there. Socio-economic condition of the family, birth order of the child, his sex, the education or profession of his parents etc., affect the development of the child.

In other words, we can say that the first phase of the child's development interlinks the biological endowments (innate abilities) of the child with his social environment. The more the social environment is conducive to the fulfillment of biological needs of the child, the more learning and development will be there.

*(b) Phase II (Secondary behaviour) :* When child is reinforced by his parents and other members of the family, and the child's biological needs are gratified, he comes to develop secondary behaviour system, *i.e.*, he has to respond to others. If his response is fine he will be motivated. If response of the child is not upto the mark, it will be corrected by others and thus the process of development of correct secondary behaviour goes on.

The secondary behaviour of children starts by imitation. If model to be imitated is good, behaviour of the child will also be fine. The secondary behaviour of children should also be reinforced by parents and others and use of punishment as a technique should be avoided as much as possible because it can create behaviour problems in the child.

During this phase when the child begins to fulfil his needs himself by learning some new behaviour, his dependency on others decreases with age till the child is grown up fully and becomes an independent member of the society.

*(c) Phase III (Behaviour motivated) :* After the age of 11-12 the social boundary of the child expands a lot. The child comes in contact with other parents and their sons and with many people in his school and thus his process of socialization is accelerated. His dependency on others is reduced further but some new dependency in the school increases also. If child is given approval by his parents and other persons of the society that his behaviour is fine, he motivated to repeat that behaviour again and thus the process of development expands.

As the number of environmental **reinforcers** increases, the child comes to identify those persons well who satisfy his needs and he accepts those people as his model.

4. **Bandura's Theory of Development :** He gives equal importance to reward and punishment in the development of behaviour. Thus Bandura is mainly concerned with the social development of the individual. He believed that responses which are reinforced are more likely to recur than those responses of children which are not reinforced. Behaviour is learned either through conditioning or observational learning. In early childhood many behaviours of children are not approved by parents. Children are rather punished for the execution of such behaviour. Due to this fear, children are conditioned not to repeat that behaviour even in the later periods of life. Thus reward and punishment both are necessary for the moral and social development of the child.

   Observation (imitation) is the second mechanism responsible for learning (or acquisition of behaviour. The child creates some models in his mind or he is impressed by the behaviour of some people and accepts them as his model. These models are imitated by the child. Imitation follows certain principles such as competency, social status, power and similarity of the model with the imitator.

5. **Jean Piaget's Theory of Development :** He has explained his theory in the context of cognitive (mental) development of the child. Before coming to various stages of development according to this theory it is better to know various related concepts to understand the theory in detail. These concept are given below:

1. **The schema :** The concept of schema is applied to the sensory motor behaviour of the infant. The infant does various activities such as sucking milk from the mother's breast, looking at the objects of the environment and pointing at it and in the process he tries to comprehend and conceptualize the objects, animals or space. This process of conceptualization depends on the sequence of behaviour employed by the infant to adapt to his environment. This is called schema which is not the same in all the individuals. Basic structure, is however the same. Although a particular scheme derives its name from the sequence of behaviour which the schema denotes yet some internal organizational disposition is there to enable the sequence to adapt itself to a number of conditions. As the development of the individual takes place, each schema is enlarged, modified and co-ordinated with other schemas. In this way, more complex schemas are formed. The sensory motor scheme develops out of reflex behaviour of the infant. When this behaviour is repeated by the infant many times and is responded by others, it is internalized and is gradually converted into cognitive schema. For example, in northern India when a child says mum and is given water by the parents the child conceptualizes mum as water. Many such defects are corrected in the later stage of life.

   Piaget believes that schemed a (cognitive structure) exists in primitive form even at conception and develops progressively with age.
2. **Assimilation and accommodation :** The schemas which are acquired in infancy period are practiced and modified in the later stages of life. This process of practice and change is called assimilation and accommodation by the cognitive field theorists. These assimilation and accumulation processes go hand in hand. For example, during infancy when infant acquires grasping schema he pick up objects and grasps them. This grasping of objects is called assimilation. But if that particular object is too big or too small to grasp it., the child changes his schema in order to manage the new situation. It is called accommodation.

   The cognitive structure (schema) changes from one stage to another by the process of equilibration. Through this process the child tries to adapt to his changing environment every time to maintain equilibrium between him and the environment.

## PIAGET'S STAGES OF COGNITIVE DEVELOPMENT

According to him, there is an orderly sequence of stages in cognitive development. Thus progression from one stage to another is always fixed. The child can not adopt the strategies of a later stage at an early stage of development. It is because he must have to acquire and exercise the strategies and schemas of earlier stages. For example, in order to understand words, the child must know letters first or we can not teach Electronic Physics to a child of primary class.

Ausbel commenting upon the development stages of Piaget writes "Piaget's stages are identifiable, sequential phases in an orderly progression of development that are qualitatively discriminable from adjacent phases and generally characteristic of most members of a broadly defined age range".

The stages of cognitive development are related in the sense that they represent forms of adaptation, but these forms are qualitatively different, that is the adaptive functions are transformed as the child moves from one stage to the next. This theory of development is quite different from the theory of associationists who emphasize the gradual accumulation of responses.

Important stages of Piaget's theory of mental development are given below.

I. **Period of sensorimotor adaptation (from 0-2 years):** The infant starts this stage by his reflex activities and then he reaches to the stage of sensorimotor schemes by practice and accommodation. The intellectual development at this stage is marked by the following characteristics.

(a) *Object concept formation :* Objects exist in the mind of an adult whether they are present before the person or not. But in the psychological world of a child, only those objects exist which have a psychological presence for the child, ie, he can look and touch it. As soon as they are removed from the eyes of the child, they cease to exist for the child. When the child experiences the same object repeatedly, he develops the concept of permanence of objects. This concept is developed in the first year of life. When this type of structure is formed in the mind, practice of concepts is started by the child.

(b) *Coordinated space :* Spatial world at first is totally uncoordinated for the child. Each sensory modality has its own space. By the end of two years, the child develops the concepts which are marked by the coordination among different objects and between objects and body of the child

(c) *Objectified causalty :* The concept of cause and effect relationship is established when action of the child brings about an effect. Then this effect is taken as the cause of that event.

(d) *Objectification of time :* By the end of two years the child is also able to objectify time.

**II. Period of symbolic and preconceptual thought (2-4 years):** Ideas begin to develop in the mind of the child at the third year. By imitation and observation, he demonstrates that he is capable of extending his physical world to metaphysics. He begins to use symbols in the 4th year. Now he can represent the environment in the absence of perceptual cues only on the basis of ideas.

**III. Period of intuitive thought (4-8 years):** At this stage the child can use various concepts in different situations, *i.e.*, he is able to generalize his past and present experiences. His thoughts are not based on logical reasoning. It is rather governed by intution. The child can talk about this and that momentary static condition in a separate manner but he can not properly integrate various sets of conditions into an integrated whole due to lack of logical weakness, *i.e.*, logical coherence is not found here. For example, a child can write fine sentences representing various topics but he can not write a compact essay.

**IV. The period of concrete operation (8-12 years):** Here the child is able to direct his attention away from the static condition, ie, he can accommodate with all the successive changes taking place in the system. It means that he can reorganize his future on the basis of his past experience as well as trends at present. Reasoning power of the child is well developed during this period. Some examples of what a child can do are handling and manipulating the numbers in various ways by various operations, arrangement of objects and materials into various groups and sub groups, ordering of objects according to one or more attributes and so on. Piaget has described a term "grouping" for this stage of cognitive development.

This period also shows some logical inconsistency in the thinking of the child. Piaget has coined a term "syncretism" for this defect. Despite this, beginning of abstract operation is seen during this stage.

**V. Period of formal (abstract) operation (12-18 years):** During this period, the thought process of the child becomes systematic, consistent and reasonably well integrated. Reality guides the contemplation process of the child. The formal operation of thinking starts with the formulation of hypothesis, (deductive reasoning) and reaches at its peak when hypothesis is tested by experiments, ie, inductive reasoning. At this stage, the boy can manipulate any abstract idea in his own way and form new idea entirely different from the old one. His wisdom lies in the expertise administration of the unforeseen. Whenever an adolescent faces any problem with the help of formal operation of thought he identifies various relevant variables which may be helpful in the solution of that problem and then all these variables are manipulated by him.

Thus, development of formal operation capacity enables the adolescent to transfer understanding from one situation to another and to evaluate the results on the basis of its pros and cons. Physical (concrete) objects are never required for thinking (operation) during this period. The thought process is completely abstract here.

**VI. Kohlberg's theory of development :** According to him moral development of the child proceeds in sequential but distinctive stages. These stages are given below:

*(a)* **Stage-I :** In the early years of a child's life (from zero-four years) the physical consequences of an action determines its goodness or badness. If fire burns the child, he does not touch it. The child is ego-centric and standards of morality are external here.

*(b)* **Stage-II :** The child gives importance to his own point of view, (his self) and is able to take account of other's roles insofar as he can use them in his own way. This is a period of make belief. Right action is what which satisfies the needs of the child. The role of others is also important in the sense that a child does only what can bring approval of others. Thus, only that behaviour is moral which can satisfy not only self needs of the child but it must please others also.

*(c)* **Stage-III :** At this stage the child adopts the view pints of others on the basis of their consequences. He does not question the views of others. The child considers only that thing as right which are considered as right by others. Thus, the child is totally conformist to the standard of the society.

*(d)* **Stage-IV:** At this stage, the child is able to make any moral decision on his own without caring for the thinking of others. Though he considers laws and regulations set by the society as the essence of morality, yet he develops his own principles of morality on various occasions. Thus, he is a non-conformist to the norms of the society to a great extent.

*(e)* **Stage-V :** Standards and norms are more internalized here. The adolescents examine various view points prepared by different societies and recognize them. They think that the laws prepared by their own society are correct. Other societies may have good moral principles that must be adopted after careful appraisal.

*(f)* **Stage-VI :** This is the last stage of moral development according to Kohlberg. Here the universality of the view points of the individual is seen. He formulates his own universal moral principles which he thinks that all societies should adhere to it. True understanding of right and wrong is developed at this stage.

**VII. Havighurst's theory of development :** According to him at each stage of development, there are certain tasks, skills and understanding that must be completed before a person can proceed to a higher level of development.

**Havighurst Says –**

"At or about a certain period in the life of the individual, successful achievement leads to his happiness and to success with later tasks, while failure leads to unhappiness in the individual, disapproval by society and difficulty with later tasks".

**LIST OF DEVELOPMENT TASKS GIVEN BY HAVIGHURST**

| S.No. | Birth to 6 years | 6 to 12 years |
|---|---|---|
| 1 | Learning to walk | Learning physical skills, ordinary games. |
| 2 | Learning to take solid food | Building wholesome attitudes towards oneself as a growing organism |
| 3 | Learning to talk | Learning to get along with age mates |
| 4 | Learning to control the elimination of body wastes. | Learning an appropriate masculine or feminine role. |
| 5 | Learning sex differences | Developing fundamental skills in reading, writing and calculating. |
| 6 | Achieving physiological stability | Developing concepts necessary for everyday living |
| 7 | Forming simple concepts of social and physical reality | Developing the ability of manipulating the ideas and concepts. |
| 8 | Learning to relate oneself emotionally to parents, siblings and other people | Achieving personal independence |
| 9 | Learning to distinguish right and wrong and developing a conscience | Developing attitudes towards social groups and institutions |

## COMPARISON OF THREE CATEGORIES OF THEORIES

| S. No. | Psycho analytic | Behaviouristic | Cognitive |
|---|---|---|---|
| 1 | Feeling is important here | Stimulus and behaviour of others are important here | Thinking is all responsible for development |
| 2 | In order to acquire moral principles, parental values are internalized | Moral values are adopted from either models or they are acquired by conditioning | Moral principles are acquired automatically with age, ie, mental development |
| 3 | Super ego, a moral conduct is formed at the age of five | Learning of morality is a life long process | Super ego is formed during the period of adolescence |
| 4 | Moral values are not free from culture | Same | Moral values are universal |
| 5 | Parents and relatives are agents of socialization | Adults and peers who give reinforcement are the main agents of socialization | People of the matured age are the agents of socialization |

## OBJECTIVE QUESTIONS

**1.** Elektra complex refers to
(*a*) daughter comes closer to the father
(*b*) son comes closer to the mother
(*c*) inferiority complex in the presence of girls
(*d*) none of these

**2.** According to Freud, super ego is properly developed during
(*a*) latency period (*b*) anal period
(*c*) phallic period (*d*) none of these

**3.** Development is a process of observable social interaction. This is the opinion of
(*a*) Erikson (*b*) Skinner
(*c*) Robert Sears (*d*) None of these

**4.** The secondary behaviour of the child according to Robert Sears starts with
(*a*) reinforcement (*b*) imitation
(*c*) modeling (*d*) none of these

**5.** The period of sensory motor adoptation of Piaget is
(*a*) 0-2 years (*b*) 1-3 years
(*c*) 3-5 years (*d*) 4-6 years

**6.** The child adopts the view points of others on the basis of consequences of these views in the
(*a*) third stage of Kohlberg's theory
(*b*) second stage of Kohlberg's theory
(*c*) fourth stage of Kohlberg's theory
(*d*) fifth stage of Kohlberg's theory

**7.** Which of the following is not the view point of cognitive theories of development?
(*a*) moral principles are acquired automatically with age
(*b*) super ego is formed during the period of adolescence.
(*c*) Moral values are determined by culture
(*d*) Mural principles are universal

## ANSWERS

| 1 | 2 | 3 | 4 | 5 | 6 | 7 |
|---|---|---|---|---|---|---|
| (*a*) | (*a*) | (*c*) | (*b*) | (*a*) | (*a*) | (*c*) |

# Learning of Concepts, Reasoning and Problem Solving

## MEANING OF CONCEPTS

Concept is the basic unit of learning. From infancy to old age, an individual accumulates different concepts through learning and maturation but level of concept formation is not the same in all the individuals. It differs with age, intelligence and chance of experiences of the learner. For example, a layman will not have the same concept of inflation as a student of economics has because the experiences of the later is wide and more sophisticated than the former.

The word "Concept" is not purely subjective and designate the mental constructs of the individual only. It is objective in nature also because it is understood on the basis of the substances and mechanism used in a particular discipline. Different concepts are identifiable, comparable and measurable because of its objectivity.

Logically, a concept refers to a phenomenon in a given field that are grouped together because of their common characteristics. For example, a square is a figure that has equal length and breath and that is why it is different from a circle or triangle.

Practically, a concept may be defined as public entities or organized information to the meaning of words which a particular society has accepted for the purpose of communication. They are the standard of which a language is judged. In other words when we say that a particular word is understood in standard form, we mean concept by that word.

Concepts are not universal. The same concept may be understood by different communities and culture in different ways. Similarly, the same word may have different concepts in different communities and languages.

### Characteristics of Concepts

1. Concepts differ in difficulty value. Some concepts are learned more easily than others. For example, concrete concepts are easier than abstract concepts and more easily perceptible concepts are learned more readily than less perceptible concepts.
2. Some concepts are used more than others in understanding communication and forming principles, e.g., symbols of numbers 1,2,3 etc, are used more than symbols of ratio or theta.
3. A concept is valid to the extent that experts agree to its meaning and definitions. Concepts of natural sciences are more valid than those of social sciences because of their objectivity.
4. The individual concept comes closer to the concept of the expert when he grows in age and attain maturity and experiences. Thus development of concepts is a dynamic process.
5. Concepts which are higher in taxonomy have fewer defining attributes than those which are lower in the taxonomy. Living things are highly general concepts in the sense that they are higher in the taxonomy.
6. Some concepts are more powerful than the other. Power refers to the extent to which a particular concept facilitates the learning of other concepts. According to Bruner (1961) every discipline has some fundament concepts which are necessary to learn the subject or discipline in the beginning.
7. Concepts must have some attributes on the basis of which they can be identified and differentiated from other concepts.

### Levels of Concept Development

Concepts do not develop in the individuals over night. There are four levels of concept development.

*1. Concrete level :* The building of concepts starts with the process of sensation. This is done by the process of perception. Concept at the concrete level is developed when an individual perceives an object next time and identifies it. Woodruff (1961) writes "All learning begins with some form of personal contact with actual objects or events. When individual gives attention to some objects through a light wave or sound wave or some form of direct contact with a sensory organ in the body, an impression is picked up and lodged in the mind"

For the purpose of developing concrete concepts, the person must be able to differentiate it from other concepts on the basis of his identification. Thus, following steps are needed for concept formation.

I. Attending to the object several times.
II. Formation of the memory image with respect to the object.
III. Differentiating from other objects.

2. *Identity level :* When the person is able to generalize the characteristics of an object in different properties it means that he is at the identity level of concept formation. He is not only able to differentiate an object from other objects on the basis of its properties, but he can identify it also on the basis of its properties. He can even recognize the object when only the properties of the object are supplied to him. This is the highest concrete level but the lowest abstract level of concept formation.
3. *Classification level :* When the person is able to classify different categories of the same object on the basis of its properties, it means that he has attained the classification level of concept formation. He is now able to treat at least two different instances of the same class as equivalent. It is the higher level of abstract concept. For example, the person can recognize an Arabian horse and an Indian horse on the basis of their properties.
4. *Formal level :* When the person is able to define a concept and name it accurately with examples it means that he has attained the formal level of concept formation. The distinctive aspect of this level is that the person is able to specify and name the defining attributes and to differentiate newly encountered instances and non instances on the basis of presence or absence of defining attributes.

### Types of Concepts

1. *Conjunctive concepts :* It is the joint presence of the appropriate value of several attributes.
2. *Disjunctive concepts :* It involves a critical combination of criterial attributes.
3. *Relational concepts :* It involves the notion of a common relation among the various elements of attribute values that define the concept.

## MEANING OF REASONING

It is the process of higher order thinking where general principles are employed to draw relevant inferences. **Gates** has defined reasoning in the following words "Reasoning is a productive thinking in which previous experiences are organized in new ways to solve a problem."

### Characteristics of Reasoning

1. It is needed when we can not arrive at the solution of a problem by applying direct approach of responding.
2. It helps in developing insight for learning or problem solving.
3. It goes in the direction given to the learner, *i.e.*, it is always goal directed.
4. It is productive thinking not a wastage of time or energy. We will get something after employing the process.
5. It works as an important tool for solving a problem
6. It is creative and reflective in nature.
7. It is a function of intelligence. A dull child is not supposed to employ reasoning process.
8. It is inductive and deductive both.
9. Reasoning ability develops gradually. It means that experiences are also helpful in developing reasoning power along with intelligence.
10. There may be more than one logic to draw an inference, ie., reasoning is multi dimensional.

**Steps involved in reasoning process :** It consists of following steps :

1. *Identification of the problem :* Problem is first identified by the person, *i.e.*, what he has to do and how.
2. *Defining the problem :* Problem in hand is defined by the person in operational terms. Analytical approach is followed to define each and every aspect of the problem one by one.
3. *Formulation of hypothesis :* Hypotheses are formulated by the person in the third step. This gives him the direction in which he will go for

collecting data. The extent of enquiry is also determined by the hypotheses.

4. *Collection of data :* In order to verify the hypotheses whether they are true or false, relevant data are collected (if needed).
5. *Tabulating and systematizing data :* Jumbled informations are tabulated and classified for the purpose of statistical treatment (if needed).
6. *Verification/evaluation of hypotheses:* It helps the person in three ways:
   - *(a)* Whether the conclusion satisfies the demands of the problem, *i.e.*, hypotheses are true or false.
   - *(b)* Whether conclusion is consistent with other known facts and principles or it is against them.
   - *(c)* Fixing the limitation of the conclusion, ie., to what extent it can be applied to different situations.

## MEANING OF PROBLEM SOLVING

It is the highest level of learning in the hierarchy according to Gagne. From application of facts and principles to their evaluation, it involves every thing. Thus, it is the highest level of thinking process. Some of the definitions of problem solving are given below.

1. Gates – Problem solving is a form of learning in which the response must be discovered.
2. Skinner – Problem solving is the framework or pattern within which creative thinking or reasoning takes place.

### Characteristics

1. It is a process of removing obstacles that appear to interfere with the realization of goals. Thus it is a perceptual and goal directed process.
2. It is a selective process in the sense that only relevant facts or informations are selected to reach the goal.
3. Problem solving ability of a person depends on his reasoning power.
4. Re-organization of experiences are also needed here.
5. It is a creative process that gives us something new.

### Approaches of Problem Solving

Psychologists have mentioned two approaches of problem solving

*(a)* Cognitive approach *(b)* S-R approach

*(a)* *Cognitive field approach :* Perception of total situation is needed here and it is done by linking various components and restructuring the cognitive field. It has already been discussed in the learning by insight theory.

*(b)* *Stimulus-response approach :* Trial and effort and regular reinforcement are needed here. By this process, problem is solved by gradually eliminating the errors and by increasing the chance of correct responses through reinforcement.

### Harlow's Approach of Problem Solving :

His approach is a combination of the two approaches given above. He (1959) says that trial and error behaviour is shown in the beginning. Later on insightful learning is developed and the subject can solve the similar problem immediately. Positive transfer of training takes place from one situation to another .

*Phases of problem solving :* Steps needed in problem solving are the same as we need in reasoning process. It is a type of research the scale of which depends on the nature of the problem.

Following are the steps which have been given by the research workers on problem solving:

| S.No. | Rossman | Dewey | Merrifield | Klaus Meier |
|---|---|---|---|---|
| 1 | Need or felt difficulty | Sensing difficulty, locating and defining | Preparation difficulty | Attending and cognizing |
| 2 | Information gathering | Suggesting hypothesis | Analysis | Stating the general requirements |
| 3 | Solution tested | Testing hypothesis | Production | Recalling existing knowledge |
| 4 | New ideas formulated, tested and accepted | — | Verification | Applying substantive knowledge |
| 5 | — | — | Re-application | Inferring possible solution |
| 6 | — | — | — | Evaluating the quality of the accepted solution |
| 7 | — | — | — | Transfer of new acquired knowledge |

## THINKING PROCESS AND ROLE OF THE TEACHER

1. The teacher should not give ready made solution to the problems. He should use inductive and deductive methods of teaching to develop reasoning power in his students.
2. Self learning is the best learning. It is possible only when students are trained to solve the problems themselves.
3. While giving problems to students for solution, the maturation level, intelligence and experiences of students should also be taken into account.
4. After giving problems to students they should be only moderately motivated. Excessive motivation is an impediment in the way of problem solving.
5. Divergent thinking is necessary for reasoning and problem solving so, confirmatory behaviour of learning should be discouraged. The teacher should be flexible in his attitude for this purpose
6. Sensation and perception both operate simultaneously for problem solving. The teacher should help the students to perceive the problem as a whole.
7. Active involvement of students is necessary for developing problem solving ability in them. Diagrams, models and figures should be used and concrete materials should be manipulated to conceptualize the abstract problems.
8. In the opinion of Harlow, practice is necessary for developing insight. The teacher should give chance of practice to his students.
9. There should be free discussion and questioning in the class.
10. Cues and prompts should be given to students only when it is very necessary

## OBJECTIVE QUESTIONS

**1.** Organization of sensory experiences about a particular object is called
 (*a*) percepts (*b*) reasoning
 (*c*) concept (*d*) none of these

**2.** The concept building in a person depends on
 (*a*) the age and maturity of the person
 (*b*) past experiences of the learner
 (*c*) intelligence of the learner
 (*d*) all of these

**3.** Agreement on a concept is possible because
 (*a*) concepts are subjective
 (*b*) concepts are objective
 (*c*) conceptss are hierarchical
 (*d*) b and c both

**4.** Which of the following statements about concepts is correct?
 (*a*) Some concepts are more powerful than others.
 (*b*) All concepts are universal
 (*c*) Concepts are differentiated on the basis of their attributes.
 (*d*) None of these

**5.** Which is the highest level of concept formation?
 (*a*) formal level (*b*) sensory level
 (*c*) concrete level (*d*) none of these

**6.** How many steps of problem solving has been given by Gates?
 (*a*) Six (*b*) Seven
 (*c*) Five (*d*) Ten

## ANSWERS

| 1 | 2 | 3 | 4 | 5 | 6 |
|---|---|---|---|---|---|
| (*a*) | (*d*) | (*d*) | (*b*) | (*a*) | (*c*) |

# UNIT-IV

★ *Intelligence and its Measurement*

★ *Memory and Forgetting*

★ *Motivation and Learning*

★ *Learning Theories and their Applications*

★ *Transfer of Training*

# Intelligence and its Measurement

## INTRODUCTION

The most important variable that affects schooling or performance on a job is intelligence. Psychologists have interpreted the term intelligence in different ways and there is no consensus among them on the term even so far. In psychology this term is treated as a construct whose structure is different in different individuals.

The vagueness of the term arises due to the fact that intelligence is not a concrete material. It is rather abstraction from the behaviour of the individual which is indirectly inferred and elaborated as an adjective.

The dictionary meaning of term "intelligence" is the capacity to acquire and apply knowledge. **Boring** defines intelliegence as intelligence is what an intelligence test measures.

## DEFINITIONS OF INTELLIGENCE

Several psychologists have classified and defined intelligence in several ways. Some of them are given below:

### 1. Vernon's Classification of Intelligence

(a) *Biological approach:* Man is an organism among millions living on earth. Environment works as a foe for him. Intelligence is the capacity to adapt to the environment or new situations of life at every moment.

This definition of intelligence can be criticized on the ground that there have been many intelligent and renowned persons who were ill adapted to their social and physical environment. Besides, if we want to study individual differences in a society, this definition serves no practical purpose.

(b) *Psychological Approach :* According to psychologists intelligence is the relative effects of heredity and environment both. An English psychologist, **C Burt** defined intelligence as the innate general cognitive ability.

In support of psychological definitions of intelligence **Hebb** and **R.B Catell** distinguished two kinds of intelligence. The first is intelligence "A" which is Fluid intelligence and which is related to genetic potentialities or innate qualities of the individual's nervous system. Second is intelligence "B" which is crystalised "intelliegence" and which is related to experiences, learning and environmental factors. These two types of intelligence in normal circumstances so much overlap on each other that they are practically indistinguishable.

(c) *Operational Approach :* These definitions help us to understand the concept of intelligence in clear and definite terms. In this approach scientific terms are first of all defined operationally and then observations are conducted with reference to these terms. For example, in order to determine a child's IQ, we first administer a test of a specific kind. Then we observe his performance on the test and finally draw certain conclusions in the context of the pre-determined objectives.

### 2. Freeman's Classification

(a) *Ability of adjustment :* An individual is intelligent to the extent to which he is able to adjust to new situations and problems of life. The more a person is intelligent, the more he is able to adapt to his environment in antagonistic conditions. The person who is low in intelliegence has less capacity to adjust to the new situations of life.

(b) *Ability of learning :* Learning ability is also an index of intelligence. The more a person is intelligent, the more he will be able to learn new things.

(c) *Ability to carry on abstract thinking* : This category of definitions of intelligence is related to the effective use of concepts and symbols in dealing with situations and solving the problems through the use of verbal and numerical symbols. According to **Terman**, an individual is intelligent to the extent he is able to carry on abstract thinking.

### 3. E.L. Thorndike's Classification

(a) *Concrete intelligence* : The intellectual ability in relation to concrete materials is called concrete intelligence. It is the ability of a person to comprehend the actual situations and react to them adequately. This kind of intelligence is measured by using performance tests or picture tests in which the subject manipulates the concrete materials.

(b) *Abstract intelligence* : It is the ability to respond to words, letters, numbers or symbols. This type of intelligence is required in all academic activities in schools or outside the schools. The highest level of abstract intelligence is manifested in the thoughts of philosophers or in the inventions of scientists and mathematicians.

(c) *Social intelligence* : It is the ability of an individual to react to social situations of life. It is the ability to understand others and to react to them in such a manner that they may not feel unjust attitude regarding them.

### 4. Intelligence as a Global Capacity

A comprehensive definitions of intelligence : **Stoddard** (1943) and **Wechsler** (1944) have defined intelligence in the following words :

"Intelligence is the aggregate or the global capacity of the individual to act purposefully, to think rationally and to deal with the environment effectively".

**Stoddard** further elaborated that intelligence is the capacity of a person to undertake such activities which are (i) difficult (ii) complex, (iii) abstract (iv) economical (v) goal directed (vi) valuable from social view points (vii) original. These activities demand concentration of energy and a resistance to emotional forces.

## CHARACTERISTICS OF INTELLIGENCE

From the above definitions of intelligence, we can draw the following characteristics of intelligence:

(i) Intelligence is the composite of several intellectual skills, such as thinking, doing, reasoning, dealing, learning etc.

(ii) Intelligence is displayed by the behaviour of the individual as a whole and intelligent behaviour is always goal directed.

(iii) Intelligence is the ability to adjust to abnormal and challenging situations of life.

(iv) Intelligence is not related to ordinary tasks of life. It is always related to extra ordinary manipulation.

(v) Wechsler has included the concepts of drive and incentive which are implied in his statement. "To act purposefully" and "to deal effectively". But many psychologists are of the view that drive and incentive are non-intellectual traits of personality and if they are included in a test of mental ability, more confusions will be created thereof.

(vi) There are seven fundamental elements of intelligence according to **Stoddard.** Intelligent person can undertake difficult and abstract tasks with ease. He can manipulate and deal the abstract ideas and concepts efficiently. Similarly, economy refers to the rate at which a mental task is done or a problem is solved. If "A" solves a problem sooner than 'B' then 'A' will be considered more intelligent than 'B'. The term social value indicates whether a mental task performed by a person is in accordance with the socially desirable and acceptable norms or not. The last term original refers to a person's, ability to discover something new and different, i.e., this term is directly related to creative potential of a person. Discovery of some new facts and principles and inventions of new concrete materials by the scientists are few examples of originality.

**Stoddard's** definition of intelligence has been criticized on two grounds :

(a) It includes social values in intelligence, *i.e.*, intelligent task must be socially desirable. Psychologists criticize this point by saying that social value is a subjective phenomenon, i.e., what is desirable for me, may not be necessarily desirable for others. So, there is no scope of subjectivity in an objective intelligence test.

*(b)* He has included two conditions of intelligent behaviour in his definition. First is concentration of energy and second is resistance to emotional forces. Psychologists say that these elements are non-intellectual traits and hence they should not be included in mental abilities at any cost.

## THEORIES OF INTELLIGENCE

### 1. Faculty theory of intelligence:

This is the oldest theory of intelligence given during the period of pre-experimental psychology. According to this theory mind is made up of different faculties like reasoning, logic, memory, imagination and discrimination. These faculties are independent of each other and can be developed by rigorous mental exercises of the difficult subject-matter.

This theory does not take the hereditary factors of intelligence into account and thus this theory was discarded by the later psychologists who believed that we can never improve the intellectual capacity of a person if he is mentally slow by birth.

### 2. Unifactor theory:

According to Alfred Binet (1916) intelligence is a general intellectual ability which is made up of several discrete abilities. These abilities include.

*(i)* to reason well with abstract material
*(ii)* to comprehend well
*(iii)* to have a clear direction of thoughts
*(iv)* to relate thinking with the attainment of a desirable end and
*(v)* to be self-critical

All these abilities combined together is called general mental ability. Thus, intelligence is a single but complex mental process which can be measured by different kinds of materials designed for the purpose.

### 3. Two factors theory:

This theory was developed by an English psychologist, **Charles Spearman** in 1904. According to him, intellectual abilities consist of two factors, general ability known as 'G' factors and specific abilities known as 'S' factors.

**Characteristics of G factors**

*(i)* It is universal inborn ability
*(ii)* It is general mental energy
*(iii)* It is constant, i.e., it remains the same in all the individuals and does not change with time.
*(iv)* The amount of G differs from person to person depending on his genes.
*(v)* It is used in every life activity.
*(vi)* Greater the amount of G in an individual, larger is the chance of his success in life.

**Characteristics of 'S' factors**

*(i)* It is learnt and hence acquired in the environment.
*(ii)* It varies from activity to activity in the same individual.
*(iii)* The amount of S also differs from person to person due to his accessibility to learning situations.
*(iv)* 'S' factors are related to the specific activity. A low correlation between two or more functions or activities indicates the presence of 'S' factor involved in the activity. A person can be expert only in one or few activities because of the specific factors involved in the activity.

According to Spearman, out of these two factors 'G' factor is more important and thus it is an important measure of intelligence. So, any intelligence test should measure only 'G' factor because it provides most important basis of predicting a person's behaviour in different situations. Raven's Progressive Matrices and Catell's Culture Fair Test both measure 'G' factor.

**Spearman** has explained his theory with the help of a tetrad equation which is given below :

rap x rbq-raq x rbp = 0

Here,

a = opposites
b = discrimination
p = completion
q = cancellation

Thus, rap means correlation between opposites and completions, rbq means correlation between cancellation and discrimination, raq means correlation between opposite and cancellation and rbp means correlation between discrimination and completion. This theory can also be explained with the help of a diagram given below :

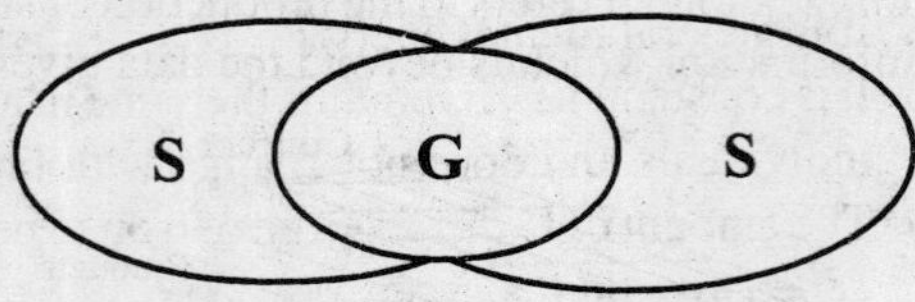


4. **Multi-factors theory :**

This theory was developed by an American psychologist, **E.L. Thorndike.** He opposed the theory of general intelligence by saying that there are specific stimuli and specific mental responses. Intelligence is nothing more than a potential specific connections between these stimuli and responses. Differences of intelligence among people are due to the different number of such connections in the neurological system. This theory is also called **atomistic theory** of intelligence. There are **four attributes of intelligence** according to him:

(a) *Level :* It refers to the difficulty of a task that can be removed by using intelligence. If different tasks are arranged in increasing difficulty order, then the height that a person can attain determines his level of intelligence. It is a kind of power test.

(b) *Range :* It refers to the number of tasks of the same difficulty value that a person can do in a certain period of time. Theoretically, an individual possessing a certain level of intelligence should be able to solve the whole range of tasks at a given level. It is a kind of speed test.

Range and level can not be completely isolated from each other. We can not measure range without altitude (level) and vice versa.

(c) *Area :* It refers to the total numbers of situations at each level to which the individual is able to respond. Area is the summation of all ranges at each level of intelligence. Area=Level × Rang.

(d) *Speed :* It refers to the rapidity with which an individual can respond to a test items. Speed and level are positively correlated. It is different from range in the sense that no specific time is given here to complete a task. Every intelligence test should consist of these four attributes.

5. **Group factor structure of intelligence (PMA Test) :**

This theory was developed by **L.L. Thurstone.** According to him intelligence is not an expression of general factor but a combination of group of traits. They are intermediate factors, i.e., they are not so universal as 'G' factor and they are not so specific as 'S' factor. This primary group of factors give the common mental abilities, a functional cohesiveness and then constitute a group. Another group of common mental abilities is said to have another primary factor and so on. In this way, there are a number of groups of mental abilities each of which has its own primary factors. On the basis of factor analysis of these groups, Thurstone identified the following seven group factors which are termed as primary mental abilities (PMA).

1. Number factor (N) : It is the ability to do numerical calculations rapidly and accurately.
2. Verbal factor (V) : They are related to the operations involving verbal comprehension.
3. Space factor (S) : It is related to the tasks in which subject manipulates an object imaginary in space.
4. Word fluency factor (W) : It is involved to the situation when the subject is asked to think of isolated words at a fast rate.
5. Reasoning factors (R) : It is used in those tasks that require the subject to discover a rule or principles involved in series or groups of letters.
6. Rote memory (M) : It is the ability to memorize a fact quickly.
7. Perceptual speed (P) : It is the ability to note perceptual (visual) details rapidly.

The point to be noted here is that these seven abilities are significantly correlated with each other.

6. **Structure of intelligence (SI) model :**

This model was given by **J.P.Guilford** in 1966 in the University of California on the basis of factor analysis of many tests. According to him human mind is composed of at least three dimensions—operations, contents and products, and each dimension of intellect is sufficiently distinct which can be detected by factor analysis. These three dimensions of mind are given below:

(A) **Operations :** Operations can be divided into five major groups of intellectual abilities.

- Cognition : It includes discovery, recognition of informations and new understanding of the facts.
- Memory : It is the ability to recognize or recall previously learnt material.
- Divergent thinking : This operation is closely associated with creative potential. It refers to the ability to search out and think in a novel out of track way.
- Convergent thinking : It refers to the generation of information from given information and drawing conclusion from the given facts.
- Evaluation : It is the ability to make judgement on the basis of merits and demerits of a phenomenon. Here value judgement on knowledge and thoughts is placed after critically examining them.

(B) **Contents :** Five kinds of contents are involved here. Operations are performed on these contents.

- Figural Content : It is the concrete material perceived through the senses. Visual materials have three properties, size, form and colour.
- Auditory content : It includes nature and characteristics of sound perceived.
- Symbolic content : It includes letters digits and other conventional signs usually organised in general pattern.
- Semantic content : It refers to those verbal meanings, ideas and concepts for which no examples are necessary.
- Behavioural content : It includes knowledge regarding other persons.

(C) **Products :** When five operations are applied to five types of contents, six kinds of products are made.

- Units : It refers to the production of a single word, definition or isolated bits of informations
- Classes : It refers to the production of a concept
- Relations : It refers to the production of any form of relationship, such as, analogy, opposite or similar ones.
- System : It refers to the production of internally consistent set of classification of various forms.
- Transformation : It refers to the production of changes in meaning, organisation or some other arrangement.
- Implication : It refers to the production of such information which is beyond the data given.

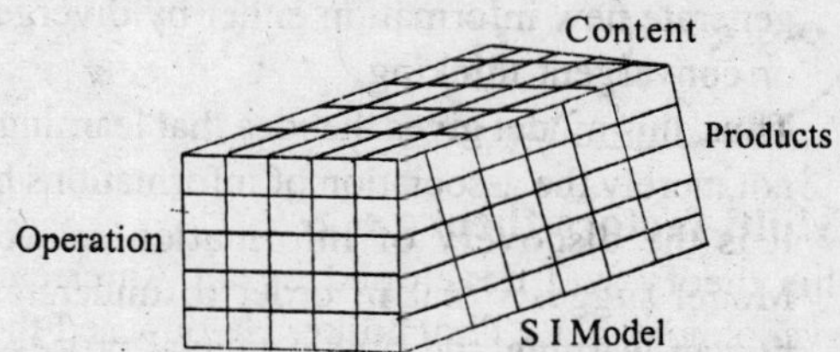

S I Model

On the basis of the model given above it can be stated that there are 5 × 5 × 6 =150 factors involved in intelligent acts.

## Educational Implication of the Model

(a) **In psychology :** This model is very much helpful for constructing various types of intelligence tests suitable to different age groups. These tests will help us to study individual differences in the society. This model is taxonomic in nature and has discovered many abilities which were not known before. If test maker has included items representing contents and operations, he can see whether products are same or different. Conversely, if products are shown by the subject through the test, the test maker can find out the content and operation and match them with the items given in the test.

(b) **In vocational testing :** This model shows that there are 150 intellectual abilities. This model predicts five kinds of mental abilities classified as content. This means that different kinds of test items are needed in vocational testing. Six types of products are also tested on the basis of items representing the products. For example, if a person is able to deal with items of figural contents, he can deal with machines, operators, engineers etc. and any or all of the six types of products can be made by him, such as , he can define a machine or any operator. He can give clear concept about how a machine is operated and so on.

(c) **In the field of education :** Conventionally, learner was considered to be a kind of stimulus response device. Once the stimulus is given to him, he will respond but the new conception of the learner in the light of S1 model is that of electronic computer which not only stores information but uses that information to generate new information either by divergent or convergent thinking.

Thus, this model gives the idea that learning is not merely the association of informations but it is the discovery of information as well. Model suggests that in order to understand human learning and higher mental processes of thinking, some drastic modifications are to be made in our theory of curriculum construction and pedagogy of instruction.

Similarly, education is no longer considered to be the training of mind. Now main emphasis on education is given to the learning of specific skills and modification of behaviour and all these materials are not taught merely for the purpose of training the mind of humans.

### 7. Two level process theory of intelligence

This theory was developed by **Jensen** in 1968. According to him intelligence is a combination of two levels of processes. One is associative intelligence and the other is abstract intelligence. Associative intelligence includes those kinds of tests that depend upon memory and simple verbal association. Abstract intelligence includes those factors as concept learning, thinking, problem solving skills, multiple discrimination, principle learning etc.

### 8. Burt and Vernon's hierarchy theory :

Burt (1940) separated four factors of intelligence by using statistical techniques :

- General factors (common to all traits)
- Group factors (common to some of the traits)
- Specific factors (limited to few traits)
- Error factors (limited to a particular trait when it is measured)

When human mind is put at the top, there will be 5 level hierarchical model of intelligence where general factors will come next to intelligence and error factors will come in the last.

Vernon, on the other hand, suggested that intelligence tests measure an overall factor G as well as two other mental abilities. First are related to verbal, numerical and educational. Second are related to practical, mechanical, spatial and physical. These two major factors can be divided into minor group factors. These minor factors can further be divided into various specific factors and so on.

## MEASUREMENT OF INTELLIGENCE

Historical development of mental testing can be divided into three periods for the purpose of convenience.

### (A) Pre-Binet period :

In the 19th century, there was a good deal of interest in the field of psychophysics in which attempts were made to develop general rule of sensory judgement. The functioning of sensory reactions of the typical individuals is actually studied in psycho-physics). Method of limits procedure was used here to measure the extent to which people were able to differentiate between stimuli. But the limitation of these experiments was that accurate generalization of the result was not possible.

**Francis Galton** was the first psychologist who took interest in studying whether individual characteristics are acquired or inherited. For this purpose, he studied the lives of prominent English men and in his book "Hereditary Genius" he demonstrated that personal characteristics, (mental and physical) of men are inherited. He developed a series of tests to measure these characteristics. It was the starting point of mental measurement.

**The first laboratory** of experimental psychology was established by **Wundt** in 1879 in Leiping. He employed two methods to test vision, hearing, reaction time and psychosomatic problems: —*(i)* psycho-physical method *(ii)* Introspection method. He also developed mental tests which could measure the keenness of vision and hearing, muscular strength, reaction time and other sensory motor functions of body.

Many of **Galton**'s ideas were brought to USA by an American psychologist **J.M.Catell.** Like **Galton** he also believed that intellectual functions can best be measured by the reaction time and sensory discrimination tests.

In the last quarter of the 19th century, many psychological laboratories came into existence and studies of individual differences in mental abilities started.

The word "**Mental Test**" was first used by Catell in 1890 but his tests were actually tests of sensory discrimination, speed of motor responses and the like.

Thus, upto this period mental ability was identified as sensory acuity of an individual. The correlation between mental abilities and academic achievements was not known at the time.

**Drawbacks of this period :**

- Psychologists were unable to identify and define the nature of intelligence. Keenness of sensory motor reactions were related to intelligence.
- They were unable to measure the complex functions of the body
- Intelligence tests developed during this period were measuring other than intelligence.

### (B) Binet Period :

An important incident led the people to think about mental measurement during this period. In the beginning of the 20th century in France, a large number of students failed in the examination. For this teachers and students blamed each other. Seeing this, superintendent of public instruction appointed a committee to device some techniques to screen out slow learners in the schools. Binet and Simon were among members of the committee. They developed a variety of paper pencil tests in their psychological laboratory established in 1889, to administer them on children of different ages. Through these tests Binet tried to measure more complex mental functions such as power of judgement and reasoning, memory, arithmetic ability, etc.

An important contribution of Binet and Simon is that they categorised their tests in terms of age levels by administering their test items to children of different ages. In this way, an age scale of intelligence was also developed. For example, if an item was correctly answered by majority of seven years old children but only few six years old children could respond it correctly, then this item was reserved for seven years old children. In this way, Binet and Simon developed separate tests for different ages.

Similarly, if an item suited to eight years old child was correctly answered by a child of 6 years and if the same trend was shown by the six years old child in most of the cases of a test, then the mental age of the child was considered to be eight years not six years, though his chronological age is six years only. Thus, the concept of mental age was also introduced by Binet and Simon for the first time in the history of mental testing and with the help of this concept we could assess the intellectual ability of a person. Some of the tests developed during this period are given below :

## BINET-SIMON SCALE

The first scale of Binet-Simon was published in 1905. This scale consisted of 30 items arranged in increasing order of difficulty. This scale was a crude measure of intelligence of school going children.

In order to remove some of its defects they revised their scale in 1908. It was the first age based scale and it created a lot of interest among the psychologists across the world. The items in the tests were grouped according to the appropriate age levels form 3 to 13 years.

Some items for three years age

- Point to your nose, eyes and mouth
- Repeat two digits 3,5
- Repeat sentences of six syllables
- Enumerate objects in a picture
- Give family names.

Some items of eight years age

- Read a passage and remember two lines.
- Add up the value of five coins
- Name four colours
- Count reverse from 20 to zero.
- Give differences between two objects.

1908 revision of Binet-Simon Scale was adopted by many psychologists of America, Switzerland and Germany and many suggestions were given by them for the improvement of the scale. Binet-Simon accepted their suggestions and revised their scale again in 1911.

Some sample items of 1911 scale are given below:

(A) Age = 8 years

- Gives difference between two objects.
- Counts reverse from 20 to zero
- Points out omissions from unfinished pictures.
- Tells the dates correctly.
- Repeats the digits

(B) Age = 10 years

- Arranges five blocks in order of increasing weights.
- Reproduces two geometric designs by using memory.
- Criticizes absurd statements.
- Comprehends and answers difficult questions.
- Uses three given words in two sentences.

## Main Features of Binet-Simon Scale

*(i)* They are really scales, i.e., items of the tests are arranged in the increasing difficulty order. Easiest items are put in the beginning and the most difficult item is put in the last. Thus, these scales measure the level or aptitude of an examinee and not their speed.

*(ii)* These tests measure the general abilities of intelligence instead of specific abilities.

*(iii)* They can also measure the mental growth of the subject because they are arranged according to different ages from 3 to 14 years.

*(iv)* They are administered on subjects individually.

*(v)* Their system of scoring is tied to age norms. A child's performance on the scale will be compared to that of children of his own age.

**L M Terman's revision of Binet –Simon Scale:** L.M. Terman of **Stanford** University revised this scale in 1916 to adapt to American situations. He introduced one new concept which was intelligence Quotient (IQ) in his revision. His scale consisted of 90 items ranging from 3 to 14 years of age. Some items of this scale are given below :

Age = 7 years

- Knows number of fingers on both hands
- Describes pictures
- Repeats five digits.
- Gives differences between paired objects.
- Ties a bowknot.

**1937 Revision of Binet-Simon Scale :** Terman along with his associate Merill revised 1916 scale again in 1937. This revision had two equivalent forms L and M. The number of items in the test was raised to 129 in each L M. forms. A new change was also introduced in the test which was the calculation of chronological age. Upto 13 years CA was taken to be as original but after 13 years CA was computed in the following manner.

At 14 years = 13 yrs+2/3 of 14$^{th}$ year = 13 2/3
At 15 years = 13+2/3 of 2 years = 14 1/3 yrs.
At 16 years = 13+2/3 of 3 years = 15 years.

Besides, 16 years was taken to be the last age for calculation of IQ. After that, CA was taken to be constant.

**LM form revision of 1960 :** Binet-Simon scale was last revised in 1960 in which items of both L and M forms were included in the scale. This revision has a range of 2 years of mental age scores to 22 years and 11 months of mental age score. This form of the test measures abilities from 7 categories namely, language, memory, reasoning, social intelligence, conceptual phenomenon, numerical, reasoning and visual motor. Test items are in the form of words, objects and pictures and the responses given by the examinees are in the form of drawing, calculating, writing and speaking. Administration of the test requires one full hour. In this revision intelligence is expressed in terms of standard scores of the deviation IQ ( See Chapter-'Preparation of Norms' in Optional).

**Wechsler Scale :** This scale may be considered an improvement over Binet-Simon scale as it can measure the intelligence of adults very effectively. David Wechsler developed this scale in 1939. This scale was developed in two equivalent forms, each form consisted of ten sub tests of which five tests were verbal and five were non-verbal or performance type. This scale was revised in 1955 and was renamed as Wechsler Adult Intelligence Scale (WAIS). It comprised of 11 sub tests of which six were verbal and five were non-verbal. This scale is used on persons above 16 yeas of age upto 64 and administration time of the scale is one hour.The detail of these 11 sub tests are given below :

**(a) Verbal sub-tests :**

1. Information : 29 questions are given here to test the recall of knowledge concerning wide varieties of information.

2. Comprehension : 14 questions are given here to test understanding of knowledge concerning a particular subject or event.
3. Arithmetic : 14 questions are given here to test numerical ability. These questions are solved orally without using paper and pencil at all.
4. Similarity : 13 questions are given here to measure abstract verbal reasoning. Examinees are required here to compare two objects and find out the relationship between them.
5. Digit span : Memory for digits are measured here. In the first half, the examinee is asked to repeat in the same order, three to nine digits presented in the forward directions and in the second half, the digits are repeated in a backward direction.
6. Vocabulary : 40 words of increasing difficulty value are presented before the examinees here and they are asked to tell the meaning of these words.

**(b) Non-verbal or performance subtests :**

1. Digit symbol : Nine digits each with different digit symbols are given to the examinees here and they are asked to give the right code for each digits or symbols.
2. Picture completion : This subtest measures the ability of the examinees to analyse the parts from the whole. Examinees are given 21 cards containing incomplete pictures and they are asked to fill the missing part of each picture.
3. Block design : Its purpose is to measure the ability to analyse the complex whole. There are only 7 designs in these blocks which have red, white and red-white sides. Examinees are asked to produce a given design with the help of these blocks.
4. Picture arrangement : Its purpose is to measure the ability to identify the whole from the parts. Here six set of pictures are given to the examinees and they are asked to arrange them in an order which tells a meaningful story.
5. Object assembly : Its purpose is to measure the ability to synthesise the whole with the help of parts. Here examinees are given some puzzle pictures each representing some parts of the human body and they are asked to assemble them in the form of a complete man.

Speed and accuracy factors are also scored in Arithmetic, digit symbol, block design, picture arrangement and object assembly. Raw scores of each subject are converted into normalized standard scores with a mean of 10 and SD of 3. This makes the scores of each sub tests comparable. Separate IQ for verbal and non-verbal subtest forms is calculated by adding up the respective sub-tests of the two forms and if we add up scores on all the 11 subtests, we obtain total scale score. These standard scores are expressed in the form of deviation IQ with a mean of 100 and SD of 15.

Wechsler developed another scale known as Wechsler intelligence Scale for Children in 1949 to test the intelligence of children from 5 to 15 years of age. It also takes one hour to administer, though there are 12 subtests in this scale. Maze test is the only test which is extra in WISC. Maze subtest has eight mazes to be traced by the examinee with a pencil. These mazes are given in increasing order of difficulty.

The scoring system of both the tests WAIS and WISC are the same. Here also the total scores are converted into deviation IQ with a mean of 100 and SD of 15.

## Advantages of Wechsler scales

*(i)* Though Binet's scale and wechsler's scale both are individual scales, yet the later can be administered on small groups of children and adults.

*(ii)* Wechsler scale is easier to administer than Binet's Scale and its scoring is also less complex than the former.

*(iii)* Wechsler has prepared separate scales for children and adults Binet's scale does not possess this advantage.

## Other differences of Wechsler scales and Stanford Binet Scale

*(i)* In Wechsler scale, items are not grouped in terms of mental age as is the case of Stanford-Binet scale. Points are given here for all correct responses. Thus, WAIS or WISC is a point scale.

*(ii)* In Stanford-Binet scale items are interpreted in terms of different age levels of the examinees but in WAIS or WISC similar types of items are grouped together to form sub tests.

*(iii)* WAIS has separate age norms for adults but in SB Scale all the individuals above 18 are

treated in a similar manner as far as computation of IQ is concerned. Thus, people of all age levels are treated as 18 years of age after 18.

*(iv)* In SB tests items are varied, unrelated and upgraded but in WAIS and WISC tests, items are graded according to various range of ages.

*(v)* SB scale is internally standardized and rigid but WAIS is externally standardized and flexible.

*(vi)* SB scale refers to qualitative evaluation while WAIS refers to quantitative evaluation.

*(vii)* Slight chance of statistical treatment is possible in SB scale but WAIS is fully subject to all statistical analysis.

### (c) Post binet period :

This period is particularly known for testing intelligence in groups and thus group test of intelligence became popular during this periods.

A group test is one that can be given to a number of subjects at a time by a single examiner. This type of test came into being during first World War for the purpose of classifying soldiers for various jobs in accordance with their mental abilities. Army Alpha and Army Beta, two tests were developed during this period. Army Alpha is a verbal group test of intelligence meant for literate people. Army beta is a non-verbal group test of intelligence meant for illiterate persons.

We will discuss here some more group test of intelligence :

1. **Catell's Culture Fair Test :** This test was developed by RB Catell and was published by IPAT (Institute for Personality and Ability Testing) in 1961 . The test has three scales and can be administered on children and adults both.

   Scale I meant for 4-8 years
   Scale II meant for 8-15 years
   Scale III meant for 15 years and above

   This test measures the general intelligence factor and takes 30-60 minutes to administer. The test has been prepared in such a manner that previously learnt skill or knowledge does not help the examinee to score more on this test. That is why, it is said to be independent of school achievement, social advantages and environmental influences.

2. **Large Thorndike's Intelligence Test :** This test is meant for primary and secondary school children graded into five different levels. The purpose of the test is to measure verbal comprehension, numerical skill and reasoning abilities. Test has verbal as well as non-verbal items. Only non-verbals items are, however, included at the lower levels. The administration of the test takes 30 minutes in all.

3. **Raven Progressive Matrices Test :** This test was developed in England. It consists of geometric figures and designs. The subjects find out the relationship between figures and select appropriate parts for completion of each pattern of relations.

## CLASSIFICATION OF INTELLIGENCE TEST

### (A) Classification from the point of view of administration

1. **Individual intelligence test :** An individual intelligence test is one which is administered to only one person at a time. Binet-Simon is an example.

2. **Group intelligence test :** A group intelligence test is one which can be administered to more than one persons at a time. Army alpha and Army Beta are two examples of such tests.

Some general characteristics of group intelligence tests are as follows :

*(i)* They have been developed on the assumption that intelligence is a general capacity and can be measured by sampling a variety of mental activities.

*(ii)* In group tests the similar types of items are pooled together in different sub tests.

*(iii)* Every group test is standardized for a special range of ages or school grades.

*(iv)* Construction of individual test is also very difficult and costly as compared to group tests. Their scoring and standardization is also time consuming process.

*(v)* It is very difficult to establish rapport between the examiner and the examinees and hence examinees can not be motivated properly in group tests of intelligence. These two limitations are not seen in individual tests.

*(vi)* Group tests are superior to individual tests in the sense that norms established here are more dependable than that of individual tests. It is because these norms are calculated on the basis of a very large sample.

*(vii)* Individual test provides qualitative performance of the individual while group tests are mostly point scale and express the performance in quantities.

## (B) Classification from the point of view of nature of items of the test

1. **Verbal test :** Verbal test of intelligence is one in which instructions and items are produced before the examinees through the written language. So, examinees must be literate to take these tests. Mohsin's General intelligence Test, Joshi's General Mental Ability test and Jalota's Group General Mental Ability Test are some examples of verbal tests of intelligence of Indian origin.
2. **Non-verbal test :** A non-verbal test is one which requires the use of language only to impart instructions. The examinees are asked to manipulate the test materials in their own way. Since language is not needed to respond to items here, it can be administered to illiterate persons as well. They are also culturally free and hence they can be applied to any situation representing any culture. Test items are usually of figured relation type. Army Beta is a good example of non-language test.
3. **Performance test :** A performance test is one in which a subject has to perform some thing or to manipulate some concrete materials without much use of the language ability. Non verbal and performance tests are useful for the following groups of people:
   *(a) Deaf and Dumb :* Those children who cannot hear or speak can be tested with the help of performance test.
   *(b) Illiterates :* Verbal test of intelligence is useless for those who can not read or write. Performance test is useful for them.
   *(c) Shy children :* Many withdrawn children are hesitant to express before others. Performance and non verbal test of intelligence will suit them very much.
   *(d) Educationally deficient children :* Verbal test of intelligence generally measure learning along with intelligence. If children are educationally poor, they will perform poorly on intelligence test too and thus they will be wrongly declared as children of below average intelligence. Such a problem can be overcome by using performance test or non-verbal intelligence test.
   *(e) Useful for children of other culture :* A particular culture dominates in every verbal intelligence test and thus the test can not be adopted by other cultures. Due to free from culture, performance test is suitable for these foreign students.

Some performance tests of intelligence are given below :

**(a) Pintner Paterson Scale :** This is the first systematic performance test. This scale was standardized in 1917. It consists of 15 subtests.

**(b) Goodenough Drawing Test :** This scale was developed by Florence Goodenough in 1926. Here child is asked to draw the picture of a man as best as possible without any time limit. This is especially useful for those children who are suspected to be mentally retarted.

*Weaknesses of performance test :*

- Here the subject can score high due to practice effect and chance success is more frequent than verbal tests. Because of this reason, reliability coefficient is very low.
- They fail to distinguish between gifted and average children due to limited scope of these tests.
- These scales fail to test fine mental abilities such as, ability to make abstraction or concept formation or evaluation abilities of mind.

**Interpretation of Intelligence Test Scores :** Intelligence test scores can be interpreted in the following three ways:

1. **Mental age :** This concept was first introduced by **Afred Binet** of France in 1908. It refers to a score that is determined by comparing a child's score with the scores obtained by younger or older children in the norming group. Here a child's score is compared with the average score of his own age. For example, if a nine year old child scores 60 on an intelligence test and suppose mental age norms for that scale are as follows:

Mental age of 8 years = 60
Mental age of 9 years = 70
Mental age of 10 years = 80

Then, in that case, mental age of the child will be considered as 8 years instead of 9 though his chronological age is 9 years.

Similarly, if another child of 8 years obtains a score of 80, then his mental age will be ten years, though his chronological age is eight years only.

Thus, we can say that the mean performance of each age level becomes the mental age for that age level.

**2. Intelligent Quotient (IQ) :** IQ is also based on the concept of mental age. It is the ratio of mental age to the chronological age multiplied by 100.

$$IQ = \frac{MA}{CA} \times 100$$

Suppose the mental age of a ten years old child is 12 years on the basis of his scores on an intelligence test, his IQ will be

$$\frac{12}{10} \times 100 = 120$$

Similarly, if mental age of a person is nine years two months and his age is 12 years 6 months, then his

IQ will be $\frac{110}{150} \times 100 = 73.3$

**General classification of persons in terms of IQ**

| IQ | Classification |
|---|---|
| 140 and above | Genius |
| 130-140 | Very superior |
| 120-130 | Superior |
| 110-120 | Bright |
| 90-110 | Average |
| 80-90 | Dull |
| 70-80 | Borderline |
| Below 70 | Mentally retarded. |

**Shortcomings of IQ:** Some of the main short comings of IQ are as follows:

*(i)* It is a well known fact that after 18 years, the mental age of a person tends to stablize. Thus, if IQ is calculated after this age, the result will be misleading, i.e., a person will be less intelligent if he grows in age.

*(ii)* Variability of IQ scores from one test to another is not the same. As a result IQ scores for different tests would not be directly comparable.

*(iii)* It has also been found that variability in IQ scores for the different age levels on the same test is not the same. In that case IQ scores would be a misleading index because it would indicate that a person's IQ may increase or decrease as he grows in age. An example will illustrate this point.

| Age | IQ | SD |
|---|---|---|
| 9 years old child | 120 | 12 |
| 7 years old child | 120 | 9 |

Here IQ of 120 of both the children is not the same due to difference in SD.

**3. Deviation IQ :** Now a days IQ ratio is converted into a normalized standard score with a fixed mean of 100 and SD of 15. This is known as DIQ. This fixed mean and SD remain constant through all the age levels. It means that if a child's score is 1 SD above the mean his DIQ will be 100+15=115. Similarly, if his score is 1 SD below the mean his DIQ will be 100-15 =85 and so on. Thus, with the help of these **DIQ** scores inter age comparison is also possible.

## Uses of Intelligence Test

Intelligence tests can be applied in the following situations.

1. **Measurement of general learning abilities :** Intelligence and achievement in schools are highly correlated. If a person is high on an intelligence test, he is expected to score high on school achievements also. Conversely if a person scores high on an intelligence test and still his school achievement is very poor, we can find out other reasons for his educational backwardness.
2. **Assessment of individual differences and categorization :** With the help of intelligence tests we can categorise a particular class into several convenient groups and plan our instructional strategies accordingly. Thus, intelligence testing is very useful for educational guidance.
3. **Exact definition of mental retardation is possible :** It is said that those who are below 70 in IQ are retarded but to what extent they are mentally retarded can further be studied with the help of higher screening. We may define the three groups of mentally retarted in the following ways.

| Category | IQ level |
|---|---|
| Morons | 45-69 |
| Imbeciles | 25-45 |
| Idiots | Below 25 |

4. **Identification of gifted children :** Gifted children are the treasure of the society. They must be

identified in the earlier stages of their lives so that they can be fully guided and helped for their better advancement which is directly related to the advancement of the society as well. Intelligence testing will help the concerned organisations to chalk out plans in the desired manner.

5. **Vocational guidance :** Some children are very forward in verbal abilities and some are superior in non-verbal abilities. This identification is possible only with the help of intelligence tests. Since academic subjects need verbal intelligence and technical subjects need non-verbal or performing abilities, hence children may be guided accordingly.
6. **Screening :** In today's age of competition and rush, screening has become a necessity. Every school has limited seats of admission and it has to select only those students who can raise the academic level of the school high and get name for it. Same is the case with appointments in jobs. For all these purposes, intelligence testing is a must.
7. **Study of mental growth :** Mental abilities develop in a sequential order onward. We can use intelligence tests for studying the trends of mental development of individuals. Intelligence tests have made it clear that mental development of children is a steady consistent process from year to year till the age of 25. Intelligence tests show that mind does not develop rapidly in the period of adolescence like the physical and emotional development, but in childhood, it develops rapidly.

## Limitations of Intelligence Tests

1. Generally intelligence test shows what a person can do at a certain point of time. These abilities are tested on the basis of certain items included in the test. In order to make the results dependable, a proper size of the sample must be selected for standardization of the test.
2. Some people may be fatigued earlier than others when take a test. This extent of fatigue may reduce their scores and hence intelligence testing will not be accurate. So scores should be taken with caution.
3. No intelligence test is fully free from cultural influences. So, home or school background may affect the intelligence test scores of subjects.
4. Administration of the test also affects the scores of subjects. If proper rapport is there between the examiner and the examinee. I Q scores may be high. On the other hand, if children are frightened with the testing situation as is case of slow learners they will perform poorly on the test.
5. Taking intelligence scores in absolute form is misleading. Intelligence tests do not reveal all the mental abilities in most of the cases. So, intelligence test must be supplemented with clinical setting and case history method to collect detailed information about a subject as is done in clinics by physician who does not entirely believe in physical investigations. He rather takes the help of clinical diagnosis before giving remedial treatment to the patients.

# OBJECTIVE QUESTIONS

1. Freeman considers intelligence as an ability
   (*a*) to adjust in an adverse situation
   (*b*) to learn better and faster
   (*c*) to manipulate abstract materials
   (*d*) all of these
2. Single factor theory of intelligence was given by
   (*a*) Alfred Binet (*b*) Thorndike
   (*c*) Freeman (*d*) None of them
3. Which of the following is not the characteristics of 'S' factor according to Spearman ?
   (*a*) It is the acquired capacity of the individual
   (*b*) Specialization in only one trade is possible.
   (*c*) It varies from activity to activity in the same individual
   (*d*) Individuals differ only in 'S' factor of intelligence
4. In multifactor theory, range is related to
   (*a*) Number of tasks that a person can do in a limited period of time.
   (*b*) Difficulty level of items.
   (*c*) General intelligence of learners.
   (*d*) None of these
5. SI model of intelligence was given by I P Guilford in
   (*a*) 1911 (*b*) 1904
   (*c*) 1966 (*d*) 1975
6. Hierarchy theory of intelligence was given by
   (*a*) Jenson (*b*) Thorndike
   (*c*) Burt and Vernon (*d*) None of them
7. In the pre-Binet period, intelligence was considered as

(*a*) Sensory acuity of the individual
(*b*) Verbal ability of the individual
(*c*) Associative ability of the individual
(*d*) All of these

**8.** An age scale of intelligence was first developed by
(*a*) Spearman (*b*) Terman
(*c*) Binet-Simon (*d*) None of them

**9.** Binet-Simon scale of intelligence measures
(*a*) General mental abilities not specific ones.
(*b*) Mental growth of the individual over a period of time
(*c*) The aptitude or level of an examinee not their speed.
(*d*) All of these

**10.** WAIS came into being in
(*a*) 1939 (*b*) 1955
(*c*) 1960 (*d*) 1964

**11.** Wechsler developed an intelligence test for children in
(*a*) 1939 (*b*) 1949
(*c*) 1955 (*d*) 1956

**12.** Catell's culture fair test of intelligence was developed in
(*a*) 1960 (*b*) 1961
(*c*) 1965 (*d*) 1955

**13.** Non-verbal test of intelligence is suitable for
(*a*) deaf and dumb (*b*) illiterates
(*c*) backward children (*d*) all of these

**14.** Intelligence testing is useful for knowing
(*a*) individual difference
(*b*) mental retardation
(*c*) educational backwardness
(*d*) all of these

**15.** Scores on intelligence tests can not be fully relied on because
(*a*) fatigue level can influence the performance
(*b*) cultural factors can influence the score
(*c*) they generally do not reveal all the mental abilities of a person
(*d*) all of these

## ANSWERS

| 1 | 2 | 3 | 4 | 5 | 6 | 7 | 8 | 9 | 10 |
|---|---|---|---|---|---|---|---|---|---|
| (*d*) | (*a*) | (*d*) | (*a*) | (*c*) | (*c*) | (*a*) | (*c*) | (*d*) | (*b*) |
| **11** | **12** | **13** | **14** | **15** | | | | | |
| (*b*) | (*b*) | (*d*) | (*d*) | (*d*) | | | | | |

# Memory and Forgetting

## MEANING OF MEMORY

Memory is the capacity to retain the learnt material for a longer period of time and reproduce it through recognition or recall when required.

### According to This Definition:

*(i)* Memory is directly related to learning. If memory is sharp, learning will last long and vice versa.

*(ii)* Memory is directly related to examination or testing of learning. If memory is good, performance in the examination will also be good.

*(iii)* Short memory means forgetting the learnt material in no time.

But now the question arises why do we forget something and why can we not retain the learnt material for longer period of time?

## THEORIES OF FORGETTING

### 1. Theory of Practice :

Traditionally it was believed that learning was the result of practice. We forget a thing when we stop practice.

**Criticism :**

1. Modern psychologists criticized this theory by saying that forgetting takes place only when some other learning takes place. If there is no learning, there will be no forgetting. Thus, forgetting is an essential element of learning. Students have to learn so many materials in the class. So, forgetting will also be a necessary evil.
2. Second reason of forgetting according to them is that if students have not learnt the matter properly, they will forget it soon

### 2. Theory of Decay :

In spite of these criticism, this theory has some value. Forgetting is a process of fading with the passage of time. Thus time factor is important here. According to this theory impressions created by learning in the cartex fade away as the time passes. For example, we forget the names of our students after some years, We sometimes forget what we ate two days ago.

**Criticism :**

1. Psychologist criticized this theory by saying that spontaneous recovery takes place when retained material is used again and feedback is given to the learner.
2. Second criticism is that we do not forget many activities of our daily life such as swimming, skating, cycling etc.
3. The third point is that quality and quantity of memory largely depends on what the learner does while he is learning something. The experiences during learning are more important rather than time factor.

In spite of these criticism, this theory has neither been proven nor disproven.

### 3. Theory of Interference :

According to this theory some intervening activities cause forgetting. This interference maybe of two types:

1. *Retroactive inhibition :* It means something works backward to block something else. It otherwise means present learning interferes to recall the past learning.
2. *Proactive inhibition :* It means the previous learning interferes the recall of the present learning.

The relation between intervening activities and retention has been systematically studied by psychologist by the transfer of training experiment

The experimental design to study proactive inhibition is given below:

| Groups | Original learning | Activity interpolated | Test |
|---|---|---|---|
| 1-Experimental | Learn A | Learn B | Recall A |
| 2-control | Learn A | Constant | Recall A |

In this experiment, the experimental group was found poor in the recall of A because of the interpolated activity of B. It further shows that greater is the interpolated activity, lesser the amount of recall A. This inhibition was not shown by the control group. It means that present learning inhibited to recall the previous learning. Moreover, greater the similarity between two types of learning, the greater will be the amount of forgetting.

The experimental design to study the proactive inhibitions is given below—

| Groups | Preceding activity | Original learning | Test |
|---|---|---|---|
| 1- Experimental | Learn B | Learn A | Recall A |
| 2-Control | Constant | Learn A | Recall A |

In this experiment, experimental group was found poor in the recall of A due to his past learning of B. This is not the case for control group.

## 4. Trace Change Theory :

This theory of forgetting is based on the perception of a person. When we see an object, trace is formed in our mind. If we see other figures different from the original one, this trace changes and we forget the earlier thing.

## 5. Retrieval Failure Theory :

In our daily life we see that we want to recall the name of a friend or any other thing and fail at that time but when condition changes, the same thing comes to our mind more or less spontaneously. This phenomenon is called tip of the tongue. Thus forgetting is a temporary phenomenon not a permanent one. When cues that were present at the time of learning are not available at the time of recall, retention suffers. Forgetting occurs because of failures in the mechanism responsible for remembering.

**Abernethy** (1948) conducted an experiment on class room learning. He found that those students who were tested in new class rooms had poor test scores as compared to those who were tested in the same class where they were taught. It shows that change of the place causes retrieval failure.

**Criticism :**

1. This theory has no practical significance in the sense that testing is generally takes place not at the place of learning.
2. Retention is automatic due to the change in the situation. But this theory does not explain the situation responsible for retention.

## 6. Pleasure Theory :

Learning which is associated with any unhappiness or suffering is often forgotten and if learning has come with pleasure or reinforcement, it will be retained. In military field, forgetting that is called amnesia appeared in soldiers is selective in nature. Due to this they are unable to recall certain war experiences. They generally forget those experiences which they are ashamed of. It otherwise means than interesting materials are retained for a longer period of time than uninteresting ones.

## 7. Consolidation Theory :

According to this theory if newly formed traces of mind are immediately disturbed and no time is given for consolidation, they will be wiped out ie, forgetting will be there. On the other hand if proper time is given for the consolidation of the traces, the learnt material will be retained for a longer period of time.

Retrograde amnesia or backward forgetting supports this theory. Human being who suffers from brain injuries display retrograde amnesia. They are unable to report what happned just before the accident even though their memory of their distant past is normal. It means that accident had disturbed the consolidation process.

## MEASUREMENT OF RETENTION

Following methods are used by the psychologists to measure the memory

1. **Recall :** In this method a person is required to reproduce correctly what he had learnt in the past such as reproduction during examination. Here students are shown some lists of words. After seeing them they recall as many words as possible. Direct questions are also asked for this purpose.
2. **Recognition :** Recognition means distinction between seen and unseen. When we take multiple choice questions in the examination, we recognize the correct answer out of the choices given.
   Rogers Shepherd conducted a series of experiments on recognition. In one such experiment 540 words on cards were presented to the subject. Student was tested with sixty pairs of words. One word in each pair was correct if students is able to pick out each correct word, it means that his recognition level is perfect.
3. **Relearning :** Here subject is asked to relearn the already learnt material. The difference between the number of trials and time taken in two occasions of learning is considered to be an index of retention. This index is often refered to as saving score. It is because time and trails are saved in the second learning.
4. **Reproduction :** Here learner is asked to reproduce what he had learnt in the past exactly and correctly. The retention is measured on the basis of errors made by the learner in the reproduction. Lesser the number of mistakes, higher will be the retaining power of the learner. This reproduction maybe oral or written or both.

### Methods of Improving Retention Power

Experimental studies show that we can not eliminate forgetting altogether, but we can take several steps to minimize the role of forgetting. Following steps must be taken by a class room teacher to increase the retention of a subject matter in the class.

1. **Over learning :** If subject matter is properly learnt, its retention will be high. Thus over learning can improve memory but how much over learning is needed will depend on the learner's mental ability, nature of subject matter, motivation level of students and so on.
2. **Meaningfulness :** If subject matter taught to the students is meaningful and it has been presented to them in an organised manner, it will be retained for a longer period of time. So, the efforts of the teacher should be to make the material meaningful and useful for students.
3. **Sequential presentation :** If subject matter presented to students is in sequential form, it can be easily memorized. For example it is very difficult to retain 1248163264 as ten unrelated digits but if some sequence is found out between these digits such as grouping these numbers into seven digits and knowing that every second digit is twice the first one ($1 \times 2 = 2$, $2 \times 2 = 4$, $4 \times 2 = 8$, $8 \times 2 = 16$ and so on) then these digits can easily be remembered. So subject matter should be well organised in increasing difficulty order or the whole lesson should be divided into different natural units. While organizing the subject matter, interrelation between different segments should also be there.
4. **Clustering :** We do not retain information in the form that we acquire it. In the process of retention some changes in the memory take place. Clustering or grouping is one of them. If one word of a group is retained, the whole textual material can be reproduced such as retention of headings can help a man to write the whole matter related to the heading. So, a teacher must try to present facts, events or principles in the form of a group rather than in jumbled or scattered form.
5. **Pairing :** Everything in the universe is in the form of matching such as woman and men, lion and lioness, birds and animals and so on. If information is presented in pairs, it will improve memory, such as hair and ear, cheeck and chin, eye and eyebrow, head and forehead etc. Similarly, if we want to crame the spelling of CAMEL we form a pair in the following way- **CA-MEL.** A teacher should use this technique in the class as much as possible
6. **Association:** If we are able to associate a material with other known materials we can remember both of them easily. For example, we can

remember the telephone number by associating it with a car number. In the class room situation if a teacher is able to associate the learning with the real life situations of the child, greater retention will take place.

7. **Use of mnemonic devices :** Use of such devices can also improve the memory of the learner. **Kidd and Segmen** (1968) conducted an experiment in this regard. A nursery jingle of words rhyming with numerals one to ten was used effectively to superimpose an order on a set of unrelated words and thus improved the retention.
   Alphabets can also be taught with the help of short poems for each letter. By this method information in the brain is deliberately transformed into a more meaningful organization and memory is improved.
8. **Practice :** Practice makes a man perfect. If learnt materials are repeated again and again at short intervals of time it will improve memory.
9. **Slow speed:** It is a new experiment conducted by MS Ansari himself in 2001. Experimental design is given below:

| Group | Fast speed | Slow speed | Duration | Tests |
|---|---|---|---|---|
| Experimental | Learning A | Learning B | One month | A&B |

   Here learning material A&B were of equal difficulty value. It was found after the tests that material B was properly retained even after 30 days and material A which was learnt at a fast speed could be retained less than 50% in oral reproduction.
   So, a teacher must keep the craming speed of his students as slow as possible.
10. **Formation of clear concepts :** If concept is made clear by a teacher with the help of audio-visual aids or in any other way by involving more than one senses, it will improve memory. Active participation of learners also helps in improving the retention.
11. **Self recitation :** Self recitation also improves retention power. So, a teacher must encourage his students for self recitation.
12. **Principle of learning by doing :** We never forget the technique of cycling or way of writing letters throughout our lives even if we stop practice. It is because doing associates with learning and with the help of habit formation and characterization (see domains of learning) forgetting never occurs.
13. **Consolidation :** If we take complete rest or sleep after learning, traces will consolidate in our mind and when we wake up we will be able to retain the learnt material. If we play or run just after learning, memory traces are disturbed and nothing is remembered after that.
14. **Dividing the textual material into parts :** If the whole material is divided into different usable parts and each part is learnt one by one, then material can be memorized. The Quran is crammed in the same manner.

## TYPES OF MEMORY

1. **Short term memory :** Those learnt material which we need immediately to recall just after the experience is called short term memory. For example, when we go to a new place we need to remember the names of the streets, places. Persons and telephone numbers of different people.
   George A Miller conducted an experiment on the span of memory. He concluded that humans can recall 7+2 items on an average as far as short term memory is concerned. Other researchers in the field were B B Murdock Junior and Jean Peterson. This type of memory we need very much in our daily life situations
2. **Long term memory :** This type of memory is called a store house where information is stored almost permanently. Many short term memories are also transformed into long term ones if they are used permanently. Over learning or repetition of the learnt material at short intervals is needed for long term memory. Tulving (1967) conducted an experiment in this regard and concluded that rehearsal improves retrieval. This type of memory is needed to pass an examination, to face a viva voce, to develop a skill and so on.
   Many psychologists are of the view that same storage and retrieval mechanisms are involved

in short as well as long term memories and principles of interference operate in both the cases in the same manner but many behaviourists and neurologists concluded that these two types of memories differ in mechanism. Long term memory was not found affected in brain damaged patients but their STM was found affected.

3. **Part memory :** In this type of the memory whatever we have to learn is divided into parts and each part is learnt separately. If every part is reproduced separately at the time of need it is called part memory.
4. **Whole memory :** Here nothing is forgotten or left at the time of reproduction and a whole texual picture is presented. Drawing a picture or diagram and their explanations are examples of whole memory.
5. **Rote memory :** In this type of memory the whole texual matter is reproduced as it is without any slightest error whether the learner understand the matter or not Learning of Quran or Vedic Hyms are examples of rote memory.
6. **Insightful memory :** Here material is not reproduced as it is but they are presented in manipulated form, however, conceptual meaning of the texual matter does not change at all. This type of memory is very much needed in school system and students take the examinations successfully with the help of this memory. Here students answer the questions in their own language but without manipulating the meaning of the concepts, laws and principles.
7. **Perfect memory :** Luria in his book **"The Mind of Mnemonists**" (1968) reports a case of an exceptional individual. He was 29 years old newspaper agent. He would remember to each and everything he once memorised. He had no difficulty to remember 70 words while normal people can learn seven words only.

   But when Luria studied this young man thoroughly, he found that consequence of having such a strong memory were not good in all respects. He had a great trouble in grasping information in simple prose passages. He had great difficulty associated with synonyms and metaphors too.

   This experiment shows that having a strong memory does not mean that a person has a perfect memory. **Signs of a perfect memory** or a good memory are given below:

   (a) *Rapidity :* It means that how rapidly a person can recall his past experiences. if he is able to do so, it means that he has a good memory.

   (b) *Accuracy :* It means that how accurately a person can recall or assimilate his past experiences. If he is able to reproduce his past learning without any mistake, it means that he has a good memory.

   (c) *Length of time :* It means that how long a person can retain his past experiences and recall them when it is required.

   (d) *Promptness :* It refers to the revival of the details of past experiences

   (e) *Serviceableness :* It refers to the recall of right things at the right time. If a student is not able to recall his learning at the time of examination, his memory will be considered weak.

**Important disturbing factors affecting retention power :**

1. **Physical environment :** If physical environment is not peaceful and conducive to learning, the learner will not be able to retain the learnt material properly. For example if there is noise or lack of proper lighting arrangement or the weather is too hot or cold to bear at the time of learning, learning will be weak resulting in low level of retention. Similarly, if physical environment is not good at the time of memory testing, the retention power will again be badly affected.
2. **Social factors :** Social factors such as aspiration level of learners, usefulness of learnt material to life situations, unconducive relations between various social stimuli etc. also badly affect memory. If a teacher is able to utilize these factors positively, retention power of his students will be high.
3. **Psychological factors:** Interests, attitudes, motivation level and attention of the learner at the time of learning also affect retention level of learners. For example, if learner is not attentive to what he learns, he will not be able to retain the subject matter.

## Types of Memory Disorders

In his book "**Disorders of Memory and Learning**" George Tolland has described a case in the following manner:

An epileptic patient under seizure stood up one day and preached a funeral sermon in Latin. He had not learnt this sermon in full before but he must have heard the bits and snatches of it on several different occasions. When the seizure was over, he could not remember even a single word of the sermon. In fact he could never understand Latin language at all. Hypnosis was tried on him but even then he could not recall anything about his performance.

Another case mentioned in the book was also an illiterate man but when he lay down in special posture, he would recite verses from Vedas and Translate them into Hindi.

These cases are examples of memory disorders. They are not normal men. The recall that they exhibit is not related to their previous learning.

Psychologists have identified two causes of memory disorders:

### 1. Neurogenic disorders

In this type of disorder the person is unable to hold any new information in his memory for more than a few seconds. He loses his belongings every time. He even forgets the way home. He cannot recognise even his own sketches and hand writings after a few minutes. This particular defect of memory is called **Korsakoff's Syndrome Mental Deficiency**. This defect is caused by the destruction of brain tissues in an area of the brain called hippocampus. This defect is of two types:

(a) *Epilepsy :* An epilepsy seizure is often accompanied by hallucination and spontaneous action. Here the patients can not recall the events that occur during fits or the events that precede the fits. The forgetting of events that occur prior to a seizure is referred as retrograde amnesia. Some of these lost memories may often emerge later on spontaneously.
The cause of this defect in the brain is genetic not environmental. Action of recessive genes in the offsprings may bring about epilepsy.

(b) *Traumatic Amnesia :* We can understand this defect by the following examples:
A motor cyclist was riding along a dark road one night. He was knocked down by a cyclist from the opposite direction and he became unconscious. When a doctor came to attend him, the victim recovered consciousness after a few minutes. On the following day, the victim blamed the doctor for the accident. He had totally forgotten about the cycle rider who knocked him down.

Thus, we see that wounds from accidents or war can cause traumatic amnesia. Similarly, if head receives any injury due to any reason, it disrupts the memory traces, preventing it from becoming it a permanent memory and it causes a traumatic amnesia.

### 2. Psychological disorders

The material we forget or remember depends on our motives. If we are emotionally attached to any thing, person or place, the material related to it will be remembered.

Psychogenic memory disorders arise out of emotional disorders. If something has happened to any person with whom a child is emotionally attached a lot, he will either remember every incident related to the person or he will forget everything about him.

**Role of image formation in memory process :**

Gordon (1971) opined that memory involves two components simultaneously :

I. **Non verbal imagery process :** It means that when we see an object, pictures or model its image is formed in our mind and when we see the object, model or picture next time we recognise it very easily

II. **Verbal symbolic process :** When we hear some words or see some of them written any where, the audio or visual picture of the word symbol is formed in our mind and when we hear or see this word again, we recognise it.

Three explanations on the basis of several experiments are given below:

- Objects or pictures are remembered more easily if some verbal explanations are attached to it.
- Objects or pictures are remembered better than concrete words.
- Concrete words are remembered better than abstract words because no clear image of abstract words are formed into our minds.

# OBJECTIVE QUESTIONS

**1.** Which of the following is the sign of good memory
- *(a)* Ability to retain learnt material for a longer period of time and reproduce it
- *(b)* Quick ability to learn any thing.
- *(c)* Ability to relate abstract materials with life situations
- *(d)* All of these

**2.** Traditional theory of forgetting believed that
- *(a)* Learning is the result of practice
- *(b)* Forgetting is the result of decay
- *(c)* Forgetting is the result of interference
- *(d)* None of these

**3.** In our daily life, we want to recall the name of a friend but we fail at that time but when condition changes, we recall the name this is
- *(a)* Trace change theory
- *(b)* Pleasure theory
- *(c)* Retrieval theory
- *(d)* None of these

**4.** In which of the following conditions we will forget a thing readily?
- *(a)* If importance has not been given to the material
- *(b)* If we are in a condition of fear or tension
- *(c)* If we have not given enough time to consolidate the material and go for physical activities immediately after learning.
- *(d)* All of these

**5.** In order to measure memory power of a person, which of the following methods can be adopted?
- *(a)* To what accurately and quickly a person can reproduce his learnt material
- *(b)* To what correctly the person can recognise his previously learnt material.
- *(c)* The time taken by the person for relearning the already learnt material.
- *(d)* Any of the above

**6.** In order to improve retention and learning which of the following methods can be adopted.
- *(a)* Over learning
- *(b)* Complete rest after learning
- *(c)* Making the material to be learnt meaningful
- *(d)* All of these

**7.** Why it is said that a teacher should relate learnt material with life situation?
- *(a)* Because association improves learning and retention
- *(b)* Because materials of life situations work as material aids
- *(c)* Because the gap between past and present is reduced to zero level
- *(d)* All of these

**8.** When learnt material is reproduced without any manipulation it is called
- *(a)* whole memory
- *(b)* rote memory
- *(c)* perfect memory
- *(d)* all of these

## ANSWERS

| 1 | 2 | 3 | 4 | 5 | 6 | 7 | 8 |
|---|---|---|---|---|---|---|---|
| *(d)* | *(a)* | *(c)* | *(d)* | *(d)* | *(d)* | *(a)* | *(b)* |

# Motivation and Learning

## MEANING OF MOTIVATION

Two elements are required to perform a job. First is the ability to perform the job. Second is the will to do the task from within. Until we do not have internal will to do a job, we will not do it in spite of having the ability to do it.

This will depend on how important and satisfying the job is for us and need of the job depends on the utility that we derive from the fulfillment of the job. Meaning thereby the utility determines the objectives of the job.

Motivation is that internal psychological process that activates the person to fulfil his needs by achieving the objectives. Until this process is not active in the psychological frame of a person, he will remain sit idle or perform below his ability.

### Definition of Motivation

1. **J.P. Guilford :** Motivation is any internal factor or conditions that needs to initiate or sustain an activity.
2. **B.F. Skinner :** Motivation in school learning involves arousing, persisting, sustaining and directing desirable behaviour .
3. **Lowell :** Motivation is psycho-physiological and internal process initiated by some needs which led to activity and which will satisfy those needs.
4. **Thompson :** Motivation is the act of stimulating interest in the pupils (individuals) where there is no such interest.
5. **Woodworth :** Motivation is the state of the individual which disposes him of certain behaviour for seeking goals.

### Nature and Characteristics of Motivation

On the basis of above definitions following nature and characteristics of motivation are established:

1. Motivation is such a psychological factor which is controlled by physical conditions. This is an internal process. When this process becomes active in the body of an organism, he starts activity. This very process furthers the activity and directs the activity as well. As soon as the process stops activity also stops immediately.
2. In school environment motivation arouses the behaviour of pupils, directs it and helps the pupils to persist on it. A teacher can make any thing do by the students in the class by it.
3. A person is motivated to do an activity only when he is driven by any internal need for that job. When study becomes the need of the pupil, he is motivated to study. If this need is not there in him, it is created by the teacher from outside. This need gets satisfied at the fulfillment of the activity. The same job is performed by all sports and games coach in fields and playgrounds.
4. Need of life depends upon the objectives of life. If the student has fixed the objective of scoring 80% marks in the examination, this objective works as a need for him. Thus, teacher, by making the aimless students sensitive to objectives of life, motivates them to do better and better.
5. Motivation is an art of increasing the interest of students. Students can not be motivated to teaching learning process just by arousing their interest without creating the needs.

In conclusion we can say that need is the main factor behind motivation. Other factors are interest, objectives of life, curiosity, intelligence etc.

**Needs :** The feeling of want of something is called need. Condition of restlessness continues until the need is fulfilled. Man manifests any specific type of behaviour because of this very tension.

### Maslow's Hierarchy of Human Needs

Abraham Maslow explained the theories of motivation in 1954 in the perspective of needs. He classified human needs in five levels in a continuum of pyramid. He termed the physiological, safety and belongingness needs as lower level needs and esteem and self-actualization needs as higher level needs.

1. **Physiological needs:** These primary needs are created in an individual by nature. Needs of air, water, food, defecation etc. are such needs. Unless these needs of the individual are satisfied, he can not even think of higher level needs. Meaning thereby, we can not motivate a hungry or thirsty pupil for learning in the class. If a child does not have even resources to fulfil these needs, he can defer these needs by his will power but only for a short duration, but ultimately these needs will have any how to be fulfilled.
2. **Safety needs:** After fulfilling the physiological needs an organism wants to be protected in the environment from his enemies whether they are his fellow being or the fury of the environment in the form of heat, cold, rain etc. In the school situation a child wants that he should not be teased by any body. If the school is unable to protect the child, the child can never be motivated for learning.
3. **Needs of belongingness:** Having the above two needs been fulfilled an individual wants to be associated with others. He wants love, affection and friendship from his fellow beings. In order to satisfy these very needs child participates in different types of programmes in the school. In order to draw the attention and love of his teachers, he fulfills the home works given to him. Those teachers who fail to satisfy these needs of their pupils, they cannot motivate them for learning as well.
4. **Esteem needs :** After the lower level of needs being fulfilled, an organism wants respects and recognition in the society. For this purpose he exhibits some extra ordinary performance on certain affairs. The organism wants some powers in his hand to use it in the society. For example, he wants to become monitor of the class or captain of football or cricket team. In order to motivate such students for learning, it is necessary that such needs of these students must be fulfilled to the maximum level possible.
5. **Needs of self actualization :** An individual comes to recognise his strengths and weakness fully before coming to this last level of needs. On the basis of potentialities he wants to do such an extra-ordinary work so that he may acquire the top place in the eyes of the people. For example, talented students after a period of time come to know that they can top the class. In order to achieve this target they try their best. If a teacher fails to recognise the abilities of these students and does not respond properly at their achievement, these students lag behind their actual level of performance.

It is clear from the above classification that there are five groups of people found in every society. The first group gets satisfied only at the fulfillment of its first level needs and does not care for the next. Second group can be satisfied only at fulfilling the two levels of needs. The next two groups are smaller than these. They can be motivated only when their higher levels of needs are fulfilled. The last group is actually never contended. It always tries its best to excel more and more.

## Types of Motivation

1. **Extrinsic Motivation :** In such type of motivation efforts are made to create such environment from outside that individual starts taking interest in the task. For example, if a student does not take interest in teaching learning process because of his hunger, thirst or lack of safety, first of all, these needs of the students are satisfied. Important other extrinsic motivations are reward and punishment, praise and blame, success and failure, competition and cooperation, and so on.
2. **Intrinsic Motivation :** These motivations are related to subject matter or activities of the students. This motivation stresses to fulfil the higher level of needs such as esteem or self actualization needs. Such type of individuals can hardly be motivated by extrinsic motivation. Here efforts are made to create such an environment from within the individual that higher performance becomes his needs and objective of

life. Unless and until these needs are fulfilled, he never sits idle. Knowledge of progress, novelty in the procedure, and higher aspiration level, goals, etc, are important intrinsic motivating factors.

3. **External Internal Motivation :** This is the joint technique of motivation and is applied simultaneously on the individual.

## TECHNIQUES OF MOTIVATION

Important extrinsic and intrinsic techniques of motivation are as follows:

### 1. Reward and Punishment

Student endeavours to do the best in order to get reward. He becomes pleased when he is given reward and greater enthusiasm on the part of the student is shown. Following things must be kept in mind while giving reward to an individual.

*(a)* The nature or amount of reward should be according to the level of performance. Additional reward is always fatal for the future progress of an individual.

*(b)* Individual must know the importance of reward. If reward is given to so many individuals at a time, the reward loses its validity.

*(c)* Reward should not be traditional or a routine activity. Different types of rewards should be given at different occasions.

*(d)* Reward should have some monetary or social value.

As far as punishment is concerned its fear leads an individual not to do unwanted jobs. The child comes to the class with full preparation in order to avoid punishment. Following things must be kept in mind before assigning any punishment:

*(a)* Punishment should not be regular. Such punishment can make the children habitual to punishment.

*(b)* Punishment should not be so severe. Such punishment can create hatred in the minds of children towards the whole system.

*(c)* Punishment should be given keeping in view the mental and physical resistance of children.

*(d)* Punishment should be judiciously distributed to all guilty persons.

Researches have made it clear that reward is better technique of motivation than punishment. Punishment is fatal to the psychological development of the organism also. So, punishment should be avoided as much as possible.

### 2. Praise and Blame

When a child is praised at his successes, he is overjoyed. As a result he works better than before. Following points must be kept in view while using praise as a technique of motivation:

*(a)* If an organism is praised at every big or small successes randomly, he will be addicted to listening the words of praise. As a result no new behaviour is created due to praise.

*(b)* Weaker children should be praised even at their small bits of successes while talented children should be praised only when they have really done something very unique.

*(c)* Praise technique should be applied according to changing ratio schedule, i.e., sometimes, it should be used and sometimes not and the subject must not know at what time this is to be given.

As far as blame is concerned, students are directly blamed for their failures and they are made ashamed. But excess use of blame as a technique of motivation may frustrate the child. Following points must be kept in mind before blaming the students on their failures:

*(a)* Positive efforts of a child must be praised first before blaming him on his failure.

*(b)* Students should not be solely made responsible for their failure. Other related factors and conditions must also be included in the list of factors causing failures in life.

*(c)* The language of the blame should not be insulting for students. The self respect of every individual must be recognised.

### 3. Success and Failure

Success creates self confidence among individuals and possibility of more successes increases. Teacher creates such an environment in the class in which all the barriers in the way of success are removed.

Failure can also work as a source of motivation. Especially the talented students accepts the failure as a challenge for them. In order to use this technique in the classroom situation, the teacher presents such problems in the class which students are unable to solve. The bright students accept this challenge for future and thus they are motivated for work.

### 4. Competition and Cooperation

The feeling of competition is universal in humans. In the classroom situations weak students compare themselves with their own group and bright students compare their achievements with that of bright group of students. In this way the whole class is motivated. In games and sports too, competitions works as the best motivator. Every sports person does harder and harder efforts to raise his performance level. Such type of competition is called individual competition. Team competition also works as a good motivating force. These two types of competitive feelings are aroused by the teacher in the class in order to motivate the pupils.

The utility of cooperation as a technique of motivation is very limited. Here. Students are asked to work with mutual cooperation so that every one in the group may get opportunity to develop. Project method of teaching is a good example of this technique.

### 5. Knowledge of Progress

It is a traditional method of motivating the students that they are regularly told about their progress on the basis of formative evaluations. When they come to know about their achievements, they work harder to raise this level due to the feedback obtained from the knowledge of their progress. Teacher and sports teacher should regularly evaluate the achievement of students and students should be informed immediately about this. If any delay is made in evaluation or its reporting, the teachers will not be able to give any feedback to his students. For this purpose, regular tests should be conducted in the class and they should be evaluated with no delay. If evaluation and its reporting takes much time, students forget their mistakes or actual activities and as a result, they do not get any feedback from these.

### 6. Novelty

Researches have proved that monotony makes a man bored. In order to motivate such persons in their task novelty and change in the approach is essential. In the class room situation a teacher brings about novelty in his method of teaching at regular intervals. This makes the students come across to new experiences at every movement. Level of students must be kept in view while introducing novelty in the situation so that this novelty may not work as a bouncer.

### 7. Aspiration Level

Level of aspiration has a direct relationship with the objectives of life. An individual can achieve the objectives of his life when his aspiration level is high. A teacher tries to raise this level as much high as possible but it is always matched with the mental or physical potentialities of the pupils. If this level of aspiration is higher than physical or mental level, student will get frustrated at their successive failures. Contrary to this if this level is lower than the physical or mental level, it will reduce the activities of students and they will develop inferiority complex.

## THEORIES OF MOTIVATION

### 1. Instinct Theory

This theory of motivation was propounded by an English psychologist **Mc Dougall**. He pleaded that every human being has some innate powers or instincts. These instincts work as motives also and influence our behaviour. Under the influence of these instincts relationship between the object and the individual is established. Sentiments are aroused as a result of this. These sentiments organise an individual's emotional life and bring about stability in his behaviour. Thus, sentiments are an important factor behind the force of motivation. He explained the importance of self respect regarding sentiments. An individual's character is evaluated in terms of the stability of his self respect. If organisation of moral sentiments is more stable than the sentiments regarding the self respect, the character of the person will be strong.

### 2. Psychoanalytic Theory : (By Freud, Young and Adler)

According to them conscious plays main role in controlling an individuals' behaviour. As against unconscious mind there is the role of repression. Repression is the elimination of painful and unhealthy experiences from the conscious mind. Thus, repression is a defense mechanism with the help of which an individual tries to adjust partially. This repression is necessary because as child grows, many of his needs and feelings are disliked by the people which were earlier liked. When these needs are eliminated from the conscious mind, they are collected into unconscious mind and affect human behaviour indirectly. Sometimes these repressed needs come to the conscious level also when they receive any stimulus from outside. Thus, according to these psychologists, human behaviour is influenced by such motives also about which he is totally unaware.

### 3. Maslow's Need Theory

This theory has already been explained under the head of Maslow's Hierarchy of needs.

### 4. Social Theory

This theory is of two type :

**(a) Cultural Pattern Theory** (by **Mead & Benedict**) **:** According to this theory, behaviour of a person is influenced by the respective culture in which he lives. For example, individuals of those castes which have strict controlling system on their members become foolish, dry and short tempered when they grow. On the contrary, the castes in which children are behaved affectionately, they manifest considerate behaviour when they grow. Thus, behaviour is very much influenced by the pattern of rearing of a person. In the classroom situation, a teacher can motivate his students by his own behaviour.

**(b) Field Theory** (by **Kurt Levin**) **:** According to this theory, the behaviour of an individual is not determined by his qualities or personality traits but all those forces which act between an individual and his environment. Thus, there is a close relationship between an individual and his environment. In the class room situation a child can be motivated by creating an environment suitable to the child.

### 5. Drive Theory

This theory is somewhat similar to need theory of Maslow. According to this theory an individual is driven to act when certain biological needs create some inner tension which is called drive. Thus drive is the primary cause of motivation.

The drawback of this theory is that it is helpless to explain why an individual, in the absence of inner drive behaves in a particular situation due to the effect of his environment as is explained by the social theory of motivation.

### 6. Incentive Theory

According to this theory, external incentives such as rewards, monetary benefits, promotion in the social status etc. can also motivate an individual to act in a certain direction.

### 7. Expectancy Theory

According to this theory an individual is not actually getting any reward or monetary benefits but the expectation of getting such a reward or benefits can motivate him to do the job in the best manner possible. In the field of games, a sportsman can be motivated to perform his best by giving him some incentive not at present but in the future.

### 8. Learning of behaviour Theory (Clark Hall)

According to this theory an individual's behaviour depends on the satisfaction or dissatisfaction of his needs. When his needs are satisfied, his psychological tensions are reduced and he retains the reaction of his learnt behaviour. When his organic needs are satisfied, he learns to link the social conditions with his primary needs and retains that particular behaviour.

### 9. Motivation Hygiene Theory (Fredrick Herzberg)

This theory was indoctrinated in the field of industry and commerce first. Herzberg interviewed farmers, account officers, nurses and house wives in Pistbarg University in 1966 and propounded this theory.

According to this theory motives enhance the efficiency by providing comforts and satisfactions to the pupils. Motives keep them delighted by increasing their achievement on one hand and pupils get satisfied by their motives on the other. This in turn enriches learning. Since the effect of motives are positive and persists for a longer period of time, as a result motives develop the following feelings in the pupils:

*(a)* Achievement
*(b)* Recognition

(c) Responsibility
(d) Advancement
(e) Personal growth

The above feeling are directly affected by hygiene factors. They are given below :

(a) Methods of supervision
(b) Condition of work
(c) Inter-personal relations
(d) Social policy and administration
(e) Status
(f) Security

If level of these factors is low, the individual becomes unhappy, and as a result, learning outcome will fall. It can also develop negative attitude among the learner. The learner can be motivated by raising the level of these six hygiene factors.

This theory has direct application in the field of education and sports along with other field of life. Performance of students of government schools is low only because of low level of some of hygiene factors. If organizational climate of the school is made good, it will automatically increase the achievement of pupils.

## 10. Operant Conditioning Model of Motivation

This model was presented by Skinner. It suggests that behaviour would change by the consequence of that very behaviour. If the result of a particular behaviour is satisfactory, it will be automatically reinforced and repeated in future. Reinforcement is given from outside also for the recurrence of desired behaviour.

Thus, this model does not give importance to the inner motivation of the individual. It ignores drives and needs of learners as well. Level of aspiration is also ignored by this model. This model is rather based on the observable and measurable overt behavioural responses which are modified slowly by giving proper reinforcement.

According to this model the desirable behaviours are first identified. Then conditions are created for the occurrence of these behaviours. And finally, once they occur, reinforcement is given for the recurrence of these behaviours.

**Techniques of motivation and students' needs, teaching objectives and learning structures**

| Need (lower needs) | Teaching structure | Teaching objectives | Techniques of motivation (Extrinsic) |
|---|---|---|---|
| 1. Physiological | 1. Signal learning | 1. Knowledge | 1. Reward |
| 2. Safety | 2. Chain learning | 2. Comprehension or understanding | 2. Praise and reward |
| 3. Belongingness (higher needs) | 3. Multiple discrimination learning | 3.Above + Analysis | 3. Success and failure (extrinsic and intrinsic) |
| 4. Esteem | 4. Cocept learning | 4.Application | 4. Competition and cooperation |
| 5. Self actualization | 5. Principle learning | 5.Creativity | 5. Knowledge of result<br>6. Novelty<br>7. Level of aspiration<br>8. Self-motivation |

**Techniques of motivation and students' needs :** The teacher should first of all find out the needs of his student's *i.e.*, at what level of needs the students are. Only then the teacher can give intrinsic or extrinsic motivation to his students. It is also likely that students do not have the capacity to think beyond the third level of Maslow's needs. In that case the teacher should create the other two needs in his students by telling the students about the goals of life and its related difficulties.

These very needs will motivate the students for effort and desired behaviour will be seen in future.

## Motivation techniques and learning objectives

While selecting suitable techniques of motivation the teacher keeps this fact into account what learning objectives he had formulated in the beginning. Thus, a teacher takes 6 × 3 = 18 objectives into account while selecting motivation techniques. We will discuss these three domains of objectives in relation to motivation techniques below :

(a) *Cognitive Domain Objectives :* If teacher has restricted his objectives to the level of application only, then for realising these three levels of objectives, a composite techniques of motivation may be proved to be successful. But if the objectives are extended to analysis, synthesis or evaluation, motivation techniques will not work much. The teacher will rather have to take the help of teaching strategies and tactics such as self study, problem solving group discussion, symposium and seminars etc.

(b) *Affective objectives :* Lower level of affective objectives like receiving, responding and valuing etc, can be achieved by using techniques of motivation. But techniques of motivation are not very much helpful for achieving higher level of objectives and in that case, the teacher should use strategies of teaching like self study, brain storming , CAI etc. more than motivation techniques.

(c) *Psychomotor objectives :* Techniques of motivation are most helpful for realising objectives of psychomotor domain and extrinsic techniques are more powerful than intrinsic techniques here.

**Motivation and Learning Structure**

Various techniques of motivation should also he selected according to different structures of learning. These five structures are given here:

(a) **Signal learning** : Stimulus and responses are directly connected here. Extrinsic techniques of motivation are most suitable here.

(b) **Chain learning** : Chain is formed between stimuli and responses here. Environment is especially significant here so, extrinsic techniques are most suitable in chain learning.

(c) **Multiple discrimination learning** : So many stimuli are presented before the students simultaneously here and they respond to these stimuli on the basis of similarities and differences. Environment and content both are important here. In this type of learning structure, both types of motivation techniques are useful.

(d) **Concept learning** : In such type of learning content and its presentation are given preference here. Therefore, only intrinsic techniques of motivation are useful here.

(e) **Principle learning** : In this structure, various concepts are presented in the form of chain here. When this is done, they take the form of laws or principles. It means that only content is important here. So, only intrinsic techniques of motivation is useful here.

## OBJECTIVE QUESTIONS

**1.** Who among the following psychologists is of the view that a learner can be motivated by satisfying his needs?
(a) Henry Murray (b) Abraham Maslow
(c) Both of these (d) None of these

**2.** Permanent change in behaviour brought about by experience or training is called.
(a) Learning (b) Motivation
(c) Assimilation (d) None of these

**3.** The book "**Theory of Motivation**" has been written by
(a) K B Madson (b) Maslow
(c) Murray (d) None of these

**4.** Motivated behaviour of a person is
(a) Well directed and well guided toward the goal.
(b) Agitated until the goal is achieved
(c) Both of these
(d) None of these

**5.** Factors affecting motivations are
(a) Physiological factors only
(b) Psychological factors only
(c) Psycho-social factors
(d) All of these

**6.** Process of motivation is affected by all except
(a) Habits
(b) Mental sets and values
(c) Physical factors
(d) None'

**7.** Which of the following does not come under the category of social motives?
(a) Prestige and status (b) Social approval
(c) Personal goal (d) Money hoarding

**8.** Our action and behaviour is motivated by the desire for getting pleasure and avoiding pain. This is the opinion of
(*a*) Thomas Hobbes (*b*) Descartes
(*c*) Kant (*d*) John Locke

**9.** Fundamental instincts of humans are inherited rather than acquired. These instincts are the spring of human behaviour. The above opinion was held by
(*a*) Charles Darwin (*b*) Mc Dougall
(*c*) Both of these (*d*) None of these

**10.** Instinct theory of behaviour was rejected by psychologists on which of the following grounds?
(*a*) Adult behaviour is guided by experience and learning also. It is not always guided by instinct
(*b*) Human behaviour is affected by the cultural factors also.
(*c*) Human being is a rational animal. He iş not supposed to be directed by instincts only.
(*d*) All of these

**11.** Central motive state was explained by
(*a*) Morgan (*b*) Mc Dougall
(*c*) Murray (*d*) None of them

**12.** Abraham Maslow was basically a
(*a*) Pragmatist (*b*) Humanist
(*c*) Realist (*d*) All of them

**13.** A self actualized person is one who
(*a*) Does not accept restrictions imposed by the society
(*b*) Always seeks perfection
(*c*) Is very good in inter personal relationship with others.
(*d*) All of these

**14.** The theory was achievement motivation was developed by Mc Clelland of Harward University in
(*a*) 1949 (*b*) 1951
(*c*) 1965 (*d*) 1944

**15.** Achievement motive in a child can be developed by
(*a*) Proper guidance and high expectation from the child
(*b*) Telling the stories of great men to the child
(*c*) Setting a realistic goal for the child
(*d*) All of these

## ANSWERS

| 1 | 2 | 3 | 4 | 5 | 6 | 7 | 8 | 9 | 10 |
|---|---|---|---|---|---|---|---|---|---|
| (*c*) | (*a*) | (*a*) | (*c*) | (*d*) | (*d*) | (*c*) | (*a*) | (*c*) | (*d*) |
| **11** | **12** | **13** | **14** | **15** | | | | | |
| (*a*) | (*b*) | (*d*) | (*b*) | (*d*) | | | | | |

# Learning Theories and their Applications

## INTRODUCTION

Every organism who comes in this world is equipped with certain inborn capacities to enable him to face and control the environment. For example, a baby sucks milk from the breast of his mother as soon as he takes birth. This inherited behaviour is known as instinct. This behaviour is not competent enough to face the hardships of the environment successfully. He needs something more thus the process of learning begins from the birth of the child and continues his death. As soon as the child takes birth, he comes in contact with the environment in which he is born and he reacts to the environment after the interaction with the environment. Thus, the foundation of learning is laid.

## MEANING OF LEARNING

A considerable change in the behaviour of the organism is called learning. When organism comes in contact with his environment certain necessary adjustment in the behaviour is needed. This adjustment in behaviour is the result of acquision of various habits, skills, attitudes and knowledge which is actually learning in simple term

Thus, learning means change in response or behaviour (modification, elimination or acquisition of responses involving some degree of performance) caused partly or wholly by conscious or unconscious experiences. This learning does not include physiological changes such as fatigue, temporary sensory resistance or non functioning even after continued stimulation.

### Definition of Learning

It is very difficult to give a universally acceptable definition of learning because psychologists have defined the concept from different angles on the basis of their experiments. The common feature among these definitions is that learning in psychology has the status of a construct which means an idea or image that can not be directly observed like electrons or genes but they are inferred from the behaviour of the organism.

**Melvin H Marx** has defined learning in the following words;

"Learning is a relatively enduring change in behaviour which is a function of prior behaviour (usually called practice)

**Explanation :** According to the definition given above learning has three attributes:

1. Learning is a some what permanent change in behaviour. Changes occurred due to illness, fatigue, maturation or the consumption of intoxicants is not learning.
2. Learning is not directly observable. It is inferred from the behaviour of the organism in the form of construct.
3. Learning is a function of practice and experience. Experiences adds learning and practice gives it an enduring nature.

Some other **definitions** of learning are given below;

"Learning is modification of behaviour through experiences." — **Gates**

"Learning involves the acquisition of habit knowledge and attitudes". —**Crow and Crow**

"Learning is any change in behaviour resulting from behaviour." —**Guilford**

"Learning includes both acquisition and retention." —**Skinner**

"Any activity can be called learning so far as it develops the individual (in any respect good or bad) and makes him after behaviour and experiences different from what that would otherwise have been."

—**Woodworth**

"The term learning covers every modification in behaviour to meet environmental requirement".

—**Gardner Murply**

"Learning is the process by which behaviour (in the broader sense) is originated or changed through practice or training."

—**Kingsley and Garry**

"Learning is the acquisition of new behaviour or the strengthening or weakening of old behaviour as a result of experience."

—**Henry P. Smith**

"Learning is an episode in which a motivated individual attempts to adapt his behaviour so as to succeed in a situation which he perceives as requiring action to attain a goal."

— **Presey, Robinson & Horrocks**

"Learning is the process by which an activity originates or is changed through reacting to an encountered situation, provided that the characteristics of the changes in activity can not be explained on the basis of native response tendencies maturation or temporary state of the organism (e.g. fatigue or drugs etc.)

—**Milgard**

## Characteristics of Learning

On the basis of the meaning and definitions given above following characteristics of learning can be derived:

1. **Learning is a relatively permanent change in behaviour :** Temporary changes in behaviour brought about due to some accidents or consuming any drugs is not learning at all. Learning is a relatively permanent change in behaviour. It is in this context we can say that reading some selected material to pass an examination is not learning. It is because learnt material is forgotten immediately after the exam.
2. **Learning is a progress or growth of the organism :** Learning is a fundamental need of life. Without it, no progress or growth is possible. This process of growth is unending also. One achievement of the organism motivates him to go for further achievement and thus excellence in many cases is achieved.
3. **Learning is a life long process :** An organism needs learning (behavioural change) at every moment of life to adjust to new situations at every moment. He can not sit idle at any time. Situations all the time force him for the acquisition of new learning.
4. **Learning is not directly observable :** How much learning has taken place in an organism can not be directly observed. It is inferred from his behaviour which is manifested by some activities, mental or physical.
5. **Learning is the result of experiences :** Experiences are gained at every moment of life. Learning is the other name of these experiences.
6. **Learning is a goal directed process :** Learning is a purposeful activity. It is a goal directed process. Learning which is the result of unconscious efforts of the individual is not learning in actual sense.
7. **Learning is retained through practice :** Practice or exercise is a must to retain learning. If practice is not made, learning will be forgotten and the nature of learning will no longer remain permanent. Thus, learning is acquisition and retention both.
8. **Learning reinforces further learning :** Learning definitely gives satisfaction to the individual which further motivates him for higher level of learning. Similarly, learning which is accompanied by reinforcement is more likely to become permanent and motivating for further learning.
9. **Learning is motivated by adjustment :** Man has to adjust himself according to the new environment. In this way learning is an adjustment.
10. **Learning is aroused by individual and social needs :** Learning depends upon our social needs, problems, desires, and ideals. There are certain persons who learn very fast whereas others are slow in learning. It should be noticed that social environment affects learning. It is impossible to learn in the absence of environment.
11. **Learning is transferable :** It means that learning may change place but the quantum of change in the place may be different. Change in the place is caused

by techniques, ideals and the process. Change of place takes place from one field of education to the other field and from one class to other class.

12. **Learning is a process not a product :** Learning is a product for public at large but a psychologist considers it a process which has got the following four shapes-Need, Goal, adjustment and change.
13. **Improvement in the behaviour through learning :** When man reacts to the environment there is progressive modification of behaviour through learning. That is why, learning is known as improvement.
14. **Learning is active and creative :** Learning is active and creative i.e. learning depends upon the active involvement of the learner. It is said that if the learner is not self active, he cannot learn.
    It is, therefore, said that learning is the result of active involvement and experience from the sender and the receiver both.
15. **Learning is universal :** Humans are not the only organism that learn ie, react to the environment for adjustment. Animals also go through the process of learning though their speed of learning may be slower than humans.

## Learning differentiated from Some Concepts

1. **Learning and instinct :** Some behaviour of every organism is reflexive or inborn, eg, breathing, breast feeding etc. All such activities take place without the process of learning. As we move to lower animals reflexes or instincts are seen more and more in their behaviour. The least example of instincts are found in humans. These instincts are not the result of any learning or experiences. They are relatively invariant in form and are reliably elicited or released by a particular and usually very simple stimulus (R Habber 1966) Thus learning is not needed for instincts or reflexive behaviour.
2. **Learning and maturation :** Maturation means physiological development of the individual according to the norms of a particular age. Learning and maturation are very closely related in the sense that for a successful learning, a definite level of maturation is a must. Thus learning is induced by maturation. For example, we can not teach quantum mechanics to a six year old child due to lack of maturation.
   Maturation on the other hand, is qualitative changes in the organism which are not induced by learning. Maturation is an increase in competency and adaptability according to Baldwin.
   Thus, we see that maturation is purely an internal process in the organism and learning is an external process more than an internal change in the behaviour of the organism. Learning and training should start only when a child must have reached an appropriate level of maturation. Maturation is actually the readiness for an activity due to physiological preparation.
3. **Leaning and cramming :** Cramming does not bring about any change in the behaviour of a student. So, cramming can never be called as learning. Despite this fact, in order to make a durable or permanent change in the behaviour of an organism, cramming will be very much helpful.
4. **Learning and acquisition of knowledge :** Acquisition of knowledge and skills is generally termed as learning but if that change of behaviour in the organism is not applied in any situation in any manner, mere accumulation of facts and information is not learning in real sense.
5. **Learning and education :** As the meaning of education suggested by the Good's dictionary of education, education is the aggregate of all the processes, by means of which a persons develops his abilities, attitudes and other forms of behaviour of positive value in the society in which the organism lives. Learning is also a process of change in the behaviour of the organism but this change may be of positive and negative value both.

## Mental Process Involved in Learning

Learning may be the result of conditioning of behaviour but following mental processes are also involved in learning:

1. **Direction :** The person must be directed to the process of learning. It means that he must be full attentive to the process. He must have a clear cut goal for learning and he must take full interest to achieve that goal.

2. **Interpretation :** Learning needs perception, reaction to the stimuli and then concepts formation. The organism must realize all these relations in his mind.
3. **Selection :** So many stimuli or experiences may be there before the organism at the time of learning. He selects and recalls only those stimuli and experiences which are relevant to the situation.
4. **Insight :** When organism comes across a number of stimuli and experiences, he tries to find out various types of relationship among them. An insight helps him to reach the correct relationship.
5. **Creation :** When learning takes place, certain new mental pattern is formed which forces the organism to think and act in a new way.
6. **Criticism :** When an organism learns something (his behaviour is changed ) he does not accept it so easily. he evaluates all workable solutions in his mind before putting it into application or practice.

## TYPES OF LEARNING

Different criteria of classification of learning are given below:

### (A) Learning according to the development of body organs

Such type of learning can broadly be classified into two categories:

1. **Motor learning :** It involves motor and muscular parts of the body. Motor learning is also of two types sensory motor and perceptual motor. Sensory motor learning is related to the acquisition of simple habits through sense organs. Learning of skills in nursery school play ground is a good example of sensory motor learning.

   Perceptual motor learning is related to the acquisition of social habits and complex motor skills. Dancing, cycling, handwriting, typing, swimming, driving, playing a musical instrument, etc, are some examples of perceptual motor learning. It is very much objective in nature.
2. **Ideational learning :** In this type of learning, muscular or motor activity is not needed. It is related to the acquisition of concepts, ideas and mental associations. This type of learning is mostly subjective in nature.

   Ideational learning can also be classified into the following categories.
   *(i)* Perceptual learning which mostly comes through senses (direct experiences with the objects). Learning through concrete materials, learning through written or spoken symbols,, drawing a picture, nature study and sight seeing are some examples of perceptual learning
   *(ii)* Conceptual learning is the other name of abstract learning. It is related to the acquisition of concepts and abstract ideas.
   *(iii)* Associative learning is learned incidentally or by connecting two different types of learning. Prescribed sequence is followed while linking one information with the other.
   *(iv)* Imaginative learning is the process by which things of the past, present and future are given a definite form. It involves the acquisition of images and understanding of things beyond the normal range of sensory experiences.

### (B) Learning according to the domains of behaviour involved

Domains of human behaviour are three, cognitive, affective, and psychomotor so, learning can also be classified into these three categories.

1. **Cognitive learning :** It is related to the acquisition of knowledge, understanding of concepts, inter-relationship of various concepts and ideas etc. This type of learning is 90% emphasized in the classroom. Here only mind is brought into action. When this type of learning is well developed, a learner is able to generalize and evaluate concepts as well as personal experiences.
2. **Attitudinal learning :** Attitudes, values and social systems are also learnt by the individual. This type of learning begins with the feeling of belongingness of a person to his group. How a person should react to others in various types of emotional situations is the result of this type of learning.

3. **Skill learning and habit formation :** Motor behaviour of the individual along with feeling is involved here. Practice is an important aspect of this type of learning. Reading, writing, playing a certain game or doing some physical job with perfection is the result of this type of learning.

## (C) Gagne's classification of learning

Gagne has classified learning into eight categories in a hierarchical order as given below.

1. **Signal learning :** This is called classical conditioning learning developed by Russian psychologist Pavlov. In this learning unconditioning stimulus (food) and conditioned stimulus, (sound of the bell are paired together and presented to a dog a number of times. Due to this paring sound of the bell (conditioned) stimulus also forces the dog to elicit the response (to salivate ) This secretion of saliva by the sound of the bell is called conditioning. Sound of the bell works as signal here.
2. **Stimulus-response learning (operant conditioning) :** This study of operant conditioning started with the work of E.L. Thorndike He placed a hungry cat in a box and dish of food was kept outside. When cat manipulated the lever of the box correctly, it opened and cat could get food. Here manipulation of lever as a response is instrumental in producing the reward (food) here hence, this learning is also called instrumental conditioning. Instrumental conditioning is more flexible than classical one in the sense that responses are conditioned here to a variety of efforts. Such experiments were conducted and improved further by Skinner to explain operant nature of behaviour in a set form with the help of reinforcement.
3. **Chain learning :** Chaining means connection between S-R is formed in sequence Chaining is of two types, motor and verbal. Using remote controller to switch on or off a T V is an example of motor sequence and greeting a guest at home is an example of verbal sequence.

   In verbal chaining, two or more previously learned verbal sequences in stimulus response form are chained. If first member or the second member word of the sequence comes, the other member will automatically come, such as mummy daddy, chhola bhatora, old, young etc. Opposite words are also used in the sequence to form a chain.

   In motor chaining, a number of related activities are tied in such a sequence that one activity will necessarily be followed by the other. Driving a car or weaving cloth on a handloom are best examples of motor chain. The driver of a car comes to the next activity taking the gear into neutral position immediately after applying the brakes. This second activity is chained in a sequence.

   It must be noted here that a chain can not be established unless the organism is capable of linking various acts in a sequence.
4. **Verbal associate learning :** In this type of learning verbal language is also used along with showing an object, ie, seeing is associated with a word. For example, we show an object to a child and say that it is monkey. Next time when the child will see an object exactly or almost similar to the object previously seen by him, he will name it as monkey.

***Two types of chaining are involved here:***

*(i)* Observing S-R connection that connects the appearance of the object and distinguishes it from other objects, i.e., the child distinguishes the object before him from the other objects not similar to it.

*(ii)* When object is clearly distinguished from the other objects it becomes next stimulus for the child and when the child say it is monkey, it is the second response. Thus, a connection between S-R is formed

In order to make this type of learning a success, the following points must be kept in mind:

*(i)* Verbal units must be presented in a proper sequence, *i.e.*, one chain must come after the other and the whole chain at a time.

*(ii)* Learner must be active enough to make responses required by every chain.

*(iii)* Cues may be used to facilitate verbal association.

*(iv)* Span of retention power of the individual determines the length of the chain. There is

however, a limit of these verbal chains. Unlimited number of chains can not be retained at all.

(v) There must be provision for the confirmation of correct responses in the learning situation.

5. **Learning by discrimination :** When specific behaviour is shown to only one given stimulus and other stimuli are totally excluded it is called discrimination. This type of learning is seen from the beginning of life of the organism. An infant does not consider all women having breast or feeding him by their breast as mothers. Only one out of so many is her mother and that is well discriminated. The child discriminates a feeding bottle and other bottles, the child of the home and the child outside the home etc. thus, a relatively higher mental operation is involved in discrimination.

   The concept opposite to discrimination is generalization. When after conditioning to a particular stimulus, other similar stimuli also cause to elicit same response, the process is called stimulus generalization. The point to be noted here is that without perfection in stimulus generalization, nobody will be able to learn by discrimination.

   Fine discrimination takes place only out of the process of stimulus generalization. Initially the infant accepts every woman as mummy but when he does not get required response from every one, he narrows down the spirit of generalization and recognizes his real mummy on the basis of her responses.

   Discrimination is also not similar to the word of differentiation. In discrimination, emphasis is placed on stimulus side, but in differentiation, emphasis is placed on the response side. In discrimination, we eliminate the unwanted responses to the other stimuli through selective reinforcement but in differenciation, we develop a very specific type of response on the basis of the stimuli presented through selective reinforcement after examining a number of related responses too.

6. **Concept learning :** Concept is developed on the basis of common characteristics of an object. When we identify an object or an idea on the basis of its common properties, which a class of objects share in common not specific to other objects or ideas, it is called concept learning. The properties of shape, size, colour, form, nature etc are used to discriminate an object from other objects of the same class. For example, trees are many but the concept of a mango tree is applied to a tree which has some very specific property. Concept learning is the pre-requisite for learning a law or principle. Learning of abstract concept is more difficult than concrete concepts ;because discrimination is done here on the basis of ideation only.

7. **Learning of principles :** Learning of principles or laws takes place only after concept learning. It is because regular and constant relationship between two or more concepts is established in a principle. Knowledge of so many principles and laws are necessary to function properly in the environment and to save our time in repeated experimentations. Most of the learning obtained in schools is concentrated to laws, principles, systems etc.

8. **Problem solving :** It is the highest stage of learning in the hierarchy. When an individual has learned all laws and principles, he evaluates them from the point of view of utility or facticity. This evaluation helps him to solve various problems of life.

## IMPORTANCE OF LEANING FOR TEACHERS

Learning is important for a teacher in the following ways:

1. A teacher can adopt learning centred approach of teaching such as, activity programme, project method, problem solving method etc., and avoid teaching centred approach. Former is autonomous process and later is a burden on students.
2. A teacher can use the whole and part learning methods alternately to benefit the poor and talented students equally in the class.
3. Verbalization on the part of the teacher along with other motor activity can explain and

clarify the concepts and remove the difficulties of students. Cue is also used by the teacher in the class.

4. A teacher will not bank upon memorization from the very beginning of teaching. Desired change of behaviour is not related to memorization,
5. A teacher can keep the maturity level and inborn capacity of students in mind for effective learning.
6. A teacher can provide varied experiences to students in such a way that they can identify similarities and differences in objects, situations and concepts. This approach of learning will facilitate learning in the class.
7. The primary objective of schooling is to bring about desirable changes in the behaviour of learners through the process of learning. A teacher must know all these approaches and operations of learning and their relative significance. A teacher can adopt a better teaching strategy in the class only after knowing different approaches and operations of teaching.
8. A teacher can accommodate his teaching according to the individual differences of students only after knowing the process and theories of learning.
9. An important contribution of leaning psychology is that it has propounded and popularized the concept of motivation and its uses on scientific lines. We are now in a better position to use different techniques to motivate the students for verbal, mental or motor activity. The teacher can motivate the students in the class according to their age levels.
10. A teacher can know various procedures of remembering and forgetting and he can utilize various techniques of learning to minimize the share of forgetting in the class. He can help the students to transfer skills and informations acquired in the classroom to daily life situations outside the school and vice versa.
11. Modern psychology of learning lays much stree on social psychology of leaning and group dynamics. A teacher can improve social learning environment of the class by putting various theories and procedures of learning into practice.

## THEORIES OF LEARNING

We may categories all these theories of learning into two groups.

1. Laboratory psychologists' theories of association or connection (S-R theories)
2. Cognitive field theories or gestalt psychology of learning. S-R theories of learning can further be classified into two categories as under

| (A) S-R theories without Reinforcement | (B) S-R theories with reinforcement |
|---|---|
| 1. Pavlov's conditioning theory | Thorndike's theory |
| 2. Watson's learning theory | Hull's theory |
| 3. Guthrie's learning theory | Skinner's theory |

As far as field theories are concerned there are three important theories which are given below:

1. Gestalt theory of learning
2. Lewin's theory of leaning
3. Tolman's sign gestalt theory of learning

Now we will describe all the above eleven theories of leaning one by one.

### 1. Classical Conditioning Theory ( Ivan P. Pavlov, 1849-1936)

Pavlov was a Russian physiologist. He was basically interested to know how the process of gastric secretion in dogs works. He was also awarded noble prize in 1904 for his contribution in medicine especially the digestive process. This theory of learning was accidentally discovered by him during his experiments on dogs.

He noticed that the dog secretes the saliva at the sight of the food or the sound of the servant's foot steps who brings the food for him. This process of salivation which was before the food was put into the mouth of the dog was called psychic secretion-a basis for classical conditioning theory.

Conditioning according to **Branald** is "The automatization of behaviour by repetition of stimuli which accompany causes for the behaviour which formally they merely accompanied."

It means that one more psychic behaviour is also linked along with the normal routine behaviour and the person becomes conditioned to the secondary stimulus also.

**Reflexes are of two types** according to Pavlov- psysiological and psychic.

Physiological reflex is an innate process which controls the amount of gastric secretion. It will actually depend upon the kind of food that the organism is going to receive, eg, pickle can bring in more secretion of saliva in the mouth than sweets.

Psychic reflexes are none else than conditioned reflexes which occur only as a result of the particular experience of the organism .

In Pavlov's experiment the dog salivates even at the sound of the bell which is rung along with giving food to the dog. This salivation is psychic (conditioned) reflex according to him.

**Pavlov's experiment:**

Pavlov based his experiment on dogs. When food is put in the mouth of the dog, it salivates. This food is called unconditioned stimulus (UCS) and the salivation of the dog is called unconditioned (natural) response (UCR). The UCR is unlearned and implies no pre-condition.

In Pavlov's experiment, when food was given to the dog, the sound of the bell was rung. The sound of the bell, a neutral stimulus evoked no response on the first and second presentation. This stimulus is called conditioned stimulus (CS). Initially CS and UCS was given to the dog together for a number of times. Then UCS was withdrawn and only CS was presented. This alone evoked response and the dog secreted saliva.

Thus if CS alone is successful in eliciting responses, this response (salivation) is called conditioned response (CR) ie,

UCS(food) → UCR (Saliva)
UCS+CS → UCR (Saliva)
CS(sound of bell) → UCR (Saliva)
CS → CR (Saliva)

Thus, classical conditioning is a process in which a neutral stimulus acquires all the properties of natural stimulus when both are repeated together for a number of times.

Since natural stimulus like food is substituted by a neutral stimulus, say sound of the bell, this theory is also called **substitution learning**.

This conditioning does not occur in the beginning. It takes time and repeated trails. The response to conditioned stimulus (sound of the bell) depends on paring it with unconditioned stimulus (food).

**Higher order conditioning** : A model of higher order conditioning is given below.

UCS(FOOD) → UCR(SALIVA)
UCS+CS (Food + bell ) → CR
$CS_1$+$CS_2$ (Bell + light) → CR
$CS_2$ (light) → CR (Saliva)

**Properties of Classical Conditioning :**

1. *Mechanical behaviour of animals :* Pavlov's theory is based on the opinion that animal's action is mechanically governed, ie, learning is mechanistic. Mind has no role to play in leaning. The response which was originally made to UCS becomes associated with CS also and thus a CS-CR bond is made, though this learning is not permanent.
2. *Intensity :* Correlation between intensity of the stimulus and magnitude of the response is positive but correlation between intensity of the stimulus and latency of response is negative. It means that higher intensity of CS will lead to higher magnitude of CR. Apart from this, if CS is very weak, there may be no CR and thus no conditioning.
3. *Nature of relations between CS and UCS :* Time interval between CS and UCS is also important 0.5 second gap between CS and UCS has been found to be most effective. from the point of view of conditioning. Similarly UCS must follow the CS for conditioning to take place. On the contrary if UCS is given first (dog is fed first) and then CS (sound of the bell) is presented, there will be no conditioning. If UCS is presented prior to CS, it is called backward conditioning and it is mostly unsuccessful. The fourth option is that if CS and UCS both are given simultaneously, conditioning will be very weak. The last option is that UCS must be stronger than CS, ie, food must be adequate enough to quench the hunger of the dog. If amount of UCS is very little, CS will not be able to bring, about conditioning ie, bond between CS-CR will not be seen.

4. *Extinction :* CR like many other learned behaviour is temporary and unstable. If UCS is not given for a longer period and only sound of the bell (CS) is used to elicit response, a stage will come when dog stops to secrete saliva due to lack of reinforcement. This is called extinction. Pavlov reported in his experiments that when the spacing of test trails was increased, the response extinguished rapidly. This extinction of CR is the result of disuse.
5. *Spontaneous recovery :* When the dog is again brought to the experimental set up and UCS is also given along with CS, the dog responds to CS by gastric secretion, This process is called spontaneous recovery. This point also clarifies that there is no complete extinction of CR seen.
6. *Inhibition :* Inhibition is defined as a process in which a stimulus inhibits a response. It means that this stimulus is so strong that it inhibits the establishment of bond between a CS and CR. Inhibition may be **external and internal both**.
   In external inhibition external factors restrict a CR to occur such as noise, fast blowing wind, earth quake etc. These factors may distract the attention of the dog. This inhibition will be stronger if there is greater degree of similarity between CS and inhibitors. For example, if we present a tone to the dog and a new stimulus (noise) is also presented to the dog, the CR will be blocked ie, the dog will not salivate.
   In internal inhibition, CR is blocked by some internal factors (physiological or mental) For example if the organism is having body temperature more than the normal, he may have poor level of concentration to CS but once this problem is over, recovery will be fast.
   Inhibitory factors are active in old people more than in young child, hence, CS-CR bond can be established more rapidly in young children than in the older people.
7. *Generalization :* Generalization in this theory is a process in which CR to a particular stimulus (CS) is generalized to other similar stimuli. Suppose the dog secretes saliva at the sound of 1400 kHz. if the same dog secretes saliva at the frequency of 1100 kHz also, it is called stimulus generalization. CR is generalized to CS within certain limits. That is why application of generalization is very limited in our practical life.

**Factors affecting conditioning :**

Important factors affecting substitution learning are as follows :

1. *Exercise :* Conditioning is the result of repetition of conditioning process. If dog is removed from the experimental set up for a longer period, bond between CS-CR will be weakened.
2. *Time :* CS must follow the UCS and the gap between CS and UCS must not be more than 0.5 seconds, otherwise either conditioning will not take place or it will be very weak.
3. *External barriers :* Role of inhibitory factors of any type should be mitigated for proper conditioning to take place.
4. *Motivation :* If organism is not motivated to elicit response, he will not be conditioned to the CS
5. *Age factor :* conditioning is easy in children than in adults. Similarly, conditioning is also easy in lower animals. Mental operation may play a negative role in conditioning.

## Application of the Theory :

1. Learning can be made easy by associating one stimulus to the other. For example, if we want to teach 'A' for apple to our children and we show them apple also, verbal operation of the mind will be associated to sight and thus children will learn the alphabet easily.
2. Conditioning can also be used for developing good habits in children and adults. Bad habits can also be removed from them by using this theory. It is because all learning is acquired according to Pavlov. If that learning is not purposeful it can be eliminated by using the process of extinction.
3. Animals can also be trained mechanically to perform different acts with the help of this theory.
4. This theory is also used by psychotherapist in deconditioning emotional fears and mental tensions from patients.
5. This theory can be used in developing positive attitudes among students. They can be moulded

to behave positively to learning, school and the society.

6. This theory is also useful in the development of concepts, learning symbols and formulae.
7. Physiological defects of the body can also be removed to some extent by using this theory. For example, if a child urinates on the bed in his sleep, this defect can be removed by using a corporal punishment technique immediately the child starts urinating.
8. Pavlov developed an objective approach to the process of learning. He for the first time, gave emphasis on the mechanical behaviour of learning which is not manipulated by the mind.
9. Elimination of superstitions : A teacher can eliminate the superstitions of children by the activity of conditioning. For example, if a child thinks that he will be punished if a cat crosses him on the way, then such superstitions of the child can be removed through conditioning.
10. Use of Audio-Visual Aids : In the class room the use of audio-visual aids can be made effective through conditioning. For example, if "an ant is to be taught to the children in the class then the picture of an 'Ant' must be shown along with the written word. Children will speak that word after looking at the picture. Then the picture of ant is removed. Children will repeat only the written word ant. In other words, the children have learnt to speak ant as a result of conditioning.

Sometimes conditioning is ceased or happens to cease itself. This is known as deconditioning. Lack of motivation, increase in interval, lack of repetition and removal of natural stimuli are the responsible elements for deconditioning.

**Criticism of the Theory :**

This theory despite its usefulness can be criticized on the following ground:

1. Pavlov conducted all his experiments on animals (dogs) and the results obtained from animals can not be so easily implemented on humans. The reason is that human is a rational being. He is not as mechanical in his behaviour as other lower creatures are. Most of his behaviour is guided by reason and intellect.
2. This theory fails to explain the higher order thought and reasoning process which is responsible for many human behaviours and it is not like a machine all the time.
3. This theory does not take the role of emotions into account and emotions also influence behaviour.
4. It does not explain the voluntary activities guided by autonomous nervous system.
5. This theory does not recognize the role of readiness, repetition, belongingness, drill, motivation, physical and mental conditions of the organism and other environmental factors in learning.
6. According to this theory learning by CS is temporary and spontaneous recovery is possible if feedback is given to the organism again. Thus, this theory does not satisfy an important condition of learning ie, permanent behavioural change in the learner.

## 2. J.B.Watson's Learning Theory

J. B. Watson (1878-1958) revolutionized the theory and practice of psychology by his radical ideas. He outrightly rejected the consciousness and introspection as methods of studying psychology because these methods and their results can not be objectively verified.

He defined psychology as the study of overt and observable behaviour which can be measured objectively. He opined that behaviour can be explained in terms of S-R connection in the brain. It is because contiguity of the brain was enough to establish connection (bond) between stimulus and response.

**Watson's Experiment :**

Watson conducted the experiment on his eleven year old son. Watson presented him a rabbit. His son Albert started loving that rabbit : He always played with it. After this Watson produced a loud sound during his son's love making and playing with that rabbit. This sound was repeated many times. The sound was produced only at the time of his playing with the rabbit. After this the sound producing process was stopped. But the child started fearing that rabbit even on looking at the rabbit. In this way the response of fear got conditioned along with the rabbit (Artificial stimulus). The result of these experiments was that learning activities are facilitated through the process of conditioning.

On the basis of his experiments Watson concluded that

*(i)* When a stimulus and a response occur at the same time in close connection, the connection or bond between S-R is strengthened. The strength of this S-R connection depends upon the frequency of S-R repetitions.

*(ii)* Law of frequency can be derived from his theory. It means that frequency of exercise has a great role in learning. We see a candid role of exercise or practice in mathematics all the time. We can not solve a mathematical sum just by knowing its formula. Various steps of solving the sum and its repeated drill are necessary here.

*(iii)* The second law proposed by him is the law of recency. It means that the most recent response is strengthened more by its frequent occurrence than an earlier response.

*(iv)* Conditioning is the basis for learning. Learning for him is the shifting of old responses to new stimuli.

*(v)* The real explanation of behaviour lies in nervous system. It means that behaviour can be objectively explained and nervous system can explain all types of behaviour with these ideas Watson convinced other psychologist that for the explanation of learning (changed behaviour) understanding of brain including nervous system and its functioning is very essential

*(vi)* He emphasised that all our behaviour is learned by interacting with external environmental stimuli.

Thus by these ideas and efforts, he motivated psychologists to conduct researches on human behaviour (conditioning) in America. His theory influenced educational system of America very much and efforts were made to provide conducive learning environment to children in schools for efficient and permanent learning as was emphasised by Watson for strengthening the S-R.

## 3. Guthrie's Theory of Learning

Edvin R Guthrie (1886-1959) belonged to Washington University. He was also strong supporter of stimulus- response theory without reinforcement. He explained S-R bond with the help of contiguity like Watson. Thus, his theory was very much similar to the theory of J.B. Watson except the law of frequency. He rejected this law and developed a new law, principle of posterity. This principle explains that only the last response in the series which was connected to the stimulus was important.

In order to explain his theory Guthrie conducted a series of experiments on cats in puzzle boxes. He proved that for connection between S-R only one trial may be sufficient to give the conditioned stimulus full strength but practice is useful because it helps to knit the S-R connection together (strengthen SR bond) to form the larger uits of behaviour desired.

He also stressed that organisms react to various stimuli either by contraction, expansion of muscles or secretion of glands. These specific responses are called movements. When a number of such movements are associated together by the law of contiguity it is called act. For example, writing is simply an act but it requires a number of muscular movements and action of senses. When these two things are combined together, action takes place. Thus, according to him learning is actually an association between stimulus and response.

**Guthries Experiment :**

In order to prove that learning is an association between stimulus and response he puts a cat in a puzzle box. There was a pole in the middle of the box. Touching of the pole from any side and in any way opened the door of the box. Food for the cat was also put outside the box, when the cat was kept inside the box, it found the solution to come out immediately. After that whenever the cat was put in the box, the cat would repeat her previous behaviour all the time.

By this experiment, Guthrie concluded that the second movement of any organism would be based on his first one. It means that the law of contiguity works there.

**Principles Developed by Guthrie :**

1. **Principle of conditioning :** The organism is conditioned to his previous experience

(behaviour) A single trial is enough for conditioning.

2. **Principle of inhibitory conditioning :** It means that responses are inhibited when any other response occurs in between the original S-R.
3. **Principle of practice :** Improvement in performance is possible if practice is made.

## Educational Implication of Guthrie's Theory:

1. According to this theory child learns due to action. Stimulus is the result of perception and response occurs at the same time due to the action of the stimulus. Whenever the stimulus reappears, response is also repeated. If students in the class are given chance to practice a learnt material conditioning will improve.
2. The principle of association by contiguity is important to analyse emotional responses in daily life. Such responses play a significant role in teaching learning process. For example, when the child generalizes the emotion of fear, he may be frightened to all teachers instead of one or two. On the other hand, if a teacher is successful in making the school situation good, the students may enjoy the whole teaching learning process of the school system.
3. Stimuli work as motives also which cause the learner to respond in many ways. The teacher should give as many stimuli to learners as possible in order to attract the attention of learners.
4. Contiguity theory says that forgetting takes place when we do something else. We forget anything not by disuse but by other inhibitory learning (stimuli). Here Guthrie minimizes the role of other learning by more and more practice and thus he does not accept the theory as it is.
5. Behaviour therapists can apply his theory for breaking bad habits and for correcting deviant behaviour in children. This is possible by providing proper stimuli for the purpose.

## 4. Thorndike's Trail and Error Theory (S-R with reinforcement)

E.L. Thorndike (1874-1949) was the first American psychologist who introduced the concept of reinforcement for learning to occur. Mere stimulus was not considered enough for responses to occur. He conducted a series of experiments on animals for this purpose. By these experiments, conclusion was drawn that responses which are followed by satisfaction or pleasure are automatically reinforced and they are likely to be repeated in future.

Second thing is that learning is nothing but the formation of bond between stimulus and response.

### Thorndike's Experiments

He put a hungry cat in a puzzle box. A hinge was so arranged at the door that a light pressure on the floor slat close to the door helped the door open. A fish was placed near the door outside the box. Seeing the food outside, the hungry cat wanted to get out of the box.

The cat in the box made several random movements of jumping, dashing and running to get out of the box but no result was seen. At last the cat succeeded in pulling the hinge. This made the puzzle box open. The cat immediately came out and ate the food Thorndike put the cat inside the box immediately for the second trail. Again the food was kept outside the box. It was also seen when cat was not hungry it did not make any trial. When the cat was again hungry, it again gave a lot of random behaviour to open the box, before succeeding to press the hinge.

Over a series of successive trails the cat became expert in getting out of the box. The number of errors committed by the cat was reduced slowly on subsequent trails. This improvement in performance of the cat was gradual but slow. The cat learned how to open the box after many trials when a connection between stimulus and response was formed.

By his experiment, Thorndike concluded that for learning to occur, two conditions must also be satisfied.

*(i)* Cat should be hungry, ie, motivation (to quench the hunger) should be there in the cat to go through the trials of opening the box.

*(ii)* Food should also be there as an stimulus to satisfy the needs of the cat.

### Essential requirements of the experiments (Assumptions of the theory)

1. **Drive :** Drive or motive must be there to work and to respond. If cat is not hungry, she will not respond.

2. **Barrier :** There must be some barrier to reach to the satisfaction of drive. Successive trails will be made to cross the barriers.
3. **Random movement :** Initially the movements of the organism is not goal directed. It is rather random and error is reduced slowly and successively.
4. **Chance success :** success is obtained by chance. It means that learning begins with chance factor and trail.
5. **Selection :** Right responses are selected from among so many responses after repeated trails.
6. **Fixation :** Right responses are fixed and drilled in order not to be forgotten by the organism.

## Laws propounded by Thorndike

E L Thorndike propounded three basic laws and five secondary laws on the basis of his trial and error theory.

**(A) Basic laws :** Three basic laws are given below :

1. **Law of effect :** This law is also known as the law of satisfaction or annoyance. Learning occurs if and only if the response has some effect on the environment. According to this law when modifiable connection between stimulus and response has been made, the connection was strengthened if it resulted in satisfaction and was weakened if it resulted in annoyance.

Thus individual repeats those experiences which provide him satisfaction or pleasure and tasks causing discomfort are avoided by him. Thus, by this law, Thorndike accepts the importance of reward and punishment in learning. Reward is satisfying and punishment is painful for children.

***Classroom Application of the law:***

The educatioinal implication of this law are mentioned below:

(i) *Increase in Memory :* Law of effect is related to remembering power. Interesting tasks are remembered by the students for a long time and uninteresting jobs or tasks are forgotten.

(ii) *Increase in interest :* Like memory, interests are also directly related to this law. The satisfaction and pleasure arousing activities give birth to the interest of the students.

(iii) *Use of reward and punishment :* The effect of reward and punishment also affect learning. Use of reward and punishment is based upon this law.

(iv) *Formation of Good habits :* The teacher can produce good habits and attractive behaviour by using stimulation efforts.

(v) *Treatment of Delinquents :* The teacher can change the behaviour of delinquent children by using this law. He can cure them by providing satisfying experiences.

(vi) *Control of emotions :* With the help of this law the teacher can control the negative emotions of children such as anger, jealousy etc.

(vii) *Improvement in teaching method :* The teacher can improve his teaching methods with the help of this law. He can see the effect of his teaching methods on students. If he thinks proper he should not hesitate to make necessary change in them.

(viii) *Care of mental level :* The teacher should show more interest in the activities being performed according to the mental level of the students.

(ix) *Satisfying experience :* classroom experiences should be satisfying and pleasant in order to strengthen the bond between S-R. If experiences are meaningful and useful to the daily life of learners they will produce a satisfying effect on learners. In order to increase satisfaction, school activities should be arranged in such a way that learners may have some degree of confidence and success by their own efforts.

(x) *Self learning :* Self learning by the students is encouraged in the class. It is because a lesser degree of success in this leaning is more satisfying than 100% success in that learning which is directly under the control of the teacher.

2. **Law of exercise :** There are two sub laws of this law (i) Law of use (ii) Law of disuse

The law of use states that the more frequently a modifiable connection between S-R is made, the stronger that connection will be. Repeated use increases the bond. Thus, an activity on repetition gets stabilized and strengthened.

The law of disuse states that when a modifiable connection between S-R is not made over a period of time, the strength of that connection is weakened. If a connection is out of use for a long period, power of that relationship decreases.

***Classroom application of the law :***

*(i)* Students should be provided ample opportunity for practice after every learning in the class. This will strengthen the bond between S-R.

*(ii)* Exercises may be oral, written or activity based. But efforts should be made to make all exercises activity based.

*(iii)* All learnt materials and lessons should be revised time and again because disuse of bond for a longer period weakens the bond.

*(iv)* Things such as pronunciation, handwriting, mathematical computations, etc., can be improved only if practice or exercise is there.

*(v)* No type of skill can be learnt without the help of this law Music, painting, field performance etc all need exercise at every stage.

*(vi)* Drill plays a special role in strengthening the bond between S-R especially in elementary classes. It is because small children use their mind and understanding power less than the powers of their muscles and motor activities.

**3. Law of readiness :** When a modifiable connection is ready to act, that action is satisfying. On the other hand, when it is not ready to act, doing is unsatisfying. Readiness depends on maturation and experiences of the learner simultaneously. This law states that if any thing is imposed on an individual, its doing will not be satisfying for him. As a result, he will not be ready for that learning.

***Classroom application of the law :*** This law is also known as the law of motivation. Its classroom implications are given below.

*(i)* If learners are not ready to learn in the class, the teacher should not teach them at all. The teacher should wait till the readiness of learning is seen.

*(ii)* The teacher should give those experiences first which enhances readiness.

*(iii)* Aptitude tests in various subjects and disciplines may be conducted in order to determine the mental readiness of learners.

*(iv)* If anything is imposed on learners to act, that action will be unsatisfying for him and unsatisfying experiences weaken the bond between S-R

*(v)* Instead of compulsion, children should be motivated to learn. The teacher should start teaching only when students are ready to learn.

**(B) Secondary laws of learning :**

**1. Principle of multiple responses :** Organism tries many responses before coming to the right response through the process of trail and error. During this process he eliminates unproductive responses and comes to the point of success gradually and sometimes randomly. Thus, the learner learns from his own mistakes

From this point of view, it is proposed that students should be given opportunity for self learning through the process of multiple responses. Help is given to them only when it is needed. It is in this sense that psychologists say that all experiences are educative.

**2. Principle of mental set :** It refers to the predisposition to act in a given way. It is directly related to one's attitude, feeding, interest and drive. Learning is possible only when positive mental set is there in learners.

The teacher should first of all make the positive attitude and feeling of pupils towards learning. Mental set of pupils can be made positive by creating interest in pupils, by making the material meaningful and creating an inner urge for learning. Emotional atmosphere of the classroom should be very congenial and satisfying for learners . It will also make the mental set of pupils positive.

**3. Principle of partial activity :** According to this principle a response is made only to parts or partial aspect of total situation. For example, a baby will respond to his mother whether she is in night clothes or in evening dress or in the bathroom. In the classroom, a student does not mind whether the teacher is in pant shirt or dhoti He will always respond to the teacher.

4. **Principle of analogy :** When an individual faces a new situation, he responds to the situation in the manner he responded to a similar situation in the past. Thus, the law of contiguity works.
   In the classroom, the teacher should help the students to identify the similarities between different situations for transfer of learning. In this way the pupils are brought from known to the unknown situation. For example, he compares the historical events with the present day situation.
5. **Principle of associative shifting :** The learner uses the learnt material or knowledge to other fields of life. One knowledge is shifted to other fields. For example, HORSE means an animal that eats grass and that is used for walking long distances on its back. The concept of grass eating animals can be used in other fields.

## 5. Hull's Theory of Learning (Drive Reduction Theory )

This theory was propounded by Clark L Hull in 1915 but it was systematically explained in his two books **Principles Of Behaviour** (1943) and **Essentials Of Behaviour** (1951)

Hull wanted to give a comprehensive theory of learning which could explain from simple trial and error learning of animals to complex social learning in humans. His theory can be summarized in the following words.

When a response ® is quickly followed by a stimulus (S) and this connection of S-R is closely and timely associated with the diminution of a need, there will be an increased tendency of that S-R to occur in the later occasions

**Hull's Experiments :**

He took a puzzle box having two compartments. The wall which divided the two compartments had a hole at the top. The rat was put in one compartment and electric current was passed. The electric current worked as stimulus and the rat started cutting bars and it also jumped in the box in all sides. Since the current was there in the wall also, it made the jumping of the rat difficult but finally the rat was able to jump into the other compartment through the hole. Then electric current was run in the second compartment also and the rat tried again to jump to the first compartment. After many trails the rat was able to learn that he should jump to other compartment whenever he feels current in the compartment. This learning is the result of law of effect.

In other experiment, hull used bell before giving electric shock. The rat learned to jump to the other compartment on hearing the bell even without feeling the current. This learning is the result of conditioning.

**Ruch** (1970) summarized the theory in four phases given below:

- It assumes that what is learnt is a connection between S-R and learning is the result of habit formation (SHR)
- Reinforcement is a necessary condition for stability in the connection between S-R and hence learning. The strength of bond can be increased only when response is followed immediately by a goal substance. It means that reinforcement given to the organism reduces his drive and mental tension.
- The connection between S-R (SHR) is increased in magnitude gradually as a function of reinforced practice and to represent a permanent change in behaviour.
- The performance of a learned response is measured through its amplitude, speed, frequency of occurrence and resistance to extinction. All these have been explained by him in the 16 postulates given by him. The factors which will influence learning are drive (D), reinforcer (k) and the amount of effect and fatigue involved in learning. The third factor is known as reactive inhibition (Ir).

Thus, the tendency of a given stimulus to evoke a particular response is a function of habit strength of that connection times level of drive times magnitude of reinforcers minus reactive inhibition.

Clark Hull was a professor of the Yale University. He developed a mathematical, deductive and testable system of S-R learning. He differed from other learning theorists especially in the following concepts:

1. **Need :** It is a state of organism in which a deviation of the organism, from the optimum of biological conditions necessary for survival,

takes places. When a need arises, the organism acts in order to reduce the need. Sometimes, Hull's theory of learning is called need reduction theory.

2. **Drive :** It is a common denominator for all primary motivations due to food, water, sex or any other cause. No individual can be motivated to any work without satisfying these drives.
3. **Reinforcement :** Whenever a reaction ® takes place in temporal contiguity with a receptor impulse resulting due to the receptor of stimulus energy (s) and this conjunction is followed by the diminution in a need, in the tendency of that stimulus to evoke that reaction. Thus reinforcement (I) according to Hall is like a stimulus. Which has the ability to alter the probabilities of R. These reinforcing stimuli are associated with the biological drive.
4. **Unlearned behaviour :** Such behaviours are found more frequently on the lower phylogenetic levels than on the higher ones. Learning is a super structure built upon the inherited connections (unlearned behaviour).
   Hull developed an elaborate symbolism for his theory. This symbol is SUR which stands for stimulus unlearned response connection.
5. **Stimulus :** According to Hull, responses are conditioned not only to the physical stimuli but to the neural effects of the stimuli. The effective stimulus in learning is the trace that is formed in the nervous system caused by the environmental objects. These stimulus traces are designated as S and learning is the result of this capital S.
6. **Response :** There is a difference within the organism to make a response and a real response. The internal response tendencies (designated as r) are not observable but inferred from behaviour. The overt response ® is actually important here. The association of S-R is represented as SHR Here, H represents as habit. According to Hull, changes in SHR constitute learning. This SHR can be understood with the help of the following figure.

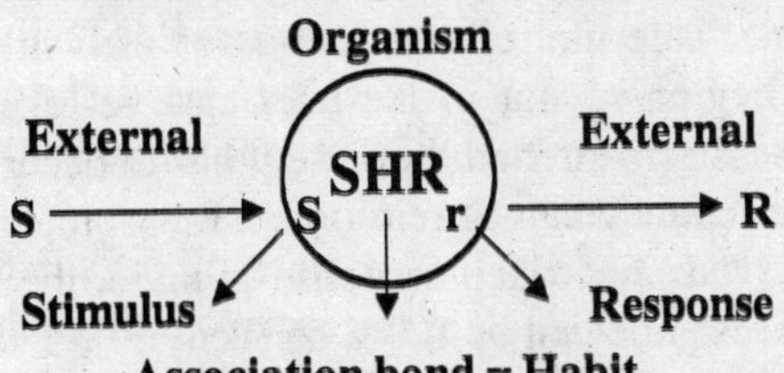


7. **Learning and performance :** Learning is different from performance altogether. Performance can be influenced by many factors such as need, drive etc but learning is affected by only one factor, the number of times a particular response occurring together has been followed by a reinforcement.

After explaining the important concepts touched by Hull, his theory of learning is given below:

"Connection between stimulus and response is not enough for learning. Some kind of reinforcements is a must to establish this connection. Once this connection is established, drive is reduced."

## Hull's Postulates

Hull has explained his theory in sixteen postulates. Only four of them are given below.

1. **Law of Habit Formation :** SHR=10-0.03N$^a$
   Here, N=Number of trials to form a habit, a= Empiral constant which is = 0.03, SHR=Habit formation
   When a stimulus (s) works on an organism (o), natural impulse in the organism forces him to make response ( R ) This R reduces the drive in the organism to some extent, ie, SRR=1-10- N$^a$
   In this way, the more the S is given, the stronger the habit becomes.
2. **Reaction Potential :**

| | | |
|---|---|---|
| SER | = | D X Vi X K X SHR |
| SER | = | Reaction Potential |
| D | = | Drive present in the organism |
| Vi | = | Dynamism in the signaling stimulus trace. |
| K | = | Reinforcement given to the organism |
| SHR | = | Habit formation |

   This reaction potential (SER) is not the same all the time. It varies from time to time in the same individual and from individual to individual depending on the stimulus.
   The second thing is that if reinforcement (of a link within a given behaviour chain) is delayed, the reaction potential will be weak. Thus, immediate reinforcement is necessary.
3. **Stimulus Generalization :** When there are two or more stimuli of similar nature, they can

evoke the same response by the organism. This is called stimulus generalization. If $S_1$ and $S_2$ are same, habit strength (SHR) generates a stimulus generalization, same as R was by the presence of $S_1$ $S_2HR = S1HR \times 10 - 0.135$ d here, d = a difference in the nature of $S_1$ and $S_2$.

4, **Primary Motivation or Drive :** According to Hull, motivation is nothing but drive (need) reduction. Primary motivation is caused by providing food, water, oxygen, opportunity to satisfy sex urges etc.

This drive (D) has two components

*(i)* Drive proper ($D_1$) It is a function of number of hours of food privation (h)

*(ii)* Negative drive ($\Sigma$) It is a positively accelerated monotonic function of "h" It slowly decreases from one to zero, i.e.,

$D = D_1 \times \Sigma$

Here value of $D_1$ = 37.824 x 10-27.49 61/h+4.001

## Conclusion:

*(i)* Drive presents in the organism creates tension. In order to reduce this tension the organism is motivated to do some acts. In the course of his action, he comes across certain stimuli. These stimuli forces him to make a series of responses. This makes a chance of association between S-R but this association is not stable unless it is followed by a reward or reinforcement.

*(ii)* Learning takes place as soon as drive is reduced to the minimum. That is why his theory is also called drive reduction theory of learning.

**Educational Implication of need reduction theory :**

*(i)* A pupil can not be motivated for learning in the class until his need or drive of any type is reduced to minimum. It means that needs of all categories of children should be incorporated in the learning process.

*(ii)* The second implication is that learning becomes meaningful for children only when it satisfies the needs of children, ie, learning should reduce the drive to the minimum. If drive is reduced, children will automatically be motivated.

*(iii)* Reward should be regularly used in the learning process because it can reduce the tension from the minds of children.

*(iv)* Secondary reinforcements can also serve as motives. For example, a child knows that he can purchase toffee, in Rs. 2, so he can do something to get Rs. 2 Thus, this Rs.2 works as secondary reinforcer.

*(v)* Hull explained learning in quantitative terms. He measured the latency of response. Latency of response means the length of the interval between a signal and a response. He explained that there should not be so much delay in the reward after the response.

*(vi)* According to this theory repetition stimulates learner. Hence, a teacher should try to revise and recapitulate the learnt materials as many times as possible.

*(vii)* Artificial incentives (reinforcers) can also he used in the class to motivate learners.

## 6. Skinner's Operant Conditioning Theory of Learning:

B F Skinner was a professor in Harward University. By studying the behaviour of organisms he said that reflex was the basic unit for analyzing the behaviour. He conducted several experiments on reflexes in rats and pigeons. He found out two types of conditioning by these experiments. In Pavlovian conditioning the reinforcing stimulus (sound of the bell) was paired with natural stimulus (food). The conditioning that emerged due to this pairing was termed as type "S" conditioning or respondent conditioning by Skinner. In this type of conditioning, subject has no control over the conditioned response. Skinner described his own procedure as another type of conditioning (type R conditioning) which he termed as operant conditioning. Here a response occurs spontaneously in the absence of any stimulus. The term operant means that the behaviour operates upon the environment to generate its own consequences.

Thus, the difference between classical conditioning and operant conditioning is that in the former case the reflexes may have zero strength in the beginning but in the later case reflexes never possess zero strength because it has to occur at least once before it can be reinforced. Reinforcement will be given only when response is there, though this response may not be 100% correct.

The second distinction is that operant behaviour is external and hence observable but respondent behaviour is internal and personal. Two experiments of Skinner with Skinner box on rats and pigeons are given below.

**Experiment-1**

The box used by Skinner is dark and soundless. The hungry rat had to pass through narrow grilled way in the box and reach the goal. Before starting the experiment rats were kept hungry for specified number of days and arrangement was made to keep them active for obtaining food. There was a lever in the box. The rat went ahead on a definite route, puts its (rats) feet on the lever and there was a sound whenever the lever was pressed by the feet of the rat. There was a light and he got some food in the bowl.

In this way the sound caused by pressing the lever and receiving of food worked as reinforcement. In this way every behaviour or activity of rat regarding the pressing of lever, the resultant sound and the availability of some food worked as reinforcement. The rat being more active got more reinforcement. It resulted in an accurate performance and accelerated the speed of reaching the goal.

**Experiment-2**

Skinner made a pigeon box for experiment on pigeons. In this experiment Skinner tried that the pigeons should learn to take a complete round rightward and strike their beak at particular places. As soon as the hungry pigeon imprisoned in the pigeon box took a rightward turn, hit the beak on a particular place, he was served with a grain. The availability of grain after striking beak worked as reinforcement and the pigeon went on repeating and correcting the performance to get more and more grain. After sufficient practice the pigeon learnt to turn its head rightward and hit beak at a particular place to get more and more grain.

Skinner by these experiments introduced his theory of operant conditioning in the field of learning. He concluded that our learning behaviour is directed by operant conditioning. Our behaviour and activity to a greater extent is the result of operant conditioning.

**Operations Involved in Operant Learning:**

Four important operations involved in operant conditioning are as follows.

1. **Shaping:** (generalization, chaining and habit competition)- In order to bring about desirable changes in the behaviour of the organism selected reinforcement is used. This process is called shaping. The behaviour of the organism is shaped by systematically reinforcing the closer approximation to the desired behaviour. Suppose, we want to train a pigeon how to peck a particular disk, we will wait the pigeon to make a correct pecking response. If his response behaviour is close to the correct response, reinforcement will be given. A chain of different closer correct responses will be prepared in such a manner that final response of the pigeon is 100% correct.

   At first we would give reinforcement to the pigeon if he merely turns slightly in the direction of the disk. This will motivate the pigeon to come closer to the correct response by and by and finally he would make a definite approach movement towards the disk. Skinner says that by using this technique, a hungry pigeon can be made to peck at the disk within a period of three minutes.

   **Three principles** are involved in shaping the behaviour of an organism—

   (a) *Generalization :* All the living organisms generalize experiences and knowledge acquired in one situation to other situations. This generalization is also of two types, the first is response generalization and the other is stimulus generalization.

   Response generalization means when responses are repeated, they are likely to vary over a range of similar acts. This type of generalization is a must for shaping. If pigeon only repeats his previous responses after reinforcement without any variation, he would never come closer to the correct response. The more his response is closer to the accuracy, the more he is reinforced and thus he learns to peck at the disk.

   Stimulus generalization occurs when a particular response is made after a particular stimulus, that response is repeated at the similar stimuli also. The boy who fears a particular teacher, generalizes his fear to other teachers also.

(b) *Habit competition:* At every point of chaining of a number of responses the correct habit must dominate over the competing habits. This is made possible when only correct habit of the organism is reinforced.

(c) *Chaining :* It is the third principle of shaping the behaviour. It means that each segment of the chain must be linked with the succeeding segment. The cues produced in one response must be linked with the next response. Suppose, we want to train a monkey to dance. We will start this training by reinforcing her even if she lifts one leg. We will then reinforce her if she lifts her next leg and so on.

Skinner also proved by his experiments that secondary reinforcers are more effective than primary ones because primary reinforcers disturbs the cues of the chain by bringing more concentration of the organism. If secondary reinforcers are used, his concentration is not so much disturbed.

2. **Extinction :** If reinforcement is not given to the organism, previously established relationship between cues is weakened and then extinguished. For example, if the rat presses the bar of the skinner box and does not get pellet of food repeatedly, his bar pressing behaviour will be extinguished
3. **Spontaneous recovery :** Skinner does not differ from the concept of respondent conditioning in this context. If reinforcement is again given after extinction, the previously learnt behaviour of the organism will return again and his performance would be better than would have been predicted. Gagne further opined that amount of spontaneous recovery of an operant habit is directly related to the length of the period since the termination of extinction. Besides, if amount of reinforcement is more, the recovery will also be greater.
4. **Role of reinforcement :** A reinforcer, according to Skinner, is any event that changes subsequent behaviour when it follows behaviour in time. So, it is used as a procedure for controlling behaviour. These events definitely raise the rate of responding.

**Types of Reinforcement:**

Reinforcement is of three types:

(a) *Positive reinforcers :* Food, money or all physical items are all positive reinforcers for which an organism works to get them. They either strengthen or at least maintain the response. Positive primary reinforcements are based on drives (needs) as food water, oxygen etc. They are essential for the survival of the organism. Positive secondary reinforcers are based on socially derived motives as money, prestige, praise etc. They are needed for social existence in the world and are attached to the recognition of the organism for a particular act.

(b) *Negative reinforcers :* They are those unpleasant stimuli which the organism will avoide by not doing a particular act. Social disapproval or condemnation are few examples. When this is used the organism terminates the annoying stimulation quickly by engaging in the required task. They strengthen the avoidance response. It means that in negative reinforcement an organism does something to avoide displeasure, discomfort or condemnation.

(c) *Punishers :* They are aversive stimuli and when they are used, the individual is afraid of doing a particular act. They are different from negative reinforcers in the sense that a negative reinforcement precedes the response (given before the response) and forces the organism to avoide an unpleasant situation by doing a particular act while a punisher is followed by a response and forces the organism to avoide punishment by not doing a particular act, both are, however, aversive stimuli .

**Schedule of reinforcement and theory of operant conditioning :** Procedure for giving reinforcement to the organism is called conditioning here. The schedule of reinforcement is either regular or intermittent. Important such schedules are as follows:

1. **Continuous schedule :** Here reinforcement is provided to the organism regularly after all correct or closer to correct responses. Linear model of programmed instruction or getting results after examination is an example of such schedule.

2. **Intermittent schedule :** Here, we sometimes give reinforcement to the organism and sometimes not even after correct responses. Intermittent schedule can be classified in tabular form as below:

**SCHEDULE OF INTERMITTENT REINFORCEMENT**

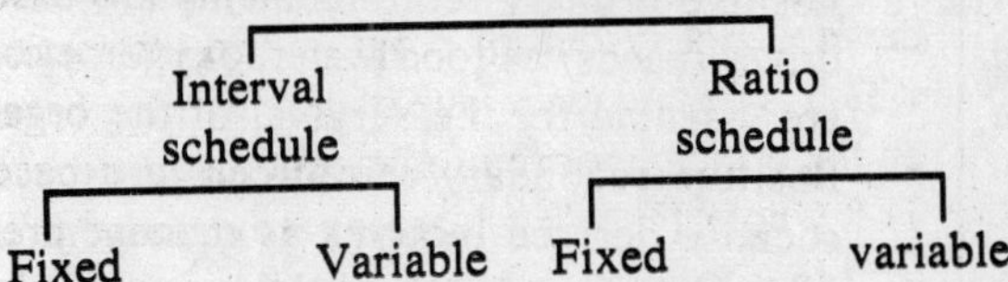


In interval schedule reinforcement is given after a gap of some hours, some days, some months or years, e.g., a worker will get Rs. 50 as his wages after 8 hours. In ratio schedule, reinforcement is given to the organism on the basis of his performance no matter after how long he gets, e.g., payment is given to a watch repairing person when he repairs the watch correctly no matter how much time he takes in repairing. The details of fixed and variable schedules are given below:

(a) *Fixed interval schedule :* Here, reinforcement is given to the organism after a prescribed interval of time irrespective of his performance, e.g., government servants draw salaries at the end of every month whether they perform poorly or nicely.
The demerit of this schedule is that organism develops time discrimination here after sometime. It means that he knows that he will get the salary at the fixed time and hence little or no response is elicited even after reinforcement.
The second problem is that if interval between reinforcement is too long, it is very difficult to maintain behaviour. As a result, no improvement in the behaviour is possible here.

(b) *Variable interval schedule :* Here the reinforcement is randomly spread over for a particular period of time, *i.e.*, sometimes, it is given after say two minutes and sometimes after three or four minutes. Steadiness of rate is the important characteristic of this schedule. The dating behaviour of American girls is an example of this schedule. In the teaching learning process if we have to give 15 reinforcements in one hour, we will not reinforce the child after every four minutes. We may reinforce the child 5 times in the first 15 minutes, 5 times in the next 40 minutes and in the last five minutes, he is reinforced 5 times at every minute.

(c) *Fixed ratio schedule :* In this schedule an organism is reinforced only after emitting a certain number of responses. For example, if he is reinforced once after five correct responses, schedule will be 5 : 1 or a child is given one toffee after solving five questions of mathematics and so on.

Important characteristics of this schedule are as follows:

(i) FRS>VIS>FIS
(ii) We can start by a low ratio, ie, 3 : 1 We can establish a very high ratio, such as 500 : 1 by increasing the ratio in graded forms.
(iii) Unlike FIS a discrimination is built. There is a break after the reinforcement is given followed by rapid rate until the next reinforcement is given. Two example of VRS are as under:
  - Commission agent receiving commission after selling a particular amount of commodity.
  - Student receiving a toffee after cramming 15 lines from a book.
(iv) Variable ratio schedule : Here, the number of responses required for reinforcement varies around some average ratio. The organism is sometime given reinforcement after two correct responses and sometime after three or four responses but the total number of reinforcements that he is to be given will not change.

Important characteristics of this schedule are as follows :

(i) The organism does not know at how many responses, he will get reinforcement. Announcement of bonus for employees by the companies on different occasions is an example of VRS. It results in steady rate of responding without break, ie, better performance all the time.

*(ii)* Very high rates can be built if the beginning ratio is small.

*(iii)* VRS>FRS>VIS>FIS Gambling is the best example of variable ratio schedule.

**Educational Implication of theory of operant conditioning :**

Theory of operant conditioning has an important place in Educational Technology. It has constructive use. Its educational uses can be justified on the following grounds :

1. Theory of operant conditioning should schedule and control the learning process and environment in such a way that the learner should be encouraged to advance ahead and he should have the least failure and disappointment.
2. Theory of operant conditioning is used effectively for the modification of behaviour. We should be aware of the suitable reinforcer for a particular child whose behaviour are to be modified. As soon as the child starts behaving in the desired way he should be immediately encouraged by suitable reward. This will enable the child to repeat the behaviour. As a result, the child will proceed faster towards the desired behaviour and attain maturity in learning by way of balanced adjustment with reinforcement.
3. On the basis of this theory of learning Skinner developed a system of programmed instruction which is a good technique of self learning based on the principle of reinforcement on all steps.
4. The whole teaching learning environment in Indian schools is surcharged by fear and unpleasant experiences. Corporal punishment is used by teachers in all schools. Due to these reasons students work only to avoide punishments. These schools can use the principles of operant conditioning to eliminate the amount of fear from the minds of children. Positive reinforcements can be used for this purpose.
5. We can immediately reinforce the positive behaviour of students in the class. The delay in

**Comparison between classical (respondent) conditioning and operant conditioning**

| | Classical | Operant |
|---|---|---|
| I | It is called type I learning | It is called type 2 learning |
| II | Conditioned response is reflexively forced by unconditioned stimulus | Response is very much spontaneous, though it can be increased by giving reinforcement |
| III | Conditioned stimulus works as signal so, it is called signal learning | Here organism has already certain responses available in its repertoire |
| IV | S-R takes place on the basis of law of contiguity | S-R takes place on the basis of law of effect produced by reinforcement schedule |
| V | It is controlled by automatic nervous system in the organism | It is controlled by central nervous system in the organism |
| VI | Reinforcement in the form of UCS (Food) is given first to elicit response | Reinforcement is given to the organism only after eliciting response |
| VII | Single bond is formed between S-R here | A chain of responses is formed here |
| VIII | Different pictures of behaviour are presented here to establish an arbitrary stimulus with a specific response. | Responses are discriminated out of a mass behaviour emitted in response to a complex stimulus field |
| X | Time controlling is important here | Success of learning depends on response modification |
| XI | Conditioned reflexes may have zero strength initially | Responses will never have zero strength. It has to occur at least once before it can be reinforced. |
| XII | Respondent behaviour is internal here | Behaviour is external here |

reinforcement may destroy the effects of reinforcing stimuli. For example, if a student performs very nicely in the class in a particular test, and he is not reinforced for a number of days, then delayed reinforcement given to him will have no effect on his behaviour.

6. If regular reinforcement is given to students on all their correct responses, they will be conditioned to the reinforcing event and their behaviour will not be affected in future. So, teachers are advised to use variable ratio schedule of reinforcement along with fixed ratio schedule and interval schedules for small kids.
7. This theory also helps us to define objectives in behavioural and operational terms. These objectives are measured on the basis of the responses of the organism.
8. This theory can also be used for the proper development of personality. We can shape the personality of any organism in the desired manner by using the reinforcement schedules .
9. According to this theory maximum learning can be achieved if learner commits minimum mistakes and this is possible when learning materials are arranged systematically in an easy manner.
10. According to this theory nothing can be achieved over night. Success in learning is gradual and step by step. So, teacher should not lose patience in the class.

**Criticism :** Some of the weaknesses pointed out by **Chomsky** in this theory of operant conditioning are given below:

*(i)* Results obtained from controlled situations can not be so easily generalized in social situations.

*(ii)* Skinner has completely ignored the structural and genetic factors in the psychological process of language development. Chomsky wrote "Skinner's interpretation of verbal behaviour were formulated in terms of metaphoric extension of the technical laboratory........in fact the terms used in the discription of the real life and of laboratory behaviour may be homonyms with at most a vague similarity of meaning".

*(iii)* Reinforcement system of Skinner does not take into account the role of spontaneity, curiosity and credivity in humans.

*(iv)* When an organism behaves after reinforcement, the role of thinking in his behaviour can not be denied. This makes the theory somewhat subjective. Humans are not machines. Mental process is also seen active in the manifestation of their behaviour.

*(v)* When a teacher fully applies this theory in the classroom, his behaviour may be undemocratic there. He will always try to control the behaviour of his pupils.

## 7. Gestalt Theory (learning by insight)

In opposition to Thorndike and Watson who were developing objective methods to study behaviour and were busy to do away with the role of mind in psychology, three German psychologists-Max Wertheimer, Kurt Koffka and Wolfgang Kohler developed a new approach of studying behaviour which considered learning as the result of organization of perception (insight) by the learner. They advocated that we perceive and think of whole not of parts.

Gestalt is a German word which means pattern, form or configuration. These psychologists believed that we react to our own pattern of perception when we face a problem. We learn not by associating bits of experiences but by forming new Gestalt in the mind and these new patterns are organized into meaningful wholes in the total situation. This mental exercise helps us to solve the problem. These psychologists also opposed the quantification of behaviour.

The basis of learning through insight are those experiments which these German psychologists conducted on animals. They made it clear through the experiments that animals can also learn through insightful observation like human beings. Kohler made it clear by experimenting, on chimpanzees. He experimented by keeping those animals in natural environment. According to Kohler everything can be learnt through insight.

"By insight is meant a good observation, perception of situations as a whole or perception of those parts of the situation that provide the goal."

—**Woodworth**

Woodworth says that before doing any task the goal should be looked at. He has called this as foresight. After making a trial, it is to be seen whether that trial is right or wrong. This is called insight hence insight includes foresight.

In the process of insight, whole unit is emphasized rather than parts. These various parts are organized but this organization is purposeful. For this law of similarity is to be followed. The perception of the whole situation and intelligent response has been named as insight by the psychologists. In other words, it is the mental ability which is found in human beings and higher order animals.

## Kohler's Experiments

The theory of learning by insight is basically associated with the name of Wolfgang Kohler who conducted a series of experiments on chimpanzees. Some of his experiments are described below.

***Experiment-1 :*** A chimpanzee was closed in a cage with a stick. Some bananas were put outside the cage. Seeing the fruit, the chimpanzee became restless and tried to get it but he failed in all his trials. Then he perceived the stick and the total situation. He got bananas by establishing relationship between the stick and the bananas.

***Experiment-2 :*** In this experiment two sticks were put in the cage. These sticks were such as they could be made a big stick by inserting one into the other. The chimpanzee first tried to get bananas with one stick but failed. Then he inserted one stick into the other and got bananas with the help of this big stick.

***Experiment-3 :*** In this experiment, chimpanzee was put in the cage and bananas were hung by the ceiling of the cage. A box was also put in the cage . when chimpanzee could not reach bananas., he used the box to raise his height and got them.

***Experiment-4 :*** Kohler conducted his experiment on 15 months old girl also. The girl was able to walk. A toy was put at a distance of 2 meters but there was some barrier between the toy and the girl. When girl could not reach the toy straight she used her insight and reached the toy by turning on one side of the barrier.

Thus, insightful learning involves the following **characteristics (Steps):**

*(i)* Survey of the problem.
*(ii)* Hesitation or pause to see the problem.
*(iii)* Repeated trial without insight.
*(iv)* If initial mode of response is failed, other modes are tried. Transition from one method to the other is sharp and sudden.
*(v)* Rethinking about the goal.
*(vi)* Appearance of critical point after insight at which the organism suddenly and definitely performs the required act.
*(vii)* Repetition of adaptive response.

Principles involved in perceptual organization (insightful learning).

Some of the basic laws propounded by Gestalt psychologists are as follows:

1. **Law of figure ground :** Everything is perceived in the context of its background. Thus, close relationship is there between figure and ground. For example, we try to solve a sum by using the ground that has been provided. It otherwise means that closed areas are more stable and satisfying than the unclosed ones. Closed areas form groups very easily. This law is also called law of closure.
2. **Law of pragnanz:** An organism is motivated to learn when there is tension or disequilibrium of forces in the psychological field. Learning is the removal of this tension. When we perceive an object, we find some gaps in our perceptions. These gaps are filled by the perceiver and a whole figure is prepared.
3. **Law of continuity :** Objects having continuity are learnt easily because they can easily make a whole.
4. **Law of similarity :** This law makes the individual to grasp things which are similar. They are picked out as they were from the total context. Similar ideas and experiences get associated. An object revives another object which resembles or looks similar to it e.g. seeing a man and remembering an intimate friend by some resemblance though never saw them together in the past.
5. **Law of proximity :** This law states that proximate or near together things are picked up first and learnt easily than distant things. In other

words, perceptual groups are favoured according to the nearness of their respective parts. Items tend to form groups if they are spaced together. For instance, a triangle or a circle is understood in this way.

Gestalt theory of perception has been summarized as below by Kohler himself.

"Our view will be that instead of reacting to local stimuli by local and naturally independent events, the organism responds to the pattern of stimuli to which it is exposed and that this answer is a unitary process, a functional whole which gives in experience, a sensory scene rather than a mosaic of local sensation"

**General Features of the Theory :**

*(i)* In this theory motivation and purpose are the same thing. Learner is motivated for action because of the goals which control his behaviour. If goal is clear and realistic for the learner, learning will be natural.

*(ii)* This theory endeavours to deal with all types of learning from very simple to most complex occurring in the organism. It is a problem solving approach of learning.

*(iii)* This theory is somewhat subjective in nature. Personal experiences of learners are important here.

*(iv)* This theory uses the term perception instead of simple knowing. The term 'know' could be used for those ;beliefs of the person that rest on adequate evidence and on highly efficient construct systems. The term perception, on the other hand, means personal beliefs that is governed by internal factors.

**Educational Implications :**

*(i)* Small children are very much able to perceive essential relations when they are given concrete materials. They have limited capacity to manipulate and draw conclusions about objects or events that are not directly present before them.

*(ii)* At higher intellectual level, students are better able to perceive abstract materials.

*(iii)* The structure and systematic organization of subject matter plays an important role in learning. The teacher should study the learner's reaction every time in order to see whether the material is organized systematically or not.

*(iv)* Purpose or goals of learning should be made clear to the students, before the teacher starts teaching.

*(v)* Past experience of children and their background should be associated with the present situation. It will develop insight in students.

*(vi)* All subjects to be taught in the class should be taught as an integrated whole.

*(vii)* According to this theory, whole is not mere summation of parts. Whole is based on the law of figure ground. Hence, the teacher should present the picture of whole subject matter in the class first, then he should come to its parts.

*(viii)* This theory is very much helpful in adopting problem solving approach in the class.

*(ix)* The insight of the learner is based upon his past experiences. So, in order to develop insight in them, the teacher should relate the previous knowledge with the present knowledge of students by proper lesson planning.

*(x)* For developing insight, motivation in the form of cues is also necessary. The teacher should use different techniques in the class.

*(xi)* Simple trial and error does not work according to this theory. Hence, the teacher should pay attention to understanding the concept and laws also.

*(xii)* This theory helps the learner to develop reasoning, thinking and imagination powers and thus their creative potentials are always encouraged.

**Criticism :**

Most of the findings of this theory and trial and error learning are the same. If we say that there is nothing new in this theory except the subjective interpretation of the behaviour of the organism by propounding different laws, it is correct.

**Comparing trial and error and learning by insight theories.**

| | Trial and error | Learning by insight |
|---|---|---|
| 1 | Learning depends on the efforts of the learner | Learning depends on the insight and intellectual use of the learner |
| 2 | Motivation is stressed here | Problem solving approach is stressed here |
| 3 | It is based on sensory motor coordination of the learner | It is based on the ability of perceptual organization. |
| 4 | It does not take transfer of training into account | Transfer of training is necessary for learning here. |
| 5 | Applicable for small children more than the others | Applicable for all groups of learners |
| 6 | In this method, physical skills are used. These physical skills help in reducing the errors | In this method perception is the main thing. The object is looked as a whole |

## 8. Kurt Lewin's Topological Theory of Learning

Lewin was also a Gestalt psychologist but the difference between Kohler and Lewin is that Kohler gives more emphasis on previous experiences of the learner for developing insight while Lewin emphasises more on the development of behaviour and makes use of motivation. According to him, learning is behaviour, a locomotion from one region of life space to another, ie, when a person moves from one region to another, the structure of his space changes. This change in cognitive structure is learning.

He classified learning into four categories

(*a*) Learning is a change in cognitive structure.
(*b*) Learning is a change in motivation
(*c*) Learning is acquisition of skills
(*d*) Learning is a change in group belonging

**Components of Lewin's theory :**

There are four main components of the theory

1. *Life space :* It refers to that environment to which individual is living, responding or reacting. It includes features of the environment to which reaction is made, the people to which the learner comes in contact, the problems he faces, the materials he manipulates, and his way of thinking. While living in the environment the individual has to cross certain barriers to reach the goal. The group of forces organizes individual's behaviour pattern and this pattern will determine his future behaviour. The perception helps the learner to distinguish between reality and unreality levels of the life space.
2. *Valence :* It refers to attraction or repulsion of a region. If the region (goal) of an activity is attractive (gives pleasure and reduces tension) it is called positive valence and if the goal is repulsive, it is called negative valence. Valence may also be strong, weak or moderate depending on the cognitive structure of the psychological field of the learner. If level of aspiration or goal changes, valence will also change.
3. *Barrier :* When individual undergoes the process of learning, he comes across a number of difficulties (barriers) to reach his desired goal. These difficulties may be physical or psychological in nature.
4. *Motivation :* Motivation is the process in which motives are related to specific goals and these motives are satisfied when goals are achieved. These motivations may be internal and external both.

   Learning is not a haphazard and unplanned process according to him. It depends on how the life space is organized and how the psychological world is constructed while crossing the barrier.

**Educational implication of the theory :**

This theory can be applied in the class in the following ways:

(*i*) Proper psychological as well as physical environment should be provided to pupils in the class in order to help them cross the barriers and develop insight in them.

*(ii)* Understanding part of teaching and comprehension of textual matter should be stressed. It will provide motivation to pupils. Actually understanding is a must for learning.

*(iii)* The teacher should help different pupils in formulating their respective goals keeping in view their needs and capacities. If goals are attainable for them, they will face no difficulty in crossing the barriers.

*(iv)* Valence can also be strengthened by making the goals attractive for learners and by raising their aspiration level.

*(v)* Total situation of the problem should be made clear and understandable for learners. If problem is clear, learner will be self motivated for learning.

*(vi)* The teacher should use reward and punishment procedure regularly.

*(vii)* Efforts should also be made to reduce tension of learners as much as possible.

## 9. Tolman's sign gestalt theory of learning

The important characteristics of Edward C Tolman's theory is that it has almost all the merits of respondent operant conditioning theories and field theories. Tolman published his work "Purposive behaviour in animals and man" in 1932 declaring his system as purposive behaviourism. He was opposed to the psychology of consciousness and introspection method of studying psychology. He advocated.

"We do not only respond to the stimuli but we act on our beliefs and strive toward goal by using our intellect".

The second characteristic of Tolman's system is that he developed molor approach to behaviour instead of molecular approach developed by Watson. Molor behaviour is purposive and goal secking all the time. It means that behaviour is guided by the goal determined by the cognitive structure of the organism. He has discussed three types of variables in his theory. They are given below:

*(a)* **Independent variables :** Behaviour of an organism is generated by five initiating causes (independent variables). They are (i) environmental stimuli (ii) physiological drives (iii) heredity (iv) Previous training of the organism (v) physical maturity or age.

*(b)* **Dependent variables :** They determine and generate the overt behaviour of the organism. Behaviour according to him is (i) active and selective (ii) purposive and goal directed (iii) guided by S-R connection though not so mechanical as Pavlov or Watson advocated and (iv) molar and trainable .

Thus Tolman's behaviour is determined by the goal directed and active perception of the totality of the situation (sign gestalt expectation of the individual) Behaviour of an organism is generated when sequence of cause and effect is combined with the goal directed perception.

*(c)* **Intervening variables :** They come in between dependent and independent variables. They are of two types:

*(i)* Purposive and cognitive determinants

*(ii)* Capacities and behaviour adjustment

These variables can not be directly observed. They can, however, be inferred from the overt behaviour. Important intervening variables are psychological deprivation related to needs, beliefs, values, motives and life spaces.

**Types of Learning Identified by Tolman :**

1. *Cathexis :* This type of learning explains final type of positive or negative objects to basic drives. It is a connection between a given type of food and drive of hunger.
2. *Equivalence beliefs .* It is a connection between a positively cathected objects and a type of sub disturbance of objects.
3. *Field expectancy :* It is developed in the organism when certain environmental set up is repeatedly presented to him.
4. *Field cognition modes :* New modes of perceiving and cramming the objects of the environment is developed.
5. *Drive discrimination :* There is always a definite relationship between type of drive and mode of response.
6. *Motor pattern :* Motor patterns' are conditioned with the help of the signs.

**His Experiments :**

One of his experiments is known as **latent learning experiment**. This was conducted in 1930. In this experiment he allowed groups of rats to run through the mazes without giving food. Later on, the food as reward was given to them. The group of rats which was given chance to explore maze learned much faster than the group which could not find the maze. By this experiment, Tolman concluded that some latent learning took place as a result of the exploration of maze.

**Other experiments proving his theoretical system :**

Tolman's students conducted series of experiments to test his theoretical system of behaviour Macfarlane (1930) trained some rats to swim across a simple maze filled with water to reach the goal box. Granted that the animals learned to reach the food, there remained the question of whether they had learned. something cognitive about the maze or had learned a series of stimulus-responses (S-R) connections. To clarify this problem, he drained the water out of the maze. Rats were put into the maze so that they could run through, instead of swimming to reach the goal box. He found that the rats could reach the goal without committing any error. He concluded that the animals learned the specific lay out of the maze. They had acquired a cognitive map of the maze.

**Reward expectancy learning experiment** was another experiment in the series. It was conducted by one of his associate M.H. Elliot in 1928. He selected two hungry groups of rats and trained them to find a reward in the form of corn. The bran mash group was called experimental group and the sun flower seed group was called control group. The experiment continued for nine days and on the tenth day these two groups were inter-changed with respect to reward. It was found that the experimental group which expected bran mash committed more mistakes than its counterpart and its learning was disrupted.

On the basis of these experiments it can be concluded that:

- behaviour is docile and hence can be moulded by experiences and training.
- learning can be improved and errors can be reduced by providing rewards to the organism
- learning is an affair of sign gestalt, formation, refinement, selection and invention.
- some objects attract and some objects repel the organism and thus behaviour is generated in the behaviour space.
- an organism is activated for an action when it has a demand for a particular goal. Demand is of two types- demands avoiding physiological disturbances and demands seeking physiological quiescences. For example, if we avert appetite by taking food first type of demand is satisfied. When these two types of demands are satisfied the organism is motivated for action (learning)

Three types of laws are needed to account for learning:

1. Capacity laws relating to traits, aptitudes and characteristics of the learner which determine type of tasks and situation which can be mastered successfully.
2. Stimulus laws which deal with conditions inherent in the material itself such as belongingness of its parts and how well it leads to insightful solution.
3. Laws related to the manner in which material is presented such as frequency of presentation, distribution of practice and use of rewards.

**Educational implication of the theory :**

*(i)* The teacher should make the behaviour of learners purposive and goal directed during the whole teaching learning process.

*(ii)* Reward and punishment should also be used for reinforcing behaviour.

*(iii)* The learning which occurs by perception should be stabilized by practice. The teacher should not rely on simple trail and error techniques only.

*(iv)* The impact of intervening variables should be reduced to the minimum.

*(v)* The teaching should be child-centred keeping in view their age needs, previous experiences and endowments.

*(vi)* The teachers should also help learners to set up their personal respective goals to avoide tension from their minds. Goal directed behaviour will work as a motivating force for learners.

*(vii)* The teacher should follow gestalt principles in order to make the teaching material meaningful.

**10. Bruner's Discovery Approach to Learning :**

J.B.Bruner also developed a cognitive model of learning. His theory explains how the subject matter can best be learnt practically. He has stressed three points that should be taken into account in the teaching learning process.

- Nature and ability of learners.
- The structure of knowledge
- Nature of knowledge acquisition process.

Thus, according to him, a learning theory, should have the following **characteristics**:

*(i)* A theory should specify the experiences which effectively implant a predisposition toward learning in the learner. Merely gaining knowledge is not learning. It should necessarily convert gained knowledge into rules for thinking about the world and oneself. It otherwise means that cultural, motivational and personal factors do play important roles in learning.

*(ii)* A theory should specify the ways how a knowledge can be structured so that it can easily be understood by learners. Any idea or body of knowledge can be presented in a form for any particular learner to understand it in the form. Once the learner understands the form of knowledge, he can apply it any where.. Three aspects of structure of knowledge affects the learner's ability to understand the form

- Mode of presentation
- Economy of time and resources
- Power

*(iii)* A theory should specify all the sequences of material to be learned. If learner knows these sequences, he can relate all the learning materials with each other and a picture of composite whole will be formed.

*(iv)* A theory should also specify the nature and procedure of reward and punishment in the process of learning.

Thus, according to Bruner, learner discovers learning himself:

## 11. Ausubel's Theory of Verbal Learning

The other names of this theory are theory of **reception learning** and theory of **meaningful verbal learning.** Ausubel says that if learners have properly internalized the material learnt, they can easily reproduce it. The more the material is presented to the learner systematically, the more the process of internalization will be facilitated.

Learning is internalized by using the following two processes:

**(a) Progressive differentiation process :**

In this process, more general or inclusive ideas of a discipline are presented first. Then concepts are differentiated in terms of details step by step. As the learning proceeds, a student organizes the content in a hierarchy. Then all these concepts in the hierarchy are differentiated.

**(b) Integrative reconciliation process :**

In the second phase of learning, after internalizing the learnt material, new ideas are also taken in and relationship between the two are explored. As a result of this reconciliation, new learning takes place. This is known as integrative reconciliation.

In the words of Ausubel " To facilitate learning and retention, it would be necessary to introduce appropriate subsumers and then a part of the cognitive structure prior to the actual presentation of the task"

**Learning of skills-specific type of learning :**

When a particular task is performed efficiently, it is called skills. Skills can be developed in any person, by providing proper guidance and techniques. Sequence of steps and their due weightage in the cue are identified and drilled. When a person becomes perfect in a particular skill, he also becomes habitual to perform the task in the similar situation with the same accuracy.

All skills are not alike in nature. Development of some skills depends on perceptual and conceptual factors. Some skills such as typing or short hand need emotional involvement along with motor coordination and some skills needs only guidance and so on.

Following factors play key roles in the development of skills:

1. **Readiness :** Unless or until one is ready for the acquisition of a certain skill one can not be made

to learn or acquire that skill. Therefore, the first step in guiding a learner towards the development of any skill is to make him ready to learn that skill. He must be given adequate incentive or sufficient motivation to start the learning of skill with great enthusiasm and effort.

2. **Utilization of the method of Transfer of training :** Phenomenon of transfer of learning may help a lot in learning new skills. A person who has learnt a wide variety of skills is able to learn new skills with greater ease. Therefore, by securing the help of positive transfer, the teacher should guide the students to acquire new skill.
3. **Knowledge of one's progress :** There must be a continuous appraisal of skill learnt so that the learner may be acquainted with the pitfalls in his learning. This can give him additional incentive to keep him on the track and help him to learn correct responses in place of incorrect ones.
4. **Adequate guidance :** The student should be given adequate amount of guidance at the proper time in learning a skill. Too much help makes the students dependent and kills their originality and initiative while denial of guidance discourages them in learning further. Therefore, an intermediate principle should be followed. They should be given help when they think they need it, but cultivate self reliance in their learning.
5. **Maintaining a proper balance between speed and accuracy :** Speed and accuracy both are important for the proper learning of a skill. Which one of them should be given more importance is a difficult question to be answered. In my opinion both are equally important as they add to the proficiency and competency of a person in a specific area. Therefore, both should be given equal weightage in learning skill.
6. **Learning method :** The unit of practice as Boring, Langfield and Weld advocate, " Must involve the entire sequence and pattern which is essential for correct performance. "Neither, the learner should involve him in peace meal learning or concentrate on minute details, nor he should choose very large units for practising in all situations. He should try to keep a proper balance between the whole and part methods of learning. In place of continued or massed practice, distributed practice should be adopted.
7. **Repeated practice :** Learning of skills require sufficient practice. So, chance of practice should be given to the learner.

**Factors Affecting Learning :**

Factors affecting learning can be classified into three categories :

(A) Factors belonging to the learner himself
(B) Factors belonging to the teacher
(C) Factors belonging to the material and human resources.

**(A) Factors relating to the child :** Important such factors are as follows :

1. Motivation level of the child : There is a proverb in Hindi that we can not arrange a market by knitting the shopkeepers with ropes. If learner is not motivated to learn, no learning can take place. If these motives are not there in him, his power of action can not be aroused. If these motives are not there in him, they are given to him from outside. Since, all learners can not be motivated by the same techniques, motives according to the psychology of learners are identified and selected.
2. Intellectual ability of the child : We can not make a mentally retarded child learn by adopting any measure howsoever, it is effective. If level of intelligence of a learner is high, his learning ability will also be high and vice versa provided that he has not become problematic or delinquent because of his superior intelligence.
3. Interest of the child : Children also differ in interests because of the differences in mental tendencies and attitudes to the environment. Interest can also be created by providing incentive to him.
4. Age of the child : Learning efficiency increases with age but to a certain extent till it reaches to the maturity level of a particular age. Maturation of an individual makes a difference in the total learning of an individual. This process is reversed in the old age.
5. Child's willingness to learn : The amount of learning very much depends on the will of the learner to learn. If an inner urge or drive is not there in the child to learn, he will not learn. This

will can be developed by raising the aspiration level of students.

6. Availability of guidance facility : Simple trial and error method of learning will not work if guidance is not provided to learners to develop proper insight for learning in them. Guidance can eliminate frustration and tension from their minds and it will work more positively for learning. This guidance should be so much as to facilitate learning. Excessive guidance is an impediment for learning.
7. Background of the child : Socio-economic status of the child's family also affects learning. If educational background of the child is poor and his low family income is a source of continuous tension for the child, a number of factors will work to reduce the amount and quality of learning of the child. Good educational background facilitates transfer of training and hence learning.
8. Physical health of the child : Physical health is a function of sensory motor coordination and development of cognitive structure. A student should be physically fit so that he may learn easily and comfortably. Attention span, concentration, interests etc all depends on the physical health of the child. Hence, health is a necessary factor affecting learning.

**(B) Factors related to the teacher:** Following factors on the teacher's side affect learning:

1. Use of psychological principles and theories : It is the teacher who creates environment for learning and proper learning environment can be created by applying psychological theories and principles in the classroom. If such principles and theories are applied, only then environment will match with the age, maturity and tendencies of the child. From the process of child's growth to the procedures of learning and motivation, everything contributes to learning.
2. Professional efficiency of the teacher: The teacher should have full command over the subject that he is to teach along with the knowledge of educational philosophy and psychology. He should be a life long student of his field in order to give more and more to his students.
3. Knowledge of educational technology : Educational technology includes application of mechanical devices into the teaching learning process for the speedy transfer of knowledge to students and use of scientific procedures and practices in the class room. Such a knowledge and his commitment to its use facilitate learning.
4. Knowledge of individual differences : No two individuals are alike with respect to physical, mental or emotional abilities so a teacher has to deal not a class of 40-50 students but 40-50 different individuals. This makes the task of a teacher very difficult and gigantic. The task of a teacher will not be over unless each and every child is satisfied with him.
5. Attitude and personality of the teacher : Teaching profession is not a physical job like that of a rickshaw puller. His job is psychological in nature because he deals with human being. Unless his attitude towards humans is not positive and his personality is not structured in the line of learning, learning will not be facilitated.

**(C) Factors related to physical and human resources:** The teacher is helped ;by the available resources for bringing desirable changes in his behaviour. How effectively such changes will be introduced in his behaviour depends much on the quality and the management of these resources. Such things and factors affecting learning may be listed as below:

1. The quality of the teacher in terms of his mastery over the subject matter, teaching skills, rich experiences and teacher like qualities and behaviour.
2. The socio-emotional climate available in the institution in the shape of teacher pupil relationship.
3. The availability of appropriate learning material and facilities in terms of teaching learning aids, text book, library and laboratory facilities project work etc.
4. Proper conducive environment and learning situation like:

*(i)* Proper seating arrangement

*(ii)* Quite calm and peaceful environment

*(iii)* Management and control of factors leading to distraction.

*(iv)* Cooperative and competitive group situation

*(v)* Learning environment at home

*(vi)* Rest and recreation facilities provided to the learner

# OBJECTIVE QUESTIONS

1. Which of the following is not a characteristic of learning?
   (*a*) Learning is a relatively permanent change in behaviour
   (*b*) Learning is a growth of the organism
   (*c*) Learning is directly observed
   (*d*) Learning is a goal directed process.
2. In the beginning of life, the baby is guided by
   (*a*) maturation (*b*) instincts
   (*c*) learning (*d*) none of these
3. Accumulation of knowledge or facts becomes learning when
   (*a*) It is applied in real life situation.
   (*b*) It is done by the learner himself
   (*c*) It is provided by the teacher
   (*d*) None of these
4. Dancing, driving, writing etc are the examples of
   (*a*) Mechanical learning
   (*b*) Perceptual motor learning
   (*c*) Psychomotor learning
   (*d*) b & c both
5. In Gagne's hierarchy, learning has been divided into
   (*a*) eight parts (*b*) nine parts
   (*c*) seven parts (*d*) none of the above
6. Match the following:

| | (A) | (B) |
|---|---|---|
| (*i*) | Classical conditioning | 1. Kohler |
| (*ii*) | Drive reduction | 2. Hull |
| (*iii*) | Sign gestalt | 3. Pavlov |
| (*iv*) | Learning by insight | 4. Tolman |

| | (*i*) | (*ii*) | (*iii*) | (*iv*) |
|---|---|---|---|---|
| (*a*) | 1 | 2 | 3 | 4 |
| (*b*) | 3 | 2 | 4 | 1 |
| (*c*) | 2 | 1 | 3 | 4 |
| (*d*) | 4 | 3 | 2 | 1 |

7. Reflexes are of two types according to Pavlov. They are physiological and
   (*a*) Psychic (*b*) Neural
   (*c*) Mental (*d*) None of these
8. In classical conditioning extinction will take place when
   (*a*) Organism is poor in generalization
   (*b*) C S is given without UCS for a long time
   (*c*) CS>UCS
   (*d*) None of these
9. Backward conditioning will take place when
   (*a*) UCS is presented prior to CS
   (*b*) CS is presented prior to UCS
   (*c*) Reward is not given to the organism
   (*d*) None of these
10. When connection is not established between a CS and CR, due to any factor, that is called
    (*a*) Spontaneous recovery
    (*b*) Extinction
    (*c*) Inhibition
    (*d*) None of these
11. When a child responds to all women who wear black suit because of the black suit of her mother, it is the example of
    (*a*) internal inhibition
    (*b*) generalization
    (*c*) assimilation
    (*d*) all of these
12. Which of the following is not a behaviourist?
    (*a*) Watson (*b*) Skinner
    (*c*) Pavlov (*d*) Lewin
13. Learning according to Watson is
    (*a*) the shifting of old responses to the new stimuli
    (*b*) the result of connection between S-R formed in the brain.
    (*c*) both of these
    (*d*) none of these
14. Which of the following points differentiates the theories of Watson and Guthrie?
    (*a*) law of contiguity (*b*) law of recency
    (*c*) generalization (*d*) law of frequency
15. In operant conditioning reward works as motives but in Guthrie's theory motives are
    (*a*) Stimuli given to the learner
    (*b*) Actions done by the learner
    (*c*) Both of these
    (*d*) None of these
16. We forget something not by disuse but by other learning. This is the theory of
    (*a*) contiguity
    (*b*) trial and error

(*c*) learning by insight
(*d*) perception

**17.** Which of the following is not an essential requirement for trial and error learning?
(*a*) Drive
(*b*) Barrier
(*c*) Chance success
(*d*) Selective movement of the organism

**18.** According to the law of trial and error, learning occurs when
(*a*) it is satisfying for the learner
(*b*) bond between S-R is strengthened by the repeated use
(*c*) drive is there in the learner to act
(*d*) all of these

**19.** Which of the following facilitates learning according to Thorndike?
(*a*) Transfer of training
(*b*) Mental set of the learner
(*c*) Law of contiguity
(*d*) All of these

**20.** In Hull's theory, for learning to occur, the S-R connection must be associated with the
(*a*) cognitive field of the learner
(*b*) diminution of the need
(*c*) both of these
(*d*) none of these

**21.** Reinforcement in Skinner's theory is similar to drive reduction in which theory
(*a*) Hull's theory (*b*) Guthrie's theory
(*c*) Lewin's theory (*d*) None of these

**22.** Which of the following theories is most quantitatively measurable?
(*a*) Pavlov's (*b*) Skinner's
(*c*) Hull's (*d*) None of these

**23.** In drive reduction theory, the effective stimulus in leaning is the trace. It is formed
(*a*) in the brain
(*b*) by the bond of S-R
(*c*) in the nervous system
(*d*) none of these

**24.** In drive reduction theory, habit formation is a function of
(*a*) stimulus potential
(*b*) stimulus generalization
(*c*) reaction potential
(*d*) all of these

**25.** Hull may be considered superior to other S-R Theorists in the sense that he was able to measure
(*a*) latency of response
(*b*) reinforcement potential
(*c*) both of these
(*d*) none of these

**26.** Which of the following points differentiates Skinner from other S-R theorists?
(*a*) His operant conditioning (type R learning )
(*b*) His schedule of reinforcement
(*c*) His way of shaping behaviour
(*d*) All of these

**27.** Skinner's theory is more objective in nature than the others because
(*a*) operant behaviour is external
(*b*) reflexes never have zero strength
(*c*) reinforcement is followed by responses
(*d*) all of these

**28.** Aversive stimuli in operant conditioning means
(*a*) individual will not do a particular act because of fear of such stimuli
(*b*) individual will not do a particular act because of the disapproval from others.
(*c*) both of these
(*d*) none of these

**29.** In Skinner's theory, reinforcement is given to the learner when
(*a*) his response is 100% correct
(*b*) his response is not correct
(*c*) his response is closer to the correct behaviour
(*d*) his response is regular and continuous

**30.** Which of the following statements regarding S-R theories is not correct?
(*a*) Man behaves like a machine
(*b*) Behaviour is overt and can be objectively measured
(*c*) Learning proceeds from simple to complex
(*d*) Things are perceived in the context of figure ground *i.e.*, in relation to other things

**31.** Which of the following statements regarding field theories are correct?
(*a*) Learning is not additive
(*b*) Molar approach of behaviour is followed here.
(*c*) Interaction between organism and the environment is essential for learning
(*d*) All of these

**32.** Operant conditioning is different from respondent conditioning in which of the following points
(*a*) In OC reinforcement is given after the response is made
(*b*) In operant conditioning, behaviour is controlled by central nervous system.
(*c*) A chain of responses is needed for shaping the behaviour (learning)
(*d*) All of these

**33.** Thorndike and Skinner do not differ at all in
(*a*) the law of effect (*b*) law of readiness
(*c*) law of contiguity (*d*) all of these

**34.** According to gestalt psychologists, behaviour can not be quantified because
(*a*) it is always changeable
(*b*) it is governed by the configuration produced in the mind
(*c*) it is rarely overt
(*d*) all of these

**35.** Law of pragnanz is the other name of the law of
(*a*) continuity (*b*) closure
(*c*) contiguity (*d*) none of these

**36.** How does the law of similarity work according to field theorists?
(*a*) Similar ideas and experiences get associated to form a whole
(*b*) Similar objects or experiences are easily learnt
(*c*) Both of these
(*d*) None of these

**37.** Learning by insight looks similar to some extent to which of the following theories?
(*a*) Need reduction theory
(*b*) R type of learning
(*c*) Trial and error theory
(*d*) None of the above

**38.** The other name of conditioned reflexes is
(*a*) psychic reflexes
(*b*) motor reflexes
(*c*) physiological reflexes
(*d*) none of the above

## ANSWERS

| 1 | 2 | 3 | 4 | 5 | 6 | 7 | 8 | 9 | 10 |
|---|---|---|---|---|---|---|---|---|---|
| (*c*) | (*b*) | (*a*) | (*d*) | (*a*) | (*b*) | (*a*) | (*b*) | (*a*) | (*c*) |
| **11** | **12** | **13** | **14** | **15** | **16** | **17** | **18** | **19** | **20** |
| (*b*) | (*d*) | (*c*) | (*d*) | (*a*) | (*a*) | (*d*) | (*d*) | (*d*) | (*b*) |
| **21** | **22** | **23** | **24** | **25** | **26** | **27** | **28** | **29** | **30** |
| (*a*) | (*c*) | (*c*) | (*a*) | (*a*) | (*d*) | (*a*) | (*a*) | (*ac*) | (*d*) |
| **31** | **32** | **33** | **34** | **35** | **36** | **37** | **38** | | |
| (*d*) | (*d*) | (*a*) | (*b*) | (*b*) | (*a*) | (*c*) | (*a*) | | |

# Transfer of Training

## INTRODUCTION

Past experiences play a key role in the life of human being. In fact, it works as base for curriculum of every next class. A student can not understand the book of class Xth without the study of the book of class IXth. Similarly whatever is learnt in the school, is applied in the real life situation in future. For example, knowledge of mathematics is used in solving the problems of banks, architecture and civil engineering. All these are the examples of transfer of training. It is believed that training in one subject is necessarily transferred to other subjects or field, *i.e.*, knowledge of mathematics is used to solve numerical problems in physics.

In common language if training in one subject is transferred to understand the other subject in any way, it is called transfer of training.

## DEFINITIONS

1. **Crow and Crow,** "The carry over of habits of thinking, feeling or working of knowledge or of skills, from one learning area to another usually is referred to as the transfer of training."
2. **Skinner,** "Transfer of training is concerned with the question of whether or not the learning of material A-say Mathematics-aids, hinders or does not affect the subsequent learning of material B-say Physics or Chemistry.
3. **Sorenson,** "A person learns through transfer to the extent that the abilities acquired in one situation help in another".
4. **W.B. Kolesnik,** "Transfer is the application of carry over the knowledge, skills, habits, attitudes or other responses from the situation in which they are initially acquired to some other situation."
5. **Peterson,** "Transfer is generalization for it is extension of ideas to a new field."
6. **Hilgard Atkinson,** (Introduction to psychology), "The influence that learning one task, may have on the subsequent learning of another is called transfer of learning."
7. **H.C Ellis,** "Transfer of learning means the experiences or performances on one task influence the performance on some other subsequent task."

### Characteristics of transfer of training

On the basis of the definitions given above following characteristics of transfer of training can be derived :

*(i)* Knowledge or skills acquired in one area is transferred to other areas for the purpose of facilitating or deteriorating the later.

*(ii)* Transfer of training may be automatic also along with the result of the efforts of learners.

*(iii)* If memory is sharp, transfer will be speedy and vice versa.

*(iv)* If intellectual ability of the person is high, he will always try to take the benefit of positive transfer.

*(v)* Transfer helps in generalization and application of ideas or principles into practice.

### Types of Transfer

1. **Positive transfer :** If performance on one task improves or facilitates the performance on another task it is called positive transfer. Past learning facilitates present learning.
2. **Zero transfer :** If there is no effect of one learning on another learning, it is called zero transfer, ie, learning of mathematics does not help in learning a language.
3. **Negative transfer :** Past learning hinders present learning and makes it difficult ie, if one is a good wrestler, he may have difficulty to become a boxer.

## Forms of Transfer

1. **Lateral transfer :** If an individual is able to transfer his learning in the same context in other situations it is called lateral transfer. Application of rules of addition or subtraction in the real life situation is an example.
2. **Sequential transfer :** If an idea taught today has relation to an idea to be taught tomorrow and both these ideas will have some relationship to an idea to be taught next day, it is called sequential transfer of learning. Here past learning facilitates present and future learning, ie, addition helps multiplication.
3. **Horizontal transfer :** Lateral and sequential both transfers are called horizontal transfer. Here, the learner does not change the track (context)
4. **Vertical transfer :** If learning of one behavioural level in the hierarchy of learning domain facilitates learning at a higher behavioural level, it is called vertical transfer, e.g., knowledge objectives help in reaching comprehension or application objectives of BS Bloom.
5. **Bilateral transfer :** Human body is divided into two parts- left and right. When training imparted to one side is transferred to another side, it is called bilateral transfer.

## Significance of Transfer of Training

1. Our reaction to future life situations depends on how we took our past experiences. If we were not serious in the past, we are not expected to transfer this learning in future.
2. All new inventions and discoveries are generally founded on past inventions and discoveries. It saves our energy and time.
3. If we are not able to apply our knowledge and experiences to real life situations eg, if history does not help us in solving present political crises, that knowledge is useless. Transfer of training helps us to apply knowledge.
4. All training is given to the trainees on the assumption that they will apply their knowledge and skills in real life situations. In fact, existence of educational institutions is based on the idea of transfer of training.
5. Teachers always create those conditions which facilitate transfer of training from one subject to another.
6. The more a child is able to transfer his learning, the more he is considered intelligent.

## THEORIES OF TRANSFER

### Theory of Mental Discipline :

There are two forms of mental discipline :

(*a*) Classicism of Plato, according to which mind can be best trained by studying classical languages.

(*b*) Faculty psychology originated in 1734, according to which mind was composed of mental faculties in the same way as body have muscular power. Mental exercises can strengthen these mental faculties. For this purpose, hard intellectual work should be provided to learners. In the olden days, languages like Greek, Latin, Sanskrit and subjects like mathematics and philosophy were supposed to be the best disciplines for training various mental faculties of the learner. According to this theory, transfer of training is automatic and these exercises will help the learner to transfer knowledge to different fields. The first psychologist who attacked this theory was William James (1890). On the basis of his experiments he concluded that practice in memorizing does not improve memory and hence he rejected the theory of mental discipline. Thorndike (1924) also found that students who studied Latin did not gain intelligence more than those who studied physical education.

### Theory of Identical Elements

This story was propounded by EL Thorndike in 1924. According to it transfer of learning from one situation to another would occur if the two situations have some elements in common. The more the similarity is there, the greater will be the transfer of training. These identical elements have the same cell action in the brain.

According to Thorndike, maximum transfer will take place when the two activities have common factors and the total situations have some important common characteristics. Two factors play a key role in the process of transfer. They are matter and method. oth of them may have some elements in common.

"Utility theory of education" has also been derived from this theory. Now, curriculum for schools is constructed from utility point of view. Those materials are included in the curriculum which have direct correlation with the life experiences of the child. While selecting and constructing curriculum for students, identity in matter or method or both are taken into account. The more the similarity is there between school curriculum and daily life situations, the greater will be the amount of transfer.

This theory can be criticized on three grounds:

*(i)* This theory assumes that life problems remain static and there are pre determined and fixed solutions to these problems. This is not a realistic assumption. Society is always changing and hence practical problems of life are also changing.

*(ii)* This theory assumes that school learning will always bring about a good result in the daily life of the people. This is also not a realistic assumptions. Many things in the school are studied just for pleasure or for facilitating the learning of other subjects hence, concept of direct utility of knowledge for practical life is unbelievable.

*(iii)* Allport is of the view that it is possible to identify elements on objective reality but in case of subjective reality (personal experiences of the learner) it is very difficult to find out identical elements in theory and practice.

**Merits of the theory:** In spite of the above criticism, we apply this theory in the field of education to a great extent such as:

*(i)* During co-curricular activities, a student who is a goal keeper in football can transfer his learning to wicket keeping in cricket.

*(ii)* On the basis of common elements in different school subjects, we can form a group of such points. This configuration will help us in developing insight for learning other elements of the curriculum.

*(iii)* Special skills are developed in trainees through professional and technical education. These special skills are transferred to real life situations to perform special type of tasks.

*(iv)* Efforts are made to include as many common elements in different subjects as possible to maximizes transfer. This reduces the load of the teacher and students both.

*(v)* A teacher can identify all common elements in his teaching material and then he can teach them in a group. Retention of one element will help the students to retain all elements of the group.

*(vi)* Pragmatist philosophy of education very much recognizes this theory and stresses the inclusion of those subjects in the curriculum which are useful to the society.

*(vii)* Practical work, assignments, field and project works etc are emphasized in the school today just to take the benefit of identical elements in theory and practice.

## Judd's theory of generalization

According to him transfer of training can be increased by teaching students general principles rather than specific solutions. It means that teaching of generalization will increase transfer of training. Attitudes, skills and activities are transferred only when they are systematized and related to similar situations.

For example, if a child is very punctual to his dinner parties, he is not supposed to be punctual to his school unless punctuality has become the attitude of the child as a result of training. Judd proved his theory with the help of experiment on two groups of children using water explaining them how to apply laws of refraction in different situations.

This theory is similar to gestalt field theories in the sense that gestalians believe that learning of a meaningful configuration presumes a kind of structural organization in the mind that modifies the organism. This organization will lead the organism to generalization,

This theory can be criticized on the ground that generalization principles can not be taught to students without giving them specific behaviour of events. So knowledge of specifics is also necessary for transfer of training.

In spite of the above criticism, this theory has following implication in the field of education:

*(i)* If teacher does not use common principle to present the subject matter in the form of totality

or group, the isolated bits of information will be forgotten soon. The principles of physics can be applied to even social science, if teacher follows this approach.

*(ii)* Teaching general rules of spelling and grammar to students can always improve their language. Grouping of words with similar spelling will surely improve spellings of students.

## Theory of Transposition

This theory was developed by Max Werthimer and other Gestalt psychologists. According to them, transfer of training occurs because of perceptual similarities between different situations and that it is in the form of generalization. Max pointed out that a number of mental operations are involved in this process. They are given below :

- Grouping, reorganization and structurization of learning material take place in the mind.
- Process of inter-relationship of form and size operates.
- Separate structure in the mind is formed
- Transfer of training needs consistent and persistent thinking also.

This theory must be understood in relation to learning by insight as far as classroom implication of the theory is concerned.

## Harlow's theory of learning to learn

Learning ability of the individual improves when they go through the practice of related or similar tasks. If a student is very expert in solving linear equations, he can easily solve other linear problems of different subjects. This progressive improvement in performance is known as transfer of learning to learn. It simply ranges from simple rote memory to complex problem solving.

**Several experiments on transfer of training :**

1. Starch asked the subject to draw the figure of a star with left hand after seeing the figure. The time taken in doing so was noted. Then the subject was asked to draw the figure with his right hand. This practice continued for ten days and it was seen after 10 days that the person was taking less time in transferring his skill from hand to hand. This is an example of transfer of skills.
2. Thorndike and Woodworth gave the subject to measure the line of a fixed length. Then he was asked to measure different lines of different lengths. They also gave the subject to compare two circles of different radii with regard to their areas. In this way subjects were tested whether they can apply the knowledge of the length, area etc from one situation to another.
3. Herbart was the first person who emphasized the need for correlating different school subjects to maximize transfer of training.

**Factors affecting transfer of learning:**

1. **Intelligence :** Transfer of training is positively related to intellectual ability of learners. Sharp minded children can transfer their experiences more effectively in different situations than average or dull children.
2. **Attitude :** If attitudes of learner towards learning is positive, transfer of training will be more. The attitude towards learning can be made positive by making the subject matter useful and interesting for him.
3. **Meaningfulness of learning elements :** The more the subject matter is meaningful for learners, the more it is possible for generalizing the principles and hence transfer of training
4. **Method of teaching :** If teacher has taught the students how to transfer matter and methods to different situations, only then transfer of learning will be more .

**Role of the teacher in maximizing transfer :**

A teacher can increase transfer of training by adopting the following methods:

*(i)* The teacher can create some similarity between teaching learning and testing situations. If students are able to identify this similarity, their performance in the exam will always be better.

*(ii)* The teacher should transfer the life experiences of students to the classroom and relate them with his teaching. The similarity between the two will increase learning.

*(iii)* The teacher can help the students to identify the similarity between matters and method of different subjects.

*(iv)* The teacher should provide maximum opportunity of practice to his students.

Excessive practice of original task increases the likelihood of positive transfer to a subsequent task.

(v) The teacher should enable the students to generalize the laws and principles by giving them example. Examples also help the students to understand concepts and they will be able to apply them in different situations.

(vi) The teacher should develop a link between different segments of tasks and experiences in order to develop concept of whole in their minds.

(vii) General principles and rules should be taught first before coming to the points of specifics.

(viii) The sequence of learning should proceed from more inclusive tasks to the more specific aspects of the task.

## OBJECTIVE QUESTIONS

**1.** Zero transfer of training helps the teacher in the class when
(*a*) He does not want one learning to be inhibited by other learning.
(*b*) He has to teach a lot in the class
(*c*) He teaches mathematics
(*d*) None of the above

**2.** Theory of generalization is similar to the theory of
(*a*) Transposition (*b*) Identical elements
(*c*) Both of these (*d*) None of these

**3.** If rules of multiplication helps in learning correlation or regression, it is an example of
(*a*) Sequential transfer
(*b*) Horizontal transfer
(*c*) Negative transfer
(*d*) Vertical transfer

**4.** Who is the chief contributor of the theory of transposition?
(*a*) Max Werthimer (*b*) Kohler
(*c*) Thorndike (*d*) None of these

**5.** If a student uses his knowledge obtained in class VIIth in understanding the subject matter of class Xth, it is an example of :
(*a*) horizontal transfer
(*b*) Vertical transfer
(*c*) Sequential transfer
(*d*) None of these.

**6.** Which of the following philosophies believe in the theory of identical element?
(*a*) Idealism (*b*) Existentialism
(*c*) Pragmatism (*d*) None of them

**7.** Democracy is a way of life not a mere political arrangement. It is based on the principle of equal freedom and equal rights for all. This definition of democracy was given by
(*a*) University Education Commission
(*b*) Seely
(*c*) Abraham Lincon
(*d*) B.R. Ambedkar

**8.** Match the following :

| I<br>*Role of the teacher* | II<br>*Philosophy* |
|---|---|
| A. Guide and helper | 1. Marxism |
| B. Instructor | 2. Existentialism |
| C. Autocrate | 3. Pragmatism |
| D. Disciplined initiator | 4. Idealism |

**Codes**

| | A | B | C | D |
|---|---|---|---|---|
| (*a*) | 3 | 4 | 1 | 2 |
| (*b*) | 1 | 2 | 3 | 4 |
| (*c*) | 4 | 3 | 2 | 1 |
| (*d*) | 4 | 2 | 3 | 1 |

**9.** Which of the following beliefs represents Gandhijee's philosophy of life?
(*a*) Education through crafts
(*b*) Request for truth
(*c*) Non violence
(*d*) All of these

**10.** Logical positivism is a philosophy which
(*a*) uses language for logical analysis
(*b*) rejects metaphysics on the ground that it can not be analysed logically
(*c*) both of these
(*d*) none of these

**11.** The role of which of the following informal agencies of education is most dominant in the life of a man?
(*a*) School (*b*) Family
(*c*) State (*d*) Library

**12.** Which of the following does not belong to five principles of curriculum propounded by Aurobindo?
(*a*) Principle of child's interest
(*b*) Principle of child's motivation
(*c*) Principle of activating child's creative potentialities
(*d*) Principle of earning a living

**13.** Which of the following is the greatest challenge before any democracy of the world?
(*a*) Regionalism
(*b*) Fundamentalism
(*c*) Castism
(*d*) Utopianism

**14.** In which of the following society's racial supremacy and state dominance over individuals were emphasized?
(*a*) Medieval societies
(*b*) Fascist societies
(*c*) Religious societies
(*d*) All of these

**15.** Which of the following is not an important characteristics of Indian society?
(*a*) A stratified society
(*b*) A closed society
(*c*) A conservative and unwelcoming society
(*d*) A class based society

**16.** Which of the following philosophies supports individual and subjective reality?
(*a*) Existentialism
(*b*) Humanism
(*c*) Both of these
(*d*) None of these

**17.** An individual can be influenced by
(*a*) Local and communal culture
(*b*) Material and non material culture
(*c*) Academic culture
(*d*) All of these

**18.** **Assertion (A) :** We can not eliminate the impact of castism from the Indian social system.
**Reason (R) :** It is caste that is giving some people high status and some low status.
(*a*) Assertion (A) and Reason (R) both are not related
(*b*) A and R are related to each other
(*c*) A is true but R is false
(*d*) A is false but R is true

**19.** Which of the following processes will make the child socially adaptable and acceptable?
(*a*) Culture formation
(*b*) Socialization
(*c*) Social synthesis
(*d*) None of these

**20.** Cultural inertia refers to
(*a*) those beliefs, customs and traditions which a man considers very great on the basis of ancestral beliefs and he is not willing to give it up
(*b*) resistance of a person to adopt another culture
(*c*) both of these
(*d*) none of these

## ANSWERS

| 1 | 2 | 3 | 4 | 5 | 6 | 7 | 8 | 9 | 10 |
|---|---|---|---|---|---|---|---|---|---|
| (*a*) | (*b*) | (*d*) | (*a*) | (*b*) | (*c*) | (*a*) | (*b*) | (*d*) | (*c*) |
| **11** | **12** | **13** | **14** | **15** | **16** | **17** | **18** | **19** | **20** |
| (*b*) | (*d*) | (*b*) | (*b*) | (*c*) | (*a*) | (*d*) | (*a*) | (*b*) | (*a*) |

# UNIT–V

★ *Maladjustment and Educational Adaptation*

★ *Personality & Its Measurement*

1

# Maladjustment and Educational Adaptation

## INTRODUCTION

Maladjustment is a relative term. It is understood only in terms of adjustment. Adjustment is again a relative term. It is understood in the context of the situation which is either favourable or unfavourable to adjustment. So we should first know the meaning of the term adjustment.

## MEANING OF ADJUSTMENT

The concept of adjustment was first used by Darwin in his theory of natural selection. At that time the word adaptation to environment was used instead of adjustment.

Man has the highest capacity to adapt to new situations among all living being. In this process of adaptation man uses his maximum capacity to fight against the adversaries of the environmental situations. When man becomes victorious, he is said to have been adapted to the environment.

Thus, the term adjustment means reactions to the demands and pressures of socio-physical environment imposed upon the individual. The same demand is also expressed by the individual in the context of his environment. This demand may be internal or external or both. Thus, there is always a conflict between the demands of the individual and the demand of the environment. Had this conflict not been there, there would not have been any problem of adjustment. The problem of adjustment arises only because we can not gratify all our needs due to the adverse condition imposed by the environment. This is technically known as maladjustment.

### Two interpretations of Adjustment

Psychologists have interpreted the term adjustment from two angles:

(A) Adjustment as an achievement.

(B) Adjustment as a process

**(A) Adjustment as an achievement :** It means how efficiently an individual can perform his duties in different adverse as well as favourable circumstances. From this point of view four criteria for good adjustment are given below:

1. **Physical Health :** It is the first pre-requisite that is needed for adjustment. If individual is not physically healthy and ailing in any way, he will face difficulty in adjusting to the environment. An ailing person may hate even his lover.
2. **Psychological Security :** The individual should have no psychological disease like obsession, compulsion, neuroses, psychoses, anxiety and depression. If any of these are there in the individual, he will have difficulty in adjustment.
3. **Work Efficiency :** The person who makes full use of his occupational or social skills can be capable of adjusting to the environment.
4. **Social Acceptability :** If a person obeys social norms and traditions and accepts its values willingly, he is likely to be acceptable to others. This acceptability will make him fully adjusted in the society. If, on the other hand, he is rejected by the society due to any of his disabilities, he will be maladjusted.

**(B) Adjustment as a process :** The adjustment of a person largely depends on his interaction to the external environment in which he lives. This interaction is not an easy process. It depends upon a number of factors such as internal as well as external, demand of the individual and the external pressure of the environment. Whatever an individual wants to do freely due to the pressure of his demand, the environment puts a check on it. For example, a young adult wants to gratify his sexual desires with a girl without marriage, the social environment will not let him do that and the conflict between the internal demand and the external environment will emerge. To what extent the adult is able to reduce this conflict, he will be adjusted to that extent in the environment. Thus, the concept of adjustment is also expressed in degrees.

When a conflict occurs between internal needs and external demand, three possibilities may arise.

- The individual may modify his internal needs
- He can alter the environment to get his demand accepted.
- He can use some mental mechanism to escape from the conflicting situation and in this way he will be able to maintain the balance of his personality. He will change his needs in accordance with the values of the society. If he is able to do so, he will be adjusted. This is the process of adjustment.

It is in this context that the concept of mental health and hygiene is also studied in the process of adjustment. The more a person is mentally healthy, the more he is likely to adjust in the society.

## MENTAL HEALTH

In order to understand mental health, we should first of all know about mental hygiene.

Mental hygiene is a science which deals with the process of attaining mental health and preventing mental illness. The process of mental hygiene is a life long process beginning with the time of birth and continues till death. The difference between mental hygiene and mental health is that the former is means and the later is the end.

The movement of mental hygiene started in the first decade of 20th century with the publication of a book **"A mind that found itself"** by **Clifford Beers** in 1908. He was a graduate of Yale University. He became mentally disturbed due to unnecessary stress and strain on his mind. Being frustrated with his life he tried to commit suicide but he was rescued and treated by doctors (psychiatrists). After recovery, he wrote his experiences and the types of treatment that he received in this book. His book revolutionarised the concept of mental ill health and created awareness in general public regarding mental hygiene.

Mental Hygiene has four underlined **objectives** :

*(a)* **Realisation of Potentialities:** After realising his strengths and weaknesses, a person is given full opportunity to develop his potentialities to the maximum.

*(b)* **Happiness :** The person is given full opportunity to develop positive attitude towards life in the context of the society and nation which is always full of problems. This freedom gives him happiness.

*(c)* **Harmonious Existence :** The physical, mental and spiritual capacities of the individual are developed in a harmonious manner and harmony of the individual with the environment is also achieved.

*(d)* **Effective Existence :** Mental hygiene enables the individuals to use his abilities effectively to exist effectively in the society.

Now the question arises what mental health actually is. It is very difficult to define mental health in definite terms. However, **Norman E. Cutts** has defined mental health in the following words:

"Mental health is the ability to adjust satisfactorily to the various strains of the environment that we meet in life and mental hygiene is the means to assure this adjustment.

The criteria of a **mentally healthy persons (teacher)** are given below :

*(i)* He can adapt himself to the changing conditions of the environment. Thus, he is accommodative in his behaviour.

*(ii)* He can participate in social activities properly even in stress and strain of emotional disturbances.

*(iii)* He is well contented person. He enjoys at what he gets but does not lament what he does not get.

*(iv)* He is not involved in any antisocial or antinational activities. Thus he abides by the laws and rules happily.

*(v)* He self evaluates his behaviour and improves it every now and then.

*(vi)* His life is full of enthusiasm. He is reasonable in his action and devoted to his profession.

*(vii)* He has good habits.
*(viii)* He is not a man of irritable temper.
*(ix)* He has his own philosophy of life and is not a blind follower of social norms.
*(x)* He tries to make the others happy .

Thus, internal happiness and frustration free life make a person mentally healthy and if he is mentally healthy, he will be fully adjusted in the society, i.e, adjustment is a function of metal health.

## CONCEPT OF MALADJUSTMENT

When the behaviour of a person intervenes not only the progress of others but his own progress also and because of this it is either opposed or hated by the people causing severe adjustment problem of the person, it is called maladjustment. For example, if a person does not keep his words in the society, he is opposed and that creates the problem of adjustment for the person.

### Definitions

1. Tyson, "Maladjustment in relation to some specific terms is such as **inadaptability**, incapacity for affection, imbalanced life, inability to profit from experiences, frustration, intolerance power, subjectivity and many things, that makes the person unhappy."
2. Eysenck, "Maladjustment is a state in which the needs of the individual on one hand and the claims of the environment on the other, are fully unsatisfied or a process by which this inharmonious relationship can be attained."

**Identification of Maladjusted Children :** Maladjusted children and adults can be identified on the basis of their behavioural symptoms and characteristics given below :

### (A) Symptom

1. **Physical symptoms :** Stuttering, stammering, scratching head, beating head and chest, facial twitching, biting nails, rocking feet, restlessness, drumming with fingers and vomiting.
2. **Behavioural symptoms :** Aggression, lying, bullying, poor school achievement, hyper activity, negativism, and sex related disturbances.
3. **Emotional Symptoms :** Excessive worry, fear, inferiority complex, hatred, jealousy, extreme timidity, temper tantrums, persistent anxiety, conflicts and tension.
4. **Other related Symptoms**
   *(i)* Adverse relationship between the individual and the environment.
   *(ii)* Unsatisfied state of mind of the individual and of those who are in touch with him.
   *(iii)* Incapacity of the person for getting affection of others.
   *(iv)* Inability to profit from his own experiences as well as the experiences of others.
   *(v)* Subjective and prejudiced thinking.

### (B) Characteristics

1. **General Characteristics**
   *(i)* They always try to go against norms.
   *(ii)* They feel that they are not being loved by others.
   *(iii)* They think that there is always injustice meted out to them.
   *(iv)* They realize that they have not been given all those human rights which are essential for the survival of man.
   *(v)* They feel that they are burden on this earth.
   *(vi)* They feel that people are jealous to them.
2. **Physical Characteristics .** See Symptoms.
3. **Emotional Characteristics :** See Symptoms.
4. **Cognitive Characteristics :** They are not mentally backward in any way but when they are tested on an intelligence test, they score less than average due to the maladjustment problems.
5. **Social Characteristics :**
   *(i)* When social environment around the child is not good, he will not adjust to that environment and thus his behaviour will be adversely affected.
   *(ii)* Maladjustment due to poverty or low socio economic status of the family is very common and in this case. child will not go to establish relations with the elite class people of the society.
   *(iii)* Maladjustment due to affluence of the family and children are not likely to adjust to poor people.
6. **Educational Characteristics**
   *(i)* They take lots of pain of the situations and thus they waste much time in balancing them.

Due to this their educational achievement is likely to be poor.

*(ii)* They change schools frequently in order to better adjust there but they fail to do so.

*(iii)* They hate their peers and teachers and principal are mostly targetted by them.

*(iv)* They feel that the total system is against them, as a result they do not try to overcome their academic problems.

## (C) Methods and Procedures of Identification

The exact categorization of these children, is not possible by the ordinary teacher. Only an expert in psychology can do so. However, a teacher can detect these children in the class on the basis of their symptoms and characteristics. He may adopt any of the following procedures for this purpose.

1. *Observation :* Here the behaviour of the child is observed when he is in the classroom, outside the classroom, in the play ground, in the library and in the laboratory and his way of participating in co-curricular activities is also observed and dimensions of conflicts are noted down.
2. *Interview :* Direct interviews are conducted to know the problems of maladjusted children. After knowing these problems, a teacher can remove at least some of them. This is, however, not an effective measure because these people generally hide the facts.
3. *Psychological Tests :* A number of psychological tests and adjustment inventories have been constructed by the psychologists to identify these maladjusted children from the lot.
4. *Situational Tests :* Here the suspected person is put to a situation in which he acts freely. His behaviour is then observed by the teacher.
5. *Indirect Methods of Collecting Data :* If we want to collect information about these suspected children, we can collect information about them from three major sources.
   - From the family where the child is being brought comprising of parents, brothers, sisters and other relatives.
   - From neighbourhood where the child lives for a certain period of time with peers and friends.
   - From the school where the child is getting education comprising of teachers, principal, other non teaching staff and class fellows of the child. These people will tell about the behaviour of the child clearly.
6. *Medical Examination :* Some of the maladjustment symptoms are such that they can be detected only by medical personnel. Besides, causes of many adjustment problems lie in physical problems and health. They are investigated by the expert in the field to give proper medical treatment of the child. Once these problems are known, their causes can also be ascertained.

# CAUSES OF MALADJUSTMENT

Before coming to the possible causes of maladjustment, it is better to give the opinion of some of the psychologist on maladjustment. These opinions will help us know the nature of the problem.

### Opinions of Psychologists

**1. Freud :** According to him, behaviour of individuals are guided by two basic principles seeking pleasure and avoiding pain. When he tries to do so, he is stopped by the environmental forces, such as social norms, traditions and religious values. It creates frustration in him. Sex and aggression are the two basic instincts causing frustration. Maladjustment is caused due to the conflicts between instincts (urges) and the environmental restrictions, and social pressure that is there in the mind of the individual.

This conflict is reduced by training the mind in the direction of the social norms and values and the person ceases to violate them. He accepts these taboos and values willingly by crushing or repressing his own urges, especially those urges which are socially reprehensible.

According to Freud, nothing happens without an antecedent cause. Every action of the individual is determined by a number of casual factors. Sex related factor is above all those factors. Most of the conflicts arising in his mind is sexual in nature. These conflicts cause anxiety and anxiety gives birth to ego which disturbs the mechanism of adjustment in all stages of human development. Thus, according to him sexual problems are the main cause of maladjustment.

**2. Adler:** According to him, even sex urges can be sublimated or minimized if the person has determined some other goals for his life. He says that a child is born helpless in the world. He depends on others for gratification of his needs. This creates inferiority complex in him which is the primary cause of stress or frustration in him. As much as the child grows up, he endeavours to reduce his dependence on others and thus his inferiority complex is gradually reduced leading him to the level of adjustment.

Thus, the desire for superiority is the universally acceptable goal of human behaviour which is nothing but the dynamic process of adjustment.

**3. Jung :** He understood personality in terms of intrapsychic conflicts. There are basically two instincts, preservation of race and preservation of self. These two instincts guide his behaviour. Since, they are always conflicting in nature, the process and mechanization of adjustment continues throughout life.

According to him, neurosis is caused by he conflicts between instinctive wishes and their conscious opposition by the environment. These conflicts are largely unconscious which ultimately causes neurotic behaviour. A normal man reduces these conflicts by sublimating his personal instincts in the interest of the social instincts and thus he becomes well adjusted to the environment.

Thus, we see that there may be so many causes of maladjustment. They can be categorised into three categories:

(A) Personal Causes
(B) Social Causes
(C) School Related Causes

**(A) *Personal Causes:***

These causes are directly related to personality characteristics of an individual. Some of these causes are given below:

1. **Physique:** It is the physique or appearance of an individual which determines the range of his interaction and hence social development of the individual. If he is suffering from any infectious disease, he is impaired in any way or he is ugly or deformed, he is likely to be rejected or shunned by others. The behaviour meted out to him by others and the remarks passed by the people in the humiliation of the child can cause a lot of adjustment problems for the child. That is why physically handicapped children are seen maladjusted.
2. **Regular ailment :** If the child is suffering from diseases for a very long period of time and is not getting well despite efforts and treatment he becomes irritable in temper. These problems adversely affect his social interaction in the neighbourhood and educational achievement in the school which will further lead him to manifest maladjusted behaviour.
3. **Economic deprivation :** Maximum number of maladjusted children are found in poor families where they are unable to fulfil even their basic needs of life due to poverty. When the legitimate demands of the child is not fulfilled by the family he becomes frustrated. He develops a negative attitude towards others in the family as well as in the society and his maladjusted behaviour becomes a routine behaviour of his life.
4. **Broken families :** Studies show that children who come from broken families either by the death of any of the parents or divorce are mostly maladjusted. The reason is that they do not get the love, affection, sympathy and security of their families as much as they should have normally got or as much as the other children are getting. These deprivations emotionally disturb them and they become maladjusted.
5. **Poor home environment :** If there is regular nagging between parents or any conflict among other members of the family, it will be a source of emotional stress for the child. He may feel insecure, disturbed and worried leading to maladjustment of the child in the neighbourhood as well.
6. **Mental or learning disabilities :** Such type of disabilities of the child will lead to poor academic achievement in the school and poor achievement is an ample source of maladjustment for the child. Besides if parents have set a very high goal for the child without regarding his abilities, it will frustrate the child further leading to higher level of maladjustment in the society.

7. **Lack of self contentment :** Many people do not get what they want to get by their efforts and sometimes they do not succeed in their effort. If spirit of self contentment is not there in them, they will be highly frustrated and hence maladjusted in life.
8. **Negative attitude :** Many people always take every matter in a negative way. They even think those people as their enemies who are their best wishers. Such people are maladjusted all the time without any reason.
9. **Parental attitude :** Attitude of parents towards their children also affect adaptability of the child. For example, rejected child develops the feeling of insecurity, isolation and helplessness. It will lead to maladjustment of the child. Contrary to this, over protection given to the child by parents is also a source of maladjustment in future because, due to lack of self-confidence, the child finds himself helpless to face the real hardship of life.
10. **Discrimination :** From family to the job opportunities in the society, discrimination is the main source of frustration and maladjustment. Discrimination is actually depriving a person of his due rights. Once it happens, it creates hatred in the person being discriminated. Person may do any thing wrong not only against the person responsible for discrimination but against the whole system.
11. **Adoption :** Adopted children are generally found maladjusted. If a child has been adopted in his infancy and he has been given full psychological security only then adoption will not prove to be a source of maladjustment.
12. **Emotional shock :** Sudden emotional shock due to the death of a relative, due to failure in any good effort or due to any other reason will bring about a permanent maladjustment for the child. The child or the person may take a very long time to recover from his mental shock.

**(B) *Social Causes :***

Important social causes of maladjustment are given below :

1. **Communal tension :** India is a country of many religions and beliefs. People belonging to different religions follow different tracks of life many times antagonistic to each other leading to communal riots and hatred. These things are great source of maladjustment for many people.
2. **Lack of social institutions :** Clubs, libraries and playgrounds are important places where people can come in contact with each other, participate in different activities and release their pent up feelings in the process. If these facilities are not available for citizens, they become vulnerable to maladjustment.
3. **Transferable services :** A person takes time to adjust in any new society. If he is frequently changing his place of work, his total family will face the problem of maladjustment
4. **Lack of equal opportunities of education and employment :** Equality leads to justice and discrimination leads to corruption. If all the people living in the society are denied the right of equality in the matters of education and employment and some of them are getting more than their due, the remaining people will he maladjusted due to frustration.
5. **Lack of social security :** Social and economic securities are connected to each other. If a student knows that he will be given unemployment allowances if he is unable to get job after education, he need not worried at all. On the other hand if no opportunity is available even after the age of 35, the person is most likely to be maladjusted. Similarly, physically handicapped people need social security measures for their placement. If such measures are not available, they will remain maladjusted forever.
6. **Religious beliefs :** Religious beliefs may be important sources of emotional adjustment. If it teaches lessons of self contentment, justice, honesty, sacrifice tolerance, perseverance and respect to others, people will be happy and adjusted. Contrary to this, if religious belief is based on superstition, unhistorical dogmas, unfounded rituals and unprincipled practices, maladjustment may be a permanent problem of the people in the society.

**(C) *Causes Related to Schools :***

Education is itself a process of adjustment. The more it is founded on principles and rules, the more it is constructive to the people as a whole leading to full social and emotional adjustment. During the teaching-learning process at schools several negative factors also work which causes maladjustment there. These factors are given below :

1. **Teaching by untrained teachers :** Teaching a student by an untrained teacher is nothing but spoiling the life of the student because such teachers are not supposed to teach on psychological lines. It may create a lot of tensions in the minds of learners. The teacher who does not know mental hygiene, how can he treat a maladjusted child in the class. Besides, defective methods of teaching will cause poor academic achievement of students which is itself a great source maladjustment in schools.
2. **Faulty curriculum :** If curriculum of the school has not been developed according to the needs, interests and abilities of students and they are gaining nothing from it to be used in their future life, they will surely be maladjusted in the school.
3. **Lack of recreational activities :** Recreational activities release tension and pent up feelings of students and thus, they are very much conducive to proper adjustment in the schools. If such facilities are not provided to children in the school, they are most likely to be maladjusted.
4. **Poor discipline :** If discipline of the school is good, everybody will feel secure in the campus and nobody is expected to be teased by other children. On the contrary, poor discipline makes the social and educational environment of the school uncomfortable, insecure and frustrating leading to severe form of maladjustment.
5. **Climate of the classes :** If social climate of the classroom is charged with negative emotions and tensions due to faulty relations between teachers and students or between students and student, it may lead to a number of adjustment problems there. Quarreling or nagging of any form in the class is fatal to the process of adjustment.
6. **Examination System :** If examinations are conducted only once in an academic session and a large number of students are failed in the examination due to poor guidance and preparation, the failed students are likely to be maladjusted. Contrary to this, formative evaluation of students at regular intervals and regular feedback given to them will reduce the incidence of maladjustment in the school.

## Adjustment Mechanism

Individual uses a number of methods and procedures to defend or escape from conflicts, frustration and depression, in order to better adjust in the society. They are known as defense or adjustment mechanism. The underlying processes of this mechanism are given below :

1. **Overcoming blocks :** Through this mechanism, the individual puts away the impediments that are there in the way of his success in future. If these blocks are not removed, he will not be able to do efforts in future.
2. **Reaching goals :** This mechanism helps the individual to reach the ultimate goal of his life, i.e., mental balance through occupational adaptation is done here.
3. **Satisfying motives :** Frustration which are caused by failure or deprivation are reduced to minimum by adopting these methods. They work as alternate source of satisfying motives.
4. **Relieving tensions :** This mechanism brings the individual into another world which is full of pleasure and thus his tension is released.
5. **Maintaining equilibrium :** Maladjustment inbalances the mind for a limited period of time. This mind is again brought to the equilibrium point through this mechanism.

One fact to be kept in mind is that defense mechanism is a sort of self deception. We deny and disguise the real cause of our behaviour in order to maintain the balance of our personality. Despite this fact adopting such a mechanism is necessary. Otherwise he will remain maladjusted for a very long period of time.

**Some Adjustment Mechanisms**

Some common mechanisms that an individual can adopt for the purpose of adjustment at least mentally are given below :

1. **Simple denial :** The simplest way to maintain the balance of the personality is to deny the fact outrightly so that conflict may not have a place in the mind. For example, when children are called by their parents and they do not heed to the call deliberately but later on they deny that they had heard for fear of punishment from the parents it is called simple denial. The same denial is shown by adults also. When they are asked, "Have you stolen the watch" ? they say "No" I have not".
2. **Aggression :** Aggression is an adjustment mechanism used as an attempt to hurt or destroy either the source of frustration or any other thing or person itself if it is not possible to destroy the source. For example, if a candidate has been denied of admission by the principal of a school as a matter of prejudice and the candidate sets the building of the school on fire, it is aggression. Aggression is always shown at the call of deep anger and frustration. Aggression may be of two types:
   (a) *Extra punitive :* Extra punitive responses are those responses in which the individual aggressively attributes the frustration to external persons or objects. It may be a physical assault on the person or his nominee responsible for frustration. It may be in the form of abusive language or it may be just intriguing against the responsible person as a matter of taking revenge in future. Direct attack against the responsible person is also seen. When the person is unable to take any revenge against the person responsible for frustration, his aggression is shifted to inanimate object, animals or wives. He can beat the table, hit the dog or abuses his wife in order to maintain balance of his personality.
   (b) *Intra punitive :* In this type of responses, the individual expresses his aggressive behaviour towards himself. He sometimes criticizes himself and sometimes hurts himself also. The rationale of these methods is that they release pent up feeling but excess use of these methods is injurious. That is why the teachers try to mould this behaviour by sympathy shown for the child or by telling him the real cause that led him to the state of frustration.
3. **Compensation :** It is a general tendency of the people. If a person is deficient in one area that is the source of frustration for him, then he might make up the deficiency by doing something excellent in other areas. This technique is especially useful for those who are having any sort of handicap. For example, if due to learning disabilities, the child is achieving very poorly in academic field, then he may work hard to increase his efficiency in the playground.

**Compensation is of the following types :**

(a) *Direct Compensation :* In this method the individual removes his specific weakness and frustration in the same field in which he is deficient by doing hard labour.

(b) *Over compensation :* In this method, special weakness is converted into outstanding strength by doing extra ordinary effort in the field.

(c) *Substitute Compensation :* When an individual finds himself weak in an area and he finds himself helpless in removing the defects, he selects another field to show his outstanding performance in that field, it is called substitute compensation.

(d) *Indirect Compensation :* When a person is unable to compensate his defect himself, he takes the help of others to do so, it is called indirect form of compensation. For example, a father who wanted to become an engineer but failed in his life, prepares his son from the very beginning to become an engineer in future.

(e) *Neurotic Compensation :* When a person fails in his attempt again and again, he develops neurotic symptoms, i.e.., he falls ill or he behaves so abnormally that he draws the attention of the whole family, it is called neurotic compensation. Regular attempts and failure of mentally retarded persons in academic fields is the best example of neurotic compensation.

4. **Sublimation :** It is actually making the desires sleep. Through this method intolerable impulses and drives are directed to socially accepted channels. If a person fails in his love, he converts his frustration into the composition of poetry and songs. It is sublimation. It is actually making the mind understand "Not to run after the thing that is beyond the reach. We see a lot of people kissing small children in order to pacify their sexual urges. Thus, socially unacceptable behaviour is converted into acceptable one and the personality comes into balance

   This technique is especially useful for those whose maladjustment problem is the result of any physical or social handicap or deprivation.

5. **Identification :** This method operates outside likes and he and beyond conscious awareness through which an individual makes himself like some one whom he has identified in any particular field. The elements identified for the purpose are thoughts, behaviour, beliefs, tasks and character. For example, adolescents identify themselves with film heroes, heroines, political leaders and scientists and they try hard to acquire the characteristics of their identified personalities. Copying the hair style of Salman Khan by children and adult is a good example.

   Identification process may be conscious and unconscious both. With the help of this method, the person removes his anxiety by doing well in the direction of his efforts and leaving everything else.

6. **Projection :** In the words of Freud, projection is a process by which we describe to the external world the rejected impulses of the Id. We defend ourselves against our repressed guilt feelings by projecting them into other things and people.

   In the classroom situation, children who do poorly are often critical of the teacher or other pupils. By this technique, they try to blame others for the loss and take credit themselves for the good. Here the individual always projects the situations in his own favour. For example, a person working in a group takes the full credit of what the group did commendable or every player of the team takes the credit of winning the game.

7. **Rationalization :** It is a mechanism by which an individual justifies his beliefs, thinking or action by giving reasons other than those which are real and motivating for the belief or action. By doing so the individual minimizes his frustration. The reason of failure given by him is so sound that his mind fully accepts it but it does not mean that others will also believe in those reasons. For example, if a child fails in the annual examination, he takes no responsibility of failure himself. He blames either the paper setter or the examiner who evaluated the answer books or his own health that was not good during examination period. Similarly, if a boy is not liked by the girl who he loves he blames either the girl or the other situations responsible for it. Thus, our own fault is shifted to others here.

   By rationalization we actually try to convince the people that we are not responsible for failure. There were many other things or persons which played active role in our failure. The team lost the match not because it did not play well but it was the referee who took wrong decisions against the team several times and as a result the team lost the match. In rationalization, the fact are actually distored by the person very cleverly in the manner that can be accepted by others.

   There are two forms of rationalization:

   *(a) Sour grapes :* When a person fails to achieve his cherished goals due to his own faults or deficits, he blames other factors that contribute to his failure, it is called sour grapes.

   *(b) Sweet Lemon :* When an individual is not fully satisfied with his achievement but in order to maintain the balance of his personality, he accepts the achievement as good, it is called sweet lemon. For example, we all are frustrated with the corruption rampant in Indian society, but we are least willing for its eradication. We accept it as good saying that we can get any type of benefit just by giving bribes to officers.

8. **Regression :** It is an unconscious back tracking either in memory or in behaviour which might have been successful in the past. An adult behaving or crying like a child in certain situations is an example of regression. The old people who always talk of their achievement in young age show the mechanism of regression.

   Some sort of regression is normal for maintaining mental health. If a teacher adopts this mechanism, he can come to the state of boyhood mentally and enjoy with his students. In this case, his age superiority will not create a problem for him. By adopting the method the teacher will be able to establish full rapport with his students. On the other hand, regression can pose a serious problem if the person is habitual to using this technique in all circumstances. It is actually a sign of mental ill health.

9. **Repression :** Repression is an attempt by the individual to push those experiences and thoughts into unconsciousness which are in conflict with the social norms or moral standard and which are painful to contemplate. The forces of repression exist within the individual. Repression may be of two forms:

   *(a)* By repression, we try to forget those things or experiences, which make us feel inferior, ashamed, guilty and anxious.

   *(b)* We try to crush those thoughts and behaviour which are unacceptable to the society in any way, i.e., crushing sexual urges in the presence of relatives. This is repression.

   An example may illustrate the point. A person was beaten by his neighbours in the presence of so many people. Due to this he felt insulted and ashamed. He did not come out of his home for several days due to this insult. By the mechanism of repression, he tried to forget this painful experience by and by and then he was again seen in the market talking to the people.

10. **Reaction formation :** It is to substitute opposite reaction formation which causes anxiety or fear. When we are frightened to a fearful situation we avoid and escape the fear by engaging in some other activity. For example, when a child fears graveyard or ghosts in a lonely situation he whistles or sings a song to escape his fear. In the classroom situation when a child fears a teacher he poses before his mates that he does not fear him. This is negative reaction formation which is injurious to a child. Contrary to this, if a child is not liked by his teacher due to his bullying or carelessness, he tries to change his behaviour in order to please his teacher. This is positive reaction formation.

11. **Negativism :** It is partially a defense mechanism and partially an escape mechanism. In this method, the person develops strong and irrational resistance to accepting the suggestion of others if the person is criticized by them repeatedly. If a person has some shortcoming which is frequently criticized by his peers then in this situation the person will resist to change due to obstinacy. This is negativism. This method is always injurious for every child. Once the tendency of negativism develops in a child it becomes very difficult for the teacher to change this behaviour. A teacher has to change this tendency by using positive remarks given to the child along with his negative points.

12. **Day dreaming (fantasy) :** It is actually roaming about in the imaginary world which is full of pleasure and satisfying stimuli for the individual. Masturbation by an unmarried man is the best example of fantasy. This helps the individual minimize frustration of the real life. Hungry men dream of food, unsuccessful men dream of success, poor people dream of richness by an unknown source are few examples. Day dreaming reduces tension immediately.

    Fantasy is useful for an individual in the following ways:

    - We can escape the pains of real life by using fantasy. It is very much soothing at least temporarily.
    - Fantasy is useful for creative thinking also provided that it is followed by action.
    - Fantasy helps the person excel in fine arts, poetry and other forms of literature.

    Excess use of fantasy without the feedback of action is harmful for the individual. He will cease doing efforts. He will just anticipate for any windfall gains. On the other hand, legitimate use of fantasy is always useful and enjoying for any body.

## Two severe cases of maladjustment

**(A) Neurosis :** The behaviour of a person that deviates from the normal behaviour to a great extent is called neurotic behaviour. This deviation is caused either due to a malfunctioning in the nervous system of the person or a disorder in his psyche. However, the deviant neurotic behaviour does not cut off from the environment. The individual remains in touch with his surrounding and develops a rapport with it.

***Causes of neurotic behaviour***

*(i)* Hysteria is the main cause of neurosis.

*(ii)* Weakness of the ego, overpowered by a super ego is another cause.

*(iii)* Hypertension is the third cause.

*(iv)* Faulty relationship of the child with his parents in the early years of his life. If the attitude of parents are critical, dominating or rejecting towards their children and they exercise excess control over their children, such children become the victim of neurotic problems. As much as they grow up, whatever behaviour they have developed with their parents is generalized in the environment and the problem becomes acute. A wife suffering from this problem will find it very difficult to adjust with her husband.

The problem of neurosis can be understood with the help of an example. A child knows that parents and other members of the family are the closest person for him. He develops close attachment with them. If these very people do not treat the child well, they reject or criticize him. They exercise undue control over him and do not like the child in any way. If this type of impression is developed in the child, he becomes deviant in his behaviour. He grows up keeping this attitude with him. He thinks that if parents who were the closests relatives did not treat him properly, how can the other people treat him in a proper manner who are definitely very far in relations. The child suspects the whole society and generalize his neurotic behaviour in the society without discrimination and thus he becomes problematic.

***Effects of neurotic behaviour :***

1. *An obsessive-compulsive reaction :* An obsession may he defined as a recurring thought or desire and this thought or desire is regarded by him as useless or false but he can not help himself to overcome this thought or desire. The person who is obsessed by any idea is unable to get rid of the idea easily.

   Compulsion is a tendency through which the person resists to do something at the advice of others. The person who is inflicted with compulsive reaction knows that whatever he is going to do is absurd and useless but he can not resist the temptation of doing so.

2. *Hypochondria :* It is a tendency in which the person in anticipation of some failure by his action pretends to he sick. He pretends so only to avoid painful situation, though , he is not actually sick. This imaginary sickness makes him the victim of failure forever. For example, if a person can not defeat a strong man , he pretends that he is sick so that he may not have to fight.

***Treatment of neurosis :*** Following methods can be adopted to treat these people:

*(i)* Yogic exercises are the best method of correcting the disorder of nervous system. Muniasan and Shirshasan are the most suited asans. In case of Muslims and Christians rituals (namaz) in the late hours of night is the best suggestive measure.

*(ii)* The ego of a person should never he damaged by superimposing a super ego on it irrationally. Moral behaviour should be taught only after telling the rational uses of it. If morning prayer is considered good by parents, they should tell their children why it is good.

*(iii)* Every person in the society has a right to live his own life, it should not be transgressed by others. Even dependent children have their own world to live in. If they are given bread at the cost of their freedom, the child will develop neurotic symptoms in future.

*(iv)* Sympathetic behaviour of people towards these people is the best suggestive measure.

Perseverance is, however, needed here. The neurotic people do not easily believe or trust anybody. It may take long time to win the hearts of these neurotic people.

(v) Such people have some real problem of life due to their persistent anxiety and they are unable to save them also. These people should be helped to solve their problem of life, only then their neurotic anxiety will come to a normal stage. Saying the statement "There is nothing to be worried about" is not simply enough.

(vi) If a person is obsessed by an idea or desire, he should be shown some emotion stirring films to change an obsessed idea. Regular treatment will be required here.

(vii) Lastly, Kali Phosphoricum, a homeopathic medicine has been found effective for such patients.

**(B) Psychosis :** Psychosis is so severe form of mental disturbance that makes a person incapable of adjusting to his environment. Two forms of psychosis are commonly seen—

1. *Organic psychosis :* This type of psychosis is caused due to a damage of brain or interference with the functioning of the brain like brain tumor, head injuries etc. Problems arises due to this disease are impairment of intellectual functions, sensory motor disturbances, (aphasia paralysis etc) and emotional problems.
2. *Functional Psychosis :* There are three main varieties of functional psychosis :

   *(a) Schizophrenia :* Mental disturbances caused by this disease are disturbance in thought process, diversion of reality, delusion, hallucination and inability to control emotions and all these cause loss of integrated and controlled behaviour. Four important levels of schizophrenia are given below:

   - **Simple schizophrenia,** marked by loss of interest, isolated behaviour, social withdrawl and flatness of emotional expressions. Other symptoms of schizophrenia are laziness, irresponsible behaviour and involvement in anti-social activities.
   - **Catatonic schizophrenia,** marked by two patterns of behaviour-stupor and excitement. In the first case, the person remains motionless in a certain posture for hours together. He may remain mute and isolated for months. In the second case, the person shows hyperactivity in walking, talking etc. He talks too loudly. He may hurt himself and others by his activities.
   - **Hebephrenic schizophrenia,** marked by childish mind in thinking and behaviour, complete disintegration of the personality, delusion and hallucination. Other symptoms are self talking, and inconsistency in thought, action and feeling.
   - **Paranoid schizophrenia,** the last stage of schizophrenia is marked by delusion of being persecuted and hallucination as if he is followed by some one. Other symptoms are complete delusion about oneself as if one is god or lord and persistent fear of enemies.

   *(b) Paranoia :* This form of psychosis is characterized by delusion, hypersensitivity, limited social functioning and limited social relations, insufficient self control and self centred behaviour. They expect too much from others but they are willing to give only a little to others.

   *(c) Affective psychosis :* Two important varieties of affective psychosis are manic and depressive. In the manic state, the person feels elated and highly energetic. Overactivity and uncontrolled behaviour are other symptoms. Depressive state is marked by loss of enthusiasm and extensive slowness in physical and mental activity. Other symptoms are defection, hopelessness, lack of enthusiasm, selfishness, guilty consciousness in abnormal situation and so on. The person feels that he/she is highly attached to others but actually he is not willing to go to that level in practical life.

## Educational adaptation of maladjusted children

1. **Regular observation :** It is the duty of the teacher to observe the behaviour of maladjusted children in order to know their problems regularly and giving their immediate solutions. Sympathetic behaviour

of the teacher towards these children will minimize their adjustment problem to a great extent.

2. **Regular Counseling :** Regular teacher generally do not know how to minimize the problems of these children. For this purpose special teachers are appointed to teach these students in integrated classes. Apart from this a full time, counsellor is also appointed in the school to serve the purpose. These children are regularly sent to the counsellor for remedial advices and behavioural training.

3. **Provision of special services :** Child study centers, separate music room, child guidance clinic, psychological bureau etc. are the important services which are arranged in the school to help these students. Relevant personnel like doctors, psychologists, physiotherapist, social workers etc. work in these departments to benefit maladjusted children.

   In child study centres the problem of students is studied by using clinical case history method or experimentation. Then these children are given proper guidance in child guidance clinics. Psychological bureau helps the child to overcome his adjustment problem and to do better in the academic field. Lastly, social workers bring the home closer to the school and thus, the child, his parents, teachers and the principal all work as an integrated force.

4. **Method of instruction :** Important special techniques applied by the teacher in the class are as follows:
   - He should come very close to these students before asking a question. He should not ask questions from his seat. If teacher asks questions from his seat, he will not be able to win the hearts of them.
   - The teacher should maintain eye contact while responding to the question of these students.
   - If such students are not willing to do a job, they should not be requested persistently. It will irritate them.
   - The tone of the teacher should be very humble, loving and pleasant while addressing to these students.
   - The teacher should give students time to comply with requests rather than expecting immediate response from their side.
   - The teacher should have full control over his negative emotions while dealing with these students.
   - The request of the teacher should not be ambiguous in any way. He should speak out in clear words.
   - The compliance of the students should be immediately reinforced. If a part of the behaviour is good, he has to be reinforced at least to that extent by ignoring the unwanted behaviour.
   - Such students should be given assignments only after dividing them into smaller units.
   - The teacher should prepare a detailed plan for these students before giving them any assignment.

5. **Integrated classes :** Special classes are not suitable for these students because in that case all students of deviant behaviour will come in the same arrangements and multiply each others' problems. Integrated classes are, therefore preferred for these children.

6. **Guardian Institutions :** Students are sent to these institutions only when it becomes impossible to improve the behaviour of these students either in schools or at home. These institutions are residential in nature and modification of behaviour rather than teaching a set academic content is stressed here. Thus, adjustment training rather than teaching is important here.

## OBJECTIVE QUESTIONS

1. A process by which conflicts between the demands of the individual and demand of the environment is normalized is called.

   (*a*) Adjustment (*b*) Maladjustment
   (*c*) Social therapy (*d*) None of them

2. Which of the following attitudes is required to remove the situation of maladjustment?

   (*a*) The individual should modify his own demand
   (*b*) The individual should alter the environment itself

(c) The individual should adopt some mental mechanism to escape the situation.
(d) All of these

3. Which of the following is an important symptom of mental ill health?
(a) He is irritated to pity situations.
(b) The person demands more from others than he pays to them
(c) He considers himself a perfect person
(d) All of these

4. Which of the following is not a symptom of maladjusted children?
(a) Aggression and bullying.
(b) Hyperactivity
(c) Sexual crimes
(d) Extreme timidity

5. Which of the following is not the social cause of maladjustment?
(a) Injustice prevailing in the society
(b) Disability
(c) Faulty social environment of the school
(d) Communal tension.

6. A science which deals with the process of attaining mental health and preventing mental illness is called:
(a) Adjustment psychology
(b) Mental hygiene
(c) Social medicine
(d) None of these

7. **"A mind that found itself"** was written by Clifford Beers in
(a) 1908
(b) 1912
(c) 1943
(d) 1945

8. The purpose of mental hygiene is
(a) to make the individual healthy and happy.
(b) to help the individual to adjust in the environment
(c) to enable the individual to use his potentialities effectively to achieve to the maximum.
(d) All of these

9. Which of the following is an important source of frustration for an adolescent?
(a) Delay in sexual gratification.
(b) Smoking prohibition
(c) Regular failure in the competitive test
(d) All of these

10. In which of the following situations conflict is created ?
(a) when individual has two equally attractive options (goals) to follow
(b) when individual wants to achieve two conflicting objectives at a time
(c) when individual comes across two equally painful or enjoying situations simultaneously
(d) all of these

11. Maladjusted children are mostly found in
(a) Broken families or unitary families
(b) Poor or joint families
(c) Both of these
(d) None of these

12. Which of the following mechanism is used by a child in the school to escape punishment?
(a) Denial of the fact
(b) Rationalization.
(c) Sublimation
(d) All of these

13. Which of the following is an important cause of mental ill health (maladjustment) of the teacher in the school?
(a) Poor service conditions
(b) Hostile attitude of students.
(c) Prejudices against him
(d) All of these

**Directions:** *There are four alternatives given below in each question. Choose the best one.*

14. Philosophy is a science which discovers the real nature of supernatural things
(a) Hegel (b) Aristotle
(c) Descartes (d) None of these

15. Which of the following statements regarding the nature of philosophy and education is correct?
(a) Philosophy determines the objectives of education which is nothing but goals of life
(b) Philosophy shapes the theoritical aspects of education

(*c*) Education gives birth to new philosophies when it interacts with practical problems of life
(*d*) All of these

**16.** The Rig Veda, the oldest of all Vedas contains
(*a*) 1028 mantras
(*b*) 2000 mantras
(*c*) 2500 mantras
(*d*) uncountable numbers

**17.** Match the following:

| List I | List II |
|---|---|
| A. Islam | 1. Jurosalam |
| B. Judaism | 2. Allahabad |
| C. Christianity | 3. Macca |
| D. Hinduism | 4. Vatican City |

**Codes**

| | A | B | C | D |
|---|---|---|---|---|
| (*a*) | 1 | 2 | 3 | 4 |
| (*b*) | 3 | 1 | 4 | 2 |
| (*c*) | 4 | 3 | 2 | 1 |
| (*d*) | 3 | 2 | 1 | 4 |

**18.** Skeptical methodology in education was introduced for the first time by
(*a*) Plato (*b*) Aristotle
(*c*) Socrates (*d*) Democritus

**19.** Idealism can be criticised on each of the following grounds except
(*a*) It takes the man into a world of dream (heaven or hell)
(*b*) Teachers are sympathetic to children to the extent of lawless in the class
(*c*) It ignores physical realities of the world at present
(*d*) It considers values and truth both as absolute

**20.** Which of the following is an important cause of class struggle according to Marxism?
(*a*) Inference of Church in the individual life of man
(*b*) Poverty and exploitation of poor by the rich
(*c*) Hightening inequalities of income and wealth between rich and poor
(*d*) b & c both

## ANSWERS

| 1 | 2 | 3 | 4 | 5 | 6 | 7 | 8 | 9 | 10 |
|---|---|---|---|---|---|---|---|---|---|
| (*a*) | (*d*) | (*d*) | (*c*) | (*b*) | (*b*) | (*a*) | (*d*) | (*d*) | (*d*) |
| **11** | **12** | **13** | **14** | **15** | **16** | **17** | **18** | **19** | **20** |
| (*a*) | (*d*) | (*d*) | (*b*) | (*d*) | (*a*) | (*b*) | (*c*) | (*b*) | (*d*) |

# Personality & Its Measurement

## MEANING OF PERSONALITY

The word personality has been derived from the Latin word Persona. Persona at that time meant the mask which the Greek actors commonly used to wear on their faces before coming to the stage for acting. These masks would hide the real faces of actors before the audience. Thus, in the olden days personality was meant the outward appearance of a person. Personality was thought to be the effect of a person on the others. Later on, the word personality came to be known the real nature of a man.

Now this word is used in a wide sense. It denotes the real as well as phenomenal nature of a man. It implies the organisation and pattern of every thing which an individual possesses.

## DEFINITIONS OF PERSONALITY

Personality has been defined by different psychologistss in different ways. Some of these definitions are given below :

**(A) Personality as a distinct feature of the individual :** Personality is the organised system, the functioning whole or units of habits, disposition, and sentiment that mark off any one member of a group being different from other members of the same group. **– Schoen**

**Comment:** This definition considers each individual of the society unique in his habits, disposition and sentiments. Personality impressions develop only when these differences are significant.

**(B) Personality as a stimulus :** Personality is determined by how an individual influences other persons in his group, whether he is impressive or repulsive, he has dominating or submissive traits. These impressions are created by physical appearance, clothing, conversation style, etiquettes etc.

**Comment :** Selection of applicants in various professional courses and jobs is done on the basis of this concept of personality.

**(C) Personality as a summation of qualities :** Personality is the sum total of all biological innate dispositions, impulses, tendencies and instincts of the individual plus all the dispositions and tendencies acquired by experience.

**– Motron Prince**

**Comment :** According to this definition, personality of an individual is determined by hereditary and environmental factors. All the qualities that a person possesses genetically or socially, personality is the sum total of these qualities.

**(D) Personality as an integration of abilities :** Personality is the integrative organisation of all the cognitive, affective, conative and physical characteristics of an individual as it manifest itself in focal distinction from others.

**– Warren's Dictionary**

**Comment :** This definition is an improvement over the previous summative definition of personality. According to this system, all the abilities of a person are organised and integrated into a whole and this makes the personality of a person distinct from others.

**(E) Personality as adjustment to environment :** Every individual through his continuous reactions tries to adjust himself to his environment. This pattern of adjustment is not the same in all the individuals. Every individual develops his own unique way of adjustment to his environment. Thus, personality and manner of adjustment differ from person to person.

Several definitions of personality as an adjustment mechanism are given below :

1. **Allport (1961) :** Personality is the dynamic organisation within the individual of those psychological systems that determine his unique adjustment to his environment.
2. **Kemph :** Personlaity is the integration of those system of habits that represents an individual's characteristic adjustment to his environment. Thus, we can say that all those characteristics which are needed for adjustment in the society determine the personality of an individual.

## THEORIES OF PERSONALITY

### 1. Type Theories

Personalities of the people have been classified by different experts in different ways. Some of these classification are given below :

**(a) Constitutional Classification :** German psychiatrist Ernest Kretschmer classified human being on the basis of physical constitutions. Human personalities are of four types according to him.

| Types | Characteristics |
|---|---|
| I. Pyknic | Stocky, Full chested, Popular |
| II. Asthenic | Weak, Sensitive, Thin |
| III. Ashleric | Strong |
| IV. Dysylastic | Mixed type |

**(b) Somatic Classification :** American surgeon William H. Sheldon divided human personalities on the basis of their physical characteristics into three categories. These physical features determine the temperamental characteristics :

| Physical Characteristics | Temperament |
|---|---|
| I. Endomorphic (soft and round) | Sociable, Extrovert, Affectionable |
| II. Mesomorphic (Muscular and strong) | Energetic, Healthy, Risk loving |
| III. Ectomorphic. (Thin and tall) | Introvert, Artistic, Restrained |

**(c) Spranger's Classification :** German philosopher Spranger divided human being on the basis of interest in the following categories:

I. Theoretical : These persons avoid social and political participations.

II. Economic : These persons are interested to earn more and more money.

III. Aesthetic :These persons are the lover of beauty and they take much interest in sensuous gratification.

IV. Political : These people want to grab political power and authority in their hands.

V. Religious : These people take much interest in religious activities and mystic stories.

**(d) Jung's Classification :** According to him human personality is of two types :

I. Introvert : These people tend to withdraw into themselves especially when they face emotional disturbance. They are lonely loving people of shy nature. They generally avoid the company of others.

II. Extrovert : These people deal with social situations very efficiently. They are conventional , social and friendly. They are generally free from worries and take the surcharged atmosphere very lightly.

Jung further stated that a person may be introvert for one function such as feeling but he may be extrovert in another function such as intuition. Thus, all humans can be divided into eight types on the basis of dominance of any one factor out of the eight factors mentioned by him.

In between these two extremes of personalities, modern psychologists have introduced a third type of people. They are neither introvert nor extrovert. They are rather ambivert.

**(e) Freud's Classification :** Sigmund Freud has classified human personalities into three categories on the basis of fixation of sexual energy at a particular stage of sex development. Thus, personalities are of three types according to him.

I. Oral Eratic : According to him sex in infancy is located in mouth. There is a membrane in the mouth which when irritated gives pleasure to the child. Sexual gratification at this stage is acquired through the mouth related activities such as sucking of milk from the breast of the mother or putting any object in the mouth. If fixation of sexual energy takes place at this stage, it will result in two types of personalities at the later stage of life.

- Passive, i.e., the person will be dependent, optimistic and immature in his thinking. He will always behave like a child.
- Sadistic, i.e., the person will be aggressive, suspicious and pessimistic. He is likely to deal the others high handedly.

II. Anal : At this stage child obtains sexual gratification through anus related activities. Here child enjoys defectation or touching the anus. If fixation of sexual energy takes place at this stage, the child will become obstinate, miserly or orderly in the later stage of his life.

III. Phallic : This is the third stage of sexual development of a child and it starts with the signs of puberty in him. If fixation of sexual energy takes place at this stage, the child will become showy in the later stage of his life. He will try to draw the attention of others by making him self-attractive. He will be the extreme lover of beauty in whatsoever form it is.

***Applications :***

These typology of personality has wide application in Education and physical Education especially. While finalizing any teaching-learning programme for a child his specific type of personality must be kept in view and child should be guided accordingly.

## 2. Trait Theories

Type and trait theories are very much overlapped to each other because type theories include many variety of traits which are specifically mentioned in trait theories and specific mode of behaviour of a person is determined on the basis of these traits.

***Meaning of Traits :***

By traits we mean a specific mode of behaviour which is manifested by a person in a number of situations consistently. This trait is so dominating that we can distinguish a person from other persons on the basis of his trait. Thus, trait is actually a unique but relatively stable reactions to environment.

In ordinary life, trait is used as a qualitative adjective. For example, Hamid is a brave boy. It means that Hamid will behave bravely in most of the situations of his life.

Some **general properties of traits** are given below :

I. They can be measured and scaled quantitatively. So, statistical analysis of traits in researches is possible.

II. Traits are not directly observable unlike physical characteristics of a person. They are manifested through activities or verbal expressions in a number of situations persistently. So, inferring a trait from the behaviour of an individual may take time.

III. Traits are not static or rigid. They are rather flexible. They may become stable with the maturity of the person in age but some variability will always be there. For example, a person may manifest his honesty trait in a number of situations but he may be dishonest in some situations too.

IV. There are certain traits which are universal such as height and weight.

V. Traits are high order habits which recur in the behaviour frequently.

VI. Traits are mental sets. They are nothing but readiness to responds to different situations in a consistent way.

VII. Traits are organised frames of references. Whatever beliefs or emotions an individual has about the environment, he responds to the environment by his traits.

VIII. Traits are not genetically determined. They are rather acquired with the interaction of the environment. Thus, personality of a person is determined by the environment in which he lives.

Keeping these characteristics of traits into account different psychologists and physiologists have classified human personality on the basis of traits in the following ways :

**(A) G. W. Allport's Classification :** He defined traits in the following words :

"Trait is a generalized and localized neuropsychic system with the capacity to render many stimuli functionally equivalent and to initiate and guide consistent forms of adaptive and expressive behaviour".

Thus, according to him traits have a real and vital existence. They are general and enduring in nature. On the basis of traits Allport has classified human personalities into three categories:

I. Cardinal Traits : Those traits which appear in most of the behaviour of the individual are called cardinal traits,. These traits do not change much in life.

II. Central traits : They are less pervasive than cardinal traits but they are quite generalized dispositions.

III. Secondary disposition : They are the attitudes or the narrow traits such as attitude towards politics, religion etc.

According to Allport, traits differ in intensity and magnitude from individual to individual. Every one in the group behaves in his own unique way and thus, he can be distinguished from others.

**(B) Raymond B Cattell's Classification :** He defined traits in the following words :

"Trait is the structure of the personality inferred from behaviour in different situations".

*Cattle has classified traits into four categories:*

I. *Common traits :* These traits are widely found among all the individuals, such as honesty, cooperation, aggression etc.

II. *Unique traits :* They are temperamental traits possessed by a particular person, such as, energy, height, weight etc.

III. *Surface traits :* These are common traits possessed by people and exhibited by them in normal situations, i.e., curiosity, honesty etc.

IV. *Source traits :* These traits are not directly observable. They are rather inferred from behaviour, such as, dominance, leadership, obedience etc.

Cattell differs from other trait theorists in the sense that he was the first man to recognise the hereditary and environmental factors both in determining the traits of a person.

**(C) H. J. Eysenck's Classification** : He was a British psychologist. He conducted an extensive research on ten thousand soldiers and isolated two dimensions of personality after applying quantitative technique of factor analysis.

I. *Introversion and Extroversion :* They are the normal people. Here his ideas are similar to those of Jung.

II. *Neuroticism & Psychoticism :* They are the abnormal people suffering from psychological problems. These two types of problems are caused due to the malfunctioning in the automatic nervous system. He thus concluded that personality is genetically determined.

**Criticism of Trait Theories:**

I. There is no agreement among the psychologists regarding the conceptual meaning of traits

II. It is believed that a behaviour determined by a trait is consistent and does not vary from situation to situation. But in actual situation we see that a person who has friendliness as his trait behave in a friendly manner to some people but becomes very unfriendly to other people.

III. Quantification of human traits is not easy due to lack of zero reference and equality of units in trait measurement.

IV. If traits are measured by using questionnaire as tool then false information regarding his trait can be given by the respondent.

V. Error in rating due to subjectivity is always there. Some people may rate an individual very high on a specific trait while others may rate him very low.

VI. The behaviour of a person can not be predicted correctly on the basis of his scores on a trait inventory. Traits are only points of reference.

## 3. Psychoanalytic Theories

These theories were developed on the basis of psychoanalysis of individuals. Some of these theories are given below :

**(a) Freud's Theory :**

He stressed very much on instincts as the determinants of human behaviour. There are two types of instincts:

I. Life instinct

II. Death instinct.

These instincts are the ultimate cause of all human activities. These instincts can be understood by studying the psychic structure of a man.

**Psychic Structure :** Consists of the following units :

I. Psychic energy : Psychic or sexual energy comes from libido. Libido is the source of energy of all life instincts. Personality is governed by the need to gratify the libido, (sexual desire)

II. Id : It is inborn and its main function is to discharge the psychic energy. If this energy is not released, it creates tension in the personality of an individual. This id can not differentiate the good and bad and operate on pleasure principle only. If sexual desire can be fulfilled with a girl then there is no need of waiting a marriage. This is id.

III. Ego : Id knows only the subjective reality of mind but ego can distinguish between the subjective reality of mind and things in the external environment. Thus, it can differentiate the good and bad and operate on reality principle. A person can not fuck a girl without her consent. Ego formulates a plan for the satisfaction of needs and executes it keeping in view the reality of the situation. Thus, ego brings a compromise between the instinctual urges of the id and demand and forces of the external environment. But such compromises are not always possible. If id is horse and ego is the rider, then rider usually determines the direction of the horse but sometimes it is the horse who leads the rider. This is generally known as sexual crimes by the society.

IV. Super Ego : It internalizes the parental influences and ideals of the society through early childhood experiences. It works in accordance with the moral standard of the society.

An example will illustrate these concepts. Suppose a person sees a beautiful girl and he kisses her without considering any thing it is id. If he does not kiss the girl because of the fear of the society, it is ego. If he does not kiss the girl even in solitude considering it immoral, it is super ego.

Thus, an individual whose super ego is well developed, refrains from bad or evils automatically. He is not expected to steal something or tell a lie or abuse someone etc.

These four units, psychic energy, id, ego and super ego are the important determinants of personality. The biological energy from food is converted into psychic energy and is manifested by id, ego and super ego. Generally individual wants immediate gratification of his impulses. So he seeks pleasure and avoids pain in order to release his tension. As a result, his id becomes active but it is interfered with the ego and super ego. Ego or super ego is always there to impose inhibition on him. These conflicts amongst id, ego and super ego will shape the personality of the individual. It will depend upon the fixation of psycho-sexual energies at any of the four stages of development-oral, anal, phallic or genital. If ego or super ego has no role to play in the life of an individual, he will become self-centred and aggressive. But on the other hand, if parental or social care is there, his ego will help him adjust in the environment very easily. (see Freud's Type Theory of Personality also).

**Criticism of the Theory :** Freud's psychoanalytic theory of personality has been criticized on the following grounds :

I. Freud collected data from his patients and propounded his theory. He did not verify his finding from other sources. Thus, these sources of information can not be relied upon.

II. He has given more emphasis to sex as an interpretation of behaviour. There are so many factors also that affect pattern of behaviour.

III. He has used a number of ambiguous concepts in his theory and meaning of these concepts is also different at different places. For example, the term libido has different meanings at different places.

IV. It is purely a descriptive theory and the data collected by Freud can not be quantified. Thus, it is very difficult to test this theory.

V. This theory is unable to predict human behaviour in different situations.

VI. The theory gives importance to internal organisation of behaviour and past experiences in the development of personality. It neglects the importance of present experiences and takes only past experiences of the individual. Thus, it is incomplete explanation of personality.

VII. Freud's conception that source of life or sex instinct is libido but it has been proved wrong by studying the cases of neurosis in soldiers in the First World War.

**(b) Jung's Analytic Psychology :**

He was a close associate of Freud in the beginning but he parted with Freud on the ground that libido (sex) is not the only driving force in life according to Jung. Personality consists of three other elements different from Freud according to him. These elements are given below :

I. Conscious ego : It determines the process of thinking, feeling and remembering.

II. Personal unconscious : It is highly individualistic in nature and is determined by personal experiences. It is formed by those repressed experiences of the individual which can reach to the conscious mind.

III. Collective unconscious : It is primitive in nature and is consisted of the materials which had never reached the conscious mind before. All humans have the same collective unconscious because of the similarity of born structure and racial experiences. It can also be good and bad both depending upon the experiences. Collective unconscious is made of universal ideas which are called archetype. For example, mother is a universal idea which is inherited from generation.

***Various concepts defined by Jung***

**I. Anima and Animus :** A man has an anima which constitutes the feminine attributes while woman has animus which represents her masculine side. It indicates that both feminine and masculine characteristics are found in humans. The reason is that man living with woman from time immemorial has become somewhat feminine and woman living with men have become masculine that is why, boys like to wear feminine dress and vice versa. Thus, all humans are bisexual in nature.

**II. Shadow :** It includes animal instincts that man has inherited from lower forms of life. This shadow is similar to Id of Freud.

**III. Self :** It is the organizing agency of the personality. It gives unity and stability to personality characteristics. Every individual tries to establish a harmonious relationship with the self.

**IV. Extrovert and introvert :** Extroversion means orientation towards the outer environment and introversion means orientation towards the inner subjective world. Both of them are present in the personality of an individual but only either of them will dominate at a time and it becomes the basis for classification of personality. (see type theory of Jung also)

**V. Psychic energy :** Unlike Freud he also considers libido as all sources of psycho-sexual energy. This libido is innate but set in the cycle of growth. It is the main point of sex also. Psychic energy flows from weaker value to the stronger value and maintains the balance of personality.

***Personality of Jung :***

Man is not merely an organism whose main purpose is to accumulate power and gratify his urges only. He is the member of a complex society who wants to achieve self-actualisation in the process. All his behaviour is directed towards the good which is determined by the person himself. Here present is determined not by the past but by the future expectations of the individual. The individual in the process of personality development is inhibited by the environment and he may become mental patient. For this very reason Jung developed a full fledged system of psychotherapy to treat mental patients.

**(c) Adler's Individual Psychology :**

He was also an associate of Freud but he disagreed with Freud on certain issues and parted with him. He was the first psychologist who de-emphasised the concept of inborn instincts and gave importance to social factors in the development of personality. According to him will power is the central force active behind all the behaviours of the individual.

He says that an individual makes three types of adjustment in his life, adjustment to the society, to his vocation and to his love. These adjustments depend on how an individual was enriched by experiences in his childhood.

Second thing is that child wants to grow, to dominate and to be superior only because he is born helpless. Poor runs after wealth or weak follows the strength only because, deprivation creates the need.

Thus, every one is pushed by the urge to develop to higher levels of life.

This striving for superiority is innate in a child. Adler quotes the examples of Beethoven who was slightly deaf from his childhood, but became a great musician and he thus, compensated his deficiency by the other quality. This is possible only by 'will to power'.

### Several other determinants of personality

According to Adler are given below :

**I. Fictional Finalism :** Fictional finalism means that man's action is governed by fictional ideas. These ideas are not necessarily to confirm to reality. When such fictions are found in a man, he is expected to cope with life more successfully. Thus, future goals of man affect his present behaviour very much and he can be motivated by these goals.

**II. Style of life :** It is a unique quality of personality that differentiates a person from others. Style of life includes everything related to living such as goals of life, tendency to strive for superiority etc. There are many ways to reach goals of life. For example, some persons seek these goals through social relation, other persons through educational achievement and many other persons through business or politics. These different ways represent a person's style of living and hence his personality.

Formulation of life style starts from the age of four or five and later experiences of the individual are assimilated into this life style. It is very difficult to change this life style in the later period of life. Thus, style is formed on the basis of childhood experiences. That is why, every child tackles his problems of life in his own way depending on his style. The unique way of tackling the problems of life is called creative self. This creative self moulds the personality structure into a unique way depending on hereditary capabilities and life experiences of the individual.

**III. Social Interests :** Social interests determine the social relation of an individual. Social relation includes cooperation, sympathy and interpersonal identification with a group. Social relation of man means to help the society to attain perfection. Adler says that social interest is latent and inborn characteristics of a man. This innate capacity will not develop without the guidance and experiences in social context. These healthy social interests are subordinated or suppressed by selfish power goals in neurotics.

### Contributions of Neo Freudians in Developing psychoanalytic Theories of Personality

All Neo Freudians rejected the concept of libido and emphasised the importance of culture and social experiences in the development of personality. The views of some neo Freudians are given below:

**(a) Erich Fromm :** He was the first psychologist who advocated the sociological approach to personality rather than individual approach of Freud and his followers. His central theme is man's feeling of loneliness and isolation which motivates him to behave in a certain way. Fromm studied the man and his needs in his own way and gave the following conclusions :

- Man is not in harmony with nature now. He has rather separated himself from nature and violated the laws of nature to gain freedom. But this has led him into trouble. Thus, there is an immense need to create new relationship between nature and man.
- Man also has a need to rise above his animality. This he achieves by love and hate.
- Man has a need to be recognised in the society.
- Man has a need to mix up in the society.
- All men seek stable relations with other fellow beings.

Development of personality depends upon the intensity of these needs. Early childhood experiences play a very significant role in this regard. The child gradually learns to distinguish between "I" and 'not I' through his contract with his environment. If child is separated from his parents, it gives birth to feelings of isolation and doubt in the mind of the child. In order to remove these doubts he seeks new relations in the environment. As a result, his personality continues to develop during adulthood also if external influences are quite intense to affect changes in adults.

**(b) Karen Horney :** She also emphasised the importance of cultural factors in the development of personality. Man is constructive rather than destructive agent according to her. She developed five principles regarding the development of personality.

- **Optimism :** Horney was a psychotherapist. She treated a number of patients in her clinic and found that man has many positive qualities.
- **Socio-cultural factors :** Socio-cultural factors very much affect the development of personality.
- **Character structure :** Genetic factors and environment play a simultaneous role in the development of character.
- **Self-concept :** It is the directing force in life.
- **Conflicts :** Conflicts are natural phenomenon while living in a society. There are three major techniques of adjustment with others. Moving toward the people, moving away from the people and moving against the people. Her theory of personality development is incomplete in the sense that she only elaborates the process and does not lead us to the outcome.

**(c) Sullivan :** He too emphasised the importance of social factors in the development of personality. He also stresses the role of energy in the body but in a different way. He says that when an individual faces with a choice between two alternatives neither of which is agreeable the energy appears as a tension in the mind. This we can call excess of energy. The child directs his energy towards social relationship with his mother first. This interaction gives him the basic pattern of personality. As soon as the interaction of the child with other members of the society increases, his personality gradually gets matured. Personality is a matter of how we see ourselves and how we are seen by others.

Thus, personality structure of a person will depend on what type of people a person has interacted with the people in the society. Company of good people can make him good and vice-versa. But future development of personality to a great extent depends on the early experiences of the child at his home. On the basis of these very experiences he will choose his company in the later parts of his life. On the other hand, if a person feels himself to be a 'bad one' relationship with other, it will create a lot of anxiety in him because people may reject him. This will slow down his development of personality.

Sullivan further states that forced rules and regulations imposed by parents and society often lead to personality problems. For examples, if a person is not given reasonable freedom to interact with the opposite sex, he is likely to become homo-sexual . It is because it may be a safer relationship for him.

**(d) Erikson :** He also emphasised social factors along with biological ones in the development of personality. He developed the concept of 'development milestone' which means those functions which vary in stability and persistence throughout life but they provide regulatory constants at different age levels. Conflicts at different age levels are resolved in accordance with the strength or weakness of the basic alternatives which are present in the environment. He introduced eight stages of personality development in which he emphasised the interaction of biological and social factors.

**Stages of Personality Development:**

| Stages | Age | Conflicts |
|---|---|---|
| 1. Oral | 0-2 Years | Trust/Mistrust |
| 2. Anal | 2-3 Years | Autonomy/Shame |
| 3. Genital | 3-6 Years | Imitative//Guilt |
| 4. Latency | 6-12 Years | Industry/Inferiority |
| 5. Adolescence | 12-18 Years | Intensity/Confusion |
| 6. Young | 18-21 Years | Intimacy/Isolation |
| 7. Adulthood | 21-50 Years | Creativity/Stagnation |
| 8. Maturity | Above 50 Years | Integrity/Despair |

Thus, we see that individual faces conflicts in every stage of his personality development. These conflicts are resolved by accepting and adapting to the change of the social situations : Erikson recognises three factors representing the personality :

I. Somatic factors
II. Ego or self
III. Social and culture factors

The personality of a person will develop by the relative influence of these Three factors.

## 4. Phenomenological Theory

### Carl Roger's Self-theory :

He presented this theory in 1947 after studying the patients in his clinic. He stresses the importance of the individual who determines his own fate. He criticized the behaviouristic theories of personality by saying that they are mechanical in nature and neglect the vitality of individuals. He believed that behaviour is not based on needs or drives but it is based on a higher driving force within the individual which impels him to behave in a different way. His theory of personality is given below :

There are two basic concepts underlying his theory :

I. **Organism :** Organism is the centre of all experiences which take place within the individual at a particular time. The totality of experiences is called a phenomenal field. It develops a person's unique outlook.

II. **Self :** It is a part of phenomenal field and is related to 'I' or 'me'. There is an ideal self also which determines what we would like to be. Each of us has a potential for self-actualisation, but many of us are not aware of it. So we must become aware of it first.

The experiencing individual reacts to his perceptual field as an organised whole when he seeks to actualize, maintain and enhance himself. Thus, behaviour is a goal directed effort of the organism to satisfy needs experienced in the field.

According to Rogers, the organism continuously strives to develop and expand his self. And in the process he becomes aware of his power of self-actualisation. This self is developed in the process of inter-personal and social experiences in the environment. In order to become aware of the potential of self-actualisation, four conditions are necessary :

I. The person must be respected and loved by others.

II. The person must respect himself and his abilities to achieve his goals.

III. The choices available to the individual must clearly be perceived. If the person is unaware of the choices, the growth of self will be hindered.

IV. The person must have clear cut description and full understanding of choices.

Rogers has not divided personality into different stages of development. He rather maintains the continuity of growth. It is because strife for the development of self continues throughout life. When a person incorporates his experiences into his self, this self may be outgoing, private, friendly, unfriendly and so on. Once the concept of self is formed, the individual allows the external things to enter into his consciousness that is fit and rejects those that are not fit. Thus, personality development is a reciprocal relationship between the ways a person perceives his experiences and the actual social experiences that he goes through. We adopt many behaviours of others when they are consistent with the concept of our self, i.e., they are in accordance with our feeling, attitude and impulses.

## 5. Cognitive Theory of Personality

### George Kelley's theory of personal construct :

Kelley propounded his cognitive theory of personality in a reaction to phenomenological theories. He believed that most of man's behaviours are influenced by thinking, judging and anticipating rather than instincts, drive, growth etc.

According to him a person anticipates events by constructing their replications. After experiencing an event a person places a structure and a meaning to the events. Thus, Kelly believes that every man is capable of constructing his own theory and is able to control and predict his own personality like a scientist.

**Personal construct** is the only element in his structure of personality. Personal construct is the way of interpreting the event or world based on his own evaluation and thinking. The development of personal constructs will depend on the relationship of the person with other significant persons in the society. These constructs will determine the present and future behaviour of the person.

## 6. Learning Theories of Personality

All learning theories agree on two basic assumptions in explaining personality :

- All behaviour is learnt by the organism in the process of interaction with external stimuli.
- Behaviour of the individual can be objectively observed.

Thus, learning theories were developed in the process of experiments. Experimental psychologists were of the view that learning theory is the most reliable and objective approach to understand personality. Two learning theories of personality are given below :

**(a) S.R. Learning Theory of Dollard and Miller :** This theory is also called reinforcement theory of personality. While developing this theory they borrowed basic ideas from psycho-analysis and converted them into Hull's theory of reinforcement.

According to them learning theory is the study of circumstances under which a response and a cue become connected. They are joined together in such a way that the appearance of the cue evokes the response in a natural manner. The connection between response and cue can be strengthened only under certain conditions. The learner is driven to make the response and rewarded for the response in the presence of the cue. Thus, learning requires four factors. These four factors are explained below :

**I. Drive :** It is related to motivation and initiates action on the part of the organism. Drive differs in strength in different organisms. The stronger the drive, the more vigorous or persistent will be the behaviour. There is a positive correlation between drive and stimulus also. The stronger the stimulus, the greater will be its drive function. Drives can also be classified into two broad categories:

- **Primary or innate drives :** They originate from the physiological needs of the individual, such as, sex, hunger, thirst etc. They are essential for the survival of the organism. They are more forceful than the secondary drives.
- **Secondary or acquired drives :** They are acquired from the process of social learning, such as, practice, status, affection, approval, money, achievement etc. They can be termed as social motives.

**II. Cue :** It is related to stimulus and guides the organism for response. Cues (stimuli) are fundamental elements for learning. They may be internal as well as external. They are also distinctive in nature, i.e., learner can differentiate them in different situations. Learning of an individual depends on the perceiving abilities of cues. Thus, it is cue that determines when and where an individual will respond and what type of response he will make.

**III. Response :** Drive and cue combined together enables the organism to respond. Response is the action of the organism which is the basis for learning. Thus, learning will take place only when appropriate response is produced. The strength of S-R. habit increases with the number of occasions on which S-R have occurred together.

**IV. Reinforcement :** When a response is followed by a reward, the connection between S-R is strengthened and the possibility of correct response increases. Reinforcement takes place in the presence of a drive. If drive is dead, reinforcement will not work.

As far as schedule of reinforcement is concerned, immediate reinforcement after the response is more effective than the delayed reinforcement. If an organism is immediately rewarded after the response, he will be able to identify the act for which he has been rewarded.

***Other Principles of S-R Learning:***

- ***Extinction :*** It is a process of weakening or eliminating previously learned responses. When a response is not rewarded for a number of times, S-R bond weakens and finally no response is exhibited due to the absence of reward. This extinction is not permanent. An extinguished habit reappears if reward is again given. This is called spontaneous recovery.
- ***Stimulus Generalisation :*** It is a process in which responses learned from one situation are transferred to a variety of similar situations. The amount of this generalization depends on the similarity between two similar situations. It increases the horizon of learning. The stronger the drive, the more stimulus generalization will take place.
- ***Habit Hierarchy Response :*** Whatever is learned by the organism becomes the part of his habit if S-R bond is repeated again and again. Early years of life for a child is important because during these years the child establishes response hierarchy for a great variety of stimulus contexts.

That is why, if a ten year old child learns aggression in home environment he can act aggressively in school and neighbourhood and attitude towards parents is generalized to other persons such as teachers, friends etc.

- ***Discrimination :*** In this process, learned responses are made to a particular and appropriate cues in the environment and not to others. This process is very essential for concept formation, such as child discriminates chair from the table.

Thus, we see that this theory of personality emphasises habit formation through learning. Habits are formed by S-R connections in the presence of reinforcement materials. These habits are not static but they change with the change in social experience of the individual. Drives in the form of tension also play important roles in the development of the personality. Secondary drives which are acquired with the help of primary drivers in a social environment plays more dominant role in shaping the personality. Whatever we learn through the process of stimulus, response, drives and reinforcement, it becomes the part of our personality in social situations.

***Merits of the theory :***

- It is purely an objective approach to explain human behaviour.
- It emphasises the role of learning from infancy onward.
- It rejects the concepts of ego and super ego developed by Freud.
- It states that appropriate habits can be formed by appropriate learning conditions.

***Demerits of the Theory :***

- Learning principles have been derived from researches conducted on rats, dogs etc. under controlled conditions. The application of these principles on humans is not a sound approach.
- This theory neglects the complexities of human learning. Here cognitive, intutive or subjective aspects of human behaviour have been completely ignored.
- This theory overemphasizes the importance of environmental factors in shaping the personality and neglects hereditary factors altogether.
- It is a molecular and fragmented approach of studying personality. Human behaviour cannot be predicted on the basis of this theory.

**(b) Social Behaviouristic Theory of Bandura and Walter :** It is also called social learned theory of personality. This theory is also based on the assumption that behaviour is learned and personality can be explained in terms of cumulative effects of a series of learning experiences.

This theory differs from S-R learning theory in the following ways:

I. It emphasises the role of observational (cognitive) learning in the development of personality.

II. It rejects the psychoanalytic theory of Freud and his followers altogether.

III. It is based on the experiments conducted on children directly rather than findings based on lower animals. Thus, it is based on real life situations.

IV. It synthesises the cognitive learning with the principles of behaviour modification given by behaviorists and says that cognitive functioning is more important in acquiring new behaviour.

## BASIC PRINCIPLE OF SOCIAL LEARNING

(Principle of reinforcement) : Most of our behaviour in social situations is acquired through the principle of reinforcement. It increases the rate of responding to a great extent. Walter also concluded from his experiments that partial reinforcement leads to greater resistance to extinction than continuous one i.e., continuous reinforcement is not very much effective.

Reinforcement becomes more important in situations where a person observes the action of other persons who is reinforced for his action. This vicarious reinforcement modifies the behaviour of the observer also. For example, when a player is rewarded for his achievement, the audience are also reinforced to do that job. This process of learning through imitation is influenced by the nature of the reinforcement given to the models or actual performers.

These models may be classified into two categories :

**(a) Real life models :** Under these models we include parents, teachers, friends, film stars, sportsmen and most successful persons in the society, in business or in any other profession.

**(b) Symbolic models :** Under these models we include verbal, written or pictorial materials, books, paintings etc.

Both types of models are equally effective in learning. It is a common experience that whatever children see in films and TV, they try to imitate them in real life. Hair style, dress, delinquency, style of conversation etc. are imitiated by adults on the ground that these things are accepted by the people in films.

Thus, positive reinforcement and reward play an important role in social learning, i.e., in shaping the personality. They strengthen our responses and develop a tendency to repeat the same responses in future.

## Factors Operating in Social Learning

*(a)* **Stimulus properties of the model :** Model's age, sex, social status etc. affect the observer very much. That is why, we see that high status models are more imitated by the people than common people.

*(b)* **Model's similarity to the observer :** The observer imitates those models more which are somewhat similar to him.

*(c)* **Type of behaviour exemplified by the model :** Three types of behaviour of the model are imitated more :

- Novel skills
- Hostile or aggressive behaviour
- Touching behaviour

*(d)* **Consequence of model's behaviour :** Rewarded or acceptable behaviour is more likely to be imitated by the observer.

***Sub-Processes in Observational (social) Learning:***

- ***Attentional process :*** Attention to the model is the first process in observational learning. If observer is not paying attention to the model, he will not learn anything from the model.
- ***Retention process :*** Whatever is learned from the model must be retained by the observer.
- ***Motoric Reproduction of skills :*** A considerable motor practice with feedback of result is needed to shape the motor skills. Seeing a good model of hand-writing is not enough. It should be imitated and practised. Imaginary practice will not work.
- ***Role of reinforcement :*** Reinforcement works as motivating factors to increase earlier learning behaviour.

## Observational Learning and Personality Development :

I. From the beginning of his life the child learns many activities by observing the behaviour of others. These activities become the part of his personality.

II. The model which the child observes also plays an important role in social learning. Child imitates the model and develops his personality.

III. While observing a model children identify themselves with the model if they like him. If they do not like the behaviour of the model, they do not copy it.

IV. Reinforcement plays an important role in shaping the personality e.g., aggressive boys who are rewarded for their behaviour in the society learn aggression and their behaviour is imitated by others.

V. If learned activities are practised by the observer, only then it will last long.

VI. A person can also be motivated by reinforcing the model. If a student scoring 90% marks is given a cash prize of Rs. 1000, the other students will also be motivated to do that.

VII. The behaviour and personality of an individual can be modified by creating good models.

Thus, we see that this theory has a direct application in the classroom situation. A teacher can mould the behaviour of his students just by moulding his own behaviour and by presenting a good model before them. He can also make some of his students as models.

## MEASUREMENT OF PERSONALITY

### Purpose of Personality Measurement

Identification of the following types of traits and their respective roles in shaping total personality of an individual is the main purpose of personality testing:

1. **Social traits :** Social traits are those traits which determine how a person interacts with others in

individual and social situations in the society, such as, friendliness, sociability, honesty, dominance, cooperation, aggressiveness, shyness etc.

2. **Motives :** They are those biological and non-biological needs which push an individual to keep himself always active, moving and dynamic. Biological drives are necessary for physical survival and non-biological drives are necessary for psychological (real) survival. Examples of biological drives are needs for food, water, oxygen, defecation etc. while examples of non-biological drives are need to earn money and prestige, need for academic achievement and affiliation, need for grabbing power etc. The second type of needs constitute personality dynamics especially.
3. **Personal Conceptions :** These conceptions include people's attitude towards self and others, personal values, interests and liking. These conceptions determine how a person is likely to behave and think in certain situations.
4. **Adjustment :** It includes traits like freedom from emotional worries and stability in thoughts and actions. Its opposite maladjustment includes traits like hallucination, imaginary illness, hysteria, psychoses, neuroses etc.

Point to be noted here is that all these four types of traits are not independent. They are rather correlated with each other. For example, a social trait such as domination is likely to influence motives, personal conception and adjustment all. Similarly, if motive of affiliation is there, the person will be very sociable, adjusted and cooperative to others.

## Important tools of Personality Measurement

(A) Self-Report inventories
(B) Observational Techniques
(C) Situational Tests
(D) Projective Techniques
(E) Measurement of Attitude, interest and values.

We will discuss them here one by one :

### (A) Self-Report Inventories

In these inventories some questions are given to examinees and they answer them in their own way. Inventories are actually self-rating questionnaires where individual describes his own feeling and reaction towards other persons and vice versa.

Limitation of this tools is that a person can report about himself in the light of the questions already given in the questionnaire and his answer may be in Yes/No or agree/disagree/undecided etc.

**Questionnaire, a tool for self report :** It is used when factual information from a respondent is needed. A number of questions in the questionnaire are given to the examinee and he answers these questions according to his own will.

Questionnaire is different from a schedule, an opinionnaire and an interview guide.

**A schedule** consists of questions which are asked by the investigator (not read by the respondent) and then answers of the respondent are filled in by the investigator himself. Thus, it is an oral communication process and it is used in individual situation.

An opinionnaire consists of questions or statement by which an attempt is made to measure the attitude or belief of an individual. That is why, the other name of opinionnaire is attitude scale.

An interview guide consists of those points which are to be covered by an interviewer during an interview.

A questionnaire is preferred to a schedule when a large number of respondents are to be covered simultaneously.

**Language of a Questionnaire :** When we are going to use questionnaire as a tool of data collection we must give special emphasis on the language of a questionnaire. Important points to be kept in mind are as follows :

1. **Simplicity of language :** While preparing a questionnaire we must ensure that the language of the questionnaire must be very close to the respondent's language and understanding level so that communication barrier is not created. Technical and sophisticated language may, however, be used if respondents are from elite and educated class. In short, language conveying the meaning has to be used. Lengthy and complicated questions should never be asked because answer of these questions will put great strain on the mind of the respondent.

2. **Clarity of language :** The language of items of questionnaire must be free from ambiguity so that different respondents may not derive different meanings from the same item. If language is not clear, different respondents will answer the items differently.
   Example : "Do you feel shy when you are in a group".
   The meaning of shy and group is not one here. If one feels shy in the group of girls, he will say yes but if he takes the meaning of group as his own company of his own sex, he may say no.
   Clarity also requires that no two things should be asked in one question and the use of phrasal verbs should be avoided as much as possible.
   Ambiguity is introduced not only by sentences but also by words like often, generally sometimes, etc. If such words are used in a sentence, the answer will also be vague and it can not be interpreted in an objective language.
3. **Inclusion of embarrassing questions :** When such private matters of the respondents are asked which they do not want to make public, they would answer the question otherwise. Such questions, if necessary to be asked, should be asked indirectly by referring any other person. The example of an indirect questioning is given below :
   Example : Do you agree with the statement "wives require fulfilment of sexual desires more than anything else." Yes/No.
4. **Use of double negatives :** Double negatives used in a question tend to cancel each other and hence create confusion. An example of such an item is given here.
   Example : "Nobody likes not to go alone" Agree/ Disagree
5. **Use of leading questions :** A leading question is one which by its virtue of content and structure lead to a specific type of answer either positive or negative. i. e., "Do you think that study is a burden on those who are very poor in intelligence. The answer to this question is most likely to be in negative and thus purpose of asking a question will not be served.
6. **Hypothetical questions :** Questions which are not yet supported by evidence are hypothetical questions and they must not be asked in a questionnaire.

**Other Characteristics of a Good Questionnaire:**

1. Questions should be framed from those topics which have direct relevance to the examinees. Purpose of the test should be explained in the questionnaire.
2. Directions as well as its wordings should be in simple language
3. The number of questions in a questionnaire should be neither less nor more than the required one.
4. Questions of the questionnaire should be presented in an order so that they look usable , such as, from general to specific.
5. Questions should be neatly printed and clearly arranged following the rules of punctuation.

**Types of Questionnaires :** Questionnaires can be classified in different categories on two bases :

**(a) Classification on the basis of responses required:**

1. ***Fixed Response Questionnaire :*** This type of questionnaire consists of questions which have fixed number of response options. Respondents are asked to check the options that are best suited to them. Responses in such questionnaires may be in the form of Yes/No, Agree/Disagree etc.
   Example : "Politics is a game that can be played by anyone" Agree/disagree)
   Framing of this type of questionnaire is based on the following two assumption :
   - Respondents know the answer of these questions.
   - The researcher has enough knowledge about the sample under investigation.
2. ***Open end Questionnaire :*** This type of questionnaire consists of those questions which require free responses on the part of the respondents. The maximum word limit may be given here.
   Example " Give two causes of degradation of educational standard in government aided schools."
   Assumptions of this type of questionnaire are also the same as given above.

**(b) Classification on the Basis of Administration**

1. ***Mailed questionnaire :*** Such questionnaires are those which are mailed to the sample for giving response. They are returned to the investigator by the respondents through mail as well. Return envelop is also provided to each respondent so that he may not have to bear the postal expenses.
2. ***Face to Face Administered Questionnaire :*** This type of questionnaire is given to the selected sample in face to face situation and responses of questions are collected in the same sitting. This type of questionnaire is preferred when subjects to be studied are readily available at one or few places.

**Advantages and Disadvantages of These types of Questionnaires:**

*Advantages of fixed response questionnaire:*

- Due to fixed nature of responses, items can be easily scored and analysed statistically.
- These items generally do not require any writing on the part of the respondents. They only check the response which they like by putting right or wrong. Thus, these questionnaires can be administered on less educated people.
- They do not require much time to complete. More than 100 questions can be answered in one hour.
- If this questionnaire is mailed to the sample, it is most likely that they will be returned to the researcher after completing it.
- Manipulation of information from the respondent's side is not possible here.

*Limitations of Fixed Response Questionnaire:*

- Only limited information can be obtained through these questionnaires.
- If none of the choices given in the questionnaire fit the respondent, he will be in dilemma and may skip the item.
  This problem can be minimized by increasing the numbers of response option such as,

| Strongly agree | Agree | Undecided |
|---|---|---|
| Disagree | Strongly disagree | |

- Here, the respondents sometimes do not read the item properly and check the options rapidly. Thus, misleading information is obtained.

*Advantages of open end questionnaire:*

- Such questionnaires are preferred when researcher has no knowledge about the sample to be studied.
- They provide large range of information to the investigator and he can know a problem better. He can also eliminate irrelevant informations from the responses.
- Construction of such a questionnaire is easy.

*Limitations of open end questionnaire:*

- In such questionnaires some respondents will give very detailed answer and others may give a very short answer of the question. As a result, educational bias will operate leading to misleading results.
- Variation in responses will make the interpretation and analysis of the results very difficult.
- It is very much time consuming to answer these questions and the respondent may avoid such questionnaires.
- Objective scoring of such questionnaires is not possible and subjectivity of scoring will cause great measurement errors.

*Advantages of Mailed Questionnaire:*

- When sample is scattered to a variety of regions across the country and is not reachable by the investigator, it is the only option left with the researcher to mail the questionnaires to the respondents.
- It is always less costly than holding an interview.
- Results of mailed questionnaire are less biased than interview. It involves less measurement errors as compared to interview.
- When sample to be covered is highly aware and educated, mailed questionnaire is a good tool of collecting data.

*Disadvantages of mailed questionnaire:*

- Non-response is the major problem here. Survey shows that about 70% of the questionnaires are not returned back to the researcher.

- When complete study of a problem or a thorough understanding of a personality is required , mailed questionnaires will not serve the purpose because complete rapport between a researcher and the respondents is needed in that case.
- When respondents find many questions irrelevant to them, they either do not answer the questionnaire or answer them wrongly.
- In mailed questionnaire, the researcher can not observe the mode of expression of the respondents, their reactions to the typical and embarrassing questions and their general attitude towards the problem.

*Advantages of face to face administered questionnaire:*

- They are less time consuming. A number of respondents can be covered at a time.
- If respondents have any doubt on any question, their doubts can be removed immediately by the researcher.
- Researcher can motivate the respondents when they are working on questionnaires.
- A researcher can know who is actually attempting the questions and who is faking the responses.
- Maximum interaction between the researcher and the respondents are seen here.

*Limitations of Face to Face Administered Questionnaire:*

- Validity of the informations may be adversely affected if respondents are very much afraid and shy of the presence of the researcher.
- If respondents can be grouped into one or two places and personal contacts with these respondents are individually required, this way of collecting data becomes very costly.
- When sample is scattered throughout the country or respondents are not willing to give time, administration of such a questionnaire is not possible.

**Types of Self Report Inventories:**

1. **Social Traits Inventories :** These inventories measure traits like self-confidence, dominance, ego strength, extroversion, sociability etc. Eysenck's personality questionnaire and differential personal scale are examples of such inventories.
2. **Adjustment Inventories :** These inventories measure the adjustment of a person in different situations and environment. Bell adjustment inventory is an example.
3. **Pathological Traits Inventories :** These inventories measure traits like hysteria, hypochondria, depression, schizophrenia etc. Minnesota Multiphasic Personality Inventory is an example.
4. **Group Categorisation inventories :** These inventories divide the persons into two or more groups on the basis of their deviant and normal personality characteristics Cornell index is an example.
5. **Attitude, Interest and Value Inventories :** These inventories measure attitude, values and specific interests of different people. Strong Vocational Interest Blank is an example.

*Some Famous Personality Inventories:*

1. **Woodworth Personal Data Sheet :** It was developed by Woodworth in 1918. It consists of 16 questions relating to neurotic tendencies. The purpose of this inventory was to screen out emotionally disturbed men so that only normal men could be sent to the front.
2. **Minnesota Multiphasic Personality Inventory:** MMPI first appeared in 1940 and its first manual was prepared in 1943. It was developed to measure abnormal psychological traits. It consists of 550 affirmative statements printed on cards and respondents are required to classify them into three piles, true, false and can not say. Although the inventory is meant for those who are 16 years of age or more but it can be applied to those also who are below 16 years.

   After scoring, personality traits are classified into 14 scales of which ten are clinical and four are validity scales.

| S.No. | Clinical | Scales |
|---|---|---|
| 1 | HS | Hypochondriasis |
| 2 | D | Depression |
| 3 | HY | Hysteria |
| 4 | Pd | Psychopathic deviate |
| 5 | MF | Masculinity Femininity |
| 6 | Pa | Paranoia |
| 7 | Pt | Psychasthenia |
| 8 | Sc | Schizophrenia |
| 9 | Ma | Hypomania |
| 10 | Si | Social Introversion |

**Validity Scales**

- Questions scores (?)
- Lie scores (L)
- Validity scores (F)
- Correlation scores (K)

Here the purpose of validity scales is to check misunderstanding, carelessness, defensiveness, test taking attitude and operation of other response sets. An atlas has also been prepared for the interpretation of scores.

3. **Bell's Adjustment Inventory :** In the construction of this inventory 223 items of Thurston Personality schedule were used along with 118 new items. Certain items were finally eliminated to make the total items as 140. It measures four types of adjustments :
   - Home adjustment
   - Health adjustment
   - Social adjustment
   - Emotional adjustment
4. **California Psychological Inventory :** It is partially based on MMPI. It consists of 400 items and is meant for 13 years old adults. Here each item is to be answered in true or false.
   There are 18 scales of the test in all out of which three validity scales have been prepared to measure various kinds of response sets. Other 15 scales measure personality traits like dominance, sociability, responsibility, self-control, self-acceptance, femininity etc.
5. **Bernreuter Personality Inventory :** It consists of 125 items measuring personality in six fields.
   - Neuroticism
   - Self-sufficiency
   - Dominance
   - Introversion-Extroversion
   - Sociability
   - Lack of self-confidence

   This inventory can be applied on children and adults both. It is very useful in identifying persons of extreme traits.
6. **Shipley Personal Inventory :** This inventory was developed to identify those people who were mentally unfit for military service during the World War II. In this inventory, items are given to the respondents in pairs and he has to check which one of the two is more true to him than the other.
7. **Minnesota Counselling Inventory :** It was developed by Berlie and Layton in 1957. The purpose of this inventory is to measure adjustment towards the family, emotional stability etc. There are 413 items and 7 scales in this inventory. Most of these items have been taken from MMPI but in an adapted manner.
8. **Singh Adjustment Inventory :** It was developed in India in 1967 to measure adjustment problems of college students. There are 102 items in Yes/No form in this inventory. Internal consistency reliability and validity of this inventory is 0.94 and 0.62 respectively.
9. **Prasad Adjustment Inventory :** It was developed in 1974 to be used on teenagers to measure several adjustments like parental, family home, social, emotional etc. There are 279 items in the inventory and norms for different sections of the population are also given.
10. **Differential personality Scale :** It was developed by Sinha and Singh in 1979 to measure nine personality traits namely decisiveness, responsibility, emotional stability, masculinity, friendliness hetero-sexuality, ego strength, curiosity and dominance. There are 165 items in this scale and it is meant for college students. The test retest reliability of the inventory is very high about 0.9.

Apart from these, a number of foreign inventories have also been adapted and rewritten in the context of Indian situation, such as

I. Mohsin and Husain (1981) adapted Bell Adjustment Inventory in Hindi. It had 134 items originally but its modified form of 1987 has only 124 items.

II. Singh V Jamuar (1971) adapted Maslow's Security Insecurity Inventory in Hindi.

**Evaluation of Personality Inventories:**

These personality inventories are not free from defects. Some of these defects are given below :

(*i*) Reliability coefficients of these inventories are very high but it is not the case of validity.

*(ii)* Many items are ambiguous in these inventories and subjects interpret them differently.

*(iii)* Respondents can not answer some of these questions due to forgetting. i.e., Did you ever have gastric trouble. The answer of this type of questions is required good retention power.

*(iv)* Subjects sometimes do not have correct understanding about his own psychological make up. In such a case he would not be able to answer a question correctly.

*(v)* No norm for ideal adjustment or behaviour is available so far. Personality is still interpreted by the researcher in his own way. Thus, informations provided by these inventories are not as reliable as it is considered.

*(vi)* When an individual works on a personality inventory he comes across certain such problems which are required to be dealt with in a socially approved direction. So instead of revealing his true behaviour or feeling, he answers the items wrongly.
For example, items pertaining to personal, social family, or sexual problems are generally hidden.

*(vii)* Personality inventories have very poor diagnostic value. These traits are most of the time hypothetical not real.

## (B) Observational Methods for Measuring Personality

**Meaning of Observation :** Observation means looking outside one self. Here the researcher observes the overt behaviour of the individual from outside. As far as observation of overt behaviour is concerned it is the manifestation of covert condition by different activities within the organism. The study of these behaviours gives the clue about the mental condition of the organism. For example, if a person is kicking household articles without caring damage of the article, it means that he is in the state of anger.

**Tools & Techniques of Observation:** Important techniques of observation are given below:

1. **Interview :** Interview is a face to face situation between the interviewer and the respondent which is intended to derive certain informations from the later and to orally read his behaviour directly. Thus, interview is a social process in which at least two persons are involved. The success of an interview lies in the interaction between the two parties. If the interviewer is able to develop maximum rapport with the respondent, he can obtain much more information about him. The next question of an interviewer very much depends on the answer given by the respondent. Similarly, the respondents also weigh his counterpart and if he thinks that he can befool the interviewer, he does so.

**Conditions required for the success of interview:**

*(i)* Maximum rapport between the interviewer and the interviewee.

*(ii)* Free from bias balanced outlook of the interviewer.

*(iii)* Sequential questioning sampled from all areas required.

*(iv)* Clear and practical language of questions

*(v)* Moderate rate of questioning.

*(vi)* Useful comments if necessary and proper feedback to the respondents.

*(vii)* Cooperative approach and congenial atmosphere.

*(viii)* Trained interviewer

*(ix)* Proper interview setting

*(x)* Fixed timing depending on the nature and propose of the interview.

**Types of interview:**

**(a) Formal interview :** Formal interview is one in which preplanned questions are asked by the interviewer and answers are recorded either by audio recorder or by a short hand master. Due to this reason they are also called structured interview. Sequence of questions and scoring methods are also predetermined.

**Merits** of this type of interview are that :

- Objectivity in scoring can be maintained due to uniformity of questions.
- Such interviews are highly valid. We can restrict ourselves to the content to be covered.
- Even a less trained person can conduct this type of interview.

**Limitations** of the formal interview are that :

- It is very expensive and time consuming.

- Sample of behaviour represented by questions is uniform and do not vary from person to person. Due to this reason exact assessment of varying personalities is not possible.
- Once questions are exposed before an interviewee, they will no longer remain secret for other examinees and thus reliable informations can not be obtained.
- Validity of such tests is lower than the other methods, such as, biodata analysis and other standardized psychological tests.

(b) **Informal Interview :** Informal interview is one in which nothing is predetermined such as

- Number and sequence of questions are not determined.
- Method of scoring is also not fixed
- Everything depends on the interviewer and the situations

**The merits** of informal interview over the formal one are that :

- The interviewer can get deeper understanding about the respondent by moulding the questions.
- It is more flexible than the formal interview and thus interviewer and the respondent get maximum opportunity to interact in a free atmosphere.
- They are very much useful for reading overt behaviour.

**Limitations** of informal interview are that :

- There is greater scope of personal bias on the part of the interviewer in this type of interview. Due to the subjectivity of the interviewer, results obtained are less reliable.
- Greater skills are required to conduct such type of interviews. Questioning with flow is not an easy task.
- Data obtained from this interview can not be quantified and analysed easily.
- Different questions are asked from different respondents and thus, inter examinees comparison is also not possible.

(c) **Fact finding interview :** Interviews to be held for the purpose of selecting persons for a job or course are of this nature. Attitudes and feelings of the respondents can also be discovered by this interview.

**Merits** of this type of interview are that :

- We can eliminate the chance of guessing or cheating by this method.
- Respondent's ability to interpret a topic or concept orally can be judged only by this method. That is why, it is widely used in the selection of school and college teachers.

**Limitations** of this type of interview are that:

- It is very time consuming and highly subjective. Supreme Court has given two ruling in this regard in order to reduce prejudices and corruption.
  *(a)* The number of marks allotted for an interview will not exceed 15% of the total marks.
  *(b)* Minimum 40% marks out of the total of interview marks will be given to all the examinees in an interview.
- In personality testing, the interview can hide individual's trait by giving wrong answers to the questions. Thus, test will become totally unreliable.

(d) **Therapeutic Interviews :** This type of interview is used for the purpose of treating psychological diseases. They are of the following two sub-types

*(a)* Counsellor directed : Here counsellor finds out the causes of the problem, its history and its symptoms etc. by asking questions.

*(b)* Non-directed : Here interviewer and the subject both take the initiative and arrives at a final conclusion.

The main advantage of therapeutic interview is that it is an important clinical method to know about the details of a disease. That is why doctors, psychologists, psychiatrists etc. use this technique.

**Factors affecting interviews**

(a) **Characteristics of interviewers** :

*(i)* If interviewer is objective in his behaviour, results will be more accurate.

*(ii)* If interviewer is subjective in nature, i.e., he has his own particular view regarding a particular problem, only that interviewee will get more marks whose views coincide with those of the interviewer.

(*iii*) If interviewer has full skill in questioning, he can readily sharpen the question, redirect and mould the questions and motivate the respondent to speak more.

(*iv*) If interviewer is able to pool together the scattered pieces of information into a uniform and integrated one, only then he can draw right conclusion.

**(b) Characteristics of the interviewee :**

(*i*) If the respondent is able to verbalize his knowledge, information and mental power, only then he can provide required information. Communication skills of young children, mentally retarded and dumbs are very very poor and therefore this technique cannot be used for them.

(*ii*) If the respondent is willing to verbalize his responses regarding the research problem, only then this technique will be successful.

(*iii*) If the respondent is in the state of frustration or depression, he will not be able to verbalize his responses. He must feel normal psychologically in order to give correct response.

**(c) Nature of the problem under study :**

(*i*) If questions are such which hurt the sentiment of the respondent they will not be responded properly.

(*ii*) If private affairs of the examinees are touched by the interviewer, it will not be correctly replied by the respondent.

(*iii*) If questions above the ability level of respondents are asked, he will again see a problem of non-response.

(*iv*) If the problem under study has not been sampled properly by the questions, incomplete information will provide misleading results.

**Errors involved in interviews:**

Though interview does not give accurate results, yet it is most commonly used method of data collection. Some important sources of errors are given below :

1. **Subjectivity of the Interviewer :** Subjectivity of the interviewer in scoring and interpreting the results is the biggest source of error. His own attitude toward a problem causes great variance in the scores.
2. **Incomprehensibility of questions :** Questions may become incomprehensible for the respondent due to a variety of reasons such as, ambiguous language, voice tone of the interviewer, high academic level of questions, speed of questioning etc. They all lead to incorrect responses on the part of the respondent.
3. **Cold interview climate :** Interview held in an atmosphere when interviewer and the respondent do not feel close to each other gives misleading results. It makes the data invalid and undependable.
4. **Problem of quantification of responses :** Some respondents answer more accurately and in an elaborated fashion of a question than the others and it becomes very difficult to differentiate the two while assigning them marks. Moreover, same questions can not be asked from different respondents and if questions differ, difficulty values of questions may also differ causing variation in scores.
5. **Long duration of the interview :** If an interview is held for a longer period of time, the respondents may become nervous and exhausted. As a result, they may score less. Moreover, if time is equally available for all the respondents, they may again score differently because some of them require less time to answer a question and some take more time.

**Advantages of interview: (see advantages of four types of interviews also)**

(*i*) It allows greater flexibility of interaction between the interviewer and the respondent. Both of them can change their behaviour any time during the process of questioning which is not possible in a written test. Questions can not be changed in a written test.

(*ii*) Any desired information can be obtained readily and without difficulty in this technique. We can cover all the aspects of personality here.

(*iii*) We can maintain a desired level of control here.

(*iv*) Validity of the verbal informations supplied by the interviewee can be checked by cross questioning and by studying his attitude towards the problem.

**Disadvantages of interview:** See the following sub-heading here :

I. Disadvantages of four types of interview
II. Factors affecting interview
III. Errors involved in interview.

**2. Rating scale :** This is the second observational technique to study behaviour. Rating scale is a tool of assessing actual behaviour ( behaviour manifested and recorded immediately) and remembered behaviour both. Rating scale is actually a technique through which the observer (rater) categorises objects, events or persons on a continuous numerals. The various points on the continuum show the level of impressions that objects, events or persons have left on the rater.

A rating scale may have five to eleven points (categories) showing different levels of traits being observed. There are two components in a rating scale:

- Stimulus variable : It consists of trait names or qualities to be rated. A number of statements (questions) representing various traits or sub-traits are given here.
- Response option : It consists of numerical or descriptive categories given on a continuum. The observer rates the objects, events or persons on the continuum scale according to his own impression and therefore provides a quantitative base of his observation.

**Example :**

| Stimulus Variable | Response option | | | | |
|---|---|---|---|---|---|
| He is allergic to girls | SA | A | U | SD | D |
| In the class | 5 | 4 | 3 | 2 | 1 |

It is an example of five points scale. Here,

SA = Strongly agree
A = Agree
U = Undecided
D = Disagree
SD = Strongly Disagree

**Nature of Rating :** Rating may be retrospective or concurrent. Retrospective rating tends to summarize all the impressions left on the rater regarding the ratee over a particular period of time. Concurrent rating tends to summarize only the immediate impressions left on the rater about the ratee.

**Advantages of rating scales :**

1. They are very easy to construct and use. A number of statements representing the traits can be framed very easily.
2. Quantification of traits is also easy and thus all statistical operations are possible.

**Disadvantages of rating scales :**

I. Traits to be measured are not distinctively defined and thus different raters derive different meaning from the statement.
To solve this problem three precautions should be taken while constructing a rating scale.
*(a)* Trait to be rated should be clearly defined and explained with suitable examples.
*(b)* Various intervals or points on the response option should also be clearly defined.
**Example :**
He is very social 1 2 3 4 5
Here I may be taken as 20% agree, 2= 40% agree, 3= 60% agree and so on.
*(c)* Overt traits like cooperation, sympathy, honesty etc. can be easily observed than covert traits like ego strength, emotional stability etc. So, rating scales should be used to study overt behaviour to the maximum level possible.

II. Mental set of the rater plays an important role here. If he is prejudiced against the ratee in any way, his rating can not be relied upon.

**To remove this problem two steps may be taken :**

I. The ratee may be rated by more than one person and then their rating may be averaged.
II. A person should be rated by the rater on different occasions and then conclusion should be drawn.

**Types of rating scales:**

1. **Numerical rating scales:** Here the rater is supplied with a sequence of numbers on the response set which is well-defined and he rates the objects, events or persons on the given sequence of numbers on the basis of his impression.

**Example :**

A sympathetic teacher can control the class very easily.

Strongly agree → 5
Agree → 4
Indifferent → 3
Disagree → 2
Strongly Disagree → 1

Generally, the numerical anchors along with their meaning are printed on the first page and a number of statements revealing various phenomenon about the objects or events are given on the subsequent pages.

**2. Graphic rating scale :** It is an improvement over numerical rating scale in the sense that it fills the gap between any two points on the scale. Here scale is presented graphically. Here statements have no blank box and rater only puts a tick mark on any of the descriptive cues to indicate his opinion.

**Example :**

Mr. Gupta delivers lectures in the class

| At a very fast speed | At fast speed | At moderate speed | At a slow speed | At a very slow speed |
|---|---|---|---|---|

Above example shows that there is no gap from one description to other on the continuum and scale is fully smooth. The only limitation of this scale is that it is very difficult to score such scales.

**3. Percentage rating scale :** This type of rating is used when many raters are to arrive at a consensus about the traits of the ratee. Here the retees are placed into different percentile groups as shown below.

- Highest = 5 %
- Second highest = 5 %
- Third highest = 10 %
- Average = 40 %
- Third lowest = 10 %
- Second lowest = 5 %
- Lowest = 5 %

This type of rating is used by class teachers in order to classify their students into different categories.

**4. Standard rating :** This type of rating is not very popular for psychological measurements. Here rater is given some standard with pre-specified scales. Rating is done on the basis of that given standard. Man to man scale is an example of this rating. This scale was developed during World War I. Here the rater was asked to give the name of a person who knows well and who is very high on the trait being rated. That person's name is noted down to define the very high point on the scale. After that rater was asked to give the names of four other persons who are high, average, low and very low on the trait being measured. In this way, a five point standard scale was prepared. Lastly, the rater would rate the other persons by comparing them with this scale. The resemblance of the person with the person referred in the standard determines his point on the scale. For example, if Mr. Gupta is very high according to the knowledge of the rater in decision making power, the person who resembles Mr. Gupta will be rated as very high in this trait.

Merits of this scale are given below :

*(i)* It eliminates the confusion arising out of abstract numerical anchors assigned to the traits being rated.

*(ii)* If different raters use the same key men in their rating, their rating is most likely to be comparable.

*(iii)* Since the scale values of all the key men are pre-established and fixed, raters can not give different rating in different times.

**5. Checklist :** When we want to assess whether some traits are present in the behaviour of an individual or not, we use this technique. Here a number of statements representing various traits of the personality are taken by the rater. He rates any person on the basis of these statements. If the trait is present in the ratee, the rater puts a tick mark and finally all these traits are quantified to know over all personality traits.

**6. Forced choice scale :** In this scale rater is given a set of verbal statements representing different attributes of a trait and then the rater decides which statement or statements is/are best suited to the individual being rated. Thus, a single trait or sub-trait may be defined by more than 5 or 6 statements. Two alternative form of items are commonly used. Here one statement of the item is favourable and other statement is unfavourable. An example of four alternative forced choice rating scale is given below Mr. Asim.

- develops full rapport in the class.
- keeps the students interested and motivated.

- takes much care of slow learners.
- accepts suggestions of his students to improve his teaching.

In the above item, the most discriminating statement is ( c) and least discriminatory statement is (a) Statement (c) may be assigned a score of 3 and statement (a) may be assigned a score of zero. A rater's total score would be the sum of all the scores on discriminating statements in each set.

The main advantages of this technique are given below :

I. This scale minimizes generosity error. Here rater is not given any chance to choose an item according to his absolute will. He will have to choose one item out of many given in the set.

II. Here the rater is generally unable to identify favourable or unfavourable choice because the items appear to be equally favourable and unfavourable. Thus, personal bias of the rater will not work.

**7. Q Sorting technique :** It was originally developed by William Stephenson in 1953 for the study of verbalized attitudes and preferences. It is actually a comparative rating method where various traits of a person are relatively studied. Here some verbal statements, pictures, words or phrases are given to an individual to sort them out into nine or eleven piles according to a fixed criteria. Types of items put in a particular pile show the preference of the person being rated. Thus, Q sorting works as a self-rating. These statements or pictures are printed on cards. The number of such cards should not be less than 60 or more than 140. The person being rated sorts a fixed number of cards into each pile so that the resulting distribution may approach to normal.

An example of 11 piles Q sorting is given below:

**Q sort distribution of 100 items**

| Piles | 10 most preferred | 9 | 8 | 7 | 6 | 5 | 4 | 3 | 2 | 1 | 0 Least preferred |
|---|---|---|---|---|---|---|---|---|---|---|---|
| No.of Cards | 2 | 4 | 8 | 12 | 14 | 20 | 14 | 12 | 8 | 4 | 2 |

In the above table pile no. 10 indicates the most preferred items which are only 2 in numbers. Next pile has four items which are next preferred items. Similarly, last pile has 2 least preferred items and undecided items are put in pile number 5.

When sorting is complete, statistical analysis is done.

**Advantages** of Q sort technique are given below:

I. It permits the subjects to make comparative responses towards a large number of stimuli. Test retest reliability of this technique is very high.

II. It is very much helpful in formulating or testing a theory because it allows the manipulation of variables in a logical and empirical manner.

III. More statistical computations like coefficient of correlation as well as analysis of variance is possible here.

**8. Behaviourally anchored rating scale :** This scale is used for measuring the performance of a person in a job. This scale is developed in three stages.

In the first stage, a group of experts decide upon the possible dimensions which can be used as the aspect of performance being evaluated. Suppose, we want to evaluate the academic performance of a college, the experts can decide upon the following dimensions:

- Sincerity of students
- Leadership ability of teachers
- Organizational ability of teachers
- Pragmatic curriculum and so on.

In the second stage, several statements regarding each dimension are prepared. These statements represent the superior, average or inferior performance of these dimensions.

Third stage consists of calculating scale value and consistency of each critical incident (statement). For this purpose statements are given to a group of experts who rate all these statements on a scale of excellence. Median value of rating of each statement is calculated. This median value is the scale value of each statement. Here only those statements are retained that show higher agreement among judges. Thus, the scale is now ready to be used.

**Errors in Rating (Validity of Rating Scales) :** Following types of errors are generally noticed in rating scales :

1. **Halo Effect :** Halo effect refers to a tendency on the part of the rater to be unduly influenced by a single favourable or unfavourable trait which colours their judgement of the individual's other traits. For example, if a teacher is very much impressed by the outstanding performance of a student in a game, he may rate him higher on academic performance also.
   This halo effect maybe in positive and negative directions both. If a teacher does not like the behaviour of a student in the class, he may underrate him while evaluating his class work. This is the negative halo effect.
   We can reduce the possibility of halo effect to some extent by defining the traits being measured in behavioural terms. The other way of reducing this effect is that a rater should first rate all the ratees on one particular trait, then he should come to the next trait. Thus, rater will pay attention to each trait separately.
2. **Error of Severity :** It refers to a constant tendency to rate the ratee too low. Those raters who are in search of perfection are usually reluctant to rate any person or object very high. This type of error can be reduced by using forced choice rating scale.
3. **Error of Leniency :** This is the opposite of error of severity. Here the rater rates objects or persons too high. Liberal nature raters have this tendency.
4. **Error of central tendency :** In this type of error the rater keeps the ratees on the middle and avoides extreme ratings. This tendency makes the rating futile. It generally happens when raters do not know the ratees well and hesitate to rate them on the extremes.
5. **Contrast error :** It was first pointed out by Murray (1938). It refers to a tendency on the part of the rater to rate the retees in a direction which is in contrast to the trait he himself possesses. For example, if a person is highly dedicated to his job, he will rate the others to be less dedicated by comparing himself with the ratees.
6. **Proximity error :** This error was first pointed out by Stock Ford Bissell in 1943. This error is seen when two close types of traits are rated simultaneously. For example, cooperation has proximity to friendliness. If rater rates a person on friendliness trait very high, he may rate him high on the trait of cooperation too.
7. **Logical error :** It was pointed out by Newcomb in 1931. Here rater gives more or less similar rating to traits which appear to him somehow related to each other. This similarity is created in the mind of the rater and error is introduced. For example, if a person is not honest in individual situation, a rater may think that he will not be honest in social situations too.

Due to these errors mentioned above the validity of rating scales is generally very low.

**Reliability of rating scales :** Reliability of rating scale is also very low (from 0.45 to 0.66) Reliability of ratings depends upon a number of factors such as nature of traits, number of traits, acquaintance of the rater with the ratees etc. Some of the important factors affecting the reliability of rating are given below :

1. **Difference in the raters ability to rate :** Some raters are more capable of rating than others. Rating capacity depends on intelligence decision making power, knowledge and consistency of the rater. So if the same person is rated by the same rater again, the result may differ.
2. **Ignorance about the ratee :** Some traits are not properly displayed sometime. So, if the rater does not know the ratee properly, he will rate him wrongly.
3. **Overlapping of traits :** It is very easy to rate general traits as compared to specific traits which may overlap with each other. Thus, we will get wrong results.
4. **Subjectivity in the traits being used :** Some personality traits are not directly revealed and their absence or presence are inferred from a number of behaviours of the ratee which is done by the investigator himself. Thus, higher level of subjectivity is involved due to a number of factors, such as, inability of the rater, lack of proper sampling of behaviour etc. All these things make the reliability of the ratings low.

**5. Lack of uniformity in the response set :** In a seven point rating scale if from superior to very poor different points are given, different raters may have different criteria for superior, excellent, good etc. It is very difficult to classify the ratees on the continuum due to lack of uniformity of standard. For example, in a group a person scoring 95% and above maybe termed as superior and in another group which is poor, a person scoring 85% and above may be termed as superior. Similarly, different raters may have different definitions of satisfactory, good, average, poor or very poor. As a result reliability of the test will be low.

**Methods of improving effectiveness of rating scales:**

**1. Refinement of stimulus variables :** Stimulus variables means the traits, dimensions or qualities being rated. Objective traits can be measured with greater accuracy and consistency than subjective traits. Following steps may be taken to improve the quality of stimulus variables :

*(i)* Each trait should refer to only one type of activity. For this purpose each trait may be divided into sub traits after careful analysis of the trait.

*(ii)* Efforts should be done to make the traits objective to the maximum level possible. For this purpose all traits should be clearly defined in behavioural terms.

*(iii)* Language of the stimulus variable should also be clear and free from ambiguity.

*(iv)* Traits should be judged on the basis of past and present accomplishment rather than on future.

*(v)* Other precautions of framing a questionnaire should also be taken into account.

**2. Refinement of response options :** High degree of subjectivity is involved here too. One rater's superior is another rater's average. For achieving objectivity in response options, various points on the continuum should be clearly defined and a clear-cut criterion must be given for each level of categories.

**3. Improvement of rating procedure :** Following steps may be taken for this purpose :

*(i)* Trained raters must be selected for the purpose of rating.

*(ii)* Rater must have close contact with the ratees and perfect rapport should be there between the two.

*(iii)* Raters should be given sufficient time to rate objects, events or persons.

*(iv)* There must be similarity between the background of the raters and the ratees.

*(v)* In order to increase the reliability of rating, ratings done by independent raters should be pooled together. It will work in the same way as we see by increasing the number of items in a test. When number of items in a test is increased reliability is increased.

## (C ) Situational Test

Situational test is a compromise between a standardized test and observational methods of assessing personality. It is a rating of what a person thinks and does in a given situations. The person being rated has usually no idea that he is being studied by some one. Here the behaviour of an individual is studied while he is in action. Following techniques are used in situational test:

**1. Sociometric Method :** This method of assessing personality was developed by J.L.Moreno in 1946. It is actually the measurement of the frequency of acceptance-rejection in a group of individuals. This method illustrates the position of a particular person in his group with respect to certain traits of personality. The following questions may be asked to assess the structure of a group :

I. With whom would you like to sit in the class.

II. Name the two students with whom you would like to go on picnic.

If question first is asked by a group of 40 individuals, each one of them will choose his mate. Some individuals may be chosen by many persons and some may be chosen by one or two. In this way, the group will be classified in the following manner :

**(a) Stars :** Stars are those who are selected by a large nuber of persons and super star will be one who is chosen by maximum number of individuals.

(b) **Isolates :** Isolates are those who are not chosen by anybody in the group. They are also called the rejected individuals of the group.

(c) **Mutual pairs :** They are chosen by each other and pairs are formed.

(d) **Chains :** The mutual pairs may be liked by third or fourth persons in the group and third and fourth persons have their liking with fifth or sixth persons and a chain is formed.

A teacher must understand the structure of his class by using this technique. It will help him plan his interactive phase of teaching. For example, he may give more attention to the isolates and try to know the causes of their isolation. Similarly, if a super star is a girl, then a teacher can find out why the girl is so much liked by her classmates. He can also take the help of mutual pairs in his teaching by motivating either of them to attend the class.

**2. Psychodrama :** Here the individual is asked to play a role spontaneously in a specified situation and then his behaviour is observed by trained persons. This method is based on the assumption that individuals project their inner feeling and conflicts in the role they are going to play. This technique is used for the following purposes :

I. To assess the personality of maladjusted persons.

II. To release the emotional conflicts and pent up feelings from the individuals.

III. To detect the criminals from the suspected people

**3. Situational tests in military :** Situational tests are used to assess the potential personality characteristics of officers suitable for military services. Here various types of tasks are given to a small group of candidates and then their activities are observed by experts.

## (D) Projective Techniques

**Meaning of projective techniques :** It is an indirect method of measuring personality which basically originated in a clinical setting. In these techniques an individual is given an unstructured situation to which he responds.

Unstructured situation means a situation whose meaning and interpretation vary from person to person. While responding to such a situation an individual projects his own feelings, needs and motives without knowing that he is doing so. Thus, he is totally unable to adopt any defense mechanism and can reveal his actual traits.

This technique differs from self-report inventories in the sense that SRI provides a direct and structured situations for assessing the traits while projective tests provide an indirect and unstructured situation for assessing these traits. Second difference is that SRI measures some aspects of personality traits while projective technique focuses attention on the measurement of personality as a whole. Third difference is that in self-rapport inventories only desirable traits are revealed but in PT person being tested does not know which type of traits he is revealing. It is the investigator who interprets the different aspects of personality of the person being tested on the basis of some rules.

**Types of projective Techniques:** (a) Frank's Classification of Projective Techniques: Frank (1939) classified projective techniques into five categories :

1. **Constitutive :** In these tests the examinees constitute or frame structures upon materials which are yet unstructured. Drawing completion is an example of this type of test. Rorschach inkblots another example where the examinee imposes his own structure (personality) upon the unstructured inkblot situation.
2. **Constructive :** Here the examinee is required to construct a specified task and he imposes his own structure upon the situation in the direction set by the examiner. For example, he may be asked to draw the picture of a male or female with certain specified characteristics.
3. **Interpretative :** Here the examinee is required to add a comprehensive meaning to the situation according to his own way of thinking and feeling. Thematic Apperception Test (TAT) and Word Association Test are two examples.
4. **Refractive :** Here the examinee is required to express his personality in the form of painting, drawing, handwriting etc. Graphology is the best example of this type of tests.
5. **Cathartic :** Here the examinee is given opportunity to manipulate a task in his own way

and thus he releases his internal conflicts. Play techniques come under this category.

The limitation of Frank's classification is that much overlapping is seen in different types of tests. For example, drawing completion test may be included in constitutive and constructive category both.

**Best's (1978) Classification of Projective Techniques:**

1. **Association Type :** In this type of test examinee is given some stimulus material, such as, pictures, inkblots, words etc. and he is asked to tell what he sees, thinks and feels. Then the structure of the examinee is interpreted. Rorschach inkblot test and word association test are some examples.
2. **Completion type :** Here some incomplete sentences are given to the examinee and he is asked to complete them in the manner he likes. These tests are very much useful for assessing traits like anxiety, guilty feeling, aggression, sexual temperament etc. An example is given here.

   I worry about.................

   This sentence can be completed by different persons in different ways depending upon the composition of personality structure of the examinees, e.g.,

   - I worry about my health :

     If this statement is given by a healthy person, it shows that the person is mesomorphic.
   - I worry about my sexual problem.
   - I worry about my examination and so on.
3. **Role Playing Type :** Here the examinee is asked to play a specific role in a group for a certain period of time. His role reveals his unique wishes, conflicts and feelings.
4. **Creative or constructive :** Here the examinee is asked to do some tasks like playing with toys, drawing a picture, writing an essay or story etc. Personality of the examinee is assessed on the basis of choice of words, colours, order of sentences. TAT also falls under this category.

Broadly speaking, projective tests are of three types. Pictorial , Verbal and Expressive. We will discuss here two tests of each type one by one in detail:

### 1. Rorschach Inkblot Test:

It was developed by Herman Rorschach in 1921 in Switzerland to study the personality of a person as a whole. It measures intellectual as well as non-intellectual traits of personality. This test consists of 10 cards each containing a bilaterally symmetrical printed inkblots. Five cards (I, IV, V, VI and VII) have black and gray shades, two cards (II and III) contain bright patches of red colour in addition to black and gray and the remaining three cards contain shades of pastel colours.

**(A) Administration of the test :** Administration of the test is comprised of three stages

- First stage- Performance proper
- Second stage-Inquiry
- Third stage- Testing of the limits

**First stage**, Rapport between the examiner and the examinee is developed first. Then first card of the test is given to the examinee and he is asked. "People see all sorts of things in these inkblots, tell me what you see and what it makes you think of "

After that examiner notes down the following events while the examinee is in action :

I. Reaction time : Time which is taken from presentation of the card to the examinee's first score :

II. Examiner notes down the position of the card when the response is given by the examinee, Symbols used here are :

-U = Card is kept upright
-U = Top is turned downward.
-< = top is kept at the left side.
-> = top is kept at the right side
-(0) = Constant rotation of the card

III. Responses are recorded verbatim. This verbal and detailed recording can help others to understand the responses.

IV. The examiner records the total time taken for each card. It is symbolized by T.

When the examinee returns the first card, he is given the second one and this process goes on till the last card. One thing should be kept in mind by the examiner at every step. If examinee is having any difficulty in answering any card, he should be motivated by the examiner to the maximum level possible.

Now the question arises for how long can an examinee keep a card. Experts have suggested that he can keep a card with him for five minutes. Thus, Rorschach test will take 50 minutes in the first stage of administration.

**Second stage :** When examinee gives vague response to any of the cards, it is clarified by the examiner in the second stage. Many experts are of the view that inquiry should be conducted immediately after the return of every card so that examinee may not forget his associations. The main purpose of inquiry is to collect all the necessary informations for scoring responses accurately. This inquiry provides the basis to know what part of the blot is the basis of the responses of the examinee and why is his response like that.

In order to make the inquiry stage a success the examinee should keep the following points in view.

- He should ask questions from the examinee only when something is not clear from the answer of the examinee.
- Questions of inquiry should be framed in a non-direct manner.
- Question asked should be precise and clear.

**Third stage :** This stage is not needed for all the examinees. Testing of the limit stage is needed only when examinee's responses are uncommon and out of Rorschach protocols. For example, an examinee may think that whole responses are better than part responses and he gives whole responses to all the 10 cards and his responses are not to the point. In that case examiner will have to limit the examinee to come to the pint.

**(B) Scoring of rorschach test :** For the purpose of scoring responses are classified into three main categories, Location, Determinant and Content:

*(a)* ***Location :*** Location refers to the part of the blot which produces a particular response. If the whole blot is producing a response, the scoring is direct and simple. If a part of the blot is producing a response scoring will not be so simple. It will depend upon whether the part is commonly used or rarely used.

Whole response is scored as W. It is considered a good response because it indicates an over all view of the entire situation.

W response is also of two types. First is cut off whole symbolized by W and second is confabulatory whole symbolized by DW. W response includes all minor details but then examinee generalizes these details to the entire blot.

As far as part of the blot is concerned D response is used which is actually related to all common or large usual details. A low percentage of D response is usually indicative of maladjustment. This D is again divided to capital D related to large usual area and small d related to small usual area. Besides, that part of the blot which is rarely used by the examinee is scored as Dd. It is called unusual detail.

When the white space area is used as the basis of response it is scored as S. This S response is called site space details. This is actually a variety of unusual detail (Dd.) This s can further be categorised as capital S related to frequently used white space detail and small S related to rarely used white space detail.

Last type of response is DdD. It refers to a response in which the examinee interprets an unusual detail of the blot and then generalizes from that interpretation to a common detail area. Such responses are rarely seen.

Out of these location scores W.D and Dd are the primary ones. The rest three are secondary ones.

## Summary of Location Scores

| Symbol | Description | Criterion |
|---|---|---|
| W | Whole response | When the whole blot is used for giving response. |
| DW | Confabulatory whole response | When primary emphasis is on detail part of the blot but secondary emphasis is given to the whole blot. |
| D | Usual detail response | When response is based on the common area of the blot. |
| Dd | Unusual detail response | When response is based on uncommon area of the blot. |
| S | White space response. | When response is given on the basis of white space area of the blot. |
| DdD | Confabulated detail response. | When secondary emphasis is given upon a usual detail and primary emphasis is given on an unusual detail area. |

***(b) Determinants :*** This scoring system is most complex of all phases. Determinants refer to the features of the blot which have produced the particular response. The success of the response category depends on how properly the inquiry has been done. Only 6 categories of determinants were suggested by Rorschach in the beginning but now psychologist have added three more categories of determinants. His categories are given below:

I. *Form determinant (F) :* F refers to the response which has occurred purely because of the form of the blot. When form is clear and good before the examinee it is scored as f– and when form looks vague before him it is scored as f-. A proper inquiry from the examinee will make this point clear.

II. *Movement determinant (M and FM) :* Movement here is related to human movement according to Rorschach which is denoted by M. This symbol is restricted to only those responses which contain human figure either complete or incomplete. Human movements are of two types active and passive. Running walking, jumping, crying, etc. are active movements which are denoted by Ma and sleeping, talking, smiling and thinking are the passive movements which are scored as Mp. Certain precautions in scoring for M are that F should not be scored when M is scored, as M automatically assumes form or shape. Second precaution is that M should not be scored when response from the examinee is not spontaneous. When M response is obtained after inquiry it will be scored as F. Take the example card VII. If examinee says that it looks like two women then he will be scored as F. But during inquiry when the examiner asks the questions.

"Are they doing something" and the examinee responds that they are talking, this change of response will not change the score from F to M because response is not spontaneous.

Apart from human movements there may be the response of animal movement which is scored as FM.

III. *Colour determinants (C, CF and FC) :* Those responses which are totally based on colour are scored as C. Those responses where colour dominates but form (shape) is also involved are scored as CF and in those responses where form dominates but colour is also involved are scored as FC.

Thus, C is scored for pure colour responses. A few examples of C is blood, ice-cream, paint etc. C is interpreted as indicative of lack of control over emotional responsiveness. In CF scoring, colour is clear but form is vague. Few example of CF are sky, lake, fire, meat, water etc. CF should not be confused with FC. For example, if an examinee emphasises that he perceives meat because it looks like a piece of meat then his response will be scored as FC not CF because shape or form dominates here. Few examples of FC are lungs, heart, red dog, red shirt, brinjal etc. FC indicates control over emotional impulses while CF indicates less control over emotions.

IV. *Shading determinants : (T,TF and FT) :* A shading response is one in which light dark features of the blot are used. Shading responses are divided into three categories. First category includes those determinants in which shading produces the impression of texture (reflection) and is scored as T, TF and FT. Here in TF texture dominates but in FT form dominates.

The second category includes those determinants in which shading creates the impression of depth or distance and they are scored as V, VF and FV. If form dominates FV is scored and if vista (depth) dominates VF is scored.

The third category includes those determinants in which responses are based on shading features (light dark features) and they are scored as Y, YF and FY. Here Y denotes pure shade. FY is dominance of form over shade and YF is the opposite of it.

V. *Form dimensional response (FD) :* In FD responses the basis of dimensionality is the form interpreted by the size of the blot area. FD is a new scoring category introduced by **Exner** in 1974. According to him FD scores are given for those responses which include dimension of the blot area and form both. Responses like "a bird on the top of a tree," a statue on the top of a hill etc. are scored as FD.

*VI. Reflection response (r Fand Fr) and Pair response (2) :* Reflection response is based on the symmetry of the blot. Reflection response is classified into two categories. First is reflection form response which is scored as rF. rF response is one in which symmetry features of the blot are primary to the formation of the responses and form is used secondarily. Usually form or shape is vague and symmetry is clear. Fr response is the opposite of it.

Pair responses are also based on the symmetry of the blot and are scored as parenthesize (2). These responses do not have form quality at all. Thus, when the symmetry of the blot evokes the perception of the pair, responses are scored as (2) Some examples of (2) responses are a pair of shoes , a pair of flags, a pair of girls etc.

***(c) Content :*** This is the third aspect of scoring. As far as content is concerned there are two types of responses-popular responses (P) and original responses (O). P response is one which occurs most frequently in the protocols and an O response is one which occurs very rarely.

Rorschach in 1921 used only six symbols for the scoring of the content. They are human (H) human detail (Hd) animal (A) animal detail (Ad). Landscape (Is) and objects (Ob). These scores were found inadequate by the later psychologists. Exner (1974) gave a list of 26 content categories out of which 22 are basic and rests are parenthesized supplementary content categories. The most common and important content categories are given below :

**I. Human response (H and Hd) :** H is used for whole human figures, Hd score is used for parts of the human body or the incomplete human form, such as, limbs, hands, feet, head etc. Similarly, H is used for fictional figures like ghosts and Hd score is used for parts of body of fictional figures.

**II. Animal responses (A and Ad) :** 'A' score is used for whole animal figures and Ad is used for parts of real animals. Similarly, A is used for fictional animals like flying horses or flying fish and Ad is used for parts of fictional animals.

**III. Anatomy (An) :** An is used for anatomy (internal organs) of humans or animals. Lungs, heart, kidney, etc. are some examples.

**IV. Nature (Na) :** Natural objects or things are scored as Na. Waterfall, storm, flood, etc. are some examples. But cloud is excluded from Na and a separate symbol CI is used for it.

**V. Botany (Bt) :** Botanical objects like plants, trees, flowers, fruits etc. are scored as Bt.

**VI. Blood (BI) :** Human or animal blood is scored as BI.

**VII. Art (Ar) :** Paintings, crest, family, seal of the authority etc. are scores as Art.

**VIII. Clothing (Cg) :** All clothing materials of human being are scored as Cg.

**IX. Food (Fd) :** All edible objects and food materials are scored as Fd.

**X. Fire (Fi) :** Electric bulb, burning candle, actual fire etc. are scored as Fi. Here responses like atomic explosion or blast etc. is given the symbol Ex while scoring the content.

**XI. Households. (Hh) :** Interior household items, such as table, chair. cot, pan etc. are scored as Hh.

**XII. Landscape. (Ls) :** It is scored as Ls. Examples of Ls are beautiful gardens, aerial view of the city etc.

**XIII. Sex (Sx) :** Responses highlighting sex organs or sexual functions are scored as Sx.

**(C) Interpretation of the Rorschach test :** There is no complete consensus among the psychologists regarding the interpretation of the data obtained. However, some attempts have been made to interpret the data in the simplest possible form.

In any Rorschach test the total number of responses ® varies from 15 to 30 (Rorschach) or from 20-45 (Klopfer). So if number of R is below 10, it indicates rejection of the test by the examinees. It otherwise indicates defensiveness, intellectual limitations or depression of the examinee. Similarly, a very high total R such as 90 or more indicates Schizophrenic tendencies.

We will discuss the normal score interpretation regarding location determinants and contents below :

***(a) Location scores :*** These scores indicates only the manner how the examinee approaches the ambiguities of the world without telling why he prefers this manner or that manner. Location scores are interpreted in the following ways:

I. W Score : It has a direct relationship with intellectual ability and capacity to organise things or objects in a meaningful manner. W is also interpreted with reference to M scores. The ratio of W : M should not be less than 2 : 1 or more than 3 : 1. If W : M is greater than 3 : 1 it means that his aspiration level is higher than ability and if W : M is less than 2 : 1 it means that his aspiration level is below the level of his ability :

II. D Scores : It indicates the ability to perceive and react to the distinct characterisıics of the world. If the number of D responses are low in a test, it indicates the stress and anxiety of the examinee along with maladjustment.

III. Dd scores : A normal adult has low Dd scores as compared to W or D. This response should not be more than 5% of the other scores. If Dd scores are more than 30% it means the examinee is either Schizophrenic or neurotic or a case of simple mental disturbance. Dd score means positive correlation with internal adjustment and negative correlation with external adjustment.

IV. S score : It indicates negativism in the examinee.

***(b) Determinant scores :*** These scores indicate psychological actions. They are interpreted in the following ways :

I. F scores : They are related to examinee's thinking and reasoning and indicate his attention and concentration. They also show the ability to discriminate judgement. When the number of F responses is very low, it indicates effective instability of the examinee and this generally occurs when the examinees are instructed to respond very quickly.

II. M scores : M indicates the phenomenon of internalization i.e., the ability of the examinee to handle the more deliberate inner experience in a way that can be controlled emotionally. It also indicates a functional relationship between inner and outer (real) world. Studies have also confirmed that there is a positive correlation between M scores and intelligence.

III. FM scores : The person scoring FM is guided by the need of immediate gain more than that of long term gains, i.e., the trait of impulsiveness. This trait is more common among children and older people than in adults. Studies have also confirmed that FM is positively correlated with aggressiveness.

IV. C , CF, FC and Cn scores : These scores indicate effectivity which has no capability for adaptiveness. Proper ratio between these scores are calculated for interpretation. (see the manual of Rorschach Inkblot test).

V. V, VF and FV scores : These vista responses are shading responses based upon dimensionality. Such responses are very rare and it is a healthy sign from the point of personality of the examinee. They indicate a painful feeling tone in which depression and inferiority complex are also involved.

VI. Y, YF and FY scores : These diffused shading responses are more common responses than texture ( C ) or vista (V). They indicate anxiety or withdrawal from the real situation and environment. Among these three Y and YF show more extreme form of withdrawal than FY and FY is a mild form of withdrawal from the environment.

VII. FD scores : They indicate internalization involving self-inspection or self-awareness. Examinees giving this response are sensitive and self-critical.

VIII. Fr, rF, and (2) scores : They indicate egocentricity of a person.

***(c) Content scores :*** These scores are interpreted in the following manner :

I. A and Ad scores : Children score A and Ad more than adults. Excess of these scores indicate intellectual constriction or emotional disturbances. A low 4% A and Ad scores indicate ideographic character of the person.

II. H and Hd scores : These responses are scored less by children than adults. High frequency of

H scores indicate better cognitive development and examinee's potential for good relations. Low frequency of H scores is associated with delinquency. High frequency of Hd responses indicates that the person is poor in inter-personal relationship due to his pre-occupation. The ratio between H and Hd should lie between 2 : 1 and 3:1 in a normal adult. Hd > H indicates anxiety, depression, constructive defensiveness and intellectual limitations.

III. An scores : These responses are also common in the test. They indicate excess pre-occupation with bodily concerns without any physiological problem. Psychosomatics usually score more An responses than neurotics.

IV. Bl and Sx scores : They indicate sexual or aggressive acts.

V. Na and Bt scores : They indicate emotional deprivation and so on.

**Note :** All the interpretations given above are only a guideline for the general students. If anybody wants to administer this personality test on someone, he must go through the manual of the test also.

***Criticism :*** Rorschach personality test of assessing personality can be criticized on the following ground:

- It talks much but gives only a little.
- All the interpretations given in the test are purely subjective which are most likely to vary from climate to climate, from country to country and from culture to culture.
- The success of this technique mostly lies in proper inquiry and interview which is really a challenging task for a researcher.
- Scoring of this test is also very difficult. Even an experienced person can commit mistakes and can give very different personality descriptions.
- Reliability and validity of the test is very poor. If the same scorer rescores the protocols, his second scoring will be much different from the first.

## 2. Thematic Apperception Test (TAT) :

This test was first devised by **Morgan and Murray** in 1935 in the course of research programme at the Harward Psychological Clinic. It may be considered as an improvement over the Rorschach test. However, a combination of RT and TAT has been found very effective in assessing personality. Thus, both of them may be considered as complementary to each other especially for the study of psychosomatic diseases. The main use of TAT is to expose the underlying inhibited tendencies which a patient cannot admit in normal situations due to his unconsciousness of them or unwillingness to admit.

The term thematic has been derived from the word **Thema**' meaning a topic on which a person think, speaks or writes. Thema according to Murray is an interaction of the need and press variables. Need, according to him, is a hypothetical process within the organism which stimulates him into covert or overt action. Press, according to him, is a force in the environment which may facilitate or interfere in the satisfaction of the need.

Apperception refers to a clear perception involving definite recognition or identification. It can never be vague. Thus, in TAT examinee not only perceives but also recognises the implication of the stimulus situation of the card. This special feature of recognition of the stimuli differentiates it from the Rorschach test.

**(a) Administration of the Test :** TAT material consists of 31 cards. Thirty of them are vague pictures in black and white and one is blank. These pictures are arranged in such a manner that they indicate four overlapping sets of 20 cards in each set, (19 pictures and one blank) one set for boys, one for girls, one for males over 14 years and the fourth set for females over 14 years. These four sets are symbolized as F for adult females, M for adults males, B for boys and G for girls. The overlapping cards will be symbolized as BM for boys under 14 and adult males both. GF for girls under 14 and adult females both and so on.

These 20 cards will be administered in 2 one hour sessions, i.e. 10 cards in each session. An interval of 24 hours is ideal between two sessions.

Instructions for these four groups in the first Session.

1. **For adults :** This is a test of imagination. I shall show you some pictures, one at a time. Your task will be to describe a story. The story must be related to the events shown in the picture, i.e.,

what is happening at the movement, what the characters are feeling and thinking etc. You can devote about five minutes to each story.

2. **For children under 14 :** I am showing you some pictures. See the pictures and tell a story about each of them. The story should include what has happened before and what is happening now. You should also tell what the people are thinking and feeling in these pictures. You can write any kind of story you want. You will be given five minutes for each card.

Similar instruction will also be given in the second session. More imaginative stories will be collected here.

**(b) Recording and Scoring :** The response of the examinee are recorded verbatim and comments of the examiner are given after every card. The purpose of the comment is to know whether outcome has been mentioned or not, whether a story is long or short and so on. (Average length of a TAT story is 300 words) A story of less than 140 words is not scored at all. if an examinee describes more than one story in a single card, he is motivated to concentrate on only one long story rather than several short stories. In this way, all the ten cards are scored and the first session is over.

Blank card is given to the examinee in the end of the second session. While attempting the TAT cards, behaviour of the examinee, his emotional expression, his tone, his way of turning the cards etc. are also recorded.

After the test is over, an enquiry from the examinee is also made to know whether the stories written by him is original or he has taken them from novels or films.

One important characteristic of this test is that scoring and interpretation go hand in hand. This makes TAT different from Rorschach test. One more difference is that the purpose of RT is to reveal the structure and organisation of personality and the purpose of TAT is to reveal the contents of the personality, such as, drive, need, fantasies, complexes, conflicts, etc.

**(c) Interpretation of the Test :**

***Assumptions underlying the interpretation :***

1. Characteristics of the hero of the story represent the tendencies of the examinee's personality i.e., he manifests his own personality in the hero.
2. Situations surroundings the hero of the story represents various facets of the examinee's life situations containing the past, present and future environment.

***Interpretations of various terms:***

1. **Hero :** Hero of the story (male and female) is the central figure around whom the entire events revolve. The examinee recognises the hero by his principal traits like superiority, inferiority, belongingness, mental abnormality, criminality etc. The examinee identifies himself with the hero by taking much interest in him. Hero is the main character of the story who dominates from the beginning of the story. There may be more than one heroes in the stories , so, sequence of heroes is taken into account.
2. **Motives, trends and feelings of heroes :** Here the interpreter analyses the overt behaviour of the hero, i.e., what the hero thinks, feels and does. These overt behaviour reflect the needs and emotions of the heroes which are actually the needs and emotions of the examinee. Murray has given a list of 28 such needs. Some of these needs are aggression, achievements, sex related needs etc. These needs are rated on a five point scale ranging from 1, representing for a mild form of needs to 5, representing intense form of needs. After all the 20 stories of cards have been scored on a five point scale a total score for each need is computed and compared with the standard score given for the examinees of a particular age or sex. High or low score needs are then carefully analysed in relation to each other. An example is given here.

   "A male examinee showing unfriendly motives and actions to females indicate that he has some troubled relations with females in his life"
3. **Forces of the hero's environment :** Here emphasis is given on environment variables which is called press. They can either facilitate or interfere in fulfilling the needs. A list of 30 press has been given by Murray in this regard. Some of these press are rejection, dominance, physical injury etc. All these forces are classified according to their effect on the hero. The strength of press in each story is also rated on a 5 point

scale out of which 1 represent the minimum strength and 5 represents the maximum strength. After rating all the 20 stories on a scale , the total scores for each press is computed and then it is compared with the standard score of the examinee of that age or sex.

4. **Outcomes :** Outcome refers to how the story ends. This ending maybe tragic or comedian. This ending shows how an examinee thinks about the future of his life.
5. **Thema :** It refers to the interaction of the hero with the forces of the environment. The purpose of thema is to study different types of forces which work for or against the hero in the story. Themas actually help us to understand the problems of the examinees.
6. **Interest and sentiments :** Here choice of the topics of the stories and ways of handling them are analysed. The assumption is that an examinee chooses a story according to his own interest or attitudes and handles them on the same line.
7. **Conclusion :** After analyzing all the above six points conclusions are drawn. But following points must be kept in view while drawing conclusions.

I. Only six out of 20 stories should fall under the impersonal category. The elements given under this category are not personal. They are rather derived from films, novels, story books etc. If more than 6 out of 20 stories fall under this category. It indicates three things.
- examinee is not involved in the test
- content is psychologically irrelevant
- administration of the test is poor

II. Murray has given three types of normal personality (-) outer layer, middle layer and inner layer.

In inner layer, personality tendencies or wishes are repressed, i.e., not expressed in thoughts.

In middle layer, personality, tendencies or wishes are expressed in thoughts, but repressed in action generally.

The outer layer consists of those wishes or tendencies which are frequently expressed in thoughts and behaviours both without any repression. The interpreter must take all these three layers of personality into account.

III. There are two levels of functioning in a person. The first level includes the physical and overt verbal behaviour and the second level includes plans, ideas, dreams and fantasies. TAT has been designed to reveal the second level not the first level.

**Limitations of TAT**

I. Limited Applicability of the test : It can be applied only on those people who are intellectually above than average. Those who are low in intelligence are not expected to form stories on the basis of cards.

II. Validity of the test : Psychometricians are of the view that validity of TAT is very low because there is lack of standardized procedure or final normative data.

III. Fantasies and real life contradiction : Every man wants to become a superman and every poor wants to become a billionaire. So ideas given by him in the stories may not necessarily reflect the real personality of a man.

IV. Reliability of TAT : Reliability of the test can be calculated only by test retest method or equivalent form method and split half method cannot be used here at all because set of pictures can not be divided into two equal halves.

## 3. Word Association Test :

This test asks the examinee to tell the very first word that comes in his mind after listening to the stimulus word from the examiner. The examiner notes down the responses along with the reaction time taken by the examinee.

This technique of testing personality was first introduced by **Jung** in 1910 in his psychoanalysis. He presented a list of 100 words (some neutral and some emotionally directed) and analysed the responses of the examinees from different angles. If examinees take longer time to respond, it is an indicative of conflicts, anxieties, repressed experiences and a sign of emotional embarrassment according to him. Similarly, a large number of unusual responses like 'pen bar' was taken to be an indicative of mental illness.

The next important Word Association test was developed by **Rapport** and his associated in 1946.

The test consisted of 60 words and its aim was to explore the areas of aggression and sexuality with special emphasis on oral, anal and genital levels of psycho-sexual development.

### 4. Sentence Completion Test :

In such tests a number of incomplete sentences are given to examinees and they are asked to complete them in their own way. No time limit is given to them for this purpose. This technique was first used by **Elbinghous** as a non-projective technique of assessing intelligence. This technique was started to be used as a personality test since 1930s. OSS is a popular word association test.

### 5. Figure Drawing test :

Here the examinee is given a sheet of paper and a pencil to draw the figures of a person. The two most common figure drawing tests are Machover Draw a Person (DAP) test and Buck House Tree Person (HTP)] test.

In the DAP the examinee is asked to draw the figure of a person. If first drawing is male, he is asked to draw the figure of a female. The examiner notes down the sequence how different parts of the body are shown. Drawing is also followed by inquiry in order to know more information about the details of the drawing.

In HTP the examinee is asked to draw the figure of a house, a tree and a person. According to Buck, the house indicates the examinees house and those living there. Tree indicates the life style of the examinee and his ability to derive gratification from the general environment and the person indicates about the person who is closely associated with the examinee.

All these figures are interpreted from three angles:

I. Analysis of the overall impression of the drawing : It is related to the posture of the figure (static or in action) facial expression and other related features.

II. Analysis of the structural features of the drawing : It is related to size of the figure, fatness, pressure of the lines, sequence of the parts drawn etc.

III. Content analysis of the drawing : It is related to the different parts of the body of the figure and its dress.

The underlying assumption of these drawings is that the examinee projects himself and his surrounding in these figures. For example, if he has drawn a disproportionately bigger head, it is an indicative of organic brain disorder of the examinee. Similarly, emphasis upon genital organs or breast is an indicative of psychosexual conflicts, emphasis on eyes or ears is an indicative of paranoid tendencies, emphasis upon lips in male drawings by male is an indicative of homo-sexual tendencies and so on.

Dress of the figure has also some meaning. For example, emphasis upon pockets on the shirt of a male figure drawn by a male is an indicative of homo-sexuality, holding of a pistol by the figure indicates hostility and aggression and so on.

### 6. Toy Tests :

In such tests toys like dolls, puppets or miniatures are given to the examinees mostly children and they are asked to play with them in the manner they like. The examiner notes down the item chosen by the examinees, the manner they handle them, their emotional verbalization and other overt behaviour. One example of a toy test is the **World Test** developed by Lovenfield in 1939. This test consisted of 150-300 miniature pieces of items like trees, cars, fences, dolls, houses, bridges, animals etc. In this test the examinee is asked to construct whatever he likes with these objects. Then the examiner notes down the objects chosen by the child, the sequence in which they are placed, his verbalized emotional expression and other overt behaviour. Then the personality of the child is interpreted with the help of the manual of the test.

## Merits of projective Techniques

The only merit of these techniques is that subject can reveal even those traits and constructs before the examiner which he would never reveal if he was directly asked to-do so. He would do unconsciously what he is not expected to do in normal setting. For example, if we ask a person if he is interested in homo-sexual relation, he would reply in negative. but by using projective techniques he can project his homo-sexual temperament unknowingly.

**Limitations :** Major limitations of projective techniques are given below :

1. **Lack of standardized instructions :**Directions for the standardized tests are not standardized and the examiner can significantly influence the subject's responses. Besides, responses of the examinees are not of the same length. This makes a difference in scoring as well.
2. **Fakability of responses :** It is said that in projective techniques, the examinees can not hide his true responses but there are many evidences against this statement too. They can fake their responses especially when they are instructed to modify their responses at the inquiry stage.
3. **Lack of objectivity :** These tests are always less objective as compared to other personality tests. It is because there is not uniform and standardized interpretation procedure in these tests. Examiner's personal experiences and training also affect the scores and interpretation. It would be more correct to say that test makers reflect their own personality in scoring and interpretation of the test. All the test makers give their own criteria of interpretation which may or may not be correct. For example, selection of red colour may be interpreted as hostility, liking for teenaged girls or vulnerability to natural calamities.
4. **Low level of reliability :** Reliability of most of the projective tests is generally very low due to two reasons (i) There is no uniform standard method of scoring and interpretation of responses. As a result scorer reliability is very low (ii) These tests do not yield consistent scores upon retesting of the same subject. Similarly, alpha coefficient of reliability can not be computed too because items are not usually comparable.
5. **Poor validity :** Validity of these tests is also very low. They claim to have criterion related validity which is inconclusive and hence debatable. In reality, most of the projective tests require construct validity to be ascertained which has never been obtained
6. **Influence of situational variables :** Situational variables like physical appearance of the examiner, emphasis upon a particular type of responses by the examiner and frequent change of instructions influence the responses. For example, if the examiner is dangerous and rude in appearance, it may badly affect the examinee's capacity to imagine, think and respond.
7. **Limited Applicability :** If the subject is blind or semi-blind, he cannot use these tests to project his personality. Similarly, subjects of low intellectual abilities also find it difficult to take these tests. Again, these tests are not expected to give dependable results if they are applied on normal people of the society. Time consuming factor is the biggest hurdle against the use of such tests in school situations.

## (E) Measurement of Attitude, Interest and Values

### (1) Interest

**Meaning of Interest :** Interest is a preference for one activity over others. According to Kelley, interest of an individual provides important information about the make up of his personality.

**W.V. Bingham** has defined interest in the following words :

"An interest is a tendency to become absorbed in an experience and to continue it."

**Characteristics of interest :**

Following characteristics of interests can be inferred from the definition given above :

I. Interests involves selection and ranking of different activities along a like-dislike dimension and its related scales. For example, a student may rank three activities, novel reading, radio-listening or cricket playing as 3, 2 and 1 on the basis of his particular interest in these activities.

II. Interest indicates the investment of a particular person in a particular activity with zeal.

III. Interest and abilities are not always correlated. An individual may take interest in such an activity which he is not capable to perform.

IV. Interest is not a permanent construct. It can change with the change of time. For example, a person may have interest in teaching profession but if he does not get that job as a profession and adopt another profession on compulsion, his interest may change. But interest does not change in a short period of time. It may change in the long run because it is acquired.

V. Excellence in an activity mostly depends on the interest that a person possesses in that activity. Larger the interest, the better will be the performance in that activity.

**Types of interest**

1. **Expressed interest :** It is the most simple and direct way of obtaining information about interest and is defined as the interest shown in the form of preference by the person involved in a particular activity.
2. **Manifest interest :** When a person voluntarily participates in an activity, it is called manifest interest. For example, when a student regularly completes his home work without any compulsion, it shows his manifest interest.
3. **Inventoried interest :** Inventoried interests are those interests which are measured by interest tests and that compare interests in different activities.

**Measurement of interest :** As far as measurement of interest is concerned, investigators are primarily concerned with interest in vocational pursuits. The easiest approach here is that subject is directly asked about his choice or preference in a particular field. But the experience has shown that responses given by the subject are mostly wrong and unreliable so, an indirect method of assessing interest was discovered and used by the psychologists to obtain dependable results. As a result, several standardized interest inventories were developed. We will discuss here some of them.

***1. Strong Vocational interest Blank (SVIB) :*** It was developed by E.K. strong in 1951. This test was revised several times to obtain accurate results. 1966 revision of SVIB includes 3999 items grouped into eight parts. Separate forms of the test are available for males and females. The first five parts are concerned with the categories like school subjects, amusement, occupation, day to day activities etc. In each of these parts, the subject indicates his preference on a three point scales-like, indifferent and dislike.

On the remaining three parts, the subject is required to rank the given activities in the test according to his preference, 1,2,3,4, etc.

All these responses are scored in terms of 54 occupations on men's form and 32 occupations on the women's form. A separate scoring key has been prepared for each occupation.

The main purpose of SVIB is to measure the extent to which the individual's interest are similar to those of the successful persons in the given occupations. In this way, the comparison between the people in a particular occupation and the people in general is made possible. The weights in these occupations range from + 4 to – 4. A positive weight means that people in given occupation mark likes more frequency on that item than the people in general. If an item does not discriminate these two groups of persons it is weighted as zero. Criterion key is used to score these two groups of persons-occupational and general. A person's total raw score on SVIB is simply the algebraic sum of this plus and minus weights on each occupational scale. These raw scores are converted into standard scores by taking mean as 50 and SD as 10.

SVIB also includes four non-occupational scales *(i)* Specialization level (SL) *(ii)* Masculinity-Femininity (MF scale) *(iii)* occupational level (OL scale) *(iv)* Academic Achievement of college and School students (AACS scale)

SL scale measures the differences between the interest of individual men or women and the general people. MF scale measures the difference between the interest of men or women and the general people. OL scale measures the extent to which interest of unskilled persons are similar or dissimilar to the interest of professional and skilled persons.

AACS scale measures the differences of interest in scientific and academic achievement among the school and college students.

***2. Kuder Interest Inventory :*** These interest inventories are available in the form of three preference records-occupational, vocational and personal and all these records are meant for the students of class IXth onwards.

Occupational records provide scores for 50 occupations. This form of the test is completed in 35 minutes.

Vocational records provide scores in 10 vocational areas namely, outdoor, mechanical, scientific, computational, persuasive, artistic, literary, musical, social service and clerical. The purpose of this vocational scale is to check certain response biases such as faking good, faking bad, carelessness, misunderstanding etc. Here relative interests in a smaller number of broad areas rather than in a specific occupation are evaluated. This form of the test is completed in 30-40 minutes.

Kuder's personal records measure five personal characteristics which are potentially significant for certain types of occupations or vocations. These characteristics are as follows:

I. Active participation in group activities.
II. Ability to exist in familiar and stable situations.
III. Ability to deal with abstract ideas and thoughts.
IV. Avoiding conflicts.
V. Directing others.

Forced choice technique is used in the two inventories given above, i.e., each item consists of three statements out of which subject is required to select any one which he prefers most and the one which he prefers the least.

## (2) Attitude

**Meaning of attitudes :** An attitude is a tendency to react in a certain way towards a designated class of stimuli or an object. An attitude is actually an enduring (stable) system of cognitive component, feeling component and the action tendency component indicating towards an object, event or person. Cognitive component relates to beliefs, feeling component relates to emotions and action tendency component (behavioural component) relates to the action readiness and all these are related to objects, events or persons.

Thus, attitude has a well-defined object of reference and the degree of a person's attitude may vary from favourable to unfavourable.

**Characteristics of attitude**

I. The deep rooted feeling on the basis of preoccupied notion and manifested in the form of action is attitude and it cannot be changed easily.
II. It is different from opinion in the following ways:
   *(a)* Attitude is generally rigid but opinion can change very easily.
   *(b)* Attitude can be graded from most favourable to most unfavourable but opinion is always in yes or no.
   *(c)* Total opinion of a person on the basis of his feeling and belief is actually his attitude.
III. Like the interest, attitude is also not related to ability
IV. Attitude provides a sound basis for individual differences.
V. Attitude may be overt or covert both.
VI. It varies from culture to culture and society to society.

**Definition of attitude**

"An attitude is a mental and natural state of readiness exerting directive or dynamic influence upon the individual's response to all objects and situations with which it is related."
**—Britt.**

**Measurement of attitude :** There are numerous types of attitude tests. The most common among them is self-report inventory. A large number of statements are given here and the person is directly asked what is his attitude toward a particular statement. They are technically called attitude scale.

There are two basic underlying assumptions behind all attitude scales :

I. An individual's behaviour with respect to object or event will be consistent from one situation to another. For example, if. Mr. Gupta likes co-education, he would continue to like it in all situations.
II. Attitude cannot be measured directly. It is actually inferred from the statements or actions of the person, i.e., it is inferred from verbal and non-verbal behaviour of the subject.

**Various measures of attitudes are given below:**

1. **Non-disguised structured test :** Direct statements regarding the objects of attitude are given to the examinees here. Thurstone scale and Likert scale are two examples of this type of test.
   **Thurstone scale :** Following are the steps in constructing this type of test :
   **Step-I :** Several hundred statements expressing various degrees of negative and positive attitude

towards the objects or events are collected. These statements can be obtained from experienced people or from popular literature on the issue.

**Step-II :** Each statement is written on a separate slip of papers or cards. These statements are given to different judges to pile them on 11 point scale ranging from favourable to unfavourable.

**Step-III :** This is the scale construction stage. These statements are put into different scale points on the basis of consensus of judges. On those statements where judges do not agree are eliminated here.

**Step-IV :** Final statement for the scale is selected here. Then the subject is asked to mark those statement with which he is fully agreed and he is then given 10 scores.

2. **Non-disguised non-structured test :** Survey interviews are the most popular techniques of these types of tests. Here as many as possible number of people are interviewed in a short period of time Fixed alternative as well as open end questions are asked for this purpose. In the former type questions, the interviewees choose answers from the given choices but in the open end questions they express themselves in the manner they like. Questions here are also non-structured and free discussion between the interviewee and the interviewer takes place. From the point of scoring and maintaining objectivity, fixed alternative questions are better but from the point of view of detailed information about the problems and context of the object of attitude, open end questions are better.

   Biographical and essay methods are also used as a non-disguised and non-structured test. In this method, attitude is assessed from the opinion of the person expressing in letters, essay, autobiographies, diaries etc. One of the biggest demerits of this method is that the person do not express the true content of an event which is humiliating for him in his diaries, autobiographies and essays.

3. **Disguised non-structured test :** Under this method projective tests to measure personality variables like want, desire, anxiety, frustration etc. are employed. We have already discussed all these projective tests in the earlier part of this chapter.

   **Proshansky** devised one such projective test for studying attitude toward labour. He collected some pictures for this purpose. In those pictures working people were shown in the conflicting situations. After showing the pictures subjects were asked to describe them in the detailed manner possible. These details were demanded in the form of the story. After that three judges rated the story from the point of view of degree of favourable or unfavourable attitude towards labour.

   Two serious limitations of projective type attitude tests are given below :

   *(a)* The descriptions of these pictures are sometimes so vague that it is very difficult to score and interpret them.

   *(b)* Judges can also be influenced by their personal biases in ratings.

4. **Disguised Structured tests :** This is also an indirect method of assessing personality like the third type of tests. This method very much resembles to the objective inventories. Error choice technique developed by **Hammond** (1948) is an example of this type of test.

   This technique requires a number of non-factual items each of which is supported by two alternative responses. Out of these, the subject selects either of these responses on the basis of his own judgement or attitude. The Hammond test which is closely connected with the attitude towards the labour management and the attitude towards Russia is used as information test. The systematic error in checking the alternative on error choice item in one or other directions were taken as a measure of attitude towards the objects. Hammond has also suggested that the number of these alternatives should be increased from 2 to 5.

   It is clear from the other discussions that the first two types of tests are direct measures of personality and the last two are indirect measures of personality variables. The advantages of the indirect method are the same as those of projective methods.

## (3) Values

The term 'values' is rooted in religion and ethics. They are first judged by human mind and then translated into action. They actually determine the future course of human action. They are actually related to what should be done and what should not be done by a person. The purpose of these values is to improve the social situations of humans.

If values are considered objective they will be defined in the following way :

"Values seem to reside in the object just as truly as do colour shape, size and temperature."

—**C.E.M. Joad.**

If values are considered as subjective they will be defined in the following manner:

"Value is an object, condition or activity which individual feels as an effect on his well-being"

—**Wood Ruff**

**Murphy** has defined values as motivation which sustain an individual's efforts to achieve a particular goal.

**Measurement of Values :** Measures of values intend to measure generalized and dominant interest based on religious beliefs and ethics. Interest tests, on the other hand, measure interest in specific activities or areas. Psychologists have taken less interest so far as the measurement of values is concerned. As a result, no satisfactory tool is available to measure generalized interests (values) However, study of values developed by Alport, Vermon and Lindzey may be considered as a popular test of values. There are six categories of values given in the test. These are the theoretical, economic, aesthetic, social, political and religious. They have elaborated these values in the following ways :

I. Generalized and dominant interest of theoretical man lies in the discovery of truth.

II. Generalized and dominant interest of economic man lies in what is useful and practical for man.

III. Aesthetic man takes interest in enjoying the beauty and unique experiences to harmonise the highest values with this value.

IV. The dominant and generalized social man is lover of the masses

V. Political man considers power and influence as the highest value.

VI. And the religious man places the highest value on the unity of all experiences in a bid to understand the cosmos as a whole.

Here items given to the subjects have either two alternatives or multiple alternative response. Their responses become the index of the relative strength of the six basic values.

On the basis of these six categories the people in a society can be categorised into more than one category, i.e., 6x6x6=216 categories on the basis of their dominant interest.

Indian psychologists have tried to develop value test to suit to Indian situations. **Prasad** is one of them. He in 1968 developed an inventory of vocational values for undergraduate and PG students. This inventory covers nine areas-altruism, physical conditions of the work, power prestige, security, economic returns, self-enhancement, social climate and traditions. The inventory consists of 72 pairs of items. The test-retest reliability of the inventory ranges from 0.80 to 0.92.

The value test based on Spranger's six Categorisation of values given above have been adapted and developed in Hindi by **Singh and Sharma** in 1975. And on the basis of their studies they have concluded that males have higher theoretical, economic and political values and females have higher aesthetic, social and religious values.

## OBJECTIVE QUESTIONS

**1.** Ectomorphic people according to Sheldon are
   (*a*) Introverted (*b*) Artistic
   (*c*) Self controlled (*d*) All of these

**2.** Spranger classified people on the basis of
   (*a*) Their physique
   (*b*) Their psychology
   (*c*) Their interest in different fields
   (*d*) None of these

**3.** Extroverts are
   (*a*) social and friendly
   (*b*) tension free
   (*c*) both of these
   (*d*) none of these

**4.** If fixation of libido takes place in the third stage of development according to Freud, the person will be
   (*a*) Extreme lover of beauty
   (*b*) Dealing people high handedly

(c) Both of these
(d) None of these

**5.** Which of the following is not the property of traits?
(a) Traits are directly observable
(b) Traits are quantifiable
(c) Traits change with time
(d) Traits are higher order habits

**6.** The trait theories are not free from shortcomings as they are
(a) Subject to subjective interpretation.
(b) Not universal
(c) Not quantified with zero reference point
(d) All of these

**7.** Match the following :
**Column A**
**Traits**
A Product of neuropsychic system
B Structure of personality
C Unconscious mind
D Determine the type of personality
**Column B**
**Psychologists**
(i) Freud (ii) Cattell
(iii) Eysenck (iv) Alport

| | A | B | C | D |
|---|---|---|---|---|
| (a) | (i) | (ii) | (iii) | (iv) |
| (b) | (iv) | (ii) | (i) | (iii) |
| (c) | (iv) | (iii) | (ii) | (i) |
| (d) | (iv) | (ii) | (iii) | (i) |

**8.** Individual psychology of personality was given; by
(a) Adler (b) Jung
(c) Eysenck (d) None of these

**9.** The process of personality development is completed in...........stages according Erikson.
(a) 8 (b) 6
(c) 7 (d) 10

**10.** Theory developed in reaction to phenomenological theories of personality is
(a) Behaviour theory (b) Cognitive theory
(c) Both of these (d) None of these

**11.** Walter's theory of personality emphasizes.
(a) Good models to be imitated
(b) Rewarded models to be immitated
(c) Both of these
(d) None of these

**12.** Which type of behaviour of the model is imitated in social learning theory of personality ?
(a) Novel and unique behaviour
(b) Aggressive behaviour
(c) Touching behaviour which is applauded by the people
(d) All of these

**13.** The purpose of personality testing is
(a) To know the causes of maladjustment
(b) To classify people into different groups
(c) To apply behaviour/psycho therapy
(d) All of these

**14.** Questions in the schedule are
(a) Read by the respondent.
(b) Asked by the investigator in a face to face situation
(c) Few in number
(d) None of these

**15.** Which of the following things should be done in order to make a good questionnaire?
(a) Language of questions should be clear and simple
(b) Private questions should be asked only indirectly
(c) Number of questions should not be very large
(d) All of these

**16.** Questionnaire for collecting data is mailed when
(a) Respondent is an educated and responsible citizen
(b) A large number of respondents are to be covered
(c) It is not easy to approach the respondents personally.
(d) All of these

**17.** Open end questionnaire is not preferred to fixed response questionnaire because
(a) they can not be statistically treated
(b) subjectivity of interpretation may distort the result
(c) respondents may ignore them
(d) all of them

**18.** Which of the following inventories is not used in schools?
(a) Adjustment inventories

(b) Pathological trait inventories
(c) Social inventories
(d) All of these

**19.** Woodworth's personal data sheet was developed in
(a) 1908 (b) 1911
(c) 1918 (d) 1924

**20.** Minnesota Counseling Inventory was developed by
(a) Minnesota (b) Berlie and Layton
(c) Bell (d) None of these

**21.** Personality inventories are criticized on which of the following grounds
(a) Their validity coefficient is very low
(b) The individual may understand a question wrongly
(c) They have very poor diagnostic value
(d) All of these

**22.** Interview is
(a) An educational process
(b) A social process
(c) A psychological process
(d) None of these

**23.** The purpose of an interview may be
(a) To gather some facts
(b) To assess and study the personality
(c) To treat a psychological disease
(d) All of these

**24.** A person can abase interview as a tool if
(a) He is obsessed by his own philosophy of life
(b) He can not mould and redirect questions
(c) He is unable to pool informations into an integrated whole
(d) All of these

**25.** Interview is preferred to personality inventories because
(a) It involves greater flexibility between the two parties
(b) It can cover maximum aspects of personality
(c) Both of these
(d) None of these

**26.** Graphic rating scale is preferred to point scale because
(a) It fills the gap between two scale points
(b) It can be plotted on a graph.
(c) Both of these
(d) None of these

**27.** Q sorting technique was developed by **William Stephenson** in
(a) 1853 (b) 1953
(c) 1974 (d) 1960

**28.** The performance of a person in a job is measured by
(a) Group performance test
(b) Behaviourally Anchored Rating scale
(c) Both of these
(d) None of these

**29.** Error of Halo Effect' is caused when
(a) rater is influenced by one single favourable or unfavourable trait
(b) rater rates the person in the middle
(c) rater is lenient in his rating
(d) none of these

**30.** The logical error in rating scale was first pointed out in
(a) 1924 (b) 1931
(c) 1961 (d) 1904

**31.** In order to improve the validity of rating scale which of the following methods should be adopted?
(a) Traits to be measured should be defined in behavioural terms
(b) Response options and different scales should be well defined
(c) Rating should be done by independent raters
(d) All of these

**32.** In socio-metric method, the super star is one who
(a) is chosen by maximum number of persons
(b) is chosen in multiple pairs
(c) both of these
(d) none of these

**33.** Situational test for assessing personality is used in
(a) military services for selecting officers
(b) police department for identifying criminals
(c) both of these
(d) none of these

**34.** Actual traits of an individual can be known by projective techniques because
(a) He is unknown to what he is doing or showing
(b) Projective techniques reveal the total personality of an individual
(c) If goes from a complex process of interpretation.
(d) a & b both.

**35.** Which of the following is the most difficult and challenging step of project method for testing personality?
(*a*) Administration of the test
(*b*) Scoring of the test
(*c*) Preparation of the test
(*d*) Interpretation of the test

**36.** In how many categories Best (1978) has classified projective techniques?
(*a*) four (*b*) three
(*c*) five (*d*) two

**37.** In how many stages the administration process of inkblot test gets completed?
(*a*) four (*b*) three
(*c*) two (*d*) five

**38.** In Rorschach test, vague responses of the examinee are clarified in
(*a*) inquiry stage
(*b*) preparation stage
(*c*) testing of limit stage
(*d*) none of these

**39.** When response is based on uncommon area of the blot , it is denoted by
(*a*) S (*b*) Dd
(*c*) DW (*d*) DdW

**40.** Natural objects or things in ink blot tests are scored as
(*a*) Na (*b*) Lm
(*c*) No (*d*) N

**41.** If number of D responses in an inkblot test is few, it indicates
(*a*) Stress and anxiety of the examinee
(*b*) Cheerfulness of the examinee
(*c*) Love for beauty of the examinee
(*d*) None of these

**42.** Projective techniques are very poor measure of personality testing because
(*a*) they are highly subjective
(*b*) their accuracy depends on the success of its inquiry stage
(*c*) both of these
(*d*) none of these

**43.** The success of TAT lies in the
(*a*) Expression power of the examinee
(*b*) Conclusion drawing power of the examiner
(*c*) Both of these
(*d*) None of these

**44.** The personality of the individual in TAT is reflected by
(*a*) the personality of the hero
(*b*) the environment in which hero lives
(*c*) both of these
(*d*) none of these

**45.** Word Association test for assessing personality was first used by **Jung** in
(*a*) 1912 (*b*) 1922
(*c*) 1848 (*d*) 1910

**46.** Underlying assumption of figure drawing test is that
(*a*) the examinee projects himself and his surroundings in these figures
(*b*) the examinee expresses his feelings through these figures.
(*c*) both of these
(*d*) none of these

**47.** Self report inventories are called
(*a*) Check list (*b*) Attitude scale
(*c*) Both of these (*d*) None of these

**48.** Which of the following theories considers personality as the product of environmental factors?
(a) Trait theories (b) Learning Theories
(c) Both of these (d) None of these.

**49.** Education can strengthen national integration in which of the following ways
(*a*) It can reduce the ill effects of caste differences
(*b*) It can minimizes regional aspirations of the people
(*c*) It can bring about justice and equality in the society
(*d*) All of these

**50.** Employment Guarantee Act 2005 is
(*a*) for landless labourers to provide 100 days employment in a year
(*b*) for educated unemployed to provide employment after graduation
(*c*) for women to provide them employment round the year
(*d*) all of these

**51.** Special provision can be made for women and children by the government under Article
(*a*) 15 (1) (*b*) 15
(*c*) 15 (3) (*d*) 19

**52.** In order to make India a modern society, a teacher should
(*a*) develop scientific temper among students
(*b*) help the students to select subjects and courses according to the modern needs
(*c*) make the students competitive to survive in a modern society
(*d*) all of these

**53.** In Psychology, we study
(*a*) group behaviour of persons in relation to their environment
(*b*) activities of an individual in relation to his environment
(*c*) factors and circumstances contributing or restricting learning
(*d*) all of these

**54. Assertion (A) :** An intelligent father is likely to have an intelligent.
**Reason (R) :** Intelligence is determined by hereditary factors.
(*a*) A is correct but R is not the correct explanation of A
(*b*) A and R are correct and R is the correct explanation of A
(*c*) R is correct but A is wrong
(*d*) Both A and R are wrong

**55.** The weight of a human baby at the time of birth is
(*a*) 2.5 kg to 3.5 kg
(*b*) 3 pounds to 5 pounds
(*c*) exactly 3 kg
(*d*) 4 kg to 4.5 kg

**56.** Erikson has divided human development into
(*a*) four stages (*b*) six stages
(*c*) eight stages (*d*) five stages

**57.** A learner is motivated to learn when there is tension or disequilibrium of forces in the psychological field of learner. It is the
(*a*) Law of pregnanz
(*b*) Law of figure ground
(*c*) Law of proximity
(*d*) Law of continuity

**58.** Highest level of concept formation is
(*a*) Concrete level (*b*) Classification level
(*c*) Formal level (*d*) None of these

**59.** In normal learning environment, forgetting is caused
(*a*) due to lack of practice for a long time
(*b*) due to the interference of other learnt material
(*c*) due to lack of consolidation of memory traces
(*d*) all of these

**60.** Which of the following terminologies is not related to Guidance?
(*a*) Group counselling
(*b*) Physio-therapy
(*c*) Psychotherapy
(*d*) Behaviour therapy

**61.** Alfred Binet's test of intelligence was first revised in
(*a*) 1908 (*b*) 1937
(*c*) 1911 (*d*) 1954

**62.** According to Heek, the minimum level of IQ that a talented child should have is
(*a*) 125 (*b*) 120
(*c*) 130 (*d*) 135

**63.** Which of following is an important perinatal cause of mental retardation?
(*a*) Pre-mature birth
(*b*) Traumatic brain injuries
(*c*) Both of these
(*d*) None of these

**64.** In order to improve work habit of learning disabled, what should be done?
(*a*) Unattending behaviour of learners should be penalized
(*b*) Close monitoring of behaviour is needed
(*c*) Prompts and cues should be regularly given
(*d*) All of these

**65.** Observation as a method of assessing personality is criticised on which of the following grounds?
(*a*) Subjectivity of interpretation
(*b*) Faking of traits by the subject
(*c*) Both of these
(*d*) None of these

**66.** Social behaviouristic theory of personality was developed by
(*a*) Bandura and Walter
(*b*) Spranger
(*c*) Eysenck
(*d*) None of them

**67.** A questionnaire should have all the characteristics except
(*a*) unambiguous language
(*b*) indirect questioning of information of personal nature
(*c*) questions of fully representing attribute
(*d*) none of these

**68.** Field experiment in education is a classroom experimental research while field study is
(*a*) Survey research
(*b*) Normative research
(*c*) Both of these
(*d*) None of these

**69.** Discovery of new truths and its application is called
(*a*) Applied research
(*b*) Pure research
(*c*) Phenomenological research
(*d*) None of these

**70.** ANOVA is used when
(*a*) we do not want to use so many *t* test in order to determine significance of difference between means
(*b*) ratio between variance within group and variance between groups are to be calculated
(*c*) both of these
(*d*) none of these

## ANSWERS

| 1 | 2 | 3 | 4 | 5 | 6 | 7 | 8 | 9 | 10 |
|---|---|---|---|---|---|---|---|---|---|
| (*d*) | (*c*) | (*c*) | (*a*) | (*a*) | (*d*) | (*b*) | (*a*) | (*a*) | (*b*) |
| **11** | **12** | **13** | **14** | **15** | **16** | **17** | **18** | **19** | **20** |
| (*c*) | (*d*) | (*d*) | (*b*) | (*d*) | (*d*) | (*d*) | (*b*) | (*c*) | (*b*) |
| **21** | **22** | **23** | **24** | **25** | **26** | **27** | **28** | **29** | **30** |
| (*d*) | (*b*) | (*d*) | (*d*) | (*c*) | (*a*) | (*b*) | (*c*) | (*a*) | (*b*) |
| **31** | **32** | **33** | **34** | **35** | **36** | **37** | **38** | **39** | **40** |
| (*d*) | (*a*) | (*c*) | (*d*) | (*b*) | (*a*) | (*b*) | (*a*) | (*b*) | (*a*) |
| **41** | **42** | **43** | **44** | **45** | **46** | **47** | **48** | **49** | **50** |
| (*a*) | (*c*) | (*a*) | (*a*) | (*d*) | (*a*) | (*b*) | (*c*) | (*d*) | (*a*) |
| **51** | **52** | **53** | **54** | **55** | **56** | **57** | **58** | **59** | **60** |
| (*c*) | (*d*) | (*d*) | (*a*) | (*a*) | (*c*) | (*a*) | (*c*) | (*d*) | (*b*) |
| **61** | **62** | **63** | **64** | **65** | **66** | **67** | **68** | **69** | **70** |
| (*a*) | (*a*) | (*c*) | (*d*) | (*c*) | (*a*) | (*d*) | (*c*) | (*b*) | (*c*) |

# UNIT-VI

- ★ *Super Intelligence and Educational Adaptation*
- ★ *Mental Retardation and Educational Adaptation*
- ★ *Creativity and Educational Adaptation*
- ★ *Learning Disabilities and Educational Adaptation*
- ★ *Backward Children and their Education Adaptation*
- ★ *Educational Guidance and Counseling*

1

# Super Intelligence and Educational Adaptation

## HISTORICAL BACKGROUND

Plato was the philosopher who concerned first to discuss the most able youth of the country so that they might be educated for state leadership and he suggested the test of native ability for their selection.

Scientific investigation of gifted individuals started after the Galton's report (1869). It was the first quantitative study of human abilities. He stressed on inherited factors responsible for natural abilities and asserted that without a particular gift for a particular kind of achievement, one would not be able to achieve well in that area. For that purpose, the person needs a high degree of general ability.

Emphasis on superior intelligence got momentum with the advent of **Binet's test of intelligence** and their application. Those scoring very high or very low on the test were termed as exceptional children. **Terman** (1925) systematized these efforts. He investigated more than one thousand gifted children and reported about their development and behaviour.

### Meaning

Children or people who are bright in intelligence, sharp in memory and quick in decision making are generally termed as gifted children. They are called gifted because they have extraordinary intellectual power given by the nature as a gift.

### Definition

It is very difficult to find out a uniform and universally acceptable definition of gifted people because different investigators have used different criteria to define such people. Some of the definitions in this regard are however, given below :

1. The term gifted is usually used to refer to those people who have superior cognitive or intellectual performance while the term talented is used for those people who manifest outstanding performance in a specific area, e.g., in performing or visual arts.
2. Gifted and talented children's education Act (1978) USA :
   The term gifted and talented children means children and youth who are identified at the pre-school, elementary or secondary level as possessing demonstrated or potential abilities that give evidence of high performance capabilities in areas such as intellectual, creative, academic or leadership or in the performing or visual arts and who by reason thereof require services or activities not ordinarily provided by the school.
3. IQ definition: In Terman's notable investigation, the minimum score originally set for the gifted was 140 IQ. Later on children scoring 135 IQ were included in this group but Heek (1953) indicated that an IQ of 125 was an appropriate, point for determining admission to classes especially meant for gifted.
4. Three ring conception : Gifted and talented children are specific in three traits :
   *(a)* They have above average ability in every field.
   *(b)* They are committed to tasks and highly motivated.
   *(c)* They are definitely creative.
   A student is identified as gifted when all the above three traits exist in him concurrently.
5. Functional definition : Gifted and talented children are those identified by professionally qualified persons who by virtue of outstanding abilities are capable of high performance. These are children who require differentiated educational programmes beyond those normally provided by the regular schools in order to realize their contribution to self and society.

6. Children capable of high performance include those with demonstration achievement or potential in any of the following areas:
   *(a)* General intellectual ability
   *(b)* Specific academic aptitude
   *(c)* Creative or productive thinking
   *(d)* Visual and performing arts.
   *(e)* Leadership ability
   *(f)* Psychomotor ability **Morland (1972)**

## IDENTIFICATION OF GIFTED CHILDREN

### (A) Need and purpose of identification

**I.** Their identification is done in a view to educate and develop them in such a planned way that is most fruitful to their self on one hand and to the society on the other. If they are not identified timely, financial, social and cultural losses are bound to occur.

**II.** It is not easy for them to adjust with normal children in schools due to their high performing ability and way of thinking. They are most likely to create problems for others.

**III.** They are deviant people. If their extra intellectual energy is not properly utilized, they can harm to the whole society by their deviations. This deviation is dangerous because it is filled with extra energy especially mental.

**IV.** If they are identified earlier, they can benefit others to the maximum level possible by their creative performance.

**V.** Ordinary curriculum will not suit these students in schools. They do need special curriculum and special methods of instruction to match with their intellectual potentials.

### (B) Methods of identification

They can be identified by using the following methods:

**(a) Standardized intelligence test :** It is the best method for identifying these children. Standardized intelligence test is administered to these children in schools and their IQ level is calculated. Those scoring high enough above the norms for their age can be considered student with superior intelligence. These students will further be examined because intelligence is not the only trait for giftedness.

**(b) Standardized achievement test :** Gifted and talented children score very high on achievement test too. Standardized achievement tests are administered to these children and their achievement is compared with the norm. If it is high enough above the average, the child is said to have high intellectual abilities. It is because intelligence and achievement are directly correlated.

**(c) Teacher's observation and rating :** The teacher consistently observes the behaviour and activities of these children and if he finds almost all the characteristics to be specific for gifted and talented children in them, he may declare that the child is gifted and talented but teacher's rating will surely be matched with the scores on intelligence test.

## Characteristics of children with superior intelligence

### 1. Cognitive

- Extraordinary quality of accumulating information.
- Advanced comprehension access to challenging curriculum.
- Varied interest and curiosity
- High level of verbal intelligence
- Early development of reading skills.
- Original in thinking and action
- Not conservative rather flexible and progressive in thought process.
- Very advanced in abstract thinking.
- Unusual capacity for processing information.
- Comprehensive synthesis.
- Hightened capacity for seeing unusual and diverse relationship among objects, events and concepts.
- Better in reasoning ability and generalization.
- High memory power.
- Early ability to use and form conceptual framework.
- An evaluative approach to themselves and others.
- Persistent and goal directed behaviour.

- Tend to excel in the academic aspects of education but tend to excel to a lesser degree in areas which are not directly correlated with intelligence.
- They are at least two years advanced from the average children in IQ, having IQ more than 125.

**2. Affective**

- Large accumulation of information about emotions.
- More advanced emotional maturity than the average child.
- Better adjusted in the society.
- Unusual sensitivity to the expectations and feelings of others.
- Sense of humour.
- Gentle and hostile both but are generally polite.
- Self-awareness accompanied by feelings of ego and being different.
- Idealism, sense of justice and honesty.
- Emotional depth and intensity.
- High expectations of self and others often leading to high degree of frustration.
- Advanced level of moral judgement.
- Observes objects and situations deeply and with keen.
- Indifferent and hostile to dishonest people.

**3. Physical**

- Advanced in physical development and health having a good height, weight and bodily development from birth onwards.
- Study shows that they walk and talk about two months earlier than the average.
- Superior in neuro-muscular capacity.
- Low tolerance for lag between their standard and their athletic skills.
- They are generally successful in sports and games (indoor and outdoor).

**4. Psychomotor**

- Have more positive attitude toward the society
- Energetic and active. Their life is so stimulating that they sleep less and have unusual physical and mental energy.
- Ability to concentrate for a longer period of time.
- They care less for quality of hand writing.

**5. Intutive**

- Early involvement and concern for intutive knowing and metaphysical ideas.
- Creativity apparent in all areas of endeavours
- High interest in the life hereafter.

**6. Social**

- Less boastful exaggeration, less cheating and greater trustworthiness.
- Excess in courtesy, cooperation and willing to take suggestions (if acceptable)
- They are more frequently chosen by their peers and age mates in schools and outside schools.
- Strongly motivated to their self-actualizing needs.
- Highly interested in solving social problems.
- Leadership quality of high level.
- Seek older companions.

**7. Academic**

- Superior achievement in one or more academic subjects, i.e., performance much above than average children.
- Ability to learn even complex content easily.
- If instructional material is not challenging enough, they may drop out of the school due to lack of motivation in the curricular activities.
- If they are not identified for providing special services, they may become the victim of under achievement.
- High organizational ability of the subject matter.

**8. Communication ability**

- There communication ability is higher than the average people.
- They take much interest in conversation in social situations
- They enjoy conversation with older people and peers more than their age mates.
- Their language ability and speech development is very advanced at least more than two years.

**9. Negative characteristics**

- Restless in the classroom.
- Disturbing in group situations.
- Inattentive to instructions if it is of low standard.

- Careless in handwriting.
- Indifferent to class work occasionally, especially when it is too easy.
- Outspokenly critical and egoistic in nature.
- Hostile towards dishonest people and athiests.

## Factors responsible for superior intelligence:

1. **Genetic and hereditary factors :** Sons of gifted parents are generally gifted but some exceptions are also seen.
2. **Environmental factors :** Following factors contribute to the development of superior intelligence:
   - Family background like education of parents, socio-economic conditions, size of the family, number of children in the family and birth order, position of the child etc. affect intelligence, positively and negatively both. For example, if socio economic status of the family is high due to high education and affluence of parents, children are likely to gain superior intelligence.
   - Educational opportunities and training also affect intelligence. If child is getting education in a highly reputed school, he is likely to show higher level of intelligence than those who are not educated properly in the school.
   - Values and expectation of culture, if it is stressing education and knowledge, the people are likely to be intelligent.
   - Occupation of the family and that of locality. If it is of manual type occupying people round the clock, people are likely to be less intelligent.

## Educational adaptation of gifted children

Gifted children are generally well advanced in almost all aspects of life, i.e., they create no classroom disturbances due to their giftedness at least in normal situations. Seeing their advanced abilities, no consulting programme is required for them. However, if any school arranges special programmes for them, it is more in the interest of the school and the society than that of these children. Following adaptive measures are employed to satisfy the special needs of these children.

### (A) Role of the teacher

I. The teacher should provide diverse instructional activities addressing diversified interest and preferences of these students.

II. The teacher has to develop higher level of thinking skills in these students by adopting problem solving approaches and brain storming techniques.

III. The teacher should recognize them in the class as they are superior in intelligence and treat them accordingly. It will satisfy the ego of these students.

IV. The students should be allowed to move through the curriculum at their own respective paces.

V. After identifying advanced content, the teacher should assign them independent reading, projects, worksheets, reports, etc.

VI. They should be encouraged to solve practical problems of life through their novel ideas.

VII. They should have full access to the participation of classroom management.

VIII. They should be given full opportunity for independent learning.

### (B) Enrichment programmes

In such programmes they are not placed in any special class or school. They remain in the regular class with average students but special attention is paid to them in the classroom by the teacher. It is directly related to teaching techniques and curricular programmes rather than administrative ones.

Enrichment activities in the classroom and in the school campus many be of the following types:

1. **Creativity fostering activities :** Open writing activities like essay writing, stylist writing, poster writing, letter writing etc. are organized in the class to benefit these students.
2. **Mathematical puzzles :** Some very difficult questions of mathematics (related to their syllabus) are given to them to solve. Mathematics teaching is also related to team and individual statistics, i.e., games and in this way they learn in the playground.
3. **Student's research activities :** Students are given opportunity to conduct surveys and collect data related to social sciences and these data are

analysed by using mathematical tactics. While doing so they formulate the hypothesis themselves and then test the hypothesis on the basis of the information collected by them. Library work can also be given to them for this purpose.

4. **Broadening the area of comprehension :** Their area of understanding is broadened by helping them to find out the new avenues of the problem and their possible solutions.
5. **Extra and tough assignment :** They should be given chance to deal with more difficult problems than what the class is doing. Apart from this, their quantity of work should also be more than others in order to engage them sufficiently.
6. **Free time activities :** These children should not be left free at any time. Important free time activities useful and necessary for them are as follows:
   - Map reading while studying social sciences.
   - Field trips and excursion for collecting novel informations and for relating theoretical knowledge with the practical aspect of life.
   - Sketching and drawing maps of the locality where the child resides on the basis of his travel experiences.
   - Organizing debate and speech competitions for them.
   - Collecting informations from the website etc.
   - Suggesting them to study some additional literature.
   - Asking them to prepare summary of lessons.
7. **Use of computers in education :** The students should use computers to find students in other cities and the schools located in other areas on the website. It will increase their range of experiences. Curricular experience can also be extended by using internet.
8. **Art enrichment :** These students are very superior in performing and visual arts both. In order to excel them in these areas they should be made involved in the following activities:

   I. If history is being taught, students should be asked to depict centres of arts and monuments of that period.

   II. They should be encouraged to write poetry and other creative works in the class.

   III. Drama and stories should be taught to them by activity not by lecture. They should play the roles of various actors in the drama.

   IV. They should be encouraged to organize various cultural and literary activities themselves.
9. **Laboratory enrichment :** Thinking process of these children is very diversified. They want to do some new experiments and prepare some new materials. They should be given full opportunity for that but once they are working in the lab, the teacher should supervise them so that they may not inflict any casualty on themselves.
10. **Integrated approach :** They should be given opportunity to relate.

    I. One area with other areas and discipline.

    II. The knowledge obtained in the class with the real and practical problems of life.

    III. What they have learnt in their previous classes with what they are learning at present.

## Advantages of the programmes

I. It can provide opportunity for each child to develop his abilities to the fullest.

II. Children of low IQ can also benefit from these students because gifted children are placed in the same class where average children study.

III. Less able pupils of the class will also be motivated to work harder after seeing the performance of more able pupils. This is true only in case of average students only. Students who are below average cannot benefit from this arrangement because after seeing the super performance of gifted children, they will be frustrated.

IV. This type of arrangement is more democratic in nature than that of acceleration or special schooling programmes where gifted child is educated separately.

## Limitations of enrichment programme

I. It is very difficult to provide so many competent teachers to teach these students in regular classes. Most of the teachers do not have sufficient knowledge and experience in diversified fields and hence they cannot deal with gifted children.

II. The teachers generally have insufficient time to work with the gifted children in the class particularly in secondary and senior secondary classes because one third of the school timetable is killed in unnecessary holidays.

III. It is very difficult to frame separate curriculum suitable for gifted children in the class.

## (C) Acceleration programme

It means students will finish 12 grades in less than 12 years or 10 grades in less than 10 school years. They take less time to complete their course than the average child. Important methods of acceleration are given below :

1. **Early admission to grade first :** Admission of gifted children is made on the basis of their mental age rather than chronological age and thus they are given admission in class first at an early age, i.e., at 3 or 4 years rather than at 5.
   The practical difficulty of this method is that it is very difficult to measure intelligence of a 3 or 4 years old child in an accurate manner.
2. **Double promotion :** Child on the basis of his performance in the school is given double promotion, i.e., he may be promoted to class Vth from IIIrd or from II nd to IVth.
   The disadvantage of this method is that the gifted child often skips some important learning materials due to skipping which are very difficult to accomplish in the next grades and it may create learning problem for him.
3. **Shortening the period of grade :** It is more effective method than that of double promotion because nothing is left here for the child to study. He is taught everything in 6 or 8 months rather than 12 months and thus he completes four grades in either 2 or 3 years. If academic year is of eight months, they will study the whole syllabus in eight months what the normal children study in 12 months and thus their time is saved.
   The difficulty of this method is that integration of any type is not possible here. The child will have to be put in special schools for education where summer vacations will also have to be used for teaching.
4. **Lengthening working days of the school :** In this arrangement summer and winter vacations are also utilized to teach these gifted children something new and extra. The curriculum of the next grade can also be taught to them in order to skip them at least one grade.
5. **Early admission to college :** Through regular skipping in schools they complete their school education in less than the usual number of years and hence they are given admission to colleges at an early age. Education policies and regulations are also changed for the purpose.
6. **Telescoped programme :** Here three years educational programmes are condensed into two years or four years syllabi are condensed into three academic years.
7. **Subject wise acceleration :** Here syllabi of various subjects are enriched according to the mental level of these children and then they are taught in a routine manner. Separate classes and separate examination system are necessary in this arrangement. In this arrangement, a child may be in class VI in one subject but he may be in class IXth in other subjects.

## (D) Placement

1. **Special classes :** Special classes are arranged for gifted children on the basis of their intelligence and age. Special grouping from among sections are done on the basis of various subjects like music, art, literature, mathematics etc. Some special grouping can also be made on the basis of degree of IQ, i.e., high achievers in English are put together in the high English section and low achievers are put in the low English section. Sometimes, an extra foreign language is taught to these gifted children in a special class for the purpose of enrichment.
2. **Special school :** When the number of such children is very high in a particular society due to large scale migration and concentration of elite class people in a particular age, special schools are started for these children. Dun public school or Our Lady Fatma at Aligarh are examples. In these schools they are taught with the help of enrichment and acceleration programmes.
3. **Team Teaching :** In this arrangement, students are not taught by one or two teachers. They are taught by a team of teachers experts in their respective fields.

### Gifted Underachievers

This concept is not new. The concept of gifted underachievers is as old as that of students with superior intelligence. They are those who are highly intelligent on one hand but their academic achievement is very poor on the other hand.

Gifted under achievement is the lag between the achievement to be predicted on the basis of the mental age of a bright child and his actual achievement in the class. If mental age is used as the criteria of estimating achievement, the brilliant child can be labeled as under achievers.

### Characteristics

The children are identified and separated from the lot with the following characteristics.

I. Poor achievement in academic content.
II. Being low in self-concept
III. Being unable to persevere when they face difficulties.
IV. Less adjusted in the society and in the school.
V. Lacking a sense of purpose or goals.
VI. Inferiority complex.
VII. Experiencing family conflicts.
VIII. Lack of leadership qualities.

### Culturally different gifted

These gifted children also come under the category of underachievers. Following factors contribute to their under achievement:

I. If sub culture to which the child belongs does not value or reinforce academic achievement then child will not give importance to education.
II. If academic achievement is regarded as feminine for boys and aggressive for girls then the achievement of gifted child in the school will be low.
III. If focus of attention of the culture is on developing only mechanical and technical skills in order to get job, students will do only what is the minimum requirement and they will not be motivated to achieve high in the class.
IV. If wide spread differences are there between their culture and the culture of those who dominate on the educational scene causing communal tension and hatreds, achievement lag will be seen.

### Educational adaptation of Gifted Under achievers

Following modification in the curriculum, method of teaching and administrative arrangement is done to bring these children to normal.

1. Curriculum should stress on cultural pluralism, i.e., no particular culture should dominate on the educational scene.
2. Community resources should supplement the school programmes in order to organize some more activities for these children.
3. Special education programmes should recruit and train those personnel who understand cultural pluralism. If they are the member of minority community, it is better.
4. State should provide facilities for all such programmes.
5. Frustration of these children should be removed by adopting whatsoever means possible. Reservation given to disadvantaged section of the society is an important measure in this regard.

## OBJECTIVE QUESTIONS

**1.** First quantitative study of human abilities was Galton's report prepared in
(*a*) 1859 (*b*) 1904
(*c*) 1869 (*d*) 1888

**2.** First systematic intelligence test was prepared by Alfred Binet in
(*a*) 1905 (*b*) 1911
(*c*) 1888 (*d*) 1904

**3.** According to Renzuli, a gifted child is one
(*a*) Who possesses above average ability in almost every field.
(*b*) Who is committed to task and highly motivated.
(*c*) Who is definitely creative
(*d*) All of these

**4.** Gifted and talented children must be identified as early as possible because.
(*a*) If their potentials are not developed by proper guidance of the teacher, it is a loss of the society.

(b) They are likely to create problems for others, if they are not given work according to their ability.
(c) Ordinary level of curriculum will not suit to these children
(d) All of these

**5.** Achievement test can be a good indicator of intellectual power if
(a) It is conducted immediately after the teaching is over.
(b) A student shows good performance consistently on different achievement test.
(c) Both of these
(d) None of these.

**6.** Which of the following skills does not require high intellectual ability?
(a) Technical skills (b) Mechanical skills
(c) Teaching skills (d) Management skills

**7.** Cognitive abilities related to giftedness are all except
(a) High comprehensive and analytical abilities
(b) High level of verbal intelligence
(c) High retention power
(d) None

**8.** A superior child is advanced to a normal child by at least
(a) 2 ½ years.
(b) Four years
(c) 1 years
(d) 1 ½ years

**9.** A gifted child is
(a) realistic in his approach
(b) highly interested in solving social problems
(c) more frequently chosen by his age mates and peers.
(d) all of these

**10.** Which of the following enrichment programmes is suitable for gifted children in the school?
(a) Mathematics or Science Olympiad
(b) Challenging home assignments
(c) Map work during studies.
(d) All of these

**11.** Which of the following does not come under the category of acceleration for gifted children ?
(a) Skipping of classes
(b) Early admission
(c) Extra laboratory work.
(d) Organizing summer camps.

**12.** Under achievers are those who
(a) Score low on intelligence tests
(b) Achieve low in the class consistently despite their superior intelligence.
(c) Are unable to correspond their achievement to the level of their innate abilities
(d) Both b and c.

## ANSWERS

| 1 | 2 | 3 | 4 | 5 | 6 | 7 | 8 | 9 | 10 |
|---|---|---|---|---|---|---|---|---|---|
| (c) | (a) | (d) | (d) | (c) | (a) | (d) | (a) | (d) | (d) |
| **11** | **12** | | | | | | | | |
| (c) | (d) | | | | | | | | |

# Mental Retardation and Educational Adaptation

## MEANING OF MENTAL RETARDATION

Children who have a condition of incomplete or less than normal mental development so that they are unable to adjust to day to day living in a normally efficient, useful, productive and harmonious manner are called mentally retarded. They are, hence, in constant need or care, protection, supervision and help.

Thus, mental retardation is a serious disability. It creates a lot of learning problems before mentally retarded children. These learning problems create obstacle in other areas of life as well. Thus, total life activities are affected by mental retardation.

### Definition

1. **American Association on Mental Retardation (1992) :** Mental retardation refers to substantial limitations in present functioning. It is characterized by significantly sub average intellectual functioning existing concurrently with related limitations in two or more of the following adaptive skill areas:
   *(i)* Communication,
   *(ii)* Self care
   *(iii)* Home living
   *(iv)* Social skills
   *(v)* Community use
   *(vi)* Self direction
   *(vii)* Health and safety
   *(viii)* Functional academics
   *(ix)* Leisure and work.
   Mental retardation manifests before the age of 18."
2. **Tredgold (1937) :** It is a state of arrested or incomplete development of mind so severe that the patient is incapable of leading an independent life.
3. **Kidd (1941) :** It refers to significantly sub average intellectual functioning which manifests itself during the developmental period and is characterized by inadequacy in adaptive behaviour."

Thus, three conditions must be satisfied in order to designate a person mentally retarded:

I. Sub-normal intellectual functioning.
II. Severity to the level of incapability leading to an independent life.
III. Impairment of adaptive behaviour

### General characteristics of mentally retarded

On the basis of the definitions given above following common characteristics of mentally retarded children (less than 18 years of age) can be derived:

1. **Limited functioning :** Their level of functioning is very limited. They have difficulty not only in learning but also doing routine life job due to significant loss of conceptual, practical and social intelligence.
2. **Sub average intellectual functioning :** Their intellectual functioning is less than average (below 80 IQ) on an intelligence test. This is the fundamental criterion of diagnosing a mentally retarded child.
3. **Poor performance level :** If someone falls short in his performance of certain tasks from the performance of the majority of children of his own age, he is said to have low mental age or sub-normal intellectual functioning. For example, If eight years old child performs equal to the child of 6 years, his IQ will be (Mental Age/Chronological age × 100) or (6/8) × 100=75
4. **Slow acquisition of skills :** Academic (content related) and non academic (action related) both

types of skills are acquired by them at a very slow rate.

5. **Low level of adaptive skills. :** They are not only slow in acquiring skills but they are always poor in adaptive skills also.
6. **Early manifestations :** Mental retardation manifests itself before the age of 18. From this perspective, mental retardation is viewed as a disorder of the life period characterized by the slow rate of development.

## Identification (Diagnosis) of mental retardation

For early detection of mental retardation of a child, the parents and the teacher refer the cases to child guidance centres so that their mental level may be ascertained and they may be classified for the purpose of placement (education and training).

Following symptoms will help the teacher and the parents to decide whether the child should be sent to child study centres for screening or not. Screening test results must be interpreted and matched in terms of following clinical diagnostic symptoms.

1. **Social adjustment criterion :** If a person is functioning adequately in all socio-economic conditions as compared to his peers or age mates, there is no need of sending the person to child guidance centres (CGC) for proper screening. Mentally retarded person will surely exhibit adjustment problem in social situations.
2. **Learning ability criterion :** Failure in educational endeavours or low level of general aptitude is another criterion of mental retardation but effects of socio-economic and physical factors should also be taken into account because poor academic achievement is caused due to these factors also.
3. **Development criterion :** The developmental history of the suspected child should also be taken into account, e.g., when the child began to sit, crawl, stand, walk and talk, whether it is normal or not. Delayed development is generally seen in mentally retarded children so, retardation in these areas is certainly helpful in diagnosing the child.
4. **Academic achievement criterion :** These children are generally very slow in academic achievement due to low level of retention power and understanding ability. When they constantly perform poorly in content related skills despite repeated remedial measures adopted by the teachers, they are suspected to be mentally retarded.
5. **Size of the family criterion :** Larger the size of the family, lower will be the IQ scores of the family. Hence, it should also be taken into consideration while taking a decision of M.R.
6. **Medical examination :** It is generally done by experts in the field in CGCs.

   Important physical symptoms of mentally retarded children are given below :

   I. He has lips fairly apart with his tongue visible in between the teeth with saliva.
   II. He has a vacant look and a clumsy gait.
   III. He has flattered skull, stanting eyes and broad nose.
   IV. He has unusually large heads.
7. **Proper screening :** After identifying all the above symptoms, suspected mentally retarded children are properly screened by using different tests.

   The description of some of these tests are given below :

(a) **Siguin Form Board Test :** This form board test was developed by Seguin a French physician in 1907 to identify and screen mentally retarded children. Here ten boards of different sizes are kept in different shelves of respective sizes in a tray. These boards are taken out of the tray at the time of testing. Then testee is asked to put these boards in the tray again in the same sequence as it was before in as less time as possible. This process is repeated three times and least time taking effort is taken for the purpose of scoring.

(b) **Developmental Screening Test :** This test is used to measure the mental development of children from the age of 3 months to 15 years. Here different types of activities are given to children according to their ages to do. Mental development of the child is calculated on the basis of performance on these activities. Children and their parents and relatives are also interviewed here to gather some more informations about the child.

(c) **General Mental Ability Test** : This test was developed by RP Srivastava and Kiran Saxena in 1985. Verbal and non-verbal both types of items have been included here. Both these sections have 50 items each. These sections have further been divided into five sub sections namely, analogy, classification, number series, reasoning problems and absurdities. Each item has four multiple choice responses out of which only one option is correct.

Time allotted for verbal and non-verbal items is 15 minutes and 10 minutes respectively. One mark is given for every correct response and thus a child can score maximum 100 marks. This test can be administered in individual and group situations both.

## Purpose of diagnosing mental retardation

Diagnosis of mental retardation serves the following purposes:

1. It provides an estimate of the individual's present level of functioning in terms of the test performance, social adjustment and so on.
2. It provides information regarding the cause of the individual's inadequacies.
3. It helps us to provide them proper care and treatment.
4. It provides some predictions of the probable outcomes in future.
5. It helps us to take decision regarding their placement in proper special educational programmes.

## Mental retardation and age

Incidence of mental retardation rises with the increasing age, reaches at its peak at about 14-18 years and then drops off sharply.

## Causes of mental retardation

Underlying causes of mental retardation can be divided into two categories :

(A) Endogenous causes
(B) Exogenous causes

### (A) Endogenous causes

Endogenous literally means originating within the body of the organism, and should refer to those forms of mental retardation that are genetically determined. Heredity is the primary casual factor here. Important genetic factors active to cause mental retardation are given below :

1. **Action of dominant gene** : The transmission of defective dominant gene from one generation to the next is very rare but in some cases some of these conditions may occur in mild form in one generation or in certain members of the family of that generation and in more severe form in another generation or in other members of the same family.
2. **Action of recessive gene** : Such defective children typically come of normal parents. This defect occurs due to child's receiving two similar recessive genes one from each parent.

### (B) Exogenous causes

They are also known as secondary, acquired or environmental causes. Some of these causes of mental retardation are given below :

(a) **Prenatal causes :** They work before the birth of the child, and are related to pregnant mothers. Important prenatal causes of mental retardation are as follows:

1. *Physical trauma :* Unsuccessful attempt at trauma and accident to pregnant mother so injure the fetus as to lower the child's mental level.
2. *Nutrition :* Malnutrition during the period of pregnancy may lower mental level of the child.
3. *Infectious diseases :* Infectious diseases of the mother during pregnancy may affect physical and mental development of the fetus and lower mental ability of the child.
4. *Blood incompatibility :* Incompatibility between maternal and fetal blood may cause the child severely jaundiced and mental deficiency is a possible accompaniment.
5. *Radioactivity :* Radiation may affect the germ cells in three ways.
   - They may be killed.
   - Their chromosomes maybe broken up.
   - They may be mutated.

All these changes may lower mental ability of the child.

6. *Toxic agents :* Toxins such as lead, nicotine, and morphine affect the developing embryo and lower the mental level of off springs.
7. *Consumption of drugs and alcohols :* Consumption of wine, LSD, heroine etc., by the mother during pregnancy is also very fatal for the fetus development and it may cause permanent mental retardation of the child after birth.

(b) **Perinatal (natal) causes :** These causes are associated with the delivery of the child. Important likely causes of mental retardation are as follows:

1. *Pre-mature-birth :* Studies have shown that a large number of people born pre-maturely are mentally retarded. The brain structure of the premature infant is more fragile and thus it can be very easily damaged.
2. *Traumatic Birth injuries :* It is estimated that birth injuries are responsible for 1.5% of the total mental retardation in western countries.
3. *Delivery Complications :* If complications have emerged during the period of delivery, it may cause mental retardation to some extent.

(c) **Post-natal causes :** Important post natal causes of mental retardation are given below :

1. *Brain injury :* Traumatic brain injury from gun shot, wounds or fall is a rare cause of mental retardation.
2. *Infections :* Brain infection causes permanent brain damage or mental retardation. They include encephalitis of various types, meningitis, hydrocephally and the like infections.
3. *Severe malnutrition :* Deficiency in any particular nutrient like vitamins or minerals causes deficiency diseases which may cause mental retardation in the long run.
4. *General health :* Mental and physical health are most of the time found associated though mental retardation due to poor physical health is not permanent. Heavy mental shock may also cause mental deficiency temporarily. However, good physical health does not necessarily mean good mental health.
5. *Cultural factors :* Low IQ does not always mean low level of intelligence. It is because intellectual level is influenced by the child's cultural background. If an intelligence test includes items representing a particular culture, children alien to that culture are not supposed to perform well on this test of intelligence and hence their IQ level will be low.
6. *Home and family background :* It also affects mental level and intellectual power but so far as mental retardation is concerned, its role is very limited.
7. *Social deprivation :* When a child is deprived of social environment for a very long period of time he is likely to become mentally retarded.

## Methods of Identification of mentally retarded children

Different criteria are used to classify mentally retarded into different categories. These criteria are given below:

1. **Normal distribution criterion :** In a normally distributed population, mentally retarded population is found beyond 2SD from the mean, i.e., about 2% of the population is generally found mentally retarded. If this population is tested on intelligence test, their IQ will be less than 90.
2. **IQ criterion :** American Association of Mental Deficiency has classified mentally retarded children on the basis of their IQ scores. Several other educationists have also classified them on this basis. Four broad categories of mentally retarded children are given below:
   (*a*) Border line cases or dullers : (IQ = 70-90)
   (*b*) Morons or feeble minded (IQ = 50-70)
   (*c*) Imbeciles ( IQ = 25-50)
   (*d*) Idiots (IQ less than 25)
   We will discuss all of them and their educational adaptation in detail in the later part of this chapter.
3. **Medical criterion :** Medical personnel and physician classify mentally retarded children on the basis of their physical/mental characteristics caused by a damage in the functioning of the

brain due to genetic or environmental reasons. Some of these categories are given below:

*(a)* Brain damaged child : It is a type of organic malfunctioning in the body which is caused by any serious disease or damage of the brain.

*(b)* Mongoloids : These slow learners are very peculiar in the physical characteristics and behaviour such as they are very humble and friendly, they are very poor in taking initiative, they are obstinate in behaviour and they are so simpleton in their behaviour that we call them as cow of the God. Mongols are moderately mentally retarded whose IQ ranges 50-70.

*(c)* Cretin child : Mental retardation in these children are caused due to any deformation in thyroid gland. They can be cured by the physician by correcting thyroid gland provided that they are identified in the early stage. They are similar to monogoloids in behaviour and characteristics.

*(d)* Phenylketonurin (PKU) : This problem is caused due to metabolic disturbances but its incidence is very rare. When body fails to metabolise phelinylenin protein, a toxic material reaches the brain and enters it through blood circulation and brain cells are damaged resulting in mental retardation.

*(e)* Microcephally and hydrocephally : The head becomes short in microcephally and large in hydrocephally, as a result cerebro spinal fluid which is responsible for mental action stops causing mental retardation permanently.

*(f)* Cerebral palsy : It is a type of disease which causes uncontrolled action of some muscles and mental retardation is caused due to inadjustability of muscles.

4. **Social deprivation criteria :** Mental retardation is also caused when a person is deprived of social environment and interaction for a long period of time. When these children comes to the environment they fail to adjust there which again increases their mental retardation.

## Types of mental retardation and Educational Adaptation

**(A) Borderline or dullers :** They are in between the morons and the normal. They generally have the IQ from 70-90 that is why they are called mildly retarded. Borderline cases and dullers are the same in physical and other characteristics but different in IQ level. Those whose IQ are between 80-90 fall into the group of dull normals and those who possess IQ between 70-80 are called borderline cases. They are identified by administering standardized intelligence test Developmental scale is also used for the identification of these children. It is because

- They are younger than their age.
- They are slow in demonstrating initiative.
- They are poor in thinking and planning.

In every population they are about one fifth of the total population as the study reveals.

They can not be termed as mentally retarded technically because they can do everything like the normals. Only their speed will be slow. They are, however, separated from the normal children from the point of view of placement. They are called educable mentally retarded (EMR).

## Characteristics of borderline or dullers

1. **Physical features :** These people possess no special characteristics nor do they vary in physical appearance in any way that can be used for the purpose of identifying these children. It is because physical and intellectual abilities do not have high degree of correlation in this case.
2. **Level of social expectancy :** It tends to be high in these children. They try to equate themselves with the normals. If they are not identified in the schools early, they will become problematic in future.
3. **Dullness and Pseudo-dullness :** Dullness does not here mean that the child is without life or spirit. They may be quite alert, self confident and active in schools, family and in the neighbourhood. Their verbal fluency may also be very high.

   True picture of these children is revealed only when we administer intelligence test to them. But poor performance on intelligence test does not always mean low intellectual ability. It may be due to emotional problems like anxiety, hypertensin etc. It is technically called pseudo-dullness. Which is actually dullness for no reason.

4. **Social behaviour :** They are more easily likely to be delinquent than the normal children as they have less capacity to understand the consequences of their actions. They may be faithful friends and trusted servants. They may show honesty in their job if they are not tempted. If they are put to a job which does not absorb their mind fully, they may become problematic for the family and the society. In spite of these none of them will be untrustworthy, lazy, uncooperative, hostile and vindictive. These characteristics affect them in the same way as they affect the normals.
5. **School Performance :** They tend to be uninterested in school and school works. As they become tired they get discouraged. When they fail in their attempts, they devalue themselves and regard themselves as failures. They can, however, be expected to be master of reading, writing and arithmetic but it is very difficult for them to learn those abstract concepts and materials that are too far from their real life situations.

## Factors causing low level of intelligence

1. **Family as a function of retardation :** Larger the family, i.e., the number of children in the family, lower will be the mean and medium scores of IQ of the child. So, size of the family should also be taken into consideration while taking a decision regarding mental retardation on the basis of IQ scores. Socio-economic background of the family also affects intelligence. The reason is that intelligence test is highly verbalised and culturally dominated. Similarly, children belonging to low income families have also been found poor on intelligence tests. It is because these families do not give much importance to educational achievement or academic excellence. Their apathy to school activities may lower their intellectual abilities.
2. **Nature of occupation and mental retardation:** These children are only slightly less than the normal children in intelligence and deviate only a little in behaviour with reference to normals but this slight deviance may lead to poor performance in academic fields. As a result of this they will not be able to get good jobs. They can not get those jobs which require more academic and professional skills and training. These factors will again lower their socio-economic status and hence intelligence.
   In short border line cases and dullers may be characterized as
   I. Lower IQ level resulting in lower educational level.
   II. Lower educational level leads to lower occupational level.
   III. Lower occupational level means lower socio-economic status.
   IV. Low socio-economic status again leads to low level of intelligence and thus vicious circle of poor intelligence continues unabated. Backward communities in India like SCs, STs, OBCs and Muslims suffer from the same vicious circle of low intellectual abilities. If special protection is not given to these sections of the society, significant social change will not be possible.
3. **Level of aspiration :** Level of aspiration is found lower in these children, as it is directly related to the concept of Self which is very limited in these children. Conversely, if level of aspiration is low, performance on intelligence as well as achievement test will also be low.
4. **Role of schooling :** Proper schooling positively affects the intellectual abilities. If schooling facilities are not properly available to a normal child, he may become duller in the long run.

## Educational Adaptation of Mildly Mentally Retarded

1. **Aims of education :** Aims of education for these children are almost similar to the normals because borderline cases have everything except a slightly minor lack in their mental abilities which can be compensated by special care and attention. However, they are expected to excel more in technical fields rather than in academics. So, it is

better to enroll them in technical or semi professional courses just after high school.

2. **Administrative arrangement:** They have some difficulty only in adjustment with the normal people so special schools or special classes may be arranged for them. However, if they remain in regular schools, attend regular classes plus partially integrated classes (some periods in regular classes and some periods in special classes) and some extra help and special attention are also provided to them, it is far better for them. This arrangement will help them more adjust with the normal people of the society.

3. **Special help provided to them:**
   *(i)* Partially integrated classes.
   *(ii)* Itinerant services like regular counseling, periodic excursion and camping.
   *(iii)* Extra curricular activities.
   *(iv)* Remedial teaching.
   *(v)* Regular checking of assignment
   *(vi)* Behaviour therapy by the psychologist.
   *(vii)* Continuous evaluation.

4. **Curriculum:** No modification in the curriculum is needed for them because they can study each and every subject but somewhat slower speed than the normals. Their academic achievement will also be lower than the average. They need only special help. They should be motivated and encouraged even if they perform poorly or fail in the class.

   They are likely to excel more in non academic, technical and semi professional subjects than the academic subjects because these subjects involve activity more than thinking process. Therefore, after high school, they should be admitted in such courses.

5. **Teaching of Special Skills :**
   I. They generally have adjustment difficulties, so, special concession must be given to them by the society. Their behaviour should be tolerated to some extent and changed by using behaviour therapy.
   II. Activity dominated skills like electric fitting, motor repairing, radio or electronic equipment repairing, decoration skills etc. may also be taught to them.

6. **Adaptive methods of instruction :** Modification in the method of teaching is needed to bring these mentally retarded children to normal. A special teacher can play following roles in this regard:

**(A) Improving functional academic skills :** Mildly or moderately mentally retarded children respond to instructional strategies almost in the same way as other normal students do. They only require more time to achieve mastery or require special instructional procedure to generalize what they have learned in the class or resource rooms. An effective regular or special teacher can improve their functional academic skills in the following ways.

I. They generally avoid tasks given to them. In order to reduce this habit random check and regular monitoring of behaviour are necessary. Reward and punishment techniques should also be used to increase incidence of wanted behaviour.

II. Since these students are a little low at their confidence level, products as well as the processes both should be rewarded. They should be helped how to start a task and how to complete it in the allotted time .

III. In order to improve their functional reading, they should be given chance to practise those materials which they already know and use in their daily life. The names of these materials, objects and persons should be written by them in a drilling manner. It will help them develop a clear concept of these materials and objects.

Thus, teaching has to be related to daily life situations of students.

IV. Once the student has learnt a list of functional words, he should be given chance to apply those words in his real life situations on his own.

V. In order to improve their functional writing, activities of daily living should be used, i.e., listing daily activities, noting down home and class works, writing the cramed materials on paper, writing messages received from others and communicating messages to others.

VI. In order to improve arithmetic and computational skills, they should be given more and more questions for drilling. Computers should also be provided to them to do some practice of geometry and algebra through the programmes fed in computers.

VII. In order to improve functional mathematics, problems related to real life situations should be given to them to solve.

VIII. When the teacher starts teaching any new skill, he should give related examples first.

IX. Modification in tests and evaluation procedures is also necessary to improve general learning. For example, short test at frequent intervals is preferable to long tests of annual or half yearly nature. Similarly, more objective type questions should be included in the test than few essay type questions.

X. Complex skills should be taught to them only after splitting them into parts and each part should have to be followed by definite steps.

Thus, we see that the focus of attention of the teacher is always on improving functional skills of students.

**(B) Improving school adaptive behaviour :** Social skills, self direction, self care, health and safety are the important school adaptive behaviours where intervention is especially needed. The teacher will address these areas in the class room in the following manner:

**I. Social skills:** Students should be engaged in those plays and activities which require maximum display of social skills and wanted behaviour of children should be rewarded regularly by the teacher.

**II. Reduction of social isolation:** They should be given opportunity to select those students as friends who have common interests and habits in order to share experiences with them.

**III. Improvement of self direction skill :** They should be given chance to discuss the problems to solve them. Many alternative solutions will help them to improve their self direction skills.

**IV. Improvement of self care, health and safety skills:** Video cassettes showing wrestlers fighting in the ring and athletes performing on the tracks and marks may be used for this purpose. TV can also serve this purpose. These demonstrations will motivate them to take care of their health.

**(B) Morons or feeble minded :** Those educationally and socially inadequate persons whose IQ s range between 50-70 i.e. they are moderately mentally retarded, come under this category. They are not custodial cases and a large number of them can study even in regular classes and in regular schools meant for the normals. They are similar to borderline cases and dullers in some ways but different in many ways. So, same teaching strategies are adopted for them as was suitable to borderline cases but placement and administrative arrangement for them differ. They are also called trainable mentally retarded (TMR).

## Characteristics of morons

**1. Physical health and growth :** Their physical growth is slow and they are also slow in thinking planning, initiative and reasoning. Some of the high grade morons very much look like the normals. They may be of pleasant nature and good looking.

Their health is considerably below that of the normals. Tuberculosis, diseases of the central nervous system, pulmonary and infectious diseases etc. are the common diseases that they are likely to suffer from. Due to these reasons their life expectancy is also found to be very low. Low health and poor physical development is also caused due to poor sanitary and hygienic conditions at home and in the environment.

**2. Social behaviour and personal adjustment :** They generally come from semi skilled or unskilled fathers who have low level of income and acquired intelligence. As a result, they are rejected by the society in general. Rejection by the community is accompanied by the familial rejection, i.e., they are neglected by the family also. All these factors have a crippling effect on the mental development of the child.

When child is rejected by the family and the society, he gets frustrated and becomes tense which further makes him poor in academic and vocational pursuits too. As a result, he is again rejected and scolded and when he is dejected and discouraged by the situation, he ceases efforts. Since, he is intellectually less capable of dealing these problems, he becomes more backward socially and educationally. The ground is thus paved for the development of autistic behaviour.

**(Autism is a symptom indicating the child to establish an unsatisfactory relation with his environment)**

Lastly, he has strong sex desires and drives but finds no girl friend due to his defects. This leads him to use animals or male children for sexual gratification.

All these conditions compel him to react in two ways :

I. He will develop a low self concept and devalue himself.

II. He will become hostile and aggressive towards the outer world. In order to remove his anxieties and cope with his frustration, he will manifest aggressive behaviour against the environment, social and physical.

3. **Cognitive abilities :** Due to low level of intelligence they are very poor in thinking, planning, synthesis and evaluation. They reach to the mental maturity level at a very very slow rate. Since they lack maturity, they can not solve complex cognitive problems.

   Memory, power of generalization and conceptualization, imaginative power and language abilities, all these are very poor in these children.

4. **Job adjustment :** Most of them can be expected to get a good job and earn a living, but their job will be restricted to semi skilled or unskilled occupations. Mentally retarded women and girls can do almost all household works like cooking, cleaning, decorating etc, reasonably well. Proper assistance is, however, needed to help them get job according to their capacity and interest. So, they need job protection from the society.

5. **Delinquency :** Moderate level of mental retardation is always associated with crime and delinquency. Women are found engaged in sex crimes and prostitution. Men also do these crimes due to higher level of sex urge. Other crimes that morons are indulged in are taught to them by the treatment meted out to them by the society. In order to save them from unsocial conditions, early identification is a must which is generally done when they are actually victimized. They are ego centric and develop bizarre cause and effect relationship.

6. **Educability :** They are not educable upto the degree of normal children any how due to their low level of intelligence and they are found backward by at least two or three years to the normals in the classes of their study. Their grasping power of the academic content is so low that they can educate others only partially, what they were educated. Their education is not expected to exceed 10+2 and in most of the cases upto tenth. Besides, they have restricted vocabulary, are inadequate in the use of abstract terms and concepts, low in test performance and deficient in quantitative thinking.

## Educational adaptation of moderately retarded

1. **Placement :** They are deviated from the normals to such an extent that they can not be educated properly in regular classes. They can be educated and trained only in special classes, or special schools exclusively meant for them.
2. **Skills based curriculum :** They approach to normals in sensory acuity and motor ability more than they do in academic persuits so, curriculum should be based on motor abilities and demanding sensory acuities. They can excel in motor abilities even more than normals. Thus, mechanical and vocational education is most suitable for them.
3. **Academic persuits :** Morons are expected to acquire academic skills ranging from grade IIIrd to grade Xth but they will reach that level at a

later period than the normals due to repeated failures and slow rate. Thus, they can obtain 7th grade education in 10 to 11 years.

4. **Academic curriculum :** At primary level, much of the school work is pre-academic. At junior level, instruction is basically provided in basic social and vocational skill areas. At secondary level, they are partially integrated with the regular students (if they have reached that level) Here more academic subjects like English, social studies, science and mathematics are taught in special classes and less academic subjects like music, arts, economics, physical education etc. are taught in regular classes. Much emphasis is given on preparing the child for life and work. Lastly, post school education is concentrated to job training only.
5. **Social adjustment and training :** Socially acceptable attitude are tried to develop in them by using social skill training and behaviour therapy. They are especially taught to face the realities of life and cope with its difficulties.
6. **Physical training :** They are not much less than normals in physical areas of life, so, such training should be started for them from an early age. It should be made a regular part of the curriculum. This type of training is a must for them because their job will mainly be restricted to those areas which involve physical labour, ie., motor abilities. Type writing, tailoring, tannery works, driving etc. are most suitable education for them.
7. **Aims of Education :**
   - Adequate social development
   - Academic achievement to the ability level.
   - Inculcation of adaptive social skills.
   - Development of vocational skills..
   - Teaching of self help skills, health and safety training, teaching of emotional control.

## Autistics—The largest group of moron category

They are also moderately mentally retarded children who fail to learn to communicate or develop social relationship in usual ways. They tend to develop anxiety (in childhood) when separated from their mothers. They do not play in normal or constructive manner. They tend to develop realistic and compulsion movements in adolescence.

**(C) Imbeciles :** Mongolism constitutes the largest category here. They are severely mentally retarded. Their IQ ranges in between 25-50. They have mental deficiency to the extent that they can not manage themselves properly. Though they can be trained to care for their own bodily needs, yet they are not supposed to be trained in complex life skills.

They can learn to do some simple jobs under supervision but they can never be self supporting. They would always need at least some care and control at home as well as in the institutions throughout life. In spite of these, they can be taught some language and some habitual behaviour.

No universally acceptable definition is available regarding these severely mentally retarded children, yet we feel convenient to give a practical definition of imbeciles given by Association of Persons with Severe Handicaps (USA 1991).

These people include individuals of all ages who require extensive ongoing support in more than one major life activity in order to participate in integrated community settings and to enjoy a quality of life that is available to citizens with fewer or no disabilities. Support may be required for life activities, such as mobility, communication, self care, and learning as necessary for independent living, employment and self sufficiency."

## Characteristics of Imbeciles

1. **Physical growth and development :**
   - Learning to sit up is often delayed upto 18 months.
   - Walking and talking are delayed upto 4 years.
   - Similar delay is also noticed in other areas of life such as feeding, dressing and washing.
   - Speech is delayed by at least three years and speaking power is always low.
   - Lack of motor coordination is a general problem exhibited in these children.
2. **Physical characteristics :**
   - Flattered skull.
   - Abnormally upturned nostrils caused by undeveloped nasal bones.
   - Abnormal toe spacing.
   - Disproportionate shortness of the fifth finger.

- Fifth finger curves inward.
- Fifth finger has only one crease instead of two.
- Short and squared hands.
- Abnormally simplified ears.
- Epicanthic fold at the inner corner of the eye.
- Abnormal size of head.

3. **Social and emotional characteristics :**
   - Withdrawn
   - Dependent in behaviour.
   - Low communication ability due to low mobility and withdrawing nature.
   - Unable to deal with people, without supervision and control.
   - Hyper tension and anxiety due to harsh behaviour meted out to them by the people.
   - Social relations restricted to the family and close relatives.

## Educational adaptation and care of imbeciles

1. **Aims and objectives of education (training) :** They are the dependent or semi-independent individuals throughout their lives. So, objectives of education for these children are restricted to only few areas given below:
   - To develop self help skills.
   - To promote socialization.
   - To teach elementary oral language.
2. **Adapted curriculum :** Physical and mental health centred content, stressing upon nutrition, cleanliness, etc.
   - Safety teaching and education of first aid.
   - Skills of listening, observing, speaking and writing.
   - Home economics and sociology.
   - Local travel skills.
   - Passive and active recreation.
   - Games involving physical activities and muscles.
   - Inter-personal and group socialization skills.
   - Concept of money, value and management of material and time.
   - Habit of work and responsibility training.
   - Habit of judgement in ordinary matters.
3. **Teaching of functional skills :** Functional skills have real application in daily life at home as well as in the community. They should be taught to participate in these activities practically so that they may be able to interact with peers and age mates, to make independent decisions and to enjoy the environment independently.
4. **Areas of special instruction :** Four areas of instruction are considered critical for these children communication, self care, mobility and community living. They should be given chance to communicate the people orally in special manner and written communication should also be encouraged. Sign language, communication boards, symbol boards and electronic communication devices should be used here.

The development cf self care skills should begin in the early years of their lives. Self cure skills consist of feeding, dressing, toileting grooming, washing, bathing, brushing, hair combing, etc.

Mobility is essential not only for general health and comforts but also to participate in school and community activities. They should be especially trained to improve their mobility by organizing various social and games activities or by using physio-therapy.

Independent and successful community living requires mastery of basic vocational and recreational skills. They should be taught such skills which can help them get some jobs in future life, such as obeying instructions, completing ordinary habitual tasks, following rules and regulations etc. They should also be helped in not only finding a job but special assistance should be given to them in learning, performing and keeping jobs.

5. **Adaptive methods of instruction :** Special teaching approach is required to teach these children in special classes. A teacher has to follow the following steps in this regard.

Step I—Assessment of current level of functioning, i.e., what the child can do at present and what he is expected to do in future after training.

Step II—Defining the skills to be taught in behavioural terms, i.e., students will be able to do this and that after the training is over.

Step III—Arranging the conditions of learning, i.e., what sequence of steps will be used to teach the desired skills.

Step IV—Prompting and cueing the responses, i.e., what verbal or material messages will show and motivate the students what to do and in a better manner.

Step V—Reinforcing good responses, i.e., what feedback system will be used in special classes to maintain and improve the desired behaviour.

Step VI—Prompting generalization, i.e., what procedure and techniques will be used to help them apply the learnt skill in practical life situations.

Step VII—Evaluating performance, i.e., what procedure and methodology will be used to judge whether the learnt behaviour is a success for the students or not.

Since they can not be taught much by way of reading or writing, learning by doing and activity centred strategies are used for them. Some of the high grade imbeciles can do some manual works, such as they can cane the chairs, they can sweep the floor, they can water the plants, they can dig grounds, they can produce some simple articles like, mats, carpets etc. under supervision. So, these functional skills are especially stressed in special schools. Farming, gardening, repairing shoes or clothes and many other similar activities are not also uncommon to these children of higher intelligence hence, they should also be given stress in schools after identifying competent imbeciles.

6. **Placement :** Following principles must be followed while placing them in any special institutions:

   I. They should be placed in those schools which are close to the schools attended by the normal children.

   II. They should be placed in age appropriate schools.

   III. They should be placed in those schools and special classes where principal and teachers support their admission.

   IV. They should not be placed in those schools where a large number of children of other types of disabilities study.

   V. They can be placed in any of the following settings depending on the nature and degree of disability.

   - Residential schools.
   - Special day schools.
   - Special classes.
   - Sheltered workshops.

   VI. They will be slowly withdrawn from residential or fully intervened system of education and integrated to regular classes in normal schooling system. This is essential for teaching them four fundamental skills namely, **communication, self care, mobility and community living.**

**(D) Idiots :** They are the profoundly mentally retarded children. They are so prone to mental retardation that they can neither be educated nor trained. They possess IQ less than 25 when measured on an intelligence test. They are totally dependent and custodial cases either in institutions or at home. They can not even dress, wash, bathe, comb, brush and so on without help. They could bubble a few intelligible words with saliva dropping from their mouths. They have vacant looks and they are not supposed to respond to any question.

**Guidelines for mentally retarded parents:** Some suggestions for parents of mentally retarded children are given below :

**I.** Parents should accept the reality that they have a mentally retarded child.

**II.** They must also accept the reality that mentally retarded will never come to normal in his life whatsoever training or treatment is given to him. Only some improvement can be brought about in them through education and training.

**III.** After proper diagnosis, parents should not waste their time, money and energy to have the child cured.

**IV.** Parents should be given regular consoling and appeasement by psychologists and social workers.

**V.** They need not worry about the opinion or remarks of others. Such a problem can happen to anybody and anyone can have retarded child.

**VI.** They should not expect from their mentally retarded child more than their mental level.

**VII.** They should take the help of custodial institutions or sheltered workshops if it is needed.

## Prevention and treatment of mental retardation

The cause of mental retardation may be genetic and acquired both. As far as genetically caused retardation is concerned, they can not be treated at all. Retardation caused due to environmental factors can be cured but only to some extent by applying medicines or surgery.

Important preventive measures to avoide mentally retarded child are as follows :

I. Close relatives should not marry each other as much as possible. Recessive or dominant genes are mostly transferred to offsprings due to this reason, which are the main cause of mental retardation.

II. Pregnant mother should not consume wine or drugs during pregnancy or she should not smoke too much during this period.

III. Infectious diseases occurred during pregnancy should be treated as early as possible.

IV. If there is any blood abnormality either in the father or mother, it should be treated first before trying for an offspring.

V. Balanced diet and regular exercise during pregnancy is the key factor to avoid a handicapped child.

VI. Delivery or ceasarian should be conducted under the supervision of an experienced doctor and nurses.

VII. Parents should follow right path and the path of justice to avoid such children. This may be an important reason of mental retardation.

VIII. Proper care of the child in the early eight years period of his life.

## OBJECTIVE QUESTIONS

**1.** Which of the following conditions must be satisfied in order to designate a person mentally retarded?
   (*a*) Sub-normal intellectual functioning.
   (*b*) Very poor adaptive ability
   (*c*) Dependability on others
   (*d*) All of these

**2.** The best measure of identifying mildly mentally retarded is
   (*a*) Administration of standardized intelligence test.
   (*b*) Administration of behaviour test
   (*c*) Administration of adjustment test
   (*d*) A combination of all.

**3.** Physical trauma during pregnancy may cause
   (*a*) Mental retardation
   (*b*) Blindness
   (*c*) Deafness
   (*d*) All of these

**4.** All of the following may cause mental retardation except.
   (*a*) Blood incompatibility
   (*b*) Action of toxic agent
   (*c*) Radio-activity
   (*d*) None

**5.** Which of the following is an important postnatal cause of mental retardation ?
   (*a*) Brain injury
   (*b*) Infection
   (*c*) Severe malnutrition
   (*d*) All of these

**6.** Dullers do not differ from normal children in
   (*a*) Physical characteristics.
   (*b*) Level of social expectancy
   (*c*) Both of these
   (*d*) None of these

**7.** Which of the following things is not required for educating mildly mentally retarded children ?
   (*a*) Regular counseling
   (*b*) Remedial teaching
   (*c*) Modification in the curriculum
   (*d*) Regular evaluation.

**8.** Teaching of which of the following skills is not suitable to borderline cases?
   (*a*) Electric fitting
   (*b*) Repairing of electric or electronic equipments
   (*c*) Oratory skills
   (*d*) Activity based skills

**9.** IQ range of morons are in the range of
   (*a*) 60-90 (*b*) 50-75
   (*c*) 60-80 (*d*) 30-50

**10.** Morons are slow in
   (*a*) Physical growth
   (*b*) Thinking and planning
   (*c*) Taking initiative
   (*d*) All of these

**11.** Unsatisfactory relation of a mentally retarded child with the environment is technically called
   (*a*) Autism (*b*) Maladjustment

(*c*) Pseudo-dullness (*d*) None of these

**12.** All of the following are characteristics of morons except

(*a*) They are restricted to unskilled or semi skilled occupations.

(*b*) They are likely to be delinquent more easily.

(*c*) They have stronger sex drives than the normals

(*d*) They are educable upto normal level but at a slower rate

**13.** Which of the following modifications in the curriculum is needed for morons?

(*a*) Activity based curriculum

(*b*) Skill dominated curriculum

(*c*) Emphasis on social training

(*d*) All of these

**14.** Which of the following things can not be taught to Imbeciles ?

(*a*) Self help skills

(*b*) Unskilled job to be performed under supervision

(*c*) Writing skills

(*d*) Social skills

## ANSWERS

| 1 | 2 | 3 | 4 | 5 | 6 | 7 | 8 | 9 | 10 |
|---|---|---|---|---|---|---|---|---|---|
| (*d*) | (*d*) | (*d*) | (*d*) | (*d*) | (*c*) | (*c*) | (*c*) | (*b*) | (*d*) |
| 11 | 12 | 13 | 14 | | | | | | |
| (*a*) | (*d*) | (*d*) | (*c*) | | | | | | |

# Creativity and Educational Adaptation

## MEANING OF CREATIVITY

Creativity is the unique aspect of intelligence which is generally seen in children above average in intelligence. Creativity is the capacity of a person to produce composition, products or ideas of any sort which are novel and unique and was previously unknown to the producer. It can be imaginative activity or thought synthesis when the product is not a mere summation. It may involve the formulating patterns and combination of information derived from past experiences and transplanting of old relationship to new situation.

Creative products must be purposeful or goal directed not mere idle fantasy, although it need not have immediate practical application or be a perfect product. It may take the form of artistic, literary or scientific production and may be procedural and methodological nature.

—(**Drevdale** 1956)

## Definitions of Creativity

Definitions of creativity are many and vary according to the particular emphasis given to the concept. The general definitions of creativity involve novelty or uniqueness of the products or thoughts. A product may be a creative one if it is novel to the individual involved provided that it is his own creation. It need be neither unique nor useful. Its social recognition or cultural impact may be zero. But those psychologists who use a cultural frame reference insist that product must be novel to the individual as well as to the society and it must be useful also.

Several definitions of creativity are given below:

1. **Ausubel :** Creativity refers to rare and unique talent in a particular field of endeavour ....Creative achievement reflects a rare capacity for developing insights, sensivities, and appreciations of a circumscribed content area of intellectual or artistic activity.
2. **Torrance :** Creativity is a process of becoming sensitive to problems, gaps in knowing missing elements, identifying the difficulty, searching for solutions, making guesses, formulating hypotheses, testing and retesting these hypotheses and finally communicating the results.
3. **Guilford :** Divergent thinking process is associated with creativity and involves such thought processes as speculation, imagination and invention. Originality, fluency and flexibility are the three important constituent of creativity.
4. **Trafinger :** Creativity is one of the most complex of human functions, it is un-realistic to expect that there ever will be a single, easily administered, simply scored test booklet that education can use to decide who is at least one standard deviation above other students in creativity.

### Characteristic/Features of Creativity or Factors Involved in Creativity or Process of Creativity

On the basis of the meaning and definitions of creativity, given above we see that following factors are involved in the process of creativity.

1. **Originality :** It has three alterative dimensions, uncommonness, remoteness and cleverness. Uncommonness is meant something infrequently produced by the individual, i.e., uniqueness. What ever thoughts or materials are produced by him are very rare and unknown to him as well as to others.

Remoteness of an associations is defined as the ability to make remote or indirect associations that are not made frequently by the individual. In Hindi it is known as "Door ki Kaudi Lana". Witty peoples have this ability.

Cleverness is the ability to produce responses that are rated above by judges i.e., responses full of wisdom and vision.

2. **Thought process :** Creative thought process consists of divergent as well as convergent thinking.

   Divergent thinking is required when one is confronted with a problem that has many possible solutions, i.e., writing an essay or doing some experiments in the laboratory. With this type of thinking one does not think on a beaten track. He rather diverges his thought process in all directions.

   Convergent thinking is involved in situations when the production of one correct response is required, i.e., multiple choice test or doing mathematical sums. In order to reach to convergent thinking one has to go through the process of divergent thinking. For example, in a sentence completion test convergent thinking is actually required but when one reads the statement, a large humber of solutions come to his mind. This is divergent thinking. He then tries out and rejects all until he reaches to only one solution which seems to be the best. This is convergent thinking. In this way, the creative process completes.

3. **Fluency :** When during a thought process, one is not hampered in the middle, it is called fluency. Original ideas are presented quickly here and no delay is seen. The individual is able to produce a new material in the least possible time. Composing poetry at the spot on a topic running is a good example of fluency.

4. **Flexibility :** In creativity, ideas and all its associations are not rigid in nature. They are flexible to the extent it is needed. Thus, anybody can manipulate them in as many ways as possible. For example, a brick can be used in many ways such as making a house or shrime, throwing it on a dog or on the enemy and so on.

5. **Problem Solving :** Creativity comes to light when society faces some particular kinds of problems. These problems are solved with the help of creative thinking and imagination. If an idea is not able to solve a problem, it is not creative one.

6. **Usefulness :** Every creative idea or product should have some purpose to serve and should be useful to at least a significant part of the society. If one is criticizing the religious books and hurting the sentiments of people in general, it is not a creative thinking. It is only a destructive idea which will serve no purpose. Creativity is always goal directed.

## Measurement of Creativity

Creativity is measured on the six lines given above, i.e., originality, thought process, fluency, flexibility, problem solving and usefulness. The person who scores high on all these six lines is said to be creative. Some important creativity tests are given below :

1. **Torrance Test of Creativity (1959 & 1962) :** The test consists of two sub tests, verbal and figural.

   The verbal section includes (i) ask and guess (ii) Product improvement (iii) Unusual uses.

   In the ask and guess questions the examinee is given a picture and asked what has led to the scenes in the picture and what might happen next.

   In the product improvement part, the examinee is given the picture of a toy and asked to suggest changes in the toy, so as to make it more fun for playing.

   In the third section, the examinee is asked to give as many unusual uses as he can of a common objects.

   The figural subtest requires the examinee to draw a picture representing an object and to tell an interesting and an exciting story associated with the picture.

   Torrance test can be administered to small children as well as adults. On the basis of this test 3 marks are given to the examinee one for originality, fluency and flexibility each for all correct responses. No norms of this test is available so far so, examinee's total scores are evaluated against a set of common criteria for creative achievement.

2. **Remote Association Test (RAT) :** This test was developed by Mednick and Mednick in 1971. This test is meant for adolescents and consists of 40 items. In each item of the test the examinee is given three words and asked to give the fourth word which is related to each of these words. These three words are thought to indicate remote association clusters and the fourth word is a mediating link for all three words. One minute time is given to the examinee to give answers of each item and thus the entire test takes 40 minutes time to complete.
3. **Getzels and Jackson's Test (1962) :** These two psychologists used different measures of creativity in their research. They are given below:

(a) **Word Association Test :** Here students are required to give as many definitions as possible of a fairly common word. The marks of the examinees depend on the absolute number of definitions and the number of different categories into which these definitions can be classified.

(b) **Things Test :** This is very much similar to the test used by Guilford while testing cognitive abilities. The subject is required to give as many uses as he can of a common object such as bricks and he is scored on the basis of number, originality and fluency of responses.

(c) **Hidden Shapes Test :** Here the subject is shown a card with a simple geometric figure on it and he is required to find that figure which is hidden in a more complex form or pattern. The score is allotted on the basis of originality, and flexibility of response.

(d) **Fabbles Test :** Here the subject is provided with short fables from which the last line is missing in each fable. He is then required to compose three different endings for each fable- a moralistic, a sad and a humorous one. Scoring is done on the basis of number, appropriateness and originality of responses.

(e) **Make up problems :** Here the subject is given a number of complex paragraphs containing so many numerical statements and then he is asked to make up as many mathematical problems as he can with the help of the information given in the para. The score of the subject depends on the number, appropriateness and complexity of the problems given by him.

## Procedure for constructing creativity tests

Construction of creativity test is simple in the sense that we can adopt any verbal and non-verbal technique to test originality, fluency flexibility and problem solving abilities. Creative products or thoughts need not be useful to the society according to many experts in the field. Problem here actually lies in scoring of test items. Following steps are followed in constructing a creative test:

**Step I :** We first of all, define creativity in behavioural term, i.e., what dimensions of creativity we will cover by our test, originality fluency flexibility, usefulness etc.

**Step II :** Problems to be assigned to the students are classified and selected. Problems are of two types- presented and discovered. Only discovered problems related to unknown situations are included in the test.

**Step III :** A problem may have different solutions. Only those solutions are demanded which are unique and useful. The students should not take much time in presenting solutions. Brain storming method is also used to test problem solving skills.

**Step IV :** Different types of test items are constructed to know the ability to discover the problems and its possible solutions. Getzels and Jackson have used five types of test items in their research. These items may be a guideline for a test maker.

**Step V :** This is the second last step which is related to scoring of test items. Items are scored on either three grounds originality, fluency and flexibility and one mark is given to each dimension, or on five dimensions originality, fluency, flexibility problems solving and usefulness and five marks are given to the examinee in all if he has given the answer correctly.

**Step VI :** Total scores of the examinee is compared with the average score of his group.

## Identification of creative individuals

It is a known fact that many young children who are creative will no longer be so in the adulthood and those who are not classified as creative children may turn into creative adults. It means that constancy of creative scores is not universal. However, in most of the cases we see that a young creative child is turned into a creative adult. So if creative traits of these children are identified in the early stage of life, it is possible to equip them with those experiences that will develop the creative potential among them.

Now the question arises how can we identify these creative children. Following method can be used here for the purpose:

1. **Nomination by peer groups, teachers and parents :** These people observe the activities of these children and so on the basis of their thought process and actions, they may nominate them to be creative.
2. **Self rating :** It can be used as a measure of creativity testing. But the results obtained by this method will not be very valid and reliable.
3. **Applying formal creativity :** This measure is more reliable and valid as compared to other measures. Creativity tests are administered to children and creative ones among the lot are identified on the basis of their scores obtained on the test.

## Important symptoms of creative adults

If we administer creativity tests to all the individuals, it will be a time consuming process. So creative individuals are isolated from the lot on the basis of their symptoms first and then they are formally tested by applying creativity tests. These symptoms are given below :

I. They are self sufficient of independent judgement, dedicated, introspective, ideationally productive and somewhat unconventional.

II. They score high in theoretical aesthetic values but low in social, religious and economic values.

III. They are turbulent and want to do something every time. Restlessness is always seen.

IV. They have openness to their feelings and emotions, have sensitive awareness to self and others and have a wide range of interest.

V. Creativity is a significant part of intelligence and all highly intelligent children are creative ones but vice-versa is not so much correct because creativity refers to certain specific dimensions of intelligence only.

VI. They possess emotional stability, ego strength, personal dominance, fearfulness of opinions and disciplined mind.

VII. They appear to be somewhat detached and distant in personal relations and prefer to deal with things rather than people, i.e., withdrawn in nature.

VIII. They are risk loving and enthusiastic people dedicated to the pursuit of their own ideas and tasks and somewhat sensitive to criticism.

IX. They are critical to others due to their non conventional nature and habits.

X. Artists, scientists and writers all are creative people but artists are more unconventional and less intelligent than scientists and writers.

XI. They have a high degree of aesthetic feeling, desire to excel, belief in themselves and are curious for distant goods.

XII. Creative adults may be destructive or delinquent in their behaviour.

XIII. They laugh at the sorrows of others.

## Symptoms of Creative Children

I. They score high on the strength of self image, ease of early recall, humour, availability of oedipal anxiety and uneven ego development.

II. They show a tendency towards unconventional responses and imaginative treatment of the materials and objects.

III. They are hyper sensitive and are independent in thinking.

IV. Highly creative boys have wild and silly ideas. They do not follow the beaten track and always choose new track for themselves.

V. They are playful and lack rigidity and relaxation.

VI. They are naughty and sometimes problematic for parents and teachers.

VII. Witty responses.

VIII. Restless and turbulent all the time.

## Educational Adaptation of Creative Children

They are deviant in many ways which may be a source of annoyance for a busy teacher in the class. And if this uniqueness of creative behaviour is not taken into account and they are rigorously dealt along with the normal children, it may be a source of tension for them.

Following modifications are made in the educational programme in order to make them fully adjustable in the school as well as the society and to develop their creative potentials to the fullest extent.

1. **Providing situations for the development and use of problem solving skills :** Brain storming method and heuristic method of teaching are used to develop their problem solving skills and divergent thinking. Children are not only given problems to solve but they are also asked to identify new problematic situations also.
2. **Reinforcement of creative achievement :** Torrance has suggested five ways by which a teacher can encourage and reinforce creative achievement.
   I. Asking unusual questions.
   II. Presenting unusual ideas
   III. Showing that their ideas are valuable
   IV. Giving credit for self initiated learning
   V. Providing opportunity to students to learn, think and discover.
3. **Psychological safety :** Acceptance of the individual is one of the important factors conducive to psychological safety. Creative children deviate from the conventional/cultural norms in ideation and overt behaviour both. This deviation should be recognised by the teacher and channellised properly and students should be made free in the pursuit of their path to educational goals, so that they may not experience much anxiety.
4. **Psychological freedom :** Freedom to explore and discover things is the main source of motivation to these children. Teacher should not ridicule and criticize their deviant behaviour in the class so that they may not feel guilty for their deviant actions. They should rather be rewarded and encouraged if they perform their task in a different and unconventional but somewhat correct manner. Their deviant behaviour must be tolerated by the teacher to the maximum level possible.
5. **Fostering flexibility :** Flexibility does not mean lawlessness or lack of values. But it implies a readiness to make change in behaviour to meet circumstances that has not been previously met satisfactorily. If creatives are weak in some areas, they should be given chance to excel in other areas to compensate the weak areas. They work in those areas more for which they are most capable of. For example, if a creative student is weak in geography due to his creative potential in science, then he should be given opportunity to excel in science to compensate the weaknesses of geography due to his creative potential in science.
6. **Time Flexibility :** Creative work sometimes needs preparation, formulation and revision. So, children should be given enough time to produce their work and to prove their strength of mind. Moderately creative children generally takes much time to produce creative thoughts and products. Creative potential will not come out if time is short for the students.

## Creativity and other related traits

1. **Creativity and Intelligence :** Positive correlation has been found between intelligence and creativity. But some psychologists are of the view that a creative person will not necessarily be an intelligent one. It is because creativity is only a part of intelligence. However, since creativity requires divergent thinking, which is an important ingredicnt of intelligence, an intelligence person will surely be creative
2. **Creativity and scholastic achievement :** Generally, positive correlation is found between creativity and scholastic achievement but negative correlation is also seen especially when creativity is restricted to only a particular area of experiences. In that case child may achieve high in that area (subject) in which he is creative but his achievement will be low in other subjects, e.g., he may achieve high in literature due to his creative potential of writing poems, stories or essays.
3. **Creativity and values :** Study shows that social, economic and aesthetic values are found in creative children but religious or moral values are rarely seen in creative people because they are generally against the norms and traditions prevailing in the society. That is why they feel pleasure to criticize religion. Examples of Tasleema Nasreen and Rushdi can be cited here.

# OBJECTIVE QUESTIONS

**1.** Creative products or ideas are
(*a*) Novel and unique (previously unknown)
(*b*) Constructive or destructive
(*c*) Flexible to be remanipulated
(*d*) All of these

**2.** Originality in creativity refers to
(*a*) Uncommonness
(*b*) Remoteness
(*c*) Cleverness
(*d*) All of these

**3.** A person can not be a creative one unless
(*a*) He is clever enough to think divergently deviated from the normal track.
(*b*) The product produced by him is a useful one.
(*c*) Both of these
(*d*) None of these

**4.** In which of the following cases divergent thinking is required?
(*a*) Attempting a multiple choice items
(*b*) Writing an essay
(*c*) Doing a research activity
(*d*) Both a and c

**5.** Remote Association test of creativity was developed by Mednick and Mednick in
(*a*) 1971 (*b*) 1965
(*c*) 1964 (*d*) 1982

**6.** Which of the following tests is similar to Guilford's test of cognitive abilities?
(*a*) Word association test
(*b*) Things test
(*c*) Hidden shapes test
(*d*) None of these

**7.** In Hidden shapes test of creativity, which of the following things is used?
(*a*) Pictures
(*b*) Words
(*c*) Things
(*d*) None of them

**8.** A creative child in the class can not be satisfied unless
(*a*) He is given freedom to manipulate ideas or things
(*b*) He is allowed to ask questions in his own way
(*c*) Both of these
(*d*) None of these

**9.** A creative child is one who
(*a*) Is ideationally productive and unconventional
(*b*) Does not stick to social and religious norms in a hard manner.
(*c*) Is all the time restless to do something uncommon and unique.
(*d*) All of these

**10.** For the development of creative potential of a child, the teacher should
(*a*) Allow him to be critical to ideas and people.
(*b*) Give them chance of problem solving
(*c*) Both of these
(*d*) None of these

**11.** Creativity is positively correlated to
(*a*) Intelligence
(*b*) Social and aesthetic values
(*c*) School achievement
(*d*) All of these

**12.** Which of the following statements about creativity is not correct?
(*a*) A creative child is conformist
(*b*) He can anticipate the problem which can emerge in future
(*c*) He does not accept religious values very much
(*d*) He may be problematic in the class

**13.** New ideas (Eureka) suddenly comes in the minds of the creative children in the stage of
(*a*) Preparation
(*b*) Illumination
(*c*) Revision
(*d*) Incubation

**14.** The technique to foster creativity in children is
(*a*) Brain storming

(b) Problem solving
(c) Both of these
(d) None of these

15. A teacher can foster creativity in children by
(a) Developing confidence in them
(b) Giving them opportunity to express
(c) Both of these
(d) None of these

16. Which is the most difficult step in creativity testing?
(a) Administration of the test.
(b) Scoring of the test.
(c) Construction of the test.
(d) None of the above.

## ANSWERS

| 1 | 2 | 3 | 4 | 5 | 6 | 7 | 8 | 9 | 10 |
|---|---|---|---|---|---|---|---|---|---|
| (d) | (d) | (a) | (d) | (a) | (b) | (a) | (c) | (d) | (c) |
| **11** | **12** | **13** | **14** | **15** | **16** | | | | |
| (d) | (a) | (b) | (c) | (c) | (b) | | | | |

# Learning Disabilities and Educational Adaptation

## HISTORICAL BACKGROUND

The term learning disabilities was first used by **Samuel Kirk** in 1962. While dealing with the term he said that these children are learning disabled not because they are deficient in intelligence, have problems in studying potentials or slow in activity but they are learning disabled due to some other reasons, such as problem in educational conditions or any problem in the dysfunction of the child.

Several educationists have tried to define the term so far but consensus is still lacking there.

In this chapter, efforts have been made to elaborate the term in the context of the views which are seen popular in the decades of 80 s and 90 s of the last century.

### Definition

According to the latest federal guideline (USA) implemented under the **Individual with Disabilities Education Act**, learning disability means a disorder in one or more of the basic psychological processes involved in understanding or in using language-spoken or written. They may manifest itself in imperfect ability to listen, think, speak, read, write, spell or to do mathematical calculations. The term includes such conditions as perceptual disabilities, brain injury, minimal brain dysfunction, dyslexia and developmental aphasia. The term does not apply to children who have learning problems that are primarily the result of visual, hearing or motor disabilities, of mental retardation, of emotional disturbances or of environmental, cultural or economic disadvantages.

The criteria of **US department of education** slightly differ from the above definition. It has given the following criteria for the identification of children with learning disabilities:

1. This decision must be taken by a team of professionals each having different experiences regarding the assessment of the child. The team must determine if the child does not achieve at a level judged appropriate in one or more areas such as listening comprehension, oral expression written expression, basic reading skill, reading comprehension, mathematical calculation or mathematical reasoning.
2. While taking this decision the team must see the discrepancy between academic achievement and intellectual ability, i.e., learning disabled are normal in intelligence. If low level of achievement is due to low level of intelligence, it is not the case of learning disability any way.
3. If low achievement is not due to hearing, visual or motor disability or due to mental retardation or emotional disturbance, or adjustment problem, only then our direction will move to the problem of learning disabilities.
4. If there is a significant difference between actual and expected achievement, only then it will be the case of learning disability. Here expected achievement is predicted using intelligence tests for measuring mental abilities and using other tests for measuring hearing, visual, motor, or emotional abilities.

### Explanation of the above definitions

1. Learning disabled are those who are performing significantly poorly in some academic areas.
2. Their expected performance is less than their actual performance
3. Their learning problems are associated with comprehension, using language, listening, thinking, reading, writing, spelling or

mathematical calculations. They will be very poor in one or more of these areas.

4. The term learning disability is also associated with perceptual (not visual) ability minimal brain dysfunction, dyslexia, etc. These problems cause learning disability in the child.
5. Those children are not learning disabled who are poor in academic achievement due to any physical, mental, sensory or behavioural retardations.

## Characteristics of Learning Disabled Children

Most of the learning disabled children are first identified in the early elementary stage when they perform very poorly in academic contents due to any hidden reason.

Learning disability is also suspected when a child performs nicely in one skill such as reading or writing skill but he performs extremely poorly in other areas such as mathematical calculations or organisation of subject matter without any visible reason.

In addition to the fundamental characteristics given above, these learning disabled children can be identified in the school on the basis of the characteristics given below :

### (A) Cognitive Characteristics

1. They have average or above average intelligence, when measured on an intelligence test.
2. They have very specific thinking, understanding and expression related problems, such as the problem of remembering things, problem of discriminating visual or auditory perceptions, problem of applying cognitive abilities such as analysis, synthesis or evaluation, in practical life situation and so on.
3. They have specific perceptual problems such as left-right orientation, figure ground differentiation, pattern discrimination, visual abstraction, symbol recognition auditory association or the like problems.
4. They are unable to organize learning tasks and systematize their learning procedures and strategies.
5. They are very poor in self monitoring and self evaluation.
6. Their problem solving skill is also very low.
7. They are unable to retain oral instructions especially.

### (B) Educational Characteristics

1. Their actual performance is lower than their expected one in the class. In this sense, a gifted child can also be a learning disabled case if he is performing average or less than average in the class.
2. He is very slow in telling exact time of the watch or giving the names of months or seasons in sequence.
3. He is poor in mathematical calculations in general. About two third learning disabled suffer from this difficulty.
4. He misses one or two lines while doing loud reading in the class or he sometimes repeats the same line without taking notice of it.
5. He is unable to pronounce the words correctly even after knowing its spelling
6. He reverses the sequence of letters when he pronounces them, e.g., he reads 'tis' instead of 'sit'
7. He is poor in memorizing words and framing sentences on the basis of words.
8. He writes the numbers in wrong manner such as 9 is written as 6 or 916 is written 196 etc. This reversing of numbers or letters is unnoticed of him.
9. He is unable to write letters in correct style even after repeated attempt and remedial coaching.
10. He is not found poor in technical and professional subjects.

### (C) Physical Characteristics

1. They look like normals in 90% situations but they are clumsy and awkward in some situations.
2. They show poor coordination of motor abilities.
3. They do not differ from the normals in height, weight, health and habits.

### (D) Behavioural Characteristics

1. They show high rate of purposeless activity.
2. They have difficulty to pay attention to teachers or sustaining attention when class activities are going on.
3. Their behaviour may be termed as inattentive, hyperactive, impulsive, overly energetic, erratic and distractable. These behaviours are, however, not general. Many students with learning disabilities do not exhibit any of these behaviours and many students without this disability do exhibit them.
4. They show lack of judgement in social situations, i.e., the habit of sharing personal informations with the strangers poorly.
5. They have difficulty in deciding how others feel about them, and have difficulty in establishing good family relations.
6. They have very low self concept.
7. They are very slow in responding to the teacher in the class.
8. They become so excited in the class on certain occasions that they are unable to control themselves.

### (E) Communicative Characteristics

1. At the pre-school level, language problem is the most common problem found in them and this problem is never removed completely due to schooling.
2. They do not very much mix up with any one due to their poor expression power.
3. They do not respond adequately to question asked or instruction given by the teacher.
4. They are very poor in defining words, clarifying concepts and formulating linguistic constructions. Elaboration of the content is also difficult for them.
5. Their oral language is more weak than their written language.

## Types of Learning Disabilities

Learning disabled children can be classified into two categories.

(A) General Learning disabilities.

(B) Specific Learning disabilities

**(A) General Learning Disabilities :** They have learning disabilities in almost all areas of academic content. Their performance will be considerably low as compared to average children. Their disability does not restrict them to get any type of education. They will take only more time to learn with special methods of instruction.

They can not be easily identified in the earlier stages of education. If they are identified in the initial stage, they can be easily helped by applying special techniques. Integrated system of education is best suited to them.

**(B) Specific Learning Disabilities :** The problem of these children are very specific in nature restricted to one or more academic or skill related areas. They can not be educated through integrated system due to the problem being very specific.

The important specific areas in which these children have problems are given below :

1. **Incompatibility of reading :** This problem is related to reading skill, reading comprehension and correctly pronounced reading. If this problem is very severe, the child can not even read four letter words.
2. **Incompatibility of writing :** This type of children have the problem of writing correctly and at reasonable speed. They are incompetent to organise the subject matter. If problem is very severe, they can not be taught this skill. Drilling will help the teacher to some extent.
3. **Communication disability :** See characteristics of learning disabilities.
4. **Mathematical incompatibility :** They are unable to do simple mathematical calculations. They can not operate symbolic language of mathematics. They are also incompetent to know the abstract relations among concepts. Existence of such a disability in a person does not restrict him to excel in other fields of education, e.g., writer of the book is himself having mathematical learning disability of mild nature but his performance in philosophical and literary areas has always been estimated to be more than average.

**Testing or Measurement of learning disabilities :** Following procedure is followed to identify learning disabled children in a class or school:

**Step-I :** Physical, cognitive educational, behavioural and communicative characteristics of suspected children are identified by observation and direct interview and they are matched with the characteristics of learning disabled children. These children are isolated from the lot. This is the clinical procedure.

**Step-II :** The expected performance of suspected children are estimated by administering standardized intelligence test to them and then the result is matched with either the previous or present actual performance of children. If expected performance of these children is far less from the actual performance, they are again separated from the lot identified in the first step.

**Step III :** Discipline wise performance (subject wise achievement) is estimated to know the specific learning disabilities.

**Step IV :** The above screened group of children are further given psychological and behaviour test to know whether poor performance is due to any emotional disturbance or due to learning disability active in the brain dysfunction. Those having emotional disturbances are discarded here and the rest of them are considered as learning disabled.

The degree of learning disability will depend upon the level of performance made by these children in different subjects.

**Learning Disability Quotient** : This quotient was-developed by Prassad and Srivastava.

$$LDQ = 1 - \frac{PASS}{IQ} + Grade$$

Here,

PAAS = Percentage Academic Achievement Quotient

IQ = Intelligence Quotient

Treatment of learning disabilities :

Following methods are used to treat these children:

**(A) Behaviour Guidance Method :** Stephense (1970) suggested four steps for this purpose:

1. Targetting the behaviour to be modified.
2. Measuring targeted behaviour repeatedly.
3. Removing those conditions from the environment of the institutions which are working as impediments in the way of desired behaviour.
4. Assessing the changes in the behaviour and ascertaining to what extent the change is satisfactory.

This method is based on the following assumptions:

I. If conditions restricting the educational achievement are removed from the learning environment of the child, the problem of learning disability will automatically be removed.The reason is that it will change the behaviour of the child in the direction of learning.

II. If model teaching is done repeatedly we can control the negative impact of conditions causing poor achievement, i.e., factors restricting the educational achievement can be identified and removed.

**(B) Cognitive Behaviour Modification :** In this method following aspects of teaching learning process are identified:

1. **Reducing emotional role and sensitivity :** Sensitivity or emotions can play an important role in affecting educational achievement. It can be controlled by using extensive training techniques, self guidance and model behaviour of teaching.
2. **Emphasizing on goal directed behaviour :** Hyper activity is the important characteristic of these children. Hence, they should be restricted to act only in the direction of goal. Thus, behaviour is guided from random to goal directed to relate it with learning or acquisition of academic content. In order to direct their behaviour in the direction of goal, the desired behaviour is reinforced.
3. **Emphasizing on processes rather than product in mathematical operations :** Learning disabilities in mathematics are basically related to processes which can be reduced by making the processes easy and processes can be made easy by using model roles and self direction skills. Processes can also be made easy by dividing the total operation in various steps.

4. **Emphasizing on study style :** Defective study style is an important cause of poor academic achievement. The teacher should first list down all these defects one by one and they should be properly removed.

## Adaptive Teaching Methods

Treatment of learning disabled and their proper adjustment in the society are easy in the sense that teachers can remove many of their problems by using direct instruction, extra instruction or remedial instruction, but it is very difficult in the sense that proper positive response is generally not shown when teacher uses the strengths of these students in order to make up their weaknesses.

A teacher will have to take the following adaptive measures in order to reduce the effects of learning disabilities on their academic achievement:

(A) **Improving Basic Skills :** Thinking, reading, writing, listening, spelling and pronouncing words and doing mathematical calculations are the important basic skills needed by every child and learning disabled are especially deficient in these skills, so, they must be improved by the teacher in the following ways:

**1. Reading**

1. Analytical approach is followed by the teacher to teach students how to read properly. In this approach, starting readers are taught systematic method for decoding words. Students are taught skills for breaking down words then they practice decoding skills with words at appropriate instructional levels.
2. Whole language programme is another strategy for improving reading skill. In this programme reading is integrated with other communication skills especially writing. Students are given chance to use the language more and more in oral and written form. Model reading of the teacher is also helpful in this regard.
3. Students are provided with lists of simple words like hear, hair, bear, bair etc. and they are asked to produce new words on the basis of them by following certain rules like heard or hearing from hear, cheery or cheerful from cheer etc.
4. Computer software like Reader Rabbit or Word Munchers or any other language programme can help the students learn decoding principles.
5. In order to improve reading rate and comprehension, the same passage is repeated again and again. Silent reading for developing reading comprehension is also promoted. High degree of accuracy is maintained by using self corrective measures, i.e., cues are supplied for self correction.
6. Use of thematic units is another measure to improve reading comprehension. In thematic units we cover topics like seasons, months, outer space, holidays, animals, birds, continents etc. and incorporate study guides, comprehension activities and reading guides into it. This will help the students to write stories, poems and essays on their own.
7. Writing can also improve reading comprehension. For example, students can be asked to identify relevant facts and list them down, they can also be asked to write a summary of the passage that they have immediately read on the basis of the fact learnt and identified by them and so on.
8. Prompt and cues can also be used to help the students focus on relevant content and improve their reading comprehension. Following questions as prompt for students can be used while they are reading the passage:
   - What is the story about?
   - Who is the central character?
   - What does the central character do?
   - What happens to the central character in the passage?
   - What happens in the end?
   - What is the effect of the character on you?
9. In order to improve reading comprehension central questions are also asked from the passage which are a bit deeper than the above questions.
10. In order to increase the interest of students in reading, they are shown how reading is valuable for them. For example, they are encouraged to speak the language, they are helped to use reading skill in other subjects like sciences, maths and social science and relating the use of the language in the real life of the student.

**2. Mathematical Operations**

1. Cues and prompts are provided to students in order to enable them not to commit much mistakes while solving mathematical sums. Answer key at the end of the exercise is also provided for the purpose. This will work as prompt for them.
2. If students are reluctant to complete so many number of problems in a period, the number of problems should be reduced. Break should also be given during the total time, i.e., a long assignment should be divided into several smaller assignments.
3. They should be provided with multiple opportunities for success to improve accuracy.
4. They should be taught mathematical sums in steps and only one step should be drilled by them at a time.
5. Those problems should be given to students to solve which have direct relevance to their daily life such as problems related to money matters, house construction, use of daily needs etc. These materials will form a cue in the minds of students.
6. Before they are taught by the problem solving procedure, the related concepts should be made clear first, by using examples and by helping the students use them.
7. To improve the performance further, structure and content of assignment should be simplified.
8. Alternate easy and tough examples should be given to students and practised before taking them to the exercise of the lesson. These easy and tough examples will help them do the exercise with minimum mistakes.
9. Mathematics should be made easy by the extra activities of the teacher. This will give self motivation to students.
10. If students are having only mathematical learning disability, then double time period should be allotted for teaching this subject, i.e., first period in the morning and sixth period after break. Here one period can be used for teaching and the other for drilling.

**3. Writing**

1. In order to improve writing work, quantity should be focused more than quality and beauty should not be taken into consideration. Emphasis on quality is not very much relevant to these children. Grammatical errors in writing works should also be checked as much as possible.
2. In order to improve written products, checklists should be used to guide students before they write.
3. Students should be encouraged to monitor their own written works and specific skills such as targetted composition skills should be taught to students.
4. In order to improve spelling, students should be allowed to use familiar words for practice. For example, they can learn the spelling of met or set with the help of the word "bet"
5. Students should be trained to crame words only after dividing them into convenient groups or pairs such as "Reluctant" word can be cramed as RE-LUC-TANT. Here rhyming period for each group of letters will be the same. This will help the students to write correct spelling of the word.
6. Computers and word processing tools may also be used for making a significant improvement in writing works.

**(B) Improving Classroom Behaviour :** Learning disabled do not generally have behaviour problem but they do sometimes exhibit those behaviours which is anti-productive in the class. Classroom behaviour is composed of work habit and study skills. These two aspects of the behaviour can be corrected in the following ways:

**(1) Work habits**

1. Students attending to the teacher to some extent should be rewarded and unattending behaviour should be penalized. Variable ratio technique of B.F. Skinner is the best technique for reinforcing the behaviour.
2. Attention of students can also be improved by three methods, self monitoring by the students through timer watches, monitoring by the teacher by direct observation method and monitoring by the principal by close circuit television.
3. Cues and prompts should also be used in order to focus the attention of students.
4. Daily report card should be used to minimize inappropriate behaviour of students.

**(2) Study habits**

1. Study habits of these students can be improved by giving them regular assignments in the class.
2. They should be taken to historical places and places of scientific research for the purpose of giving them motivation.
3. They should be motivated to study novels, short stories and biographies of esteemed personalities of the world. This will also increase their study habits.
4. Students should be shown how to set up an assignment book and how to arrange a notebook. Periodical checking of notebooks and assignment is also necessary.
5. Regular assignments given to students increase their study habits. So, assignment should be given to students regularly.
6. Project works should be given to students periodically so that students can work to complete the project in a group.

**(C) Improving Social Behaviour :** Social relation is the most affected area that these students come across due to their disability, i.e., low level of interactive ability and the humiliating behaviour meted out to them by others damage their social relations. It can be improved in the following ways:

1. Words and actions provide a model for students behaviour. Problem of disability should be shared with other classmates.
2. Students with learning disability resist classroom discussion and inter-personal interactions because they are afraid of failures or doing mistakes in such situations. The teacher can help them to reduce this problem by providing them different techniques of communication.
3. Group co-curricular activities in the class should be organised in the school to foster socialization. These activities will help them learn social rules and regulations.
4. Students should be forced to participate in all structured activities of the school either in a passive or active manner for the purpose of getting motivation.
5. Appropriate behaviour should be demonstrated in the class by the teacher himself or by using films and cassettes. When students see the rewarded behaviour in the film, they will learn and copy them in their lives.
6. The teacher should, first of all, identify the skills, hobbies and individual interests of students then he should plan and organise various types of group activities for them.
7. Progress report of improvement in social skills and behaviour should be periodically sent to parents for feedback. Parents-teachers meet should also be organised.

Attention Deficit Hyper-Activity Disorder (ADHD)

3% of school going children suffer from the problem of attention deficit and hyperactivity disorders and all the students of learning disabilities do have this problem, so both these problems may be studied together.

ADHD students basically suffer from three main problems-lack of attentiveness, hyperactivity in the school and neighbourhood and impulsiveness.

In this way they are similar to learning disabled children. Details are given below:

**Inattentivity Symptoms :** Inability to give close attention to details, committing mistakes in class works, difficulty in sustaining attention in tasks, inability to listen when addressed directly and hence not following instructions, difficulty in organizing activities, reluctance to engage in tasks, frequent distraction from tasks etc.

**Hyperactivity Symptoms :** Leaving seats in the classroom frequently, frequently teasing other students, engaging in leisure activities quietly, restlessness, excessive talking, damaging school property etc.

**Impulsivity Symptoms :** Bluring out answers before the completion of the question, difficulty in awaiting turn, butting into the conversation or games etc.

**Remedial measures :** All those remedial and adaptive measures are suitable to these children which can be applied to children with learning disabilities.

# OBJECTIVE QUESTIONS

1. Learning disabled children are
   (a) Deficient is using potentials
   (b) Low in intelligence
   (c) Slow in activity
   (d) None of these
2. Learning disability is related to
   (a) low listening and comprehension power
   (b) poor ability of expression
   (c) poor ability of mathematical operation
   (d) all of these
3. Learning disabled children perform very poorly in
   (a) academic areas (b) technical areas
   (c) both of these (d) none of these
4. Problem of learning disability is more complex than that of other disabilities because
   (a) Its causes can not be easily ascertained by applying usual tests
   (b) It is associated to behaviour problems
   (c) Both of these
   (d) None of these
5. Educationally, learning disabled look similar to
   (a) dullers (b) backward children
   (c) both of these (d) none of these
6. In which of the following physical characteristics learning disabled children differ from the normal ones?
   (a) They are all the time clumsy and awkward
   (b) Poor coordination of motor abilities
   (c) Height, weight and health
   (d) All of these
7. Which of the following methods is most suitable for learning disabled children?
   (a) Behaviour guidance method
   (b) Remedial teaching
   (c) Brain storming
   (d) None of them.
8. In order to improve work habits of learning disabled what should be done?
   (a) Unattending behaviour should be penalized
   (b) Close monitoring of the behaviour is needed
   (c) Cues and prompt should be given
   (d) All of these

# ANSWERS

| 1 | 2 | 3 | 4 | 5 | 6 | 7 | 8 |
|---|---|---|---|---|---|---|---|
| (d) | (d) | (a) | (a) | (b) | (b) | (a) | (d) |

# Backward Children and their Education Adaptation

## Meaning

The term backwardness can be applied to any field of life. If the performance of a person is poor as compared to most of his colleagues, in social, economic, religious or any other field, he is said to be backward in the field.

The term educational backwardness refers to consistent below average performance of a child in the academic content to the extent that he is alienated from the rest of population for psychological and educational treatment. This backwardness is generally seen in one or two subjects and sometimes it is seen in all the school subjects.

It is a general problem in nature. The reasons of backwardness may be many ranging from psychological to social causes via physical factors and they are studied separately to adapt separate intervention procedures but general causes of backwardness are studied by all teachers to remove them from the environment of backward children and bring them to normalcy to some extent.

## Definitions

1. Warton Hall : Backward child is one who in mid school career is unable to do the work of the class next below that which is normal for his age.
2. Shonell : Backward student is one who when compared with other pupils of the same chronological age shows educational deficiency.
3. Burt : He has used the term educational quotient for separating backward children in the class. According to him the children who have EQ less than 85 are backward. Education quotient is calculated by the following formula:
   EQ = (Education achievement/Chronological age) × 100

## Characteristics of Backward Children

On the basis of the definitions given above, we can arrive at the following conclusions regarding the characteristics of backward children:

1. Their rate of learning as well as power of retention is very low.
2. They feel frustrated due to their low achievement in the school.
3. The IQ of these children is low, i.e., less than 80 when measured on an intelligence test. Low IQ leads them to low academic achievement. Since intelligence is a composition of 150 factors (6 × process × 5 contents × 5 products) and no mentally retarded child lacks all these factors at a time, so, low intelligence will not lead to poor academic achievement in all the subjects simultaneously. Their backwardness may be restricted to one or few subjects only.
4. These children are slow in emotional and social development also.
5. He is slow learner and feels difficulty in keeping pace with the normal school work.
6. Educationally, he is unable to attain what he should. In other words his educational attainment falls below his natural abilities.
7. He falls far behind other children of his age in matters of education. Usually such children remain in the same class for a number of years., i.e., backwardness leads to stagnation.
8. Not only he is unable to learn in his class with the children of his own age but also feels difficulty in learning with the children of lower classes, who are younger than him in age.
9. He is necessarily a failure in the academic field and shows poor educational performance.

10. According to Burton Hall, "A child may be both dull and backward but he is not necessarily backward because he is dull." Therefore lower IQ does not make a child backward. Consequently, the backward child should not misunderstood and leveled mentally retarded or dull.

**Causes of Educational Backwardness :** The causes of educational backwardness are internal (lying within the child) and external (related to environmental factors both)

**(A) Internal causes :** Causes of backwardness lying within the individual are as follows :

1. **Physical causes :** There may be some physical defects in the body of the child. This defect may be to the extent of disability too. Due to these defects learning and retention of learnt material may be adversely affected. Some of these defects are given below :
   - Sensory defects like visual or hearing impairment.
   - Motor defects like defects in legs, feet, hands or speech.
   - Mental retardation due to any disease or brain injury.
   - Defective working of glands.
   - Poor health condition of the child
   - Infection of a chronic disease like tuberculosis, malaria, AIDS etc.
2. **Mental causes :** Low educational quotient is most of the time due to low IQ and low IQ is directly related to poor functioning of mind which maybe due to so many reasons. Moreover, many intellectual abilities like, thinking, reasoning, manipulation, evaluation, concentration and observation etc. are not properly arranged in these children, so, they perform poorly in the class.
3. **Emotional disturbance :** If child is suffering from any emotional disturbance, his emotional development maybe faulty and delayed. It will lead to further complication in emotional and social adjustment. The child may also develop faulty self concept. All these factors will create problems before the child in the school.

**(B) External causes :** Environment also plays an important role in making the child educationally poor. Important environmental factors are as follows :

**1. Family**

*(a)* If economic conditions and social status of the family are very low, the family will not be able to cater to the basic needs of the child. If family is not providing proper educational facilities and guidance to the child, the child will perform poorly on academic skills.

*(b)* Similarly, poverty in the family may lead to malnutrition of the child. If it is so, the child's poor health will affect his educational achievement negatively.

*(c)* If background of the family is very backward and child is deprived of elementary general knowledge and life experiences, he is expected to perform poorly.

*(d)* If students do not get sufficient time to devote to educational tasks given to them because of their excessive engagement at home in occupational tasks, their educational performance will be low. The girls engaged in the care of young brothers and sisters generally perform poorly in the school.

*(e)* If parents are illiterate and child is not helped in the family in completing his school assignment, he will perform poorly.

*(f)* Lastly, emotional climate of the family also affects learning and achievement. If there are strained relations between the child and the family, he belongs to a broken or nagging family, or any of his parents is addicted to drugs or habit of gambling, harsh attitude is meted out to the child in the family and child feels insecure, unwanted and a burden on the family, all these factors will contribute to low achievement of the child.

**2. School environment**

*(a)* The most crucial factor is the school where the child receives education. If due to poor economic condition, the child is educated to a school where educational environment is polluted, he is not supposed to show higher educational achievement there.

*(b)* School discipline and good school administration is a function of good

educational achievement. If discipline is poor due to poor and defective administration, the performance of the school in general will be low.

(c) If method of teaching is defective, uninteresting and lacks innovation and novelty, achievement will be low.

(d) Lack of adequate resources and materials, ignorance to experimentation and creative work, disregard of co-curricular activities and so on will lead to poor educational achievement of the child.

(e) If guidance services are not provided in the school and curriculum is not revised for a long time leading to uninteresting curriculum, it will also lead to low educational achievement of the child.

(f) If sufficient options are not made available for children and they are forced to select only few subjects, they will perform very poorly in the school.

(g) If school lacks healthy inter-personal relationship and the environment of the school is surcharged with communal or any other tensions, educational achievement of the child will be low.

(h) If physical facilities available in the school is not sufficient according to the needs of children and more than 100 children are accommodated in a class where only 50 students can be accommodated, all of them will perform poorly.

(i) If school has not fixed any academic standard and everything is going on in an aimless manner, the performance of the whole school will be low.

**3. Neighbourhood**

(a) Friends selected by the child from neighbourhood and from the school shape his behaviour. If they are not having interest in schooling, the child is also expected to be poor educationally.

(b) Press, mass media, and socio-religious institutions also affect educational achievement. If they are playing a poor role in the interest of the child, he will perform poorly in the school.

(c) Late admission is another problem related to low educational achievement. If society is reluctant to giving education to children, they are sent to school late by two or three years. When these children attend the classes, they study curriculum below their age which may be uninteresting to them. For example, if a ten year old child is reading a story which has been written in the context of those children who are six or seven years old, the child is not supposed to take interest in that story. As a result, he will perform poorly when he is tested.

(d) General attitude of the people towards education also affects educational achievement of the child. If attitude of the people is not positive, they will not motivate their wards for achieving high in the class.

(e) If job expectancy and job security are very low after education, students are not likely to study hard resulting in low educational achievement of the child.

(f) Stagnation unattended by the society is the major environmental cause of educational backwardness. If child remains in a class for two or three years and the causes why he fails repeatedly in a particular class are not identified and removed by the society and the family as a combined, effort, his educational achievement will remain low.

## Corrective measures and educational adaptation

The only way to overcome educational backwardness is to remove the underlying internal as well as external causes of educational backwardness. If the problem is due to any physical disability upto the level of handicap, it can not be removed by a regular teacher through general techniques of teaching. Only a specially trained teacher can do this job. But if educational backwardness is due to minor physical reasons and major social reasons, it can be removed by the teacher, parents and the society by a combined effort.

Following adaptive measures can be taken to minimize the problem of educational backwardness:

1. **Regular health check up and treatment :** If educational backwardness, is due to physical and health related reasons, it can be removed only by

adopting medical measures. Team of doctors should be regularly sent to the school for regular check up, vaccination, immunization and treatment of students. Adequate medicine should also be supplied to them by the hospitals because they can not purchase it due to their poverty. (Educationally backward children are mostly seen in children belonging to poor families) Mid Day Meal programme of the government is a good initiative in this connection. It is likely to reduce malnutrition in children making them less vulnerable to infectious and deficiency diseases. Thus, it is a good preventive measure adopted by the government.

Apart from these, if child needs some equipments to overcome his disability, he should be supplied it either from the government or from school organisation.

Besides, the services of at least one regular and permanent doctor must be hired by the school for diagnosing the general problems of students and treating them.

2. **Special educational programmes and role of the teacher :** In integrated education system, a special teacher can do following things to remove educational backwardness of these children:

## Problems of Backward Children

Backward children generally face three types of problems:

1. **Educational problems :** They are slow in learning and slower in retention. The result is that they can not get along with the learning pace of other children of the class. Normal children find it difficult to work with them. From educational point of view also, they are not successful in their achievements. They lag behind in studies to the children of their age group. Sometimes they cannot work even with the young children. As a result, they do not succeed in various examinations. For the same reason stagnation occurs in the schools. Backward children cannot adjust themselves under these circumstances.
2. **Social problems :** Backward children suffer from inferiority complex. They find themselves unable to adjust to the social environment. They remain isolated from the society. They have a fewer friends. Some times they show anti-social behaviour as they easily fall in the clutches of anti-social elements. The backwardness persists in the nature of anti-social elements and in the persons with the background of criminal nature. This great problem can be a challenge for a teacher to deal with the backward children in the society and make them good citizens.
3. **Emotional problem :** Backward children feel frustrated and disappointed when they repeatedly fail in their social and educational life. When they have to bear insult in society and school they are mentally disturbed. As a result, many types of problems stream out. They do not concentrate in any activity. They do not get love and respect from society and colleagues. In order to make their identity they indulge in undesirable activities and cause indiscipline in schools.

(a) **Increased attention :** Special attention is paid by the teacher to these backward children to know their specific problems and to remove them. Individual guidance is given to them by the teacher in the class with remedial measures. Backwardness also develops inferiority complex in children. The task of the teacher is to remove this complex from them as much as possible. It is necessary for emotional and social adjustment too.

(b) **Diagnosing the causes of backwardness :** A teacher can not remove the educational backwardness of his children unless he knows the causes behind it. So, it is essential to diagnose the responsible causes prior to the remedy by adopting clinical and observation methods or by administering standardized achievement and intelligence tests and attitude inventories to them. Child's educational history and his socio-economic status will also help the teacher to know the causes of poor achievement. After this inquiry, proper educational planning for these children can be made by the teacher and the principal.

(c) **Adjustment training :** Such children find it very difficult to adjust in the school as well as at home because of the humiliating situations that they face everywhere. The teacher fully helps them in this regard by using verbal and behavioural reinforcement techniques. He gives them love, affection, sympathy and security. He behaves them in such a decent manner (which is generally not done by teachers in schools) that they become closely attached to the teacher emotionally. He develops smooth and healthy environment in the class by controlling other normal students of the class so that they may not create any problem for backward children.

(d) **Checking of truancy :** Tendency of truancy is generally seen in these children. The teacher motivates them to attend the classes regularly by his sympathetic attitude and habit of truancy is severely dealt with sometimes. They generally miss classes because they are unable to complete assignments given to them and they fear that they will be punished. Teacher helps and motivates them to complete their home works also.

(e) **Special teaching strategies :** These children are not expected to be benefited by general methods of teaching. So, adaptive methods of instruction are used to teach these children. (see optional paper special education chapter 2 also). The teacher uses direct instructural strategy and takes the help of concrete materials and hardware technology to teach these students.

Some other adaptive measures are as follows:

- Teaching by small step.
- Frequent but short assignments
- Regular checking of assignments
- Frequent revision of the text
- Drilling of learnt material.
- Examination free teaching.
- Regular reinforcement for wanted behaviour.
- Concept based teaching.
- Illustration with examples.
- Regular prompting and cues.
- Conditioning of study habits by artificial as well as natural stimuli.
- Writing work should be emphasized more than reading one.

3. **Special arrangement :** Following special arrangements can be made for these children to remove their educational backwardness:

(a) **Specified curriculum :** Backward children generally lag behind the normals in academic subjects that is why they are not successful in achieving higher education. In order to overcome this problem, handicrafts and some technical subjects should be included in the curriculum. These subjects will involve more activities and these activities will help them to learn. This will also help them to get job in future and they will be self motivated for learning. Thus, academic content from the curriculum should be reduced and writing work should be emphasized.

(b) **Stress on co-curricular activities and varied experiences :** Co-curricular activities are required by gifted and normal children to satisfy their extra need. Backward children require their involvement in these activities in the school to compensate their academic deficit through games (indoor and outdoor) and through community services. These activities help them to restore their emotional balance in the school. These activities also increase their interest in the school.

(c) **Controlling negative environmental factors :** There are many factors of the environment which work negatively for the child and cause slow educational achievement such as unsanitary condition of neighbourhood leading to infectious diseases, bad company of children leading to apathy towards education, poor socio-economic status leading to frustration, aimless life of the child leading to undirected efforts etc. These factors are controlled to the maximum level possible by providing scholarship to students and by integrating them to NSS programmes.

(d) **Itinerant services :** Backward children regularly need the services of doctors for medical treatment, the services of psychologists for psychological treatment, the service of counsellors for guidance and counseling and the services of behaviour therapists to modify their behaviour. Various types of resource rooms are prepared for this purpose and regular feedback is taken from these students.

**4. Administrative arrangements :** To benefit backward children, some modification in the administrative arrangement is also needed. They are given below :

**(a) Special schools :** Special schools for educationally backward children are required when

- backwardness lies in any physical handicap.
- backwardness is very serious problem and it can not be remedied in regular schools.
- Number of backward children are very high in a particular society

In these cases only special schools are suited to these children. The reason is that their disability restricts them to learn through usual methods in normal schools. Such severely damaged children need special teaching methods and materials, special curriculum and special activities to follow and these can not be arranged in regular schools.

**(b) Special classes :** In those schools where the number of backward children is very high and due to their severity of the problem they can not be educated in regular classes, special sections are arranged for them in the school and all the necessary facilities are provided to them. When separate classes are arranged for them, they do not have the problem of adjustment with normal children academically and socially.

But this is not a healthy approach as the experience of the writer shows. When I was the Principal of a school. I did the same but I found that these children remained backward for two years in spite of all special services provided to them due to the stigma attached to these sections. Only 25% students benefited from this arrangement. As a result, this arrangement was withdrawn after two years.

**(c) Special curriculum :** Special curriculum is also developed for these children to be followed in special schools or special classes. In this curriculum, activities, rather than academic subjects are stressed. Bookish knowledge is replaced by handicrafts and technical subjects.

**(d) Special teacher :** The problem of these children is so diverse in nature that they cannot be taught by regular teachers. Special teachers trained for the purpose are required to teach them in special classes. These teachers know not only the psychological problems of these children but they are also cognizant of tackling these problems through special adaptive measures.

**(e) Modification in school time table :** Backward children can not concentrate for a longer period of time in the class due to their mental, physical or psychological deficits, so , modification in the time table becomes also necessary. The duration of the period is shortened according to their needs and various types of tasks required in a subject are given away among many teachers instead of few. Sometimes they take longer time to understand even a little problem, hence, time table should be flexible enough to adjust to the problem of these children.

**(f) Modification in the examination system :** Sometimes defective examination system makes the students educationally backward so, improvement in the system is a must. For example, essay and objective type written and oral test must be supported by regular assignments and project works.

Similarly, these students take much time to complete their answers in the examination, hence extra time is needed to be given to them. Lastly, one annual exam is not suitable for them because they can not prepare the whole syllabus for this purpose. In order to avoid this problem at least four or five short examinations should be conducted in a year and one examination should cover only one unit.

# OBJECTIVE QUESTIONS

1. Those who are normal in intelligence but slow in academic achievement due to psycho-social reasons are called
   - *(a)* Backward children
   - *(b)* Gifted under achievers
   - *(c)* Both of these
   - *(d)* None of these
2. Consistent low achievement leads to low intelligence because
   - *(a)* 50% intellectual ability is expressed in verbal form
   - *(b)* Learning develops thinking and reasoning power
   - *(c)* Both of these
   - *(d)* None of these
3. Which of the following situations may lead to educational backwardness?
   - *(a)* Sensory impairment
   - *(b)* Motor disability
   - *(c)* Long diseases and health problems.
   - *(d)* All of these
4. Emotional disturbances may lead to educational backwardness because
   - *(a)* Proper emotional development is necessary for social interactions
   - *(b)* Emotions will develop intellectual power, i.e., emotional intelligence.
   - *(c)* Both of these
   - *(d)* None of these
5. Which of the following factors will not lead to educational backwardness?
   - *(a)* Poor socio economic status of the family.
   - *(b)* Poor educational environment of the school.
   - *(c)* Occupation of the family.
   - *(d)* Poor emotional climate of the family.
6. Which of the following is an important cause of educational backwardness at primary level of education in India?
   - *(a)* Poor school organisation.
   - *(b)* Lack of accountability
   - *(c)* Attitude of the masses towards education.
   - *(d)* All of these
7. Which of the following measures should be adopted by the teacher to check educational backwardness?
   - *(a)* Continuous evaluation and regular feedback.
   - *(b)* Remedial teaching
   - *(c)* Adjustment and behaviour training.
   - *(d)* All of these
8. Teaching by small steps and frequent short assignment techniques are useful for
   - *(a)* Slow learners
   - *(b)* Learning disabled
   - *(c)* Educationally backward children.
   - *(d)* Children of all types of disabilities.
9. Special schools are required for backward children when
   - *(a)* Backwardness is due to any serious physical handicap.
   - *(b)* The size of population of backward children in the society is very large as is the case of Gujarat where the achievement of students in mathematics is always seen very low.
   - *(c)* Both of these
   - *(d)* None of these

## ANSWERS

| 1 | 2 | 3 | 4 | 5 | 6 | 7 | 8 | 9 |
|---|---|---|---|---|---|---|---|---|
| *(a)* | *(c)* | *(d)* | *(c)* | *(c)* | *(d)* | *(d)* | *(d)* | *(c)* |

# Educational Guidance and Counseling

## INTRODUCTION

Guidance is a universal and automatic phenomenon in the sense that every person who is more experienced than his counterpart endeavours to guide him even without seeking guidance from him. Parents guide children, older members of the family provide guidance to younger ones, teachers guide students and so on. These are few examples of guidance. These are unorganized and unscientific form of guidance.

Professional guidance on scientific lines started only in 1908 in Boston (USA) with the establishment of **Parson's Vocational Bureau** to help the young generation to choose profession in accordance with their needs, interests and abilities. All relevant informations were provided to the people here. The study of vocational guidance as a course started in 1911 first in the Harward University (USA). Then other countries of the world including India followed America and now guidance services are provided to the people by the professional workers in the field. The concept of guidance has now been extended to every aspect of life to minimize the problems of life and avoid wastage of energy, time and money. For example, if guidance services are available in the school which guide the students to select courses after school education by administering interest and intelligence test, a child of below average mental ability will not dream and struggle for becoming an IIT or medical practitioner.

### Meaning of Guidance

Guidance is a process by which individuals are assisted in the making of their life and career to better adapt to the environment and enjoy temporary worldly life. Following steps are involved in guidance

I. Individual is first helped to recognize his abilities, interests and needs by administering standardized tests.

II. After appraisal of the individual, he is now motivated to face the realities of life without being frustrated or overwhelmed

III. Necessary informations are provided to the individual in the third step where he can make his career and how. In this way a harmony between him and the outer world is brought about.

IV. In the last step the individual is guided to find a placement after completion of course or training.

**Rath Strang** has defined guidance in the following words.

"Guidance is a process of helping the individual through his own efforts to discover and develop his potentialities in order to better adjust to the environment".

There are four important characteristics included in the process

I. It is a process of knowing oneself.

II. It is a process of knowing the relationship between him and the environment *i.e.*, what he expects from the environment and vice versa.

III. It is the process of utilizing the potentialities in the best manner possible, making decision about oneself.

IV. Self effort in the direction of goal.

Thus, guidance is a process by which individual solves his problems by his own efforts. The guide or counsellor only shows him the way how to solve the problems.

In the school environment, guidance is a process of helping the students to know their potentialities and weaknesses, to know their tendencies and to achieve the best in the environment from the available potentialities by their non efforts.

## Characteristics of Guidance (Advantages)

I. It is a process by which individual is helped to choose the best alternative available in accordance with his potentialities and interest.

II. It is a process by which individual is helped to solve his educational, vocational and personal problems efficiently and accurately, by his own efforts.

III. It helps the people to adapt to the antagonist environment and to enjoy it.

IV. It makes the people realistic in thinking and approach as a result, people avoid running after dreams

V. It helps the people to come to know their potentialities and shortcomings and to try their efforts in the direction of their interest

VI. It provides relevant information to the individual to choose a better career.

VII. It motivates the individuals to contribute most to the society by their creative works.

VIII. It helps the individuals to satisfy their needs and enjoy the life.

IX. Guidance helps the people to avoid wastage of time, energy and money

X. It removes the psychological problems of the people in the best manner possible and they are guided in accordance with their psychological needs and tendencies.

## Some other Concepts Related to Guidance

1. **Counseling :** It is a face to face relationship between the guidance worker and the person who seeks a special kind of guidance. The area of guidance is predominantly psychological, ie, problems related to self concept, adjustment, anxiety, hyper-tension, ego formation and the life. Thus, counseling is related to personality correction.

**Rogers** defined counseling in the following words. "Counseling is a series of direct contacts with the individual with a view to offer him assistance in changing his attitudes and behaviour".

Thus, counseling may be differentiated from guidance in the following manner

I. Guidance is broader in scope than counseling

II. Guidance is a group process while counseling is a one to one relationship in nature

III. If counseling covers psychological aspects, guidance covers mostly social aspects.

IV. Counseling is a learning oriented process and may reduce learning problems of the individual. Guidance is an adjustment oriented process and helps the individual to exploit the environment to the maximum.

V. Personnel involved in guidance may be counselors, career masters, social workers, psychologists, psycho-therapists and so on but in counseling only trained professionals trained in behaviour therapy or psychology works.

**Shaw (1973)** defined counseling as an intimate inter-personal relationship which one person by virtue of his special training and skills is reorganized as the helper while the other person is reorganized as an individual or group with a problem who can benefit from the former"

2. **Group counseling :** It is a situation in which more than one individuals having common problems are put in a single group and assisted together. The members of the group often discuss their problems in the presence of the counseller themselves and find the solution. The counselor goes deeper into the psyche of the group and reduces their tension and anxiety together.

   It is different from group guidance where only needed information of the environment is supplied to the group.

3. **Advising :** Giving formal or informal advices to the people on any matter without any professional training behind the advice is called advising. These advices are very general in nature. In fact if professional degree is there behind the advice, it is counseling otherwise it is advice.

4. **Psychotherapy :** It is a technique of treating mentally ill persons and of those who suffer from any behaviour problems in a medical setting. It does not deal with normal people as the counseling or guidance does. Persons needed in

psychotherapy are trained in psychopathology, abnormal psychology and psychiatry. Generally a team of experts in these fields are needed here.

## Need and importance of Guidance and Counseling

The basic purpose of guidance and counseling is to strengthen the individual by optimum development of his personality. Potentialities of the individuals are developed to the maximum through these services. These services are needed by the individuals because of the following reasons:

1. Human being is the most dependent being of all the existing living things on earth. From birth to death, he needs guidance and counseling at every moment. If such guidance is not made available to him, he will be corrupted by the ill effects of the society.
2. No individual is fully fit for all purposes. Each human is different from others in capacity, interest and tendencies. If he is not guided to go to the direction of his needs, interests and capacities, he might fail in his efforts. In such a case it will be a loss not only for the individual but also for the society as a whole. For example, everyone can not become an engineer or doctor due to his specific aptitude. If he tries to become an engineer without engineering aptitude, he will fail.
3. Individuals differ in physical strength also. It is necessary to guide them to select job according to their respective physical fitness or strength also. If jobs are not matched with the people according to their physical or mental level, results obtained will not be satisfactory.
4. From economic point of view, optimum utilization of resources is essential for optimum production and full employment in the economy. Individual and group both types of guidance are necessary for this purpose.
5. Psychological problems of complex nature can not be tackled by laymen. Services of expert counsellors and therapists are needed for this purpose.
6. Failure in life situations creates tension and frustration. Such frustration will result into behavioural problems and hence further failures. Such a vicious circle can be broken only by taking the services of guidance workers and counsellors.
7. Guidance and counseling are also needed for making proper adjustment of the individual in the society as much as for making the children fully adjusted to the environment of the school.
8. A child comes to the school with his background. A counsellor brings him at par with other children by raising his motivation level if his background is poor.
9. Counseling is needed to remove barriers of learning every time. Guidance and counseling strengthen the process of education on social as well as psychological grounds.
10. In a democratic country where everyone is free without disregarding the freedom of others, guidance and counselling services help the people to be considerate in their attitude and approaches.
11. The society is changing very fast today resulting into fast changing pattern of jobs and employment opportunities. An individual on his own can not cope with this situation. He needs immediate informations of various types at every step of life. Such information can be supplied to him by professional workers in the field.
12. Adolescents need guidance at every moment due to their unique psychological and social problems. Such guidance can be provided to them only by experts in the field.

## Objectives of Guidance and Counseling

Guidance and counseling services are provided in order to serve the following purposes:

I. To assist students to make educational and vocational choices in order to build up a better career.

II. To help the students to make the best possible adjustment in the school and in the society.

III. To develop the personality of the child according to his inborn tendencies, traits and capacities.

IV. As a continuous process it assists all the individuals as a whole not a few deviants of the society.

V. To help the students to cope with their emotional problems by reducing their anxiety and by making them realistic to the situation.

VI. To provide all necessary information to the people to choose a better career and to get success in no time.

VII. To help all the individuals to gain the most with least available resources.

## Principles of guidance and counselling

Following principles will help the persons involved in such programmes to run them efficiently and effectively.

1. **Principle of universality :** According to this principle, all students irrespective of their psychology or physical limitations need guidance and counselling services so, it should be provided to all of them. The only thing that is needed is that deviant people need it more than the normal ones. The philosophy behind such programmes is the development of total personality of all the students in the school not to restrict such programmes to few problem groups of the society.
2. **Principle of continuity :** Guidance and counselling services are needed by all the individuals from birth to death. Hence, it should be run as a continuous process from the school scenario to the society in general. Counselling maybe voluntary but it should be made clear to all the students that they can avail it any time when needed. Timely guidance is made effective by timely follow up, evaluation and recounselling or new guidance.
3. **Principle of individualism :** Such programmes have to develop each and every individual of the society. Even guidance and counselling in groups are evaluated in terms of individual performance of students. Guidance is actually a self making process and it will be a success only when all individuals are touched by these services individually. These services are basically client centred.
4. **Principle of flexibility in methods and procedures :** Everyone can not be punished with the same stick or rewarded with the same type of foods. The success of these programmes lies in the uniqueness in their procedures just according to the need and variety of the individuals. Only those methods and procedures are considered the best which satisfy the people to the maximum. The reason is that some methods which suit to some people will not necessarily suit to others. It has also been seen that the same method does not work even if the problems of different individuals is the same. It is because different people react to different situations differently. Due to the above reasons, novelty and flexibility in procedures and methods are needed every time.
5. **Principle of complexity of problems :** The problem that a counsellor or guide faces is not any time simple. Problems are always complex in nature and a counsellor cannot solve them without analyzing or going deep into them. He should give proper time to every person who approaches him and guide him very carefully. Even physical or vocational problems should be tackled with care.
6. **Principle of cooperation from the concerned people :** A guide or counsellor should keep this fact in mind that he can not solve the problem of any person on his own. He will have to motivate the counsellee to take help from the concerned people like parents, family members, teachers, principals, religious persons etc. These concerned people can provide him necessary information and data about the counsellee. If counsellor fails to harness the cooperation of the people he will fail in his efforts.
7. **Principle of self pacing :** A guide or cousellor does not work like a physician or surgeon who uses medicines to cure the patients. He motivates the people to work and find the solution of their problem by their own efforts. He only guides them to go to the right path. His success totally lies in the efforts of the counselees. The more he is able to encourage them, the more he is successful in his job.
8. **Principle of voluntary counselling :** According to this principle, no student or person can be forced to go to a counsellor or guidance worker for seeking solution of his problem. Solution of the problem needs that the person having a problem should contact a counsellor or guidance centre himself at the call of his inner urge. If the situation is so, only then full rapport between the two parties will be seen.

## Types of guidance

1. **Educational guidance :** It deals with those problems of students which are related in any way with the educational progress and learning

experiences, ie, low achievement in any subject, difficulty in learning a particular subject, inability to select a subject or paper, and so on. Excellence in the field of education is also brought about through such guidance. Other areas covered by educational guidance are improvement of study habits, adjustment problems in the class or school, language difficulties, excessive school work load, lack of co-curricular activities and other issued related in any way to the normal development of students in the school.

2. **Vocational guidance :** Guidance in which students are assisted to choose a better career and to solve their vocational problems is called vocational guidance. In this guidance students are tested first from different angles and then they are suggested to opt a career on the basis of their potentialities and trends. Necessary informations are also supplied to them to find a proper vocation.

In India Kolkata University was the first which introduced guidance as a section of its department of psychology in 1938. **Batlibox Vocational Guidance Bureau** (Bombay) was the second established in 1941 to provide vocational guidance to the people. UP government too on the recommendation of Acharya Narendra Deo Committee established a Bureau of Psychology at Allahabad in 1947 to provide educational and vocational guidance to school going children.

Thus, vocational guidance implies a process of assisting individuals to choose an occupation, prepare for it, enter and progress upon it. **International Labour Conference** (1949) defined vocational guidance as "Assistance given to an individual in solving problems related to occupational choices and progress with due regard for the individual characteristics and their relation to occupational opportunity." It means that guidance is psychological as well as socio-economic in nature. Once such services are provided total development of the individual becomes a reality.

In the beginning, it was thought that such services should be provided to the students when they reach in secondary classes. Now it is believed that guidance should start at the primary stage.

**Vocational guidance at primary level :** Following things can be done at this stage:

I. An insight into the world of work and favourable attitude towards work can be developed. It helps the students to take interest in any work which is assigned to them
II. Occupational informations of basic nature are provided to students activity method of teaching is also used for this purpose
III. Curriculum touching the practical aspects of life are especially included to enable them to live a competent life.
IV. Healthy attitude towards work is developed through co-curricular and recreational activities.
V. General occupational ability is developed in children.

**Vocational guidance at secondary level :** Following things can be done at this stage.

I. It is concerned with the development of positive vocational attitudes.
II. Students are assisted to choose subjects according to their tendencies and worth.
III. Every student wants to get good job after education but he does not know exactly what is required to get that particular job. Complete informations are provided to him regarding that job and the real challenges that the student will have to face.

**Vocational guidance at the higher education level :** Following things can be done at this stage

I. Students are systematically tested to know their interest and aptitude and test scores are interpreted for the use of pupils.
II. Students are suggested to choose a particular vocational course and information regarding admission in that course is also given to them.
III. Proper guidance is provided to them for the preparation of entrance test.
IV. While discussing the suitability of these occupations with the students several other factors like socio-economic factor, parents aspirations, job value, pay scale in the job, etc are also taken into account.

3. **Personal guidance :** It is concerned with the problems of the self ie, the problems which occurs within the individual. These problems are related to the personality and behaviour and unless they are not solved, adjustment of the individual in the society will not be possible.

Anxieties, tension, aggressiveness, adjustment difficulties, lack of confidence, shyness etc are some examples of personal problems. If these problems are not tackled professionally educational and vocational progress will also be retarded.

Thus, personal guidance maybe defined as helping students with psychological difficulties, conflicts, problems of daily life, behaviour and adjustment problems and so on.

Guidance and counselling to deal with personal problems need deeper understanding of the individual, so, a counsellor not only holds interviews with the individual and conducts standardized tests, but he also develops rapport with those persons who are in touch with the individual in any ways. The procedure adopted by the counseller is given below.

I. As soon as problematic cases are referred to the counsellor he tries to collect as many informations as he can from these cases.

II. Needed informations about the personality, behaviour or emotional disturbances are also collected from the relatives, mates and teachers of the problematic cases.

III. Informations about the cases are also collected by conducting standardized psychological tests.

IV. Counselling interviews are also arranged to collect more comprehensive information .

V. These informations are tabulated and analysed to interpret the behaviour of the case and to suggest relevant remedial measures.

## Tools of collecting information in guidance

Before providing any guidance to an individual, guidance worker needs a lot of information about him and about the environment in which he lives. These informations help him to understand the problem and its possible causes. These informations can not be collected all of a sudden. A number of techniques are used for a long time to collect these informations.

The collection of information about the individual is called diagnostic or appraisal services of guidance and counseling. **Two types of informations** are generally collected for this purpose.

1. **Psychological informations :** It includes information regarding intelligence, aptitude, attitude, skills, interest, personality traits, needs, values etc., of the individual concerned. Informations regarding behaviour of the individual in different situation are also collected here.
2. **Social data :** It includes information regarding home and school environment, social pressures on the individual, adjustment problems and so on.

The above two types of informations are collected by using the following **methods and techniques.**

I. **Records :** It refers to the qualities and abilities of the individual in relation to his background, i.e., informations related to his past. Interview is conducted for this purpose. Records are of three types.

(a) *Anecdotal records :* These records provide information about the behaviour of the individual in concrete situations. They illustrate some specific personality traits of the individual. For example, if an individual manifests honesty in a number of situations, he is said to be honest. These behaviour are described by using qualitative adjectives. In anecdotal records, short stories about the incident of behaviour indicating a characteristic of one's personality are written. Analysis of behaviour with the help of these incidents is very difficult.

(b) *Personal record :* It is the same as we see in factories where a comprehensive record of a worker indicating his qualification, date of appointment, nature of job, achievement of the worker, level of proficiency, his job related personal and social qualities, his negative output etc. is maintained by a personal officer. In guidance it indicates the total qualities of the individual in the context of his present and past assignment. For example, in the school situation, the punctuality of the child, his sincerity to class work, his achievement in tests, and exams etc., are recorded.

(c) *Comulative record :* They are more comprehensive than personnel records in the sense that they reflect the total personality of the child, i.e., his performance in co-curricular and curricular activities both. Important things included in this record are physical characteristics, health status, Intelligence, special aptitude and interest of the child, achievement in various school tests and examinations along with its trend, participation in games, sports and cultural programmes and performance trend in these fields, emotional status, level of self concept, his relationship with others, adjustment problems, personality traits, background of the child etc. All these informations are either stored in a file or in the computer disk to be used in future.

**Uses of records :** All these records help the guidance worker in the following manner.

I. Reason of why progress of an individual is slow or blocked can be found out

II. The points through which optimum progress can be achieved is identified.

III. Solutions of the problems can be suggested on the basis of the possible causes.

IV. Records can provide a good knowledge of potentialities and weaknesses of the individual as a result, measures to exploit potentialities and remove weaknesses can be suggested.

V. A brief discussion of records with the pupils can develop in them a more realistic perception of the situation in relation to their worths.

**II. Rating scale :** Such scales are of two types-
The informations supplied by the individual himself which is known as **check list** and the individual rated by others on the basis of observation of overt behaviour which is known as **outside rating.** A mixture of the two will help us understand an individual and his specific problems Rating scales have been discussed in detail in the chapter "Personality and its Measurement".

**III. Tests :** Tests play an important role in the educational life of the individual. When psychological tests are added to achievement tests., we can obtain a very objective and accurate information about an individual. Guidance work starts with diagnostic tests such as intelligence, aptitude or interest tests. Then behaviour or personality tests help the counsellor to analyse the personality of an individual in an objective manner and finally achievement tests complete the process by providing specific post training information to the cousellor. Readers are advised to go through the second part of the book, paper-Measurement and Evaluation, chapter first.

**Interpretation of diagnostic results :** Results of these tests for the purpose of guidance can be interpreted in three ways given below—

(a) *Directive interpretation :* In such interpretation, test results, abilities and achievement of the individual are interpreted in terms of his background and final decision about a career choice is made by the counsellee himself. The alternative career may be suggested by the counsellor if counsellee's decision does not exactly match with his potentialities and barriers. For the purpose of interpreting the results accurately, the counsellor should explain the significance of any test and its vocational implication to the counsellee before conducting any such tests. After the test is over, the counsellor should explain each and every point before the counsellee and help him to take his own decision.

(b) *Non-directive interpretation :* Problem of test interpretation has two aspects.

(i) Presenting test results to the clients in such a way that they can easily understand them

(ii) Dealing with the client in such a way that he can use these informations easily.

In non directive interpretations nothing is explained to the client. He is helped to understand the data in the following manner:

(i) Statistical predictions based on test results are communicated to him eg, the counsellor can say that only those scoring 90% in a particular test can compete an IIT test.

(ii) The counsellee is allowed to evaluate the prediction himself, ie, to what extent he is reaching to the prediction level.

(iii) Reactions of the client about the prediction after evaluation are noted down.

(iv) Client is allowed to take his own decision. He is not persuaded at all what he has to do and what he should not do.

(c) *Eclectic interpretation* : In this approach, results are interpreted on the basis of relevance to the client. Here, neither directive nor non-directive approach will serve the purpose but a combination of the two following pragmatic philosophy should be adopted to interpret the test results.

(d) *Essays and autobiographies* : Free association of thinking and imagination is seen in essays and autobiographies which help the counsellor to understand a client very thoroughly. In these two projective techniques the client projects himself in his own way without hiding his thinking, attitude or self. Readers are advised to go through the chapter, personality and its measurement.

(e) *Questionnaire* : (see the same chapter.)

(f) *Interviews* : (see the same chapter.)

## TECHNIQUES AND APPROACHES OF GUIDANCE AND COUNSELING

Based on varying nature of problems, clients are guided by using different techniques. Important such techniques and approaches are given below:

### 1. Rational Approach

In this approach the client is trained to think and evaluate his worth rationally and advised not to run after the dreams. A decision about career choice is taken here on the basis of logic and reasoning. In this approach diagnosis or appraisal of the client is made first and then on the basis of potentials and weaknesses, treatment is given.

According to this approach, counselling is a cognitive process where client's own thought process is manipulated and then on the basis of rational understanding of the problem, the individual is directed to go to a certain path. In this way, client finds a solution to his problem himself.

This approach is analytical in nature in the sense that clients are first made to recollect and realize those experiences, factors and conditions which created troubles for them and measures are suggested to remove those obstacles and this is done by the clients themselves. For example, suppose a client is having adjustment problem, he is first brought to retrieve from his those subconscious memories of experiences that really troubled him and is the major cause of maladjusted behaviour at present. The therapist probes the subconscious of the patient through transfer of his suppressed aggression. By this process, client comes to know that some of his basic urges were blocked. He also comes to know that if these urges get satisfied, he will behave normally. As a result of this counselling, confidence is developed in him and he will handle the similar situation in future without the help of the therapist.

Chief contributors of this approach are Thorne (1961), Ellis (1962), Weitz (1964) and Williamson (1965). The advocates of this approach use explanatory, persuasive, logical and directive techniques of counselling. Some of these techniques are given below:

(A) **Williamson's directive technique :** According to him counselling involves discussion, analysis, reasoning and other cognitive process. It should never be impersonal and formal in nature. Perfect rapport between the client and the counsellor should be established first then counselling should begin. This technique is based on the following assumptions:

(i) The aim of counselling is to help the individual achieve optimum development of personality by having a complete understanding of the self

(ii) Each individual is unique in many ways and all his unique qualities can be developed in the group, ie, interaction with other is necessary for development.

(iii) Counseling is a voluntary process. Nobody can be compelled to go for guidance, though non willing persons can be benefitted occasionally.

(iv) Counselling is a remedial process. A person comes to take guidance when he is unable to solve a problem himself.

*(v)* Counselling is an unbiased and neutral process, i.e., counsellor does not impose his personal opinions on his clients.

*(vi)* Counselling is a self made process based on the self perception of the problem by the client. He will take initiative to solve his problem himself.

*(vii)* Counselling is a cognitive process based on reason and logic.

*(viii)* Counsellor will have to back on the resources that he has in the form of worths and weaknesses of his clients and he will develop them to the fullest extent after careful appraisal.

## Steps of counseling according to williamson

Six steps to be followed in Williamson's techniques are given below:

**First step:** Analysis : Here, data about the counsellee are collected by using various tools and thorough appraisal of the client is done.

**Second step:** Synthesis : Here, the data collected are organized and summarized in order to draw a clear picture of the individual, ie, what the individual is at present and why he is so. In order to answer why part of the question interviews and discussions with the client and his associates are also conducted.

**Third step:** Diagnosis : The data organized are used in order to identify the problem and its possible causes Williamson used three methods for this purpose:

Clinical method where results of each test are interpreted separately or in relation to other tests attempted by the client in different situations.

Psychometric method where scores are compared with occupational norms in order to know the level of the client.

Psychometric index method where client's scores are converted into the total score or index.

**Fourth step:** Prognosis : Here, prediction of the consequences of the problem and its dynamism is made, ie, what will happen if client does not take remedial measures. It is generally expressed in the form of a hypothesis.

**Fifth step:** Counselling : Here the measures to solve the problem are identified and suggested to the client after discussion with him.

Several methods of counselling described by Williamson are as follows:

*(i)* Forcing confirmity, The client is motivated to accept the norms of the group to which he belongs.

*(ii)* Changing the environment. The client is suggested to choose new environment to avoid the recurrence of the problem.

*(iii)* Learning needed skills : The client is suggested to learn those skills which he does not have at present and which is the cause of the problem.

*(iv)* Changing the client himself, The client is suggested to change his attitude and behaviour in order to remove his difficulties.

**Sixth step :** referring to other experts : If problems of the client is beyond the reach of the counsellor, the client is sent to other persons for further counseling and guidance.

Rogers has criticized the above directive counselling technique by saying that in this technique, the counsellor poses himself as an expert who can solve any problem of the client and the later totally becomes dependable on the former.

**(B) Ellis' directive technique :** This is also known as Rational psychotherapy. It is very much useful for dealing with personal and emotional problems. Stresses and anxieties can be removed by this technique. According to him, most of the emotional problems are due to irrational thinking. If such thinking is removed by making the client a rational person, emotional disturbance will be over. The client can be made a rational being in the following manner.

*(i)* The client is made aware of his irrational thoughts by discussion

*(ii)* Client is told that irrational thinking causes emotional disturbances and behaviour problems

*(iii)* Client is made aware of his illogical verbalization.

*(iv)* Logical thinking is developed in the client.

**(C) Thorne's directive technique :** Thorne is eclectic more in his approach than directive because he says no technique is applicable always and everywhere. Clients differ in their perception of the self and of the environment. They also differ in speed in solving their problems, so, methods of counselling should vary according to the demand of the particular situation and person. In spite of this his technique is called directive because it uses medical model of therapy, ie, personality disorders can be corrected in the same way as any physical ailment is cured Thorne classified problems into different categories and suggested relevant techniques to remove these problems under each category, though some methods maybe suitable to more than one category

Thorne has given the following counseling methods that should be used according to the nature of the problem.

*(i)* Method used for dealing with complaints

*(ii)* Method used for dealing with emotional and adjustment problems

*(iii)* Method used for dealing with problems of therapeutic nature

*(iv)* Method used for dealing with intellectual power of the client.

Thorne further said that the distinction between directive and non directive technique is unreal. So, only those methods should be used by the counsellor which suit to the situation. In addition to suggestion and persuasion, Thorne supports the use of other measures also, such as, pressure, coercion and punishmen.

## 2. Leaning Theory Approach

According to this approach the purpose of counselling is to modify the behaviour of the client which is actually learning in technical term. Thus, counseling and learning are the same thing. Since theories of learning are many, counseling techniques will also be many more. Broadly, counseling techniques can be classified into two categories according to learning theory approach.

(A) S-R Techniques of counseling

(B) Cognitive field techniques of counseling

**(A) S-R techniques of counseling :** Exponents of these techniques say that behaviour of the individual is the result of stimulus (external forces) exerted upon him. If these forces are manipulated, behaviour will change. So, counseling should be directed to the manipulation of the stimuli. This way of counseling has been termed as "Behaviour therapy" by Eysenck (1960). Among so many approaches of counseling here, **Skinner's** operant conditioning is more popular than Pavlov's respondent conditioning though all these approaches are very much successful in modifying the behaviour.

Behaviour therapy assumes that a behaviour or motion is not necessarily the result of some inner problem that has to be worked out in therapy. It may rather be a superstitious behaviour, one conditioned through chance contingencies of the environment not recognized by the person himself but still effective in producing a behaviour. If those chance contingencies are eliminated, behaviour will be correct. If we are able to identify the unknown stimuli responsible for that and remove them, behaviour problem will be over.

Another approach of correcting behaviour is that the person is desensitized for that stimulus which is the cause of unwanted responses. For ;this purpose weak form of stimulus similar to the real one is given and response is seen. This process is repeated till the original response is extinguished.

Operant conditioning approach of counseling is that in which responses closer to accuracy are reinforced and behaviour is shaped step by step.

**Applied Behaviour Analysis (ABA)** which came into being in 1965 is another approach. It drops out some features of operant conditioning and adds some new ones. ABA therapists prefer to work in educational setting rather than in a clinic. They follow the maxim "prevention is better than cure". Thus, they do not approve medical model of treatment for behaviour problems. In the words of **Goodall** "if a person manifests deviant behaviour, it is due to the defect prevailing in the physical and social environment that determines his behaviour not in the individual. "It means that if environment is rectified, behaviour will also be rectified. Goodall further states "the best person to provide the treatment are parents, teachers, friends, not the medicos. Ogden Lindsley, Florence Harris, Vance Hall, Montrose Wolf, Donald M Baer, etc. are some other psychologists who support this view.

**(B) Cognitive field techniques of counseling :** In such techniques behaviour of clients is changed and corrected by changing his perception of the total environment through goal centred approach of living. According to perceptual theorists, learning is not simply a matter of motivation, repetition, presentation, stimulation or conditioning. Learning is the result of total personality that a person possesses. Anything that has no personal meaning for the person is not learned by him at all. In other words we can say that learning is the discovery of personal meaning.

According to perceptual theorists, factors that determine the colour of an individual's perceptual field are his needs, values, goals and his self concept. It is the perceptual field that determines how the person will behave in a particular situation. Combs has listed seven such factors determining perceptual field.

*(i)* Physical nature of human organism

*(ii)* Length of time he has lived

*(iii)* Opportunities of perception got by him in the past.

*(iv)* Need of the person at present

*(v)* The goals and values held by the individual at present

*(vi)* Self concept of the person.

*(vii)* Perception hindering factor that is experience of threat or anxiety.

Thus the basic difference between this approach and S-R one is that in the S-R system, the forces outside the organism are manipulated to correct the behaviour while in perceptual field approach, forces inside the personality of the individual are manipulated. We will manipulate the above seven factors and modify the behaviour. There are two therapies based on perceptual reorganization very famous and popular. First is Roger's **client centred therapy** and second is Kelley's **Personal construct therapy**

Client centred approach of counseling is also known as **phenomenological approach**. To Carl Rogers, phenomenal field of the individual means the totality of his own experiences. Thus, he places great importance to self. That is why his theory is also called self theory of counseling. Some features of this theory are as follows:

I. It considers individual as an organised whole and basic aim of his life is self actualization. This is possible only through the interaction with the environment.

II. Total experiences of the individual at a given time constitute his phenomenal field.

III. Every individual wants to develop his self concept through self perception.

IV. Behaviour is determined by the concept of self. Complete matching between phenomenal field and self concept results into a balanced personality which is free from stress and strain.

Roger's client centred therapy is based on the following **assumptions:**

I. Man is not a machine to be manipulated at will. Man is rather creative, rational, constructive, forward moving and a social being. Man is capable of solving his problems by developing his self and by taking some help from outside.

II. Human being functions as an organized whole in the direction of satisfying its needs. He reacts to his phenomenal field on the basis of his own experiences. The experiences which are inconsistent with the self concept are denied symbolization and thus they are ignored.

III. Human being always creates his self in a forward moving manner.

**Procedure or technique** of counseling followed by client centred therapy is given below:

I. Inherent potentialities are first taken out by holding interview of the client. This helps the client solve his problems himself through the maximum exploitation of the self.

II. Relevant needs of the client in relation to his environment are identified in the second step. This helps him improve his self concept and discover the nature of his difficulties. When self concept is improved positive change in behaviour takes place.

III. The counseller accepts the self report of the client as the direct and the correct source of information. Counsellor always shows warmth of feeling and sense of understanding without showing any biased reaction to what the client says. His permissive behaviour for the client makes him more expressive and more active. Client is very much valuable for the counsellor whatever maybe his shortcomings

IV. After knowing the strengths and weaknesses of the client no direct advice is given to him. He is rather given full freedom to discuss his matter of concern further. Then in the context of perception of whole, the client is brought to the state where the client is capable of matching his self concept with the phenomenal field.

The second therapy which is very popular is Kelley's **personal construct therapy**. In this approach Kelley has drifted to some extent from the position of perception to development of conception for the purpose of changing behaviour (though conception depends upon perception) He believes that deviant behaviour has its routs into the constructs of the individual which maybe defined as organized way of thinking about things, events and persons and consistent belief about the world and the people. If any deviance is seen in the behaviour of an individual, it is due to his faulty constructs formed. For removing the behaviour problems, thinking of the person will have to change. He further says that in order to understand people and their behaviour, we will have to see things as they do by placing our own constructs over theirs rather than just observing their overt behaviour. It is said "Hamraz Ban Kar Raz Lena" in Urdu.

Kelley's approach is also known as **fixed role therapy** which uses active counseling method and emphasizes rational processes and diagnostic techniques. It first analyses and explains the feelings and constructs of the client and then replaces the irrational constructs by rational ones. Kelley's approach requires the counsellor to help the client try out a different picture of himself through acting out a planned role for a specific period of time. Thus, his approach is very close to Williamson and Ellis. The task of the counsellor here will be to form new personal construct by loosening old constructs. Thus, outlook or the attitude of the client toward the environment is changed here. According to Kelley a problem client is he who discovers and lives with unsatisfactory constructs. If he is helped to rediscover some satisfying constructs and practise them in life, his problem will be cured. So, counseling will begin from the point how the client looks at the other people and the world, i.e., how he interprets the norms and values. After that the causes of inadequate looking of the world is analysed.

## 3. Psychoanalytic Approach

Freud was the first physiologist who used this approach for the purpose of changing the behaviour of the people. Jung and Adler were other medical men who used psychoanalysis for treating maladjusted and deviant people.

According to psychoanalytic theory, all kinds of mental illness and behavioural disorders are due to the blocking of expressions of psychic energy system. Sexual instinct, (libido) is the main of all neurotic disorders. Psycho-anylysis deals with unconscious mind of the patient and is based on the assumption that individual in the society has to repress many desires due to social and familial restrictions. These repressed desires are dragged into unconscious of the individual and causes a deviant behaviour shown by him thus, "repression" is one of the defence mechanisms of the ego ie, adjustment is made by repressing the ego and reconciling the social pressures. When this mechanism is excessively used, mental illness develops.

According to psychoanalysts, mind is a kind of conflict solving instrument. When mind is unable to solve these conflicts, psychological disorders are caused. For example, we need sexual gratification after puberty, if it is not availed for long, constant repression of the desire will create a conflict in our mind, and if mind is unable to cope with this conflict, mental disorders will be the result. In order to solve this type of problem, the origin of defense mechanism (repression of ego) should be located first. Sex is not the only cause of such conflicts according to later psychoanalysts. Social factors like self respect, status, inter-personal relations etc are also the cause of conflicts and hence mental disorders.

Important techniques of counseling used in this approach are as follows:

(a) *Free association and dream analysis (Freud):* In free association technique patient is asked to lie on a bed in an easy mood. He is then asked to verbalise his feeling without any fear or restriction. The doctor keeps himself away from the client at that moment. The doctor gives his comment if necessary during the expression from a distance. In this way, the patient brings his repressed desires from unconscious state of mind to the conscious mind and causes of behaviour problems comes to light.

**Dream analysis was the second techniques developed by Freud**

This technique is based on the assumption that our repressed desires, feelings and motives appear in our dreams in disguised form and can provide lots of information to understand the behaviour problem of a client. When dream is reported by the client, the psycho-analyst listens to him very carefully and observes the emotional tone of the client also. Lastly all these things are analysed to come to the causes of the problem.

Following points should be kep. in mind by the doctor while using the above two techniques.

I. The patient should be encouraged to express himself freely and frankly.

II. The doctor should discover family style of the patient which will lead him to know the life style of the patient.

III. Goals and motives of the patient should also be discovered.

IV. He should be so careful that the patient may not subterfuge him and give him wrong information.

V. A congenial and friendly atmosphere at the time of counseling is also necessary.

(b) *Persuation :* Through this techniques, the client is explained about his irrational thinking and behaviour and trained to face the realities of life. As a result, the client gets rid of his irrational thoughts and misconceptions. The client is also told that the solutions of his problem lies in the exercise of his will power and in the release of his pent up feelings.

## Other techniques of Psychotherapy or Counseling

As we know, in psychotherapy psychogenic diseases are treated by psychological methods rather than by using medicines. Mental problems are first diagnosed here by using various techniques or tools and then curative measures are applied to the patient. Apart from the above techniques some more techniques are also used in psychotherapy. They are given below:

1. **Play therapy :** It is a technique of modifying the behaviour of small children, who suffer from any sort of emotional disturbances. In this technique of counseling, child is given full freedom to play in the manner he likes. He expresses his emotions through play activities and materials. His pent up emotions and conflicts are released through these plays. Guidance is given to the child after the end of the play on the basis of his emotional reactions and by and by the child becomes more adaptive to the situation he is in.Play therapy may be used in two ways:

   (a) *Non directive play therapy :* In this method, child is given full freedom to do anything whatever he likes in the play room. He can manipulate any play material in his own way and his behaviour is observed by the therapist.

   (b) *Controlled play therapy :* In this method, the therapist selects the play material for the child himself and plans the sessions of play in standardized situation keeping the age of the child and nature of his problem into account.

Play therapy is based on the assumption that the child may acquire new feelings and attitudes by his plays which maybe generalized to life situations.

2. **Shock therapy :** There are two methods commonly used in shock therapy First is **insulin coma** and second is electric **shock therapy**.

   (a) *Insulin coma :* In this method, insulin injection is given to the patient. This technique was developed by Sakel in 1928.

   (b) *Electric shock :* In this method, current of different voltages is passed through the brain of the patient in order to produce convulsion. This method is less painful for the patient than insulin coma.

These two methods are generally opposed by the psychologists on the ground that no one knows how and why they work. In spite of that, shock therapy is used even today. Assumptions underlying the shock therapy are given below:

I. Shock therapy alters the brain metabolism causing changes in oxidation.

II. It acts as sedatives and hence it reduces the over activity of the central nervous system. Sedatory effects can reduce the emotional pressure also.

III. When this therapy is applied, some organic changes in the brain are produced which interrupt the path from the cerebral cortex to the thalamus and reduce the transmission of emotional impulses from one to the other.

3. **Occupational therapy :** It works in the same way on adults as play therapy works on children. Here, therapist organises various occupations for the client through which he can expresses his creative and emotional feelings. These occupations are selected keeping in view the age, interest and educational status of the client. When the client is engaged in his occupation, his suppressed and repressed motives are released.
4. **Transaction analysis :** This approach of counseling was developed by Eric Berne. TA is actually a theory of personality and social action and a clinical method of psychotherapy based on the analysis of all possible transactions between two or more people. This theory wants to turn the people into a real, and autonomous people free from the chain of the past. Autonomous people are, aware of their environment. They perceive the people and the world in their own personal way. They know their own feelings and fantasies and they are always willing to act accordingly. These autonomous people behave according to their own impulsive feeling. They choose their life style and career as their impulses dictate them. Thus, real people have mainly three qualities awareness, autonomy and intimacy.
   Four types of analysis is done in this approach.
   *(a)* Structural analysis
   *(b)* Transactional analysis
   *(c)* Game analysis
   *(d)* Script analysis
5. **Eclectic approach :** When a therapist banks upon all the sources and systems for counseling, it is called eclectic approach. The purpose of this approach is to solve the problems of the client in whatever manner it is possible. Here selection of method depends on the nature of the problem and demand of the situation.
6. **Aversion therapy :** The aim of this therapy is to eliminate deviant behaviour and replacing it by developing satisfactory behaviour in the client. Therapists generally use two methods for this purpose.
   I. Punishment is given for eliminating conditioning
   II. Classical conditioning method for developing desired behaviour.

**Differences between Freudian psychotherapy and behaviour therapy**

| S.No. | Freudian therapy | Behaviour therapy |
|---|---|---|
| 1 | It is based on inconsistent theory | It is based on consistent theory |
| 2 | It was derived from clinical observations | It was derived from experimental studies on learning |
| 3 | It considers the symptoms visible upshot of unconscious causes | It considers symptoms as unadaptive conditioned response |
| 4 | It regards symptoms as evidence of repression | It regards symptoms as evidence of faulty learning |
| 5 | It believes that symptoms are determined by defense mechanisms | It believes that symptoms are determined by faulty learning |
| 6 | All treatment of neurotic disorders must be historically based. | All treatment of neurotic disorders is concerned with habit existing at present. |
| 7 | Cures are achieved by handling the underlying dynamics, not by treating the symptom itself | Cures are achieved by treating the symptom itself |
| 8 | Interpretation of symptoms, dreams etc. is an important element of treatment | Interpretation even if not completely subjective and erroneous, is irrelevant |
| 9 | Symptomatic treatment leads to the elaboration of new symptoms | Symptomatic treatment is permanent recovery |
| 10 | Transference relations are essential for cures of neurotic disorders | Personal relations are not important for cures of neurotic disorders, although they may be useful in certain circumstances. |

## Organizing guidance services at different levels of education

Guidance services aim at making such individuals who are personally well adjusted, occupationally well adapted and socially and emotionally mature in their thinking and action. It is in this sense that the task of guidance services do not essentially differ from the task of education in general. Both of them differ only in their approach, techniques, and specific programmes meant for the clients. Guidance and counseling may be considered as complementary to education because attainment of educational goals are facilitated through such services. Such services may be a regular part of school programme and may be organised separately. These services are provided by professionally trained specialized persons who have specialization in different fields of guidance and counseling. They are concerned mainly with the personal, social and emotional development of the students.

One more difference between a guidance worker and a teacher is that former does not have any touch with the school curriculum and a teacher is tied up with the school curriculum.

## Need for guidance services

1. Our society has become very complex in nature today. Its fast changing requirement cannot be fulfilled by traditional education only. A variety of professional training and education is needed by the individual to adjust fully in the society. Guidance services provide us such information in an specialized manner.
2. Materialism and consumerism have increased our personal and social adjustment problems many times. Stress and strain have become a part of our lives today. Such problems can be solved only by those who are especially trained in the field of guidance and counseling.
3. Every individual is not able to measure his strengths and weaknesses on his own and if efforts on to achieve a particular goal of life without knowing the capacity or interest, wastage of time, money and energy will be the result.
4. Such services help in the optimum utilization of potentialities of an individual which is indirectly contributive to the society also.
5. No two individuals are alike in the world. From mental to physical or social aspects they differ in many ways. Best choices are made available to these individuals through guidance services.
6. Humans are capable to solve their problems themselves. The only thing that is needed is that they should be given opportunities in a proper setting. Guidance services provide such opportunities to them and self confidence created in them helps them in many ways.
7. An important problem that every students in the secondary school faces is the selection of subject or course of study. Guidance services provide him such vocational and technical guidance by testing him in different ways.
8. Information about the nature and status of job after education and training is also given to students by guidance workers.

## Objectives of Guidance Services in the School

**(a) General objectives :**

I. Helping the underachievers and low achievers in the school.
II. Helping exceptional and deviant groups of students.
III. Treating juvenile delinquents
IV. Helping the students to select suitable subjects and course of study.
V. Helping them to adjust properly in the school.
VI. Helping them to choose the best career
VII. Helping the pupils to develop their potentialities to the maximum'
VIII. Guiding the pupils to solve their own problems themselves
IX. Helping the students know their potentialities and shortcomings and the nature of their personality.
X. Providing them information about the world of work.

**(b) Specific objectives :** In order to realize the general objectives, they are divided into functional activities carried out by the guidance workers and counsellors. These activities are as follows:

I. Interpreting various educational programmes running in the country and in the world including their basic requirements for admission.
II. Reorienting the students to all school activities and guiding them to choose the best as specialization.

III. Adopting theraputical measures for helping the students to adjust in the society properly.
IV. Informing students about their potentialities and weaknesses including their personal interests and personality characteristics by conducting standardized tests and interviews and helping them to utilize these potentialities to the maximum.
V. Assisting students to make plans for their career on the basis of their needs, interests and abilities.
VI. Helping the people in getting better placement after education.
VII. Devising suitable techniques and measures to be used by teachers to cope with the problem of under achievement
VIII. Assisting exceptional children by using suitable materials and methods and guiding them to occupational adjustment.

## TYPES OF GUIDANCE AND COUNSELING SERVICES IN THE SCHOOL

To achieve the objectives mentioned above various types of programmes and guidance services are organised in the school. There is no maximum limit of such services. It depends upon the resources available with the school and objectives it was founded with. However, five basic programmes are essentially needed in guidance and counseling.

### 1. Orientation Services

These services are organised to achieve two basic objectives.

I. to motivate the students to learn and achieve more in the class room.
II. To acquaint the students with the basic philosophy, objectives and traditions of the school itself and to help them best utilize the facilities available in the school.

These services are mainly forwarded through dialogues but other measures like the use of psychotherapy are also used. Such services may be provided to parents also and they can be enlightened about the educational and social scenario of the country and the efforts made by the school to achieve highest level of educational objectives. If parents are well informed about what the school is doing for their wards, they are expected to cooperate more with the school personnel and maximum development of the child will be seen.

### 2. Information Services

Students need various types of informations in the school. They need information about themselves to develop their potentialities to the maximum. They also need information about the world of work to choose a better career. Thus, information services provide two types of informations.

(a) Personal information
(b) Occupational information

**(a) Personal information :** It means information about the pupil, i.e., what he is and what he is likely to be in future. Socio-economic background of the pupil is also taken into account while communicating these informations to pupils. Here information regarding personality, intelligence, interest, creative potentials, adjustment problems, interpersonal relationship and needs of pupils are accumulated and supplied to pupils and concerned personnel. These informations are collected by conducting tests, interviews and observation schedules. These informations help the pupil to adopt a realistic attitude towards education and life.

**(b) Occupational information :** This information maybe considered as base for educational and career guidance. Choice of course after high school and selection of career after 10+2 depend mostly on this information. For example, if a student wants to become a doctor, he will study biology along with physics and chemistry at 10+2 level. Then he will appear in pre-medical test after 10+2. For this purposes , he must also know the places and institutes where medical education is given and what are the criteria of admission in MBBS course. Before communicating such informations to students they should be systematically collected, stored and disseminated. These works are done by the career information centre of the school. **Procedure followed in occupational information** is given below:

**First Step—Collection of Information :** Informations regarding institutions of professional and academic learning courses available in those institutions, criteria and procedure of admission in those courses and nature and status of job after the completion of course are collected from different sources, such as booklets, pamphlets, newsletters, career book and information voucher published by various agencies and educational institutions themselves. Some of these literature are also published by the government agencies such as state educational and vocational guidance Bureau, Directorate general of Resettlement and Employment, (Ministry of labour govt, of India ) etc. Daily and weekly newspapers and monthly magazines are other sources of occupational information, where advertisements about various courses are published. These informations need to be updated every year due to fast changing educational and occupational scenario of the country.

**Second Step—Filing and upkeeping the Information** If collected informations are filed and maintained properly only then it can be supplied to students on demand timely and readily. For the purpose of proper filing, the information received are first classified into categories on the basis of its nature and importance. Those informations which are frequently needed may be kept in a separate file. After preparing required number of files of various types of informations, they are alphabetically arranged . Nowadays computers are being used for storing occupational informations and they can quickly be made available to the user. Use of internet has also come into practice and website created for the purpose provides complete information about a particular course or job.

Following **methods** are commonly **used for filing informations.**

I. **Alphabetical system :** In this system, names of occupations are arranged in alphabetical order. Eligibility criteria for different occupations are also given with the name . The different occupations are also given with the name. The demerit of this method is that if a person is eligible for different occupations he can not find them without going the whole lot.

II. **National classification of occupation *(NCO):*** In NCO, occupations are classified into families. Then families are combined into groups and groups are classified into divisions.

III. **Filing based on school subjects :** Here, occupations related to different school subjects are filed in separate groups such as occupations related to literature, Mathematics group science subjects, biology group science subjects, occupations related to fine arts and so on. It is very comfortable for students who have to select occupation on the basis of their qualification and stream of education.

**Third Step–Disseminating information :** Filed informations are communicated to students at their demand . The necessary informations reach them any how in whatever manner it is possible. It should reach to those students also who do not take much interest in these informations in the beginning. This is the process of disseminating information. It is done by using any of the following mediums.

I. **Display centre :** Posters, charts, leaflets, news letters, notification and advertisement of jobs etc. are used to display information about jobs and courses of study in the display centre. Bulletin board, display racks, display windows etc. may be used for the display of these materials. Posters may be displayed at the gate of the school or in the library. Leaflets, monographs and news letters should be kept in racks in such a way that students may have access to them easily. Every display material should have an attractive title or headline. Some bulletins and booklets may be issued to pupils to study them thoroughly at home. Right in the beginning of the session the guidance worker should invite all the pupils to visit career information centre and see all the materials available there. Photo copy of the material maybe given to students on demand

II. **Career talks :** For disseminating informations, career talks is the most popular and easy method. The guidance worker makes arrangement for such talks according to the educational qualifications and courses of study selected or to be selected by students. In India such talks are needed at the end of either class $10^{th}$ or $12^{th}$ which are bifurcation points for further education and training. Through this method, complete information about the eligibility criteria and admission procedure in a particular course is given to students. Students are also told how they can go to that level and what level of preparation is needed to achieve the goal. Career talks may also be organised after graduation because different varieties of career is available after BA, B.Sc, B Com. MBBS, B Tech, etc. During such career talks, students are also motivated to come to the career master for free discussion at the end of lecture. Question answer session may also be arranged for clarification of points. Experts in various specialized field such as leading industrialists, government officers, managers of private or public companies may also be invited to deliver a lecture on career building in the school. The purpose of such talk should always be to guide the students from beginning of preparation to all minute details about the career. No point should be left by the speaker. Relevant written materials may also be supplied to students at the end of final session.

**III. Career conference :** Such conferences are generally organised by educational institutions once a year in which experts in different fields are invited to speak before the gathering on career issues. Special arrangement is made for the conference in the college as a result, students take much interest in career guidance programmes. Parents and local people are also invited to attend this conference. Even students of other schools are also be invited here. The most suitable time for such conferences is the first week of November. In such conferences separate sessions should be organised for different classes and courses of study. Officers from state Bureau of educational and Vocational guidance should also be invited to speak in such conferences. If there is any local guy who has gained success in any particular field, he should also be invited to share his experiences with the local students. It will be very much motivating for all local boys.

Topics for such conferences should be selected according to needs and interest of pupils and demands of the local people and their economic and social background. Mind that if occupational preparation is very costly and local students can not afford guidance about this type of career, it is of no use.

Lastly, complete information should be given to students about a particular field. For this purpose, its allied branches should also be covered. For example, all students can not become MBBS. Hence, they may be given details about its allied fields such as nursing, dentistry, pharmacy, pathology, radiology ophthalmology etc.

**IV. Career visits :** The purpose of such visits is to have first hand experience and information about a particular career. Pupils are taken to the places where the job is actually done by professionals. An informal discussion between the career master and the pupils is also followed after such visits. While organizing such visits, the guidance worker should have a list of leading industries and institutions of higher learning. Prior appointment from management of concerned establishment is also necessary before such visits. Complete adherence to social etiquettes and disciplinary rules is necessary during such visits.

**V. Practical job experience :** In order to provide work experience to students, they are taken to the place of work (factories and establishment) in their summer and winter vocations. Students come to know through such experiences about the practicability and vitality of the work. This drags them from the world of dream and enables them to face the realities of life. They can test their abilities in the job also.

**VI. Meeting with old boys of the college :** Those old students of the college who are already placed in different types of jobs can give a lot of informations to the existing students. Such meetings are arranged by the guidance worker in the college when these old students come to their homes on vacations.

A list of old boys along with their complete bio data is always kept ready for this purpose. Personal contact with such old boys is necessary for the purpose. These old boys of the college may give upto date occupational information to the students at present .

**VII. Information through school subjects :** Many types of occupational informations can be included in school subjects and teachers who teach these subjects are invited by the guidance worker to enrich the career information centre with these informations. Teachers are also encouraged to collect more such information and supply it to the centre.

**VIII. Publication :** Many career informations may be published in guidance news letter or monthly bulletin of career information centre. These materials are provided to students either free of cost or on nominal charges. Guidance worker can make a survey of local employment opportunities and the training facilities available in the locality and these things may be published in the newsletter. Achievement of local students in different fields along with their interviews can also by published and communicated to students.

## 3. Testing Services

The purpose of this service of the guidance centre is to collect information about the pupil in order to guide him according to his strength and psychological tendencies. Interest, values, personality, intelligence, adjustment etc. regarding a pupil is tested here through standardized measures and tests. These psychological tests are prepared either by the guidance worker himself or purchased from the market. These tests are administered to students in different sessions and then they are scored and analysed either manually or by a computer. The records of these tests are kept by the guidance worker all the time.

## 4. Guidance and Counseling Services

After collecting so many informations about the pupil through tests and interviews, proper guidance or counseling services are provided to him. It is the stage of real help provided to students. Normal and deviant both types of pupils need these services to get rid of their personal and behavioural problems and to choose a better career on the basis of their capability. Guidance and counseling services may be personal, vocational or education depending on the requirement of the pupil.

## 5. Follow up Services

In order to know the results and progress of guidance and counseling services, follow up is needed. It tells us to what extent, students have been benefited from these services. and what further measures are required to be taken. It is, thus, evaluation stage of guidance and counseling. It helps the guidance worker and the counsellor to bring about change in strategies and improvement. Follow up services may be periodic and unscheduled both and organised according to the need. Interview method is generally used to review the progress of guidance and counseling.

## Guidance and Counseling at different Levels

**(A) Guidance and counseling at secondary level of education :** Following services are provided at this stage:

1. Individual records of pupils are maintained which includes their educational achievement in the past, their trend of progress and change of interest, their intelligence, their personality characteristics, their values, their socio-economic status, goals of life etc.
2. Various types of orientation services are provided to them and efforts are made to increase their achievement in curricular and co-curricular programmes.
3. Behaviour of pupils with reference to their adolescent needs and problems is closely monitored and efforts are made to get them adjusted fully in the society.
4. Special exploratory programmes are organised for them in order to explore their hobbies and specific interest.
5. Necessary occupational as well as personal informations are supplied to them to get them acquainted with the social needs and personal requirements. It should be noted that at this age, they cannot stick to their missions constantly. So regular feedback is necessary. Besides, occupational information helps them select best subjects and streams at the 10+2 level in order to build a good career.
6. They need regular counseling in secondary class because of their specific demand created by their physiological changes in the body coupled with emotional problems. These services are provided to them.

7. Students with special problems are referred to other specialized agencies for career guidance and behaviour counseling.
8. Personal records specifying their strengths and weaknesses are supplied to pupils. This makes them realistic in approach and pupils will not waste their time, money and energy in non-reachable occupational pursuits.
9. Parents of pupils are also informed about the courses running in the school and prospects of different types of courses available in the country.
10. Occupational informations in detail are given to all the pupils through display centres, publications, lectures by experts, occupational visits etc.
11. Pupils are given guidelines how to prepare and take different types of examinations and tests.
12. Follow up services are also organised in order to see to what extent these students have benefited from guidance and counseling services.

**(B) At senior secondary level :** At this level of education, streams and sub streams of subjects are already clear. Students take admission in arts, commerce, science (Bio group) and science (maths group) and some students offer vocational courses like ITI, polytechnic etc. Guidance and counseling programmes are arranged for these students in the following manner—

1. They are given complete information about medical and Para medical courses, technical courses, course of engineering and technology, courses related to business and industry, courses related to clerical jobs and all are meant for 10+2 passed students.
2. Students are guided how to take admission in the above courses and what are the pre-conditions for that, e.g., no student below 60% marks in 10+2 can appear in IIT entrance test.
3. Intelligence and personality of pupils are again tested in order to give them a realistic suggestion whether they are capable for competing a particular exam. or not.
4. Individual record is prepared and maintained here also and progress reports of pupils is communicated to parents also.
5. Pupils are suggested about different options which are available for them on the basis of their abilities and efforts.
6. Regular counseling programmes are organised for under achievers and for those who have any behaviour problem either due to physical reasons or mental ones.
7. Orientation programmes are organised for pupils for developing interest in a particular stream and for increasing scholastic achievement.
8. Parents and pupils are given assistance in changing options within the stream if possible.
9. Orientation of employment opportunities after the completion of a particular course are given which is necessarily based on the study of particular subjects or stream at 10+2 level.
10. Students are helped in making proper planning for their career and course of study. Informations regarding inter-connection of different courses are also given to them

**(C) At higher education level :** Higher education can be bifurcated into two groups, higher education (technical) and higher education (general). Technical graduate of any field do not need much guidance or counseling because they know about all the PG courses available in their respective field. They need only guidance about the place of work, ie, where they can get job after their education.

As far as graduates in general and non technical/ professional courses are concerned they need guidance in a proper way. Following types of guidance services can be made available to these students.

1. They are given information about the job opportunities after graduation or post graduation and how they can get those jobs
2. Selection tests are conducted in most of the jobs. Students are guided how to prepare for such tests and how to take them.
3. Every country needs a lot of clerical and assistant staff and selection in all these jobs is done on the basis of a competitive exam and interview. Full guidance is given to students for this purpose
4. Many creative potentials become evident at this stage. Pupils are guided to exploit their potential to the maximum
5. Intelligence and personality of students are tested to guide them to opt for a particular job on the basis of their abilities and interest.

# OBJECTIVE QUESTIONS

1. Directive therapy was developed by
   (*a*) Carl Roger (*b*) Ellis
   (*c*) Skinner (*d*) None of the above
2. Directive technique of counseling puts emphasis on
   (*a*) Knowing the causes of the problem first
   (*b*) Applying direct remedial measures
   (*c*) Developing counseling on the basis of learning theories
   (*d*) None of the above
3. Counseling based on learning theories and principles is known as
   (*a*) Shock therapy (*b*) Eclectic therapy
   (*c*) Behaviour therapy (*d*) Play therapy
4. The term behaviour therapy was coined by Lazaraus in
   (*a*) 1994 (*b*) 1956
   (*c*) 1932 (*d*) 1950
5. According to Watson and Rayner learnt fear can be removed by which of the following techniques?
   (*a*) Experimental extinction
   (*b*) Constructive activities around the feared objects
   (*c*) Reconditioning through feeding the child in the presence of the feared objects.
   (*d*) All of the above
6. Bringing desirable changes in the behaviour of the client by reinforcing the behaviour close to the point of correction successively is called.
   (*a*) Generalization (*b*) Shaping
   (*c*) Fading (*d*) Extinction
7. Which of the following is the best method of treating neurotic patient?
   (*a*) Eclectic method
   (*b*) Electric shock method
   (*c*) Gradual desensitization
   (*d*) Play method
8. The method used to release the blocked emotions and pent up motives is
   (*a*) Desensitization (*b*) Psycho drama
   (*c*) Socio drama (*d*) None of these
9. Which of the following terms is close to guidance?
   (*a*) Professional advice
   (*b*) Group counseling
   (*c*) Psycho therapy
   (*d*) All of these
10. Which of the following statements about counseling is not correct?
    (*a*) Every child needs counseling
    (*b*) Counseling is a continuous process
    (*c*) Same counseling procedure is needed for all the pupils
    (*d*) Counseling helps the pupil to solve his problem himself
11. Which among the following tools of collecting psychological informations about the pupil is the most objective?
    (*a*) Rating scale (*b*) Interview
    (*c*) Standardized tests (*d*) Projective devices
12. Which of the following is the contributor of rational approach of counseling?
    (*a*) Thorne (*b*) Ellis
    (*c*) Williamson (*d*) All of these
13. In Williamson's directive technique of counseling, which of the following is the third step?
    (*a*) Synthesis (*b*) Diagnosis
    (*c*) Counseling (*d*) None of these
14. Learning theory approach of counseling is based on the assumption that
    (*a*) Behaviour is acquired and hence can be modified
    (*b*) Behaviour is genetic
    (*c*) Behaviour changes with age
    (*d*) None of these
15. In behaviour therapy
    (*a*) The desired behaviour is conditioned
    (*b*) Undesirable behaviour is desensitised
    (*c*) Present behaviour is modified
    (*d*) All of the above
16. Psychoanalytic approach of counseling was first introduced by
    (*a*) Adler (*b*) Jung
    (*c*) Freud (*d*) None of these
17. According to psycho analysis theory of personality neurotic disorders are caused by

(a) Repression of desires
(b) Inactivity of libido
(c) Role of unconscious mind
(d) All of these

18. If a child fails again and again in a class, which of the following services will be most suitable to him?
(a) Orientation services
(b) Follow up services
(c) Information services
(d) Testing services

## ANSWERS

| 1 | 2 | 3 | 4 | 5 | 6 | 7 | 8 | 9 | 10 |
|---|---|---|---|---|---|---|---|---|---|
| (d) | (a) | (c) | (d) | (b) | (d) | (c) | (b) | (d) | (a) |
| **11** | **12** | **13** | **14** | **15** | **16** | **17** | **18** | | |
| (c) | (d) | (b) | (a) | (d) | (c) | (a) | (d) | | |

# UNIT–VII

- ★ *Research and Educational Research*
- ★ *Research Problem*
- ★ *Sampling*
- ★ *Hypothesis*
- ★ *Research Proposal (Synopsis)*
- ★ *Analysis of Data*

# Research and Educational Research

## MEANING OF RESEARCH

Research and scientific enquiry both are generally considered as synonymous. The only difference between the two is that it is possible to employ scientific method without research but it is not possible to conduct any research without employing scientific method (enquiry)

Thus, research is a more specialized form of scientific enquiry which is the result of thinking process.

**Meaning of thinking process :** The normal human mind works in terms of problem situation. If these problems are familiar to the people and their solution is well known, people react to them without applying any thought process. This is called tradition. If, on the other hand, problem is complex and require additional thinking to solve it, reflective thinking is applied.

**Steps in reflective thinking** ( by John Dewey)

1. The occurrence of a felt difficulty
   - In the lack of adaptation of means to ends.
   - In identifying the nature of the problem
   - In explaining an unexpected event.
2. Definition of the difficulty in terms of a problem statement.
3. Occurrence of a possible solution, i.e., hypothesis formulation.
4. Rational elaboration of an idea on the basis of the data collected.
5. Corroboration of the idea and formation of a concluding belief through experimental verification of the hypothesis.
6. Appraisal of the solution in the light of future needs, i.e., generalization and formulation of laws and principles.

**Meaning of scientific method :** Science refers to an organized knowledge but this knowledge and facts are seldom final truth. The new experiences and additional informations constantly change them. They are replaced by generalizations that confirm the latest bodies of findings.

Same is the case with social sciences also. Scientific method can be applied to subjects of social sciences also.

**Steps in scientific method** (by Milton Fairchild)

1. Collection of data on the problem in hand according to some adequate plan and their systematic observation.
2. Observations are done with a well defined purpose and they are recorded in definite terms.
3. Classification and organization of data on the basis of similarities, variations, activities, causes and results.
4. Generalization of data for the purpose of formulating principles and theories. The principles should be able to solve the problems in the related field.
5. Verification of generalizations by controlled experiments, by tested prediction of results and by repetition of experiments. Correlation coefficient of original and verification results is also calculated and probable errors are estimated. It is also determined whether the error lies in procedure or apparatus.
6. Assumptions and limitations are noted down on the basis of verification of results.
7. Reporting the research in full.
8. Announcement of the results before the general public for practical use.

**Steps in Scientific Process :** (by E.R. Downing)

1. Purposeful observation : Observation should be accurate and extensive and it must be done under variety of conditions.

2. Analysis-Synthesis :
   - The essential elements in a problematic situation must be picked out by analysis.
   - Similarities as well as dissimilarities must be isolated.
   - Exceptions are to be given special attention.
3. Selective Recall :A wide range of experience is essential.
4. Hypothesis : It is nothing but tentative solution of the problem. It may be more than one depending on the nature of the problem.
5. Verification by inference and experiment.
6. Reasoning by method of arguments and difference : Here only one variable is manipulated and judgement is made on the adequacy and accuracy of data.

## Definitions of Research

1. **Clifford Woddy of Michigan University :** It is a careful and critical enquiry or examination in seeking facts or principles and diligent investigation to ascertain something"

   Thus, research is not merely a search for truth but a prolonged, intensive and purposeful search.
2. **Phi Delta Kappu :** "Research is an honest, exhaustive and intelligent searching of facts and implications with reference to a given problem. The findings of research should be an authentic verifiable contribution to knowledge. Research is of two types, fundamental research and service research. Former is responsible to the development of science of education and later is usually pursued as a means of solving immediate local problem".

## Meaning of a scientific theory

Theories are systematic statements that explain a particular segment of phenomenon by specifying certain relationship among variables.

**Kerlinger** has defined a theory in the following words:

"A theory is a set of interrelated constructs (concepts), definitions and propositions that present a systematic view of phenomena by specifying relationship among variables with the purpose of explaining and predicting the phenomena".

## Explanation of the definition

I. Theory is a set of inter-related concepts, definitions and propositions.

II. These inter-related concepts and definitions help us to understand the phenomena in a systematic manner.

III. Theory establishes relationship among various variables in a systematic manner. With the help of this relationship we can predict about the future nature of the phenomena.

IV. A theory helps us to formulate hypothesis for further researches.

## Characteristics of Research

Research is a systematic process for developing a theory by applying scientific methods. It is an impartial, objective, empirical and logical analysis and recording of controlled observation that will finally lead to the development of a theory, principles, laws etc. and will help us to predict about the phenomenon in future.

Best and Kahn (1992, pp. 18-20) have summarized the main characteristics of research as under.

1. Research is directed towards the solution of a problem. It may attempt to answer a question or to determine the relation between two or more variables.
2. Research emphasizes the development of generalizations, principles, or theories that will be helpful in predicting future occurrence. Research usually goes beyond the specific objects, groups or situations investigated and infers characteristics of a target population from the sample observed. Research is more than information retrieval, the simple gathering of information. Although many school research departments gather and tabulate statistical information that maybe useful in decision making. These activities are not properly termed as research.
3. Research is based upon observable experience or empirical evidence. Certain interesting questions do not lead themselves to research procedures because they cannot be observed. Research rejects revelation and dogma as methods of establishing knowledge and accepts only what can be verified by observation.

4. Research demands accurate observation and description. The researcher uses quantitative, numerical measuring devices, the most precise means of description. The researcher selects or devises valid data gathering instruments or procedures and employs appropriate mechanical, electronic, or psychometric devices to refine human observation, recording, computation and analysis of data.
5. Research involves gathering new data from primary or first hand sources or using existing data for a new purpose. Teachers frequently assign a so-called research project that involves writing a paper dealing with the life of a prominent person. The students are expected to read a number of encyclopedias, books, or periodical references and synthesize the information in a written report. This is not research, for the data are not new. Merely reorganizing or restating what is already known and has already been written, valuable as it may be as a learning experience, is not research. It adds nothing to what is known.
6. Although research activity may at times be somewhat random and unsystematic, It is more often characterized by carefully designed procedures, always applying rigorous analysis. Although trial and error are often involved, research is rarely a blind, shotgun investigation-trying something to see what happens.
7. Research requires expertise. The researcher knows what is already known about the problem and how others have investigated it. He has scratched the related literature carefully. He is also thoroughly grounded in the terminology, the concept and the technical skill necessary to understand and analyse the data that he has gathered.
8. Researcher strives to be objective and logical, applying every possible test to validate the procedure employed, the data collected, and the conclusions reached. The researcher attempts to eliminate personal bias. There is no attempt to persuade or to prove an emotionally held conviction. The emphasis is on testing rather than on proving the hypothesis. Although absolute objectivity is as elusive as pure righteousness, the researcher tries to suppress bias and emotion in his or her analysis.
9. Research involves the quest for answer to unsolved problems. Pushing back the frontiers of ignorance is its goal, and originality is frequently the quality of a good research project. However, previous important studies are deliberately repeated, using identical or similar procedures, with different subjects, different settings, and at a different time. This process is replication, a fusion of the words repetition and duplication. Replication is always desirable to confirm or to raise questions about the conclusions of a previous study.
10. Research is characterized by patient and unhurried activity. It is rarely spectacular and the researcher must accept disappointment and discouragement as he pursues the answers to difficult questions.
11. Research is carefully recorded. Each important term is defined, limiting factors are recognized, procedures are described in detail, references are carefully documented, results are objectively recorded, and conclusions are presented with scholarly caution and restraint. The written report and accompanying data are made available to the scrutiny of associates or other scholars. Any competent scholar will have the information necessary to analyze, evaluate and even replicate the study.

**Educational research :** Educational research refers to a systematic attempt to gain a better understanding of educational process, generally for the purpose of improving its efficiency. It is actually an application of scientific method to the study of educational problems. The main concerns of educational researches are to understand, explain, predict and control human behaviour in individual and social situations so that events or situations can be improved further.

**Purpose of Educational Research:** Researches in education are conducted for fulfilling the following purposes:

1. To solve the immediate local problems in education.

2. To ascertain principles and develop procedures for use in the field of education to determine to what extent we should go in educating children and adults.
3. To answer the questions related to education through reflective thinking to determine what should be on the basis of what is as presents, and what was in the past.
4. To discover new application of principles and laws in the field of education.

## Need and importance of researches in education

Research in education is needed because of the following reasons:

1. Education has direct link with History, Philosophy, Sociology, Psychology and Economics. It is through an intensive process of scientific enquiry about the philosophical, sociological, psychological, economic and the like impact on various aspects of education that scientific theories can be establish.
2. Education is science and arts both. So, there is a need to add scientific knowledge to it for enrichment and improvement. This will help in adjusting educational programmes according to the situation. Researches will also give suggestions of what to do and what not to do
3. Introduction of democratic principles into the field of education has given rise to numerous problems like the problem of individual differences, expansion, of relations, building, discipline etc. Solution of these problems needs systematic research and experimentation so that defects of traditional methods may be avoided.
4. Meaning and application of many concepts of education have changed today. So the limits of educational research have to be extended from the formal and conventional modes of education to the non formal and innovative system based on ecological and cybernetic models.
5. Many new changes have taken place in the field of knowledge in the 21st century due to scientific and technological development. Education has to play a convincing role here too so that we can accept these changes with pleasure and adapt to these changes. Educational researches will help us in this regard to construct curriculum, to prepare new textbooks and to adopt new methods of teaching.

## Steps in Educational Research

Following steps are followed in all educational researches:

1. Selecting the field, topic or subject for research.
2. Surveying the field to identify the problem
3. Developing a bibliography after studying the literature.
4. Isolating the problem and its various dimensions.
5. Defining the problem and its various terms.
6. Differentiating or outlining the elements in the problem.
7. Classifying the elements in the problem on the basis of their relation to the data to be collected.
8. Determining the data or evidence required on the basis of elements in the problem
9. Ascertaining the availability of the data required.
10. Determining whether the problem can be solved with the help of the data collected.
11. Collecting the data relevant to the problem.
12. Systematizing and arranging the data.
13. Analyzing and interpreting the data and evidence.
14. Arranging the interpreted data for presentation.
15. Classifying the data into facts and opinions.
16. Deriving inferences and testing the hypothesis.
17. Giving suggestions to the concerned people.
18. Selecting and using references and footnotes.
19. Giving assumptions and limitations of the study.
20. Developing the form and style of the research expansion.

The above steps can be condensed into the following six steps:

1. **Identification and definition of the problem :** Research problem is selected either by surveying the literature or by the experience when the researcher comes across a problem in actual situation. This problem is actually a question that is to be answered by using scientific enquiry and procedure. After defining various concepts, problem is stated in definite and clear terms. The problem is stated in such a manner that it becomes clear what data or evidence will be required to solve this problem.
2. **Formulation of hypothesis :** Hypothesis is formulated in the second step. Hypothesis is

nothing but tentative solution of the problem. The relationship between various variables is understood by these hypotheses. They determine the direction of collecting data.

3. **Clarification of research procedure :** Procedure and method of research are clarified here. It refers to the general strategy to be followed in collecting and analyzing the data. The research method depends on the nature of problem under study and type of data required.
4. **Collection of data :** The method or technique to be used for collecting data is clarified here. Here, first of all, sample is chosen and then research tools such as questionnaire, test, interview etc. are used on the sample.
5. **Analysis and interpretation of data :** At this step, data are first arranged in systematic form, then they are analysed and interpreted in the context of hypothesis. Appropriate quantitative as well as qualitative techniques are used for processing the data. This step helps in testing the hypothesis.
6. **Drawing conclusions and development of theory and principles :** This is the final step where conclusions are drawn on the basis of results and laws or principles (generalizations) are developed for wide use of the result.

After doing all these things the research report is now written in sequential form.

## Characteristics of a Good Research

1. The research should contribute to human knowledge and human welfare
2. A research should never be an ending process. It must open the new avenues of research.
3. It is a deliberate effort not a flash of intution, though it starts with sudden sparks of ideas.
4. A research is a specialized process rather than a generalized one.
5. It must be able to solve local or national problems.
6. A research is more than compiling or analyzing the data. It must be able to develop theories or principles.
7. A research is a creative process that can question the authority.
8. It must be objective and free from bias.

## Types or Nature of Research

1. **Pure or fundamental research :** The purpose of this kind of research is to develop theories, laws or principles by observing broad generalizations or phenomena. These theories or laws were previously unknown to anybody, e.g., discovery of law of gravitation by Newton, law of operant conditioning by Skinner, and so on.
   The researcher here selects the problem from any source which is generally not traditional. Generally, the problem automatically comes into the mind of the researcher. When researcher comes to the solution of the problem through his research, then he comes to know that he has done something useful economically or socially.
2. **Applied research :** It is an application of pure research and its new interpretation in a different situation. Sometimes two pure laws are compared and third new law emerges. This is called applied research. Both the above researches use scientific method of reflective thinking but their objectives are different. Problems involved in applied research have definite relevance to human aspirations but pure research is not directly related with specific human needs at least in the beginning.

## Steps in Applied Research

1. A growing concern is studied and points of weaknesses in the system are isolated.
2. Some of these weaknesses are selected for investigation.
3. Investigation is followed by solution either in the laboratory or in the field.
4. Solution is modified and installed so that it may work in practice.
5. Solution must be maintained by planning it in the organization so that it may become a permanent part of the system.

3. **Action research :** It is the research during action like observation of students in the class. Its findings are to be related in terms of local applicability. It means action research is generally used to solve local problems. As a result, its findings can not be generalized beyond a particular setting. Its purpose is generally to improve the school practices and educational outputs.

## Scope of Educational Research

The field of educational research can be classified into the following categories :

1. **Educational Psychology :** Researchers in this field help the teacher to understand the child in the class room in order to improve teaching learning process. These researches provide the following informations :
   - (*a*) Relative effectiveness of socio-cultural forces on the development of children.
   - (*b*) Usefulness of learning theories in various educational setting.
   - (*c*) Relative effectiveness of various learning theories by field experiment.
   - (*d*) Identification of factors conducive to learning.
   - (*e*) Role of physical/intellectual efficiencies and defects in learning.
   - (*f*) Understanding the personality of children in the class.
   - (*g*) Effects of parental and teacher's attitude toward children on learning.
   - (*h*) Understanding the problems of physically and socially handicapped children in the school system.
   - (*i*) Role of teachers and text books in removing delinquency in adults and so on.
2. **Philosophy of Education :** Researches in this field can provide us the following informations:
   - (*a*) Role of logic in various areas of education from concept formation to theory development.
   - (*b*) Role of knowledge, beliefs and values in developing educational theories.
   - (*c*) Role of ideologies and religion for improving educational practices.
   - (*d*) Development of a practical philosophy in Indian context.
   - (*e*) Finding new implication of ancient Indian Philosophies in the present scenario.
   - (*f*) Determining the contributions of various Indian philosophers and their implications at present.
   - (*g*) Reorganization of social structure and educational system in India.
3. **Sociology of Education :** Various dimensions of research in this field are given below :
   - (*a*) Effects of changes in the demographic structure on education.
   - (*b*) Effects of New Education Policy (1986, 1992) on expansion of education and employment.
   - (*c*) Role of educational institutions in bringing about social change and vice versa.
   - (*d*) Role of social and cultural factors in bringing about social and educational equity.
   - (*e*) Role of teachers as agents of social change, modernization and social equity.
   - (*f*) Education in disadvantaged sections of the society.
   - (*g*) Minorities and their problems.
   - (*h*) Reservation policy and its impact on the social system and so on.
4. **Educational Management and Administration:** Educational researches in this field can help us to understand the following aspects.
   - (*a*) Problems of educational administration in India and its impact on performance
   - (*b*) Impact of educational planning and legislations on performance.
   - (*c*) School plant as a function of output.
   - (*d*) Development of management theories and its implications on educational institutions.
   - (*e*) Role of teachers and principles in enhancing performance of students.
   - (*f*) Impact of recruitment policies on output.
   - (*g*) Supervision and performance.
   - (*h*) Contribution of NGO's in education.
   - (*i*) Liberalization and privatization of higher education in India and so on.
5. **Comparative Education :** Educational researches in this field can help us to understand the following aspects of education :
   - (*a*) Administrative and educational policies of different countries and their impact on the society as a whole.
   - (*b*) Impact of various systems of education in the world on each other.
   - (*c*) Comparison of educational progress in various countries of the world.
   - (*d*) Impact of economic progress on education.
   - (*e*) Allocation of budget on education in different countries and its impact on educational progress and so on.
6. **Curriculum Development :** Nature and scope of research in this field can be understood by the

following topics:

(a) Structure of curriculum in India from primary to higher level.
(b) Analysis of psychological demands of learners at different stages of education.
(c) Analysis and organization of curriculum in various subjects.
(d) Curriculum in relation to needs of the learner and the society.
(e) Analysis of text books at different stages of learning.
(f) Modernization of curriculum in relation to changing needs.
(g) Inculcation of national values through curriculum development.

7. **Guidance and Counseling :** Researches in this field help us to understand the following aspects of education:

(a) Role of family and neighbourhood in making the children adjusted in the society.
(b) Construction of tools for diagnosing adjustment problems of students.
(c) Methodology of vocational guidance for children belonging to different strata of society.
(d) Identification of factors contributive to success in the life of students.
(e) Adaptation of foreign tests and inventories to Indian situations.

8. **Educational Technology :** Educational researches in this field will contribute to the following aspects of knowledge :

(a) Development of new teaching strategies by action researches
(b) Role of technology in teaching learning process.
(c) Application of psychology to solving teaching problems.
(d) Application of technological equipments and laws in education.
(e) Development of new audio-visual aids and so on.

9. **Problems of Indian Education:** Researches in this field covers the following areas:

(a) Pre-primary education.
(b) Primary education.
(c) Secondary education.
(d) Higher education.
(e) Vocational and technical education
(f) Non formal education.
(g) Distance education.
(h) Recommendations of commissions and committees on education.

10. **Special Education :** Physical handicap is genetic and acquired both 34 million handicapped children in India invite the researchers in India to do something in their interest. From diagnosis to their rehabilitation, we come across a number of problems that are to be investigated scientifically to arrive at a definite solution.

## OBJECTIVE QUESTIONS

1. No research is possible
   (a) without applying scientific method.
   (b) Without using statistical techniques.
   (c) Without formulating a hypothesis.
   (d) All of these.
2. Research is an honest, exhaustive and intelligent searching for facts and implications with reference to a given problem who said this.
   (a) Best (b) Kappu
   (c) M. Fair Child (d) Dewey
3. Problem of a research can be identified and selected.
   (a) by surveying the literature.
   (b) by comming across a real problem in the field.
   (c) by studying fundamental researches.
   (d) All of these.
4. A research is
   (a) a goal directed activity.
   (b) An effort to formulate new laws and principles or their applications
   (c) A solution to the problem, local or universal.
   (d) All of these.
5. When a pure research is applied to new situation after careful inquiry it is called.
   (a) applied research (b) action research
   (c) both of these (d) None of these.

## ANSWERS

| 1 | 2 | 3 | 4 | 5 |
|---|---|---|---|---|
| (a) | (b) | (c) | (d) | (a) |

# Research Problem

## INTRODUCTION

The first step in reflective thinking (research) is the selection of a suitable problem for investigation. Research starts with a felt difficulty (problem) and solution of this problem is found out through the process of research.

But before the identification of the problem, it is necessary for a researcher to choose a broad field within which he has to conduct his study. He should select only that field for study in which he is expert to exercise his reflective thinking.

### Selection of the problem

After selecting a broad area, the researcher now isolates his problem of study. Important sources for selection of the problem are as follows :

1. **Professional experiences :** Class rooms, school, community etc. are the places where researcher might have come across a number of conflicting experiences and difficulties. He will find the solutions of these problems through his research.
2. **Inference from the theory :** Many varieties of inferences can be derived from various theories New Implications of these inferences are possible. A researcher selects problem in order to find out new implications of these researches.
3. **Social changes :** Technological and social changes bring forth new problems and thus new apartment for research.
4. **Doubt about present practices :** The investigator may be dissatisfied with many of the present practices and tradition. He may select such a problem that can help him to adopt new practice after research.
5. **Survey of the literature :** The investigator can study a number of related literature like books, journals, news paper, research reports etc. to find out a problem. Educational surveys will also help to find new topic for research.
6. **Discussion :** The investigator can discuss his teachers, seniors, classmates etc. on various topics and find out a problem.

**Procedure for selection of a problem :** J.C.Almack

I. Analyse what is known including historical records.

II. Look for deficiencies or gaps in explorations or the area of darkness. It is the point that is not clear so far by the researches done in the field.

III. Watch for incongruities and contradictions, i.e., the points of controversy among educators, untested conclusions and so on.

IV. Follow clues and suggestions obtained from readings, discussions, conferences thinking and so on.

### Procedure to discover experimental problem

I. The best way to find experimental problem is that the person should become a scholar in one or more specialities.

II. Reading, listening and working critically.

III. Applying reflective thinking even in normal situations.

IV. Reasoning of obstacles on the way of solution.

V. Doing informal and trial experiment for discovering a research problem.

VI. A researcher should not miss those points which have already been discovered by others.

**Defining the problem :** Once a problem for study is isolated, the next task is to define it in operational term. According to **Whiteny** (1964) "To define a problems means to put a fence around it, to separate it by useful distinctions from like questions found in related situations of need."

Defining the problem is the first level of analysis of the problem. If a problem can be successfully defined, it will take the form of an individuality that will make the solution of the problem possible. Reflective thinking actually starts from this point when a researcher tries to define a problem in operational term.

Following rules should be followed by a researcher in putting down on paper the final definition of a problem. These rules have been given by Hillway (1964):

1. Be sure that the topic chosen is neither too vague, nor too broad in scope.
2. To make the problem clearer and more understandable, state it as a question which requires a definite answer.
3. Carefully state the limits of the problem, eliminating all aspects and factors which will not be considered in the study.
4. Define any special terms that must be used in the statement of the problem.

Thus, at this step, the researcher defines all his variables in clear and definite terms. If difference of opinions is seen regarding a concept, the researcher defines the concept according to his own need, ie, he takes only that meaning of the concept with which he has used it in his study.

Any concept can be defined in three ways:

1. Conceptual definitions : Here origin of the concept and its related meaning are emphasised.
2. Idealistic definition : What a term technically means is emphasised here.
3. Operational definition : This is the meaning with which the term has been used in study. Here, the researcher defines the term in his own way without deviating much from the real meaning of the concept.

## Evaluation of the problem

Before starting the actual research, the researcher finds the answers of the following questions. If answers of all these questions are in affirmative, only then he goes further to his research.

1. **Is the problem researchable :** There may be many problems that can not be solved through the process of research, e.g., is it good to provide sex education to secondary class students" is a problem that is based on personal value. Science can not provide answer to such a philosophical or ethical questions. Hence, this problem can not be selected for research. A problem must establish relationship between two or more variables. The above problem can be studied in the following manner—
"Effects of sex education on social life of girls and boys."
2. **Is the problem new :** A problem that has already been studied by others must not be selected for study. Problem must be new in all respects. To avoid duplication, the researcher must examine the records of previous researches in that particular field. A research may be repeated on two grounds only.
   I. To verify the previous conclusions.
   II. To extend its applicability in an entirely new situation
3. **Is the problem significant :** The problem under study must be useful to the society in any way. It means that it must add new knowledge to the existing one and this knowledge must be valuable.
4. **Is the problem feasible for the researcher :** A problem may be a good one from the above view point but if it is not feasible for the researcher due to its high cost, too lengthy to complete in the stipulated time, incompetency of the researcher to study the same, and due to lack of administrative facilities etc, it must not be selected by the researcher for study.

## Criteria of evaluation given by Carter Alexander

1. It must be within the field of the particular branch of study.
2. It must be unsolved so far so that its solution may be a contribution to education.
3. It must be real in the sense that its solution is a felt need and it is capable of definite solution based on adequate data.

4. It must be worth while and significant for practical purposes.
5. It must be able to evaluate the previously discovered techniques and principles.
6. It must be sufficiently limited to time, energy and money available.
7. It must be valuable to justify the efforts and time employed in the research work.

### Criteria of social value given by H.H. Abelson

1. How wide effect the solution of the problem may have in terms of geographical area, number of persons reaching and duration of applicability.
2. How profound effect the solution is likely to have on the individuals as well as on the society as a whole.
3. To what extent the solution is likely to fill the gap in the organised body of knowledge.
4. How much value the solution is likely to have for practical uses.

### Problem statement

Research problem is nothing but a statement explaining the relationship between two or more variables. It is always written in question form. It should be written in such a form that it may be easily evaluated on the basis of the criteria given earlier :

**Example :** "Is transparency in recruitment of teachers conducive to better academic performance".

There are two variables in the above example. These two variables are defined separately.

1. Transparency in recruitment of teachers-Independent variables
2. Better academic performance-dependent variable.

### Types of Variables

1. **Independent variables :** The values of these variables can be manipulated by the researcher at his will. Sometimes, they are not too obvious to be identified.

   **Example :** Effects of lecture and text book methods on learning. Here, lecture and text book methods are independent variables.

2. **Dependent variables :** Where values cannot be changed by the will of the researcher are called dependent variable. They are the variables on which the study is based 'Effects on learning' is dependent variable in the above example.

3. **Continuous or discrete variables :** When there is a possibility of any more point between the two points (variables given above) it is called intervening variable.

   **Example :** "Aptitude of visually handicapped children and their achievement". In this example, visually handicapped children are of two types-Partially blind and fully blind. This is the example of discrete variable.

### Importance of defining the problem

Each and every variable and concept in the problem is defined operationally. They are helpful for us in the following manner:

1. It determines the philosophical background of the entire research because the ultimate objective emerges from it.
2. It directs the whole research procedure and helps the researcher to concentrate on required points only.
3. It makes the generalization of the research possible.

### Final decisions in research work

After defining and evaluating the problems, some more decisions are also taken. They are as follows :

1. Decide the stream and field of work -Science or Social Science Stream and philosophy of education, psychology of education, measurement etc. All these things will depend upon the ability and interest of the researcher.
2. Whether the research undertaken will be pure or applied.
3. Whether the research will be general or specific. Specific research will concentrate into a small corner of the field while a general research will cover a large field of study.
4. Whether the research will be new or a repetition of previous research for verification or finding new applications.

# OBJECTIVE QUESTIONS

**1.** Which of the following situations will motivate a researcher to conduct a fresh study?
- *(a)* When pace of social change is much faster than the pace of education causing adjustment problems.
- *(b)* When he finds a gap in two researcnes conducted in the field.
- *(c)* When some doubt is there in the mind of the researcher regarding a particular practice.
- *(d)* All of these

**2.** All of the following are characteristics of a research problem except
- *(a)* Problem is new
- *(b)* Problem will satisfy the mind of the researcher
- *(c)* Problem is feasible for the researcher
- *(d)* Problem is socially significant.

**3.** Which of the following is the best method of defining a problem?
- *(a)* Conceptual definition
- *(b)* Logical definition
- *(c)* Operational definition
- *(d)* Idealistic definition

**4.** Which of the following variables is manipulated by the researcher?
- *(a)* Independent variable
- *(b)* Dependent variable
- *(c)* Continuous variables
- *(d)* Discrete variables

**5.** Why is definition of the research problem necessary ?
- *(a)* It determines the direction of research.
- *(b)* It limits the study to a particular boundary
- *(c)* Both of these
- *(d)* None of these

**6.** Which of the following things is first done before the selection of a problem?
- *(a)* Selection of area of study.
- *(b)* Discussion with experts
- *(c)* Both of these.
- *(d)* None of these

## ANSWERS

| 1 | 2 | 3 | 4 | 5 | 6 |
|---|---|---|---|---|---|
| *(d)* | *(b)* | *(c)* | *(a)* | *(c)* | *(a)* |

# Sampling

## INTRODUCTION

Most of the researches are based on samples rather than population. The reason is that it is impracticable to observe the total population or to apply a questionnaire or any other tool on the total population under controlled condition. Shortage of time or money is another problem. Study of the total population is neither possible nor needed because if sample is representative to the population, it will give the same result. For example, when we go to the market to buy rice we do not check the total quantity of rice there. We only take a handful of rice and check it. If it is found good, rice is bought. Same is the case in researches also. We study only a sample and then generalize the results to the population.

### Meaning of sampling

Sampling is the process by which a relatively small number of individuals, objects or events is selected and analysed to find out something about the total population from which the sample was drawn. It helps to reduce expenditure, time and energy of the researcher and can produce greater precision and accuracy due to better controlling.

### Meaning of the sample

Representative proportion of the population is called sample. This proportion is not fixed sometimes. Less than 1% proportion of the population may provide a representative sample but sometimes a bit larger sample is needed.

### Steps in sampling

(A) Defining the population
(B) Listing the population
(C) Selecting a representative sample
(D) Obtaining an adequate good sample (Proper size of the sample)

**(A) Defining the population :** A population refers to any collection of specified group of humans and non humans, such as objects, institutions, time units, geographical area or events. It is also called universe.

The population may be finite or infinite both. Population may be existent (like the population of concrete individuals) and hypothetical (like the collection of all possible ways in which an event can be materialized) both.

Exact definition of the population is necessary before selecting any sample. For example, if we want to survey the achievement of students in mathematics, the researcher will have to specify the following things:

I. Age and grade of students
II. Type of school—public or government.
III. Place of the population.
IV. Socio-economic status of students.
V. Academic year for which data is to be collected.

Exact definition of the population will help the researcher to select truly representative sample.

**(B) Listing the population :** After defining the population, a comprehensive and accurate list of the population is also prepared. It is technically called sampling frame. It is very difficult to prepare a perfect sampling frame in large scale surveys. In such cases special care is necessary so that no unit or group of the population is left out.

**(C) Selecting a representative sample :** After preparing a list, sample is selected from the frame. A sample must have at least the following characteristics:

1. It must be unbiased and true representative of the population.

2. It must be adequate enough to represent the entire population.
3. It must provide all the informations about the population from which the sample is drawn.
4. It must have all the characteristics of the populations.
5. Sample must adequately represent all the units or groups of populations from which it is drawn.
6. It must be adequate enough to provide statistical treatment of the data.

(D) **Obtaining an adequate sample :** If population is homogeneous, a relatively small sample may serve the purpose. But if population is heterogeneous, larger sample will be needed. Similarly, if study is clinical and experimental, small sample is needed because we can control them easily and since each subject is measured repeatedly, so, it will be less time consuming. Large sample is needed when the differences between variables **under study** are small and variables are not highly correlated. The size of the sample will also depend upon the method used in drawing the sample.

## METHODS OF SAMPLING

### (A) Non Probability Method

In this method, sample is selected by the discretion of the researcher and no theoretical basis is taken into consideration here. While selecting the sample, the researcher only thinks where he will get the required data to serve his purpose. That is why it is also called **purposive sample**. For example, if a researcher wants to study the relationship between socio-economic status and achievement, he will select those schools purposefully where rich and poor students study. This selection will be done on the basis of personal experience.

Other types of non probability samples are as follows:

(a) **Quota or chunk sample :** In this method quota of sample from different units of the population is fixed and thus total sample is selected.

(b) **Incidental sample :** In this method, whosoever is available to cooperate for providing information is selected and thus the required number of sample is obtained.

### Advantages of non probability sample

These methods are very useful in the situation when.

I. The sample to be selected is small and researcher wants to get some idea about the population characteristics in a very short period of time.

II. The researcher wants to understand the problem by contacting with only informed people.

III. Different units of the populations have total characteristics of their respective units, then selection of few units out of so many is considered sufficient.

### Limitations of non probability methods

1. Such sample can be biased and hence generalization of results for the entire population may be misleading.
2. Sampling errors in these samples can not be determined because they can affect variance within the group as well as between groups.
3. Such samples depend on uncontrolled factors and researcher's insight which can not be relied on all the time.
4. Such sampling frame does not adequately cover the population.

### (B) Probability Methods

In this method of sampling, each unit of the population has equal chance of being selected. That is why they are also called **random samples.**

According to Good (1966, p. 217)probability samples have the following characteristics:

1. Each unit in the sample has some known probability of entering the sample.
2. Weights appropriate to the probabilities are used in the analysis of the sample.
3. The process of sampling is automatic in one or more steps of selection of units in the sample.

In probability sampling, a researcher designs the sample in a way that ensures that each unit in the population has a fair chance of being selected and numerical value of that chance can also be calculated. These methods can help the researcher in the following ways :

I. The researcher can know the size of the sample which is needed for a desired level of accuracy.

II. He can tell the chance of each unit being selected.
III. He can calculate sampling error.
IV. He can determine the level of confidence.

## TYPES OF RANDOM METHODS

### 1. Simple or Unrestricted Random Sampling

In this type of sampling, each unit of the population has equal chance of being selected. The law of chance operates here. Several devices are used here to draw samples from population.

(a) **Lottery method :** If there are X numbers in a population, each unit is assigned numbers from one to last. Then they are properly mixed up. After that required numbers of units are taken out from the lot one by one. This method is applied when size of the population is small and numbering of all the units of the population is possible.

(b) **Use of random table :** Fisher and Yates have prepared a random table. After assigning consecutive numbers to all units of the population the investigator starts from any point on the random table and reads consecutive numbers in any direction, horizontally, vertically or diagonally. He reads the number on the table and picks up that very number of unit one by one and in this way the required number of units is selected. If the number of population is less than 999 (of three digits only) investigator takes only three digits of the random table from the left and matches the numbers of the table to the number given to different units of the population.

**Example :** Following random numbers are given in the table in five columns

| 1 | 2 | 3 | 4 | 5 |
|---|---|---|---|---|
| 10480 | 15011 | 01536 | 02011 | 90700 |

If we have to select a sample out of 280, we will select the following units 104th, 150th, 15th and 20th only. The last 907 will not be selected because it is more than 280. the remaining sample will be selected by using the table in the same way.

Besides, if the number of units of the population is less than 99, only two digits from the numbers of random table will be taken into account.

**Limitation :**

1. Simple random sampling procedure is an ideal plan theoretically but practically it is very tough job if number of units of population is very large.
2. Simple random sampling procedure fails when lists of units of the population are not available
3. This procedure fails when population is infinite.
4. It is again not good to use this method when different units of the population is very much heterogeneous in characteristics.

### 2. Stratified Random Sampling

This method is used to overcome the above four problems. Here the researcher first divides his whole population into different strata on the basis of certain characteristics and random sample is drawn from each stratum. This stratification of the population makes different small homogenous groups of the population and simple random sampling technique can be applied to each group to select required number of sample. This makes the sample more representative to the population. For example, we can divide the whole population into upper class, upper middle class, middle class, lower middle and lower class first and then we can select sample from each group.

A population can be stratified on many grounds such as age, sex, grade, economic condition, place of residing, occupation, castes etc. The efficiency of stratified random sample depends on the allocation of sample size to strata. Percentage method is the best method of allocating sample size among strata .

**Example:**

| Economic Strata | UC | UMC | MC | LMC | LC |
|---|---|---|---|---|---|
| N of Population | 1000 | 500 | 400 | 2000 | 1500 |
| Sample size 5% | 50 | 25 | 20 | 100 | 75 |

Lottery method or random table may be used to obtain this 5% sample from each strata.

We can stratify a sample on more than one ground like age + sex or age + economic condition and so on. The more we stratify a population on different grounds, the more the different units of the population become homogeneous and standard deviation of each group decreases. Moreover, if two characteristics of the population are perfectly correlated, stratification on the basis of one characteristic will lead to perfect stratification on the basis of the other characteristics. If this correlation is weak, stratification will also be imperfect.

## Advantages

1. It can overcome most of difficulties of simple random sampling.
2. It can make different units of population homogeneous and small and thus we can use lottery method for each stratum very easily.
3. It can be used when lists of all units of the population is not available.
4. This method is especially useful in opinion surveys when we have to cover a large and scattered population.

## 3. Systematic Sampling

When a population is finite and can be properly listed, this method is used. Here, all the units of the population are listed in an alphabetical order first. Then if we have to select 100 units out of 1000 units of a population, we will keep interval of 10 units throughout the population. For example, if we have selected 4$^{th}$ unit, then we will select 14$^{th}$, 24$^{th}$, 34$^{th}$, 44$^{th}$ and so on and thus required sample will be drawn.

If population is homogeneous, this method of sampling is as good as simple random method and the researcher can not apply his own bias here.

**Limitations :** This method will not work properly in two situations.

1. If population is showing some trend in its characteristics, then trend will not change from beginning to end and thus sample may be biased to a particular trend. For example selection of 2$^{nd}$, 12$^{th}$, 22$^{nd}$, 32$^{nd}$ etc. may not have the same characteristics as 10$^{th}$ 20$^{th}$, 30$^{th}$, 40$^{th}$ etc. may have.
2. This method will also not work in case of cyclic variables. If attendance of students of a school is generally very low on Mondays due to certain reasons, and we select only Monday of the week for the whole year as a sample for studying the attendance of students, our sample will not give the correct result.

## 4. Cluster Sampling

This method is used when

I. Population is infinite

II. List of all units of population is not available

III. Population is scattered over a wide geographical area

IV. Individuals have to be studied as a group

V. Individual units can not be sampled due to administrative reasons.

For example, we can not list all the students of class VIIIth or IXth of the whole state, so, we will form cluster of students. In this method we form different clusters of whole population due to large area of the population. That is why it is also called **area sampling**. The individuals in these clusters have almost all the characteristics of their respective groups. Suppose, we want to study any problem of secondary class students in UP, we will not select all the secondary schools. We will select only few representative schools and study their problem. Then the results will be generalized to the whole state.

## 5. Multistage Sampling

It is used in large scale surveys for making the study more comprehensive. Sampling here is done in two or three or four stages. In large scale surveys we generally use mailed questionnaire to collect data. The missing data due to incomplete response or non return of the questionnaire might introduce a bias. In such cases double stage or triple stage sampling is used to make the sample representative to the population. The researcher draws a second sample at random from non respondents and contacts them personally to collect the required information with the help of interview. Then generalizes the information to the entire non-respondent population. One more example is that if we want to study the attitude of teachers across the country towards a particular text book, we will first sample states from across the country. Then sample of few districts will be selected from each state. Finally sample of few schools will be selected from each district and thus survey will be undertaken

## OBJECTIVE QUESTIONS

**1.** Multistage sampling is recommended in large scale surveys because
*(a)* It is convenient.
*(b)* It is less time consuming
*(c)* We may overcome the problem of non-response here.
*(d)* All of these

**2.** Cluster method is employed when
*(a)* It is easier to form groups of individuals
*(b)* Lists of all units of populations is not available
*(c)* Both of these
*(d)* None of these

**3.** Sampling is preferred to studying the entire population because
*(a)* Sample may have the same characteristics of the population
*(b)* It is possible to control a sample as compared to the entire population
*(c)* Both of these
*(d)* None of these

**4.** Population differs from sample in which of the following respects.
*(a)* Sample is always finite.
*(b)* Sample can never be hypothetical.
*(c)* Both of these
*(d)* None of these

**5.** Sampling technique is based on
*(a)* Inductive method
*(b)* Deductive method
*(c)* Analysis method
*(d)* None of these

**6.** Non probability sample is used when
*(a)* Researcher wants to collect information only from informed people.
*(b)* Researcher wants to get some idea about the population in a very short period of time.
*(c)* Both of these
*(d)* None of these

**7.** Which of the following does not belong to the category of non-probability sample?
*(a)* Quota sample *(b)* Multi-stage sample
*(c)* Purposive sample *(d)* Incidental sample

**8.** Which of the following methods of study will need a very small sample?
(a) Clinical studies *(b)* Field Experiment
*(c)* Surveys *(d)* All of them.

## ANSWERS

| 1 | 2 | 3 | 4 | 5 | 6 | 7 | 8 |
|---|---|---|---|---|---|---|---|
| *(d)* | *(c)* | *(c)* | *(d)* | *(a)* | *(c)* | *(b)* | *(a)* |

# Hypothesis

## MEANING

Hypothesis etymologically means less certain than a thesis. It is actually a proposition or a reasonable guess based on the available evidences. This tentative solution to the problem guides the researcher to go into a certain direction for collection of data. Once data are analysed and hypotheses are tested, final hypothesis (theory) is formulated.

### Definition

Hillway (1964) has defined the term in the following words:

"From the research scholar's point of view, the hypothesis may be conveniently considered as a tentative or working assumption, and the theory as the surviving or final hypothesis which is most defensibly supported by all the evidence. But since knowledge arrived at through the scientific method is subject to revision in the light of new data, a theory is only a working assumption, so that the conventional distinction between hypothesis and theory (on the basis of increasing adequacy of evidence and hence a greater certainty) is a relative one. For all practical purposes, the duality of the term hypothesis need not concern the research scholar except to serve as a salutary reminder that no conclusion reached by the scientific method is necessarily a fixed and final truth."

### Need and importance of hypothesis

Hypothesis serves the following purposes in research works:

1. It is a tentative solution of the problem and helps the researcher to relate theory to observation and vice versa.
2. It enables the researcher to locate the independent and dependent variables involved and defined in the study.
3. Hypothesis is required in those studies which aim at predicting some outcome on the basis of the data collected. It is not required in fact finding studies where the researcher is investigating the history of a phenomenon to determine the status quo.
4. Objectives of the study are determined on the basis of hypothesis and vice versa.
5. Hypothesis provides tentative explanations of facts and phenomenon and once they are tested and validated, they become permanent (generalized )
6. The elements included in the hypothesis are expressed logically so that relationship between variables may not look absurd. Thus, hypothesis enables the researcher to relate logically known facts to intelligent guesses about unknown conditions. It is in this sense that use of mind starts from the formulation of hypothesis.
7. Hypothesis gives direction to the research work and enables the researcher to avoid unnecessary efforts. It helps him to determine the type of data required and the sample from which such informations can be collected,
8. Hypothesis also determines the statistical techniques needed for the analysis of data.
9. Research tools are also determined on the basis of hypothesis.
10. There may be more than one hypotheses depending on the nature and scope of research.
11. Hypothesis provides the basis for reporting the conclusion of the study. These conclusions are drawn after testing the hypothesis.

### Formulation of hypothesis

Imaginative power and logical thinking are required while formulating a hypothesis. They are based partly on known facts and partly on conceptual knowledge. Following things help a researcher while formulating a hypothesis:

1. **Background knowledge of the phenomena :** The researcher must know the general facts and trends, nature of relationship between different variables and the experiences of others in the field. Background knowledge will help the researcher to identify the possible relationship between variables and thus hypothesis will be formulated by him.
   Background knowledge before formulating the hypothesis is essential because of two reasons.
   *(i)* New knowledge, discoveries and inventions should form continuity with the existing knowledge, inventions and discoveries.
   *(ii)* It will help the researcher to avoid the repetition of a study which has already been done by others.
2. **Use of intellect and deductive reasoning :** Deductive reasoning is needed to derive a hypothesis from known theories so, selection of these required theories is first needed. All these things require creativity and intellect.
3. **Analogy and other practices :** Analogy will also help the researcher to find clues in formulating a hypotheses. Analogy enables the researcher to establish relationship between old and new situations and find resemblance in the context of facts.

## Criteria of Formulating a Hypothesis

Following points must be kept in mind by a researcher while formulating a hypothesis.

1. Hypothesis must be stated in clear and precise terms. General terms such as personality, intelligence etc. should not be used here. Specific terms such as personality as measured by 16 PF or intelligence as measured by Binet will be used here. It means that terms used in the hypothesis should not create any confusion in the minds of others.
2. Hypothesis should be testable on the basis of the data collected. Conclusion is drawn only after testing the hypothesis. If data collected are in accordance with the hypothesis, then it is accepted otherwise rejected.
   For example, if we formulate a hypothesis that cultural activities will increase the aesthetic sense of students, we will select two groups of students, one is given exposure to cultural activities and other is not. Then we will conduct a test of aesthetic sense and then performance of both the groups will be compared. If the performance of the group involved in cultural activities is significantly better than the other group, hypothesis will be accepted otherwise not.
3. Hypothesis must express logical relationship between variables.
4. Tools must be available to measure the variables mentioned in the hypothesis. If such tools are not available, they have to be constructed by the researcher himself. It is in this sense that variables should be identified where construction of tools is possible.
5. Hypothesis should define variables operationally not conceptually. Operational definition is that definition with which the variable has been used in the study.
6. Hypothesis should be limited in scope. Hypothesis of global significance are not usable because they are not specific and hence they can not be tested. If area of study is wide, more than one hypothesis will be needed to be formulated.
7. Hypothesis should be consistent with most known facts. They should be grounded on well established theories and laws. If hypothesis is far from known fact, nothing will come out by research. Some deviations are, however, essential here so that something new can be brought out.
8. The scope of hypothesis should be limited to a reasonable time. For example, if we have formulated a hypothesis which requires huge data to be collected and this collection takes more than 6 or 7 years, that hypothesis will not be considered sound.

## Types of Hypothesis

1. **Research hypothesis :** It is a tentative or possible solution to a research problem which is tested on the basis of research. Once, the hypothesis is proved, it becomes a fact.

### Research hypothesis is of two types

**(a) Directional hypothesis :** The hypothesis which stipulates the direction of the expected differences is called directional hypothesis.

**Example :** There is a positive relationship between socio-economic status and scholastic achievement.

This hypothesis stipulates that if socio-economic status of students is high, scholastic achievement will also be high.

(b) **Non-Directional hypothesis :** This does not stipulate the direction of relationship between two variables.

**Example :** "Girls of different I Q s differ in anxiety level."

This hypothesis does not stipulate that high anxiety level is found in intelligent girls, average girls or dullers. Thus, direction of difference is not specified here.

2. **Statistical hypothesis :** To establish relationship between variables, statistical terms are used here.

   **Example :** "IQ level and behaviour of adolescents are positively correlated"

3. **Declarative form of hypothesis :** When the researcher makes a positive statement about the outcome of the study it is called declarative form of hypothesis.

4. **Null hypothesis :** Null in mathematics means zero. This hypothesis indicates statements which suggests no relationship between variables $r = 0$ Research as well as statistical hypothesis are tested on the basis of null hypothesis. If it is zero, it means research hypothesis is meaningful and vice-versa.

   **Example :** "There is no significant different between academic achievement of boys and girls".

Thus, a null hypothesis challenges the assertion of a declarative hypotheses and denies it altogether. It states that even if there is some difference between two subjects or phenomena, it is due to mere chance. If difference is really significant, null hypothesis is rejected. The criteria of rejecting null hypothesis may differ at different levels of significance, e.g., 0.01, 0.05, or 0.10 levels.

0.01 level of significance means that there is only one chance out of 100 of the incident to occur and 0.05 level means there is 5 chance out of 100 to occur.

**Practical problems of testing the hypothesis :** Once, the hypothesis is formulated, data are collected and analysed to test the hypothesis. But mere empirical testing is not enough. Logical testing is also needed in most of the cases. Some practical problems of testing the hypothesis are given below :

1. Some hypotheses are very simple and can be tested directly. But there are some hypotheses which are very complex and reflective thinking is needed to test these hypotheses. For example, if there is an hypothesis that " Affluence leads to immorality", we can not test this hypothesis directly. Indirect method of testing this hypothesis will be used here. We will study the habits of high consumption of the rich person which might go in purchase of liquor, prostitution, spending money in night clubs and in gambling and on the basis of these habits we will be able to conclude that affluence leads to immorality.

   Thus, intellectual and logical efforts are also needed for the deduction of consequence. Once, all the deduced consequences after testing come out to be true, the hypothesis is verified and confirmed. If some of the deduced consequences are true and some are false, hypothesis is examined afresh.

2. If tools used for collecting data are not free from errors or there is some defects in sampling techniques, the results will not be dependable and confirmation of hypothesis will not mean that result is true. In that situation, the researcher will have to admit his limitations regarding research tools and samples

3. The researcher predicts something after testing the hypothesis and gives some generalizations. If those generalizations are practically true and prediction is successful in real life situation, there remains no doubt about the outcome of the study. So, practical aspect of the research must also be taken into account while testing the hypothesis.

# OBJECTIVE QUESTIONS

1. Which of the following methods of writing hypothesis is correct?
   (a) They are formulated before the collection of data.
   (b) They are formulated before defining the problem.
   (c) They are always written in directional form.
   (d) None of the above.
2. In a research, conclusions are drawn
   (a) After testing the hypothesis
   (b) Before testing the hypothesis
   (c) After verifying the results
   (d) None of these
3. All of the following purposes are served by hypothesis except
   (a) They determine the direction of research
   (b) They help to relate theory to observation and vice versa
   (c) They help to determine the sample
   (d) None of these
4. Which of the following is an important characteristics of hypothesis?
   (a) They should be testable
   (b) They should express relationship between variables.
   (c) They should be limited in scope
   (d) All of these
5. Hypothesis is related to all of the following except
   (a) Research tools
   (b) Research objectives
   (c) Sample
   (d) None

## ANSWER

| 1 | 2 | 3 | 4 | 5 |
|---|---|---|---|---|
| (a) | (a) | (d) | (d) | (d) |

# Research Proposal (Synopsis)

## INTRODUCTION

Research proposal is the detailed written plan and procedure of research. It consists of statement of the problem, hypotheses, objectives, methods and procedure, tools and techniques used and method of data analysis and their interpretation etc.

Before going to the actual research work, a researcher plans his entire programme of research, how he has to go through the problem.This is called research proposal. This initial draft of the agendum is subject to modification in the light of further analysis by the student and his supervisor and then it is submitted to the concerned institution.

### Need and importance of research proposal

In many institution, the research scholar is required to submit a detailed synopsis for approval by the Research Committee of the department. This proposal helps to determine the following things:

I. Whether the researcher is able to conduct the research in that particular field by studying the bibliography, hypothesis in relation to the tools and samples used in the research and methods of analysis and interpretation of data.

II. Whether the project is significant and valuable socially and whether it can adds something to the existing knowledge.

III. Whether the project is feasible for the researcher in terms of time, money and competence.

IV. Whether synopsis is correct in all respect or some modifications at any step are needed.

### Types of Research projects

Research projects can be broadly classified into the following categories :

1. **Research proposal for the purpose of degree :** Such synopsis is submitted by the individual for taking admission in Ph.D. or D. Lit. Such research proposals are evaluated by experts in the departments of the university and then admission is given to the candidate.
2. **Proposals submitted to research institutions for getting financial assistance :** These institutions may be private and public both and proposals are scrutinized by experts and then grant is given to the researcher for conducting his research.
3. **Large scale surveys :** They are conducted by universities or institutions by taking the help of so many researchers.

### Steps in Preparing research proposal

1. **Title of the project :** It is written at the top in bold letters and language of the title is kept simple and clear. It is the catch word, the slogan that makes it possible to determine the ultimate objectives of the research.
2. **Name of the researcher :** Name of the researcher is written just below the title.
3. **Statement of the problem :** It is not the repetition of the title. It is actually an expansion and elaboration of the title. It is generally written in question form. Major questions may be followed by some minor questions.
4. **Type of the problem :** The researcher describes the type of the problem that he is going to investigate and clarifies which field of study the problem belongs to, whether it is related to curriculum, method of teaching, psychology of learning or whatsoever. He states the angles of his study also.

5. **Analysis of the problem :** Important terms used in the problem are clearly defined in operational terms and then problem is evaluated from different angles. The researcher also points out how solution of the problem can influence educational theory and practice.
6. **Objectives of the study :** Here the researcher describes the purpose of his study. Objectives should be written in clear and behavioural terms so that they can be evaluated at the end of the study. If the researcher is able to achieve the objectives that were stated in the beginning, research is passed.
7. **Formulation of hypothesis :** It is a probable theory which is tested on the basis of the data collected. Hypothesis is sometimes obvious and sometimes not. A proposal can have more than one hypotheses if needed.
   Hypothesis actually expresses the relationship between different variables used in the topic of research. In research proposals only research hypothesis should be written.
8. **Delimitation of the study :** Boundaries of the study should be made clear with reference to
   (*a*) Scope of the study : Here area to which the conclusion is to be confined will be written. It will restrict the generalization of the study to a particular limit.
   (*b*) Procedural treatment : Here sampling procedure, tools and methods of data collection and procedure of data analysis will be specified. It will restrict the application of the study to the population from which the sample is drawn.
9. **Assumptions of the study :** Assumptions are those statements which are accepted as true. They are actually written to indicate those factors which can affect the study in any way and the researcher is unable to control them. Assumptions tell us that the findings will be applicable only when these assumptions are fulfilled.
10. **Review of the related literature :** The theoretical and empirical framework from which the problem has been derived is stated here. A number of research and other literature in the field are studied by the researcher first and a bibliography is prepared. The latest research trend related to the problem in hand is also mentioned here. Through the review of the literature, the researcher finds out the gap that has motivated him for further exploration. This step is useful in the following ways:
    (*a*) It provides evidence that researcher is familiar with what is already known in the field and what is unknown so far. Thus, he is saved from the process of duplication or repetition.
    (*b*) It provides a sound basis for formulating hypothesis.
    (*c*) It provides a sound basis to judge the capacity of the researcher to do research in the field.
11. **Methodology and Procedure :** Here the researcher determines the entire method to be used in his study. It includes the following things:
    (*a*) Sampling : The population from which the sample is to be drawn is first selected. Then according to the nature and scope of study, size of the sample is decided. Then sample is finally selected by applying suitable sampling techniques. All these things are clearly mentioned here.
    (*b*) Research tools : Keeping the hypothesis in mind, the researcher decides which tool he will use in his study for collecting data. Whether these tools are available in the market or whether the researcher will construct them is also mentioned here. The researcher will also give reason why he is using a particular tool.
    (*c*) Collection of data : Here the researcher writes in detail with reference to each section of the problem how and where he expects to find the needed data upon which a solution can be made. He also clarifies how he will apply the tools on the sample and what precautions he will take in gathering the data. He states advantages and disadvantages of each source and his criteria of priority.
    (*d*) Manipulation and Interpretation of data : How data are arranged on the basis of the proposed research is stated here. Whether data will be presented in tabular or graphical form, which statistical method will be used to treat the data and at what level of significance he will test his hypothesis, all these things are stated here.

The researcher will also give reason why he is going to use a particular statistical technique to analyse and interpret the data. Actually the nature of data will determine the technique.

(e) Checking data for reliability : The researcher describes here how he proposes himself and others to examine the facts that he has presented and to what extent it is reliable.

12. **Implications :** The researcher states here what practical use he expects from his study and who will probably read his thesis.

13. **Probable rate of progress :** The researcher here indicates how much time will he need for each section of his work and when will the research work be completed. Proper allocation of time for collection and analysis of data is essential here.

14. **Budgeting :** How much money needed for different portions of the work is stated here and total expenses are also given here. Cost of the following things is included here.
    1. Cost of paper and stationery
    2. cost of books and journals
    3. cost of tours to various places.
    4. photo copying cost.
    5. cost of typing the thesis
    6. daily allowance and so on.

## OBJECTIVE QUESTIONS

1. Review of the related literature helps the researcher
   - *(a)* To avoide duplication
   - *(b)* To find the gap between different facts.
   - *(c)* To determine the limits of his field of research.
   - *(d)* All of these
2. Which of the following is an elaborated form of the title?
   - *(a)* Statement of problem.
   - *(b)* Hypotheses
   - *(c)* Objectives
   - *(d)* None of the above.
3. Evaluation of the research proposal is necessary because
   - *(a)* It determines the significance of the study.
   - *(b)* It can determine the competence of the researcher.
   - *(c)* It can determine the method and procedure of research
   - *(d)* All of the above.
4. The research proposals sent to research institutes for financial assistance must have
   - *(a)* The whole plan and procedure
   - *(b)* Budget requirements and time schedule
   - *(c)* Definite objectives of research
   - *(d)* None of the above
5. Selection of research tool depends
   - *(a)* On the nature of hypothesis'
   - *(b)* On the nature of sample selected
   - *(c)* Both of these
   - *(d)* None of these

## ANSWERS

| 1 | 2 | 3 | 4 | 5 |
|---|---|---|---|---|
| *(d)* | *(a)* | *(d)* | *(b)* | *(c)* |

# Analysis of Data

## QUALITATIVE ANALYSIS

### Qualitative Data

When we use open end questionnaire, observation, unstructured interview, rating scales etc. they provide verbal and qualitative data. These data indicate the wordings of the people about the phenomena on the basis of their own experiences. The qualitative data provide depth or detail about the phenomenon. If questionnaire or interviews are open ended in nature, the responses will be more detailed and comprehensive. They are though not systematic, yet they help the researcher to understand the problem in hand more comprehensively. They also enable the researcher to understand the attitude and values of the people, their emotions and their way of organizing the views. Participant observation also serves the same purpose. These qualitative data are to be organized, analysed and interpreted in the manner given below :

### 1. Organization of Qualitative Data

The data gathered by open end questionnaire, participant observation and non-structured interviews are voluminous and haphazard. They need to be classified and organized into specific patterns, categories and units on the basis of similarities and differences in opinions, values, attitudes and perceptions.

Steps in organizing the data are given below :

I. Four copies of the whole data are prepared. One copy is kept into a store for the purpose of safety. Second copy is used for further treatment and scrutiny of the data. Third copy is used to fill the missing gaps in the information (if any) identified during scrutiny of data. Fourth copy is used for cutting and pasting the data at suitable and needed places.

II. Meaningful form is given to the data in the second step. This is done on the basis of differences and similarities of the respondents. The researcher also notes down his own comments on the margin of papers.

III. The data is then arranged into topics and sub topics.

IV. Index of topics and sub topics are prepared in the fourth step.

### 2. Analysis and Interpretation of Data

Here organized materials (data) are studied analytically in order to discover facts and opinions. These data are studied from different angles in order to explore new facts or to reinterpret the already known facts. Three types of analysis are used here to analyse qualitative data.

(*a*) Content Analysis

(*b*) Inductive Analysis

(*c*) Logical Analysis

### Content Analysis

According to **Bereison** "Content analysis is a research technique for the objective, systematic and quantitative description of the manifest content of communication". Content analysis is concerned with the classification, evaluation and comparison of content of communication or information. That is why it is also called information analysis. Content may be in the form of personal responses (opinion, perception, values etc.) or in the form of official records (census, birth, death, accident, crime etc.) or in the form of financial records cumulative records, content of text books, reference works and so on. Three broad approaches are followed for content analysis.

**(a) Characteristics of the content :** The researcher may find out the following things in the characteristics of the content.

I. Trends in the information content.

II. Comparison of content materials coming from different sources.

III. The role of different agencies like mass media, school, family etc. in moulding public opinion.

IV. Evaluation of the content against standard set by the researcher or any other body.

Apart from identifying these characteristics, form of the content is also taken into account. Its value is measured in terms of difficulty of comprehension, (such as number of new words used, nature and length of sentences etc.) eloquence style and so on.

**(b) Causes of content :** Here the researcher tries to draw valid inferences about the nature and causes of the content (why it is so) **Cartwright** (1970) has highlighted four uses of content analysis which illustrate the ways which the researcher tries to construct a picture of the content producer from his symbolic or verbal materials.

I. The attitude and intention of the communicator (producer) is inferred.

II. Psychological state of the producer is assessed.

III. Detecting the existence of propaganda is the third use.

IV. Obtaining political emotional or social intelligence of the producer.

**(c) Audience and effects of content :** In this approach of content analysis, the researcher interprets the content in order to reveal something about the nature of its audience, i.e., what effects will it cause on audience. The audience for whom the material has been produced are isolated first then their characteristics are inferred on the basis of the content produced .

**Steps in Content Analysis**

1. **Defining the unit of analysis :** The unit or material may be in the form of words, phrases, sentences, paragraphs or a full chapter. Which form of the unit is taken for content analysis should be defined first. However, this unit should be comprehensive enough to provide meaningful information but not so large as to introduce subjectivity on the part of the researcher.

2. **Specifying variables and categories :** The purpose of researcher is to obtain objective data for scientific treatment and generalization. For converting symbolic materials into objective data he specifies variables explicitly in terms of which description can be made. The variables here refer to dimensions or attributes into which the data are to be categorised. There are many ways in which these variables can be categoried.

   i. Unqualified confidence
   ii. qualified confidence.
   iii. confidence and mistrust
   iv. qualified mistrust
   v. unqualified mistrust
   vi. questions not asked by the interviewer.
   vii. responses not classifiable

3. **Frequency, direction and intensity :** In the third step different units of data are classified in terms of frequency, direction and intensity.

   Frequency refers to number of times a particular unit has occurred, i.e., how many people are giving a particular statement in favour or against the statement. For example, if we are going to study the policy of the government on higher education, we can count the people (units) favouring privatization of higher education.

   Similarly, if majority supports privatization of higher education, the direction will be in favour of it. The direction refers to favorableness unfavourableness or indifference toward a particular unit of variable intensity refers to the emotional impacts of the units on the producers, i.e., to what percentage a unit is favoured or opposed by the producers whether it is supported by 90% people, 80% people and so on.

4. **Contingency analysis :** It aims at considering the content within which the unit of information is found, i.e., whether the support or oppose within the framework of the unit or the producer(respondent) is speaking something else outside the frame of the unit.

5. **Sampling :** The unit which a researcher is going to analyse must be representative of the total material (topic of research) so that results can be analysed. At this step, the researcher discards the irrelevant parts of units and concentrates to his actual topic. If producer is speaking something irrelevant on a particular unit, is must be discarded. In fact, selection of universe (different units covering the topic) will depend on the purpose of research. The research should never deviate from its purpose.
6. **Preparing the content analysis outline :** Here the researcher first specify and isolate the required data that he actually needs in his research. Then this data is tabulated properly to make it understandable. Then he lists down the variables in terms of which the content is to be understood. **Berelson** has given the following list of variables in terms of which a particular unit of the content will be analysed.

**What is said :**

- Subject matter (what is the communication about)
- Direction (favourable or unfavourable)
- Base on which it is said
- Values (goals revealed)
- Methods to achieve the goals
- Traits of persons revealed
- Actor (person initiating action)
- Authority (In whose name it is said so)
- Origin (where the statement came from)
- Target (the person who is targetted)

**How it is said :**

- Form of the content (is it news, fiction, opinion etc.)
- Intensity (the force with which statement is made)
- Device (style of communication)

After listing down the variables, they are matched with the units of the content and categories are filled in.

7. **Mechanics of coding :** Meaning or inferences are drawn from each units of the universe here. Efforts are made here to eliminate the biases on the part of the researcher. It is also ensured that all; the materials get coded (interpreted) only once. At the final stage of coding, the researcher can add new categories to some of the variables of the outline if he comes across a recording unit for which no category is there.

## Inductive Analysis

In this analysis, patterns, theme and categories are analysed and researcher looks for natural variation in the data.

According to **Patton** (1982) "For evaluators, the study of natural variation will involve particular attention to variations in programme processes and how participants respond to and are affected by programmes. Two ways of representing the patterns emerge from analysis of data. First, the analyst can use the categories developed and articulated in the programme studied to organize presentation of particular themes. Second, the analyst may also become aware of categories or patterns for which the people in the programme did not have tabels or terms, and the analyst develops terms to describe these inductively generated categories.

- In order to understand the opinions of a particular group of people, the researcher should analyse the whole of experiences in the context of their concepts. The verbal categories used by the participants are labeled and given names so that they can be separated from others. Then characteristics and attributes of these names are identified. Finally, these categories are turned into themes which are used while reporting the research.

Similarly, the patterns into qualitative data are also converted into meaningful categories. These categories are further judged by two criteria. Internal homogeneity and External homogeneity. Using these two criteria the researcher develops several different classification system of categories and then establishes some priorities to determine which category system is more important than others.

## Logical Analysis

It is sometimes felt that cross classification of different

dimensions of data is needed to generate new insight about the nature and pattern of information. Logical analysis aims at creating potential categories by crossing one typology with another so that some more logical conclusions can be drawn from the data **Patton (1982)** writes creating cross-classification matrices is an exercise in logic. This procedure involves creating potential categories by crossing one dimension or typology with another, and then working back and forth between the data and one's logical construction, filling in the resulting matrix. This logical system will create a new typology all parts of which may or may not actually be represented by the data. Thus, the analyst moves back and forth between the logical construction and the actual data in the ongoing search for understanding through description.

### 3. Validation of Qualitative Analysis

This is the last step of qualitative analysis of data. Important strategies employed for validation of data are given below :

(a) **Rival Explanation :** Through this method the researcher goes in other ways and tries to reject his results in all the manner possible. Here the researcher tries to find out all other logical possibilities supported by the data. He gives answer of the question, "can it not happen so". However, these rival explanations should be based on supportive evidence from the data available. If it is not supported by evidence, it is rejected and original interpretation is considered true.

(b) **Triangulation :** (Matching qualitative data with quantitative ones) : In this method, data are collected through quantitative method also then both the results are compared. It is likely that both these types of data will lead to different findings. It is because qualitative data are used for generating or describing the hypothesis while quantitative data are used for verifying the hypothesis. However, if findings of both the researchers match in some respects on some points, findings of qualitative data are considered valid.

(c) **Design checks** (keeping methods and data in context) :

The defects in research design and methodology can also distort the results. Sampling may give rise to three types of errors:

I. Errors due to distortion in the situation that were sampled for observation.

II. Errors due to distortion introduced by the time period during which observation was made.

III. Errors due to biased selection of the sample.

If a researcher is capable in controlling these errors during his research process, his findings will be valid.

(d) **Controlling the effects of the researcher :**

The presence of researcher during the process of data collection can distort the results in the following ways:

I. Reaction of the respondent or observant may be far from facticity due to the presence of the researcher.

II. Changes in the researcher himself during the process of data collection.

III. Incompetence of the researcher.

If we are able to control these variables to the maximum level possible, only then findings will be reliable and valid.

## QUANTITATIVE ANALYSIS

Quantitative data collected by using different tools are organised, analysed and interpreted in the following manner:

### 1. Organization of data

It consists of editing, classifying and tabulating the informations collected.

Editing refers to checking of collected data whether they are accurate, useful and complete.

Classifying refers to dividing the information into various categories and groups. This process is guided by the nature of problem in hand, nature of hypothesis to be tested and the characteristics of sample selected. For example, if we are going to study the attitude of people towards sex education in schools following four categories can be made

| Attitude of people | Men | Women |
|---|---|---|
| Upper class people | | |
| Lower class people | | |

Tabulating is the process by which classified data are transferred into various columns and rows of the table so that they can be systematically analysed. This tabulation may be manual and computerized both.

Tabulation needs marking and counting of frequencies for different items one by one and then final figure is put on the table.

## 2. Analysis of data

Analysis of data means studying the organised and tabulated material in order to discover inherent facts by drawing conclusions. For this purpose, data must be studied from as many angles as possible to discover as many facts as possible.

Data analysis is guided by the hypothesis formulated, statistical techniques available and the number of categories into which data has been classified. The researcher must also know the strengths and weaknesses of various statistical techniques and their applications and limitations.

## 3. Interpretation of results

Once data are analysed by using suitable statistical techniques, they are interpreted by the researcher in terms of the hypotheses and objectives formulated for the study. Interpretation answers the following questions:

I. What inferences and conclusions can be drawn from the results

II. To what extent, the results are significant and match to the objectives of the study.

III. Can the results solve the problem in hand.

IV. Are they able to open new avenues of research in the field.

All these things clarify that interpretation of results is not a mechanical process. It requires careful, logical and critical thinking and evaluative power on the part of researcher. Apart from these, the researcher must eliminate the subjectivity on his part while interpreting the results. He should keep the following factors in view while interpreting the results—

(a) **Ignoring of unstudied factors :** The researcher thinks that whatever changes have been brought about in experimental variable are the results of treatment given to it only and he ignores many others factors that did operate and contributed to change. Thus, ignoring the effects of unstudied factors while interpreting the results will lead the researcher to go to over generalization. This is a fault. It is nothing but misinterpreting the actual truth.

(b) **Ignoring of selective factors :** This type of misinterpretation occurs when a selective group is made the subject of investigation. For example, if we ask the views of the people about current fiscal policy of the government by contacting only the teachers or businessmen and on the basis of their opinions we conclude that fiscal policy of the government is very good, this conclusion will not be correct.

Similarly, a number of selected factors actually operate during the process of our investigation but if we ignore those factors at the time of interpretation, the findings will be far from facticity.

(c) **Interpreting extra results :** If a researcher does not stick to the limit of his study and interprets the data in terms of expected results in future, he is again caught for not being objective. Speculations may be given in separate chapter but not in the chapter of interpretation.

(d) **Interpreting negative results :** When interpreter develops a sort of defense mechanism and says that he could not find the desired result due to a number of other disturbing factors such as biased response of the sample, faulty research tools, physical condition at the time of observation etc, he may interpret the results in a very wrong manner. It is not correct to get those results which could confirm the hypothesis. If our results contradict the hypothesis and they are rejected after the study, even then our research is correct because it can save us from wrong notions and beliefs.

(e) **Interpreting the results when null hypothesis is retained :** Null hypothesis may be retained in two situations also:

I. When there may be no relationship between two variables or the experimental variable may not be more effective than the control variable.

II. Null hypothesis is false but internal validity problem of the data contaminated the results so badly that actual relationship between variables could not be established.

Hence, it is not always correct to understand the retention of a null hypothesis as evidence of no relationship between variables under study. The above two conditions must also be scrutinized.

(f) **Ignoring of unhypothesized relationship :** If the researcher has come across any unhypothesized relationship between variables during his study, he should not ignore it. It should be recognized and analysed also. This relationship should also be reported by the researcher to guide the others for further research but they should not be considered as a part of present study. They are only incidental.

### 4.Drawing conclusion and formulating generalization

This is the last step of quantitative data analysis. This is nothing but summarizing of the study in the form of final result. It also requires critical and logical thinking and reflective power. The researcher should not draw those conclusions which are inconsistent among themselves or with external forces.

Similarly, generalization and laws drawn from findings should not contradict with the known laws of nature or universal facts. Apart from these, the researcher should give suggestions and points for further researches.

The research thesis of the researcher will be evaluated by experts in terms of objectives he formulated in the beginning and in terms of its practicability and novelty.

## OBJECTIVE QUESTIONS

1. Classification of quantitative data into categories is not needed when
   (*a*) The group is highly homogenous
   (*b*) Tool is faulty and defective
   (*c*) Experimental studies are conducted
   (*d*) None of these

2. Which of the following is not an approach of analysis of qualitative data?
   (*a*) Logical analysis
   (*b*) Criterion analysis
   (*c*) Content analysis
   (*d*) Inductive analysis

3. Which of the following will provide qualitative data?
   (*a*) Open end questionnaire
   (*b*) Non structured interview
   (*c*) Observation
   (*d*) All of these

4. Qualitative data are preferred when
   (*a*) A researcher wants to study a problem more comprehensively.
   (*b*) A researcher wants to study the attitudes and values of the population.
   (*c*) It is not possible to collect quantitative data.
   (*d*) All of these

5. Index of topics and sub topics is prepared in which of the following stage?
   (*a*) Data organizing stage
   (*b*) Data analysis stage
   (*c*) Interpretation stage
   (*d*) Conclusion stage

6. The purpose of content analysis is
   (*a*) To express data quantitatively
   (*b*) To express data objectively
   (*c*) To give a systematic description of data.
   (*d*) All of these

7. Variables and categories are specified in
   (a) The first stage of content analysis
   (b) The second stage of content analysis
   (c) The third stage of content analysis
   (d) None of these

8. Data analysis is guided by
   (a) Hypothesis formulated
   (b) The number of categories into which data has been classified
   (c) Statistical technique available
   (d) All of these

## ANSWERS

| 1 | 2 | 3 | 4 | 5 | 6 | 7 | 8 |
|---|---|---|---|---|---|---|---|
| (a) | (b) | (d) | (d) | (a) | (d) | (b) | (d) |

# UNIT-VIII

- ★ *Historical Research*
- ★ *Descriptive Research*
- ★ *Experimental Research*
- ★ *Qualitative Research*
- ★ *Hypothesis Testing and Use of 't' Test*
- ★ *Chi Square ($X^2$) Test and Goodness of fit*
- ★ *Measure of Correlation*

1

# Historical Research

## HISTORICAL METHOD OF RESEARCH

**Meaning of History:** When our attention is directed towards the uniqueness, the individuality of past social facts, they interest us because of their importance for the unique evaluation of man in his activities as a social being in selecting the facts and in proving them into a complex evolving whole, we employ the historical method, the result of our work is history".

**F. M. Fling**

Thus, history is a meaningful and systematic record of past events and facts related to social, cultural, economic and political matters in such a manner that it becomes very easy for us to understand the period and age.

**Meaning of historical research :** It is the application of scientific method of enquiry to historical problems. Here we investigate a particular problem in the past, i.e., curriculum in the Mughal period, Kingdoms of South India in the pre Mughal period and so on.

### Importance of Historical Research in Education

1. Knowledge of history of schools and other educational agencies is an important part of professional training of the teacher.
2. It helps the teacher as well as the administrator to introduce and adopt new methods and curriculum in schools on the basis of past experiences. Thus, history is an important base of system analysis.
3. Present educational problems can be viewed and understood in the light of its origin and their growth
4. History of education is an ally of the scientific study of education. It can help the educational workers and educator to avoid the mistakes of the past.
5. The study of historical facts inspires us to show respect for sound scholarship and reverence for great teachers.
6. The history of education shows how functions of social institutions have shifted from a very simple arrangement to a very complex one of today.

### Purpose of Historical Research

1. On the basis of these researches, past incidents are interpreted in the light of the incidents that took place just before and after them and thus, a sequence is prepared from past to present chronologically. This perspective and trend help us to forecast about what may happen in future.
2. Second purpose of historical research is to avoid the mistakes committed in the past by studying the consequences of different actions. Thus, repetitions of experimentation can be avoided and new experimental approaches can be adopted.
3. Taking the benefits of experiences of our forefathers is the third purpose of historical research.

### Problems (Difficulties) Related to Historical Research

We come across following problems when we conduct any historical research.

1. It lacks control over treatment and measurement of data.
2. We have less control over sample. We generally rely on whatever source is available.
3. Replication of the study is not possible here. It is based on the report of observation of the past which can not be repeated. The data of the historian is always unique.
4. If data included in a historical research are inadequate, correct and valid conclusion can not be derived.

## Types of historical researches in Education

1. **Bibliographic Research :** It aims at determining and presenting, the life, character and achievements of important educators chronologically. Their impact on educational system at present can also be studied here.
2. **Legal researches :** It aims at studying the legal bases of educational institutions run by different religions and castes, educational administration at the central and state level, laws passed by parliament and state assemblies, legal status of teachers and others attached to the field of education, affiliation rules framed by department of education, etc. Thus, legal aspects of education are studied here.
3. **Study of history of ideas :** It aims at studying the philosophical and scientific thoughts from their origin through their stages of development, theories and laws propounded by educational thinkers, evolution of current concepts such as use of technology in education, micro teaching, use of computer in evaluation etc.
4. **Study of educational institutions :** It aims at studying prominent educational institutions and their contribution to their respective ages, their problems etc. This study is carried out in the perspective of their contributors.

## STEPS INVOLVED IN HISTORICAL RESEARCHES

Historical research consists of the following steps :

### A. Selection of the problem

It consists of the following sub steps :

1. **Identification of the problem :** When a researcher is not satisfied with the current interpretation of data and he wants to give a more convicting explanation of the past events, he isolates and selects it for further analysis and interpretation. He can also select a problem when he wants to study a data from other angle.

   **Precautions :** While selecting a problem for study the researcher must see that
   - Problem must be of historical significance
   - Solution of the problem must have some practical significance
   - Problem must be answerable by available methods of research and by available sources of data.
2. **Definition of the problem :** At this stage, different terms used in the problem are defined operationally, the period of study is specified and various aspects of the problem are elaborated.
3. **Delimiting the problem :** Here the researcher delimits his study to an era or age of events in a local, regional or national setting. If this delimiting is not done, the researcher can go to any extent of study and it will be very difficult to evaluate the study after it is over.
4. **Analysis of the problem :** To ascertain whether the problem is suitable to historical research, i.e., whether data for the solution of the problem can be collected or not, different dimensions of the problem are separated to prepare content of the total study.
5. **Objectives of the study :** What is the practical use of the solution of the problem? These objectives of the study are written by the researcher one by one. They clarify that his study is not just waste of time.

### B. Formulation of Hypothesis

Hypothesis for historical researches may not be formal hypothesis to be tested. They are, rather, stated as explicit statement that tentatively explain the occurrence of events and conditions. They may also be formulated in question form, eg, Was Babar a tolerant emperor of India?. These hypotheses give direction to the gathering and analysis of data.

Regarding hypothesis in historical researches **Van Dolen** (1973) has given the following opinion.'

"An explicit statement or a systematic awareness of the hypothesis is used in determining what facts were significant, clarifies the relationship between the investigator's ideas and facts reported by him and it minimizes the possibility of employing trivial, biased conflicting, faulty or archaic hypothesis?

### C. Collection of Data

This is the third step of historical research where data is collected in the direction of the hypotheses. There are two sources of collecting data:

1. **Primary sources :** They are eye witness account and reliable sources. They are the records kept and written by the actual participants, ie, the person who has actually seen the event as an observer or a participant, such as,

- Personal records- certificates, diaries, autobiographies, declaration, letters, wills, deeds, contracts, original draft of the articles, manuscripts, books, pamphlets etc.
- Religious record- holy scriptures and traditions narrated by saints.
- Official records- judicial or legislative documents, data collected by religious or social organization, report of the commissions and committees, minutes of school's committees, constitutions, newspaper and magazine reports of that time, etc.
- Oral testimony of traditions-myths, folk tales, family stories, spoken account of a witness of an account, interviews with the persons involved, etc.
- Pictorial records-photographs, movies, micro films, drawings, paintings etc.
- Remains- monuments, fossils, skeleton, tools, weapons, clothes, furniture, etc.
- Mechanical records-interviews, speeches, meetings recorded in tape or incidents tapped in CDs etc.

2. **Secondary sources :** They are the account of an event provided by a person who did not directly observe the event. The person may have directly contacted an actual observer or he may read an account by an observer. Thus, the reporter is neither a participant nor an eye witness of an original event. History text books and encyclopaedia are the examples of secondary sources.

The more the data has been collected from primary sources, of the more the research is reliable. Moreover, some data may be of primary sources for some persons but of secondary sources for others, e.g., high school text book is a secondary source but if we are going to study the cultural or mythical factors in the text book, it will become a primary source for the researcher.

In many cases, it is not possible for the researcher to collect data from primary sources, then he will have to rely on secondary sources, e.g., all Hadises of Prophet Mohamad have been collected from secondary sources and then they were compiled in books.

As far as location of resource materials are concerned, card catalogues, periodical indexes, bibliographies, reviews, research journals etc. are very much helpful.

## (D) Criticism of data

The process of appraisal which is used to derive the usable and trust worthy data is called historical evidence which is derived by the process of historical (data) criticism. This tells us whether the source is trustworthy or not. It is of two types:

1. **External criticism :** It is aimed at establishing the authenticity of data. It answers the questions whether a document or record as a source of information is true or not. It is also called **lower order criticism.** External criticism can be done by verifying signature, handwriting, scripts, calligraphy, carbon dating of metals, rocks, stones, papers, ink, cloths, bones etc. For example, if we want to establish the genuineness of the age of the documents, we may test the signature, scripts, hand writing, language style, usage etc. For this purpose other aspects of the same period may also be studied and compared with the historical aspects of that period and logical relationship between the two aspects can be established.
2. **Internal criticism :** It is aimed at establishing the accuracy of the documents (source) collected. A document may be authentic but it is not necessary that it is accurate too. For example, if the author is testified, the document will be considered authentic but if it is not revealing true picture of the time or event due to lack of competence on the part of the writer in reporting the indecent or the author was biased when he reported it or the author was under fear, pressure or vanity when he actually reported the incident, then the document will be considered inaccurate and hence unreliable. This way of criticizing the source is an example of negative internal criticism. Internal criticism is also called **higher order criticism**.

Internal criticism is also done by comparing a document with the statements of other authors and hence validity of content of a document is established.

### Internal Criticism is of Two Type

(a) **Positive internal criticism :** When researcher seeks to discover true and literal meaning of the text by comparing it with other possible sources, it is called positive internal criticism.

**Negative Internal criticism :** When the researcher seeks every possible reason for disbelieving the documents by suspecting the truthfulness, competence, honesty, and boldness of the author, it is called negative internal criticism. Both the criticisms are needed to arrive at an accurate and reliable information.

Some of the questions listed by Good (1941) will be very much helpful for the researcher in the processes of internal as well as external criticism.

- Who was the authorie, not merely what was his name but what were his personality, character, position, and so forth.?
- What were his general qualification as a reporter-alertness, character, bias?
- What were his special qualifications and disqualifications as a reporter of the matters here treated?
- How was he interested in the events related?
- How was he situated for observation of the events?
- Had he the necessary general and technical knowledge for learning and reporting the events?
- How soon after the events was the document written?
- How was the document written, from memory, after consultation with others, after checking the facts, or by combining earlier trial drafts?
- How is the document related to other document?
- Is it an original source, wholly or in part?
- If the latter, what parts are original, what borrowed, whence? How credible are the borrowed materials?
- How accurately is the borrowing done?
- How is the borrowed material changed?

## E. Interpretation and Synthesis of Data

It is the stage when final data collected are arranged in the light of the research problem and hypothesis formulated by the researcher. This is called tabulation of data. Then various similar informations and facts are grouped together for the purpose of interpretation on the basis of cause and effect relationship. This is called synthesis of data. In the third sub step data are interpreted in the light of cause and effect relationship or in the light of present relevance. The most popular theory of interpretation is the "collective psychology of the whole period theory" which can explain all phases of historical development.

Investigator must, however, be very cautious while dealing with any cause and effect relationship. Here, his position is very different from that of the researcher of physical science. Historical causes are very complicated and consequence of an event may have a variety of causes not caught by the researcher in his study.

The aim of a historical research is not only to establish facts but to determine the trends of the events also. So, sequence of events must be there while interpreting the data.

## F. Writing Research Report

The research report must be written in a style that is dignified, simple and objective. Any addition at this stage will be fatal to the whole study. However, a historian is given a little more freedom to write his research in attractive and literary style but he should never distort facts or hide any part of it at his own will. Generally descriptive cum narrative style is followed in writing research report. Creativity on the part of the research is needed here.

Apart from these, if there is a gap in the historical data any where, the researcher should not fill this gap by mere speculations. He should, first of all, point out the gap and then give possible alternative explanations to fill the gap.

Lastly, a historical research report must be written in logical, topical and chronological order. Reference of overlapping incidents should be given in the footnotes, not in the main body, so that continuity is not disturbed.

## G. Implications

It means implications of the facts findings in the field of education. The scope and area of generalization should also be mentioned at the end of the research report.

## H. Footnotes and Bibliography

This is the last chapter of the thesis. Here all references and footnotes are given point wise. Footnotes and reference may be given on each page by drawing a cut line but the bibliography from which these references have been derived are given at the end. This will help the reader to go for further and detailed study again if he desires so.

## Criteria for Evaluation of Historical Research

1. Problem should be worthy of investigation. Its solution should contribute something to the society. It should not be just waste of time, i.e.,

Pragmatic approach of evaluation.
2. The sources should be assigned to definite places, authors and times i.e., objective approach of evaluation.
3. The study should he limited and feasible in terms of research ability and availability of time and money.
4. The report should be logically organised, narrative and expository. It must reveal some hidden facts.
5. The interpretation of data (facts) should be convincing and adequate.
6. The sources should be original secondary sources should be relied on only when primary sources are not available.
7. The report should guide other researchers to go for further researches. Proper suggestions should be there for this purpose.
8. The facts on which the study is based should be verified by at least two independent witnesses.

## OBJECTIVE QUESTIONS

**1.** The study of history is useful to us in which of the following ways?
*(a)* To avoide the mistakes of our forefathers.
*(b)* To take the benefit of past experiences.
*(c)* To predict future on the basis of the trends available
*(d)* All of these

**2.** System analysis in curriculum development applies
*(a)* Historical researches
*(b)* Survey researches
*(c)* Both of these
*(d)* None of these

**3.** Findings of historical researches can be criticized on which of the following grounds?
*(a)* The investigator does not have control over treatment of data.
*(b)* The investigator can not manipulate the source of information.
*(c)* The investigator's dependence on secondary sources of data
*(d)* All of these

**4.** Which of the following is the best approach of writing historical findings?
*(a)* Descriptive *(b)* Narrative
*(c)* Expository *(d)* A combination of all

**5.** Restricting the study to a particular age or region is called
*(a)* Delimiting the problem
*(b)* Defining the problem
*(c)* Analysing the problem
*(d)* None of these

**6.** Which of the following is secondary source of data?
*(a)* Relics
*(b)* Novels written in the past
*(c)* Will and deeds
*(d)* None of these

**7.** Internal criticism is done
*(a)* to verify the accuracy of the source
*(b)* to verify the authenticity of the source
*(c)* both of these
*(d)* None of these

**8.** If researcher notices a gap in his historical studies, what he should do?
*(a)* He should fist of all point out the gap.
*(b)* He should give all possible explanations of the gap.
*(c)* Both of these
*(d)* None of these

## ANSWERS

| 1 | 2 | 3 | 4 | 5 | 6 | 7 | 8 |
|---|---|---|---|---|---|---|---|
| *(d)* | *(c)* | *(d)* | *(d)* | *(a)* | *(b)* | *(a)* | *(c)* |

# Descriptive Research

## MEANING

They are designed and conducted to obtain information about the current status of the phenomena or about the phenomena of immediate past. They are fact finding studies and help to formulate certain principles and to give solutions to the problems concerning local, national or international issues. Use of statistical treatment of data is necessary here. They provide three types of informations:

*(i)* What exists at present or in the immediate past with respect to variables?

*(ii)* To what extent present conditions is above or below the norm?

*(iii)* What are possible suggested ways to achieve the goals on the basis of experiences and opinions of experts?

### Characteristics

1. They are fact finding studies and to what extent these facts are reliable will depend on the reliability of the source, competence of the researcher to treat the data statistically and the representativeness of the sample.
2. Sometime, formulation of hypothesis is not needed in descriptive researches, eg, "Number of students from different sections of the society failed in 10+2 CBSE exam in 2001-2002". Here only figure of pass and fail is needed and researcher is not interested to know why they failed.
3. They study phenomena in a natural setting. Variable is not manipulated here.
4. They can provide informations for the solution of local and national problems.
5. They are different from historical studies in the sense that historical studies deal with past and descriptive studies deal with present phenomenon, or those events that have already taken place in the immediate past.

### Importance of descriptive studies in Education

1. It can explain the present condition of education and its standard.
2. It can point out the defects in the educational system after comparing the results with the norms or criteria.
3. It can tell us about the trends of performance of students and teachers.
4. Descriptive survey is the only means through which we can know the opinions and attitudes of the people and can have information regarding the suggestions of improving educational procedures and practices.
5. They are very helpful in solving the problems of students, school organization, curriculum, teaching methods and evaluation by knowing the cause of the problems and taking adaptive measures.
6. We can compare one school system with others quantitatively and improve the system if there is any defect in it.
7. Change is an important characteristic of any social system. Descriptive researches help us to know these changes and the impact of these changes on educational system.
8. With the help of these studies we can develop many data gathering tools like questionnaire, checklist, schedule, rating scales etc. and these tools can be standardized to be used in future in a wise manner.

## TYPES OF DESCRIPTIVE RESEARCHES

Descriptive studies are classified into the following categories from the point of view of operation:

(A) Survey studies

(B) Inter-relationship studies

(C) Developmental studies

## (A) Survey Studies :

They describe the status quo of educational variables . They are conducted to collect three types of informations:

(i) Data concerning existing status.
(ii) Comparing the existing status with the standard norms.
*(iii)* Means of improving the existing status.

Survey studies may have different forms depending on the nature and scope of the problem. They may restrict to one region and encompass the whole country. In survey studies, the data maybe collected from the whole population and a representative sample may also be approached to collect relevant data.

Important **types of survey** studies are as follows :

1. **School surveys :** It includes testing aptitudes, intelligence and achievement of students, appraisal of school status and performance, study of financial position of schools, infrastructure of the school and its impact on performance of pupils, curriculum and text book studies, service conditions of teachers in different types of schools etc.
2. **Job Analysis :** It is basically used in business enterprises and industries. In the field of education, it is used to collect information about duties and responsibilities of school personnel, working condition of teachers and other staff, qualification of teachers, appraisal of performance of teachers, administrative decisions taken by principals and other administrators etc.

**Purpose of school surveys :** The purpose of school surveys is to determine the effectiveness of the school programmes and activities and to suggest the measures that can improve the overall situation.

### Types of School Surveys

(a) **Investigative surveys :** They are conducted to know the status quo (existing condition). They are also called evaluative surveys.
(b) **Developmental or planning surveys :** They are conducted to give proposals for development or improvement on the basis of experiences of others.
(c) **Implementive surveys :** They are conducted to create suitable conditions in which suggestive measures will be implemented.

**Scope of school surveys :** School surveys cover all aspects of school system from teaching and administration to finance, building and school community relationship.

### Purpose of Achievement Testing in School Surveys

1. To compare the achievement of pupils at present with the achievement of previous year's, pupils to know the trend and to know the causes of unsatisfactory achievement.
2. To compare the achievement of pupils belonging to different schools which are being run with different philosophies and resources in order to know the causes of unsatisfactory achievement.
3. To compare the performance of pupils with the standard norms.
4. To know the effectiveness of innovative programmes and methods and to know the usefulness of additional resources making available to schools. This is done by comparing the present result with the previous one.
5. To introduce remedial measures for weak students after testing their achievement.
6. To determine to what extent educational objectives have been realized.

### Purpose of Building Surveys

They are conducted to collect information regarding the site and location of the school, accommodation facilities, classroom and library facilities available in the school, infrastructure of the school etc. Suggestive measures are given on the basis of these surveys.

### Purpose of Consultant Surveys

They are conducted by the specialists who are not the part of school system in order to give expert opinion on the problem and to give recommendations for the solution of these problems. These surveys are very comprehensive in nature and if school administration does not cooperate the surveyors, such surveys are not possible.

### Uses of Job Analysis

**Van Dalen** (1971) has pointed out that they are advantageous in the following ways:

1. They can detect weaknesses, duplication or incompetency in the personnel.

2. They are helpful in preparing wage or salary schedule for various types of jobs (according to the performance of workers).
3. They are helpful in employing personnel in various jobs for their best utilization.
4. They are used in preparing in-service training programmes for teachers and other personnel.
5. They are used to take decision regarding the transfer or termination of a personnel.

3. **Documentary analysis :** It is also called content, activity or information analysis. Here the investigator studies and analyses text books, syllabi, pupils' diaries, teacher's diaries, prospectus of the school, financial records of the schools and other school records. By the analysis of these documents, their defects are isolated and suggestions are given to remove them.

4. **Public opinion surveys :** These surveys are conducted to know what people feel about education and activities of the school and what are they interested in. These surveys help us to know what type of education people want. Interview, questionnaire and schedule as research tools are used in these surveys.

   One difficulty here is that if data have not been collected from representative sample of the population, results will not be reliable.

5. **Social surveys :** They are more general and comprehensive than school surveys. They are conducted to know overall social situation of a particular region such as health services available to the public, employment opportunities, juvenile delinquency, housing and sanitation problems, conditions of roads and transport etc.

## (B) Interrelationship Studies

They are conducted to know the relationship between various facts of the existing phenomena. They are of the following types:

### 1. Case study

It is an intensive investigation of a social unit or an individual. They are sometimes conducted for the purpose of hypothesis testing and thus it takes the form of experimental research.

In case study, the researcher gathers intensive information about an individual or a social unit in relation to the environmental forces that contribute the individual or social unit to behave in a particular manner. This method was originally used in medical sciences to know the health status and development of the individual from the very beginning in order to ascertain the possible causes of the disease. Psychologists use this method to treat maladjusted people and those who have any behaviour problem. This method is also used by counsellors and guidance workers in the school system.

- Case study is different from social surveys in the sense that social surveys collect information about few factors from a large sample but in case study a wide range of intensive informations from a limited sample on an individual basis are gathered here.

## Steps Involved in Case Study

Following steps are involved in case studies :

1. The present status of the individual or the social unit is determined through observation, physical investigations or measurement. Standardized tools and techniques are used here for this purpose. For example, if we want to conduct case study of a delinquent child, we will administer intelligence and personality tests to know his cognitive ability and behaviour. His physique and other physical problems are also examined to know exactly what he is at present.
2. In the second step hypothesis is formulated by determining the most probable antecedent of the case. For example, the researcher can formulate the hypothesis that delinquent behaviour of the child is due to poor academic environment of the school.
3. Hypothesis is verified in the third step on the basis of the informations collected by the researcher. Interview and questionnaire are also used as research tools along with observation for gathering data here. In order to prepare a comprehensive report about the case, data are also collected from teachers, friends and relatives and then on the basis of these data hypothesis is either accepted or rejected.

4. Some remedial measures are suggested to the individual or the social unit in the fourth step. These suggestions are given in the light of the possible causes of the problem.
5. Follow up study is conducted in the last step to know whether the treatment suggested to the individual or social unit is producing desired result or not. If the change is significantly positive, remedial measures are considered correct.

### Limitations of Case Study

(i) Role of subjectivity involved on the part of the researcher can give very prejudiced results.
(ii) If exceptionals have been targetted in case studies, no conclusion can be drawn about normal people. If sample is not representative, conclusions will be misguiding.
(iii) Conformation of a case study is not possible by other empirical methods of study.

## 2. Causal Comparative Studies

Through these studies a researcher explains not only the status quo but also how and why it is so. This method is used when experimental method is impracticable or costly. Through such studies similarities and differences among different phenomena or systems are discovered. For example, "a comparative study of achievements of students of GGIC and Arya Kanya School in terms of infrastructure available".

In this example, following procedure will be followed—

Achievement of pupils in these schools in 10th and 10+2 will be compared. If difference between the two is significant, then infrastructure and other facilities like availability of class rooms, library, laboratory, playground, required number of teachers etc. will be compared. if both schools are similar in every respect except the administrative arrangement then difference in administrative arrangement will be considered the function of achievement.

Causal comparative studies are conducted when a researcher can not manipulate independent variable by controlling the dependent one, *i.e.*, laboratory experiment is not possible.

### Limitations of the study

(i) The results obtained by this method can be criticized on the ground that so many factors contribute to a particular effect and it is very difficult to isolate the real factors responsible for that effect.
(ii) Classification of subjects into dichotomous group is very difficult.
(iii) Control of variable is not possible here.
(iv) When relationship between variables is established, it is very difficult to determine which is the cause and which is the effect.

## 3. Correlation and Prediction Studies

These studies help us to know the extent of relationship between any two variables at present and to what extent one variable is expected to affect the other one in future. Coefficient of correlation gives us this magnitude and direction of relationship. For example, if coefficient of correlation is 0.70 between academic achievement and socio economic status, it means that if socio economic status of the child improves in future, his achievement will also increase. The direction of relationship between two variables may be positive or negative and degree of relationship may range between zero to one. Negative sign means inverse relationship. Positive sign means direct relationship. Zero coefficient means no relationship. Coefficient in the range of 0.45-0.55 means average relationship and coefficient above 0.70 means high level of relationship between two variables. High degree of positive correlation means if subject scores high in one field (intelligence) he is expected to score high in the related field (achievement).

### Types of Correlations and Corresponding Types of Scales

1. **Pearson's Product Moment Correlation :** Here variables are expressed in interval scale.
2. **Spearman's Rank Order Correlation :** Here variables are expressed in ordinal scale.
3. **Point Biserial :** Here one variable is expressed in interval scale and other variable is expressed in nominal scale.
4. **Tetrachoric Correlation :** Here artificial dichotomy is used for both the variables and they are expressed in nominal scale.

5. **Biserial Correlation :** Here one variable is expressed in interval scale and the other on an artificial dichotomy.
6. **Phi Coefficient of Correlation :** Here both the variables are expressed in nominal scale and genuine dichotomy is used in both the variables.

## VARIOUS CORRELATION STUDIES

1. **Multiple correlation :** This is used when the researcher wants to know the relationship between one independent variable and two or more dependent variables.
2. **Partial correlation :** This is computed when the researcher wants to eliminate the effects of other intervening variables on variables under study.
3. **Use of $r^2$ in correlation studies :** $r^2$ shows the proportion of variance in one variable that can be attributed to its linear relationship with the other variable. For example, if coefficient of correlation between tests of physics and chemistry is 0.80, $r^2$=.8x.8=0.64. It means that 0.64 variation in chemistry will be attributed to the variation in scores in physics.

### Application of Correlation Studies

These studies are used to predict what may happen in future on the basis of the present relationship between two variables. One variable can be predicted from the other variable with the help of coefficient of correlation.

Four types of predictions are possible according to Guilford—

(a) **Prediction of attributes from other attributes-** i.e., predicting intelligence on the basis of caste or race.

(b) **Prediction of attributes from measurements-,** i.e., predicting criminality on the basis of scores on personality traits.

(c) **Prediction of measurement from attributes-** i.e., predicting achievement scores on the basis of socio-economic status.

(d) **Prediction of measurement from other measurement-** i.e., predicting achievement scores on the basis of scores on intelligence test.

### Limitations of Correlation Studies

1. Coefficient of correlation is only a number representing degree of relationship but they should not be taken arbitrarily. 0.70 coefficient is not double the degree of 0.35 coefficient.
2. A high degree of correlation between any two variables does not necessarily mean that there exists a cause and effect relationship between them. Other factors may also be at work that might have influenced both the variables.
3. Some logical relationship must be there in advance between the two variables. Merely correlating the numerals on two variables is wrong. For example, if we correlate anxiety with food habits, it will be wrong.

## (C) Developmental Studies

These studies are used in investigating those characteristics of children which change with age (growth). Thus, time factor is important here. They are also called genetic studies because gene has fixed the limit of growth of various organs and attributes for different levels of development of children, *i.e.*, from infancy to old age. Important types of developmental studies are as follows :

1. **Growth studies :** There are two approaches of growth studies .

(a) **Longitudinal studies :** Here the same subject or group of subjects is studied for a long period of time. Thus, it is a kind of extended case study, e.g., study of personality of a child from six to ten years of age. Whatever changes take place at different age levels are noted down here. Such type of research is mostly used in clinics and laboratories but it can be used in education especially to study the growth pattern of exceptional children.

### Limitations

1. Sampling error is very common in these studies because data is collected from a single individual or limited number of individuals and if this result is generalized, consequences may be absurd. Similarly, if sample is selected from a limited area in order to keep them in touch throughout the year, a bias in the finding will be introduced because the sample does not represent the total population.
2. It is very difficult to maintain rapport between the researcher and the subject for such a longer

period of time. Non cooperation on the part of the subject will affect the findings.

3. The researcher can not improve his tool any time in the middle of the study. He will have to bank on the same tool that he used in the beginning.
4. It suffers from all those defects that observation as research tool possesses.
5. If a group of researchers are observing wide range of behaviour of the individual or the behaviour of large number of subjects for the sake of convenience, subjectivity on the part of researchers will again affect the result.

**(b) Cross sectional studies :** Here random sample of individuals of successive ages are selected and traits of individuals of different age levels are measured separately. Then growth norm is prepared on the basis of traits after comparing the traits of individuals of different groups.

### Limitations

(i) The researcher can not control other variables except age, eg, intellectual level, socio-economic factor, aspiration level etc. may also affect the trait to some extent.

(ii) Chance of differences between samples may also disturb the results in both directions.

(iii) Such studies lack continuity. They can be mere statistical games.

2. **Follow up studies :** Such studies are conducted to know the subsequent changes that have taken place after being given specified treatment. It helps us to know whether the treatment given to the subject is suitable and giving desired results or not.
3. **Trend studies :** They are conducted to predict what may happen in future on the basis of trend of development at present. An example can illustrate this point.

| Year | 1999 | 2001 | 2003 | 2005 |
|---|---|---|---|---|
| % age of Marks | 48% | 54% | 58% | 60% |

On the basis of this trend available, we can predict that Mr. X can score more than 60% in 2007.

Such studies are conducted either through documentary analysis or surveys. The rate and direction of growth of the individual or the institution help the researcher to predict what may happen in future.

## Common Steps Involved in Descriptive Researches

Following steps are common in all descriptive researches—

1. Selection of the problem is the first step.
2. Definition of the problem is the second step. All variables that are to come in the study are defined operationally.
3. Preparing the list of data to be collected is the third step. Nature of data and its source are also specified.
4. Selecting or developing the required tools of research is the fourth step. It will depend upon the nature of data to be collected. If tools are not available in the market, they are constructed and standardized by the researcher. Tests, interviews, rating scales, questionnaire, schedules etc. are such tools.
5. Selecting the sample that adequately represents the population is the fifth step.
6. In the sixth step, tools are applied on the sample and required data is collected.
7. Analysis and interpretation of data is the seventh step. Appropriate statistical techniques are also used to interpret the data. Conclusions are drawn on the basis of these results.
8. Writing the research report is the last step.

# OBJECTIVE QUESTIONS

1. Which of the following studies is used for prediction?
   (*a*) Correlation studies
   (*b*) Trend analysis
   (*c*) Both of these
   (*d*) None of these
2. Which of the following researches provides information about status quo of a phenomenon?
   (*a*) Survey studies
   (*b*) Follow up studies
   (*c*) Case studies
   (*d*) All of these

**3.** School surveys are conducted
   *(a)* To know the real position of the school at present.
   *(b)* To compare the performance of the school with that of other schools.
   *(c)* To give recommendations for improvement.
   *(d)* All of these

**4.** Consultant surveys are conducted
   *(a)* To give expert opinion on the problem.
   *(b)* To give recommendations for solution of the problem
   *(c)* Both of these
   *(d)* None of these

**5.** Which of the following statistical techniques is used in opinion surveys for analysis of data.
   *(a)* $X^2$ TEST *(b)* R
   *(c)* T test *(d)* None of these

**6.** Causal comparative studies are similar to
   *(a)* Social surveys *(b)* Correlation studies
   *(c)* Both of these *(d)* None of these

**7.** Formulation of hypothesis is not necessary in
   *(a)* Survey studies *(b)* Growth studies
   *(c)* Both of these *(d)* None of these

**8.** Which of the following is similar to case studies?
   *(a)* Longitudinal studies
   *(b)* Social surveys.
   *(c)* Follow up studies
   *(d)* None of these

## ANSWERS

| 1 | 2 | 3 | 4 | 5 | 6 | 7 | 8 |
|---|---|---|---|---|---|---|---|
| *(c)* | *(d)* | *(d)* | *(c)* | *(a)* | *(b)* | *(c)* | *(a)* |

# Experimental Research

## Meaning

It is the classical methodology of science laboratory and is probably the most difficult but exact method of research. If variables under study can be controlled in such a way that experimental factor is isolated and change in the factor is measured after treatment, it is called method of experimental research.

## Definition

"It is the description and analysis of what will be or what will occur under carefully controlled condition"

**-Best**

## Characteristics of Experimental Research

Important characteristics of experimental research are as follows :

1. **Method :** There is only one dependent variable on which the effects of one independent variable are studied.
2. **Control :** Here all extraneous factors are first of all controlled for achieving equivalence among groups. Following methods are used to control extraneous factors—

## Experimental Control :

It is done by any of the following procedures—

**(i) Elimination :** Unnecessary factors affecting the experiment are eliminated. This method is used when sample of study is too small. For example, if we are going to study the effects on audio visual aids on learning and break down of light can affect the result, we use generator from the very beginning and thus the effect of break down of light is eliminated.

**(ii) Equalization (matching) :** Individual subjects are matched on as many extraneous variables as a researcher can identify. If he is going to compare the achievement of two groups of pupils in English, he will equalize both the groups in intelligence, motivation, age etc. It is done by any of the techniques given below—

*(i)* Subject to subject matching.

*(ii)* Matching of mean scores and SD.

*(iii)* Matching by ranking all the subjects on the basis of their scores on extraneous variables.

**(iii) Randomization :** This method is based on probability theory. Group or groups of subjects are selected randomly (using random table) without any consideration. In this way all extraneous factors active in both the groups will not create any special impact. Both the groups will be affected equally here. This method is used when sample is large and matching will take time.

## Statistical Adjustment

This is the second method of controlling extraneous variables. Following techniques are used here—

(i) Analysis of variance.

(ii) Correlation coefficient.

(iii) Multiple regression analysis.

## (C) Using subjects as their own control

Here same subject is selected for experiments. Two experimental treatments are given to him and then difference of the two experiments is calculated. For example, two teaching methods are applied on the same class and difference of achievements of the class is computed.

3. **Manipulation :** This is the third characteristics of experimental research. Here, a predetermined set of conditions are imposed on the subject selected for study. This set of varied conditions is called independent variable, treatment variable or experimental variable. This variable is manipulated by the experimenter. For example, if a researcher wants to compare the performance

of boys and girls, then variable of sex will be manipulated by applying a particular technique on both the sexes.

4. **Observation :** Here, the effects of treatment are seriously observed by the researcher. Other characteristics of the experimentee is also observed by him.
5. **Replication :** This is the characteristics that makes experimental research different from and superior to other researches. Since one single experiment can not provide perfect result, same study is repeated again and again to arrive at final result. In this way the discrepancies arising out of the experiment will be removed.
6. **Role of validity :** Two types of validities are determined in experimental researches.

(a) **Internal validity :** It is computed to determine whether the variables that have been identified bear a systematic effect on the dependent variable and whether the experimental results have not been affected by extraneous factors(variables)

(b) **External validity :** This is necessary to determine whether the systematic relationship that has been identified after experiment can be generalized outside the experimental setting. If results can be generalized, the research is said to be externally valid.

## Importance of Experimental Research in Education

1. Experiment is the only means by which disputes found in the field of education can be settled. Any body can be convinced here by replication of the study.
2. Treatment given in the direction of solution to the problem can be verified here.
3. Various methods and strategies can be applied on different groups of subjects and their relative effectiveness can be ascertained with the help of experiments.
4. Experimental research is used to determine and evaluate the adequacy and effectiveness of educational and instructional objectives.
5. The results of experimental researches are so accurate that they can not be questioned by any one.

## Assumptions

Experimental research is based on the following assumptions—

1. Law of single variable must be satisfied. It means that if two situations are similar in every respect and one element is added or subtracted, the changes that will occur is the result of the operation of that element.
2. All other variables are kept constant except one that is to be manipulated.

## Limitations

1. Experimental findings in the field of education are not as exact as we see in natural sciences because some variables such as teacher's enthusiasm, his competence in using a particular strategy, regularity of attending the variable, mental or emotional state of the experimentee etc. are very difficult to control and hence their effect can not be eliminated.
2. Control group and experimental group are never as identical as they ought to be for experimentation.
3. Intervening variables which are out of the preview of the experiment also affect the independent variable. Thus, a margin of error is always possible to occur.

## Procedure of Experimental Research

1. **Planning the experiment :** It consists of the following sub steps :
   - Related literature are studied for investigating and identifying the problem.
   - The need and importance of experimenting the problem are stated.
   - Problem is defined operationally.
   - Experimental factor in the problem is isolated and delimited.
   - Methods of experimentation are determined. The whole procedure of experiment is formulated, ie, determining the time, place, duration and materials of experiment.
   - Experimental group is selected
2. **Formulating a working hypothesis :** Hypothesis is formulated after a preliminary try out of the problem. Hypothesis suggests that an antecedent condition (independent variable) is related to

dependent variable or event. Hypotheses are formulated in such a way that they can be verified by the result of the experiment. Once they are verified, they can contribute to the development of new knowledge and theories.

3. **Conducting the experiment :** It consists of the following sub steps :
   - Controlling all extraneous variables (non experimental factors)
   - Applying the experimental factor on the dependent variable
   - Keeping a careful record of all steps of the experiment
   - Measuring the experimental results.
   - Classifying, analysing and interpreting experimental findings.
   - Drawing conclusions from the findings.
   - Verifying the hypothesis.
4. **Reporting the results :** Following points should be kept in mind here—
   - It should be written in an analytical and systematic manner.
   - Different steps of the experiment should be written in an orderly manner.
   - Ambiguous language should never be used in writing research report.
5. **Verifying the result (replication) :** This is the final step of experimental research and it is necessary for application and generalization of findings. At this step, the same procedure of experiment is repeated by another person. If results are again the same, finding is generalized.

## Experimental designs

There are various experimental designs and the researcher can use any one of them. The criteria that can help a researcher to select an appropriate experimental design for conducting the research are given below :

1. **Appropriateness :** The design must be appropriate for testing the hypothesis that has been formulated by the researcher, ie, design should match the hypothesis.
2. **Suitable to control extraneous factors :** The design must help the researcher to control all irrelevant factors that can affect the experiment in any way.

## Validity

The design must be internally as well as externally valid. This is necessary for testing the hypothesis. **Camphel and Stanley** (1963) have pointed out two types of validity here—

*(a)* **Internal validity :** The extent to which extraneous variables are not affecting the results of the experiment is a measure of internal validity of experiment. Those extraneous variables that can affect the internal validity of the research design are given below—
   - If subject has gained something extra in between the period of first and second measurement, it will affect the experimental results.
   - Physiological changes in the subject due to maturation due to long period of experimentation can affect his performance in the second measurement.
   - The subject can use his pre test experiences in his post test performance.
   - Different measuring instrument used in the first and second test will also affect the actual result.
   - Group chosen on the basis of extreme scores can cause statistical regression effect. When treatment is given to this extreme group of population, it will move toward the population mean.
   - The groups selected for experiment may differ significantly on variables that are related to dependent variable even before the application of experiment.

*(b)* **External validity :** It is related to whether the relationship that has been identified and measured can be generalized outside the experimental setting or not. The extent to which this objective is achieved is the measure of external validity.

## Types of Experimental Designs

The selection of a particular experimental design depends on a number of factors such as purpose of study, nature of independent variables, nature of data, facilities available for experiment and the competence of the researcher. Important types of experimental designs are discussed below :

**1. Individual experimentation :** It is basically laboratory experimentation either in the natural setting or in an especially arranged situation. The experiments of Pavlov, Skinner and Thorndike were all conducted in especially arranged situation. Experimental condition of this design is given below:

**Hypothesis :** It is very difficult to formulate any special hypothesis here. Exploration is done open mindedly and whatever findings appear is reported objectively. Thus, ultimate objective need not be written here.

**Assumption :** It may be in the form of concrete long period behaviour sequence such as the wishes and priorities of the individual, his experience, his beliefs etc.

**Experimental materials :** What type of materials are needed in the experiment will depend upon the nature of experiment and its duration.

**Observation :** After applying treatment to the experimentee, the experimentee is constantly observed and changes in his behaviour (result) is recorded.

**Generalization :** Whatever changes have been recorded in the behaviour of the experimentee is generalized.

2. **Single group experimentation :** It involves the application of an experimental factor to a group in such a manner that certain changes in him can be determined. Its main steps are as follows :
   *(a)* Group is first of all measured with regard to certain factors under study.
   *(b)* All factors are kept constant except the experimental factor and treatment is given to the group.
   *(c)* Experimental factor is applied for some definite period of time.
   *(d)* When the experiment is over, the group is measured again to determine the changes brought about by the treatment.
   *(e)* The result is reported in terms of gains or losses in achievement.

Example, if a topic "The effect of small size of the class on achievement" has been selected for experiment, the experimental design can be presented symbolically in the following manner:

**D = CS-CL,** here,

D = Difference in achievement
CS = Change in achievement in small room (initial-final test)
CL = Change in achievement in large room (initial-final test)

If D is positive, the results of the experiments will be in favour of small room. If D is negative, the results will be in favour of large room.

## Advantages

1. This type of research is very simple to plan and its operation is also very easy.
2. Matching of two groups is not required here.
3. It is very much adaptable to classroom situations.

## Limitations

(i) Carry over effect of attitude and maturation may change the result.
(ii) Practice effect of the group on measuring tool can also affect the result.
(iii) Variation in learning speed at various stages of learning processes may also change the result.

## Equivalent group experimentation

This design is used when the purpose of experiment is to determine the superiority of one experimental factor over other and when these variables are observed in identical conditions. This design is more accurate than single group experimentation. Here two equivalent groups is of subjects are selected. One group is called control group and the other group is called experimental group on which the experimental factor is applied.

This experimental design consists of the following steps :

**(a) Topic :** "Rative value of text book study in the class and field trip in general science"

**(b) Selecting two groups equal in all respects :** Both these groups should be equal in age, size, intelligence, sex, socio-economic background, previous educational experiences, health etc. Teachers dealing these two groups should also be equal in competence. If the same teacher deals with these groups, he should not be biased to any particular method. Curriculum to be taught should also be the same for these two groups of students.

(c) **Applying experimental factor on both the group :** One group is taught by text book method and the other group is taught by field trip method.

Comparing the results : D = CC – CF

D = Achievement difference

C C = Change in achievement in classroom group (initial – final test)

CF = Change in achievement in field group (initial-final test)

If D is positive, result of the experiment is in favour of text book study in the classroom. If D is negative, the result is in favour of field trip.

(d) **Reporting of results :** This is the final step. When results are reported, they can be used by others, ie, result is generalized. All the assumptions and limitations that are involved in the findings should also be reported so that they may not mislead the people who generalize the findings.

## Advantages

(i) It is free from many defects of single group experimentation. It is because here both the controlled and experimental factors are applied simultaneously

(ii) In order to arrive better and more accurate result, the groups of experiment can be reversed. Those who were taught in the class room will be taught by field trip method. In order to avoid practice effect, curriculum of study will also be changed.

## Limitations

It is very difficult to equate groups and control all extraneous variables.

4. **Rotation Group Experimentation :** In this method, either control group or experimental group or both are rotated. It is in fact a combination of design No2 and 3. This design is used when it is very difficult to equalize the two groups. Through this procedure the role of extraneous factors can be eliminated.

**Procedure of research**

**Topic supposed :** "Relative value of text book and question answer methods for teaching geography".

**Time period :** 6 weeks divided into three equal sessions.

**Size of sample-** One dozen in each group A and B (total 24 pupils) Experimental group and the second group both are rotated each week.

## Procedure

I week A is experimental and B is controlled group

II week B is experimental and A is controlled group

III week A is experimental and B is controlled group

IV week B is experimental and A is controlled group

V week A is experimental and B is controlled group

VI week B is experimental and A is controlled group

**Computation of results :** The result of the experiment is computed in accordance with the following formula:

CAQ When A used question answer method (initial-final test).

CBQ When B used question answer method (initial-final test)

TCQ Total change=CAQ + CBQ

CAT When A used text book method (initial-final test)

CBT change when B used text book method (initial-final test)

TCT Total change =CAT-CBT

D Difference=TCQ-TCT

If D is positive, the result will be in favour of question answer method. If D is negative the result will be in favour of text book method.

## Advantages :

This method is superior to equivalent groups experimentation in many respects.

5. **Randomized control group Pre test, Post test method :** In this design, random procedure is followed for both experimental and controlled groups and treatment is given only to the experimental group only. A pre test $T_1$ is administered on both the groups before the start of the experiment. At the end of the experiment a post test $T_2$ is administered on both the groups. Then difference between means of $T_1$ and $T_2$ is calculated for each group. If this difference is significant the changes brought about are considered to be the consequence of experimental treatment given to the control group.

## Procedure of Research

**Topic proposed :** Relative value of discussion and lecture method for teaching English.

**Time period :** 3 weeks.

**Groups :** Group C is controlled group and group E is experimental.

**Size of sample :** 30 in each group

Experiment : Here treatment (discussion method) is given only to group E.

**Step I-** Pre test $T_1 = T_1E + T_1C$

$T_1E$= pre experiment scores of experimental group.

$T_1C$ = Pre experiment scores of controlled group.

**Step II-** Discussion method is used for group E by replacing the lecture method but group C is still taught by lecture method.

**Step III-** Post test $T_2 = T_2E + T_2C$

$T_2E$ = Post experiment scores of experimental group.

$T_2C$ = Post experiment scores of controlled group.

**Step IV-** Calculation of DE and DC

$DE = T_1E - T_2E$

$DC = T_1C - T_2C$

**Step V-** D = DE-DC

If D is significantly positive, the result is in favour of discussion method otherwise not.

## Advantages

1. Randomization ensures equivalence between two groups.
2. The researcher's control over the pre test scores provides an additional check on the quality of two groups on the dependent variable.

**Limitations :** This design is criticized because of its poor external validity.

6. **Factorial designs :** So far we have discused those research designs which operate on the law of single variable. In all these designs the experimenter manipulates one independent variable to study its effect on the dependent variable. But in behaviour sciences the effect (change) which is noticed due to experiment is never the result of only one factor. This makes the findings of experimental research almost meaningless. For example, teaching strategy depends on a number of factors such as change in motivation level of students, their level of intelligence, type of teacher teaching the group and so on. In such a situation one variable design will not reveal the true result.

This difficulty was realized by **R.A. Fisher** first. He developed factorial designs and analysis of variance (ANOVA) to overcome this difficulty. A factorial design enables an experimenter to manipulate two or more variables simultaneously in order to study their effects on dependent variables individually as well as collectively.

We are giving here the model of simple factorial design of 2X2.

In this design there are two independent variables and each one has two values. The first variable which is manipulated is experimental variables. The second variable works as a control variable.

## Procedure of Research

**Topic proposed :** "Relative effectiveness of seminars (S) and lectures (L) in raising study habits of students"

**Number of Activities :** Five seminars and five lectures on "Education since Independent" will be conducted.

**Step I-** From the study of the literature of psychology and education we know that study habits of students are affected by motivation. So, the experimenter divides the population into two groups-highly motivated and low motivated groups on the basis of a test.

**Step II-** Each group of subjects is randomly divided into two equal parts. For example, if there are 50 students in each group, then two groups of 25 each from high and low motivation group will be formed as A1, A2 and B1 B2 sub groups.

**Step III-** A1 and B1 will be exposed to S and A2 and B2 will be exposed to Lectures (L)_ alternately as shown in the following table—

| A | | B | |
|---|---|---|---|
| A1 | A2 | B1 | B2 |
| (S) | (L) | (S) | (L) |

**Step IV-** At the end of the experiment study habits test was given to all these four groups of subjects and scores were arranged in the respective categories to compute mean scores for each group. The assumed scores for all of them are given below :

| Motivation level | Seminars(S) | Lecture(L) | Mean |
|---|---|---|---|
| High (A1A2) | 80 | 70 | 75 |
| Low (B1B2) | 61 | 65 | 63 |
| Mean | 70.5 | 67.5 | |

**Step V-** (Illustration) The experimenter can first determine the effectiveness of two variables, S and L on both the groups separately with the mean score of 70.5 and 67.5 respectively. If the mean difference (70.5 – 67.5 = 3) is significant the result is in favour of seminar.

In order to determine the effectiveness of motivation level on study habits, the mean scores of group A (A1A2) and group B (B1B2) is compared which is 75 – 63 = 12. If this difference is significant, it can be concluded that motivation level of students is a strong factor determining study habits, irrespective of the techniques applied to them for determining study habits.

**Step VI -** (Conclusion) In this experiment, Seminars and Lectures as strategies do not play an important role in developing study habits because mean difference between the two strategies is only 3. however motivation level is an important factor determining study habits where mean difference is 12. Significance of difference between means is determined statistically here.

### Advantages

1. More than one variables can be studied here simultaneously with the help of factorial design.
2. We can also know the relative effectiveness of two variables and conclude which one of the two is more determining than the other. In the above example motivation level is more important than teaching strategies.

## OBJECTIVE QUESTIONS

**1.** Field experiment differs from field studies in which of the following respects.
   *(a)* Former is a controlled study and later is a status quo study.
   *(b)* Formulation of hypothesis is a must in field experiment but it is not always needed in later case.
   *(c)* Both of these
   *(d)* None of these

**2.** Which of the following statements about experimental research is not correct?
   *(a)* Only single variable can be manipulated by using factorial design.
   *(b)* More than one variables can be manipulated by using factorial design.
   *(c)* Controlling of extraneous factors is a must here.
   *(d)* Ail of these

**3.** Which of the following statistical techniques is not used in controlling extraneous factors?
   *(a)* t Test
   *(b)* Correlation coefficient.
   *(c)* ANOVA
   *(d)* Multiple Regression analysis

**4.** Which of the following is an easiest method of matching the two groups of subjects?
   *(a)* Subject to subject matching
   *(b)* Matching by means and SD of scores
   *(c)* Matching by ranking
   *(d)* None of these

**5.** Criterion for formulating a hypothesis is that
   *(a)* They can be verified after experiment.
   *(b)* They should specify the dependent and independent variables.
   *(c)* They should be closer to the known facts
   *(d)* All of these

**6.** In single group experimentation which of the following is not needed?
   *(a)* Matching of subjects
   *(b)* Keeping all variables constant except the experimental one
   *(c)* Calculation of D (final test-initial test)
   *(d)* Observation

**7.** Experimental researches are superior to other studies because

(*a*) They can be replicated to verify the result

(*b*) They will always give correct result.

(*c*) Subjectivity does not have any role to play here.

(*d*) All of these

8. Who gave the idea of Factorial design?

(*a*) Best

(*b*) R A Fisher

(*c*) Skinner

(*d*) None of them

## ANSWERS

| 1 | 2 | 3 | 4 | 5 | 6 | 7 | 8 |
|---|---|---|---|---|---|---|---|
| (*c*) | (*a*) | (*a*) | (*b*) | (*d*) | (*a*) | (*a*) | (*b*) |

# Qualitative Research

## Characteristics of qualitative research

1. It is actually an explanatory activity. Phenomenon is explained on the basis of observation or open end interviews. Here effort is made to isolate the strengths and weaknesses of a phenomenon.
2. In a qualitative research, data are usually collected in a real life natural setting and they are, therefore, rich, descriptive and extensive.
3. Here, human being involved is the main research instrument.
4. When we go along a qualitative research the design of the study emerges or evolves sometimes leading to broadening or blurring of focus and sometimes leading to narrowing or sharpening of focus.
5. Important research tools in qualitative researches are observations, open end and unstructured interviews, video recording and collection of documents.
   Development of teaching skills in pupil teachers through micro teaching cycle is a good example of qualitative research.
6. Qualitative research can never be complete function. It must depend on certain inter-subjective reality, i.e., reality lies within the mind of the researcher. But this reality is so luminous that it can guide the others also

## Difference Between a Qualitative and Quantitative Research

The differences between two types of researches have been given in the following table.

| Points of Difference | Quantitative | Qualitative |
|---|---|---|
| 1. Guiding Principles | – Theory laden i.e., theory determines practice. | – Grounded theory |
| | – Hypothesis is deductive | – Inductive approach is followed |
| | – Hypothesis testing | – Research is descriptive |
| | – Replication | |
| | – Objective study | |
| | – Value free study | – Value laden study |
| | – Neutral | |
| | – Search for generalization | – Subjective study |
| 2. Methods of data Collection | – Numerical evidence (Hard data) | – Textual evidence (image based) |
| | – Observations are temporal and situational | – Researcher is the key instrument him-self and situated in the world being studied, i.e., he is thus part of the situation. |
| | – Researcher is detached from the situation | |
| | – Outcome are central | – Processes of research rather than outcomes are central |
| | – Social world is like the natural world | |

| Points of Difference | Quantitative | Qualitative |
|---|---|---|
| 3. Data analysis | – It is independent of the researcher /analyser | – It is dependent on the researcher.<br>– Inductive and interpretative approaches are followed for interpretation. |
| 4. View of the world | – Reality is objective | – Reality is subjective and constructed by the researcher. |
| | – Facts are external | |
| | – Researcher is neutral/objective | – Researcher is central and part of the investigation |
| | – Findings are independent of the researcher. | – Reflexivity is vital |
| 5. Methods associated with Tools | – Questionnaires<br>– Surveys<br>– Experiment<br>– Structured interviews | – Case studies<br>– Observation<br>– Participant observation<br>– Non structured interviews. |
| 6. Sampling | – Based on probabilities | – Opportunistic<br>– Purposive |

## Types of Qualitative Research

1. **Naturalistic Research:** This is exactly antagonistic to experimental research in the sense that it is conducted in a natural setting where no control or equalization is required, while experimental research is a clinical laboratory experiment.

Important characteristics of a naturalistic research are given below.

Table: Some features of 'naturalistic' research

| | |
|---|---|
| 1. Setting | Research is carried out in the natural setting or context e.g., school, home classroom, playground. |
| 2. Primary data gathering instrument | The researcher |
| 3. Background Knowledge | Personal, tacit, intuitive knowledge is a valuable addition to other types of knowledge |
| 4. Methods | Qualitative rather than quantitative methods will be used but not exclusively |
| 5. Sampling | Purposive sampling is likely to be preferred over representative or random sampling |
| 6. Design | The research design tends to unfold/ emerge as the study progresses and data is collected |
| 7. Theory | Theory tends to emerge from (be grounded in) the data |

2. **Practitioner Research:** This is also a type of qualitative research and conducted in a natural setting. This is why it is considered very close to naturalistic research. This is a research conducted by a practitioner or professional in any field like law, medicine, nursing, management etc. Important advantages and possible problems related to this research are given in the following table.

Table: Practitioner/Insider research: potential advantages and problems

| Potential advantages | Possible problems |
|---|---|
| Prior knowledge and experience of the setting /context (insider knowledge) | Preconceptions, prejudices |
| Improved insight into the situation and people involved | Not as open-minded as an 'outsider' researcher |
| Easier access | Lack of time (if working inside the organization) and distractions/constraints due to being 'known' |
| Better personal relationships, e.g., with teachers, pupils | 'Prophet in own country' difficulty when reporting or feeding back |

| Practitioner insight may help with the design, ethics and reporting of the research | Researcher's status in the organization e.g. a school |
|---|---|
| Familiarity | Familiarity |

**3. Phenomenological Research:-** It is a kind of research based on direct perception of an incident or object. It is a qualitative research in the sense that its reporting is directly influenced by the subjectivity of the researcher. Simply reporting an incident as a news reporter does is not a phenomenological research. But when the reporter goes into the background of an incident and finds out the possible causes of the occurrence of the incident and its possible consequences on the society and humans, it becomes a phenomenological research.

# Hypothesis Testing and Use of 't' Test

## DIFFERENCE BETWEEN MEANS

Statistical inference refers to the process of selecting and using a sample statistic to draw inference about a population parameter based on the very sample drawn from the population. Statistical inference deals with following types of problems :

**Hypotheses testing :** To test some hypotheses about percent population from which sample is drawn.

**Estimation :** To use the statistics obtained from the sample as estimate of the unknown parameter of the population from which the sample is drawn.

We will discuss here only the first.

**Hypothesis testing:** Hypothesis testing begins with an assumption that we make about a population parameter. This supposition is based on reasoning and logic.

According to **Morris Hamburg**, hypothesis is simply a quantitative statement about a population.

An example will illustrate this point. If we study the average marks obtained by 110 students in English in a particular college and get the results as 85, we may test the hypothesis that the sample has been drawn from a population with an average marks of 85.5. Similarly we may study about two attributes, study habits and achievement or intelligence and aptitude etc. and inter-relationship between the two can be known.

### Procedure for testing hypothesis

Following procedure is followed in testing hypothesis:

1. **Formulation of hypothesis :** Here hypothesis about a population parameter is formulated. Then we collect sample data, use sample statistics and make use the result to decide how far our hypothesized population parameter is correct. In short, in hypothesis testing the difference between the assumed value and the actual value of the sample mean is determined. After that we judge by using tables whether the difference is significant or not. For this purpose the observed value and the table value are compared. Two hypotheses are simultaneously formulated for this purpose—

(a) **Null hypotheses :** (Ho) This type of hypothesis asserts that there is not any difference in the sample and the population in the particular matter under study. The word null actually means invalid, void, zero or not considerable. If there is any difference found, it is accidental or unimportant arising out of fluctuations of sampling. For example, if a hypothesis that achievement of students from higher and middle class does not differ is formulated and achievements of these two groups of students are compared, we see that if the difference of achievement is not significant, null hypothesis is accepted. It means that there is really no difference between these two groups of students. If slight difference is there, it is due to the fluctuation in sampling or due to other reasons than economic status.

Similarly, if we want to know whether extra coaching has benefited the students or not. Null hypotheses will be, "extra coaching has not benefited the students.:

Thus, rejection of null hypothesis indicates that difference is statistically significant and vice versa.

(b) **Alternative hypothesis :** (Ha) It specifies those values that the researcher believes to hold true. For example, he may hold the assumption that drill technique enhances achievement. For this purpose, he will select two groups controlled and experimental and apply the technique on experimental groups finally he will compare the achievement of these two groups. If difference is significant, hypothesis will be accepted. In that way null hypothesis will be rejected.

One more example will make the difference between these two hypotheses clear.

If a researcher is interested in testing the difference between the mean IQ of two groups, null hypothesis will be that the two groups have equal means $\mu_1 - \mu_2 = 0$ and alternative hypothesis will be that the two groups are not equal in means, i.e., $\mu_1 - \mu_2 \neq 0$

$$Ho = \mu_1 - \mu_2 = 0$$

$$Ha = \mu_1 - \mu_2 \neq 0$$

2. **Fixing a suitable significance level :** In the second step, the validity of Ho against Ha is set up at a certain level of significance. The significance level is generally expressed as a percentage, such as, 5% or 1% is the probability of rejecting the null hypothesis if it is true. When a hypothesis is accepted at 5% level of significance, it means that in the long run the researcher will be making wrong decision about 5 times on every hundred occasions.
3. **Formulating a test criterion :** Formulating a test criterion is the third step of testing hypothesis. Here an appropriate probability distribution for the particular test is selected. If distribution is normal 't' or F test is applied and in other cases non-parametric tests are applied.
4. **Computation :** After formulating a test criterion, a number of computations are donev. These computations include testing statistic and standard error of testing statistic.
5. **Making Decisions (Drawing conclusions) :** A statistical conclusion is a decision either to reject or accept a null hypothesis. This decision is make on the basis of level of significance. If 5% level of significance has been fixed and observed set of result has probabilities less than 5% (the value of the test is more than table value), we consider the difference between the sample statistics and the hypothetical parameter significant.

On the other hand, if at 5% level of significance, the observed set of result has probability more than 0.05, we come to the conclusion that the difference is there due to chance factors or chance variations. As a results Ho is accepted and Ha is rejected and we state that sample observations are not inconsistent with the null hypothesis.

## Types of errors in testing hypothesis

While testing a hypothesis, two types of errors are seen—

Hypothesis is true but our test rejects it (Type I Error)

Hypothesis is false but out test accepts it (Type II Error)

Type I error is committed by rejecting the null hypothesis when it is true, i.e.,$\alpha$ = Prob(type I error)

Similarly, when type II error is committed following equation is seen, i.e., $\beta$ = prob ( type II error)

While testing hypothesis a researcher reduces these two types of errors. But due to fixed sample size, it is not possible to control both errors simultaneously. If we want to kept $\beta$ low , we will have to put up with a high $\alpha$ and vice versa. Technically, it is more dangerous to commit type II error than that of type I error. Hence, we keep the probability of comprising type I error at a certain level of significance.

## Two types of test for testing the hypothesis

1. **Two tailed test :** A two tailed test of hypothesis will reject the null hypothesis, if the sample statistic is significantly higher or lower than the hypothesized population parameter.

   Thus, in a two tailed test the rejection region is located in both the tails (directions). If we are testing a hypothesis at 5% level of significance the size of acceptance region on either side of the mean would be 47.5% and the size of rejection region will be 0.025 (2.5%) on both the sides. If sample mean falls within this area, the hypothesis will be accepted.

   The acceptance and rejection region for testing a hypothesis at 0.05 level of significance are given in the following normal probability curve. If, on the other hand, we want to reduce type I error we will reduce the size of the rejection region from 0.05 to 0.01 (1% level of significance). The acceptance region at this level of significance will the 2.56 σ from mean.

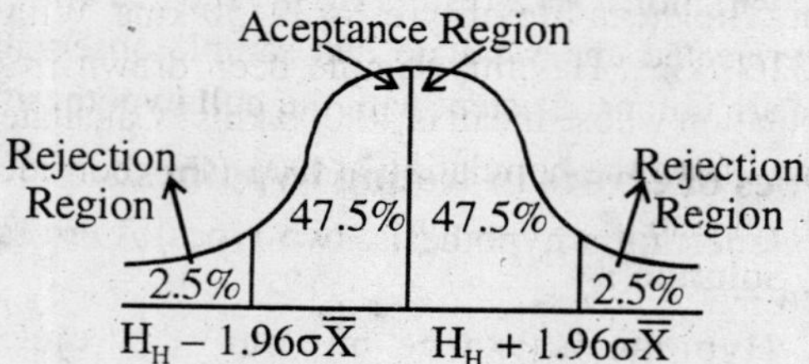


2. **One tailed test :** In this type of test, the rejection region will be located in only one tail either left or right depending on the alternative hypothesis formulated. For example, if we want to test a hypothesis that average income per household is more than Rs. 1000, the whole sample will be concentrated on only the right side and the test will be called one tailed test.

To sum up if we want to test the hypothesis that the population has a specified mean, null hypothesis will be

$$Ho = \mu = \mu 0$$

Alternative hypothesis may be any of the following

I. $Ha = \mu > \mu a$

II. $Ha = \mu < \mu a$

## DIFFERENCE BETWEEN LARGE AND SMALL SAMPLES

Technically, a sample is said to be large if its size is greater than 30. The sample is otherwise small.

The test of significance used in dealing with these two types of samples are different for the reason that the assumptions that we make in case of large as well as small samples are entirely different.

### Test of Significance for Large Sample Assumption

1. The random sampling distribution of a statistic is approximately normal.
2. The values given by the samples are almost close to the population value.

**(A) One tailed test of significance :** While testing the significance of a statistic of large samples the, concept of standard error is used. Some formulae in this regard are given below :

(i) When standard deviation of the population is given :

$$SE_{\bar{X}} = \frac{\sigma_P}{\sqrt{N}}$$

$\sigma_p$ = standard deviation of the population.

N = Number of observations in the sample.

(ii) When standard deviation of the sample is given:

$$SE_{\bar{X}} = \frac{\sigma(sample)}{\sqrt{N}}$$

(iii) When value of median is given :

$$SE_M = 1.52331\frac{\sigma}{\sqrt{N}}$$

$SE_M$ = Standard error of median.

(iv) Standard error of quartile deviation

$$SE_{QD} = 0.78672\frac{\sigma}{\sqrt{N}}$$

(v) Standard error of mean deviation

$$SE_{MD} = 0.6028\frac{\sigma}{\sqrt{N}}$$

(vi) Standard error of SD.

$$SE_{\sigma} = \frac{\sigma}{\sqrt{N}}$$

(vii) Standard error of variance

$$SE_{\sigma^2} = \sigma^2\sqrt{\frac{2}{N}}$$

(viii) Standard error coefficient of correlation

$$SE_r = \frac{1-r^2}{\sqrt{N}}$$

(ix) Standard error of rank correlation.

$$SE_{rn} = \frac{1}{\sqrt{1-N}}$$

### Numerical Examples

**Example 1.** The mean value of 225 students in a test of History is 40 and standard deviation is 12. How dependable is this mean and also estimate the population mean from which sample is drawn?

**Solution :**

$$SE_{\bar{X}}(\sigma\bar{X}) = \frac{\sigma}{\sqrt{N}} = \frac{12}{\sqrt{225}} = \frac{12}{15} = 0.80$$

Since SD of the population is not known here, SD of the sample will be taken as the SD of the population which is equal to 12.

## Computation of the population Means

1. At 95% confidence interval (fiduciary limit) :

X ± 1.96 σ M
40 ± 1.96 x 0.80
38.43 - 41.57

Thus, we see that the upper limit of the population mean= 41.57 and lower limit=38.43

2. At 99% confidence interval (Fiduciary limit) :

X ± 2.58 σ M
40 ± 2.58 x 0.80
37.97 - 42.06

It means 99% chances are there that the population mean will fall between 37.94 to 42.06. It otherwise means that only one sample out of 100 will get the value less than 37.94 or more than 42.06.

## The probable error

1. At 95% confidence interval ±1.57 (40 – 38.43)
2. At 99% confidence interval ±2.064 (40 – 37.97)

**Example 2.** Mean height of a random sample of size 100=64 inches. The standard deviation of the population is known to be 3 inches. Test the hypothesis that mean height of the population is 67 inches at 0.05 level of significance. Calculate the population mean set up at 99% also.

**Solution :**

$$\sigma X = \frac{\sigma}{\sqrt{N}} = \frac{3}{\sqrt{100}} = 0.3$$

$$\frac{Diff}{\sigma\bar{X}} = \frac{67-64}{0.3} = 10$$

10 > 1.96 SE at 5% level of significance So, hypothesis is rejected. It means that height of the population can not be 67 inches.

Computation of population mean at 99% level of significance :

X ± 2.58 SE x
64 ± 2.58 x 0.3
63.2 – 64.8

It means that there is only one percent chance that the population will get less than 63.2 inches or more than 64.8 inches.

**Example 3 :** A sample of 100 tyres is taken from a lot. The mean life of tyres is 39350 kms. With SD of 3260 kms. Has this sample been drawn from a population whose mean is 40,000 kms? Calculate the mean life of the population at 0.01 (1%) confidence interval also.

**Solution :**

$$\sigma X = \frac{\sigma}{\sqrt{N}} = \frac{3260}{\sqrt{100}} = 326$$

$$\frac{Difference}{\sigma\bar{X} =} = \frac{40,000-39,350}{326} = 1.994$$

Since 1.994< 2.58 (at 1% level), so null hypothesis is accepted. It means that the difference which is there between the sample and the population regarding mean is due to the fluctuation of sampling.

Mean of the population at 1% level of significance:

X ± 2.58 $SE_M$
39350 ± 2.58 x 326
38509 - 40191

**(B) Two tailed test for difference between the means of two samples :** If two independent random samples both $N_1$ and $N_2$ numbers respectively are drawn from the same population and standard deviation is σ, standard error of the difference between the sample means is given by the following formula

$$\sigma X_{\bar{1}} - X_{\bar{2}} = \sqrt{\sigma^2\left(\frac{1}{N_1}+\frac{1}{N_2}\right)}$$

If two random samples with $\bar{X}_1$, $N_1\sigma_1$ and $\bar{X}_2$, $N_2\sigma_2$ respectively are drawn from different populations then $SE_{\bar{X}}$ will be computed by this formula.

$$\sigma\bar{X}_1 - \bar{X}_2 = \sqrt{\left(\frac{\sigma_1^2}{N_1}+\frac{\sigma_2^2}{N_2}\right)}$$

In such a case null hypothesis to be tested will be that there is no significant difference between the means of two samples, i.e.,

## Numerical Examples

**Example 1.** The results of intelligence test of two groups of students are given below:

| | Mean | SD | N |
|---|---|---|---|
| Group A | 75 | 15 | 150 |
| Group B | 70 | 20 | 250 |

Is there a significant difference between the mean scores of these two groups?

**Solution :**

$$SE_{\bar{X}_1-\bar{X}_2} = \sqrt{\frac{\sigma_1^2}{N_1}+\frac{\sigma_2^2}{N_2}}$$

$$= \sqrt{\frac{(15)^2}{150}+\frac{(20)^2}{250}}$$

$$= \sqrt{\frac{225}{150}+\frac{400}{250}}$$

$$= \sqrt{\frac{3}{2}+\frac{8}{5}} = 1.761$$

$$\frac{Difference}{SE_{\bar{X}_1-\bar{X}_2}} = \frac{75-70}{1.76} = 2.84$$

At 1% level of significance 2.84 > 2.58 so, null hypothesis is rejected. It means that there is a significant difference between the means of these two groups.

**Example 2 :** Two samples of 100 electric bulbs have mean life of 1500 hours and 1550 hours with standard deviation of 50 and 60 respectively. Do these two brands of bulb differ in life at 0.01 level of significance?

**Solution :**

$$SE_{\bar{X}_1-\bar{X}_2} = \sqrt{\frac{50^2}{100}+\frac{60^2}{100}}$$

$$= \sqrt{\frac{2500}{100}+\frac{3600}{100}}$$

$$= \sqrt{25+36} = \sqrt{61}$$

$$SE_{\bar{X}_1-\bar{X}_2} = 7.81$$

$$\frac{Difference}{SE_{\bar{X}_1-\bar{X}_2}} = \frac{1550-1500}{7.81} = \frac{50}{7.81} = 6.4$$

6.4 >2.58 (at 1% level of significance) Therefore, null hypothesis is rejected. It means that there is a significant difference between the mean life of two brands of bulbs.

**Example 3 :** Two groups of students 100 in sample size were taught by two different methods. The mean scores and SD of group A was 40 and 20 respectively while the mean scores and SD of group B was 50 and 10 respectively. Is there any significant difference between two means at 1% level of significance?

**Solution :**

$$SE_{\bar{X}_1-\bar{X}_2} = \sqrt{\frac{20^2}{100}+\frac{10^2}{100}}$$

$$= \sqrt{\frac{400}{100}+\frac{100}{100}}$$

$$= \sqrt{4+1} = \sqrt{5} = 2236$$

$$\frac{Diff.}{SE} = \frac{50-40}{2236} = \frac{10}{2236} = 4.47$$

Since 4.47> 2.58 at 0.01 level of significance so, null hypothesis is rejected. It means that difference between means is significant.

## Test of Significance for Small Samples

When the size of the sample is small the above formulae can not be used because of the lack of fulfilment of two assumptions given in large samples. Due to this reason separate testing techniques are needed to be used to test a hypothesis. It should also be noted that methods and theory of small samples are applicable to large samples as well, though the reverse is not applicable at all.

It should be noted that investigator who works with small samples must know that his estimate will vary widely from sample to sample. So, he should take his results very carefully due to greater possibility of sampling error.

Parent population is assumed normally distributed here also. It otherwise means that our results will be true only when the population is normally distributed. If in any case, population is not normal, it is clarified how much skewed it is and in what direction.

Two types of tests are generally used while dealing with small samples—

(i) t test—by William Gosset 1905

(ii) z test—by Fisher

These two tests are based on t and z distributions respectively. We will discuss here only t test.

**t Statistic :** The other name of t distribution is student's distribution.

$$t = \frac{X - \mu}{S}\sqrt{N}$$

$$S = \sqrt{\frac{\Sigma(X - \bar{X})^2}{N-1}}$$

't' distribution has been derived mathematically under the assumption of a normally distributed population.

$$f(t) = C\left(1 + \frac{t^2}{v}\right)^{-(v+1)/2}$$

C = A constant required to make the area under the curve equal to unity.

$v = (n - 1)$ = degree of freedom.

## Properties of 't' distribution

(i) 't' distribution ranges from minus infinity to plus infinity.

(ii) Constant C actually a function of v so that for a particular value of v, the distribution of f (t) is completely specified. Thus f (t) is a family of functions, one for each value of v.

(iii) Like the standard normal distribution the 't' distribution is symmetrical and has a mean zero.

(iv) The variance of 't' distribution is greater than one but slowly approaches to one as the number of degree of freedom and hence size of the sample increases.

## Procedure for using 't' table

't' value is evaluated with reference to 't' table with a certain degree of freedom.

This t table consists of five columns. The first column indicates the degree of freedom from 1 to 100. The remaining four columns show the 't' value at four levels of significance, i.e., 0.10, 0.05, 0.02 and 0.01. Out of which 0.10 and 0.02 levels of significance are used for correlated means. It is also called one tailed test.

$df = (N - 1)$

0.05 and 0.01 levels of significance are used for unrelated means. It is also called two tailed 't' test.

$Df = (N_1 + N_2 - 2)$

Here, $N_1$ and $N_2$ are the number of observations in the two samples.

## Applications of the 't' distributions

### (A) Testing the significance of mean of a random sample

It is used to determine whether the mean of a sample deviates from the population mean or not. When variance of the population is unknown we calculate 't' by the following formula:

$$t = \frac{(X - \mu)\sqrt{N}}{S}$$

Here, $\bar{X}$ = Mean of the sample

$\mu$ = Actual mean of the population

$N$ = Size of the sample

$S$ = Standard deviation of the sample

$$S = \sqrt{\frac{\Sigma(X - \bar{X})^2}{N-1}}$$

$$\text{or} = \sqrt{\left(\frac{1}{N-1}\right)\left(\Sigma d^2 - \frac{\Sigma d^2}{N}\right)}$$

d = deviations from the assumed mean.

If calculated value of 't' value exceeds the 't' table value at 0.05 level of significance, the difference between $\mu$ and $\mu$ is said to be significant at 5% level of significance.

Here, fiducial limit of the population mean $\mu$ will be calculated by the following formula.

$$\text{At 95\% limit} = \bar{X} \pm \frac{S}{\sqrt{N}} \text{ to } 0.05$$

$$\text{At 99\% limit} = \bar{X} \pm \frac{S}{\sqrt{N}} \text{ to } 0.01$$

## Numerical examples

**Example 1 :** Calculate 't' value of the following data and compare the mean at 1% level of significance.

Table value for 5,6 and 7 degrees of freedom are given 4.032, 3.707 and 3.489 respectively. The claim of the product is that his bulbs have a mean life of 25 months.

Life of bulbs in month.

24, 36, 30, 20, 20, 18

**Solution :**

**Null hypothesis :** There is no significant difference between the mean life of the bulbs given in the sample and population mean, (Applying 't')

| X | X − $\bar{X}$ (x) | $x^2$ |
|---|---|---|
| 24 | 1 | 1 |
| 26 | 3 | 9 |
| 30 | 7 | 49 |
| 20 | −3 | 9 |
| 20 | −3 | 9 |
| 18 | −5 | 25 |
| ΣX = 138 | 0 | $\Sigma x^2$=102 |

$$\bar{X} = \frac{138}{6} = 23$$

$$S = \sqrt{\frac{\Sigma(X-X)^2}{N-1}} = \sqrt{\frac{\Sigma x^2}{N-1}}$$

$$= \sqrt{\frac{102}{6-1}} = \sqrt{\frac{102}{5}} = \sqrt{20.4}$$

$t = 4.517$

$$t = \frac{(\bar{X}-\mu)}{S}\sqrt{N}$$

$$t = \frac{23-25}{4.517} \times \sqrt{6}$$

$$= \frac{2 \times 2.449}{4.517} = \frac{4.898}{4.517} = 1.084$$

Degree of freedom ($v$) = $N - 1 = 6 - 1 = 5$ (± sign ignored)

$v = \pm 5 t = 4.032$

Since the value of t (1.084) <table value (4.032) , so null hypothesis is accepted. It means that producer's claim is not valid at 1% level of significance.

**Example 2 :** A random sample of size of 16 has mean value of 53. Sum of the deviations from mean if squared is 135. Is this sample representative to the population having mean 56. Calculate mean of the population at 95% and 99% levels of significance. $v$= 15 t 0.05 =2.13 and $v$ =15 t 0.01=2.95

**Solution :**

$$\text{Calculation } S = \sqrt{\frac{\Sigma(x-\bar{x})^2}{N-1}}$$

$$= \sqrt{\frac{135}{15}} = \sqrt{9} = 3$$

$$t = \frac{(X-\mu)}{S}\sqrt{N}$$

$$t = \frac{53-56}{3}\sqrt{16}$$

$$= \frac{-3 \times 4}{3} = -4 = 4 \text{ (± sign ignored)}$$

Here 't' value (4)> table value (2.13 and 2.25) at v=15 't' 0.05 and v= 15 't' 0.01 respectively. Hence, hypothesis is rejected. It means that sample does not represent the population.

Population mean at 95% level of significance

$$= \bar{X} \pm \frac{S}{\sqrt{N}} t \ 0.05$$

$$53 \pm \frac{3}{\sqrt{16}} \times 2.13$$

$$53 \pm \frac{3}{4} \times 2.13$$

53 ± 6.39/4

53 ± 1.6

51.4 – 54.6

Population mean at 99% level of sig

$$\bar{X} \pm \frac{S}{\sqrt{N}} t \ 0.01$$

$$53 \pm \frac{3}{4} \times 295$$

53 ± 2212

50.788 – 55.212

**(B) Testing difference between means of two independent samples**

Independent sample is one which has been selected randomly from the population and its study is not affected by the study of other sample. If we want to test that the two samples have come from the same normal population, t will be calculated by the following formula.

$$t = \frac{\bar{X}_1 - \bar{X}_2}{S} \times \sqrt{\frac{n_1 n_2}{n_1 + n_2}}$$

$\bar{X}_1$ = Mean of the first sample.

$\bar{X}_2$ = Mean of the second sample.

$n_1$ = number of observations in the first sample.

$n_2$ = number of observations in the second sample.

S = Combined SD.

S = will be calculated by using the following formula.

$$S = \sqrt{\frac{\Sigma\left(X_1 - \bar{X}_1\right)^2 + \Sigma\left(X_2 - \bar{X}_2\right)^2}{n_1 + n_2 - 2}}$$

## Numerical examples

**Example 1 :** Two types of medicines were used on two independent samples to treat tuberculosis. Numerical responses of the medicine are given below:

| Drug A | 10 | 12 | 13 | 11 | 14 | | |
|---|---|---|---|---|---|---|---|
| Drug B | 8 | 9 | 12 | 14 | 15 | 10 | 9 |

Is these a significant difference in the efficiency of the two drugs and also determine which of the drugs is more effective and why?

**Solution :**

**Hypothesis :** There is no significant difference in the effectiveness of the two medicines.

$v = n1 + n2 - 2 = 5 + 7 - 2 = 10$

$v = 10\ 0.05 = 2228$

$\bar{X}_1$ and $\bar{X}_2$ will be Calculated first from the data

$$\bar{X}_1 = \frac{\Sigma X_1}{N_1} = \frac{60}{5} = 12$$

$$\bar{X}_2 = \frac{\Sigma X_2}{N_2} = \frac{77}{7} = 11$$

| $X_1$ | $(X_1 - \bar{X}_1)$ | $(X_1 - \bar{X}_1)^2$ | $X_2$ | $X_2 - \bar{X}_2$ | $(X_2 - \bar{X}_2)^2$ |
|---|---|---|---|---|---|
| 10 | –2 | 4 | 8 | –3 | 9 |
| 12 | 0 | 0 | 9 | –2 | 4 |
| 13 | 1 | 1 | 12 | 1 | 1 |
| 11 | –1 | 1 | 14 | 3 | 9 |
| 14 | 2 | 4 | 15 | 4 | 16 |
| | | | 10 | –1 | 1 |
| | | | 9 | –2 | 4 |
| $\Sigma X_1 = 60$ | | $\Sigma(X_1 - \bar{X})^2 = 10$ | $\Sigma X_2 = 77$ | | $\Sigma(X_2 - \bar{X}_2)^2 = 44$ |

$$S = \sqrt{\frac{\Sigma\left(X_1 - \bar{X}_1\right)^2 + \Sigma\left(X_2 - \bar{X}_2\right)^2}{n_1 + n_2 - 2}}$$

$$= \sqrt{\frac{10 + 44}{10}} = \sqrt{5.4} = 2.324$$

$$t = \frac{X_1 - \bar{X}_2}{S} \times \sqrt{\frac{n_1 n_2}{n_1 + n_2}}$$

$$= \frac{12 - 11}{2.324} \times \sqrt{\frac{35}{12}}$$

$$= \frac{1.708}{2.324} = 0.735$$

t 0.735 < vt 2.228. Hence hypothesis is accepted. It means that the two drugs do not significantly differ in efficiency. Choice A or B drug will depend on factors other than efficiency

**Example 2:** Two groups of students A and B were taught by two teachers for a weak. One teacher used stimulus variation and the other did not. Marks obtained by these students are given below. Determine the validity of stimulus variation in teaching.

| | | | | | | | | | | |
|---|---|---|---|---|---|---|---|---|---|---|
| Group A | 10 | 8 | 7 | 12 | 13 | 13 | 14 | | | |
| Group B | 11 | 9 | 7 | 5 | 8 | 5 | 8 | 10 | 7 | 10 |

Note : Group A was taught by stimulus variation.

$$\bar{X}_1 = \frac{\Sigma X_1}{n_1} = \frac{77}{7} = 11$$

$$\bar{X}_2 = \frac{\Sigma X_2}{n_2} = \frac{80}{10} = 8$$

| $X_1$ | $(X_1-\bar{X}_1)$ | $(X_1-\bar{X}_1)^2$ | $X_2$ | $X_2-\bar{X}_2$ | $(X_2-\bar{X}_2)^2$ |
|---|---|---|---|---|---|
| 8 | –3 | 9 | 11 | –3 | 9 |
| 10 | –1 | 1 | 9 | 1 | 1 |
| 7 | –4 | 16 | 7 | –1 | 1 |
| 12 | 1 | 1 | 5 | –3 | 9 |
| 13 | 2 | 4 | 8 | 0 | 0 |
| 13 | 2 | 4 | 5 | –3 | 9 |
| 14 | 3 | 9 | 8 | 0 | 0 |
| | | | 10 | 2 | 4 |
| | | | 7 | –1 | 1 |
| | | | 10 | 2 | 4 |
| $\Sigma X_1 = 77$ | | $\Sigma(X_1 - \bar{X}_1)^2 = 44$ | $\Sigma X_2 = 80$ | | $\Sigma(X_2 - \bar{X}_2)^2 = 38$ |

$$S = \sqrt{\frac{\Sigma\left(X_1 - \bar{X}_1\right)^2 + \Sigma\left(X_2 -- \bar{X}_2\right)^2}{n_1 + n_2 - 2}}$$

$$= \sqrt{\frac{44+38}{7+10-2}} = \sqrt{\frac{82}{15}} = 2338$$

$$t = \frac{\bar{X}_1 - \bar{X}_2}{S} \times \sqrt{\frac{n_1 n_2}{n_1 + n_2}}$$

$$= \frac{11-8}{2338} \times \sqrt{\frac{7\times10}{7+10}}$$

$$\frac{3}{2338} \times \frac{2029}{1} = 2603$$

From the $t$ table $v = 15$ $t\,0.05 = 213$

$v = 15$ $t\,0.01 = 2.95$

t 2.603>t 0.05=2.13. Thus, the difference is significant and hence hypothesis is rejected. It means that stimulus variation has really affected the achievement if other things being the same. On the other hand, this very difference is not significant at 1% level because t value is less than the table value.

**Example 3 :** In a test given to two groups of students, the marks obtained by them are as follows:

| | | | | | | | | | |
|---|---|---|---|---|---|---|---|---|---|
| Group A | 18 | 20 | 36 | 50 | 49 | 36 | 34 | 49 | 41 |
| Group B | 29 | 28 | 26 | 35 | 30 | 44 | 46 | | |

Examine the significance of difference between means of the marks scored by the students in the group A and B . Apply 't' test for this purpose here?

| Group A $X_1$ | $(X_1-\bar{X}_1)$ | $(X_1-\bar{X}_1)^2$ | Group B $X_2$ | $X_2-\bar{X}_2$ | $(X_2-\bar{X}_2)^2$ |
|---|---|---|---|---|---|
| 18 | −19 | 361 | 29 | −5 | 25 |
| 20 | −17 | 289 | 28 | −6 | 36 |
| 36 | −1 | 1 | 26 | −8 | 64 |
| 50 | 13 | 169 | 35 | 1 | 1 |
| 49 | 12 | 144 | 30 | −4 | 16 |
| 36 | −1 | 1 | 44 | 10 | 100 |
| 34 | −3 | 9 | 46 | 12 | 144 |
| 49 | 12 | 144 | | | |
| 41 | 4 | 16 | | | |
| $E X_1=333$ | | $E(X_1-0_2)^2=1134$ | $E X_2=238$ | | $E(X_2-\bar{X}_2)^2=386$ |

$$\bar{X}_1=\frac{\Sigma X_1}{N_1}=\frac{333}{9}=37$$

$$\bar{X}_2=\frac{\Sigma X_2}{N_2}=\frac{238}{7}=34$$

$$S=\sqrt{\frac{\Sigma\left(X_1-\bar{X}_1\right)^2+\Sigma\left(X_2-\bar{X}_2\right)^2}{n_1+n_2-2}}$$

$$=\sqrt{\frac{1134+386}{9+7-2}}$$

$$=\sqrt{\frac{1520}{14}}=10.419$$

$$t=\frac{37-34}{10.42}\times\sqrt{\frac{63}{16}}=0.571$$

Here t value is less than table value at v= 14 t 0.05=2.14. Hence, hypothesis is accepted. It means that two means do not differ significantly.

**(C) Testing differences between means of two dependent samples (Paired Observation)**

Two samples are said to be dependent when the elements in one sample are related to those in the other sample in a significant manner.

The two samples may be dependent under the condition that pair of observation is made on the sample object or individual. Thus, sample may be the same but observation will differ.

For example, when we study the effects of a particular training on employees, we study the effect of training by finding out the difference between the performance of employees before and after the training. The following formula of t test will be used here.

$$t=\frac{\bar{d}-O}{S}\sqrt{N}\ \text{ or } t=\frac{\bar{d}\sqrt{n}}{S}$$

$\bar{d}$ = Mean of the differences = $\frac{\Sigma d}{n}$

$S$ = Standard Deviation of the differences.

$$S=\sqrt{\frac{\Sigma\left(d-\bar{d}\right)^2}{n-1}}\ \text{ or } \sqrt{\frac{\Sigma d^2-n\left(\bar{d}\right)^2}{n-1}}$$

Degree of freedom $(v)=n-1$

**Numerical examples :** A new course was introduced in a school. A test was given to 12 students before and after the course. Marks of these students in the first and second tests are given below :

| First test (Before course) | Second test ( After course) |
|---|---|
| 44 | 53 |
| 40 | 38 |
| 61 | 69 |
| 52 | 57 |
| 32 | 46 |
| 44 | 39 |
| 70 | 73 |
| 41 | 48 |
| 67 | 73 |
| 72 | 74 |
| 53 | 60 |
| 72 | 78 |

Calculate the usefulness of the course by applying 't' test.

**Solution :**

**Hypothesis :** There is no significant difference in the marks obtained by students before and after the course, i.e., course is not at all useful.

$t$ formula $= \bar{d}\sqrt{n}$ will be used here and degree of freedom $v$ will be $n - 1 = 12 - 1 = 11$

| I st test | IInd test | II-I test (d) | d² |
|---|---|---|---|
| 44 | 53 | 9 | 81 |
| 40 | 38 | -2 | 4 |
| 61 | 69 | 8 | 64 |
| 52 | 57 | 5 | 25 |
| 32 | 46 | 14 | 196 |
| 44 | 39 | -5 | 25 |
| 70 | 73 | 3 | 9 |
| 41 | 48 | 5 | 25 |
| 67 | 73 | 6 | 36 |
| 72 | 74 | 2 | 4 |
| 53 | 60 | 7 | 49 |
| 72 | 78 | 6 | 36 |
| | | $\sum d=60$ | $\sum d^2=578$ |

$$\bar{d} = \frac{\Sigma d}{n} = \frac{60}{12} = 5$$

$$S = \sqrt{\frac{\Sigma d^2 - n\left(\bar{d}\right)^2}{n-1}}$$

$$= \sqrt{\frac{578 - 12(5)^2}{11}} = \sqrt{\frac{578 - 12 \times 25}{11}}$$

$$= \sqrt{\frac{278}{11}} = 5.03$$

$$t = \frac{\bar{d}\sqrt{n}}{S} = \frac{5\sqrt{12}}{5.03} = 3.443$$

$$v = 11 t\ 0.05 = 2201$$

Here, 3.443 > 2.201. Hmlence hypothesis is rejected and the course is useful.

## Advantages of 't' test

1. We can test the significance of difference between two means of the two groups. We can thus find out whether there is really a difference between means or it is due to chance factors.
2. We can easily find out the effectiveness of a treatment given to two different groups or to a single group.
3. We can also find out the mean of the population from which the sample is drawn.
4. 't' test can be applied to even large samples and we will get very dependable result.

## Limitations of Hypothesis Testing

While testing hypothesis the following points must be kept into account.

1. **Mechanical use of testing is absurd :** There may be situations where huge difference between means exist. In such situations too we can not say whether difference is significant or not without going through such tests. Even after testing the significance, results should be interpreted very carefully.
2. **Conclusion is to be drawn in terms of probabilities not in terms of certainties :** When test of significance shows real difference between means, it can not be definitely stated that this difference will always occur. It only shows the 99% or 95% probability of occurring such difference and this is real difference not a difference due to chance factor. At 95% level, there is 5% chance that this difference between two means will not be seen.
3. **Testing does not respond the question of why the difference between means is there :** Hypothesis testing is only a statistical treatment of the data. It does not deal with those factors responsible for the difference.
4. **Precautions regarding assumptions :** Many hypothesis are tested even though the

assumptions regarding the procedure are not fulfilled. For example, samples are not drawn from the population about which study is being conducted or the population and hence sample is not normally distributed, or sample is biased in any way etc. Hypothesis testing does not touch these problems.

**5. Limitations of behavioural Sciences :** No testing is direct and hence perfect in all behavioural sciences. So, degree of imperfection should always be taken in view. It means that chance of error is always there due to indirect nature of measurement in behavioured sciences.

## OBJECTIVE QUESTIONS

**1.** Variation of sample mean from the population mean is due to
*(a)* sampling error
*(b)* wrong method of data collection.
*(c)* biased attitude of the researcher
*(d)* all of the above

**2.** According to central limit theorem, if large sample is selected randomly from an infinite population then
*(a)* the distribution of sample mean is normal
*(b)* the average value of the sample means will be the same as that of the population mean
*(c)* standard deviation of the sample mean will be the standard error of means (SEn)
*(d)* all of the above

**3.** 1.96 level of significance for a large sample means:
*(a)* 2.5% on each side of the normal curve out of range of the investigation
*(b)* 5% chance is there that the result obtained will not match the population mean
*(c)* both of these
*(d)* None of these

**4.** 't' formula has been given by
*(a)* Fisher *(b)* Best
*(c)* Karl Pearson *(d)* None of these

**5.** In the formula of 't' = $\frac{M_D}{SE_{MD}}$ . $SE_{MD}$ is
*(a)* standard error of mean of difference
*(b)* standard error of mean deviation
*(c)* both of these
*(d)* None of these

**6.** If we have five random samples and we want to determine whether there are significant differences among their means, we would have to use:
*(a)* $5\frac{(5-3)}{2} = 5$ *t tests* *(b)* $5\frac{(5-1)}{2} = 10$ *t tests*
*(c)* $\frac{5\times5\times4}{2} = 50$ *t tests* *(d)* None of the above

**7.** Formula for standard error of Z ($\sigma_z$) is
*(a)* $\frac{1}{N-3}$ *(b)* $\frac{1}{\sqrt{N-3}}$
*(c)* $\frac{1}{\sqrt{N-2}}$ *(d)* None of the above

## ANSWERS

| 1 | 2 | 3 | 4 | 5 | 6 | 7 |
|---|---|---|---|---|---|---|
| *(a)* | *(d)* | *(c)* | *(a)* | *(a)* | *(b)* | *(b)* |

# Chi Square ($X^2$) Test and Goodness of Fit

## Meaning

There are many situations in which it is not possible to make any rigid assumption about the distribution of the population from which samples are drawn, i.e., the distribution is not definitely said to be normal. Non-parametric tests are used in such cases. Chi square test is one of them. The reason why such tests are used so popularly are given below :

I. These tests are distribution free, i.e., they can be used with any shape of population distribution.

II. They can be easily computed, handled and understood.

III. They can be used with those types of measurements that prohibit the use of parametric test.

$X^2$ test was first used by Karl Pearson in 1890. The quantity $X^2$ describes the magnitude of the discrepancy between theory and observation.

## Definition

$$X^2 = \frac{\Sigma(O-E)^2}{E}$$

O = Observed frequency
E = Expected frequency

## Step in the calculation of $x^2$ test

1. Expected frequencies (E) are calculated first by using the following formula :

$$E = \frac{RTxCT}{N}$$

RT = The row total for the row containing the cell

CT = The column total for the column containing the cell.

2. Get the difference between observed and expected frequencies and then find the value of $(O-E)^2$

3. Divide this value by E and then find the sum total. The value of $X^2$ ranges from zero to infinity. Zero $X^2$ means observed and expected frequencies completely coincide. Greater the discrepancy between O and E, greater will be the value of $X^2$.

**Level of Significance:** The calculated value of $X^2$ is compared with the table value of $X^2$ for given degree of freedom at a certain specified level of significance. Generally 5% level of significance is selected for this purpose. If the value of $X^2$ >table value of $X^2$, the distribution between theory and observation is considered to be significant.

The value of $X^2$ is a random variable which takes on different values from sample to sample and its value will always be positive. Besides, $X^2$ is derived from observation, so it is a statistic not a parameter.

**Points to remember: Following points must be remembered regarding $X^2$ test**

I. Sum of the observed and expected frequencies is always zero i.e.,

$$\Sigma = (O-E) = N - N = 0$$

This equation provides a check on the computation of $X^2$.

II. $X^2$ test depends on only the set of observed and expected frequencies and degree of freedom. It is a distribution free test.

III. $X^2$ distribution is a limiting approximation of the multinomial distribution.

IV. Though $X^2$ distribution is essentially a continuous distribution, yet $X^2$ test can be applied to discrete random variables whose frequencies can be counted and tabulated.

## Conditions for applying Chi square test

I. N must be reasonably large to ensure the similarity between theoretically correct distribution and sampling distribution of $X^2$. $X^2$ test should not be used when N is less than 50.

II. The theoretical cell frequency should not be small when expected frequency are too small. In that case the value of $X^2$ will be overestimated resulting in two many rejection of Ho. To avoid making incorrect inferences, a general rule is that expected frequency of less than 5 in one cell of a contingency table is too small to use. When the table contains more than one cell with an expected frequency of less than 5, we pool such frequencies with the preceding or succeeding frequency so that the resulting sum is five or more. In doing so we reduce the number of categories of data and will gain less information from contingency table.

## Uses of $X^2$ test

1. **$X^2$ test as a test of independence :** With the help of $X^2$ test we can find out whether two or more attributes are associated or not. Suppose we have N observation classified according to some attributes, we may find out whether the attributes are related or independent. In order to test whether attributes are related or not we take the null hypothesis that there is no association in the attributes under study. If the value of $X^2$ is less than the table value at a certain level of significance (5% level) we say that the results of the experiment provide no evidence for doubting the hypothesis, i.e., attributes are not related. On the other hand, if value of $X^2$>table value, null hypothesis will be rejected, i.e., attributes are related.
2. **$X^2$ test as a test of goodness of fit :** It enables us to ascertain how appropriately the theoretical distribution fit empirical distribution. When an ideal frequency curve is fitted to the data, $X^2$ test find out how well this curve fits with the observed facts.
3. **$X^2$ test as a test of homogeneity :** Tests of homogeneity are designed to determine whether two or more independent random samples are drawn from the same population or from different populations.

### Numerical examples

**Example 1 :** In an experiment on immunization of cattle from tuberculosis the following results were obtained.

| | Affected | Non affected |
|---|---|---|
| Inoculated | 12 | 26 |
| Non-inoculated | 16 | 6 |

Now calculate $X^2$ and discuss the effect of vaccine in controlling susceptibility to TB (5% value of $X^2$ for one degree of freedom= 3.84)

**Solution :** Hypothesis : Vaccine is not effective in controlling susceptibility to TB applying $X^2$ test

$$\text{Expectation of } AB = \frac{(A \times B)}{N}$$

$$= \frac{38 \times 26}{60} = 17.7$$

$A = 12 + 26 = 38$

$B = 12 + 16 = 28$

| Table of expected frequencies | | |
|---|---|---|
| 17.7 | 20.3 | 38 |
| 10.3 | 11.7 | 22 |
| 28 | 32 | 60 |

Since one of the expected frequencies is less than 10, we would use Yates correction then apply $X^2$ test.

| $O$ | $E$ | $(O-E)^2$ | $(O-E)^2/E$ |
|---|---|---|---|
| $12 + 0.5 = 12.5$ | 17.7 | $(5.2)^2 = 27.04$ | 1.528 |
| $16 - 0.5 = 15.5$ | 10.3 | $(5.2)^2 = 27.04$ | 2.625 |
| $26 - 0.5 = 25.5$ | 20.3 | $(5.2)^2 = 27.04$ | 1.332 |
| $6 + 0.5 = 6.5$ | 11.7 | $(5.2)^2 = 27.04$ | 2.311 |

$$\Sigma(O-E)^2/E = 7.796$$

$$X^2 = 7.8$$

$$V = (r - 1\ (c - 1) = (2 - 1)\ (2 - 1) = 1$$

(V = Degree of freedom)

Here 7.8 is significant at 1 degree of freedom. Ans.

**Example :** Two investigators study the income of a group of persons by the method of sampling. Following results were obtained by them.

| Investigator | Poor | Middle | Upper | Total |
|---|---|---|---|---|
| A | 160 | 30 | 10 | 200 |
| B | 140 | 120 | 40 | 300 |
| Total | 300 | 150 | 50 | 500 |

Show that the sampling technique of at least one of the investigator is suspected.

**Solution :**

**Hypothesis :** There is no suspicion about the sampling technique of the two investigators.

$$E_{11} = \frac{200 \times 300}{500} = 120$$

$$E_{12} = \frac{200 \times 150}{500} = 60$$

| Table of expected frequencies | | | |
|---|---|---|---|
| 120 | 60 | 20 | 200 |
| 180 | 90 | 30 | 300 |
| 300 | 150 | 50 | 500 |

**Calculation of $X^2$**

| O | E | $(O-E)^2$ | $(O-E)^2/E$ |
|---|---|---|---|
| 160 | 120 | 1600 | 13.333 |
| 140 | 180 | 1600 | 8.888 |
| 30 | 60 | 900 | 15 |
| 120 | 90 | 900 | 10 |
| 10 | 20 | 100 | 5 |
| 40 | 30 | 100 | 3.333 |

$$\sum (O-E)^2/E = 55.554$$

$$X^2 = 55.554$$

$$v = \text{(row-1) column-1)}$$

$$(2-1(3-1) = 2$$

$v = 2X^2$ 0.05 = 5.991. From the table 55.554 is much greater than the value of $X^2$ from the table. Which is only 5.991. Thus, difference is significant (hypothesis) is rejected). It means that sampling technique of at least one of the investigators is suspected.

## Analysis of Variance

If we have more than two samples under study to calculate significance of difference between various means, we will have to use many 't' tests Analysis of Variance (ANOVA) saves us from this difficulty and only one ANOVA is needed to be calculated to study the significance of difference between means for example, if there are six samples under study at a time, the number of 't' test required at a time will be

$$\frac{6(6-1)}{2} = 15 \ t \text{ tests.}$$

This burden can be used by using one F test.

$$F = \frac{\text{Variance between groups}}{\text{Variance within groups}}$$

## Assumptions of ANOVA

1. Population distribution should be normal.
2. All the groups of a certain criterion should be randomly selected from the sub population having the same criterion.
3. The sub groups under study should have the same variability (SD)

## Steps in the calculation of ANOVA

Step I : Calculate correction, i.e., $\frac{\Sigma X_2 + \Sigma X_2 + \cdots \Sigma X_n}{\Sigma N}$

Step II : Calculate total sum of squares, i.e., $\sum X^2$ - Correction

Step III : Calculate sum of squares between means of various groups, i.e.,

$$\frac{(\Sigma X_1)}{N_1} + \frac{(\Sigma X_2)}{N_2} + \cdots \frac{(\Sigma Xn)^2}{Nn} - \text{Correction}$$

Step IV : Calculate sum of squares within means of all groups, i.e.,

Total sum of Squares – Sum of Squares

Step V: Calculate F ratio.

Step VI : Determine level of significance.

**Example :** Calculate analysis of variance of the following data.

| Groups | Scores | | | | |
|---|---|---|---|---|---|
| A | 5 | 6 | 7 | 3 | 2 |
| B | 4 | 7 | 8 | 4 | 1 |
| C | 1 | 3 | 2 | 0 | 3 |

**Solution :**

| Group A | | Group B | | Group C | |
|---|---|---|---|---|---|
| $X_A$ | $X_A^2$ | $X_B$ | $X_B^2$ | $X_C$ | $X_C^2$ |
| 5 | 25 | 4 | 16 | 1 | 1 |
| 6 | 36 | 7 | 49 | 3 | 9 |
| 7 | 49 | 8 | 64 | 2 | 4 |
| 3 | 9 | 4 | 16 | 0 | 0 |
| 2 | 4 | 1 | 1 | 3 | 9 |
| $\Sigma X_A = 23$ | $\Sigma X_A^2 = 123$ | $\Sigma X_B = 24$ | $\Sigma X_B^2 = 146$ | $\Sigma X_C = 9$ | $\Sigma X_C^2 = 23$ |

I. Correction : $\dfrac{(\Sigma X_A + \Sigma X_B + \Sigma X_C)^2}{N_A + N_B + N_C}$

$$\frac{(23+24+9)^2}{5+5+5} = \frac{3136}{15} = 207.06$$

II. Total sum of Squares = ($åX^2_A + åX^2_B + åX^2_C$) – Correction

= (123 + 146 + 23) – 207.06

= 292 - 207 = 85

III. Sum of Squares between means

$$= \frac{(\Sigma X_A)^2}{N_A} + \frac{(\Sigma X_B)^2}{N_B} + \cdots \frac{(\Sigma X_C)^2}{N_C} - \text{Correction}$$

$$\frac{(23)^2}{5} + \frac{(24)^2}{5} + \cdots \frac{(9)^2}{5} - (207)$$

= (105.8 + 115.2 + 16.2) – 207

= 30.2

IV. Sum of Squares within means of various groups = Total sum of squares – Sum of squares between means

85 – 30.2 = 54.8

V. $F = \dfrac{30.2}{2} \div \dfrac{54.8}{12} + \dfrac{15.1}{4.57} = 3.30$ **Ans**

Note: Here 12 = (5 – 1) + (5 – 1) + (5 – 1)

## OBJECTIVE QUESTIONS

**1.** The other name of non-parametric tests is
*(a)* distribution free test *(b)* X test
*(c)* both of these *(d)* none of these

**2.** Non parametric tests are used when
*(a)* the population from which sample is drawn is not normal
*(b)* Variables are expressed in nominal form, i.e., represented by frequency counts
*(c)* variables are expressed in ordinal form
*(d)* All of the above

**3.** The test used with discrete data in the form of frequencies is
*(a)* $X^2$ test *(b)* 't' test
*(c)* Z test *(d)* ANOVA

**4.** In a 2 × 2 table comprised of four cells with (2 – 1) (2 – 1) = 1 formula used for calculating $X^2$ is

*(a)* $X^2 = \dfrac{N(AD-BC)^2}{(A+B)(C+D)(A+C)(B+D)}$

*(b)* $X^2 = \dfrac{(AD-BC)^2}{(A+B)(C+D)(A+C)(B+D)}$

*(c)* $X^2 = \dfrac{N(AD-BC)}{(A+B)(C+D)(A+C)(B+D)}$

*(d)* None of the above

**5.** Median test is used for testing whether
*(a)* two independent samples differ in SD
*(b)* two independent samples differ in central tendencies
*(c)* two samples differ from the population mean
*(d)* none of the above

**6.** Significance of contingency coefficient is calculated by the formula

*(a)* $C = \sqrt{\dfrac{X^2}{N+X^2}}$ *(b)* $C = \dfrac{X^2}{N+x}$

*(c)* $C = \dfrac{\sqrt{X^2}}{N+X^2}$ *(d)* none of the abvoe

## ANSWERS

| 1 | 2 | 3 | 4 | 5 | 6 |
|---|---|---|---|---|---|
| *(a)* | *(d)* | *(a)* | *(a)* | *(b)* | *(a)* |

7

# Measure of Correlation

## Meaning of Correlation

If two quantities vary in such a way that movements in one are accompanied by movements in the other, these quantities are said to be correlated. For example, there is direct correlation between achievement and intelligence. How much the two variables are correlated is determined by the degree of correlation. This degree of relationship is measured through the correlation analysis. This is called correlation coefficient.

One important point to be kept in mind is that two independent variables are never correlated because they will have nothing for interpretation. For example, if we correlate diagnostic test with interest test, we will get nothing but an aptitude test has direct correlation with achievement.

The degree of correlation will always vary from –1 to +1 i.e. from perfectly negative to perfectly positive and zero degree means no correlation at all.

## Definitions

1. **L.R. Conner :** If two or more quantities vary in sympathy so that movement in one tends to be accompanied by the corresponding movements in the other, then they are said to be correlated.
2. **Ya Lun Chou :** Correlation analysis attempts to determine the degree of relationship between variables.

   Thus, correlation is a statistical device which helps us in analyzing the comparison between two or more variables. Correlation helps us to determine four things.

   I. Whether a relationship exists between variables, i.e., measurement of relation.
   II. Whether correlation is positive or negative.
   III. Whether the degree of correlation is significant or not.
   IV. Establishment of cause and effect relationship between variables.

## Significance of Co-relational Studies

I. With the help of one single coefficient of correlation, we can measure the degree of relationship existing between two or more variables.
II. The prediction based on correlation analysis is likely to be more viable and near to reality.
III. It helps in locating such variables on which other variables depend. Once these dependent factors are known, that can either be controlled or eliminated to escape the effect.
IV. This helps us to get rid of false beliefs that we have about different things. For example, anxiety will increase or decrease achievement, can be studied only with the help of correlation analysis.

## Type of Correlations

1. **Positive and negative correlation :** If both the variables are varying in the same direction, i.e., if intelligence is high, adjustability is also high and vice versa, the correlation is said to be positive. It is denoted by + sign.

On the other hand, if values of two variables move in different directions so that with the increase in the value of one, the other value decreases and vice versa, the correlation is said to be negative. it is denoted by minus sigh.

### Example of positive correlation

| Variable X= | 5 | 8 | 10 | 12 | 18 | 20 |
|---|---|---|---|---|---|---|
| Variable Y = | 25 | 40 | 50 | 58 | 63 | 80 |

### Example of negative correlation

| Variable X= | 10 | 20 | 35 | 50 | 80 |
|---|---|---|---|---|---|
| Variable Y= | 80 | 70 | 60 | 35 | 20 |

Zero coefficient of correlation, on the other hand shows no relationship between the variables.

2. **Simple, partial and multiple correlation :** This type of distinction of correlation is based on the number of variables studied.

When only two variables are taken into consideration, it is an example of simple correlation, e.g., relationship between study habits and achievement.

In multiple correlation three or more variables are studied simultaneously, e.g., we try to correlate socio-economic status, adjustment and achievement.

In partial correlation, we recognize more than two variables at a time but consider only two variables to be influencing each other. Here the effects of other variables are kept constant.

3. **Linear and non-linear correlation :** When the variations in the values of two variables are in a constant ratio, correlation is said to be linear. For example, if there is 10% increase in the variables X all the time which causes 20% or 25% increase in the variable Y all the time, the relationship is said to be linear and positive. In such a case the curve showing this relationship will be a straight line rising from left to right upward. Here, relationship will be maintained at a constant rate till the end.

**Example :**

| | | | | | |
|---|---|---|---|---|---|
| **Variable X** | 2 | 4 | 6 | 8 | 10 |
| **Variable Y** | 5 | 10 | 15 | 20 | 25 |

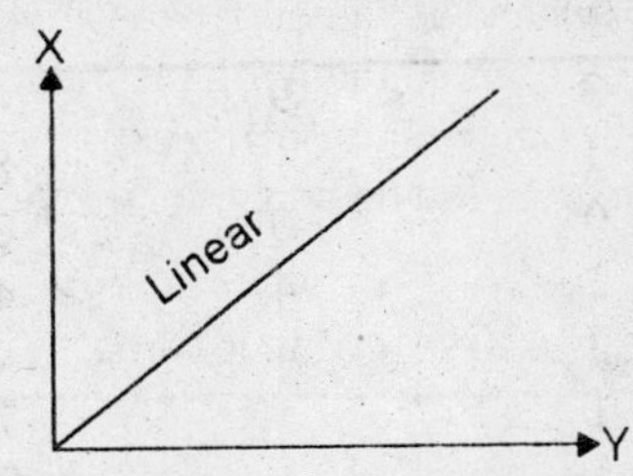


On the other hand, if percentage change in X and Y are not constant all the time, it is rather fluctuating, the relationship is said to be non-linear or curvi linear.

**Example :**

| | | | | | |
|---|---|---|---|---|---|
| **Variable X** | 2 | 4 | 6 | 8 | 10 |
| **Variable Y** | 5 | 8 | 12 | 17 | 24 |

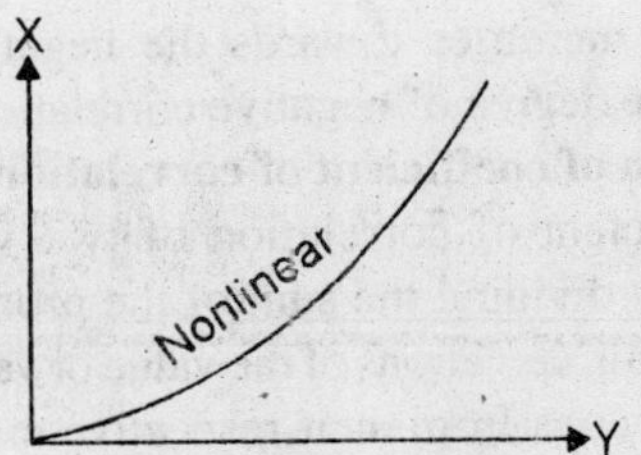


**Method of studying correlation :** Some of the methods of studying correlation are as follows :

1. Scatter diagram
2. Correlation graph
3. Product moment coefficient of correlation
4. Rank difference correlation method
5. Coefficient of concurrent deviation
6. Method of least Square

We will discuss here only few methods :

### (A) Product Moment Coefficient of Correlation :

This method was developed by Karl Pearson. That is why, it is also called Pearson's coefficient of correlation. The purpose of calculating coefficient here is to study the extent or degree to which the two variables are correlated with each other.

This coefficient of correlation would vary from perfectly positive +1 to perfectly negative –1.

Perfectly positive correlation is that correlation in which an increase in the values of one variable causes an increase in the value of the other variable in a fixed proportion. Here variations will be proportionate. In perfectly negative correlation, the proportional relationship will be inverse. Relationship of such a perfect nature is not seen in behavioural sciences.

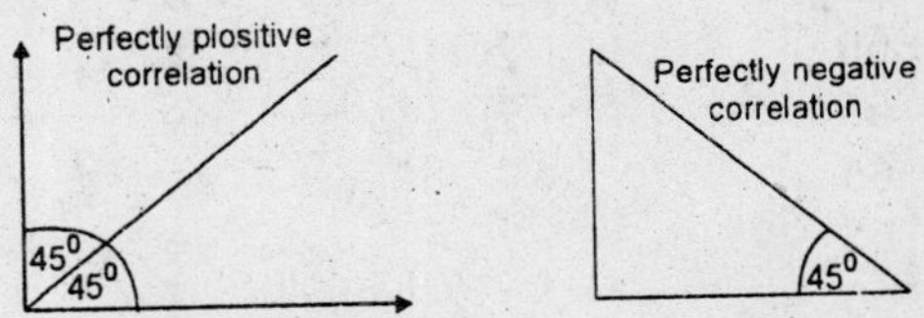


The mid point between +1 and –1 degree of correlations is zero which shows no correlation between the two variables at all. When this coefficient increases from zero to positive direction like 0.20, 0.35 etc. it shows some degree of positive correlation.

When this increases towards the negative side, it shows some degree of negative correlation.

**Calculation of coefficient of correlation**

The coefficient of correlation of two variables is obtained by dividing the sum of the products of the corresponding deviations of the value of various items of the two series from their respective means by the product of their standard deviations and the number of pairs of observation i.e.,

$$r = \frac{\textit{Covariance of the two series}}{\sqrt{\textit{Variance of series } 1 \times \textit{Variance of Series } 2}}$$

$$r = \frac{\textit{Covariance}}{\sigma_1\sigma_2} = \frac{\sigma xy}{\sigma_1\sigma_2}$$

Here,

Covariance = $\Sigma xy \div n$

There are different methods of arriving at this formula. They are given below :

**Direct method No 1:** Calculation of r involves the following steps here—

I. Find the means $\overline{X}$ of the two series X and Y.

II. Find the mean deviation of series X and Y separately. Mean deviation of X series $(X - \overline{X})$ is denoted as $x$ and mean deviation of Y series $(Y - \overline{X})$ is denoted as y.

III. Square these deviations, of $x$ and $y$ and then summed them up i.e., å $x^2$ and å$y^2$.

IV. Multiply the respective deviation of the two series and total them, i.e., åxy.

V. Calculate r by using the following formula given below :

$$r = \frac{\Sigma xy}{n\sqrt{\frac{\Sigma x^2}{n}} \times \sqrt{\frac{\Sigma y^2}{n}}}$$

$$= \frac{\Sigma xy}{n\sigma_1\sigma_2} \text{ or}$$

$$r = \frac{\Sigma xy}{\sqrt{\Sigma x^2 \Sigma y^2}}$$

**Example 1.** Calculate product moment coefficient of correlation between the scores of a student in mathematics and Hindi in ten different tests.

| Tests | Maths | Hindi |
|---|---|---|
| 1 | 50 | 11 |
| 2 | 50 | 13 |
| 3 | 55 | 14 |
| 4 | 60 | 16 |
| 5 | 65 | 16 |
| 6 | 65 | 15 |
| 7 | 65 | 15 |
| 8 | 60 | 14 |
| 9 | 60 | 13 |
| 10 | 50 | 13 |

**Solution : (Direct method)**

| Scores in Maths (X) | $X - \overline{X}$ Deviation from mean 58 ($x$) | $x^2$ | Scores in Hindi (Y) | $Y - \overline{X}$ Deviation from mean 14 ($y$) | $y^2$ | Product of deviations $xy$ |
|---|---|---|---|---|---|---|
| 50 | –8 | 64 | 11 | –3 | 9 | 24 |
| 50 | –8 | 64 | 13 | –1 | 1 | 8 |
| 55 | –3 | 9 | 14 | 0 | 0 | 0 |
| 60 | 2 | 4 | 16 | 2 | 4 | 4 |
| 65 | 7 | 49 | 16 | 2 | 4 | 14 |
| 65 | 7 | 49 | 15 | 1 | 1 | 7 |
| 65 | 7 | 49 | 15 | 1 | 1 | 7 |
| 60 | 2 | 4 | 14 | 0 | 0 | 0 |
| 60 | 2 | 4 | 13 | –1 | 1 | –2 |
| 50 | –8 | 64 | 13 | –1 | 1 | 8 |
| $\Sigma x$=580 | $\Sigma x$=0 | $\Sigma x^2$=360 | $\Sigma y$=140 | $\Sigma y$=0 | $\Sigma y^2$=22 | $\Sigma xy$ =70 |

Here mean of X and Y series are calculated first separately. Then deviation scores are obtained as we see in column 2 and 5.

$\overline{X}$ of $X = 580 \div 10 = 58$ and

$\overline{X}$ of Y = $140 \div 10 = 14$

$$r = \frac{\Sigma xy}{\sqrt{\Sigma x^2 \times \Sigma y^2}} = \frac{70}{\sqrt{360 \times 22}} = 0.786 \textbf{ Ans.}$$

**Interpretation :** This high degree of correlation only shows constancy in scores obtained in mathematics and Hindi. The trend of the students in his scoring does not change. He had started from high scores in Maths and low scores in Hindi. He is following the same pattern of scoring in both the subjects in all the ten tests. High correlation does not mean high achievement in one subject will lead to high achievement in the other subject necessarily.

**Example 2.** Calculate product moment coefficient of correlation from the following data?

| **No. of students** | 1 | 2 | 3 | 4 | 5 |
|---|---|---|---|---|---|
| **Marks in History** | 48 | 35 | 17 | 23 | 47 |
| **Marks in English** | 45 | 20 | 40 | 25 | 45 |

**Solution :**

| X(H) | X− $\overline{X}$ (x) | ($x^2$) | Y (Eng.) | Y− $\overline{X}$ (y) | $y^2$ | *xy* |
|---|---|---|---|---|---|---|
| 48 | 14 | 196 | 45 | 10 | 100 | 140 |
| 35 | 1 | 1 | 20 | -15 | 225 | -15 |
| 17 | -17 | 289 | 40 | 5 | 25 | -85 |
| 23 | -11 | 121 | 25 | -10 | 100 | 110 |
| 47 | 13 | 169 | 45 | 10 | 100 | 130 |
| ΣX=170 | Σx=0 | Σ$x^2$=776 | ΣY=175 | Σy=0 | Σ$y^2$=550 | Σxy=280 |

$\overline{X}$ of $X = 170 \div 5 = 34$ and $\overline{X}$ of Y = $175 \div 5 = 35$

$$r = \frac{\Sigma xy}{\sqrt{\Sigma x^2 \Sigma y^2}} = \frac{280}{\sqrt{776 \times 550}}$$

$$= \frac{280}{10\sqrt{4268}}$$

$$= \frac{280}{10 \times 65.3} = \frac{280}{653} = 0.428$$

**Example 3.** Calculate r from the following informations given about two series :

| Series X | Series Y |
|---|---|
| 7 | 7 |
| 4 | 8 |
| — | 76 |

I. Number of items (N) =

II. Arithmetic mean X =

III. Sum of squares of deviation from $\overline{X}$ = 28 and 76

IV. Sum of the products of deviation (Σxy) = 48

$$r = \frac{\Sigma xy}{\sqrt{\Sigma x^2 \Sigma y^2}}$$

$$= \frac{48}{\sqrt{28 \times 76}} = \frac{48}{46.13} = 0.997$$

**Points to be remembered**

1. From the above examples we see that if value of Σ xy is very high in relation to $\Sigma x^2 \Sigma y^2$, then correlation will be high and vice versa. Moreover, if value of Σxy is in negative, negative coefficient of correlation will be there.
2. Degree of r only shows the degree of variations on the two series. If ΔX is 10% and ΔY is also near to 10% such as 9%, 11% or 12% etc. correlation will be high.
3. If correlation is less than 0.40, it does not necessarily exhibit any relationship between the two variables. This low level of relationship may be due to some other factors.

   Direct method no. 2 : Coefficient of correlation can be calculated without finding out deviations from means of the two series with the help of the following formula

$$r = \frac{n\Sigma XY - (\Sigma X)(\Sigma Y)}{\sqrt{N\Sigma X^2 - [\Sigma X^2]}\sqrt{N\Sigma Y^2 - [\Sigma Y^2]}}$$

This formula is based on the facts that :

I. Sum of the products of corresponding deviations of the two series from their respective means is equal to the sum of the products of the values if corresponding items less the products of the total values of the two series is divided by the number of items.

II. Sum of the squares of the deviations of items from their means is equal to the sum of the squares of the value of items less the square of the total values divided by the number of items.

**Short cut method of calculating r :** Here we do not calculate the actual mean for the purpose of obtaining mean deviations *x* or *y*. Here we take assumed means of series X and Y and use the formula in the following ways :

$$r = \frac{\Sigma dxdy - \frac{(\Sigma dx)(\Sigma dy)}{n}}{\left(\sqrt{\Sigma dx^2 - \frac{(\Sigma dx)^2}{n}}\right)\left(\Sigma dy^2 - \frac{(\Sigma dy)^2}{n}\right)}$$

Here,

I. dx and dy refer to deviations from assumed means $X - \overline{X}$ and $Y - \overline{X}$ respectively.

II. $\Sigma$dxdy= sum of the product of the deviations of X and Y series.

III. $\Sigma dx^2$= sum of squares of deviations from X series.

IV. $\Sigma dy^2$ = sum of the squares of the deviations of Y series.

We can simplify the above formula in the following manner.

$$\frac{n\Sigma dxdy - (\Sigma dx)(\Sigma dy)}{\sqrt{n\Sigma dx^2 - (\Sigma dx)^2}\sqrt{n\Sigma dy^2 - (\Sigma dy)^2}}$$

Steps involved in the calculation of coefficient of correlation by short cut method are given below :

I. Deviations of assumed mean of X and Y series are obtained in the form of dx and dy and then they are totaled as $\Sigma$dx and $\Sigma$dy.

II. Square dx and dy and find the sum of these squares $\Sigma dx^2$ and $\Sigma dy^2$.

III. Multiply dx and dy and find the sum of the these products $\Sigma$ dxdy.

**Example 4.** Calculate coefficient of correlation between X and Y from the following data.

| Values of X | 15 | 16 | 17 | 18 | 19 | 20 |
|---|---|---|---|---|---|---|
| Values of Y | 80 | 75 | 60 | 40 | 30 | 20 |

**Solution :**

| X | dx if AM = 17 | $dx^2$ | Y | dy if AM = 40 | $dy^2$ | dx dy |
|---|---|---|---|---|---|---|
| 15 | −2 | 4 | 80 | 40 | 1600 | −80 |
| 16 | −1 | 1 | 75 | 35 | 1235 | −35 |
| 17 | 0 | 0 | 60 | 20 | 400 | 0 |
| 18 | 1 | 1 | 40 | 0 | 0 | 0 |
| 19 | 2 | 4 | 30 | −10 | 100 | −20 |
| 20 | 3 | 9 | 20 | −20 | 400 | −60 |
| | $\Sigma$dx = 3 | $\Sigma dx^2$= 19 | | $\Sigma$dy = 65 | $\Sigma dy^2$= 3735 | $\Sigma$dxdy =−175 |

$$r = \frac{n\Sigma dxdy - (\Sigma dx)(\Sigma dy)}{\sqrt{n\Sigma dx^2 - (\Sigma dx)^2} \times \sqrt{n\Sigma dy^2 - (\Sigma dy)^2}}$$

$$r = \frac{6 \times -175 - (3 \times 65)}{\sqrt{6 \times 19 - 9 \times \sqrt{6 \times 3735 - 4225}}}$$

$$r = \frac{-1050 + 195}{\sqrt{114 - 9 \times \sqrt{22410 - 4225}}}$$

$$r = \frac{-855}{\sqrt{105} \times \sqrt{18185}}$$

$$r = \frac{-855}{1381 - 819} = -0.618 \textbf{ Ans}$$

**Example 5.** Calculate coefficient of correlation between X and Y from the following data.

| **X** | 2 | 4 | 6 | 8 |
|---|---|---|---|---|
| **Y** | 5 | 9 | 13 | 17 |

**Solution :**

| X | dx if AM = 5 | $dx^2$ | Y | dy if AM = 10 | $dy^2$ | dx dy |
|---|---|---|---|---|---|---|
| 2 | −3 | 9 | 5 | −5 | 25 | 15 |
| 4 | −1 | 1 | 9 | −1 | 1 | 1 |
| 6 | 1 | 1 | 13 | 3 | 9 | 3 |
| 8 | 3 | 9 | 17 | 7 | 49 | 21 |
| | $\Sigma$dx=0 | $\Sigma dx^2$=20 | | $\Sigma$dy=4 | $\Sigma dy^2$=84 | $\Sigma$ dxdy=40 |

$$r = \frac{\Sigma dxdy - \frac{(\Sigma dx)(\Sigma dy)}{n}}{\left(\sqrt{\Sigma dx^2 - \frac{(\Sigma dx)}{n}}\right)\left(\sqrt{\Sigma dy^2 - \frac{(\Sigma dy)^2}{n}}\right)}$$

$$r = \frac{40 - \frac{(0)(4)}{4}}{\sqrt{20 - \frac{(0)^2}{4} \times 84 - \frac{(4)^2}{4}}}$$

$$= \frac{40}{\sqrt{20} \times \sqrt{80}} = \frac{40}{\sqrt{1600}} = \frac{40}{40} = 1 \textbf{ Ans}$$

Here, r = 1 or unity. It means that relationship is linear. Linear relationship can also be understood from the raw score of X and Y. Where Y= 2X every where.

### (B) Rank Difference Correlation Coefficient

When quantitative measurement of a variable is difficult, rank difference correlation coefficient is used. For example, a teacher can arrange his students qualitatively on the basis of their intelligence in ascending or descending order without measuring their intelligence quantitatively. There are many attributes which are incapable of quantitative measurement, i.e., honesty, morality, trustfulness etc. This method is most suitable for these attributes. This method was developed by British psychologist Charles Edward Spearman in 1904.

If we want to study the correlation between intelligence and beauty, we will select the required number of individuals and arrange them in the order of their rank in intelligence. The rank of most intelligent individual will be I and next most intelligent individual will be 2 and so on. Similar procedure will be followed in case of beauty also. If there are 10 students in all, we will have rank from 1 to 10. Then rank correlation will be calculated by the following formula

$$R = 1 - \frac{6\Sigma d^2}{n\left(n^2 - 1\right)}$$

Here,

R = Rank difference correlation.

d = Difference of the ranks of the same individual in the two attributes.

n = Number of pairs.

### Interpretation of results

I. +1 means complete agreement in the order of the ranks between the two attributes, i.e., the person who is most intelligent is most beautiful. Opposite will be the case if R= -1.

II. If R is very low such as 0.30, 0.35 or 0.45 etc, such degrees are not significant to establish a relationship between the two attributes.

**Example 6.** Values of 15 students on two attribute A and B in the brackets are given here. The first figure denotes the attribute A and second figure denotes attributes B of the same individual.

(1,10) (2,7) (3,2) (4,6) (5,4) (6,9) (7,3) (8,1) (9,11) (10, 15) (11,9) (12,5) (13,14) (14,12) (15,13)

Calculate rank difference correlation using Spearman's formula.

| Rank of A $R_1$ | Rank of B $R_1$ | $R_1$-$R_2$ (d) | $d^2$ |
|---|---|---|---|
| 1 | 10 | – 9 | $d^2$ |
| 2 | 7 | – 5 | 25 |
| 3 | 2 | 1 | 1 |
| 4 | 6 | – 2 | 4 |
| 5 | 4 | 1 | 1 |
| 6 | 8 | – 2 | 4 |
| 7 | 3 | 4 | 16 |
| 8 | 1 | 7 | 49 |
| 9 | 11 | – 2 | 4 |
| 10 | 15 | – 5 | 25 |
| 11 | 9 | 2 | 4 |
| 12 | 5 | 7 | 49 |
| 13 | 14 | – 1 | 1 |
| 14 | 12 | 2 | 4 |
| 15 | 13 | 2 | 4 |
| | | $\Sigma d = 0$ | $\Sigma d^2 = 272$ |

$$R = 1 - \frac{6\Sigma d^2}{n^3 - n}$$

$$= 1 - \frac{6 \times 272}{15 \times 15 \times 15 - 15} = \frac{1632}{3375 - 15}$$

$$= 1 - \frac{1632}{3360}, = 1 - \frac{17}{35} = 0.51 \textbf{ Ans}$$

**Example 7.** Two ladies were asked to rank 7 different types of perfumes. Their rankings are given below:

| **Perfumes** | A | B | C | D | E | F | G |
|---|---|---|---|---|---|---|---|
| **Lady A** | 2 | 1 | 4 | 3 | 5 | 7 | 6 |
| **Lady B** | 1 | 3 | 2 | 4 | 5 | 6 | 7 |

**Calculate rank correlation.**

**Solution :**

| Rank of A $R_1$ | Rank of B $R_2$ | $R_1$-$R_2$ (d) | $d^2$ |
|---|---|---|---|
| 2 | 1 | 1 | 1 |
| 1 | 3 | – 2 | 4 |
| 4 | 2 | 2 | 4 |
| 3 | 4 | –1 | 1 |
| 5 | 5 | 0 | 0 |
| 7 | 6 | 1 | 1 |
| 6 | 7 | –1 | 1 |
| | | $\Sigma d = 0$ | $\Sigma d^2 = 12$ |

$$R = 1 - \frac{6\Sigma d^2}{n^3 - n} = 1 - \frac{6\Sigma d^2}{n(n^2-1)}$$

$$= 1 - \frac{6\times 12}{7(49-1)} = 1 - \frac{72}{336}$$

$$= 1.321 = 0.79$$

## Calculation of Coefficient of Rank Correlation (R) from Quantitative Data:

If we are dealing with variables which can be measured quantitatively, product moment method is the most suitable method of establishing correlation. But rank difference formula can also be used to calculate R. For this purpose we will have to convert the numerals into ranks first, then we can use Spearman's formula for calculating correlation.

**Example 8.** Calculate coefficient of rank correlation from the following data.

| Marks obtained in History | Marks obtained in Science |
|---|---|
| 60 | 78 |
| 34 | 32 |
| 40 | 34 |
| 50 | 42 |
| 45 | 45 |
| 41 | 33 |
| 24 | 18 |
| 43 | 30 |
| 42 | 36 |
| 66 | 72 |
| 63 | 41 |
| 46 | 57 |

**Solution :**

| History | R | Science | $R_2$ | $R_1$-$R_2$ (d) | $d^2$ |
|---|---|---|---|---|---|
| 60 | 3 | 78 | 1 | 2 | 4 |
| 30 | 11 | 32 | 10 | 1 | 1 |
| 40 | 10 | 34 | 8 | 2 | 4 |
| 50 | 4 | 42 | 6 | –2 | 4 |
| 45 | 6 | 45 | 4 | 2 | 4 |
| 41 | 9 | 33 | 9 | 0 | 0 |
| 24 | 12 | 18 | 12 | 0 | 0 |
| 43 | 7 | 30 | 11 | –4 | 16 |
| 43 | 8 | 36 | 7 | 1 | 1 |
| 66 | 1 | 72 | 2 | –1 | 1 |
| 63 | 2 | 41 | 5 | –3 | 9 |
| 46 | 5 | 57 | 3 | 2 | 4 |
| | | | | $\Sigma d = 0$ | $\Sigma d^2 = 48$ |

$$R = \frac{6\Sigma d^2}{n(n^2-1)} = 1 - \frac{6\times 48}{12(144-1)}$$

$$= 1 - \frac{288}{12\times 143} = 1 - \frac{288}{1716} = \frac{1716-288}{1716}$$

$$= \frac{1428}{1716} = 0.82 \text{ Ans}$$

**Example 9.** Calculate rank coefficient of correlation from the following data.

| **X** | 40 | 32 | 19 | 35 | 50 |
|---|---|---|---|---|---|
| **Y** | 13 | 28 | 15 | 35 | 40 |

**Solution :**

| X | $R_1$ | Y | $R_2$ | $R_1 - R_2$ (d) | $d^2$ |
|---|---|---|---|---|---|
| 40 | 2 | 13 | 5 | –3 | 9 |
| 32 | 4 | 28 | 3 | 1 | 1 |
| 19 | 5 | 15 | 4 | 1 | 1 |
| 35 | 3 | 35 | 2 | 1 | 1 |
| 50 | 1 | 40 | 1 | 0 | 0 |
| | | | | Ed = 0 | Ed² = 12 |

$$R = 1 - \frac{6\Sigma d^2}{n(n^2-1)} = 1 - \frac{6\times 12}{5(24)}$$

$$= \frac{72}{120} = 1 - \frac{9}{15} = \frac{6}{15} = 0.40 \text{ Ans}$$

**Equal ranking and calculation of R**

When there is more than one item with the same value, a common rank is given to such items. This rank is the average of ranks which they would have got separately in case of difference in values. For example, if three items of the respective values 40, 45, 50 are given 4,5 and 6 ranks respectively, these ranks will change in the following ways if values coincide.

| **Values** | **Ranks** |
|---|---|
| 40 | 4 |
| 45 | 5.5 |
| 45 | 5.5 |

Apart from this modification, some correction in the formula will also be made.

If in a series there are 'm' items whose ranks are common, then for the correction in the coefficient of rank correlation, $1/12(m^3\text{-}m)$ is added to the value of $\Sigma d^2$.

If there are more than one such groups of items with common ranks, this value is added as many times as the number of such groups.

$$R = 1 - \frac{6\left[\Sigma d^2 + \frac{1}{12}(m^3 - m) + \frac{1}{12}(m^3 - m) + \cdots\right]}{n(n^2 - 1)}$$

Here,

m = number of items whose ranks are equal.

**Example 10.** Calculate coefficient of rank correlation from the following data.

| **X** | 48 | 33 | 40 | 9 | 16 | 16 | 65 | 24 | 16 | 57 |
|---|---|---|---|---|---|---|---|---|---|---|
| **Y** | 13 | 13 | 24 | 6 | 15 | 4 | 20 | 9 | 6 | 19 |

**Solution :**

| X | Rank $R_1$ | Y | Ranks $R_2$ | $R_1 - R_2$ (d) | $d^2$ |
|---|---|---|---|---|---|
| 48 | 3 | 13 | 5.5 | –2.5 | 6.25 |
| 33 | 5 | 13 | 5.5 | 0.05 | 0.25 |
| 40 | 4 | 24 | 1 | 3 | 9 |
| 9 | 10 | 6 | 8.5 | 1.5 | 2.25 |
| 16 | 8 | 15 | 4 | 4 | 16 |
| 16 | 8 | 4 | 10 | –2 | 4 |
| 65 | 1 | 20 | 2 | –1 | 1 |
| 24 | 6 | 9 | 7 | –1 | 1 |
| 16 | 8 | 6 | 8.5 | –5 | 0.25 |
| 57 | 2 | 19 | 3 | –1 | 1 |
| | | | | Σd=0 | Σd²=41 |

**Note :** In the X series figure 16 occurs three times. If these figures were different, they would get the rank of 7, 8 and 9. The average of 7, 8 and 9 in 8. so all the three figures have been given the rank of 8.

In the Y series figure 13 occurs twice. So they have been given the equal rank of 5.5 instead of 5 and 6. Similar is the case with figure 6.

**Correction :**

In the X series value of 16 has occurred three times so $\frac{1}{12}(3^3 - 3)$ will leadded to $\Sigma d^2$. In the *y* series, there are two such groups of common ranks. So, $\frac{1}{12}(2^3 - 2)$ will be added to $\Sigma d^2$ two times. Thus, required formula will be as follows.

$$R = 1 - \frac{6\left[\Sigma d^2 + \frac{1}{12}(m^3 - m) + \frac{1}{12}(m^3 - m) + \frac{1}{12}(m^3 - m)\right]}{n(n^2 - 1)}$$

$$= 1 - \frac{6\left[41 + \frac{1}{12}(3^3 - 3) + \frac{1}{12}(2^3 - 2) + \frac{1}{12}(2^3 - 2)\right]}{10(10^2 - 1)}$$

$$= 1 - \frac{6\left[41 + \left(\frac{1}{12} \times \frac{24}{1}\right) + \left(\frac{1}{12} \times \frac{6}{1}\right) + \left(\frac{1}{12} \times \frac{6}{1}\right)\right]}{10 \times 99}$$

$$= 1 - \frac{6[41 + 2 + 0.5 + 0.5]}{990}$$

$$= 1 - \frac{6 \times 44}{990} = 1 - \frac{264}{990}$$

$$= \frac{990 - 264}{990} = \frac{726}{990} = 0.73 \textbf{ Ans}$$

**Example 11.** Calculate coefficient of rank correlation from the following data :

| **Marks in Geo. X** | 20 | 20 | 25 | 13 | 18 | 24 |
|---|---|---|---|---|---|---|
| **Marks in Scie. Y** | 19 | 18 | 12 | 19 | 19 | 22 |

**Solution :** In the X series 20 occurs twice so its rank will 3.5 and 3.5 and $1/12(m^3\text{-}m)$ will be added to Ed² (value of m=2). In the Y series 19 has occurred three times. So $1/12(m^3\text{-}m)$ will again be added to Ed² and the value of m will be 3.

| X | $R_1$ | Y | $R_2$ | $R_1\text{-}R_2$ (d) | $d^2$ |
|---|---|---|---|---|---|
| 20 | 3.5 | 19 | 3 | 0.5 | 0.25 |
| 20 | 3.5 | 18 | 5 | –1.5 | 2.25 |
| 25 | 1 | 12 | 6 | –5 | 25 |
| 13 | 6 | 19 | 3 | 3 | 9 |
| 18 | 5 | 19 | 3 | 2 | 4 |
| 24 | 2 | 22 | 1 | 1 | 1 |
| | | | | Σd = 0 | Σd² = 41.50 |

$$R = 1 - \frac{6\left[\Sigma d^2 + \frac{1}{12}(m^3 - m) + \frac{1}{12}(m^3 - m)\right]}{n(n^2 - 1)}$$

$$R = 1 - \frac{6\left[41.50 + \left(\frac{1}{12} \times \frac{24}{1}\right) + \left(\frac{1}{12} \times \frac{6}{1}\right)\right]}{6(35)}$$

$$R = 1 - \frac{6[41.50 + 2 - 0.5]}{210} = 1 - \frac{6 \times 44}{210}$$

$$R = \frac{1}{1} - \frac{264}{210}$$

$$= \frac{-54}{210} = \frac{-9}{35} = -0.26 \textbf{ Ans}$$

## Merits of Rank Difference Correlation (R)

1. This method is easier to compute and simpler to understand as compared to Karl Pearson's method and R and r will not differ if there is no repetition of values.
2. When the items are qualitative in nature like beauty, honesty, preference etc, this method can be used with great advantage.
3. This is the only method to study correlation if we are not given numerals of the actual data, i.e., we are given only ranks.

## Limitations

1. This method can not be used for finding correlation in a grouped frequency distribution (in a continuous series)
2. When the number of items exceeds 30 or 35, the calculation becomes a tedious task. In those cases this method would not be applicable or least convenient.

## (C) Bisserial Correlation

This is a method of studying relationship between dichotomous variables. Dichotomy means cutting into two almost equal parts. For example, if we want to know the relationship between intelligence and adjustment and we divide either of these two variables into normal and sub normal intelligence or socially adjusted or socially maladjusted, then dichotomy will be formed and Bisserial Correlation will be used. Here dichotomy is formed in only the second variables.

Formula for Bisserial Correlation is given below.

$$r_{bis} = \frac{M_p - M_q}{\sigma t} \times \frac{pq}{Y}$$

$M_p$ = Means of the group in the first category

$M_q$ = Means of the group in the second category.

$\sigma t$ = Standard Deviation of the entire group.

p = Proportion of the entire group in the Ist category

q = Proportion of the entire group in the IInd category

Y = Height of the normal curve ordinate dividing the two parts P and Q

**Example 12.** Suppose intelligence of 200 students of a school was tested. Out of them 80 were maladjusted and 120 were socially adjusted. It was found that mean scores of adjusted children were 110 (superior category) and mean scores of maladjusted children (inferior category) were 100 only and SD of the whole group was 10.

Calculate $r_{bis}$ if height of the normal curve ordinate is 0.3984

Here, Mp = 110, and Mq = 100

$\sigma$ t = 10

$$P = \frac{120}{200} = \frac{3}{5} = 0.60$$

$$Q = \frac{80}{200} = \frac{2}{5} = 0.40$$

$$Y = 0.3984$$

$$r_{bis} = \frac{110-100}{10} \times \frac{0.60 \times 0.40}{0.3984}$$

$$= \frac{11 \times 0.24}{0.3984}$$

$$= \frac{0.24}{0.3934} = 0.61 \textbf{ Ans}$$

## (D) Point Bisserial Correlation

When the variable which has been classified into two categories has real and genuine dichotomy (this dichotomy is not arbitrary) we make use of point bisserial correlation. Example of such dichotomous variables are male-female, living dead, abnormal-normal etc. Such dichotomies are not artificially formed.

$$r_{pbis} = \frac{M_p - M_q}{\sigma t} \times \sqrt{pq}$$

Thus, in point bisserial correlation, height of the ordinate does not have any role to play.

**Example 13.** A test was administered on 15 students. Point bisserial correlation between total test scores and item scores is to be calculated from the following table. Here score 1 means student has passed the item and zero means he has failed in that item. There are

25 items in the test and the first item has to be correlated to the total test score?

| Students | Total test scores | Item score |
|---|---|---|
| 1 | 25 | 1 |
| 2 | 23 | 1 |
| 3 | 18 | 0 |
| 4 | 24 | 0 |
| 5 | 23 | 1 |
| 6 | 20 | 0 |
| 7 | 19 | 0 |
| 8 | 22 | 1 |
| 9 | 21 | 1 |
| 10 | 23 | 1 |
| 11 | 21 | 0 |
| 12 | 20 | 0 |
| 13 | 21 | 1 |
| 14 | 21 | 1 |
| 15 | 22 | 1 |

Thus, this item has been passed by 9 students

Mp = 25 + 23 + 23 + 22 + 21 + 23 + 21 + 21 + 22 ÷ 9

$$= \frac{201}{9} = 22.33$$

Mq = 18 + 24 + 20 + 19 +21 +20 ÷ 6

(Six students could not pass one item)

$$= \frac{122}{6} = 20.33$$

σt = It will calculated as 1.82

$$p = \frac{9}{15} = 0.60$$

$$q = \frac{6}{15} = 0.40$$

$$r_{bis} = \frac{22.33 - 20.33}{1.82} \times \sqrt{0.6 \times 0.04}$$

$$\frac{2}{1.82} \times \sqrt{0.24} = 0.54 \textbf{ Ans}$$

## (E) Tetrachoric correlation ($r_t$)

This correlation is used when we want to find out the relationship between variables neither of which can be measured in scores. In that situation both these variables are artificially classified into two separate categories and $r_t$ will help in that case. For example, if we want to study the relationship between socio-economic status and achievement, we will separate the first variable as poor and rich and the second variable as under achievers and high achievers and $r_t$ will be used. These dichotomous divisions will be artificial.

$$r_t = cos\left[\frac{180° \times \sqrt{BC}}{\sqrt{AD} + \sqrt{BC}}\right]$$

Here, A,B, C and D represent frequencies in the four fold table as shown below

| | | | Total |
|---|---|---|---|
| Y Variable | B | A | A + B |
| | D | C | C + D |
| Total | B + D, | A + C | |

## (F) Phi co-efficient of Correlation

This type of correlation is used when the two variables are genuinely dichotomous, ie, classification is real

$$\phi = \frac{AD - BC}{\sqrt{(A+B)(C+D)(B+D)(A+C)}}$$

## (G) Partial correlation

Through this method of correlation, we partial out or nullifies the effect of third variable or a number of other variables upon the two variables that are actually under study.

For example, if we want to study the relationship between height and weight which might be disturbed by age factor, this age factor is nullified by partial correlation.

If we want to partial out only third factor out of three factor 1,2 and 3 the following formula will be used.

$$r_{1,2,3} = \frac{r_{12} - r_{13}(r_{23})}{\sqrt{(1 - r_{13}^2)(1 - r_{23}^2)}}$$

**Example 14 :** Correlation between intelligence and achievement = 0.80

Correlation between intelligence and age = 0.70

Correlation between Achievement and age = 0.60

Find out correlation between intelligence and achievement.

**Solution :** Age will be nullified in the following manner.

$r_{12}$ = 0.80

$r_{13} = 0.70$
$r_{23} = 0.60$

$$r_{1,2,3} = \frac{0.80-0.70(0.60)}{\sqrt{\left(1-(0.70)^2\right)\times\left(1-(0.60)^2\right)}} = 0.67 \text{ Ans}$$

**(H) Multiple Correlation**

When one variable is correlated with more than one variable at a time, multiple correlation is used. Here the first variable is called dependent variable and the other variables. ($X_1$, $X_2$, $X_3$ etc.) to which it is correlated are called independent variables. The multiple correlation clarifies the relationship between dependent and independent variables on one hand and inter-relationship among independent variables on the other.

If there are three variables $X_1$, $X_2$ and $X_3$, the formula for calculating multiple correlation will be as follows (here $X_1$ is dependent variable)

$$R_1 = 1-\sqrt{\frac{\sigma^2_{123}}{\sigma^2_1}}$$

Here, $\sigma_1$ = SD of $X$ measures

$$\sigma_{123} = \sigma\sqrt{1-r^2_{13}}\ \sqrt{1-r^2_{132}}$$

**Uses of Multiple Correlation:** This type of correlation is generally used in action researches where a number of factors are to be correlated to study the effect of independent variables on one or two dependent variables.

## OBJECTIVE QUESTIONS

**1.** The degree of relationship between a bivariate data is called
(*a*) regression (*b*) correlation
(*c*) data analysis (*d*) none of these

**2.** If a group of students having low intelligence has low level of achievement, it is an example of
(*a*) positive correlation
(*b*) positive high degree correlation
(*c*) zero correlation
(*d*) none of the above

**3.** Coefficient of correlation ranges from
(*a*) 1 to 2 (*b*) –1 to +1
(*c*) 0.7 to –0.7 (*d*) None of these

**4.** Direction of relationship between two variables is expressed by
(*a*) the sign of the coefficient
(*b*) percentage of the coefficient
(*c*) degree of the coefficient
(*d*) none of the above

**5.** The other name of Pearson is
(*a*) rank difference correlation
(*b*) product moment correlation
(*c*) phi coefficient of correlation
(*d*) none of the above

**6.** Partial correlation is calculated when
(*a*) we want to nulify the effect of third variable on other two variables
(*b*) we want to know the partial relationship between two variables
(*c*) both of these
(*d*) none of these

**7.** Coefficient of correlation is used to
(*a*) make predictions
(*b*) evaluate the degree of reliability and validity of tests
(*c*) analyse factors
(*d*) all of these

## ANSWERS

| 1 | 2 | 3 | 4 | 5 | 6 | 7 |
|---|---|---|---|---|---|---|
| (*b*) | (*b*) | (*b*) | (*a*) | (*a*) | (*a*) | (*d*) |

# UNIT-IX

- ★ *Universalisation of Education*
- ★ *Educational Administration in India*
- ★ *Distance Education in India*
- ★ *Vocationalization of Education in India*
- ★ *Educational Administration in the USA*
- ★ *Distance and Continuing Education in Australia*

# 1

# Universalisation of Education

## History

Gurukul system was the earliest form of elementary education in India which started in Vedic period and continued till the end of medieval period. It began with Upnayan Sanskar at the age of 8, 11 and 12 for children of Brahmins, Kshatriyas and Vaishyas respectively. The subjects of study at this stage were Ved, Vedang, literature, grammar, Nirukti, kalp jyotish and mathematics. Tuition fee was paid at the end of education in the form of Guru Dakshina. At the completion of education pure water was dropped on to the pupil. In Gurukul, emphasis was given to rote memory. Takhti was also used for writing practice in the beginning.

Attention was diverted to religious education during medieval period and education of Quran, Hadis and Fiqh was especially emphasised. Education of a child started with Bismillah ceremony at the age of four years, four months and four days. Primary education was given in maktabs and higher education in Madarsahs. Mediums of education were Arabic, Persian and Urdu. Education was completely free and its cost was borne by the local people and the community.

The structure of education that we see today is mostly derived from British period. For example, state controlled and private education both go hand in hand, medium of instruction is Hindi or English or a regional language upto primary level, curriculum for education is prepared by the state and so on.

## Structure of Elementary Education

There are two forms of elementary education in India—

1. **Primary Education :** It is general in nature and concentrated to the development of intellectual skills. This education is called by different names in different states. It has been stated in Article 45 of the Indian Constitution that state shall endeavour to provide within a period of 10 years from the commencement of the constitution for free and compulsory education for all the children until they attain the age of 14. This commitment of the constitution has not yet been realized even after 56 years of the enactment of the constitution and the result is that literacy rate in India is just 64.8% even today.
2. **Basic education :** This scheme of education was proposed by Gandhi Jee in order to provide education to children in the age group of 6-14 through crafts. Many states in India adopted this stream. This scheme of education was adopted with great enthusiasm during 1950-65 but after that it was almost given up by all states of India. Important education policy documents.

National policy on education was framed and announced by the government for the first time in 1968 but it could not be implemented properly.

In 1986, another policy on education was framed and announced by the government This policy was again revised in 1992 by Janardhan Reddy Committee . It stressed on the reorganization of Education at different levels along with education for equality. According to this policy education was structured in the following ways—

| | |
|---|---|
| Pre-school education | Age group 2 ½ -5 yrs. |
| Elementary education | (Class I-VIII) Age group 6-14 yrs. |
| *(a)* Primary education | (Class I-V) age group 6-11 |
| *(b)* Middle education | (Class IV-VIII) age group 12-14 |
| Secondary education | ((IX-X) |
| Senior secondary | (XI-XII) |
| Graduation | 3 yrs. education. |
| P G | 2 yrs education |

## Problems of elementary education

Important problems of elementary education are given below:

1. **Administration :** Primary education is administered partially by the local government and partially by the state government. Lack of coordination between these two bodies has made the situation poor. Education Director in the municipal board and committees in Panchayats along with sub Deputy Inspectors and Education Development Officers perform the administrative function of primary education. Functions of these bodies are not classified systematically. Every thing is going on in an as it is manner. No proper monitoring, no proper controlling, no accountability to the community and no proper planning are the major administrative problems.
2. **Inadequacy to the needs :** The number of primary schools in towns and villages is not in accordance with the local requirement. Insufficient number of teachers and kachcha buildings magnifies the problem. Thousands of one or two teachers schools can be seen in all parts of UP.
3. **Finance :** Only 2.3% of the GDP is spent in India on education which is 6% in Japan, 4.5% in USA and 4.1% in China. This is leading to paucity of teachers and school building. More than 85 students in one section of a class can be seen in almost all government schools in UP. How can a teacher control and teach such a huge number of students in a period of 35 minutes.
4. **Curriculum:** Whatever is taught in these schools is not according to the needs and interest of pupils. Two languages, mathematics, science and social sciences are unable to attract the attention of pupils and no fail policy at primary level of education has made the teacher free from teaching accountability.
5. **Ancillary Services :** Ancillary services include arrangement for books, supply of free text books, mid day meals, hostel facilities and medical care. None of these services has attained 50% success due to lack of will power on the part of state government.
6. **Lack of lady teachers :** Small children must be taught by lady teachers but the percentage of lady teachers to teach primary classes is less than 25% and recruitment policy is still not in favour of women teachers.
7. **Problem of wastage :** Wastage refers to dropping out of the child from the educational process before completion of the course. Wastage here is the wastage of human and financial resources coupled with the wastage of time and energy on the part of pupils. Major causes of drop out in schools are lack of teachers to teach pupils, lack of facilities to accommodate pupils, earning responsibility of the child at home, unattractive school environment, excess holidays leading to lethargy on the part of teachers and pupils.
8. **Problem of stagnation :** If a pupil stays in a class for more than one year due to failure or any other reason, it is called stagnation. It is a type of wastage in Indian context because classes are already packed with pupils and there is zero chance of accommodating a failed pupil in the class again. Stagnation at primary level in India is about 33%. Important causes of stagnation are defective implementation of education policy by the state, poor administration, lack of accountability on the part of teachers and head masters and all the causes of wastage.

## Integrated Approach in Primary Education

Integrated approach can be seen as an attempt to integrate education with life in order to make education a powerful medium of socio economic and cultural transformation. The term was first coined by **Kothari Commission** (1964-66). For linking education to life, education from primary to higher level should also be integrated in such a way that there is no gap between any two classes in the context of knowledge and experience.

The main plank of the integrated approach is that knowledge is a single unit not divided parts. Even the specialized knowledge is integrated to general education. All the subjects that are taught in schools are only the various branches of knowledge and each of them aims at human development. The medium of this integrated approach will be curriculum and nothing else.

## Objectives of Primary Education

Objectives of primary education formulated in the Conference of Education Representatives of Asian Government held at Karachi in 1980 are given below:

1. It should provide opportunities for further learning.
2. It should bring about comprehensive and integrated development of the child's development through physical, mental, moral, emotional, aesthetic and spiritual development.
3. It should prepare the child for good citizenship and instil deep love for national culture and traditions in him.
4. It should evolve the attitude of international brotherhood.
5. It should create scientific attitude and open temperament in him.
6. It should arouse respect for labour in him.
7. Education should prepare the child for life by giving him practical and work experiences.

## Universalisation of Education—An Unachieved Target

Dictionary meaning of universalisation is extending education opportunities to all youths irrespective of their caste, creed, colour, or sex. Nobody can shoulder such a huge responsibility except the state. It is the state that can perform this gigantic task on welfare ground. Article 45 of the constitution directed the state to take this responsibility and finally free and compulsory education to children upto the age of 14 years was enacted as a fundamental right in 2001.

Steps to be taken by the government in the context of universalisation of elementary education :

- Opening schools within the reach of the child (not more than one mile away from home)
- Making required number of teachers available in the schools to teach.
- Ensuring 100% enrolment for school education and removing economic and social barriers in the way of enrolment.
- Retaining the child in the school till the completion of education by providing adequate facilities to the child and by providing good educational environment to the child.
- Controlling wastage and stagnation by adopting suitable measures like mid day meals, free books and stationery and adequate amount of scholarship to children.

## Universalisation and National Policy on Education 1986 :

1. **Early Childhood Care and Education :** Proper investment should be made by the government for the development of young children especially on those children who are first generation learners in their family. For all round development of the child education should integrate with the child development services programmes. Day care centres are to be provided as a support service to enable the girls taking care of siblings to attend school and as a support service to poor working women. Full integration between child care and pre primary schooling will be brought about. School health programme will also be strengthened in this regard.
2. **Improvement in Elementary Education :** Elementary education will stress on universal enrolment and retention of children upto 14 years of age and a substantial improvement in the quality of education. A child centred activity based process of learning will be adopted for this purpose. The first generation learners will be provided supplementary remedial instruction. Cognitive learning will be increased stepwise along with drill of skills.
3. **Child Benefiting Steps :** Corporal punishment will be completely abolished from the education system. School timing and vacations will be adjusted according to the convenience of children. Efforts will be made to bring the earning children to school through additional support.
4. **Operation Black Board :** Under this operation essential facilities will be provided to schools such as two large rooms usable in all seasons, toys, black board, charts, maps and other learning materials. At least two teachers one male and one female will work in every school and efforts will be made to raise the number of teachers to one teacher per class. Private agencies and NGOs will also be involved in this operation.
5. **Non Formal Education :** Systematic non formal education programme will be launched for drop outs, working children and for those girls who can not attend whole day schools. Modern technologies will be used to improve learning

environment at NFE centres. Talented men and women from the local community will be recruited to serve as instructors. They will be given special training for this purpose.

Curriculum of non formal education will be need based. Learning materials of high quality will be developed and provided free of cost to learners. Games, sports, cultural programmes and excursions will also be organised for learners.

### Universalisation and Recommendations of Acharya Ram Murti Committee :

The committee gave the following suggestions in 1992—

1. Day Care Centres will work for the children in the age group of 0-6 under Angan Vadi Centres.
2. Ungraded system of education will be implemented in primary schools.
3. Assistant teachers (Shiksha Mitr) will be appointed on probation for two or three years on a salary one third of the normal salary of teachers Headmasters of schools will do this job.
4. Para schools will be established in all those villages where population is 300 or more by 2000.

### Universalisation of Girls Education

Universalisation of education caters to the needs of all boys and girls but girls have been especially targetted to increase their enrolment and retention in schools such as—

1. Making the girls free from care of brothers and sisters by creating awareness among the masses and by providing extra help to girls.
2. Providing drinking water facilities, mid day meals and free books to girls.
3. Increasing the admission of girls in schools by motivating the community.

### Universalisation of Education and Role of the Government :

1. For the tenth five year plan (2002-07) Rs. 4280 crores have been provided for education sector out of which about 1/3 will go for primary education.
2. Universalisation of elementary education has been accepted as a national goal. Sarva Shiksha Abhiyan will be launched to cover all children of 6-14 years by 2010. Operation Black Board has also been merged in Sarva Shiksha Abhiyan from 2002-03. 94% of India's rural population have primary schools within a reach of one km from their houses at present.
3. Non Formal Education has been revised as Education Guarantee Scheme (EGS) and Innovation Education Scheme (IES)
4. In order to ensure quantitative growth in primary education District Primary Education Programme (DPEP) was started in 1994 with the financial assistance of World Bank. At present, it is covering 273 districts of 18 states of India.

The Times of India on August 15, 2001 reported the following achievement of the Department of Elementary Education and Literacy, Govt. of India—

- Literacy rate-65.39%
- Female literacy increased to 52.21%
- Male literacy increased to 75.8%
- Absolute number of illiterates went down for the first time in Indian history.
- 95% districts now covered under Adult Education Programme
- 92 Jan Sikshan Sansthan have now been opened to promote vocational and skill development programmes for neo learners.

### Pledge of the Government (in 2001)

- All children in the age group of 6-14 will be in school by 2003.
- All districts will be covered by Sarva Shiksha Abhiyan by 2002.
- Special focus will be given on promotion of literacy among women, SCs and STs.

### Performance of National Open School (Times of India report Sep 5, 2001)

- It is the largest open school in the world having more than 5 lakhs learners on its role at secondary, Sr. secondary and vocational levels.
- Mahila Samakhya Programme for educating women for women's equality in 9000 colleges.

### National Literacy Mission

NLM was started in 1988. 84 million people had been made literate by 2000. UNESCO has appreciated this programme very much. 560 districts of India have been covered by this programme so far.

### Suggested Remedies for Eradicating Wastage and Stagnation

1. Education at the primary level should be free and compulsory and the principle of the universalisation should be implemented in letter and spirit.
2. The principle of equality with regard to the age group of children should be observed.
3. School should not be beyond a specified distance from children's homes.
4. The behaviour of teacher should be of love, sympathy and co-operation towards the students.
5. The date of admission should be specified.
6. Students teacher ratio should be proper.
7. The school environment should be healthy, attractive and congenial for learning.
8. Student should get individual attention.
9. The curriculum should be easy, practical and useful.
10. Suitable arrangement for the education of girls should be made.
11. Facilities of games should exist in schools.
12. Poor children should get milk, mid-day meal, books, etc. free of cost.
13. The methods of teaching and examination system should under-go radical changes.
14. Supervision and inspection should be revitalized and made much more useful and effective.

### Major Problems and Challenges of Education in India.

1. Schemes for promoting education is launched, relaunched and then forgotten. For example, deadline for total literacy and education for all was 2001. Now it has been shifted to 2010 Similarly, Sarva Shiksha Abhiyan was relaunched but again only Rs 25 crore out of Rs 325 crores could be spent by 2001.
2. States which do not have 100% enrolment at primary level even today are UP, Bihar, MP, Rajasthan, Orissa and West Bengal. UNESCO says that India is world's largest illiterate nation.
3. The position of India is not only poor in village, but in cities also. Many urban children in all states of North India do not go to school. For example, 30% children in Delhi do not go to school. (Times of India Sep. 12, 2003)
   In India, about 45% children in the age group of 6-14 are out of school even today. They have either not seen the school or they are dropped out before class VIIIth. Thus universalisation of elementary education is still an unrealized dream.
4. The conditions of primary schools in India is very poor. They are ill equipped with irresponsible and insufficient teachers. The educational environment there is so bad that children prefer to going to the factory for work and pleasure both.
5. Literacy rate in India has no doubt increased by 5.2% since 1991 but readership grew only by 0.3%. It shows that real education is still far far away from the target of a democratic nation.

## DESCRIPTIVE QUESTIONS

**Directions :** *Answer the following questions in 50 words only.*

1. What is Surva Siksha Abhiyan.
2. What do you mean by Stagnation.
3. What factors are responsible for wastage in the school.
4. How can wastage and stagnation be controlled.
5. Why is universalisation of education necessary in India.
6. Give the structure of elementary education in India.
7. Whom do you hold responsible for poor primary education in India and why?
8. What is National Literacy Mission (NLM)?

**Directions :** *Answer the follwing question in 500 words.*

Evaluate the problems and aspects of primary education in the context of

*(i)* Constitutional Provisions

*(ii)* NPE (1986, 1992)

*(iii)* Programmes of the government and lethargy of people in general

# Educational Administration in India

We can divide the total education system in India into the following categories :

- Primary education
- Secondary education
- Higher education
- Technical and Vocational education
- Medical education
- Teacher education

Before coming to the administration of these levels of education, it is better to know about ministry of Human Resources Development at the central level and Education Ministry at the state level—

1. **Ministry of HRD :** Education department of the central government is controlled by this ministry. This department takes all decisions related to education. Secretariat of this department is headed by Education Secretary, Additional Secretaries and education advisors are also there to assist him.

Education department has been divided into different bureaus and divisions. Every bureau is headed by joint secretary who is assisted by division officers. Education advisor is the administrative head of the department of education.

A number of advisory boards and commissions have been created to organise education in the country from primary to higher level.

Since education is in the concurrent list of subjects, this makes ministry of HRD more powerful than the state education ministries. Education was put in the concurrent list in 1976 by 42nd amendment of the constitution. At present both centre and states can make laws on matter related to education and if there is any controversy and contradiction between the two, only the law made by the Indian Parliament will prevail. Generally centre does not interfere in the affairs of states as far as education is concerned but in order to create a unified and symmetrical system of education throughout the country, it is the ministry of HRD that gives guidelines to states.

2. **State's Education Ministry :** Education minister and one or two deputy ministers look after this ministry. Education minister is responsible to all levels of education in the state. Education minister is assisted by two officers-education secretary and director of education.

Education secretary is the head of secretariate of education. He is assisted by deputy secretaries. Group officers work under deputy secretaries and section officer assist group officer.

Education secretary is an IAS. He issues directions to implement education policies of states formulated by education minister. He also gives advices to the minister regarding the matters of education. Decisions regarding the recognition of a school or about the salary of teachers can not be taken without the consent of the education secretary. As far as UP is concerned the office of secretariat is at Lucknow.

Orders of the secretariat (state govt.) are enforced by the directorate of education. If secretariate is policy making body, directorate is an executive body. It works as a link between state's school and colleges and secretariate. Director of education is assisted by joint directors and education officers. The office of directorate of education is at Allahabad in UP. It consists of three divisions

- Directorate of higher education.
- Directorate of secondary education.
- Directorate of primary education

All three officers are headed by separate directors but director, higher education works as a coordinator.

As far as UP is concerned, the whole state is divided into nine mandals as (i) Agra (ii) Meerut (iii) Allahabad (iv) Varansi (v) Gorakhpur (vi) Bareilly (vii) Lucknow (viii) Faizabad (ix) Kanpur. Mandals are further divided into districts and district inspector of schools (DIOS) controls the matters of secondary education here. Basic Shiksha Adhikari is the in-charge of primary education at district level. He is assisted by SDI at the block level.

DIOS is responsible for appointment and transfer of third grade teachers and JD is responsible for appointment and transfer of second grade teachers.

## 1. Administration of Primary Education

Primary education is mainly controlled and administered by the state department of education through Basic Siksha Parishad and local government (Municipalities and Panchayat). The role of central government is only advisory here.

**Important functions of Basic Shiksha Parishad are given below :**

1. Controlling over primary teachers and other related staff.
2. Appointment and transfer of primary teachers and other related staff.
3. Arrangement of examination materials and declaration of results.
4. Developing curriculum for primary education and preparing text books for children.
5. Doing arrangement for training of teachers.
6. Recognizing private primary schools.
7. Organization and control of basic schools, normal schools and units of basic certificates.
8. Development of primary education in the state.
9. Receiving grants from the state govt. and distributing them to different schools.
10. Construction and maintenance of primary schools.

As far as role of central government for promotion of primary education is concerned, it is performed by All India Council of Primary Education (AICPE). It was established in 1957. The purpose of establishment of this council was to take necessary steps to provide free and compulsory education to children in the age group of 6-14. Whatever action is taken by the central government in this regard, it is taken by this very council.

The main functions of AICPE are as follows :

1. Giving suggestions to all primary education institutions managed by the central and state governments regarding primary education.
2. Conducting researches on the administrative, financial and educational problems related to primary education and publishing the results and conclusions.
3. Preparing literature and text books for the improvement of primary education.
4. Giving the declaration of free and compulsory education upto the age of 14 a practical shape through its policies and suggestions.
5. Giving suggestions to central government for the development of primary education and for bringing cooperation between the centre and states.
6. Preparing programmes for the development of primary education in the states and forcing the states to implement them.

## 2. Administration of Secondary Education

We can divide the administration of secondary education into two sections—

### State Administration

All educational institutions that impart secondary education in states can be classified into the following categories—

- Schools maintained by universities for practice teaching of B.Ed. trainees. State government does not have any direct control over them.
- Government Inter Colleges and Government Girls Inter Colleges maintained by the state government.
- Government aided colleges managed by private organizations and societies. 100% grants are given to these schools by the state government and appointment of teachers and other staff is also done by Madhyamic Siksha Parishad.
- Hindi and Sanskrit colleges maintained by the state government.
- Minority colleges maintained by the state government by giving them 100% grants but they are managed by minorities. Appointment of teachers and other personnel is done by the management committee here. They are autonomous institutions.

- Unaided but recognised schools.
- Unaided and unrecognized schools like Madarsahs and Pathshalas. Their certificates are recognised by some universities of India. For example, a semi graduate of Darululum-Deoband can take admission at A.M.U. Aligarh in graduate classes (BA).

Administration of all recognised schools is the responsibility of state department of education (Madhyamic Siksha Nideshalay) through Madhyamic Siksha Parishad . Parishad performs the following functions here—

1. It prepare norms for the recognition of schools with the Madhyamic Siksha Boards and gives its recommendation after the inspection of a school to the directorate for recognition.
2. It prepares secondary school curriculum and text books for secondary classes.
3. It also determines the limits of grants in aid or its curtailment for a particular school.
4. It prepares programmes for in-service training of teachers.
5. It publishes magazines and journals for the improvement of education system.
6. As far as examinations of high schools and intermediates are concerned, they are conducted by Madhyamic Siksha Board and results are also declared by it.

## Administration by the Centre

A number of central schools for central government employees, army schools, railway schools, Navodaya Vidyalays and a large number of private schools affiliated to CBSE or ICSE are administered by the central government through its agencies. All these schools were opened to bring about uniformity in the pattern of secondary education throughout the country to benefit those employees whose jobs are transferable across the country and change in boards for their wards was really a problem for them because of the following reasons—

- Standard and quality of education were not uniform in all state boards.
- Standard and quality of education were very poor in many states and government employees could not afford this loss.

**Central Board of Secondary Education (CBSE)** was established by the central government to solve this problem and a number of schools were affiliated with this board. At present, there are 6200 schools affiliated with this board, out of them about 50% are private schools.

In order to provide quality education to rural pupils free of cost from class VIth to XIIth our Late Prime Minister Mr. Rajeev Gandhi started hundreds of Navodaya schools across the country. Provision was made that at least one Navodaya Vidyalaya will be opened in every district and admission in these schools will be given on the basis of an aptitude test.

Important agencies working at the central level for the administration and improvement of secondary education are given below :

**(a) National Council of Educational Research and Training (NCERT) :**

It was established in 1961 at the recommendation of Secondary Education Commission (1952-53). The purpose of establishment of NCERT was to lead the nation in the field of research in education and teaching and in the preparation of text books for all classes from Ist to 12th. Following departments were established by the government for this purpose.

- National Text Book and Research Bureau (1954)
- National Elementary Education Institute (1956)
- National Fundamental Education Institute (1956)
- National Education Extension Directorate (1959)
- National Audio Visual Education Institute (1959)

However, irony of the fact was that all the above institutes could not realize the objectives identified by Secondary Education Commission. As a result NCERT was established in 1961 and in order to lessen its work loads State Council of Educational Research and Training (SCERT) were also established in states. NCERT is an autonomous body of the central government and it has been set up in order to achieve the following objectives—

1. To study the problems of school education in the country.
2. To organize extension programmes in the field of secondary education. Such programmes consists of pre-service and in-service training programmes.
3. To lead every field of secondary education at the central level such as preparation of text books, teaching strategies, evaluation etc.

4. To provide extension services to teachers in teacher training colleges across the country.
5. To help the states to establish Model Teacher Training Centres.
6. To conduct educational surveys across the country and publish the results.
7. To work as a distribution centre for innovative educational concepts.
8. Discovering best teaching strategies and techniques and introducing them all over the country.
9. To prepare standard text books, to publish and distribute them from its counters. All schools affiliated to CBSE New Delhi prefers these text books to the books published by private agencies.

The functions of NCERT can be divided into four units—

(a) **Organizational committee :** This committee manages all the four regional colleges of NCERT. These training colleges are in Ajmer, Mysore, Bhopal and Bhuvanesvar. These colleges run B.Ed., BPEd., M.Ed., Ph. D. and integrated three year, courses. They provide training to teachers of their respective regions and guide them in the field of secondary education.

(b) **National Educational Institute :** There are 12 departments in this institute. The main function of this institute is to further research, training and extension programmes.

(c) **Secondary Education Extension Directorate :** This directorate is controlled by NCERT but it has been affiliated to Delhi University for degree and other formalities.

(d) **Educational Administration Board :** This board has three permanent committees. First committee considers research projects and gives its report to the main body. Second committee coordinates different programmes, projects and researches. Third committee takes care of the four regional colleges of NCERT.

## Contribution of NCERT

1. **Education of Science and Technology :** NCERT has collected and prepared a lot of text materials of science and technology on its own as well as with the collaboration of UNESCO. It has also guided students in various fields of science and technology. Council has organised a number of seminars and workshops for the advancement of knowledge.
2. **Teacher Training :** Contribution of NCERT in the field of teacher education is also commendable. Through its regional training colleges Council maintains good relationship with the training colleges of the state and gives them informations about new researches in the field of education.
3. **Extension Programmes :** In service training camps are organised by the NCERT in the summer vacations for the benefit of secondary teachers. In these extension programmes teachers do researches in teaching strategies of their respective subjects themselves.
4. **Teaching competition :** In order to make the teaching of secondary teachers effective, competitions are regularly organised among teachers across the country. Successful teachers are awarded in these competitions.
5. **Talent Search Programmes :** In order to guide and help talented students across the country National Talent Search Test is conducted every year. Thousands of selected students are not only given heavy scholarship but they are also guided to study in good schools of the country. Every student studying in class Xth can participates in these tests. These tests are conducted at three stages. At first stage, candidates are to pass state level examination. Second stage is related to the test conducted by the NCERT itself. Those who cross the first stage are eligible for the second stage and interview is conducted for final selection. Questions asked in these examinations are from Science, Mathematics and English
6. **Publication works :** The main job of the NCERT is the preparation of text books and its publication. Books of all classes are prepared and published here and they are considered the best text books in the country.

Apart from text books NCERT also publishes educational surveys and studies. Five educational surveys have been published so far. Council also publishes the following educational magazines and research journals.

- Indian Education Review.
- Journal of Indian Education.
- Journal of National Institute of Education.
- School Science
- Modern Indian Teachers
- Primary Teachers

## All India Council of Secondary Education

This Council was established in 1955. The purpose of this council was to bring about qualitative improvement in secondary education. It is an advisory body. It studies the problems of secondary education across the country and gives relevant suggestions to states for the solution of these problems. Education Advisor of the government of India is the head of this council. There are 22 other members in the Council who come from the following departments—

- Representatives of ministry of HRD.
- Representatives of the finance ministry.
- One representative from Indian Council of Pravidhik Shiksha.
- One representative from All India Council of Primary Education.
- One representative from University Grants Commission.
- One representative from All India Teachers' Community.
- One representative from All India Council of Teachers Education.
- Representative of the States

## Central Board of Secondary Education (CBSE)

It is an autonomous body of the central government which controls 6200 schools across the country and overseas and conducts examinations for them. Thus character of CBSE is global in nature. The headquarter of CBSE is in New Delhi. It has six regional offices which are located at Allahabad, Ajmer, New Delhi, Chennai, Gauhati and Chandigarh Administrative functions are performed by these regional offices. Even examination for class Xth and XIIth are conducted by these regional offices and results are declared. Its chairman Ashok Ganguli has declared to open two more regional offices at Orissa and West Bengal. CBSE affiliated schools of UP and Bihar are controlled by regional office of Allahabad.

The main functions of CBSE are as follows—

1. Determining affiliation norms for affiliating private schools to CBSE.
2. Inspecting CBSE schools even after affiliation.
3. Giving affiliation to new schools after inspection.
4. Preparing necessary text books for CBSE affiliated schools. This work is done by the academic cell of the board.
5. Conducting examinations for all CBSE affiliated schools and declaring results.
6. Developing curriculum for its affiliated schools.
7. Awarding talented teachers every year after appraisal of their performance.
8. Organising in service training programmes for teachers and principals both.

## Administration of Higher Education

As far as administration of higher education is concerned, University Grant Commission is the main and autonomous body. It controls all the 343 universities, 18 Central and 325 State Universities by preparing curriculum for them and by sanctioning or restricting grants for them. Universities are also autonomous bodies at their own level. They are responsible not only for the maintenance and advancement of university education but they also control the education imparted by affiliated degree and PG colleges of the states whether they are government aided or private colleges.

**University Grants Commission (UGC)** was established in 1945 on the recommendation of Sargent Report (1944). Higher Education Commission (1948-49) recommended to develop it as an autonomous body. Consequently a bill regarding this was passed in Indian Parliament in 1954 and University Grants Commission (UGC) was made an autonomous body.

UGC had 9 members apart from chairman and vice chairman at that time. Out of these 9 members, three of them were university Vice Chancellors, two of them were government representatives and remaining two were prominent educationists of the country. The number of these members were raised to 12 in 1966. They are nominated by the government for a period for six years.

### There are six sections working in UGC as-

- Humanities and Social Science Department
- Science and Technology Department

- Central Universities, Coordination, Administration and Finance Department'
- Higher Studies Centre and Scholarship Department
- Statistics, Publication and Information Section
- Pay Scale Section.

## Main Functions of UGC

1. Determining the norms and standard of education for colleges and universities.
2. Coordinating among the higher education institution of states.
3. Granting funds to universities for performing different types of functions.
4. Preparing norms for pay scale
5. Evaluating the performance of universities and colleges through National Accreditation and Assessment Council (NAAC)
6. Conducting JRF/NET exams and sanctioning fellowship to research scholars.

In order to improve the quality of education in universities and colleges UGC has taken several other measures also such as:

- College Humanities and Social Science Institute Programme
- College Science Institute Programmes
- Universities Leadership Programme
- Setting up committees for assessment of different programmes
- Establishment of Examination Reform Cell in Universities in order to improve quality of examination.
- Implementing the recommendations of pay commissions for improving the pay scale of teachers and other personnel.
- UGC has also stressed on setting up and development of Women's Studies Centres. For this purpose it has given the status of autonomous college to 111 Women's colleges.

Grants by the UGC are given for the following purposes—

1. Grants for development such as appointment of additional staff, establishment of libraries and laboratories, purchase of books, furniture and equipments, construction of hostels and buildings.
2. Grants for improvement in the standard of education such as setting up of advanced studies centres in universities, research works, in service training programmes, establishment of resource centres and academic staff colleges etc.
3. Grants for regional studies such as study of historical, social and economic conditions of the country and abroad.
4. Grants for exchange programmes of teachers.
5. Special grants given to retired teachers in order to take the benefit of their long experiences.
6. Grants given to universities and colleges for the construction of staff quarters.
7. Grants given for the purpose of student's welfare Programmes, i.e., constructing health care centres and hostels for them, arrangement of fellowship, sanction of research project etc.

Apart from giving grants to universities, UGC is also giving special grants to 62 colleges of science and technology, 19 higher studies science centres and 35 higher studies centres of humanities and social sciences.

As far as appointment of teachers are concerned UGC, Central or State government do not interfere in the affairs of universities and autonomous colleges. However, teachers in government aided colleges are appointment by Higher Education Commission of States and pay scale is determined by the State department of education. For the convenience of administration, these colleges are affiliated to any nearby university of the state.

## Administration of Technical and Vocational education

Norms for technical education in India are prepared by All India Council of Technical Education (AICTE). Some of the technical institutes in India are autonomous bodies like IITs and IIMs and remaining of them are affiliated to universities.

## Medical Education

Norms for medical education are prepared by Central Council of Indian Medicine (CCIM) and norms for Unani medicines are prepared by Central Council of Unani Medicine (CCUM). Some of the medical colleges are autonomous like King George Medical College Lucknow and other colleges are affiliated to Universities for the convenience of administration.

## Administration of Teacher Education

Teacher education is only a part of total education in universities and colleges. In order to control the quality of teacher education in the country, **National Council of Teacher Education (NCTE)** was established in 1999 under Parliament Act of 73. The main objectives of establishing NCTE are as follows:

- To develop teacher education in the whole country in a systematic and coordinated manner.
- Determining the norms and rules of teacher education to be followed by the whole country.
- To control adult and continuing education and give it adequate directives. NCTE has four administrative units across the country as,
- Eastern Regional Committee- Bhuvaneshwar.
- Northern Regional Committee-Jaipur
- Southern Regional Committee-Banglore
- Western Regional Committee-Bhopal

The establishment of such a body like NCTE is very necessary in the present scenario because thousands of private B Ed. Colleges have been recognised across the country to distribute B.Ed. degree. Only CCS University Meerut has 131 private B.Ed. Colleges to look after. NCTE can enforce the rules and regulations on these colleges and compel them to follow norms. But irony of fact is that NCTE is not fulfilling its responsibility honestly. I know dozens of B.Ed. colleges which do not have even a single qualified **teacher** to teach but they have been given clearance by the NCTE.

Important functions of regional committees of NCTE are as follows—

1. Preparing norms for teachers training colleges and giving them recognition after inspection.
2. Establishing coordination among B.Ed. Colleges, concerned universities and the state government.
3. Having control over B.Ed. colleges.
4. Developing curriculum for teacher education in India.
5. Determining eligibility of teachers to teach in B.Ed. and M.Ed. classes.
6. Determining eligibility for admission in B.Ed. BTC etc.
7. Determining fee structure for private colleges.
8. Restricting material professionalism in teacher education.
9. Implementing the orders of the central government.
10. Supervising the research works in the field of teacher education.

# Distance Education in India

## INTRODUCTION

As a modern system of non formal education, distance education is imparted through mass media, correspondence courses, contact programmes and other audio visual materials. Open learning, open schooling, continuing and life long education, home tution, independent learning etc. are synonymous concepts of distance education. Above all, it is a non-conventional type teaching-learning programme

**Peters** has defined distance education in the following words

"Distance education is a method of indirect instruction implying geographical and emotional separation of teacher and taught. In mainstream education the relationship between a teacher and students in the classroom is based on social norms. In distance education it is based on technological rules"

### Characteristics of Distance Education

Distance education is different from formal system of education because of its following characteristics:

1. It is a non-formal system of education, which is provided through correspondence courses, contact programmes and electronic media.
2. It is a method of indirect instruction applying geographical and emotional separation between teacher and taught.
3. Distance education is applicable to all levels of learning and degree can be awarded to the learner, which is generally not done in non-formal system of education.
4. It is a systematically organised form of self-learning in which student's counselling, presentation of learning material and student's success is carried out by a team of teachers. All these activities are performed without a direct contact with learners.
5. It is a part time study and it is done when it is not possible for a learner to continue his full time courses due to some reasons.
6. Wider sections of adult population can have access to this education very easily and they can compensate for their lost opportunities in the past. This will enable them to require new skills.
7. Here only indirect interaction between the teacher and taught is seen either on television or on computer. If it is provided through teleconferencing, then learner can ask questions through telephone or electronic mail and they will listen their answer on radio, TV or computer.
8. It is provided through written communication more than oral communication.
9. Classroom is not needed here and a large number of population scattered in a wide area can be covered through distance education. This makes the education very cheap.
10. Learning is very much individualistic here and its success will depend on the motivation level of learners.

### Basic Philosophy Behind Distance Education

No one in the world can have complete knowledge in his life. His thirst for learning must be quenched through distance education. This will help him to improve himself on one hand and to improve the society on the other.

### Objectives of Distance Education

1. To bring the school/college to the home of the learner.
2. To provide opportunities to the learner for higher education and to continue his education that got a break in the past.
3. To provide cheap education to learners without depriving them of their jobs or business.
4. To help the learners to improve their professional and social skills.

5. To enable the learner to join regular colleges and universities again after getting necessary qualifications through distance learning.
6. To increase reading rate of the population.

## People Benefiting from Distance Education

Following categories of people can be benefited from distance education—

1. People who live in remote areas where there is no institution of higher learning.
2. People who discontinued their formal education due to certain reasons.
3. People who are unable to join a regular college due to their engagement in various activities-productive, social or political.
4. People who do not get admission in regular colleges or universities due to limited number of seats.
5. People who need some additional training in their vocation for updating their knowledge.
6. People who are retired or elderly in the society but want to keep themselves busy in learning.

## Merits of Distance Education

1. It is a flexible system of education which is free from time or place restrictions.
2. In distance education a learner can progress at his own pace because learning materials are prepared keeping in view the principles of programmed instruction.
3. Self learning is considered the best learning. Distance education provides this opportunity in full.
4. A learner can improve his social and vocational skills through distance education.
5. Those who live in very remote areas of the country can easily benefit from this system of education.
6. Distance education can especially benefit those who discontinued their education in the past. Thus it can supplement regular studies.
7. We can cover a large section of population through distance education by spending less money.
8. Distance education can be used at any level of education from primary to higher.
9. Distance education can introduce new courses to learners more frequently than colleges or universities.
10. It can also help in achieving the objectives of universalisation of elementary education.
11. Talents and creativity can be nourished through this education.
12. We can be benefited from the teaching of very effective teachers on TV or internet which is not so easily possible in formal education.

## Limitations of Distance Education

1. Education is stereotyped here.
2. Complicated science subjects can not be taught through distance education.
3. There is least chance of practicals here.
4. Distance education is mostly examination oriented and learners do not give stress on acquisition of knowledge here.
5. Lack of required number of study centres can increase the problem of learners.
6. No direct interaction between the teacher and taught is seen here. Hence, learners can not be motivated here.
7. Feedback procedure is also very weak here. Only in tele-conferencing, learners can ask questions and get feedback but teachers still get very limited amount of feedback.
8. Learning without activity is the method of instruction here.
9. Costly learning materials are beyond the capacity of poor learners in distance education.
10. It is not so much job oriented as it is claimed.

## Growth of Distance Education in India

1. **Delhi University :** Distance education through correspondence was first started in Delhi University in 1962 under the Directorate of Correspondence Course and Continuing Education. The materials were also supplemented by radio broadcast and Delhi Doordarshan telecasts.
2. **Patiala University :** Distance education in Panjabi University started in 1967. Correspondence course in B.Ed. was also started in 1988.
3. **Mysore University :** Mysore University started Institute of Correspondence Courses and Continuing Education in 1969.

4. **Punjab University Chandigarh :** Here Directorate of Correspondence Courses was opened in 1971. Shimla University also started the same course in the same year.
5. **Jammu University :** Distance education in Jammu University was started in 1976 Kashmir University Srinagar also opened Institute of Distance learning in the same year.
6. **Andhra Pradesh Open University :** The first open university in India APOU was opened in Andhra Pradesh in 1982.
7. **Delhi Open School :** This school was opened in 1983 to meet the requirement of secondary education on a non formal basis.
8. **Indira Gandhi National Open University :** IGNOU was established in India September in 1985 in order to achieve the following objectives.
   - To provide access to the masses to higher education.
   - To provide opportunities for continuing education to the people
9. **Nalanda Open University** established in 1987
10. **Kota Open University (Rajasthan) :** (established in 1988): At present there are nine open universities and 64 directorates of distance education in conventional universities.

## Methods of Imparting Distance Education

Following methods are used to impart distance education—

1. **Supply of study materials :** Study materials in the form of written sheets or audio/video cassettes prepared by subject experts are supplied to the learner. There should be adequate illustrations in these materials in order to make them understandable by the learner.
2. **Response Sheet :** It is an assignment given to the learner from each unit/lesson of their syllabus. These sheets are regularly submitted by the learner after completing the assignment. These sheets are evaluated by the study centre and remarks and grades are sent to learners for feedback.
3. **Personal Contact Programme (PCP)** : PCP is organised at such places where maximum number of learners can come. It may last for several days to benefit the students. The number of PCPs will vary with the resources available.
4. **Guided Study Centres :** Guided study centres are opened at various places to provide face to face learning and counselling opportunity to learners. Library and laboratory facilities are made available at these centres for further study and practical training. Such services are provided either weekly or fortnightly.
5. **Radio and TV counselling :** Discussion on different topics of the syllabus by the experts are arranged on the radio and TV both. Learners can hear these discussions and enrich their knowledge.
6. **Teleconferencing :** In this arrangement local telephone is connected with the STD lines and a bridge is prepared by joining different radio or TV lines. Experts at different places of the country discuss topic and learner can ask any question by using his local telephone.

## Open University System of Education

Open system of education is the latest in the field of distance education. IGNOU established in 1985 offers a number of degree and diploma courses to fulfil the educational requirements of the masses. Objectives of open university system of education are as follows:

1. To provide access to higher education to a larger section of population.
2. To provide educational opportunities for those who discontinued their education due to some reasons.
3. To make education a life long process.
4. To equip the people with new skills and knowledge while in service.
5. To provide specialized knowledge to learners in different fields.
6. To provide in –service training to professional workers.
7. To reduce the per-capita cost of higher education.

## Methods of Imparting Open University Education

*See* method of imparting distance education.

Advantages of Open University system of education

1. The objective of equality of educational opportunity can be realized. Even those people

can have access to higher education who are denied admission in regular course in universities and colleges.

2. Attendance is not compulsory in such universities. Students are only required to return the response sheets after completing the assignment to the study centres and to attend practical classes (if needed) arranged at study centres time and again.
3. Learners can get jobs and admission in regular courses after receiving degrees from open university.
4. Learning materials (written/audio/visual) are prepared by very experienced and talented teachers here. Thus, it can improve the standard of education no doubt.
5. Admission policies in open universities are liberal. Age does not become a bar here. Even prior academic qualifications are not required in getting admission in some courses.
6. Higher education is very costly if it is imparted through formal system but if it is imparted through an open university, its per capita cost will be very low because an open university can cover lakhs of students with the help of less number of teachers by using educational technology.

## Criticism of Open University Education

Open university system of education can be criticized on the following grounds :

1. Some of the courses run by open universities are not need based.
2. Standard of education goes down when evaluation is not done properly.
3. Some of the learning materials supplied by IGNOU is very cheap and mere translation of English writers.
4. Audio/Video cassettes supplied here can be utilized only by those who have proper access to modern technology.
5. A learner can not learn the ideals of a teacher. His behaviour will not be influenced by the high character of a teacher here. Thus, open university system of education is a lifeless and mechanical process.
6. Sometimes materials prepared by experts are not edited properly. This creates problem before the learner.
7. Cost of printing materials become very high if only few students are there and only few copies of the materials need to be printed.
8. Lack of infrastructure like printing press, movie camera, photo copier etc. is another problem which is the major cause of delay in supplying learning materials to the learner.
9. Proper guidelines how to go through the learning materials are not given to the students and hence they fail to take benefit of these materials.
10. Assignments sent by pupils should be immediately checked and graded and pupils should be communicated about the results immediately. Delay in feedback is the major defect of this system and hence learners are never motivated to study by the system.
11. Many topics of the syllabus needs personal contact programmes which is not arranged by the university.
12. Number of study centres are not opened according to the requirement of learners. Long traveling to the study centre by the learner increases his cost of education.
13. Time schedule of use of electronic media is not supplied to the lerner. Counselling and discussion programmes are only announced on the radio and television. If a learner misses the announcement, he will surely miss the programme.
14. University system of education can not be run privately only which is generally the trend across the world 50% grants should be given by the government to meet the cost of education. Education from the "University in the Air" is really very expensive for learners. For example, two years B.Ed. course from IGNOU costs more than Rs. 20000 at present.

## Indira Gandhi National Open University (IGNOU)

It was established in 1985 with the following objectives—

1. To coordinate distance education system in the whole country.

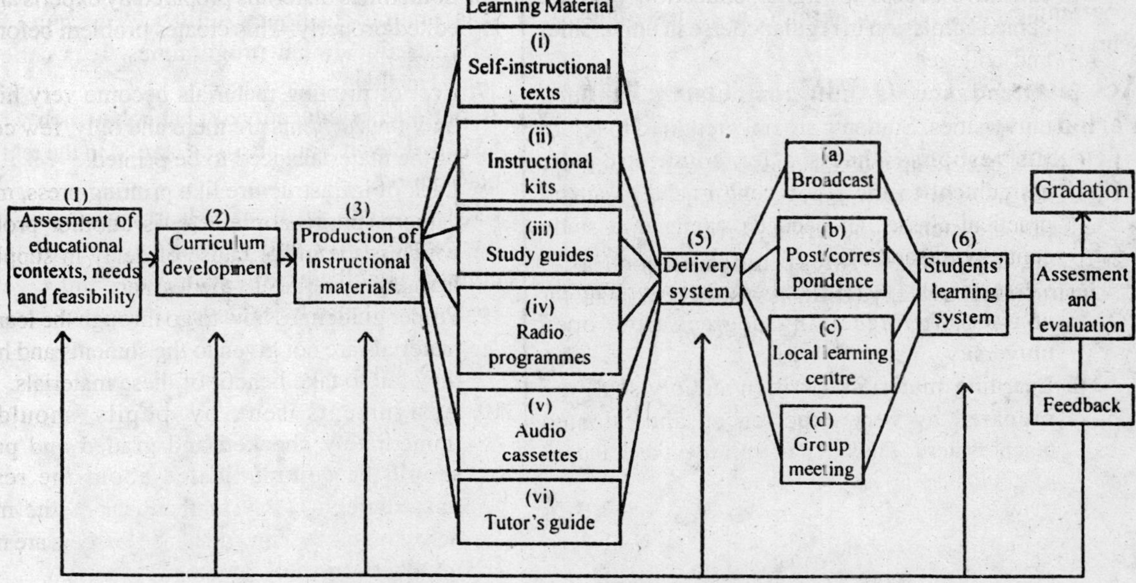


*Fig. The Operational Model of Distance Education*

2. To determine and maintain the standard of education.
3. To fulfil the requirements of distance learning in the country.

At present IGNOU is running a large number of degree, diploma and certificate courses in the field of sciences, informations technology, management, commerce, business, mass communication, etc. All these courses are recognised by all 343 universities of India and these courses have the same status as those of any other university of the country.

Contributions of IGNOU can be understood by the following points

1. It has widened the access to higher education by providing opportunities to learners from backward population especially women, rural people, people of hilly and remote areas.
2. The total enrolment of IGNOU has crossed 15 lakhs and the number of courses offered by IGNOU is about hundred.
3. IGNOU has 50 regional offices and 770 study centres across the country.
4. At present, there are nine open universities in the country (2004-05) and IGNOU is the biggest of all. These nine universities are fulfilling the requirement of the people that can be fulfilled by at least 500 universities.

## Open School System

In Aug. 1974 director, NCERT appointed a working group to examine the feasibility of setting up an open school in Delhi. A joint meeting of CBSE, NCERT and ministry of HRD were again held in 1978. These recommendations were approved in 1979 by the ministry and open school system of education came into being.

## Objectives of Open School System

1. To develop bridge/preparatory courses for working adults and women who do not have any qualification from a formal school.
2. To provide education to children belonging to weaker sections of the society.
3. To provide continuing education facilities to drop outs who have passed class VIIth or VIIIth.
4. To enroll those students who have failed in class Xth or XIIth.
5. To provide vocational and life skills to adults especially from SCs, STs and OBCs.

## National Open School

It was first affiliated to CBSE and became an autonomous body in 1989. It is not only providing education upto class XIIth but it has also introduced a number of vocational courses for adults. National

Open School (NOS) is also expected to provide programme and resource support to states' open schools.

## Activities of IGNOU in the Tenth Plan Period

1. IGNOU has set up a distance education Council (DEC) to act as a nodal agency for distance education system at the tertiary level.
2. It has adopted an integrated multimedia instructional strategy (IMIS) consisting of print and audio visual materials.
3. It is running 24 hour satellite TV channel to telecast educational programmes. It is called Gyan Darshan.
4. About 40 FM educational channels which will be called Gyan Vani are to be started in the tenth plan period.
5. IGNOU would open more learning centres in backward, hilly and remote regions of the country. Facilities of Gyan Vani and Gyan Darshan will also be extended to these regions.

# Vocationalization of Education in India

## INTRODUCTION AND MEANING

In order to relate education with life and productivity, the concept of vocationalization of education was coined. The basic philosophy behind the scheme was that all students could not go to the level of higher academic education due to poverty, low intelligence, immediate need of earning livelihood and due to non-availability of higher education opportunities for such a huge population. Besides, in the 21st century of today, industry, agriculture and service sectors need professionals of different specialized fields not thinkers of BC era. Even specialized fields of today require thinking but that thinking is always contributive to bread and butter needs of the common people today not the mental sensuality of elite class of the past.

### Need for Vocationalization

In the opinion of Education Commission 20% students who have passed class VIIIth should get vocational education and 50% class Xth and XIIth passed students should get vocational/professional education. In this way only 30% students who have passed class XIIth will go for higher education in the academic areas from graduation to Ph.D.

Regarding the vocational education at the school level views of Education Commission are as follows:

1. **Variety of courses :** Government should introduce a variety of courses for boys and girls in the age group of 14-18.
2. **Intensive courses :** Instead of putting outstanding students in special courses they should be allowed to work intensively within the same syllabus so that the deficiency can be made up.
3. **Establishment of technical schools :** A large number of technical schools like polytechniques, ITI etc. should be opened for tenth class passed students. The name of Junior Technical schools should be changed to technical high schools. This will make education production oriented.
4. **Part time vocational training :** Many students after passing class VIIIth adopt their family professions or engaged in small scale business or industry. A part time vocational training should be given to these students in order to make them excellent in their respective fields.
5. **Domestic (Home) Science education :** A large number of girls get married soon after leaving school education. So, home science should be taught to them during their stay in schools.

### Work Experience as an Integral Part of Vocational Education

Work experience may be defined as the productive activity which contributes to productive works in schools, field, laboratory and factory. Commission suggested that work experience should be introduced at every level of education. If work experience is related to actual life situations, it is better, e.g., taking the students to the field at the time of sowing or harvesting is real work experience of agriculture.

**Suggestions of Education Commission** regarding work experience are given below.

1. At the lower secondary level one workshop should be arranged for every school.
2. Regular workshops should be arranged for senior secondary schools in order to provide work experience to students.
3. Work experience relating to the production of materials should be made available in schools.
4. In some selected institutions science students should be engaged in full scale production.
5. Work experience should be introduced at every level of education in order to bring social and cultural transformation of the society.

## Objectives of Work Experiences

Introduction of work experience in the school system is needed in order to fulfil the following objectives—

1. In order to develop the ability and respect for physical labour in the child.
2. To enable the child to earn something by his physical labour while in school.
3. To enable the child to bear the cost of education through this earning.
4. To acquaint the students with the world of employment, industry, business and agriculture.
5. Not to prepare the child for a particular profession but to develop in him the abilities which may facilitate his choice of profession.
6. To increase the total production of the country by the small contribution of students.
7. To reduce the social differences between rich and poor students of the school.

## Guiding Principles of Work Experiences

Following principles must be followed by schools while introducing work experience in the school system—

1. **Less expensive :** Only those work experiences should be selected in the school which are less expensive and the purpose is always maximum utilization of resources available with the school.
2. **Profit oriented :** Income or production obtained from work experience must be more than the expenditure incurred on it. This will help the students to earn something.
3. **Employment oriented :** Work experience given to students should be such as they can get self employment after school education. At least poor students should take the benefit of these experiences.
4. **Students' profit :** Whatever profit is obtained at the sale of products produced in workshops should go to the students directly.
5. **Optional nature :** Work experience should not be made compulsory in the school. It should be optional and should be left on the personal choice of students.
6. **A part of extra curriculum :** Work experience should not be made a part of the curriculum. It should not be introduced by disturbing the regular time table of the school.
7. **Work based time schedule :** The time allotted for work experience should be in accordance with the nature of the activity. For example, agricultural activity may need 48 or 72 hours regularly at the time of sowing or harvesting while carpentry will need not more 60-120 minutes in a week.
8. **Help from retired persons :** School should take the help of retired ITI personnel for providing work experience to students.
9. **Close to family occupation :** Only those work experiences should be provided to students which are similar to their family occupations so that they can improve their family occupation after school education.
10. **Complete knowledge :** Student should be given complete knowledge of all steps of production so that he make the product on his own without taking any outside help.

## National Policy on Education 1986 and Vocationalization

1. Vocational education will be a distinctive stream intended to prepare students for identifying occupations spanning several areas of activity. These courses will ordinarily be provided after the secondary stage, but keeping the scheme flexible, they may also be made available after class VIII. In the interests of integrating vocational education better with their facilities the Industrial Training Institutes will also conform to the larger vocational pattern.
2. Health planning and health service management should optimally interlock with the education and training of appropriate categories of healthy manpower through health-related vocational courses. Health education at the primary and middle levels will ensure the commitment of the individual to family and community health, and lead to health-related vocational courses at the +2 stage of higher secondary education. Efforts will be made to devise similar vocational courses based on Agriculture, Marketing. Social Services, etc. An emphasis in vocational education will also be on development of attitudes towards knowledge and skills for entrepreneurship and self-employment.
3. The establishment of vocational courses or institutions will be the responsibility of the government as well as employers in the public and private sectors. The government will, however, take special steps to cater to the needs

of women, rural and tribal students and the deprived sections of society. Appropriate programmes will also be started for the handicapped.

4. Graduates of vocational courses will be given opportunities, under predetermined conditions, for professional growth, career improvement and lateral entry into courses of general, technical and professional education through appropriate bridge courses.
5. Non-formal, flexible and need-based vocational programmes will also be made available to neo literate, youths, who have completed primary education, school drop-outs, persons engaged in work and unemployment or partially employed persons. Special attention in this regard will be given to women.
6. Tertiary level courses will be organised for the young graduates from the higher secondary courses of the academic stream.
7. It is proposed that vocational courses will cover 10 per cent of higher secondary students by 1990 and 25 per cent by 1995. Steps will be taken to see that a substantial majority of the products of vocational courses are employed or become self-employed. Review of the courses offered would be regularly undertaken. Government will also review its recruitment policy to encourage diversification at the secondary level.

## Structure of Vocational Education in India

1. **Pre High School (Xth) level :** In India education upto class Xth is general in nature whether it be the case of girls or boys. Work experiences in the form of crafts and agriculture for boys and home science for girls or Socially Useful Productive Works (SUPW) have been introduced in secondary classes no doubt but no specific vocational education is given to students.
2. **Post High School level :** Vocational education in India starts after High School. A number of polytechniques institutes, Industrial Training Institutes, Diploma in Engineering Institutes and certificate courses in para medical fields are running in the country where high school passed students are given admission. All these courses are generally of three years duration. Admission to these courses are given after a competitive tests because of limited number of seats in these courses. Apart from these, CBSE have introduced Information Technology and Computer Applications as regular subjects at 10+2 level to meet the job requirement of IT sector.
3. **Post 10+2 level :** Those students who do not join any vocational course after high school and complete their 10+2 in science, Arts or Commerce streams are given admission in post 10+2 level vocational/professional courses. Four years engineering course is available for Science students of PCM group and 4 ½ years medical course (MBBS, BUMS, BAMS, BHMS etc.) are available for science students of PCB group. Similarly, commerce students can go for company secretary, ICWA or Chartered Accountancy courses and Arts students can opt for stenography, journalism, BALLB, B. Com Computers, B.Sc Home Science, and the like courses. A large number of para medical courses are also available for PCB students. As far as students of 10+2 in agriculture are concerned, many courses in agricultural science including BSc in agriculture are available for them.
4. **Graduation level professional course :** These courses make the people fully professionals. Hundred of such courses are running in the country in which students can take admission after graduation and can get job after the completion of the course.

Thus, we see that from high school to graduation about 60% students go to vocational/professional field and only 40% students are left for academic fields to work as teachers or lectures after their educations.

**Advantages of vocationalization :** Vocational education is advantageous to us in the following ways:

1. There will be a direct relationship between education and employment and educated class will not have to run for job hither and thither.
2. They will help the individuals to become self employed if job is not easily available after the completion of vocational education.
3. Economic conditions of the country will improve if every educated person is engaged in any productive work either in an industry or at his home.
4. Students will be convinced that education is purposeful for them.
5. Through vocational education, educated individual will be given a job along with certificate.

6. Vocationalization of education will make the best utilization of country's resources possible because this type of education gives specialized knowledge which can increase the productivity per head.
7. Science and technology will be accepted as the foundation stones and hence modernization, religion and work will be harmoniously blended together.

## Five Year Plans and Vocationalization

- **First Plan 1951-56 :** A number of diversified courses were introduced to give base to vocational education. Agriculture was mainly targetted in the first five year plan, so these courses have agricultural bias.
- **Second plan 1956-61 :** A large number of multi purposes schools were started. Scholarships were offered to students for opting vocational training after high school.
- **Third Plan 1961-66 :** Institute of Manpower and Planning was established and vocational/technical education was developed according to the needs of the country.
- **Fourth Plan 1969-74 :** Diversified courses were given impetus and scholarships were granted to students. Medical education and para medical courses got momentum during this period.
- **Fifth Plan 1974-79 :** Vocationalization of secondary education was taken as a policy to solve unemployment problems in the country.
- **Sixth Plan 1980-85 :** Vocationalization of education was started as a movement and a number of new professional courses were introduced in the country. Plan also emphasized to do some research work in vocational education.
- **Seventh Plan 1985-90 :** 5000 schools were selected for vocationalization of secondary education.
- **Eighth Plan 1992-97 :** 10+2 vocational courses were started during this period. This period was the start of globalization and privatization. Govt. encouraged those vocational courses which could provide jobs in private sectors. India achieved excellence in IT sector and IT professionals were recognised across the world.
- **Ninth Plan 1997-2002 :** Scholarship amount and its number were increased for those students who opted for vocational education. Private schools and vocational colleges were encouraged.
- **Tenth Plan 2002-2007 :** National Open Universities and National Open School have been instructed to introduce more vocational courses for the benefit of adult learners.

## Problems of Vocational Education and Their Solutions

Some of the major problems of technical and vocational education and their tentative solutions are given below :

1. **The problem of creating favourable attitude toward manual work :** The person engaged in manual work is looked down upon in India. Due to this reason people opt manual jobs only as last option. Since vocational education is directly related to manual work, students who go far this education considers themselves to be inferior.
   This problem can be solved only by engaging students, teachers and principals in manual works since the very beginning. More time should be allotted for practicals in the time table.
2. **Defective curriculum :** Curriculum in vocational courses does not match to the local needs and interests of children. In India where two third population are engaged in agriculture, work experience and agricultural science should be the regular part of the curriculum. Similarly, practicals in vocational curriculum does not stress the production of units for sale in the market. If practical is associated with the earning of students, they will take much interest in it.
   This problem can be solved by raising the number of teaching and technical staff for practical works and by making all equipments available for practical work.
3. **Problem of medium of instruction in vocational courses :** When student take admission in any technical or vocational course, he is given education in English medium because good books are not very much available in regional languages of India. It is really a problem for student, for they have generally been educated in regional language upto high school. Thus, they have to devote much time in learning English rather than knowing the technical subjects and skills.
   This problem can be solved in two ways (i) Reading materials should be prepared in regional languages also so that language may not be a bar for them (ii) If English medium is the

compulsion, knowledge rather than language should be emphasised. If a student is able to express himself it is enough. Knowledge of correct language is not needed.

4. **Problem of administration of vocational education :** Union ministry of HRD should take full responsibility of administration of vocational and technical education as was recommended by Indian Education Commission 1964-66. This is not the case in India. Various departments of the States look after this education. In some states Education Department is taking the responsibility of administration while in some states labour department is looking after technical and vocational education.

   This problem can be solved by attaching vocational education to nearby state universities by creating a separate cell there. Every university should also have polytechniques so that other vocational colleges may be administered with the help of the real experience there.

5. **Lack of research works in vocational education :** Survey and researches are needed to know the real utility of this education to the masses and fundamental researches are needed to make it more fruitful to the masses. In India, the case is just opposite. We are only copying the West without making any innovation.

   This problem can be solved by involving the universities in research works. This will make the education adaptive to the domestic industries and agriculture. We should also make such researches with the help of which we may employ our manpower to the maximum extent.

6. **Problem of post technical education and training :** If trainees do not get job immediately after receiving vocational education, they forget everything after sometime. If they get jobs after eight or ten years even then they face adjustment problem in the industry because whatever they learned ten years ago has become obsolete in the industry today. It is because students have not got any chance to acquaint themselves with the latest techniques and devices.

This problem can be solved in the following ways—

(*a*) Correspondence courses should be made for those students who have passed any vocational course. This will help them update their knowledge.

(*b*) Pass out students should be given chance to work in the workshops of industries as an apprentice on contract basis and they should be paid out of the products made by them.

(*c*) In service training should also be given to workers in order to update their theoretical knowledge.

(*d*) A technical journal should also be published by the government of India and it should be sold in the market at subsidized rate. This will help the students to know new techniques and innovations in the field and to know the places where students can get job.

7. **Problem of coordination between training facilities and job opportunities :** We have been able to establish a lot of vocational education centres since the last 50 years but we have not been able to give jobs to millions of trainees. The reason may be that either the number of vocational institutions in India is very large or the training given by these institutes is not according to the domestic needs of the industry. This problem can be solved by developing proper coordination between vocational institutes and domestic industries. An intensive research work is needed for this purpose.

# Educational Administration in the USA

## INTRODUCTION

There was no centralized system of education in the USA before 1789 and education was mostly in individual hands. In 1789 American Constitution was formulated and adopted and powers of states and federal government regarding education were clearly classified and defined.

Initially, the system of education in America was mostly a copy of British system but constant reforms and changes in the system in order to make it adaptable to the American environment made it a different system. As in the case of India, educational organization in America mostly lies in the hands of the state governments. Federal government has very limited role to play in the matter of education. Role of private agencies in education is also recognised whole heartedly and no restriction is imposed on them. Federal government does not have any direct control over education system but it influences the system by making policies.

### Role of the Federal Government

1. It prepares education policies from time to time to have a control over education indirectly.
2. It provides land grants to state governments from time to time.
3. Financial grants for technical and industrial education are also given to states from federal government.
4. Grants for agricultural education is also given by the federal government.
5. After the end of the Second World War land grant system was completely handed over to states by the federal government and states were given full powers to preserve these lands for education purposes.
6. Federal government performs its educational responsibilities through Education Office. This office has been established to conduct and control educational programmes in the country. In 1939 Education Office which was independent then now attached to Federal Security Agency (FSA)
7. Different department (ministeries) of Federal governments also give various types of grants to states for education purposes.
8. In 1917 federal government established Federal Board of Vocational Education. This board formulated programmes for technical and vocational education and gave financial help. In 1920 education for retarded children was also attached to this board.
9. Federal government collects informations regarding the progress of education in states and publishes them in its bulletins.
10. Federal government endeavours to bring uniformity in the education of states but it does not exert any pressure on them. States are not bound to follow the directions of federal government.

### Education Office

Central department of education which was established in 1867 was renamed as Education Office in 1930. It was an autonomous body to implement education programmes and policies but it was attached to FSA after World War II

**This office is headed by Education Commissioner appointed by the president.** Important functions of Education office are as follows:

1. Administration of projects related to improvement of education.

2. Organising education for non-European communities.
3. Coordinating education facilities and organisation in various states.
4. Administration of vocational and technical education in the USA
5. Collecting data regarding progress of education in states and publishing them.
6. Initiating activities related to education reforms in the country.
7. Exercising powers related to the number of subjects in the states.
8. Controlling all types of education concerning war or defence of the country.
9. Expansion of industrial education.
10. Controlling National Youth organisations and providing work for unemployed persons by giving them vocational training and unemployment allowance.

Education office could not get much success in its efforts because of the non cooperation of states.

## State Education Board

It is the most powerful body in the states to control and organise education. This board is headed by Education Commission. SEB is an autonomous body to organise education in the states. Since federal government has very limited power regarding education according to the constitution, SEB is given full power for the purpose. Education Commissioner is assisted by State Education Department under SEB. We also see Country Board working at district level. Country Board is headed by Superintendent of Schools. Local boards work under country boards. In the beginning, States were fully responsible for education of masses. Powers were delegated to local boards by the amendment of the constitution in the beginning of 20th century.

## Functions of SEB

1. Framing general education rules for the schools.
2. Determining education programmes.
3. Exercising control over schools by giving them financial help
4. Determining qualification of teachers
5. Recognizing private schools and affiliating them with State Education Department.

## Local Boards

These boards administer and manage all local schools and colleges whether they are public schools or run by private agencies. These boards are constituted by the elected members of the people. These members elect the administrative officer of the board who is called superintendent of schools. There are nine members in the board. Local Boards formulate the curriculum of schools to be taught. State government has very limited control on these boards. SEB has control over vocational subjects only. If members of local Boards are religious, they can allow to teach even Bible in the school. Subjects which can increase patriotic feelings in citizens occupy an important place in the curriculum of schools.

## Characteristics of American System of Education

American system of education is distinct and unique as compared to India or any other Asian nation in the following ways:

1. Only one medium of instruction (English) is followed throughout the country.
2. Educational literature prepared in the country manifest national character.
3. Education is imbibed with democratic ideals and values.
4. Education is graded into four stages:
   - Primary stage
   - Secondary stage
   - Higher education stage
   - Vocational stage
5. Education upto secondary stage is administered by local boards.
6. Vocational education begins after secondary stage. This training is not given in private schools. State government takes full responsibility of this education.
7. Apart from the above four stages general course, industrial course, and professional specializations are also available there.
8. The provision of education in the USA is secular and free. Every child belonging to any community, race or culture can receive education free of cost. Equality of educational opportunities is there in America.

9. Education imbibes children with feeling of patriotism and nationalism.
10. Elected members constitute the local board to run the schools. If people of the locality are religious and they want to maintain their sub culture, their representatives can advocate for religious education in the schools too.
11. Single ladder system of education from primary to higher prevails in the whole country.
12. Subject wise grading is in vogue in America. A student can be in class Vth in science but he can be in third or fourth class in maths at the same time due to poor performance in mathematics.
13. Most of the educational expenditure upto secondary level is borne by the local people State government only gives partial financial aids.

## Contribution of federal government in Education

Educations system in America is not centralized. States have more powers regarding education than federal government. They can even ignore any of the instructions of the central government. Even then federal govt. is doing a lot for the development of education, it has no direct control over education but it can influence the state policies of education.

# Distance and Continuing Education in Australia

## External Studies

This is the term used for correspondence education in Australia. However, for the school level correspondence course, the word correspondence teaching is used.

It is actually a mode of study which seeks to minimize the need to attend an educational institution by a learner. The other terms used as synonyms for this word are distance education, off campus studies.

## Tertiary Education

This education starts after secondary education which is provided by three sectors, namely, (i) Universities, (ii) Colleges of Advanced Education (CAEs), and (iii) Colleges of Technical and Further Education (TAFE). The education provided by universities and CAEs is termed as higher education and technical and continuing education are provide by TAFEs. Before coming to this education, it is better to understand the structure of education of Australia up to higher education (upper) level, which is given below.

**Structure of schooling in Australia**

| *Age* | *Level* | *Grade* | |
|---|---|---|---|
| | | — | To professional courses in |
| | | — | universities |
| 17+ | Upper | 12 | and CAEs |
| | | | To paraprofessional and |
| 16 | Secondary | 11 | }–Preparatory courses (TAFE) |
| — | | — | |
| 15 | | 10 | |
| 14 | | 9 | To trades and preparatory courses (TAFE) |
| 13 | Secondary | 8 | |
| 12 | | 7 | |
| — | | — | |
| 11 | | 6 | |
| 10 | Primary | 5 | |
| 9 | | 4 | |
| 8 | | 3 | |
| — | | — | |
| 7 | Infant | 2 | |
| 6 | | 1 | |
| 5 | | K | |
| — | | — | |
| 4 | Pre-school | | |

**Notes:**

— mature age entrance schemes (21+) cater for entry to selected courses in all three sectors: universities, CAEs, TAFE.

— adult education (hobby) programmes (TAFE) usually have no school level prerequisites.

— Preparatory courses (TAFE) include Higher School Certificate (HSC); Tertiary Orientation Programme (TOP) and certain technical subjects at the secondary level.

## Characteristics of Australia

1. Australia is a highly urbanised country about 4/5 population lives in cities.
2. Population density is very low. Population is highly scattered.
3. Per capita income is high and people can afford the cost of education.
4. Shift workers, handicapped etc of urban areas can not attend local educational institution and external studies is the only option open for them.
5. It is very difficult to accommodate all scattered population in regular institutions due to high level of conveyance cost borne by learners.

## Beginning of Correspondence Education

External studies in Australia started in 1910. Many more correspondence schools were established during 1914-1922 to provide primary and secondary education to children. The important features of this system of education were as follows:

(i) Role of home supervisor (mother) was significant.

(ii) Lesson assignment scheme (assignment after every lesson).

(iii) Role of the correspondence teacher was also highlighted.

(iv) Library and text books services were provided to students.

At the tertiary level, external studies were first offered in the University of Queensland and University of Western Australia in 1913 and 1921 respectively. The University of New England adopted this programme as late as in 1955. This university received recognition from across the world for its work in external studies (correspondence courses). In 1960 about 65.7% of the total were external students in this university.

**Royal Melbourne Institute of Technology (RMIT):** This institute first started external studies in 1919. Now it offers a large number of external courses at the CAE and TAFE levels of education.

## Role of TAFE in Distance Education

TAFE conducts a large number of courses in six streams. These streams are (1) Professional (2) Semi-professional (3) Basic and post trade, (4) Skill development (5) Preparatory (6) Adult Education

These streams cover 10 fields which are (1) Applied sciences (2) Arts and design (3) Building (4) Business studies (5) Engineering (6) Rural development and horticulture (7) Music (8) Para-medical (9) Industrial and personal services (10) General studies.

## Post Secondary System of Distance Education

After World War II three important development with regard to tertiary education is indebted to Murray Report (1957), Martin Report (1964) and Tertiary Education Commission Act 1977.

Murray Report recommended that a commission should be established on the line of University Grants Commission of Britain. Under this system states will be given grants from federal government for educational purposes. Report also recommended that there is a need in Australia for university courses to be given on a part time and on an external basis. Federal government accepted these recommendations and the number of universities rose from 9 to 19 within 20 years. With this arrangement, the influence of federal government in imparting tertiary education increased to a great extent. When Murray Report came into light, only two universities, University of Queensland and University of New England were major providers of external studies (distance education) programmes. After the implementation of the report three more universities came to light to provide such programmes with the financial assistance of federal government. These universities are Macquarie University, Sydney, Murdoch University Perth and Deakin University, Geelong. They started distance education in 1964, 1970 and 1977 respectively.

As for as Martin Report is concerned, Advanced Education Centres (CAEs) grew out of the recommendations of this report. Its purpose was to create new educational opportunities for students. For this purpose, it started a number of vocational courses and applied studies for part time students. These courses were in accordance with the community needs and CAEs awarded diplomas rather than degrees. But external students (students taking education through correspondence) could not take the benefit of these courses because Martin Report was unsympathetic to external studies.

The third landmark in the field of external studies at tertiary level is Tertiary Education Commission Act 1977. According to this Act, federal government should finance and coordinate tertiary education across the country.

## Tertiary Education Commission (TEC) and Expansion of Distance Education

TEC emphasizes on the following points:

(i) Balanced development of tertiary education.
(ii) Coordination among sectors providing tertiary education
(iii) Providing quality materials and sharing of materials among various agencies.
(iv) Study centre networks
(v) Rationalization

Other developments that took place after TEC's coming into being regarding expansion and improvement of distance education at tertiary level are as follows:

(i) Attention was diverted to increasing external courses in universities to benefit external students.
(ii) Coordination among various agencies of education increased and duplication of courses were avoided.
(iii) The role of CAE's increased for providing specialist courses through distance learning.
(iv) An examination to check the quality of external courses was undertaken
(v) Economies of scale were utilized to benefit more students with less costs.

## Major Institutions Providing External Courses as Recognised By TEC 1981

1. Capicornia Institute of Advanced Education (Rockhampton)
2. University of Queensland, (Brisbane)
3. Darling Downs Institute of Advanced Education (Toowoomba)
4. The University of New England (Armidale)
5. Macquarie University (Sydney)
6. Mitchell College of Advanced Education (Bathurst)
7. Riverina College of Advanced Education (Wagga Wagga)
8. Deakin University (Geelong)
9. Warrnambool Institute of Advanced Education (Warrnambool)
10. Gippsland Institute of Advanced Education (Churchill)
11. Royal Melbourne Institute of Technology (Melbourne)
12. Murdoch University (Perth)
13. Western Australian Institute of Technology (Perth).

## Characteristics of Distance Education of Australia

Important characteristics of Australian system of distance education are as follows.

1. It is need based and prepares the learner to take part in productive life. Skill training is given for this purpose.
2. It can suit to all learners irrespective of their nature of occupation, physical and mental potentialities and the place of residing.
3. Mixed mode is followed in this system, i.e., students study some subjects by the off campus method and some subjects by on campus method. Thus, education is flexible.
4. The use of media and multimedia in education is very common. From simple audio cassettes to home and micro computers everything is used to disseminate and process information.
5. The education through correspondence courses is imparted from upper primary to tertiary levels, to benefit millions of learners, across the country. We in India have also copied down their model at upper primary grades and in adult education centres.
6. Vocational and general both types of education are provided through distance learning in Australia.

## Criticism of External Studies of Australia

Australian system of distance education can be criticised on the following grounds.

1. One of the major problems that Australian tertiary distance education is currently facing is the problem of coordination of course production, course delivery and students support services at the state and central levels both. Different agencies work for these three purposes and lack of coordination among them creates administrative and technical problem. The agency which has produced a course does not

know how the progress of students will be evaluated by the evaluation agency.

2. Lack of diversity of organizational approaches to suit regional and institutional needs is another drawback of this system. Many such courses are introduced by the institutions which are not required in that particular region.
3. Australian system of distance education is tilted to vocational courses that make the standard of general education in the country at low level. It is purely service oriented and administrative in nature. Though it is the need of the hour but it is not the mere need of a nation.
4. This system is very averse to modification of curriculum with the changing needs of the society.
5. The same academic staff in universities and CAEs teach and examine both the on campus and off campus students enrolled in different courses. This results into a bias in favour of on campus students.
6. Finance to these courses is provided by the federal government and courses are controlled by the states. This dyrchy sometimes leads to lack of coordination between the centre and the states.

# UNIT-X

## Development of Curriculum

# Development of Curriculum

## Meaning of Curriculum

All the experiences that are provided to learners in order to bring about desirable changes in their behaviour and mental set is technically known as curriculum. These experiences may consist of a part of knowledge, skills or values. They are pre-determined in order to guide the teacher not to deviate from his line of action.

## Definitions

1. **T.P.Nunn :** Curriculum should be viewed as various forms of activities that are grand expression of human spirit and that are of the greatest and the most permanent significance in the wide world.
2. **Cunningham :** Curriculum is a tool in the hands of the artist (teacher) to mould his material (pupils) according to his ideals (aims) in his studio (school).
3. **Payne :** Curriculum consists of all the situations that the school may select and consciously organise for the purpose of developing the personality of its pupils and for making behaviour changes in them.
4. **Secondary Education Commission :** Curriculum does not mean only the academic subjects traditionally taught in schools but it includes the sum total of experiences that a pupil receives through the manifold activities that go in the school, in the class room, library, laboratory, workshops, playgrounds and in the numerous informal contacts between teachers and pupils. In this sense the whole life of the school become curriculum which can touch the life of the students at all points and help in the evaluation of a balanced personality.

## Characteristics of the curriculum

On the basis of the definitions given above, the following characteristics of the curriculum can be derived—

1. All the experiences that students receive through different types of activities is curriculum
2. Curriculum is the means through which educational aims and objectives (desirable changes in the behaviour of learners) are achieved. Any defect in the curriculum will reflect an undesirable change in the behaviour of learners.
3. Teachers' (principal's ) attitudes towards students are also a part of the curriculum .
4. Curriculum helps the teacher in determining educational aims and objectives.
5. Curriculum may reflect local needs and conditions which are also taken into account by school authorities. Thus, some modification in the curriculum prepared by the school board are allowed. For this purpose, curriculum should not be rigid. It should be flexible enough to suit local needs.

## Different types of curriculum

Some of the major types of curriculum which have evolved in the course of time and ages are given below:

(A) **Subject centred (traditional) curriculum :** It is a written statement of the subject of study to be taught in a specified period of time. Each subject is a separate entity and its scope is clearly defined. The purpose of study is intellectual development of learners only.

### Defects of Traditional Curriculum

1. Here emphasis is given on the study of subject matter only and no stress is put on the activities

of students. Thus, only intellectual development of the child is possible here.

2. Knowledge of different subjects is divided into water tight compartments here and no correlation is seen among different subjects.
3. Such a curriculum is rigid and it does not take needs, interests and abilities of children into account. It can not be modified according to local condition.
4. This curriculum is prepared by a centralized authority and then it is imposed from above.
5. Schools do not have any say when curriculum is prepared by the authority.
6. Craming of subject matter is stressed here without knowing its implications in the day to day life. Subject matter is memorized only to pass the examination and nothing else.
7. This curriculum does not make adequate provisions for the diversity of tastes and talents. It is not varied in any way.

**(B) Activity Centred curriculum :** This curriculum is based on the ideas of Rousseau, Froebel, Montessori and Dewey which emphasise activity in the school rather than rote learning. In this curriculum, whatever is to be taught in the school in respective classes is translated into activities and knowledge is obtained by the method of learning by doing . Activity rather than language becomes the medium of instruction here.

This curriculum can remove most of the defects of subject centred curriculum.

According to **John Dewey** "Activity curriculum is a continuous stream of child's activities, unbroken by systematic subjects springing from the interest and personality felt need of the child" **Basic Education Scheme** proposed by Gandhijee is based on activity centred curriculum.

This curriculum is preferred to subject centred curriculum because of the following reasons—

1. Language does not become a barrier here.
2. Students solve their problems themselves by mutual help.
3. It is very much helpful for personality development of the child.
4. It is very much child centred and takes the abilities and interests of children.

**(C) Experience Centred Curriculum :** The experience which gives varied variety of knowledge, skills, attitude and appreciations is called experience centred curriculum. Since activity can not be separated from experiences, so, this curriculum is activity centred also. Experience is an interaction of the organism with his environment-social and physical both. Thus, this curriculum helps the child to adjust in his surrounding in an amicable manner.

**(D) Undifferentiated (Integrated) curriculum :** A curriculum which does not emphasize specialization of knowledge, which integrate different subjects at a particular level and a particular subject at all levels (from first to say XIIth ) and which can relate school with life is called integrated curriculum. Subjects and activities are unified here and thus it is very much helpful for all round development of personality.

**(E) Balanced (Core) curriculum :** This curriculum is constructed by taking all the principles of curriculum construction into account. Such a curriculum will include all the aspects of human activities differenciated by age level of children. It caters to the needs of the child and the society both, it helps in performing cultural and social functions of education and it makes the child visionary, creative, spontaneous and adaptive. In this type of curriculum specialized knowledge and experience will be given to the child progressively and approach will be from general to particular from first grade to the last. The purpose of this curriculum will be to make a child a self reliant adult in future.

## Principles of Curriculum Construction

1. **Principle of child centredness :** Curriculum should be constructed keeping in view the needs, interests, attitudes and abilities of children at a particular age. Thus curriculum is founded on personal and psychological grounds. What experiences we want to give a child will be correlated to his age and activities along with subject matter will be emphasized to get the child involve in the activity not in meditation. In this curriculum, individuality of the child will always be recognized.

2. **Principle of community centred :** Requirements of the community (society) must also be reflected in the curriculum. A child belongs to the society and he will remain in the society so, curriculum must enable the child to adjust in the society properly. This is possible only when purpose of the society is fulfilled. Thus, sociological foundations of education must also be taken into account while developing curriculum for the child.
3. **Principle of Integration :** Different activities of the child determined by different subjects must be integrated with each other and with the environment in which the child dwells. This will enable the child to adopt a holistic approach towards life. Integration is not opposed to specialization. Specialization will be transferred to the child when he actually needs it and can digest it.
4. **Principle of cultural preservation :** The culture to which the child belongs must be preserved by him. This is possible only when curriculum reflects culture. However, only that part of culture or traditions should be included in the curriculum which is healthy, democratic and based on scientific values. This culture must unite the people in a group not separate them from each other.
5. **Principle of Individual Differences :** Some children are talented and creative and some are handicapped in some respects apart from normal children of the society. Curriculum should be constructed in such a manner that children may develop their creative potentials. Similarly, needs of disabled children should also be reflected in the curriculum.
6. **Principle of Vision :** A society can never be static in any way. It has to go ahead by the change of time. While constructing curriculum for children, future needs of society must also be taken into account. Subject matter and experiences given to child must help him to make visionary and foresighted.
7. **Principle of activity :** Curriculum must be based on the principle of learning by doing. It should not be based on the principle of rote memorization alone. It should involve the students in different types of mental and physical activities. These activities will enable the child to prepare working models in science and picturise the society while studying social sciences.
8. **Principle of flexibility :** A rigid curriculum is not supposed to meet the changing requirements of the society. If it is flexible, and broad based, it can incorporate new subjects and activities every time. A dynamic society needs a flexible curriculum all the time. Flexibility can also help the teachers to incorporate their own ideas in the experiences given to children. Curriculum should be flexible enough to be moulded according to the local needs and aspirations.
9. **Principle of Comprehensiveness :** Curriculum should reflect all aspects of life. Wide variety of subject matter and experiences must be included in the curriculum. Comprehensiveness does not here mean a very vast curriculum but a curriculum that can transform a child into a full man.
10. **Principle of balance :** Balance at every grade of learning and balance among different grades are necessary pre-requisite of a good curriculum. If subject matter and experiences included in Hindi is completed in six months and the same thing is not completed in mathematics even after nine months, it is a great defect of the curriculum. Similarly, if curriculum for class VIIIth is very short as compared to class IXth and it can be completed in eight or nine months, it is also the defect of the curriculum. For example, syllabus of Hindi of class Xth in CBSE is very short as compared to other subjects. It is an example of imbalanced curriculum.
11. **Principle of organisation :** Curriculum may be organised in a number of ways. It may be organised topic wise or unit wise. Different subjects may have horizontal correlation. Out of so many types of organizations which one is to be selected is a question that can be answered by adopting different angles for the same curriculum. This should be done by the person who has developed the curriculum. It should not be left on the ability of teachers or principals.

12. **Principles of utility:** Curriculum constructed for students must be useful for them as well as for the society. It must be able to change the child into a useful and productive citizen in future.

## Evaluation of the Curriculum

Curriculum of any class is evaluated in terms of the criteria given in the principles of curriculum. Some part of evaluation may be direct and some may be indirect. In direct evaluation, content or topics of the curriculum are evaluated directly in the context of its usefulness, adaptability and utility. In indirect evaluation, behavioural changes in learners and their contribution to the society are evaluated which is not an easy task. Studying the effects of curriculum on learners and the society requires an extensive data from different sources such as from the school where child reads, from the family and neighbourhood where the child stays and from the place of work where the child after becoming an adult performs to earn his livelihood. Sense of responsibility and feeling of patriotism are also tested to know to what extent citizen is willing to do something for his nation. Two approaches of evaluation are adopted for this purpose.

**(A) Formative Evaluation :** In this approach of evaluation, curriculum is evaluated round the year by studying and interpreting the reaction of students, teachers, parents and social workers. Direct evaluation is also done here to know whether the curriculum is producing desired result or not. Agencies involved in this types of evaluation are experts and education boards of respective states.

Formative evaluation is not an easy task because of the following reasons :

1. Effects of any experience on learners cannot be studied in such a short span of time.
2. Reactions of teachers, students, parents etc. can not be obtained in such a short span of time by using a questionnaire.
3. Curriculum includes all the experiences of learners. If we are able to study all these experiences anyhow, we can not compare the results with the previous experiences of learners so easily. And thus we can not use system analysis procedure here.

**(B) Summative Evaluation :** This evaluation is done at the end of the course for which curriculum was developed. The duration of course may be from two years to five or six years. Here utility of the course is mostly taken into account which is done by studying the placement value of the course. Besides, Education Board also evaluates its curriculum after every five or six years to know to what extent the curriculum is able to satisfy the needs of learners and the society. This type of evaluation is necessary because society and its needs change with the passage of time. Hence, curriculum must be modified and adapted according to the changing needs of the society. This evaluation is also done keeping in view the 12 principles of curriculum construction.

## Different Approaches and Models of Curriculum Development

Important approaches of curriculum development are given below:

1. **Tyler's Means-end approach (Rationale Approach) :** This approach was given in 1950. It is based on Dewey's work of 1929. This approach addresses four basic questions.
   — What educational objectives should the school seek to achieve?
   — What educational experiences can be provided that are likely to realize those objectives?
   — How can these educational experiences be effectively organized?
   — How can it be determined whether these objectives are being attained?

Thus according to this approach four things have to be kept in mind.

(i) Determination of objectives
(ii) Selection of experience
(iii) Organization of curriculum
(iv) Evaluation of experiences

Thus, according to this approach curriculum (experiences) are the means to achieve the ends.

This model was enlarged by Taba in 1962. He proposed eight steps in developing curriculum.

— Diagnosing needs.
— Formulating specific objectives

— Selecting content at several levels of education.
— Organizing content.
— Selecting learning experiences.
— Organizing learning experiences.
— Evaluation of learning
— Checking for balance and sequence.

2. **Naturalistic Approach (by Schewab 1969 and Walker 1971) :** It emphasizes on the planning process based on the descriptive studies of the total process as it naturally covers in both national planning groups and in individual classrooms.

For planning within a group context deliberation is the key concept in curriculum development. It is the process by which developers decides upon which relevant facts generate alternative solutions. They also traces the consequences, weighs the cost of experiences and consequences of different alternatives. In this way, he chooses the best but not necessarily the right one.

It curriculum development is considered something individual, teachers do as they plan their course of study. Here descriptive studies of teacher's planning is also necessary.

**Two models of teacher's planning**

**Model No. 1 :** This model is consisted of four levels of teacher's planning.
— Planning goals of curriculum development
— Information sources used in planning
— Forms of plan used
— Criteria used for judging the effectiveness of planning.

**Model No. 2 :** This model consists of three stages of planning.
— Problem finding stage in which teacher's good conception general knowledges and experiences, knowledge of available resources etc. are included.

Solution of the problem stage through proper planning.

Implementation of the plan stage and its evaluation.

3. **Epistemological Approach :** It is also called the art of practical knoledge approach. This practical calls for large scale empirical study of what is occuring in the class room and a continuing sophisticated assessment of students when they leave elementary, secondary or higher classes as well as the assessment of the reactions of the community, employers, co-workers, teachers and families of students. This model is also called grass root model of curriculum development. Practicals require knowledge to detect failures and frictions of the machine. Thus pragmatic approach of curriculum development is needed here.

The arts of practical also requires knowledge of attractive solutions of problems.

4. **Analysis of experience approach :** This approach was given by conceptualists. They pointed out the terms like objectives and the learner are objectionable because they focus only on the instrumental and technical aspects of education and ignore the ethical, moral, aesthetic and political dimensions.

According to them, the knowledge of curriculum is concerned not only with the destination and completion of the journey on time but it must be concerned with the experience of the journey also. Approach and procedure should also be good to reach the goal.

5. **Preconceptions Approach (by Piner 1975) :** The most important knowledge necessary for curriculum development is the knowledge of students, i.e., what beliefs, facts and concepts students possess. Without this knowledge curriculum may not be development effectively. Thus, according to this approach,

*(i)* Individual school is the satisfactory unit for curriculum development. A number of such schools may be coordinated by means of a central planning committee, but decision on curriculum problems should be in the hands of local units working within the framework of the central or state committees.

*(ii)* Curriculum should be developed keeping in view the individual needs of the students. System analysis approach should be followed to know the needs and interests of students.

6. **Correlated approach :** Efforts are made to establish relationship between different subjects here and knowledge of one subject helps the students to understand the other subjects. For example, some topics are included in literature

who help the students to know history and culture.

7. **Integrated Approach :** This approach is based on the principle of Gestalt psycholog. Efforts, are made to provide the concept of whole to students here. The procedure is that different elements of knowledge are integrated into one subject to develop a 'Whole' concept. Experiences and activities of students are emphasized here. Through these experiences and activities, they come to know about a single subject. The course of study is also related to real life situations. Individual needs and interest of students are taken into consideration here.

8. **Concentric Approach :** In this approach, curriculum is developed from easy to difficult from primary to higher level in a hierarchy. keeping in view the abilities and age of students. Concrete knowledge is given first. Then knowledge of abstract concept is given to students step by step. Learner gets deep knowledge step by step at various grades. For example, students get elementary knowledge of history at class VIth level but this kowledge is broadened and deepened at higher levels of study.

9. **Unit Approach :** This approach is antagonistic to the older atomistic conception of learning according to which learning was a matter of adding one small bit of knowledge to the previous one step by step. This approach is based on the assumption that effective learning takers place only when objectives are clearly perceived and every-phase of the operational procedure is viewed as relational part of the total learning situations.

According to Wesley unit is an organized body of information and experience designed to affect outcomes of the learner.

James High defines unit approach in the following words.

"It is more than a mere technique and is often called the unit approach rather than method. The primary requisite is a point of view that will allow the imaginative instructor to arrange and organize all available and pertinent information around a nuclear idea and then select and provide references, aids and activities that will enable his students to master the basic material."

*(i)* A good teaching unit possess the following characteristics. It consists of meaningful elements combined in a group.

*(ii)* It arranges all elements in such a manner that students can understand the whole concept.

*(iii)* It provides the starting points of teaching activities and also ending points.

*(iv)* It has a broad and comprehensive structure.

*(v)* This approach is practical from the point of learning.

*(vi)* Proper interaction can be developed between teacher and taught through this approach.

*(vii)* It gives a sound basis for evaluation of learning and performance of students.

*(viii)* It is economical from the point of view of time.

10. **Chronological Approach :** When subject matter is arranged according to the sequence of dates on which incidents occurred, it is called chronological approach. Change and continuity in informations are maintained through this approach. We can see the continuity between past, present and future here also. Time sense and its importance is developed in students through this approach.

# UNIT-XI

## Measurement and Evaluation

1

# Measurement and Its Related Concept

## MEANING OF MEASUREMENT

In order to attain accuracy of an effort in our daily life or to compare objects, events and phenomena, measurement is carried out everywhere. We measure height, weight or area by using a universally acceptable scale of centimeter, inch, yard, feet etc, and everyone of us arrives almost at the same conclusion. Such an accurate measurement is not possible in psychology or education due to the absence of such a scale on one hand and due to the metaphysical nature of the objects, events or phenomena on the other.

For example, we do not measure the intelligence or achievement of a person just by taking an inch tape as we do in measuring a land. All the measurements in psychology and education are only indirect. In order to measure the intelligence or achievement of a child, the child is first of all made do some activities related to the phenomenon, then these activities are measured by using some scales and conclusions are drawn on the basis of norms prepared after long experience.

Thus, mathematics is necessarily used in all these measurements. **Guilford** has rightly said,

"Measurement means description of data in terms of numbers and this, in turn means taking advantage of many benefits that operations with numbers and mathematical thinking provide."

Why the use of mathematics is so essential in measurement? The reason is very simple. Its terminologies are well-defined and universally acceptable. If there lies any error in results, it is only due to the defects lain in scales. Meaning thereby, objective description of data on the basis of observation and experiment is but measurement. Since such an objectivity in psychology or education can not be maintained to the fullest extent, the measurement or testing that we are discussing here is more or less subjective, indirect and imperfect in nature.

## HISTORICAL PERSEPECTIVE

We will discuss here the history of psychological measurement and its related development in chronological order.

1. **Moivere** discovered normal probability curve in 1733. **Gauss** (1777-1855) refined the phenome-non and discovered the practical utility of this curve. He told how it can he applied to distribution of measurement and errors in scientific observation. Due to this very reason N P C is also known as Gaussian curve.
2. **Quetelet** (1796-1874) pointed out the importance of statistical methods for elaborating the data of biology and social sciences. He told that one would always get normal distribution of measurement taken from a random population. The role of NPC in all measurements is so evident that a hypothesis is tested on this very basis.
3. The history of educational and psychological measurement dates back only to 1850. Before this period, psychology was non-experimental and only a branch of philosophy. Every attempt to measure human behaviour was ridiculed by philosophers. In 1850 psychology parted with philosophy and began to form a new alliance with biology. In this decade experimental method in psychology was adopted and thus began the era of quantification of behaviours.
4. Three important developments are attributed to the second half of the nineteenth century—
   (I) Development of experimental psychology in Germany. It can be described as psycho-physics.

(II) Darwinian Biology.

(III) Treatment of maladjusted and abnormal individuals in France. It can be described as clinical practices. During this period, biologists and physicists were pioneers in conducting experiments for measuring human behaviour. Now we discuss each of these developments separately.

**(a) Psychophysics** :

*(i)* **Theodor Fechner** (1801-1887) who was actually a scholar of physics and chemistry, was basically concerned with the application of exact methods of natural sciences to the study of man's inner world, i.e., relation of mental processes to physical phenomenon.

*(ii)* **Johannes Miller** (1801-1858) who was a professor of physiology was basically interested in the application of the senses and in reflex actions. In his experiments in space perception, he tried to reconcile the contradictory theories of nativism and empiricism.

*(iii)* The third most important name in this context is that of **Alexander Bain** (1818-1903) who was a professor of logic, mental philosophy and English literature in Aberdeen University. His two important works are *Senses and the Intellect* (1855) and *Emotions and the Will* (1859).

*(iv)* During this period scientists were of the view that physical methods could be successfully applied to measurement of psychological properties. As a result, psychophysics was born and experimental psychologists studied the relationship between physical stimuli (intensity of light, sound etc.) and the sensations produced by these stimuli. As a result, the first laboratory for studying psychological reactions was established by **Wilhelm Wundt** in 1879 in the university of Leipzig (now Karl Marx University). This university gradually developed into an excellent centre for measuring human reactions with reference to different physical stimuli given.

**(b) Darwinian Biology** :

Darwin published his famous book **Origin of Species** in 1859. His theory of evolution provided a big motivation to the growth of psychological measurements. One important notion of that theory was that members of the same species are not alike. **Francis Galton** (1822-1911), a half cousin of Darwin quickly picked up the idea of individual differences. He was the first scientist to undertake systematic and statistical investigations of individual differences. For this purpose he also laid the foundation stone of psychometrics. Important works of Gatton were **Genius** (1869), **Natural Inheritance** (1889) and **Noteworthy Families** (1906).

The movement of studying individual differences got momentum when **Karl Pearson** developed his famous statistical method of Product moment coefficient of correlation.

**(c) Clinical Methods** :

Clinical method of measuring human behaviour was adopted by those working in the field of medicine, Psychiatry and social welfare. Clinical interests in feeble minded and insane children were first seen in France in 1900. Psychologists tried to measure maladjustment and its causes. These maladjusted children were either found mentally retarded or had a very low level of intelligence. The pioneer of this movement was Alfred Binet. He tried to measure the mental abilities of those children who fail to adjust properly in the school and whose performance was very poor in the classroom. This movement was later turned into measurement of intelligence.

The second name in this context can be referred to that of **Cattell** of America who worked in the Leipzig University with Galton. He came back to America in 1888 and started working in the field of individual differences. His disciple **E.L.**

**Thorndike** also made this movement popular in USA. He popularized objective measurement there. **Terman** was the third important American who not only popularized objective measurement in USA but adapted Stanford Binet test to American situation.

5. The history of psychological and educational measurement in the first 75 years of educational measurement of the 20th century can be divided into five equal spans namely (a) 1900-1915 (b) 1915-1930 (C) 1930-1945 (d) 1945-1960) (d) 1960-1975.

(a) **1900-1915** : In the first span **Binet-Simon** scale of intelligence was constructed by Binet and Simon in 1905 and this test was adapted to American situations also. It was revised twice firstly in 1908 and secondly in 1911 and he died in the same year. Binet and his co-workers were mainly interested in the classification of the individuals on the basis of variation of mental processes from one individual to another and in the determination of the inter-relationship of various processes within the individual.

Standardized achievement tests also began to appear during this period. **Stone's** Arithmetic test, **Buckingham's** spelling, **Thorndike's** hand-writing scale etc. are some of the development during this period. Group intelligence test was also developed by **Ottis** during this period.

(b) **1915-1930** : This period can be regarded as the rapid development period of the psychological testing. Standardized tests were developed for all the school skills during this period. Group intelligence tests especially Army Alpha and Army Beta tests were constructed for the purpose of selecting competent army men during World War I. Former was verbal and the later was non-verbal in content and nature. Personal Data Sheet of **Woodworth** also came into being to test personality of the individual. It was in the form of Questionnaire.

(c) **1930-1945** : It was a period in which centre of attention shifted from measuring limited range of academic skills to evaluating the whole range of academic achievement and behavioural changes. Objective tests which were considered a true measure were severely criticized. The well-known controversy between heredity and environment became bitter during this period. It was a healthy sign for all the processes of measurement. People started weighing their tests critically after constructing the test.

In 1937 Binet-Simon Scale was further revised and improved by M.E. Merril. Projective techniques to measure the whole personality were also developed during this period. Two tests are worth-mentioning here. Rorschach Inkblot test by a Swiss psychologist **Rorschach** and Thematic Apperception Test (TAT) by **M.A.Murray** and **C.D.Morgan** both in 1935 are these two tests.

(d) **1945-1960** : The main feature of this period was the excessive use of test batteries and testing programmes. A number of aptitude tests and test for special ability were produced during this period. Administration of tests and scoring were also clarified by test producers. Because of these reasons this period is also known as **golden age** of psychological and educational testing. It was during this period that Edward developed a personality inventory based on personality theory of Murray.

(e) **1960-1975** : A number of new tests were developed and old ones were revised during this period especially to measure frustration, creativity, special needs, self-concepts etc.

## GENERAL THEORY OF MEASUREMENT

**Camphel** defined measurement as "The assignment of numerals to objects or events according to certain rules." Guilford raised objection against the use of the term numerals and said that it should be replaced by numbers. According to him numerals are merely symbols or scratches on papers while numbers are definite and fixed. The use of numbers to identify categories is the lowest form of measurement.

These numbers are assigned according to certain rules. These numbers as well as rules are derived from mathematics. Thus, nature of measurement can not be understood without understanding the nature of mathematics as both are closely inter-related to each other and measurement is exclusively dependent on mathematics.

## Nature of Mathematics and General Theory of Measurement

The nature of mathematics can be understood by the following points :

1. **Postulates and Theorems** : Mathematics begins with a set of postulates. A postulate is a statement taken to be granted and does not need any proof to be accepted. It states some assumptions about relationship between objects, e.g., a + b= b + a. Postulates simply state that two objects of the similar type can be combined without regarding to their order. No conclusion can be drawn without these postulates.

   Statements derived from logical deductions are called theorems. Theorems are true if the reasoning is consistent with the postulates. It is because postulates are considered true. This truth is only logical not empirical. Because of this reason no experimental proof is needed for theorems.
2. **Mathematical Models** : Mathematics is an invention of man not a discovery. Because of this reason nature can never be described exactly and with 100% accuracy by mathematical models. All such descriptions are only approximation.
3. **Isomorphism** : The properties of the nature of structure are parallel to the structure of logical system in mathematics. There exists an equivalence form between the two which is called isomorphism. This equivalence may be perfect in some cases and rough in other cases. There is no need to test a logical/mathematical system but its applications can be tested empirically. For example, we can apply normal distribution curve to any set of population and test 'goodness of fit' by making a chi-square test. If chi square ($X^2$) is small we can accept NPC model as applicable to the data, otherwise not. If the goodness of fit is acceptable, the mathematical properties of NPC can be utilized in drawing out conclusions and predictions can be made.
4. **The nature of numbers :** Numbers are actually the basis of measurement. Bertrand Russell says that number is the class of classes. For example, four men four pens, four toffees etc, all belong to the same class four and classification can be made on the basis of this common elements.

   Thus, main properties of number are basically three :

   (a) Identity

   (b) Rank order

   (c) Additivity

   Out of the nine postulates mentioned by Guilford which are basic to measurement, the first three belong to identity, next two belong to rank order and the last four are concerned with additivity. These nine postulates are given below :

   *(i)* Either $a = b$ or $a \neq b$

   *(ii)* If $a = b$ then $b = a$

   *(iii)* If $a = b = c$ then $a = c$

   *(iv)* If $a > b$ then $b \ngtr a$

   *(v)* If $a > b$ and $b > c$ then $a > c$

   *(vi)* If $a = p$ and $b > a$ then $a + b > p$

   *(vii)* $a + b = b + a$

   *(viii)* If $a = p$ and $b = q$ then $a + b = p + q$

   *(ix)* $(a + b) + c = a + (b + c)$

## Definitions of Measurement

1. **J.P.Guilford :** "Measurement means description of data in terms of numbers and this in turn means taking advantage of the many benefits that operation with numbers and mathematical thinking provides".
2. **Steven :** "Measurement is the process of assigning numbers to objects or events according to certain rules."
3. **Nunnally** (1970) : "Measurement consists of rules for assigning numbers to objects in such a way as to represent quantities of attributes."

## General Properties of Measurement

On the basis of the definitions given above we can derive the following properties of measurements.

I. In the process of measurement an investigator assigns numbers to objects or events. It means that it is not enough to say that a particular student is good or poor in his studies. But measurement tells that how much marks the student has scored in a particular test i.e., how far he is good or bad.

II. When we assign numbers to objects or events we follow certain, fixed and explicit rules for this purpose. Numbers are not given arbitrarily in measurement. For example, inch tape is used to measure clothes.

## Characteristics of Physical Measurement

I. Units can be referred to a zero point, e.g., 5 kg. weight means 5 kg. above zero, absolute zero temperature means total absence of heat and so on. Thus, zero point represents the absence of the trait being measured.

II. The basic assumption of quantitative measurement is that units bearing the same name must have the same value, i.e., these names are universally accepted with the same weightage. For example, 5 feet is just half of 10 feet.

III. Physical measurement is complete in itself. No further explanation is needed to signify the meaning, such as, 10 kg. sugar or 10 acres of land etc. give complete information about the object.

IV. Measurement conveys a definite sense and this sense can not be manipulated by the investigator.

V. Quantitative measurement is objective in nature.

VI. Physical measurement is more accurate and predictable than psychological measurement.

## Characteristics of Mental Measurement (Measurement in Behavioural Sciences)

Mental or qualitative measurement is subjective, indefinite and non-precise. Suppose, we want to judge the quality of a student's work, we will first of all, predetermine some standard in our mind and then we will compare that quality with that standard. This standard exists in the mind of the evaluator which may not be very accurate. Moreover, total work of the student is also not evaluated, only some samples of the total behaviour is evaluated.

Similarly, if that student is evaluated as average, this term average has no definite meaning for all the people. It may differ from person to person. For example, if we evaluate the hand writing of a student, we can evaluate it in terms of slant, legibility, speed, accuracy etc. but these concepts are not definite and universal.

Thus, mental or behavioural measurement has the following properties :

1. Units are not definite and fundamental here. They are rather derived and coined. In an achievement test a score of 70 or 80 percent has no meaning at all unless we know the scores of other students in the group or the standard of teaching for the group. Thus, raw scores obtained from a test will have to be converted into standard score to interpret them.
2. It is the evaluator who fixes the standard which may vary from person to person.
3. There is no zero point to be referred in mental measurement. For example, an IQ of 80 or 120 is compared with the average IQ of 100 not with zero. Scoring zero on a numerical ability test does not mean total lack of knowledge of numerical operations.
4. All measurements in behavioural sciences are only indirect. We can not measure the interest of a child by using a foot scale. The child does some activity and we measure the performance of his activity. Same is the case with achievement or intelligence testing.
5. This measurement is relative not absolute. Poverty has any significance only when there is richness in the society.
6. Error always lies in all types of psychological measurements. This error is seen in all the steps of measurement, i.e., construction, operation, scoring and interpretation.

## Scope of Measurement in Behavioural Science

Measurement in psychology and education especially answers three basic questions.

1. What an individual has done in a particular field (Achievement test). This is related to the past abilities of the individual.

2. What a person is actually able to do (Aptitude test). This is related to the future abilities of the individual.
3. What a person is not able to do (diagnostic test). This is related to the past and future both and is expressed in terms of present abilities of the individual.

## FUNCTIONS OF MEASUREMENT

The scope of educational measurement is actually elaborated by its functions which are given below :

1. **Prognosis :** This is related to administrative functions of measurement. Measurement performs the following three functions here in order :
   (a) *Classification :* After testing, measurement classifies the individuals on the basis of the scores obtained by them. (Grouping in a class is also done on the basis of measurement of abilities of children).
   (b) *Selection :* After preparing the merit list on the basis of measurement, the required number of students or applicants are selected from the top either for selection in a jobs or admission in a course. Aptitude test is also used for the purpose of final selection.
   (c) *Grading :* Selected students are then put into different grades according to scores obtained by them. Grading in jobs is done in order to treat them differentially by the employer. Class-room grading is used for the purpose of guidance, counselling or remedial teaching.
2. **Prediction :** When same type of tests is given to two groups of students, we can come to know the relative difference of achievement of these groups. On the basis of their performance on the test it can be predicted which group will show better performance in future. Similarly, if high degree of correlation is found between two tests, say intelligence and achievement tests, administered on the same group, it can be predicted that if the group is high in performance in the first test, he will be high in the second test also.
3. **Comparison :** No two individuals are alike in the world in any respect, such as, they differ in intelligence, achievement, behaviour, personality etc. These variations and their degree of variations can be found out by measurement and teaching or training tasks can be arranged accordingly.
4. **Diagnosis :** The specific learning problems of students can be found out by measurement especially, by using diagnostic tests. Once the difficulties are known, remedial measures can be adopted accordingly. Diagnosis is needed at every step of teaching in the class. Even achievement tests are also diagnostic tests as they help the teacher to change his programme of action for better achievements next time.
5. **Research :** In all types of clinical and experimental researches measurement has very important role to play. For example, two groups of students are first of all equalized in intelligence or achievement and then experiment is conducted on them. This equalization is possible only by measurement. If two groups of students are equal in intelligence and they are taught by two different methods and tested after the teaching is over, whatever difference is seen in their achievement will only be due to the difference in the methods of teaching. Measurement will be needed in all the steps of all these researches. Only philosophical and historical researches do not require measurement or testing.

### Steps Involved in Measurement

Measurement is not so easy as it is generally understood. Some measurements may be easy as the length of a stick which can be measured by applying an inch tape. It is because the concept of inch or foot has been made clear through the long passage of time. But this is not so easy in case of complicated concepts, such as durability of a machine or furniture.

Second thing is that we actually do not measure a person or object. We rather measure the attributes of a person or an object and attributes may have different meanings for different persons.

Third thing is that the more we try to make our description precise and quantitative, the more role of measurement will be there.

Suffice it to say following steps are involved in all types of measurement.

**1. Identification and the definitions of the attributes to be measured:** We have not to measure an object or a person. Only attributes of objects or persons are measured. We should first of all identify the attributes that are to be measured. Then these attributes are defined in behavioural terms. Two examples are given here to illustrate the point. The first example is related to physical measurement and second one is related to psychological testing.

**Example I:**

Suppose we want to assess the quality of an auto tire. We first identify the attributes related to the quality of the tire, such as, durability of the tire, cost and durability ratio, service of the producer, buying conditions of the tire, guarantee period etc.

These concepts may have different meaning for different persons. For example, durability is a dubious concept. It may accrue the following meaning :

I. Resistance to wear and tear.

II. Abrasion from contact with road.

Similarly, resistance is also not a universal phenomenon. It may accrue the following meanings:

I. Resistance to puncture by pointed objects, nails or stone.

II. Resistance to deterioration and decay.

III. Resistance to heat or water and so on.

**Example II :**

Suppose we want to measure intelligence of a person, intelligence means different things for different persons. We will have to decide first what kind of behaviour we characterize as intelligent behaviour. We may include the following attributes in intelligence:

I. Memory and power of recall.

II. Quickness of recall.

III. Ability to deal with ideas and abstract concepts.

IV. Ability to deal with concrete objects or events.

V. Decision making power.

VI. Ability to manipulate the object or situation.

VII. Speed and accuracy of response etc.

While dealing with these situations at the time of measurement following decisions need to be taken :

I. One should decide which particular attribute/ is/are relevant and important to measure at present that can satisfy the present needs.

II. Attribute should be defined in clear, objective and behavioural terms.

III. Purpose of measurement should also be made clear.

**2. Selection of set of operations or behaviour to express the attributes** : After defining the attributes in operational term, we select only those operations or behaviours which will manifest the attributes to be measured. Suppose, we want to measure the distance from New Delhi to New York, we will select the method to measure the distance. The possible methods may be land route or going New York from New Delhi by plane or using sound wave method.

The operation will always depend upon the definition that one has given to the attribute. Thus, operations must coordinate and interact with the definitions.

Second problem is that if operations are not available, they are invented (constructed) by the investigator and in order to make them acceptable to all, they are standardized properly. Take the example of Stanford-Binet Test of intelligence. It not only provides operational definitions of intelligence but it is also standardized and hence universally acceptable under constant conditions.

**3. Quantification of attributes and interpretation of results** : This is the last step of measurement in which attributes are quantified by counting the number of correct responses or the number of overt behaviour. For example, if we want to measure reading ability of a person, we first assign marks to accuracy and fluency of reading and same operation is repeated several times in calculated time period.

This raw score still does not have any significance unless it is converted into standard score. Here scores of different attributes are compared with the norm or the standard to give it a meaning. This is called interpretation of scores.

## Levels (Scales) of Measurement

There are basically four levels of measurement :

I. Nominal or classificatory scale.

II. Ordinal or ranking scale.

III. Interval scale.
IV. Ratio scale.

**1. Nominal Scale** : Here numbers or symbols are used to identify an object, person or group and its characteristics. For example, different players are given different numbers for the purpose of identification. Big classes of a school is classified into different sections A,B,C or A1, A2, A3 etc for better management of the class. The main feature of the scale is that once a person leaves the group, he immediately loses this number. Some imminent persons are remembered with their numbers or symbols even after their leaving the group but this identification is not related to nominal scale. It is called nick name in literature. Classification of persons into males and females, objects on the basis of its colours, classification of people on the basis of their communities, numbers given to vehicles showing a particular district or state etc. are some other examples of nominal scale.

In a nominal scale a particular class is divided into a sct of sub-classes. Members within a sub-class are equivalent in the properties being referred.

Mathematically, if a = b and b = c then a = c. It means that one to one transformation exists in the nominal scale, i.e., symbols designating different groups on a nominal scale may be interchanged without altering the essential properties in the scale. Only **frequency distribution and mode** can be used in this scale as statistical measure.

**2. Ordinal Scale** : When various groups of the population are divided according to a certain order or serial keeping in view the properties being measured, it is called ordinal scale. Classification of students into various groups-bright, average or poor, classification of the society into upper, middle and lower classes, ranking football, tennis or cricket players and teams as first, second, third etc on the basis of their performance, assigning different grades to students keeping their particular attributes into account, arranging the students in a line according to their height from the tallest to the shortest etc are some examples of ordinal scale.

In ordinal scale a transformation which does not change the order of the classes is completely admissible. For example, if a student getting distinction marks is given Rs. 500 and another student scoring just first division is given Rs.300 only as prizes, it means that a distinctioner is greater than first divisioner.

The limitation of this scale is that they are neither absolute quantities due to lack of incorporation of absolute zero point nor do they convey the equal distance between different rank values, due to lack of equal interval measures.

An example will illustrate this point. If in a class of 15 students the rank of Mr. A is fifth and Mr. S. is tenth from the top, it does not mean that the achievement of Mr. A is double that of Mr. S The later may be less than Mr. A by only a few points. The statistics used in this scale is median, percentile and rank correlation.

Because of the two limitations mentioned above ordinal scale can not be subjected to arithmetical calculations, such as mean, SD, correlations etc.

***Difference between nominal and ordinal scales:***

I. Nominal scale incorporates the relation of equivalence only (within the group) while ordinal scale incorporates the relation of equivalence and greater than both.

II. Nominal scales can be changed very easily without creating any frustration for the individuals of the group but ordinal scale cannot be changed at a point of time.

**3. Interval scale :** When a measurement conveys meaningful information with respect to distance or degree of difference between different points on the scale, it is called equal interval scale. Equal distance of the scale indicates equal distance in the properties being measured, i.e., units of measurement is constant and equal. Zero point (absence of the property) is also found on the scale (zero point in education does not, however, mean absence of the property). Zero point is only arbitrary in behavioural sciences but it is true in all physical measurement.

Measurement of temperature, achievement or aptitude tests of objective nature etc. are some examples of interval scale.

Equality and constancy of unit of measurement and existence of zero point can be explained with the help of an example.

Temperature is measured by Celsius, Fahrenheit and Kelvin. These scales covey the same kind of information. As a result, linear tr1`ansformation of values from one scale to another is possible and essential properties of an interval scale remain unchanged by any linear transformation. F° can be transformed into C° with the help of the following formula,

$$F = 32 + \frac{9}{5} \times C^{\circ}$$

Following table gives some of the equivalent temperature difference on both the scales.

| **Celsius** | 0 | 10 | 20 | 30 | 40 | 50 | 60 | 70 | 80 | 90 | 100 |
|---|---|---|---|---|---|---|---|---|---|---|---|
| **Fahrenheit** | 32 | 50 | 68 | 86 | 104 | 122 | 140 | 158 | 176 | 194 | 212 |

Here C shows equal interval of10 degrees while F shows equal interval of 18 degrees on each point.

Thus, we see that numbers in interval scale can legitimately be added to or subtracted from each other. If four students A,B,C and D have scored 20, 16, 8 and 4 marks respectively on a test of mathematics of 20 marks, their marks can be subjected to addition or subtraction and Mean, SD, t-test, F-test etc. can also be calculated here, e.g.,

A – C = 20 – 8 = 12
B – D = 16 – 4 = 12
A – B = 20 – 16 = 4
C – D = 8 – 4 = 4
A – B + C – D = 4 + 4 = 8 and so on.

In spite of this property, the process of additivity can not be carried out in the absolute sense. The reason is that zero point is not true but only arbitrary in all behavioural sciences. Zero point here, does not tell the real absence of the property being measured. It is adopted only for the purpose of convenience.

Limitation of this scale is that the statistics of coefficient of variation can not be applied in interval scale of measurement.

**4. Ratio scale** : It is the highest level of measurement and has all the properties of nominal, ordinal and interval scales plus an absolute or true zero point. In ratio scale, the ratio of any two scale points is independent of the unit of measurement. In this scale all the nine postulates of measurement can be applied and hence all the statistical operations are possible without exception. Height, weight, length, loudness, vision etc. are common examples of ratio scale.

## Difference Between an Interval and Ratio Scales

I. In interval scale zero point is only arbitrary while in the ratio scale zero point is true. Temperature measured in terms of Celsius or Fahrenheit is an example of interval scale while height measured in terms of inch or feet is an example of ratio scale. For example, if we measure the two sticks and find that one stick is 6 feet long and the other is 3 feet long we can say that one stick is twice in length as against the other. This is because 6 feet means 6 feet from 0 and 3 feet means 3 from 0. On the other hand, a temperature of 40° C can not be called twice the temperature of 20° C due to absence of true zero. Almost all behavioural measurement suffer from this problem.

II. Ratio scale is unique upto the multiplication by positive constant and interval scale is unique upto the addition by a constant number. An example will illustrate this point. If we add a given number to each value of the variable, we can not maintain the original ratio, e.g., 10/5 = 2 If we adds 2 to each of these variable, the result will be different, e.g.,
10+2/5+2 = 12/7
On the other hand, if values are multiplied by a given constant number, the ratio would not change, e.g.,
10/5 = 2 and 10x5/5x5 = 2 Here, 5 is a constant number.

## Limitations of Measurement

The progress of any science or discipline today is judged by the extent to which it has been able to make quantitative description of objects, events or persons. That is why, even social sciences are coming closer to the process of measurement day by day. It allows extremely accurate and objective description of events. As we have seen measurement is not an easy task. A behavioural scientist has to face a number of problems when he goes through the process of measurement. Even natural scientist is also found to face these problems to some extent. They are given below :

1. **Indirect measurement :** Almost all the psychological and educational measurements are indirect in nature. Suppose a teacher wants to measure the intelligence of his student, the intelligence can not be directly seen, touched or experienced. As a result the teacher will have to measure those behaviours or acts which can represent intelligence. These measures can not be 100% correct because they may not be fully reliable, valid, practical, objective or fully representative of the actual behaviour being measured.
2. **Incomplete measurement** : Psychological and educational measurements are generally incomplete. Suppose we want to measure the attitude of the people towards corruption in the society. For this a scale is constructed in which a number of behaviours expressing such an attitude are incorporated. We can not incorporate all the behaviours here due to lack of time and knowledge. Such a sampling set of behaviour may give incomplete, dubious and sometimes misleading index of attitude.
3. **Errors due to dependence on the person being measured** : Whosoever is measured in psychology or education is a living object whose traits or attributes can not be manipulated independently. The person being measured can manipulate or hide his traits or attributes on his own will and the investigator can not fully control it. Such an uncontrolled factors may either increase or decrease the scores.
4. **Errors of Measurement due to extraneous factors** : If a child is nervous, he is disturbed by the sound of high pitch or tone, he is highly under pressure and so on, he will not be able to take the test properly and all such factors will decrease his actual score. Such a problem is very common in all psychological and educational measurements.
5. **Unreliable Measurement :** All behavioural measurements are relative in nature, so they can not be 100% relied upon. 60% marks of a student in English has no meaning at all unless it is compared with his group or other groups of students. Such a group of reference differs in performance from place to place or from community to community. For example, the value of 80% score in board Examination in CBSE, UP board or Bihar board is not the same. Same individual may obtain different scores on intelligence test if he is given different sets of intelligence scale prepared by different persons. In such situations, how can we say that measurement in psychology or education is fully reliables.
6. **Subjectivity of interpretation** : The investigator may interpret the scores in a wrong manner deliberately or unknowingly and the result and the scores will be different from those of the actual ones.
7. **Overlapping of human behaviour** : In psychology or education traits are measured with the help of the behaviour manifested by humans. These behaviours are limited. A particular behaviour may be expressed for denoting so many traits or characteristics. Reverse position may also be there. One single behaviour may be related to so many traits. Thus, the items of a test measure a trait only partially or more than trait. For example, an achievement test also measure intelligence, interest, motivation, learning ability and so on. In such a situation no test can be termed as perfect test.
8. **No Consensus on the Nature of a Trait** : Different people define and understand a particular trait differently, e.g., study habit means studying books without a particular choice, studying novels and stories, studying only course books and so on. Thus, a particular test is designed and constructed in the light of the definitions that is there in the minds of the test constructor.

## MEANING OF EVALUATION

Evaluation is the criteria of success or failure of a task done. If it is done at the end of a task, total efforts, including the investment of time and money may be a failure but if it goes side by side of the task, immediate feedback received might alarm the performer to rectify his mistakes and thus there is 100% chance of success of the programme.

Education is also an investment in the sense that time, energy and money are spent to bring about behavioural change in learners. That is why when a teacher performs his teaching works in his class, he also simultaneously finds out whether the changes in behaviour of learners are in concurrence with the learning objectives or not. If it is not so there, then what types of modifications are needed and at what steps of teaching. He also finds out whether the problem lies in his teaching strategies or techniques or it is there in the students itself. Thus, teaching and evaluation run-hand in hand. Evaluation determines the behaviour of students on one hand and testifies to the teaching of the teacher on the other. This very purposeful behaviour of the teacher is called evaluation in education.

**Definitions :**

1. **NCERT** : Evaluation is any systematic continuous process which determines
   - The extent to which specified educational objectives previously identified and defined are attained.
   - The effectiveness of learning experiences provided in the class room.
   - How well the goals of education have been accomplished.
2. **Quillen and Hanna :** Evaluation is the process of gathering and interpreting evidences on changes in the behaviour of pupils as they progress through school.
3. **Goods** : "Evaluation is a process of ascertaining or judging the value or amount of something by careful appraisal."
4. **Bradfield and Moredock** : "Evaluation is an assignment of symbols to a phenomenon in order to characterize the worth of value of the phenomenon usually with reference to some social, cultural or scientific standards."

In one sentence evaluation is an educational programme concerned with the measurement of all the three domains of learning-cognitive, affective and psychomotor. Process as well as product is evaluated to arrive at a final conclusion. The results of evaluation is always expressed in terms of behavioural changes of the person being evaluated.

## Characteristics of Evaluation

On the basis of the definitions given above, the following characteristics of evaluation can be derived.

1. **A Comprehensive Process :** All the three domains of human behaviour, cognitive, affective and psychomotor, can be accurately measured by evaluation. Apart from student's behaviour, teacher's behaviour (his task of teaching) is also evaluated.
2. **A Systematic Process** : Evaluation is a preplanned and systematic process which goes ahead keeping in view the pre-determined objectives. By this process we find out how much change has occurred in the behaviour of students and teachers and how much change is yet to be brought about by the task ahead.
3. **A Continuous Process** : Evaluation process can not be separated from teaching and both go side by side. By this process whatever changes take place in the behaviour of learners, its proper record is maintained and on this very base students are either ranked in a particular class or decision is taken to promote them to the next higher class.
4. **A Social Process** : Education is a purposeful activity fulfilling the requirements of learners and the society. Evaluation tells us to what extent teaching is fulfilling the requirements of both.
5. **An information Collection Process** : When students progress step by step in the school system, all the informations regarding their progress are gathered by using a number of tests and by going through various techniques of measurement. After that these informations are interpreted in terms of predetermined objectives.
6. **A Combined Process :** While taking the final decision regarding a student and declaring him fail or pass, the reports of all the concerned teachers of school are taken into account. No such decision is taken by the evaluation report of one or two teachers. Thus, evaluation becomes a comprehensive process.
7. **A Process of Value Judgement** : Scoring 60 or 70 percent in any subject by any of the students in a class does not have any meaning unless the scores of the student is compared either with other students of his own class or it is presented with

reference to any outside criterion. When it is done and stated that student has secured first division by scoring 60% or more marks or his rank is third or tenth in his class it becomes evaluation. Thus, evaluation is a value judgement process and tells how far a student is away from his destination.

8. **Evaluation Includes Measurement** : Evaluation actually starts from some sorts of measurement then symbols are assigned to students by comparing the performance with cultural or scientific standard. It shows that evaluation reports may vary from culture to culture.

## Purpose of Evaluation

**Evaluation has following purposes to serve:**

1. **Giving Details of Students' Progress** : Evaluation tells where a student is standing on the way to his destination of learning, how much he is ahead or behind his classmates, to what extent the behavioural changes occurred in him are acceptable, how far he can apply his present acquired knowledge to his future life or learning situations, at what point he is facing any difficulty and why and so on. Thus, evaluation here works like the diagnostic function of measurement.
2. **Predicting future achievement** : When evaluation covers the aptitude aspect of behaviour, it can predict the future performance of a student or a teacher on the basis of his present performance.
3. **Guidance and Motivation** : When a student comes to know about the actual position of his achievement, he gets motivated to do better. Besides, strengths and weaknesses of students become manifest through evaluation and a teacher can guide them accordingly.
4. **Improvement in the system** : Once proper guidance is given to students by the teacher after evaluation, teaching-learning process gets improved. A teacher can also come to know his own strength and weakness by the process and can change his own behaviour accordingly. Once he gets acquainted with his own shortcomings, he can remove them. Thus, process of evaluation is concerned with inputs and output both.
5. **Discovery of effective teaching strategies** : Evaluation opens the new avenues of action researches in the class. When a teacher does not get the desired result by adopting a particular combination of teaching strategies, he adopts another combination and this process continues until a final effective combination of teaching strategies is discovered.
6. **Classification of Students** : By evaluation process we can classify students into different groups like talented, bright, average, slow learners and poor and adopt different strategies of teaching for different groups. We can also give remedial treatment to weak students in the class only after thorough evaluation of them.
7. **Providing feedback to students and teachers both** : When a teacher comes to know the results of his efforts he gets feedback. If result is good, he is motivated if result is not satisfactory, feedback pushes him to change his behaviour. Similarly, knowledge of progress and the feedback received thereof motivate the students also.

## Steps in Evaluation

An evaluation is comprised of the following steps to be followed in order :

1. **Identification of Objectives** : First of all, a teacher decides which domain of behaviour of a student and upto which level he has to cover by his tests and what advantages he wants to gain by these tests.
2. **Matching the objectives with the content:** After identification of objectives a teacher matches the objectives with the subject-matter that he has to teach in the class. He also determines the level of teaching accordingly.
3. **Writing objectives in terms of behavioural change of learners** : In the third step objectives are written in such a language which is clear and represent the change of students' behaviour.
4. **Taking the students to the environment of testing** : Teacher takes the students from teaching environment to the testing one very smoothly so that students express their behaviour freely.
5. **Selection of tools and techniques** : At this step the teacher decides whether the test will be written, oral or practical and if written test is to be administered, it will be objective or subjective.
6. **Construction of the test** : Here teacher constructs the test keeping in view the objectives already determined by matching them with the content.

7. **Administration of the test :** Students are given the test constructed by the teacher and they take the test in stipulated time.
8. **Scoring :** Whatever changes have occurred in the behaviour of students are converted into numerals or grade by scoring.
9. **Interpretation of Result :** At this stage the marks obtained by the students are analysed by the teacher in order to see whether the changes in behaviour are in accordance with the objectives or not.
10. **Value judgement :** At this step, teacher compares the behaviour of students with any internal norm or outside criteria in order to give it a value judgement, i.e., upto what level the achievement of students is satisfactory, average, excellent or poor.
11. **Feedback :** After preparing the result, it is sent to students and their guardians in order to give them feedback. Teachers also get feedback by the results and they come to know the strengths and weaknesses of their teaching.

## Techniques of Evaluation

Evaluation is broader concept than measurement but no exact evaluation is possible without going through the process of measurement. All the three domains of behaviour are covered by evaluation, e.g.,

1. **Cognitive domain :** Oral, written, essay type, objective type tests, practical examinations and observation techniques etc. are used for evaluating cognitive domain.
2. **Affective domain :** This domain is evaluated by interest inventory, attitude scale, check list, rating scales and observation techniques.
3. **Psychomotor domain :** Performance tests, practical examinations and observation techniques are used to evaluate this domain (See optional paper II for Educational Objectives).

There are basically two techniques of evaluation:

**A. Quantitative :** These techniques are highly reliable and valid. Important such techniques are as follows:

1. **Oral :** These techniques are basically used at lower grades of teaching. At higher level of education too viva voce is used to test the lower levels of cognitive behaviour. Debates or drama can also be used for this purpose.
2. **Written :** Objective type tests, essay type tests and short answer questions are important written techniques to evaluate cognitive achievement of students. They give more accurate results than oral tests.
3. **Performance tests :** Here some works are assigned to students to accomplish them. Students practically do these works and then output is evaluated.

**B. Qualitative :** These techniques evaluate the quality of attributes and hence they are highly subjective. Important such techniques are given below:

1. **Cumulative Records :** Such records are prepared by the school to show all-round development of students individually. They reflect the total personality of the child, i.e., marks obtained by students in sessional tests and examinations, their participation in games, sports cultural programmes and other co-curricular activities, their regularity, punctuality, their etiquette.
2. **Anecdotal Records :** These records maintain the description of significant events or works of students. Here informations regarding the behaviour, attitudes or interests of students are systematically cumulated.
3. **Observation :** This is the most common technique of qualitative assessment of students. It is mostly used at lower grades of education. This is the only technique for the evaluation of classroom interaction.
4. **Check list :** This technique is used for evaluating attitude and affective domain of students. Here questions are given to students and they are asked to answer them in yes or no, e.g.,
   Item : 'Do you like doing mathematical sums-Yes/No.'
5. **Rating Scales :** Here some statements are given to students and agreed, indifferent or disagreed are written before the statements. Then students are asked to tick the option according to their own choice.

## Types of Evaluation

**1. Formative Evaluation :** The purpose of formative evaluation is to monitor instructional process to know whether learning is taking place or not. It is designed to enhance and improve teaching-learning process and thus it becomes a continuous process in the school system.

These tests diagnose the weaknesses of students as well as teachers and thus, both of them can get feedback from these tests. Students and teachers both after identifying their difficulties change their behaviour and remove these difficulties. Thus, function of this evaluation is remedial in nature.

The second function of this evaluation is that if evaluation finds teaching-learning process satisfactory, it motivates the teachers and students to work harder for better results.

**Tanner** (1972) has defined formative evaluation in the following words :

"Formative evaluation refers to the use of tests and other evaluative procedures while the course and instructional programme is in progress."

Both criterion referenced and norm referenced tests are used to take the students to the mastery of the content. These tests are given in the following stages of learning.

I. At the end of each unit of the lesson.
II. At the end of each whole lesson.
III. At the end of each unit of the total course.

***Advantages of Formative evaluation :***

I. It provides sufficient information to teachers for modifying teaching.
II. It helps in formulating individual and group remedial programmes.
III. It provides feedback to students as well as teachers.
IV. It facilitates retention and transfer of training.
V. It enables the teacher to readjust his teaching according to the needs of the students.
VI. Students can also modify their behaviour after getting feedback from this evaluation.
VII. It gives reinforcement to high achievers.
VIII. It can work as a self-evaluation device for learners.

**2. Summative evaluation** : This evaluation takes place at the end of the session to measure over all achievement of pupils. Annual, internal or external examinations are the examples of summative evaluation. The purpose of this evaluation is to certify fail or pass of the product. If formative evaluation is related to the process of teaching, it is related to the product of teaching. Here students are evaluated from the whole syllabus. On the basis of this evaluation, a decision is taken whether a student should be promoted to the next class or he should be kept in the same class again.

On the basis of above discussions we can say that summative evaluation works as a complement to formative evaluation and both of them combined together are necessary for all educational system.

**Difference between Measurement and Evaluation:**

1. Measurement process may be included in evaluation but evaluation may not necessarily include any measurement.
2. Evaluation is quantitative and qualitative both but measurement is always quantitative.
3. Evaluation is a comprehensive concept while measurement is a narrow concept. It means that measurement has no meaning without involving evaluation at least in psychology and education.
4. Evaluation is a continuous process in education while measurement is only a part of evaluation.
5. Evaluation always aims at improving the situation but measurement does not involve this purpose.
6. Evaluation provides descriptive as well as quantitative data regarding behavioural changes of pupils while measurement converts behavioural changes of pupils into numerals only.
7. Base of remedial teaching is evaluation not measurement.
8. Evaluation is more reliable, valid and objective than measurement.
9. Evaluation covers all the three domains of human behaviour while measurement covers only the cognitive aspects of human behaviour.
10. Evaluation is a value judgement process but measurement has no significance in itself unless data is compared with the criteria or norm.
11. Evaluation is basically concerned with the educational process while measurement is a universal phenomenon.

## TESTING

### Meaning

Testing means the subjection to condition that shows the real character of a person or thing in a certain particular situation. In practical term test is a series of questions or exercises that represents the attributes to be measured of an individual or group.

In psychology or education tests are the means by which evaluation or measurement is done and end is achieved. If we define a psychological test we can say that "a psychological test is a standardized instrument developed to measure objectively one or more aspects of a total personality by means of samples of verbal or non-verbal responses or by means of other behaviour. In the words of **Bean** (1953) "A test is an organised succession of stimuli designed to measure quantitatively or qualitatively some mental process, trait or characteristics."

The following characteristics of a test can be derived from the above definitions :

1. **Standardized instrument :** It means that data obtained from these tests can be transformed into standard scores or norms and can be developed to interpret it systematically. In standardized test, validity and reliability of the test are already well-calculated and it is very safe to use them due to minimum possibility of errors.
2. **Objectivity** : Personal errors are to the maximum extent eliminated in such tests. As a result whosoever use them will arrive at the same conclusion. Maximum objectivity can be maintained if test is highly valid and reliable.
3. **Measure of personality aspects** : Traits and attributes of personality are measured by these tests. A test generally measures one specific attribute but other attributes are also directly or indirectly measured by these tests. For example, intelligence test also measures knowledge, achievement, attitude and so on.
4. **Sampling** : Sampling of responses means designing appropriate verbal or non-verbal items of responses to manifest the desired attribute to the maximum level possible. Sampling of population means the test is designed and constructed to be used on a specific population of subjects to which the sample represents. Such tests are not universal at all.

   Thus, we see that psychological or educational tests measure quantitatively or qualitatively one or more of verbal or non-verbal behaviours and they are standardized for the purpose of maintaining accuracy. These tests aim at serving two-fold objectives.

   I. Comparing the same individual on two or more traits or attributes.

   II. Comparing two or more persons on the same traits.
5. **An organised succession of stimuli** : It means that stimuli (items) in the test are organised in a certain sequence and are based upon some principles of test construction. Usually they are placed in increasing order of difficulty and difficult items may be put in the middle in a speed test.
6. **Quantitative as well as qualitative nature of measurement** : The purpose of all these tests is either measurement or evaluation of comprehensive nature. Even qualities of the person can be converted into quantities for realisation of better accuracy. Thus, these tests are actually means to reach to ends, i.e., measurement or evaluation or both as the case may be.

## Characteristics of a Good Test (Evaluation)

If we want to measure an attribute accurately or we want to bring about an improvement in the evaluation process of pupils, we will have to keep this while constructing a test, i.e., test must possess the following characteristics. Good evaluation should also possess these very characteristics.

1. **Objectivity :** Objectivity means two things :
   (a) Whosover takes the test, attempts its items in the same manner. It is called objectivity in the test construction. The items of the test should not create any confusion in the minds of person being measured by the test.
   (b) Items (stimuli) are such that whosover evaluates them arrives at the same conclusion. It is called objectivity of scoring. It means that if marks are not influenced by the subjectivity of examiners, such tests are called objective tests.
2. **Reliability** : If the same test is given to the student again and again at different times, the examiner does not find any variation in the scores obtained by the examinee. It means that a test should assess a situation accurately free from any error.

   The basic difference between objectivity and reliability is that same test is evaluated by different examiners with no variation in scores in the former case but in the later case the same test is evaluated by the same examiner at different times but no variation is seen in the scores obtained.

3. **Validity** : A test should measure only what it is intended to measure, e.g., if a test wants to measure extroversion-introversion of the personality, it should measure nothing other than extroversion-introversion. Thus, purpose is always involved here. The test fulfils the purpose for which it has been designed.
4. **Discriminatory** : A test should be such as to discriminate poor, average and high achievers significantly. This is essential for giving proper guidance to students. It otherwise means that the scores obtained by a group of students in a given test should be such as to lay on normal probability curve.
5. **Comprehensive** : The items included in a test should fully represent all the aspects of a particular attribute so that complete information about a particular trait may be obtained. For example, if we are constructing an achievement test, it should cover all the three domains of human behaviour representing the whole course content or curriculum.
6. **Diagnostic** : A test should enable us to find out all the weaknesses of pupils' behaviour with reference to the course content. If we are able to diagnose the pin pointed difficulties of students, only then we can adopt remedial measures.
7. **Usability** : A test should be very easy to use for the person whosever wants to use it. Following points should be kept in mind for this purpose.
   I. Items included in the test should have the same meaning for different persons taking or evaluating the test. For example, Mr. B should also mean the same thing by the word " Natural instincts" as Mr. A means. It means that questions included in the test should have clear and objective language.
   II. Clear guidance should be given for administration of the test, e.g., maximum time limit should be specified beforehand.
   III. Methods of scoring and interpretation should also be made clear in advance in order to avoide subjectivity.
   IV. Norms or criterion should be given beforehand for the purpose of clear interpretation.
   V. No test in psychology or education can be universal in nature. Hence, its limitations such as the population to which sample belongs should be given.

## Classification of Psychological and Educational Tests

Different types of psychological and educational tests can be classified on different basis. Some of these basis are given below :

**(A) On the basis of mode of administration :** Following types of tests are included under this category :

1. **Speed Test :** In this test examinees must answer all the questions of the test within time limit or in the shortest time possible. He should not commit any mistake in attempting the item. Items included in such tests are equal in difficulty level. Clerical aptitude test is an example.
2. **Power Test :** Sufficient time is given to answer all the items in this test. Here items are arranged in increasing difficulty order and ability to solve all these questions are tested. Intelligence test is an example.
   The categorization of speed or power test is only arbitrary. Otherwise, speed test measures power when all the items are correctly attempted in the least time possible and power test becomes a speed test when easy items are correctly attempted in lesser time and the time thus saved is utilized to attempt difficult items. Once a time limit is fixed for a power test, it becomes a speed test.
3. **Individual Test :** This test can be administered to only one person at a time. Cube construction Test or any type of performance test is the example of such tests. If we examine the performance of more than one persons at a time, no exact evaluation of the process will be possible, though evaluation of the product may be there at the end of the performance.
4. **Group test :** These types of tests can be administered to more than one persons at a time. Group intelligence tests, achievement tests etc are some examples. In these tests directions are so clear that no explanation is needed in the middle of the test.
5. **Oral Test (Viva Voce):** Here instruction as well as questions to be answered are presented to the examinees orally and they also give oral response

to these questions. Thus, direct interaction is seen between the examiner and the examinees.

6. **Written test:-** Here, written answers are giving by the examinees.

**(B) On the basis of Scoring** : Following types of tests are included under this category :

1. **Essay (Free answer) type test :** Such items are included in these tests which require free thinking and presentation to answer the questions in whatsoever manner the examinee likes. Organizational ability of the content is needed in these tests. When these tests are evaluated, we always see subjectivity in scoring. If one examiner puts the examinee below the fail border, the other examiner may give him 60% marks.
2. **Objective (New) type test :** Items in these tests are constructed in such a manner that only one correct response is possible of these tests and no involvement of subjectivity is possible when these tests are evaluated and scored by the examiner. Whosoever scores these tests will arrive at the same conclusion.

**(C) On the basis of usability** : Such test can be classified into two categories :

1. **Standardized tests :** These tests must have gone through the procedure of standardization, i.e.,
   (a) There is standard manner of instructions in these tests so that uniformity can be maintained in the standard of those who take the test.
   (b) Reliability and validity of the test are calculated in advance.
   (c) Norms of the test is also prepared.
   (d) There is uniformity and clear guidelines in scoring.
   (e) These tests are constructed by specialists and they are administered and scored under uniform and standard testing condition so that results obtained from different samples may be easily compared.
2. **Teacher made tests :** They are constructed by the teacher who teaches the class for classroom purposes. The effectiveness of such tests depends upon the skill of the teacher and his experience of test construction. Rules for administration and scoring are also determined by the teacher. These tests are evaluated by the teacher himself.

**(D) On the basis of nature or content of items :** Following types of tests are included in this category:

1. **Verbal tests :** Items of these tests require reading, writing and oral expression. Language is needed for communication here. **Jalota's Group intelligence test** is an example. Such tests are called paper pencil tests also because examinees are required to use pencil to write on a paper.
2. **Non-verbal test :** Symbolic materials like figures, pictures, lines etc are used in these tests but instructions are given by using language itself. **Raven Progressive Matrix** is an example of this test. These tests are used to measure special relationship or in those conditions when language may be a problem for the examinee.
3. **Non-language tests :** They are those tests which do not depend upon any form of written or spoken language or reading communication. Language is not used in any way in these tests. Instructions to the examinees are given by gestures and they respond these gestures by manipulating the objects. These tests are generally used for deaf and dumb persons.
4. **Performance tests :** In these tests examinees are required to perform a task rather than answering some questions. Instructions in these tests are given by using language as well as gestures. For example, an examinee may be asked to put different kinds of pictures in correct sequence, he may be asked to draw the picture of a cow or to prepare the model of a house and so on. Generally, product not the process is evaluated here.

**(E) On the basis of specific purpose of test construction** : These tests are designed and constructed to serve very specific purpose such as, to measure a particular trait or attribute of the examinee. Some of these tests are given below :

1. **Diagnostic Tests :** They are constructed to find out the difficulty areas of learning faced by the pupils to give them remedial measures. Difficulty areas can also be divided into different sub-categories and separate items are used for each area.
2. **Aptitude test :** Such tests measure what a person can do in future on the basis of his present abilities. Thus, they actually serve a predictive function. On the basis of these tests such abilities are identified which are essential to perform a

particular task. Able and non-able persons are differentiated by these tests.

3. **Achievement tests :** Such tests are designed to measure the extent to which the objectives of a particular course content have been achieved. Objective or essay type tests in written or oral form is used for this purpose.
4. **Proficiency test :** These tests aim at measuring the general ability of a person at a given time. It can tell us about those abilities which a particular person, e.g., a graduate or an engineer should posses regarding his field. This test is not restricted to any specific course content that a degree holder has passed. In this sense it is different from achievement test. Competitive tests for the purpose of selecting persons who can do varied nature of jobs are examples of such tests.
5. **Intelligence test :** These tests measure only one attribute (intelligence) of the person being measured just in order to know whether the person can achieve cognitive objectives of teaching or not.

**(F) Personality inventories and adjustment tests:** Some of these tests are given below :

1. **Personality inventories :** Some personality inventories measure only one aspect of the personality and some of them measure more than one. For example, Maslow's 'Security Insecurity Scale' measures 16 aspects of the personality.
2. **Interactive methods :** Questionnaires, interviews and rating scales are included in this category. Sometimes, in order to measure the patience of the examinee, irritating questions are asked from them and then they are rated by the examiner.
3. **Projective techniques :** Psychologists have developed these tests in order to explore the inner structure of the personality. Important such tests are word association test, sentence completion test, TAT, CAT, Rorschach Inkblot tests and so on. Here the examinees do not know that their personality is being measured by some one.
4. **Situational tests :** Here examinee is taken to a particular situation and he is observed participantly or non-participantly. He is required to do such a task, the purpose of which is not known to him.
5. **Interest inventories :** Interest is also an important aspect of personality. Interests of person in a particular field are measured by these inventories. Chaterjee's non-verbal interest profile is an example of this test.

# Aptitude and Achievement Tests

## MEANING OF APTITUDE

What a person can do at present and is expected to do in future under certain circumstances after a learning or training is related to aptitude. It indicates the capacity of an individual to acquire specific knowledge, skills or set of organised experiences. Ability to speak a foreign language after training is an example of language aptitude.

Aptitude has a close link with 'S' factors of intelligence not G factor. It helps us to determine whether a person can do a particular job or not. If a person is very poor on a teaching aptitude test, he is not expected to perform well on teacher training course. He may rather fail in it.

### Definitions of Aptitude

1. **Warren :** Aptitude may be defined as a condition or set of characteristics regarded as symptomatic of an individual's ability to acquire with training some specified knowledge, skill or set of responses such as, the ability to speak a language or to produce music and so on.
2. **Bingham :** Aptitude is a condition symptomatic of a person's fitness of which one essential aspect is his readiness to acquire proficiency, his potential ability and another is his readiness to develop an interest in exercising his ability.

### Characteristics of Aptitude

I. Aptitude includes inborn as well as acquired capacities of an individual. But if a person is deficient in a particular aptitude by birth, he can not be compensated with this aptitude just by training.

II. Aptitude is readiness to acquire proficiency or skill and learner's readiness to learn can be increased by conditioning the learning of the learner. Conditioning makes a person habitual to do a job almost mechanically and situation is generalized later.

III. A specific aptitude in the form of talent may show itself early and respond readily to training in future.

IV. Aptitude is an abstract phenomenon but can be inferred from the behaviour of a person even if he deals with concrete materials.

V. It is the present condition of a person with a future reference and it is symptomatic of potentialities.

VI. There are individual differences in potentialities. Hence, people differ not only in different kinds of aptitudes but they also differ in degrees for the same aptitude.

VII. The aptitude of a person is fairly stable but it can be improved by giving proper training.

VIII. Aptitude implies the prediction about the future performance of an individual. If a person scores high on numerical aptitude test, he is likely to score high in the subject of mathematics in future and vice versa.

IX. Individual differences in the society implies that certain aptitudes are unevenly distributed among individuals.

X. Aptitudes can be measured by employing various aptitude tests. These tests are very much helpful for the selection of people in a job. It is because aptitude means an individual's aptitude for a given type of activity. If aptitude is there, individual will be able to do that activity otherwise not.

## TYPES OF APTITUDE TEST

Aptitude test may be classified into two categories :

1. **Multiple Aptitude Tests (MAT) :**
   They are those tests which intend to measure several aptitudes at a time. Thus, MAT are not tests but they are rather batteries of tests.
2. **Special Aptitude Tests (SAT) :** They are those tests which intend to measure only one aptitude of a person. Among the earliest aptitude tests was the mechanical aptitude test. Such type of tests were developed when special emphasis was given on the general intelligence test and it was thought that for describing the individual measurement of intelligence, it must be supplemented by the measurement of special aptitude. But later on Thurstone and Guilford revealed that intelligence itself consists of several independent special aptitudes. As a result people shifted from special aptitude tests to multiple aptitude tests again.

### Important Multiple Aptitude Tests

Some representative multiple aptitude tests are given below :

1. **Differential Aptitude Test (DAT) :** This battery of multiple aptitude test was published in 1947 by **Bennett, Seashore** and others. It has been revised several times since then and fifth revised edition of the battery came in 1973. It comprises eight subtests—verbal reasoning, numerical ability, abstract reasoning, mechanical reasoning, clerical speed and accuracy, space relations, spelling and language usage. The battery is especially meant for educational and vocational guidance for students ranging from class VIIIth to XIIth. The whole battery has two equivalent forms S and T and administration time of the test is three hours.
   Scores on each sub-test are converted into percentile ranks for their proper interpretation. The composite scores of all these sub-tests are also transformed into percentile ranks.
2. **General Aptitude Test Battery (GATB) :** It is also an important multiple aptitude test developed by the United States Employment Service in 1962 to scrutinize the people for armed services. In this battery, 59 tests were correlated by factor analysis and 10 factors were chosen. In the later revision of the tests, these factors were reduced to 9 to be measured by 12 tests. These nine factors are as follows :
   I. General Intelligence (G)
   II. Numerical aptitude (N)
   III. Verbal aptitude (V)
   IV. Spatial aptitude (S)
   V. Form perception (P)
   VI. Clerical Perception (Q)
   VII. Motor Coordination (K)
   VIII. Finger dexterity (F)
   IX. Manual dexterity(M)
   Out of 12 tests developed for the purpose 8 are verbal and 4 are non-verbal. The scores obtained on the nine tests of GATB can be converted into a standard score with a mean of 100 and SD of 20 for the purpose of interpretation.
   The only limitations of the battery are that these tests are highly speeded and some important aptitudes have not been included in the battery, such as mechanical aptitude is not there in the battery.
3. **Flanagan Aptitude Classification Test (FACT):** It is the third multiple aptitude test. This battery was developed by Flanagan for the purpose of providing vocational counselling and selection of employees. He identified 21 job elements that discriminated significantly between successful and unsuccessful workers on each job. He developed verbal tests for measuring 19 job elements and remaining two elements were measured by performance tests. The complete administration of the test requires more than 10 ½ hours in three testing sessions.

### Important Special Aptitude Test

Special aptitude tests are preferred to multiple aptitude tests today due to the following reasons :

I. Special aptitude tests provide more flexibility in the choice of the relevant test than the multiple aptitude batteries.
II. There are certain areas of aptitudes which are rarely covered by multiple aptitude batteries. For example, artistic talents, musical talents, creative potentials etc are generally not included in the test batteries.

III. It is safer to select people for a job or admission in a particular course on the basis of special aptitude tests than that of multiple test batteries due to the specificity of the areas needed to be tested.

**Some important special aptitude tests are given below :**

1. **Sensory Tests :** Sensory tests were first devised by Galton and others to measure intelligence though in vague form. With the development of standardized intelligence tests sensory tests have lost its value as a measure of intelligence. They are only used now as a measure of sensitivity of sense organs like ear, eyes, nose etc.
   Take the example of vision. It is not a unitary capacity. It has several dimensions and a person who is normal in one dimension may be handicapped in another dimension. For example, a person is normal in vision (6/6) but he may be a colour blind or night blind. Similarly, near or far visual acuity are also two important dimension of vision. The most common method of measuring far acuity is the wall chart which is technically known as **Snellen Chart.** It consists of row of letters of gradually decreasing size as we see in any eye hospitals. It is generally placed at a distance of 20 feet and the person is asked to read the letters. If the person is able to read only the first line his vision will be 6/60. Sixth line reading capacity shows visual acuity of 6/6. Near acuity of vision is measured by giving the person to read a book at a distance of 15 to 18 inches and his near vision is calculated.
   Audition is also considered as being multi-dimensional. The most important dimension is auditory acuity which is generally measured by pure tone audiometers. Different points of sound frequencies are presented to the person and his reactions are noted down. In testing auditory acuity by this instrument only one ear is tested at a time. The investigator first starts with a sound frequency too low to be heard by the testee. Then frequencies are gradually increased until the testee perceives the sound clearly. **Massachusetts Hearing Test** is now used to measure auditory acuity in children.
2. **Artistic Aptitude Tests :** Two types of artistic aptitudes are commonly investigated here. One is related to artistic appreciation and other is concerned with the productive ability of the person. Due to this distinction, two separate types of tests have been developed. The assumption here is that a person may have a better sense of appreciation of artistic figures but he may or may not have the ability to draw a picture himself. So, separate tests of artistic aptitude are essential.
   **Meier Art Judgement Test** Developed by Meier in 1929 is an important artistic aptitude test. According to him this aptitude consists of six inter-related traits. ie., manual skill, aesthetic intelligence, volitional perseverance, cognitive imagination, perceptual ability and aesthetic judgement. In this test each item consists of two very identical paintings or drawings. One of the paintings of each pair was produced by reputed painter and another was produced by ordinary painter. Now the examinee is asked.to choose the most appealing painting out of the two and give his comments. He is now evaluated on the basis of the extent to which his opinions are in agreement with the opinions of the specialists. This is known as the judgement of aesthetic organisation, an important factor in artistic ability.
   **Hom Art Aptitude Inventory** is another important aesthetic aptitude test. The test is a measure of the ability to produce graphic arts. It measures the ability to produce original drawing or painting. The test is consisted of two parts. In the first part the examinee is asked to draw 20 drawings of very common objects and of geometric figures in a specified period of time. This is known as scribble and doodle test. The second part consists of 12 rectangles each containing a few stimulus lines. The examinee is required to make a drawing in each rectangle and his drawing must include these stimulus lines. This is known as imagery test. Then the drawings of the examinee are scored by one or two experts subjectively.
3. **Mechanical Aptitude Test :** This type of test is widely concerned with mechanical information, mechanical reasoning and mechanical

comprehension. This aptitude is further sub-divided into two parts—perceptual aptitude and spatial aptitude. **Minnesota Paper Form Board** Test is an example of mechanical aptitude test.

4. **Teaching Aptitude Tests :** It is very difficult to device such tests because of the following reasons:
   I. Teaching properties and skills are not well-defined.
   II. Teaching encompasses a very wide range of subject-matter and educational levels.
   III. Suitable personality traits are also needed for a successful teaching.

**Generally teaching aptitude tests cover the following areas :**

I. General mental ability.
II. General awareness and general knowledge of all school subjects.
III. Language and communication ability.
IV. Numerical ability and logical reasoning.
V. Spatial relation.
VI. Specialization of subjects at the graduation level.

**Two teaching aptitude tests are very common:**

I. Teacher Education Examination Programme
II. Graduate Record Examination Advanced Test

## MEANING OF ACHIEVEMENT

Achievement refers to what a person has acquired or achieved after being imparted specific training or instruction. In other words, learning outcomes or end products are the other name of achievement. Aptitude tests is conducted prior to training or instruction and achievement test is conducted after the training or instruction.

### Meaning of Achievement Tests

"Achievement test is constructed to measure the effects or efficiency of a specific programme of instruction or training". **(Anastasi 1968)**

Thus, the performance of a person on an achievement test indicates his performance under known and controlled conditions because this performance is the end product of specific training or instruction given to him in a specific field and it can be evaluated by oral or written achievement tests. The achievement of students are first quantified with the help of the responses given by them and then this quantitative data are converted into qualitative ones by assigning grades or by comparing them with the criterion measure or by comparing them the objectives formulated prior to training or instruction. Finally, the results of the examinees are declared for the purpose of giving feedback to teachers, students and guardians.

### Distinction between Aptitude and Achievement Tests

I. Aptitude test is a person's ability innate or acquired to learn or develop knowledge of a skill in some specific areas. Here his present ability is measured to determine his future achievement. Achievement test refers to what a person has acquired or achieved after a specific training or instruction. Here a person's past is measured to determine his future—successful or unsuccessful.

II. The performance on the achievement test indicates the performance under known and controlled conditions. Performance on the aptitude test indicates the performance which is the product of multiplicity of experiences of everyday life, ie, the effects of learning under unknown and uncontrolled conditions.

III. Aptitude test is future oriented while achievement test is present and past oriented dealing with the proficiency of a person in certain training or instruction. Thus, the primary purpose of an aptitude test is to predict what a person can learn whereas the primary objective of an achievement (proficiency) test is to evaluate what a person has learned after training or instruction. In other words, aptitude tests are psychometric tests and proficiency tests are endumetric tests. A psychometric test is one whose major function is to measure individual differences and an endumetric test is one whose major function is to measure the gain or growth of an individual.

IV. A psychometric test can also function as an endumetric test and vice versa. For example, when a numerical aptitude test is used for the purpose of producing the future numerical ability of a person, it would be considered as psychometric test but when the same test is used to measure the numerical ability of a person as a function of some training or instruction, it would be considered as endumetric test.

V. Achievement tests are constructed by taking the learning objectives into account but aptitude tests are constructed by taking the products' objectives into account.

As far as the distinction between intelligence test and achievement test is concerned, they are also the same as given above. It is because aptitude test and intelligence test differ only in their functioning not in their scope or objectives.

## Uses of Achievement Test

1. **Diagnostic use :** Achievement test is an effective measure to detect the weaknesses of the instruction (teacher's defects) and the shortcomings of the learner (students' defects). If weakness is found in the instruction, the teacher is asked to change his strategy or behaviour. If weakness is found in the learner, the teacher is again asked to find out the probable causes for future improvement. If low achievement of learners is associated with low level of intelligence, teacher is not blamed for the defect. He is rather asked to pay more attention to these students.
2. **Matching use :** Educational objectives are first formulated before starting an instruction or training. Achievement tests are constructed in the light of these objectives and they are matched with these objectives by the process of scoring. If educational objectives are not realized, we critically examine the content and methods of instruction both. In this way, we can find out the adequacy of the content (syllabi) with reference to age of children and suitability of teachers' behaviour in the class.
3. **Guidance to students :** Achievement or proficiency tests can classify a particular class into several groups like poor, average and high achievers. After doing this we can adapt our instruction according to the individual needs of students. We can also provide systematic guidance to different groups of learners on the basis of results on achievement tests.
4. **Qualitative categorization of students :** On the basis of performance on achievement test, the students of particular class can be qualitatively classified into different categories by assigning grades to students in different subjects. For example, a student may score 70 marks in Hindi and 95 marks in Mathematics but he may have A grade in both the subjects if range of scores in Mathematics is very high.
5. **Decision of pass or fail :** If achievement test has been conducted at the end of the session, the scores obtained by students on achievement test will determine their future. They will either be promoted to the next class if they are passed or they will be retained in the same class if they are failed.
6. **Vocational Guidance :** Marks obtained by students in different subjects determine their specific interests and aptitudes in different subjects. On the basis of these scores we can guide them to select a particular subject in the next class or choose a course after Xth and XIIth or after graduation or PG.

## Classification of Achievement Tests

Achievement tests can be classified into two major categories:

1. **General Achievement Batteries :** These batteries tend to measure the general educational achievement in several areas of the school curriculum. They can be used from primary to the higher classes. Some of the important achievement batteries are **Iowa** Test of Educational Development, California Achievement tests, **Iowa** Test of basic skills and SRA Achievement Services. All these batteries emphasize, numerical skills, reading and writing skills, spelling, map and graph reading skills etc. Adult Basic Learning Examination is also an important battery of achievement tests especially meant for undergraduate adults. It consists of four

subjects vocabulary, reading, spelling and arithmetic.

2. **Special Achievement Test :** It is meant for measuring the achievement of students in some selected areas. It can be sub divided into two categories— diagnostic tests and standardized end of course examination.

A diagnostic test is one whose primary purpose is to identify the educationally retarded pupils and to suggest remedial programmes for them accordingly. Such tests are available in special areas like reading skills, mathematical skills, grammatical skills and so on. Stanford Diagnostic Reading Test is an example. It is a group test and is meant for elementary school children. Different dimensions of the reading skills like reading speed, comprehension, vocabulary and word recognition skills are measured by this test.

Standardized end of course examinations are the coordinated series of achievement tests for different subjects taught at high school or college level. These series provide the system of comparable norms for all the tests. In this way, a direct comparison of scores obtained by the same examinee in different subjects is possible here. For the purpose of comparison, raw scores are transformed into standard scores with a fixed mean and SD.

## Limitations of Achievement Tests

I. They can not be taken as the sole basis of taking a decision to promote a student to the next higher class because most of the achievement tests are not fool proof measures of achievement. There are many other determinant factors of class-room achievement tests.

II. The standardization of the achievement tests is a tedious and complex job. So, they are very difficult to construct as compared to intelligence or aptitude tests.

III. Results on achievement tests are sometimes taken as measure of teacher's effectiveness but this is not the correct interpretation of the result because factors affecting pupils' performance are many of which teacher's quality is only one.

IV. It is very difficult to eliminate the influence of personal factors of the test maker. So, reliability of the test is always questionable.

## Two Written Forms of Achievement Tests

**(A) Essay Type Tests :** Expression and organizational abilities of students, their writing beauty, speed and their language abilities are evaluated by these types of tests. In such type of tests much importance is given to logical, sequential and creative presentation of subject-matter. The question here are formed in such a manner that their answers take the form of essays. The evaluation of organizational abilities and logical presentation of subject-matter is most important here and writing beauty and speed are emphasised by those examiners who are poor in evaluation skills and give more emphasis on these skills.

In such type of tests, the mood of the examiner, his attitude and way of thinking towards the purpose of the test and his personal opinion about the examinees play very important role and hence affect the scoring. Consequently, if an examiner gives 70% to an examinee on any essay type answer, another examiner may allot 40% marks or less on the same response, that make the essay type tests highly subjective and unreliable.

**Advantages of Essay type tests :**

1. **Easy Construction :** The construction of these tests need not require high level of skills in test construction and they can be constructed in less time also. The test maker should only know how to frame a question from the given content.
2. **Development of study habits :** In order to answer these tests, students have to know about the facts, informations and principles in detail and in a deep manner. They can not answer these questions just by guessing, recognition or simple recall. All these things develop their study habits.
3. **Measurement of high mental abilities and higher levels of educational objectives :** Logical thinking, creative, analytical, critical and evaluative mental abilities of students can be measured by these tests very effectively which is not possible by applying objective type tests. Thus, highest level of cognitive and affective domains can be measured by these tests very effectively.

4. **Measurement of expressive organizational abilities and presentation style** : Different students may organise and present a subject-matter in different ways. Out of them some presentation may be more impressive than the others. The examiner can measure all these abilities very easily through these tests which is not possible with the help of objective type tests.
5. **Improvement of writing style and language abilities :** Language abilities and writing style improve slowly and this is manifested in the answer of essay type tests. An examiner can measure through these tests how much improvement in the language and writing style has taken place.
6. **Measurement of teacher's proficiency** : A teacher presents his subject-matter in the class in the form of lectures, narrations, descriptions and discussion. So, the performance of students on essay type tests reflect the performance of a teacher in the class. How seriously a teacher has taken his teaching and what abilities he has developed in his students can be easily measured through these tests.
7. **Control of cheating in the examination hall :** The answers of these questions are so long that students do not have time to copy them from the answer-books of other students. So conduct of examination is very easy here. If a student takes the help of any unfair means to copy down his answers, he will not be able to complete the tests in the stipulated time. So he can not get good marks just by cheating.
8. **Qualitative assessment** : Essay type tests emphasize more on qualitative assessment of students than quantitative one. Every student writes the answer in his own way and gives as many arguments as he can.

**Demerits of Essay type tests**

1. **Difficult to match them with the objectives:** Whatever objectives are formulated and defined before the construction of such tests can not be totally incorporated in the test because of the long answers of questions. Similarly, sometime students are unable to understand till the last what they have been asked by a particular question due to vague nature of evaluation objectives. However, they are most suited to teaching objectives in the class.
2. **Lack of representation of the whole syllabus** : Generally five or six questions are given to the examinees to answer in three hours. These little number of questions can not represent the total syllabus. Many of the lessons and sometimes a full unit are entirely left untouched.
3. **Emphasis on craming** : In order to pass these types of tests students cram some selected questions from the total syllabus without comprehending the total syllabus. They even leave out the questions asked last or before last year and thus they have very limited knowledge of the subject-matter.
4. **Emphasis on writing beauty and speed :** These tests measure many other things such as writing beauty and speed along with the knowledge of the subject-matter. Many examiners allot good marks to those students whose writing is fine though their knowledge of the subject-matter is very poor. Thus, validity of essay type tests are always at stake.
5. **Subjectivity :** These tests are highly subjective in the sense that examiner's thinking, attitude, mood and his own attachment with the examinee, etc. affect the scoring. For example, if his mood is good in the morning he may give good marks to the examinees but if his mood is disturbed in the evening due to some reasons, he may fail many students by his scoring. Similarly, different examiners score the examinees differently.
6. **Invalid :** Such tests measure many other things than the subject-matter learnt by the students. For example, his way of presentation and organizational ability of the subject-matter, his language ability and writing speed etc are also measured. Hence, essay type tests are not valid tests in real sense.
7. **Not reliable :** These tests are not reliable in the sense that the same examiner may score the same examinee in different ways at different periods of time.
8. **Incomplete answer :** Sometimes students do not give complete answers to the questions even then

their answers are considered complete due to non-specificity of questions.

9. **Difficulty in Evaluation :** The construction of these tests are easy but their evaluation is very difficult. It takes much time and energy to evaluate these tests. Besides, specific and clear cut norms are also not available for the evaluation of these tests. Faking from the part of the examiner is another problem when he scores these tests just by counting of pages not by reading the material.
10. **Costly :** Since mechanical scoring or scoring by computer is not possible here, the administrative and evaluation costs of these tests are very high. No examiner can evaluate more than 40 copies of essay type test a day.

**How to improve Essay Type Tests**

1. If questions are divided into different segments and each segment covers only one learning objective, then most of the subjectivity of this type of tests can be reduced. Even teaching process can also be improved later with the help of these tests.
2. Questions should be asked from every lesson and unit of the syllabus. These questions may be divided into segments. This will reduce the problem of guessing on the part of the examinees and will compel them to study the whole syllabus.
3. Questions should be asked in a clear and behavioural language and limits of each part of the question should also be fixed.
4. A mixture of easy, average and difficult questions should be included in the test so that all types of students may get feedback from them.
5. Maximum marks for each part of the question should be fixed in advance so that these questions may be evaluated properly.
6. Key of essay type tests should be prepared by the test maker in advance and it should be supplied to all those who evaluate the test.
7. Marks obtained by the students in essay type test should be according to the pattern of normal probability curve. If it is not so, it should be considered the defects of evaluation.
8. The examiner should be honest and free from bias. His personal opinion should not be reflected in the scoring and he should not assign marks on the basis of counting of pages.

If all these suggestions are taken into consideration, many of the defects of essay type tests can be removed.

**(B) Objective Type Tests :** These tests are called objective because whosoever evaluates them, will arrive at the same conclusion. There is a definite answer of each questions here and examinee can not manipulate them according to his own wish. If answer is right, he will get full marks and if it is wrong, he will be assigned zero, i.e, no variation or manipulation of scoring is possible here.

Objective type tests can be classified into two categories. (a) Recall type (b) Recognition type.

**(a) Recall Type :** Important recall type questions are given below :

1. **Simple recall type :** Students answer these types of questions on the basis of their memory, previous knowledge and experience. Every question has a definite answer here :

   **Examples :**

   I. Where was Akbar born ( )
   II. Who conquered South first ( )
   III. Where is Indian Parliament located ( )

2. **Completion Type :** Here, incomplete statements are given to students, i.e., some words or phrases are deliberately left here, and students are asked to fill the gap on the basis of their knowledge.

   **Examples :**

   I. The sum of all the three angles of a triangle is..........
   II. There are ..............domain of behaviour isolated by the psychologists.
   III. All metals are hard except...............

***Merits of recall type questions :***

I. The answer of these types of questions can not be given on the basis of guessing or idea. They require the recall of real knowledge or experience.
II. The construction and scoring of these questions are also easy.
III. Subjectivity has no role to play. Whosoever evaluates them will arrive at the same conclusion.

IV. Faking is not possible here either on the part of the examiner or the examinee.

*Demerits of such tests :*

I. Only knowledge or understanding objectives can be evaluated by these tests.

II. If more than one blanks are given in an item, it creates confusion.

III. The attitude and thoughts of students can not be assessed by these tests. They answer only what they were taught earlier. Thus, independent manipulation and free association of answers is not possible here.

**(b) Recognition Type :** Important recognition type tests are given below :

**1. True/False Type :** In such type of tests, a number of statements are given to students and true and false are written against each of them. Students are then asked to mark (v) against true items on the basis of their acquired knowledge.

**Examples :**

I. The name of Akbar's father was Humayun. (True/false)

II. Software technology of teaching is related to teaching strategies. (True/false)

III. The success of the principal in a school lies in his power of controlling and supervision. (True/false)

*Merits of the Test:*

I. The construction of these test is very easy and they can be used for all school and college subjects.

II. These types of questions can be answered hurriedly and their scoring also takes less time with the help of machines.

III. Upto second level of educational objectives can be evaluated by these tests.

*Demerits of the Test :*

I. The major defect of these types of tests is that one option is to be chosen out of two given options. So, there is 50% probability of the answers being correct. An examinee can score 50% marks in these tests without knowing any facts.

II. These tests are suitable only to small children who need motivation by high percentage of marks.

III. It reduces study habits of students.

**2. Multiple choice questions :** These questions are framed either in the form of statement or in interrogative form. Every question or statement is followed by four alternative responses out of which only one response option is correct. The examinee selects the best option on the basis of his memory or understanding.

**Examples :**

I. An aptitude test differs from an achievement test in the process of
(a) objectives involved
(b) learning involved
(c) administration
(d) all of the above

II. Which of the following teaching aids is most suitable from the point of view of costs?
(a) Computer (b) Internet
(c) TV (d) Radio

*Merits of the Test :*

I. Objectives upto analysis level can be evaluated by these tests. The only conditions is that test maker is fully trained in constructing such tests.

II. Chances of giving correct answer on the basis of guessing only is reduced here as compared to true/false type tests. There is only 25% chance that a guessed item is correct. If options are increased to five, then guessing will be reduced to 20%.

III. Scoring of the test can be done very rapidly here with the help of machines or computers.

IV. If response options has been constructed skillfully, they can not be answered without right knowledge.

*Demerits of the Test :*

I. These type of questions can not be used in all subjects covering all types of contents. For example, construction of a geometrical figure is not possible by these tests.

II. The construction of these tests is very difficult and time taking. Besides, try out is also essential here for the purpose of item analysis and calculation of norms.

III. Chance of 25% guessing is here because of the four alternative responses. This problem can be overcome by assigning minus marks for all the wrong answers.

**3. Matching type tests :** Two columns A and B are given in this type of tests. Questions are generally given in column A and their responses are given in column B but in a haphazard way. Then students are required to match the items of column A with those of column B.

**Example :**

**Q. Match the following.**

| A | B |
|---|---|
| I. The biggest country in the world (in area) | (a) Aptitude test |
| II. Fruit of least nutritive value | (b) Kukamber |
| III. Ancient physicist of India | (c) Charak |
| IV. Predicting future ability of students | (d) Russia |

**Note :** If every column has at least five items then the test can evaluate the achievement of students very accurately.

***Merits of the Test :***

I. A number of knowledge and understanding areas can be evaluated simultaneously by this test.

II. These questions are very suitable for why, when, where, what, and who situation.

III. The possibility of guessing can be reduced to less than 10% by increasing the number of items in column A or B.

***Demerits of the Test***

I. Only knowledge and understanding levels of objectives can be evaluated here.

II. The scoring and analysis of test scores are very difficult here.

III. In such questions one answer helps the examinee to give right answer of other items. For example, if we know three facts and does not know the fourth one, even then we can attempt the question correctly.

**4. Classification type tests :** In such test such a group of words, numbers or facts are presented before the students that one of them looks odd among the group. The examinee finds the odd one out on the basis of his knowledge or experience.

**Example :**

Q. Find the odd one out from among the following.

1. 144, 169, 27, 196, 225
2. But, shut, hut, put, nut,

**Answers :**

1. 27 is the only cube (3) here. Others are squares.
2. Put differs in the pronunciation here.

***Merits of the Test:***

1. The cognitive thinking and logical ability of students can be developed by these tests.
2. Upto synthesis level of objectives can be evaluated by these tests.
3. The interest and attitudes of the students can also be evaluated and measured by these tests.

***Demerits of the Test :***

1. Questions based on all types of subject-matter can not be framed here.
2. Sometimes more than one logics can be applied in selecting the odd item from the test. In that case a correct answer may be wrong if it does not match with the key available.
3. The construction of these questions is very difficult.

**5. Analogy Tests :** Here the relationship between the two terms is established on the basis of the relations given in the question.

**Example :** If LIKE is written as IKLE, how will you write BIKE

Answer = IKBE

## Other Features of Objective Type Tests

Some important and common characteristics of objective type tests are as follows :

1. **Objectively :** Whosover evaluates these tests will arrive at the same conclusion, i.e., the marking of students will not differ with the change of the examiner.
2. **Validity :** These tests measure only that situation or trait which they intend to measure. Non-desirable situations are not measured here.

3. **Reliability :** If the same examiner repeats the assessment of these tests again and again the results of the examinee do not differ at all.
4. **Economy of time :** The scoring of these tests can be done very accurately and at a very fast speed with the help of the computer. One thousand copies can be evaluated in one hour.
5. **Discriminatory :** It can discriminate the slow learners from the bright ones very easily. In essay type tests, on the other hand, baring a few students all the students of the class give the same type of answer and hence they get almost same marks.
6. **Representative to the whole course content :** Questions from the whole syllabus can be asked by using objective type tests.

## Common Demerits of Objectives Type Tests

1. **Limited applicability :** Only some objectives of cognitive domain can be covered by these tests and they are helpless to measure the objectives of affective and psychomotor domains. Moreover, they cannot be applied on all the subjects of the curriculum.
2. **Chance of mass copying :** We can not control cheating and copying in the examination hall in such types of tests. Students tick the right answers by taking the help of their neighbours. If more than three sets of papers are prepared to eliminate copying, validity of the test may be very poor.
3. **Difficulty in construction :** The construction of these tests is very difficult and it requires special skills on the part of the test maker. It is also very time consuming to construct them. If we have to construct 100 items of a test it may take more than 10 hours to construct.
4. **It can not measure organizational ability :** The organizational ability of the examinees can not be evaluated by these tests. If essay type tests are completely eliminated from the examination system, students will forget how to present the subject-matter in a logical and convincing style.
5. **Chance of Guessing :** If options are available here, students can answer a question without knowing any thing about the item just by the technique of guessing. For example, if an examinee has selected all the (b) option in a multiple choice test, about 30% of his answers may be correct.
6. **Incomplete evaluation :** The answers which are given by the students in these tests are so incomplete that complete information about the students can not be obtained.
7. **Reduces study habits :** If students know that they will be evaluated by only objective type tests, they do not go through the books or texual material seriously and thoroughly. They only memorize those facts which can be included in an objective type test and hence their study habits are badly affected.

# Validity and Its Estimation

## MEANING OF VALIDITY

The process of gathering evidence to determine what a test score implies is known as validation. If a test measures only what it intends to measure, the test is said to be fully valid.

Every test is constructed keeping certain objectives in mind. This test is valid only for that purpose to the extent it measures the same thing for which it was constructed. In this sense no test is 100% valid. The validity coefficient of a test may vary from place to place, from situation to situation and from time to time. But if it fulfils the purpose for which it has been constructed, it is called valid and the degree of validity will depend upon the degree of fulfilling the purpose.

**Definitions**

1. **Gulliksen :** "Validity is the correlation of the test with some criterion".
2. **Freeman :** "The first necessary condition of a valid test is that it must have an adequate degree of reliability. If reliability coefficient of a test is zero, it can not correlate with anything."
3. **Lee Chronbach :** "Validity is the extent to which a test measures what it purports to measure."
4. **Thorndike :** "A measurement procedure is valid so far as it correlates with some measures of success in the job for which it is being used as a predictor."

### Characteristics of a Valid Test

On the basis of the definitions given above we can derive the following characteristics of a valid test :

I. It measures exactly what it wants to measure. For example, an intelligence test should not measure anything other than intelligence.

II. A test can be valid only when it has high degree of reliability. If it is not giving almost the same result again and again, it can never be valid. It does not, however, mean that a highly reliable test is always valid. It may be totally invalid.

III. A valid test can be compared with some accepted criteria and high degree of correlation means the test is valid. This external criteria may be success in a job, ability to study a particular course and so on.

IV. It is the degree to which it measures what it intends to measure. No test in psychology or education can be perfectly valid due to indirect nature of measurement of human attributes or behaviour.

V. Validity ensures reliability also. If a test is valid, it must be reliable.

## CLASSIFICATION OF VALIDITIES

**1. Cronbach's classification**

(a) Content Validity
(b) Concurrent Validity
(c) Predictive Validity
(d) Construct Validity

**2. Freeman's classification**

(a) Operational Validity
(b) Functional Validity
(c) Factorial Validity
(d) Face Validity

**3. Ross's classification**

(a) Predictive Validity
(b) Concurrent Validity
(c) Content Validity
(d) Construct Validity

**4. Green's classification**

(a) Curricular Validity
(b) Statistical Validity
(c) Logical Validity

We will discuss some of these types of Validities below :

## 1. Logical Validity

Logic means consistency of thoughts. There are two methods of ascertaining this validity.

(a) Deductive method : We proceed from general to particular here. In this method we cross-examine whether the items of the test correspond to the definition of the trait being measured. If traits are defined in behavioural terms and items of the test match to each segment of the term, the test is said to be logically valid.

(b) Inductive method : Here we proceed from particular to general. In this method, we assign the name of the trait on the basis of the items included in the test. Thus, items defining the trait are constructed one by one and a group of items measure a particular trait.

**Factors affecting logical validity :** Certain intervening factors affecting logical validity are as follows :

**(a) Advance knowledge of a particular area :** If we have constructed a test for measuring calculation power of the examinee but examinee is taking the test by using table or calculator, this will reduce the logical validity of the test.

**(b) Cultural factors :** If items included in a test represent a particular culture, the person who does not belong to this culture will not be able to take this test in spite of being highly intelligent. In that case logical validity will be low.

**(c) Mindset :** Mindset is a habit which causes a person to score differently at different times on the same test. In that case it will be very difficult to ascertain logical validity.

**(d) Craming by the examinee :** If a test includes only those items which require only memorization of the fact and application of these facts in life situation is not required, a fact once crammed will be utilized in other situations and logical validity will be low.

Thus, we see that logical validity largely depends upon the judgement of an expert in the field. In order to measure this validity, the specialist does the following things :

I. He defines the trait to be measured in behavioural terms.

II. He breaks up the total area defined into different categories before matching it with the items.

III. He decides whether sufficient number of items are there in each categories in order to discriminate between those persons who have that particular characteristics and those who do not have.

## 2. Content (Curricular) Validity

According to Anastasi (1968) content validity involves systematic examination of the test content to determine whether it covers a representative sample of behaviour domain to be measured. Thus, if a test represents objectives of the curriculum, it is said to have content (curricular) validity. This test is always curriculum-centred.

Content analysis is required to ensure this validity. If we want to measure proficiency in a particular trade, test is constructed after the job analysis of the trade.

Content analysis is relevant in achievement testing, general and special ability testing and proficiency testing.

Suppose we want to measure grammatical ability of students in English language, we will construct a test whose items will represent adequate sample of English grammar. Content validity is, however, not suited to aptitude or personality tests because these tests are not based on prior instruction.

**Following points should be kept into consideration while ensuring content validity:**

I. Level of examinees must be taken into consideration. It means that test should not be above or below the standard. Grammar test for high school students will be different from those which have been constructed for 10+2 students.

II. The language of the test should also be according to the level of examinees.

III. Nothing should be asked beyond the curriculum.

IV. Each part of the curriculum should be given appropriate weightage. No part of the course content should be left altogether. Essay type tests used by MJP University, Bareilly have very low level of content validity because it represents only half of the syllabnus.

V. Test should be constructed according to the nature and level of instruction given.

VI. Test items should represent all the levels of educational objectives.

**Methods of ensuring content validity**

(a) **Inter-collection method** (Gulliksen) : This is an objective method of ensuring content validity. In this method different types of tests sampling the area of the content are designed and comparison is made between pre-training and post-training performance of the examinee on parallel tests. If a significant improvement is seen on the test after training or instruction, the test may be called valid in content. 't' test method may also be used for this purpose.

As far as aptitude tests or personality inventories are concerned, they do not require content validity in a very hard sense. The reason is that they are not constructed for a standardized course of prior instruction. Variation in scores will mean variation in attributes already possessed by the examinee.

(b) **Criterion related method:** In this method test scores are correlated with that of criterion scores. The obtained coefficient of correlation is the degree of validity of the test. Pearson's product moment coefficient of correlation is generally used for this purpose. Multiple correlation is used when there are more than two measures involved.

Following formula is most popular and commonly used in calculating validity.

$$rxy = \frac{N\Sigma xy - \Sigma x \cdot \Sigma y}{\sqrt{\left[N\Sigma x^2 - (\Sigma x)^2\right] x \left[N\Sigma y^2 - (\Sigma y)^2\right]}}$$

N = size of the sample

$x$ = (X-Mx) = Deviation of test scores from assumed mean Mx

$y$ = (Y-My) = Deviation of criterion scores from assumed mean My.

## 3. Face Validity

Face validity refers not to what a test actually measures but what it appears to measure on the basis of subjective evaluation of the items. If a test content appears irrelevant, inappropriate, silly or childish, it can not be described as having face validity. For example, if a test constructed for children is administered on adults, the result will be absurd and test will have very low level of validity. A valid test for army purposes must include army situations in it. Similarly, if a test has been constructed to select suitable personnel for civil services, it must include those items which could find out the abilities required to perform civil service activities, e.g., "How Akbar dealt with the situation when his son Salim rebelled against him". This type of item must be included in the test.

**Mosier's Classification of Face Validity**

(a) Assumption based : An assumption is made that a given test book as if it ought to measure a characteristics.

(b) Definition based : Valid definition makes a test valid.

(c) Appearance based : Test looks apparently valid.

(d) Hypothesis based : Test constructor believes that further research will provide necessary materials to make the test more valid. At present, it is valid in the hypothesis stage only.

## 4. Concurrent Validity

A test has concurrent ability when test gives an estimate of certain performance. The procedure of obtaining this validity is that a test is administered and scoring is done. Then scores from some other performance is obtained and finally these two scores are correlated. For example, scores obtained from a group intelligence test may be correlated with the scores obtained from individual intelligence test. If correlation is high, it means that first test concur the second one.

The validity of a new test can be calculated by finding their correlation with standardized tests. That is why, concurrent validity is also called **criterion related validity.** For example, if any one constructs an intelligence test, he compares it with the Stanford Binet Scale by correlation method.

## 5. Predictive Validity

A test is said to posses predictive validity if scores obtained in a test can predict how the examinee will perform in future. In order to find this validity, a test is administered and scored and sometimes later performance of the same examinees are tested again. If high degree of correlation is seen between these two tests, the test is said to have predictive validity. For example, scores on a premedical test may be compared with the scores obtained by students in any of the achievement tests after admission in the medical course.

This type of validity is required in aptitude tests, vocational selection tests and special ability tests. If a person scores high in these tests, he must score high in the next related course or job. This validity may be interpreted in terms of standard error of estimate. Its formula is given below :

$$\sigma e = \sigma y\sqrt{1 - r_{xy}}$$

Where,

$\sigma e$ = standard error

$\sigma y$ = standard deviation of criterion scores.

$r_{xy}$ = validity coefficient

Concurrent validity and predictive validity combined together are called **empirical validity.**

## 6. Convergent (Discriminant) Validity

In order to make a test to be valid, it is essential that the test must not correlate with those variables which are not to be measured by it. If it is so , the test is said to have convergent ability. If an achievement test of history measures grammatical ability of students, it will not be called valid. If correlation between these two variables is very low, the test is said to have divergent validity.

Campbell and Fiske (1959) have proposed a systematic experimental design for convergent and discriminant validity. The example of this method is not available.

## 7. Empirical Validity

Concurrent and predictive validities combined together are called empirical validity. It is also called criterion related validity because it is obtained by comparing the test scores with an external and independent measure (with an standardized test).

**Cureton (1965)** has defined empirical validity by saying that it is an estimate of the coefficient of correlation between the test score and the criterion score.

In computing criterion related validity two types of correlation are required.

(a) Full correction which includes correction in both the tests original as well as the criterion.

(b) One way correction which includes correction in the criterion only.

**Case A :** Sometimes both the tests which are to be correlated are unreliable due to faulty methods of test construction. In that case correlation coefficient will automatically be low. In order to face this problem a general formula which takes into account the measurement errors in the test as well as in the criterion is applied.

$$r_c = \frac{r_{xy}}{\sqrt{(r_{tx})(r_{ny})}}$$

$r_c$ = corrected validity coefficient

$r_{xy}$ = obtained validity coefficient between test x and criterion y

$r_{tx}$ = reliability coefficient of test x

$r_{ny}$ = reliability coefficient of criterion y

An example will illustrate this formula. If reliability coefficient of a test (x) is 0.87 and that of criterion (y) is 0.80. Validity coefficient between the two is 0.50. Then corrected validity coefficient ($r_c$) can be calculated in the following way.

$$\frac{0.50}{\sqrt{.87\,.80}} = \frac{0.50}{\sqrt{0.696}} = \frac{0.50}{0.834} = 0.60$$

**Case B :** Sometimes criterion is found less reliable than the test itself. In that case correction should be made in the criterion (y) only not in both by using the formula given below :

$$r_c = \frac{r_{xy}}{\sqrt{r_{ny}}}$$

## 8. Construct Validity

The other names of this validity are psychological validity, factorial validity and trait validity. This validity means that test scores are examined in terms of a construct or trait. According to Anastasi (1968) construct validity is the extent to which a test measures a theoretical construct or a psychological trait.

Construct actually means those ideas which are developed in one's mind in order to define, identify or explain objects or phenomena. For example, if we assume that pupils belonging to higher socio-economic strata of the society are more intelligent than those who represent lower socio-economic strata and expected level of difference between these groups is not established by the test scores, we will say that the intelligence test used for the purpose did not have construct validity. It means that the construct which was there in the mind of the investigator was wrong. On the contrary, if a hypothesis is accepted after investigation, the test is said to have construct validity.

From this point of view, this type of validity is useful only for research purposes. Its academic use is very limited. A researcher can accept or reject a hypothesis. So, a construct may change after observation.

**Steps involved in construct validation :**

**First step :** Specification of the different possible measures of the construct.

**Second step :** Determining the degree of correlation between all these measures of the construct.

**Third step :** Determine whether all these measures act as if they were measuring the construct.

**Last step :** Isolating a factor by employing a method of factor analysis.

Thus, we see that factors are underlying forces in the test. A particular behaviour in a specific situation is manifested by the factor. If factors are isolated, we can come to know the real cause of a problem.

The term construct validity was for the first time introduced in 1954 in the technical recommendations of American Psychological Association. Since then this term is frequently used in measuring traits. Computation of this validity is a very complex process. That is why, it is computed only when the scope of criterion related validity or content validity is totally blocked.

## Some More Statistical Methods For Calculating Validity

**1. Cross Validation of a test :** It is actually not a type of validity but a method to ensure higher level of validity of a test. Cross validation means taking another independent look to verify and improve the first look.

In this method, proper evaluation scores, prediction equation, cut of scores etc. are derived from one sample of information and then the same test is administered on the second sample of subject from the universe for further analysis of the scores. If data are usable in the second trial also, the test is said to have cross validity. Failure in the second trail, however, means that test is not so valid as it was claimed and further modification in the content (items) is needed.

In order, properly, to evaluate the usefulness of a test, the prediction equation or cut off scores are derived from one sample of the subject and validated on the second sample from the same universe. If test has high degree of correlation, it is said to have cross validity.

***Need and importance of cross validation :***

I. Cross validation is especially important in the selection of items for a test and in discovering psychometric signs-score characteristics empirically derived distinguished between two or more groups. Items are valid, if two groups are found identical.

II. This validation provides more accurate information about the usefulness of a test in a particular situation than it was obtained from the original group of subjects.

III. Cross validity provides a refined cut off score in such a way that constant error is minimized for the specific data at hand.

IV. It is actually a try out of the test in new situations on a completely new group which is exactly identical in traits to that group for which test has been constructed.

V. If a test is found to have cross validity it can be generalized for a wide range of use. It is called validity generalization.

VI. Cross validation is very much helpful in item analysis. Many items can be modified after this validation.

VII. This validation is very much helpful in choosing the best test out of many to make up a battery to be used on so many groups. Statistical data obtained from empirical findings give us accurate results.

*Processes of cross validations*

(a) **Psychometric signs :** It is especially used in the selection of suitable items for a test. Psychometric signs are discovered for this purpose (see the first point of need and importance of cross validation)

(b) **Validity Generalization :** If a test is found valid in a new try out situation, it is generalized for wider use.

(c) **Validity Extension :** If the additional information is obtained by checking the effectiveness of the test on different populations using the new criterion this process is called validity extension.

**2. Expectancy Table :** It is a new method of studying the relationship between a test score and the criterion measure. In expectancy table expectancy in terms of percentage of the criterion measure for each examinee is given against the test score. Validity coefficient is calculated on the basis of this bivariate distribution of test and the criterion scores. Validity estimates are usually based on the probability that an examinee will secure in the next test. On the basis of these tables, the probabilities of scores on a performance test of an examinee is predicted when the actual score is known. An example of such a table is given below :

**Expectancy Table: Relationship between an aptitude test and performance in B.Ed. Number of Students in the sample=200**

| Net Scores | Number of Students | Percentage of performance test in B.Ed. | | | | |
|---|---|---|---|---|---|---|
| | | Very poor | Poor | Average | Good | Superior |
| 120-139 | 10 | | | | 20 | 80 |
| 100-119 | 20 | | | 10 | 20 | 12 |
| 80-99 | 35 | | | 40 | 50 | 8 |
| 60-79 | 80 | 5 | 20 | 20 | 7 | |
| 40-59 | 25 | 10 | 30 | 15 | 3 | |
| 20-39 | 18 | 25 | 40 | 10 | | |
| 0-19 | 12 | 60 | 10 | 5 | | |
| | 200 | 100 | 100 | 100 | 100 | 100 |

It is clear from this table that :

*(i)* 10 students secured marks between 120-139 marks in the aptitude test, out of them 80% were rated as superior and 20% were rated as good.

*(ii)* 20 students securing 100-119 marks in the aptitude test, 12% were rated as superior, 20% were rated as good and 10% as average.

*(iii)* In the lowest segment of 0-19 marks in the aptitude test, there were only 12 students in this range. Out of them 60% were rated as very poor, 10% poor and only 5% were rated as average.

The above table shows that %age of poor students is more on low range of scores and majority of bright students scores high marks.

**3. Cut off scores (Locating qualifying point)** : It is the score on the test which separates the highly superior examinees from the highly inferior ones. This cut off score is essential for usability of a test. For example, if a test is designed for a sample and we have to select only 100 students after the test and 5000 students take this test. The criterion of 80% marks is fixed for the selection. If more than 200 students secures this percentage, we will have to change and raise the cut off point in order to select just 100 students finally.

## Factors affecting Validity of a Test

Validity of a test is influenced by a number of factors. Some of these are given below :

1. **Length of the Test :** Homogeneous lengthening of a test increases reliability and validity both. The longer the test, the higher will be coefficient of the reliability and validity. The increased validity of the test after homogeneous lengthening is calculated by the following formula.

$$r_{cnx} = \frac{(n)(r_{cx})}{\sqrt{(n+n)(n-1)r_{11}}}$$

$r_{cnx}$ = correlation between criterion and the test lengthened $n$ times

$r_{cx}$ = correlation between criterion and original test

$n$ = number of times the test has been lengthened

$r_{11}$ = reliability coefficient of the test

**Example :** A test has original validity coefficient of 0.50. Its reliability is 0.40. If it is lengthened four times, compute the new validity of the test.

$$r_{cnx} = \frac{4 \times .50}{\sqrt{(4+4)(4-1)(0.40)}} = \frac{2}{\sqrt{9.6}} = 0.645$$

Thus, we see that lengthening of a test increases its validity also. If a test is lengthened indefinitely its reliability will be perfect. But it does not means that validity will also be perfect. It is because the variance of the test will still have some distinctives.

2. **Heterogeneity of the sample :** If subjects have limited range of ability (low range of scores) validity will be low. It means that if items are discriminatory (subjects have a very wide range of ability) resulting in scores ranging from very high to very low, validity will be high. For example, if minimum score obtained by students is 40% and maximum score is 60% validity will be low due to low range of scores. Similarly, if majority of subjects taking a test scores 80-90 percent and they are homogeneous in ability, validity again will be low.
3. **Ambiguous directions :** If directions given to students regarding the test are not clear, it will be understood by them differently. In such a case validity of the test will be low.
4. **Methods of estimating Validity :** There are seven types of validities already discussed in this chapter. Apart from these, statistical methods of estimating validity are also many. In all these cases validity coefficient will be different depending on the types and methods followed.
5. **Criterion of Validation :** A test is validated by correlating its scores with any external criterion measure. If there are so many external criteria available to be correlated with the test, validity in each case will be different.

6. **Time factor :** If time given to take a test is increased, majority of the students will be able to reach the last item and higher scores with wide range of variation will increase the validity of the test.
7. **Difficulty level of the item :** If items included in the test are homogeneous resulting in very low or very high difficulty values of items, validity coefficient will be low.
8. **Guessing by the examinees :** If examinees are attempting items by guessing not by proper efforts, it tends to affects the total test scores secured by the examinees, resulting in a hike in the degree of validity irrationally. This can be controlled by increasing the number of distracters and assigning minus marking on wrong answers.

## Relationship between Validity and Reliability

I. If a test is homogeneous in nature, poor reliability of the test will yield poor validity also. But in case of heterogeneous test, validity may be high even without high reliability. Thus, validity may be high without having high reliability. In short, we can say that reliability is attributed by factor variance.

II. A highly reliable test is theoretically valid but may be practically invalid. It is because validity coefficient is calculated on the basis of some independent criteria.

III. A highly valid test ensures reliability. It can never be unreliable because its correlation with a criterion is limited by its own index of reliability.

IV. If a test is lengthened indefinitely its reliability would be perfect but validity would never be perfect even in that case because variance of the test scores may still have some specific variance.

V. High reliability high degree of validity both require items of different difficulty values.

VI. The validity of the test may be higher than reliability but may not be higher than the index of reliability it is because index sets the maximum limit of correlation that the test can yield with a standardized test.

VII. Maintaining high reliability and high validity simultaneously is not needed at all. The reason is that high reliability requires items of varying difficulty values that is more essential for differentiating poor and talented examinees or applying cut off score method. Thus, moderate level of reliability and more than average level of validity are ideal conditions.

## Criterion—A Measure of Validation

If a test is validated by an outside criterion, its validity may be affected in the following manner. These factors will have to be taken into account while improving the validity of a test.

1. **Averaging of the criteria :** Validity coefficient of a test depends to a great extent upon the criterion against which the test was validated. For example, if many employees are employed by a company at different areas of the country they may perform differently due to various reasons. So, which area will be taken as a criterion is a matter of great concern. This problem is solved by averaging different criteria.
2. **Different nature of criteria :** Criteria have three basic levels—immediate, intermediate and ultimate. Immediate criterion is used in case of validating an aptitude test, ultimate criterion is used in case of an air force selection test and intermediate criterion is used for validating an achievement test. These factors must be taken into account while taking the decision of validation.
3. **Maturity with age :** If scores on a test show a progressive trend, the test is considered to be valid as is the case of intelligence test. So age factor must be taken into account while selecting a criterion.
4. **Final impression of the performance :** Mechanical aptitude test or physical performance test should be validated against the final achievement of the task given which has left a good impression on the observer.
5. **Validity of the criterion :** If the criterion against which a test is validated does not have high

coefficient validity, the newly constructed test will also show low level of validity.

6. **Follow up the criterion :** A test once validated is not final in any way. High validity of a test at present does not mean that it will remain high in future also. It is because cultural or social changes and flexile nature of human performance may change the scores of the criterion test. A test which was standardized some 50 years ago, if tried out today, it will surely show some variation in the scores. Thus, no criterion should be considered final. Take the example of divergent thinking (Creativity) whose dimensions have increased due to fast development of science and technology. Therefore, even criterion need to be revised over a period of time.

## Limitations of Validity Coefficient

1. Validity coefficient will depend upon the criterion against which a test is validated. If there is some defect in the external measure, validity coefficient will also be inaccurate.
2. Validity coefficient of correlation are influenced by the variability of the group. Homogeneous group will give low coefficient and heterogeneous group will give high coefficient.
3. Validity is also influenced by time due to change in social or cultural factors or due to flexibility of human abilities.
4. Comparison of validities of two different types of tests is not possible, i.e., validity of an objective type test will be different from an essay type test.

# 4 Reliability

## MEANING OF RELIABILITY

Reliability practically refers to the accuracy of the measurement. If a man measures a rod by an inch tape several times and he gets the same result every time without the slightest degree of error, inch tape is said to be reliable. Several measures are used in psychology and education in testing attributes. Reliable measures will give us accurate idea of the attributes if used again and again.

Reliability, on one hand, refers to the extent to which a test is internally consistent, i.e., scores are consistent throughout the test after administration of the test and on the other hand, reliability refers to the extent to which a test yields consistent results (scores) upon testing and retesting.

In short, we can say that if a test accurately or perfectly measures whatever it does measure, it is said to be reliable. It means that there should not be any measurement error in testing an attribute. If attributes are well represented by the test item (test is valid) and if they are measured without error (test is reliable).

### 1. Statistical Meaning

Extent of reliability statistically computed is called reliability coefficient $r_{11}$. If reliability coefficient is high (close to unity)variable error will be low and vice versa.

**Reliability coefficient refers to three phenomena :**

(a) *Stability* : It refers to temporal consistency, i.e., when the same test is administered on the same individual again and again and no variation in scores is seen.

(b) *Internal consistency* : When the two parallel forms of a test are administered on the same individuals and no variation in the scores is seen, it is called alpha coefficient or internal consistency. The individual who secures high marks on one set of items also scores high on an equivalent test.

(c) *Self correlation* : When coefficient is calculated by splitting the test into two equal halves, it is called self-correlation.

### 2. Logical Meaning

When we measure something in physical or behavioural sciences, several kinds of errors are involved in measurement like sampling errors, constant errors and interpretative errors. If measurement is free from all these kinds of errors, the test is said to be perfectly reliable and in that case $r_{11}=1$. It is an ideal situation which is never seen in practical situations of any types of measurement. This involvement of error in the measurement makes $r_{11}$ of the test always less than unity. Thus,

Total scores = True score + Error score.

Here positive error score will increase the total score and negative error score will reduce it.

$$r = \frac{\text{Variance of true score}}{\text{Variance of obtained score}}$$

$$r = \frac{\sigma t^2}{\sigma x^2} = 1 - \frac{\sigma e^2}{\sigma x^2}$$

$r_{11}$ = reliability coefficient

$\sigma t^2$ = variance of true scores

$\sigma x^2$ = variance of total scores

$\sigma e^2$ = variance of error scores.

## DEFINITIONS OF RELIABILITY

1. **Anne Anastasi :** "Reliability refers to consistency of scores obtained by the same individuals when re-examined with the same test on different occasions or with different sets of equivalent items or under other variable examining conditions."

2. **Garrett :** "The reliability of a test or any measuring instrument depends upon the consistency with which it gauges the ability to whom it is applied."
3. **Ghiselle :** "Reliability of measurement is defined as the extent of unsystematic variation in scores of an individual on the same traits when they are measured a number of times."

## CHARACTERISTICS OF RELIABILITY

On the basis of the definitions and the interpretations given above we can derive the following characteristics of reliability :

1. Reliability refers to consistency (variation free) of scores.
2. It is the measure of variable, biased or sampling error. High reliability means low error and vice versa.
3. It is the function of a test length. We can not expect a high coefficient of reliability on a small test.
4. Reliability refers to the stability of a test for a certain population.
5. It is a self correlated coefficient. It does not have any outside criterion measure to compute coefficient.
6. It is the reproducibility of the test scores, i scores can be reproduced at the time of need.
7. $r_{11}$ refers the characteristics of the test on the basis of which we can decide to use it in future or not.
8. A poorly valid test may be very highly reliable. Thus, reliability in an isolated form has no practical meaning at all.
9. Reliability does not mean error free test, i.e., perfect reliability is a myth.

### Sources of Variance in a Test Scores
### Or
### Causes of Errors in a Test Scores
### Or
### Factors Affecting Reliability

1. **General abilities of the Individuals:** Performance of an individual on any test depends on his general abilities. This is actually a systematic (true) variance and we should not be bothered at this variance in determining the reliability of a test. Some of these factors are given below :
   (a) General skills, i.e, reading, writing etc.
   (b) General ability to understand instructions, language and techniques of taking a test.
   (c) General ability to solve problems of the test.
   (d) Attitudes, emotional reactions and habits generally operating in test situations.
2. **Specific abilities of the individual :** Some students have very specific characteristics and they can not answer more than this. In such a case if two tests equivalent in all respects but different in items are administered, then they will not be able to secure the same score in both the test. Word meaning with spelling is an example.
3. **Psychological factors causing variance :** The performance of an individual on a test depends on his mood, motivational level and other psychosomatic factors. If there are some variations in these factors on different tests, scores obtained will be different. Important such factors are given below :
   *(a)* Mood of the individual which depends on health, fatigue, anxiety, disturbance, etc.
   *(b)* Motivation level of the examinee on two occasions.
   *(c)* Rapport with the examiner and test instructions.
   *(d)* Effects of heat, light, cold etc on the performance.
   *(e)* Attitude of the examinee towards the test.
   *(f)* Habits acquired after a number of tests and test situations.
4. **Methods of estimating reliability :** There are a number of methods estimating reliability and each method may give different coefficient of correlation. For example, if split half method gives $r_{11} = 0.65$, the same reliability may be less than 0.50 if test retest method of estimating reliability is used.
5. **Length of the test :** If length of the test is increased, it increases reliability. In that case reliability can be calculated by the following formula :

$$rn = \frac{nr^1}{1+(n-1)r^1}$$

Where,

$n$ = number of times a test has been lengthened

$r^{1}$ = reliability coefficient of the test

**Example :** If original reliability of the test is 0.8 and test is increased by 5 times, the new reliability will be as follows

$$\frac{5\times 0.8}{1+(5-1)0.8}=\frac{4}{1+3.2}=\frac{4}{4.2}=.95$$

However, the following precautions should be taken into account while using this prophecy formula given by **Spearman Brown.**

(a) New added items should cover the same ground and represent the same content.

(b) These items must be comparable exactly to the items in original test. Thus, the role of validity is very dominant here. If we want to increase reliability, we must have to increase validity.

6. **Heterogeneity of the group :** The error of measurement depends on the heterogeneity of the group. If group of examinees are homogeneous, reliability will be low and vice versa. Thus, a test will have low coefficient of reliability if it is administered on creamy layers of the society as well as on very poor performers because in these cases, test will not be able to differentiate the weak and the superior.

7. **Possibility of guessing :** Lesser the number of distractors more will be the chance of guessing, e.g., in case of true/false questions, chance of guessing is 50%. If alternative responses are increased to 5, the chance of guessing will reduce to 20%. The lesser the chance of guessing, the more reliable the test will be.

8. **Lowering the time limit :** The reliability of a test can be increased by lowering the time limit and in this way by making it as speed test. This will make the items discriminatory and will increase the heterogeneity of the group.

9. **Construction of the items :** Some of these factors affecting reliability are given below :

(a) If there is wide range of difficulty value among items and easy items are placed near the beginning of the test it will prevent the examinees from wasting time on items beyond their abilities and they will not reach those items which are very difficult. In that case $r_{11}$ will be low.

(b) If questions are highly objective and negative marking is used for wrong options of multiple choice questions, reliability will be high.

(c) If instructions given in the test are not clear for the examinees, reliability will be low.

## TYPES OF ERRORS IN MEASUREMENT

### 1. Measurement Errors

Measurement error is directly related to lack of efficiency of measurement. This error sometimes inflates the scores and sometimes depresses it. Thus, it works in both directions, positive and negative. The main reasons of this error are as follows :

I. Inability to include adequate number of items in the test.

II. Inability to administer the test on the correct sample of examinees.

III. Inability to avail the services of large number of examiners to arrive at the right decision.

If sample in these three respects is large enough, the positive and negative errors would tend to cancel each other and therefore total error of measurement would be zero. An example will illustrate this point.

| Subject | True Score(T) | Error Score(E) | Total Scores (X) |
|---|---|---|---|
| 1 | 5 | -2 | 3 |
| 2 | 15 | 2 | 17 |
| 3 | 20 | -4 | 16 |
| 4 | 25 | -2 | 23 |
| 5 | 25 | 2 | 27 |
| 6 | 25 | 0 | 25 |
| 7 | 25 | 10 | 35 |
| 8 | 30 | -4 | 26 |
| 9 | 35 | -2 | 33 |
| 10 | 45 | 0 | 45 |
| $\Sigma$ | $\Sigma T = 250$ | $\Sigma e = 0$ | $\Sigma X = 250$ |
| Mean | 25 | 0 | 25 |
| $\Sigma X^2$ | 1050 | 152 | 1202 |

$$\sigma x^2 = \sigma t^2 + \sigma e^2$$

$$\sigma t^2 = \frac{1050}{10} = 105$$

$$\sigma e^2 = \frac{152}{10} = 15.2$$

$$\sigma x^2 = \frac{1202}{10} = 120.2$$

$$\sigma x^2 = 105 + 15.2 = 120.2$$

$$r_{11} = \frac{\sigma t^2}{\sigma x^2} = \frac{105}{120.2} = 0.88$$

## 2. Sampling Errors

Measurement errors disturbs the individual scores while sampling errors inflate or depress the scores of the group as a whole. Since, a test can not be administered on a whole population, sampling technique is used for estimating true means of population. If size of the sample is large enough, it is expected to represent the population, otherwise not, i.e.

Sample mean = True mean +Error mean

$M_S = M_T + M_E$

If sample is large enough, sampling errors may tend to zero. Thus, mean of a large sample may be equal to true mean. Sampling error can be measured by the following formula.

$$SE_n = \frac{\sigma}{\sqrt{N}} = \frac{\text{Standard deviation of population}}{\sqrt{\text{Size of the Sample}}}$$

This formula shows that larger the sample lower will be the sampling error.

## 3. Systematic (biased)errors

This type of errors always work in any one direction, i.e., it inflates the scores, and this trend will be seen till the last. The main reason of these errors are given below:

I. Failure to breakdown the factor attributed to be measured by the point of its homogeneous property.

II. Failure to score the items measuring the correct attributes.

III. Failure to score the response sheet correctly.

IV. Failure to give proper weightage to the test items.

# RELIABILITY COEFFICIENT

Reliability of a test is expressed in terms of the coefficient of correlation between two measures obtained in the same manner or in terms of standard error of measurement. Four basic principles are applied for this purpose.

1. **Coefficient is the proportion of the test variance to non-error variance :** If an individual is tested on several trials, then the mean of these trials will be true score (T). The deviation of scores on trials is error (E). Obtained or total score is a combination of these two, i.e. X = T + E and

$$\text{Reliability} = \frac{\text{True variance}}{\text{Total variance}}$$

If reliability estimated in this way is 0.77 then error variance will be 23%.

2. **Coefficient is a function of length of the test :** Lengthy tests are more reliable because they are least affected by chance factors and well representative to the content as well as the attributes being measured. For example, an individual may solve all the five questions by guessing but he can not solve fifty questions by guessing. Spearman Brown formula will help us to understand this fact that has already been discussed in this chapter.

3. **Coefficient depends on the range of scores obtained by the group :** If individual in the group can not be discriminated on the basis of their abilities, reliability will be low. Thus, a test which has a high coefficient for a wide range of pupils may be least reliable if administered on a selected homogeneous group.

4. **Coefficient can not exceed the square root of the reliability coefficient :** Correlation between a test and a criterion measure can not be higher than the square root of the correlation between the two forms of the test.

For example, if reliability of a test is 0.64, its validity can not exceed $\sqrt{0.64}=0.8$. Thus, two correlations taken together can give us more accurate result.

The reason is that if a test is so highly valid, it must be highly reliable equally.

## Types of Reliability Coefficient Or Methods of Estimating Reliability

### 1. Test-retest Method

In this method single form of the test is administered twice on the same sample with a reasonable time gap.

Correlation coefficient is calculated between the two sets of score. This type of reliability is also called coefficient of stability. It tells us to what extent an individual is able to retain his original position. Dispersion of obtained score on both the occasions is called random variance. Pearson's product moment coefficient of correlation is used for this purpose.

***Assumptions :***

I. Number of items in the test should be large enough to avoid the role of memory or practice.

II. Innate abilities of the individual should not be affected by growth or maturity of the individuals.

III. It is useful for speed test only.

***Limitations :***

This method is criticized because of the following reasons :

I. It is less accurate than the other methods.

II. Assumptions of this method are irrational and thus variance is naturally seen.

III. It is a time taking method of calculating reliability.

IV. Psychological and motivational factors do not work equally in both the administration of the test.

**2. Alternative or parallel form method :** It is an improvement over the first method in the sense that role of memory and practice is minimized here. Here the same group of individuals are given, two tests equivalent in all respects and correlation between two sets of scores are calculated. This coefficient measures two things—temporal stability and consistency of response to different items. Standardized tests can also be used to equate the newly constructed test with the criterion test. The higher the similarity between two forms of the test, higher will be the coefficient. Pearson's *r* is used for calculating reliability here.

Gulliksen has defined parallel tests as having equal mean, equal standard deviation and equal inter correlation.

## Other conditions of equivalence are given below:

*(i)* Number of items in both the test should be equal.

*(ii)* Content equivalence, i.e., types and nature of items, range of difficulty value etc. should also be the same.

*(iii)* Items variance, i.e., MD and SD should also be similar.

*(iv)* Means of scores in both the tests should be equal.

*(v)* Instructional and administrative procedure should be similar.

***Assumptions:***

*(i)* Memory, practice and carry over factor do not affect the scores.

*(ii)* The two forms of the tests are equal in at least five respects given above.

***Limitations:***

*(i)* It is very difficult to construct two exact parallel forms of a test that can satisfy the above five conditions.

*(ii)* If the second form of the test is given immediately after the first form, we can not eliminate the role of fatigue, memory, practice and carry over factors altogether. If, on the other hand, time gap is very big, new learning and maturation will come into effect.

*(iii)* It is almost impossible to construct two parallel forms of the test in certain situation. Such as when the test is of special type (Rorschach) or when change in the individual takes place due to maturation.

**3. Split half Method :** It is the most commonly used method of determining reliability of a test. Its coefficient is the measure of stability and equivalence both.

In this method the whole test is divided into two equal and comparable halves by pooling the odd and even items in each half of the test. Before doing this item analysis of the test is done and items are arranged in increasing order of difficulty. After doing this splitting is done.

One practical problem that is seen here is that by splitting the test, the length of the test is reduced that will lower reliability coefficient. In order to escape this problem the original length of the test should be large enough.

***Procedure for splitting the test:***

**Step I** Calculating difficulty value of items and arranging them in increasing difficulty values of items.

**Step II** Pooling of items in the two halves is done in the following way

First half-1,3,5,7,9..................97,99, etc.

Second half-2,4,6,8,10............98,100. etc.

**Step III** The scoring of each answer sheet is done separately and obtained scores are arranged in the following way :

| Subject/ Examinees number | I half odd items | II half even number items | Total scores I and II |
|---|---|---|---|
| 1 | Xa | $X_A$ | X1 |
| 2 | Xb | $X_B$ | X2 |
| 3 | Xc | $X_C$ | X3 |
| 4 | Xd | $X_D$ | X4 |
| 5 | Xe | $X_E$ | X5 |
| - | - | - | - |
| - | - | - | - |
| N | $X_{N1}$ | $X_{N2}$ | $X_N$ |

Here, $Xa + X_A = X_1$ and

$X_{N1} + X_{N2} = X_N$

**Step IV :** Coefficient of correlation is calculated in the fourth step. This will give the reliability of half test.

**Step V :** The reliability of the whole test is calculated by using Spearman Brown prophecy formula.

$$r_{11} = \frac{n(\text{reliability of half test})}{1+(n-1)(\text{reliability of half test})}$$

Here $n = 2$ because test is split into two halves.

This formula can be simplified as,

$$r_{11} = \frac{2r \text{ half}}{1+r(\text{half})}$$

**Example :** If reliability of half the test is 0.70, the reliability of the whole test will be as

$$\frac{2\times 0.70}{1+0.70} = \frac{1.40}{1.70} = 0.82$$

**Guttman's formula :** While using the Spearm an Brown formula given above, this fact should be kept in mind that variance of both odd and even items should be equal. If it is not possible, then Guttman's (1945) formula should be used which is as under.

$$r_{11} = 2\left\{1 - \frac{\sigma^2 a + \sigma^2 b}{\sigma x^2}\right\}$$

Here,

$\sigma_a^2$ = Variance of firs half

$\sigma_b^2$ = Variance of second half

$\sigma_x^2$ = Variance of total scores

This formula does not require the calculation of correlation between the two halves.

***Assumptions:***

I. Test should be homogeneous, i.e., all the items should measure the same attribute.

II. All the items should have same difficulty value. If it is not so, they should be arranged in increasing order of difficulty.

III. The condition of using Spearman Brown Formula and Pearson's formula must be satisfied.

***Merits:***

I. All the shortcomings that were there in the earlier methods are eliminated here.

II. This method is useful for almost all types of tests used in psychology and education.

***Limitations:***

I. It is not exactly possible to divide a test into parts in such a way that each half is perfectly equivalent.

II. This method is not applicable for calculating the reliability of power test.

III. When we measure a number of sub-traits through a single test in order to give the picture of a whole trait, the division of the test into two halves is not possible. For example, intelligence is a composite whole of many sub traits. So, different items are needed for different sub-traits. In such case, if we divide the items into two halves it will not be possible.

**4. Rational equivalence method :** This method was developed by Kudar Richardson (KR). This coefficient actually measures the internal consistency of a test. If this method is systematically used, it can remove all the shortcomings that were found in the earlier methods.

KR believed that all the items are always homogeneous. The difficulty value of an item depends on the knowledge of a person. If he knows the answer, the item is easy for him, otherwise it is difficult. Thus, all the items are equal in difficulty value all the time.

KR has given the following formulas in calculating reliability :

## Formula First

$$r_{11} = \left\{\frac{n}{n-1}\right\}\left\{1 - \frac{\sigma_x^2 + \Sigma pq}{\sigma_x^2}\right\}$$

Here,

n = number of items in the test

p = proportion of right responses

q = 1 – P or proportion of wrong responses

$\sigma_x^2$ = variance of test scores

**Example :** There are 60 items in a test. SD of the test scores = 8.50. Sum of the product of proportion of right and wrong responses is 12.43.

**Calculate $r_{11}$**

$$r_{11} = \left\{\frac{n}{n-1}\right\}\left\{1 - \frac{\sigma_x^2 + \Sigma pq}{\sigma_x^2}\right\}$$

$$\frac{60}{59} \times \frac{(8.50)^2 - 12.43}{(8.50)^2} = 0.84$$

## Formula Second :

$$r = \frac{n\sigma x^2 - M(n-M)}{\sigma x^2 (n-1)}$$

here,

$n$ = number of items in the test

M = mean of the test scores

σ = SD of the scores

## Characteristics of the method

I. This method does not take much time to calculate reliability. Test is administered only once and then statistics are used.

II. The result obtained by this method is always accurate.

III. Under this method reliability coefficient obtained will not vary much whether the test is long or short.

**5. Analysis of variance method (Hoyt) :** This method considers item variation also. Variance is caused due to three reasons.

I. True variance II. Item variance

III. Error variance

Thus total variance

$$\sigma x^2 = \sigma t^2 + \sigma i^2 + \sigma e^2$$

$$r_{11} = \frac{\sigma t^2}{\sigma x^2 - \sigma i^2}$$

## Advantages

1. bcThus, Hoyt's coefficient is different from Guilford in the sense that Guilford takes only true variance into account, i.e.,

$$r_{11} = \frac{\sigma t^2}{\sigma x^2}$$

2. Hoyt's method is very easy to use as compared to other methods of ensuring reliability.
3. Third advantage is that it can be applied to all types of tests in psychology and education.

# Preparation of Norms (Usability of a Standardized Test)

## CONCEPT OF RAW SCORE

Raw scores are numbers obtained on a test in the original form. It has no meaning in itself unless it is interpreted in other ways. For example, a score of 80 obtained by a student is meaningless unless the scores of other students are also known. Similarly, 70% marks in Hindi does not have the same meaning as that of same percentage in Maths. Thus, a score becomes meaningful only when it is comparable with other scores.

**Smith** has defined raw scores in the following words:

"Raw scores are direct counts of the number of times, a specified event has occurred, such as the number of test items answered correctly, number of books read, the number of errors made in solving a problem, the number of statements endorsed on a questionnaire etc.

Thus, an important feature (limitation) of raw score is that they carry no meaning unless additional data and statistical measure are made available to them. In fact, raw scores are made meaningful only with the help of test norms.

## ERRORS IN MEASUREMENT

When we go through the process of measuring a trait four types of errors are commonly seen :

1. **Personal error :** This error is caused due to the poor construction of the test and its subjective scoring. This error can be minimized by constructing objective type tests.
2. **Constant error :** If items are irrelevant in the context of the trait being measured, constant error is caused. This error can be minimized by adopting two techniques.
   (a) By analysing the items and by selecting only those items which have appropriate difficulty values and index of discrimination along with the proper functioning of distractors (in case of multiple choice items)
   (b) By validating the test statistically, i.e., by matching the items with the trait being measured.
3. **Variable error :** This error is caused due to the poor construction of the test and not selecting representative sample for try out. This error can be minimized by choosing a highly reliable test.
4. **Interpretive error :** This error is caused due to lack of adequate interpretation of the test scores by the test maker. This error can be reduced to the minimum by developing test norms which makes the process of standardization of a test complete.

We have already discussed the first three types of errors and their minimization in the chapter number 3, and 5, so we will deal here only with the last. Raw scores are made meaningful with the help of test norms.

### Absolute and Relative Measurement

In physical sciences almost all measurements are absolute and hence they can be interpreted very easily. The reason is that reference point (zero point) is there to compare score with this zero. For example, if height of a boy is 173 cm, it has real meaning in itself because we can say that he is 173 cm high from zero level.

In social sciences, on the other hand, all measurements are relative due to lack of zero reference point. The term relative measurement means the performance (scores) of a person in the context of the group to which he belongs. Raw scores in itself can not be interpreted. They will have to be transformed into derived scores in order to locate the reiative position of the person in his group to make the performance comparable.

## MEANING OF NORMS

1. It is a statistical procedure to minimize the interpretive error of a test scores. Raw scores are transformed into percentile rank or standard scores here. With the help of norms, the position of a particular person (score) is determined.
2. Norms are the average scores or values determined by actual measurement of a group of persons who are representative to a specified population. On the basis of these norms we say who are good, poor or average achievers in the group.
3. A norm is the criterion level against which the value of certain activity is compared or evaluated. The performance of an individual can also be compared with that of the individual in other groups. Thus, exact comparison between individuals of different groups is possible only with the help of well-prepared norms.
4. Norms of the psychological test represents the test performance of the standard group or sample selected from a specified population. Norms are empirically established by determining what a representative group of persons actually performs on the test. In this way, an individual scores can be easily compared with the standardized sample also.
5. Norms may be defined as the average performance on a particular test made by a standardized sample. Standardized sample is one which is the true representative of the population and takes the test to provide information for comparison and interpretation of test scores.
6. The term norm should not be confused with the term standard. A standard is the desired goal which may be above the obtained norms and can he achieved only under special conditions. Thus, the term norm refers to the present performance while the term standard refers to expected future performance. If the desired standard is attained, it may be the norms of the performance at that time.

   Etymologically, norms are the minimum criteria needed at a particular period of time and standard is the criterion above or below norms.

## DEFINITION OF NORMS

1. **Frank S. freeman :** A norm is the average or standard scores on a test made by a specified population.
2. **Thorndike and Hagen :** Norms are defined as the average performance on a particular test made by a standardized sample.

### Norm Referencing and Criterion Referencing

There are two reference points that are applied in interpreting test (raw) scores. The reference points with reference to tests scores tell us about the examinees with respect to the characteristics being measured. One reference point is called norm referencing and the other is called criterion referencing.

**Meaning of norm referencing :** Here the examinee's test score is compared with the scores of other members of the same group to which an examinee belongs. When raw scores are compared to the norms (average) of the same group, raw scores become meaningful.

In norm referencing, raw scores are first converted into derived scores because of two reasons.

I. To provide opportunity for direct comparison of person's own performance in different tests. It is possible because scores of different tests are expressed in a uniform unit.

II. To determine the person's relative position in the standardized sample. In that way we can exactly determine the relative position of the person in his group and his performance can be compared to those of other persons in the group.

**Meaning of criterion referencing :** Here the performance of an individual examinee is compared with an external criterion or standard which is already fixed and does not change in the short run. If an examinee passes some pre-determined number of items (that is the criterion fixed for him) it is said that he is capable of the total performance demanded by the test. For example, in an achievement test if an examinee scores 33% marks in an examination, only then he is declared pass. This 33% is the criterion of pass marks and the achievement of every examinee is compared to this criterion to declare him pass or fail.

Now the question arises, who fixes these criteria. According to **Cox and Vargas** (1966) a major criteria for referencing a test is the training which results in an increase in the skill or proficiency. For example, if a group of individuals is given a particular training and group is tested before and after the training then better results in post training test will mean the effectiveness of training. This repeated training given to different samples and their testing help us to determine criteria for different levels of achievement. Even this criteria can change over a period of time due to improvement in the situation.

## Characteristics of a Criterion Referenced Test

1. The test is usually based upon a behavioural referents which it intends to measure, i.e., behaviour of the test measure and behaviour of the criterion measure do not differ.
2. The test represents the samples of actual behaviour, i.e., total behaviour is tried to be represent by sampling.
3. The performance on a criterion referenced test can be explained in terms of pre-determined cut off scores, *i.e.*, if an individual reaches that cut off score, only then he is declared pass.

## Similarities between Norm Referencing and Criterion Referencing

1. Content, types of items, purpose, duration, scoring etc are similar in both the tests to a great extent.
2. In some cases these two types of tests are regarded as complementary to each other.
3. Administration of both the tests is also the same though a criterion referenced test need not standardized.

## Difference between The Two

1. A criterion referenced test is always based on a pre-determined cut off score whereas a norm referenced test is always based on the performance of a normative group or standardization sample.
2. Criterion referenced test is used to determine which of the pre-determined objectives of instruction, have been achieved by a particular pupil. Norm referenced test is used to determine how much over all knowledge of the same subject a particular pupil has achieved.
3. Criterion referenced test is used in taking categorical pass fail decision with reference to certain level of competence. Norm referenced test is useful in measuring a student's general level of knowledge or understanding of a particular subject.

## Steps in Developing Norms

Preparation of norms is certainly a difficult task. Following steps are followed in developing norms :

1. **Defining the target population :** The composition of the target population is first of all defined clearly. Composition of the target population which is also called normative group is determined by the intended use of the test. For example, a test maker has constructed a test of Mathematics for IXth class selected students of elite class society and he has included all the objectives of Bloom's taxonomy in his content of the test, then the same population will be selected for preparation of norms. This target population must be well-defined by the test maker.
2. **Selecting the sample :** After determining the target population for which test has been constructed, a suitable size of the sample representing the population is selected for final try out and preparation of norms. Cross sectional representation is needed here which may be defined as the sample in which people from all sections of the target population are represented. Such a sample should be large enough and random sampling technique should be used here to select a representative sample. Besides, if it is not possible to use random sampling technique, cluster sampling method should be adopted.
3. **Standardizing conditions for proper implementation of the test :** Condition of test administration are standardized here. Unless this is not done, valid and proper comparison of individual scores to test norms is not possible. Physical conditions like lighting, sound, ventilation, space for examinees, temperature of working place etc. are properly controlled. Apart from physical factors, psychological factors, test

timing, test security, adherence to test manual instructions, behaviour of the invigilator etc are also standardized.

## TYPES OF NORMS AND TEST SCALE

There are basically six types of norms that can be prepared with the help of raw scores. They are given below :

### 1. Age Equivalent Norms

Concept of age norms was introduced by Alfred Binet in 1908. He talked about mental age at that time. Age norm is defined as "the average performance of a representative sample of a certain age level on the measure of intelligence or any other ability or trait."

Age norms are suitable for those traits or abilities which increase regularly with age. Age norms can be prepared for physical abilities like height, weight etc and psychological abilities like intelligence, creativity etc because these traits and abilities change with age. In such cases scoring of correct responses are done in terms of years and months. How age norm is prepared has been discussed in the chapter. "Intelligence and its Measurement" in the compulsory section of the book.

**Advantages of age norms**

*(i)* It is very easy to calculate and easier to interpret. Only averaging of traits is needed here.

*(ii)* It is very useful for calculating IQ and it can be used to some extent in achievement testing also.

*(iii)* It is very much suitable for those traits which increases or decreases systematically with chronological age.

*(iv)* Age norm is very much applicable in the field of health and preventive medicine.

**Limitations of Age Norms**

I. Age norms lack a standard and uniform unit throughout the period of growth of physical and psychological traits. For example, growth in the level of general intelligence from age 8 to 9 is not equal to the growth from 3 to 4 years or from 14 to 15 years. This is because growth at the earlier level is faster than the growth at a later level and growth of intelligence becomes almost constant after 17 to 18 years. Due to this problem no uniform scale can be prepared for all the ages.

II. There is high degree of variation of many physical or psychological traits during the period of adolescence. For example, height of many persons increases very rapidly during the period of 13-15 and many persons show rapid growth in height during the period of 11-13. Averaging of height of these persons will definitely inflate or deflate the score and thus norms may be poorly usable.

III. Baring intelligence testing, the use of age norms is very limited in psychology and education.

IV. Growth rate of some traits is not comparable. It is because some traits grow throughout life and some traits stop growing after 20 years.

V. Many physical and psychological traits do not grow with age i.e., vision, motivation, etc. So, age norms for these traits can not be prepared.

### 2. Grade Equivalent Norms

It is the average performance of a representative sample of a particular grade or class. The test whose norms are to be prepared is given to the sample selected from each of he several grades. Then average performance of each grade or class is calculated. This $\overline{X}$ is known as grade equivalent norms. For example, if average performance of Xth class students in mathematics is 50, then this 50 raw score becomes the grade norm for class Xth.

Grade norm is also known as educational age norms and index of achievement quotient is used to specify grade norms, ie.,

$$AQ = \frac{EA}{MA} \times 100$$

Here,

AQ = Achievement quotient
EA = Educational achievement
MA = Mental age

This quotient is very much popular in USA where courses of various subjects are divided into many grades from first to say 15th. Achievement test in each subject for each grade is constructed and then they are standardized gradewise. When a student thinks that he is well prepared to qualify a particular grade in a particular subject, he takes the test. If he qualifies the test, he is promoted to the next grade in that subject. Thus, he may be in grade VIth in English and in grade IXth in computers due to subject wise open grading system.

Grade norms can also be expressed in terms of educational quotients.

$$EQ = \frac{EA}{CA} \times 100$$

Here,

EQ = Educational quotient

EA = Educational age or class.

CA = Chronological age.

For example, if 10 years old child can pass, a test of 12th grade in a particular subject, his EQ will be

$$\frac{12}{10} \times 100 = 120$$

**Advantages of Grade Norms :**

I. It is widely used in educational institutions for assigning grades to students, CBSE is using the method of grading by score conversion. Here answer-sheets of students are first scored and scores are then arranged in descending order. Those who score below 33% marks are given grade E, i.e., fail grade. The remaining pass students are equally divided into 8 categories. The top 12 ½ % pass students are given grade A1, next 12 ½ % students are assigned grade A2, next 12 ½ % students are assigned grade B1 and so on. Thus, grading is done on equal interval scale.

II. Grading is very easy to interpret and it is easily understandable for laymen as compared to Z scores.

III. Grade norms may be 5 or 7 or 9 only as compared to percentage of marks which has 100 divisions. For example, a student scoring 50-60% marks may be given grade B2 so he will not have much tension whether he scores 50% or 55%. Thus, grading can reduce mental pressure in students.

IV. Educational abilities increase systematically with age. Thus, grade norm is preferred to age norms in achievement testing.

V. Grade norm is very much applicable in open schooling system.

**Limitations**

*(i)* Its applicability at higher level of education is very limited because very accurate and exact measurement is required at that level.

*(ii)* Though grade norms of different subjects can be made comparable by applying the CBSE system of grading discussed earlier, yet it is very difficult to compare different students, if they have been assigned different grades in different subjects.

This problem can be solved by assigning numerals to different grades and then averaging these numerals. An example will make this point clear.

**Example :** Two students obtained different grades in five different subjects. These grades are given below:

Subjects

| Student | Social Studies | English | Hindi | Science | Maths |
|---|---|---|---|---|---|
| Student A | B2 | C1 | A1 | B2 | C2 |
| Student B | B1 | C1 | D2 | A1 | B2 |

Find out which of the two students has performed well in the examination?

**Solution :** Assign numerals from 1 to 8 to these grades in the following manner.

| A1 | A2 | B1 | B2 | C1 | C2 | D1 | D2 |
|---|---|---|---|---|---|---|---|
| 8 | 7 | 6 | 5 | 4 | 3 | 2 | 1 |

Value of grades of student A

$$= 5 + 4 + 8 + 5 + 3 = 25$$

Value of grades of student B

$$= 6 + 4 + 1 + 8 + 8 = 27$$

Over all grade of student A = Grade value/ Number of subjects = 25/5 = 5 = grade B2

The over all grade of student B
= 27/5 = 5.4 = grade B2

Thus, there is no overall difference between student A and B. **Ans.**

*(iii)* The assumption of grade norms is that students of a particular class have similar curricular experiences and thus the difference in grades is due to low or high achievement in different subjects. This assumption is superfluous. It is because many students differ in achievement due to background differences also.

*(iv)* Grade norms do not suit to those areas of knowledge where students show wide range of variation in growth at different grades. For example, rapid growth is seen in the world power at the elementary grades but it slows down at higher grades. Averaging and comparison is not rational in such cases.

## 3. Standard Score (Z) Norms

A norm which is based on standard score is called standard score norms. This norm is preferred to percentile norms because of the uniformity of units throughout the scale. Thus, inter group comparison is very easy here.

In this norm raw score are converted into standard scores. Standard scores is that derived score which has a fixed mean and fixed standard deviation. Other forms of standard score norms are T score norms, stanine score norms, deviation IQ norms etc.

**Conversion of raw scores into Z Scores :** Raw scores can be converted into Z scores by two methods .

***(a) Linear transformation method :*** When raw scores are transformed into Z scores by this method, all characteristics of the original distribution of the raw scores are retained.

Following formula is used for this transformation.

$$Z = \frac{X - \overline{X}}{\sigma}$$

Z = Sigma or Z score
X = Raw score of the individual
$\overline{X}$ = Mean of the distribution
σ = Standard deviation of the data

Thus, Z score indicates how many standard deviations of a score lie below or above the mean of the distribution. Suppose a person has obtained 50 marks in a test given to a group of persons whose mean score and SD is 30 and 10 respectively. Find the Z score of the person.

$$\frac{X - \overline{X}}{\sigma}$$

$$= \frac{50 - 30}{10} = 2$$

It means that his score is 2 sigma above the mean.

Similarly, if another person has scored just 5 marks in the same test his Z score will be

$$\frac{5 - 30}{10} = -2.5$$

It means that his score is 2.5 sigma below the mean. By assuming the mean = 0, the Z scores of two persons given above can be easily compared.

Thus, we see that linear transformation retains all the properties of original distribution, i.e., standard scores are related to raw scores through a linear function.

***(b) Normalized transformation method :*** One important demerit of Z scores based on linear transformation method is that they can be compared with other groups only when they have been derived from distributions of the same form. If one distribution of observation is skewed and the other is normal, the Z scores from one distribution can not be compared with the scores of other distribution. Such a problem can be solved by using normalized standard scores.

Here raw score distribution is first of all normalized and then new mean and new SD is calculated to find out standard scores i.e.,

$$Z = \frac{X - \text{New}\overline{X}}{\text{New } \sigma}$$

Marshall and Hales (1972) have defined "Normalized standard scores as scores which have been adjusted to produce a normal frequency distribution and then converted to a standard base with a pre-assigned mean and standard deviation". A normalized score of +1 indicates that the examinee has surpassed 84% of his group and –1 Z indicates that he has surpassed only 16% of his group.

There are mainly three types of normalized standard scores, i.e., T score, stanine score and deviation IQ scores. We will discuss them one by one in the later part of this chapter.

**Advantages of Z scores norms**

*(i)* When the performance of the same person in different tests (subjects) is to be compared, Z score can best serve this purpose.

*(ii)* Scores have equal units of measurement throughout the scale and their size does not change from distribution to distribution. It makes intra group comparison easy. Because of this reason it eliminates the limitation of inequality of percentile norms.

*(iii)* Linear transformation of raw score into Z score is very easy.

*(iv)* If sample is very large, the distribution curve is most likely to be normal and hence Z score derived on the basis of standard deviation are very much dependable.

*(v)* By knowing the plus minus signs of Z scores, any body can understand them very easily. Plus sign means above the mean and minus sign means below the mean.

**Limitations**

*(i)* They are obtained in plus as well as minus forms and Z scores in minus form are very difficult to handle. In order to remove this difficulty, the score is made larger by adding to each Z score a constant such as 50 or 100, so that minus may not exist such as if Z = –1.5 then by adding 100 to it, Z will become 98.5 and no minus sign will be there.

*(ii)* Z scores may be in decimal form also which again makes its handling difficult.

This difficulty is removed by using a larger standard deviation, i.e., we can multiply every Z score by 10 or 100 and thus decimal will not exist there. For calculating new standard score we can use the following formula.

New standard score = Z (new SD) + mean.

Here SD = 100 and $\overline{X}$ = 50 may be taken as a constant value. A table given here can illustrate this point.

Transformation of Z score into New Standard Score

| Students | Raw Score | Mean & SD | Z score | New Standard Score Constant X=50,σ =10 |
|---|---|---|---|---|
| A | 80 | 60, 15 | 1.33 | 63 |
| B | 50 | 60,15 | -0.66 | 44 |

$$Z_1 = \frac{X-\overline{X}}{\sigma} = \frac{80-60}{15} = 1.3$$

$$Z_2 = \frac{X-\overline{X}}{\sigma} = \frac{50-60}{15} = -0.6$$

New standard score first = 1.3(10) + 50

13 + 50 = 63

New standard score second = – 0.6(10) + 50

= – 6 + 50 = 44

*(iii)* Third limitation is that raw scores are not normally distributed always. If one distribution is skewed and the other distribution is normal we can not compare the two groups with respect to their performance.

This difficulty can also be removed by using normalized transformation method of Z calculation.

*(iv)* Z score is interpreted with reference to mean score. Thus, it may have all those drawbacks which are related to mean itself.

## 4. T Score Norms

In order to avoide decimals and minus signs form Z scores, T scores norms are prepared. T score is an improvement over Z score. In T scores Mean is kept 50 and standard deviation =10 while in Z scores mean is zero and SD is one.

$$T = 10\frac{\left(X-\overline{X}\right)+50}{\sigma}$$

$$T = 10Z+50$$

**Example :** Mean score of a distribution is 40, standard deviation is 7.5. Transform the following raw scores into T scores.

**Raw Scores:** 10, 20, 30, 40, 50, 60 and 70

**Solution :**

| Raw score | Z score | T score |
|---|---|---|
| 10 | Z=(10–40)/7.5=–4 | T=10(–4)+50=10 |
| 20 | Z=(20–40)/7.5=–2.6 | T=10(–2.6)+50=24 |
| 30 | Z=(30–40)/7.5=–1.3 | T=10(–1.3)+50=37 |
| 40 | Z=(40–40)/7.5=0 | T=10(0)+50=50 |
| 50 | Z=(50–40)/7.5=1.3 | T=10(1.3)50=63 |
| 60 | Z=(60–40)/7.5=2.6 | T=10(2.6)50=76 |
| 70 | Z=(70–40)/7.5=4 | T=10(4)+50=90 |

In this way, instead of Z scores, T scores are provided in the manual of a test. It neither has minus sign nor value in decimals. If distribution of any two groups are normal, these two groups can be compared very easily. If one distribution is normal and the other is skewed, then skewed distribution will have to be normalized for the purpose of comparison. As far as comparison within the group is concerned, T scores provide a uniform basis of the comparison throughout the scale.

The only assumption for calculation of T score is that the standard deviation of the original distribution should not be very small otherwise we will not be able to escape minus signs.

**Advantages of T scores**

*(i)* T scores are really an improvement over Z scores and they can be easily understood by a common man.

*(ii)* We can compare the performance of persons within the group and performance of persons belonging to different groups with the help of T scores.

*(iv)* Calculation and interpretation of T scores are very easy.

*(v)* It is a linear transformation of raw scores conversion.

*(vi)* T scores are applicable in all types of tests except intelligence tests.

**Limitations**

*(i)* Interpretation of T scores is done with reference to mean taken as 50. Thus, exact position of an individual in the group can not be located as is done in percentile ranks.

*(ii)* If the distribution is not normal inter-group comparison will not be accurate without normalizing the distribution.

*(iii)* If we calculate Z scores in two decimal points, T scores will not be free from decimals and its handling will again be difficult.

## 5. Stanine Score Norms

It is regarded an improvement over T score norms. Many of the errors and limitations of Z scores and T scores can be minimized through stanine scores. The word stanine is actually derived from two words standard plus nine which was first of all used by American Air Force During Second World War. In this norm standard scores are expressed in numbers from 1-9 where mean score is 5 and total standard deviation is equal to 1.96. When raw scores are converted into stanine scores, the distribution of scores takes the shape of a normal probability curve.

Nine point stanine scale was first prepared and used by Cornfield (1951). This is actually an example of normalized standard scores. Here the area of normal probability curve is divided into nine standards with fixed percentage in each standard. For example, 4% of the bottom scores are given stanine 1, next 7% of the scores are given stanine 2 and so on as has been shown in the table given below. When these stanine scores are plotted on a diagram, they take the shape of a normal distribution curve.

### Stanine Scale Table

| Division of distribution | Stanine value | Value of standard deviation |
|---|---|---|
| Bottom 4% | 1 | –1.75 σand below |
| Next 7% | 2 | –1.23 to –1.75σ |
| Next 12% | 3 | –0.74 to –1.23σ |
| Next 17% | 4 | –0.25 to 0.74σ |
| Middle 20% | 5 | –0.25 to +2.05σ |
| Next 17% | 6 | 0.25 to 0.74σ |
| Next 12% | 7 | 0.74 to 1.23σ |
| Next 7% | 8 | 1.23 to 1.75σ |
| Top 4% | 9 | 1.75 σ and above |

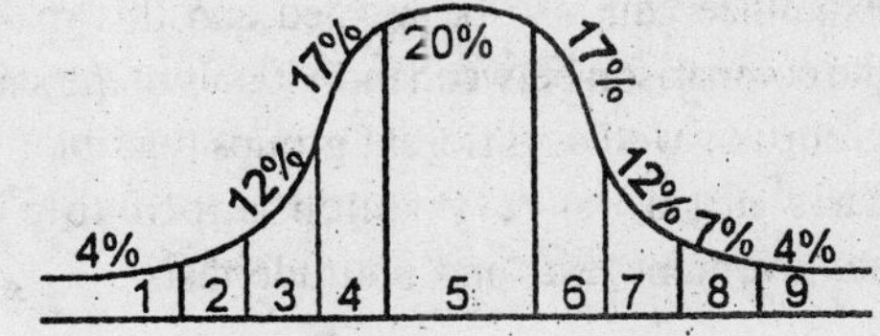

**Example :** In a sample of 400 students, the mean of the distribution is 60 and standard deviation is 15. Calculate the limits and intervals of stanine scores.

**Solution**

$X1 = \overline{X} - 1.74\ \sigma = 60 - 1.75 \times 15 = 33.75 = 34$

$X2 = \overline{X} - 1.23\ \sigma = 60 - 1.23 \times 15 = 41.55 = 42$

$X3 = \overline{X} - 0.74\ \sigma = 60 - 0.74 \times 15 = 48.90 = 50$

$X4 = \overline{X} - 0.25\ s = 60 - 0.25 \times 15 = 56.25 = 56$

$X5 = \overline{X} + 0.25\ \sigma = 60 + 0.25 \times 15 = 63.75 = 64$

$X6 = \overline{X} + 0.74\ \sigma = 60 + 0.74 \times 15 = 71.10 = 71$

$X7 = \overline{X} + 1.23\ \sigma = 60 + 1.23 \times 15 = 78.45 = 78$

$X8 = \overline{X} + 1.75\ \sigma = 60 + 1.75 \times 15 = 86.25 = 86$

While preparing a stanine score norms raw scores (limits) are transformed into stanine scores. These values are provided in the manual of the test in tabular form.

| Range of Raw Scores | Stanine Scores |
|---|---|
| 0–34 | 1 |
| 34–42 | 2 |
| 42–50 | 3 |
| 50–56 | 4 |
| 56–64 | 5 average point |
| 64–71 | 6 |
| 71–78 | 7 |
| 78–86 | 8 |
| 86 and above | 9 |

**Advantages of Stanine Score Norms**

*(i)* They can be easily used by OMR sheets of computers. Computer can analyse raw scores very easily with the help of the stanine provided on OMR sheets.

*(ii)* The interpretation of stanine scores are very easy because total range of scores are classified into nine standard only.

*(iii)* With the help of stanine the position of an examinee can also be located and this makes the comparison between individuals of the same groups as well as different groups possible.

*(iv)* This norm is very much applicable in achievement tests and aptitude tests.

**Limitations of Stanine Scores Norms**

*(i)* Calculation of stanine score is a lengthy process. Computation of stanine range with the help of normal distribution table is really a lengthy process.

*(ii)* Stanine scores are interpreted with reference to mean score rather than with reference to the specific position of an individual in the group. It is a limitation of stanine score in the sense that exact position of an individual in the group can not be known. But it is an advantage in the sense that results are not affected here by the extreme scores. Stanine score is actually a normalized standard score like T scores.

*(iii)* Stanine points are not uniform throughout the scale. The range of point 2 is 42–34 =8, range of point 4 is 56 – 50 = 6 and so on.

*(iv)* It assumes normal distribution of scores which is not always seen even in large samples.

## 6. Deviation IQ Norms

This type of norm is developed for intelligence test. Here raw scores on an intelligence test are transformed into IQs. Here again we take the help of standard scores. If sample is large, the distribution will be normal and mean score and standard deviation are expected to be 100 and 16 respectively. Conversion formula is given below :

$$\frac{IQ - 100}{16} = \frac{X - \overline{X}}{\sigma}$$

$$(IQ - 100)\sigma = \left(X - \overline{X}\right) 16$$

$$IQ - 100 = \frac{\left(X - \overline{X}\right)16}{\sigma}$$

$$IQ = \frac{\left(X - \overline{X}\right)16}{\sigma} + 100$$

**Example :** If mean score of a distribution is 50 and standard deviation of the scores is 20, calculate IQs of raw scores 0, 20, 30, 40, 50, 60, 70, 80, 90 and 100.

**Solution :**

| Raw Scores | Calculation of IQs | IQs |
|---|---|---|
| 10 | 16(10–50)/20+100 = –32+100=68 | 68 |
| 20 | 16(20–50)/20+100 = –24+100=76 | 76 |
| 30 | 16(30–50)/20+100 = –16+100=84 | 84 |
| 40 | 16(40–50)/20+100 = –8+100=92 | 92 |
| 50 | 16(50–50)/20+100 = 0+100=100 | 100 |
| 60 | 16(60–50)/20+100 = 8+100=108 | 108 |
| 70 | 16(70–50)/20+100 = 16+100=116 | 116 |
| 80 | 16(80–50)/20+100 = 24+100=124 | 124 |
| 90 | 16(90–50)/20+100 = 32+100=132 | 132 |
| 100 | 16(100–50)/20+100 = 40+100=140 | 140 |

In this way, the deviation IQ, score table for each raw score can be prepared and be given in the manual.

### Advantages of IQ Norms

*(i)* It can be easily computed and interpreted and even a layman can understand it.

*(ii)* Its application in guidance and counselling is widely seen.

*(iii)* Calculation of IQ by this method in intelligence testing is very easy as compared to the formula based on age norms given by Binet.

### Limitations of IQ Norms

*(i)* Its applicability is limited to intelligence testing. If it is used in EQ, results will be misleading because fixed mean=100 is not found in any educational testing.

*(ii)* It is also based on the assumption of normal distribution of scores. But if sample is small, distribution is not expected to be normal.

## Precaution in Using Norms

Norms are actually the average with the help of which we interpret the scores of individuals obtained in any test. When we convert raw scores into any derived score, relative level of performance of an individual is known. Thus, norm referencing provides a complete picture of the whole group.

Though these interpretations tell what an individual is in respect of his particular performance, yet what he is expected to be in future on the basis of his present level of performance can also be estimated from these derived scores. Moreover, if there is a change in the performance of an individual next time, whether this change in the performance of an individual is significant or not can also be estimated from these norms.

In spite of these merits, norm referencing should be taken cautiously as well due to the following reasons.

1. **Norms provide only relative informations rather than absolute ones :** Norms tell us only whether an individual is good, poor or average in his group and in other related groups or not but they do not tell us whether his present level of performance is satisfactory or poor. Besides, these norms are unable to explain how much improvement in the performance is possible, if system is improved. In today's age of surplus educated human capital, we have to select only few out of the lot and it is done on the basis of absolute performance of individuals rather than a relative one.

   Due to introduction of modern technology in education, absolute performance of individuals is continuously improving and new norms are needed every time in order to make a test usable. Therefore, norms prepared ten years ago should not be regarded as relevant today as it was ten years before.

2. **Norms do not provide information about the inputs:** Norms provide complete picture of an individual or group in relation to his present performance but we can not know through norms where did the individual or group start from, i.e., inputs used for preparation of output). Similarly, learning also differs from individual to individual due to a variety of reasons, such as motivation level of the child, educational facilities of the child, and competence of teachers to teach him. Once there is a difference in inputs, output is also expected to be different. Therefore, penalizing a student on the basis of his norms score is not a correct approach. Inputs must be measured before measuring output and that we do not exactly know how to measure inputs. If

inputs and outputs both are measured in relative context, only then norms prepared will be dependable.

3. **Norms are prepared in relation to objectives of testing and instruction :** Once we are going to prepare norms for the standardization of a test, we set certain testing objectives in advance and test is prepared from the content in relation to those objectives.

   These objectives vary from persons to person across the globe. So, norms prepared in one situation can not be regarded fully relevant to other situations. Generally national pattern and outlook are reflected in a standardized test. The extent to which a particular school system deviate from this national pattern, norms will also differ to the same extent. For example, if précis writing of a texual material has been delayed by the school beyond the grade at which it was expected to be introduced by the test maker who has made a test in the national framework, relative standing of different individuals in the group will differ.

   If a test maker keeps all the above points in his mind and he is considerate enough to accommodate all of them in his test, results are more likely to be dependable.

## Preparation of the Test Manual and Reproduction of The Test

This is the last step in the standardization of a test. Whatever we have achieved so far from planning to preparation of norms are summarized in the test manual. It is actually a guide book for the test user. Without this manual, no body can use this test with confidence. The test user can compare his own results with the results of manual and make sure about his own competency.

Preparation of a manual is really a difficult task. It must be so clear and exact enough that any qualified test user can comprehend it and use the test properly. So, while preparing a test manual, a test maker should not miss any relevant point that he came across while standardizing the test. It means that assumptions, limitations, precautions etc. should be provided along with the statistical details in relation to objectives of testing.

### Functions of a test manual

(i) It works as a guide for those who construct and standardize the similar tests.

(ii) A standardized test possesses all statistical indices which are made available in the manual and the user need not go through all these operations again.

(iii) Users can evaluate the quality of the test i.e., reliability, validity and norms.

(iv) Test scores are interpreted with the help of norms provided in the manual. Thus, drawing conclusions on the basis of the test become easy.

(v) Further review of the test results is also possible with the help of the manual.

## Types of Manuals

**A. User manual:** It provides following informations about a test :

(i) Detailed instructions for test users.

(ii) Duration for administering the test.

(iii) Answer key and scoring procedure of the test scripts.

(iv) Information about standardization, such as, reliability, validity, P values, D values and norms.

(v) Summary about the nature and quality of the test.

(vi) Norms table for the homogeneous groups.

**B. Technical manual:** It provides following information about a test.

(i) Procedure (steps) of the construction of the test.

(ii) Procedure of preliminary and proper try out of the test, size of the sample on which the tests was tried out.

(iii) Method and procedure of item analysis and its values.

(iv) Methods and criteria of preparing final draft of the test.

(v) Methods of estimating reliability and validity including the size of the sample on which final try out was done.

*(vi)* Determining cut off score and way of cross validation.

*(vii)* Development of norms table and its procedure.

*(viii)* Final instruction for administering and scoring of the test.

In short, manuals provide those facts and informations on which the quality of a test can be judged. They help in easy administration and scoring of the test and finally they provide solid bases why the review of the test is essential. These are the **three important objectives** with which a test manual is prepared.

## Criteria of Usability of a Test

The important criterion for selecting a test is its usability. Usability of a test can be judged on the following grounds:

*(i)* A test, having high reliability and validity coefficient are not the criteria of judging the quality of a test. A test of low reliability and validity coefficient if it has been used in several studies and is giving consistent and purposeful results can be termed as usabie and of high quality. There are several psychological tests which has never been validated and their reliability has never been calculated, even then they are constantly used in psychological and educational measurement such as projective tests of personality measurement.

*(ii)* If norms provided by a test are consistent with norms table provided by the test of similar nature and low variation is found there, a test is used with ease and confidence.

*(iii)* There are several methods of standardizing a test from item analysis to norms calculation. Easier is the methods used, greater will be the usability of a test. It is because nobody likes complicated procedures and formulae especially when results do not differ significantly.

*(iv)* In spite of above points, a test must have adequate degree of validity and reliability and its items should discriminate between good and poor students.

# Construction of Objective Type Test and Its Standardization

## INTRODUCTION

The main purpose of constructing objective type test is to reduce interpretive and scoring errors. Such tests would always give the same result whosoever scores them. They are more precise and definite than the other types of tests. An important advantage of such tests is that they can be standardized to be used in future with accuracy and objectivity. Due to these merits they are used in the following fields by the researchers, educators, guides and counsellers.

1. In the field of achievement testing
2. In the field of aptitude testing
3. In the field of intelligence testing
4. In the field of diagnosis

From the point of usability and procedure adopted they can be classified into two categories.

## A. STANDARDIZED TESTS

Standardized tests are used in research work, guidance and counselling and also for screening the candidates for admission in a particular course or appointment for a job. In such tests, raw scores are converted into standard scores and norms are prepared. Individual items of the test are also analysed statistically and record is maintained.

Statistically, a standardized test is one in which minimum level of personal, variable, constant and interpretive errors are kept at the minimum by preparing standard scores and norms.

In the words of **Cronbach** "a standardized test is one in which, the procedure, apparatus and scoring are fixed in advance so precisely that the same test can be given at different times and places". One point to be noted is that if a test is highly valid and reliable but its norms have not been prepared, it can not be considered as a standardized test. Norms must be prepared for being a test standardized. Thus, standardization refers to usability of a test.

### Characteristics of a Standardized Test

1. The first condition for a standardized test is that there must be a standard manner of giving instruction so that uniformity can be maintained in the evaluation of all those who take the test.
2. Second conditions is that there must be uniformity of scoring and an index of fairness of correct items by analysing the individual items.
3. Third condition is that reliability and validity of the test must be established and the individuals for which the test is prepared must be clearly mentioned.
4. As far as fourth condition is concerned educators are not at consensus on this conditions but majority is of the opinion that a standardized test must have well-prepared norms. Informations regarding standard scores should also be there.
5. Manual of the test must have been prepared to provide required information for the test users.

## B. TEACHER MADE TESTS

Objective type tests are prepared by subject teachers as well. The other name of this type of tests is new type tests. A teacher makes such tests in order, accurately, to evaluate effectiveness of his teaching and to know the progress of his students on a routine basis. They are not standardized and hence they can not be used by other teachers with the same accuracy and objectivity. The teacher who knows his subject well and has expertise in constructing such tests can do this job now and then. It is the teacher himself who determines the rules of administration and scoring of such tests.

## Characteristics of Teacher Made Tests

1. In teacher made test also students responses are objectively scored and personal errors are eliminated to the maximum level possible.
2. In order to cover the whole course content, a large number of items are included in the test.
3. Administration and scoring of such tests and its responding by the students are very economical.
4. Organizational ability of the subject-matter on the part of the students is not needed here.
5. They are reliable and valid upto a limit needed by the teacher.
6. They are not standardized but difficulty value of items can be calculated. Besides, items in the test are arranged in the ascending order of difficulty level.
7. They can be used for the purpose of prognosis and diagnosis both.

## STEPS IN THE CONSTRUCTION OF AN OBJECTIVE TYPE TEST

Following procedure is followed while constructing an objective type test.

## (A) PLANNING OF A TEST (FIRST STEP)

Before constructing a test a detailed plan regarding the nature, objectives and length of the test is made. The more comprehensive the plan is, the greater will be the accuracy in the test items.

Different types of planning is required for different tests. In planning an achievement test, content and objectives are more important. In aptitude test, job analysis is the main focus of the plan. As far as intelligence test is concerned identification of intelligent behaviours of the examinee is the centre of activity of a test maker and so on.

In general, following things are done in the planning step :

1. **Determining objectives and its level :** A test maker first decides what are his objectives of using a particular test. The knowledge about objectives and various levels attached to them can be obtained from three domains of behaviour. Test maker also finds the answer of the question why he is going to conduct a test. Knowing the effectiveness of teaching, differentiating the poor and talented students from the average and ironing out learning difficulties of students by remedial teaching maybe some other purposes and these objectives will differ from subject to subject, i.e., objectives will largely depend on the content.

   Test maker also decides upto what level of knowledge a particular group of examinees should have to be taken and hence he prepares the items accordingly. He, however, takes this point into account that he has to cover the whole course content for which the test is being prepared. Proper and judicious sampling is needed for this purpose.
2. **Writing objectives in behavioural terms :** After determining the objectives, they are further written in behaviour terms (change of behaviour of the examinee) so that result of the test can be analysed. There are different approaches of writing objectives. RCEM approach is most popular among them. (See Optional Paper-II)
3. **Content analysis :** After writing the objectives, books and other source material from which the test is to be constructed are analysed. Through this analysis, efforts are made to fully represent the whole content by the items of the test. Important materials to be analysed are as follows:
   - **(a) Test books and notes :** They are the primary source. How many and what type of questions are to be prepared are decided first then they are matched with the objectives. Such items are to be constructed which possess originality and appropriate departure from the text. Bookish questions without changing their language are not desirable at all.
   - **(b) Lectures and discussions :** Some learning materials are also provided by the teacher to students through discussions and lectures. Test items should represents these materials also along with the personal experiences of learners from the environment.

(c) **Self-study materials and reference materials:** A certain percentage of items are also to be constructed from this source to increase the knowledge and study habits of students.

4. **Determining the sub types and number of items:** It is statistically proved that the larger the test, the higher will be the reliability. but time limit will restrict the test maker to prepare test of a particular length. Besides, it is very difficult to construct all good items in the first attempt. hence, double than required number of items are constructed for final sorting.
   The number of items will also depend on the length and nature of items. If content is very large, large number of items will be needed to represent the content. Similarly, if content is very tough, only few items may serve the purpose.
   As far as sub types are concerned, multiple choice items with at least five distractors are considered the best. If there are five options to respond an item, there will be only 20% chance of guessing by the students. Other types of objective type tests are not considered suitable here.
5. **Preparation of the Blue Print :** After taking all the previous decisions a blue print of the test is prepared. It will guide the test maker from beginning of the process to the end. Here educational objectives are matched with the content and items are matched with the final objectives of test maker. A specification table covering cognitive domain of learners in terms of number of questions is given below.

| Objectives | Number of questions | | | | | | |
|---|---|---|---|---|---|---|---|
| Chapters | 1-2 | 3-4 | 5-6 | 7-8 | 9-10 | Other Materials | Total |
| Knowledge | 5 | 5 | 4 | 6 | 5 | 3 | 28 |
| Comprehension | 4 | 4 | 6 | 3 | 2 | 3 | 22 |
| Application | 2 | 3 | 1 | 2 | 3 | 1 | 12 |
| Analysis | 3 | 2 | 3 | 4 | 2 | 3 | 17 |
| Synthesis | 2 | 1 | 3 | 2 | 2 | 1 | 11 |
| Evaluation | 2 | 1 | 2 | 2 | 2 | 1 | 10 |
| Total | 18 | 16 | 19 | 19 | 16 | 12 | 100 |

## (B) ITEM WRITING (SECOND STEP)

After planning stage comes the item writing stage in which three persons experts in three respective fields are required.

*(i)* **Subject expert :** Who knows the content well.

*(ii)* **Expert in psychology and education :** Who knows the psychology and educational needs of the examinees.

*(iii)* **Expert in measurement :** Who knows how to measure a particular trait or behaviour with minimum error.

A person who is expert in the above three fields can only construct a good test otherwise the services of three experts will be required.

While writing a test item, a decision is taken whether test maker has to construct essay type items or objective type items. Here we are dealing with objective type test only which can further be classified as recognition type and recall type. They can further be categorised as under:

| **Recall type (supply type)** | **Recognition type (selection type)** |
|---|---|
| Simple recall | True/false type |
| Completion type | Multiple choice type |
| Short answer type | Matching type |
| | Classification type |
| | Analogy type |
| | Arrangement type |

**Points to remember :** Following points must be kept in mind before writing any test items :

*(i)* More than one type of objective items should be included in the test, so that test may not be boring for the examinees.

*(ii)* The number of items in the preliminary draft should be about double the final draft of the test.

*(iii)* Test items should be clearly phrased so that their content may be clearly understood by the examinees. Words like always, about, never etc. should be strictly avoided.

*(iv)* In order to reduce guessing the number of distractors should not be less than four, i.e., five options in the response set are better.

*(v)* One item should not lead the answer of other items.

*(vi)* The items of one type should be grouped at one place.

*(vii)* There should not be any sequence in responses. If sequence of a , b b a and a d a d is repeated,

it will lead to guessing in multiple choice items.

*(viii)* The test should fully represent the content at hand.

*(ix)* Each item of the test should carry equal weightage.

*(x)* Items should be put in ascending order of difficulty value. It means that easy items should be placed in the beginning and most difficult items should be placed in the end.

*(xi)* Items should be discriminatory. If all items are difficult, it will not be possible to discriminate good and poor students and the purpose of measurement will be defeated. Such situations will again happen when items are very easy.

*(xii)* The difficulty value of items should range from 30-70.

## (C ) EXPERIMENTAL TRY OUT OF THE TEST (THIRD STEP)

The main purpose of this try out is to improve and modify the language ambiguity and difficulty. For this purpose, a sample is selected from the population for which the test has been designed. This try out is done individually or on very small samples one by one to locate item difficulty or ambiguity of language.

**Following rules are followed at this stage :**

*(i)* Preliminary draft of the test should be prepared on separate cards.

*(ii)* The preliminary draft should have more items than required in the final draft, i.e. almost double number of items.

*(iii)* The items should be in the form of statements.

*(iv)* Similar type of items should be pooled together to avoid confusion. It should be noted that number of items is not reduced after first try out only the language of the items are modified.

## (D) PROPER TRY OUT AND ITEM ANALYSIS (FOURTH STEP)

Proper try out is done on a sample drawn from the same population for which the test has been constructed. This is done for the purpose of systematic analysis of the item. After the items have been carefully reviewed and edited in the first try out, they are subjected to a procedure called item analysis. It is a procedure applied to know the truthfulness or validity of items. Through this analysis items which are valid and suited to the purpose are selected and \remaining items are either eliminated or modified according to the purpose.

In order to select appropriate, valid and discriminating items, the individual item performance by a group of examinees is compared to their performance on the whole test. Since validity of the whole test depends on the validity of individual items, only valid items are selected for the final draft.

## ITEM ANALYSIS

### Objectives of Item Analysis

1. The main purpose of item analysis is to select suitable items for the final draft of the test and reject the poor ones.
2. To find the difficulty values of all the items given in the preliminary draft is the second objective. The item whose difficulty value (Easiness value) is very high say 0.90 or above need not he included in the test because more than 90% students can answer this question. Thus, the purpose of measurement is defeated. Item analysis indicates which item is easy or difficult or moderately difficult.
3. Item analysis helps us to discriminate weak and talented students of the group. Only those items which are positively discriminating are selected and items of negative or zero discrimination are rejected.
4. To rectify the function of the distractors is the fourth purpose. If any of the distractors is not functioning at all, it is changed in the final draft.
5. Calculation of the reliability and validity of the test becomes easy by this process.
6. It provides a logical basis for selection of items for the final draft. After calculating difficulty value, items in the final draft can be arranged in increasing difficulty order.

## STEPS IN ITEM ANALYSIS

### 1. Administration of the Test

Once the first draft of the test is well prepared after first try out, it is administered on a sample representing the same population for which it has been prepared. Conditions of administration are kept standard in a bit to avoid cheating or faking the responses. Sufficient time is also given to attempt the items by the examinees. Clear instructions are given to examinees to attempt the items.

## 2. Scoring

Before scoring the items, answer key is prepared before hand. In order to make scoring procedure simple, one mark is given to every correct answer and zero mark is allotted to every wrong one. Scoring machines can also be used for this purpose. If answers are crossed on a separate OMR sheet, computer can score more than one thousand OMR sheets in one hour.

## 3. Analysis of items

Following information are obtained by item analysis:

**(a) Difficulty value of Items :** Difficulty value of an item is defined as the percentage of the examinees who answer a particular . item correctly. If 80% students have answered an item correctly, it will mean that the item is comparatively easy and it is not discriminating well at the bottom of the scale of the trait being measured. Contrary to this, if an item has been answered correctly by 5% students only (DV=0.05), it means that item is a very difficult one and it is not discriminating well among the examinees at the highest level of the trait being measured. One thing is clear that higher the index of difficulty, the easier the item.

There are basically two statistical methods of estimating the index of the difficulty of an item.

First method determines the index on the basis of the responses of all the examinees and second method determines the index on the basis of the responses of only a portion of the examinees.

***First method of calculating difficulty value :*** For a dichotomous item (items where correct answer in the test is given 1 mark and wrong response is given zero), the index of difficulty can be determined by the following formula :

$$P = \frac{R}{N}$$

P = Index of difficulty.

R = Number of examinees who attempt the item correctly.

N = Total Number of examinees who take the test.

P values are practically significant for two reasons.

(i) P value directly indicate the total test scores as well as their standard deviation. If P values of all the items in the test are generally very high(test consists of easy items), the distribution of the curve would be negatively skewed and the standard deviation would be very small. Reverse will be the case if the test is very difficult but SD would again be very small. Items whose values are close to 0.5 p values will procure symmetrical distribution as well as larger SD. A test consisting of items giving P in the range of 0.4 to 0.6 is called **peaked test.**

(ii) P also affects reliability of the test. Reliability is statistically defined as the self-correlation of the test. If the items have extreme P values like 0.05, 0.10, 0.20, 0.95, 0.90,0.80 etc. they may not correlate with each other resulting in low inter-item correlation. It otherwise means lower internal consistency reliability coefficient. High reliability coefficient is possible when P values of items are close to 0.5. Since, items having high item correlations are expected to correlate with the total test scores, majority of items having P= 0.4 to 0.6 are selected for the final draft of the test.

***Second method of calculating difficulty value :*** In this method, total number of examinees are ranked from highest to lowest or vice versa on the basis of their total scores. Then upper 27% and lower 27% of the examinees are separated naming them as upper and lower groups. Thus, middle 46% of the examinees are kept aside. Index of difficulty (P) is calculated by using the following formula.

$$P = \frac{R_U + R_L}{N_U + N_L}$$

Here,

Ru = number of examinees in the upper group answering the item correctly.

$R_L$ = number of examinees in the lower group answering the item correctly.

$N_U$ = Number of examinees in the upper group.

$N_L$ = Number of examinees in the lower group.

**Example :** In a test $N_U$ and $N_L$ is 200 each. In the upper group an item was correctly answered by 120 examinees and the same item was correctly answered by only 30 examinees in the lower group. Calculate difficulty value of the item.

**Solution:**

$$P = \frac{120+30}{200+200} = \frac{150}{400} = 3/8 = 0.375$$

***Problem of guessing and difficulty value :*** Sometimes examinees answer the item correctly just by guessing. It inflates the actual score on one hand and increases measurement error on the other. If we want to reduce guessing we will have to increase the response option. Larger the alternatives, lesser is the chance of guessing. In order to reduce measurement error due to guessing, correction formula is used. This formula is based on the following assumption.

I. Examinees give wrong answers due to absence of knowledge .

II. All response items are equally attractive for such examinees who do not have knowledge.

***Guilford's formula correction for guessing :*** The formula for correcting the total score due to guessing is given below.

$$S = R - \frac{W}{K-1}$$

Here,

S = corrected score.

R = number of correct responses of particular item.

W = number of wrong responses.

K = number of response option used in the item.

Suppose an item is correctly responded by 300 examinees out of four hundred and each item have five response options a,b,c,d and e the corrected score will be

$$S = R - \frac{W}{K-1}$$

$$S = 300 - \frac{100}{5-1} = 275$$

So, the number of right responses taken as 275 instead of 300. Now p value which was 300/400 = 0.75 before correction will go down to 275/400 = 0.689

***Purpose of introducing Correction :*** Correction in calculating difficulty value is introduced with the following objectives :

*(i)* To discourage guessing by the examinees.

*(ii)* To give an advantage to the examinees who guess over those who don't.

*(iii)* To make the score meaningful and dependable.

*(iv)* To make even those items comparable which have different number of distractors.

Guessing can also be minimized by increasing the number of response options and by introducing negative marking for wrong options.

***Optimum difficulty value for a reliable test :*** Difficulty levels producing higher reliability are the optimum levels. A test constructor should keep the following suggestions in his mind in this regard.

I. He should select maximum number of those items whose difficulty values are close to 0.5.

II. When the number of items in a test is very large, scattered indices of P are preferred, though such items do not yield high inter-item correlation.

III. At least two third of the total items should have P around 0.40 and 0.60 in order to discriminate the poor and talented groups of examinees.

IV. True/false items or agree/disagree items should have difficulty value of more than 0.70.

The P values necessary for the final draft of 100 items test is given in the following table :

| Range of P values | Number of items | Types of items |
|---|---|---|
| 0.25 to 0.35 | 5 | Most difficult |
| 0.35 to 0.45 | 20 | Difficult |
| 0.45 to 0.55 | 50 | Moderately difficulty |
| 0.55 to 0.656 | 20 | Easy |
| 0.65 to 0.75 | 5 | Most easy |

**(b) Discriminating power of items:** Index of discrimination is also known as its validity index. Index of discrimination is that ability of an item by which the discrimination between the inferiors and superiors is possible. **Bean** (1953) has defined this index "as the degree to which the single item separates the superiors from the inferiors in the trait or group of traits being measured." From the point of view of discriminating power all the items of a test can be categorised into three types:

I. Positively discriminating items.
II. Negatively discriminating items.
III. Non discriminating items.

A positively discriminating item is one in which the proportion of correct responses is higher in the upper group. A negatively discriminating item is one in which the proportion of correct responses is higher in the lower group. It means that poor group is able to attempt the item correctly and superior group fails to do so which is absurd logically. A non-discriminating item does not discriminate the upper and lower group at all. Here the proportion of right responses is equal in both the groups.

After this analysis only positively discriminating items are selected for the final draft of the tests and other items are dropped.

***Methods of determining index of discrimination :***

1. Test of significance of the difference between two proportions.
2. Correlational techniques.

We are discussing these two methods one by one.

**1. Test of significance of the difference between two proportions or percentages** : In this method examinees are first divided into two equal groups on the basis of the total scores arranged in order. **Kelley** has suggested that top 27% and bottom 27% of the total examinees should be selected for the purpose of comparison and testing the significance of difference. Although Kelley's dichotomy has no theoretical argument behind it, yet it has been proved the best dichotomy so far empirically.

His dichotomy can be illustrated with the help of an example. A test was administered on a group of 100 students. After scoring the answer sheets, scores were arranged in descending order. For the purpose of getting top 27% $P_{73}$ was calculated. For the purpose of getting bottom 27% 27 percentile point was calculated. His dichotomy is shown in the figure of normal distribution curve given below :

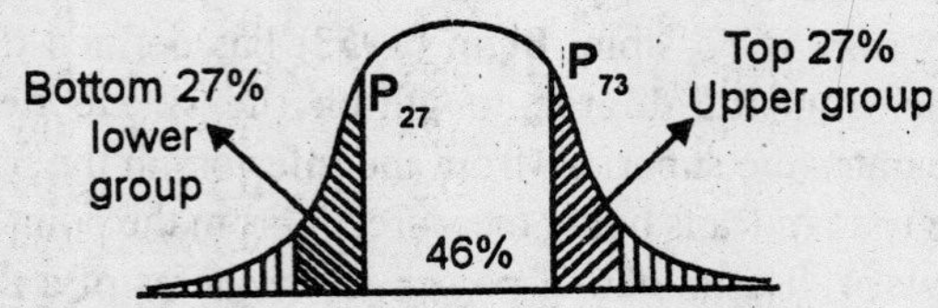


*Below 27% lower group, top 27% upper group*

After preparing this dichotomy, the answer-sheets of high and low group examinees will be recorded separately item-wise and thus scores of each item will be noted down one by one. Here right responses on each item are calculated separately for high and low group examinees. Thus, separate difficulty value of item for top and bottom groups of examinees will be obtained which will be $P_U$ and $P_L$ respectively. Davis has given the following formula in this regard.

$$P_U = \frac{R - \frac{W}{n-1}}{R+W} \text{ and } P_L = \frac{R - \frac{W}{n-1}}{R+W}$$

$P_U$ = Proportion of right answers of upper group of students, i.e, difficulty value of an item for the upper group.

$P_L$ = Proportion of right answers of lower group of students, i.e., difficulty value of an item for the lower group.

R = Right responses of an item in respective groups.

W = Wrong responses of an item in the test in the respective group.

$n$ = number of response options.

**Example :** An item was attempted correctly by 20 out of 30 top 27% students while only 10 students in the lower group could answer it correctly. The item has 5 alternative responses (multiple choice). Find the proportion of correct answers in the upper and lower groups separately?

**Solution:** $P_U = \frac{R - \frac{W}{n-1}}{R+W} = \frac{20 - \frac{10}{5-1}}{20+10}$

$$= \frac{20-2.5}{30} = \frac{17.5}{30} = \frac{35}{2\times 30}$$

$$= \frac{7}{12} = 0.58$$

$$P_L = R - \frac{\frac{W}{n-1}}{R+W} = 10 - \frac{\frac{20}{4}}{10+20}$$

$$= \frac{5}{30} = \frac{1}{6} = 0.16$$

One point to be kept in mind is that if some students have not reached some of the last questions while taking the test, then not reached responses will not be counted. Only attempted questions right or wrong will be counted here. Moreover, if any examinee has not attempted any of the item in the middle, it will he counted as wrong response because it shows difficulty value for a particular examinee.

On the basis of $P_U$ and $P_L$ we can calculate difficulty value and discriminating power of an item.

$$P = \frac{P_U + P_L}{2}$$

$$DP = P_U - P_L$$

In the example given above difficulty value of the item will be

$$\frac{0.58+0.16}{2} = \frac{.74}{2} = 0.37$$ and discriminating power of the item will be 0.58 – 0.16 = 0.42

Discriminating power of an item can be calculated by the following formula also.

$$DP = \frac{P_U - P_L}{\sqrt{\frac{P_U Q_U}{N_U} + \frac{P_L Q_L}{N_L}}}$$

$P_U$ = Percentage of students attempting the item correctly in the upper group.

$P_L$ = Percentage of students attempting the item correctly in the lower group.

$Q_U$ = Percentage of students attempting the item wrongly in the upper group.

$Q_L$ = Percentage of students attempting the item wrongly in the lower group.

$N_U$ = Number of students in the upper group.

$N_L$ = Number of students in the lower group.

If DP value>1.96, the item is said to be discriminatory

**Example :** An item was correctly attempted by 80% students in the upper-group and by 30% in the lower group. If number of students in both the groups were 10 each, calculate DP.

$$DP = \frac{80-30}{\sqrt{\frac{80\times20}{10} + \frac{30\times70}{10}}}$$

$$= \frac{50}{\sqrt{370}} = \frac{50}{19.23} = 2.6$$

2.6 > 1.96, so item is able to discriminate the superiors and inferiors and hence it must be included in the final draft.

**2. Correlational technique for determining index of discrimination :** In this technique each item is correlated against the internal criterion of the total score. **Lindquist** has called it internal consistency item discrimination index, if correlation is high of a particular item, it means that item of the test is serving the purpose for which it is intended to serve, i.e. item is difficult for poor group and easy for superior group. There are different methods of calculating correlation coefficient, selection of which will depend on the nature of the test. When multipoint items are employed, product moment correlation is the most appropriate method. When items are in two response option like true/false, biserial correlation is the most appropriate method and so on.

Since, the calculation of all these correlation coefficient is a very cumbersome task and lengthy procedure, we take the help of item analysis work sheet table especially to calculate biserial co-efficient of correlation. This table was prepared by Flanagan. It is actually a short cut method of finding r of a particular item. If we know the proportion of the examinees passing an item in the upper 27% criterion group and proportion of the examinees passing an item in the lower 27% criterion group, we can directly read the value of Biserial r from the table.

The only assumption regarding the use of the table is that the number of examinees in each group should not be less than 100. Thus, size of the sample should he 100+100+170 (27%+27%+46%)=370 at least.

**Item Analysis Work Sheet**

| 1<br>Item no. | 2<br>N=100 Correct Proportion in the upper 27% | 3<br>N=100 Correct Proportion in the lower 27% | 4<br>Index of difficulty | 5<br>Index of discrimination |
|---|---|---|---|---|
| 1 | 0.8 | 0.2 | 0.5 | 0.6 |
| 2 | 0.65 | 0.35 | 0.5 | 0.3 |
| 3 | 0.9 | 0.4 | 0.65 | 0.5 |
| 4 | 0.4 | 0.6 | 0.5 | –0.20* |
| 5 | 0.65 | 0.85 | 0.75 | –0.25* |
| 6 | 0.55 | 0.25 | 0.4 | 0.3 |
| 7 | 0.5 | 0.5 | 0.5 | 0.00* |
| 8 | 0.7 | 0.7 | 0.7 | 0.00* |
| 9 | 0.75 | 0.05 | 0.4 | 0.7 |
| 10 | 0.95 | 0.9 | 0.92 | 0.05* |

The items on which stars are there, will either be dropped or modified. If items are modified, further try out will be needed.

In the above table, the index of difficulty of items have been calculated by averaging the values of column 2 and 3 ie. $\left(\frac{P_U + P_L}{2}\right)$

And discrimination power in the fifth column is $P_U - P_L$ on each item. This is exactly in accordance with the table prepared by Flanagan.

***Relation between difficulty value and discriminating power:***

*(i)* P and D both values are complementary to each other. If an item is comparatively easy even then it must discriminate between superiors and inferiors. If $P_U$ of an item is 0.60 and $P_L = 0.50$, its $P = 0.60 + 0.50/2 = 0.55$ which is satisfactory but $D = 0.60 - 0.50 = 0.1$ which is very low. It means that item is very poorly discriminatory. Thus, selection of an item for the final draft of a test will not depend only on difficulty value but item must be discriminatory as well.

*(ii)* If an item has negative or zero index of discrimination, it will surely be eliminated from the draft even if it has sufficient level of difficulty value. Contrary to this, if an item has a very high or very low difficulty value it must be eliminated even if it has sufficient level of discriminating power.

*(iii)* The difficulty value depends on item variation and subject variation both whereas, discriminating power depends on the item variation only and groups are formed on the basis of subject variation only and hence P and D both are inter-dependent on each other.

*(iv)* If an item is correctly answered by the middle 46% examinees only and upper or lower group is not able to answer that item, that item will be **out rightly** rejected by the test maker due to low level of D.

**(c) Effectiveness of distractors (Distractor Analysis) :** If a test consists of multiple choice items, effectiveness of distractors is also to be analyzed. If an item is not functioning well in the test, possible reasons of why it is so are examined and examining distractibility of incorrect options is one of them. This is technically called distractor analysis.

Here the number of examinees answering each distractor of an item in both the upper and the lower groups is counted first. If a distractor is opted by more examinees in the lower group and less ones in the upper group, the distractor is said to be good. if opposite is the case, the distractor is said to be poor. In that case it is modified by the test maker to make it more attractive to the lower group.

If any distractor of an item is not functioning at all, i.e., it is not touched by any examinee in the lower or middle group, it must be either dropped out or modified. It is because its absurdity is very clear to the examinees and they are only thinking about the other response options while leaving this distractor aside.

Third type of distractors are those which are equally attractive for the lower and upper groups. They are also modified by the test maker to make it more attractive to the lower group.

These modifications in distractors are necessary because poor distractor tends to lower the difficulty value of an item and hence affect the reliability of the total test.

Distractors can also be analysed statistically by computing discriminating index of each distractor by using the same formula of D. An example will illustrate this point.

**Table for item No. 9 in a test**

| Response options | Upper 27 N=100% | Lower 27 N=100 | P value | D value |
|---|---|---|---|---|
| A | 75 | 25 | 0.5 | 0.5 |
| B | 0 | 0 | 0 | 0 |
| C | 5 | 10 | 0.075 | –0.05 |
| D | 20 | 65 | 0.425 | –0.45 |

In the above table correct option is A which shows that it is a good item because its difficulty as well as discrimination is 0.50. Distractor B is not functioning at all, so it must be removed and modified. Distractor C is also a poor distractor because it is attracting only 10% examinees in the lower group. Only distractor D is effective here which fulfills all the three conditions mentioned earlier. So, it must be retained. A good distractor must have high (close to 0.50) negative discrimination index.

***Item analysis for speed tests :*** A power test is that test in which examinees are given enough time to attempt all the items. Here speed of the examinee is not taken into consideration.

In such tests items of different difficulty values are selected and they are arranged in increasing order of P and the reliability of the test will depend upon the number of items in the test. Larger the number of items in a tests, higher will be the reliability of the test.

In a speed test a time limit is fixed within which an examinee is expected to reach the last item of the test. In such tests, items of uniform difficulty values are generally included in the test. Because of the time factor examinees attempt the items speedily as a result indices of difficulty and discrimination can not be determined in the same way as it is done in case of a power test.

***Item analysis for speed test :*** Following modification is made in the formula of determining difficulty value of an item as far as speed test is concerned.

$$P = \frac{R}{N_E}$$

P = index of difficulty

R = number of examinees attempting the item correctly.

$N_E$ = number of examinees who actually reach that item whether right or wrong.

Suppose there are 100 items in a test. 80 items were attempted by all the examinees say 100 but $81^{st}$ item was correctly answered only by 45 examinees and this item was attempted only by 80 examinees. In that case

$$P = \frac{45}{80} = \frac{9}{16} = 0.56 \text{ and not } 45/100 = 0.454$$

In order to reduce guessing factor, following correlation is introduced in the formula.

$$P = \frac{R - (W/K - 1)}{N - HR}$$

Here

R = Number of right responses.

W = Number of wrong responses.

K = Number of response options in a particular item.

N = Number of total examinees.

HR = Number of examinees who could not reach the item within the time limit.

As far as determination of index of discrimination is concerned, it can not be determined by correlational techniques. It is because in a speed test items are arranged in an arbitrary manner without any order as is done in power test where easiest item is put in the beginning and the most difficult item is put in the end in increasing difficulty order. Limitation of time is another problem which restricts at least some of the examinees to reach the last item. As a result, items put in the beginning of the tests will have higher difficulty value as against those items which are put in the last of the tests.

As far as reliability of the speed test is concerned, it depends upon the reasonable time limit given to examinees to attempt all the items. A reasonable time limit will ensure a high degree of reliability.

Nunnally (1970) has given a useful method for establishing the time limit of a speed test.

The test should be tried out on different samples of equal level belonging to the same population for which test is constructed. Different time limit is given to different sample here to take the test. The ideal time limit would be one which gives us largest standard deviation of scores. For this SD of scores of all the samples will be calculated. Larger the SD, higher will be the reliability of the test.

***Factors affecting item indices:*** Difficulty value of an item (P), Discriminating power of an item (D) and effectiveness of distractor are affected by a number of factors. They are given below.

1. **Ambiguity and complexity of an item :** If an item is complex and ambiguous in structure, it will become difficult for the examinees resulting in low P value and D may also be low. Similarly if distractors are not functioning properly and they are not evenly distributed in the middle and lower group, P may be high and D may be low.
2. **Non-familiarity of the examinees about the forms of the tests :** If examinees are not familiar with the forms of the test they would commit many mistakes resulting in low level of P.
3. **Methods of estimating the indices :** There are more than a dozen methods of estimating P and D values and all of them give different results.

4. **Techniques of dichotomizing low and high groups :** Some people take top 25% and bottom 25% for the purpose of dichotomy. Kelley has raised this limit to 27%. There are some educators who divide the whole group in the following way

   | **Top** | **Middle** | **Bottom** |
   |---|---|---|
   | 33% | 34% | 33% |

   all the dichotomies will give different Ps and Ds.
5. **Correction formula :** In order to reduce the influence of guessing, correction formula are used. It surely affects those students badly who do not adopt guessing technique for attempting the test. Similarly, there are several formulae used for guessing correction and each of them gives different Ps and Ds.
6. **Ability level of the examinees :** If the group of examinees is homogeneous, very talented or very poor, the index of discrimination will be low. Similarly, high ability level of examinees increase P values of items and vice versa.
   Contrary to this, if group is heterogeneous, D value will be high and reliability of the test will also be high due to high standard deviation.
7. **Skill of test construction :** The more skilfully a test has been constructed, the more valid and reliable the test will be resulting in P values ranging from 0.25 to 0.75 and desired degree of D values. Similarly, if distractors are very close to the right option, difficulty value will be very low. They will all depend on the skills and experience of a test maker.
8. **Lack of time for attempting the items. :** If reasonable time is not made available and a power test is made a speed test at least some of the examinees will not be able to reach the last 10% to 15% items. It will lower the P and D values both.

***Difficulties and limitations of item analysis :*** A number of techniques and methods have been developed for the purpose of item analysis so far which are used by a test maker and a test is standardized. Despite this fact some basic problems still remain unsolved which are to be discussed below.

1. **Problem of spurious correlation in item total correlation:** Whenever an individual item is correlated with the total score for the purpose of validating the item, the obtained coefficients are spuriously high. This problem becomes more serious when all items in the test measure almost the same function. Two things may be done for the purpose of minimizing this problem.
   I. The number of items in the test should be kept large.
   II. Heterogeneous items rather than homogeneous ones should be included in the test, i.e., extreme indices of items should be there.
2. **Problem relating to dichotomous items :** Items with true/false, agree/disagree and yes/no responses are generally used in non-ability test like personality test, interest inventory, attitude scale etc. Suppose a test maker has constructed 100 dichotomous items for an anxiety test and in the test 50 items are positive statements and 50 ones are negative statements.
   Key says that all agreements to the statements are given +1 mark each and disagreements to the statement means zero score. In that case all item total correlation will be close to zero and all positive statement would correlate negatively with the negative statements. Thus, item total correlation techniques will fail here.
   This problem can be solved by giving a score of +1 to all positive statements when agreed and one same score to all negative statements when disagreed. In such a case item total correlation will be positive.
3. **Problem of controlling unwanted factors :** In homogeneous tests all items are said to measure only one factor. Consequently all items should correlate with each other only. But it does not happen practically. Take the example of an aptitude test. It not only measure quantitative or mechanical aptitudes of the examinees but it also measures the factor of verbal comprehension and thus the test is likely to correlate with this factor also. This problem can be minimized by increasing the number of items in the proper try out test four times the final draft. In this way, only those items will be selected for the final draft which highly correlate with the total scores and items of low degree coefficient of correlation will be eliminated. Here KR formula (20) is used

for estimating the reliability of the final test form. If $r_{11}$ is greater than the correlation of the total scores with scores on the unwanted factors (which is computed separately), the effects of unwanted factors is said to have minimized.

4. **Problem of guessing:** Problem of guessing is very common in all types of objective type tests. It inflates the scores and increases the P values and Ds both. This problem can be minimized by introducing minus marking in the scoring procedure. For every wrong answer ¼ extra marks are deducted from the total score. For example, if an examinee has attempted 20 questions wrongly out of 100, his total score will be $100 - (20 + \frac{1}{4} \times 20) = 75$

   Formula for guessing correction is also used to reduce the effect of guessing. But this idea of correction is opposed by many technicians on the ground that correction formula does not make correction for guessing only but it also makes correction in those cases when wrong option of a response set is opted due to lack of information or poor construction of items.

5. **Problem related to time limit :** No power test is purely a power test in itself. Examinees are required to complete the test in reasonable time. Thus, it becomes speed test for about 25% of the examinees. In this way their scores are affected by time limit resulting in low P values and High D values.

## (E) FINAL TRY OUT (FIFTH STEP)

After item analysis, items for the final test are selected. Here only those items are selected to be included in the final draft of the test which have appropriate P and D values and whose distractors are functioning properly. In this way, final length of the test becomes one third or one fourth of the initial draft.

This test is tried out on a sample again for further statistical operations like calculation of reliability and validity of the tests and preparation of norms for the final tests.

We have already discussed reliability and validity in detail in the second and third chapter. We have also discussed how norms of a test are prepared in order to make a test usable in future. Once this process is completed, a test are standardized and it can be used by any person in future with ease and results of the test will be the same if all assumptions related to the test are fulfilled.

# Modern Trends in Evaluation

## (A) GRADING SYSTEM

### Arguments Against the Marking System

Assignment of marks to examinees are not liked by some educators on the following grounds

I. At least ± 7% error is always possible in every measurement in behavioural science. If a student has scored 60% marks in any achievement test, then his actual score will lie between 53-67%. This is not the case only in subjective tests. Even objective tests can have this error due to guessing on the part of the examinee. So, classifying students into 100 categories on the basis of their percentage of scores is not a sound approach.

II. Criteria of evaluation differ from board to board and from university to university. For example, students doing B.Ed. from MJP university score more than 80% marks when they top the class but in A.M.U., Aligarh toppers normally score less than 65% marks in B.Ed. So, if merit list of all B.Ed. passed candidates is prepared for selection in any job, AMU students will suffer. Conversely if 7 or 9 point scale is prepared and students are graded on these scales on the basis of Normal Probability Curve, no talented student will suffer.

III. Classifying students in 100 categories by assigning marks is neither justified nor needed. Classifying students in six categories only as we see in a normal distribution schedule is enough. All students scoring in the range of 43% 57% are average students. It does not matter whether they have scored 45% or 55% because a number of physical and psychological factors also work at the time of examination and achievement of a student is sure to be affected by these factors. Low score on an achievement test does not mean low achievement in real sense.

IV. Cut throat competition among students for scoring high and high in board examinations is benefiting only few and disturbing millions of them. Many students suffer from stress and strain at the time of examination and some of them often commit suicide in frustration. Besides, such a heavy spirit of competition is not conducive to nourishing creative potentials. Such potentials are developed in tension free environment only. So, if 7 or 9 point grades are allotted to students, they will not mind whether they have secured 90% or 93% because both of them may have the same grade.

V. The biggest argument against marking system is that 1% difference of marks changes the total status of an examinee. For example, the student who scores 59% is considered second divisioner and the student who scores 60% is considered first divisioner. Is this categorization genuine? Can 1% marks really change the position of a student? May it not be due to the involvement of error. There are four divisions seen in percentage of marks, ie, first division, second division, third division and distinction. Here 1% variation in marks can change the position of a child. But in grading system, if nine point scale is being used ie, A1, A2, B1, B2, C1,C2, D1,D2 and E, then 1% variation of marks may not necessarily change the position. If any how position changes, there is less difference between A1 and A2 as compared to first and second division.

VI. Different subjects measure different abilities and it is very absurd to aggregate all of them on the basis of marks obtained in different subjects.

## Meaning of Grading

The strongest argument in favour of grading system is that it is a qualitative assessment of achievement of a student not a quantitative one. The strength of personality of a person is determined on the basis of his quality not quantity. Desirable change in the behaviour of a learner is determined on the basis of its quality and grades assigned to behavioural changes is the best parameter of determining quality.

In grading system, grades instead of marks are assigned to the examinee on the basis of quality of his answer. Various grades referring to various qualities are pre-determined. An example will illustrate this point in which various grades ranging from excellent to very poor are given.

| *Quality* | *Grades* |
|---|---|
| 1. Excellent | O |
| 2. Very Good | A |
| 3. Good | B |
| 4. Satisfactory | C |
| 5. Average | D |
| 6. Poor | E |
| 7. Very Poor | F |

On the basis of the quality of the question, the examiner gives various grades to different examinees by keeping the parameters from excellent to very poor into account.

## Methods of Grading

There are basically two methods of grading used.

**1. Direct grading :** In this method grades are allotted to questions directly on the basis of their quality. If answer written by the examine is of very fine quality almost uncomparable to any other answer, it will be considered excellent and grade 'O' will be assigned to it. If the quality of the answer is very very poor, F grade will be assigned to it on a seven point scale as is the example given above.

If there are more than one question in a question paper say seven and each question is graded differently by the examiner, then final grade of the examinee will be calculated by using the following formula.

$$\text{Overall grade} = \frac{\Sigma \text{ grades}}{\text{No. of questions}}$$

An example will illustrate this point. Suppose seven questions were graded by an examiner in the following manner on a seven point scale. Find the over all grade of the examinee.

Grades allotted to different questions from first to seventh = A, C, C, D, O, F, C

**Solution :**

**Step I :** Numerals are assigned to different grades from 1-7 in the following manner.

| Grades | O | A | B | C | D | E | F |
|---|---|---|---|---|---|---|---|
| Numerals | 7 | 6 | 5 | 4 | 3 | 2 | 1 |

**Step II :** These numbers are put below the grades in the following manner.

| Assigned grades | A | C | C | D | O | F | C |
|---|---|---|---|---|---|---|---|
| Assigned Numerals | 6 | 4 | 4 | 3 | 7 | 1 | 4 |

**Step III :** These numerals are summed up and total is divided by the number of questions in the following way. Overall grade = 6 + 4 + 4 + 3 + 7 + 1 + 4 = 29/7 = 4.14 = grade C

***Limitations of direct grading:***

*(i)* Determination of quality of an answer is a subjective phenomenon. It lies in the mind of the examiner which varies from examiner to examiner. Thus, different persons will grade the examinee differently. Even the same examiner can not grade the same examinee in the same way because criteria of quality may change over a period of time.

*(ii)* An examiner can not judge the quality of a question without evaluating at least some considerable number of answer books of different examinees. It will take much time. And if all the examinees in the group are very poor, the exact quality of a question can not be determined.

*(iii)* The examiner compares the quality of the examinee with his own quality. If he has a high quality of response in his mind, he will evaluate the examinee at low grade.

**2. Grading by Score Conversion :** It is a mid way approach between grading and marking and thus, it can remove some of the defects of both the systems, ie.

*(i)* It classifies the students into less number of categories and thus creates less confusion.

*(ii)* Qualitative assessment which is advocated by philosophers is possible here.

In this method, answer sheets of students are first scored in usual manner, then these scores are converted into grades on the basis of any of the two criteria given below:

(a) **Determination of grades by fixing range of scores :** In this method different grades are allotted to students on the basis of range of scores, e.g., seven point scale can be prepared in the following manner.

| Grade | Scores |
|---|---|
| O | Above 91% |
| A | 81%-90% |
| B | 61%-80% |
| C | 51%-60% |
| D | 41%-50% |
| E | 33%-40 |
| F | Below 33% |

(b) **Determination of grade by preparing merit list of all the students :** This method has been exactly adopted by CBSE in India Answer sheets of all the students are evaluated in a usual manner. Then subject wise merit list of all students is prepared. Those students who score less than 33% in a particular subject are considered failed in that subject and they are allotted grade E. The remaining pass students in that subject are equally divided into eight section. 12½% passed students who are on the top of the merit list are allotted grade A1, next 12½% students are allotted grade A2, next 12½% students are allotted grade B1 and at last bottom 12 ½ % are allotted grade D2 and in this way a nine point scale, A1, A2, B1, B2, C1, C2, D1, D2 and E are prepared.

***Practical problems of grading system :***

*(i)* Grading system can be adopted by any board or university provided that all the boards and universities in India adopt this system and with the same criterion out of three given above. If consensus is not there among them regarding a particular criterion or method, acceptability of candidates from one board or university to other board or university will not be possible.

*(ii)* In a country like India where opportunities for admissions or jobs are few and candidates are 100 times more than the opportunities, grading system can not be used as the basis of admission or recruitment. We can not accommodate all the candidates in any situations even if they have got A1 because of the limited number of opportunities.

*(iii)* Conversion of marks into grade is easy but vice versa is not possible in any way. As a result, we can never know the exact marks obtained by a candidate.

*(iv)* Grades given to students by preparing subject wise merit list will not work if examination is internal and purpose of examination is to remove the weaknesses and improve the situation. The students getting grade A1 may be below average if range of marks is 0-50% and not above. We can not convince such students that they need improvement. In such a case either direct grading should be adopted or grade should be determined by fixing the range of scores.

*(v)* In certain systems marks are fixed to appear in the competition as is the case of IIT, JEE where no student can appear in JEE who has scored less than 60% in 10+2. In such cases this system will fail.

***Practical approach :*** No system is completely free from shortcommings. Neither marking system is fully free from limitations nor so the grading system. So, both these approaches should be adopted simultaneously and marks obtained in different subjects by candidates should not be aggregated in order to clarify aggregate percentage of marks. This is being done by CBSE for the last 11 years. Now CBSE has decided to mention only grades on the mark sheet. This will definitely create many problems before students.

***Merits of grading system :*** In spite of many limitations of grading system, this system is advantageous to students, authorities and the schools in the following manner.

*(i)* Error of measurement is reduced to minimum here.

*(ii)* Inter-subject comparison of the same examinee and inter-examinees comparison in a particular subject both are possible here.
For example, if an examinee has scored 75% marks in Hindi and the same percentage of marks in mathematics, it does not mean that his ability in both the subject is the same due to variation in the nature of questions and variation in the criteria of marking but if grades

are also there along with marks and they have been allotted by preparing merit list, then the candidate may have grade A1 in Hindi but B2 in mathematics. In this way we can compare the performance of the examinee in both the subjects.

Similarly, different examinees can be compared on the basis of their grades obtained in different subjects. Over all grades can be calculated for this purpose.

*(iii)* With the grades given in board examination a school can know at what level of teaching it is at present. If majority of students have got grade C or D in a particular subject, then it will be concluded that teaching and preparation in that subject was definitely poor.

*(iv)* Grading system classifies students into less number of categories and hence the tendency of cut throat competition among them for solitary marks is checked. They will not have stress or strain for want of marks.

*(v)* Grading system is a boon for weak students more than bright students. It reduces the frustration level of weak students very much.

## (B) SEMESTER SYSTEM

When a particular course of study is divided into different equal parts not on the basis of the session but on the basis of months and examination is conducted after the completion of every part it is called semester system. For example, if course of study is of two years, four semesters may be there. A professional course which is of long duration, e.g., 4 ½ years, may have only three semesters of 1 ½ years durations each as we see in medical and engineering courses.

**Need and importance of Semester System :**

*(i)* If it is not possible to divide the course on yearly basis due to technical reasons, the total course of study is divided into different semesters.

*(ii)* If there is no internal evaluation prevailing in the system, two semesters are arranged in one academic session in order to keep the student alert for their studies.

*(iii)* When duration of course is very long, ie, 4 ½ years and first part of the course can not be completed in one year, then a semester of one and half years is arranged for the students.

*(iv)* When so many subject papers are to be taught to students and every subject or paper needs only five or six months to complete, semester system is the best option.

*(v)* In semester system no arrangement for long vocation is made. Classes are held round the year without giving any break to students except for the period of examination. When course of study requires round the year study, semester system is the best option.

**Limitations :** Replacing annual system by semester system is nothing but old wine in a new bottle. Its demerits are as given below :

*(i)* Hectic examination activities are seen very frequently here if duration of a semester is short. It means that purpose of learning is to pass the examination and nothing else.

*(ii)* It suffers from all those defects which annual system of examination suffers Students starts their study only when the examination is near.

*(iii)* After the examination is over, students do not start their fresh study before they gets feedback from their examination results. Since declaration of results takes time, at least 20-30 working days are wasted after every semester.

*(iv)* In semester system papers are not set by internal teachers. They are sent to other universities for setting. This increases clerical work and may cause delay in the examination.

## (C) CONTINUOUS INTERNAL ASSESSMENT

Continuous Internal Assessment (CIA) is a system in which the teacher who teaches the class sets examination papers, evaluates the answer sheets of students, declares the result in the class and gives, feedback to his students. This assessment procedure is not time bound. It goes side by side of teaching as a continuous process for regular improvement of the teaching-learning process. Five or six sessional tests conducted by school in an academic session is an example of CIA. Oral examinations are generally added to written ones in CIA.

**Procedure of CIA :**

I. The date of test is announced by the teacher who teaches the class. Total syllabus is divided into different units for the purposes of convenience. It should match the number of tests to be conducted in a year.

II. Subject teacher prepares the test paper from that part of the syllabus that he has already covered.

III. The number of such tests in a year is decided by the principal of the school. All subject teachers must have to conduct at least the required number of tests in a year. They can, however, conduct more tests than required but marks obtained by students in these extra tests are not added to total marks.

IV. Test is conducted in the class in the period which is allotted for teaching that particular subject. Thus, duration of test is 40 minutes.

V. Test copies are evaluated by the subject teacher and returned to students after scoring. Mistakes committed by students in their test copies are encircled for the purpose of giving feedback to students. These mistakes are later discussed in the class in the form of recapitulation.

VI. Marks obtained by students in these tests are noted down in the test register so that final result may be prepared at the end of the session.

VII. Progress report card is prepared and sent to the guardian from time to time to give immediate feedback to students and guardians.

**Advantages of CIA :**

I. It gives regular feedback to the teacher who teaches the subject and he can remove his mistakes and weaknesses every time.

II. CIA can give us the trend of progress of a student, whether he is going up or he is coming down or he is stagnant at his progress. This will help the teacher to modify his strategies every time.

III. With the help of CIA the teacher can classify his students into different categories on the basis of their scores in tests and can adopt different strategies for different categories. Thus, backward students will be given more attention by the teacher.

IV. CIA goes along with teaching and only a small part of the syllabus is covered. Thus, it reduces the burden of examination from the shoulder of students. It does not create any stress or strain in the minds of students. They can take the test in an easy manner.

V. CIA motivates the students to study on a regular basis in order to improve achievement at every level. Thus, there is less chance of students', failure in the class. Problem of stagnation at the primary level can be solved by adopting this method.

VI. It is less time consuming. Teaching is not disturbed in CIA because only one test is conducted on a day and other periods are utilized in teaching as usual.

VII. CIA does not make teaching examination oriented. Acquisition of knowledge or skills becomes the purpose of teaching learning process.

VIII. Maximum number of working days can be utilized in teaching while adopting CIA system. One or two months need not be wasted exclusively for examination, its preparation and declaration of results.

IX. In CIA system, tests conducted are very short and hence immediate feedback can be given to the learner.

X. In annual examination system if a student is failed, his whole year will be wasted but in CIA, if he is failed in one test, there is a chance to recover in the second or third test.

## (D) QUESTION BANK SYSTEM

In this system a large number of questions from each topic or unit of the syllabus are prepared in advance and required number of questions from each topic or unit of the syllabus at the time of examination or test are taken out from the pool. They are separately printed and test is conducted, with the help of these questions.

Making question bank is a regular process in the sense that different varieties of questions of definite number are regularly constructed by experts and added to the bank. All these questions are standardized by adopting systematic procedure of item analysis and total reliability and validity of the test can also be calculated before administering it to the examinees.

If question bank is stored in a computer disk then we give programme to the computer to bring out the required number of items from each topic. We can also get items of required difficulty value by using computer programme and computer can also calculate the reliability or validity of the test which consists of those items.

**Steps in the preparation of question bank :**

*(i)* The whole syllabus for which question bank is to be prepared is divided into different convenient topics.

*(ii)* Different topics are given to different experts for constructing questions from each topic.

*(iii)* Experts construct at least three times the number of questions required from each topic and then after item analysis the required number of questions are selected. Thus, first step of preparing question bank is completed.

*(iv)* The above three procedures are repeated again and a large number of questions are again constructed and added to the pool.

*(v)* This unending process of adding the questions to the question bank and taking some of them for use goes on intermittently.

**Advantages of question bank system :**

1. There is least chance of leakage of question paper here because experts who have constructed the questions do not know whether their questions have been included in the test or not. Thus, secrecy of examination can be maintained here.
2. Question papers can be set immediately by using question bank. There is no need of sending the syllabus to paper setter and waiting for his response. Even a layman can select the required number of questions from the question bank and get it printed for administration.
3. If question bank is published for wide use, learners can be benefitted from it very much. They can know the pattern of questions and different angles from which questions are constructed. It will definitely facilitate learning.
4. Question bank can help in recruiting the best candidates on the basis of test. Recruitment boards and agencies use these question banks very comfortably. All Railway Recruitment Boards in India have a variety of such question banks and required number of items are included in the test to select suitable candidates from the lot.
5. Question bank is also used in admissions. When we have to select only few out of so many candidates, we prepare a test by taking out items from the bank and thus a test of required validity and reliability can be prepared in no time. This test will definitely discriminate poor and good students positively and only able candidates will be selected for admission. IIT and IIM both uses the same procedure for selecting students for various courses.

## (E) USES OF COMPUTER IN EVALUATION

Computer can be used in the evaluation process in the following ways :

1. **Storing of Items :** A large number of items (Question Bank) can be stored in the Compact Disk of the computer. Difficulty values of items, discriminating power and efficiency of destractors can also be given against each items. We can increase the capacity of question bank by increasing the number of items constructed by experts.
2. **Printing of the test :** We can give a programme to the computer to print out such and such items of such and such difficulty value from such units and topics. Thus, a test covering the whole syllabus can be prepared and printed by the computer. If we want to maintain higher degree of secrecy and do not want to go to the printing press, we can print out the required copies of the test by the computer. All these things do not require the services of an expert. Even a layman can do all these jobs.
3. **Analysis of Records :** While conducting large scale competitive examinations, agencies use OMR sheet where informations are supplied by the candidates. Computer records these informations and match them with the eligibility criteria. In this way, informations of thousands of students can be analysed and entertained in one hour. Such a fast speed of operation is not expected by a man or a group of men.
4. **Scoring of items :** If answer sheets are to be evaluated by using computers, then OMR sheets is used. In case of multiple choice items, candidates mark and darken a,b,c, or d options as the case may be and OMR sheet is scored by the computer. More than one thousand such sheets can be scored by the computer in one hour.

Computer also prepares merit list after the scoring is over and required number of candidates are selected on the basis of cut off scores of the merit list.

5. **Item analysis :** Item analysis is an important procedure in standardization. If this is done manually it will take much time. Computer can perform this function very accurately and at a very fast speed.
6. **Preparation of mark sheet :** On the basis of achievement of a student in various subjects computer can prepare mark sheet of the student and print it out. It was done manually some ten years ago but now all the universities and boards have adopted computer system for this purpose.
7. **Use in internal assessment :** If a number of internal tests are conducted by an educational institution, then results of all the students in all the tests can be stored in the computer. Computer can provide us the trend of achievement of a student graphically in no time. It will help the principal to study the efficiency of a subject teacher. He can also know whether the teacher adopted remedial measures in case of poor performance of students or not.
8. **Analysis of results :** Computer can analyse the results of any examination not only quantitatively but also qualitatively. We can compare the performance of a section with other sections of the class and by using t test we can also come to know whether the difference is significant or not.
9. **Grading :** Computer can convert marks into grades very easily. We will have only to give the criteria of conversion to the computer.
10. **Transfer of results :** If networking facility is there in an educational institutions, one department can get the information of other departments and all of them can get feedback from the results of students.

Besides, internet system has narrowed the whole globe. We can transfer any information to any place by using internet.

# Administration (Conduct) of a test

## INTRODUCTION

Administration of a test is the second important task before a test maker after constructing a test. Extensive training and special skills are required for administration of a test. From management of the examination hall to the scoring of the test questions many varieties of skills are to be used. Knowledge and experience of these things are necessary for any test maker (examination in charge in case of annual or terminal exams).

There are many tests which are used across the globe and then performance of examinees of different countries are compared. Due to this reason examinees of one test centre should not be given extra advantages in relation to the examinees of other countries. All examinees must have to be tested in an ideal condition everywhere.

### Ideal Physical Conditions for Testing

Testing is done in an examination room. Following facilities are necessary for the examinees :

1. Ventilation and lighting either natural or man made should be proper not to tax the examinees physically.
2. There should be sufficient place for sitting. Table and chair should not have loose fitting or they should not be unbalanced.
3. Sufficient space should be there to spread the writing materials on the table.
4. Directions of the invigilator should reach to the last examinees of the room and if room is very large loud speakers may be used.
5. If something is to be demonstrated by the invigilator, the examinees must be able to see them. It means that examination room should not be more than 50x25 in size.
6. The room where the test is to be administered should be quiet and free from any outside noise pollution. Invigilators too should not disturb the examinees by their own gossiping.
7. Test room should not be over-crowded by so many examinees. More than double space is required for examination than for studying in the class.
8. Seating arrangement should be such as to avoid copying.
9. If weather is very hot and humid, electric ceiling fans should be used to give comforts to examinees.
10. If it is raining outside, it may create a lethargic atmosphere for the examinees. Its effects may be reduced by closing the windows and by drawing the curtains on them.
11. A wall clock should be there in the examination hall to help the students to adjust the test with time in a speed test.

### Time Schedule and Other Related Factors

1. If test is very lengthy having items 200 or more, intermission may be given in the middle to avoid fatigue. A light breakfast may be supplied to students during this period. If long tests are conducted in two or three sitting, it is better.
2. Proper rest should be given to students before taking a test. They should come to the exam-hall at least 30 minutes before the commencement of the test. This time should be utilized to develop rapport with them.
3. Time of the day is also an important factor. The best testing time is 8 AM to 11 AM and the worst timing is 2 PM to 5 PM. It is because fatigue and frustration are caused less in the morning and more in the afternoon.
4. The best testing time of the year in Indian climatic conditions is February to March and Oct. to November.

5. Every test requires a certain time limit. It should be very judiciously estimated by the second and third try out for regular use of the test.
6. An examinee should be tested only when he feels easy and comfortable.
7. Test of short duration should be given first if more than one tests are to be conducted on a day.
8. If we are going to conduct a speed test, time allowed should be short enough so that most of the students taking the test may not be able to finish up the test within the prescribed time limit. If it happens so, discrimination between poor and good will be possible.
9. Time actually depends upon the nature and number of items. If all items are difficult and require lengthy calculations and long thinking process, longer time will be needed to take the test. Due to this reason it is the test maker who can actually calculate time limit of a test. As a general guiding rule, the items from knowledge to evaluation in cognitive domain has the following time ratio:

| Level of objectives represented by items : | Knowledge | Comprehension | Application | Analysis | Synthesis | Evaluation |
|---|---|---|---|---|---|---|
| Time ratio in minutes : | 1/2 | 1 | 3/2 | 2 | 5/2 | 3 to 4 |

Here, 1/2 minute is for knowledge items.
1 minute is for comprehension items.
3/2 minutes are for application items and so on.

10. Timing also depend on the ability level of examinees.

## Seating Arrangements and Control of Copying

In group testing, adequate control over the group is very much needed to avoid copying. This control should not, however, be a military like manner. Effective command and control may be established by establishing rapport with the examinees. Larger the group, the more will be the problem of controlling.

Lack of adequate control over the group leads to cheating and mass copying on the part of students. Cheating or copying raises the actual scores of examinees in achievement or intelligence tests.

## TYPES OF CHEATING

### A. Cheating to Raise Actual Scores

This type of cheating is done by applying the following methods:

**1. Copying from the neighbours :** In group tests such type of copying is very common. Examinees copy from their neighbours from sides or from back and front.

This type of cheating can be controlled by proper seating arrangements and by other measures such as:

(a) Distance between the examinees should be large enough in rows as well columns both. No two rows should have a distance less than three feet and some space should be left after every five seats to make the cross of the row by the invigilator.

(b) If different grades of students are taking a test in the room in case of achievement test (x) should be there in the seating arrangement of these examinees in the following ways.

VIth ——— IXth
IXth ——— VIth

(c) This type of cheating can also be checked by supplying different sets of question papers like set A,B,C and D. The same items are arranged in different serials in these sets so that students may not be able to copy the answers from the answer-sheets of their neighbours.

(d) Different equivalent form of tests can also be used especially in achievement testing.

(e) Proper search should be made so that students may not use scraps for cheating.

(f) Invigilator should not allow the examinees to talk among themselves.

(g) The seats of well-known defaulters should be kept on the front and near the main doors.

**2. Prior knowledge of test items :** Examinees may collect information about the items of the test from those who have already gone through such tests. They can also consult the printer or photocopier holder to get knowledge about the items

This type of cheating can be checked by adopting the following measures.

(a) Proper orientation should be given to students regarding the purpose of the test and its advantage in the field of education and research. In this way, they will not go to seek for unfair means.

(b) Testing materials should be safeguarded properly and secrecy should be maintained.

(c) Such students should be selected as sample who belong to a school of high repute.

(d) Test materials should be kept into locker with the bank or the library and only the authorized person should have access to these materials.

(e) New test forms should also be developed from time to time in order to prevent previous acquisition of knowledge about the test.

(f) Test booklets after use should be destroyed properly.

(g) Examinees must not be allowed to take the help of any book or notes to attempt the items.

**3. Extension of time limit :** Sometimes students start attempting question before the signal to begin is given and they may continue to attempt after the expiry of the time. In this way they can attempt more items correctly.

This type of cheating can be checked by adopting the following measures.

(a) Only question booklet should be given to students first for filling up names and other details. Answer-sheet should be supplied to them only when the bell to begin rings. If there are sufficient numbers of invigilators in the room, the distribution and collection of answer-sheets will not take more than 30x2=60 seconds for supplying the materials and taking them back.

(b) Sometimes searching is done in the middle of testing period which takes not more than 2 minutes but extra time of five minutes is given to examinees. This is wrong. Only that amount of extra time should be given to students which was consumed up for searching.

## B. Faking of Responses

Sometimes subjects give fake or wrong answers in order to look better in a particular psychological trait. It happens when questionnaire is used to test a trait and examinees try to give socially approved answers rather than answers corresponding to their own typical behaviour. Such type of faking is done due to lack of interest in the test.

This type of cheating can be avoided by adopting the following measures.

(a) The purpose of the test may be disguised from students so that they may not hide the truth but this is possible only in projective techniques of testing. In other tests, purpose of testing should be clarified before them.

(b) Examinees should be motivated properly before taking a test.

(c) Students should be taken into confidence that their answers will be kept secret at all costs and it will not be disclosed to any body.

(d) Sometimes students avoid giving any answer and leave the item blank. Forced choice technique should be followed to escape this problem with the clear instruction that not responding means negative trait.

(e) Problem of faking can be eliminated by administering the test on two samples and thus by using Chi square test, significance of difference can be obtained.

(f) If students are taking objective type achievement test, faking should be controlled by assigning negative scores on wrong responses.

## Instructions Regarding the Test and Its Administration

Clear-cut directions need to be given to the examinees regarding how to attempt the items and to the test administrator regarding how to deal with the examinees and how to score the test. Some of these directions to develop proper rapport are given below:

1. Administrator should have thorough knowledge about the directions of the test so that he may clarify any point before the examinees if they are unable to understand it.
2. He should ensure that examinees turn over the pages only when they are instructed to do so.
3. Instructions to be followed by the examinees should be in clear and understandable language. The administrator (invigilator) should demonstrate important instructions in the exam-hall if needed.
4. General instructions about the test should be given on the first page of the test booklet.

5. While simplifying any instruction before the examinees, the administrator should not add any new point to lead them to the correct answer.
6. Queries of the examinees about any item or its directions must be normalized by the administrator without giving them any hint regarding the right answer.
7. Separate instructions are necessary for each type of items. Sample questions may also be given if necessary.
8. Educational level of the examinees and their age must be kept in mind while finalizing the time limit.
9. Instructions regarding how to answer an item must be clearly given.
10. Instructions regarding how to handle the computerized OMR sheet must also be given otherwise the purpose of scoring will be defeated.
11. If invigilator clarifies any point to any testee, it is wrong. He should rather generalize the clarification in the hall.

## Techniques of Avoiding Guessing in Answering Objective Questions

Guessing a correct option by the examinees without knowing the answer is an important problem that is common everywhere when items are of multiple choice type. In multiple choice objective type questions, four or five options are given for each item and only one option is the correct answer of that item. If examinees do not know the answer they guess it and attempt the item.

Guessing is also seen in matching type or true/false items. In true/false type items, there is 50% probability to be a guessed answer correct due to only two options there. Similar is the case of a matching item. If four informations are to be matched in an item with four relevant factors or events given there and an examinee knows two facts out of four. He will again guess the remaining two and again there is 50% chance to be an answer correct. Problem of guessing is very common in all non-achievement tests.

All these types of guessing inflate the actual score of an individual and thus whole purpose of the test will be defeated.

## Guessing Can be Avoided by Using the Following Techniques

1. **Instruction and introduction of minus marking:** In this technique 25% minus marks are allotted to the examinees for each wrong answer along with the deduction of marks for that item. If an item is such that 1 score is allotted for the answer being correct and zero is given to the examinee if answer being wrong and if an examinee has attempted 60 right items and 40 wrong ones out of 100, his actual score will be $100 - (40 + {}^{25}/_{100} \times 40) = 100 - 50 = 50$ marks instead of 60 in minus marking technique. Due to this penalty, no examinee would dare to attempt any question whose answer he does not know.
2. **Raising the number of response option :** If there are only two response options, there is 50% chance to be a guessed answer correct. If we increase the number of response items to five, only 20% chance will be there to be an answer correct. In such a case if minus marking system is there, no examinee would like to guess the right answer without knowing it, because 80% chance is that his answer will be wrong. Thus, guessing can be reduced by raising the number of response options.
3. **Introducing a supplementary short answer test:** A supplementary short answer test of the same weightage can also be introduced to avoid guessing on the part of students. If correlation coefficient between the two tests is high, it will be stated that there is no role of guessing in the pure objective type tests. If correlation coefficient is low, the individuals should be tested again. Individual scores will determine the names of defaulters here. These tests should, however, have only one definite answer.
4. **Avoiding computerized scoring :** Multiple choice questions can be scored with the help of the key programmed in the computer. Thus, just and fast scoring is possible here. If we give up mechanical scoring and introduce very short answer type questions to be scored manually, the problem of guessing will automatically be removed again.

5. **Taking the help of guessing correction formula :** Inflated scores are brought to the actual level by using guessing correction formula. But honest and really talented students are also penalized here.
6. **By developing rapport with the examinees :** If examinations are conducted by developing rapport with them and it is made clear to them that whatever is being done that is entirely in their interest to a large extent, examinees would avoid doing guessing. They will attempt only those items whose answers they actually know.

## Maintaining Rapport with the Examinees

Rapport means a relation free from all formalities between two persons or groups. Subject is made to do his best by maintaining rapport by the test administrator with him. Techniques used to develop rapport with the examinees depend on the testing situation and nature and composition of the group taking the test. However, certain points must be borne in mind by the person administering the test.

1. Standing over the examinees every time, giving unnecessary directions, telling time after every 10 or 15 minutes, criticizing the examinees, appreciating some of them in the presence of others, passing unhealthy remarks for the examinees, taking much interest in female examinees by the male invigilator, helping some of them beyond the rule, extra attention to some examinees and so on adversely affect the group behaviour and rapport.
2. Preliminary suggestions and necessary explanations should be given to examinees to raise their confidence level. It will also help them to understand the directions.
3. Surprising elements must be eliminated to reduce anxiety among them.
4. Students should be properly motivated to take the test with confidence.
5. Distraction, negativism and shyness before the strangers are the major problems of lower primary school children. Efforts should be made to create direct affiliation of these examinees with the person administering the test.
6. Getting the physical and psychological needs of the examinees fulfilled is another measure to develop rapport.
7. A democratic and sympathetic behaviour on the part of the invigilator will surely increase rapport between the invigilator and then examinees.
8. Examinees should be properly convinced that testing is in their own interest. The purpose of the test may also be explained to then along with the procedure of taking the test.
9. If physical atmosphere of the room is painful, it may increase tension in the minds of the examinees. Unless this problem is not reduced, proper development of rapport is not possible.Rules and regulations about the test situation should also be properly explained before the examinees.

## How to Motivate the Examinees

High level of motivation is seen among the students in some tests especially in those tests which are conducted for the purpose of screening the examinees for selection in a job or for admission in a particular course. In such tests there is no extra need to motivate the students for the test. But when a test is conducted for the purpose of evaluation or research, motivation given by the test administrator to the examinees becomes essential. Since the test has no direct significance for the examinees, they do not take much interest in the test. In such cases extra motivating factors are used to motivate the students. Some of these factors are given below :

1. **Welcoming the ego of the examinees :** If an administrator of a test is somehow able to convince the examinees that they are an important asset not only for the test maker or researcher but for the whole society and findings based on the test will be utilized for improvement in the educational system, they will take full interest in attempting the test items. They should also be told that their contribution in the field of research will be recognised.
2. **Praise and Reward :** Studies have shown that praise and reward help improvement of a scores of school going children on Arithmetic and intelligence tests. Rewards may be monetary or non-monetary both. It will surely motivate the students to take the test seriously.
3. **Other motivational techniques :** Other motivational techniques such as raising the

aspiration level of students high, creating group competition, knowledge of results etc also motivate the students for the test.

4. **Long preparation :** If students are being prepared mentally so that they may not skip the test, they will be mentally ready to take the test.
5. **Elimination of tension and suffocating situations:** Tension and threat reduce motivation. Tension may be caused due to the attitude of the teachers or parents or due to the teasing situations created by other students. Some tests phobia already exists in all the examinees. For the purpose of motivating the students these phobias and fear psychosis should be reduced to the minimum and tension should be released from the minds of students. The test administrator can do it by making the environment easy and friendly.
6. **Extra precaution for abnormal children :** Students who are physically and psychologically normal and adjusted are normally motivated for the test. But if there are maladjusted, deviant, delinquent and emotionally disturbed children found in the group, they can not so easily be motivated. These things affect their performance on the test. The invigilator should motivate these students by using special techniques and by recognizing their valuable contribution.
7. **Cultural factors :** Students belonging to high socio-economic strata of the society are well motivated for any test but students of poor or uneducated background may think all these processes to be a wastage of time. These students should be told about the world scenario of education and the reason why India is so backward in the field of education. If these things are told to them, they will be motivated also.

## Discretionary Power of the Person Administering the Test

Even in standardized tests many things are not mentioned in the manual and the discretion is left on the administrator how he has to tackle a situation. Some discretionary powers given to him are as follows:

1. He can give extra time to late comers, physically challenged examinees and the person who has somehow wasted some part of his time.
2. He can provide the facility of writers to some examinees in abnormal situations. This is, however, not mentioned in the manual.
3. He may allow the examinees to attempt 90-100 items first, then come to 40th to 50th item. But the answer-sheet will not be disturbed here.
4. When examinees are up set or disturbed due to some unavoidable situations, he may postpone the test. But in annual examinations he will have to take the permission of the centre superintendent to do so.
5. He has the right to change the language of any directions given at the beginning of a particular type of items but sense of the directions should not change.
6. He has the right to encourage the examinees of tender ages by adopting methods such as, a sympathetic smile, a word of appreciation, demonstration of an instruction etc.
7. He may change the seating arrangement of the examinees in the examination hall any time if he needs so.
8. He may clarify some questions in easy language.
9. He has the right to allow the examinees to go out of the ball for different purposes as many times as possible but his exit entries will be maintained.

# UNIT-XII

## Educational Technology

1

# Educational Technology : Nature and Scope

## MEANING OF TECHNOLOGY

Before coming to the meaning of educational technology, we should, first of all, know what the word technology signifies? In common language, the application of scientific laws and principles for the purpose of making daily life easy and comfortable is technology. By these applications, we construct such machines and devices which accelerate and systematize our daily life. Thus, technology refers to two aspects — theoretical, based on ideas and practical, based on putting ideas into practice.

## EDUCATIONAL TECHNOLOGY

When technology is used for the purpose of accelerating and facilitating educational processes with certain objectives in view, that technology is called educational technology. But this is the incomplete meaning of educational technology. As it has already been stated that technology is not limited to the construction of machines and other devices (hardware). Designing, modeling and organisation of hardware are needed before their construction which are primarily based on well-testified laws and principles (software). Thus, in educational technology, humans and machines both have their respective roles and both work as complements to each other in the process of education. It means that man uses his intellect and experiences along with the machines and devices and by using his arts he organises the teaching-learning process in the best possible manner.

Educationists have understood educational technology in different ways. Some of these dimensions are given below :

### First Meaning of Educational Technology

**J. K. Galbreth,** in his book "New Industrial State" has stated that every type of technology implies two important characteristics.

First—Application of scientific laws and principles for practical works. Second—Dividing the practical works into steps and sub-steps and then completing them systematically.

These two techniques are followed in educational technology too. Functional analysis of the task is done first and then each section of the task is completed by applying relevant scientific laws and principles. This functional analysis requires formulation of objectives which is actually the tasks of philosophers and thinkers. When a teacher uses educational technology in the class, he provides (physical)concrete structure to these mental (abstract) objectives.

Thus, educational technology is that science of strategies and techniques which leads us to the educational goals. Thus, educational technology refers to teaching strategies and techniques. In other words, by using educational technology, after preparing the environment, all inputs (Hardware and Software) are organised in such a manner that students learn themselves what they want to learn. This whole process completes in four stages.

(a) **Analysis of teaching tasks :** Identifying all the components of inputs, process and output related to teaching-learning process.

(b) **Observation of relative impacts of all these components :** Doing action research in order to study the utility of any component in the class.

(c) **Drawing conclusions :** On the basis of his observation a teacher draws the conclusion to what extent a particular strategy or combination of strategies and behaviour is successful in the class.

(d) **Translating the experiences :** Whatever conclusion a teacher arrives at is translated into usable language for the benefit of other teachers.

Thus, this meaning of educational technology, makes teaching a process of research which is carried out in the field on dependent variable (students) for the use of other independent variables (teachers).

### Second Meaning of Educational Technology

Mechanization of teaching-learning process for the benefit of the big masses is educational technology. It is related to hardware technology. This is applicable to all the three stages of human knowledge.

(a) **Preservation of knowledge :** Preserving the present knowledge of humans is the first function of education. This knowledge was preserved orally or in the form of manuscripts before the invention of printing press. Now this is preserved in printed books, tape recorders, CDs, films and digitals.

(b) **Transmission of knowledge :** Whatever knowledge is acquired is transmitted to others at other places. In the classroom situations this task is done by the teacher to transmit knowledge to limited number of students. But when this knowledge is to be transmitted to a large number of students simultaneously TV, Internet or Printed books are used. Besides, this knowledge can be tapped to be communicated to the learners again and again. This special type of technology can help the students to remove their doubts by listening or reading any educational programme pacing with their abilities, and convenience.

(c) **Advancement of knowledge :** Machines or hardware technology has no direct role to play in the advancement of knowledge. But when a part of knowledge reaches to a large number of learners through these machines they apply this knowledge in their life situations and many new problems of life arise. When any of these learners takes the initiative to search the solution of these problems, the knowledge advances automatically. Knowledge which was imprisoned by some selected well off people is now open to reach to the masses. This universalisation of experiences has accelerated and multiplied the research works too. People of new skills and intelligence are now giving many new dimensions to knowledge by using their creative potentials. As far as computer application is concerned, nobody can deny its role in the analysis and presentation of data in all research works.

### Third Meaning of Educational Technology

Educational technology unites the science of learning with the art of teaching and leads to the development of teaching theories and principles. While doing so, educational technology does the following activities.

*(a)* Analyses teaching/instructional problems.

*(b)* Selects suitable teaching strategies and techniques for the purpose of preparing desired output (students).

*(c)* Constructs relevant tests and applies them to students to evaluate their behaviour. Thus, inputs and processes are evaluated in terms of output.

## DEFINITIONS OF EDUCATIONAL TECHNOLOGY

Educationists have defined educational technology in different ways. Some of the representative definitions are given below :

1. **Leth :** "Educational Technology is the application of scientific knowledge about learning and conditions of learning to improve the effectiveness of teaching and training."

   **Explanation :** According to this definition, purpose of educational technology is to improve the process of teaching and training. For this purpose, it uses all those research findings which have been done in the field of learning and its conditions.

   **Criticism :** This definition is very slightly different from the definitions of educational psychology which puts greater emphasis on the behaviour of learner and learning conditions and makes the teacher subservient to those conditions.

2. **Richmond :** "Educational technology is concerned with providing appropriately designed learning situations which holding in view the objectives of teaching or training bring to bear the best means of instruction."

   **Explanation :** According to this definition, the purpose of educational technology is to create suitable learning conditions in the class. For this purpose the teacher uses the best means of instruction out of so many available with him. In this way, he reaches the objectives which he formulated in the beginning. Thus, educational technology is related to goal based teaching.

   **Criticism :** This definition talks about selecting the best means of instruction but it does not tell the criteria on the basis of which the best means of instruction can be selected.

3. **R.A.Cox :** "Educational technology is an application of practical study which aims at maximizing educational effect by controlling such relevant facts as educational purposes, content, teaching materials, methods, educational environment, conduct of students, behaviour of instructions, and inter-relation between students and instructors".

   **Explanation :** According to this definition the purpose of educational technology is to increase the effectiveness of teaching to the maximum level possible. This is done by controlling all the relevant factors such as, the teaching process, content, strategies, material aids, behaviour of students, behaviour of the teacher, educational environment etc. Thus, this definition emphasises the role of educational technology in teaching as well as educational administration. It treats the learners as experimentees in the class who are given least opportunity to manipulate.

   **Criticism :** This definition is very much against the democratic concept of teaching and talks about fully controlled atmosphere in the class. This strict nature of controlling may be a burden for the students and the teacher both. A teacher cannot transform his teaching into entertainment under this controlled environment and everything goes on in the class only mechanically.

## Other Definitions

1. Educational technology can be understood as the development of a set of systematic techniques and accompanying practical knowledge of designing, operating and testing schools' educational system.

   **–Robert M.Gagne**

2. Educational technology has to be seen as part of persistent and complex endeavour of bringing pupils, teachers and technical means together in an effective way. **– J.K.Gass**

3. Educational technology can be defined as the application of laws and discoveries of science and technology to the process of education.

   **– S.S. Kulkarni**

**Practical Definition :** The composite form of material and non-material strategies and techniques used by classroom teachers and school principals in order to increase the learning speed of students in the class is none but educational technology.

## CHARACTERISTICS OF EDUCATIONAL TECHNOLOGY

On the basis of the definitions given above, following characteristics of educational technology can be drawn:

1. Here inputs are integrated and assimilated to the output in such a manner that the application of science and technology in education becomes an automatic process.
2. Here learning theories, art and science of teaching both go hand in hand. Thus, it removes the defects of educational psychology.
3. It emphasises on the development of new strategies and techniques for an effective and result oriented learning. Thus, it is a constant process of research which can benefit all the future teachers of the society.
4. It first defines the objectives in behavioural terms. Then it creates suitable teaching learning environment to realize those objectives.
5. It endows too much responsibility on a teacher and asks him to control the situation in the best manner possible.

6. In order to evaluate the learning objectives, it constructs the relevant tests so that all the efforts may go in the direction of goals only.
7. It can speed up the process of learning by controlling educational environment, the behaviour of students, contents, strategies etc.
8. It emphasises on the systematic approach of teaching where task is analysed first. Then relevant strategies are selected for each unit of tasks.
9. Educational technology considers school as a system where plants, equipments, furniture etc are inputs, various strategies and techniques of teaching are process and these two things are used to produce output (students).

## Need and importance of Educational Technology:

Use of educational technology is needed in the process of education because of following reasons :

1. **Population Explosion :** Population of Asian countries are increasing at a very fast speed and we can not educate all these people just by using teachers in the class. Modern media of communication like TV, Internet, CDs etc. can impart education to millions of people together in one setting.
2. **Fast Generation of New Knowledge :** New knowledge is expanding at a very fast speed. It is almost doubling in just three years. A teacher is not supposed to impart this huge amount of knowledge by tutorial or classroom teaching. Educational technology can perform this function very easily.
3. **Development of New Strategies :** It is the educational technology that has helped to develop new strategies in the field of education like micro teaching (inculcation of teaching skills among teachers), programmed instruction (preparation of instructional materials in written or CAI forms for individualized learning). Instructional analysis (analysis of teaching materials into convenient parts to be presented to students one by one) and use of hardware technology in education etc.
4. **Controlled Atmosphere :** Education can not be treated as plaything by some teachers. After the introduction of educational technology, it has made the whole process of defining teaching objectives, clear, scientific and interesting. The teacher controls the classroom environment in his own favour but his performance is evaluated simultaneously by applying tests.
5. **Importance of the Teacher's Role :** It emphasises theories and principles of teaching more than those of learning. Thus, it has removed many of the defects of educational psychology and has raised the significance and relevance of a teacher in the class.
6. **Mass Extension of Model Teaching :** The facilities of radio, television and internet are now available at a large scale. By demonstrating the effective teaching of renowned teachers on these media, we can benefit millions of students together. Even the less effective and less skilled teachers can take the benefit of these demonstrations and improve their teaching.
7. **Beneficial to Private Students :** Many universities have given permission to students for private examinations, even in higher education. These students do not attend classes. In order to maintain standard of education in higher education, the use of educational technology becomes a necessity.
8. **Beneficial for Teacher Training Colleges :** Even teacher training colleges can not produce good teachers without the use of educational technology. It is because, this branch of education puts emphasis on the modification of teacher's behaviour. For example, we can develop teaching skills in students with the help of micro-teaching techniques.
9. **Improvement of School Administration :** Educational technology helps us to analyse the problems of school administration scientifically leading to improvement in the system. This is done by applying various combinations of inputs or adopting the procedures followed by the other school systems.
10. **Preservation of Knowledge :** By using hardware technology, we can preserve knowledge in audio video cassettes, CDs and floppy disks.

11. **Development of Teaching Models :** When a definite combination of inputs and strategies gives good result repeatedly in a number of class room situations, it can be translated into teaching models to be used universally. It can also lead to the development of teaching theories.
12. **Creation of Interesting Learning Situation :** Educational technology can transform the teaching learning process from burden to enjoy which is psychologically very sound for students, e.g., use of material aids in teaching increases the interests of students.

## Assumptions of Educational Technology

Knowledge of all social sciences are not as stable and universal as those of natural sciences. They are applicable only when certain conditions are fulfilled. Educational technology is also based on the following assumptions :

I. Human is such a biological system which is influenced by communication. If communication is effective, he will receive it without difficulty. Thus, humans are not rigid like stones. They are flexible. We can change the behaviour of the teacher as well as students by adopting suitable communication strategies. It otherwise means that different situations affect the humans differently.

II. When we sue any physical object for a human, his biological system unique to him improves his communication. For example, use of tap recorder in the class makes the communication speed favourable to him and barriers of communication are automatically removed.

III. Educational technology is a science more than an art, i.e., its results can be verified in other situations. It means that teachers are not only born. They can rather be produced in teacher training institutions. Teachers will make drill of different strategies and techniques and they will become effective teachers by habit formation.

IV. Teaching theories can also be developed in the long run by doing action researches or by applying psychological principles and theories. Once this happens, teaching will no longer remain an individual activity or monopoly of a teacher.

V. Suitable communication strategies and techniques can increase learning.

VI. Media of communication can also be helpful in solving the educational problems. But when some problems are solved by them, some new problems are also created by the media. So selection, application, analysis and evaluation of these means must be done very carefully.

## USE OF EDUCATIONAL TECHNOLOGY FOR TEACHERS

Until recently, the teachers used to be the sole interpreter of knowledge to the learners and the text-books the sole resource. Educational technology has affected the conventional roles of the teachers and equip them with technical mindset to perform various activities related to teaching in the following manner.

1. Educational technology has provided a scientific base to educational theory and practice.
2. It has helped teachers to use scientific and systematic approaches to conduct action research in the classroom situation to overcome the classroom problems, related to classroom environment, content, curriculum etc.
3. It helps the teacher to modernize and mechanize the teaching learning process. It also helps the learners to study at their own rate with the help of programmed instructions on video or computers.
4. Educational Technology supplements teachers in their instructional programmes through the structured lessons for remedial, enrichment or drill purposes. The learners get the training of self-instruction and teachers are relieved of the burden of routine repetition for exercise and revision purposes.
5. Educational Technology supplements the teacher with audio-video aids to make the teaching-learning process more effective. Audio-visual aids do not supplant the teacher.
6. Through analyzing the content and organizing it in a systematic, logical and psychological order in their lesson plans teachers, especially

prospective teachers, visit the classroom with confidence and put up a high profile performance due to their total control on content and process.

7. Helps in teacher's professional growth.
8. Adds to their teaching competence, modify their teaching behaviour and style, inculcate a scientific outlook, approach and attitude and helps them transfer these to their learners.
9. It helps in realising pre-specified learning objectives by incorporating available procedures and techniques.

### Misconceptions about Educational Technology

Educational technology is sometimes misunderstood by the people in the following ways :

I. All engineering technology is considered educational technology by some people. It is not so in fact. Only those machines and equipments prepared by engineering technology which can be applied in the process of education in any way come under the category of educational technology.

II. Some people think that audio-visual aids are educational technology. They too are not educational technology. They are only inputs which when used along with the process keeping certain objectives in view produce the output.

III. Programmed instruction is also not educational technology. It is only a self-learning written technique which is used in some contents in order to realize the limited level of objectives. Thus, it may be only a part of educational technology.

IV. Some people think that micro-teaching in itself is educational technology. It is rather a micro approach of making the teaching strategies effective in which teaching skills are taught to teachers by drill.

V. Educational technology can not solve all the problems of education. It can only solve those problems of education which are related to classrooms or schools.

VI. Educational technology is misunderstood by some people as applied form of educational psychology. Though the fact is that when we use psychological principles for improving teaching-learning process, it is called educational psychology but when we apply the same principles for realising certain predetermined objectives and pour teaching principles into it, it also becomes educational technology.

## FUNCTIONS/OBJECTIVES OF EDUCATIONAL TECHNOLOGY

1. **Determination of Objectives :** Objectives are, though formulated by philosophers and thinkers, yet defining the objectives in behavioural terms so that they can be evaluated objectively is the function of educational technology.
2. **Identification and Categorization of Students:** Use of similar type of teaching strategies is not successful for all types of students. Educational technology helps us to identify the students and their ability levels by testing their entering behaviour and by arranging the subject-matter accordingly.
3. **Effective Presentation of Subject-Matter :** After knowing the entering behaviour of students, the subject-matter is now presented to them according to their needs, interests and abilities. This presentation is sometimes logical and sometimes psychological. Various communication strategies and devices help the teacher to present the subject-matter effectively.
4. **Bringing Novelty in Teaching Strategies :** If the same strategy or technique is used throughout the lesson, it bores the students a lot. For this purpose, change in strategies is needed every now and then. Educational technology helps the teacher to bring about change and novelty in them in an unnoticeable manner.
5. **Modification in Teacher's Behaviour :** If a teacher knows educational technology, he is always alert to the ongoing effect of his behaviour on the students. He modifies his behaviour by novel experiments and drill and makes his teaching effective.
6. **Making Teaching-Learning Process Effective:** The ultimate aim of educational technology is

to make the teaching-learning process effective. For this purpose the teacher not only changes his process off and on but he also uses new technological equipments in his teaching.

7. **Evaluation of Teaching :** Whatever a teacher has taught is evaluated by the teacher at the end of his teaching. This process helps the teacher to know to what extent the educational objectives have been achieved. He uses measuring instruments for this purpose. If such instruments are not available, he constructs them and then he matches the results with the objectives already formulated.
8. **Guiding the other Teachers :** The quality of output produced after teaching helps the teachers to decide to what extent he is successful in his efforts. If results are good, the model is supplied to other teachers for improving learning. If results are otherwise, other teachers are made cautions against the strategy and thus educational technology becomes a living subject.

## Three Approaches of Educational Technology

1. **Hardware Approach (Educational Technology I ) :** The very use of different types of machines in teaching is known as hardware approach. It is also called mechanization of education through the use of teaching machines, TV, radio, computer etc. It has also been given the name of audio-visual aids provided that they have been prepared by applying scientific and technological principles. It should be noted that all audio-visual aids are not educational technology first. Educational technology I is such an application of science and technology in teaching and education by which maximum number of students can be benefited by incurring minimum costs. This application makes the teaching so impressive that it can save time and energy as well. For example, application of radio, television, computer, internet etc. in teaching and education not only makes the tasks easy and effective but we can also teach millions of students together by using the teaching of an effective teacher on TV and internet repeatedly. Similarly, nobody can deny the use of hardware technology as material aids in the class.
2. **Software Technology (Educational Technology II) :** It is the application of laws of behavioural sciences or principles of psychology, philosophy and sociology coupled with the general laws and principles of natural sciences in education and training. Here, instead of using machines, principles of learning and teaching are used to bring about desirable changes in the behaviour of learners. If machines are ever used, they are used only for the clarification of concepts and principles, i.e., principles involved in the construction of the machine are only applied in education. Thus, this technology is related to the mental aspect of the task and it deals with writing educational objectives in behavioural terms, selecting suitable strategies for the presentation of the subject-matter, proper use of reinforcement devices and evaluation of educational outcomes. **Silcherman** has termed this technology as constructive educational technology. It consists of the following steps :

   I. Analysis of instructional problems
   II. Writing objectives in behavioural terms.
   III. Selecting suitable teaching strategies.
   IV. Reinforcing the students on right responses.
   V. Selecting or constructing measuring instruments for evaluating instructional outcomes.
   VI. Decision making and improvement.

   It is clear from the above discussion that hardware and software both the technologies are supplementary to each other. A good instructional material needs both of them simultaneously.
3. **System Analysis or Educational Technology III:** This technology is exclusively related to the problems of educational administration and management. Problems of school administration and management are analysed and studied scientifically and quantitatively under this technology. This study is based on mathematics. Then solution of these problems is also arrived

at by taking the help of quantitative interpretations. Thus, this technology can make educational administration effective. Procedure of system analysis is given below :

I. The number of inputs involved in a school system is calculated first. Then it is interpreted in terms of educational outcomes.

II. Some modifications in the inputs are made. For example, if in any school teacher-students ratio was 1 : 40 and result of the school was 80%. Now this ratio can be decreased to 1 : 30 to achieve 100% results in the school.

III. The effects of change in output are studied and they are matched with objectives of system analysis.

IV. The input-output ratio of one school system is compared with that of other school systems.

V. The best alternatives are chosen on the basis of the conclusions drawn.

## SCOPE OF EDUCATIONAL TECHNOLOGY

(A) Teaching Technology
(B) Behaviour Technology
(C) Instructional Technology
(D) System Analysis

### (A) Teaching Technology

Teaching is such a classroom activity which is completed by the interaction between teachers and students. This activity leads to complete development of students. It differs from instruction in the sense that only teacher is active and communicative in instruction while in teaching, students fully participate in the learning process and outcome is the result of interaction between teachers and students.

Teaching technology refers to the application of laws and principles of science and philosophy for realising certain objectives in education. Teaching which is an art in itself is made a science when technology gives it a practical, objective and goal based shape.

**Content of Teaching Technology**

**1. Planning Teaching :** A teacher makes proper plan to what he is to teach in the class. In planning he does three things :

(a) He analyses the content and arranges each sub content into systematic manner. It is called task analysis.

(b) Then he identifies the objectives i.e., what changes he has to bring about in the behaviour cf his students.

(c) Finally, he writes the objectives in the language of behavioural change of learners so that they can be evaluated at the end of the task.

**2. Organizing Teaching :** This is the second stage of teaching. This stage is particularly related to the presentation of the subject-matter. In organizing stage, a teacher does the following things :

(a) He selects suitable teaching strategies and techniques.

(b) He selects or prepares suitable material aids for making the presentation of the subject matter effective.

(c) He matches the strategies and material aids with the nature of the sub content to give such an experience to his students which is conducive to the realization of learning objectives.

In order to make this stage of teaching a success, teacher trainees are taught lessons like principles and theories of teaching and learning, behaviour development, strategies and devices of teaching, methods of evaluation etc.

**3. Leading Teaching :** This stage is related to communication strategies and reinforcement devices. Teacher motivates the students in such a way as learning becomes their necessity and they take full interest in the process. In order to learn various techniques of motivation, teacher trainee is taught lessons like techniques of behaviour development, motivating devices, classroom behaviour model, observation of classroom behaviour etc.

**4. Controlling Teaching :** This stage is related to evaluating teaching tasks. At this stage teacher evaluates organizing and leading stages separately and tries to ascertain whether the objectives formulated in the planning stage are achieved or not. If objectives are not found realized, the teacher will find out at what stage—organizing or leading he is doing mistakes and consequently he modifies his behaviour. A teacher does the following things here :

(a) He decides which form or procedure of evaluation he has to use.
(b) He selects suitable measuring instruments.
(c) If instruments are not available, he constructs them.
(d) He scores the tests by following certain rules.
(e) He interprets the scores in relation to objectives formulated in the beginning.

In order to make this stage a success, a teacher must know the techniques and procedure of evaluation.

**Assumptions of Teaching Technology :** Teaching technology is based on the following assumptions :

1. Teaching is a science more than an art and it can be learnt by efforts as is done in teacher training colleges.
2. Modification and improvement can be made in teaching activities according to the situation, i.e., there is no general formula applicable to all circumstances.
3. Teaching and learning are mutually inter related, i.e., they are affected with each other. It otherwise means that better teaching leads to better learning environment which in turn leads to better teaching.
4. Desired learning situations can be created by suitable teaching situations. It means that the role of the teacher is very significant in the class.
5. If teaching is effective, objectives will surely be realized i.e., a teacher will not be unsuccessful if he desires so.

**Characteristics of Teaching Technology**

I. This technology can make the teaching effective.
II. This technology also takes the help of sociology, philosophy and psychology from planning to controlling stages.
III. Here inputs, process and output work together and result in the form of behavioural changes coming to the fore every moment.
IV. All the three domains of objectives, cognitive, affective and psychomotor can be achieved by this technology.
V. Teaching can be organised on any of the three levels—memory, understanding and reflective levels by the use of teaching technology.
VI. New teaching theories can be developed by the use of teaching technology.
VII. This technology is equally effective to all grades of learning, i.e., primary, secondary, post secondary etc.

## (B) Behaviour Technology

This technology emphasises the application of teaching and learning principles into teaching so that behaviour of students as well as teachers may be modified in accordance with the objectives of teaching. Because of this reason, this technology is also known as training technology.

This technology is closely related to psychology. Psychology is the science of behaviour and learning is the modification of behaviour through activities and experiences. Behaviour technology applies all these principles of psychology to bring about desirable change in behaviour. We can train the behaviour of any person by reinforcing his desirable responses **(Skinner).**

This technology puts more emphasis on the behaviour of the teacher than that of students and whatever changes we want to bring about in the behaviour of learners can be brought through the behaviour of the teacher only. For this purpose, behaviour of the teacher is closely monitored and reinforced by expert observers.

**Content of Behaviour Technology :** A teacher learns the following subject-matter (topics) under this technology :

I. Meaning, assumptions and principles of teacher's behaviour.
II. Methods of observing teacher's behaviour and its rating.
III. Analysis of teacher's behaviour.
IV. Manifestation of behaviour under different situations.
V. Evaluation of teacher's behaviour and its manifestation.
VI. Different models of teacher's behaviour.
VII. Different techniques of developing teacher's behaviour, i.e., reinforcement models.

VIII. Micro teaching, team teaching and stimulated teaching.
IX. Social skill training.
X. T group training.

**Assumptions of Behaviour Technology :** This technology is based on the following assumptions:

I. The behaviour of the teacher is social as well as psychological. It means that psychological and social conditions directly affect teacher's behaviour.
II. Teacher's behaviour can be observed and measured.
III. Teacher's behaviour is relative. It means that some teachers are good and some are not good.
IV. Teacher's behaviour can be modified by training and by using reinforcement devices.
V. There is always a possibility of improvement in teacher's behaviour. Behaviour can be made good by imitating good models.

**Characteristics of Behaviour Technology :**

I. Psychology is the base of this technology. By using psychological principles and methods teachers' behaviour can be modified in the desirable way which will lead to the desirable changes in the behaviour of the learner.
II. Teaching skills can be developed in teachers with the help of this technology. It means that teachers' behaviour in the class can be observed and suggestions can be given by experts for improvement.
III. Reinforcement is the backbone of this technology which is used at all desirable responses.
IV. Here teaching activities are evaluated objectively. This makes the evaluation free from bias.
V. This technology emphasises more on the realization of psychomotor objectives.
VI. This technology is based on the use of software technology and role of machines is negligible here, though video recording devices can be used for observation and reproduction of behaviour.
VII. This technology is especially useful for teacher training institutions where modification of teacher's behaviour in the desired direction is needed.
VIII. This technology is also useful for principals of schools who can observe the classroom behaviour of their teachers and suggest remedial measures.
IX. This technology can tell us how teaching can be made successful by keeping the individual differences of students into account.
X. Content and methods of communication both can be used in order to improve teaching aspects in the class.

## (C) Instructional Technology

Instructional technology refers to the communication of content or informations to the learner. Content can be presented on all the three levels—memory, understanding and reflective levels. Instructional technology, can however, present the content to the second level of teaching only and we will have to take the help of teaching technology for reflective level of teaching.

Similarly, communication also has two elements—verbal and non-verbal. For example, questioning by the teacher and its responding by the students in the class is verbal communication. But in non-verbal instructions teacher uses his body actions gestures, stimulus variations and material aids for communicating the content. For example, if a teacher wants to convey the meaning of jump to the class, he jumps slightly and say it is jump. This is non-verbal instruction.

Instruction can be given either by the teacher or by the machine and it does not make any difference. For example, open universities use TV, radio or Internet for instructing thousands of students in a single setting and whosoever is interested can take the benefit of this programme. Thus, instructional technology is based on hardware approach i.e., here teaching-learning material can be communicated to learners by using audio-video recorders, radio, television, or computers. Direct interaction between the teacher and the students is not seen here as is the case of teaching or behaviour technologies. Instruction can not be termed as teaching due to lack of participation on the part of students. Even a teacher becomes an instructor when he does not invite the students to participate in the lesson. In spite of that if an instructor is very much effective in his communication skills, he can make the instructions living and interesting. This technology basically refers to communication of contents in an effective manner either by a teacher or by a machine.

In instructional technology too, instructional materials are prepared keeping in view the objectives formulated in advance. Then subject–matter is presented by using different strategies, techniques and material aids. Finally the outcomes are evaluated in terms of the objectives in order to ascertain whether instructional process is successful or not. In order to make instructional technology a success, knowledge of psychological and scientific principles and laws and awareness of social values and norms is a must, i.e.,. Maxims and principles of teaching must be kept in mind while preparing instructional materials.

**Content of Instructional Technology :** Following subject-matter are studied in this technology :

I. Meaning and definitions of instructional technology.
II. Meaning and principles of programmed instruction.
III. Linear programmed instruction, meaning, concept, principles and models.
IV. Branching programmed instruction, meaning, concept, principles and models.
V. Computer assisted instruction, its nature and various models.
VI. Construction of programmed instruction in various subjects.
VII. Adjustment procedures of individual differences and development of suitable equipments.
VIII. Media and printing equipments and their functioning.
IX. Principles of learning and instruction.
X. Devices of feedback and their uses.

**Assumption of Instructional Technology :** This technology is based on the following assumptions:

I. If we divide the whole subject-mater into parts, then each part can be taught separately. If it is not possible to divide the subject-matter into natural parts, this technology can not help to make the presentation of the subject-matter effective. In this way, learning situation can be created from outside by reorganizing different elements of the lesson.
II. A student can learn only according to his needs and rate of learning. It means that an instruction cannot benefit all the students equally, howsoever it is good.
III. A student can learn by machines (radio, TV, computers, etc.) without the help of the teacher provided that instructional materials are prepared after dividing the content into different natural elements.
IV. Students can be given feedback by instructional activities also, i.e., effective communication can provide feedback to learners.
V. Learning objectives can be achieved with the help of instructional objectives. For this purpose instructional techniques will have to change again and again.

**Characteristics of Instructional Technology**

1. Objectives of cognitive domain can be achieved by the use of this technology.
2. This technology can fill up the deficiency of effective teachers because we can communicate the instructional materials to thousands of learners at a time by recording the teaching of an effective teacher into machines.
3. By the use of this technology, students can learn according to their own ability and needs, e.g., if the rate (speed) of learning of a student is very slow, he can rebound the tape recorder or log on the website more than once until the topic is clear to him. Thus, with the help of this technology, we can control the problem of individual differences to a great extent.
4. Right responses of students can be reinforced regularly which will lead to further right responses to occur.
5. This technology is also based on principles of psychology and social values and instructional

materials are prepared by following these principles and values.

6. By using this technology into researches instructional principles can be developed.
7. Comprehensive analysis of the subject-matter is also possible with the help of this technology and it can make the presentation easy and logical.

## (D) System Analysis

This approach of instructional design is related to management technology. By its decision making processes, this technology has greatly influenced the fields of industry, trade, administration and military.

The assumption of this system is that every human behaviour works as a component of an organised system and since no system is perfect in itself, we can come to know the defects, of the system by analysing various components of the system. And after knowing the defects improvement can be made. For example, administration of a school is not an independent entity in itself but it is only a part of the whole educational administration as well as the society. So, administration of the school is definitely influenced by these two greater systems. If we want to remove the defects of any school system, it is necessary to analyse all its internal and external elements separately and quantitatively.

Thus, system analysis is the application of scientific and mathematical techniques into various elements of organizational activities. The purpose of this analysis is to improve the system.

**Procedure of system analysis :** System analysis is comprised of the following steps :

*Step I :* (Formulation of objectives) : This is the most difficult step of the system analysis where objectives are determined keeping in view the budgetary and human resources, plants, equipments, rules and regulations imposed by the education department of the state and the output produced by other schools and so on.

*Step II :* (Assessment of activities) : Here we find out the areas where the defects lie after making quantitative assessment of all the activities of the system.

*Step III :* (Collection of data) : After identifying the problems relevant data are collected to know whether they are really problems and if they are really problems, then to what extent they are affecting the system. Statistical methods are used for collecting data.

*Step IV :* (Analysis of data) : Sometimes we consider those things as problems which are not problems in real sense. Analysis of data helps us to verify or deny a problem. Thus, this is the step of hypothesis testing.

*Step V :* (Determination of the problem) : Here, problem is defined in clear and behavioural terms.

*Step VI :* (Explanation of the scope of the problem) : After knowing and ascertaining the problem, its various aspects are explained comprehensively. Then each of these aspects are studied in detail in the context of other school systems.

*Step VII :* (Outlining the solution ) : Here, a new outline is prepared for the solution of the problem. This solution is based on different models of the system working in the society.

*Step VIII :* (Use of the new model ) : For the purpose of reaching the solution of the problem, new model is introduced in the system.

*Step IX :* (Evaluation of the new model) : After applying the model into system, its outcomes and effects are evaluated every now and then. This process continues till the model coincides with the objectives decided in the beginning.

*Step X :* (Comprehensive generalization) : If this model is found fit for successful functioning of one system, it is published for extensive uses in other systems.

**Criteria of a Good Model :** How far a particular model is relevant to a system is determined on the basis of the following criteria. Effectiveness of a model is determined on the basis of this.

1. *Ability and devotion :* Whether all the components of the system are functioning skillfully and devotedly or not.
2. *Economy :* If a model is giving good results at low expenses then model is considered satisfactory and good.
3. *Utility :* Model must be useful to all involved directly or indirectly in the system.

4. *Time* : If good results are coming out in lesser time, then model is acceptable.

If we apply the above criteria in a school system we will say that a good system model implies four things.

I. All its components should work effectively and skillfully.
II. It should be economical.
III. It should be time saving in its use.
IV. The results of the system (school) should be useful for the students and the society both.
V. It should be simple to administer.

**Items of System Analysis :** We can analyse the system of a school on the basis of the following items and improvement can be made accordingly :

I. Teacher-students ratio.
II. Classroom students ratio.
III. Library and lab facilities.
IV. Facilities for co-curricular activities.
V. Working hours and working days in a particular session.
VI. Number of homework and class work given to students.
VII. Number of unit tests in a year.
VIII. Regular checking of CWs and HWs.
IX. Number of punishment given to defaulters-(teachers and students both can be defaulters).
X. The number of teacher-parents meet in the school in one session and so on.

# Multimedia Approach in Education

## CLASSIFICATION OF AUDIO-VISUALS

(A) Mechanical and Projected Aids
(B) Electronic Aids
(C) Software Aids
(D) Non-Projected Aids

Mechanical and projected aids are those aids which can not be directly introduced into a lesson. They rather depend on some mechanical devices to make their use possible in a class. If these equipments are not available, they can not be displayed and used in the class. Supply of electricity will also be needed here. These aids come under hardware technology of education. These aids can further be classified into the following categories given in tabular form.

## MECHANICAL AND PROJECTED AIDS

**Table : Projected and mechanical aids**

| Film | Photo Slides | Picture | Television |
|---|---|---|---|
| (i) 16 mm<br>(ii) 35 mm<br>(iii) 70 mm<br>(iv) Super 8<br>(v) Film strips | (i) 2 × 2 inches<br>(ii) 4 × 4 inches<br>(iii) Hand made Slides | (i) Magic lantern<br>(ii) Epidiascope | (i) Telecastes<br>(ii) Cassettes<br>(iii) CDs |
| Device used here is picture projectors | Device used here is OHP | Device used here is OHP | Device used here is projector and TV |

### Characteristics of Projected Equipments

I. Projected and mechanical teaching aids depend on some kinds of special equipment only then they can be used in the class. Thus, the medium through which projected aids are used in the class is called projector.

II. They are the mechanical devices assembled by certain technical parts such as lens, motor, photo-electric cell etc. The material is put here in inverted position but the image formed by this material is normal.

III. Projected film materials are based on the principle of persistence of vision, i.e., no gap is seen between images and continuity is perceived. This continuity between images creates an illusion of motion.

IV. A film is consisted of fixed frames divided by a very thin line. If a film is moved at a speed that the next image reinforces the first, the two frames would look as if moving.

V. Projectors are the devices through which materials are projected on a white wall or a screen.

VI. If film is audio and visual both, a fine beam of light from the photo electric cell (PEC) moves along the sound track and thus, reproduces the sound also along with the picture. Thus, sound and pictures are synchronized here with the help of mechanical devices.

VII. The source of energy of these projectors is light produced by a very high power bulb. Focal length of the projection lens would help in focusing as well as enlarging the image.

## IMPORTANT PROJECTED DEVICES

### I. Slide Projector

Simple 'slide projector' was known as "magic lantern" in the olden days. The principle here is that when we put the transparent slide on the socket and throw light from behind, the light passes through it and projects the image on the screen.

A slide projector typically consists of a quart, three halogen lamps, light to be reflected by the reflector, a heat filter and lastly, condenser lenses. The heat filter is a thermo crystal which absorbs most of the heat produced by three lamps. A cooling system is also needed which consists of a fan for convecting off the heat, filter and other components. The fan is thermostatically controlled. When projector is switched off, the fan is also switched off.

**Working of a Slide Projector :** When light passes through the slide, it projects an upside down and laterally inverted image on the screen because of the objective lens placed between the slide and the screen. If we want a bright image, we can use a focusing knob. In order to change this inverted image into a normal image on the screen, we will insert the slide in the inverted position.

In automatic slide projectors following components are needed :

I. Magazine facility.

II. Remote control switches, one for fan and projector each.

III. Automatic timing devices.

IV. Synchronized projection (sound and sight) both. This recorded textual matter makes the projector an effective means of communication.

Slides are single frame 2 × 2 mounted ones or in a roll of about 20 frames to be shown one by one. These slides are put into the socket one by one. These slides are projected through slide projectors especially designed for the purpose. When they are supplemented with synchronized audio-recording, they become audio-visual.

**Classroom uses of the Slide Projector :** Slides are prepared for selected topics and the informations contained by them may be in the form of written words, pictures, graphs, sketches, etc. The topic selected should be arranged frame by frame. The ideal ratio of length and breadth of slides is 2 : 3. Each frame should have only one concept for the ease of understanding.

The slides and the film strips are arranged in a sequential order. This arrangement is also coordinated with the teaching learning activity of the class. When slides are shown in the class, curtains are drawn on the windows in order to reduce the entry of natural light in the class.

Before showing these slides, teacher elaborates important points. Once the film is over, the teacher gives his own comments and relates the aid with the lesson to be taught.

### II. Film Strips

They are used before a large group of students either for introducing a lesson or for elaborating some minute object not seen in ordinary situations. Film strips are projected on a big screen through a film projector and then the projector is switched on. Here, very minute objects look very big on the screen and we can study their parts. For example, knowledge about bacteria and viruses can be given to students through these film strips. Sometimes, sound recording is also used along with the film to clarify important points.

**How to use film strips in the class :**

I. A teacher should first of all see whether all the equipments are working properly.

II. These films should be shown only by relating them with the lesson. They should not be shown in isolation.

III. A teacher should determine his own role in the film also as to when and what point is to be explained by him in the class and when and what question he is to ask here.

IV. Proper review of the film is also necessary after it is over.

V. In order to see whether desired results have been achieved, comprehensive questions must also be asked after the review.

**Advantages of Film Strips :**

I. The order or sequence of film strips is fixed and a teacher can prepare the relevant material to supplement the film according to the sequence.

II. We can have any part of the film on the screen as long as we desire so. As a result, a teacher can discuss a single topic as long as he needs. Thus, complete control over the equipment and the material is possible.

III. Handling of film projectors is also not complex. There is no problem of storing them because of their small size. Precautions are, however, needed against fungi or physical damage.

IV. They have become very cheap today and any school can afford the cost of these projectors.

V. They do not require complete darkness in the room as we do in using epidiascope or motion film projectors.

**Limitations of Film Strips:**

I. They can be used only in small sized classes because of limited focal length. Modern projectors are, however, having large focal length.

II. Slide projection is not as effective as film projection. Inventions of 3D films have reduced the use of slides even further. In spite of this, fixed order of the film strips creates problem in handling individual frames.

III. Many schools do not have audio-visual workshops and thus, they depend on the cheap and unstandardized materials available in the market.

**Difference between handmade photographic slides and computer made slides :** Photographic or handmade slide is one which is 4 × 4 in size. They are projected either through slide projectors or through epidiascope and its socket also coincide this slide. These slides are made of glass which is covered by another plain glass of the same size and bound on all four sides for protection. They are put into the socket in an inverted position in order to have normal image on the screen.

Computer made photographic slides aré of the size of 2 × 2.

**Superiority of Slides over Film Strips :** Slides can be presented in whatever manner we like, i.e., its order can be changed but the order of film strips is fixed and we can not change its order. From the point of view of classroom teaching, use of slides may be more useful when order of the topic is to be changed by the teacher but it happens very rarely in modern teaching.

## III. Film Projector :

16 mm films are generally used for the purpose of training or teaching. These films are planned and executed by a pannel of experts who endeavour to prepare films of good quality.

Motion picture is comprised of a number of frames separated by a thin line between each frame. Projector is run at a certain speed to match the sound with the persistence of vision. In place of 16 or 35 mm films, video cassettes can also be used in the classroom to teach 50-80 students because they can also give a fairly big image on the screen.

As far as use of film projector for classroom teaching is concerned, it is very easy. Everything is automatic here. If electricity supply is not restricted, the film will not stop in the middle, after it is put on the projector.

**Three steps** are involved to use motion pictures in the classroom teaching.

(a) **Preview :** Before showing any film in the classroom, the teacher should, first have a view of the film in advance in order to tell the students about the main features and gist of the film. After knowing all about the film, the teacher can direct the attention of the pupils to such salient points which he considers to be essential. He can also guide his students to concentrate on linguistic or technical aspects of the subject matter by preview. This preview is also essential for the determination of educational objectives to be realized by viewing the film.

(b) **Screening :** Screening is actually a sort of proper checking of the film. By screening the film, the teacher helps his students to concentrate on only those points which are essential. If any important point has been missed or skipped in the film, the teacher comes to the mike to tell about that point by stopping the film. Screening helps the teacher to discuss the topic minutely also.

(c) **Review :** After the process of screening is over, the teacher would review the film by highlighting its salient features, its implication in the practical life and by giving his conclusions. Pupils also participate in these discussions and success of the review session depends on the comprehension level of pupils. Comprehensive questions are also asked here. Home assignment can also be given by the teacher after review.

**Advantages of motion pictures :**

I. Motion pictures can especially be used for training purposes. Take the example of games and sports. If some actions of a player is wrong leading to defeat in the game, it can be corrected by viewing the films. After the game is over, the film of the game is later analysed to be discussed by the experts to bring in new strategies and tactics to counterplay. In this way the defective action or mistakes of any player can be removed by the coaches. When Kapil Dev broke Richard Hadley's record of 431 test wickets and the comparative action play of the two great bowlers were seen on the film, it was found that Kapil Dev's arm swing was defective. That was why he took longer time to reach 431 wicket record than Hadley. This defect could have been removed earlier by using motion pictures.

II. In all training courses, perfection is needed everywhere. If action is recorded on films, we can see our own performance and remove our defects.

III. In the classroom teaching, motion pictures can highlight those aspects also that would have otherwise been missed. For example, by enlarging, close up and action replay techniques, motion pictures can highlight those movements also which are very minute and can be missed in ordinary situations.

IV. Motion pictures are **multi-sensory technique** of instruction. It is because a combination of light, sound and actions are seen here.

V. Motion pictures can develop imaginative and observational capacities of students simultaneously.

VI. Whatever ideals are shown by the models in motion pictures are imitated by pupils and thus, good ideals and etiquettes can be developed in them.

VII. The highest level of objectives of affective domain can be realized through these pictures.

VIII. They are helpful in giving clarity of concepts through concreteness and accuracy.

IX. Students can be motivated through these pictures all the time.

X. Facts and events related to industry, politics, history and geography and knowledge about scientific inventions, discoveries, laws and principles can be communicated to pupils very effectively through these motion pictures.

XI. It can solve the problem of size, time and space in the sense that a large sized class can be taught through motion pictures anytime when they feel convenient for that.

XII. Motion pictures can work as a permanent source of recreation which is not possible by the teaching of a teacher in ordinary setting.

XIII. Since films are produced after careful planning and many more editing is also done to organise and present the content accurately, a greater degree of perfection can be maintained here.

XIV. They can initiate the students for self-activity. What they see in the film can be repeated by the pupils later on.

XV. Once a motion picture is shown, hall is kept in full darkness. Thus, no disturbance or outside interference is possible.

XVI. Watching a film is actually an experience in itself which pupils need all the time.

**Note :** *Video Cassettes or television also have similar advantages as the motion pictures possess.*

**Use of motion pictures as material aids :**

A teacher follows the following steps while using motion pictures as material aids.

***Step I*** Determination of objectives : Clear specific objectives must be there while showing motion pictures in a class.

***Step II*** Selection of the film : Films are selected keeping in view the objectives that the teacher has decided.

***Step III*** Sending demand : Order of the films is booked in advance to purchase the film from the market.

***Step IV*** Setting of equipments : Before viewing the film, the necessary equipments are fixed in the class and room is made dark by drawing the curtains on the windows.

***Step V*** Preview : Teacher watches the film before showing it in the class so that he can analyse different aspects of the film.

***Step VI*** Screening : It has already been discussed.

***Step VII*** Introduction of the film : The teacher introduces the film to the students in detail before actual showing. Aims and objectives of the film are also made clear here.

***Step VIII*** Actual show : At this step film is shown properly in the class.

***Step IX*** Review : Finally, the film and its subject matter is evaluated keeping in view the educational objectives determined in the begining.

## IV. Kinescope :

It is a sight and sound recording that can be made in the studio from the television screen for repeated use. What transcription is to radio, the kinescope is to TV. They are used for the following purposes :

I. For delayed telecast.
II. For retelecast of the same programme.
III. For repeating the telecast when programme could not be seen due to failure of network.
IV. For sending programmes abroad.

Only limitation of kinescope is that live element or spontaneity does not exist here.

It can be used in teaching learning process in the same way as television is used. We will discuss television later in this chapter.

## V. Epidiascope :

Epidiascope is an equipment that can project all types of materials whether transparent or non-transparent (opaque). It has thus a twin facility and separate mechanism for projecting transparent and opaque materials.

In epidiascope, the word epi means 'upon' dia means 'through' and scope means 'projected material to be seen'.

While projecting a slide, beams pass through the slide and projects its image on the screen. In this way, transparent material is projected.

While projecting the opaque material the light bits upon the object which reflects the image on a very sensitive mirror and reflects the image of the opaque objects on the screen.

Despite the multipurpose functioning of this device, it is not very popular in educational institutions because of its poor quality image, total room darkening, very high need of energy, complexity of its use and poor range. It is to be installed in the middle of the class due to its low range, therefore, causing more interference than aiding something to the lesson. Because of its ability to project opaque objects on the screen, it is also known as opaque projector.

## VI. Overhead Projector (OHP) :

In OHP, the transparent object to be projected is placed upon a glass platform of 25 square inch in size. The light from a halogen bulb (put below the platform) passes through the head which is a system of lens and mirrors to project the image on the screen. A thermostatically cooling fan is provided in the lamp house to blow air near the source of light. The image on the screen is focused by turning a knob which raises or lowers the projection head. The projection head can be titled upward or downward in order to centre the image on the screen.

Built on the basic principle of periscope, OHP is an important audio visual equipment. In the classroom it is placed in front of the teacher above his head to reflect an image on the screen (blackboard). This device consists of a strong energy source, (bulbs), fixed reflectors (mirrors), projection lens and a platen. This projector is called over head because the image goes over the head of the teacher and falls on the screen behind him. The teacher puts one slide over the other in order to give a sense of continuity of the subject matter projected on the screen.

**Advantages of OHP :** Its advantages lie in its special characteristics given below :

I. They have a very high source of energy and hence total darkening of the room is not needed.
II. Its screen does the function of a blackboard also. Generally, place of the blackboard is made as screen.
III. Its equipments last long. Only fused bulbs are replaced. Thus, any school can afford them because of its low cost of maintenance.
IV. The teacher need not look back while using OHP. Projector is put before him and he writes on the platen (with a glass pencil) to show

material on the screen. Thus, he always remains facing the class and can control the students very easily.

V. No special training is required by the teacher to operate a projector.

VI. OHPs are not very costly as compared to computers or film projectors.

VII. It is handy and portable.

VIII. The image formed by the projector is also very bright and every pupil can see it. A 4 × 4 inches slide gives an image of 4 × 4 feet. This enlarged image is very easy to understand.

IX. It can create interests in pupils and hence it is a good motivator.

X. It is the best visual aid available to a teacher to supplement his oral teaching. He uses the screen of OHP as a blackboard without looking back. Transparencies, drawing, diagrams, figures and outlines etc. can be shown on the screen.

**Limitations of OHP:** If OHP has any limitations, it lies in the teacher himself. The teacher must know to write on the platen with a glass pencil. This pencil should not be very much pointed otherwise writing will be very poor. Even a small defect in writing a letter will look very big on the screen.

The second limitation is that the range of OHP is very limited. We can not see the screen from more than 4 yards due to limited focal length of the lenses. Thus, it is not applicable for large sized classes.

## ELECTRONIC AIDS

Many electronic devices are used in the teaching learning process today in and outside the class. Some of them are audio equipment like radio, tape recorder, public address system, gramophone, walkman, linguaphone and some of them are visual ones like TV, Computers, CD players etc. Descriptions of some of them are given below :

### I. Television

TV differs from the radio in the sense that it is audio and visual both. We can see the incident occurring round the globe on it immediately after the occurrence of the incident through telecast. Thus, it is bisensory (multisensory) media. We get news, views and recreation through television in the same way as we do through the transistor but in a more compact and concrete way due to the facility of vision here.

As far as application of TV in education is concerned, it is still in the stage of infancy in India. It was only in 1961 that Indian television (Doordarshan) started a special service for schools in collaboration with the directorate of Education. This programme aimed at supplementing the regular classroom teaching in selected subjects. By 1972 only 400 schools of the capital received this telecast and two lakh students benefited from them. These programmes were telecast in the evening and on Sundays but there was no mechanism developed at that time to measure the effectiveness of such transmitting programmes.

After the introduction of distance education system in India, television is now regularly used as an instructional media. The enactment of Prasar Bharti Act is expected to boost the role of TV in the teaching learning process.

**Advantages of television :**

I. It heightens the reality more than the physical presence. For example, if someone is watching a cricket match in a stadium, even then he can not see certain situations despite being present there. On the other hand, if he is viewing a match on a TV, he can see and analyse every situation by close up action replay. Thus, television experience may be more real than the actual one. It can show even those details which we can not see with the help of direct experiences. Thus, television can be used for all training programmes and behaviour of the trainees can be modified in the desired manner.

II. It can overcome the barriers of time and space. A very large number of students representing a wide range of area can be covered through teaching on television.

III. TV experiences are new and versatile. So, they can bring variety to classroom teaching by breaking monotony and strengthening the learning structures by its multisensory approach.

IV. It widens the horizon of pupils' experiences by giving them upto date knowledge of the real situation and by making them conversant with the opinions of others.

V. It can motivate the pupils for learning by arousing and retaining their interest in the learning situation.

**Television is superior to motion picture** in the following ways :

I. It does not require darkening of the room.
II. It is handy and portable.
III. Action replay is possible here for clarifying a situation.
IV. It does not require any helper for its operation.
V. Recurring expenses of TV are also negligible.
VI. Video cassettes and CDs can also be used in a television. Thus, any educational programme presented by an expert can be recorded on CDs and Video cassettes which can benefit millions of students at a time.

**Limitations of Television:**

I. Speed of a television can not be changed as we can do in motion pictures.
II. A TV programme can not be adjusted to teaching and vice versa will have to be done. A teacher can take the help of video recording in such cases.

## II. Tape Recorder and Audio Cassettes

Cassette type audio taps are available now which can play for 90 minutes on both sides. We can listen to our own recorded voice, recorded speeches of politicians and learned people, recorded poems of great composers, songs, music etc by the tape recorder.

Audio cassette recorder is used for the following purposes :

(a) **Audio recording for feedback :** When one listens to his own voice, he can find out mistakes in it and feedback is received. It can motivate the person if his recording is fine.

(b) **Audio recording for information :** A variety of informations in prose, poetic or rhythmic form can be obtained by audio recording. It requires the following steps of planning and production.

- Identify the purpose of such presentation.
- Identify the audience for whom the presentation is to be made i.e., their age, interest and attitude.
- Decide the strategy of presentation, i.e., forms of presentation, number of voices, melody etc.
- Prepare a content outline.
- Develop a script according to the order of content outline.
- Organise the recording of the presenters.
- Actual recording of the presentation in a controlled situation.
- Editing of the audio-tapes by selecting the required material and mixing extra voices and background with it.
- Preparing short notes on the recorded materials.

(c) **Audio recording for instruction and training :**

*Instructional recording is of two types :*

(a) For group listening and discussion as is the case of classroom.
(b) For individual self-paced learning as is the case of a computer or music laboratory.

*Such types of recording serve the following purposes:*

I. **Analysis of verbal messages :** Accuracy, speed and tone of verbal messages are studied here and if perfection is seen, reinforcement to the presenter is given.
II. **Drill and practice :** Accurate verbal messages are presented before the trainee for drill and practice.
III. **Teaching of specific skills :** Impressive oral presentation is actually a skill. This skill is taught to students through audio-recording in the individual and group situations.
IV. **Speech improvement :** Style of speaking and phonetics can also be improved by using this technology.
V. **Improvement in vocabulary :** Recorded verbal messages are full of many new words which pupils can learn by listening to the message.
VI. **Recreation :** Many recorded songs and music entertain the listeners and remove their fatigue.

*Instructional formats of such audio recordings are of three types.*

(a) **Audio notebook :** It consists of a study guide plus a worksheet. Study guide introduces the topic and then audio cassette describes the content and periodically directs the learner to the activities given in the workbook. The workbook includes the following things :

- Question for discussion.
- Experiences to be worked out.
- Objective items.
- Numerical problems.

The answers and discussions are provided in the audio cassette.

(b) **Audio tutorial :** The system based on the audio cassettes to conduct the tutorials consists of the introduction of the lesson, related information and instructional material. It also directs the learner to undertake various learning activities themselves. No study guide is made available here. Help is taken from text books, newspapers and journals. For example, audio cassettes may direct the pupils in the following manner : "You are advised to study the text book from page. No. 25-30 before listening to the cassette."

(c) **Audio vision :** Here visual materials are given either in the study guide or in the text book and audible materials are given in the cassette and both of them go side by side.

## III. Radio

It is an important and easily accessable audio aid serving three important general purposes "news, views and recreation". It is the cheapest equipment of all and radio broadcast is now reachable to 100% population of the country. Pupils can get information about the incidents in any part of the globe immediately through radio. This increases their general awareness of the world. Students listen the ideas of learned people, politicians and educationists from across the world on the radio. This extends their own views and way of thinking. Apart from these, there are hundreds of programmes of music, songs and plays broadcast on the radio which entertain them round the clock.

**Instructional Value of the Radio :**

I. It is a powerful means of developing listening comprehension.

II. It can also help the pupils to acquire correct pronunciation and phonetics like tape recorders.

III. Conversational style and language can be learned on the radio.

IV. It improves word power of learners.

V. Valuable radio programmes may be recorded on audio cassettes and played back any time.

VI. Mass education goals can be achieved through radio broadcast. It was the realization of the people when radio came into being in 1917.

VII. The lectures by the eminent persons like scientists, historians, politicians and other professionals can be broadcast on the radio.

VIII. Its role in broadcasting stories, dramas and commentaries is also very commendable.

IX. The effectiveness of radio programmes and lessons is also increased by the introduction of sound effect of rain, thunder, waterfall, chirping of birds and background noises.

X. Radio broadcasts can reach to almost 100% population of the country and thus even laymen can be educated by them.

XI. News listened on the radio can improve our general knowledge.

XII. Radio listening does not require literacy. Even illiterates can take the benefit of it.

**Radio Broadcast in India :** The first radio station was established in India in July 1927 in Mumbai followed by one more station in Kolkata in the same year. This media is now able to penetrate to the remotest villages of the country and is covering more than 99% of the population.

School broadcasting in India was started in 1937. Radio broadcasting is now very much used for mass education as well as the education of school going children in selected areas. Central Institute for educational technology (CIET) under the supervision and control of NCERT produces quality radio broadcast programmes. Adult education Radio Programmes also started in 1956 to educate the adults in the age group of 15-35 in the vicinity of Pune as a project sponsord by UNESCO. Today, broadcast of adult education programmes are many under different titles. When Consumer Protection Act was passed in 1986, consumer education through radio was also given recognition. Today, it is a regular programme of all the radio stations in India. One more regular radio programme is the radio counseling programme of IGNOU which is broadcast from 4-5 pm on every Sunday.

Apart from these, radio broadcast is also making the people aware about various social and economic problems and people are also educated about how they can solve these problems.

**Characteristics of a good radio programme :**

1. **Coverage :** Radio broadcast may cover not only a country but the entire world. So, radio programmes should be prepared in such a manner that maximum number of listeners may be benefited by the programme.
2. **Speed :** The speed of radio programmes should be arranged according to the receiving capacity of listeners and target group.
3. **Beneficial for the target group :** The target group for whom the programme is prepared must be benefited by it.
4. **Accessibility :** It should reach the people for whom it has been prepared. Power of the frequency should be set so as to take the programme to the target group.
5. **Cheapness :** Radio programme should not be so costly as to adjust the cost by boring advertisement.
6. **Ease of listening :** We can listen to a radio programme while doing something else such as taking food, working in a farm or taking rest in the bed. Thus, it is not an extra burden on the listeners.
7. **Extending thoughts :** Radio programmes should be such as to extend our thoughts in many directions without visualizing the facts or events.
8. **Easy production :** The production of radio programme is very easy as compared to television items.
9. **Interesting :** Radio programmes should be made interesting to attract the listeners. Even educational programme should be attractive and entertainable.
10. **Educative and informative :** Radio programmes should also have some direct or indirect educational value. Even music and songs can educate the people if they are supplemented with other informative materials.

**Limitations of radio:** Certain inherent limitations of radio programmes are given below :

I. It is a one way communication. Talk back telephone lines are being introduced in order to make it a bipolar communication. Without this facility, feedback can not be received from either side.

II. It is only unisensory. The material obtained by aural sense organs can not be retained very much.

III. It is rigid in the sense that no modification can be introduced in the middle of the programme.

IV. Uncontrolled and unevaluated learning received by radio broadcast is ineffective and temporary.

V. Learners of poor background can not be satisfied with the inputs of the programme.

VI. Recorded radio programmes are generally not available in the market. If a teacher wants to use them in the class, he will have to record them first.

VII. Teachers and students are not showing much interest in educational programmes broadcast by the radio due to their poor quality.

**How to use radio programme in the class :**

Before broadcast of any educational programme, its information regarding its timing, nature and the class for which it is designed etc, is given to listeners in the midst of other radio programmes. The teacher notes down this advertisement and arranges his class accordingly. After presenting the programme before the students in the class, the teacher discuses it by asking questions from his students. He also removes doubts of his students if any about the radio lesson. Since these lessons are presented by the experts, the teacher can also take the benefit of them.

Following steps are followed in using a radio lesson in the class :

1. **Selection :** Lessons related to the curriculum are selected. It should be recorded by the teacher also so that he may carry out necessary preparation before presenting the radio lesson in the class.
2. **Introduction :** Before presenting a radio lesson in the class, it should be properly introduced by the teacher so as to clarify its aims and objectives and its relevance to the course.

3. **Elaboration :** Whatever graphs, charts, notes etc. the teachers has prepared in the context of the programme, should be used properly in the class during the radio lesson to elaborate the necessary points and to give his comments.
4. **Discussion :** Once the radio lesson is over, it should be discussed by the teacher with his students through comprehensive and evaluative questions. It will help the teacher to elaborate the missing points of the lesson.
5. **Directions :** Once the radio lesson is on, the teacher should instruct his students to note down the important points. If a radio lesson is trapped, he can stop the tape in the middle as many times as required.

**Evaluation of a radio lesson :**

Radio lesson is evaluated by students and teachers both in their respective ways. Students evaluate the lesson from the point that to what extent the lesson was useful for them and what part of the subject-matter they have learnt by the presentation of the lesson. Teacher evaluates the lesson by asking comprehensive questions from his students. If they are able to answer all these questions, the lessons is said to be a successful one. Internal criticism of the subject matter is also done by the teacher. If he finds any fault in the content or in the presentation, he informs about it to the concerned radio station.

## IV. Public Address Equipment

This equipment is used to increase the range of voice from few people to many thousands. Supply of electricity is needed for its working. It consists of the following equipments:

I. Speakers-one, few or many
II. Microphone-one or few
III. Amplifier
IV. Transformer

Speakers are of two types, horn type and box type. Its output is given in ohms. It is based on Ohm's law i.e., strength of electrical current is directly proportional to electromagnetic force and inversely proportional to resistance. Transformer changes this ohm loudness into its maximum capacity. That is why additional speakers can be put into the system only after taking the ohm capacity of the transformer into account. Microphones can also be of two types—unidirectional and multidirectional, out of which later is more sensitive than the former. If microphones and speakers are in proper working condition, there will not be any humming or feedback effect there.

## V. Computer

It is the latest electronic device that is audio and visual both. It accepts data, performs operations on that data in sequence (decided by a programme) and outputs the results. Computers are termed according to their size and thus we come across terms like mainframe computers, mini-computer and microcomputers. Besides size, specialization of the electronic devices (that differ from computer to computer) are also used to identify computer-types. The specification includes details about the amount and type of the nature of the peripheral equipment (such as disc storage) that can be connected to the computer.

The basic micro computer system consists of an input device (e.g., the keyboard), the central processing unit of the computer and storage devices (e.g., cassette tape player, floppy disc device) and the output device (e.g., computer screen and TV) display unit, or a monitor and/or printing terminals. The actual equipment of storage, the capabilities of the central processing unit, and the type and the computer system is called the hardware, while the term software refers to the instructions or the programmes that the computer carries out.

**Characteristics of computers :**

1. **Automation :** It is a speedy electronic device which is designed to accept and store data and to process the same automatically to produce results to the given programme. If programme is given to the computer once, it will perform the same job repeatedly and with the same accuracy.
2. **Speed :** Computer can perform any job at a very fast speed. Its speed is calculated in nano seconds whereas the speed of humans is calculated in seconds only.
3. **Storage capacity :** A very heavy amount of data and informations can be stored in computers. If the same amount of information is written on papers, it will fill a big room to store the material.

4. **Ability :** Computer can work for hours without being tired or without losing its concentration. A human being is not supposed to do that amount of work in any way. It is because the capacity of humans is limited.
5. **Accuracy :** Computer is not supposed to commit error in doing any job. If any error is seen any time, it is because of the wrong commands given to the computer.
6. **Universality :** Computer can do any job however complex or difficult it is at ease. The conclusions drawn by the computer on the basis of the data stored is not supposed to be wrong. The results given by the computers are universally accepted.
7. **Privacy :** We can store many such informations in computers which we do not want to be seen by others. Nobody can have access to those informations without knowing the password.

**Applicability of computers :**

Application of computers is seen in almost every field of life. Some of them are given below :

1. Routine job handling.
2. Traffic control.
3. Automatic Teller Machine (ATM) in banks for limited money transaction.
4. Electronic office routine e.g., fax, internet, telex, e-mail.
5. Controls and checks production in industry, brings efficiency and reduces wastage.
6. Computerized telephones for automation.
7. Trade, banks and Stock Exchange, controlling stocks and accounts.
8. Scientific Research where it helps store and analyse data fast and accurate. Helps sharing of data and results globally.
9. Extremely useful for diagnostic purpose in medical science e.g., ECG, CT-scan, Ultra-sonography etc wherein the equipment is computerized.
10. Space Science and astrophysics wherein all instruments, data and commands are computerized.
11. Printing and Publication.
12. Communication e.g., telex, fax, e-mail, internet, etc. for faster, accurate and multiple communication.
13. Videography and films, especially for animation wherein computer introduces multi-media approach.

**Computer in education :** From input devices to output and its storage, computer has a wide range of applicability in education. In computers inputs are converted into output by a programme. Thus, input (data) plus programme form software or instructional programme. Inputs are converted into output in the CPU of the computer.

Computer always works according to the programme given to it. Whatever instruction or programme the students gives to the computers, it will always act accordingly and output will also come out on the same line. Application of computers in education can be understood by the following lines.

**(a) Application of computers in instructional situations :**

1. Pre-testing of students knowledge for admission.
2. Planning and printing individualized programmes like CAI, CAL etc.
3. Monitoring students' progress.
4. Compiling tests for evaluation.
5. Scoring of test items.
6. Storing data files and informations for future use.
7. Using internet for distance learning.

**(b) Advantage of computers for learners :**

Gaining knowledge through computer is a new experience for learners. They can be benefited from computers in the following ways.

1. Computer motivates the students to deal with complex situations and reinforces them. Thus, we see a direct interaction between a student and the computer.
2. When students go on right direction on a computer, computer gives them reinforcement.
3. Learning process becomes individualized and flexible through computers. It means that every student gets chance to learn according to his own ability.
4. Computer removes loneliness of those students who are learning through distance education. They can contact to their study centres through

internet by logging on the website of their study centres.

5. Computer motivates the students for new experiments and to deal with novel problems every time.
6. Students can increase their educational achievement through computers.
7. Computer develops the critical thinking power of students. When a student progresses on a computer programme, he is compelled to think why it is happening so.
8. Computer provides them chance how to progress on an instructional programme by avoiding mistakes. As soon as a student commits a mistake, he is immediately instructed by the computer what mistake he has done and how can it be removed.
9. Computer also provides them the opportunity of recreation together with gaining knowledge.
10. Computer assisted instruction is never dull. Thus, acquired knowledge is always stable and fixed in the minds of learners.

**(c) Advantages of computers for researchers :**

Research is the highest level of teaching learning process. Computer is helpful in this process in the following ways:

1. Computer can store large amount of informations (data) which can be taken out in a moment when required.
2. Computer can analyse the data very accurately and speedily. It can change the quantitative values of attributes into graphs, charts or tables.
3. With the help of statistical operations, computers can derive conclusions and the results given by the computers are not supposed to be wrong.
4. Researcher can explain the results given by the computer with much accuracy.
5. Computers have converted the books in CDs resulting in the reduction of library loads and costs.
6. A researcher can search out any book from the library on any topic, if internet facility is available, and any information on any topic can be obtained in no time from any part of the world.

## VI. Videodiscs

This system is comprised of videodisc, where the information is stored, a video player and a TV set. Microscopic pits put on the disc contain these informations. The disc rotates on the player at a high speed and the information of videodisc is read by a stylus or laser. The information read from these pits is displayed on a regular TV set. In common language, this system is called CD player.

It is helpful in teaching learning process in the following ways :

I. Students can get more informations through effective way of presentation.

II. By forwarding or reversing the CD player, learners can have access to any informations as many times as possible. This repeated action is necessary in understanding complex materials.

III. Live coverage given by the CD player can provide higher degree of motivation.

IV. Auto stop system provided in the system can help those learners who study till late hours of night.

V. The materials prepared by the effective teachers can be made available in the market for wide use.

**Limitations of CD players**

Here information is stored in the same way as it is done in a gramophone and thus it can not be erased or rerecorded. In video or audio tape we can do so as many times as we need. In this way CD player is only one time recording system and hence very expensive.

## VII. Videotext

This system provides an interactive information retrieval service. It allows the home television to work as a computer terminal, which retrieves the textual material and graphic information from a remote data base. It is also known as website.

This system consists of a keyboard, a TV set, a decoder, a telecommunication link and a computer containing a database. Videotext uses television and local telephone in order to have access to the computerized information. Keyboard is used to give command to download the required information from a remote computer.

In order to display the recording on the videotext, television is connected to the local telephone line and adapted by means of a decoder. Thus, home TV is turned into a terminal.

**Advantages of Videotext:**

I. It is useful for downloading the required information from a remote data base.

II. It raises the general awareness of learners.

III. The principal of a school can have access to any information about his or other schools any time if this system is available in the school.

IV. It is especially useful for distance learning. A learner can connect himself with his study centre or regional office any time.

V. It is free form time schedule. We can have any information any time.

VI. Two way interaction between the teacher and the taught is possible here with the help of alphanumeric keyboard. The learner can address to his tutor by typing questions and sending it to the tutor. Once he receives the answer, he gets immediate feedback.

VII. It is faster than telephone or telegram because user need not wait here in queue.

## SOFTWARE AIDS

These aids are produced by using different types of hardware equipments. They are used in the process of instruction. Some of these aids are given below :

### I. Teleconferencing

Teleconferencing is a two way broadcast system in which learners can interact with the programme through a local telephone. It is a powerful medium of instruction for distance education. In this system three or four subject experts sit at different places and participate in the discussion on the given subject matter. Here learners do not take part in the teaching-learning process directly. They only hear the programme on their radio set or TV. They can however, interact with the experts through telephone which is connected to the radio or TV station where the discussion is being organised.

Thus, teleconferencing involves the use of many media and allows interactive group communication by means of a two way broadcast. All such conferencing need good quality audio device to facilitate immediate interaction among the participants for exchange of views.

**Types of Teleconferencing :**

1. **Audio teleconferencing :** Here several telephone or radio lines are inter-connected. These multi lines are also connected with the local telephone lines in order to facilitate the learners to talk to the experts through local telephones. Thus, a bridge is built among these lines. After that, programme is organised from one place through radio or telephone. In order to solve the problems of listeners organising radio or telephone station centre is connected to several places where experts of the subject take part in the discussion and answer the queries of learners. Learners only need to contact with the organising centre and get immediate feedback by hearing the answer on their radio or telephone. When this type of conferencing is organised through radio, it is called radio bridge programme.
2. **Video teleconferencing :** Here, all the above processes are done through facilitating visual interaction. Learners ask questions through their telephone and listen the answer of experts on their television.
3. **Computerized teleconferencing :** This process of bridging a programme is more convenient than the above two because computers are already connected here through internet. Only experts are needed to be arranged at different places for discussing the topic at a fixed time. Learners can ask question from experts either through e-mail or internet telephone system.

**Advantages of Teleconferencing :**

1. **Effective for distance learning :** When groups of students are scattered over a large area of the country and it is not possible for them to interact with their teachers personally, then learning through teleconferencing is the best option for them.
2. **Low cost approach :** Many more number of students can be taught through this approach. Seeing the large coverage of students, it is a cheap means of instruction.

3. **Time-table adjustability :** In this approach time-table can be adjusted according to the availability and suitability of learners scattered over wide range of area. If such programme is available on website, students can hear and read them any time.
4. **Interaction between the teacher and the taught possible :** As far as interaction between teachers and learners are concerned, this approach does not differ in any way from classroom teaching.
5. **High quality instruction :** Since, very learned people and experts of the subject take part in these discussions, the quality of the programme is never questionable.
6. **Immediate feedback :** Learners get answer of their questions immediately from the experts and their problem is solved. In this way, they get immediate feedback.
7. **Flexibility :** Experts do not teach here on a pre-determined track. Their instruction and its way of presentation always changes according to the questions asked by learners. Thus, this approach is very flexible.

## II. Internet

It is the abbreviation of international network. The computers connected to this system are automatically connected to world wide website(www). Due to this we can hear and see any programme available on website any time when we want to do so. If we have missed any television or radio programme, we can not have access to that programme again but if that programme is loaded on the website, we can repeatedly hear and see the programme. We will only have to log on the website of the programme producer and it will be available for us. The major advantage of this system is that it has made 24 hour communication possible especially between those countries which have great differences in their local timings such as India and America have a time difference of 10 ½ hours. When there is day time in India, offices are closed in America.

The popularity of internet can be assessed by the fact that about 50 million people of the world have internet connection. This media facility started in India by BSNL on Aug. 15, 1995. Now this facility is being provided by private companies and cable operators also and every district of the country have internet gate ways at present.

**Applications of internet in education :**

1. We can get any information any time at home through internet on one hand and we can store the information by creating our own website on the other. Thus, it is not necessary to have immediate print out of the textual matter.
2. The two talking persons can see each other in face to face situations also through internet. Thus, a teacher can teach millions of students scattered across the world together.
3. Many educational institutions have created their educational websites. We can download any information about them any time by logging on these websites.
4. Internet has also its role to play in classroom teaching. Teacher can show any educational programme through internet any time according to his own convenience and he will not have to adjust his time table according to the programme as he does while using radio or television as aids.
5. Examination results are now loaded on the website of the universities and boards. Students can see their results on internet and they will not have to wait for their mark sheet for many days.
6. Many radio and television programmes can also be heard on the website of respective broadcasting stations.
7. Latest teaching strategies and latest researches in different fields can be obtained through internet immediately and we need not have to wait for their publication in magazines and journals.
8. Many teaching skills can be learned just by watching their demonstration on internet.
9. Books, magazines and newspapers are also published on internet and it has made our access to them easy. Any Indian living in Canada even can read "Amar Ujala" or "Times of India" daily.
10. Research material and encyclopaedias are also published on internet to facilitate learning process.

## III. Language laboratory

Language laboratory consists of the facility of CCTV, Computer Aided Learning (CAL) and objective based instructional programmes with regard to language teaching. Here the main equipment console works as a controller and regulates the programme. Each student is connected with the programme machine with a headphone. If he gets a stuck, he klicks a button and console comes on the line and students may seek advice and clarification how to manage and handle the programme. Once a student is doing so, other students of the group are not disturbed at all due to separate control system. If console is engaged any time, the student will have to wait his turn. Console also monitors the output of each student also and checks him if he is committing error. In this way a language laboratory is a two way teaching-learning process.

**Robert Lado** has defined language laboratory in the following words :

"Language laboratory is the centre of language teaching and teacher helps its operational activities by providing suitable materials and leaning situations".

Language laboratory is actually a teaching room equipped with all electronic devices for recording and reproducing speech sounds with correct pronunciation, phonetics, intonation and articulation to teach a language. Here students interact with the console individually and follows the instruction given by it.

**Limitations of a language laboratory :**

1. Language teaching is the main aspect of teaching-learning process in schools and it is not possible for them to arrange so many language laboratories in the school to teach different languages. It will incur heavy cost.
2. It is a time consuming process to teach the whole language and all its aspects through language laboratory. Only certain peculiar language skill can be taught through this system, otherwise, novelty aspect of the lab will wash off. Thus, it is not the central component of language teaching. The role of the teacher is always central.

## IV. Computer Assisted Instruction (CAI)

CAI does not mean to train the learners how to operate computers. It rather means that students will take the help of computers in their learning. Thus, the first condition of using CAI strategy is that students must have computer literacy. Because of this limitations, CAI is essentially used only in those countries where computer literacy is satisfactory. In a country like India where computer literacy is below 2%, this technology is only in the stage of experimentation.

The second reason why this system is not popular in India is that even teachers in India are not fully aware about computer technology. Due to this reason, they can not prepare good CAI lessons.

**Focus of CAI :** To achieve cognitive objectives of learning.

**Principle :** The strategy is based on the principle of machine on one hand and principles of programmed instruction on the other. A machine involves a system and a system always goes through three main stages—input, process and output.

**Purpose:** The main purpose of CAI programme is to provide individual instruction to students keeping in view their personal abilities and interests. A special device is needed for this purpose. This device should be so flexible as to store huge amount of organised informations on one hand and to provide the user with the selected information when he desires so on the other hand. Computer fulfils these two conditions so, assistance is taken from the computer to provide instructions to students.

Thus, CAI may be defined as the use of computers as an integral part of an instructional procedure in which the learner is engaged in two way interaction with the computer via terminal.

One more characteristic of CAI is that whatever knowledge a learner obtains through CAI is well organised and maximum according to the needs of learners and learning which takes place by these informations is always perfect.

**Structure :** Linear and branching both types of instructional programmes are used in CAI. Students are directly connected with the computer via instructional material. Whatever response is made by the student after studying the programme is also recorded by the computer. On the basis of this very response, the computer takes decision as to which information is to be made available to the learner next. If learner's answer is correct, computer gives him feedback as well.

**Steps involved in CAI :**

(a) *Pre-tutorial phase :* The main purpose of this phase is that student must achieve the objectives by using a specific type of instruction. Here objectives of instruction are first determined and then instructional programme is prepared and feeded in the computer.

(b) *Tutorial phase* : Its main focus is to select an appropriate instruction and present before the learner. It will control the learner's responses also. The learner may select one or more than one instructions at a time.

**Instructional modes of CAI :** When a lesson is presented in a CAI, direct interaction between the learner and the computer is seen. Computer makes the instructional material directly available to learners. The learner reads the lesson in the way it has been programmed in the computer and gives his reactions. If reaction or response is correct, he gets feedback by the computer and if response is wrong, he is given another instruction to follow. This process goes on till the end of the lesson. Computer records the responses of students also and final evaluation of the learner is given.

**Various models of CAI :** In order to apply a CAI programme in learning process following methods of instruction are used.

1. **Tutorial method :** In this method, information are presented in small units and questions are asked at the end of every unit. Computer evaluates the responses of students and gives them immediate feedback. Thus, in this method students are given chance to learn according to their respective abilities and speed.
2. **Drill method :** In this method, computer teaches the students through examples. Students try to learn the concept through these examples and retain them. If they are unable to learn the concept by one example, they are given another example. This drilling continues till the students acquire full mastery over the concept or fact. When correct response is given by the student, he is reinforced by the computer and instructed to go ahead.
3. **Discovery method :** Problem is presented before the student here and computer asks him to discover the solution of the problem by trial and error. Since problem is presented here through examples, this method is based on inductive method of teaching.
4. **Play method :** In this method knowledge is imparted to students through recreational activities like games. This method is especially suitable for small children.
5. **Problem solving method :** Here computer presents the problem before the students in such a manner that students are compelled to reflect on it and they arrive at the solution after applying reflective thinking. Some prompts are also given by the computer to solve these problems.
6. **Enquiry method :** In this method, computer answers those questions of learners which are already stored in the computer.
7. **Logo :** By this method students are taught to draw pictures or sketches on the screen or to write letters on the screen in a stylish manner.

**Experts needed in CAI :**

Experts from three respective fields are needed to prepare a CAI programme :

(a) *Computer engineer.* A technical person who knows the physical principles and procedure of programming.

(b) *Lesson producer.* A teacher or educator who knows how to develop a lesson logically on psychological ground.

(c) *Computer operator.* The person who operates the computer. For CAI programme to be a success, students must operate the computer themselves.

**Importance of CAI :**

1. It is an important source of collecting facts and informations for students as well as teachers.
2. Students are given the opportunity of drill through it.

3. It is also useful for seeking the solution of administrative and educational problems.
4. It is useful in the process of evaluation also.
5. It can be helpful for preparing a good school time-table.
6. It is also used for preparing pay bills.
7. It is very much useful for developing various types of skills.

**Advantages of CAI :** See "Advantages of computers for learners"

**Limitations of CAI :** The underlying limitations of CAI are given below :

1. That sensitive and emotional climate cannot be created by CAI which a teacher of the class can do. Thus, CAI is indifferent to human emotions.
2. CAI does not solve the psychological or educational problems of students in the manner that a teacher can do.
3. CAI has been proved to be incompetent in developing verbal ability among students. Students only follow the pre-determined language of the computer.
4. It has also been noticed that students get tired earlier in CAI than in classroom instruction because they have their connection with a non-living machine.
5. CAI is also indifferent to artistic practices of students.
6. Good CAI programme is not available in India and it has also been noticed that programme prepared for one computer does not work properly in other computers.
7. In a country like India where classes are over-crowded and even basic facilities are not available in schools, how can we think of a computer assisted instruction here.
8. Teachers are also not well trained to develop good CAI programmes.

## NON-PROJECTED AIDS

These aids are actually visual in nature and they are generally prepared by the teacher to facilitate his teaching-learning process. They do not need any projector to use them in the class. Teacher uses them on his own and creates good learning environment in the class. Some of these aids are given below:

### I. Chalkboard

It is the closest friend of a teacher in the class and about 50% teaching task is completed with the help of the blackboard. Advantages of using a chalkboard in the class are as follows :

1. It is a cheap material aid which does not cost much on its maintenance.
2. When a teacher writes important points of the lesson on the chalkboard along with his oral teaching and lectures, aural and visual both the senses of students work simultaneously. It increases learning many times.
3. Writing meaning of difficult words, drawing graphs or diagrams, solving the sums of mathematics, preparing the summary of the lesson, all these works can be done on the chalkboard and they help the students understand the facts, events or terminologies.
4. Blackboard works as a model for students. This can help the students mend their ways if they imitate the model.

**How to use a chalkboard :**

1. The chalkboard work should be so clear and so big in size that all the students can see it from their seats.
2. Teacher should also utter words while writing them on the chalkboard, so that there may not be complete calm in the class.
3. If chalkboard is black or green in colour, only white chalk should be used on it.
4. Coloured chalks should be used while drawing pictures, graphs or diagrams.
5. The teacher should write only important points on the chalkboard.
6. The teacher should write beautifully on the chalkboard and in a straight line.
7. After blackboard work is over, the teacher should stand at such a distance from the blackboard that he can himself see his work clearly. It is not proper

to stand in front of the chalkboard and shuffling in the class on demand.

8. How the students have to note down the blackboard work on their copies, clear instructions should be given to students regarding it.

## II. Real objects

Material aids are especially used to clarify the concepts. Real objects as material aids can best serve this purpose. For example, if a teacher is to teach the structure of a plant, he must bring that plant to the class and show it. It will facilitate in clarifying each and every part of the plant before the students. The objects which can be brought to the class in real form, it is wrong to show them in the class on charts in the form of diagrams or pictures.

## III. Models

Models are the reflection or copy of the real objects. They are used in the class to clarify the concepts when either real objects are not available or it is not possible to bring real objects to the class. They are also the abbreviated version of real objects. Elephants, lions or other animals or birds can not be brought to the class, hence, it is better to use the models of these objects. Globe is the best example of model to be used in the class.

Through models knowledge of all types of historical, geographical and scientific facts and concepts can be given to students. Models are especially useful for teaching visually handicapped children who perceive the objects by touch. Since, clear dimensions of length, breadth and height are given in the model in a proportionate manner, they are more useful for concept formation than pictures.

**How to use models :**

1. Scale should be used for showing size, shape or structure of the real objects. Apart from this, teacher should also clarify the real shape, size or structure of the real object.
2. Students should be given opportunity to have a critical view on the model and their views on it.
3. All students should be given chance to have a close look at the model in the class.
4. Models should have direct relevance to the lesson and they should develop scientific temperament among learners.
5. Models should be properly explained in the class in order to make the use of models effective.

## IV. Pictures

Pictures are used in the class as material aids when neither real objects nor models can be arranged. They are cheap and easily available in the market, therefore, a teacher should not be miserly in using them. Pictures are actually the outlines of the real objects and when they are shown in the class, they give clear concepts about the colour, physique, shape and size of the real objects. Attention of students can easily be drawn to the lesson through them. If pictures related to the lesson are not available in the market, the teacher should sketch them by using pencils and water colours. Pictures are used as material aids for teaching all the school subjects.

## V. Diagrams

They are another option and used when even pictures can not be arranged. They can also clarify the concepts like models or pictures but at a lesser degree. Diagrams are drawn on the chalkboard by using coloured chalks and then students copy it on their notebooks. The biggest advantage of this material aid is that teacher need not spend even a single pie in using this material aid.

They help in clarifying the concepts, laws and principles of science and social sciences. Their role in teaching languages is very limited.

## VI. Graphs

Graphs are especially used in history, geography, science and mathematics. They help the teacher and the students to study, analyse and compare the data, facts or events. Whenever action research is made by a teacher in the class, graphs are used to show the data.

## VII. Maps

Maps are the flat representation of the surface of the earth on a paper where many informations are presented through lines, symbols dots, points or letters. They have special significance in teaching history and geography. We can also get information about the size and physical features of a country, state or continent through these maps and distance between different parts of the country or the world can also be read from them. Though printed maps of all states or countries are available in the market yet a teacher draws them also on roler boards. This will enable the students to draw such maps themselves.

**How to use graphs, diagrams, maps etc:**

1. As far as possible, the teacher should prepare all these material aids himself.
2. He should not prepare these aids in the class. They should rather be prepared in advance along with the plan of the lesson.
3. He also ensures that all the informations given in these aids have reached to the students.
4. The teacher should have clear objectives of using these aids in his mind.
5. The teacher should give appropriate time to his students for understanding these aids. They should be explained and analysed by the students as well.

# Modalities of Teaching

## MEANING OF TEACHING

Teaching is such a social process which is directly influenced by socio-political system, culture, philosophy and value to a great extent. Because of this reason, it is very difficult to give a universally acceptable definition of teaching. It has been defined in different ways on the basis of socio-political systems prevailing in the world.

### 1. Autocratic Meaning of Teaching

In autocracy, the law is what an autocrate frames. When this socio-political philosophy is implemented in the school, a teacher behaves like an autocrate in the class. He inserts the knowledge into the minds of learners without heeding to their needs, interest and abilities. He considers himself as an ideal and fully matured and treats the learners like a rough clay.

This system is based on task-centred traditional theory of organisation. In this system only teacher is seen active in the class and learners receive instructions fearfully in a passive manner. What to talk of criticising their teacher, they are not even given permission to ask any question in the class without the permission of the teacher.

**H.C. Morrison** (1964) has defined this type of teaching in the following words :

"Teaching is an intimate contact between a more mature personality and a less mature one which is designed to further the education of the later."

### 2. Democratic Meaning of Teaching

This system is based on relation centred theory of human organisation. Here people's representatives work according to the wishes of the people. When this philosophy is implemented into a school system, a teacher teaches in the class by keeping in view the needs, interests, abilities and feelings of his students. As a result, a free interaction between the teacher and learners is seen in the class, i.e., both are equally active in the class and influence each other. Learners can openly ask questions and express their difference of opinions. Teacher, on the other hand, modifies his behaviour in respect of his students and welcomes happily to what comes from them.

**N.L.Gage** (1962) has defined this type of teaching in the following words :

"Teaching is a form of inter-personal influence aimed at changing the behaviour potential of another person."

### 3. Laissez Faire Meaning of Teaching

This system is based on the relation-centred modern theory of human organisation. Here ruler does not impose any restriction on the subject. When this philosophy is implemented in school organisation, a teacher works like a friend and guide in the class. His task in the class is not to teach but to create a conducive learning environment only and rest of the learning job is performed by the learners themselves. Thus, this system makes the students more active. Teachers present facts and information before them in such a manner that some gaps are left. Learners fill these gaps by their own efforts. It means that teacher provides them opportunity to find out the solution of the problem themselves.

Activities and relations both are given importance here but these activities are performed by the students not by the teachers.

**Brubacher** has defined this teaching in the following words :

"Teaching is an arrangement and manipulation of a situation in which there are gaps and obstructions which an individual will seek to overcome and from which he will learn in the course of doing so.

## Other Definitions of Teaching

1. **Edmond Emidon :** Teaching is an interactive process primarily involving classroom talk which takes place between a teacher and pupils and occurs during certain definable activities.
2. **Thomas Green :** Teaching is the task of a teacher which is preformed for the development of a child.
3. **Clark :** Teaching refers to activities that are designed and performed to produce desired changes in pupils' behaviour.
4. **Smith :** Teaching is a system of action to induce learning.

## NATURE AND CHARACTERISTICS OF TEACHING

Following characteristics of teaching can be inferred from the definitions given above.

1. Teaching is an interaction between a teacher and his pupils.
2. Teaching is a social and professional process in which teacher applieds his professional skills on the students (society).
3. Teaching is a purposeful activity which ends at desired changes of learners' behaviour.
4. Teaching is a process leading to the development of learners.
5. Teaching is the name of giving scientific shape to the art of teaching with the help of strategies and techniques.
6. Teaching is a communicative process which furthers by verbal as well as non-verbal mediums.
7. Teaching is a bipolar process where a teacher ensures the participation of learners in the task through the medium of the content.
8. Teaching is diagnostic as well as remedial process. We first of all, find out the weaknesses of students and then suggest remedial measures.
9. Teaching is a logical activity centering around planning, presentation and evaluation in a logical sequence.
10. Measurement of teaching is possible, i.e., teachers' behaviour can be observed and rated quantitatively.
11. Improvement in strategies of teaching and reinforcement can lead to better learning all the time. Thus, teaching is a learning process also. Search from good to better is a continuous process that makes the task a challenging one.
12. Teaching is a tripolar process also in which teaching objectives (teacher) learning experiences (content) and changes in behaviour (students) all work together in a unified form.
13. Teaching is a guiding activity by which students are guided in the class to learn according to their interest, abilities and needs.
14. Teaching becomes formal when it takes place in the form of a regular class. Teaching outside a school system is only informal which is mostly dominated by instruction.
15. Teaching is a controlled activity where nothing is done by the teacher without proper deliberation.
16. Teaching is that activity which removes the barriers from the path of learning. The task of the teacher does not complete until the students complete the activity of learning.
17. Teaching is an activity of furthering the generalization of knowledge.

### Structural Elements of Teaching

Teaching consists of three structural elements.

1. **Signal or Symbol :** Signals or symbols make the teaching economical. We get these signals or symbols after we analyse different elements of teaching. A teacher starts using these symbols from the very beginning of his teaching and students follow them. Then the use of these symbols continues till the last process of teaching, i.e., evaluation. Students also use these symbols to communicate their knowledge to others. For example, teaching of trigonometry starts with the symbol θ and all trigonometric relations are taught by using this symbol.
2. **Language :** In order to communicate ideas and concepts to students, a teacher takes the help of linguistic elements also. Even the communication and recognition of symbols are not possible without language. Alphabets of a language are also symbols. When letters are organised into words to denote some pre-determined meaning, they become linguistic elements. Thus, use of language in teaching serves the following purposes.

I. For the purpose of explaining ideas and concepts.

II. For the purpose of discussing events and facts.

III. For the purpose of motivating the students.

IV. For verbal interaction in the class.

V. For supporting non-verbal communication.

3. **Logic :** A teacher must have logical power in order to make his teaching effective. A teacher first weighs various elements of a content on logical parameter and then he presents each or these elements in a natural sequence. Logical elements in teaching serve the following purposes:

I. For positive transfer of training in the class.

II. For systematic organisation of the subject-matter.

III. For drawing right conclusions.

IV. For making summarizations.

V. For synthesizing the analysed parts of subject-matter.

VI. Logical elements are needed in all the four stages of teaching from planning to controlling.

## TEACHING DIFFERENTIATED FROM SOME CONCEPTS

### Teaching Differentiated from Instruction

1. If a teacher does not get his students involved in his teaching and only inserts titbits of knowledge into their minds like an autocrate, it is called instruction. But if full interaction is there between a teacher and students and the teacher leads the students to learning objectives, it is called teaching.
2. Good communication skills can lead to good instructions in the class but teaching requires a good communication skills on the part of students also. Thus, a teacher gives primary emphasis to the development of these skills.
3. All the three domains of behaviour-cognitive, affective and psychomotor can be developed by teaching but the role of instruction is restricted to the development of cognitive domain of learning only.
4. Teaching necessarily consists of instruction but vice-versa is not correct.
5. Instructions can be given by using machines (hardware technology)but teaching is not possible without an effective teacher.

### Teaching Differentiated from Learning

1. Modification and improvement in the behaviour of students brought about through responses and experiences is called learning. It otherwise means that learning is the outcome of teaching. (if a learner has not learnt, a teacher has not taught). Thus, teaching is done for creating learning. Even mere instruction can do this job but only at a lower level.
2. Learning is affected by the acts of teaching and instruction. It otherwise means that teaching consists of learning as well. But all learning is not the result of teaching or instruction, i.e., learning can also take place by experiences, maturation and motivation.
3. Learning refers to activities and experiences. Teaching is also done on the basis of activities and experiences. But the difference between the two is that learning, activities and experiences are more stable than teaching ones.

### Teaching Differentiated from Education

1. Education is a social process but teaching is only a method to further that social process.
2. Education is a life long process not confined to the boundaries of an educational instruction. While teaching is an activity performed in a controlled environment of the class. Later is the result of interaction between students and teachers to create learning curiosity among students.
3. Process of education is not always a deliberate efforts, e.g., we learn many things by viewing a film, though the purpose of viewing the film maybe amusement only. Teaching on the other hand, is a formal activity that is performed after well deliberation and it has pre-determined objectives.
4. Education can be formal and informal both but teaching is always a formal activity of the class.

### Teaching Differentiated from Training

1. Training refers to shaping of habits and behaviour while teaching refers to constructing

of habits and behaviour. It means that training starts only after preliminary form of teaching.

2. Training is technically a part of teaching which is restricted to enable the students to acquire a particular skill. Teaching, on the other hand, is the foundation stone of all skills. Thus, skills are developed through training and knowledge is inculcated through teaching.
3. Training is the lower level of teaching which is given only to those who have particular ability or interest in a definite field.
4. An idealistic society gives importance to teaching while a pragmatic society prefers training. It is because training is directly related to livelihood.

## VARIABLES OF TEACHING

### Meaning of Variables

Any reaction or behaviour which is manifested in different categories under different situations is called variable.

There are three types of variables in teaching :

1. **Independent Variable :** This variable can be manipulated according to our will. By the manipulation of this variable, we can manipulate the dependent variable. Teacher is an independent variable in the class, If he modifies his behaviour, the behaviour of students is also experted to change.
2. **Dependent Variable :** Independent variable is applied to this variable to bring about desirable changes in the behaviour of learners. Students are dependent variables in the class. A teacher can not manipulate this variable directly.
3. **Intervening Variable :** This works as an impediment in the way between dependent and independent variables. Content to be taught in the class is an intervening variable. Direct interaction between a teacher and a student is interfered by this variable.

### Functions of Variables

(A) Diagnostic function
(B) Remedial function
(C) Evaluative function

Just as a doctor diagnoses the disease of a patient first, then he suggests and prescribes medicines for the cure of the disease and finally he studies the effects of the drugs on the patient and changes the treatment if the response of the medicine is not positive. Similarly, a teacher (independent variable)also goes through these processes in the class. He diagnoses the learning problems of learners (dependent variable), then he suggests and adopts remedial measures and finally he evaluates the behaviour of students to know the effectiveness of his measures. Intervening variable does not have any role to play here except providing some content of feedback to the other two variables.

Now we will discuss all the three functions here one by one :

### (A) Diagnostic Functions

These functions are related to pre-active phase of teaching. This prepares the foundation of how a teacher prescribes remedial measures in the class. Diagnostic functions of a teacher are given below:

1. **Analysis of teaching tasks :** Teacher first analyses the subject matter to know whether the teaching task concurs the ability level of students or not. This analysis is also necessary to divide the subject-matter into different homogeneous segments and match the teaching strategies and hardware technologies according to the nature of the task.
2. **Determining the entering behaviour of students :** Teacher determines the entering behaviour (previous knowledge) of students by asking some questions from them. New knowledge is given to them on the basis of this very behaviour. In this way, he fills the gap between old and new knowledge by relating the two by using proper tactics. The number of such introductory questions should not be less than five or more than six.
3. **Determination of individual differences :** Every student is different in his interest, ability needs and attitude. A teacher has to satisfy each of them in the class. Due to this reason, he will have to guide the weak students and talented ones very systematically during his teaching along with keeping his teaching at average level. Thus, collective teaching will be supplemented by individualized teaching also.

4. **Analysis of activities :** A teacher has to perform many activities in the class. By keeping the total subject-matter into account, a teacher decides in advance what learning and teaching activities he will do in the class in order to make his teaching effective. Thus, teaching strategies and techniques are determined here according to the nature of the sub content. He also takes decision about the nature and the number of material aids that he has to use in the class to clarify the concepts.
5. **Determination of teaching objectives :** The teacher formulates the objectives of teaching according to the level and grade of students. Then these objectives are written in behavioural terms so that evaluation may be easy.

   It should be kept in mind that all the above five functions are not separate from each other. They are inter-related to each other and are done simultaneously.

## (B) Remedial Function

These functions are related to interactive phase of teaching. Under these functions teacher puts all the variables of teaching into practice in such a manner that objectives are realized. He takes the help of action researches in order to solve the problems related to techniques and strategies of teaching. Remedial functions of a teacher are as follows :

1. **Putting teaching strategies and skills into practice :** What strategies and techniques the teacher had selected for the presentation of different units of the subject-matter during the pre-active phase are now used here. The teacher changes them along with his teaching skills according to the nature of the subject-matter and does not allow the students to get bored in the class.
2. **Arrangement of reinforcement and feedback devices :** Proper application of strategies and techniques are not simply enough. Regular feedback and reinforcement to students at correct responses are also needed. These techniques and devices increase the rate of responses of students because students get motivation from them. These devices are decided and prepared in advance in the diagnostic function of the variables.

## (C) Evaluative Functions

These functions are related to post-active phase of teaching. Here the effects of remedial measures on diagnostic functions are studied by the teacher. Realisation of the objectives is the criteria of evaluation. If objectives are achieved, then the remedies suggested by the teacher will be considered correct. Otherwise, either diagnosis will be stated as wrong or modification in the remedity or treatment will be suggested. Evaluative functions of a teacher are as follows:

1. **Construction of a Criterion Test :** In order to know the exact information about the changes brought about in the behaviour of learners, evaluation becomes necessary. This requires criterion test relevant to the situation. If such tests are not available, they are constructed by the teacher himself. These tests must be reliable, valid and objective to the maximum level possible.
2. **Evaluation of Behavioural Change :** After constructing the test, the teacher administers it to the students to know as to what extent the changes in the behaviour of learners have taken place. These behavioural changes are evaluated on the basis of the responses given by the students.
3. **Analysis of Results and Improvement :** After scoring the answers given by the students, results are now analysed to see as to what extent the teacher is successful in his efforts. Further improvement measures are also taken on the basis of this analysis.

# PHASES OF TEACHING

This is also called **Philip Jackson's** analysis of teaching. The three phases of teaching are not very much different from the functions of variables given above, yet a brief account of them is given below :

There are three phases of teaching given by Philip Jackson :

(A) Pre-active phase
(B) Interactive phase
(C) Post-active phase

## (A) Pre-active phase

This phase is exclusively related to the analysis of the teaching task at the time of planning. Activities which are included here are done by the teacher before entering the class. Preparing lesson plans by the pupil-teachers is pre-active phase of teaching. The success of interactive phase entirely depends on it. A teacher does the following five things here.

1. **Formulation of Teaching Objectives :** The preliminary task is related to why a teacher is to teach in the class. What knowledge students will receive in 40 or 50 minutes period is called objectives for the teacher. These objectives are determined by keeping the three domains of learning into account. Then these objectives are written in the language of behavioural change of learners. These objectives are formulated by keeping the following points into consideration.
   I. Mental level and socio-economic background of students.
   II. Standard of the lesson and the class.
   III. Resources available in the class.
   IV. Environment and its aspirations.
   V. Needs of the students and the society.
   VI. Socio-political philosophy of the nation.
2. **Selection of the subject-matter :** After determining the objectives, the subject-matter through which these objectives will be realized are selected. Sometimes teacher selects the subject-matter first then objectives of teaching are formulated because formulation of objectives does not become possible without seeing the subject-matter and matching the objectives according to the curriculum and directions of Education Board. A teacher takes following points in view while selecting the subject-matter.
   I. Previous knowledge of students.
   II. Need and utility of the lesson for the students.
   III. Educational and mental level of students.
   IV. Level of teaching to be adopted by the teacher in the class.
   V. Nature of feedback and reinforcement applied to students.
   VI. Methods and procedure available for evaluating the lesson.
   VII. Needs of the students and the society.
3. **Analysing the subject-matter and arranging its segments into logical sequence :** Here the teacher first analyses the subject-matter and divides it into different parts. He then arranges these parts into logical sequence. While doing so he keeps the psychology of students into account also.
4. **Selection of teaching strategies and techniques :** A teacher has to present the subject-matter by using suitable strategies and techniques and material aids are also selected accordingly. Different strategies and techniques are selected for different elements of the subject-matter and sometimes a combination of strategies are applied for the purpose. Selection of strategies and techniques also depends on the age and psychology of students. For example, a content can be explained by story telling and opposite word techniques both. The first is useful for children of smaller age and later is effective for those of higher age.
5. **Distribution and arrangement of strategies and techniques :** Here teacher decides when and what strategies he will use and how. When he will ask questions and when he will explain the content. When and where he will use blackboard, roller board, chart and models and how many times a particular techniques is repeated in the lesson and so on.

## (B) Interactive Phase

In this phase of teaching those activities of a teacher come which are done by him after entering the class. Generally these activities go on according to the plan of pre-active phase. Some modifications are, however, allowed if need arises. This phase consists of the following three varieties of activities:

1. **Measuring the size of the class :** As soon as a teacher enters the class, he throws a bird's eye view on the class and comes to know in a moment the following things :
   (a) What is the size of the class.
   (b) Who are those students who will cooperate him during teaching.
   (c) Who are those students creating problems for him.

   On the other hand, students also try to weigh his teacher visually, i.e., what is the worth of their teacher.

2. **Identifying students :** After a teacher has assessed his students visually, the teacher asks a number of questions in order to know the abilities, interests, attitudes, needs and entering behaviour of his students so that students may be prepared for learning. The maximum number of these questions will be six.
3. **Teacher's initiative and student's and teacher's activities :** These two activities are called interactions. When a teacher does some activities by asking questions or by showing some material aids in the class, students react to these stimuli leading to some responses from the teacher also, i.e., reinforcing the students at proper responses. Thus, this process of action and reaction goes on in the class unabatedly.

   A teacher does following activities in this sub-phase of teaching :

(a) **Selection of Stimuli :** Stimuli are necessary for creation of responses. These stimuli can be verbal and non-verbal both. The teacher selects only effective stimuli of these two types so that response may be maximum.

(b) **Presentation of stimuli :** After selecting the stimuli, the teacher presents them in such a manner that students are motivated for learning. At the presentation stage of stimuli, the teacher keeps this fact into mind, which stimulus is to be presented and when.

(c) **Regular reinforcement :** When students react to the stimuli in a desired manner, the teacher reinforces them. As a result, students' responses get direction and energy. If students' responses are not correct, the teacher rearranges the stimuli again and presents them to the students. This helps the students not to commit the same mistakes again.

(d) **Extension of teaching strategies :** For the presentation of stimuli and reinforcement of students, different teaching strategies are adopted by the teacher. Continuous change in teaching strategies leads to increase the number of responses.

### (C) Post-active Phase

When teaching task is over, the teacher asks written or oral questions in order to measure the changes in the behaviour of learners. Only after the evaluation, the teacher comes to know whether the objectives are achieved or not. This phase of teaching consists of the following activities by the teacher.

1. **Defining the dimensions of behavioural change:** Here the teacher defines the different dimensions of behavioural change on the basis of the criteria of desirable behaviour. For example, after teaching the lesson of **'Parliament'** to students, the teacher expects that students must have learnt about the functions, houses and officers of parliament. The teacher compares the real behaviour change of the students with their expected behaviour. If there is greater similarity between the two, it is assumed that objectives are achieved.
2. **Selection or construction of measuring instruments :** For the purpose of comparing the expected and real behaviour, the teacher either selects or constructs the measuring instruments. These instruments are either oral or written, essay type or objective type.
3. **Application of these tests :** The selected tests are applied to students. By these tests, teacher comes to know about the achievement of students on one hand and on the other hand he can also know the effectiveness of his own teaching strategies. These instruments can also help the teacher to know his shortcomings.

## THEORIES OF TEACHING

### Need of Teaching theories :

1. The main functions of the teacher is to create suitable learning situations in the class. This can be done with the help of teaching theories. It is because the task of teaching planning and control can be made effective by the application of these theories.
2. We come to know about the variables of teaching by these principles. The theories tell us about the action of independent variables on dependent ones.
3. These theories give the knowledge of assumptions and laws to teachers and improvement in the behaviour of learners can be brought about by them.

4. We come to know about the multidimensional nature of teaching with the help of these theories, e.g., what are the different levels of teaching and what can be the suitable model of teaching concurrent to the level.
5. Learning theories explain the correlation between teaching and learning. In this way, a teacher comes to know about the common factors of teaching and learning.
6. It makes the development of instructional design and its application into teaching easy.
7. Teaching skills can be developed by the application of these theories. It means that effective teachers can be prepared by training.
8. These theories provide scientific base for the investigation of teaching problems and their verified solution.
9. Nature and form of teaching can be prepared with the help of these theories.
10. Teaching theories put more emphasis on understanding learners than content. This makes the scope of the teacher more wide and comprehensive.

## Difficulties in Propounding Teaching Theories

Teaching is a well-defined technique of a social process but since social factors continuously change so, a universally acceptable definition of teaching is not possible. This very difficulty makes it very difficult to propound a teaching theory e.g., :

1. Educational system and policies also change with the change in political system and its policies. In such a situation, change in teaching philosophy (theory) is but natural.
2. There is great difference in the subject-matters of science, mathematics, literature etc. Due to this reason different teaching theories are required for different subjects.
3. Level of teaching also changes with the change in the stages of child's development. Therefore, the application of teaching theories will also have to change.
4. Most of the teaching theories and principles are based on learning theories which have been propounded by doing experiments on rats, dogs, cats and other lower animals. The application of these theories to humans is not a sound approach because they use intellect also in learning and their learning is not confined to the result of conditioning only.
5. Communication has special significance in teaching process and the form and nature of communication vary from person to person, culture to culture and society to society .
6. No two teachers can teach a class together. They teach different classes separately. So, no group experiment or observation is possible on them.

In spite of these difficulties, educationists are constantly doing efforts in developing universally acceptable theories. Whatever teaching theories have been propounded by them so far are mere propositions. We are discussing here some of them.

## (A) General Theories of Teaching

**Important general theories of teaching are given below :**

1. **Maeiutic theory :** The propounder of this theory is Socrates. He believed that spirit has a feeling of all types of knowledge. But when it takes birth into a human body, it forgets it. Teacher brings this forgotten knowledge to the conscious mind again by recognition. Socrates propounded questioning method to bring this knowledge to the conscious mind again. These questions are asked in such a manner that they help the person being questioned to regain the knowledge, i.e., questions aid some new knowledge themselves.
2. **Communication theory :** According to this theory teachers communicate new knowledge, facts, events and concepts with the help of a language. Thus, this theory gives more importance to classroom interaction by using a language.
3. **Moulding theory :** According to this theory teaching is such a process by which desirable changes in the behaviour of learners is brought about. Relations between the teacher and the students become close by classroom interaction between them and this makes a positive change in the behaviour of learners. Teacher takes the

help of the content also for changing the behaviour of his students.

4. **Mutual inquiry theory :** According to this theory, the task of a teacher in the class is not to teach but to create a congenial learning environment. For this purpose, he guides his students in such a way as they reach to the solution of the problem themselves. Teacher and the taught both further the task of teaching by mutual questioning and discussion.

### (B) Cognitive Theory of teaching

This theory was propounded by Gaze. He was of the opinion that no single theory of teaching can fulfil the objectives of teaching. So, teaching work should be done after getting so many theories of teaching combined.

**Gaze** has analysed teaching in the following way:

1. **Teaching objectives :** Objectives can be divided into three categories—cognitive, affective and psychomotor. Specific teaching activities are required for realizing each of these objectives. Hence there must be at least three theories of teaching.
2. **Teaching activities :** A teacher does so many types of activities in the class, eg., philosophical, guiding, instructional, activities related to classroom management and evaluation related activities. Hence, only a bunch of teaching theories can explain all these activities. Process of teaching is mostly mental supported by physical activities.
3. **Learning theories :** Teacher's activities itself can not create congenial learning environment in the class. These activities are based on psychological, scientific and social theories and principles. Thus, so many learning theories and principles will lead to the development of so many teaching theories.
4. **Elements of learning :** There are four elements of learning.
   I. Drive
   II. Response
   III. Cue and
   IV. Reinforcement

All these four elements will need different types of teacher's activities, i.e., teaching activities.

Thus, Gaze has emphasized much the understanding aspect of leaning in his teaching theory. According to him, all teaching activities are expected to increase the understanding level of students. The nature of teaching is mostly cognitive.

## PRINCIPLES OF TEACHING

Due to the evolution problems of teaching theories, educationists are now mostly concerned with the development of teaching principles rather than theories. These principles are only tested guidelines for a teacher because they are mostly based on learning theories and principles.

1. **Principle of Activity :** This principle states that teaching should mostly go in the direction of students' activities, i.e., teacher should get the students involved physically in his teaching as much as possible. Knowledge which is obtained by the involvement of activity is never forgotten. According to **Mc Dougal**, every child has some natural instinct of construction. Because of this instinct he is always in action doing one thing or the other. If a teacher does not get him involved in any activity, he will himself do something without purpose.

   Activities are of two types- physical and mental. Both these activities are important in teaching. However, physical activities are preferred to mental ones because acquisition of knowledge is already concerned with mental activities.

   The introduction of physical activity into teaching learning process can be understood with an example. We can forget a story read in a book after one or two years but we do not forget the skill of cycling after we have learnt it once. The reason is that activity is involved in the second type of knowledge. So, if a teacher wants to make a knowledge fixed into the minds of learners, he must supplement the theoretical knowledge with the practical one. Even history can be taught by doing activity, by dramatizing the incidents and staging it in the class. Due to the utility of this principle many modern methods of teaching such as Montessori Method, Project method, Kinder Garten method, Problem solving method etc are based on it.

2. **Principle of Interest :** According to this principle, a teacher should teach in the class only when students take interest in it and if this interest does not exist, it should first be created by the teacher. Interests in learning can be created in the class in so many ways. Some of them are given below :
   I. Tell the students the aims of their life.
   II. Tell them how useful they are for the country.
   III. Develop curiosity of learning in them.
   IV. Clarify the objectives of the lesson before the students.
   V. Teach the subject-matter to students by relating it with their daily life situations.
   VI. Principles of leaning by doing and motivation should be followed.
   VII. Clear cut relation must be established between content, aims and students.
   VIII. Lesson should be made interesting by using proper material aids and engineering technology and so on.
3. **Principle of linking with life :** It has been seen that every child lives in his own world. Thus, children take interest in those activities and subjects only which have a direct link with their lives. Thus, according to this principle, subject-matter should be taught to students only after it has been linked with the daily life of the child. This enables them to learn at faster rate and with ease. The reason for this is simple enough. When new experiences are integrated with old ones, they also become the part of old experiences. For example, if we want to teach consumer's surplus to students we first of all tell them why or how a commodity is cheap or dear for persons of different incomes. Then we inculcate the concepts of ability to pay and willingness to pay and finally, the concept of consumer's surplus becomes clear to them. If a teacher is fully acquainted with the background of his students only then he can use this principle.
4. **Principle of definite Aim :** Teaching objectives must be clear before the teacher prior to teaching because only on the basis of these objectives he selects suitable teaching strategies and techniques. For example, if the purpose of a poetry teaching is the appreciation of the poem, then pronunciation and rhythm will be emphasized and if understanding is the aim of poetry teaching, then vocabulary and sense perception will be emphasized. Thus, a teacher must know why he has to do an activity in the class before doing the activity.
5. **Principle of Selection :** Content is selected keeping in view the larger objectives of education. There may be many irrelevant materials in a lesson which are not useful for students. Similarly, many such things may be there in a text-book which do not pace with the level of learner. So, teacher selects only that part of the subject-matter which match the objectives and are meaningful for learners. For example, if a teacher decides that his students should score at least 90% marks in the examination, he selects all those parts which enable the students to score 90% marks in the exam.
6. **Principles of Planning :** A teacher must prepare a lesson plan of the lesson which he is to teach. Planning helps him to identify the expected problems of teaching and select suitable strategies to overcome them. If such a problem arises during teaching about which teacher had not even thought of while preparing the lesson plan, this type of the problem is solved by the teacher on the basis of his experiences. Planning is actually the name of taking benefit of the experiences of others.
7. **Principle of Division :** If a teacher teaches a lesson after dividing it into different natural parts, his presentation will be effective. But the teacher should keep this fact in mind that every unit of the lesson should be complete in itself and should be able to arouse curiosity for learning of the next unit. This makes the whole lesson easy and systematic for learners. When a teacher teaches a lesson in this way, he synthesizes these units in a logical sequence also.
8. **Principle of Revision :** Whatever lesson is taught to students, it must be revised by them as well. If it is not done, it will be forgotten soon. Tough subject-matter needs more revisions and easy one needs comparatively less revisions. Home work is given to students only on the basis of this very principles.

**9. Principle of democratic dealing :** The behaviour of the teacher should be democratic in the class. It means that he should give full opportunities to students to develop their self thinking and self-expression by respecting their personalities. In democratic dealing teacher is guided by the students and vice-versa. Thus, the teacher develops the lesson with the cooperation of students. He questions them and answers their queries. He also invites them for criticising him at the end of the teaching. All these activities increase the self-confidence of students.

**10. Psychological principles of teaching :** These principles are based on psychological researches conducted on lower animals and children. Some of these principles are given below :

(a) ***Principle of Motivation :*** The task of a teacher becomes very easy if he is successful in motivating his students for learning. Since, motivation is directly related to needs, the teacher must take steps to satisfy their needs. Reward and punishment, praise and blame, arousing and quenching the curiosity of learners, using material aids in teaching, competition and cooperation etc are some important techniques of motivation.

(b) ***Principle of Recreation :*** Lengthy and dull teaching tasks bore the students and proper enthusiasm on both sides can entertain both of them. In order to reduce the fatigue and boredom of students, teaching task is made interesting. A teacher must make his teaching a means of recreation not a burden on students.

(c) ***Principle of Individual Differences :*** No two learners are alike in the world in their abilities and interest. So, teaching work is done keeping in view the individual differences of learners. Thus, a teacher has to satisfy at least four groups of students by his teaching simultaneously.

- Talented and superior students.
- Weak and dull students.
- Students of average performance
- Students with special problems.

(d) ***Principle of Remedial Teaching :*** It has generally been seen that only those students shun the classes who are educationally backward in any way. This problem of backwardness lies in defective method of teaching and unsystematic classroom management. A good teacher is one who diagnoses his faults of teaching by applying standardized test and adopts remedial measures thereon.

(e) ***Principle of Sympathy :*** Those teachers who are sympathetic to their students can easily motivate their students for learning. If a teacher is able to develop a feeling in his students that there is none more sympathetic to them than him, the teacher will always be cooperated by his students.

(f) ***Principle of Reinforcement :*** Reinforcement refers to removing barriers from the way of students and presenting such stimuli before them which increases the rate of responses by learners. The teacher reinforces his students off and on during teaching sometimes verbally and sometimes by giving rewards in order that their enthusiasm for more correct responses increases.

(g) ***Principle of training to senses :*** Five sense organs play a very important role in the acquisition of knowledge. Teacher initiates those activities in the class which are conducive to the development of these senses.

## MAXIMS OF TEACHING

In order to make the teaching successful, a teacher must know the following four things.

I. What to teach—knowledge of the subject-matter.
II. How to teach—knowledge of the teaching strategies.
III. Whom to teach-knowledge of the students
IV. Why to teach-knowledge of the society and the nation.

Apart from these four fundamental elements of teaching, he must also know the experiences of the educators in respective field. These experiences of educators are called **maxims of teaching**. They are given below :

1. **From easy to difficult :** A teacher should first divide the subject-matter into two categories—easy and difficult matters. Then he should teach the easy matter prior to difficult one. This division of the content into easy and difficult ones is done from the point of views of students by keeping their background and previous knowledge into

account. For this purpose the teacher studies his students for several days by observing them, by conducting standardized tests and by going through their previous academic records.

2. **From known to unknown :** A teacher first finds out the previous knowledge of his students and then he should give new knowledge to them by making their old knowledge as the base. This maxim has two advantages.
   I. Shifting from known to unknown facts is done in such a cautious manner as it is not noticed by the students.
   II. Students do not feel that they are learning something new. Every thing goes on in an automatic and natural way.
3. **From seen to unseen :** Material aids in the class are prepared only on the basis of what a child has already seen in his environment. Then the child is taught to what he has not seen so far. The reason is that a child lives in his present day world not in the past or future. The lesson becomes easy when experience of the teacher integrates with that of students.
4. **From concrete to abstract :** Concrete objects are experienced directly by students. Because of this reason the mental development of a child starts from the experiences of the concrete materials. A teacher should give the knowledge of concrete materials first. Models as material aids are prepared for this very purpose and abstract knowledge is given on the basis of these models or pictures.
5. **From particular to general :** Specific examples are given to students before clarifying the facts. Then rules and principles are derived on the basis of these very examples. This is actually the inductive method of teaching. Demonstration method of teaching is also based on this very maxim. This maxim leads to the simplification of the lesson because students observe and test the rules and principles themselves.
6. **From whole to part :** Gestalt psychologists are of the opinion that we observe the whole of an object first then we come to different parts of it. For example, when we look at an elephant, the picture of the whole elephant comes to our mind first. Then we analyse its trunk, tusk, feet etc. Parts of an object are also remembered or recalled on the basis of whole. The teacher in the class should also present the outline of the whole lesson before the students first. Then he should later explain each part of the lesson one by one by integrating it with the whole, e.g., sentence should be taught prior to words in language teaching because vocabulary can be remembered with the help of these sentences.
7. **From indefinite to definite :** When a teacher starts teaching, the knowledge given by him is not definite in any way. it becomes definite only after experiment. This experiment is also based on theoretical knowledge. Thus, a teacher should teach theoretical part first and practical aspect should be taught later on.
8. **From psychological to logical :** When teaching task is done by keeping in view the age, grade, interests and curiosity of a child, it is called psychological teaching. But when the lesson is presented to students in a logical sequence by dividing it into different parts it is called logical teaching. The first type of teaching is child-centred and the second one is lesson-centred. The teacher shifts from students to the content very silently unnoticed by the students.
9. **From empirical to rational :** Empirical knowledge is that knowledge which is obtained by a child by observation, e.g., observation of converting water into ice, historical knowledge obtained from the archeological excavations and so on. Rational knowledge is that knowledge which is based on science and reason. For example, if we want to test age of a particular archeological object, we use carbon dating for the purpose. This is the knowledge based on science. But when we compare the result (object) with the other objects of the same period and draw a final conclusion, this is the knowledge based on reason. Thus, in rational knowledge, no importance is given to belief or dogmatism, e.g, Ram Temple of Ayodhya belonging to the period of Rama is not a matter of belief. The question of its ownership is settled on the basis of logical and scientific reasoning.

10. **From analysis to synthesis :** Construction is difficult and destruction is easy even in practical life. Dividing a problem into different parts on the basis of logic and studying these parts one by one for the purpose of arriving at the solution is called analysis. The role of analysis is very significant in teaching history, geography, mathematics and science.

    Synthesis refers to studying different aspects of a problem one by one and arriving at the solution by synthesising these parts, e.g., writing an essay or story, doing experiments in the lab or proving a theorem in Geometry. A teacher starts his teaching by analysis and furthers it by using synthesis.

11. **From Naturalism to Idealism :** In Naturalism, children are educated according to their physical and mental development in a free environment while educating the students according to the ideals and values of life and society is idealism. A teacher starts his teaching in a free environment and provides enough opportunities to students to develop on their own. Then he comes to those ideals which have been accepted by the majority of the society. When these ideals do not match with the thinking of students, they are taught to follow these ideals by telling them the utility of restriction(discipline).

12. **From teaching to self-study :** A successful teacher is one who teaches less but motivates his students to study more themselves. Self-study is a life-long process which can help a student even after leaving the school or college. For achieving this objective, the teacher guides his students during teaching how to go through the books and how to take benefit of them. For motivating them he himself presents the summary of different books during teaching.

## Characteristics of Good Teaching

Good classroom teaching lies in the application of teaching theories, principles and maxims. If a teacher is sincere to these things, his teaching is most likely to be good and effective. So, a teacher must follow all maxims, principles and theories of teaching in order to make his teaching effective.

# Levels of Teaching

## INTRODUCTION

Teaching affects learning directly and indirectly both. If we disregard the self-efforts of learners, learning and its extent will depend on the level of teaching of the teacher. What a teacher wants to make his students by his teaching depends on what the objectives of his teaching are? It means that as soon as level of teaching changes, its objectives and way of attack also change and evaluation of students also changes accordingly. Educators have determined three levels of teaching and a teacher selects these levels according to the ability and mental levels of students.

(A) Memory level of teaching (MLT)
(B) Understanding level of teaching (ULT)
(C) Reflective level of teaching (RLT)

It must be kept in mind that only one level of teaching is selected at a time. When one level of teaching completes and the teacher receives feedback by the process of evaluation only then he skips to the next level. All these three levels of teaching can be arrived at either in one period or it may take several periods to reach all these levels. Determination of the level of teaching depends on the following factors:

I. Mental and academic level of students.
II. Nature of the content (subject-matter).
III. Skill of the teacher to use different strategies of teaching.

## (A) MEMORY LEVEL OF TEACHING (MLT)

This is a thoughtless teaching level. This level is concerned with the mere reproduction of learnt material by students through recognition and recall. If subject-matter presented by the teacher is crammed by students, task of this level of teaching is said to be complete. The subject-matter which is easy, interesting and purposeful is learnt by students easily and retained for a longer period of time. On the other hand, difficult, dull and purposeless subject-matter is learnt with difficulty and forgotten hurriedly.

At this level of teaching, without regarding interests, attitudes and freedom of students, the teacher inserts the facts and informations into the minds of learners like an autocrate and learners receive them like a mute audience. This attitude of the teacher makes the teaching teacher centred and low level of interaction is seen between teachers and students. This instructional type of teaching can develop only limited level of cognitive domain and if students are able to reproduce the learnt facts or events in written or oral form, teaching is said to be successful.

In spite of some shortcomings, the advantages of this level of teaching is that this is the foundation stage of understanding or reflective levels of teaching, i.e., we can not adopt any other level of teaching without completing teaching at this level.

### Model of MLT

This model was presented by **Herbart.** Like other two models this model is also based on the following four points :

I. Focus (Objectives)
II. Syntax (Methods and Strategies)
III. Social System (learning environment)
IV. Support system (Evaluation)

1. **Focus :** This level of teaching focuses on the following points :
   I. Craming facts and principles by students and their proper retention.
   II. Presenting the crammed materials when needed in written or oral form.
   III. Presenting subject-matter to students like an autocrate.
2. **Syntax :** Herbart has divided the memory level of teaching into five categories. A teacher adopts

these five steps one by one in order to create proper learning environment.

I. **Preparation and statement of objectives :** In the preparation stage, the teacher asks few questions in the class in order to check previous knowledge of students and arouse their curiosity. The teacher brings the students to the main topic gradually and when topic is clear to students, teacher repeats the topic orally and writes it on the blackboard.

II. **Presentation :** At this stage, the teacher presents new knowledge before his students on the basis of their previous knowledge in such a manner that a bond is established between new and old knowledge. The teacher keeps the following four points into his mind :

(a) The teacher does not deviate from the subject-matter slightly.

(b) The type of knowledge which is to be given to students, is prepared by the teacher in advance, i.e., advance lesson planning is made.

(c) The teacher gives such a knowledge to his students that can be evaluated.

(d) At this stage the teacher tries to gather maximum information from his students.

III. **Comparison and Association :** At this stage the teacher associates different facts, events and subjects in such a manner that they can be easily compared with each other, e.g. giving the knowledge of antonyms and synonyms, comparing the similarities and dissimilarities of the life incidents and characters of gentlemen-real or created ones. This makes the knowledge fixed into the minds of learners.

IV. **Generalization :** At this stage the teacher teaches how to develop new rules and principles on the basis of given facts and information, i.e., obtained knowledge is generalized in similar situations. For example, if a child learns BUT and HUT, he also learns SUP and NUT himself.

V. **Application :** In the last stage the learnt knowledge is applied in real life situations, i.e., use of words in sentences or making stories with the help of sentences etc.

The above stages given in the syntax show that memory level of teaching also needs abundant use of intellect and creativity. Mere cramming of facts or principles without understanding is not enough.

3. **Social system :** The social system of MLT is that teacher's behaviour dominates over students' one. He enjoys full commands over his students. Almost no freedom is given to students to express themselves. Teacher gives them chance to take part in the lesson through the use of motivation techniques only, i.e., the freedom of students lies in the wishes of the teacher.

4. **Support system :** In MLT, whatever knowledge students have gained is tested using written or oral tests. Tests may be objective and essay type both. Exactness of the response from the side of students is important. Full marks is given to students only when he reproduces exactly what he is taught by his teacher.

## Suggestion for Improving MLT

A teacher must heed to the following suggestions in order to make this level of teaching a success.

I. Presented material should be meaningful and interesting for students only then it will be retained by them.

II. Subject-matter should be presented to students systematically in a logical sequence only then proper relationship can be established between new and old knowledge.

III. When students are tired physically or mentally, they should never be taught.

IV. Feedback and reinforcement must be given to students regularly for motivating them.

V. Recall and rehearsal of the learnt knowledge should be done at short intervals. Delay leads to decay.

VI. Students should not only cram the subject-matter but they should also rehearse it in writing and these should be done by using part memory method.

VII. There must be full control on cheating in the examination hall. If students are able to produce the material just by copying, the evaluation of teacher's effectiveness will not be possible there.

## (B) UNDERSTANDING LEVEL OF TEACHING (ULT)

Successful accomplishment of memory level of teaching is the assumption of ULT. We may call it a necessary supplement to the first level of teaching. By understanding level of teaching the teacher develops the mental capacities of students in such a manner that the students can now understand and apply the laws and principles in a confident manner. Their potentials developed by this level of teaching enable them to solve the problems themselves. The roles of the students do not lag behind the teacher. For example, students can answer the comprehensive questions from the para themselves. They can write the summary of the paragraphs and can draw conclusions on the basis of the facts given in the extract or subject-matter. Doing long mathematical sums by using the numerical tables is also the example of understanding level of teaching.

### Model of ULT

ULT model prepared by **Morrison** is given below. This model is basically based on unit approach of lesson planning.

1. **Focus :** Getting complete mastery over the subject-matter by the students is the focus of teaching here. The learning of students should be so perfect that students are not less than the teacher at least for the subject-matter taught to them. Students clearly understand what they are being taught in the class.
2. **Syntax :** Syntax of the model is divided into five sub stages of teaching :

**(a) Exploration :** Three activities are performed by the teacher here :

I. He finds out the entering behaviour of students by asking questions from them. The teacher especially sees whether memory level of teaching is complete or not.

II. He analyses the content and divides it into different units. Then he arranges all these units in a logical sequence so that lesson can be understood easily.

III. He selects different teaching strategies suitable to the presentation of each unit so that different units of the content may be presented by different strategies and techniques.

**(b) Presentation :**

The teacher does the following three activities here :

I. He presents the subject-matter unit by unit and maintains the logical sequence in between these units.

II. While presenting the units of the subject-matter, he receives the feedback from his students whether each unit has been clearly understood or not.

III. He recapitulates the subject-matter till it is clearly understood by almost all students of the class.

**(c) Assimilation :** This is the third stage of teaching. After presenting the subject-matter to students the teacher provides them opportunities for the assimilation of the acquired knowledge. It requires the following activities on the part of the teacher.

I. The teacher provides the opportunities of generalization to his students through the process of assimilation. For example, after teaching a paragraph to the students, he gives another para of the same difficulty level to his students and ask comprehensive questions from it. Unseen passages in language teaching are used for this purpose.

II. He takes the students to the depth of the subject-matter by the process of assimilation, e.g., different meanings of an extract are given for the purpose.

III. He provides opportunities to each of his students to understand the content according to their respective leaning capacities.

IV. When students do self-study during the activity of assimilation, the teacher supervises them.

V. After self-study, the teacher tests the students whether they have got mastery over the subject-matter or not. If students have acquired the capacity of generalization, the assimilation process is said to be completed. In history teaching, generalizing the causes of failure of other rulers on the basis of a particular ruler is a good example of assimilation.

(d) **Organisation :** After assimilation, the students either enter organisation stage or recitation as the nature of the subject-matter demands.
In the organisation stage, the students are expected to reproduce the subject-matter in his own language in written form without taking help from any body. If students are able to do so, the understanding level of teaching is said to be accomplished.

(e) **Recitation :** If after assimilation subject-matter is to reproduce orally by the students instead of written form, it is called recitation.The teacher must be very careful in organising the activities of recitation or organization, otherwise the students will reproduce the learnt material by craming. The material reproduced in organisation or recitation should be in the learner's own language not in the language of the text-book.

3. **Social System :** The teacher is more active in the class than the students at the time of exploration and presentation. This is necessary to control the behaviour of students. During the process of assimilation both of them are equally active. After that learners are required to be more active than the teacher. Teacher motivates his students also during all these five stages of teaching. Thus, we see a fully democratic environment in the class.

4. **Support System :** Examination system constantly changes at this level of teaching. Sometimes written and sometimes oral tests are conducted and the tests may be objective and essay type both. Organizational ability of students and their expression is much emphasized here as compared to mere recognition or recall, hence, objective type tests are least applied.

## Suggestions for improving ULT

Following suggestions are given for the benefit of the teacher to improve understanding level of teaching :

I. Students should not be brought to the understanding level without passing the memory level of teaching. If they do not know the fundamentals of a concept, teaching at this level will only be a waste of time.

II. Children shoulc be brought to different stages of teaching from exploration to recitation in a sequential order. It means that once the teacher has not accomplished the presentation stage, he should not take his students to the assimilation stage.

III. Teacher should motivate his students in all the stages of teaching. Reinforcement techniques should be regularly applied to motivate the students.

IV. The teacher should take initiative himself to solve the individual problems of his students. It is because all learners can not learn at equal speed. It requires that teacher should test his students at short intervals and change his strategies accordingly.

V. The teacher should have full command over the subject only then he can enable his students to comprehend the subject-matter to the desired extent.

VI. The teacher should raise the aspiration level of his students as high as possible.

VII. The teacher should be able to develop comprehensive questions from the texual matter. These questions will open new avenues of learning.

VIII. While evaluating the understanding power of his students, the teacher must be very careful so that answers are not supplied on the basis of memory.

## (C) REFLECTIVE LEVEL OF TEACHING (RLT)

This is the highest level of teaching which starts when understanding level of teaching is over. It is a child centred approach of teaching where students are more active than the teacher and they deliberate consciously over the understood material. By doing so the students present their original views.

**M. Bigge** has elaborated it in the following words:

"Reflective level of teaching tends to develop classroom atmosphere which is more alive and exciting, more critical and penetrating and more open to fresh and original thinking".

Thus, this level of teaching increases the thinking power of students and when this ability is developed in students fully they can solve the real life related problems by applying reflective thinking and logic. This teaching is basically problem-centred. The teacher extracts the problems from within the text and presents them before his students. After looking at the problem, they become excited and tense. Then they reach to the solution of the problem by applying critical judgement techniques. The knowledge which is obtained by this reflection is original and permanent.

## Model of RLT

This model was prepared by **Hunt.** The summary of the model is given below.

1. **Focus :** The focus of the reflective level of teaching is to develop following abilities among learners.
   - I. To develop the ability of problem solving among students.
   - II. To develop creative and critical abilities among students.
   - III. To develop original and free thinking power of students.
2. **Syntax :** Syntax of the model is comprised of four stages of teaching.

(a) In the first step the teacher presents the problematic situation before his students. For example, after teaching the lesson of 'Akbar' in history, , he can present before them a problem like that "Had Akbar not propounded the religion of Deen-e-Ilahi, what would have happened".

(b) Students formulate the hypothesis after pondering over the problem seriously. In the example given above, they formulate one or two hypothesis on the basis of the consequences of this religion in the following ways :

(I) Had Akbar not propounded this religion, orthodox Mullas would not have stood against him.

(II) Had Akbar not done it, liberal Hindus and Hindu rulers would not have come closer to Akbar.

(c) In the third step students apply reflective thinking and collect relevant data for testing the hypothesis. In the above example, they categories the positive and negative consequences of the propagation of Deen-e-Ilahi separately and then ponder over these consequences one by one. On the basis of these reflections they find out some more effects of the religion which would have incurred if Akbar had not propounded this religion.

(d) Hypothesis is tested in the last stage of teaching and conclusions are drawn. If reflective data do not support the hypotheses, they are rejected.

In medieval period, this level of teaching was greatly emphasized in the madarsahs of Arabia, Turkey and Central Asia and Logic and philosophy were especially taught to students to develop reflective power.

RLT is different from problem solving method in the sense that in reflective level of teaching only imaginary problems are taken while problem solving method takes real problems of life to solve. The second difference is that former is a mental approach while later is a practical approach of teaching.

3. **Social system :** The learning environment is fully laissez faire at this level of teaching. The atmosphere of the class is so open and free that students can express themselves fully in the manner they like. Seminars and group discussions are also organised in the class for reaching the solution of the problem. Thus, we see that students are always more active in the class than the teacher. The task of the teacher is only to guide them.
4. **Support System :** Objective type questions are not asked at all for evaluating the achievement of learners at reflective level of teaching. Evaluation is done either through essay type tests or through discussion, seminars and speech competitions. The more the views of a student are logical and convincing, the more he is given marks.

## Suggestions for improving RLT

A teacher should keep the following suggestive points in view in order to make this level of teaching a success:

1. After creating the problem to be solved, the teacher should not interfere the thinking process of students at all. students should reach the results themselves.

2. A teacher should raise the aspiration level of students as high as possible. High aspiration level can only lead to high level of reflection.
3. The teacher himself should be creative and highly intelligent.
4. The teacher should extract only such problems for reflective thinking which have direct relevance to the career of students. It means that problems must be useful for students.
5. Hypothesis which is the tentative solution of the problem should be formulated by students with the help of the teacher. Such hypothesis should never be formulated whose testing is not possible by the collected data.
6. In the evaluation process, if the teacher involves the students also, it is far better. It will help the teacher to critically examine the views. It means that the achievement of a student is evaluated not by his teacher only but his class fellows also evaluate him and criticize his views. Then final marks are allotted by the teacher on the basis of the total assessment

# Modification of Teaching Behaviour

## (A) MICRO-TEACHING

### Meaning of Micro-Teaching

Educational technology believes that teachers are not only born but an ordinary person can be made a successful teacher by giving him training in teacher training institutions. Meaning thereby teaching of any teacher can be improved by drilling different strategies, techniques and skills of teaching. In this way, many teaching skills and techniques have been developed by the science of educational technology in order to transform teaching from art to science. Micro teaching is one of such attempts.

By micro-teaching, teachers are taught teaching skills in such a manner that the application of these skills in teaching not only becomes the habit of the teacher but it also becomes the part of his character. In short, micro teaching is a special technique to bring about a desirable change in the behaviour of the pupil teacher.

In micro-teaching, a pupil teacher teaches a single unit of the lesson for five to ten minutes to a small group of students comprised of 5 to 7 students and manifests only one teaching skills repeatedly during his teaching. His teaching is observed by his classmates and the teacher trainer. After the teaching is over, they tell the pupil teacher at what points did he commit mistakes, how many times and to what extent of accuracy and effectiveness he used a particular skill during his teaching and how he can improve his teaching by the effective use of this skill. This process continues till the pupil teacher is fully practiced with that skills.

### Definitions

1. **M.B.Bush (1968) :** Micro-teaching is a teacher education technique which allows the teacher to apply clearly defined teaching skills to carefully prepared lessons in planed series of 5 to 10 minutes encountering with a small group of real students often with an opportunity to observe the result on video tape.
2. **Allen and Eve (1968) :** Micro-teaching is a system of controlled practice that makes it possible to concentrate on specific teaching behaviour and to practice teaching under controlled conditions.
3. **Chift (1976) :** Micro-teaching is a teacher training procedure which reduces the teaching situaiton to a simpler and more controlled encounter achieved by limiting the practice teaching to a specific skill and reducing teaching time and class size.

### Characteristics of micro-teaching

Following characteristics of micro-teaching can be drawn on the basis of the definitions and meaning given above:

1. Micro-teaching is done in a controlled environment of a small sized class of five to seven students.
2. The time period of this teaching is also very short, i.e., five to ten minutes, in which the teacher manifests only one teaching skill repeatedly in order to get it practiced.
3. Video tape facility is also provided in order to give proper feedback to the pupil teacher. With the help of video tapping, the pupil teacher can observe his activities himself and after receiving criticisms from his classmates and the teacher trainer, he can mend his behaviour.
4. In micro-teaching the pupil teacher concentrates on only one teaching skill and this skill is especially shown by him.

5. In micro-teaching the pupil teacher teaches only a small portion of the lesson plan. Thus, teaching behaviour is important here rather than content.
6. In this teaching, class size and teaching time both are reduced thus, all pupil teachers get proper time for the practice of teaching skill.

**Assumptions :** Micro-teaching is based on the following assumptions:

1. The complexities of teaching can be reduced by micro-teaching.
2. Reform in teacher's behaviour can be brought about by micro-teaching.
3. It is completely an individualized programme of training.
4. When reinforcement is given at desired behaviour, teaching practice is controlled.
5. Feedback is the key concept in developing desirable teaching skills. Feedback can be given to pupil teachers in many ways. For example, video film of micro teaching can be prepared and shown to the pupil teacher, the classmates of the pupil teacher can criticize the teaching of the pupil teacher and so on.

## Components of Micro-Teaching

1. **Controlled Environment :** Here only 5 to 10 students are kept in the class and duration of teaching does not exceed to 15 minutes. In such a short span of time only a small unit of the total lesson is taught to students. In this way, the pupil teacher exerts full control over his students and the subject-matter.
2. **Teaching Skills :** Only one teaching skill is concentrated upon by the pupil teacher in micro-teaching. He may use other skills but they are neglected by the observer.
3. **Pupil teacher :** He is the person in charge of the teaching activity.
4. **Feedback :** Feedback is given to the pupil teacher only after the teaching is over. For this purpose either video recording of the teaching is done or the classmates of the pupil teacher observe his lesson on a set format.
5. **Laboratory :** This teaching is done in a laboratory situation not in the classroom. All the necessary equipments are made available there.

**Micro-Teaching Cycle :** Micro-teaching consists of the following steps :

1. **Defining the particular skill :** Whatever teaching skill is to be developed by this type of teaching in pupil teachers is first identified and then defined in clear unambiguous language. Take the example of blackboard writing. After identifying this skill we define the skill, i.e., what are the activities in black-board writing expected from a teacher and what are the benefits that a teacher can take from these activities. All these things are told to the pupil teacher.
2. **Preparation of the micro lesson plan :** The micro lesson plan is prepared in advance with special emphasis on the skill to be developed in the pupil teacher. The teacher practices the skill with the help of the content.
3. **Observation of the lesson :** Before demonstrating the skill by the pupil teacher, observers are told about the methods and procedures of observation and criticism of the lesson. Separate observation formats are given to all the observers here.
4. **Demonstration of skills :** In the fourth step, the pupil teacher demonstrates the required teaching skill again and again with the help of the lesson plan that he is teaching. The duration of this teaching session is from 5-15 minutes and only 5-10 students are taught here.
5. **Feedback :** For the purpose of giving feedback to the pupil teacher, either video recording is done or his classmates note down the critical comments on observation proforma on the basis of their observation. These critical comments are analysed after the teaching is over and feedback or suggestions are given to pupil teachers on the basis of these points.
6. **Repetition of the cycle :** After getting feedback at the end of teaching, the pupil teacher does reteaching if necessary by preparing fresh lesson plan and in the second round, he tries his best to escape those mistakes that he did in the first round.

The cycle continues till the pupil teacher has fully practiced the skill.

## Advantages of Micro-Teaching

1. In this type of teaching the whole lesson is divided into different units and skill is selected according to the nature of unit. It makes the task of the teacher easy.
2. There is no problem of discipline in micro teaching due to controlled atmosphere and small size of the class.
3. Pupil teacher gets feedback immediately after the teaching is over.
4. In micro teaching if one pupil teacher learns skills by practice, other teachers learn the skill by imitation. Thus, all the teachers need not practise the skill by formal teaching in the class.
5. The pupil teacher can evaluate his teaching himself by microteaching when it is tapped on a video.
6. Critical thinking power and observation ability can be developed in all the pupil teachers by micro teaching.
7. Special teaching skills can be developed in all the pupil teachers by it and thus desirable changes in their behaviour can be brought about.
8. This is a successful method for individualized training and thus, individual weakness of teachers can be found out.
9. It can bring professional maturity in students (Pupil teachers).
10. This type of teaching can also be used for research purposes and new teaching strategies and techniques can be developed.

## Important Teaching Skills

1. **Set Induction :** By this skill old knowledge of students are related and inter-twinned with the new knowledge in such a manner that there is no gap or zero left for the students. They are brought to the topic very silently. All the introductory questions are connected in series and the last question has direct link with the topic to be taught.
2. **Stimulus Variation :** In this skill, the teacher changes the movements of his hands, legs, mouth, eyes, voice, etc, at regular intervals to eliminate monotony from the class. For example, instead of standing at one place for a longer time, he goes to the back-bench of the class and returns back. Similarly, smile of the teacher at any good response from the students is also an example of stimulus variation.
3. **Probing Questions :** Through these questions the teacher compels the students to go to the deep of the lesson so that their thinking power may be easily developed. When students sometimes find it difficult to answer these questions, the teacher provides them clue to reach the right answer.
4. **Illustrating with Examples :** When students find it very difficult to understand facts and concepts, the teacher clarifies them by giving suitable examples. These illustrations are given only after relating them with life of students.
5. **Closure :** The word, closer here means ending the lesson in such a manner that curiosity of the new knowledge does not end. When the teacher ends the lesson, he creates the feeling by his closure that students were getting something very important. Now they will get it again soon. Summary of the lecture, seminar or demonstration is also presented with the help of this skill.
6. **Lecture :** The success of this skill lies in the effectiveness of communication. That is why it is also called communication skill. By this skill, the teacher fully absorbs the students in the lesson and they do nothing except listening to his lecture.
7. **Skill of Explaining :** By this skill the teacher explains facts, concepts, principles and laws in such a manner that they are able to answer the questions of what, why, how etc.
8. **Use of Black-Board :** Black-Board work is the simultaneous activity of teaching. Following things are included in blackboard work :
   I. Writing neatly and beautifully on the black-board, ie., legible and straight writing.
   II. Drawing figures, maps, charts or diagrams on the blackboard, i.e., neatness or exactness of the figure or diagram.
   III. Supplementing the teaching with blackboard work all the time whenever needed.
   IV. Drill of spellings or words on blackboard (Writing main headings on the black board in all subjects).
   V. Number of times a blackboard is used in every five minutes (Writing more and more on the black board).

VI. Motivating the students to note down the black board work on their copies.

By all these activities, the teacher does not let the attention of students be away from the blackboard and students take full interest in these activities. They go to learn all the skills of their teacher especially accuracy, neatness, beauty and speed of writing.

9. **Use of Audio-Visual Aids :** By this skill the teacher uses audio-visual aids in the lesson in such a manner that they look us if they are the part of the lesson and if they were not used by the teacher, the content would be incomplete. Thus, these material aids provide complete form of the content to the students.

10. **Skill of Class Management :** Classroom management is a big skill in itself. By this skill, the teacher engages his students all the time in one activity or the other. The result of this is that students, in spite of being fully free, do not do anything without the permission of their teacher.

11. **Skill of Increasing Pupils' Participation :** Students' participation refers to that overt behaviour of students which can be observed. By this skill, teacher does some activities in the class which increase the activities of the students automatically. For example, he slightly smiles at any activity of students showing his approval or pleasure, he looks pleased in the class at any right response from the part of students or he praises any of his students in the class on any success secured by him and so on. Participation of students can also be increased by the teacher by creating personal attachment with them.

12. **Recognizing Attending Behaviour :** An effective teacher is always very sensitive. He tries to pay his attention to each and every behaviour of his students. When he is responded by his students in the class, he recognises those attending behaviour without delay. Thus, no student of his class feel unattended any time.

13. **Silence and Non-verbal Cues :** Sometimes teacher becomes silent for four or five seconds while speaking in the class. The silence is maintained at a place where students come to understand next point without being told. One more advantage of this skill is that when any students is not attentive to teaching in the class, the teacher can know about that student by keeping silent for a while. This skill is used in the class all of a sudden and students can not know when the teacher will use this skill.

14. **Fluency of Questioning :** The teacher who knows how to frame questions well in the class is half teacher and if he is able to ask these questions fluently, he can be called a full teacher. By this skill, the teacher asks questions non-stop and students respond to these questions without break mechanically. The teacher is so much competent in questioning that he frames the next question before the answer of the first question completes. This skill is especially demonstrated for recapitulating the lesson taught.

15. **Giving Assignment :** The teacher gives two types of assignments to his students—class and home assignment. Home works are generally considered a burden by the students. but if the teacher is competent in using this skill, he can make these home assignments a challenge and a source of motivation for his students. For example, he can relate the home or class assignment with the pleasure and displeasure of the teacher or the guardian, the teacher can make the assignment useful for practical life of students and so on.

16. **Planned Revision and Repetition :** Sometimes the teacher repeats the difficult points or any part of the concepts or any good response of his students again and again. This is definitely useful for students because repetition or revision creates the atmosphere of conditioning.

## Application of Some Important Teaching Skills

**(1) Probing questions :**

These questions are used under the following circumstances :

*(i)* When students are unable to answer a particular question or his answer is not upto the mark the teacher tries to take the students to the correct response through probing questions.

*(ii)* Sometimes the answer of the students is very much correct but it is not according to the level of the answer that the teacher demands. The teacher tries to get the desired answer through these questions.

(iii) When students are not taking much interest in the lesson, these questions are asked to create interest in the lesson.

(iv) When knowledge level of students is not so deep as the teacher desires, the teacher increases the depth of knowledge of his students through these questions.

(v) These questions are also asked by the teacher in the class in order to focus the attention of students on a particular problem.

(vi) Different dimensions of a problem can also be found out through these questions.

***Components of probing questions:***

1. *Prompting :* Prompting is given to students to help them to reach the correct answer.
2. *Seeking more information :* When answer of the students is not according to the expectations of the teacher, the teacher asks some additional questions from the students to take them to the correct response.
3. *Refocusing :* When a teacher is failed in both the attempts given above, he refocuses the attention of his students to another problem similar to the previous one and asks questions on the basis of that problem, and students reach the correct response.
4. *Redirecting :* Here the teacher asks some additional questions from his students in order to develop their logical power. These questions redirect the thinking power of students.
5. *Critical Awareness :* This is the ultimate aim of probing questions. Here the teacher asks questions of why and how in order to provide them a deep knowledge of the subject-matter. These questions develop the critical and evaluative awareness among the students.

**Supervision and Evaluation of the skill :** When the pupil teacher demonstrates this skill in the class, the teacher trainer and other classmates of the pupil teacher observes his teaching on the basis of these very five components given above. They rate the pupil teacher on a seven point scale from zero to 6 and note down how many times each of these components have been included in 5-10 minutes span of teaching, e.g., how many prompting questions have been asked, how many questions belong to seeking more information, how many redirecting questions have been asked and so on. Maximum six questions can be asked from each component. If pupil teacher is asking one or only one question of a particular component, he will be kept at the minimum on the rating scale. If he has asked 4 or more questions of a component, he will be put at the maximum. The example of the rating scale is given below :

**Skill A**

| Components | Minimum | | Average | | Maximum | | |
|---|---|---|---|---|---|---|---|
| | 0 | 1 | 2 | 3 | 4 | 5 | 6 |
| Prompting | — | — | — | — | — | — | — |
| SMI | — | — | — | — | — | — | — |
| Refocus | — | — | — | — | — | — | — |
| Redirect | — | — | — | — | — | — | — |
| Critical Awareness | — | — | — | — | — | — | — |

Before translating a component into rating scale a rough total of the number of questions must be made.

**(2) Use of Black-Board :** Black-board is used by the teacher for many purposes. That has already been discussed in the chapter second.

***Components of the Skill***

1. Legible writing.
2. Straight writing
3. Drawing of figures, diagrams or charts.
4. Writing with teaching of words, concepts and numbers etc.
5. Noting down the blackboard work by the students.

The same seven point scale is used here for observation of micro teaching. If pupil teacher uses a component of the skill only once during his short span of teaching, he will be rated at the minimum. If he is using every component twice or three times, the level of using the skill will be average and if a particular component is being used more than 4 times, he will be rated at the maximum.

**(3) Stimulus Variation :** By this skill the monotony of the environment is removed and its dullness is reduced. The logic behind the use of this skill is that a man becomes bored while living in the same environment for a longer period of time. It causes not only fatigue but staleness also. This staleness and fatigue of the man is removed by changing the environment, .e.g., if a teacher delivers his exposition standing at the same place, it may bore the students but if he shuffles his position occasionally, the boredom of the students will be less.

***Components of stimulus variation :***

1. *Changing the movements of the body :* Roaming about the class like a top or standing at a place for a longer period like a statue both are practically wrong. So, a teacher should adopt the middle path. He sometimes goes to the black-board to write something on it and sometimes goes to the students to draw their attention. He sometimes goes to the last bench to establish rapport with the backbenchers also. All these are the examples of changing the movements of the body.
2. *Gesture :* Gestures are actually the variation in the outer organs of the body like smiling, laughing, glaring, gazing, expanding or contracting eye brows or nose, nodding head for approving the response, shaking hands to instruct the students to keep quite or to stop the work etc. These gestures are very effective when verbal communication becomes difficult doe to noise pollution or any other reason.
3. *Change in speech pattern or tone :* The teacher sometimes increases or reduces the pitch of his voice in the class. He sometimes changes the speed of his speech pattern. Frequency of loudness is also changed by the teacher to eliminate monotony. All these are the examples of change in speech pattern.
4. *Focusing :* In order to focus the attention of his students on the same point or event, the teacher utters the same words or sentences repeatedly. For example, three battles, three battles were fought in the field of Panipat-first in1526, .... Third in 1761. He repeats the words "three battles" two or three times here. Sometimes the teacher gives clear instructions to his students by saying "Now I am going to tell you a very important point. Please be attentive".
5. *Change in interactional style :* There are many styles and techniques of interaction e.g, questioning, getting the black-board work done, showing any material aid, explaining the concept in simple language etc. When students get bored with one style, the teacher adopts another style and this change of style is so creeping that it is not noticed by students.
6. *Change in the sequence of audio-visual aids :* In order to remove the monotony of the environment, the teacher sometimes shows visual aids and sometimes audio materials. These audio-visual materials are also many and they are demonstrated one by one. For example, he sometimes uses models, and sometimes graphs or charts. He occasionally uses TV or radio also in order to reduce monotony of the environment.
7. *Pause :* Pause refers to the inactivity of the teacher in the class. It works as an activity and motivating force because constant activity bores the students. This pause, however, should not be for more than five seconds.

***Observation and Evaluation :*** The classmates of the pupil teacher and the teacher trainers observe and evaluate the skill of stimulus variation on the basis of seven components given above. The number of times a particular component demonstrated in 5-10 minutes of teaching is the criteria of rating. The same 7 point scale is used for the purpose. The observers also note down on a separate sheet to what extent the monotony or boredom of the environment is removed after use of this skill. The rating scale is given below :

| Components | Minimum | | Average | | Maximum | | |
|---|---|---|---|---|---|---|---|
| | 0 | 1 | 2 | 3 | 4 | 5 | 6 |
| CMB | — | — | — | — | — | — | — |
| Gesture | — | — | — | — | — | — | — |
| CSP | — | — | — | — | — | — | — |
| Focus | — | — | — | — | — | — | — |
| CAV Aids | — | — | — | — | — | — | — |
| CIS | — | — | — | — | — | — | — |
| Pause | — | — | — | — | — | — | — |

In the above example, if a teacher has used say pause seven times during his teaching, he will be allotted maximum rating on the scale. Similarly, if he has used focus component only once, he will be rated at minimum.

**(4) Reinforcement Skill :** Reinforcement skill refers to those activities or events on the part of the teacher which can increase the possibility of future response on the part of students.

***Reinforcements are of three types***

1. *Positive reinforcement :* They increase the possibility of a good response. If they are given, the respondent is likely to give more correct responses in future due to the internal motivation received, e.g., teacher says, yes, good, very good, fine, excellent etc. on correct responses of students.
2. *Negative reinforcers :* They reduce the possibility of a bad or wrong response on the part on the students. For example, the teacher says no, wrong, very bad, mistaken, aim etc. on wrong responses of students.
3. *Punishers :* By using these reinforcement devices, the teacher gives corporal punishment or mental torture to his students on wrong responses. Beating the students by stick on wrong responses or rusticating the child from the class for the whole period on non-completion of the homework are few examples of punishers. The rule of thumb for a teacher is that he should avoid punishers as much as possible, he should use negative reinforcers only occasionally and take full benefit of positive reinforcers to the maximum level possible.

***Components of Reinforcement Skill :***

1. Use of positive reinforcement.
2. Accepting the advices of students.
3. Positive reinforcement by non-verbal activities.
4. Writing the responses of students on the black-board.
5. Use of negative reinforcers.
6. Use of non-verbal negative reinforcers.
7. Attempting to reinforce maximum number of students.
8. Novelty in reinforcing words and sentences.

***Suggestions for using reinforcement skill :***

1. As far as possible, the teacher should reinforce all the students of the class.
2. As far as possible, the teacher should avoid negative reinforcers and punishers.
3. Reinforcement should not be given on every right activity of students. Variable ratio schedule of reinforcement is the best technique used by the teacher.
4. Suitable words and activities should be selected for the purpose of giving reinforcement.
5. New reinforcing words and activities should be used every time, e.g., sometimes fine, sometime nice, sometimes good and sometimes excellent should be used as reinforcing words.

***Observation and evaluation :***

The reinforcing skill of a pupil teacher is observed and evaluated on the basis of the components given above and same 7 point scale is used for the purpose.

## (B) FLANDER'S INTERACTION ANALYSIS

### Meaning of Interaction

His analysis is also known as reciprocal category system. When a teacher goes to a class for teaching he interacts with his students there. The behaviour pattern of a teacher is guided by the behaviour pattern of pupils. And in this way regular interaction between the two takes place.

The behaviour of a teacher can be divided into two categories.

**(a) Dominant behaviour :** It is seen when the teacher speaks to elaborate some points. Pupils' freedom is restricted here.

**(b) Integrative behaviour :** It is seen when teacher directly comes in contact through questioning, commands or accepting and repeating pupils' ideas.

The interaction which takes place between the teacher and pupils in the class through integrative behaviour is called teaching.

### Meaning of Interaction Analysis

The observation and coding of the verbal communications which takes place between the teacher and his pupils is known as interaction analysis.

**Ober** has defined interaction analysis in the following words.

"Systematic observation represents a useful means of identifying, classifying, studying and measuring specific variables as they interact within the instructional learning situation".

**Characteristics of interaction analysis :**

1. It is a research oriented method in the sense that scientific and sequential study of all events and behaviour (variables) of the class room is made here.
2. Subject matter is not measured by this analysis. Only the interaction between the teacher and pupils are studied here.
3. Here observable behaviours of the teacher is first identified, then they are classified into different convenient groups for the purpose of systematic study and finally the specific behaviour is analysed by observation method.

### Reciprocal Category System

**Objectives :**

1. To identify specific behaviour of the teacher in the class.
2. To collect relevant data of teacher's behaviour by observation and recording them.
3. To find out remedial strategies after knowing the defects in the behaviour.

**Meaning of RCS :** In RCS only the social and affective environment of the class is taken into account.

In order to classify the verbal behaviour of pupils and the teacher interaction analysis functions as observational tool. Verbal communication between teacher and pupils are recorded here.

**Teacher's talk**

| *Direct talk* | *Indirect talk* |
|---|---|
| I. Lecturing or explaining | I. Accepting feelings |
| II. Giving commands | II. Praise or reinforcement. |
| III. Criticising | III. Accepting ideas of pupils |
| | IV. Asking questions |

The two categories, relating to the pupils' behaviour are classified as under.

**Pupil's talk**

- Responding to the Question of The teacher
- Asking question by students and expression of ideas.

Flander classified the classroom behaviours of the teacher and pupils into ten categories. The first seven are related to direct or indirect behaviour of the teacher in the class. The next two are related to pupils behaviour and the last one is the state of silence or confusion, i.e., an environment in which none is seen showing any communication.

**Assumptions of RCS Model :**

I. Classroom environment is most important in the entire learning process.

II. Teacher's behaviour influences pupils' behaviour and hence teaching.

III. Democratic classroom environment is appreciated by pupils.

IV. Classroom behaviour (environment) can be modified by using feedback mechanism.

V. Objective observation of teacher's behaviour in the class is possible and it can be recorded by video disk and camera.

VI. The interaction between the teacher and pupils is the most important aspect in the entire teaching process.

VII. Verbal behaviour can be recorded more objectively than non-verbal behaviour.

**Explanation of RCS categories :**

**(A) Categories related to indirect impact of the teacher.**

The first four categories are related to indirect talk of the teacher. They are given below :

1. **Accepting Pupils' feeling :** Here teacher recognises and accepts the feelings of pupils. He also directs these feelings in the manner conducive to learning. The teacher believes that pupils are not to be punished for exposing their feelings and emotions.
2. **Praise or reinforcement given to pupils :** The teacher uses many reinforcement words like good, fine, excellent, fantastic, correct, very good etc. for this purpose. He can also encourage them by saying carry on, try again or think once more etc. He maintains very democratic and enjoying atmosphere in the class for this purpose. By this behaviour the teacher praises the tasks of pupils and motivates them to do more.
3. **Accepting the ideas of pupils and using them into his teaching :** In this category the ideas expressed by pupils are accepted by the teacher if they are correct. If a pupil gives any suggestion that is good, that suggestion is repeated by the teacher in his own style and then these ideas and suggestions are applied into teaching.
4. **Asking questions :** Questioning is an important weapon that a teacher has and it can be used to win the battle in many ways. He asks developing questions, evaluation questions and recapitulatory questions in the class to increase the comprehension level of students and these questions are answered by pupils. Questions which do not require answers and they are asked during the lecture just for the emphasis or elaboration are not included in this category.

**(B) Categories related to direct behaviour of the teacher :**

1. **Lecturing :** This is the fifth category of the system. It is a verbal communication that is used by the teacher to communicate facts, informations or principles to pupils. Explanation of various concepts is also given by the teacher through this behaviour. Students are not given freedom at all during this process. They only listen to what the teacher says.
2. **Giving commands or direction :** Whatever is asked by the teacher to do on the part of pupils is called giving directions. This communication is also direct in nature. When pupils follow these directions, interaction between the teacher and pupils take place.
3. **Criticising :** In order to correct incomplete or unsuitable responses (behaviour) of pupils, the teacher criticizes them in the class. He dominates the scene by asking questions with why, how, when etc.

**(C) Pupils' behaviour :**

1. **Pupils' responses :** The pupils fully participate in the teaching-learning process by responding questions asked by the teacher. Limited freedom is given to pupils for this purpose.
2. **Pupils' initiation :** In this category, pupils ask questions themselves and the teacher responds to these questions. They express their ideas regarding any matter and full freedom is given to them for this purpose.

**(D) State of confusion or silence :**

This is related to the last category of RCS. The state of confusion occurs when communication is not understandable either by the teacher or by the pupils. The duration of this behaviour is very short.

**Procedure for observing RCS :** In order to evaluate the interactive behaviours of the teacher and pupils in RCS system, the observer occupies his seat in the class in such a manner that he can perceive the whole class clearly and hear their voices. He notes down the activities of the teacher and pupils under the ten given categories. One behaviour is observed in three second here. After the expiry of three seconds the observer decides to which of the ten categories the behaviour belongs and it is noted down. The serial number of the category is also recorded on the given sheet. Thus 18-20 behaviours are recorded in one minute. After the observation is over, the observer prepares the details on the basis of those serial number of the categories. Writing of serial numbers of the ten categories is called coding and writing details of behaviours on the basis of serial numbers of the categories is called decoding.

**Rules of observation :** The observer must remember the following rules while observing the RCS categories :

1. When it is not clear to which category the behaviour belongs then serial number of the farthest category from the fifth one is noted down. For example, when it is not clear whether behaviour belongs to category No 3 or 4, then category No 3 will be recorded.
2. When the trend of teacher's behaviour is continuously direct or continuously indirect, then the observer should restrict himself to first to fourth categories or fifth to seventh categories unless observer finds a clear indication for that. He should not come from direct to indirect or vice-versa categories in hurry.
3. The observer should be completely objective in his observation.
4. If more than one categories dominates in a span of three seconds, then all these categories are recorded. If even after three seconds no change in the category is seen, then the same serial number of the categories is repeated in the next three seconds.
5. If silence period is for more than three second, i.e., no interaction is seen, then category No 10 is noted down.
6. If a teacher addresses a pupil by his name, then category No 4 is recorded.
7. If a teacher repeats correct answer of a pupil, then category N o2 is recorded.
8. When a teacher listens to a pupil or accepts his ideas, then category No 3 is noted down.
9. If a teacher starts his talk after the talk of the pupil is over, then category No 10 is also recorded in between 8 and 9.
10. Reinforcing words belongs to the category No 2.
11. When a teacher jokes without aiming any pupil, this behaviour is also recorded as category No 2. But if jokes are made by aiming at any particular pupil then it is recorded in category No 7.
12. When students respond a question collectively, then category No 8 is recorded.

**Advantages of RCS :**

I. This method can also be applied on those who are regular teachers and their behaviour can be evaluated and modified.

II. If observer is not present in the class, the video recording along with the computer can perform the function and matrix can be prepared by the computer.

III. It can provide feedback to pupil teachers.

IV. This is an analytical method of knowing what activities are going on in a class in an objective manner.

V. This method can be very well applied in micro teaching and stimulated teaching.

VI. It is an effective instrument to measure the socio-emotional environment of a class.

**Limitations of RCS :**

I. This method is very complicated and costly in terms of time and money.

II. It is not a complete research tool in itself. Several other factors must also be identified by using factorial analysis method.

III. Regular concentration is needed for observing the behaviour here which is not practically possible.

IV. This method does not touch the content aspect of a teacher at all.

V. Preparation of matrices takes a very long time and output is very little.

VI. Pupils' talk is given less importance here. Teacher fully dominates in the class.

VII. Training of observers to observe the behaviour is also a difficult task.

## STIMULATED TEACHING

### Meaning of Stimulated Teaching

Stimulated teaching is a training technique like micro-teaching. This technique is used to change the behaviour of trainees in industry, military services and education. In education, it is used before the actual practice teaching.

It is a role playing technique. In this technique, the pupil teacher plays double role, the role of a pupil and the role of a teacher. One pupil teacher teaches in the class a particular topic and his other colleagues play the role of pupils. This teaching takes place for a period of 10 to 15 minutes. After the teaching is over, a discussion on teaching strategies and techniques is organised. After this discussion another pupil comes to the blackboard for teaching and the cycle is repeated again. The feedback that a pupil teacher receives from his teaching helps him to modify his behaviour. The learning obtained from this artificial teaching situation is applied in the actual classroom situation during practice teaching.

## Assumptions of Stimulated Teaching

The concept is based on the following assumptions :

I. Teaching behaviours can be identified.

II. Behaviour of the pupil teacher can be modified by two methods.
 (a) by the use of role perception.
 (b) by the use of actual role playing.

III. The behaviour essential for effective teaching can be drilled.

IV. Feedback mechanism works in the modification of pupil teacher's behaviour.

V. Social skills can be communicated.

## Steps of Stimulated Teaching

Pupil teachers are trained in the artificial teaching situations in their own B.Ed. class through this technique. These pupil teachers are sent to actual class room situations only after they have got mastery over some teaching behaviour like introduction of the topic, use of blackboard, way of questioning, ways of giving reinforcement to pupils, method of giving exposition etc.

Steps involved in stimulated teaching are as follows :

**Step I :** Roles are assigned to all pupil teachers, i.e., when they have to play the role of a teacher and when they have to play the role of pupils.

**Step II :** Some specific teaching behaviours are selected. Topics through which these social skills will be manifested is also selected here.

**Step III :** Following decisions are taken at this step :
- Which pupil teacher will initiate the teaching.
- When it will be summed up.
- Who will initiate the discussion after the teaching is over.
- How many pupil teachers will teach in the stipulated time.

**Step IV :** How will the teaching be observed is decided in the fourth step. It is also decided which data they will record and how the data will be interpreted. Thus, all pupil teachers excepts the active teacher play double role—role of students and the role of observers.

**Step V :** After making all the above preparations, the practice session is started and feedback is given to all pupil teachers for their teaching tasks at the proper time. The informations regarding the first practice session is recorded by the other pupil teachers. Evaluation of the required teaching behaviour is done on the basis of these records. Once the first session is over, the second session starts after the discussion of the first session completes.

**Step VI :** After the first session is over, necessary changes in the procedure can be made, e.g., topic of teaching, required teaching behaviour, observers etc can be changed.

This cycle of stimulated teaching is repeated till all the pupil teachers get adequate chance of teaching and practice their behaviour.

## Characteristics of Stimulated Teaching

1. It is a type of rehearsal before the start of actual practice teaching in schools.
2. Its feedback mechanism improves behaviour at a faster rate.
3. It is an artificial setting and if pupil teachers commit mistakes here, they will not be ridiculed by students.
4. It is an easy method of teacher training.
5. This technique helps the pupil teachers to apply their theoretical knowledge of education and training.

## Limitations of Stimulated Teaching

The underlying limitations of stimulated teaching are given below :

1. This technique can not be used for teaching all the topics of all the subjects because all pupil teachers are not supposed to know all the school subjects.
2. This technique needs video recording and hence regular electricity supply is also required.
3. Baring the active teacher, all pupil teachers play double role-the role of students and the role of observers and hence they can commit mistakes in recording the behaviour.
4. Regular concentration of mind on teaching is a tough task.
5. Some pupil teachers take longer time to learn a particular teaching behaviour. It might bore the others.

**Advantages (Merits):** Main advantages of this teaching technique are given below :

I. Theoretical knowledge of education can be given a practical shape through this technique.

II. Some serious teaching problems and behaviour can be identified and analysed through this technique.

III. Pupils can learn how to ask different types of questions in the class and how to mould the same question when needed.

IV. It improves the teaching behaviour of pupil teachers through feedback mechanism.

V. It creates confidence of teaching in pupil teachers..

VI. Different types of role played by pupil teachers make them diverse, creative and energetic.

VII. It supplements the demonstration teaching and thus, it can save the energy of the teacher trainer to repeat the demonstration again and again.

VIII. It helps in acquiring real classroom behaviour and pupil teacher will not be hesitant when he goes to teach actual classes.

IX. Learning through stimulated teaching enhances learning and increases the interests of pupils. So, it can be used as a technique of teaching also.

X. This teaching makes a person more conscious about his role.

# Programmed Instruction

## INTRODUCTION

This technique of instruction was basically developed by **B.F.Skinner**. This technique is fundamentally based on the principle of reinforcement and self-learning, i.e., based on the theory of trial and error and operant conditioning. This is a technique of learning in which learner goes forward himself in the process of learning. Thus, it has contributed a lot in reducing the load of a teacher in formal education system.

### Meaning

"Programming refers to the arrangement of the stimulus material in an order of presentation that would maximize the rate of leaning resulting in optimal behaviour modification on the prescribed lines". It gradually shapes learner's responses to the desired level or refinement. Origin of programming may be credited to **Pressey** but he soon dropped out this effort as his interest was restricted only upto developing testing devices.

### Definitions of Programmed Instruction/ Learning

1. Programmed learning/instruction is the change in the response of the behaviour brought about through the use of material built into a carefully organised sequential system. It refers to utilization of teaching machines, programmed text and computer programming, in order to achieve prescribed learning or behavioural modification objectives.
2. Programmed instruction has been defined as a method of giving individualise instruction, in which the student is active and proceeds at his own pace and is provided with immediate knowledge of result. The physical presence of teacher is not essential in this strategy.
3. **Sussan Markle** gave a wider definition of programmed instruction. "It is a method of designing a reproducible sequence of instructional events to produce a measurable and consistent effect on behaviour of each and every acceptable student".
4. Programmed learning is a designed strategy in which various kinds of intellectual, emotional and motor experiences are provided to the learner in a controlled situation through a variety of devices like a book, teaching machine, teacher, radio and television etc.

### Assumptions of Programmed Instruction

Programmed instruction is based on the following assumptions :

I. A student learns better when he himself is active.

II. A student learns better if he is motivated to learn by confirming his responses.

III. A student learns better if subject-matter is presented to him in small steps (units).

IV. A student learns better if sequence of the content is psychologically workable.

V. Learning may be effective if the pre-requisite on the part of the learner are specified.

### Characteristics of Programmed Instruction

1. It is a part of educational technology in the sense that programmed material can be presented with the help of machines or computers.
2. It is a new strategy of teaching and learning. Here learner learns himself without the help of the teacher. Thus, the problem of the dearth of effective teachers can be overcome.
3. It is a technique for the solution of educational as well as teaching problems. We can supply programmed instructional materials to lakhs of students at a time and can help them to have

access to the latest knowledge and its dimensions.

4. It is a technique for the modification of learner's behaviour. Thus, it is opposite of micro-teaching where teacher's behaviour is modified. Learner's behaviour is modified by confirming the right responses immediately.
5. It can not replace the teacher from the field of teaching altogether. It is because only an effective teacher can prepare a good programmed material.
6. It requires more creativity and imaginative efforts to develop such individualized instructional material. Every individual learner learns at his own speed here.

## TYPE OF PROGRAMMED INSTRUCTION

(A) Linear or Extrinsic programming by B.F. Skinner.

(B) Branching or Intrinsic Programming by Norman Crowder.

## (A) LINEAR OR EXTRINSIC PROGRAMMING OF INSTRUCTION:

A linear programming of instruction is one in which the learner is allowed to study only one frame at a time. A frame is the smallest bit of information that is supplied to a learner at a time. The frame is followed by a question. When learner gets feedback by the confirmation of his answer, he is supplied the next frame. This process goes on till the last part of the subject-matter. Here learner goes ahead in a straight line fashion. Every learner is supplied the same series of tasks and each of them fulfils the task according to their individual rate of learning.

This programmed material is based on Skinner's operant conditioning theory of learning where contingencies of reinforcement are properly arranged which shapes up the behaviour of an organism in a desirable manner.

This programmed instruction was first systematically prepared by B. F. Skinner of Harward University. In this programming the effort is made to give only one information by one frame and if the learner is unable to answer the question of the frame or he gives wrong answer, he is asked to repeat the frame again. A key is also supplied along with the frames for the purpose of confirmation, i.e., whether the answer is right or wrong.

### Principles of Linear Programming

The linearly programmed instruction propounded by Skinner is based on the following five principles given by the very Skinner. They are given below :

1. **Principle of small steps :** The subject-matter which is to be programmed is divided into hundreds of meaningful bits after analysing the subject-matter comprehensively. Only one piece of information (unit) is presented before the students at a time. This bit of information is called frame.
2. **Principle of immediate confirmation :** When the student answers the question after reading a frame, his answer is immediately confirmed with the help of the key If his response is correct, it is confirmed by the key. This gives immediate feedback to the learner and the reinforcement obtained by him increases the possibility of further correct responses. On the contrary, if the answer given by the learner is wrong, he is corrected by the key. This makes the learner more cautious in future and he reads the frame more carefully next time.
3. **Principle of active responding :** In this type of instruction one frame is attached to the next frame in such a manner that student is compelled to answer the question of the frame and go ahead. In this way, he is never able to separate himself from the learning process. It is not possible for him to skip any frame even if he desires so. For example, if we present any such frame before the student that is very tough or boring for him and the student ceases to go ahead, this will be considered the failure of the programme. We have anyhow to transform difficult frames into easy ones.
4. **Principle of self pacing :** In programmed instruction all the learners do not learn collectively and with the same speed. Every learner rather learns according to his own speed and ability. No restriction is put on the leaning process of students in this method.

5. **Student testing :** To what extent the instructional programme is successful depends on the progress and achievement of students. When learners go on the programmed material, the teacher constantly observes and assesses them. Through this process he finds out the weakness or strength of his programme. For example, if there is such a frame in the programme on which no learner is successful, this frame will be considered a bad frame and it will be eliminated from the programme. This elimination is necessary because if all the students are unsuccessful on a frame, they will stop going ahead on the programme and thus the whole purpose of programmed instruction will be defeated.

## Edward F.A. Day's Modification in the Principles of Programmed Instruction

Prof. Edward F.A.Day in his book "Programmed Instruction, Techniques and Trend" has classified these principles into two categories only:

(I) Mandatory Principles
(II) Optional Principles

**(I) Mandatory Principles:** The mandatory principles given by Day are as follows:

1. **Determination of norms and objectives :** What is the purpose of that instructional material that has been prepared and what behavioural changes are expected from the completion of the programme, all are determined first". Then these objectives are defined in behavioural terms. Next step is to decide to what extent. The ultimate behaviour demonstrated by the learner at the end of the programme is acceptable and matches the norms prepared by the experts. For this purpose, criteria and procedure of evaluation are also decided in advance.
2. **Observable testing (Standardization of programmed material):** Whatever material has been prepared for the purpose of programmed instruction is tested and tried out in three stages given below :
   (a) In the first stage the preliminary draft of the programme is tried out on an individual learner in a face to face situation and reactions of the learner on all the frames are noted down. Here, effort is made to find out to what extent the learner is able to attempt all these frames.
   (b) In the second stage modification in the frames are made on the basis of the reactions made by the learner. Then this modified form of the programme is tried out on a small group of students ranging from 5 to 10 of the same grade for which the programme has been prepared and reaction of these students are noted down.
   (c) Final modification in the draft is made in the third stage and thus final draft of the programmed material is now prepared for wide use.
3. **Principle of Self-Pacing :** At this principle, B.F.Skinner and F.A. Day do not differ at all.

**(II) Optional Principles (preparation of norms):** Optional principles propounded by Day are as follows :

1. **Clear Response :** While going ahead on the programme, the learner gives clear response of the question followed by each frame. He does not hide his reaction. Thus, he remains active throughout the programme and gets feedback from the key after every response.
   If about 50% of the students remain silent on any frame that frame is considered to be useless and it must be modified by the programme maker.
2. **Principle of Immediate Feedback :** When learner goes ahead on the programme, he is immediately given feedback by the key and he comes to know whether his response is right or wrong. For this purpose he matches his response with the response given in the key.
3. **Principle of Small Steps :** The whole instructional material is presented to students by dividing it into a number of small frames and only one frame is given to the students to read. If more than one question can be framed from a frame, that frame is considered to be wrong. It is reduced by the maker after the first try out.
4. **Sequence :** All frames of the programme are put in the increasing difficulty order in a sequence and all frames must be connected with each other.
5. **Rate of Errors :** Rate of errors is tried to be kept at the minimum level by this programme. It means that frames are presented before the students in

such a manner that there is least chance of committing mistakes on the frames.

It has been recommended that the rate of error in linear programming should not be more than 5% and in branching programming, the error rate should not be more than 20%. Skinner believes that if any frame is responded wrongly by any more than 5% students of the class, that frame is considered to be wrong and it must be modified by the maker.

6. **Prompting :** Sometimes the teacher gives prompting to students in order to take the students to the right response. But this is done only in the try out stages and when final draft has got prepared, prompting is not needed at all.

## Assumptions of Linear Programming Model

According to **Lysaught and Williams** basic assumption of the linear programming is that each stimulus (frame) should be designed to elicit the correct response by the student and that his own construction of the response is an integral part of the learning situation.

Susan M. Markle has given three basic assumptions of linear programming:

I. A student learns the way how the programme leads him to learn. An active response is not necessarily a small one nor is it necessarily an overt one.

II. A student learns better if he commits minimum errors in going through the instructional material.

III. A learner learns effectively if correct responses given by him are immediately reinforced. It means that his responses must be confirmed at once.

IV. The previous knowledge of students is considered to be zero.

## Rationale of Linear Programming

(a) According to **David Cram** the rationale of the Linear Learning programme are as under :

- Recall is more effective in the learning process than recognition.
- The act of responding tends to cause learning hence, no incorrect responses should be there as they affect learning adversely.
- As the act of responding tends to cause learning, each step should be small enough to elicit correct response.
- Too many errors would be discouraging, hence small steps should be there and it would be more likelihood of correct responses.

(b) Originally called **Skinnerian programme**, the Linear programme has many variations having different sets of rationale, such as the one devised by Pressey and it is called multiple choice linear programme and has the following rationale :

- The student may sometime get wrong answer, He ultimately gets a correct answer in each frame. By law of frequency he would get more correct than wrong answers.
- Number of wrong answer in response to a question is of no consequence, as the correct answer is always the last one, and it is more likely to be remembered because it comes close to the reinforcement. Having intensity of response, it helps in more lasting learning.

(c) Skinner gave following rationale :

- Student learns better if he makes less errors, errors erode and influence learning adversely.
- Learning process is effective if the learner's responses are continuously reinforced.

## Various Types of Linear Programme

1. Construct Response Type : Skinnerian.
2. Multiple Choice type : Pressey.
3. Conventional Chaining type : Horn Barlow.
4. Skip-Linear, for brilliant students who can skip frames
5. With Criterion-Frames : Criterion frames direct the learner along the linear path according to their responses.
6. Rules System : Here content is organised in terms of rules first and examples are given later on.
7. Egrule System : Here examples are given first then rules are taught on the basis of those examples.

## Characteristics of Linear Programming

1. In linear programming of instruction the total subject-matter is first broken into small frames. The information given in one frame does not exceed to 30 words. Thus, students get small piece of knowledge at a time and do not feel any problem of learning.
2. In this type of programming students go forward in a straight line, i.e., one frame is connected to the next frame in ascending difficulty order. Thus, students do not get deviated at all for giving responses.
3. In this programming the answers of questions and the sequence of answers are definite and pre-determined. Thus, students do not get any chance to respond on the basis of their own understanding and reason. It means that the behaviour of students are fully controlled along with the control of the content.
4. Every student is bound to answer every frame for the purpose of learning. If he skips any frame deliberately or by mistake, he will not be able to learn the next frame at any cost.
5. As soon as the learner responds he immediately gets feedback whether his response is right or wrong. Thus, no skepticism is left to survive in the mind of the learner.
6. In the initial stages of the programme, when students start reading it, prompting is also given to take them to the right response. When students ponder over this clue, they easily reach the correct response.
7. Linear programming instructional material can be prepared and applied to any class of students. Even students of primary classes can be taught through programmed learning.
8. This programme emphasizes the individual differences of learners. It means that it can be beneficial for weak and talented students alike.
9. The knowledge here is presented in a logical sequence, hence, it is more permanent in nature.
10. Learners are reinforced here at every correct response. Thus, this programme can play a very special role in shaping the behaviour of learners.

## Limitations of Linear Programming

The main disadvantages of this programmed instruction are given below :

1. In linear programming every learner has to follow the same linear (straight) path. Thus, a programme which is very suitable for average learners may be dull and useless for talented learners.
2. It can be used to achieve the lower level of objectives of cognitive domain only. As far as objectives of affective or psychomotor domain is concerned, it has almost nothing to do with them.
3. The freedom of learners is restricted here by giving pre-determined feedback. If the response of a learner is slightly deviated, it is not confirmed at all.
4. It is very difficult and time taking to prepare such a instructional material. Learners do a lot here but get very less.
5. It cannot be used for remedial or diagnostic purposes.
6. It is based on those principles or theories of learning which were formulated by conducting experiments on lower animals. Thus, these principles cannot be relied upon in toto as far as human beings are concerned.
7. Linear programming gives stress on environment and stimulus-response mechanism and thus the role of mental processes and abilities is reduced to the minimum.
8. It is a time consuming method of learning. This makes the students bored very soon.
9. The preparation cost of this material is also very high. In a country like India where millions of teachers are available to teach on a monthly salary of just Rs. 1500, how can this self-learning technology be an effective or useful method of learning.
10. The application of this programme is possible only to those areas where behaviour can be observed and measured.
11. Linear programming assumes that previous knowledge of students is zero. Thus, it is not possible to test the pervious knowledge of learners by this instruction. Every learner is treated on equal footing.

12. This programme is totally proved to be worthless when students starts looking at the key without reading the frame and we do not have any mechanism to control this dishonest behaviour of learners.

## Application of Programmed Instruction or Scope of Linear Programming

B.F. Skinner has developed this strategy to improve the teaching-learning process. It can solve the problems of teaching and instruction at different stages. Education Commission (1964-66) has recommended to use the strategy in schools and colleges for teaching various subjects. The commission also recommended to use this strategy in correspondence education organised at various levels. This strategy can be used effectively in the following areas :

1. **Elementary Education :** At this stage there is an urgent need to prepare text-books on Linear model. Generally there are single teacher schools where a teacher is required to teach all subjects. This strategy will be very helpful to them. It may raise the academic standard of primary education.
2. **Secondary Education :** The major feature of secondary education is the diversified curriculum. The teacher may be assigned a subject other than of his interest. The diversity of interests and curriculum necessitates the application of self-instructional strategy. It may be used as remedial teaching. The classroom teaching may be followed by this strategy. It maybe helpful for non-science teachers to prepare for science which is a compulsory subject upto high school.
3. **Correspondence Education :** The correspondence education has been introduced at various levels. Programmed learning has great application at all levels.
4. **Hindi and Other Languages :** With the present methods of teaching languages, the task seems to be unsurmountable. The programmed material for language learning will be presented in a book format or through tap recorder or language laboratory. It will help in achieving the objectives of language teaching.
5. **Programmed Material in Science and Mathematics :** It may also be noted that as science and mathematics are growing rapidly it is becoming harder and harder for school teachers to keep pace with the changes. In this regard, the programmed instruction material should be developed on new topics which will be helpful to the teachers to equip themselves with latest content and they will be able to keep pace with time.
6. **Medical Education and Health Education :** There is rapid advancement in medical education. In these circumstances, programmed learning material may be used in medical colleges and for doctors.
7. **Teacher Education :** Those teachers who completed their B.Ed. several years ago do not generally know about the modern strategies and techniques of teaching. Special instructional material can be prepared for these teachers to update their knowledge. They will study these materials themselves to update their knowledge. Thus, programmed instruction can be very effective for inservice training of teachers.
8. **Non-formal Education :** Non-formal education programmes can also be improved with the help of programmed instruction. The reason is that many non-formal education centres are running only on papers in India and no teaching task is going on there despite many teachers appointed for the purpose. In such a situation money saved from the salary of these teachers can be diverted to the preparation of these materials.
9. **Character Formation :** Programmed material of instruction can also be used to bring about desirable changes in the behaviour of children and this is possible by reinforcement obtained by students during learning. Many bad habits of children can be made rid of by using these materials effectively.
10. **Education of Exceptional Children :** Exceptional children are those who are either very superior in intelligence or mentally very weak. Special instructional material can be prepared for both these deviant groups separately.
11. **Useful for Writers :** If writers of text-books write their books by keeping all the principles of programming into consideration, they can write very good text-books. These principles can make

the presentation of the book easy, systematic and to the point.

Thus, there is great scope for the application of programmed learning material in education (teaching and remedial instruction) industry, defence and health. This strategy will not replace the teacher but it will help the teacher to make teaching effective and purposeful.

One more point to be kept in mind is that these applications are not restricted to linear programming only. Branching programmed instruction has the same application as has been given above. The only differences between the two is that linear programming is useful for learners of younger age and branching programmed material is useful for learners of older age in general and former is more effective technique than the later.

### Construction of frames in Linear Programming

In linear programming the frames are constructed very carefully. The language of the frame is kept easy almost to the level of students and analytical style is used for expressing thoughts. The structure of the frame can be of three types :

I. *Stimulus contential form*-where content is used as stimulus.

II. *Response-desired behaviour form*-where response is constructed in the form of desired behaviour and questions are framed accordingly.

III. *Reinforcement confirmation form*-where confirmation given to learners motivates them to learn more.

**Types of frames used in Linear Programming:**

1. *Introductory frames*-used before the actual start of the lesson.
2. *Teaching frames*- used to give some new knowledge to students.
3. *Practice frames*- used for the purpose of drilling already acquired knowledge.
4. *Testing frames*- used to test the understanding of the frame already given to learners.

## Steps in Developing Programmed Material

Various steps for developing programmed material are given below :

**(a) Preparation of the programme :** Following activities are undertaken under this step :

1. Formulation of objectives-for what purpose the programme is to be prepared.
2. Defining the objectives in behavioural terms-it will help the teacher to evaluate his programme.
3. Identifying the terminal repertoire- what students are able to do at present.
4. Identifying entering behaviour of students.
5. Constructing a test of terminal behaviour after it has been used on the population.
6. Constructing a test of entering behaviour-it will help the teacher to establish new behaviour (knowledge) upon what the learners already know. This is actually the point where to start the programme.
7. Selection of units or topics on the basis of the entering behaviour.
8. Identification of sub-topics in relation to the objectives formulated-these sub-topics must be inter-related with each other.
9. Dividing the sub-topic into a number of frames-it will help the teacher in writing the frames.
10. formulating criterion achievement measures-how the responses of learners will be evaluated, whether the test will be essay type or objective type and what variety of objective type test is to be selected for measuring achievement.

**(b) Writing the programme :** It consists of the following sub-steps :

1. Writing the frames one by one.
2. Constructing tests after each frame.
3. Requiring active responding from the students.
4. Providing confirmation to students if answer is correct or correcting the responses of learners. For this purpose the teacher must speculate all possible mistakes to be committed by learners.
5. Using prompt to guide students' responses.
6. Providing careful sequences of frames.
7. Preparing answer keys.

**(c) Try out and Revision :**

1. Preparing the initial draft of the programme.
2. Editing the draft by internal criticism.
3. First try out on a single student and modification of frames.

4. Second try out on a small group of learner and second revision of the draft.
5. Final administration of the programme on a large sample and preparation of manual.

**(d) Publication of the programme :**

1. Prepraration of norms, i.e. difficulty level of frames for a particular class of students, calculation of time and its application in life situation.
2. Publication of the programme for a wide use-frames are printed in a sequence one in every page of a spiral bound book so that pages can be turned with speed.

## Terminologies Used in Programmed Instruction

1. **Frame :** The small bit of information or a single step of instruction given to students at a time and responses from them is called a frame. It provides immediate feedback to learners.
2. **Prompt or Cue :** Additional information contained in a frame to help the learners to respond the frame correctly.
3. **Fading :** A method of vanishing the presence of cues during the sequences of frames before the learner has mastered the frame. It eliminates the effects of cues.
4. **Linear model :** Programme prepared in a straight line from easy to difficult where no additional response from a frame is possible.
5. **Branching :** Sequencing of frames in relatively big form depending upon students' responses.
6. **Chaining :** Sequence of frames based upon mastery of pre-requisites. Frames are connected by this chain/chains.
7. **Terminal Behaviour :** Terminal behaviour refers to all those responses and behaviour which are helpful for achieving desired objectives. They refer to what a learner can do. This is post test behaviour.
8. **Stimulus :** It refers to the content or information presented in frames.
9. **Feedback or reinforcement :** It is the knowledge of the result of a learner's response whether it is right or wrong.
10. **Internal criteria of Programme Evaluation :** The internal criteria of evaluating a programme are given below. They refer to the inherent characteristics of the programme.
    (a) *Error rate*-What percentage of students have attempted the frame correctly.
    (b) *Programme density*- To what extent frames are inter-connected.
    (c) *Sequence progression*- How far the sub-topics have been presented in a logical sequence./
    (d) *Frame Inventory* : To what extent the language and style of frames are understandable to learners.
11. **External criteria of programme evaluation :** These criteria are related to the performance gain and change of attitude of learners. They are given below :
    (a) *Performance level* : How much learning has been gained by learners.
    (b) *90.90 Standard :* It means that 90% of the learners do 90% of the frames correctly. Here 90% is the mean performance of the group, i.e., programme must be able to elicit 90% responses correctly.
    (c) *Attitude Coefficient :* It refers to the positive attitude toward the programme

**Nature of frames in the above examples :** In the above example, the frames 1 to 4 are introductory frames. The frames from 5 to 8 are teaching frames. Frames from 9 to 11 are testing frames and the last one is the practice frame.

## Class VI Lesson:- Square Root

**Entering Behaviour :** Knowledge of squared figures:

1. When length and breadth of an object are equal, it is called squared. It otherwise means that there are two dimensions in a square—length and breadth and both are equal.

Q. How many dimensions are there in a square and how are they related to each other?

2. If any person is so bulky in size that he lays in a cot of six feet in length and six feet in breadth, then the area of the cot is the area covered by the man.

Q. How much square feet area of the cot the man has covered?

3. This very 36 square feet space is the area of the cot.

Q. It we draw lines at a distance of 1 feet each from both the dimensions of the cot, how many such squares will be formed in the cot?

4. Thus, we see that area of the cot is what the number of unit squares are there in a cot. It also clarifies that the length and breadth of a square is always equal.

Q. Can you tell what is the unit of 'Area'?

**Prompt :** Area is expressed in terms of number of square units in an object.

5. If you are given the area of a figure and asked to find out the value of one side of the square, then you will calculate the square root of the area. This very square root will be the length or breadth of the figure. (Length=Breadth in a square).

Q. What is the square root of a given square (digit)?

6. In order to find out the square root of a digit, we divide or break up the digit into a number of factors by dividing the digit by 2, 3, 5 and 7 etc. This break up is done in such a manner that the number of factors on length and breadth both sides are equal. Pairing of factor is done for this purpose and only one factor is selected from each pair. Finally all these factors are multiplied to find out the square root of the digit.

Q. We can take either length or breadth in calculating square root. Why?

7. Thus, we see that in order to calculate square root, the digit is first broken up into factors. The digit is first divided by the smallest digit like 2 or 3. If digit is indivisible by these two numbers, we take the help of larger numbers like 5,7, 11 or 13. In this way, the process of factorization gets completed.

Q. How is factorization done?

8. After the process of factorization is over, we arrange these factors in the form of pairs. Then we take one factor from each pair and finally all these factors are multiplied to find out the square root.

Q. Can you tell why do we arrange factors in the form of pairs?

9. Factorise 36?

10. Which factors will be multiplied to find out the square root of 36?

11. What do you call the obtained multiplicant?

12. Find out the square root of 144?

**Answer key :**

1. Two and equal.
2. $6 \times 6 = 36$
3. 36.

4. Square
5. The length or breadth of a given square.
6. It is because both are equal.
7. Factorization is done by dividing the digit by various other numbers.
8. So that we can put these numbers in the form of squares.
9. $2 \times 2 \times 3 \times 3 \times 3$
10. $2 \times 3$
11. Square root
12. $2 \times 2 \times 3 = 12$

## (B) BRANCHING OR INTRINSIC PROGRAMMING OF INSTRUCTION

This model has been developed by Norman A Crowder. The greatest characteristic of this model is that it has been developed by keeping the individual needs, interests and attitudes of learners. It is called branching or intrinsic programme because of the following reasons:

1. More than one informations are given in a frame here and students take a decision internally which information is according to their needs.
2. Similarly, the questions which are asked on a frame are also multi-dimensional and of multiple choice. Learner answers these questions only after

free thinking and divergent deliberation. Thus, every frame is divided into a number of branches.

3. Here student is guided through sub-steps in order to respond the frame. If his response to a multiple choice item is incorrect, he is directed to a frame to explain why his answer is not correct. Thus, before he is allowed to proceed to the next main frame, he is allowed to follow a different route of subsequences. Due to this reason branching programme is also known as **scrambled programme.**

## Superiority of Branching Programme Over Linear One

Crowder is different from Skinner in the following ways :

1. Linear programme is based on experiments on rats, pigeons etc. and when the same analogies are applied to human behaviour, quantitatively different learning is seen. Branching programme, on the other hand, directly deals with the behaviour of humans.
2. The linear programming always results in slow learning due to the process of learning through small steps. It may be just wastage of time. The branching programme does not follow the principle of small steps.
3. Linear programme is fixed. All learners have to go on the same track irrespective of their entering behaviour or intelligence. Branching programme is free from this demerit.
4. Linear programming considers errors as obstacle to learning and allows only 5% errors on any frame. Branching programme allows upto 20% error on any frame and opines that errors can also stimulate learning. If there are not errors committed by learners there is no scope for its remedy for removing the weaknesses of learners.
5. Linear programme has construct response while branching programme has multiple choice response.
6. Linear programme provides only psychological motivation to learners while branching programme can provide social motivation also along with psychological one.
7. Linear programme is least concerned with individual differences whereas branching programme suits to all types of students alike. Thus, even children of superior intelligence can be satisfied with this programme.
8. Linear programme is suited to achieving lower objectives of cognitive domain only whereas the branching programme is suitable to achieve higher level of objectives also.
9. Only one information is given in one frame in linear programming but branching programme has many informations in one frame.

## Assumptions of Branching Programme

This type of programming is based on the following assumptions :

1. A students learns better if he is exposed to whole concept. Thus, concepts must be comprehended at all costs. That is why this programme is also known as expository programme.
2. The second assumption is that the wrong responses do not necessarily hinder in learning but they help in diagnosis and providing remediation for their weakness.
3. The third assumption is that a student learns better if remediation is provided simultaneously for his weakness. The teaching and remediation should go side by side for effective learning.
4. This is essentially based on the psychology of individual differences. This provides an opportunity to choose the learning path according to one's need and requirement. Thus, it is highly individualized instruction.
5. The fifth assumption is that a learner can select best or correct response easily from multiple-choice responses. It facilitates the process of discrimination and generalization.

**Branched Programming as an Intrinsic-Process :**

As against extrinsic process of linear programming branched programming is an intrinsic process because of the following reasons.

1. Discrimination of the correct answer by the learner from among the multiple options given is internal to the learner and the programme both.
2. Learners control their responses internally by reading the bigger sized frames.
3. Here learner detects the improbable responses and avoids them to escape errors. This is also an internal process.
4. Discrimination in the process of learning occurs at the stage of presentation too in a natural manner, i.e., many informations are given in one frame. This again makes the programme intrinsic.
5. Here remediation is given by perceiving the internal difficulty of learning manifested through wrong responses of the learner.

**Characteristics of Branched Programming :**

Branched programme of learning has the following characteristics :

1. It is particularly suitable for dealing with materials that involve complex problem solving.
2. It works effectively for realising higher cognitive objectives and teaching students of higher classes.
3. Frames are relatively bigger in this programme consisting of more than one paragraph and thus it includes many informations in a frame.
4. It can provide better chance of free thinking and imagination to students. Thus, it is very suitable for creative and talented students.
5. Learners are asked multiple choice questions in branched programming. Learners select the best alternative from among the choices available. Answer keys are also made available on different pages of the programme. Students confirm their responses from these keys and get immediate feedback.
6. Teaching is mainly a communication process according to Crowder. The more the communication is effective, the more the teaching will be effective. That is why Crowder stresses more on the improvement of communication. It means that subject-matter must be presented to students in such a manner that it is easily understood by them.
7. In this model of instruction, the learners can use even their previous knowledge to respond the stimulus. Thus, role of entering behaviour is important here.
8. Here learner proceeds to the process of learning in a very careful manner because he has to deal a number of informations at a time.
9. Crowder is of the view that a man learns by committing errors also (Close to Thorndike). That is why upto 20% mistakes on a frame is allowed here. When learner commits errors, he also comes to know why he has committed this mistake. This enables him to escape the errors in future.
10. This model is very suitable for concept learning because more words and examples are needed to clarify the concepts.

## Principles of Branched Programming

1. **Principle of Exposition :** Here the learner is exposed to the whole concept with the help of suitable illustration and chosen words. The learner reads the frame to have a mastery over the concept.
2. **Principle of Diagnosis :** Weaknesses of the learner is diagnosed with the help of multiple choice questions. When learner attempts wrong options, his weaknesses come to knowledge.
3. **Principle of Remediation :** After diagnosing the weaknesses of the learner, he is provided with fresh frame to come to the right response, it is called remediation. Thus, we see that frame structure of branching programme consists of exposition,- diagnosis-remediation.

## Major forms of Branched Programming

1. **Constructed response question :** Such questions are used when we do not want to give any choice to learners. They rather construct the response after reading the frame. They write down the responses in their own language and it is then matched with the response key.

2. **Constructed choice question :** Here the student is asked to write down the response of a direct question and then he turns a page to check whether his answer is right or not. When he reaches that page, he is again reminded of the question along with a set of alternative responses from which he chooses the one that resembles his own answer. If he choose an incorrect answer, remedial help is given to him in the usual manner.
3. **Block questions :** These are very similar to comprehensive questions which are asked at the end of the paragraphs in text-books. The purpose of these questions are to test the understanding of the passage by the students. In such forms several questions are asked on the basis of the frame given. The learner responds to these questions after analysing and processing the total informations given to him. In such questions neither immediate feedback is given to students nor is there any provision for remedial help.
4. **Linear Sequence :** Such sequence is used when learners do some memorizing acts, formulate symbols, relate technical terms and evaluate a problem.

## Limitations of Branching Model

The main disadvantages of this model are given below:

1. Guessing is the main problem in multiple choice questions. Students can answer questions correctly by guessing without reading the frame thoroughly. Thus, this model may have all those shortcomings which are seen in multiple choice questions.
2. When long frames followed by several questions are used in this model, it looks like general text-books. And if level of students is low, this programme will not work at all.
3. It is very difficult to speculate how many branches of knowledge a student needs. Thus, we can not fulfil the needs of all types of students-average, poor and superior by this programme. Thus, branched programming may have all those shortcomings which are generally seen in text-books.
4. The preparation cost of this programme is also very high, probably higher than that of linear programming model.
5. This model depends on the planning and imaginative power of the programmer. It is he who decides the level of the frame and standard of questions asked from the frame.
6. This programme is useful for higher classes only because only the students of higher classes can understand the complexities of the programme.
7. The major limitations of the model is that we can not ask the questions from the whole frame. Only limited sampled questions are asked here.
8. This is also a time consuming approach of learning. Use of wrong pages for redirecting the learner makes the programme very bulky.

**Difference between Linear and Branching Programme of Instruction.**

| Contents | Linear | Branching |
|---|---|---|
| Exponent<br>Source of origin | B.F.Skinner (1954)<br>From Psychological laboratory experiments on pigeons | Norman A.Crowder(1954)<br>From semi-industrial situation with emphasis on efficient instruction to improve job performance. It has originated from "human training techniques". |

| Contents | Linear | Branching |
|---|---|---|
| Learning Theories | Based on operant conditioning learning theory. It is a response-centred approach of learning (R-S) | Based on configuration theory of learning. It is a problem solving approach. It is stimulus centred approach of learning.(S-R) |
| Principles | I- Based on five fundamental principles.<br>1. Principle of small steps<br>2. Principle of active responding<br>3. Principle of immediate confirmation<br>4. Principle of self-pacing<br>5. Principle of student testing. Besides these, optional or mandatory principles may be there :<br>Mandatory principles:<br>1. The principle of objective specification<br>2. The principle of empirical origin<br>3. Principal of self pacing<br>Optional principles<br>1. Principle of over-responding.<br>2. Principle of immediate feedback<br>3. Principle of small steps. | Based on three basic principles<br>1. Principle of exposition.<br>2. Principle of diagnosis.<br>3. Principle of remediation. |
| Assumption | 1. Student learns better if content is presented in small units.<br>2. Students' response if immediately confirmed, results in better learning.<br>3. Students errors create hindrance in learning.<br>4. Students learns better in laissez faire environment. | 1. Student learns better if he is exposed to whole situation/content.<br>2. Students errors help in diagnosis.<br>3. Student learns better if remediation is provided side by side.<br>4. Student learns better in democratic environment. |
| Frame Size | 1. Small steps/frames.<br>2. Include only one element of the topic at a time. Each step is complete in itself. It can be taught independently and can be measured independently. | 1. large frames or steps.<br>2. There may be a para or page in the frame. |
| Frame structure | Stimulus-Response-Reinforcement | Exposition-Diagnosis-Remediation |
| Types of Frames | There are four types of frames :<br>1. Introductory frames (or priming frames)<br>2. Teaching frames (or full prompt frames)<br>3. Practice frames (or Half prompt frames)<br>4. Testing frames (or unprompted frames) | There are two types of frames :<br>1. Home page (for teaching and diagnosis)<br>2. Wrong page (for remediation) |

| Contents | Linear | Branching |
|---|---|---|
| Responses | 1. Structured responses (e.g. recall or recognition type)<br>2. These responses are controlled by programmer and not by learners. | 1. Responses not rigidly structured. (e.g. multiple choice frames)<br>2. Responses are selected by the learners and not by the programmer. |
| Reinforcement | 1. Immediate confirmation of correct responses provides reinforcement<br>2. Wrong responses are ignored | 1. Confirmation of correct responses provides reinforcement.<br>2. Wrong responses also help in diagnosis of weaknesses of the learner.<br>3. Remedy is provided on the basis of diagnosed weaknesses. |
| Errors | Hinder in learning | Helps in diagnosis of the weaknesses of the learner. |
| Error rate | Less than 10% in criterion programme is acceptable but not beyond that. | More than 20% error rate can be accepted |
| Individual differences | Only in working at their own pace i.e., time is the factor for individual differences | In choosing their own path according to their needs and requirements. |
| Form of the programme | 1. Conventional booklet of six inches to four inches.<br>2. Includes instructions regarding use of the programme.<br>3. Introduction of the content matter.<br>4. Presentation of small content units | 1. Scrambled booklet.<br>2. Includes instructions in the beginning.<br>3. Content is presented in the form of paras or pages.<br>4. These paras are not in a sequence. |
| Teaching Machines | Very simple and cheap model of teaching machine is | Difficult to use teaching machine. A complex, costly model of machine required |
| Purpose | 1. Modification of learner's behaviour.<br>2. To stimulate learner for self-learning, no teacher is required<br>3. Continuous stimulus flow motivates the student throughout the programme. | 1. To draw out weak points of learners.<br>2. To provide remedy for removing these weaknesses. |
| Uses | 1. Used for secondary level students.<br>2. Used for achieving lower objectives of learning especially for recall and recognition.<br>3. Useful for students of average and below average intelligence.<br>4. Can be used in distance education programmes | 1. Used for secondary as well as higher classes.<br>2. Higher objectives can be achieved such as multiple discrimination etc.<br>3. Useful for students of above average and high intelligence.<br>4. It can also be sued in distance education programmes. |

| Contents | Linear | Branching |
|---|---|---|
| Limitations | 1. No freedom for students to respond. | 1. It does not consider learning process whether learning is taking place or not. Main emphasis is on diagnosing the weaknesses of learners and providing remedy to them. |
| | 2. Based on learning theories which are formulated by experiments conducted on animals. A human being is more intelligent than animals, he has got an intelligent brain. | 2. There is not sequencing of pages. Student finds it difficult to follow the steps. He does not find it exciting or motivating therefore he does not want to go through these pages. |
| | 3. Every learner has to follow the same path. | 3. More emphasis on remediation rather than teaching. Hence, it is only a tutorial approach. |
| | 4. Wrong responses are avoided in the programme. No remedy is provided for them. | |

# 7

# Models of Teaching

## INTRODUCTION

Teaching is such a social process which aims at maximizing learning. But teaching and learning is not related to each other in a bipolar manner. It otherwise means that where there is teaching, there is learning but where there is learning it is not necessary that it is the result of teaching. This learning may be due to any other factor. This is the reason that learning theories have been proved to be unsuccessful in solving teaching problems. Teaching theories are all the time needed to solve teaching problems. The only progress in this regard is that many teaching models have been developed so far. These models have been propounded by keeping learning theories as base and hence they can not be substitute of teaching theory. They, however, work as hypotheses for propounding teaching theories in future. Whenever experiments verify these hypotheses in future, universally acceptable teaching theories will come into effect.

### Definitions of Teaching Model

1. **B.R. Joyce :** Teaching models are just instructional designs. They describe the process of specifying and producing particular environmental situations which causes the students to interact in such a way that specific changes occur in their behaviour.
2. **Cronback and Gagne :** Development of teaching model is brought about by keeping in view the learning theories so that the teaching theories may be indoctrinated by using these theories.

### Characteristics of Teaching Models

1. **Based on assumptions :** These models are based on the following assumptions :
   - *(i)* Appropriate learning environment can be created by teaching models.
   - *(ii)* The teacher and the students interact each other through the content and the teaching skills. These interactions will lead to specific changes in the behaviour of learners.
   - *(iii)* These models have been developed on the basis of learning theories but they can help in developing teaching theories in future.
   - *(iv)* Different elements of teaching can be explained in different ways and objectives can also be realized accordingly.
   - *(v)* Teaching models present a real and practical outline for learning.
2. **Activities involved in teaching models :** Six types of activities are mainly included in the format of teaching models.
   - *(i)* Giving practical shape to learning situation.
   - *(ii)* Selecting suitable conditions of stimulus so that learners may respond in the desired manner.
   - *(iii)* Observing the response of learners.
   - *(iv)* Determining the criterion behaviour of teachers and pupils.
   - *(v)* Selecting appropriate teaching strategies and techniques for creative conditions of interaction between learners and the environment.
3. **Introducting suitable experiences :** Teaching models provide suitable experiences to learners and the teacher both. By selecting the subject matter, the teacher presents these experiences before the learners in such a way that they become an enjoying experience for them.
4. **Giving answers to basic questions :** These teaching models give the answers of some basic questions related to teaching-learning process such as,
   - *(i)* How does a teacher behave?
   - *(ii)* Why does he behave so?
   - *(iii)* What will be the effect of his behaviour on his students?

5. **Based on individual differences :** These models have been developed keeping in view the individual differences of learners. So, every type of learner can be benefitted from them.
6. **Influenced by individual philosophy :** Different educationists have propounded different teaching models on the basis of their own philosophy of life, e.g., Realist tries to make his pupils a realist, a pragmatist tries to make him a pragmatist and so on.
7. **Based on maxims of teaching :** All these models are based on different maxims of teaching. The reason is that these maxims very well explain the behaviour of the teacher and the students.
8. **Product of practice :** These very models have got recognition only after continuous and long practice.
9. **Recognise teaching as an art also :** All these models recognise teaching as an art also.
10. **Based on learning theories :** All the models have been propounded by keeping learning theories as base.

## Fundamental Elements of Teaching Models

Four fundamental elements are found in any teaching model :

1. **Focus :** What objectives are to be realized by teaching is called focus. Thus this element is related to planning phase of teaching and all the other three elements revolve round this.
2. **Syntax :** In this element, teaching strategies and techniques are selected and their sequence is determined so that suitable learning situations may be created and objectives are achieved.
3. **Social system :** This element is related to class interaction. Here the desired activities between the teacher and pupils and mutual relationship between them are determined. This leading of teaching will lead to desirable changes in the behaviour of learners and objectives will be achieved.
4. **Support system :** Here behaviour is evaluated objectively to see to what extent the objectives have been achieved. This element determines the effectiveness of syntax and social system. If objectives are not realized, modification in these two elements are made.

Since, every teaching model is propounded with different objectives, difference is also found in their focus, syntax, social and support system. That is why it is not possible to compare a model with other model.

## CLASSIFICATION OF TEACHING MODELS

All teaching models can be classified into the five categories given below :

1. Historical teaching models.
2. Philosophical teaching models.
3. Psychological teaching models.
4. Teaching models for teacher education.
5. Modern teaching models.

We will describe here one representative model of all the five categories given above:

1. **Socrates Teaching model :** Socrates was of the opinion that no knowledge can be imparted from outside. It is hidden already in the soul of the child. The teacher has only to bring it out through questioning.

   Socrates did not formulate any teaching objectives (focus element does not exist in his model) because be opined that the task of the teacher is not to impart knowledge to students but his task is only to create conducive learning condition and this is done by question answer method. Thus we see that social system of Socrates is fully democratic and permissive but his support system is not clear from his model.
2. **Impression model :** This model was propounded by **John Locke.** He believed that the mind of the child is like a plane slate at the time of his birth. Whatever experiences are provided to him through teaching put a direct impression on his mind. This very impression is called learning. Thus sense organs as well as communication skill of the teacher both play their respective roles in the teaching-learning process. Powers of recognition, diversification, communication and perception are developed through practice and experience.

   As far as his social system is concerned, teacher is active at the time of communication and pupils are active at the time of practice.

3. **Basic teaching model :** This teaching model was propounded by **Robert Glasser** in 1962. In this model, teaching objectives are realized by using psychological powers. Four basic elements of this model are as follows :
   (a) **Instructional objectives :** It refers to those activities of the teacher which he does before the start of his teaching, i.e., analysing the content, determining the teaching objectives and writing objectives in terms of behavioural change of learners. Thus, objectives of the teacher and pupils are known as instructional objectives.
   (b) **Entering behaviour of learners :** It refers to those fundamental abilities of pupils which are essential to follow the subject matter. Interaction between the teacher and pupils starts only when entering behaviour is established. Before taking the students to the objectives of the lesson their entering behaviour (background knowledge) is found out.
   (c) **Instructional process :** It refers to those activities of the teacher which are done to present the subject-matter in the class, e.g., use of teaching strategies and techniques, devices or reinforcement, application of audio-visual aids in teaching and regular feedback techniques.
   (d) **Assessment of achievement :** It refers to those activities of the teacher through which he takes decision to what extent the learners have gained mastery over the subject-matter, i.e. to what extent the objectives have been achieved. Whatever may be the technique of evaluating the achievement of students but technique must be objective, reliable and valid.
4. **Taba's teaching model :** Taba's teaching model is related to teacher training programme. This model helps the pupil teacher in developing thinking power and skill. According to this model, following three activities are included in the curriculum.
   (a) Formation of the concept.
   (b) Explanation of concepts and their generalization.
   (c) Explanation of facts with the help of laws and principles.

In order to carry out all these three activities, the pupil teacher uses external activities and internal reflection both. The teacher first determines important concepts of the lesson. Then he explains these concepts one by one and helps the students to generalize them. Then, on the basis of these concepts, laws and principles are formulated. In order to do all these activities successfully, the pupil teacher presents the subject-matter in a sequentional manner. He takes the help of questions for increasing interaction and besides all these he gives the students opportunities for analysis, synthesis and generalization.

5. **Modern teaching model : B. R. Joyce** has classified all modern teaching models in four convenient groups:
   (a) Social interaction models
   (b) Information process models
   (c) Individual development models
   (d) Behaviour modification models

In the first category of models development of social skills of learners has been stressed. It will develop capacity of social adjustment among learners.

In the second category of models preference has been given to make the students understand facts, informations and principles. It will develop cognitive abilities of learners.

In the third category of models emphasis has been given on developing individual capacities of learners. It will help them excel to the maximum level possible.

In the fourth category of models, it has been stressed what measures can be adopted to increase the scope of knowledge of learners. These models are directed to bringing about desired changes in the behaviour of learners.

We will discuss here one teaching model from each category.

a. **Social Interaction model**-Group heuristic model:

—John Dewey and Kilpatric :

- **Focus :** The purpose of this model is to develop social competencies among learners. These capacities will help them adjust in the society.
- **Syntax :** Here problem is presented by the teacher before students. After going into the details of the problem and its relevant aspects, the students seek the solution of the problem. After they have

got the solution, they evaluate the solution by discussing with other pupils. The solution is presented before the teacher only after evaluation.

- **Social system :** The classroom environment is democratic here. Students are given full freedom to learn and teacher works in the class only as a guide or helper. From beginning to the end pupils are completely free to think and act under the guidance of a democratic teacher.
- **Support system :** Solution of the problem is evaluated on the basis of its practicability and meaningfulness. If it is so, the solution is accepted otherwise rejected. Discussion is the best technique of evaluation here.

**(b) Information process model**-inductive model: This model has especially been prepared for teacher education. Here, pupil teacher analyses learning problems and reaches the solution one by one.

1. **Focus :** This model aims at developing social processes and making the principles understood by learners. In order to achieve these activities special emphasis is given on the comprehension of facts, events, concepts, laws and principles.
2. **Syntax :** Situations are created by the teacher here to develop interactive activities. For this purpose teaching activities are arranged in such a manner that pupils understand the concepts very easily, e.g.,
   *(i)* First of all, list of teaching activities are prepared.
   *(ii)* Then these activities are classified into different groups.
   *(iii)* Then these teaching activities are exposed before the students one by one.
   *(iv)* Then direction of teaching activities are determined.
   *(v)* The directions and relations of various teaching activities are explained.
   *(vi)* Then conclusions are drawn on the basis of these explanations.
   *(vii)* Then in order to test the consequences of these activities, hypotheses are formulated.
   *(viii)* Then these hypotheses are explained. For this purpose, help is taken from facts and relevant concepts.
   *(ix)* Then hypotheses are verified and generalization is arrived at.
   *(x)* Finally, conclusions are practised.
   In this way, the pupils come to understand facts and concepts very clearly.
3. **Social system :** Here students are given full freedom to act in the class. Teacher also initiates his activities from the activities of students. He works in the class only as a guide or helper. Questions are continuously asked in the class in order to maintain democratic environment there.
4. **Support System :** Only objective type test is used here to evaluate the comprehension ability and intellectual power of students.

**(c) Individual development model**-Creative teaching model :

—W. Garden

1. **Focus :** This model aims at developing creative potentials for the purpose of solving practical as well theoretical problems.
2. **Syntax :** Five steps are followed here :
   *(i)* In the first step students are helped to understand facts and concepts.
   *(ii)* Analogy (similar experience) is presented by the teacher in the second step.
   *(iii)* In the third step, students try to apply that analogy in other situations.
   *(iv)* In the fourth step they learn to establish relations between the analogy and the content.
   *(v)* Various analogies are mutually compared in the last step.
3. **Social system :** Here teacher initiates his activities in a sequential manner. He helps the pupils to develop their mental abilities.. Pupils also get full freedom for their counter activities. They are given deliberate motivation by the teacher to develop their creative abilities.
4. **Support system :** Creativity tests, testing originality, fluency, flexibility and usefulness is conducted here and achievement of pupils is evaluated by using creativity tests.

**(d) Behaviour modification model**-conditioned response models :

—B.F.Skinner

1. **Focus :** This model aims at bringing about desirable changes in the behaviour of pupils.

2. **Syntax :** Three steps are followed in this model of teaching.
   - In the first step, subject-matter is presented before the pupils in the form of verbal or non-verbal stimuli. It means that subject-matter is presented in such a way that it will necessarily lead the students to respond.
   - Pupils are motivated to respond to the stimuli in the second step and their responses are accepted.
   - In the third step, reinforcement is given to students to increase their rate of responses. Positive reinforcement are generally given and punishers are ignored altogether.
3. **Social system :** The teacher exercises full control over the behaviour and responses of pupils here. Besides, equal opportunities are given to all learners according to their abilities, interests and needs. It means that freedom of students works under the guidance and supervision of the teacher.
4. **Support system :** The assumption of this model is that the rate of pupil's mistakes should not be more than 10% at any cost. In order to evaluate the achievement of pupils, internal as well as external criterion measure are used here. The attitude of learners towards instructional programme is also included in the evaluation process here.

# Instructional Objectives and Task Analysis

## L.K. DAVIES MATRIX

Davies and Thomas have given the concept of management of teaching. This concept is based on modern theory of human organization. According to him, teacher works as a manager in his class in the following manner.

1. He plans his teaching learning process keeping in view the objectives formulated by him.
2. He organizes the human and physical resources, hardware and software both to achieve the objectives in his plan.
3. He leads his teaching process by utilizing all the techniques of motivation and leads his students to the level of objectives.
4. He controls his teaching learning process by applying various techniques of measurement and evaluation from the very beginning to the end.

These four steps are cyclically used in the teaching learning process repeatedly.

Glaser is somewhat different from Davies. He says that relationship among those steps are not cyclic. It is rather linear.

Davies matrix is shown below :

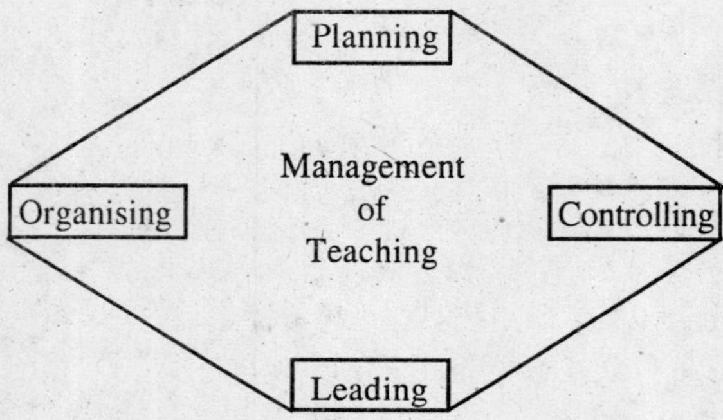


We will discuss only the first step in this chapter. Planning (Pre-active phase of teaching):

It is the first step in the teaching learning process. It is the most important step of all in the sense that success of all other steps depends on it. If planning is accurate and practical, it is likely that it can be properly implemented in the class.

Davies has defined planning of teaching in the following words:

"Planning of teaching is the work which a teacher performs to establish learning objectives".

## ACTIVITIES INVOLVED IN PLANNING

Three activities are involved in the planning stage :

A. Task analysis
B. Formulating educational objectives
C. Writing objectives in behavioral terms, i.e., in the language of change of behaviour of learners.

## A. TASK ANALYSIS

It is related to what to teach or do in the class and on what foundations. It has been discussed in detail in the Previous Chapter.

This concept was given by **Ryle.** It has its origin into training psychology and is based on the assumption that once task is analysed into its various convenient segments, it can be easily performed by choosing suitable strategies.

Task, according to Devies is a unit of performance which collectively constitutes a function.

Task analysis can be classified into three categories.

### 1. Content Analysis

It is the analysis of the topic or unit of a subject-matter to be taught in a 40 minutes period. The analysis of the content helps to arrange all its constituents into logical sequences so that suitable strategies and techniques may be selected to teach each segment and the change of learner's behaviour can be evaluated.

Davies has developed a matrix for the analysis of the content. According to this matrix, content analysis is completed into four steps :

I. In the first step, the whole content to be taught in a period is divided into different units, and sub-units. For example, we can divide "Akbar's extension of Empire" in the following manner.

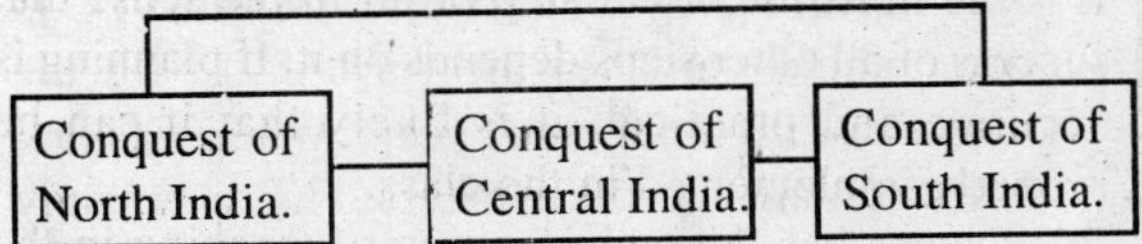


II. In the second step, all those sub-units are arranged in a logical as well as psychological manner. Maxims of teaching and relevant principles are taken into consideration while doing so.

III. These sub-topics are again divided into different convincing elements in the third steps again in the form of 1, 2, 3 etc. heading and these elements are taken one by one. For example, we can analyse the above topic in the following manner.

**CONQUEST OF NORTH INDIA**

| Wars | Social Relation |
|---|---|
| *(i)* Conquest of Rajasthan | *(i)* Marriage relations. |
| *(ii)* Conquest of Gujarat | *(ii)* Recognition of scholars and artists |
| *(iii)* Conquest of Bengal | *(iii)* Tolerant attitude towards religions |
| *(iv)* Conquest of Bihar | *(iv)* Unbiased role of administration |

IV. These elements are again synthesized in the fourth step in such a manner that they look like a whole integrated unit. This process gives a clear and composite picture of the total lesson to the students. It means that these topics, sub-topics and elements of the lesson are linked by a chain.

**Sources of content analysis :**

The sources on which content analysis is based are given below :

*(i)* Valid content material available any where.
*(ii)* Entering behaviour of students.
*(iii)* Needs and interests of students and the society.
*(iv)* Objectives to be determined.
*(v)* Availability of audio-visual aids.
*(vi)* Pattern of examination system.
*(vii)* Criteria of promoting students to the next higher class.
*(viii)* Teaching skill competency of the teacher.

**Assumptions of elements in the content analysis :**

I. An element is complete in itself and can be taught to students separately.
II. An element can be evaluated independently.
III. An element can bring about at least one change in the behaviour of learners.
IV. An element can be easily understood by students as compared to a big sub-unit or unit.

### 2. Job Analysis

In job analysis some social and professional activities and roles of the person are analysed. It also involves the following four steps given below :

I. *Diagnosis :* Here the inherent power of the learner is found out.
II. *Treatment :* Here various techniques to complete a particular job are taught to students.
III. *Rehabilitation :* This step is related to the active participation in a particular job.
IV. *Prevention :* This step is related to maintaining the job for a longer period without losing it.

### 3. Skill Analysis

Different types of skills are involved in different jobs. For example, teaching job requires teaching skills and sub-skills such as skill of presentation, questioning, illustration, black board writing, probing questions etc. These skills are analysed step wise and each step is taught to learners one by one.

## (B) DETERMINATION OF OBJECTIVES

While constructing any type of tests, content is first analysed, i.e., how many and what type of questions are to be asked from a particular lesson or content. After content analysis, teaching or testing objectives are determined. Since this taxonomy of objectives is mainly related to teaching-learning process, it is exclusively concerned with the achievement testing.

Objectives are mainly concerned with "why to teach". It is a philosophical process which goes on keeping in view the needs and aspirations of students, teachers, school, community and the nation. Determination of objectives is essential in any activity because it determines the direction of the activity on one hand, and enables the person to remain on the track all the time. Besides, achievement tests are constructed on the basis of these very objectives.

**NCERT** has defined objectives in the following words:

"Objective is a point or end in view of something towards which action is directed and a planned change sought through the activity what we set out to do".

**Explanation :**

According to this definition, objectives include the following three points :

(ii) *Action :* Action is a must in order to achieve any objective.

(iii) *Direction :* Objectives determine the direction of action. They keep the person in action on the track all the time.

(iv) *Planned modification :* When action is done in a definite direction, desired changes in the behaviour of learners is brought about.

## Educational Objectives

B.S.Bloom has defined educational objectives in the following words.

"Educational objectives are not only the goals towards which curriculum is shaped and towards which instruction is guided, they are also the goals that provide the detailed specification for the construction and use of evaluation techniques".

**Explanation :**

**Curriculum :** It means what type of experiences are to be provided and to what extent it is to be provided to the students.

**Instruction :** It means what procedure and strategies are to be adopted to provide experiences to learners.

**Evaluation :** Whatever experiences have been received by learners, they are evaluated, i.e, to find out whether these experiences have reached to learners or not and if they have has reached them, then what portion of it they have received.

## Teaching Objectives

These objectives are related to teaching-learning process in the class. A teacher does his teaching acts keeping these very objectives in view. On the basis of the very objectives, he evaluates his teaching whether it is effective or not.

Educational objectives referred by B.S. Bloom are actually teaching objectives.

## Difference between Teaching and Educational Objectives

1. The nature of educational objectives is comprehensive. They are formulated for the whole session or for many years. While teaching objectives are marrow in nature. They are mainly concerned with the classroom teaching and formulated for a period or for a particular unit of the lesson.
2. Educational objectives take its origin into philosophy while teaching objectives are determined on psychological grounds. A classroom teacher also tries to coordinate these two bases.
3. Teaching objectives are only a part of educational objectives which are restricted to a particular lesson/subject and a particular class. It means that these very objectives are the medium of attaining educational goals. Educational objectives, on the other hand, are related to the whole educational system. Their attainment or evaluation is impossible for a single teacher.
4. Educational objectives are general. They point out to the goals of education. It means that ultimate aim of teaching of all subjects to learners is one and the same, i.e., turning a man into a useful human. Teaching objectives, on the other hand, are very specific. They change with the change of subject, lesson, topic and sub-topic.
5. Educational objectives also change with time when socio-political system changes but teaching objectives do not change in 40 minutes period.
6. Educational objectives are called goals or general objectives while teaching objectives are specific objectives. Thus, goals and objectives have the same difference as we see between educational and teaching objectives.

7. Curriculum is constructed keeping the educational objectives into account. This very curriculum is transferred to learners by formulating, teaching objectives. Learners are also taken to the evaluation stage through these objectives.

## Taxonomy of Educational Objectives

Teaching is a process which goes ahead in a phased manner. The curriculum is constructed according to the level at which students are to be taken. But only construction of the curriculum is not enough here. The taxonomy has an important role to play in the presentation of the content. A teacher teaches his students according to the level that he has decided to take his students at. For example, if a teacher wants to keep his students at the knowledge level, he will emphasize more on cramming and drilling in his teaching. But if he wants to take his students to the application level, he will first help the students to comprehend the knowledge and then he will teach them how to apply the acquired knowledge in different situations. Thus, teaching of a teacher goes up step by step Taxonomy of objectives tells us these very steps and levels.

One more problem is that we can evaluate our students only according to the levels of teaching objectives that we formulated in the beginning. For example, if we have made the students crame the definition of social stratification and we are asking them to analyse and correlate different concepts of the definition, then students would not be able to answer the question.

Thus, taxonomy table determines the direction and nature of teaching and evaluation both. Besides, this table plays an important role when we write objectives in behavioural terms. This table provides information about all the three domains of behaviour. These domains are given below :

1. **Cognitive domain :** This domain is related to cognitive (mental) abilities of human behaviour. This taxonomy was given by B.S. Bloom in 1956.
2. **Affective domain :** This domain is related to feeling aspect of human behaviour. This taxonomy was given by Maseea in 1964.
3. **Psychomotor domain :** This domain is related to physical abilities and skills of human behaviour which are manifested when process is over. This taxonomy was given by Sympson in 1969.

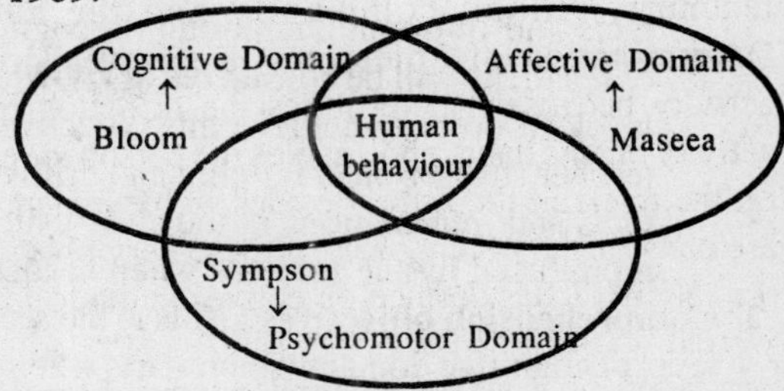


The above diagram clarifies that all the three domains are not seen all the time simultaneously in the behaviour of a human. Sometimes, only one domain manifests and sometimes a composite of two or three domains are seen.

Cognitive domain of learning is given much importance in the classes but other domains are not neglected altogether.

**Taxonomy Table**

| Cognitive domain | Affective domain | Psychomotor domain |
|---|---|---|
| 1. Knowledge | 1. Receiving | 1. Impulsion |
| 2. Comprehension | 2. Responding | 2. Manipulation |
| 3. Application | 3. Valuing | 3. Control |
| 4. Analysis | 4. Conceptualization | 4. Coordination |
| 5. Synthesis | 5. Organization | 5. Naturalization |
| 6. Evaluation | 6. Characterization | 6. Habit formation |

## Explanation of the Table

**I. Cognitive Domain :** Cognitive (intellectual) abilities of students are developed by this domain. Its base is cognition. This domain starts with recognition and recall abilities of mind. Following six objectives are included here in hierarchical manner.

1. **Knowledge objectives :** This is the first level of cognitive domain. It has three sub-levels given below :
   *(a)* Knowledge of specifics, i.e., knowledge of words, concepts, facts, events, dates, persons, places etc.
   *(b)* Knowledge of methods and procedure to know the specific, i.e., knowledge of traditions, trends, norms, strategies, classes, classification etc.
   *(c)* Knowledge of laws, principles and generalization, i.e., knowing the laws and

principles of science, knowing how to generalize these laws and principles etc.

If a student is able to present all the above facts and informations through recognition or recall, he will be considered at knowledge level. In order to achieve this objective the teacher stresses on cramming and drilling of facts and informations in the class which is reproduced by the students when needed.

2. **Comprehension objectives :** This is the second level of cognitive domain which starts when first level of objectives is achieved. It also consists of three sub-levels :

   *(a)* Translating the facts, events, laws and principles into easy language.

   *(b)* Interpreting the facts, events, laws and principles into common words and simple language.

   *(c)* Extrapolating facts, events, laws and principles, i.e., drawing additional conclusions from the given conclusions.

   If a student is able to do all three activities mentioned above, we will say that he has proper understanding of the knowledge gained. For example, elite class means very rich class of the society. This is knowledge level of learning. If students can identify the people belonging to the elite class in the society, it is comprehension level of learning. Answering paragraph based questions in languages is also the example of comprehension level of behaviour.

   In order to realize this objective, the teacher stresses much on the depth of knowledge obtained. He also teaches the students how to manipulate a subject-matter in other ways.

3. **Application objectives :** After getting maturity at the comprehension level, students are taught to apply the knowledge in new and unfamiliar situations. It also consists of three sub-levels:

   *(a)* Generalizing the laws and principles and seeking new uses of facts.

   *(b)* Finding faults in the laws and principles.

   *(c)* Applying laws and principles in new situations to expand the horizon of knowledge.

   If a student can do all the three activities given above himself, he is said to have acquired application level of learning. Once this objective is achieved students can use words in their own sentences, they can write the summary of the lesson, they can do experiment in the laboratory and so on.

   In order to achieve this objective, the teacher creates new situations every now and then to enable the students to apply the acquired knowledge.

4. **Analysis objectives :** Analysis of any fact, event, law or principle is possible only when a student has already crossed the application level of learning. Analysis means dividing a subject-matter, laws or facts into different feasible parts following certain rules. This level of objectives also has three sub-levels:

   *(a)* Analysing the elements of events, laws or principles.

   *(b)* Analysing the inter-relationship of different facts, events, laws or principles.

   *(c)* Analysing the underlying principles and rules of facts, events or laws.

   In order to achieve this objective, the teacher creates new situations every now and then to enable the students to apply the acquired knowledge.

   If a student is competent to carry out all these operations, he is said to be at analysis level. For example, before writing an essay, the student finds out different headings and sub-headings and completes the essay on the basis of them.

   In order to achieve this objective, the teacher presents new problems before his students in the class. Then he teaches them how to analyse them from different angles on the basis of certain rules. He himself presents the lesson in the class only after analyzing it.

5. **Synthesis objectives :** Synthesis means joining the divided parts in such a novel manner that a new useful structure is formed. This ability is developed only after mastery at analysis ability. This helps in developing the creative potential of students.

   Synthesis is the fifth level of behaviour in the hierarchy of cognitive domain. It also consists of three sub-levels.

   *(a)* Producing unique communication material.

   *(b)* Producing new useful structure by synthesis on the basis of divided parts.

(c) Finding out abstract relationship among different concrete elements.

If a student can do all these three types of activities, we will say that he has the potential of synthesis. Writing, stories, poems, essays etc, by students or drawing map of a place on the basis of recall etc. are some examples of synthesis level of learning.

6. **Evaluation objectives :** This is the top level of cognitive domain. Evaluation refers to throwing critical views on facts, events, laws and principles and their generalization and testing these facts, laws and principles on new criteria in such a manner that all their positive and negative aspects becomes manifest. The examinations which are conducted for administrative services consist of more than one third questions of this type. Evaluation ability is very rare which is found in only 3% to 6% people of the society.

Evaluation level of learning has no limit at all. Evaluation provides criterion standard to check facts, events, laws and principles on one hand and on the other, this ability helps to develop new laws and principles. Scientists, writers and administrators do possess this ability.

In order to achieve this objective, the teacher teaches his students to criticize facts, events, laws and principles in a healthy manner. For this purpose, they are taught rules and procedure of healthy criticism.

The above six levels of cognitive domain will help a teacher to construct items of achievement tests. Certain proportion of questions are constructed from each level given above depending upon the nature and level of examinees.

**II. Affective Domain :** Affective domain is concerned with attitude, emotions, interest, mental sets and values of students. The development of this domain is not easy because every student differs in attitudes, tendencies, emotions and values and it is very difficult for a teacher to understand each student of the class. Despite this difficulty, every teacher must try to develop this domain of behaviour also in order to develop cognitive domain. Hierarchy of this domain is comprised of six levels given below :

1. **Receiving :** This level is directly related to that sensitivity of the child which is created in him when stimulus is given. The teacher presents the stimulus in the class either by questioning or showing any material aid. Three interrelated activities come under this level.

   (a) Sensitivity to the stimulus.

   (b) Willingness to accept the stimulus.

   (c) Control on stimulus.

   An individual will receive a stimulus only when the above conditions are fulfilled.

2. **Responding :** A student responds when he is motivated by the stimulus and acquires new knowledge in the process. This level also consists of three sub-levels.

   (a) Obedient behaviour for response.

   (b) Willingness to respond

   (c) Getting satisfaction by responding.

   If a teacher is able to develop these abilities in his students only when he can improve his cognitive domain of learning.

3. **Valuing :** Valuing refers to those values which a student gives special importance in his life. He succeeds to manifest stable emotions in his behaviour by these values even in changing situations. In order to achieve this objective, a teacher teaches some imitable values by his teaching. For example, attending the blackboard work is a value. Accepting this value is always in the interest of the student so teacher teaches this value to the class by adopting various strategies. It consists of the following three activities on the part of the students.

   (a) Accepting the values.

   (b) Preferring the values

   (c) Standing firm by the values.

4. **Conceptualization :** When many values are accumulated in a child and he comes to the conclusion that more than one values are good simultaneously, then he selects few values out of many on the basis of his liking. Selection of a group of values by the students on the basis of his choice is called conceptualization. It forms a clear concept in the mind of the child and he behaves in future according to this very concept. It also consists of the following three levels.

   (a) Liking good values.

   (b) Hating the bad values.

   (c) Transmitting the good values to others.

5. **Organisation :** This is the fifth level of affective domain where different concepts and ideas are organized in order to form a system. Here student does the following activities with different types of values and concepts :
   (*a*) Sorting out various values on the basis of different concepts formed by these values and arranging the concepts in the form of a system.
   (*b*) Determining inter-relationship among values and concepts to distinguish one system from the other.
   (*c*) Formation of the most acceptable concept suitable to a system.
6. **Characterization :** This level comes at the top of the affective domain. Here student gets specialization in one or two value systems after knowing so many of them. The student is so perfect in that value system that he is identified by it. For example, punctuality to the class is a system which consists of lots of values. If a student has got specialization in this system, he will be described as punctual student. When this stage of learning comes, the student can do the following activities.
   (*a*) Seeking the solution of the problem.
   (*b*) Working efficiently with no burden.
   (*c*) Concentrating fully in the task.

Suffice it to say, with the help of these levels of objectives, a teacher can mould the character of his students in a manner which is very conducive in playing positive role for making teaching learning process a success.

**III. Psychomotor Domain :** In this domain skill is developed in students by using physical activities. Since use of mind (psyche) is included in all these motor activities, this domain is called psychomotor. The development of this domain is especially emphasized in training institutions. It also consists of six levels of hierarchy.

1. **Impulsion :** This is the first and the lowest level of the domain. Here the student tries to do in the same manner as he sees. It is totally based on imitation. For example, pupil teacher imitates the demonstration teaching of the teacher trainer. Copying the alphabet from the book or drawing a picture from another book or improving the handwriting by seeing the blackboard writing of the teacher are some other examples of impulsion.
2. **Manipulation :** It is an indicative of the creative potential of the pupil. Here, he not only imitates the others but endeavours to do something new. For example, he introduces some new points in his teaching which are not given in the book. This manipulation is, however, not necessary to be correct. We may call it the initial effort of a trainee.
3. **Control :** Control is achieved by the coordination of various motor organs i.e., the learner does not commit mistake here. He can draw the picture of a cow without looking at it, he can write the correct spelling of a word and so on.
4. **Coordination :** Here full coordination is obtained between mind and other motor organs. This is the perfection stage of the control. Whatever a student does here is perfect in every respect. He works so nicely that his task is liked by the people, e.g., excellence in games activities, decoration job, effective teaching by a pupil teacher, driving a motor bike or cycle etc.
5. **Naturalization :** At this stage he can do a work in whatever manner he likes. Here, perfection is shown without using the mind fully or without doing any deliberate efforts, e.g., jumping 1 feet as a target, writing correct spelling without using the power of recall and so on.
6. **Habit formation :** This is the last level of psychomotor domain. This stage shows full maturity and habitual action on the part of students. Mind is not used here at all. For example, we sometimes, think something while going on a bicycle on the road even then our bicycle goes in a right manner and we do not fall. This is called habit formation. Speaking a foreign language fluently is another example of habit formation.

The above discussion shows that psychomotor domain exclusively depends on practice and drill. The more the practice is made, the greater will be the habit formation.

## (C) WRITING OBJECTIVES IN BEHAVIOURAL TERMS

This is the third and last stage of planning of teaching. Once the objectives are formulated, it is also necessary to write them in behavioural change of learners only then teaching tasks can be evaluated correctly. Why objectives are to be written in behavioural terms can be understood by the following points :

I. In order to check the teaching work to be deviated from the main track.
II. In order to create coordination between teaching and learning process.
III. In order to select suitable teaching strategies and techniques.
IV. In order to construct a reliable and valid achievement test.
V. In order to evaluate the objectives objectively to make sure whether objectives are achieved or not.
VI. In order to modify some strategies if some objectives are not achieved.
VII. In order to compare the behaviour of the teacher and the taught.

## Methods of Writing Objectives

If we have to write objectives of the lesson "Metals and Non-metals" of class VIIIth and we have to include knowledge to analysis objectives in our teaching, these objectives will be written in the following manner.

1. *Knowledge :* (I) Students will know the definitions of metals and non-metals (II) Students will know the features of metals and non-metals.
2. *Comprehension :* Students will learn to classify the metals and non-metals on the basis of their definitions and characteristics.
3. *Application :* Students will learn to use these metals and non-metals in their life on the basis of their uses.
4. *Analysis :* In order to know the similarities and differences between metals and non-metals, students will study the characteristics of metals and non-metals separately.

Thus, we see that action verbs are used to write the objectives in behavioural terms. There are, however, five historical bases of writing objectives in behavioural terms.

1. **Drecker (1954) :** He is of the view that managing of teaching is a dynamic concept. So, activities of management should be explained in the light of objectives only. It means that teaching strategies should coincide with the teaching objectives.
2. **Bloom (1956) :** The evaluation system of B.S. Bloom stresses more on objectives than content. Here objectives are written in the form of action verbs and every question evaluates any one of the specific objectives.
3. **Robert Mager (1962) :** He has stressed the need to concentrate on cognitive and affective domains both. He also gives importance to action verbs instead of mental processes. He has given the following methods of writing objectives:

   I. First, behaviour should be identified with specific name.
   II. Then by interpreting and Analysing the situation, the desired behaviour should be defined in clear terms.
   III. Lastly, the teacher should see to what extent the behaviour which is manifesting, is acceptable. It means that modified behaviour is to be compared with the criterion measures.

   Mager's scheme has some defects such as,

   - Actions have been over stressed here. Thus, it has ignored mental processes altogether.
   - The same action verb is included in more than one level of objectives. T his creates a confusion before the teacher e.g.,
     (i) Student will learn to define atom.(knowledge objective)
     (ii) Student will learn to analyse atom (Comprehension objective)
4. **Robert Miller (1962) :** He has stressed more on writing objectives of psychomotor domain. This scheme analyses the skill first, then stresses to develop each segment of the skill. He has given the following method of writing objectives.

   I. An indicator should be created first. Action will take place on this indicator, e.g., determining the length or height of a jump, formulating the criterion of a good hand writing etc.
   II. Then stimulus is to be applied on this very indicator (criterion).
   III. After that action will be performed.
   IV. Lastly, if the action (performance) is according to the criterion already fixed, then feedback will be given.
5. **RCEM Scheme (1972) :** The method given by Regional College of Education, Mysore, India is

called RCEM scheme. This scheme stresses on processes rather than output (reverse of Bloom's scheme). Objectives of all the three domains can be written by this scheme. Here, Bloom's taxonomy of cognitive domain has been classified into four broad categories only. Then these categories have been sub-divided into 17 groups in the manner given below :

| Categories of objectives | Processes involved |
|---|---|
| 1. Knowledge | I Recognition |
| | II Recall |
| 2. Comprehension | III Seeing relationship |
| | IV Giving examples |
| | V Differentiating |
| | VI Classification |
| | VII Explanation |
| | VIII Verification |
| | IX Generalization |
| 3. Application | X Logical power |
| | XI Formulation of hypothesis |
| | XII Establishing (testing) the hypothesis |
| | XIII Drawing conclusion |
| | XIV Perfection |
| 4. Creativity | XV Analysis |
| | XVI Synthesis |
| | XVII Evaluation |

Thus, we see that this scheme is more practical in writing objectives in behavioural terms. Important characteristic features of this scheme are given below:

I. It is very easy to write objectives in the language of behavioural change of learners by this scheme.

II. The objectives which are written by this scheme are more clear and definite.

III. Objectives of all the three domains can be written by this scheme.

IV. This scheme stresses the process rather than output. Thus, it is more comprehensive than other schemes given above and modification in the teaching learning process can be made at any stage here.

**Cognitive objectives and Associated Action Verbs**

| Objective | Associated Action Verbs | | |
|---|---|---|---|
| 1. Knowledge | Define | Write | Underline |
| | State | Recall | Select |
| | List | Recognize | Reproduce |
| | Name | Label | Measure |
| 2. Comprehension | Identify | Illustrate | Explain |
| | Justify | Represent | Judge |
| | Select | Name | Contrast |
| | Indicate | Formulate | Classify |
| 3. Application | Predict | Choose | Construct |
| | Select | Find | Compute |
| | Assess | Show | Use |
| | Explain | Demonstrate | Perform |
| 4. Analysis | Analyse | Select | Justify |
| | Identify | Separate | Resolve |
| | Conclude | Compare | Break-down |
| | Differentiate | Contrast | Criticize |
| 5. Synthesis | Combine | Argue | Select |
| | Restate | Discuss | Relate |
| | Summarize | Organize | Generalize |
| | Precise | Derive | Conclude |
| 6. Evaluation | Judge | Support | Identify |
| | Evaluate | Defend | Avoid |
| | Determine | Attack | Select |
| | Recognize | Criticize | Choose |

# Methods and Strategies of Teaching

## INTRODUCTION

The biggest challenge before a teacher is the presentation of a lesson. If this presentation is effective, students can reach the goals of life by the acquisition of knowledge and if the teacher is unsuccessful in his presentation, it is impossible to reach the educational objectives. Therefore, how to teach is the biggest problem before a teacher.

Three terminologies are used with reference to the problem of how to teach.

### 1. Method of Teaching

Method of teaching is directly related to the presentation of the lesson. Which method of teaching a teacher should use depends on the nature of subject-matter and the tacts of the teacher. There are four methods of presenting a subject-matter generally used.

(a) *Telling methods* : Lecture method, discussion method, story telling method and so on.

(b) *Doing methods :* Project method, problem solving method, text-book method and so on.

(c) *Visual methods :* Demonstration method, supervised study method and so on.

(d) *Mental methods :* Inductive, deductive, analysis, synthesis methods etc.

### 2. Strategies of Teaching

Strategy is the art and science of directing and controlling the movements and activities of the army. If strategy is good, we can get victory over our enemies. In teaching this term is meant those procedures and methods by which objectives of teaching are realised in the class.

**Stone and Morris** have defined teaching strategy in the following words :

"Teaching strategy is a generalized plan for a lesson which includes structure, instructional objectives and an outline of planned tactics, necessary to implement the strategy".

It is clear from the above definition that :

I. Teaching strategy is the generalized plan of the whole lesson plan.

II. It consists of structure of teaching, objectives of teaching and techniques of evaluation of teaching.

III. In strategy of teaching, realization of objectives is given more importance than presentation of the lesson.

IV. A strategy does not follow a single track all the time but it changes according to the demand of the situation such as age, level, needs, interests and abilities of students. Thus, strategy is more comprehensive than method.

V. It is directional in nature. It refers to goal directed activities of the teacher. Thus, it is more close to science than arts.

### 3. Tactics of Teaching

It is that procedure by which new knowledge is fixed in the minds of students permanently. For this purpose, a teacher does extra activities in the class. These activities help the teacher to take shift from one strategy to another. Thus, teaching tactics are related to that behaviour of the teacher which he manifests in the class, ie, the development of teaching strategies, giving proper stimulus for timely responses, drilling the learnt responses, increasing the responses by extra activities and so on.

### Difference between Teaching Method and Teaching Strategy

Strategy and method both are similar in procedure and format but even then they are different from each other in the following ways :

1. Teaching method is limited to the presentation of the subject-matter but when we try to achieve some objectives by any method, it becomes strategy.
2. No single method can never be described as teaching strategy. Strategy is actually a combination of different methods. For example, lecture or text-book or question answer methods can never be used separately. In order to make a strategy successful, other strategies will necessarily be included in it.
3. Teaching method is a macro approach while teaching strategy is a micro approach.
4. Teaching method considers teaching as an art while strategy considers it as science. That is why it prefers the application of psychology, natural science and technology in teaching.
5. The purpose of teaching method is effective presentation of the subject-matter while the purpose of teaching strategy is to create conducive learning environment in the class.
6. Teaching method is based on the classical theory of human organisation while strategy is based on modern theory of human organisation. For example, lecture is a teaching method but when this method is used to achieve certain predetermined objectives, it becomes strategy of teaching.
7. Work is important in methods while in strategy of teaching behaviour of teachers and students and their mutual relationship are important.

Thus, we see that methods and strategies, despite being the same are different. In Educational Technology the terminology of strategy is used in place of method.

## TYPES OF TEACHING STRATEGIES

Selection of strategies for teaching depends on the nature of organisation of human activities. We can divide different teaching strategies (methods) into two categories.

**Note :** We will use the word "Method" instead of "Strategy" for the sake of convenience here.

## (A) AUTOCRATIC TEACHING STRATEGIES

These methods are also called teacher-centred methods. Here teacher exercises full control over his students and they are given least chance to act freely in the class. They can do in the class only what they are allowed to do. Teacher tries to insert the titbits of knowledge in the minds of pupils and pupils listen to what the teacher says almost silently. They are not given liberty to express themselves.

Important autocratic methods of teaching are given below :

### 1. Story Telling Method :

In this method the teacher tells the students any real story or anecdote about the great men or women like rulers, social reformers, prophets, saints, artists, scientists, discoverers, etc in order to develop the qualities of truth, honesty, perseverance, courage, cooperation, humbleness or creativity in them. These stories and anecdotes are directly or indirectly related to the lesson. Teacher colours the story by his tacts or communication skills and presents it before his students in such a manner that students are completely absorbed in the story for the time being. They are so absorbed in the story that they consider themselves an important part of the story by identifying any of its characters. What type of stories should be told to the students in the class depend on the mental and chronological age and interest of students and the nature of the lesson.

**Suggestions :** In order to make this method a success, a teacher must keep the following points into consideration:

I. Story should be interesting to the students.
II. There should be natural sequence in the incident while telling the story. Sequence break or skipping should not be there in the story.
III. Incidents should be narrated in such a manner as they look real for the listeners.
IV. Characters of the story should be properly elaborated and compared to the present life situation.
V. The story should be full of actions and these actions should be expressed by the teacher.
VI. The method of telling the story should be interesting and living and phrases and figures of speech should also be used here and there.
VII. The story should be purposeful and not waste of time.

**Advantages :** Important advantages of this method are as follows :

I. It increases the interests of pupils in the lesson.
II. It increases and improves the vocabulary of pupils.
III. It becomes easy for the pupils to understand the lesson after the story.
IV. Imaginative powers of students also increase.
V. Good qualities, manners and etiquettes can be developed in students through the stories.
VI. The dullness of the environment can be removed.

**Application :** This method can be especially used in teaching languages and subject of social sciences.

## 2. Textbook Method :

In this method, the teacher reads the text-book loudly and explains the difficult points wherever necessary. Sometimes student are also asked to read the text-book and their reading skill is developed by rectifying their pronunciations. The main purpose of this method is to enable the students to get mastery over the textual matter.

In teaching languages the teacher first read a para from the book loudly, then he writes the difficult words on the blackboard to be pronounced by the students. He can give some clue to them to pronounce these words correctly. After that students imitate the reading of the teacher. Then meaning of the difficult words are given to students by suing devices such as using antonym or synonym or using the word in an easy life related sentence or showing a picture that is clarifying the meaning of the word. After that para is explained in easy understandable language line by line. Lastly, comprehensive questions are asked from the para and their satisfactory answers is technically known as effective teaching provided that almost all levels of cognitive domain have been covered by these questions.

**Suggestions :** A teacher should take the following points into account in order to use this method effectively.

I. Text-books are only means not ends. So, in order to realise the objectives the teacher should not rely and depend on text books only. He should take the help of other materials also.
II. A teacher should also take the help of reference books for teaching a particular subject.
III. Comprehension of the textual material should be stressed while reading the text-book.
IV. Comprehensive questions must be asked after explaining the textual matter.
V. Students should be given proper time and chance to write down the important points in the midst of teaching.
VI. Model reading of the teacher must be very effective and attractive.

**Advantages :** Merits of this method are given below:

I. Text-books are prepared keeping in view the specific needs and interests of students. Thus, this method can fulfil the needs of students.
II. Text-books present the facts and informations correctly and their presentation is also logical and systematic.
III. Students learn the application of subject-matter through revision exercises given at the end of each lesson.
IV. Text-books give clear direction and guideline to a teacher regarding what to teach in the class without deviating from the main content and topic.
V. Comprehension abilities and skills which are developed in students by teaching them through this method help the students to learn other subject also.
VI. It increases the vocabulary of students.
VII. They come to know the way of presentation of any subject-matter.

**Application :** This method of teaching can be used in teaching any school subject but if the teacher is not highly competent, it will prove to be the most abused method.

## 3. Lecture Method

It is an old teaching method. In this method a teacher delivers a lecture on different points of any topic in a serial order and asks several questions from the students in the middle of his lecture in order to draw their attention properly. He comes to the class with full preparation for lecture and lays much stress on the logical and sequential presentation of the content during lecture.

**Suggestion :** A teacher must keep the following points in mind while using lecture as a successful method of teaching in the class:

I. The content of the lecture should be systematized in a logical and sequential manner and listeners should not find any gap in the content.

II. The language of the lecture should be easy, clear and understandable to students and questions should also be asked by the teacher during lecture for seeking concentration of pupils.

III. In order to make the presentation of the content effective, material aids such as chart, graph, map, picture etc should also be used along with lecture and important points should be written on the blackboard.

IV. Illustrations should also be given in order to clarify the difficult points of the subject-matter.

V. There should be a sufficient flow in the lecture and for this purpose no help should be taken from books or notes during lecture.

VI. Lecture should not be too long to be boring. Only short lecture is recommended for school boys.

VII. Lectures make the classroom environment dull and serious. A teacher should minimize this seriousness and dullness by light and humorous talks also here and there.

VIII. There should be complete peacefulness in the class.

**Advantages :** Important advantages of this method are given below :

I. It is the incumbency of the teacher to use this method in his teaching. He can not avoid this method whatsoever other method he is using.

II. For introducing any new lesson in the class, lecture is an easy and effective method.

III. Cognitive as well as affective domain of pupil's behaviour can be developed through this method.

IV. More content can be presented to students in lesser amount of time through lecture method.

V. It lays much stress on presentation. So, it can develop the ability of presentation in students also.

VI. If lecture is living, it can motivate the students for self-study.

VII. Habit of concentration for a longer period of time can be developed in students by this method.

**Application :** All the school subjects including mathematics can be taught through this method.

**Precaution :** Lecture method should not be used in an isolated manner. It should rather be used as a supplement to other methods.

## 4. Demonstration Method

In this method, teacher shows all the activities given in the lesson to the students as an action and explains the important points before them during demonstration. A teacher follows three steps here.

(a) In the first step he introduces the lesson by question-answer or lecture method.

(b) In the second step he demonstrates each and every aspect of the lesson and develops it by his activities. For example, if he is teaching the characteristics of $CO_2$, he will show how it extinguishes the fire or how it turns lime water milky.

(c) In the third step, he makes the students drill of the subject-matter for the purpose of assimilation. He asks evaluative questions here. Thus, desired skill is developed in students by imitation of action.

**Suggestion :** A teacher while using this method of teaching should keep the following suggestions into his mind.

I. Teacher should prepare well what and how he has to demonstrate in the class.

II. Students should be given enough chance to remove their doubts after the demonstration of the lesson is over.

III. After the teacher's activity is over, students should be asked to repeat the demonstration for the purpose of drill.

IV. Important points should be explained by delivering short lectures during the process of demonstration.

V. The total demonstration process should be divided into different phases and students should be continuously evaluated after every phase.

**Merits :** This method is used in teaching because of its following merits :

I. It is very much helpful in teaching skills in training institutions.

II. The lower and middle level of objectives of cognitive and psychomotor domains can easily be achieved through this method.

III. This method is especially useful for teaching science subject in schools because laws, principles and concepts of these subjects can not be clarified without demonstrating them in the class.

IV. Every practical work in craft, science or agriculture needs demonstration.

V. Observation and thinking capacities of students can be developed by this method.

VI. Senses of students can also be trained by this method.

**Application :** This method is especially applicable in teaching, science, crafts, arts and agriculture.

## 5. Tutorial Method

In this method, the whole class is divided into different groups of common features. This bifurcation is made on the basis of difficulty level of different subjects. Then every group is handed to different teachers separately. Here teacher finds out the individual problem of students and then he individually guides them to remove these problems. If difficulties of the whole group are similar, group teaching and group guidance can be given.

**Suggestion :** In order to make this method a success, the following suggestions must be taken into account:

I. Students of same capacity or same weakness should be kept in the same group in order to minimize the number of groups in the class.

II. The behaviour of the teacher should be unbiased at the time of guidance so that every student may get equal chance of progress.

III. Tutorial teaching should be done by experienced and expert teachers so that the problem of students can really be removed.

IV. Every student should be motivated to tell his problems frankly. Only then they can get the benefit of this method.

**Types of Tutorial teaching :**

(a) *Supervised tutorial teaching :* In this method bright students discuss their problems with their teacher and weak students are asked to do drill work after removing their difficulties. This system is more close to democratic method of teaching than autocratic ones.

(b) *Group tutorial :* In this technique, a teacher tries to remove the difficulties of average students. This is needed when level of classroom teaching is low or unsatisfactory from the point of view of students.

(c) *Practical tutorial :* In this system students work with their teacher in the laboratory. Psychomotor domain of students' behaviour is especially developed through this approach.

**Advantages :** Main advantages of this method are as follows :

I. This is a type of remedial teaching which is especially useful to bring the weak students to the average level.

II. In this method teacher can teach in the class keeping the individual differences of learners due to very small size of the class.

III. The absence of previous knowledge of students can be compensated through this method.

IV. Here every student can get chance to express his problems openly and individually.

**Application :** This method can be used in teaching all the school subjects. This method is especially useful for teaching natural science and mathematics.

## (B) DEMOCRATIC TEACHING STRATEGIES

These strategies (methods) are child centred in which a teacher teaches in the class keeping the interests, attitudes, capacities and needs of learners into account. These methods of teaching can develop the affective domain of students along with cognitive domain. In these methods maximum interaction between teachers and students in the class is seen. Here students as well as teachers are equally active in the class. The purpose of these methods is all-round development of learners. Teachers works as a helper and guide for his students here. Important methods are as follows:

## 1. Question-Answer Method

The propounder of this method is famous Greek philosopher, Socrates. In this method subject-matter is presented before the students through questioning. Here some questions are framed on the basis of previous knowledge of students first. Then these questions are asked from the students in such a manner that interest and curiosity of students increase by the answer of these questions. All these questions are inter-related and effort is made by the teacher to give a small bit of knowledge through these questions also.

The assumption of this method is that knowledge can be drawn out from within the individual by asking questions in sequence.

**Suggestions :** A teacher should take the following points into consideration also if he wants to make this method a success:

I. Questions should be so framed that they give some new knowledge to students on one hand and students can easily answer them.
II. Questions should be asked from the whole class. Targetting some students for questioning is wrong.
III. Every question should be answered by at least two students and then both of them should be reinforced together.
IV. When no student is able to answer a question, exposition must be given immediately. If all questions are answered without difficulty, there is no need of giving exposition.
V. The questions should be interesting and full of curiosity.
VI. Language of questions should be easy and direct. No question should have more than one answer.
VII. Feedback should be given to students at every correct answer.
VIII. Every question should be directly related to the next one, i.e., there should not be any gap between questions.
IX. Students should also be given chance to ask questions from their teachers.
X. No such questions should be asked whose answer starts with yes or no.
XI. There should not be any repetition of questions.

**Advantages :** Main advantages of this method are given below :

I. While asking questions, needs, interests, mental level and feelings of students are taken into account. Thus, the method is based on psychological principles.
II. Students and teachers both are active here and maximum interaction is possible in the class.
III. Here students can get more chance of self-learning.
IV. If a teacher teaches any class by this method, there will be no problem of indiscipline in the class. It is because questioning makes the students alert all the time.
V. Cognitive as well as affective both types of objectives can be achieved by this method of teaching.

**Application :** It can be applied to all school subjects except music, art, dance etc.

## 2. Discussion Method

It is also an oral method like question-answer and maximum interaction between a teacher and students can be seen here. Discussion can be formal as well as informal. Formal discussion are arranged for the purpose of achieving pre-determined objectives. In that case rules of the discussions are also pre-determined. On the other hand, informal discussions are neither objectives oriented nor rules are pre-determined. Teacher and students discuss the issue in the class whenever it becomes necessary.

In formal discussion teacher divides the class into different groups and gives the topic of discussion to each group. Every group has a leader to anchor and conduct the discussion. It is the leader who raises new topics of discussion. In the end, teacher draws the conclusion of the discussion with the help of leaders.

Thus, we see that students are more active in the class in this method of teaching. The teacher plays the role of a guide or helper only.

**Suggestions :** The success of this method lies in the adaptation of the following points :

I. Efforts should be made to motivate all the students to take part in the discussion. Even mute students should be encouraged to actively take part in the discussion.

II. Students criticize one another during discussion in the class. A teacher should accept only those criticisms which are really logical and meaningful.
III. Students should anchor the discussion themselves. Teacher should be there in the class only as a guide.
IV. A teacher should select the topic for discussion only with the help of students.
V. Students who have leadership qualities should be selected for anchoring.
VI. Only those topics should be selected for discussion which have any relevance to the life of students.

**Advantages :**

I. Thinking and communicating powers of students can be developed through this method.
II. Leadership qualities can be developed in students.
III. The expression abilities of students can be developed through this method.
IV. Here students find out the solution of the problem themselves. It develops the creative potentials of students.
V. The attitudes and interest of students can be drawn out towards learning though this method.
VI. Higher level cognitive and affective objectives can be realised through classroom discussions.

**Application :** This method can be used in teaching all the subjects except mathematics, arts, music, dance etc.

## 3. Heuristic Method

Heurism literally means "I discover". In this method of teaching students learn themselves. Teacher raises problematic situation before the students. He also guides them from where they will get materials to the solution of the problems. Every student discovers the solution of the problem individually by trial and error method. Five steps are technically involved in this method.

(a) Presentation of the problem by the teacher to be solved in the class individually.
(b) Giving information by the teacher about the materials and techniques that is helpful in the solution of the problem.
(c) Formulation of the hypothesis by the students themselves.
(d) Collection of data by the students for testing the hypothesis.
(e) Testing the hypothesis-accepting the true hypothesis and rejecting the false one.

**Suggestion :** A teacher should keep the following suggestions into account while using this method :

I. Teachers should help the students in formulating the hypothesis.
II. Teacher should also help the students in gathering the resources for the solution of the problem.
III. Doubts of the students should also be removed by the teacher in all the five steps mentioned above.
IV. Students should be given chance to go further themselves on the basis of trial and error theory of learning.

**Advantages :**

I. In this method students obtain knowledge through self-study and self-learning. As a result, knowledge obtained is stable and permanent.
II. In this method students learn something through investigation and research. This gives a direction to scientific attitude of students.
III. This method increases the self-confidence of students. This can help them to solve the real problem of life later on.
IV. It motivates the students to accept newer and newer challenges.
V. Highest level of cognitive objectives can be achieved through this method.

**Application :** This method is especially useful in teaching mathematics and science subjects.

## 4. Discovery Method

This method differs from heuristic method in the following ways :

I. This method is used in social science subjects to clarify the facts and concepts before the pupils while heuristic method is used in science subjects to formulate or testify laws and principles.
II. In this method, facts and concepts are explained in an objective manner while in

heuristic method subject-matter is comprehended subjectively.

III. Discovery is related to the past events while heurism is concerned with the phenomenon at present.

For example "Causes of Aurangzeb's failure in South India" is a discovery and "causes of low productivity of agricultural lands in India" is a heuristic method.

In spite of the differences given above the forms and procedures of both the methods are the same. Hence, merits and demerits of these two methods of teaching are also the same.

## 5. Project Method

This method was propounded by **W.H.Kilpatric.** Here pupils are assigned such a project to be done which has direct utility for students as well as teachers. Students work on the project under the guidance of their teacher and find out the solution of the problem on the basis of their own experience.

The difference between heuristic method and project method is that in heuristic method students solve the problems individually while in project method collective approach is followed by the students.

The second difference is that the problem given in the form of the project is real while the problem of heurism may real as well as imaginary.

The third difference is that the approach of heurism is analytical while that of project method is productive. Here something useful is created in physical form.

**Types of Projects**

(a) ***Constructive Projects :*** In such type of projects pupils work physically in or outside the class, such as writing letters or essays on given topics, preparing fields for games, playing drama, preparing models and so on.

(b) ***Aesthetic Projects :*** Appreciation powers of students are developed through such projects, such as presentation of music programmes, decorating a hall, beautification of lawn and so on.

(c) **Problematic Projects :** Students learn the solutions of life related problems through such projects, such as studying the effects of balanced diet on health, advantages of physical exercises on body fitness, causes of family disputes and their solutions and so on.

(d) **Drill Project :** Working capacities and automation of students are increased through such projects such as filling in the map, colouring the arts and pictures, solving mathematical sums and so on.

**Principles and Characteristics of Project Method :** A teacher should keep the following principles into account before assigning any project to his students :

1. ***Principles of Purpose :*** A project must have some educational purpose to be served. A project without purpose is only wastage of time.
2. ***Principle of Utility :*** A project must have some utility for students as well as the society.
3. ***Principle of Freedom :*** Students should be given full freedom in the selection of the project as well as working on a project.
4. ***Principle of Activity :*** A project must involve some activity on the part of students. They should learn something only by doing.
5. ***Principle of reality :*** The problem given in the project should be real and directly related to real life situations. Imaginary problems are not taken up in such projects.
6. ***Principles of Prior Planning :*** Teacher should do proper planning in advance as to how the project is to be completed to benefit the students and the society.

**Steps involved in Project method :** Project method of teaching consists of the following steps :

1. ***Creating Situation :*** Teacher creates such a situation in the class that students propose themselves to work on the project, i.e. high level of motivation is found in students. After that the teacher tells them the method and procedure of the project.
2. ***Selection of the Project :*** Project is selected only after taking above six principles into consideration. Teacher helps the students to select a project on the basis of their interests.
3. ***Planning :*** At this step, teacher discusses the students about the various points of the project.

Students openly take part in the discussion. After the discussions is over, teacher writes down the whole programme of action stepwise on the black-board Grouping is also done here.

4. ***Execusion :*** At this step students, first of all, collect relevant facts, information and material. Then each group works on the project separately and completes it within time limit.
5. ***Evaluation :*** When a project gets completed, it is first criticized and evaluated by the students themselves in their respective groups. When they are fully satisfied with their job it is reported to the teacher.
6. ***Reporting :*** In the last step, the students write down each and every step of the project, i.e., how they did it is noted down in words. After that the project and the report are submitted to the teacher.

**Advantages :** The main advantages of the project method are given below :

*(i)* ***Based on Principles of learning :*** This method of teaching is based on three important principles of learning :

*(a)* Law of readiness- A student should be assigned a work only when he is ready to do it.

*(b)* Law of exercise- If a learnt material is repeated again and again, learning becomes stable.

*(c)* Law of effect- When students complete some tasks themselves in suitable learning conditions, they get satisfied.

*(ii)* ***Related to real life situations :*** Through this method of teaching students learn how to solve the problems of real life.

*(iii).* ***Work experience :*** Students get the real experience of working by their projects and the learning which is associated with doing is more stable and meaningful.

*(iv).* ***Inculcation of democratic values in students :*** Students learn cooperation, tolerance and mutual acceptance through this method.

*(v).* ***A boon for weak students :*** Here students work on a project in groups collectively. As a result, weak students also get chance to rise academically.

**Demerits**

*(i)* The main demerit of this method is that it is very much time consuming.

*(ii)* Every subject-matter can not be taught through this method, i.e, its applicability is very limited.

*(iii)* Individual evaluation of students' performance is not possible here.

**Application:** Limited applicability of this method is possible in almost all the subjects.

## 6. Role playing Method

In this method students are given chance to play the role of the teacher in the class. Thus, it becomes a dramatic method. Teacher first of all teaches the topic then he calls out the students on the blackboard one by one to teach the same topic to the class. When a student teaches, all his class-mates answer his questions. They also note down the shortcomings of the student teacher. This teaching is criticized later and suggestions for improvement are given.

Dramas in literature can also be taught through this method where various students play the roles of different characters and lesson is comprehended by other students.

Role playing method is especially used in teachers training colleges. Here six steps are followed by the teacher :

*(i)* In the first step outline of the role playing programme is prepared.

*(ii)* In the second step the pupil teacher decides as to when and how he has to play the role of a teacher, role of a student and role of an observer.

*(iii)* Topic to be taught is selected in the third step. Teaching strategies, techniques and skills to be used in teaching that particular topic are also determined in advance.

*(iv)* Observation procedure and techniques are selected in the fourth step.

*(v)* In the fifth step, the outline of the observation is prepared and observation is noted down in that format.

*(vi)* Lastly, after the teaching is over, teaching of a particular pupil is criticized and suggestions for improvement are given.

**Suggestions :** In order to make this method a success, a teacher should keep the following points into account:

*(i)* Subject teacher should also be present in the class at the time of role play.

*(ii)* Subject teacher should also be there in the class at the time of criticism so that he may give appropriate suggestions to students.

*(iii)* The topic of teaching for the purpose of role playing should be the same for all students so that comparison is possible.

*(iv)* All the observers should note down the shortcomings of all teachers selected for the purpose. Discussion based on memory and recall is not recommended.

**Advantages :**

*(i)* Repeated teaching of the same topic increases learning.

*(ii)* Practice makes a man perfect and critical observation makes a man alert.

*(iii)* It increases the social skill of students.

*(iv)* Students learn the methods of analysis, synthesis and evaluation.

*(v)* It develops the critical powers of students.

*(vi)* Students can remove their own mistakes through imitations.

## 7. Brain Storming

The assumption of this method of teaching is that a group of people can give more ideas than a single person. In this way, the problem can be analysed and evaluated more comprehensively.

In this method of teaching, a problem is given to students and they are asked to put forward their views on this problem one by one. Thus, many views regarding the nature of the problem, its causes and possible solutions come to light. Conclusion can be drawn after evaluating these jumbled ideas.

**Suggestions :**

*(i)* This is a problem-centred method. Hence, the problem should be meaningful and related to real life situations.

*(ii)* All types of views of students should be welcomed and relevant views should be isolated from them later on.

III. The views of students should either be written or tapped.

**Merits :**

*(i)* Cognitive and affective both types of objectives can be achieved through this method.

*(ii)* Good ideas can be inculcated in students through this method.

*(iii)* Imaginative power of students can be developed through this method.

## 8. Bloom's Mastery Learning Strategy

This method was developed by B.S. Bloom. The purpose of this method is to take the students to that level where they do not lag behind their teacher for the topic taught to them. It means they have got mastery over the subject-matter. All the strategies, techniques and tactics of teaching are used here simultaneously and additional time is given for the remedial teaching of weak students.

Following steps are involved in this method of teaching :

*(i)* First of all subject-matter is divided into different learning units.

*(ii)* Separate objectives are formulated for separate learning units in the second step.

*(iii)* In the third step mastery level of each learning units is determined. In order to reach this level every student must score 80%-85% marks.

*(iv)* General teaching for every unit is done in the fourth step.

*(v)* In the fifth step achievement of students is tested after teaching is over. This test will reveal that how many students have reached the mastery level.

*(vi)* Diagnostic test is conducted for those students in the next step who have not reached the mastery level. This test will reveal and locate the difficulty points for these students.

*(vii)* In the seventh step remedial teaching is arranged for weak students who have not reached the mastery level. Extra time is also given to them. Sometimes tutorial classes are arranged for these students.

*(viii)* In the last step all the students are tested again and they are now categorised on the basis of their performance.

## 9. Seminar

This is an effective device to increase the self-study of students and to bring depth in their studies and knowledge. In this technique all the students are given a topic first. Then they are asked to prepare detailed matter on that topic. Students prepare a detailed paper after reading different types of books, or carrying out experiments in the laboratory or through a survey. Every student reads his paper in the seminar. All the other participants raise critical questions after the completion of each paper in the seminar. If paper reader is successful to answer all the questions here and he is able to satisfy all the listeners, his paper is considered good. In this way, all the students present their papers one by one and finally the conclusion of the seminar is presented by the expert.

**This method of self-learning has the following advantages :**

I. Students get inspirations for learning.

II. The critical and evaluative powers of students increase.

III. It increases the depth and comprehensiveness of knowledge of students.

IV. They come to know how they can put their views before the people in a logical manner.

V. They are also practiced to hear the criticism of others. Thus, tolerance which is an important quality for a teacher becomes the part of his behaviour.

# 10

# Communication Process

## MEANING OF COMMUNICATION

The process of understanding what is in the minds of others when expressed and making the others understand what we express is called communication. The communicator used either words or symbols or a combination of both for this purpose along with logic. This requires suitable techniques and strategies and thus communication becomes possible.

### Definitions

1. **Newmar and Summer :** Communication is an exchange of ideas, facts, opinions or emotions by two or more persons.
2. **Meferland :** Communication is the process of meaningful interactions among human being.
3. **Theo Haiman :** Communication is the process of passing information and understanding from one person to another. It is the process of imparting ideas and making oneself understood by others.
4. **Louis A Alen :** Communication is the sum/total of all those things which a person does in order to make his ideas well understood by others. It is personal but continuous process to tell, to listen and to understand.

### Characteristics of Communication

1. Communication is a bipolar process. One person speaks or writes and the other person listens or reads.
2. Emotions are also made understood by communication along with ideas and facts. Thus, communication is a psychological process.
3. Communication is a meaningful interaction among humans. It means that whatever we speak or does, it is understood by others.
4. Sometimes additional activities are also required to make communication possible. These activities are also parts of communication.
5. Communication is a continuous and comprehensive process. It means that speaking listening and understanding, all three activities go together. If any of these activities stops, communications will stand still.
6. Communication process is fulfilled only when receiver of the message takes the same meaning from the message as was taken by the sender. This requires that receiver must send his reaction after receiving the message.
7. Communication can be written, oral and symbolic. Immediate feedback is possible in case of oral communication but it will take time to react to written or symbolic communication. Due to this reason it is necessary that written communication must be performed with great care. If receiver of the message has derived some other meaning from the message, the very purpose of communication will be defeated.
8. Communication is an instinctive process. So, no prior assessment of the process is possible. It is clear from other characteristics that communication as an interactive process is very close to teaching. Success of teaching lies in the success of communication.

## TYPES(MODES) OF COMMUNICATION

There are basically two modes of communication :

### 1. Non-Verbal Communication

In this type of communication, instead of using words only symbols are used. The receiver of the message necessarily knows these symbols, so he reacts to them at proper time. Raising hand by the teacher to instruct the students to keep quite and sign language used in shorthand are few examples of non-verbal communication.

Non-verbal communication uses body language like blinking eyes, gestures, smiling, weeping etc.

Non-verbal communication uses signs and symbols, e.g., triangle is denoted by D, a is understood as the first alphabet of English etc.

**Characteristics of non-verbal communication:**

1. This type of communication is sometimes proved more powerful and effective than verbal communication. For example, if it is not possible to send our oral message to a crowd which is creating a lot of noise, we can instruct them to keep quite by just raising our hand.
2. If non-verbal communication is used along with verbal communication, we can win full attention of the receivers and thus, it can reduce the problem of communication barrier to a great extent.
3. Non-verbal communication is very useful to make the message precise. Thus, it can save time too.
4. When we want that no other person except the person in target should understand our message, we uses symbols and signs.
5. Symbols in the form of punctuations give us the real meaning of the text and hence confusion is overcome. For example, if we don't use full stop sign at required place, the textual matter will give us different meaning.
6. Those signs which are created by sounds such as telegraphic language have no other option than to use non-verbal signs for communication.

## 2. Verbal Communication

Verbal communi-cation can be oral or written. Here, use of language is a must.

**(a) Oral Communication :** Mouth and tongue are used for exchange of ideas here. This process of communication can take place either in a face to face situation or on the telephone or on internet. Here sender and receiver both get immediate feedback.

***Characteristics of Oral Communication :***

1. In this method, communicator can at once know whether receiver has understood him or not. Thus, this form of communication has very special role to play in extension of relations. It is, in fact a powerful weapon in the hands of a teacher.
2. This form of communication can be formal and informal both. Here both the parties have full chance of exchange of views here.
3. It is an effective method of impressing the listeners. Politicians very much use this method to befool the public. Teachers uses this method to maintain discipline and pin drop silence in the class.'
4. Confusion is not created in this mode of communication. If it is somehow created, it is removed immediately.
5. It is an effective mode of giving reinforcement to pupils.
6. Oral communication is faster than written one.
7. It is the base of discussion in the academic field.
8. Secrecy of informations can be maintained here. It can not leak out like written communication.

***Limitations of oral communication :***

1. This mode of communication is not possible without direct contact between the sender and the receiver.
2. Both the parties have less time to think here. As a result, matter is altered sometime, which is very harmful for the sender.
3. No pat of oral communication can be presented as a witness in future. Even statements tapped in audio cassettes are not acceptable to the courts as witness. Thus, denial of the statements creates problem.
4. If understanding power of the receiver is poor, he can not understand oral communication at once and thus, the very purpose of communication is defeated/

**(b) Written Communication :** This form of communication uses words and signs both in written form. All print materials and media depend on it. E-Mail is the latest version of written communication.

Since written messages are sent after careful consideration, so, they are more reliable and they can be read again and again.

***Characteristics of written communication :***

1. This mode of communication is generally formal, so it is not ignored. If anybody ignores them, it means that he has deliberately done so.
2. This communication can be presented as proof in future. As a result, nobody dares to ignóre it.
3. Direct contact between sender and receiver is not needed here.
4. Written informations are mostly reliable and clear because they are sent after careful consideration.
5. Messages in written communication can be sent through messengers. Thus, high officials can keep themselves at a distance from their subordinates with the help of this communication.
6. The revolutionary growth in human knowledge that we see today is mostly indebted to invention of printing press which increases written communication.

***Limitations of written communication:***

1. This communication takes much time and energy to reach to the person concerned.
2. It is very difficult to maintain secrecy here.
3. It can create a lot of confusion if something is missing in the matter by mistake.
4. The success of this communication requires that both the parties should be literate

## PRINCIPLES OF EFFECTIVE COMMUNICATION

If whatever is in our mind reaches to the receiver exactly in the same way, communication is said to be effective. This is possible only when seven principles given below which are also known as seven Cs are followed :

1. **Completeness :**The message should be complete in all respects before it is sent. It should give complete answers to all the relevant questions like what, when, who, where, etc. If something can not be clarified without giving examples, then examples must also be given.
2. **Conciseness :** The message should be sent in minimum needed words in order to avoide wastage of time and money. Sign language can also be used for this purpose but completeness should not be compromised.
3. **Consideration :** The messages should always be sent keeping in view the ability, status and emotions of the receiver. It means that language and style of the message will vary according the varying abilities and nature of persons receiving the message.
4. **Concreteness** : The message should be based on concrete facts and informations. If any thing can create confusion in the mind of the receiver, it should be avoided.
5. **Clarity :** The message should be in clear and unambiguous language. Different paragraphs should be used for different facts and informations. Clarity also requires that the language of the message should be close to the language of the receiver. Such words should never be used in communication which have more than one meaning.
6. **Courtesy :** The address of the message should be courteous and should not hurt the self respect of the receiver.
7. **Correctness :** The language of the message should be correct in all respects. If professional language is used in the message, it is better.

### Other principles of effective Communication

Following points must also be kept in mind while making a communication effective :

1. **Multimedia approach :** Multimedia approach should be used by the teacher in order to make communication effective. This approach will attract more than one senses and message will be understood easily.
2. **Improving the listeners :** The success of oral communication will depend upon the listening capacity and attention power of listeners. hence, efforts should be made to improve the audience first. If material is interesting and fulfilling to the needs of the audience, their attention will surely improve.

3. **Belongingness :** Rapport should be developed first before sending any message to the receiver. The message should speak closeness between the sender and the receiver.
4. **Freedom to make choice :** The message should never be imposed on the receiver. The receiver should have choice either to accept it or not. The receiver's own ideas should also be given weightage.
5. **Selection of appropriate mode :**There are different modes of communication. The same mode is not suitable for all types of messages. Hence, suitable mode of communication should be selected keeping in view the objectives of communication.
6. **Selecting appropriate time :** A message becomes important for a receiver only when it reaches to him at proper time; Even a good message, if it reaches at bad time will have opposite result. Suitable time should be selected first before sending any message to the person concerned.

## COMMUNICATION BARRIER OR MISCOM-MUNICATION

When a message does not reach to the receiver in the same way as it was supposed, this is called miscommunication. Such a problem is very common in classroom teaching and pupils understand the message in other way than it was sent to them.

**Definitions :**

1. **Jin Kushal :** Miscommunication is a ruined form of communication in which what is to be communicated does not get communicated and an obstructed form of the message is transmitted.
2. **Mittal and Garg :** Due to various barriers of communication when the message from the sender is not received by the receiver in its original form, such ruined and obstructed form of message is called miscommunication.

### Causes of Miscommunication

1. When proper rapport is not there between the sender and the receiver, and sender is unable to judge the emotions, interests and needs of the receiver, miscommunication is created.
2. When meaning of the message is not clear due to fault on the part of the sender, different people (pupils) will take the message differently.
3. If grammatical mistake like the mistake of punctuation, syntax etc. is there in the message, then it will be very difficult to derive the correct meaning from the message.
4. If sender or receiver or both are biased in any way, then receiver will take out the prejudiced meaning from the message.
5. If receiver is indifferent to the messages he receives due to physical or psychological reasons, the message will not be communicated properly.
6. If receiver is receiving many message at a time, confusion will be created.
7. Lack of sequence in the message also creates miscommunication.
8. If speed of communicating the message is very fast, the receiver will not be able to follow it correctly.

### Chief Barriers of Communication

We can classify important barriers into the following categories :

**1. Semantic Barriers :** Such barriers are created due to language related mistakes such as,

*(i)* Using a particular word in the message with different meaning at different places.
*(ii)* Using a sentence which may have more than one meaning.
*(iii)* Using highly technical words in the message.
*(iv)* Using such technical words which have different meaning in different sciences and disciplines.
*(v)* Using too many phrases and proverbs.
*(vi)* Doing grammatical mistakes.
*(vii)* Using very long and complicated sentences and paragraphs.

**2. Presentation Barriers :** The message must be organised logically, and systematically before it is to be sent. If there is any fault in the organizational structure of the message, miscommunication will be the result, such as,

(i) Including too many facts and information in one para.

(ii) Lack of logical sequence among different facts and informations.

(iii) Preparing the whole message without heading or sub heading.

(iv) The message being very lengthy and boring.

(v) Objectives of communication not clear before the sender etc.

**3. Personal barriers :** These barriers are especially related to either sender or receiver such as

(i) If high officials (teachers) are not treating their subordinates (pupils) properly, the later will not be able to understand the message due to fear or any other reason.

(ii) If rapport is not there between the sender and the receiver, they will not understand each other correctly.

(iii) If medium or source of the message is not efficient or reliable, misunderstanding will be created.

(iv) Lack of confidence between the sender and the receiver also creates miscommunication.

(v) If message has not been sent after careful consideration or preparation due to heavy load of work on the sender, mistakes are possible.

(vi) If receiver is not sensitive to the message, miscommunication will be created.

(vii) Lack of motivation on the part of the receiver is also a type of communication barrier.

**4. Emotional Barriers :** These barriers are related to the emotions of sender and receiver such as,

(i) Mood of the sender at the time of sending the message

(ii) Mood of the receiver at the time of receiving the message.

(iii) Love relationship between the sender and the receiver.

**5. Physical Barriers :** These barriers are related to physical conditions and environment of the sender and the receiver such as,

(i) Noise at the time of oral communication.

(ii) Lack of proper lighting at the time of written or non-verbal communication.

(iii) If the same message is to be sent in different shifts orally as is the case of a teacher, physical barrier will be there.

(iv) If physical distance is there between the sender and the receiver at the time of oral communication.

(v) If there is any defect in the equipment used for communication.

(vi) Sudden noise or explosion at the time of communication.

(vii) Fatigue or staleness on the part of the receiver.

(viii) Health, of the receiver, etc.

**6. Organizational barriers :** These barriers are created due to complexity in the organizational structure of the institution such as,

(i) So many layers of subordinates and officers,

(ii) Inefficiency of the medium who takes the message to the receiver.

(iii) Very rigid and strict disciplinary rules of the institution.

(iv) Lack of availability of communication equipments.

(v) Malfunctioning on the part of the operator or clerks.

## CLASSROOM COMMUNICATION

Verbal and non-verbal both types of communications are used in the classroom. In order to send the message successfully to the pupils, a teacher adopts the following communication strategies in the class.

### 1. Continuous Prose Strategy

This is simple, useful and general method of communication used in every aspect of life. No other methods of communication can be used without taking the help of this strategy. In this method, facts and informations are presented orally. Language and style are especially important here. A teacher should use only that language and style for instruction which are close to the style and language of students on one hand and increase their vocabulary on the other.

Thus, this method is used to teach the students how to speak and write a sentence correctly.

**Suggestions :**

I. This strategy should be used when the structure of the lesson is easy and non-complicated.

II. In order to communicate complex facts and informations, simple and unambiguous language should be used.

III. As far as possible, the teacher should avoide negative sentences.

IV. The teacher should speak the sentences in active voice as far as possible and use of passives should be avoided.

V. Either simple or compound sentences should be used. Complex sentences should be used only when it is needed.

## 2. Heuristic Method of Communication

This is an experimental strategy of communication based on the trial and error theory which is especially used in solving the problems. **Dankur** is the propounder of this strategy. In this strategy, the teacher presents many options (problems) before the students. Students select the best option after careful consideration. For arriving at right conclusion, students can discuss among themselves also and they are also given chance to study the relevant material in this connection.

The major limitations of this strategy is that wrong options are also drilled and retained by the students while using the strategy and arriving at the right option.

## 3. Algorithms

The word 'Algorithms' has been derived from Arabic language which means the order of counting. That is why this method is especially used in mathematics. This method was developed by **Wassons and Jone** of the University of London. Initially this method was used for the presentation of laws and principles of administration and governance. Later on, this method found its application in Education and commerce also.

The major advantage of this method is that laws, principles and elements of content are presented through this method in a logical manner and in order and students follow these very steps(order) in order to solve a problem. For example, if we are going to solve a sum of mathematics, we will have to follow certain pre-determined steps to reach the answer of the sum. When teacher knows algorithms, he clarifies each step pin pointedly and then comes to the next step.

In this method, the teacher uses questioning technique in order to find out the weaknesses of his students. And when next question is asked students come to know whether their answer is right or wrong.

Thus, we see that this strategy is especially suitable for chain learning.

## 4. Decision Table

This decision table was prepared by **Grade** in 1961. It has been proved to be very useful in computer programming so far. **Paker and Davies** used this table in 1969 for solving complex problems, explaining laws and principles and communicating instructional materials. In this method, first a table of correct answers is prepared and then questions are asked from the students. The students match their responses with this table after giving answers. If their response is correct, they get reinforcement. In the text books of mathematics and science answers of all numerical problems are given at the end of the text book. This system is totally based on this strategy of communication. Important characteristics of this strategy are as follows :

*(i)* In this strategy, subject-matter is presented to students in such a manner that students commit least number of mistakes. It means that sources of errors are taken into consideration here and efforts are made to simplify them as much as possible. Following this very principle some solved examples are also given in each lesson of mathematics text-books.

*(ii)* Students are helped to define the problems here and definitions are made clear by illustration.

*(iii)* While preparing decision table, informations are considered the base no doubt but efforts

are made to minimize the complexities of the problem also by taking the background knowledge and weakness es of students. For example, the teacher can give some hints for solving the problems so that the problem can easily be solved by students.

## Limitations of Communication Strategies

It is clear from the above discussion that no communication strategy is complete in itself. Selection of communication strategy basically depends on the nature of the content, e;g.,

*(i)* It task or the content is easy, continuous prose method is suitable.

*(ii)* Heuristic method of communication is used if task is tough and based on discovery or problem solving.

*(iii)* If sequential presentation of the task is required, algorithms method is most suitable.

*(iv)* If task is related to diagnosis, decision table may be used.

*(v)* Major limitation is that until we use a suitable combination of these strategies, there is little chance of getting success.

# UNIT-XIII

## Special Education

1

# Meaning and Scope of Special Education

## INTRODUCTION

Normal people of the society consider those persons as exceptionals who deviate significantly from the normal people mentally, physically, socially or emotionally and they are considered exceptionals to the extent they become problematic to the family and the society in all social situations. They deviate positively and negatively both from the average or normal people. On a normal distribution curve they are beyond $\pm 2\sigma$, i.e., 100-95.45% = 4.5% in every random population.

If we talk only about disabled in India they are about 35 millions in India which is more than the total population of many countries of the world. If we include the figure of superior exceptionals in the total, the figure will be very much alarming requiring huge investment on teaching and rehabilitation of these people.

### Historical Perspective

In the olden past, the demonological conception of the nature of ailment was accepted by the prehistoric man, i.e., mental deviation was considered to be the ill impact and controlling of evil spirits over the body of man.

Greek Philosopher **Diogenes** was the first man who developed a naturalistic concept of mental illness. **Aristotle** also followed the same track. Mind, according to him, was an attribute or organisation of nature itself, not something above or beyond it. On the basis of these ideas, modern naturalistic concept of mental problems was developed and **Hippocrate** went to the extent of saying that epilepsy which had once been known as a divine disease is no more divine or sacred than any other disease. Its cause as well as effect is natural. Contribution of some more thinkers in this regard are given below.

*(i)* Galen : He located psychic function in the brain and said that its operations and resulting activities are determined by the dryness and softness in the nerve tissues.

*(ii)* Christian Philosophy : Its attitude towards mental problem was also super naturalistic. Psychotic symptoms were thought to be the work or wrath of devil or God.

*(iii)* Late Medieval Period. Towards the end of the middle ages the attitude towards the deviant people changed a little. The people suffering from mental or psychic problems were admitted to the hospital. But many of them were still treated by religious ceremonisers using mantras and Quranic verses.

*(iv)* 19th Century : The first successful school for the treatment of mental defectives was established in 1837 and the difference between mentally deficient and mentally ill was for the first time recognised on experimental ground and differential treatment was given to these two groups of people. It is with this background that exceptionals (abnormal) can be differentiated from normals. Abnormality can not be understood without understanding the concept of normality.

### Meaning of Normality

Normality is a relative concept. A person is said to be normal if he behaves like the majority of the people in majority of social situations. The perception of normality or abnormality is not static. It, however, changes over the period. The more a society becomes deviant, the more the concept of abnormality is recognised.

## MEANING OF EXCEPTIONALITY

1. **Qualitative Concept :** Exceptionals are the separate categories of people who have unique traits and characteristics genetically determined by the environmental factors which make them fundamentally different from the normals. These people are supposed to learn, perceive and adjust in ways which are unique to them.
2. **Quantitative Concept :** The difference between the deviant group and the normal one is only the difference of degree and not of kind. The perceptual, conceptual and learning process of both the groups are fundamentally the same. The differences lie only in the speed. It means that disabled learn slowly as compared to normals.

   This concept is not acceptable to those who believe in qualitative conception of exceptionality. They claim that to the extent these traits are unique to these groups, the differences will become qualitative, e.g., an intellectually gifted child scores very high on intellectual aptitude tests. He scores almost equally high in academic achievement, he is slightly better in physique and motor abilities and is more adjusted to the norms than the normal people. The case of mentally retarded is just reverse of it. All these things make the exceptionals different from normals qualitatively also.
3. **Statistical Concept :** Statistical conception of exceptionality is also quantitative but more accurate and operational. For example, mentally retarded are those whose IQ is below 70 as measured by Stanford-Binet Intelligence Test, blindness is typically defined legally as visual acuity of 20/200 or less in the better eye after maximum correction and so on.

   Normal curve gives us numerical basis of how many abnormal persons can be there in a given population in terms of probability. For example, the definition of mental retardation is based on the assumption that intelligence is normally distributed. It is in this context that IQ scores which are 2 standard deviation below the average (beyond –2s) used to identify students with mental retardation. Reverse is the case of giftedness. Scores 2 standard deviations above the mean (beyond +2s) are referred as representing gifted children. The pattern of other areas of exceptionality does not exactly function in the same way and to the same degree. Their percentage in the total population may be less than $1\frac{1}{N}+2.5$ s but normal probability curve definitely tells the nature of abnormality.
4. **Social Concept :** Social usefulness is the only criteria here. For example, if an IQ of below 70 is accepted as the arbitrary criteria of mental retardation for placement in special classes but it is later found that many children with IQ 75 can equally be benefitted by placement in such classes, 70 limit loses much of its usefulness as a criterion. It then becomes necessary to change the criteria for the purpose of special education. The same rule is also applicable with other types of disabilities or giftedness.

   Thus, the term exceptional individuals usually refers to those who usually differ from the average ones to such an extent that they are perceived by the society as requiring special educational, social or vocational treatment. These people are not supposed to read, write, compute or behave to the accepted or adopted standards due to lack of proper social or emotional adjustability.

   This criteria of exceptionality lacks specificity and accuracy and vary from culture to culture, from place to place, from time to time and from the point of availability of resources. These criteria are generally fixed by social needs and political commitment.
5. **Medical Concept :** This concept of exceptionality was developed after examining many people and preparing norms. For example, medical standard for normal human body temperature is 98.6° F. It was established only after evaluating many healthy people. The

temperature above or below this point is considered to be an indicator of illness. In this way medical science has prepared standard of many physiological traits and characteristics. Any deviation from these standards produces physical and biological abnormalities. Genetic abnormalities, prenatal problems,,infections and physical trauma can cause special learning problems and needs. Retardation is caused not only by genetic abnormalities, but it is also caused by infectious diseases like German measles, encephalitis, etc. Similarly, anoxia (insufficient supply of oxygen to the fetus during pregnancy) destroys brain cells causing cerebral palsy or other mental retardation. As far as role of malnutrition causing physical, mental or sensory retardations is concerned, it is an established fact today. Thus, causes of disabilities are many.

Medical standard gives us a benchmark against which the degree of abnormality is measured. Specific symptoms are given here to elaborate specific exceptional problems and decision about imparting special type of education to these children is taken after matching the symptoms with the social criteria of exceptionality.

## Definitions of Exceptionality

1. **Crow and Crow :** "The term exceptional is applied to traits or to a person possessing the traits, because of it the individual receives special attention from his fellows".
2. **S.A.Kirk :** "An exceptional child is he who deviates from the normal child in physical, mental and social characteristics to such an extent that he requires a modification of school practices or special educational services in order to develop to his maximum capacity".
3. **Heward :** The term exceptional children includes children who experience difficulties in learning or behavioural, emotional or social problems, children with physical disabilities or sensory impairments and children who are intellectually gifted or have a special talent so that special education is necessary to help them to fulfil their potential."
4. **Operational Definition :** Exceptional individuals are those who differ from the average to such degree in physical or psychological characteristics that the school programme designed for majority of children does not afford them the opportunity for all round adjustment and optimum progress and they, therefore, need either special instructional programme or in special cases social ancillary services or both to achieve a level commensurable with them in accordance with their respective abilities.

## Characteristics of Exceptional Children

On the basis of the concepts and definitions given above following characteristics of exceptional children are inferred.

1. Exceptional children are those for whom uniform educational programmes do not suit. Hence, they need special instructional programmes or ancillary services or both.
2. Exceptionality is manifested by performance that is superior or inferior to that of the average children.
3. They deviate from the average (normal) people in both directions, plus and minus of mean physically, psychologically or socially and these deviations are significant to such an extent that their adjustment with the normals in some situations becomes difficult. Thus, exceptionality creates adjustment problem.
4. They come across learning difficulties in normal setting due to the defects and sometimes due to their superior qualities. These difficulties can be removed only by providing special instructional procedures unique to them.
5. If they are retarded or disabled in any area, their performance will be lower than the normal children and if they are superior in any trait significantly, the performance will be higher. Disabled children, however, come to the average performance when they are fully grown up and matured in their experience and drill.
6. The exceptionals are found in every society and culture almost in the same percentage of the total population. Sudden medical factors can,

however, increase their numbers all of a sudden, e.g., spread of epidemics can increase their number.

## Classification of Exceptional Children (Scope of Special Education)

**(A) Classification on the basis of area or mode of deviations:** This classification is more qualitative than quantitative. Exceptionals can be classified into the following categories on the basis of area of deviation.

*1. Intellectual Deviance :* Intellectual deviance may be in both directions from the mean. Mentally retarded comes on the minus side and gifted and creative come on the plus side from the mean. These two deviations are given below:

(a) **Mental Retardation :** They are less than 90 IQ on any intelligence test. They have special learning needs in areas requiring functional use of intelligence and adaptive behaviour. About 0.96% of the school going children is classified in this category.

(b) **Giftedness and Creativity :** These children possess IQ more than at least 110. Creatives differ from gifted in the sense that creative children perform in superb manner in one or two selected areas in original manner. These two types of children have special learning needs in areas requiring functional use of intelligence and artistic ability. About 3% of school going children come under this category.

*2. Sensory Deviance :* Here comes the hard of hearing, the deaf and dumb and visually impaired. There may be the people without the sense of taste or touch but we are not concerned with these people because they don't pose any social problem and hence they are not discussed in the category of exceptionals. Two important types of sensory deviance are given below:

(a) **Visual Impairment :** Under this category only those children legally come whose visual acuity is either zero (blindness) or less than 6/60 after correction (semi blindness). These children have special leaning needs in areas requiring functional use of vision. About 0.4 to 0.6 percent of school going children have been detected as visually impaired.

(b) **Hearing Impairment :** Audible capacity of these children are very low. Due to this reason, they have special learning needs in areas requiring functional use of hearing. About 0.11% school going children suffer from this problem across the world.

*3. Motor Deviance :* Crippled, orthopedically handicapped, speech and adjustment defectives, epileptics etc. come under this deviance. Two types of motor lisabilities are given here:

(a) **Speech Impairment :** Speech impairment is closely associated with hearing impairment because speech learning requires hearing. If speech development is nill or very close to nill, speech therapy or lip reading or reading on fingers is required.

(b) **Orthopedic Impairment :** These children have special learning needs in areas requiring functional use of hands, arms, feet, legs or other locomotive body parts. About 1% of the school going population is found to be orthopedically handicapped in India.

*4. Personality deviance :* Here children suffering from behavioural disorders and learning disabilities are included. For example, children suffering from neurosis or psychosis face serious problem of adjustment in social situations. Personality deviance can be classified into two categories:

(a) **Leaning Disabilities :** These children have special learning needs in areas requiring functional use of listening, speaking, reading, writing, reasoning and arithmetic skills. This is the largest category in special education in terms of percentage. About 4% school going children suffer from this problem. These children are normal in intelligence, even then they are very poor in learning.

(b) **Emotional Disorders :** These children lack proper emotional and social skills. When these children are treated by their peers, mates and teachers in a prejudiced manner, they become more disturbed emotionally and hence they need special attention by the teacher.

*5. **Educational Deviance :*** They are significantly different from the normals in academic achievement due to a variety of reasons in both directions. They can be classified into three categories:

(a) **Educationally bright :** Achievement level of these students is very high due to very high level of adaptability to learning, assimilation of thoughts, understanding and memory. They can learn any subject matter in no time and they can retain it for a longer period of time. They are hardworking children in the field of learning.
Though educational achievement is directly related to intelligence yet intellectually gifted and educationally bright children are not the same. The reason is that high achievement in schools may be due to some other reasons also like future aspirations of students, high motivational level, hard labour done by pupils, guidance by parents etc.

(b) **Educationally Backward :** These children are backward by their age mates by 2 to 4 years or grades in the field of education due to repeated failure in different classes. This backwardness may be due to a number of reasons such as defective teaching learning process, low intellectual ability of learners, adjustment or emotional problems in the school. etc. These children need special treatment by the teacher in the classes and if problem is very serious, special classes should be arranged for them.

(c) **Communication Disorders :** These children are very poor in understanding the views of others and equally deficient in communicating their opinions to others either due to low level of intelligence or due to poor level of concentration power to the subject matter.

*6. **Social Deviance :*** Juvenile delinquents, (adult criminals) and maladjusted students come under this category. Ethnic minorities and the culturally suppressed people also come under this category. They deviate from the social norms due to a variety of reasons and constitute educational and social problems:

(a) **Maladjusted Children :** These children fail to adjust in their family, in the school and in the society and create the problem of adjustment for others also. If they are not properly dealt with, they will remain maladjusted leading to an isolated life.

(b) **Deprived Children :** Feeling of derivation develops in such a child only after seeing social, economic and cultural inequalities.

(c) **Juvenile Delinquents :** These adult criminals are antisocial elements in the sense that they violate the social norms and legal structure. Committing crime is a fun for them.

*7. **Traumatic Brain Injury :*** These injuries are caused by an external physical force or by an internal problem such as strokes. Children who are born with brain injuries are not included in this category.

*8. **Multiple Deviance :*** Many exceptional people deviate from the normal in more than one areas like a blind man is deaf also or personality deviance is associated with educational deviance etc. Such a multiple exceptionality is an automatic process also. For example, a sensory handicapped child is very badly treated by some people in the society. The exceptionals react to these behaviours very negatively and in a hateful manner and thus social deviance is slowly developed. These students have special learning needs in more than one areas.

***Why do we concern more to handicapped than to gifted children?***

Some reasons are given below :

*(i)* Physically superior people do not constitute any social problem while handicapped may be a burden if not rehabilitated. Special protection given to them will help them to live an independent life.

*(ii)* Due to fast technological and scientific development, the difference which lies between gifted people and the average ones has become relatively unimportant today such as computers, telecommunication etc. can work more than a superior man and with a fast speed.

*(iii)* Every society takes much interest in narrowing down the difference rather than heightening it. That is why handicapped are brought closer

to the normal people in abilities. If, on the other hand, gifted are given much importance, the gap between the average and the gifted will increase.

**(B) Classification on the basis of degree or intensity of exceptionality :** On the basis of degree of exceptionality, such exceptionals can be classified into the following categories:

1. **Profoundly Handicapped or Gifted :** This is the highest degree of deviation from the mean. If both the legs of a person are damaged altogether and he is unable to use any of them, he is said to be profoundly handicapped. Contrary to this, if a child is superior in intelligence, he is said to be gifted.
2. **Severely Retarded :** They are less than the first group in degree. They are also very problematic cases in learning and other social situations. For example, an individual having IQ 25-50 may by put under this category.
3. **Moderately Retarded :** Only special attention is enough in order to bring these handicapped to the normal. Their retardation do not cause social problems very much. For example, a person having IQ in between 50-75 will be put under this category.
4. **Mildly Retarded :** Their problem of deviance is so insignificant that they are generally neglected in social situations and in the environment of the school. For example, if a person is only 10% handicapped in motor abilities, he can do every job but a bit slower speed than the normals. This problem is not given any significance in developing or poor countries due to paucity of funds. They are least touched in special education as well.

Thus, intensity refers to the degree of individual differences not only between the exceptionals and the normals but also within the deviant group itself. This very degree of deviation determines the nature of adaptive educational or rehabilitation programmes and their relative significance.

**(C) Classification on the basis of extensity or breadth of exceptionality :** This classification refers to the degree of specificity or generality of the handicap or assets in terms of which the individual is considered as exceptional. It is indicated by the extent or degree to which the primary deviation affects other aspects of one's personality and behaviour. For example, if a mentally retarded child is misbehaved or ridiculed, he is likely to become a criminal. Similarly, deaf children are thought to be withdrawn, unsocial, suspicious and unhappy. Same is the case with orthopedically handicapped who is considered to be mental as well as physical cripple. Thus, we see that one area of disability also affects other areas and this effect is sometimes very intensive as well as extensive.

***Psycho-somatic Problems :*** *It is the relationship between the possession of an atypical physique and the resulting psychological and social adjustment. It is concerned with the effect of variation in physique on the psychological situations and the adjustment of the person. And from the sociological point of view, the individual is judged and evaluated by his peers in terms of the social significance attached to his deviating traits. It means that reason is psychological but problem is physical.*

***The distinction between Disability and Handicap :*** Objectively defined impairment of structure or function is a disability i.e., loss of vision is one eye or loss of hearing in one ear. This problem, however, may not constitute a handicap.

A handicap arises from the cumulative effect of the disability and the personal and social consequences which have a detrimental effect on the individual's functional level.

A handicap is defined in terms of the situation. For example, a blind person is not handicapped in the dark. It is because all of us are blind in the dark. Similarly, a person confined to a wheel-chair is not handicapped for a bench job which does not require locomotion.

A disability becomes a handicap when the lack of an aptitude makes an individual less able or less competent in carrying out a job. It is in this context, a normal person may also feel himself as handicapped as is the case of sports persons who are unable to perform well sometimes due to certain reasons. Likewise, big feet or big nose may be an asset for a male person but it is a serious disability to a common female. Thus, it is the situation or ground that makes a disability handicap, e.g., a blind is handicapped in jobs requiring functional use of vision but he is never handicapped in playing with musical instruments like Sitar, Tabla, Shahnai etc.

This distinction has, however, been made from the point of view of functionality in particular jobs, otherwise, in general life situations, a disability is always a handicap because disability always puts hurdles on the way to day to day life activities. For example, if a person is blind or partially blind, he is not supposed to travel and visit alone to cosmopolitan cities safely and his disability may be fatal for him. Similarly, even 10% locomotion problem may cause social problems.

### Abbreviations used in Special Education

| | |
|---|---|
| DB | Students who are deaf blind. |
| ECSE | Early childhood special education. |
| GT | Gifted and talented |
| HH | Hard of hearing |
| POHI | Physical and other health impairment. |
| HI | Hearing impaired |
| MR | Mentally retarded |
| EMR | Educable mentally retarded |
| SLBP | Specific learning and behaviour problems. |
| SLD | Specific learning disabilities |
| LD | Learning disabled |
| MI | Mentally impaired |
| MH | Mildly handicapped |
| MMMR | Mild to moderate mental retardation |
| SMR | Severe mental retardation |
| TMR | Trainable mentally retarded |
| MH | Multi handicapped |
| PMR | Profoundly mentally retarded |
| PH | Physically handicapped |
| OI | Orthopedically impaired |
| SED | Seriously emotionally disturbed |
| BD | Behaviour disordered |
| ED | Emotionally disturbed |
| SM | Socially maladjusted |
| CD | Communication disordered |
| VH | Visually handicapped |
| VI | Visually impaired |

## SPECIAL EDUCATION, CONCEPTS AND PROCEDURES

### Meaning

**Bob Algozzine** defined special education in the following words : Special education is instruction designed for students with disabilities or gifts and talents who also have special learning needs. Some of these students have learning difficulty in regular classrooms. They need special education to function properly in schools. Others generally do well in regular classrooms but they need special education to help them master certain skills to reach their full potential in the school".

### Need and Importance

Provision of special education is a must to fulfil the following requirements in democratic countries.

1. When individual differences in learners are found to such an extent that all of them can not be benefitted in normal classes, they are put into the category of exceptionals for special learning arrangement. This is the responsibility of every democratic country to do its best for the maximum development of all its citizens. The handicapped can not be left unnoticed at the mercy of normal people for begging alms.
2. A severely deviant child is not supposed to take part in the routine activities meant for normal children. He will either be frustrated there or frustrate the others. Thus, the whole teaching learning process will be disturbed. Their proper adjustment of the society needs special leaning arrangements for them.
3. Gifted and talented children are the assets of the society. If they are not given proper opportunity to flourish in their own way, it will be the loss of the society itself.

***Myth of Compensatory Aptitudes :*** *It is believed by the people that if some one is deficient in one area of motor-sensory or mental ability, he is compensated by God in other areas. it is totally wrong. Vice versa is rather correct. If he is weak in visual acuity, he is likely to be deficient in hearing or smelling perceptibility also. The reason is that if certain nerve cells in the brain are affected during pregnancy or at the time of delivery, it may affect many part of the body.*

4. Exceptional can not take the benefit of regular classes due to their unique needs and abilities. They need special curriculum, special teaching strategy and special teacher to develop them to the fullest extent.
5. Creative and positive deviants are likely to turn into juvenile delinquents in future if they are not treated properly by the family, school and the society resulting in-law and order problem in the society.
6. Handicapped children will become a liability for the society if efforts are not made to educate and rehabilitate them. They can be proved to be productive in those areas where they are not disabled. For example, a blind person can he a good musician or a good teacher (communicator) though he is unable to perform in those areas which require activity of vision.
7. Deviant children generally feel problem of adjustment in normal educational setting. It will create tension in their minds and they may become deviant in other areas also.
8. Special education helps teachers, guardians, researchers and educational administrator to understand the special problems of these children.
9. Blind, deaf and dumb children are not supposed to learn properly in normal educational setting due to their unique respective problems. For example, normal children can learn more if visual aids are used in the class but such aids are useless for a blind child. He will rather need audio aids for increasing his rate of learning and it can not be provided in regular classes.
10. Educational and rehabilitational needs of these children are also different. If they are not properly educated or trained by applying special measures, their rehabilitation will not be possible.

## Origin of Special Education

It began first with the work of Jean Mark Gaspard Itard (1774-1838). He was a French Physician who worked for five years on a retarded wild boy named Victor in 1801 and tried to train him but failed.

## Historical Development of Special Education

**1. First half of the 19th Century:** It was the era in which several public and private schools for handicapped were first established in America and France. In France, this credit goes to **Edward O Seguin**, a student of Itard (1812-1880). He was an environmentalist. He established the first public residential institution for treating and educating the handicapped. He succeeded in his efforts in modifying the blocked nervous system of the retarded children and thus they could be re-educated to normalcy by such trainings.

In the USA, it was **Reverend May** who first opened a school for retarded children in 1834 in New York. Then clergymen and the physicians also came forward as the leaders of the movement to provide care and training to the handicapped.

First residential school for deaf was opened in Hartford in 1817. Then in 1824 the New York House of Refugees for delinquents was opened. In 1829 the New England Assylum for the blind was also founded in Water town.

In 1841 **Dorothea Dix**, a social reformer started appealing to state legislators for providing funds to build more such schools and to intervene to stop the abuse of handicapped individuals in jails, almshouses and primitive institutions.

Efforts in the direction of educating and rehabilitating handicapped people intensified in 1846 when **Seguin's** book "Idiocy and its treatment by psychological method" was published in France in 1846. The ideas behind special education during this period were as follows :

I. The individualized instruction in which child's characteristics rather than prescribed course content provided the basis for teaching techniques.
II. A carefully sequenced series of educational tasks were needed to be designed.
III. Stimulation and awakening of the child's senses were emphasized.

IV. Meticulous arrangement of the child's environment was made so that the structure of the environment and the child's experience of it lead mutually to learning.

V. Immediate reward for correct performance was given to provide reinforcement for desirable behavioural changes.

VI. Accommodation, education, adjustment and rehabilitation of handicapped individuals were realized as the responsibility of the society and the nation for the fist time.

VII. In order to make the child as self-sufficient and productive as possible in day to day life they were tutored in favourable and productive skills.

VIII. There was the belief that every child should be educated and trained to the greatest extent possible. Even handicapped children are not exceptions.

IX. Many deviant behaviours can be psychologically treated. Such behaviours are not the product of evil spirits.

X. All types of deviance can be rectified to some extent by applying physiological measures.

2. **Second half of the 19th century :** During this period, the focus of efforts changed from cure or rehabilitation of physically handicapped to their permanent segregation from the majority community. Social policies and political philosophy also changed accordingly. Some of the efforts made in this direction and development occurred during this period are given below:

   *(i)* Separate residential and day schools were established exclusively for handicapped.

   *(ii)* Compulsory school attendance was introduced in many schools.

   *(iii)* Ungraded system of schooling began for mentally retarded and for those suffering from behaviour disorders.

   *(iv)* American Association of Instruction for Mentally Deficient was founded in 1876 and Dr. Seguin was made its president.

3. **Early 20th century**

   *(i)* American Congress realizing the need for speedy care for retarded children established the **children Bureau** in 1912.

   *(ii)* Chifford Beans founded the vocational committee for mental hygienes in 1909 to combat delinquency.

   *(iii)* Training programmes for teachers teaching in special schools meant for the handicapped started in teacher training colleges and universities.

   *(iv)* State provided extra funds for educating deviant groups of the society.

   *(v)* State department of Special Education was established in several countries like America, England, France and Belgium.

**Late 20th Century**

*(i)* **National Association of Retarded Children** (NARC) came into being in America in 1950.

*(ii)* Association for children with learning disabilities was established in 1963.

*(iii)* International Council for the Education of Exceptional Children (ICEC) was also founded with the following objectives.

   (a) To unite those interested in the educational problems of exceptional children.

   (b) To emphasize the education of special child rather than his identification or grouping.

   (c) To establish professional norms and standard for teachers teaching in the field of special education.

## Special Education in India

So far as special education in our country is concerned, we are interested more in looking after the normals rather than the abnormals. We are still far behind in catering to the educational needs of the normal people and enrollment of school going children is not more than ¾ of the total even today. Only few educational institutions exist to educate exceptional children. Where there are 35 million exceptionals found in the country, less than 0.1 million exceptionals are being educated in specials schools. For example, in the whole Western Uttar Pradesh there is only one school for blinds-Ahmudi School For Blinds Affiliated to Aligarh Muslim University, Aligarh. Same is the case with other states also.

***Reactions to Exceptionality***

*The nature of our reactions to exceptionals depends on three factors.*

*I.* ***The nature of Individual Tolerance*** *: The teacher can accommodate to these students to the extent of his tolerance. For example, students who are outspoken in the class can be encouraged, tolerated or punished.*

*II.* ***The causes of Exceptionality*** *: Infection, physical trauma, genetic abnormalities etc. can cause different types of disabilities. The attitude of the teacher towards these children may vary from very sympathetic to very hateful.*

*III.* ***Label Assigned to the Condition*** *: If the label assigned to the handicapping condition is negative, our behaviour will be inappropriate to these people. Students may be labelled in the school as slow, disruptive, bullying etc. This labeling is bad. It creates negative attitude among the handicapped on one hand and cause the people to think against such people negatively. Thus bad labeling can cause personality deviance also.*

As far as rehabilitation of handicapped people is concerned, much more is running on paper in India but nothing is seen on the ground. So many vocational rehabilitation centres have been opened to feed some government officials. Three percent reservation given to physically handicapped in government jobs is far from facticity. The writer of the book is also physically handicapped and is qualified for the post of lecturer for the last ten years but he has not yet been given chance to teach in any university despite several attempts in last ten years. Even interview letter is not issued to appear before the selection committee by the normal people of the university. It will take very long time to change the attitude of these people towards the exceptionals.

## SPECIAL EDUCATION WITH REFERENCE TO FAMILY AND COMMUNITY

Practical shape of special education is given below:

### A. Special Education in the Context of the Family

A handicapped child first belongs to his family. He is made in future in the manner how he is responded and behaved by the family. The role of special education in the context of the family is being discussed below:

**1. Effects of Handicapping Situation:** The handicapping situation can influence and thus mould a child in the following ways.

**(a) Psychological effects :** It may cause the child to be deprived of certain abilities, e.g., the emotional and intellectual development of a two years old normal child will be more than that of a handicapped child. He may several times come to feel that his disability is a punishment and develop feeling of guilt. He may also develop feeling of hatred against his maker and thus he may hate whole human being. In this way he may either be aggressive to the environment or fearful of it.

**(b) Physical Effects :** Emotional outrage burst in the handicapped may cause physical illness, i.e., psychosomatic or neurotic problems are very commonly seen. Similarly, if child is maladjusted in the family or in the society, his parents may also face the difficulty of adjustment. If he is given more attention in the family than the normals, then the unique relationship developed between the parents and the handicapped child can create new problems for normal children in the family also. Moreover, if the material environment of the child is impoverished as we generally see (handicapped are mostly found in poor families), then the perceptual conceptual bricks with which he should build the whole framework of cognition will be very weak. Apart from these, due to impairment, physical and psychological changes of puberty and growth in height, weight and sexual traits may be delayed.

**(c) Parental Reactions to a Defective Child and Development of the Child.** Parents react to these children in the following ways:

*(i)* ***Realistic (coping with the situation) :*** They may adopt a realistic attitude towards the problem and does not try to hide anything. This type of reaction is useful for parents and the child both. They will help and

guide the child in the desired manner. They will not put extra burden on the child due to extra expectations.

*(ii)* ***Denial of the reality of handicap :*** Handicap if occurred in the family is a reality but in most of the time denied by parents due to shame or stigma attached to the disability in the society. It is useful for parents to some extent as it helps them in bringing the mind into balance but excess denial of reality is fatal.

*(iii)* ***Self pity-more than the desired care for the child :*** This is a type of over protection given to the child on account of pity. He may start questioning or suspecting God, why he has made a blind or paralysed child for him or 'what wrongs did he do that made him liable to be punished in this way' etc. Thus parents may either become atheistic or they may take solace in their religious beliefs.

*(iv)* ***Ambivalence-toward the child:*** Additional responsibilities, anxieties and irritations caused by such children which become a routine part of their life produce ambivalent parental reactions. Parents accept and love their children due to the natural love created by the blood but they also reject and hate them at the same time.

*(v)* ***Projection of the difficulty:*** Anxiety relating to unacceptable feelings of resentment, hatred and hostility can be minimized by blaming someone else for the handicapping situation of their child, e;g., other children, doctors, teachers, or the marriage arranged by their elders in blood relations can be blamed resulting in a handicapped child in the family. This is known as projection. Handicapped are mostly found in muslims due to probably the marriages between close relations.

*(vi)* ***Feeling of Guilt and Shame :*** Shame involve\s the expectation of ridicule or criticism from others while guilt involves self blaming or personal regret. When such feelings develop in parents, they try to avoid social situations resulting in slow social development of the child also.

*(vii)* ***Pattern of Mutual Dependency :*** The future development of the child depends upon the experiences that he receives at home and in the school. If he is fully cared by the parents and given chance to be exposed in social situations, his experiences will hike. Contrary to this if there is big distance between the child and his parents, the child will lose self confidence, though, he will try to develop self confidence in him.

(d) **Sexual Adjustment :**Sexual adjustment to a large extent depends on the social relationship ranging from love and friendship to increasing social horizons. If the child is not getting proper chance of socialization, his sexual adjustment with his/her life partner will always be at stake.

(e) **Economic Adjustment :** Economic self reliance is necessary for self respect and may be essential to lead a married life also. If he is not given extra educational facilities by considering his specific impairment, he will not be fully adjusted in the society vocationally or economically.

**2. Guidance and Counselling of Parents of a handicapped child :** The family counsellor, the expert in education, paedriatist and the psychologist have their respective role to play in this regard. The service of these experts are needed for proper development of the child. As we know, the influence of the family on the over all development of the child is three times powerful to any other institution. Due to this reason, the idea of a continuous consultative relationship between a well qualified person and the family has been advocated. The major areas of counselling are as follows :

(a) **Intellectual Area :** Here the parents need information concerning the nature and the degree of the exceptionality of the child, i.e., diagnostic information. They are also supposed to know the cause of the handicap to avoid future occurrence of disability in the family, i.e., etiological information. They also need information about how to treat the problem to the maximum level possible and how to educate the child, i.e., remedial informations. Parents need all these three informations together.

(b) **Emotional Area:** The counsellor must remove the parents' fear and anxieties and also their feeling of guilt and shame. He should also endeavour to minimize the emotional vulnerability of the family members though he can not eliminate all these types of tensions altogether. If only the counsellor is able to increase their ability to tolerate them, his job is over.

(c) **Behavioural Area :** The counsellor uses the techniques of psychotherapy to mould the behaviour of parents, to understand the problems and to deal with them more adequately. They are also told by the counsellor how they will behave their handicapped child so that he may properly adjust in the society.

**Principles involved in Parental Counselling :** In order to get counselling a success, following principles must be followed:

1. **Principle of Listening :** Parents should be permitted to talk freely about their problem child and the nature of the problem with which they wanted help from the counsellor and their statements should be listened to attentively by the later. Relevant information should be supplied to parents only after the parents are completely exposed.
2. **Principle of Behavioural Terminology :** Communication should take place in terms of understandable language and use of professional terminology should be deliberately avoided. The counsellor has not to show his professional efficiency here. He has rather to listen to the problems of parents and provide them the needed informations and advices.
3. **Principle of Acceptance :** The counsellor must keep this fact in mind that he is dealing with the parents of exceptional children who may also be emotionally disturbed like their sons/daughters. In order to remove tensions from their minds, it is necessary that they should be given full regard and acceptance by the counsellor. The counsellor must rise above his professionalism and deal with them with sympathy and love.
4. **Principle of Counselling the Entire Family :** Since all members of the family are disturbed and affected by a deviant child, so counselling process should reach to all of them. Counselling of parents only is not sufficient. For example, if only the father or the mother is counselled, it will be very difficult for them to communicate these ideas to other members of the family due to lake of professional skills Collective counselling will help the family to make effective planning for the exceptionals.
5. **Principles of Attitude Consideration :**The attitude of the whole family toward the problem should first be taken into consideration before providing any information to them. If their attitude toward the problem is already negative, the counselling will do nothing in reducing guilty consciousness among parents and to remove tension from the minds of family members.
6. **Principle of proper Interpretation :** Interpretation in counselling takes place at several levels. At one level, the parents are only given information about the type and nature of the problem. At the second level, its importance is communicated to parents at all these and the other levels. The counsellor should interpret the problem and its solutions through discussions and questioning and in this way he will be able to remove wrong conceptions of parents.
7. **Principle of Total Information :** At the time of counselling, nothing is left for parents. Parents are provided all the three types of informations, especially, diagnostic, etiological and remedial. In this way, they are given complete lesson about how they will bring up their handicapped child after knowing the nature and causes of the problem.
8. **Principle of Effective Planning :** Effective and specific plans for exceptional children should be programmed by parents as early as possible and the counsellor will help them to prepare a comprehensive plan for the child. Late planning sometimes spoil the personality of the child and

his emotional adjustment in future becomes impossible.

9. **Principle of Real Experience :** It has been proved very useful to arrange parents and their handicapped child to stay for short duration in specialized clinics or schools. It will help them come across real experience of the situation and its perceptibility.

10. **Principle of Group Counselling :** Meeting between parents of different handicapped children should be organised by the counsellor to help them exchange their views and understand the problem more thoroughly. In such meetings decision about important matters like transporting the handicapped children to and from the school in a collective manner or organising games activities for them can be taken.

## (B) Special Education In the Context of the Community

Democratic base of special education-Equal opportunities of education and employment for handicapped.

Equality of opportunities for handicapped means right to education. It is a human right approved by the UN Charter and it is in this context that handicapped children should be assured the facilities to attain equality and to make them at part with other people. For this purpose, they may be provided with special facilities for assistance, protection and rehabilitation.

This concept is developed on the belief that if they are given the right opportunities and the facilities commensurable with their deviance, they are fully capable of developing their residual capacities, powers and traits to the fullest extent and of becoming economically independent and socially self reliant. They need only special care not alms.

If the above concept is applied to education, they will have the equal right to get education in the same manners as normals have. In Indian context, it has been enshrined in our constitution that each and every child in the age group of 6-14 years has the fundamental right to receive free and compulsory education in the country. Before 2002 it was only a directive principle of the state policy under Article 45(A) of the Indian constitutions.

Since, handicapped lag behind the normals due to a variety of reasons, they are given three percent reservation for the admission in schools and colleges and for employment in government run installations and offices. This reservation is not against the principle of equality because of the following reasons.

*(i)* They are deficient in some respects leading to poor academic achievement. This deficiency cannot be overcome even by providing facilities to the maximum level possible.

*(ii)* They need special protection for their economic independence. If such protection is not given to them, they will not be able to survive in today's age of competition and hard struggle for means of livelihood.

*(iii)* Many backward and deprived communities in India have been endowed with reservation facilities and handicapped are the most backward of all the backwards.

*(iv)* It is their right to get extra facilities for their education and employment from the state. It is not their fault in any way that they have become handicapped. It may be the fault of their parents or other people of the society. In this sense, if special provisions are not made for them, they will be penalized for no guilt.

*(v)* If special provisions are not made for them, they may become a burden on the society.

## OBJECTIVES OF SPECIAL EDUCATION

Through special education we can serve the following purposes:

1. **Personal and Emotional Adjustment :** Handicapped are generally disliked, disregarded and misbehaved by the normal people in India. Thus, exceptionals have to perform double function. On one hand, they have to rise above their disability and do something to make themselves productive members of the society and on the other hand, they have to fight the social wars waged against them. Through special education they are told how they will adjust socially and emotionally in a society antagonistic to them.

2. **Placement :** What they can not learn in normal setting, they can learn it if special arrangements

are made for them. This helps them excel in those areas of learning which can prove for them to be productive in future. Once they are economically settled, they will not remain a burden or parasite on the society. Thus, special skills are taught to them through special education for earning livelihood. This will require which type of educational institutions they should be placed in. They should either be put in residential school, vocational school or day school.

3. **Social Integration :** The purpose of special education is not to segregate them from the rest of the society but to integrate them with the society. They have, after all, to live, remain and die in the society. So, efforts are made to integrate them with the normal people slowly by removing the special facilities given to them and by developing self confidence in them.
4. **Intellectual growth :** Intellectual development of handicapped people is affected by the social and behaviour problems that they face. Efforts are made to solve these problems through special education and intellectual growth of handicapped individuals are ensured.
5. **Vocational Adjustment :** Through this education the handicapped are taught which vocation is suitable to them keeping in view their limitations. They are also trained to acquire certain necessary skills suitable for that profession or vocation.
6. **Mass Mobilization :** Through special education the handicapped people are taught how they will convince the masses in their own favour and how they will change their behaviours in the interest of the exceptionals.
7. **Fulfilment of Educational Needs :** Exceptionals are not less than 4% of the total population in any community or country. They also have the right to get education like others. If they can not be educated in normal setting, it is the duty of the state to educate then, through special education programmes. Once this is done properly, only then the concept of universalisation of education will turn into reality.

## Special Education Process

Special education process involves three steps given below :

1. **Determining Eligibility :** In the first step eligible candidates for special education are selected. If disability is present in the person, it is decided whether it requires special education services or not. This decision is taken by the child-study team on the basis of the special learning needs of deviant children and the legal structure made by the state in this regard.
2. **Delivering the Special Education Services :** After selecting eligible candidates for the provision of special education, special education is delivered to them in the second phase by engaging trained professionals. These professionals can also work as consultants with general education personnel, to design intervention programmes to be used in regular classrooms. This phase of the process is guided by a formal document called individualized education programme prepared by the child-study team in consultation with other professionals.
3. **Evaluation :** This is the final phase of the process. Students' progress is evaluated here to determine the need for continuing, changing or ending the special education services. Here all disabled students are evaluated at least once in a year and comprehensive evaluation is also done after two or three years in order to determine whether the student is still eligible for special education services or not.

## Varieties of Special Education Programmes

Different types of special education programmes are provided to different exceptionals on the basis of the area and extent of their disabilities. The more a person is handicapped, the more he is segregated from the rest of the people for his proper education and care but as he progresses in his respective field with the help of education and care, he is slowly integrated to the normal people through integrated education programmes. Thus, the channel of special education programmes is directed from residential institutions to regular class rooms. The underlying philosophy here is not to segregate the exceptionals but to integrate them to the mainstream. Important special education plans are given below:

1. **Residential Institutions :** These residential institutions in the form of hospitals, asylums and boarding schools are managed and administered privately and by the government both.

The residential institutions ranges all the way from schools which provide relatively short term care, rehabilitation, education and training for the mildly or moderately retarded to such asylums which provide life long custodial care for the totally dependent individuals. These institutions can also be classified into three categories.

(a) **Multipurpose and Special Purpose Institutions:** The first type of institutions serve persons of all ages and sexes and all degrees of disabilities while the second type of institutions are meant to serve only one purpose, e.g., deaf assylum, orthopedic hospital, blind school etc. This speciality is fixed either in terms of mode of exceptionality or in terms of degree of impairment or on the basis of age or sex.

(b) **Short Term Facilities :** These residential institutions provide such facilities as diagnosis, short term care, treatment, training or rehabilitation to exceptionals. Once the purpose is fulfilled, these facilities are withdrawn. Individuals of the following categories may take advantages of these services.

- Those awaiting admission to those institutions which provide long term facilities.
- Those transferred from the long term facilities who have recovered upto a great extent in the custodial centre and are expected to be released soon.
- Those who temporarily suffer from a crisis or a handicapping situation.
- Those whose primary need is diagnostic or short term medical, surgical or educational in nature.

***Demerits of Institutionalization***

*(i)* Under this system child is segregated from his family for a long period of time and it will be very difficult for the child to adjust with the normal people at home as well as in the community, after the returns from his long institutionalization.

*(ii)* In such institutions life revolves about one's disabilities rather than his abilities. This shatters the confidence of handicapped people.

In order to remove the above two defects of institutionalization following modification can be introduced:

*(i)* **Cottage Plan :** IN this arrangement group of handicapped children live with a married couple in separate cottages on institutional grounds and enjoy a family life, though it is not their own family.

*(ii)* **Colonies :** Here colonies of handicapped children are established at some distance from parents. Groups of individuals live and work on farms or on industrial projects, under the supervision of one or two married couples. Colonies differ from cottage plan in terms of the size of the group (In cottages, the size of the group is 8-20 children while the size of the group in colonies is 35-40 children).

(c) **Residential Schools :** They are pure educational institutions especially meant for educating the exceptional children but medical and other facilities are also provided in these institutions. Only profoundly or severely handicapped or gifted children are admitted to these schools. In these institutions, children are not restricted to classroom teaching only but they are also taught everything which can help them live an independent life in future. Knowledge of life related skills is also given to children.

***Advantages of Institutionalization***

*(i)* It is the only option for severely handicapped children to educate and train them in residential institutions.

*(ii)* Clinical and treatment facilities can best be provided in these institutions.

*(iii)* They can serve as training centres for those personnel who work as nurses, doctors, psychologists and social workers.

*(iv)* Round the clock vigilance and supervision of handicapped children is possible in residential institutions only and behaviour of exceptionals can be moulded accordingly. It is not possible through days schools or OPD services.

**2. None Residential Institutions:** Non residential institutions can be classified into the following categories.

(a) **Day Hospitals or Day Care Centres :** Such hospitals were initially used exclusively for psychiatric patients. Now these hospitals are run for all those handicapped who need intensive treatment and regular counselling. They keep the patients attached to their homes and the community rather than isolating them. The first such hospital was established in Moscow in 1932 during the communist regime.

Day hospitals reduce the dependence of the institutional life of the handicapped. They are very essential for reducing the hospitalization process.

Besides medical facilities and psycho-therapy, occupational training is also provided in such day care centres. From these day care centres patients are also transferred to a custodial (residential) institution if their case is very serious.

***Advantages of Day Care Centres***

*(i)* Parents are relived of the 24 hour job of caring a handicapped child at home because these children remain in the centre for at least six hours daily.

*(ii)* Non handicapped children are generally neglected in the family because of the excessive demand of the handicapped child in the family. Such problems are reduced by day care centres or special day schools.

*(iii)* They reduce the emotional strain of the family and the family can live a more normal and social life.

*(iv)* They provide vocational training to handicapped children also which can help them to get a job in future. It is very essential for making handicapped self reliant.

*(v)* Those who do not like institutionalization will always like day hospitals for the care of their handicapped child.

*(vi)* The training received in such centres may raise the child's level of functioning to the point where he can attend special classes which is second stair of integration and can become partially self supporting.

Thus we see that

- Day care centre is a mid way between indoor patients hospital services and out door clinic.
- Special day school is a mid way between a residential school and special classes arranged in a normal school.

**(b) Outpatient Clinic :** No hospitalization or limited hours placement is needed here. These clinics serve as diagnostic centres, where limited treatment facility is also provided. It also refers the cases to day care centres.

**(c) Foster Home Facilities :** This type of placement is particularly advantageous for those children who can not live in their own respective homes but they have the potential to live semi-independent life in the community with other families. Families providing homes for such children are paid by the state. Once the child becomes self reliant, he is removed from these services.

**3. Half way Houses :** It is typically an intermediate step for those individuals who will soon return to the family following a period of long institutionalization. When patients are discharged from the hospitals, they are temporarily kept in these houses before sending them to their respective homes. Thus, they can also serve as an alternative to institutionalization. Half way house is designed to help the discharged patients to become fully adjustable in the community. Half way houses are generally used for alcoholics, criminals, mentally ill and the juvenile delinquents.

**4. Vocational Rehabilitation Centres :** These centres are opened to provide vocational training to handicapped individuals. They are first registered in these centres and then professional vocational trainers train them in their selected field. They are also given information about where they will get job after training. To be eligible for such state sponsored services, a person must

*(i)* be substantially handicapped

*(ii)* be of employable age by the time the training completes.

*(iii)* be interested in such services and their importance.

These requirements restrict the programme to older adolescents only and to those whose handicap is of mild or moderate degree.

**5. Sheltered Workshops :** In these workshops employment oriented training and jobs are provided to those handicapped who can not be trained or employed in normal competitive situations because of their unique nature of disabilities. They are also meant for adults only. These workshops provide training and employment both.

These workshops serve somewhat the same function for adults as the day care centres do for children. People in these workshops may make new things, repair or recondition used articles for resale. They can also take contracts from private factories for making articles on unit payments basis and then these articles are supplied to the concerned factories.

**6. Special Day Schools :** Special schools for different types of handicapped children are opened exclusively for the purpose of educating them. In such schools special facilities and equipments are provided and the services of special teachers who are especially trained to teach these handicapped children are hired to provide care and education of these children. Only severely or moderately handicapped or highly creative and talented students are kept in these schools. Separate schools are established for different categories of handicapped., e.g., school for blind, school for deaf and dumb etc. These children are so unique in their needs and abilities that they are unable to adjust in normal schools. They require special teaching strategy, equipments and curriculum.

While constructing the building of such schools or organising classes for these handicapped, their unique needs are taken into consideration. Doctors, counsellors and social workers are also appointed in these schools for proper care of the child.

***Advantages of Special Day Schools***

*(i)* It is easier for the administrative officer to administer a separate school for handicapped children than to administer and supervise a number of special classes arranged in a normal school.

*(ii)* Differential supervision is possible only in such schools. It becomes very difficult when handicapped and non-handicapped are mixed up in a school.

*(iii)* It is easier to utilize the aptitude of specialized teachers and other professionals in such schools.

*(iv)* The unique needs of handicapped or highly talented children can be fulfilled very easily here.

***Disadvantages of Special Day Schools***

*(i)* The problem of transporting handicapped children is magnified in the special school arrangement.

*(ii)* When children comes back from these schools after education, it becomes very difficult for them to be adjusted with the normal children.

*(iii)* Stigma is also attached to the children attending these schools, i.e., school for mentally retarded, school for blinds etc. Thus, these schools are identified with the name of disability.

**7. 'Special classes in normal schools :** When sizable number of exceptional children are enrolled in the school and school maintains high academic standard, then special classes are arranged for these children where they are taught by specialized teachers using special teaching equipments. The teacher is fully considerate here to the unique needs of these children.

This arrangement suffers from the same drawbacks which the special schools suffer. In order to minimize some of its demerits following modification have been introduced:

**(a) Partially Integrated Classes :** In such, arrangement, children are guided and taught by special teachers for few periods a day in special classes and they are taught in regular classes for the rest of the day. Such type of classes are suitable to gifted and handicapped both.

**(b) The Resource Room Facility :** It is a special room in the school building in which the special teacher serves the exceptionals in the specific areas where they need help, e.g., in resource room for the blind, the teacher will help and guide them in reading and writing on braille. Children are also supplied with readers, braille books, talking books and so on. Other varieties of handicapped children are also supplied with the materials required for their specific needs.

It differs from partially integrated classes in the sense that here the students come to attend these classes from their regular class rooms and teachers do not go anywhere.

**(c) Provision of Itinerant Teacher or Consultant:** He typically serves a number of schools simultaneously and assists the regular teachers, of the school, and every student in the same manner as the resource teacher does. The exceptional individuals who need special help are enrolled in regular classes in their home school and the consultant is sent to these schools to help the teachers and the students there. Such arrangement can be used in all types of schools.

Thus, we see that efforts are always made to integrate the exceptionals with the rest of the society rather than segregating them from it.

## Integrated Educational Programmes for Handicapped Children

Integrated educational programme is such a programme in which the services of medical personnels, social workers, psychologists, specialized subject teachers special teachers, trained in teaching exceptionals in their respective modes and the consultant are integrated in the same campus to teach exceptionals in accordance with heir unique needs. Thus, special arrangement are made in normal schools to teach exceptional children.

In the medical setting we find doctors, nurses, occupational and physical therapists, physician, surgeon, speech therapist and so on. When these services are integrated with social, educational and vocational services, it is known as integrated programme of education. Such a programme is very essential for achieving the objective of providing equal educational opportunities for all handicapped children. This type of programme is also very helpful for social integration of the child and he will not have any difficulty in adjusting with the rest of the society after the education is over.

In integrated educational programme, the exceptional child is not segregated in a residential or special day school. He is rather kept in the regular school and all needed services are provided to him by using the professionals mentioned above. In this way, the child doe not face any problem of adjustment in future. Post- education adjustment will not be a problem here as well.

## Administrative Arrangement for Facilitating Integrated Educational Programme

I. Only selected schools possessing all necessary equipments and buildings should be given permission for introducing integrated education.

II. Varieties of exceptionals differ widely which will require huge amount of physical and human resources to educate all these categories of exceptionals. So, no school should be allowed to deal with more than two disabilities at a time.

III. Seating arrangement should be made in the classes according to the specific needs of handicapped children.

IV. Resource room should also be there in these schools along with itinerant services.

V. Consultating facilities should be there in such schools so that teachers and students both can take benefit of these facilities.

VI. Such schools should take necessary support and financial help from the government as well as from other philanthropic personalities and NGOs.

VII. The school should also be equipped with three facilities regarding the problem of exceptional children. There should be proper identification of exceptional children, proper diagnosis of the type and the nature of exceptional children and facilities for proper educational adaptation of the child.

**Assumptions and Principles of Special Education:** There are wide differences of opinions among the educationists regarding the procedures and details involved in the education of exceptional children. However, we will try to summarize all these opinions which are basic and common.

1. **Goals of Special Education are not Unique :** The purpose which we apply on education are equally applicable to special education also. Special education attempts to provide exceptional children with educational programmes which are equivalent and applicable to normal children. It is committed to the proposition that each child should be enabled to learn as much as he can on the basis of his capacity and skills. Thus, education and special education do not differ in objectives.
2. **Special Education is Different in Procedure :** Because of the deviation of the exceptional children from the average, special legislation, special facilities and resources, special teaching methods and strategies, special teachers and other resource persons are necessary to deal with deviant groups of children. Such an education is

imparted to enable the exceptionals to realize and exploit their potentialities and to minimize their handicaps.

3. **Special education Entails Selective Placement:** Similar type of special education is not suitable to all types of handicapped children. Various organizational plans for different varieties of exceptional children such as residential schools, special day school, special classes and the like are required here. Such selective placement involves the complete assessment of the child as well as the social environment around him.
4. **Heterogeneity :** The education of a handicapped group of children involves all the problems of heterogeneous groups of non handicapped children plus all the special problems related to their handicaps. Thus, much more individual attention is needed here by taking all varieties of individual differences into account.
5. **Special Education Requires Many Ancillary Services :** Many exceptional children may be under constant medical care and supervision, Periodic examination of eyes, ears etc. may also be necessary for them so that problem may not rise further.
6. **Special Education is very expensive :** Special equipments, resource room, special training for teachers, special schools and classes and adequate medical personnel etc. are needed here that make the special education very expensive. However, ignoring a handicapped child and leaving him on the mercy of cruel society is more expensive than the cost of their training and education. This cost automatically comes to zero when they become independent and productive members of the society.
7. **Integration Rather than Segregation is Recommended :** The purpose of special education is not to segregate the deviant groups of children from the rest of the society but to integrate them with the normal children as much as possible. It means that such children will be institutionalized less. Majority of them will attend regular classes in normal schools sooner or later. Efforts will always be made to integrate the child with the family and the community to the maximum level possible.

# Visual Impairment and Educational Adaptation

## INTRODUCTION

The major part of the chapter is based on

I. The personal experience of the writer himself as he himself is technically a blind (Visual acuity = 3/60 after maximum correction, *i.e.*, 75% blindness)

II. A research conducted by the writer in 1999on 40 blinds and partially blinds of Faizabad and Ambedkar Nagar districts of UP by applying stratified sample technique and using observation and direct interview techniques for data collection.

## Persepective

In the olden days blindness unlike other disabilities was considered as a curse or wrath of nature as a result of the sins committed by parents of blinds. Blindness was thought to be a punishment from God given to sinful people. This myth has now changed and the disability is considered as the result of several malfunctioning in the body due to genetic or environmental factors. Students with visual impairment were among the first who received special education services in America. The two starting instructional programme. The New England Assylum for the blind and the New York Institution for the blind opened in 1832. This programme got popularity only in 20th century and several special residential and day schools were opened for partially sighted children in various parts of America.

In India the case of special education of blinds or partially blind is different in the sense that only few schools are running for them even today though the population of visually handicapped is more than 12 millions.

## Meaning

Visual impairment is a problem related to visual acuity. The person whose visual acuity is less than 6/60 after glass correction may be termed as visually impaired. But this term does not include with normal or near normal vision. This term rather refers to those people whose visual acuity is so defective (less than 6/60 after correction) that they can not perform their routine life activities independently either **in the school, in the society or at home**.

## Categorization of Visually Impaired

For the purpose of convenience, we can classify visually impaired children into four categories.

1. **Profoundly Impaired :** They are totally blind people having zero acuity in both eyes.
2. **Severely Impaired :** They are partially blind people whose visual acuity in the better eye is less than 6/60 after maximum correction. They can read only the second letter on the visual acuity test board (Snellen chart) by their better eye.
3. **Moderately Impaired :** Their impairment is not very serious. They have visual acuity in between 6/24-6/60. They can do each and every thing if proper help is given to them.
4. **Mildly Impaired :** Such a visual problem is very general in nature. This does not disturb the person in any way in doing any visual task. Such people have a little less than normal acuity, i.e., 6/9-6/12. They generally do not have any restriction in the visual field. People after the age of 45 generally suffer from this problem. Such people will not be discussed in this chapter at all.

## Definitions

1. **Encyclopedia of Special Education :** All those people are visually impaired who deviate from the normal even after using the glasses.
2. **Legal Definition** : (Social Security Act 1935, USA) : A person who has no vision or who has central visual acuity of 20/200 (6/60) or less in the better eye with corrective glasses or a limitation in the field of vision such that the widest diameter of the visual field subtends an angular distance no greater than 20 degrees is blind.

   This very concept of visual handicap has been accepted in India too.

   According to this definition, a blind child reads from a distance of 6 meter a line or a word which a normal child with normal vision can read from a distance of 60 meter. These children are technically called partially blind. It otherwise means that their vision is less than 6/60 or 10% of the normal vision. It is in this sense that they are differentiated from partially sighted children whose visual acuity is less than 50% of the normal vision. Due to this reason partially blind people (people having less than 10% of the normal vision) are also considered blind in India. Such a low level of visual acuity is not very much helpful for normal functioning of life. They have not only difficulty with detailed visual tasks, but also perform them at reduced level of speed, endurance and accuracy even with assistance.
3. **Functional Blindness :** It varies according to the purpose it is intended to serve like travel vision, shadow vision, near vision, distance vision, educational blindness, occupational blindness, and so on. Children under this category do not required Braille for learning (reading or writing) but they need only large print to read.
4. **Educational Blindness :** Their vision is so defective that they cannot be educated via vision in normal classroom. These children must be taught through auditory and the kinesthetic senses and they must read or write on Braille. It means that they are totally blind.
5. **American Medical Association (1976) :** Blindness is central visual acuity of 20/200 (feet) or less in the better eye with corrective glasses or central visual acuity of not more than 20200 (feet) if there is a visual field defect in which the peripheral field is contracted to such an extent that the widest diameter of the visual field subtends an angular distance no greater than 20 degrees in the better eye.

   The last definition given by AMA (USA) adds one more point in visual impairment, i.e., the concept of visual field. A person with a normal field of vision is able to see objects within a range of approximately 180degrees. If this visual field is 20 or less the person will be able to see only a limited area at a time, even though his visual acuity may be quite good. Looking through low visual field is like looking though a narrow tube or tunnel.

## EFFECTS OF VISUAL IMPAIRMENT

### (A) Perceptual Area

Blindness affects the perceptual areas of life in the following ways :

1. Vision provides a detailed, precise and continuous source of information about objects and people. Impairment of vision restricts this direct source of information.
2. It is the vision which helps the people in locating sounds, in producing objects, grasping the objects and identifying the previously perceived objects. Blinds are very poor in these respects.
3. Blinds also have difficulty in perceiving things in space or the third dimension, because the knowledge of qualities of objects is acquired by blinds largely through touch and kinesthesis which require direct contact with the object. Thus, distant objects such as heavenly bodies, clouds, etc. and large objects such as mountains, elephants etc. can not be perceived by them. These objects are only conceived by them by analogy and extrapolation from objects actually perceived.
4. In the first year of child's life it is vision which guides the behaviour of hands, feet, crawling, walking and the like. A blind infant does not have such facility. He has only auditory information available which is neither continuous nor precise like visual informations.

### (B) Non-Perceptual Areas

Blindness affects the non perceptual areas of learning in the following ways.

1. **Conceptual Area :** In the area of conceptual development vision helps the person in the identification of objects, events and persons. it consolidates various perceptual attributes into a single, integrated concept which is lacking in a blind child.

   Vision is also helpful in the dequisition of the concept of the structure of physical space and of the individual's spacial relationship with the rest of the world.

2. **Social development :** Vision is also helpful in the development of social interaction and socially oriented behaviour through identification. It is in fact the mediator of social interaction.

   Vision also facilitates the acquisition of many social skills like dressing, eating, bathing, personnel hygiene etc. Blinds are very deficient in these social skills.

3. **Development of Abstract Elements :** They have very poor concept of depth, distance or time, e.g., they cannot have clear concept about how deep a river or tank is or how far is America from India.

## Characteristics of Visually Impaired Child

We are dealing here only those children who are either absolutely blind (Zero Visual Acuity) i.e., profoundly impaired, or legally blind (visual acuity of less than 6/60 after maximum correction) i.e., severely impaired and those who are moderately handicapped in visual acuity. Mild retardation is not discussed in special education.

People with visual impairment receive special education because their vision even after correction remains so limited that it may affect their development and achievement, if they are not properly intervened.

Important characteristics of these visually impaired children are as follows.

1. **General Characteristics :** Some thinkers are of the opinion that due to lack of vision or due to poor vision they are endorsed with greater capacities in the remaining sensory areas by nature. This idea is generally held by those who believe that nature does not discriminate any one on any ground. Researches, however, done in the field do not endorse this notion. On the contrary, there is evidence that they may be deficient in other areas also upto some extent but capacities for focal and sustained attention may be better developed among visually impaired people than in the case of sighted normal ones.

2. **Cognitive characteristics :**

   *(i)* Cognition is largely a matter of development of concepts and concepts in more than 50% cases are learnt through visual means. Thus, visually impaired children may have poor cognitive power in general. They will not be intellectually poor in any way but when they are tested through an intelligence test, they are very likely to perform below the average.

   *(ii)* Many visual items in intelligence tests require seeing the stimuli before responding. They can not be explained by a reader or writer or by using Braille. In such cases blind children will definitely perform poorly. Thus we see that visual impairment produces hindrance in the course of cognitive development.

   *(iii)* They have to count on auditory or tactual abilities in order to get information which is very limited in its value and nature, ie, we can not have all the informations by touch or hearing.

   *(iv)* Visual impairment delays the child in reaching the objects or persons which will reduce his experience also. For example, when I was a child, I did not know how the goats look like because there was not goat at home and I could not see those goats properly which were seen grazing in the streets, because it required to go to the goats at close distance and whenever I did so they fled .

   **Stephens and Simkins** (1974) are however, of the view that when these children reaches the age of 18, they come almost to normal level of cognitive development in spite of their slow rate of cognitive development in the beginning. I also agree with this idea on the basis of the research conducted by me in 1999.

*(v)* They are not slow in non spacial concepts with respect to normals. Most of the differences in this area occur in early school grades but at later stages of life they come almost to normal.

**3. Educational Characteristics**

*(i)* As far as absolutely blinds are concerned, touch and audition are the two important sources of information for them, i.e, they learn through tactual and auditory perceptions. Lack of vision produces a significant defect in the conceptual development of spacial relations for the child. Tactual and auditory perceptions are also adopted by them for discriminating objects.

*(ii)* Learning based on touch and audition is limited due to limited nature of experience.

*(iii)* As far as partially blinds are concerned they bring hands under their visual guidance in the very first year of life though the use of vision is restricted to few meters only. They do not have visual experience of those objects which are either very far from them or very small in sizes, e.g., they can not read a book of less than 12 points in size of letters without using magnifying glasses and constant use of such glasses will exert strain on their eyes. Once they read a book, they bring it very close to their eyes.

*(iv)* Due to their limited range of experiences, they learn in parts rather than in whole by using their tactual perceptions.

*(v)* They have to rely more on their memory and hearing power in order to learn and retain the material because they cannot easily repeat it by reading.

*(vi)* Informations obtained by normal children through incidental or unintended learning through observation maybe unavailable for severely impaired children.

**4. Physical Characteristics :**

*(i)* In terms of size and appearance, people with impaired vision do not differ from normal people though their health may be somewhat poor due to less mobility.

*(ii)* Their motor skills are also found poor due to poor mobility power. Mobility is the ability to move in the environment safely and efficiently. Due to limited mobility(exercise) they are prone to viral and infectious diseases.

*(iii)* Perceptual and non perceptual both factors are involved in mobility. Delayed development of locomotor behaviour is seen due to inefficiency or poor efficiency of perceptual factors. Since, it is very difficult for them to see either distant or near objects due to the problem of vision, they take less interest in moving from one place to another.

*(iv)* They differ form the normal in terms of physical strength due to lack of exercise of the body parts while doing different types of works.

**Signs of Visual Impairment**

*(i)* *Frequent experience of watery eyes.*

*(ii)* *Regular red and inflamed eyes.*

*(iii)* *Irregular eye movements*

*(iv)* *Difficulty in moving around the classroom.*

*(v)* *Difficulty in reading letters of small points.*

*(vi)* *Difficulty in reading the book from normal distance.*

*(vii)* *Difficulty in identifying small details in pictures*

*(viii)* *Complaint of dizziness after reading a passage*

*(ix)* *Tilting head or squanting eyes for better focus*

*(x)* *Using one eye more than the other while doing any visual work.*

*(xi)* *Frequent eye infection*

*(xii)* *Blurred vision*

*(xiii)* *Sitting in the first row persistently for seeing black board works.*

*(xiv)* *Putting hands on one eye while reading some thing.*

**5. Behavioural characteristics**

*(i)* Since they do not perceive intensive visual stimulation, they are motivated to make up the deficiency by increasing the stimulation available from other sources. This is called

stereotype behaviour. This behaviour is also caused by social deprivation and neglect. In the educational setting such behaviour interferes with the child's attentiveness to educational activities which in turn, lead to poor learning and hence backwardness.

(ii) Non academic skills affected by visual impairment are social skills, affective understanding and non verbal (body language) behaviour. Social skills are necessary for overall success in life. If chance of social interaction is dim, social skills will be retarded. Similarly, many non verbal body language such as looking, nodding, smiling, shaking hands etc. are less developed in these children because they do not receive stimuli from others due to lack of vision or poor vision.

(iii) They are very irritative in nature. The reason is that they are badly treated or ridiculed by others and in response they adopt the same attitude towards others.

(iv) They possess very poor self confidence due to their disability. Due to this reason they try to avoid people and situations. Their withdrawing nature further makes them poor in confidence.

(v) Legally blinds look at the objects from a very close distance as they have less than 10% visual acuity.

**6. Social development and Adjustment**

(i) They are ridiculed and devalued by normal children and thus they begin to develop inferiority complex which leads to maladjustment in the school and neighbourhood.

(ii) They can participate in many play activities like swimming, dancing, wrestling, etc. Partially blind people can participate in all the athlete activities without difficulty and can increase their social development.

(iii) Process of socialization will be low in case of absolutely blind children as it much depends on the responses of others. Since visually handicapped children are either neglected or rejected in the society, they have less chance of socialization.

(iv) Even a small amount of vision is helpful for social development. So, partially blinds do not lag behind the normals in social development and adjustment.

**7. Communication Abilities :**

(i) They have difficulty in reading. They need either large print of the books or Braille. They use recorded materials and readers for reading. Many visually impaired children use magnifying glasses, contact lens and telescope in order to perform better on reading.

(ii) Writing and its speed is not very much affected in these children. Even a small amount of vision, i.e., 3/60 visual acuity is helpful in developing this skill and applying the skill in the real life situation.

(iii) Their communication may be poor in the initial periods of their lives but after 18 they were found to be almost normal in communication skills.

(iv) They prefer oral to written communication and do not like to read or write too much.

## EYE PARTS AND VISUAL ERRORS

### (A) Protective Part

It consists of socket in the skull in which the eye ball lies. Eye brows and tear glands are around it. Any defect in it could cause serious visual handicap.

Trachoma is one of the major diseases related to this part. It sometimes causes total blindness. It is a disease of the eye lids in which certain granules are produced. They irritate the eye by some secretion. This disease can also affect the cornea and conjunctiva of the eye.

### (B) Refractive Part

This part is designed by nature to focus the light on the retina in which the cornea, the crystalline lens and the humour are involved. Any defect in this part may cause the following diseases.

1. **Myopia.** (Short Sightedness) It is a condition in which rays of light focus in front of the retina (not at retina) when the eye is at rest. Concave lens is used to correct this disease.
2. **Hypermetropia (Far Sightedness).** In this case, the rays of light focus behind the retina

forming a blurred and unclear image. It can be corrected by using convex lens.

3. **Astigmatism.** It is the result of irregularity in the curvature of the cornea or the lens of the eye. In this case, horizontal and vertical rays are focused at two different points on the retina. This defect can be corrected by using cylindrical lenses.
4. **Cataract :** It is caused by the opaqueness of the lens of the eye, i.e., lens becomes opaque which prevents the light rays from passing through the lens. It can be corrected only by operating the lens.
5. **Glaucoma.** It is caused by increased pressure on the eye due to the accumulation of aqueous fluid. This is marked by increased tension within the eye ball. As a result, vision slowly grows dim day by day. It can also be corrected by surgeory. If this disease is not remedied timely, it can cause total blindness.

## (C) Directive System

It consists of the six cilliary muscles of the eye which control its movements either upward or downward or in either direction.

The defective muscle functioning of the eye may lead to the following diseases.

1. **Strabismis :** In this case, crossed eye is caused by lack of coordination of the external eye muscles. In this disease, the two eyes do not simultaneously focus on the same object.
2. **Heterphoria.** In this case, insufficient action of one or more muscles of the eye takes place causing double vision which develops a tendency in the eyes to deviate from the normal position of the eye ball. Because of this deficiency the two eyes fail to form the images of the object into one image and the person sees two objects at a time instead of one. This defect is different from strabismis in terms of treatment given. Otherwise, the defect is almost the same. It can be corrected by proper eye exercises.
3. **Nystagmus.** It is involuntary movement of the eyeballs affecting clear vision. It is cussed due to weakness of eye muscles or brain injury.

## (D) Receptive System

It depends on the retina, the optic nerve and brain cortex, when vision takes place. Important defects lying in this system are as follows.

1. **Reterolental Fibroplasias.** It is caused by the excessive oxygen given to the immature infants. It causes blindness in future if not cured.
2. **Atrophy of the Retina :** It is caused by a misplaced pigment.
3. **Optic Atrophy.** It is also called degeneration of the nerve fiber which connects the retina to the brain. It is the optic nerve which goes from each eye to the visual centres in the brain and visual messages are received by the brain. In this defect, this function is totally disturbed.

## Causes of Impaired Vision

Visual and hearing impairment and mental retardation all have common casual factors behind the problem. (See chapter, mental retardation)

### (A) Hereditary causes

1. When I studied 40 students suffering from visual impairments, I found that they were all the offsprings of those parents who had close blood relations with each other, i.e, mother was found to be either the cousin or niece of the father, Marriage in the close blood relations is the main cause of transfer of recessive or dominant gene probably.
2. Vision is very much related to heredity or gene. If father or mother is visually impaired, he/she is very likely to have visually impaired child.

### (B) Environmental Causes

1. Diseases of the central nervous system like epilepsy, meningitis, hydrocephaly or brain trauma affect the visual process and causes visual impairment.
2. Small pox was an important cause of visual impairment in India.

3. Malnutrition is the major cause of visual impairment in poor countries.

## Identification of Visually Impaired Child

**(A) Behaviour Symptoms.** Visually impaired children are first identified on the basis of their physical and behavioural symptoms. This is the first step of screening these children. Important behavioural symptoms are given below :

*(i)* He is over cautious in walking, runs very infrequently for no apparent reason.

*(ii)* He is normally inattentive during blackboard work or map work.

*(iii)* He generally poses as he is seeing the written material but actually, he does not see it at all.

*(iv)* He complains of visual blurring and attempts to brush away the visual impediments.

*(v)* He habitually holds the book very close to the eye while reading.

*(vi)* He may tilt the head to either side in order to focus the light on the retina when he reads or writes.

*(vii)* He can not sit for reading or writing for a longer period at a time.

*(viii)* He uses the magnifying glasses to see smaller objects and telescope to see distant objects.

*(ix)* He shuts one eye while reading or writing.

*(x)* Irregular eye movement or blinking of eyes.

*(xi)* He complains of dizziness when he reads a passage.

*(xii)* He uses one eye more than the other while doing any visual work.

*(xiii)* Sitting in the first row persistently for seeing blackboard works.

**(B) Physical Symptoms :** Important physical symptoms of visually impaired are given below:

1. Chronic eye irritations indicated by watery eyes or swollen eyelids.
2. Experience of nausea, double vision, or visual blurring following reading or writing.
3. Constant headache at visual works.
4. Rubbing of eyes, frowning or screwing up the face when looking at distant objects.
5. Frequent eye infections.
6. Blurred vision
7. Constant redness in the eyes.
8. Difficulty in reading small print.
9. Difficulty in identifying small details in pictures.
10. Regular blinking of the eyes.

**(C) Medical Examination :** After identifying suspected children, they are brought to the eye hospital for formal and systematic checkup in order to know to what extent their eye is damaged. It is done by ophthalmologists and eye technicians. A chart is used for this purpose. If the child is able to see only the letter at the top of the chart, his visual acuity will be 6/60 (meter). It means that he can see an object from a distance of 6 meters and the same object can be seen by a normal man from a distance of 60 meters.

If he is able to read the second line also, his visual acuity will be 6/36, i.e., 17% of the normal vision. If he is able to read the second last line on the chart, his vision will be considered as normal, i.e., 6/6, and finally if he is able to read the last line also, he will be extra normal in vision.

His visual field in degrees is also ascertained along with the visual acuity in the hospital. The visual acuity and field both will determine which type of placement or intervention the child needs in his learning process.

## EDUCATIONAL ADAPTATION

We will discuss here the educational adaptation of blinds and partially blinds separately.

### (A) Educational Adaptation of Blinds

1. **Teaching materials required-** Braille, Tape recorder, embossed and relief map, graphs, guide dogs, typing material and type writer.
2. Administrative Arrangement for Blinds

*(i)* Especially constructed schools with plane floors and lawns.

*(ii)* Fully covered electric appliances.

*(iii)* Audio recording room and record players in required number.

*(iv)* Special playgrounds.

*(v)* Teachers experts in Braille reading and writing.

*(vi)* Resource room for medical examination.

*(vii)* A large variety of teaching aids for clarifying concepts.

*(viii)* Music and dance rooms for training them in these fields.

*(ix)* Workshop for producing materials.

*(x)* Integration with normal children through co-curricular activities.

3. **Developing Reading and Writing Skills :** In order to develop reading and writing skills among them braille is the greatest single curricular modification for blinds. This technique was developed by Louis Braille of France, in 1929. He was a blind student who became a teacher of blind school in Paris.

   In 1932 a modified British Braille became the standard Braille and is continuously in use since then. UNESCO has adapted and developed a Braille system for all languages in 1950.

   It is the most effective system for teaching reading and writing to blinds even today. Special braille Rotation system is used to teach mathematics. Scientific and short hand symbols have also been converted into braille language in recent years. On brailles, a blind reads the written material through touch. He moves his hands horizontally through the lines and reads.

   The limitations of braille system are that only slow speed of reading is possible on brailles and only limited materials are available on brailles even today. The thickness of the braille book is another problem which incurs heavy cost to prepare a braille book for reading.

   When writing is taught on braille, it is written by hand using a special slate and stylus. Writing is made by punching holes with the stylus in a paper inserted between two metal strips. Since the material is written by the underside of the paper, so it is written in reverse form. A good braille typist can type 40-60 words per minutes. Teaching of braille skill generally starts from class VIth and oral teaching is done upto primary level.

4. **Teaching Through Auditory Materials :** Tap recorders and record players are generally used for reproducing the taught materials. It supplements braille reading because all materials can not be presented on braille. Recordings are generally done at the speed of less than 150 words per minute so that blinds can easily understand them.

5. **Teaching of Arithmetic :** At the primary stage only mental mathematics is used, i.e., all mathematical calculations are done orally. From junior level onwards use of calculators, slides, rulers, protractors etc. are allowed along with the braille books available on different topics. They are also taught to construct geometric designs through clay modeling and sheets of papers.

6. **Mobility Training :** In order to make the child self dependent adequate mobility is necessary. When they have learnt all these things, they can move about the environment, find the objects, locate the places, and interact with others. Blinds are also trained to use guide dogs to move in the environment freely. Mobility is also harnessed by motivating them through psychological techniques. It is necessary because they generally lack motivation for walking. They are taught by the psychologist that there is nothing to be afraid of moving and it increases self experiences as well.

   In order to increase mobility further they are trained to be sensitive to the pressure of air when any object comes in front of them. The pressure of air changes when the object is removed from their way. Once they are trained enough in this respect, they are least likely to collide to any object and they will have mastery of the environment in the process.

7. **Physical Training :** Since, the mobility of these children is generally restricted which hampers their physical growth and causes ill health. These

problems of blinds can be minimized by motivating them to do more and more physical exercise. They are also given chance of wrestling, running and brisk walking on field tracks and these activities are made regular part of their daily life.

8. **Vocational Training :** In order to make them self reliant and help them earn their living, vocational training for these children is a must. They can be taught any of the following vocational skills to earn their livelihood in future.
   *(i)* Stenography through braille.
   *(ii)* Chair and cot canning.
   *(iii)* Weaving carpets.
   *(iv)* Type writing.
   *(v)* Teaching in elementary or higher classes.
   *(vi)* Music training
9. **Behaviour Training :** They also have some behaviour and adjustment problems so, their behaviour need to be modified by using behaviour therapy and verbal counselling.
10. **Curricular adaptation :** Curriculum for these children does not differ much from the sighted children. Modification is done only in those areas where they face special problems like conceptualization of abstract and distant concrete materials and higher mathematics. They take more interest in literature, music and philosophy, so these subjects are stressed more in the total curriculum. They can also have specialization in the areas of social studies also.
11. **Placement :** Following administrative arrangements are made for them:

**(a) Residential Schools :** Residential schools are most suited to those children who are completely blind. This type of setting is useful for them because of the following reasons.

*(i)* They have adjustment problem with the normal children. So, it is better for them to develop a homogeneous learning and social environment for their education and living.

*(ii)* Trained teachers can be made available for them to teach in these institutions easily. It will incur less cost on the part of the school because if one special teacher is hired to teach five or six blind children in a regular school, it will be very costly.

*(iii)* They will feel more secure here than their homes and parents will not feel regular burden to take care of these children.

*(iv)* Due to conveyance problem special day school or special classes do not suit them. Safety precautions are very high when these children attend schools from their homes and go back.

*(v)* They need special materials and special resource room for their training in different areas. Such arrangement is not so easy in regular schools.

**(b) Sheltered workshop:** Sheltered workshops are the second option for these children where they learn different trades and then get permanent employment there. They produce different types of articles to be sold in the market and they are paid out of the profit. Advantages of this type of arrangement are given below :

*(i)* Sheltered workshops work as training centres for these children and different types of vocational training are given to them here.

*(ii)* Students need not bother about their job placement after training. They are employed in the workshops itself.

*(iii)* Emotional security and adjustment opportunities can be given to blind children here.

## (B) Educational Adaptation of Partially Blinds

They face less problems in the areas of education and training than blind children. Following intervention procedures are adopted for them:

1. **Training of Sight Saving Techniques.** They should use their other sense organs more than their vision that is already damaged because of the following reasons.

   *(i)* Visual acuity of 6/60 (10%vision) is not a much amount of vision that will last long. For example, when I was a child, I had a

visual acuity of 6/36 in both eyes. Now it is only 3/60 at the age of 40. In such a situation, these semi blind children should use their vision as less as possible and they should take the help of classroom teaching, radio and tap recorders instead of book reading.

*(ii)* These children find it very difficult to read letters of less than 12 points in prints and books are generally printed in 10 point. Thus, if they read these books by bringing them closer to their eyes, it will put heavy strain on their eyes and damage them very soon.

Due to these reasons, they should rely more on their auditory organ rather than visual organ.

2. **Teaching Materials.** These children need following teaching materials in the school.

*(i)* Tap recorders.

*(ii)* Talking books

*(iii)* Radio

*(iv)* Books printed in large size of the letter, i.e., more than 12 points in size.

*(v)* Magnifying glass to read small print.

*(vi)* Telescope to see distant objects.

3. **Administrative Arrangements in the Class and in the School:** Following administrative arrangements are required in the school system to make them suitable to these children.

*(i)* Their vision is so weak that they can not see the words written on the blackboard even if they sit in the first row of the class. So small sized classes comprising of 10-12 students are suitable to them. In this arrangement students will sit very close to the blackboard and teacher will write letters in bigger size than the normal. The gap between the students and the blackboard should not be more than two feet.

*(ii)* In case of mathematics or science even the above arrangement will not work. The size of the classes will have to reduce further.

*(iii)* Audio recording facility should also be there in the class to record the lectures of teachers. This will reduce the dependence of these children on books and save their vision.

*(iv)* Books of large prints should be especially prepared for them so that they can easily read them.

*(v)* Distracting glare of vision should be reduced as much as possible.

*(vi)* Regular eye check up to these students is also necessary to ensure whether glasses and other visual aids are functioning properly.

4. **Methods of Teaching :** Adaptive methods of teaching suitable to these children are as follows:

*(i)* The teacher should use auditory cues while referencing to the objects in the class during presentation of lesson.

*(ii)* While presenting visually dependent materials, the teacher should verbalize written informations describing pictures and narrating non-verbal sequences in videotapes also, i.e. he should speak while writing something on the blackboard.

*(iii)* The teacher should use complete sentences to provide additional context.

*(iv)* The teacher should train the students to keep the instructional materials at the same place so that they can locate them easily.

*(v)* The teacher should spell difficult words also in the class.

*(vi)* Direct instruction is most suitable to them.

*(vii)* The teacher should sketch the diagrams and figures in hold lines, to enable the students to see them properly.

5. **Curricular Modification :** They need no modification in the curriculum upto class VIIIth. Only change in instructional procedure is enough. They can be taught each and every subject in the class upto high school except higher level of physics, chemistry and biology. They can not study these subjects because these subjects can not be understood without practical and partially blind children can not carry out practicals.

With the exception of these subjects they can excel in each and every discipline but they can take special interest in literature, social sciences, music, philosophy and psychology. hence, these subjects should be given more weightage in the curriculum.

6. **Vocational Training :** It is as essential for them as for the blinds to enable them to earn their living. They can be trained in those areas which require less visual functioning or visual power of short distance. In spite of that they are not supposed to reach the level where normals can reach, i.e., their academic performance will always be somewhat lower than normal children.
7. **Placement :** Integrated schools are most suitable to these children. In this setting, the child lives at his home, attend a normal regular school daily and in that school special and integrated classes are arranged for him. He studies some subjects in regular classes and some subjects in special class. Resource room is also made available for him to enable him to excel in a particular area chosen by him. This settlement is advantageous to them in the following ways.
   *(i)* Higher social maturity scores have been found in such setting than residential schools. Socialization is most possible here.
   *(ii)* It develops among them the feeling of self sufficiency and self dependence.
   *(iii)* They will be able to adjust in the society more adequately after schooling.
8. **Use of Optical Character Recognition (OCR):** Visually impaired children use a computer based scanning device e.g., Kurz veil Personal Reader. This device converts printed words into synthetic speech Advanced techniques have now been introduced in using this type of device. This OCR is suitable for blinds also.

# Instruction and Assessment Procedures

As we have seen in the previous chapter, the goals of special education do not differ from those of general education. The goal of both the teachers, is to help the students develop their potentialities to the maximum level possible by providing them the necessary skills to be used in the society. Both these types of education differ only in instructional and assessment procedures. Students who are exceptional in any way require specialized methods of instructions and instructional materials that are adapted to their unique learning needs. For example, students with visual impairment need larger sized printed material to read.

## Components of Effective Instruction (Principles of Instructions)

Four basic components of effective instructions are as follows :

1. Planning instruction
2. Organizing instruction
3. Delivering instruction
4. Evaluating instruction

**Note :** Readers are advised to refer to the second optional paper "Essentials of Educational Technology.

## 1. PLANNING INSTRUCTION

It refers to determining objectives keeping in view the needs of students and the prescribed curriculum before hand. Planning helps us to do the right things at the right time. But all the students are not alike. So, objectives of instruction will not be the same for all of them. This very diverse nature of objectives require to do planning so that maximum number of objectives can be realized through instructions.

In planning, following decisions are taken.

*(i)* What part of the content is to be presented in the class.

*(ii)* What will be the objectives of presenting the content.

*(iii)* What material and activities will be used to present the content, i.e., how the content will be presented.

Thus, planning aspect is based upon three underlying principles

*(a)* Deciding what to teach

*(b)* Deciding how to teach

*(c)* Communicating realistic expectation

**(a) Decision of what to teach:** This decision is taken by the teacher by analysing the following facts.

*(i)* The teacher identifies the skills that students possess and those that they do not. The acquisition of new skills depends on the learning of lower level skills.

*(ii)* The teacher analyses the teaching task by assessing needs, interest and abilities of students.

*(iii)* A logical sequence of instruction is established here. The students will learn the material only when the teacher presents it in a logical sequence.

*(iv)* Relevant variables of instruction such as the place and duration of instruction, length of the content, methods of motivating pupils, and ways of interacting with students etc. are considered by the teacher in planning.

*(v)* Lastly, the gap between actual and expected performance is identified, i.e., what a student can do at present and what he is expected to do after learning.

Thus, we see that first part, the planning stage is mostly diagnostic in nature.

**(b) Decision of how to teach:** It refers to teaching strategies and tactics. Following decisions are taken by the teacher here.

*(i)* Instructional objectives are determined by the teacher.

*(ii)* There are various alternative approaches and materials. Which approach or combination of approaches and materials will take the teacher to his instructional objectives is decided here. This educated guess will depend on the experiences of the teacher himself or the experiences of others.

*(iii)* Standard rate of success by using different approaches is also determined in the third stage.

*(iv)* Students performance will be regularly monitored by using different types of tests in the fourth step. This step is related to actual teaching learning situation.

**(c) Communicating Realistic Expectations:**. What a teacher expects from his teaching is communicated to students here. A teacher takes following decisions in this regard.

*(i)* Students have to take active part in learning. If students do not take active part in learning activities, they are not expected to demonstrate high level of performance. Separate standards are fixed by the teacher for different types of students.

*(ii)* Students with disabilities have generally low level of motivation for performance in the class. A teacher has always to maintain high level of performance by adopting various techniques of motivation. Regular feedback is also to be given to students for this purpose.

*(iii)* In the third step, the instructional goals, performance criteria and the standard for mastery will either be written on the board or communicated orally to students.

## 2. ORGANISING INSTRUCTION

This component is related to interactive phase of teaching. The three principles of effective classroom management are given below:

(a) Preparing for instruction.

(b) Using time productively

(c) Establishing a positive classroom management.

**(a) Preparing for instruction :** Following things are involved here:

*(i)* Teacher establishe and communicates rules for classroom behaviour. Students are also told about the consequences of not following these rules in the beginning of the academic session.

*(ii)* If disruption occurs any time in the class, it is handled immediately in an effective manner. It is very necessary because the teacher is to deal deviant groups of children not the normal one who always have behaviour problem because of their disability.

*(iii)* Teacher also teaches the students to manage their own behaviour.

**(b) Using time productively :** Following strategies are adopted by the teacher to sue his time in a productive manner, i.e., more results in less time.

*(i)* Uses well established procedures of teaching.

*(ii)* Organises physical space to facilitate learning, i.e., each students is given adequate space to act properly in the class.

*(iii)* Interruptions are avoided by adopting adequate motivation techniques and by using proper seating arrangement.

*(iv)* The teacher properly allocates his time for various teaching activities in the class.

**(c) Establishing positive classroom environment.** It refers to interactive activities in the class. students must feel better in the class by these activities of the teacher. He follows following principles in this regard:

*(i)* He makes the environment of the class pleasant and friendly by praising and rewarding the students, by playing nicely with them and by sympathizing them.

*(ii)* He accepts their deviant behaviour and listen carefully to the individual problems of students.

*(iii)* He keeps the interaction positive by smiling on every positive behaviour of students.

*(iv)* He encourages the students to get involved in the lesson by questioning or by using proper material aids.

## 3. DELIVERING INSTRUCTION

This is the proper interactive phase of teaching. It is a three stage process:

(a) Presenting instruction.
(b) Monitoring instruction
(c) Adjusting instruction

**(a) Presenting Instruction:** It consists of the following aspects.

I. After reviewing the basic skills of students and drawing their attention, the content is now presented to them to teach them new skills and knowledge. The teacher should also make the lesson relevant to learning by adopting various techniques. It is also important that students should understand what is being taught to them. For this purpose, language of communication should be clear understandable and effective.

II. The second principle of effective instruction is to teach thinking skills to students which they can apply in completing various types of assignments given in the class. Thinking skills can be taught in different ways such as, a model can be presented before the students showing how to complete a task or elaborating procedures of accomplishing a task or directly telling to them or monitoring the students while they are doing something and rectifying their mistakes timely.

III. The third principle is that students are motivated regularly during the process of presentation. It will help them understand the content. A teacher can motivate his students in different ways such as he should show enthusiasm himself in presenting the content, he should reward his students at their nice performance or he can do any thing what he thinks better.

IV. Students learn better when they are given opportunity to practice the learnt material. This is the last principle of instruction. For this students should have ample time to practice the skill independently. It will develop automaticity, i.e. an index of complete learning in them.

**(b) Monitoring Instruction :** Good teacher is he who gives immediate, frequent and explicit feedback to his students at their performance. If students do something rightly, they are rewarded and if they do something incorrectly, they are corrected. This step is based on the following principles.

I. Different types of feedbacks are used for different types of contents, and learners, i.e., tying them to a specific job, supportive feedback to tell the students about rightness of a task, corrective feedback to correct the wrongness of a task and so on. Revision is also a type of corrective feedback which is frequently used while dealing with handicapped children.

II. Second principle is that students should actively respond to the instruction if they are asked something by the teacher during instruction. Students should be fully busy in listening to the instruction or doing what they are asked to do.

III. Timely needed help should also be given to students. This is the third principle of monitoring instruction. If help is given late, wrong conditioning will take place.

**(c) Adjusting Instruction.** All students do not learn in the same way or at the same pace. Hence, a teacher has to adjust his instruction according to the individual differences of learners. A teacher is expected to do the following things in this regard.

I. He adjust his lesson according to the individual's unique needs of learners.

II. He tries so many instructional methods and procedures in the class and selects the best one. The criteria of selection is that the more an option is satisfying to maximum number of students in the class, the better it is.

III. Finally, the teacher adjusts his speed of instruction to the pace of learner's abilities. Extra instruction can also be provided for this purpose.

## 4. EVALUATING INSTRUCTION

This is the last component of teaching. It is the process by which other three components given above are evaluated, i.e., the teacher comes to know whether the materials and methods used in teaching are effective on the basis of student's performance.

Evaluating instruction is based on the five principles given below:

(a) Monitoring students' understanding.
(b) Monitoring engaged time.
(c) Monitoring records of students' progress.
(d) Informing students about their progress.
(e) Using data to make final decision.

**(a) Monitoring students understanding:** Three strategies are involved here:

I. The teacher monitors the extent to which they understand his directions.
II. Students must understand the process they need to go through to complete the assignments given in the class, i.e, their approach of doing the task must be correct.
III. The teacher evaluates the success rate of his students, i.e, how much percent of mistakes they are committing. This error percentage should not be more than 20. If error rate is more than this. modification in the strategy will be required.

**(b) Monitoring engaged time:** Students who answer direct questions in the class and who actively participate in the discussion are called engaged students and they are expected to learn more than the others. Three strategies are involved here:

I. The teacher measures the amount of time that students have really engaged in the lesson by counting the number of times that a student has raised his hands for asking questions or responding questions asked by the teacher.
II. Students are trained to monitor their own behaviour in the class, i.e., they themselves record the number of times they have raised their hands for different purposes in the class.
III. The teacher scans the behaviour of the class as a whole on the basis of the data collected in the first two steps.

**(c) Monitoring records of student's progress.** Record of student's progress is prepared to know to what extent the students have profitted from the instruction. Two underlying principles regarding the monitoring of records are given below :

I. The teacher monitors the trends of the progress of all his students individually, i.e., whether they are going upwards or downward on the line showing their progress. This record is prepared on the basis of the task completed by students individually, though their performance may be collective.
II. The students are trained to study their own chart of progress themselves. Each individual student prepares his own chart of progress here.

**(d) Informing students about their progress :** It is a feedback process that keeps the students informed about their own progress. It also helps them to modify their behaviour if it is not satisfactory. The teacher must take following principles into account while informing students about their progress:

I. Students learn better when they know what they are doing. So feedback should be frequent and quick.
II. If mistakes are corrected regularly, they will not be conditioned to them. Thus, feedback should be regular.
III. If performance is satisfactory, motivation should also be given. Task specific praise is more effective here than random praises.
IV. Students should be helped by the teacher to correct their mistakes themselves.

**(e) Using data for decision making :** ON the basis of the records prepared by the teacher as well as the students, final decision about any student can be taken, i.e., whether he should be taught next lesson or the same lesson is to be repeated again. Decision of pass, or fail can also be taken on the basis of the submitted progress records. The teacher can also change his teaching strategies or materials if progress of students is not satisfactory.

## INDIVIDUALIZD EDUCATION PROGRAMMES (IEP)

An individualized education programme (IEP) is a written statement that describes what teachers and other professionals will do to meet the special learning needs of a student who is exceptional in any way. An IEP is written for only one particular student and at anytime only one IEP is used to guide the special education of that student. It is also a source of information for parents of the students and other professionals to know about the student.

**Items included in IEP are as follows :**

1. **Special education and related services.** Here the programme lists the following things.
   *(i)* Special education condition exhibited by the student, i.e., mental retardation, deafness, visual impairment etc.
   *(ii)* Name of the person responsible for the programme.
   *(iii)* Name of the school where the programme is being held.
   *(iv)* Related services provided to the student such as reader for a blind student, counsellor for an emotionally disturbed child, hearing aid for a deaf child and so on.
   *(v)* Name of the people involved in the special education process of the child.
   *(vi)* Description of transition services to be provided to a student who is older than 16 years.
2. **Participation in regular education :** Exceptional child is also given opportunity to take the benefit of a regular education programmes as much as possible. Lists of following informations is given here.
   *(i)* Duration of time the student will spend in regular education classes.
   *(ii)* Name of the subjects and the periods studied in regular education classes.
   *(iii)* Name of teachers teaching the student in regular education classes.
3. **Time frame for IEP's Implementation :** Following informations are given here.
   *(i)* Date of commencement of the IEP.
   *(ii)* Total duration of the IEP
   *(iii)* Review dates, i.e., in which month the programme will be reviewed after its completion.
   *(iv)* The dates on which parents teachers meet will be held during the programme.
4. **Functioning level of the student at present:** The IEP should also identify areas of special learning needs of the students on the basis of his present level of functioning. Following informations are given here:
   *(i)* Current level of performance of the student and the source of that information, e.g., dealing with mental deviance IQ scores and the name of the test which has yielded that result is given, It shows what the student is able to do.
   *(ii)* Name of the special difficulties, learning, behavioural or otherwise, of the student is given, i.e., what the student is not able to do at present.
5. **Goals and objectives of special education programme :** It is related to a verbal description of what the student is expected to learn after the end of the programme. Following informations are given here.
   *(i)* Annual Goal, i.e., what the student is expected to do after a year in the special education programme.
   *(ii)* Short Term Objectives. These objectives elaborate the steps that should be mastered to reach the annual goal, on daily basis, e.g., the student will be able to do multiplication operations of three digits at the end of lesson No. 3 or 4.
6. **Evaluation procedure and criteria :** The Programme and the progress of the student is evaluated periodically keeping in view the short term objectives and at the end of the session objectives keeping in view the annual goal. It needs the following informations to be given.
   *(i)* How the progress of the student will be measured, i.e. achievement test, skill test, essay type test, or objectives type test etc, which test will be used to measure the progress and so on.
   *(ii)* Upto which level the student must reach to match the criteria or standard, e.g., pass mark will be 33% or 40% and second division will be 45% or 50% of the total marks.
7. **Signature:** After the completion of the programme, the teachers and other professionals who prepare the programme put their signature on it. Parents and the students also sign it to

indicate that they were in the meeting when the programme was developed and finalized.

8. **Other relevant informations:** These informations are also useful from the point of view of its practicability.
   - *(i)* Nature and procedure of participation of parents in the programme.
   - *(ii)* Language spoken at the student's home.
   - *(iii)* Health condition of the student.
   - *(iv)* Management strategies to control student's behaviour.
   - *(v)* Special requirement of the student from high school onward.
   - *(vi)* Details of extra curricular activities organised for the student.
   - *(vii)* Self study or practice schedule of the student and so on.

## SPECIAL TEACHING METHODS

Common teaching strategies does not suit to exceptionals in the class. Some modifications are needed to be made in them to achieve the objectives of special education.

Important special teaching methods are given below :

### 1. Precision Teaching

It is the method in which teachers plan, use and analyse the effects of instructional methods to improve the performance of students. In this method, student's progress is constantly evaluated in terms of objectives and efforts are always made to improve the skills. Five steps involved in precision teaching are given below :

- *(i)* The teacher identifies the target behaviour pinpointed in the first step.
- *(ii)* The teacher or the student counts and records the baseline rate of the behaviour, i.e., entering behaviour of the student is evaluated before the actual teaching begins in the class.
- *(iii)* By relating the baseline behaviour with the content, the teacher writes short term objectives.
- *(iv)* Then the teacher tries an instruction method or combination of methods and regularly evaluates and records the changes in the behaviour of students.
- *(v)* If student's performance is found inadequate after evaluation, necessary changes in the instruction approach are introduced.

One point to be noted here is that progress of each student is recorded here on a special record called **"standard behaviour chart".**

### 2. Ability Training

Ability training is used by the teacher when students need instruction in pre academic skills. For example, if a student is unable to differentiate between a geometric shape of figure and a letter, the teacher gives him different types of figures to match with each other. Similarly, if a student cannot differentiate between a and e in speaking, he is given recorded sounds of these vowels for practice. Ability training is also given in those areas where students face difficulty. The underlying assumption here is that students will perform better if they are made cognizant about their potentialities. This is actually a type of remedial teaching.

### 3. Direct Instruction

In this method, instruction is directly related to the teaching goals. Here instructional procedure is divided into certain steps on the basis of various skills used in doing a job, then each of these skills are taught to students one by one. The next skill is taught to them only when the first skill is mastered by them. This is also known as Attack Strategy Training. The steps involved in this method are as follows.

- *(i)* Skill to be taught is identified first.
- *(ii)* Small steps involved in the mastery of the skill are analysed.
- *(iii)* Rules for putting the steps together are formulated.
- *(iv)* Students are taught all these steps one by one.
- *(v)* Students are evaluated on the basis of various steps that they follow and performance on the skill in accurate form.

### 4. Learning Strategies Training

This training teaches the students how to learn the content and how to demonstrate their knowledge like direct instruction, Step by step procedure is followed here also.

This strategy is based on the two assumptions given below :

(a) Students monitor themselves. Here student acts as an observer for his own behaviour and records the mistakes committed by him. If they are told how to minimize their mistakes, they will learn better.

(b) Self correction is possible. He can correct his own mistakes by comparing them with the model supplied to him.

If we apply the method in writing an essay on the basis of the words or phrases given, following steps will be followed:

*(i)* Essay will be read after writing is over.

*(ii)* Sentences relating to personal beliefs or opinions will be isolated.

*(iii)* Two reasons why we believe so will be given.

*(iv)* Then all the sentences given in the essay will be scanned one by one.

*(v)* Non sense sentences will be isolated from the essay.

*(vi)* Those sentences which do not match with our belief will also be picked out from the lot.

*(vii)* Necessary changes will be introduced in the essay after necessary sorting.

*(viii)* Essay will be read again. This is the last step.

## 5. Study skills Training

Handicapped students generally lack organizational and study related skills needed to respond to academic tasks and they also feel difficulty in the acquisition of these skills. Study skills are systematic procedures that students follow to complete such complex tasks as skimming, picking answers of questions from the text, taking notes etc.

**Archer and Gleason** (1989) developed a set of training exercises to teach study skills to students. Some of these exercises are given below.

*(i)* Gaining information from a textual material.

*(ii)* Self questioning from the text.

*(iii)* Attending to maps and graphs that accompany the content.

*(iv)* Answering comprehensive questions from the text.

*(v)* Writing summaries of materials read.

*(vi)* Organizing informations of the text in other ways.

## 6. Cognitive Skills Training

Benjamin S Bloom has identified six levels of cognitive objectives-knowledge, comprehension, application, analysis, synthesis and the last and the highest one is evaluation. These six skills will be taught to students in the following ways:

*(i)* To teach knowledge skill, teachers expose students to aesthetic, economic, political, social and educational aspects of the environment and also to people with similar interests and give them the chance of self experience.

*(ii)* To teach comprehension and application skills, students are asked to collect information to use in decision making, to work with those people who share common interest and to develop and make original products.

*(iii)* Analysis and synthesis skills include examining creative items, changing way of thinking, moulding thinking pattern, comparing thinking patterns with others and integrating knowledge through conversion or diversion of thoughts.

*(iv)* To teach evaluation skills students are trained to identify standard for making comparison, develop decision making skills and to make choices.

## 7. Behaviour Therapy

Behaviour therapy is very much needed when we deal with gifted or retarded children. It is the process of arranging environmental events systematically to influence the behaviour of a child. It is based on the assumption that environmental events that occur just before a particular behaviour and its consequences which happen just after the behaviour can be used to mould behaviour in the desired manner. The teacher can change the antecedents or consequence or both to change the behaviour of the child. (See section A, chanter 'Counselling' for detail)

Behaviour therapy is based on two types of conditioning, respondent and operant.

**Principles of Respondent Conditioning :** This type of conditioning is based on two principles:

*(i)* Innate responses (reflexes) follow specific stimuli. For example, if we see someone hitting us, we try to escape.

*(ii)* New stimuli can come to trigger innate responses through the process of conditioning. If we pair a response causing stimulus with a new stimulus (which does not generally evoke a response), the new stimulus will also come to evoke a response for some time even if it is presented alone as we see in Pavlov's conditioning theory of learning. When food is given to the dog along with ringing the bell, the dog salivates but when only bell is rung the dog still salivates.

**Principles of Operant conditioning :** It is the systematic application and gradual removal of reward and punishment to increase wanted behaviour and decrease unwanted one. Five steps are systematically followed here:

*(i)* A target behaviour and its plan of measurement is specified.

*(ii)* Different levels of behaviour are identified and isolated.

*(iii)* Reinforcers are selected to systematically apply them on these occurrence of behaviour.

*(iv)* Reinforcement plan is implemented

*(v)* Effects of the intervention is evaluated in the end.

Any of the above two techniques can be applied to change the behaviour of the student. An example of respondent conditioning of behaviour is given below.

**Example :** Mohan was a student who suffered from the problem of examination phobia. He would become very nervous when he was given any test. His problem was reduced by the teacher by giving him test repeatedly. A packet of toffees was also given to him each time along with the test. When the first test was given, it caused anxiety in him. In order to reduce anxiety it was taken back immediately. Next time, test was given for a longer period and then taken back. In this way he was trained to take a test without fear. This desensitization technique improved his performance on the test.

### 8. Social Skills Training

Handicapped children generally lack social skills **Sobornie** (1991) indicated that it is important for social skills teachers to teach those behaviours which students can learn easily, that they use readily and that are powerful enough to elicit positive responses from others. The social skills taught should increase the social competence of learners as well.

Important such social skills are given below :

*(i)* Friendship skills-greeting, joining and leaving activities.

*(ii)* Social maintenance skills-helping, cooperating, competing etc.

*(iii)* Conflict resolution skills.

*(iv)* Classroom etiquettes.

*(v)* Family norms.

## SPECIAL INSTRUCTIONAL ADAPTATION

Different instructional adaptations can be used by the students with disabilities to modify their way of participation in the teaching learning process and hence to enhance their learning. These adaptations help the handicapped students to improve their communications and some of them increase their mobility also. Two inportant adaptations are given below:–

### 1. Communication Improving Adaptation

A disabled student must be able to communicate properly with his teachers and school fellows in order to succeed in his school life. Because of his disabilities, he will be poor in this process. In order to improve his communication horizon and effectiveness, following adaptive measures can be used:

**(a) Communication Boards :** Communication boards are used by students who are unable to speak. Different letters and symbols are given here on the board. The student points at these letters and symbols and communicates his desire. Speech can also be added to these boards by using electronic communication devices.

**(b) Hearing Aids:** It is a device that amplifies the sound and used by those who are hard of hearing. Hearing aids are worn behind the ear or in the ear.

**(c) Classroom Amplification System (CAS) :** CAS is used to increase the communication abilities of those students who have special communication needs. Here students are connected with one microphone system and they hear voices of the teacher on their respective headphones. They can communicate with their teachers also by using microphones.

**(d) Telecommunication Devices:** Written communication is the only effective means for those who are deaf. Starting from paper and pencil to tele-communication devices there are different techniques used for this purpose. The deaf reads the material written on the screen and answers verbally.

Telecommunication devices are small keyboards and receivers which are connected with a normal telephone by an acoustic coupler. To make a call, we book our phone to the device and call another person with a similar device. When connection is established, a message appears on the screen. Then we type what we want to say which is translated and printed on the printer connected to the other person's phone.

**(e) Braille:** Louis Braille developed a system of reading and writing that uses arrangement of six raised dots to represent letters, words and numbers. This system is widely used by blinds to read and write even today.

The blind children who need braille are introduced to it at an early age of schooling. They are taught to read and write on braille at an early age. Generally students take about two years to read braille proficiently. Similarly, a six keyed device is used to write on a braille. This device creates a raised dot words. Instead of six keyed device, some students use a slate and stylus to punch out braille dots.

**(f) Computers.** Computers are very much used by physically handicapped as a helping device today. For example, a professional musician who is paralysed or having speech impairment uses a computerized music system to compose and play his work. An architect who can not use his arms or legs due to cerebral palsy can produce elaborate maps just with the help of a mouse of the computer.

## 2. Mobility Improving Adaptation

Important adaptive measures that can improve the mobility of orthopedically or visually handicapped are given below:

**(a) Guide Dogs :** Guide dogs are sued by those people who are fully blind to help them move freely. But individuals below 16 years are not allowed to use guide dogs because they are not supposed to care the animal properly. These guide dogs are, however, not liked by blinds because they run or walk too fast. Canes are preferred to dogs due to this reason.

**(b) Wheel Chairs :** When Mobility of an orthopedically handicapped is restricted due to a problem in his legs he uses wheel chairs to move about. Modern wheel chairs are made of a light weight metal. The large back wheel of the chair have a special rim that helps the chair to move freely. Instead of ordinary wheel chairs, motorized and computerized wheel chairs are being used today.

**(c) Prostheses :** Artificial replacement for missing body parts is known as prostheses. These devices help the handicapped people to move in the society freely.

## ASSESSMENT PROCEDURE IN SPECIAL EDUCATION

The assessment is the process by which teachers and other school personnel collect information to make decision of pass or fail of student or to modify an instructional programme in the school system. If we want to know the progress of a student, we will have to go through the process of assessment which will require testing of the behaviour. Assessment also helps us know to what extent students are making progress.

## Objectives and Steps of Assessment in Special Education

From diagnosing the handicapped children to their permanent rehabilitation, assessment is an integral part of each and every phase of special education process. Assessment is actually a decision making process. It helps to take the following decisions:

1. **Screening :** Students with learning difficulties are separated from the lot on the basis of screening. It is a process of collecting data to decide whether more intensive assessment of the child is necessary or not. Screening is thus a process of picking out suspected people from the lot.

   Screening takes place at all levels of educations. Pupils are screened before giving them admission in any class. Screening test is also conducted to measure visual or hearing acuity of students. After the process of screening is over, screening results are then compared with the standard norms to make final decision. For this very purpose, the test makers provide cut off scores to help educators to make decision. These cut off scores are called norms. Because of this reason, when a student scores less than the cut off scores in an admission test, he is denied admission in that class or course.

   Screening is used in the teaching-learning process also. It is used in the school system to identify those students who need extra attention or remedial coaching. This decision is taken only by comparing their scores with the norms or average performance of students at various age or grade levels.

   Thus, we see that cut off scores are essential while taking any decision on the basis of a screening test. When screening test indicates a special need or problem of a student, only then the student is refereed for any further test.

2. **Decision to provide special help :** Teachers generally uses class tests, observations and interviews to decide whether a student is in need of a special help. Screening is used as a decision making process in this perspective. When the problem is found serious, special help is given to the child.

   The special help does not necessarily mean special education to be provided to students. It may be in the form of extra coaching, remedial teaching or modification in the instructional strategies. All these things will help the students to correct their defects or remove their difficulties.

3. **Decision to refer to an intervention assistance team :** When a student is not showing a satisfactory progress even after the special help given to him he maybe refereed to an intervention assistance team (IAT) for further screening and guidance. This team will assess the student's minutes and necessary action will be taken thereof.

4. **Decision to provide intervention assistance :** The IAT will gather data about the student through observation, interview and testing and on the basis of these assessment, the IAT decides which type of special help will suit to the student. Whether he needs medical services, or he should be sent to the physician for further check up or the help provided by the IAT is sufficient for him.

5. **Decision to refer for psycho-education evaluation :** When the student is still not progressing satisfactorily even by the help of intervention assistance team, he is refereed to psycho-educationist for formal evaluation. In that case, a formal request is made by the IAT to the Child Study Team (CST) saying that the student is sufficiently abnormal and entitled for special education, so he should be thoroughly evaluated. The CST consists of regular education teacher, special education teacher, at least one administrator, parents and related service personnel, such as psychologist, nurses, social workers, expert in measurement and counsellors. The **child study team** takes two types of decisions here:

   (a) Decision of exceptionality, whether the child is handicapped or gifted.

(b) Verification of special learning needs of the child pointed out by intervention assistance team.

6. **Exceptionality Decision :** On the basis of its assessment the CST decides whether the child fulfils the criteria of being exceptional and eligible for special education services provided by the state or not. Here the child's assessment report is matched with the legal structure prepared by the state regarding exceptionality and its placement. For example, if a child scores less than 80 IQ score on an intelligence test, he will be considered as mentally retarded. The CST not only decides the type or mode of disability of a child but it also provides sufficient information regarding the degree of exceptionality of the child-profound, severe, moderate or **mild.**
7. **The decision about special learning needs :** The decision regarding special learning needs of the child is also taken by the child study team. For example, after deciding the degree of visual impairment of a child, the CST points out important learning needs of the child, whether he needs braille for reading or writing or he needs only books of large print and so on. On the basis of these learning needs, the CST also suggest which type of special education services the child requires.
8. **Decision of eligibility :** After specifying the exceptionality, its degree and special learning needs of the child, the Child Study Team can declare which type of special education services (placement) the child will need.
9. **Decision about instructional planning :** Three kinds of decision are made in instructional planning.
   *(i)* Decision of what to teach.
   *(ii)* Decision of how to teach.
   *(iii)* Communicating realistic expectation.
   The decision of what to teach is a content decision made on the basis of systematic analysis of skills that the student of a particular age may possess. The decision of how to teach is taken on the basis of trial of different methods of teaching or its combination. Students' progress is monitored in terms of instructional goals while trying these methods. Lastly, the realistic expectations are communicated to students on the basis of these decisions.
10. **Evaluation decision :** Evaluation decision is taken in order to know whether the students are making progress satisfactorily or not. Unit tests, terminal tests, observations or interviews are conducted for this purpose. Total skills learned by students are not tested through these evaluation techniques but only a sample of the skills taught is tested to know the progress of a student.
11. **Decision about programme evaluation :** Assessment also helps us know to what extent a specific special education programme or the curriculum is meeting the objectives of the school. School personnel use this information for school-wise curriculum planning. For example, they can compare two approaches of teaching in one content area followed in different schools and decide which one is the better.
    By evaluating the effectiveness of different instructional methods, we actually evaluate the effectiveness of the teacher also and can take decision whether the teacher is competent or he needs further in service training
12. **Accountability decision : Assessment** report can also help the authorities know whether the schools are functioning properly.
    School personnel conduct regular tests, and interviews to know the progress of students and send the same to the higher authorities for further analysis. Accountability of these schools and their personnel is thus determined on the basis of these informations.

## Techniques of Assessment in Special Education

Information (data) about exceptional children can be gathered by using following assessment techniques.

(A) Testing

(B) Observation
(C) Interview
(D) Work sample assessment

**(A) Testing :** It is a process of administering a set of items sampled from the behaviour of the child to obtain a score. It is generally designed to measure cognitive abilities of students in a particular content area.

These tests can be classified into the following categories:

1. **Formal versus informal tests :** Formal tests have standardized administration and scoring procedures. They are generally designed to be used on large group of children. Annual examination at the end of the academic session is an example of formal test.
   Informal test is developed by the teacher of the class to measure cognitive abilities in an area that was recently taught. Unit tests, weekly tests, monthly tests pre board examinations etc are examples of informal tests. Neither administrative nor scoring procedure is standardized here.
   Thus, formal tests are standardized while informal tests are teacher made.
2. **Individual versus group tests :** Individual tests are administered on individuals one by one in an individual situation and the information about the testee is collected. Group tests are administered on the whole class simultaneously to collect immediate information about the whole group. The directions given here are so clear that they do not face any problem in understanding them and hence no assistance is needed in the middle of testing period.
3. **Written versus oral tests :** In written tests, informations are gathered in written form but in oral tests informations are collected by conducting interviews or viva voce in a face to face situation.
4. **Objective versus essay type tests :** In objective type tests, only those items are included in the test which require only one exact response and whosoever evaluates them assign the same score to the examinee.
   In essay type tests questions are asked in such a manner that their answers take the form of an essay. The students' ability to organize the subject matter and its elaboration is tested here.
5. **Screening versus Diagnostic tests :** Screening tests are used to spot pupils who are making progress either too little or too much as compared to others.
   Diagnostic tests are designed to provide more specific informations about the pupils in the form of strengths or weaknesses on the development of a particular skill.
6. **Norm referenced and criterion referenced tests:** Norm referenced are those tests in which the students performance is compared with the performance of other students of the same group to which he belongs. Norm referencing is actually a comparison between obtained score and the average score. These norms (average) are prepared with the help of standardized procedures. Students who perform below the norm are said to be deficient in the area being tested and those who perform more than average are said to be superior. This type of tests are very much needed in special education.
   Criterion referenced tests tell us to what extent an individual or group have mastered specific curriculum, content or skill. Here the performance of the testee is compared with an outside criteria to know whether he has reached the criteria or not. For example, if a student scores 60% on an achievement test, he is considered first divisioner.

**(B) Observation :** See chapter "Psychology and Educational Psychology" of the book.

**(C) Interview :** Interview is a face to face situation of collecting data. Questions are directly asked here from the respondent, what he knows, thinks and feels.

Interview can be structured and unstructured both. In structured interviews, questions are framed in advance and same questions are asked from all the interviewees and data on the basis of their responses are analysed to know the causes of a problem. In unstructured interviews, free exchange of views takes place between the interviewer and the interviewee and no prior preparation regarding the number or nature of questions is made.

***Advantages of interview :***

1. Maximum rapport between the two parties is seen here.
2. Personality and behaviour of a person can be tested on the basis of his way of responding..
3. As a measure of achievement test, it compels the students to study hard because guessing will not be possible here.
4. History of the patients and the deviant children can be taken by this method very easily here.

***Disadvantages :***

1. The interviewer can manipulate the responses and results of the interviewee very easily here and thus objectivity can not be maintained.
2. If same questions are asked from all the interviewees again and again, it discloses the secrecy of the examination.
3. The respondents can hide their real behaviour very easily here.

**(D) Work sample assessment :** Here some tasks are given to students to complete or they are asked to make some products and students' work is evaluated to see whether they have performed the task correctly, and if they have done some mistakes in doing the job, to what extent they are correct.

Behaviour or abilities assessed in special education :

Following abilities are tested by using different techniques of assessment in special education:

1. **Intellectual abilities :** School personnel regularly use intelligence tests for following purposes.
   (*i*) To identify the extent to which students demonstrate normal thinking and problem solving skills.
   (*ii*) To spot out those students who deviate from the mean performance on an intelligence test, i.e., whether they are gifted or mentally retarded.
   (*iii*) To classify mentally retarded or gifted into different categories on the basis of their IQ scores.

   Gifted and retarded both types of students are a challenge for regular classroom teachers. It is because, due to their unique learning needs they do not easily adjust with the normal students of the class.

   Intellectual abilities can also be assessed through observation. A student is asked to do such a task in which thinking process is involved. The teacher observes the student in performing the task or solving the complex problem. This is the work sample assessment of cognitive domain of learners.

   Interview is the fourth source of collecting data regarding the intellectual abilities of a student. Direct questions sampling intelligent behaviour are asked from him and decision is taken on the basis of total scores secured by him.
2. **Academic achievement :** It refers to the progress made by students in academic or curricular areas. Achievement test is generally used for this purpose but the interview technique can also be used to know to what extent a student has progressed after a certain amount of instruction. Achievement tests and interviews both measure skill development in academic content area. For example, different skills are needed in writing an essay along with the mastery of the content. These skills are assessed through achievement tests and interviews.
3. **Sensory Acuity :** This behaviour is basically related to five senses, e.g., sense of taste, sense of touch, sense of smell, sense of hearing and visual sense. But only two senses, hearing and visual are studied in special education because other senses do not have any relevance in the teaching learning process.

   Poor academic achievement is sometimes caused by problems of vision or hearing. So, regular tests of sensory acuities are conducted in the school to know which student has a visual or hearing problem and to what extent. **Snellen Chart** is a common test of visual acuity. Here the individual reads the chart from a distance of 20 feet. Similarly, an audiometer is used to assess hearing acuity

Sensory acuities can also be assessed by watching how children read and how they act when asked questions. If they read books from very close distance and they do not leave this habit due to their inability to read from normal distance, they are said to be visually impaired. Similarly, if they are unable to hear low tone questions and come closer to the teacher for hearing, they are declared as students having hearing impairment. However, whatever data is collected by observation or interview, it must be verified by proper testing.

4. **Adaptive behavior :** American Association on Mental Deficiency (1973) defined adaptive behaviour as "effectiveness or degree with which the individual meets the standard of personal independence and social responsibility expected of his age and social group."

In order to know the adaptive behaviour of a child we use interview techniques and parents, teachers and others associated with the child are interviewed. These adaptive behaviour scales provide following informations.

*(i)* About student's self help skills like eating, dressing and toileting.

*(ii)* About communication skills like using money, playing games, greeting people etc.

The best method of assessing adaptive behaviour of a child is observation which provides accurate information about deviant or adaptive behaviour of a child.

Since adaptive behaviour of a child is assessed in the context of the environment, we must understand the environment first. The extent to which the behaviour of a person is adaptive, i.e., (normal) in an environment, is evaluated in the context of the environment where it must be acceptable by the majority of the people either for the whole society or for the culture or the community to which the person belongs. A number of other factors also affect adaptive behaviour such as the context in which the behaviour is exhibited, status of the person exhibiting the behaviour, the situation of the environment at the time when behaviour was shown and so on. For example, if there is communal tension in an area, none is expected to show an adaptive behaviour.

5. **Language development :** Poor academic achievement is also seen due to deficient language development. The tests measuring language development of a child possess four components of a language phonology, morphology, syntax and semantics.

For testing the language development of a child language samples of behaviour are given to the child to respond.

Language development can also be assessed by observing a child using a language. We can count the number of specific clauses of speech problem, number of mistakes committed in sentences and the number of sophisticated words used and can come to know roughly about the language development of a child. Some teachers use video tapes, audio tapes or written transcription to study the speech potentialities of their students Interview technique can also be used for assessing the language development of a child but standardized tests are the best and the most reliable technique to provide information on selected aspects of language ability and to know the strengths and weaknesses of a child regarding a particular language.

6. **Perceptual-motor development :** It is believed that if a person is able to translate sensory informations into meaningful action only then he succeeds in his school life. For example, if a child can copy a geometric design like squares or rectangles, only then he can copy letters or numbers. This ability to copy designs in the exact manner is related to perceptual motor development of the child. Here he perceives the stimuli first then by using his motor capacities, he imitates the stimuli given. This aspect of

human development plays very crucial role in all the aspects of teaching learning process.

***The Bender Visual Motor Gestalt Test :*** It is a good example of a perceptual motor measurement device. It consists of nine geometric shapes which the student is asked to copy on a plain sheet of paper.

The reproductions are scored in relation to four types of errors:

*(i)* Shape distortion. *(ii)* Preservation
*(iii)* Integration *(iv)* Rotation

Shape distortion error is scored when design is distorted to such an extent that a representation of original figure is lost.

Preservation error is scored when child fails to stop even after the completion of the figure.

Integration error is scored when parts of a design overlap.

Rotation error is scored when the student shifts the design more than $45^0$ from the way it is was presented.

The other methods of assessing perceptual motor development is observation where mistakes committed by the performance are noticed and noted down immediately. Poor perceptual motor development is associated with learning disabilities, mental retardation and multi-handicapping situation.

# Hearing Impairment and Educational Adaptation

## Perspective

Hearing and speech play a joint role in communication. When former is defective it is likely that later will also be defective and when speech is defective, verbal intelligence will automatically be low. It is in this sense that hearing impaired children face double problem, one in the area of reception and other in the area of communication.

## Meaning and Definitions

Hearing impairment is of two types-deaf and hard of hearing. Deafness is a severe disability. Those people who are deaf have a hearing loss to the extent that it prevents understanding speech through the ear. On the other hand, people who are hard of hearing can process information from sounds and they can be benefitted by hearing aids.

## CLASSIFICATION OF HEARING IMPAIRED

The above two groups of people can be categorised further into sub groups on the basis of the following criteria.

(A) Degree of Hearing Impairment
(B) Causes of the deficit.
(C) Age of the person at the time of onset of the disability.

### (A) Degree of Intensity of Threshold

Conference of executives of American schools for Deaf (1974) defined aurally handicapped children in terms of threshold and in terms of their educational adaptability.

1. **Mildly Retarded (26-54 db loss):** These children need full integration with the regular classes with special services and materials provided under the guidance of the specialists. These people have difficulty in hearing distant sounds and require hearing aids or microphones with loud speakers.
2. **Moderately Retarded (55-69 db loss):** They need partial integration in regular schools with some classes in regular setting and some classes in special setting. They have difficulty in hearing distant sounds as well as near sounds of low frequency and pitch. They require special training and hearing aids both. They can be benefitted by them.
3. **Severely Retarded (70-89 db loss):** They need self contained programme in partially integrated system of education. They do not benefit much by using hearing aids.
4. **Profoundly Retarded (db loss of 90db and above):** Their hearing impairment is so profound that they can not be benefitted by integrated classes in any way. They always need special classes and special schools to study by using very special materials and techniques. It is because they can neither hear distant nor near sounds even if they are produced with above normal frequency. They require lip reading and American sign language for learning.

Thus, a deaf person is one whose hearing is defective to such an extent that he is unable to understand the sound from a distance with or without hearing aids. For legal and administrative purposes, such a definitions is accepted.

### (B) Causes of Hearing Impairment

Aurally handicapped children are also categorised according to whether the hearing loss is conductive or neural. Conductive hearing loss is caused due to blockage or damage in the outer or middle section of the ear. Neural loss occurs when there is a damage in the inner ear or auditory nerves. If it is conductive, it can be treated by sound amplification and if it is neural, it can not be treated at all.

## (C) Age of aurally handicapped at the time of onset

The definition proposed by the White House Conference on Child Health and Protection categorised them in the following way.

1. **Born Defectives :** They are those who are born with sufficient hearing loss to prevent the spontaneous acquisition of speech. The speech of these children will always be defective and they will be dumb forever.
2. **Prelingual Deafness :** Those who become deaf before the development of language and speech come under this category. Their speech is also retarded throughout life.
3. **Post Lingual Deafness :** They are those who become deaf after the development of language and speech.

The above criteria of deafness are very important from the point of view of education and placement of these children.

**Definitions :**

1. "Deafness means a hearing impairment that is so severe that the child is impaired in processing linguistic information through hearing with or without amplification that adversely affects a, child's educational performance.
   Individual with Disabilities Education Act 1990 (USA)
2. A deaf is one whose hearing is disabled to an extent (usually 70 db or greater) that precludes the understanding of speech through the ear alone with or without the use of hearing aid.
3. A hard of hearing person is one whose hearing is disabled to an extent (usually 35-70 db) that makes difficult but does not preclude the understanding of speech through the ear alone with or without hearing aid **(Moores 1987)**

## CAUSES OF HEARING IMPAIRMENT

In 48% hearing impaired cases no definite cause of impairment can be ascertained. Some of the possible causes of hearing impairment are given below :

### (A) Hereditary or Genetic Causes

About 35% deafness found in the society is of congenital origin. More than 5 genetic syndromes have been identified so far due to which hearing loss may occur. Three of them are given below.

I. Pendred's Syndrome
II. Usher's Syndrome
III. Jervell Syndrome

**Preventive Measures**

*(i)* Constant medical check up during pregnancy.
*(ii)* Parents should consult the etiologists to avoid such defective children in future.

### (B) Exogenous Causes

1. **Prental Causes :** Prental assault to the fetus due to viral infections may result into deafness. German measles in early pregnancy, influenza, mumps etc. are some important viral infections that can cause deafness. These are basically congenital causes. Some acquired causes are given below.
   (a) Maternal Rubella. It is the most common cause of deafness. Due to this disease in mothers, children maybe born deaf. This hearing loss is sensory neural in nature.
   (b) Toxoplasmosis. It is caused by a virus, affects the fetus and causes sensory neural hearing loss.
   (c) Intoxication. Intoxication during pregnancy may also damage auditory sense of the forthcoming baby.
2. **Perinatal causes.** Important such causes related to delivery are given below:
   - birth injury.
   - Anoxia at the time of delivery.
   - Adoption of birth control measures.
3. **Post Natal Causes :**
   **(a) Meningitis.** It is a disease of central nervous system that causes sensory neural hearing loss. This disease is the common cause of deafness or hearing loss.
   **(b) Otitis Media.** It is the infection of middle ear and the accumulation of fluid behind the ear drum. It is conductive hearing loss.
   **(c) Other Causes :** Tuberculosis, mumps, measles, throat infection, influenza,

whooping cough etc. are some other possible causes of hearing impairment.

**Preventive Measures**

*(i)* Immunization of mother during pregnancy.
*(ii)* Prevention of possible diseases.
*(iii)* Avoidance of drugs and alcohols.
*(iv)* Early diagnosis of infectious diseases and their proper treatment.
*(v)* Proper and balanced diet during pregnancy.
*(vi)* Regular check up of mother during pregnancy.
*(vii)* Early identification of deafness and providing proper medical and educational advices so that the situation may not be worsened.

## Identification of Aurally Handicapped Children

They can be identified first by seeing their behaviour and the symptoms they exhibit. Important such symptoms are given below:

1. **General Symptoms :** Some of these symptoms are as follows:
   - Poor articulation of sounds.
   - Delayed speech.
   - Lack of responsiveness.

   But since these symptoms are seen in mentally retarded and sometimes in normal children too, so these symptoms alone can not help us much to identify hearing impaired children. We will have to see some more things in their behaviour. These specific symptoms are given below.
2. **Specific Symptoms**

   *(i)* Apparent chronic inattention.
   *(ii)* Frequent failure to respond when he is talked to.
   *(iii)* They come closer when they are talked to or when they listen to a radio or T.V.
   *(iv)* They tune the volume of radio or TV up more than the normal sound when they listen them.
   *(v)* They generally avoid the company of friends because it becomes very difficult for them to enjoy it with the help of conversation.
   *(vi)* Speech of the child is delayed.
   *(vii)* They do not pay attention to what the parents say during infancy period.
3. **Behaviour in the School**

   *(i)* Experiences difficulties in following oral presentation and directions of the teacher.
   *(ii)* Watches lips of the teacher very closely when the teacher speaks.
   *(iii)* Leans towards the teacher to listen.
   *(iv)* Uses limited vocabulary.
   *(v)* Uses speech sounds poorly.
   *(vi)* Shows delay in language development.
   *(vii)* Does not respond when called from behind.
   *(viii)* Inattentive in the class during oral presentation.
   *(ix)* Frequent cold and ear infection.
   *(x)* Discharging fluid from the ear.

## Characteristics of Hearing Impaired Children

They have some characteristics common with visually impaired children but some unique, characteristics are also seen in them. Some important characteristics related to these children are given below:

1. **Intellectual Abilities :**

   **I.** The environment of hearing impaired people is qualitatively different from that of the normal people. Since about one third of intellectual development depends upon what we listen in the environment and use it in our life. As a result, their intellectual functioning is obviously limited almost less than average. This low level of intellectual ability is not due to any deficiency in their cognition but due to inadequate development of a conventional language system.

   **II. Pintner and Paterson** on the basis of their studies found that severely hearing impaired have a mean IQ of 63 and medium IQ of 91 and they found no significant difference between the deaf and the normal in 12 studies. This shows that they are not intellectually low as compared to the normal children.
2. **Educational Achievement:**

   I. Children and adults who have mild hearing loss generally achieve more in academic subjects than those whose hearing losses are severe.

   II. Those who are deaf by birth tend to have more difficulty in acquiring academic skills than those who become deaf after 8 or 10 years from the life.

III. Those hearing impaired children who belong to high socio-economic status experience fewer academic difficulties than those who belong to poor families.

IV. They do not perform well like normals on reading and writing tests but their ability in performing arts or fine arts is no less than normals in any way.

V. Absolute amount of educational retardation in these people increase with age. It is more retarded in pure academic skills such as mathematics, natural sciences and writing than in the more intellectual areas such as paragraph understanding, language, communication and the like.

**3. Social Development and Adjustment**

I. They show a very high degree of emotional instability causing maladjustment but it is not apparently visible.

II. They take shelter in isolation due to poor communication ability and frustration. As a result, their social development is adversely affected.

**4. Behavioural Characteristics.**

I. People with hearing impairment are deviant from the norms and traditions of the society.

II. Some deaf people cope with the reality of deafness as a life long condition and they lead normal productive lives. Thus, deafness has no negative impact on the development of a mentally healthy person. Thus, we see that findings are contradictory regarding this aspect of hearing impairment.

III. Deaf people mostly prefer to have the company of the hearing impaired people and in this way groups of hearing impaired people are formed. Deaf culture is developed due to this clustering of deaf or hard of hearing people.

IV. People who are deaf teach each other how to function in the society and how to get along with others.

**5. Physical Capacities**

I. People who are deaf or hard of hearing are no more or less than normal people in other sensory abilities like sight, smell, taste and touch.

II. They basically differ in functional hearing from their peers or other normal people. Functional hearing refers to a person's ability to understand information presented orally and it is related to how a person might be taught. For example, a person with a moderate functional hearing loss may not be able to profit from a normal classroom presentation and would require some instructional adaptation to be successful.

***Functional hearing loss is categorised in decibel grouping in the following way.***

*(i) Less than 25 decibel loss (normal). No difficulty faces in speech.*

*(ii) 26-40 decibel loss. Faces difficulty only in faint sound. i.e., sound spoken at low pitch.*

*(iii) 41-55 decibel loss. Understands face to face speech and conversation.*

*(iv) 56-70 decibel loss moderate level of impairment). Frequent difficulty in special conversation and speech.*

*(v) 70-90 decibel loss (severe handicap in hearing). Understands only shouted speech and speech used through amplification devices.*

*(vi) More than 91 decibel loss (profoundly retarded). They face difficulty in hearing even if amplification sound or hearing aid is used.*

*Thus, we see that unique physical characteristics are seen in these children.*

**6. Communication Abilities.**

I. Language development is delayed if hearing loss is of moderate type and these people have less vocabulary power than the normals. However, if hearing impairment is severe in nature verbal communication ability may be almost zero.

II. Language and communication abilities depend upon the interaction between people individually and collectively. Since, hearing impaired people avoid to interact with others, their language abilities are retarded further.

III. Normal people also neglect hard of hearing people because later require sounds of high frequency and pitch and normal people do not like to talk at such a loud voice. The result is that deaf and hard of hearing people have less chance of interaction with others.

## Testing and Measurement of Auditory Acuity

Hearing impaired children can be identified on the basis of their symptoms and characteristics but to what extent their ears are damaged can be ascertained only after administering proper test to them. This testing is necessary because intervention programme for them can be arranged only after knowing the exact amount of hearing loss.

While determining the level of hearing impairment we consider two factors:

(a) Intensity (b) Frequency

(a) **Intensity.** Intensity refers to the relative loudness of the sound. Loudness is expressed in decibels. Greater the decibels, the louder the sound.
The individual may have difficulty in hearing sounds at a distance but when distance is reduced, the sound becomes audible for him. A comfortable listening requires an intensity level of 50-60 decibels above threshold in a normal environment. If loss of intensity is 70 db in a person he would require 70+(50-60)=120-130 db of intensity of sound to hear it which is painful for normal people.

(b) **Frequency.** By frequency , we mean the number of vibrations of sound waves occurred at a given pitch. Greater the frequency, higher the pitch is needed, i.e., an individual may have difficulty in hearing sounds of certain frequency but when frequency is increased, the sound becomes quite audible for him.

Following tests are used to measure intensity and frequency in order to determine the degree of hearing loss.

1. **Watch test:** Normal person can hear the tick of an ingersoll pocket watch at 48 inches. In this test, one ear is plugged and the watch is placed close to the other ear. Then the watch is withdrawn from the ear slowly until the person ceases to hear its tick. The reverse procedure is then followed and the average of the two procedure is calculated which provides a rough auditory acuity of the person.
2. **Whisper Test:** Here the person being tested stands 20 feet away with his back from the tester, and repeats what is whispered. If he fails, the tester gradually moves closer to the testee until the testee is able to repeat the words whispered by the tester. Auditory deficit is measured in terms of the relative reduction in distance.
The above two tests are used for preliminary screening especially when audiometric equipment is not available.
3. **Pure Tone Audiometer:** This device produces tones of variable frequencies (pitch) and intensity (loudness) over a wide range. The person being tested hears the tones through earphones and responds by saying "Alow" whenever the tone is heard by him. The test results are plotted on an audiogram which provides the graphical representation of acuity of each ears.
4. **Speech Perception Test:** These tests are standardized test materials which are presented in commercial recordings and monitored and controlled for measuring intensity and the index of the degree of difficulty in ordinary communication is estimated.
5. **Phonographic Audiometer:** These devices are phonographs with the desired number of telephonic receivers attached. Calibrated recordings of voices of males as well as females are played first. Then voices become less and less distinct gradually till spoken materials are audible. This last level can be heard only by normals. In such tests, each ear is tested separately.'
6. **Conditioned Response Method:** Here, only the appropriate responses from the child is taken into consideration. The child looks into a dark house. A device is also given to him. When he hears a tone, he pushes the button of the device. This pushing of the button illuminates the interior of the house and thus a group of dolls revolves.
How to use these tests : Hearing impairment is measured in terms of the db above zero level of hearing. The two ears of a person have different levels of audition, so, both the ears are tested one by one and an audiogram is prepared. This audiogram shows the frequency of sounds of both the ears. Then the results are compared with the normal people, i.e., those who are able to hear speech sound in the range of 50-100.

## CONCEPT OF DEAF BLINDNESS

When the problem of visual impairment is accompanied by that of hearing one, the combined situation is called deaf blindness. These children need very special programme of education because of their complexity of the problem. The reason is that audio and visual, both types of materials are useless for them.

### Definition

"Deaf blind means concomitant hearing and visual impairment, the combination of which causes such severe communicative and educational problems that they can not be accommodated in special education programmes solely meant for children with deafness or children with blindness."

### Individual with Disabilities Education Act 1990, USA

As far as characteristics of these children are concerned, they have all the characteristics of visually impaired and hard of hearing children in addition to the following characteristics.

I. They have very severe communication (written or oral) disorder. The reason is that those who are blind can profit from verbal and audible stimulations and those who have hearing loss (to the extent of deafness) can profit from visual stimuli but those who are both i.e,, they are deaf blind, how can they benefit from the stimuli given to them.

II. Their academic or social skills will be almost zero without proper individualized help. The only way to teach them any skill is that the teacher will catch their hands and will try to mould their behaviour in a step by step manner.

III. If their visual or hearing acuity is not zero, it is something more than zero, only then they can be taught something by suing special techniques and materials.

### Educational Adaptation of Hearing Impaired Children

Separate intervention programme is needed for those who are deaf and for those who are hard of hearing. The details of these programmes are given below.

1. **Oral Communication :** Oral communication methods emphasize the development and use of skills in the areas of speech, speech reading and residual hearing. This approach is essentially important because these children, have very special speech and communication defects. Whatever hearing acuity the child has is fully utilized here. If it is zero, then child is trained in lip reading i.e., the message is understood by seeing the movement of lips. Thus, vision is used here for making the child trained in speech. The child is also trained to study the body gesture and read the message thereof .If child has any amount of hearing acuity he will listen the oral communications in the environment and utter them on the basis of his own reactions.
2. **American Sign Language :** In this method people with severe hearing loss express their ideas by using manual and non-manual body movements instead of speech. Mannul form of communication is displayed by shaping, moving and positioning hands. Non-manual form of communication is displayed by using other parts of the body like moving or positioning of legs, blinking of eyes, moving lips or thumping cheeks.
3. **Finger Spelling :** It is a special form of sign system in which each letter of the alphabet has a finger sign. By using these signs with the help of fingers, spelling of words are spoken or written and thus, process of conversation goes further. The whole lesson can be taught by this method. In finger spelling method, all five fingers are arranged in such a way that spelling of words are formed and the word is understood.
4. **Total Communication Method :** In this approach, all modes of communication are used, i.e., oral system, sign language and finger spelling all are used simultaneously. When it happens the communication becomes very effective. It is also called **Rochester** approach of communication.
5. **Cued Speech :** It is also a method which involves oral communication and sign language both. In cued speech right hand shapes are used in four positions on or near the face to accompany speech. Each hand shape represents a group of consonants and each facial position represents a group of vowel sounds that are used as cues to assist listeners who are doing speech reading.
6. **Auditory Method :** Here the emphasis is put more on the development of listening skills. This method is most suitable for those who are mildly

or moderately impaired. Auditory training and training of using hearing aids are given to the child for this purpose. Residual auditory capacity is exploited here.

7. **Appropriate use of Assistive Listening Devices:** These devices help the child to use his residual hearing to the maximum level possible. Important such devices are given below:

   (a) **Hearing Aids :** They can help all those who are mildly or moderately impaired. They are worn in the ear, behind the ear, on the body or in eyeglass frames.

   (b) **Amplification System:** Here a microphone is used to link the teacher to his students and the voice of the teacher which is magnified many times by the system is heard from the speaker and sound box. Students can be given earphone receiver instead of using speaker. Here each receiver is connected to a small earplug in one or both ears depending on the degree of hearing loss. When the teacher speaks, children directly listen him in their ears with the help of these earphones.

   (c) **FM Transmission :** It is also used to increase the frequency of auditory material.

   (d) **Telecommunication Devices :** They are small keyboards with screens or printers that are connected to telephone. Telecommunication devices help the hearing impaired children to make and receive telephone calls. When a call is made using this device the incoming and out-going conversation appears on the screen or printer.

8. **Placement :** Students with severe hearing loss can not be educated in regular classes in any way because of their specific needs. They have to be placed in special schools of special classes where they will be taught by using special techniques and the materials used by the special teacher.

9. Special Arrangement and Techniques used in the Class:

   I. If amplification is not being used in the class, small sized classes will suit these students so that the distance between the students and the teacher is minimum.

   II. The teacher should speak slowly in the class. He should stress clear articulation rather than loudness.

   III. The teacher should reduce the background noise as much as possible. Air conditioned room is the standard measure.

   IV. The teacher should use face to face contact as much as possible.

   V. The teacher should use complete sentences to provide additional context during conversation or instructional presentation.

   VI. He should use visual cues while referring to any object in the class.

   VII. The students should note down all what is given to them orally.

   VIII. The teacher should make sure whether the hearing aids or amplification system are functioning properly.

10. **Social skills Training :** These children especially lacks in social skills due to deficiency of social experiences. These skills can be developed in them by adopting following measures:

   (a) Organizing games and sports activities in the school along with formal teaching.

   (b) Helping them avail the facility of T.V. film projector and video disk in the class for interacting with the outer environment on the screen.

   (c) Project method of teaching involving activity, survey and group discussion.

# Physical and Multiple Disabilities and Educational Adaptation

## PHYSICAL DISABILITIES

Under physical disabilities, we discuss orthopedic impairment, autism, traumatic brain injury and other neurological disorders that have physical effects in any way.

Physical disabilities are problems that are caused due to any physical or brain injuries or conditions directly affecting the central nervous system. According to the federal guidelines of American government, only three types of problems come under the category of physical disabilities—orthopedic impairments, traumatic brain injury and autism.

### (A) Orthopedic Impairment

The condition of orthopedic impairment involves the muscular or skeletal system and sometimes the central nervous system. The problems existing in these systems restrict or retard the mobility and movement of the person. In the context of India orthopedic impairment problem is very serious because hundreds of children are being paralysed every year due to the onset and infection of poliomyelitis in small children. Such children have problem either in their legs or in their hands. They are also called crippled children in general terms. Accident is the second cause.

Orthopedic impairment limits muscular movement and mobility but these problems will vary according to the degree of disability. Student, with mild impairment can function very well in teaching-learning process and in their life situations. They need little or no special help. Students with severe disabilities will necessarily need special furniture, devices, materials or help.

#### Causes of Orthopedic Disabilities

1. **Crippling Caused by Poliomyelitis:** Poliomyelitis is an acute communicable disease caused by polio virus. The disease can be very mild causing no apparent symptom and so severe causing acute paralysis and muscular atrophy. The incidence of Polio in India was on peak two years ago but it has gone down in the year 2005. Only 17 cases of polio were found that year. Treatment. No treatment of the disease is possible. Oral polio vaccination is the only preventive measure.
2. **Muscular Dystrophy :** It is actually a group of birth disorders in which the skeletal muscles progressively atroph. Diagnosing muscular dystrophy depends on finding elevated levels of cratine kinase (CK) in the ;blood. This enzyme is released by dying muscle cells. Muscular dystrophy has four main forms.
   - (a) **Pseudohypertrophic:** It accounts for 50% of the cases and is found only in boys. The disease is diagnosed in the early age when child begins to walk. The disorder progresses day by day and reaches at its peak in the adolescence when victim is seen in the wheelchair.
   - (b) **Facioscapulohumeral** : It occurs in males and females both. It weakens shoulders and arms more than the legs. Its early symptoms are inability to whistle, abnormal facial movements when laughing or crying, etc. Since, legs are affected less by this disease, the victim live normally throughout his life.
   - (c) **Limb Girdle Dystrophy :** Its progress is very slow. It often causes only slight disability. Muscle weakness first appears in the upper arms and pelvis. Poor balance and inability to raise arms are other symptoms of the disease. It occurs at the age of 6.

(d) **Mixed Dystrophy :** It occurs between the age of 30-50. It affects all voluntary muscles. Rapid deterioration in muscles is seen within a year.

**Treatment :** We can not stop the progressive impairment associated with these forms of dystrophy by giving any treatment. The victims are ultimately given walkers or wheelchairs but the use of these appliances should be avoided as long as possible in order to maintain the remaining strength of muscles.

3. **Juvenile Rheumatoid Arthritis :** There is no known cause of the disease. It is the disorder of those tissues which connect bones. Due to this, pain in all joints of the body is experienced. The three major forms of the disease are given below:

(a) **Systemic :** Here individual develops sudden fever, rashes, chills, enlarged spleen and liver, tender and stiff joints. Those who have severe form of this disease may be crippled for a very long period.

(b) Polyarticular. Excess articulating disease.

(c) Pauciarticular. Articulation less than required.

**Treatment:** All these forms of the disease can be treated by using Ayurvedic medicines.

4. **Osteogenesis Imperfecta :** It is a hereditary disorder that makes the bones of the child or adolescents very brittle. This disease also occurs in two forms. In one rare form fractured bones are present at birth and the infant generally dies within few weeks. In the common form the child develops fractures after the first year of his life. If form of the disease is severe, children can not participate in sports activities in any way.

**Treatment.** Preventing injury is the only precautionary measure so far.

5. **Osteomyelitis :** It is an inflammation of the bone marrow that occurs more often in children than in adults. Its incidence is more in boys than girls. It begins when a child is bruised in some way and at the same time he has an infection. The infection enters the hematoma caused by the injury. Then this infection spreads through the bones to other parts of the body. Bones of arms and legs are especially affected. This disease can also cause underdeveloped bones.

**Treatment**. Control of spreading infections by giving high antibiotic medicines.

6. **Legg-Calve Perthes :** It affects the head of the femur, the upper bone in the leg. The interrupted blood flow causes the head of femur degenerate. The disease mostly occurs in boys at the age of 4. Those who suffer from this disease show a persistent limp that becomes more severe over a period of time. In severe form of the disease, the children can not participate even in the routine classroom activities.

**Treatment:** It is not curable at all.

7. **Limb Deficiencies :** It is the ;loss of one or more limbs even at the time of birth or later. Limb deficiency can occur due to accident or illness. The severe form of the disease affects the participation of children in routine classroom activities badly.

**Treatment:** It is curable to a little extent through surgery provided that the deficiency is not by birth.

8. **Neurological Disorder :** Nervous system coordinates and directs various functions of the ;body. This system consists of nerves, central nervous system (brain and spinal card) peripheral nervous system and automatic nervous system. Each of these components controls various aspects of our behaviour. If there is any impairment in any of these four components we will be less able to adapt to the environment. The disorder in these parts can affect the physical structure of the body, brain, spinal card etc. and neuro muscular problems may emerge. Some causes of this disease are genetic and some are related to infection or injury but many more causes are yet to be known.

**Treatment.** No known treatment of the disease is available.

9. **Epilepsy :** Its incidence is very high (about 1% of the population). It is characterized by recurring seizures which are actually abnormal discharges of electrical impulses of the brain. The seizure is followed by a brief loss of consciousness. The grand mal seizures typically begin with a loud

cry. Then the person falls to the ground, he becomes unconscious and his body stiffens. Tongue biting, loss of bowel control, laboured breathing, temporary stop of breathing followed by rapid breathing and blue to purple colouring of the skin etc are some other symptoms of this seizures. It can last for few minutes and can frighten the others.

**Treatment:** No permanent cure of the disease has been seen so far by the use of medicine. The problem is automatically reduced after the age of 25. Undiagnosed seizures can be mistaken for daydreaming or temper tantrum. There are many side effects of epilepsy medications seen such as drowsiness, lethargy, intellectual dullness, behavioural and sleep disturbances etc., so school teachers should take all these symptoms into account.

10. **Multiple Scelrosis:** It is a disease of adults in which the membranes of the brain and the spinal card progressively deteriorate. Incapacity is the main symptom of the disease

11. **Cerebral Palsy:** It is actually a type of neuro-muscular disorder that results from a damage in the central nervous system, before or after the birth of the child. There are three major forms of the disease.
    (a) **Spastic Cerebral palsy:** It is the most common form of the disease. It can be detected only by a neurologist. Severe spasticity leaves the individual rigid and with tense and contracted muscles and difficulty in body movements is seen.
    (b) **Athetoid Cerebral Palsy:** Results in involuntary movements of body parts, like grimacing, writing etc.
    (c) **Ataxic Cerebal Palsy:** It is the rarest form of the disease and characterized by disturbed balance, lack of coordination, under-active reflexes, constant involuntary movements of the eyeballs, muscle weakness and tremour About 40% of those suffering from the above diseases suffer from mental retardation and same number of people suffer from speech impairment.

    **Treatment:** People suffering from this disease can not be cured. Only proper management will help the child a little.

12. **Spina Bifida :** It is related to the development of embryonic neural tube and the child is born with this disease. Usually the defect occurs in the lower back area but it can occur at any point along the spine.

    **Treatment :** If disorder is minor in nature, no treatment is required. The serious form of the disorder is myelomeningocele a sak like structure that consists of spinal cord and spinal fluid. Surgery is the only method to get rid of the disease but rate of success is very low.

13. **Spinal Cord Injuries :** It occurs when spinal cord is traumatized fully or partially due to car or motor bike accident, gun shot wounds, falls etc. People experiencing these injuries suffer from partial or total paralysis. If spinal cord is completely damaged, complete paralysis will be seen. If spinal cord is partially damaged, partial paralysis will occur. Important types of paralysis due to this disease are as follows.
    *(a)* Monoplegia. In this disease only one limb is affected.
    *(b)* Paraplegia. In this disease, lower part of the body and both legs are affected.
    *(c)* Hemiplegia. One side of the body is affected.
    *(d)* Triplegia. Three limbs usually two legs and one arm are affected.
    *(e)* Quadriplegia. All extremities and the trunk are affected.
    *(f)* Diplegia. Legs are more affected than arms.
    *(g)* Double Hemiplegia. Both sides of the body are affected.

    Treatment. No significant improvement is seen after medication.

## (B) Traumatic Brain Injury

Traumatic brain injuries may be defined as acquired injury to the brain caused by an external physical force resulting in total or partial functional disability or psycho social impairments or both that adversely affects a child's educational performance. The term applies to open or closed head injuries resulting in impairment in one or more areas such as cognition, memory, language, attention, reasoning, abstract thinking, judgement, problem solving sensory-personal-motor abilities, psycho social behaviour, physical functions, information processing and speech.

**Causes of traumatic Brain Injuries :** Falls, sports and recreation related accidents, vehicle accidents, and personal assault including child abuse. etc, are the main causes. If these injuries are severe, they affect neurological system of the body. We, thus do not study those traumatic injuries which are congenital in nature. Important traumatic injuries are skull injuries, cerebral contusions hematomas (blood clots), concussions (loss of consciousness) etc. We are giving here only two:

1. **Skull Injuries :** As far as scalp injuries are concerned, they generally do not affect neurological system even if considerable loss of blood due to injury is seen. The situation becomes worse when the skull is broken or fractured. Important types of skull fractures are given below:
   - (a) **Linear Fracture :** It is a crack in the skull bones that is visible through X Ray or USG. They are usually not associated with any neurological disturbances.
   - (b) **Depressed Fractures** In this fracture skull bone is broken and presses the underlying brain tissue. It may affect the total system of the body in severe cases.
   - (c) **Contusions of the Brain.** They are the bruises of the brain tissue resulting in direct adverse effect on the functioning of the brain.
   - (d) **Hematomas.** Swelling is caused in the brain due to blood clots. If the effect is severe, it may affect locomotion system also. As the hematoma enlarges and creates increasing pressure on greater areas of the brain, headache, confusion, vomiting and neurological deficits in strength and movements occur. If problem is not timely treated, it may be fatal.

     **Treatment:** Surgeory and timely medical help can reduce these problems to a large extent.
2. **Concussions:** It is a brain injury causing a brief loss of consciousness or amnesia. Normally complete mental functioning is seen after the consciousness is returned but severe problems may also be noticed if the attack is severe.

### (C) Autism

Autism is a rarely occurred problem that affects multiple areas like thought, communication and behaviour. It may be defined as a biological syndrome manifested before thirty months of the age causing the following problems in the child.

I. Poor rate of development.
II. Low ability of responding to sensory stimuli.
III. Poor capacity to relate people, objects and events.
IV. Frquent unconsciousness.
V. Poor educational performance
VI. Stereotyped movements.
VII. Resistance to environmental change or change in daily routines.

Thus, we see that autism is a mental problem more than a physical problem.

**Other characteristics of autism are as follows:**

I. Delayed speech and language development.
II. Repetition of words and phrases over and over again.
III. Inappropriate social and emotional behaviour.
IV. Inappropriate behaviour related to play, recreation and leisure.

**Goals of Treating Autism:**

I. Fostering normal development'
II. Promoting learning
III. Reduction of stereotyped behaviour.
IV. Reducing family stress.
V. Eliminating problem behaviour.

## MULTIPLE DISABILITIES

Two types of students are generally seen having multiple disabilities.

I. Those with more than one disability like hearing, visual, emotional and the like disabilities simultaneously.
II. Those having primary disability in one area and secondary disabilities in other areas.

### General Characteristic Symptoms

Students facing this type of disability do not demonstrate a precise set of common characteristics.

These characteristics are generous specific to their specific nature and degree of impairment. However, some general characteristics are given below :

1. **Cognitive Abilities:** It depends upon their particular disease and impairment that they suffer from. For example, the student who has mental retardation will be very poor in cognitive skills. In spite of this if mind is not very much affected by the impairment, normal cognitive development will be seen.
2. **Academic Achievement :** Poor academic achievement of students with multiple disabilities is a common phenomenon. The reason may be due to behaviour problem, poor school attendance due to orthopedic disabilities, poor mental and physical health, problem of adjustment etc.
3. **Physical Characteristics:** They may suffer from chronic illness, pain in any part of the body, weakness and poor health, lack of proper coordination or muscles etc. But it does not mean that their whole body is weak. A person on a wheelchair may be very strong by his upper part of the body.
4. **Behavioural Characteristics :** No specific behaviour is noted in children due to this problem. Negative social stimuli are the main causes behind their deviant nature of behaviour. They participate in social activities very infrequently resulting in low level of social development. Social development is also badly affected by orthopedic impairment due to low level of interaction. Limited motor skills and self help skills also limit social interaction of students, resulting in poor social development. Social development is also adversely affected by autism in students. They may show aggressive behaviour, self injurious behaviours, temper tantrums and repetitive stereotyped behaviour. These behaviours tend to isolate the victims from others, resulting in poor social development.
5. **Communicative Abilities :** Many students with cerebral palsy have little language problem. Their speech and language skills are normal. If the problem of cerebral palsy is very severe, language development will be affected. Similarly, students suffering from autism develop language very slowly. Saying words or phrases out of the context and voice disorders are also very common. Their language comprehension is also found to be very poor.

## Educational Adaptation of Crippled Children

Crippled children have limited motor functioning due to their handicap which is associated with low interaction and hence low level of social and language development, emotional problem due to maltreatment by others and low educational achievement due to poor attendance and low level of concentration. All these problems require some modification in the total educational set up. Important adaptive measures are given below :

1. **Modification in the Curriculum :** Crippled children do not lag behind the normals in cognitive abilities. So, no modification in the curriculum is needed. The only thing that is needed is that they should be given those experiences which require less motor functioning. If special facilities are provided to them, they can learn each and every thing.
2. **Emotional and Social Adjustment :** These children are generally rejected by their peers and mates and thus they face adjustment problem in the school. Adjustment training is given to them in order to enable them to adjust in the society properly. Efforts should be made to make them self-dependent and self reliant. It will develop self confidence in them which is very essential for emotional adjustment.
3. **Removing Architectural Obstacles :** Architectural obstacles impede instruction by restricting motor functioning. Instruction can be facilitated by removing these obstacles. For example, if a crippled child is coming to the class on a wheel chair, the room will have to be architecturally designed and the furniture set in such a manner that the student can reach to his desk without difficulty. Students should also be placed in the class in such a way that it is easy for them to move in the class. Adaptive design of floors and doors are especially important here.

**4. Development of Physical Efficiency :** They are prone to many diseases due to lack of motor activities. Special activities are to be organized for them to adapt to their motor abilities. Yoga and other related activities are the examples here.

**5. Classroom Adaptation :**

*(i)* Seating arrangement according to the crippling effect of children.

*(ii)* Writing in a spiral bound notebook or pad of paper rather than on a single loose sheet.

*(iii)* Limiting response options to a single word or multiple choice items that require minimal writing if there is any defect in their writing hands.

*(iv)* Pacing rubber strips or pads on work materials to prevent slipping during use.

*(v)* Using word processor, computers, type writers and calculators in order to facilitate writing and mathematical calculations.

*(vi)* In order to facilitate reading, adaptive measures used are book holders, reading stands, automatic page turners, books on tape recorders, etc.

**6. Fostering Independence :** They have to be made self dependent any how. Following adaptive measures can be adapted for this purpose.

(a) Prosthesis. It is an artificial replacement of a missing ;body part, e.g., an artificial leg or hand. This is supplied to them to make them self reliant.

(b) Orthesis. It is a device that enhances partial functioning of a body part, eg. Leg brace.

(c) Adaptive Device. It is an ordinary item used for daily living, found in school, home or office, e.g., a plate with suction cups to hold it to the table and a rim around it to keep the food from being pushed off it.

**7. Maximum use of Residual Functioning:** What amount of functioning they have should be utilized to the maximum level possible. Prosthesis or orthesis helps them use this residual functioning. These things help the orthopedically handicapped people to focus on what they can do rather than what they can not do.

**8. Special Methods of Instructions**

*(i)* The teacher motivates the students to talk about their limitations on one hand and help them exhibit their abilities on the other. This will help the teacher to study his students and teach them according to their specific needs.

*(ii)* He should come to the physical level of his students during teaching-learning process.

*(iii)* He has to modify the assignment also according to the specific needs of these students.

*(iv)* The teacher should also be concerned with the physical problems of these students and show full sympathy with them. He should be considerate enough to accept their tasks even if they are not upto the mark.

**9. Providing Medical Facilities :** They are very much prone to accidents and falls. In such cases immediate medical facilities should be made available for them in order to give them timely help. Similarly, orthopedic problem itself needs regular medical check up and follow up. School should provide this facility also.

**10. Placement:** They cannot be taught in regular schools in any way due to their motor problems because if they are placed here, normal children may hit them due to their fast movement and mobility. So, residential schools especially meant for them are the best option. Since they need special seating arrangement, special architectural design of the building, special equipments and materials and special health care services, all these things can be made available only in special schools.

## Educational Adaptation with Traumatic Brain Injury

**1. Role of the Teacher:** A teacher has to play the following role in educating these children.

*(i)* They are especially impaired in cognition, language, attention, reasoning, perception and motor abilities, so the teacher will have to adopt all those measures suitable for crippled children plus some special measures to improve their communications, achievement and behaviour.

*(ii)* The teacher should also know the process of their treatment in order to give them timely help.

*(iii)* Most of the head traumas are minor and do not require special treatment. A little tender loving care can cure minor injuries.

*(iv)* If a child develops a severe headache, loses consciousness, shows significant changes in speech or other bodily functions following a head injury, it is the teacher who helps the child first to provide first aid and then takes him to the hospital for proper treatment. Usually a neurological investigation is required after such injuries.

*(v)* The teacher has to keep a regular watch on the behaviour of these children and immediately notices if any sign of complications develops such as confusion, difficulty in grasping, problem in awakening from sleep (in case of residential schools where teachers also work as a warden) and so on.

2. **Preventive Measures:** The key to prevent such head injuries is effective education given to the child in the school and the key to effective education is the organisation's. **Head Smart School Programme.** It teaches safe and constructive behaviour to students and effective coping strategies before unsafe behaviour are manifested.
3. **Head Smart Programme:** It covers the following areas.
   (a) Pedestrian Safety. Such as how to walk safely in a crowded neighbourhood or across a busy street and what are those factors that especially cause a person to fall.
   (b) Occupational Safety. Such as proper use of safety belts, precautions in using electric appliances etc.
   (c) Tricycle, Bicycle and Skate board Safety. Such as responsible bike riding in traffic and use of safety helmets.
   (d) Playground Safety. Such as proper surfaces and safe sports equipment.
   (e) Avoidance of Violence. Such as child abuse and shaking of babies, avoiding the scenes of fighting of normals etc.

## Educational Adaptation with Autism

Following adaptive measures are used for teaching students suffering from autism:

1. **Development of Language and Communication Abilities:** They exhibit impaired speech and delayed language development. They often repeat words and phrases again and again. Severe cases of Autism never develop functional speech. Seeing these problems much more emphasis is to be given on the development of language and speech. For this purpose assistive programme in the context of language development should start very early in life.
2. **Teaching of Functional Activities and Skills:** They are mostly dependent on others due to lack of functional skills. These skills should be taught to them through specific recreational activities.
3. **Teaching Strategies:** Punishment given by the teacher to these children is fatal to them. Strategies based on reward for engaging them in appropriate behaviour or refraining from inappropriate behaviour should be used as the first line of intervention for students with autism.

## Educational Adaptation with Multiple Disabilities

The students with multiple disabilities need intervention in those areas where they dominate, i.e., disability is severe. As far as the rest of the areas are concerned, some additional measures are also needed to make them self dependent and self reliant. To what extent a teacher will succeed, will depend on the degree of disability and special measures used for the purpose.

The students with multiple disabilities must be identified before their entry to school. If it is so, only then they are supposed to learn something through the process of education either in special or integrated schools. Sometimes, they are admitted to schools without their proper identification. If teachers are not sincere, their problems will increase manifold. He studies the behavioural signs of these children and matches these signs with the standard criteria. Then on the basis of his report, they are sent to the concerned department for further investigation. Important such signs are limited energy, frequent absence from the school, poor coordination, frequent accidents, speech or language difficulties, hearing or visual problems, mental lapses, adjustment problem in the classes, nagging with other children, frequent failure in the class and acute complaints of pain.

In order to know what the special needs of these children are, the first step that a teacher takes is that he asks a number of questions to know their problems and needs. He also motivates them to respond correctly and not to hide their deficits. He also observes them in doing tasks and notes down their behaviour. The teacher shares these informations with other teachers in order to provide full guidance and help to these children. The teacher not only diagnoses the disabilities of these students but he also finds out their potentialities and these potentials are used to overcome the disabilities by them. Key areas in which a teacher can assist children with multiple disabilities are as follows:

*(i)* The teacher may give assistance with their medication while they are at school. Some schools may have distinct medication policies for these children.

*(ii)* They may require assistance in mobility if they are having any motor or visual problem.

*(iii)* The teacher can help them in taking them to the concerned doctors, therapists, nurses etc. for providing them information and training in concerned areas.

*(iv)* The teacher can take the help of intervention programmes to accommodate the individual needs of these students, to facilitate communication and to foster independence.

# Communication Disorders and Educational Adaptation

## MEANING

If the person is unable to communicate properly due to a problem of producing a speech or using language symbols, it is called communication disorder. It is actually a loss of oral expression on which the development of a language basically depends. The person suffering from this disorder is unable to express his emotions, ideas and experiences at least orally and thus, he can not release his temper tantrum and pent up feeling through oral technique. Communication disorder is of three forms- articulation disorder, voice disorder and fluency disorder.

## DEFINITIONS

Articulation disorder is defined as the abnormal production of speech sound. For example, if a person says young ma von din, he may be using spoken language but he is not producing sound correctly.

Voice disorder is defined as the absence or abnormal production of vocal quality, pitch, loudness, responses and duration.

Fluency disorder is defined as abnormal flow of verbal expression characterized by impaired rate and rhythm which may be accompanied by struggle behaviour.

## CAUSES OF COMMUNICATION DISORDER

Before coming to types of the communication disorders one fact to he kept in mind is that communication disorders are primarily caused by impairment in auditory acuity or absence of this power altogether. Some other physiological causes are deformation of lips, tongue or mouth or any defect in the throat. In such cases the person is not able to articulate speech and he utters the words wrongly, e.g., say cuth instead of cut or pronouncing gluth instead of blood.

Apart from the above two reasons of speech or language disorders some social, psychological and intellectual factors are also responsible for communication disorders, Socio-economic factors and climatic conditions also affect pattern of speech, articulation and voice. For example, people in Arabian peninsula can not pronounce t, d,, ch etc. due to climate condition or they pronounce at least six words by using their throat just to avoid sand effect of the desert climate on the throat.

Important causes of delayed or poor speech or lack of communication ability are given below:

1. **Mental retardation :** If child is mentally weak or slow, he is likely to have slow rate of language development. He has less power to learn new words due to low mental power or mental retardation. If the child is severely mentally retarded his language ability may be almost zero. Vice versa is also correct. If a ;child is learning new words or sentences very rapidly, it is a sign of fast intellectual development and high mental power.
2. **Hearing problem :** If child is having any hearing impairment of at least moderate level, his language development will be delayed because acquisition of new words 75% depends on hearing. If, on the other hand, the child is completely unable to hear words or sentences, he will not be able to speak at all and he will be dumb. If child is looking mentally fit by his activities and yet he is very slow in acquisition of new words, he must be brought to the physician for diagnosing his problem and its causes.

3. **Physical health and functioning of central nervous system:** Delayed speech is also related to poor physical health and malfunctioning in the central nervous system. If physical development of the child is normal, he is likely to have normal speech development. Since physical development depends on the proper functioning of the central nervous system, so any defect in this system is likely to have delayed or defective speech development. Nervous system directly affects speech development as well. If a person is late in receiving nerve message through his mind, he will surely be late in learning and applying new words.
4. **Aphasia :** It is also an important physical cause of delayed speech Aphasia is either due to any brain injury or high fever. Under the impact of this disease complete loss of understanding the meaning and importance of a word is seen in the victim. Thus, he can not learn new words due to the impairment of understanding ability. This lack of understanding will lead to impairment in speech.
5. **Adverse environment :** Conducive environment is also necessary for learning and applying new words and sentences. Some examples of adverse environment is also given below.
   *(i)* If both parents are busy in employment or business and they are unable to give time to their children, these children will get less chance of talking or communication and their speech development will be delayed.
   *(ii)* If child is persistently ridiculed or chided at his lingual mistake, and he is compelled to pronounce the words correctly, they avoid speaking or responding and lack of use of words in real life situation delays their speech development.
   *(iii)* If social atmosphere is charged with communal or any other tension, people will get less chance of rapport and their language development will be retarded.
6. **Emotional disturbance :** If the child is emotionally disturbed and in order to show his anger or frustration he ceases to say even a single word to any body, he will get less chance of using a language. If such a tendency is repeated again and again, the child's speech development will be retarded.

## TYPES OF COMMUNICATION DISORDER

Communication disorder can be classified into two categories.

### 1. Speech Disorder

This problem is caused due to three reasons.

**(a) Articulation disorder :** This problem is related to speech sound. Whatever words a person produces can not be understood by others due to poor articulation of sound. For example, a person may say "y ain dong" instead of saying 'I am going.' Pronunciation defect is also an example of articulatory disorder but this defect is very common in Indian people, so, it is not discussed in special education. About 90% people say haj instead of has, bajar instead of bazaar.

Causes of this disorder are many such as defective socio educational environment, lack of proper guidance, deformation of lips, teeth, tongue or any other part in the mouths. Climatic condition also causes this defect.

For example, people living in China or Arabian countries can not pronounce T and D consonants. Such defects are very common in Indians but it is 100% curable by speech therapy, speech games, group discussion and by use of tap-recorder or gramophone. One more feature of people living in Indian subcontinent is that they can utter and pronounce each and every letter of whatsoever language they represent.

**(b) Vocal disorder :** It is nothing but poor controlling of sounds that is being produced. When there is absence or abnormal production of vocal quality, pitch, loudness, resonance etc it is called vocal disorder. Individual suffering from this problem speaks in a hoarse voice or speak very loudly or in a low or very high pitch or he speaks at such a fast speed that nothing is understood. They chew some words when they speak or they skip letter or words and thus the words becomes meaningless for others. The actual problem is that these people do not know that they are doing so. Once they hear their tapped voice on the recorder only then they know what they are speaking. These people are the victim of vocal disorder. This problem is seen in adults more than in children. Even normal people can suffer from this problem temporarily if they are very much tired of physical work and they are breathing excessively or they are absent minded due to any reason.

These people can overcome this problem by adopting the following measures.

I. They should speak very slowly and at a normal pitch and be sure that each and every word is coming out clearly.

II. They should hear their speech on the tape recorder and find out which vowel or constant they are missing or repeating more. Then by using drill technique they can remove their defect.

III. Singing and song practice method can also be used to remove this defect.

**(c) Fluency disorder :** It is poor controlling of the rate and rhythm of speech. Here flow of verbal expression is so abnormal that the person is unable to speak out the word clearly. Stuttering is an example. It is caused due to imbalance between the continuity of the sound and its rhythm. It is basically a psychological problem in which the child or adult repeats a word or takes too much time to start a particular word. Sometimes delay in vowels are also seen in speech. When a person feels highly insulted or he is very aggressive at a particular moment, he can suffer from the problem of stuttering temporarily, though he is normal in other situations. Stuttering generally develops in children due to generalization of fear or phobia. For example, if a child is very much frightened of his father, he may stutter not only in his presence but also in the presence of others. If child is not encouraged by others when he speaks, his problem will become permanent. Stuttering is also caused due to physiological break down of brain mechanism and excessive tension in the vocal cards.

This problem is caused due to physiological reasons such as tension in the muscles, or jaundice or malaria. Some other causes of fluency disorders are increased level of dissatisfaction in the child, emotional disturbances, malnutrition, indifferent or cruel behaviour of parents towards the child and so on. Example of stuttering is given below :

I want to see you is the rightly spoken sentence with correct fluency but the person suffering from stuttering problem says. I I I- W-am-t-t to to sss you.

This problem can be treated by applying following methods:

I. First the child is brought and attached to a person who he fears and respects too much. Then the counterpart of the child develops a friendly relation with the child. When the child talks with his friend, he forgets stuttering. Then, this learning is generalized in other situations and thus the problem of the child is removed.

II. Fluency practice is another method when the child is trained to co-ordinate his rhythm with the continuity of his sound.

III. Group dynamics is also applied to treat these children.

## 2. Language Disorders

Language disorders can be sub divided into three categories.

(a) Form disorders.

(b) Content disorders.

(c) Functional disorders.

**(a) Form disorders:** Form refers to utterance (sentence structure) of what is said i.e., phonology, morphology and syntax. Phonology refers to the smallest unit of a language, i.e. speech sound. Morphology refers to the smallest unit of a meaningful language, i.e., words or parts of words. Syntax refers to combining language units into meaningful phrases, clauses or sentences, i.e., grammatical correction.

Suffice if to say when a person is unable to differentiate speech sounds, and words and is unable to use a language correctly from grammatical point of view, he is said to have form disorder.

**(b) Content disorder :** It refers to the inability of a person to derive the meaning of words and sentences including abstract concepts, i.e., semantics. Problems related to vocabulary, comprehension and following directions are included in content disorder. When students are unable to identify pictures when word names are provided, they are unable to answer simple questions and they can not properly follow the directions given by their teachers, they are said to have content disorder.

(c) **Functional disorders :** Functions refers to the context in which the language is used. Purpose of communication is also included here. If Mr. A wants to say something to Mr. B and Mr. B is unable to understand what Mr. A says to him due to the absence of conventional rules followed by Mr. A the problem of Mr. A will be described as functional disorder. With this problem what is said by a person is understood in another way by others and thus the purpose of communication is defeated. Functional disorder is thus seen when :

*(i)* A language is not used in its context.

*(ii)* A language is not used according to the social conventional rules set for the language.

*(iii)* A language is not used in order to fulfil a purpose.

## Identification of persons with communication disorders

Those having any sort of communication disorder can be identified on the basis of following criteria:

1. **Efficiency of receiving a language :** A person receives different types of communicative materials from morn till night. To what extent he is able to receive (retain) these materials is the basic criterion of knowing his communicative ability. If he is having any mental retardation or hearing impairment, he will not he able to receive these materials properly. Once reception is not proper, its reproduction will also be defective, i.e., If hearing acuity is zero, the person will be dumb.
2. **Oral reading :** Speed, accuracy, pronunciation, rhythm etc, are taken into consideration here. If the speed of reading of a person is slow despite regular practice and drill and if he does the same mistake in reading despite giving regular feedback then the person is said to have communication disorder.
3. **Extempore speech test :** Unlike oral reading, it is also concerned with expressive problems. Language as well as speech elements both are taken into consideration here. Thus, we can identify the above six types of defects of a person just by hearing his speech.
4. **Asking direct question orally :** Direct oral questions are asked from the students in order to know the degree of their communication disorder.
5. **Language ability test :** They are written standardized tests conducted to test the language ability of a person. If the performance of a person is poor on such tests, he is said to have communication disorder.
6. **Oral and written school works :** They are the common methods used by teachers as their routine exercises to know the language efficiency of their students.

## Characteristics Associated in the People with Communication Disorders

As we have seen, two types of problems are associated with communication disorder. One is related to speech and the other is related to language. Speech problems are evidenced in the production of speech, i.e., mis-articulation, abnormal flow of expression etc. and language problems are evidenced in the production of form, content and grammar. Despite this distinction, most of the characteristics of these people are the same. Some important common characteristics associated with this disability are given below :

(a) **Cognitive abilities :**

*(i)* Verbal intelligence is found to be low in such people due to poor language development.

*(ii)* Their development of cognitive skills, such as identifying similarities among objects or concepts, understanding words and sentences and reproducing these elements of the language etc. are generally very poor.

*(iii)* The fact is that intellectual disabilities can cause language and communication impairment and communication disorder is responsible for low intellectual power. To what extent, they affect each other is yet to he ascertained but their mutual dependence is beyond doubt.

(b) **Physical Characteristics :**

*(i)* Cerebral palsy, left palate deformed lips or tongue or other kind of oral facial disorders are not uncommon in these people.

*(ii)* Haunt look due to severe mental retardation is also seen in some people.

*(iii)* In spite of these no specific relationship between communication disorders and physical characteristics has been identified by studies in the field. This disorder does not correspond to any peculiarity in physical functioning or appearance. In most of the cases, they are found to be normal.

**(c) Academic Achievement :**

*(i)* Most of the school activities are centred around verbal symbolic environment. Throughout the school years especially at the primary level academic achievement is most likely to be affected by communication disabilities. The reason is that these children are poor in listening, concentration, following directions and comprehending the textual materials.

*(ii)* Students with speech and language problems usually experience difficulties in reading, answering, studying social studies, languages, arts and literature. The reason is that these subjects depend to a large extent on verbal and written communication skills.

**(d) Behavioural problems :**

*(i)* Communication is actually a social function. Students with speech or language difficulties often call attention to themselves. The reason is that when these students have different nature of speech or language in social situations, they are behaved by others very indifferently or in a very humiliating manner and thus, social withdrawl becomes the compulsion of these students.

*(ii)* The ridiculing or humiliating behaviours meted out to these people by others can also cause severe maladjustment. These people may lose self confidence also.

**(e) Communication abilities :**

*(i)* They have difficulty in understanding words or sentences.

*(ii)* They have poor articulation power. They can either omit sound or distort sounds.

*(iii)* They have difficulty in pronouncing words.

*(iv)* They may have defective voice in terms of quality, loudness and pitch.

*(v)* They may have fluency disorders, i.e., demonstrating interruptions in the timing or rhythm of their speech. Stuttering is a common fluency disorder.

*(vi)* They may have difficulty in combining sounds to form words or difficulty in combining words to form sentences.

*(vii)* They generally have difficulty in expressing themselves and understanding the expressions of others.

*(viii)* In severe cases, they are unable to utter even a single word.

## EDUCATIONAL ADAPTATION

### A. General Guidelines to Deal Children with Delayed Speech

These guidelines are addressed to parents and teachers both. They should follow the suggestions given below to deal with such children:

I. If there is any infant at home who is not grasping words spoken to him or he is very slow in his speech and language development then the first duty of parents is to take the child to specialist physician for proper medical check up and diagnosis. Once the physical causes of the disorder are known, remedial measures can be adopted. These doctors will attend the child from three angles.
   - To see if there is any mental retardation associated with the child.
   - To see whether there is any problem of hearing impairment that the child is having.
   - To see whether there is any problem in the vocal cord, lips cleft palate or tongue.

II. If mental problem of the child is not too serious to be diagnosed by a doctor, the child should be brought to a psychologist to administer intelligence test to him and calculate his IQ.

III. If physical problems of these children are known to parents they should follow the advices of doctors and psychologists in order to remove or minimize the speech defects of these children.

IV. Parents should motivate the child to speak more. The child should be asked to repeat the words and sentences spoken by others.

V. If child is demanding something just by pointing the object again and again he should not be given the object without uttering it vocally and verbally. Even the wrong form of the words may be accepted by parents.

VI. If it is known that child is defective in his speech or language, parents should talk before these children at a slower rate of speech so that these children can understand their conversation.

VII. When a child commits mistake in his speech, he should immediately be corrected otherwise child will be conditioned to wrong pronunciations, rhythm and tone.

VIII. Such children should never be insulted or ridiculed. They should rather be treated sympathetically.

IX. These children should have access to reciting poems or singing songs.

X. If the case is severe the child should be brought to speech pathologist regularly.

## B. Special Services

Students with severe form of communication disorder receive special education from those especially trained in the field. These experts are technically known as speech language pathologists. These people have a master degree in communication disorder plus a diploma in clinical competence. They conduct assessments and provide therapy to affected children based on their results. When they work as a regular teacher in schools, they also function as itinerant specialists spending one or two days in a week to each school they are assigned. They generally work in collaboration with class teacher and subject teachers of the school and guide these teachers also.

## C. Role of the Teacher

The special roles that the regular teachers have to play in dealing students with communication disorders are given below:

I. They should integrate appropriate language development activities into all curricular areas. Even social science, science and mathematics are to be taught with a language bias.

II. They should create supportive environment when communication is fostered. Students should be given chance to speak more and more.

III. Students should be given opportunities during regular instructions to practice skills learnt by the therapy.

IV. The teacher should arrange activities in which students can use language for different purposes, for example, oral book report, more job interview, speech therapy, speech survey and many other activities can be arranged.

V. The teacher should have to provide good speech model before his students. The students will imitate the model and remove their defects.

VI. The students should be given opportunities for exchange of views and discussions about what is being taught to them.

## (D) Reducing Speech Problems

Following techniques will help the teacher to improve areas of speech production in students:

1. **Providing good models of speech :** The teacher should speak with correct pronunciation in order to give good models to students. His model reading as well as way of explanation should be impressive and effective. He should read out the poems with an impressive style, i.e., in the tone it was written.
2. **Focussing on quantity rather than quality of speech :** Students with speech disorder will definitely have poor quality of speech but if quantity produced by children is correct they should be reinforced. At this level adequate and correct quantity of speech produced is enough.
3. **Drilling of speech :** Children learn may things from speech language pathologist. Whatever they have learnt there, they should be given opportunity to practice it in the class. In this way these children will improve very quickly.
4. **Special techniques used :** The teacher can take the help of word games to improve speech production of his students. He can also take the help of tap recorder and films to give students more chance of listening conversation.

## (E) Reducing Language Problems

Following tactics will help the teacher to improve the use of language in students:

1. **Focussing on word meaning :** Researches have shown that only that word can be remembered of which we know the meaning. It is very difficult to retain meaningless words. So teacher should focus on giving the word meaning first, then he should come to its explanation. It is also a fact that only those words can be retained and applied which we read in a sentence. Isolated words can not be remembered easily. So teacher should give the meaning of all the words that have been used in a sentence and then he should give the meaning of the full sentence. Students should learn words in a sentence not in isolation.
2. **Focussing on grammar :** Sentence meaning is influenced by the use of punctuation and intonation. Word games and sentence games will help the students to understand punctuation and intonation. Students should also be trained to use sentences of the same meaning in at least two different ways. So, teaching of transformation is necessary here.
3. **Using gesture along with verbal language :** Students with language problems may have difficulty in understanding the use of prepositions, action verbs and adverbs. By acting out the meaning of the sentence we can give a clear meaning of a word to students. For example, if a teacher wants to convey the meaning of sit, to his students, he should sit in the class for a while and then he should say it is sit.
4. **Stressing on writing :** It is said that writing makes a man perfect. In order to improve the language ability of students, the teacher should encourage the students to write as much as possible. Writing work should be three times more than reading one. For example, the teacher can give a picture to his students and ask them to write about it in as many words as possible without minding the mistakes. Then he should ask these students to read all the sentences they have written one by one.
5. **Using of familiar words as building block :** No teacher can teach all new words at one time. He takes the help of those words first which students already know and then new words are taught to them on the foundation of these familiar words. Students also make new words by these familiar words. For example, if they know the meaning of 'justify' they can form other new words like justification, justifying etc. and the change in meanings of these words is also conveyed to them.

### (F) Reducing Interpersonal Problems

Following tactics will help the students with communication disorder to overcome their social and emotional problems:

1. **Praising the accomplishment :** If these students have accomplished something genuine, they must be praised. However, all types of accomplishments should not be praised by the teacher. In applying praise technique, the teacher should also keep the students', past history and their previous performance in mind. If current performance is more than the previous one, only then praise technique should be applied. This technique will improve the relation of students with the teacher and he will perform better in future.
2. **Conveying information with praise :** Simply telling a students that he has scored 20 marks in a test is not a good approach. The teacher should rather, say that he has performed very well by scoring 20 marks in the test given to him. Similarly, regular cues and prompt should also be given by the teacher to improve the behaviour of his students.
3. **Reducing anxiety and fear :** More than half of the stuttering problems are caused due to anxiety and fear in the minds of students. The teacher should, first of all, remove all these problems by his decent and sympathetic behaviour and then he should expect that these students will come to normal a day.
4. **Praise at proper time :** If accomplishment of a task is immediately followed by praise, only then it is better. It is because child needs motivating words immediately not in the near future. If reinforcement is given late, it is useless.
5. **Reduction of embarrassment :** These children are generally ridiculed or insulted by others which makes them irritated and sometimes aggressive. Such situations should be eliminated

first before giving them any remedial measure. Strict control and discipline in the school are needed for this purpose.

6. **General praise for the entire class :** Students with communication disorders have very low level of self concept and it is very difficult for them to believe that praise is true. It is in this context that the teacher should also praise the whole class if students have done something good along with the individual praise.
7. **Organising activities :** The teacher should organize different types of activities for these students in order to improve their inter-personal and group relations. Role playing in the class or participating in games and sports outside the class are few examples.

## (G) Special Equipments Needed

If communication disorder is due to hearing impairment and it can be **rectified** ;by using hearing aids or loudspeakers, these equipments must be used by the teacher in the class to improve hearing and language abilities both. Other equipments are tap recorders, game box etc.

7

# Delinquency and Educational Adaptation

## INTRODUCTION

Crimes committed by teenagers are not new today. We find many incidents of juvenile delinquency in madarsas of Muslim period. These incidents have tremendously increased today because of the negative role played by mass media especially T.V. or Internet. These incidents have made all of us concerned. Teachers, parents, psychologists and law enforcing agencies are really disturbed because of these crimes committed by adults and every body wants to minimize the incidents of these crimes. These adult criminals not only damage the national or public properly but they also spoil their own lives. It is actually a barrier in the way of personality development of young generations of the society. It is because these delinquents spoil many young boys and children as well.

## MEANING OF DELINQUENCY

There is no consensus regarding the meaning of the term Juvenile delinquent. The reason is simple enough. There are so many types of behaviour which are not approved by the society. These socially disapproved behaviour vary with the times, place or culture. All these behaviours are not put under the category of juvenile delinquency.

Second reason of luck of a universal definition to the concept is that each group of the society sees the problem with different angles.

One point at which every one is agree that every society prescribes a set of norms or ethics of living. Those who do not abide by them willingly and behave in an anti social manner are called delinquents.

### Definitions

Several view points regarding the concept are given:

**1. Psychological view points :**

(a) **Delinquency is holes in superego :** Delinquency is actually a deficiency in the formation of superego (see chapter personality). Delinquent child fails to internalize the primitive taboos and code of conduct set by the family and the society and works on either pleasure principle or he is guided by his ego. Delinquency is actually holes in the superego of man according to **Johnson and Szurek.**

(b) **Delinquency is functional psychiatric disorder :** The fundamental intrapsychic pathology is attributed to faulty relations between parents and children in the early years of life. Disturbances in these relations create neurotic, psychotic or behavioural disorders. Some of which are manifested in the form of anti social behaviour.

(c) **Delinquency is aggression : Bandura and Walters** are of the view that delinquency is the manifestation of frustrated needs of the child which lead him to behave aggressively.

(d) **Delinquency is the under activity of CNS :** According to some psychologists delinquency is caused due to the under activity of central nervous is system. Due to which, the person is unable to respond to social situations properly. Their CNS is genetically so weak that they are not rectified even by punishment measures.

(e) **Delinquency is crime under age :** According to **New Meyer** a delinquent is a person under age who is guilty of anti social act and whose misconduct is an infraction of the law.

2. **Religious view point :** In order to seek ego related pleasures and avoid pains whatever crime is committed by adults while defying the religious boundaries are called delinquent acts. Thus, delinquency is transgression of religious norms.
3. **Biological view points :** Anti-social behaviour arises from organic or pathological causes located in the nervous system. These delinquents fail to adjust to social environment too. These acts are genetically caused, i.e, if parents or any of the forefathers was delinquent, the offsprings are likely to become so.

   One more biological reason of juvenile delinquency is that if mother is behaved very high handeadly during pregnancy by her husband she develops some disorders in the CNS, and her offspring is likely to be delinquent. This hypothesis is at experimental stage at present.
4. **Sociological viewpoints :** According to this approach, social condition and family attitude toward the child are solely responsible for juvenile delinquency. Social norms are violated here by the adults.

   **Richard A Cloward** has defined delinquency in the following words. "Delinquent act is a behaviour that violates norms of the society and when officially known it evokes a judgment by agent of criminal justice that such norms have been violated.

   Sociologists have pointed out the following causes of antisocial behaviour.

   I. Socio-economic or political stress leads to breakdown of power in the social system which is exploited by the adults.

   II. When an individual finds no avenue to realize his immediate goals and to satisfy his immediate needs, he is compelled by the circumstances to reach these goals by antisocial methods. Thus, delinquency is an expression of dissatisfied needs of the individual. He tries to satisfy his needs by his anti social activities, when he fails to gratify them by socially acceptable behaviour. These needs may be physical and psychological both (see **Maslow's** hierarchy of needs).

   III. When extra energy of the adult is not properly utilized, this energy is used in destructive works resulting in antisocial behaviour.
5. **Legal definitions :** Herbert Quay in his book **'Juvenile Delinquency'** has defined the concept in the following words.

**"Delinquent** would be a person whose misbehaviour is relatively a serious legal offence which is inappropriate to his level of development.........and is alien to the culture in which he has been reared"

According to **C Burt** "A child is to be regarded as technically delinquent when his antisocial tendencies appear so grave that he becomes or ought to become the subject of official action."

**Ohio code of the USA** defines the term in the following ways, "A juvenile delinquent is one who breaks the law, is a vagrant, persists in disobeying orders, whose behaviour endangers his own moral life as well as the moral life of others."

It is clear from the above definitions that unless a young man is brought to the court and his delinquency is not proved, he is not a delinquent. As far as age for delinquency being a delinquent is concerned, it varies from country-to-country ranging from 16-20. In India the maximum age for a juvenile delinquent is fixed at 16 years. It is applicable in most of the states in India.

## Identification of a Delinquent Person

Identification of a delinquent person on the basis of his characteristics and activities.

**(A) Characteristics :** Important characteristics of juvenile delinquents identified by **Sheldon and Gulecks** are given below :

1. Physical : Mesosomarphic in constitution, muscular, energetic and bold.
2. Temperamental : Restless, impulsive, extroverted, aggressive and destructive.
3. Attitudinal : Hostile, defiant, resentful, suspicious, unconventional and non submissive to authority.
4. Psychological : Direct and concrete intellectual expression, less methodical in their approach to the problem, and disregard to elders.

5. Socio-cultural : Lack of affection and stability and low moral standard of parents and elders.

**(B) Activities of Delinquents :** Types of delinquent's acts are many because of socio-economic and cultural variations. Some common delinquent acts are listed below:

1. These boys want to satisfy their immediate social or biological need. For this they start stealing money or articles first from home. Then this tendency is generalized to other situations like neighborhood, school etc.
   The second important act related to fulfillment of need is harassing the other boys in order to attain supremacy in his group. Such activities release sexual and other types of tensions in adolescents.
2. Forgery is another important act committed by adults. They may forge the signature of their parents and draw some money from banks. They may forge the signature of their teachers in their copies and manipulate marks allotted to them on their progress report card.
3. They behave very aggressively and rudely to others. Aggression may be shown against animate or inanimate objects of the environment. Aggressive behaviour is manifested in different ways such as
   - Using abusive or filthy language all the time.
   - Damaging school property.
   - Bullying and mockery.
   - Torturing of dumb animals, young children, strangers and beggars.
   - Committing suicide.
   - Behaving rudely and insulting to old or respected people.
   - Throwing excreta or dung in the houses of neighbours etc.
4. Sexual crimes are very common committed by delinquents. They exploit the other younger boys for their sexual satisfaction i.e., homosexuality is practised. Other sexual crimes committed by them are
   - Hetro sexuality
   - Fucking the animals like goats or bitch.
   - Sex related conversations.
   - Naked drawing or paintings.
   - Seeing nude photographs or living people. (pronography)
   - Enjoying the intercourse of animals.
   - Prostitutions.
   - Abducting and raping girls.
   - Exhibiting the hidden parts of their body.
   - Masturbation.
   - Giving sexual explanations to everything etc.
5. Extreme form of delinquency is murder or robbery. Delinquents get involved in these crimes when they are irritated by others.
6. Some delinquents work on pleasure principle only and they are unable to face the reality of the situation. They become truants and escape from the place. Some such acts are
   - Truancy from the school.
   - Running from home.
   - Leaving the place immediately after committing crime. One important point to he kept in mind is that most of these delinquent acts are given up after marriage. It has been seen in more than 90% cases. Only few delinquents frustrate the society in their later periods of life.

## Difference Between Crime and Delinquency

A Delinquent and a criminal can be differentiated in the following ways:

1. **Difference of Age :** Both of them indulge in antisocial activities but a delinquent is one who is in the age group of 15-20 while a criminal is above this age level.
2. **Difference of Activities :** In spite of many similarities between the activities of a criminal and a delinquent, they differ in many respects. Because of this, many activities of delinquents do not require legal action such as cruelty, obstinacy, keeping away from home for a long period of time without permission, roaming about the streets late at night etc. On the other hand, activities of criminals always require legal action. They definitely breach the code of law and are brought to the court. Delinquents are brought to the court only when they resemble to criminals in their activities but even then they are not treated so harshly as criminals are treated.

3. **Difference of Characteristics :** Many of the characteristics between criminals and delinquents are common except few that are given below :
   (a) A criminal may not necessarily be muscular or strong.
   (b) Only a few criminals have been found impulsive, destructive and restless.
   (c) Criminals are not generally resentful. Most of them are very cool minded and a good planner. Delinquents lack these qualities.
   (d) Criminals are generally very methodical to the problems.
   (e) A criminal does not do anything without purpose but delinquents are generally unaware of the objectives of his own action.
   (f) A delinquent generally commits crimes with only an intension to enjoy the situation. He does these acts just for fun but a criminal commits a crime for material benefit or physical satisfaction.

One more thing is that only a few delinquents become a criminal in their later age. Those delinquents who are brought to the court and jailed for one or two months get criminal training in jails.

## Methods used in Detecting Juvenile Delinquents

There are three methods used in detecting the juvenile delinquents:

**(A) Statistical method:** Cyril Burt has listed some specific situations that are taken into account in preparing the inventory for this purpose.

1. Hereditary circumstances : Such as physical health of the boy and his parents, mental health, temperament etc.
2. Environmental circumstances especially :
   (a) Family background such as poverty, broken family, discipline, bad character in the family etc.
   (b) Moral environment outside the family, neighborhood and in the society. These situations are taken into considerations while observing or testing the delinquents.

   In statistical method, different types of psychological tests such as behaviour tests, inventory, rating scales etc, are used and conclusion is drawn on the basis of statistical analysis of the data.

**(B) Case history method :** It directly studies the personal life of the delinquents. In this method efforts are made to collect all informations concerning every aspect of the subject's personality from the very beginning of his life and causes of delinquency are found out. Informations regarding the ambitions, frustrations and problems of the subject are collected here. Interview technique is mostly used here. Here not only the subject is interrogated but his parents, relatives and friends are also interviewed and then final conclusion is drawn.

**(C) Psychoanalytic method :** Here the subconscious mind of the subject is especially studied using dream analysis, word association or other psychological techniques. On the basis of this method, submerged or hidden causes that compel him to become a delinquent are brought to the surface. To understand the criminal mentality of a person, psychological process, which are in the background of human behaviour, are studied here. Out of the three methods given above no method is absolutely successful enough to study a delinquent. For this reason, all the three methods combined together can give us a real picture of a juvenile delinquents.

## CAUSES OF DELINQUENCY

### (A) Heredity

Many psychologists hold the view that crime or delinquency is inherited from parents and ancestors. Several studies in proof of this view are given below:

1. Studies of family trees of Kalikaks and Edward families have shown that crime as well as intelligence are inherited from generation to generation.
2. **Obruso** studied a number of criminals and their physical characteristic in general. He found that many inborn **physical** characteristics are found in all criminals, such as strong chin, protruding ears, abundant hairs, enormous jaws, smaller number of lines in the palms, swift movement of eyes, healthy bones etc.

3. **Goring** established the facts that intelligence was more associated with criminal tendencies as compared to physical characteristics of the subject. Low intellectual ability of the person may be an important cause of delinquency.
4. **Smith** found that thief and murderer suffered from the disturbance of gland cells and central nervous system.
5. **According to Sheldon** the mesomorph is more vulnerable to delinquency than endomorph or ectomorph.
6. **Healy and Bruonner** found that 37% of the delinquents were in the subnormal range of intelligence. Borderline cases are especially prone to delinquency. They also concluded that delinquency is found five times more in mentally handicapped as compared to normal group of adults.
7. **Goddard** in his Gook "Mental efficiency and levels of intelligencer" has stated that the greatest single cause of delinquency is mental weakness.
8. Many psychologists are of the view that a criminal is a kind of mentally ailing person who is in as much need of treatment as in need of punishment. For example, psychopathic personality is a cause of crime. Such children are born in those families where there is complete absence of love, affection and control.

## (B) Environment

Social environment starts from home and stretches to the whole society. Such factors can be categorized into four parts:

1. **Ecology :** It means the effect of physical surroundings and climate on the growth and development of the organism. **Abbott** on the basis of his studies concluded that
   (a) Delinquency comes from densely populated areas especially from congested wards of the city.
   (b) High percentage of delinquents comes from manufacturing commercial plants and highly industrialized parts of the city.

**R.S.Clifford** related situational conditions and distribution of delinquency and concluded that
   (a) Nearer a locality to the center of the city, higher will be the rate of delinquency.
   (b) Slum areas of the city breed higher percentage of delinquency.

2. **Home:** Inter relationship of family members shapes the personality of each member in the family. Following conditions are associated with the delinquent tendencies of a person.
   (a) **Broken families:** Highest percentage of delinquents come from broken families where father and mother are living apart. It is because if there is a quarrel between parents, it will badly affect the mental health of the child. On the other hand, if both parents are employed and children are left in the supervision of servants, servants in most cases are responsible for initiating young children to delinquent acts at very early stage. The reason is that such children do not get the care and attention of their parents and are inclined to delinquency in frustration.
   (b) **poverty:** Due to poverty, parents are unable to fulfil the legitimate needs of their children. Poor children are also inclined to delinquency when they see that civil administration is favouring the people of rich families in several ways.
   Several studies on delinquency shows that higher percentage of delinquents come from lower or lower middle socio economic strata of the society.
   (c) **Disability of parents :** If any of ;both the parents are physically handicapped in any field, they cannot keep full control over their offsprings and these children may become delinquents in their later stage.
   (d) **Discipline of the family :** If discipline of the family is poor and each member of the family is selfish, and self centered, the young boys of the family may become delinquents, due to lack of control and supervision on them.
   (e) **Lack of affection :** Neglected children are more prone to turn into delinquents than those who are loved and cared by their parents.
   (f) **Undue favour by parents :** If children are given undue support by their parents and are encouraged to do whatever they like, such children are more likely to become delinquents in their later age. Similarly, partiality shown to any son may motivate the others to become antisocial and aggressive.

**(g) Family tension :** In case of joint families if tensions are there between different members, the child seeks emotional satisfaction outside home and he may become anti social, aggressive and rude.

**(h) Lack of recreational facilities :** Recreational activities are important source of releasing pent up feeling. If such facilities are not available for the child at home and high restrictions are imposed on him, he will become truant and delinquent in search of pleasure and emotional satisfaction.

**(i) Lack of moral code :** Good moral code regulates our lives in a positive manner. If good moral code is there in the family, the child will not commit delinquent act even in adverse, hostile situations.

**3. Neighborhood:** Most of the delinquent acts are learnt from the society and neighborhood. Important factors associated with delinquency are given below:

**(a) Crime dominated areas :** In those areas where criminals and delinquents are found in large numbers, these areas are good places for breeding delinquency. It is because these activities are imitated by the young generation.

**(b) Bad company :** According to **Edwin H Sutherland,** criminal behaviour is acquired through close interactions with other criminals. That is why it is said that jails are good breeding places for criminal behaviour. If a good boy is having the company of a delinquent, he is more than 50% likely to become a delinquent.

**(c) War and postwar situations :** The rate of delinquency has been found increasing during war and post war situations. It is because people talk too much about such situations and scene of the battlefield is also highlighted by the media.

**(d) Displacement :** Delinquency is seen in those areas very much where enforced displacement is seen again and again. This is due to back of adjustment.

**4. School :** After family and neighborhood, school is the third important centre of shaping personality and character. Following factors in schools may lead to delinquency in children.

**(a) Discipline :** Poor and weak discipline is very conducive to turn the children into delinquents. If school does not care about the presence or absence of pupils, the absentees utilize the chance in learning delinquent acts.

**(b) Emotional climate :** If climate of the school is not conducive to satisfy the emotional needs of children by curriculum, behaviour of teachers, co-curricular activities etc, some of these children may become delinquents.

**(c) Prejudiced treatment :** If some students are given special weightage by their teacher at due negligence of others, it might turn some students into delinquents. Showing their hostility against the teachers and their pets, children want to draw the attention of others by these acts.

**(d) Lack of recreational facilities :** If recreational facilities are available to children in the school to release their pent up feelings, they will not become delinquents in the later age.

**(e) Lack of guidance and counseling facilities :** If students are not given proper guidance and counseling at the manifestations of unwanted behaviours, they are likely to become delinquents.

**(f) Unfulfilled needs :** If basic biological or psychological needs of students are not fulfilled, they are more likely to become hostile to the whole system. Their frustration will lead them to indulge in anti-social activities.

**(g) Curriculum :** If curriculum has not been developed according to the age related needs and interest of students, their dissatisfaction with the situation may make them anti social.

**(h) Defective examination system :** If a student continuously fails in a class and remains in the same class for more than two years, he will loose interest in the subject matter. As a result, he may become truant due to lack of interest in the class.

## Measures Adopted to Prevent Delinquent Tendencies from Adults

In order to check antisocial behaviour, it is a must to adopt preventive measures first. Family school and the society all have their respective role to play to prevent delinquency. Following measures can be adopted for this purpose:

I. All the possible causes, which are responsible for delinquency in adults, should be checked and removed as early as possible. (See the causes of delinquency).

II. Majority of parents in India is illiterate and uneducated. They do not know how to deal and behave with their children. An agency should be created to educate these parents Mass media can play a very important role here.

III. School can play a very important role in preventing delinquency. Its role should be increased by utilizing the services of good charactered teachers and counsellors.

IV. Moral code of conduct should be strictly adhered to in the society.

## TREATMENT OF DELINQUENCY

These delinquents are deformed in their behaviour. These deformed behaviours need be modified and improved to properly get the delinquents adjusted in the society. Following measures can be adopted to reform these delinquents.

1. **Verbal therapy :** These delinquents have acquired many unwanted behaviour in the course of time. They are told about the evil consequences of these habits by citing numerous examples. They are also told what the other people of the society think about them.
2. **Marriage :** Most of the delinquents become so due to their lonely feeling and uncared sensitivity. If they are given a life partner to look after and care them, they will become normal in a few days. Besides, sexual satisfaction received after marriage can also mend their behaviour.
3. **Abreaction :** Abreaction means providing opportunity to the child to express his pent up and suppressed feelings through discussion and speeches. Therapist also uses free association, psychodrama and play techniques for this purpose. For example, they are given chance to play different games and their pent up feelings are released through these games.
4. **Persuasion :** Therapist persuades them not to do such acts in future but this persuation is made in the form of appeal not in the form of suggestions. This techniques has not been proved very effective so far but it can be used along with other techniques.
5. **Counselling :** In this technique, therapist first of all finds out the causes of delinquency by interviewing the patient. Then he removes the causes by developing super-ego of the patient verbally. Different techniques of counselling are used for this purpose.
6. **Environmental treatment :** In this technique, home and school environment are improved on positive line. Parents and teachers are advised to change their attitude and behaviour in order to give better treatment to delinquents. Delinquents may be shifted to other places of better environment for a temporary period of time, i.e., they may be kept in foster homes. In this way the delinquent child may give up his anti social activities after a few periods of time.
7. **Probation :** In this method, the delinquent is kept under the supervision of a probation officer whose job is to look after the delinquent round the clock. The officer checks his anti social activities and helps him to live a normal life.
8. **Finger painting :** In this technique the delinquent is given art papers and colours. He is allowed to draw the sketches and paint in his own way by means of his fingers. In this way the repressed emotions of the delinquent is relieved.
9. **Establishment of special schools :** In order to rectify the behaviour of delinquents, they are admitted in special schools meant for them. They are taught special curriculum by special teachers and they are evaluated in special manners also.
10. **Modern techniques of behaviour modification:** Many psychologists are of the view that human behaviour is acquired not born. If there is any deformation in the behaviour, it can be reformed by behaviour training, conditioning and using re-enforcement techniques. The behaviour of delinquents can also be reformed by using principles of programmed learning., Some of the contributions of the psychologists in this regard are given below :

    1. Burhard (1967) launched a programme for mildly retarded delinquents. These delinquents

were kept in residential schools and their behaviour was punished or reinforced systematically.

2. Cohen (1965) used the method of programmed instruction on 16 delinquents to reach specific targets of academic achievement. If a learner completed a unit of the programme by scoring 90%, he was eligible to take examination on which he could earn reinforcement in the form of point. In this way he was able to generate desirable educational activities in delinquents.
3. Reinforcement in the form of approval by a loved one can also change the unwanted behaviour of delinquents.

## Educational Adaptation of Delinquent Children

New Meyer (1961) believed that school has an important role to play to control and prevent delinquency. Ross is of the opinion that school is not composed of four walls but of trained personnel that are collectively responsible for the behaviour of children.

These delinquents are deformed in behaviour. They do not behave normally even in the schools and create problems for others. So special care and attention must be paid to deal with them in the school environment. Following measures must be adopted to these delinquents to get them adapted educationally:

1. They should be admitted in normal schools and their number should not be more than one or two in a class so that they may not influence other students of the class. They will rather be influenced by normal students.
2. They should be taught by especially trained teachers who can handle them properly. If there case is in any why serious, they should be sent to the counsellor of the school.
3. Curriculum meant for them should be slightly different in which moral lessons should be included.
4. Meditation and yoga is a must for these children. It will give them mental peace.
5. They should be given ample opportunities for co-curricular activities arts, painting and music. All these things will help them release their repressed emotions and develop their super ego.
6. At least one counselling period should be allotted for these students separately in a regular manner.
7. Their cumulative record should be maintained by the teacher.
8. Practicals and assignments should be given more weightage than theory papers while evaluating these students.
9. Special attention must be given on behaviour modification of these students.
10. Parents should also be convinced by the school to treat these students differently at home. Regular suggestions should be communicated to parents by teachers.
11. Efforts should be made to get them involve in those activities which demand muscular power.
12. They should be assisted to choose a good friend in the school. Good company will improve their behaviour in future.
13. They should be motivated to participate in religious activities as much as possible.
14. Causes of delinguent behaviour are many. First of all, these causes must be identified by the counsellor using interviews, or standardized test, then these causes must he removed one by one.